797,885 Books
are available to read at

Forgotten Books

www.ForgottenBooks.com

Forgotten Books' App
Available for mobile, tablet & eReader

ISBN 978-1-333-66093-2
PIBN 10532443

This book is a reproduction of an important historical work. Forgotten Books uses state-of-the-art technology to digitally reconstruct the work, preserving the original format whilst repairing imperfections present in the aged copy. In rare cases, an imperfection in the original, such as a blemish or missing page, may be replicated in our edition. We do, however, repair the vast majority of imperfections successfully; any imperfections that remain are intentionally left to preserve the state of such historical works.

Forgotten Books is a registered trademark of FB &c Ltd.
Copyright © 2015 FB &c Ltd.
FB &c Ltd, Dalton House, 60 Windsor Avenue, London, SW19 2RR.
Company number 08720141. Registered in England and Wales.

For support please visit www.forgottenbooks.com

1 MONTH OF FREE READING

at

www.ForgottenBooks.com

By purchasing this book you are eligible for one month membership to ForgottenBooks.com, giving you unlimited access to our entire collection of over 700,000 titles via our web site and mobile apps.

To claim your free month visit: www.forgottenbooks.com/free532443

* Offer is valid for 45 days from date of purchase. Terms and conditions apply.

English
Français
Deutsche
Italiano
Español
Português

www.forgottenbooks.com

Mythology Photography **Fiction** Fishing Christianity **Art** Cooking Essays Buddhism Freemasonry Medicine **Biology** Music **Ancient Egypt** Evolution Carpentry Physics Dance Geology **Mathematics** Fitness Shakespeare **Folklore** Yoga Marketing **Confidence** Immortality Biographies Poetry **Psychology** Witchcraft Electronics Chemistry History **Law** Accounting **Philosophy** Anthropology Alchemy Drama Quantum Mechanics Atheism Sexual Health **Ancient History** **Entrepreneurship** Languages Sport Paleontology Needlework Islam **Metaphysics** Investment Archaeology Parenting Statistics Criminology **Motivational**

THE
VICTORIA HISTORY
OF THE COUNTY OF
HERTFORD

EDITED BY

WILLIAM PAGE, F.S.A.

VOLUME THREE

LONDON

CONSTABLE AND COMPANY LIMITED

1912

CONTENTS OF VOLUME THREE

		PAGE
Dedication		v
Contents		ix
List of Illustrations		xiii
List of Maps		xx
Editorial Note		xxi
Topography	General descriptions and manorial descents compiled under the superintendence of WILLIAM PAGE, F.S.A., the General Editor; Heraldic drawings and blazon by the Rev. E. E. DORLING, M.A., F.S.A.; Charities from information supplied by J. W. OWSLEY, I.S.O., late Official Trustee of Charitable Funds	
Hitchin Hundred	Architectural descriptions (Domestic) by A. WHITFORD ANDERSON, A.R.I.B.A. (except Hitchin Priory by S. C. KAINES-SMITH, M.A.). Architectural descriptions (Ecclesiastical) by S. C. KAINES-SMITH, M.A.	
Introduction	By LUCY M. SANDERSON	1
Hitchin	General descriptions and manorial descents by LUCY M. SANDERSON	3
Ickleford	,, ,, ,, ,,	21
Ippollitts	,, ,, ,, ,,	25
Kimpton	,, ,, ,, ,,	29
King's Walden	,, ,, ,, ,,	33
Lilley	,, ,, ,, ,,	37
Offley	,, ,, ,, ,,	39
Pirton	,, ,, ,, ,,	44
Broadwater Hundred	Architectural descriptions (Domestic) by A. WHITFORD ANDERSON, A.R.I.B.A. (except Hatfield House by S. C. KAINES-SMITH, M.A.). Architectural descriptions (Ecclesiastical) by S. C. KAINES-SMITH, M.A.	
Introduction	By MABEL E. CHRISTIE, Hist. Tripos	52
Aston	General descriptions and manorial descents by MABEL E. CHRISTIE	54
Ayot St. Lawrence or Great Ayot	,, ,, ,, ,,	59
Ayot St. Peter	,, ,, ,, ,,	63
Baldock	,, ,, ,, ,,	65
Benington	,, ,, ,, ,,	73
Datchworth	,, ,, ,, ,,	78
Digswell	,, ,, ,, ,,	81
Graveley	,, ,, ,, ,,	85
Hatfield or Bishop's Hatfield	,, ,, ,, ,,	91
Knebworth	,, ,, ,, ,,	111

CONTENTS OF VOLUME THREE

PAGE

Topography (*continued*)—
   Broadwater Hundred (*continued*)—

Letchworth . .	General descriptions and manorial descents by MABEL E. CHRISTIE	118
Great Munden	,, ,, ,, ,,	124
Little Munden	,, ,, ,, ,,	129
Sacombe .	,, ,, ,, ,,	136
Stevenage	,, ,, ,, ,,	139
Totteridge	,, ,, ,, ,,	148
Walkern . .	,, ,, ,, ,,	151
Watton-at-Stone	,, ,, ,, ,,	158
Welwyn .	,, ,, ,, ,,	165
Weston .	,, ,, ,, ,,	171
Willian . .	,, ,, ,, ,,	177
Great or Much Wymondley	,, ,, ,, ,,	181
Little Wymondley	,, ,, ,, ,,	186
Odsey Hundred	Architectural descriptions (Domestic and Ecclesiastical) by A. WHITFORD ANDERSON, A.R.I.B.A. (except Ardeley Church by S. C. KAINES-SMITH, M.A.)	
Introduction	By LILIAN J. REDSTONE, B.A.	192
Ardeley .	General descriptions and manorial descents by LILIAN J. REDSTONE, B.A.	194
Ashwell . .	General descriptions and manorial descents by CICELY WILMOT, Oxford Honours School of Modern History	199
Broadfield	General descriptions and manorial descents by MAUD F. EDWARDS, Oxford Honours School of Modern History	209
Bygrave .	General descriptions and manorial descents by LILIAN J. REDSTONE, B.A.	211
Caldecote .	General descriptions and manorial descents by LUCY M. SANDERSON	217
Clothall . .	General descriptions and manorial descents by LILIAN J. REDSTONE, B.A	220
Cottered . . .	General descriptions and manorial descents by MAUD F. EDWARDS .	226
Hinxworth . . .	,, ,,	232
Kelshall . . .	,,	240
Radwell . . .	,,	244
Reed . . .	,, ,, ,, ,,	247
Royston . .	General descriptions and manorial descents by LILIAN J. REDSTONE, B.A.	253
Rushden .	General descriptions and manorial descents by MAUD F. EDWARDS	265
Sandon . . .	General descriptions and manorial descents by LUCY M. SANDERSON	270
Therfield . . .	,, ,, ,, ,,	276
Wallington . .	General descriptions and manorial descents by LILIAN J. REDSTONE, B.A.	284

x

CONTENTS OF VOLUME THREE

PAGE

Topography (*continued*)—
Braughing Hundred . . Architectural descriptions by A. WHITFORD ANDERSON, A.R.I.B.A.

Introduction . . .	By ALICE RAVEN	289
Bishop's Stortford	General descriptions and manorial descents by ALICE RAVEN	292
Braughing . .	,, ,, ,, ,,	306
Eastwick . . .	General descriptions and manorial descents by CICELY WILMOT, Oxford Honours School of Modern History	317
Gilston	General descriptions and manorial descents by ALICE RAVEN	319
Hunsdon . .	General descriptions and manorial descents by CICELY WILMOT	323
Sawbridgeworth	General descriptions and manorial descents by ALICE RAVEN	332
Standon . . .	,, ,, ,,	347
Stanstead Abbots	,, ,, ,, ,,	366
Thorley . . .	,, ,, ,, ,,	373
Thundridge .	,, ,, ,, ,,	377
Ware	,, ,, ,, ,,	380
Westmill .	,, ,, ,, ,,	397
Widford . . .	,, ,, ,, ,,	402

Hertford Hundred . . Architectural descriptions except where otherwise stated by A. WHITFORD ANDERSON, A.R.I.B.A.

Introduction	By LILIAN J. REDSTONE, B.A.	407
Parts of All Saints' and St. John's, Hertford, including the liberties of Brickendon and Little Amwell	General descriptions and manorial descents by LILIAN J. REDSTONE, B.A.	409
Great Amwell	,, ,, ,, ,,	414
Bayford .	General descriptions and manorial descents by MABEL E. CHRISTIE, Hist. Tripos	419
Bengeo . . .	General descriptions and manorial descents by ELEANOR J. B. REID, B.A.	423
Little Berkhampstead	,, ,, ,, ,,	427
Broxbourne with Hoddesdon . . .	General descriptions and manorial descents by MABEL E. CHRISTIE	430
Cheshunt St. Mary	General descriptions and manorial descents by ELEANOR J. B. REID, B.A. Architectural descriptions of Waltham Cross and Theobalds by S. C. KAINES-SMITH, M.A.	441
Essendon . . .	General descriptions and manorial descents by ELEANOR J. B. REID, B.A.	458
Hertingfordbury .	General descriptions and manorial descents by MABEL E. CHRISTIE	462
St. Andrew Rural	General descriptions and manorial descents by HELEN DOUGLAS-IRVINE, M.A. Architectural description of Panshanger by Rev. E. E. DORLING, M.A., F.S.A. .	468
Stanstead St. Margaret's	General descriptions and manorial descents by MAUD F. EDWARDS, Oxford Honours School of Modern History	472
Stapleford . . .	,, ,, ,, ,,	476

CONTENTS OF VOLUME THREE

PAGE

Topography (*continued*)—
   Hertford Hundred (*continued*)—
      Tewin . . . . . General descriptions and manorial descents by MABEL E. CHRISTIE 480

      Wormley . . . . General descriptions and manorial descents by ELEANOR J. B. REID, B.A. 487

      Hertford Borough . History of Borough and manorial descents by A. F. H. NIEMEYER, Oxford Honours School of Modern History. Architectural description of Hertford Castle by A. W. CLAPHAM. Domestic Architecture by JOHN QUEKETT, B.A. . 490

LIST OF ILLUSTRATIONS

	PAGE
Ashridge Park from the Bridgewater Monument. By William Hyde . . . *frontispiece*	
Hitchin : View in Bancroft	4
,, Old Houses in Bancroft } . . . . *full-page plate, facing*	4
,, Church : The Nave looking East }	
,, The Three Tuns Inn, Tilehouse Street	6
,, Coopers' Arms Inn, Tilehouse Street . . . . *full-page plate, facing*	8
,, Church : North Chapel Screen } . . . . . ,, ,, ,,	12
,, ,, South Chapel Screen }	
,, ,, Plan	14
,, ,, South Porch	16
,, ,, South Porch Interior } . . . . *full-page plate, facing*	16
,, ,, The Font }	
,, Minsden Chapel, Ruins	18
Ickleford Church from the South	24
Ippollitts : Little Almshoe : The Wyck	25
,, ,, ,, ,, West Wing . . . *full-page plate, facing*	26
,, Church from the South-east	27
,, ,, The South Porch } . . . . *full-page plate, facing*	28
,, ,, The Nave looking East }	
Kimpton : Stoneheaps Farm } . . . . . ,, ,, ,,	30
,, Church from the South-west }	
,, ,, Plan	32
,, ,, The Nave looking East } . . . . *full-page plate, facing*	32
,, ,, The South Aisle looking East }	
,, ,, Old Desk in the Chancel } . . . . . ,, ,, ,,	34
King's Walden Church : The Nave looking East }	
,, ,, ,, from the North-west	36
Offley Church from the South-east } . . . . *full-page plate, facing*	40
,, ,, The Nave looking East }	
,, ,, The Font . . . . ,, ,, ,,	42
Pirton, Old Hall : Ground Plan	44
,, Grange from the South-west } . . . . *full-page plate, facing*	44
,, High Down from the East }	
,, Hammond's Farm : Plan	45
,, High Down : Ground Plan	45
,, Grange, Ground Plan	45
,, High Down : Panel with Arms of Sir Thomas Docwra . . .	46
,, Grange : East Front	47
,, Old Hall	47
,, Hammond's Farm showing Porch	48

LIST OF ILLUSTRATIONS

		PAGE
Pirton Grange : East Porch }	full-page plate, facing	48
,, High Down : The Porch }		
,, ,, ,, Entrance Gateway	. . . .	49
,, Hammond's Farm, Dovecote		50
,, Church from the South	. . full-page plate, facing	50
Aston Bury : Ground Plan	. . . .	54
,, ,, Attic Plan	. . . .	54
,, ,, Attic Gallery	. . . .	55
,, ,, from the North-west	. . . .	56
,, ,, The North Porch	. full-page plate, facing	56
Aston Church from the South-west	. . . .	57
Aston Bury : Oak Grill and Staircase	. full-page plate, facing	58
Ayot St. Lawrence Old Church : Plan	. . . .	61
,, ,, ,, ,, ,, from the South-east	. . . .	62
,, ,, ,, ,, ,, Remains of North Chapel and Aisle }	. full-page plate, facing	62
,, ,, ,, ,, ,, 15th-century Tomb }		
Baldock Village	. . . .	66
,, Cemetery Road : Old House .	. . . .	67
,, View in Hitchin Street }	. full-page plate, facing	68
,, Old House in White Horse Street }		
,, Church : Plan	. . . .	70
,, ,, The Nave looking East }	. full-page plate, facing	72
,, ,, South Chapel Screen }		
Benington Church from the South-east }	. . ,, ,, ,,	74
,, ,, The Nave looking East }		
,, ,, Tomb in the Chancel	. ,, ,, ,,	76
Datchworth : Whipping Post on the Green }	. . ,, ,, ,,	78
,, Church : The Nave looking East }		
,, ,, from the South-east .	. . .	80
Digswell Church from the North-east	. full-page plate, facing	82
,, ,, Plan	. . . .	84
,, ,, North Aisle showing Recess with Tracery	. . . .	84
Graveley : Chesfield Manor House, Ground Plan	. . . .	86
,, ,, ,, ,, from the North-east .	. . . .	88
,, Church from the South-east	. . . .	89
,, ,, The Chancel }	. full-page plate, facing	90
,, Ruins of Chesfield Church }		
Hatfield House : Plan in 1608 .	. . . facing	92
,, Old Palace : Plan of Hall .	. . . .	94
,, House : Ground Floor Plan	. . . facing	96
,, ,, First Floor Plan .	,,	98
,, ,, South Façade	. full-page plate, facing	100
,, ,, West End of Long Gallery .	,, ,, ,,	102
,, Church : The Chancel and Brockett Chapel }	. ,, ,, ,,	106
,, Salisbury Chapel }		
,, ,, from the South	.	108
,, ,, Plan	. . . .	109

xiv

LIST OF ILLUSTRATIONS

	PAGE
Knebworth House : Ground Plan in 1805 112
,, ,, West Lodge Arches from the West 113
,, ,, from the South . . . . . *full-page plate, facing* 114
,, ,, West Lodge 115
,, ,, West Lodge, 16th-century Window ⎫ . *full-page plate, facing* 116
,, Church : The Chancel Arch ⎭
,, ,, from the South-east 117
,, ,, The Pulpit . . . . . *full-page plate, facing* 118
Letchworth Hall : Ground Plan 119
,, ,, Part of Stair 120
,, ,, West Front 121
,, ,, Part of Screen in Hall ⎫ . . . *full-page plate, facing* 122
,, ,, Fireplace on First Floor ⎭
,, ,, from the East ⎫ . . ,, ,, ,, 124
,, Church from the North ⎭
Great Munden : Old Farm 125
,, ,, Church from the South-east 128
Little Munden : Lordship Farm 130
,, ,, Church from the North-east 131
,, ,, Old Cottage at Dane End 133
,, ,, Church : Plan 134
,, ,, ,, Tombs in the Chancel . . . *full-page plate, facing* 134
,, ,, ,, The Nave looking North-east 135
Sacombe Church from the South-east 138
Stevenage Bury : Back View 140
,, ,, Front View ⎫ . . . *full-page plate, facing* 140
,, Chells Farm from the South ⎭
,, ,, ,, from the North 141
,, Main Road, showing 17th century House 142
,, ,, ,, ⎫ . . *full-page plate, facing* 142
,, Old House, now Gas Company's Offices ⎭
,, Church from the North-east ⎫ . ,, ,, ,, 144
,, ,, The Nave looking East ⎭
,, ,, Plan 146
,, ,, The Font . . . . . *full-page plate, facing* 146
Walkern Rook's Nest, Ground Plan 151
,, Bridgefoot Farmhouse, Ground Plan 152
,, Rook's Nest, East Front 153
,, Old Cottage 153
,, Bridgefoot Farm from the South-west ⎫ . *full-page plate, facing* 154
,, Church : The Nave looking East ⎭
,, Rook's Nest from the South-west 155
,, Church : Plan 156
,, ,, Tomb in South Aisle . . . *full-page plate, facing* 156
,, ,, from the South-west 157
Watton Place : Front View 159
,, ,, Back View 161

xv

LIST OF ILLUSTRATIONS

	PAGE
Watton Church from the North-east } *full-page plate, facing*	164
,, ,, The Nave looking east }	
Welwyn Church from the South } ,, ,, ,,	168
,, ,, Interior looking South-east }	
Weston Church from the South } ,, ,, ,,	174
,, ,, Capital of Impost of South-east Pier of Tower }	
,, ,, Interior looking East	176
Willian Church from the South-east .	180
,, ,, Chancel Screen . *full-page plate, facing*	180
Great Wymondley : Delamere, Ground Plan	182
,, ,, ,, Drawing Room Chimney-piece } *full-page plate, facing*	182
,, ,, Church : South Doorway }	
,, ,, ,, from the North-east . ,, ,, ,,	184
,, ,, Delamere : South Front	185
Little Wymondley : Buck's Head Inn	187
,, ,, Bury from the East .	187
,, ,, Hall : Entrance Doorway	188
,, ,, ,, from the South-west } *full-page plate, facing*	188
,, ,, Priory from the North-west }	
,, ,, ,, Ground Floor Plan .	189
,, ,, Bury : Ground Plan .	189
,, ,, Priory : North Front .	190
,, ,, ,, Barn } *full-page plate, facing*	190
,, ,, Church from the North-west }	
Ardeley Church : The Nave looking East } ,, ,, ,,	196
,, ,, The Roof of the Nave }	
,, ,, from the North } ,, ,, ,,	198
Ashwell : Old House near Church }	
,, View in Village .	200
,, High Street, the 'Rose and Crown' .	201
,, House in the Main Street (dated 1681) *full-page plate, facing*	202
,, Church : Plan .	205
,, ,, from the South-east } *full-page plate, facing*	206
,, ,, The Nave looking South-west }	
,, Lychgate to Churchyard .	207
Broadfield : Old Oak Entrance Door from Broadfield Hall *full-page plate, facing*	210
Bygrave : Plan of Parish .	213
,, Church from the North-west	216
Caldecote Church from the North-west	219
,, ,, 15th-century Stoup in South Porch *full-page plate, facing*	220
Clothall Church from the South-east } ,, ,, ,,	226
Cottered Church from the South }	
,, The Town Houses	227
,, The Lordship, Ground Plan	227
,, ,, ,, from the North-west	229
,, ,, ,, Entrance Front } *full-page plate, facing*	230
,, ,, ,, Jacobean Chimney-piece in the Dining-room }	
Hinxworth Place : Ground Plan	233

xvi

LIST OF ILLUSTRATIONS

	PAGE
Hinxworth Place : Principal Entrance Doorway	234
,, ,, from the North-east } *full-page plate, facing*	236
,, ,, from the South-west }	
,, ,, Part of South-west Front	237
,, Church from the South-east	238
,, Place : Heraldic Glass Window in Drawing Room } *full-page plate, facing*	240
Kelshall Church : The Nave looking West }	
,, ,, from the South-west	243
,, ,, Locker in North-west Angle of North Aisle *full-page plate, facing*	244
Radwell Church from the South-east	246
Reed Church : Plan	252
,, ,, from the North-east } *full-page plate, facing*	252
Royston Church : 14th-century Effigy in Chancel }	
,, High Street, Old Houses	256
,, Cave : Sculptured Figures on Wall below Cornice (two views) *full-page plate, facing*	258
,, Church : The South Arcade } ,, ,, ,,	260
,, ,, The Pulpit }	
,, House in the Churchyard	262
,, Church : Plan	263
Rushden Church from the South-east	269
,, ,, The Nave looking East } *full-page plate, facing*	270
Sandon Church : Easter Sepulchre, North Side of Chancel }	
,, ,, and Cottages from the South-west } ,, ,, ,,	274
,, ,, The Nave looking East }	
,, ,, Tower and South Porch	275
Therfield Rectory : Plan	277
,, ,, 15th-century East Wing from the North-west	277
,, ,, North Window of Kitchen } *full-page plate, facing*	278
,, ,, South Window, now partly doorway }	
Wallington Church : 15th-century Altar Tomb ,, ,, ,,	286
,, ,, from the South-east	287
Bishop's Stortford : St. Joseph's, formerly Wind Hill House *full-page plate, facing*	292
,, ,, The White Horse Inn	294
,, ,, The Black Lion Inn	295
,, ,, Church : The Nave looking East } *full-page plate, facing*	296
,, ,, Waytemore Castle, South Wall of Keep from Enclosure }	
,, ,, Waytemore Castle, Plan	298
,, ,, Castle Cottage	299
,, ,, Piggotts, Back View	300
,, ,, ,, from the West	301
,, ,, ,, Ground Plan	302
,, ,, Church from the South-west	303
Braughing : Rose and Crown	307
,, The Maltings	308
,, Upp Hall : Ground Plan	312
,, ,, ,, Old Barn from the South-west	313
,, ,, ,, ,, Plan	313

xvii

LIST OF ILLUSTRATIONS

		PAGE
Braughing : Upp Hall from the West	*full-page plate, facing*	314
,, Church from the South		
,, ,, Monument to John and Charles Brograve	,, ,, ,,	318
Eastwick Church : 13th-century Effigy		
Gilston Church from the South-east .	.	322
,, ,, Piscina and Credence	*full-page plate, facing*	322
Hunsdon House : Plan .	.	324
,, ,, from the South-east	.	325
,, ,, from the North-east	.	326
,, Church : 17th-century Oak Screen to South Chapel	*full-page plate, facing*	328
,, ,, Plan .	.	330
,, ,, Tomb of Sir Thomas Foster	*full-page plate, facing*	330
,, ,, from the North-west .	.	331
Sawbridgeworth : Three Mile Pond Farm	.	332
,, Hand and Crown Inn .	.	333
,, Tharbies	.	334
,, Bursteads : Ground Plan	.	342
,, South-west Front .	.	342
,, Interior of Great Barn .	.	343
,, Church from the South-east	.	344
,, The Nave looking East	*full-page plate, facing*	344
,, The Chancel		
,, ,, Tomb of Sir John Leventhorpe and his Wife	,, ,, ,,	346
Standon : High Street	.	348
,, The School	.	349
,, Friars Farm : Old Barn .	.	350
,, The Hermitage, Old Hall Green	*full-page plate, facing*	352
,, St. Edmund's College, Old Hall Green		
,, Lordship : West Front .	.	355
,, Sutes Manor House .	.	357
,, Church : The Nave looking East	*full-page plate, facing*	362
,, ,, Plan	.	364
,, ,, Monument to Sir Ralph Sadleir .	*full-page plate, facing*	364
Stanstead Abbots : Stanstead Bury from the North-west	.	370
,, ,, Church : South Porch	.	372
,, ,, Old Church from the South-west	*full-page plate, facing*	372
,, ,, ,, ,, The Nave looking East		
Thorley Hall : West Front .	.	373
,, Church from the South-east	.	376
,, ,, The South Doorway	*full-page plate, facing*	376
Thundridge : Wades Mill	.	378
,, Old Church : The Tower	*full-page plate, facing*	380
Ware Church from the North-east		
Plan .	.	393
,, ,, The Font, East Face	*full-page plate, facing*	394
,, ,, ,, ,, West Face		
Westmill Church from the South-west	.	400
,, ,, The Nave looking West	.	401

LIST OF ILLUSTRATIONS

	PAGE
Widford : Old Gateway in Churchyard Wall 404	
,, Church from the South-east 405	
Hertford : Balls Park from the South-east } . . . . *full-page plate, facing* 414	
,, ,, ,, The Entrance Front }	
Great Amwell Church from the South-east . . . . . ,, ,, ,, 416	
,, ,, ,, Plan 418	
,, ,, ,, The Nave looking East . . . . *full-page plate, facing* 418	
Bengeo Church from the South-east . . . . . . ,, ,, ,, 424	
,, ,, Plan 426	
,, ,, Chancel Arch looking from the Nave . . . *full-page plate, facing* 426	
Little Berkhampstead Church from the North . . . . ,, ,, ,, 428	
Broxbourne Church : The Font } . . . . . ,, ,, ,, 436	
,, ,, Tomb of Sir William Say }	
,, ,, from the North-east 438	
Cheshunt College : Older Part 441	
,, The Great House, Ground Plan 442	
,, ,, ,, ,, Basement Plan 442	
,, ,, ,, ,, Staircase } . . . . *full-page plate, facing* 442	
,, ,, ,, ,, Vault }	
,, ,, ,, ,, North End of the Hall 443	
,, Street : Old House 444	
,, Waltham Cross . . . . . . *full-page plate, facing* 444	
,, Goff's Oak 445	
,, Temple Bar at Theobalds Park . . . . . *full-page plate, facing* 450	
,, The Great House from the North-west 453	
,, ,, ,, ,, from the South-west } . . . *full-page plate, facing* 454	
,, Church from the South-east }	
,, Almshouses, Turner's Hill 457	
Essendon Church : West Tower 461	
Hertingfordbury : Old Parsonage 463	
,, Church : West Tower 467	
St. Andrew Rural : Panshanger House from the South-east *full-page plate, facing* 470	
Stanstead St. Margaret's Church from the South-west . . . ,, ,, ,, 472	
,, ,, ,, ,, The Chancel . . . ,, ,, ,, 474	
,, ,, ,, ,, Plan 475	
Stapleford Church : North Doorway 479	
Tewin : Queenhoo Hall from the South-west } . . . *full-page plate, facing* 482	
,, ,, ,, ,, ,, North-west }	
,, ,, ,, Ground Plan 484	
,, ,, ,, First Floor Plan 484	
,, Lead Sundial, formerly at Queenhoo Hall (two views) . *full-page plate, facing* 484	
,, Church : Plan 485	
,, ,, from the South-east 486	
Wormley Church from the North-west . . . . *full-page plate, facing* 488	
Hertford : Plan of the Town . . . . *facing* 490	
,, Old Coffee House Inn } . . . . *full-page plate, facing* 492	
,, Old Houses in Bull Plain }	
,, 17th-century pargeted House in Fore Street . . ,, ,, ,, 494	

xix

LIST OF ILLUSTRATIONS

			PAGE
Hertford : Bayley Hall	}	*full-page plate, facing*	496
,, Cottage at North-east of St. Andrew's Churchyard			
,, Christ's Hospital		,, ,, ,,	498
,, in 1611		,, ,, ,,	500
,, Castle : The Gatehouse			504
,, ,, Plan		*facing*	506
,, St. John's Church : Plan			508
,, Tile from St. John's Church			509

LIST OF MAPS

					PAGE
Index Map to the Hundred of Hitchin					1
,, ,, ,, ,, Broadwater					52
,, ,, ,, ,, Odsey					192
,, ,, ,, ,, Braughing					289
,, ,, ,, ,, Hertford					407

EDITORIAL NOTE

THE Editor wishes to thank the following, who have kindly assisted him by reading the proofs of this volume and have otherwise helped in passing the pages through the Press :—the Hon. H. C. Gibbs, M.A., Mr. R. T. Andrews, the Rev. Edwin Burton, D.D., Mr. J. L. Glasscock, Mr. H. R. H. Gosselin-Grimshawe, J.P., Mr. C. E. Johnston, Mr. William Minet, M.A., F.S.A., J.P., and Major F. Skeet. The assistance thus afforded has added much to the completeness of the various parish histories given in this volume.

The Editor desires further to acknowledge the courtesy he has invariably received from all those to whom he has applied for information. He would more especially mention in this respect the Most Hon. the Marquess of Salisbury, P.C., G.C.V.O., C.B., the Rt. Hon. the Earl of Lytton, the Rev. Lord William Cecil, M.A., Sir Edgar C. Boehm, Bart., Mr. W. F. Andrews, the Rev. H. Athill, M.A., the Rev. H. A. Barker, M.A., the Rev. F. R. Blatch, M.A., the Rev. A. R. Buckland, M.A., Mr. H. G. N. Bushby, J.P., the Rev. L. C. Chalmers-Hunt, M.A., Mr. B. L. Cherry, the Rev. C. W. Clarke, M.A., Miss Cotton-Browne, Mr. Septimus Croft, J.P., Mr. Arthur W. Cross, Mr. R. H. Gamlen, Mr. Charles Gayton, Mr. T. T. Greg, M.A., F.S.A., J.P., Mr. R. T. Gunton, Mr. H. R. Wilton Hall, the Rev. A. C. Headlam, D.D., the Hertford Corporation, the Rev. A. B. Hobart-Hampden, M.A., the late Canon H. Jephson, M.A., the Rev. A. G. Langdon, B.A., the Rev. H. A. Lipscomb, M.A., the Rev. J. Traviss Lockwood, Mr. C. J. Longman, J.P., Mr. C. E. Longmore, the Rev. F. W. Low, M.A., Mr. W. E. Maclean, Mr. V. A. Malcolmson, the Rev. J. Mearns, M.A., Mr. Walter Millard, the Rev. W. Mitchell-Carruthers, M.A., Mr. William Morris, the Rev. R. S. Mylne, M.A., B.C.L., F.S.A., the Rev. A. Nairne, M.A., Mr. J. Phillips, J.P., Miss Pollard, Mr. J. R. Pulham, Mr. F. C. Puller, J.P., the Rev. J. E. I. Procter, M.A., Mr. J. H. Round, M.A., LL.D., Mr. Thomas U. Sadleir, Mr. Abel H. Smith, M.A., J.P., the Rev. E. A. Smith, M.A., the Rev. S. M. Stanley, M.A., the Rev. W. T. Stubbs, M.A., the Rev. M. S. Swatman, M.A., the Rev. G. Todd, M.A., Mr. J. Allen Tregelles, Mr. C. J. Veasey, M.A., and the Rev. P. M. Wathen, M.A.

For illustrations and plans the Editor is indebted to the Marquess of Salisbury, Mr. R. T. Andrews, the Editor of the *Architectural Review*, the Editor and Proprietors of *Country Life* (for photographs of Hatfield House, Knebworth House, the Wyck and Balls Park), Mr. V. A. Malcolmson, Major F. Skeet, and Monsignor Bernard Ward.

A HISTORY OF
HERTFORDSHIRE

TOPOGRAPHY

THE HUNDRED OF HITCHIN

CONTAINING THE PARISHES OF

HITCHIN	KINGS WALDEN [1]
ICKLEFORD	LILLEY
IPPOLLITTS	OFFLEY
KIMPTON	PIRTON [2]

This hundred was generally called the 'half hundred of Hiz (Hitchin),' its Domesday assessment working out at about 40 hides. During the 15th, 16th and 17th centuries it is sometimes referred to as the hundred of Polettes (Ippollitts).[3]

All the places above named are mentioned in the hundred in 1086 except Ickleford and Ippollitts; Ickleford was then included in Pirton, and Ippollitts is represented by the manor of Almshoe. The Domesday Survey also places within the hundred Westoning (Bedfordshire), Welei, Wilei, Flesmere, Hexton and Bendish, a hamlet in St. Paul's Walden.[4] Though Westoning was attached by its tenure to this hundred, its 'wara' or place of assessment was in the hundred of Manshead in Bedfordshire.[5] Welei is possibly Wedelee in Preston, but both this and Welei cannot be identified with certainty.[6] Flesmere[7] or Flexmere[8] remains unidentified, also Leglega, where there was 1 virgate of land (although the latter may possibly be Ley Green to the north of King's Walden); Hexton was transferred to the hundred of Cashio before 1286.[9] Bendish was also added to the same hundred soon after the Survey, probably by the Abbot of St. Albans, to whom Cashio belonged.[10]

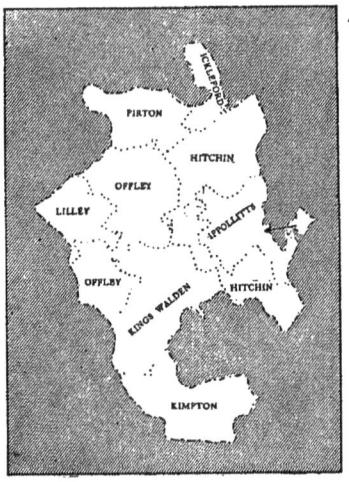

INDEX MAP TO THE HUNDRED OF HITCHIN

The hundred of Hitchin appears to have always belonged to the Crown.[11]

---

[1] St. Paul's Walden is in the hundred of Cashio.
[2] According to *Population Returns* of 1831.
[3] Chan. Inq. p.m. 4 Edw. IV, no. 38; (Ser. ii), ix, 67; xxxiii, 5; Ct. of Wards, Feod. Surv. 17.
[4] *V.C.H. Herts.* i, 302, 304, 316.   [5] Ibid. 302*b*.
[6] Ibid. 297.   [7] Ibid. 304*a*   [8] Ibid. 338*a*.
[9] Ibid. ii, 320.   [10] Ibid. 480.
[11] *Pipe R. 21 Hen. II* (Pipe R. Soc.), 77, &c.; *Rot. Cur. Reg.* (Rec. Com.), i, 164; Assize R. Herts. 323; 325, m. 18d.; *Hund. R.* (Rec. Com.), i, 188 et seq.

A HISTORY OF HERTFORDSHIRE

The three-weekly hundred court[12] was probably originally held at Hitchin, and perhaps later at Ippollitts, judging by the alternative name. There is also record of 'the full hundred court' having been held at Kimpton,[13] and a view of frankpledge was held at Oughton's Head in Pirton in the 14th century.[14] The jurisdiction of the sheriff was limited by the franchises of the lords of various manors within the hundred, including Hitchin,[15] Lilley,[16] Offley St. Ledgers,[17] Wells in Offley,[18] Oddingselles in Pirton,[19] and Dinsley.[20]

In the 17th century a grant of court leet was made to Ralph Radcliffe, lord of Hitchin, in Maidecroft, Ippollitts and Gosmore[21] and to St. John's College, Cambridge, in the manor of Ramerick in Ickleford.[22]

A survey was taken of the hundred as part of the king's possessions in 1651. Within the hundred all waifs, strays, goods of felons and fugitives belonged to the lord if his bailiff seized them first; but if they were first seized by the bailiff of the lord of a manor having a court leet the profits went to such lord. The lord of the hundred also had the return and execution of all writs within the hundred. A three-weekly court was held, and the whole value was £3.[23]

[12] Chan. Inq. p.m. 3 Edw. III (1st nos.), no. 7.
[13] Assize R. 340, m. 1; *Cal. Pat.* 1324–7, p. 135.
[14] Chan. Inq. p.m. 15 Edw. II, no. 4.
[15] *Plac. de Quo. Warr.* (Rec. Com.), 288; *Hund. R.* (Rec. Com.), i, 194.
[16] *Hund. R.* (Rec. Com.), i, 188.   [17] Pat. 4 Edw. VI, pt. ix, m. 35.
[18] Chan. Inq. p.m. 16 Ric. II, pt. ii, m. 34.
[19] Assize R. 325; Pat. 29 Hen. VIII, pt. ii, m. 18.
[20] Assize R. 323, m. 36, 48; *Plac. de Quo. Warr.* (Rec. Com.), 281.
[21] Pat. 14 Jas. I, pt. xii.
[22] Ibid. 15 Jas. I, pt. xviii, no. 12.
[23] Parl. Surv. Herts. no. 2.

HITCHIN HUNDRED

HITCHIN

Hicche, Hiz (xi cent.); Hicche (xiii cent.); Huthe, Huche, Huchine, Hytchen (xiv cent.); Lutchon[1] (xv cent.). The parish of Hitchin includes besides the town the three extensive hamlets of Walsworth on the north-west covering 1,051 acres, Preston, a straggling village in the south, having an area of 1,118 acres, and Langley still further south, which extends over 1,626 acres.[2] The parish of Ippollitts, which was a chapelry to Hitchin, lies between the main portion of Hitchin and the almost detached hamlet of Langley and is inclosed by them on three sides. The parish of Hitchin exclusive of its hamlets covers the upper portion of the basin of the River Hiz, which rises at Well Head just beyond the south-west border of the parish and flows north-east. The River Oughton, rising at Oughton Head on the west, flows north-east, forming the parish boundary and joins the Hiz. The River Purwell, which has its source at Nine Springs in the parish of Great Wymondley, flows across Walsworth Common and joins the Hiz. The surface of the land near these streams is only some 190 ft. above the ordnance datum, but the ground rises to the south, east and west, gradually reaching a height of 300 ft. on the north-east border of the parish. The greater part of Preston hamlet is considerably higher and lies on a ridge of the Chilterns. In the centre of this hamlet at its highest part the ground has a height of 507 ft., and from here there is a slight incline towards the south-east which continues through the hamlet of Langley down to a height of 309 ft.

The soil is chalk,[3] and is mentioned by Norden as 'a kinde of chalke which they call Hurlocke, a stonie Marle more fit to make lime then to soyle the grounde, yet beeing mixed with a more fragile and gentle Marle, which also aboundeth there, they find it very helpfull to their corne fields.'[4] The common fields of Walsworth hamlet were inclosed in 1766–7,[5] and those of Hitchin called Bury Mead and Cock Mead in 1877 and 1886,[6] but there are several open fields in Hitchin to this day.

In the 16th century a great quantity of malt was made at Hitchin,[7] and brewing is still an important industry of the town. Corn is the chief product of the district, and there has been a famous corn market here for more than 300 years.[8] Potatoes, peppermint, and lavender are also much cultivated. Lavender is grown in the fields to the north of the town and is distilled by two large firms, Messrs. Perks & Llewelyn and Messrs. W. Ransom & Son.

Palaeolithic implements have been found in and near Hitchin,[9] and pottery of the late Celtic period has also been found in the neighbourhood.[10] A barrow of pre-Roman date to the south of the Icknield Way was opened and found to contain burnt bones, a blade of copper, and a clay urn.[11] Coins of Offa have been discovered and Roman objects have been found.

Place-names which occur in records of this parish in the 17th century are Cleypitts, Conigre, Ladder Peece, Pattens, Hyover, Toyes, Saffron Close and Silverstreet Close.[12]

The original plan of Hitchin followed that usual in country market towns. It stands on an important road and clusters around a large triangular market-place formed by the widening of the road. The market-place originally extended from the south side of Tilehouse Street on the south to Bancroft on the north, and from the east side of Sun Street on the east to the west side of Bucklersbury and High Street on the west. The actual market-place is now restricted to the small middle portion of this area, the remainder as at St. Albans, Berkhampstead and elsewhere having been built over at first by permanent stalls and then by shops. These encroachments began probably in the 13th or 14th century, but by 1470 we have evidence of continuous tenure here by the lease of two stalls for forty years.[13] By 1603 the market-place had evidently been built upon for some time,[14] the courts being held in one of the so-called 'stalls.'[15] Facing the market-place stood the numerous inns which formerly existed in the town,[16] and the houses of the townsfolk with their back premises extending as now to the river on the east side and to Paynes Park and Grammar School Walk on the west. On the east side of the market-place stands the church of St. Mary with its large churchyard. The extension of the town along Bridge Street and Tilehouse Street, and a little later along what is now Queen Street, is of mediaeval date, and was possibly made at the time of the founding of the priory in 1317. The town has been developing rapidly of late years. Houses have been built on the higher land on the east and south sides and near the railway station, which lies about half a mile to the east of the town.

Hitchin is fortunate in having retained so many of its ancient houses, though most of them have been refronted and much altered in the 18th and 19th centuries. In Bancroft or Bancroft Street,[17] at the north end of the market-place, are many old houses. On the west side is a house now known as the Croft, which was built early in the 15th century, although since much altered, and was occupied until recently by the Tuke family. A little to the south on the same side is 'The Brotherhood,' probably the hall of the gild of our Lady, founded in 1475. It is a building of the 15th century, covered with rough-cast, with a tiled roof. It was originally rectangular in plan, and the ground floor, which was divided by

---

[1] *Cal. Papal Letters*, iv, 349.
[2] In the 16th century it was said 'Hitchin is a market town and the parish is dispersed in diverse hamelettes distant from the parish church 3 miles some more, some less' (Chant. Cert. [Augm. Off.], 27, no. 17).
[3] *V.C.H. Herts.* i, Geol. Map.
[4] Norden, *Spec. Brit. Pars* (1903), 19.
[5] *Dep. Keeper's Rep.* xxvii, App. 2.
[6] *Blue Bk. Incl. Awards*, 64.
[7] Norden, loc. cit.
[8] Ibid.
[9] *V.C.H. Herts.* i, 228, 230, 234.
[10] Ibid. 236.
[11] Ibid. 244.
[12] Add. MS. 16273.
[13] Ct. R. (Gen. Ser.), portf. 177, no. 40.
[14] Exch. Dep. Hil. 45 Eliz. no. 9.
[15] Parl. Surv. Herts. no. 22.
[16] Besides the inns hereafter mentioned the following appear in the Hitchin parish registers: the 'Vine' in 1617–18, the 'Bull' in 1645 and the 'Rose and Crown' in 1652 (MS. marked Hitchin in Lewis Evans Coll.).
[17] This name is found as early as the 15th century (Ct. R. [Gen. Ser.], portf. 177, no. 40).

3

transverse partitions, is now used for shops, whilst the upper floor, which formed the hall 48 ft. by 17 ft., with a fine open timbered roof, now ceiled, is divided into rooms. Four trusses of this roof still remain in position. They are of oak and have moulded wall-posts with moulded capitals and bases, wall-plates and purlins, cambered tie-beams and queen posts, with curved spandrel pieces and wind-braces. The timbered mullioned windows have apparently been renewed, as has also a great part of the outer walls. At the apex of each of the two gables are terra-cotta figures of a man on horseback, which have been copied from the originals still remaining in one of the shops.

On the east side of Bancroft is a large 15th-century house[18] of timber and plaster, with a tiled roof. It is L-shaped in plan with a hall in the main wing facing the street. To the north was a solar wing, beyond which was a high archway. During the latter half of the 16th century an upper story was formed in the hall by the insertion of a floor projecting on the west front and a gable built at the north end, the roof being raised to give additional height. At the same time a chimney-stack was added at the north end. Nothing beyond one tie-beam of the oaken hall roof now remains, with mortise holes for curved angle brackets. A little further south is the 'Hermitage,' now a portion of the residence of Mr. Frederic Seebohm, LL.D., which mainly consisted of two houses converted into one in the 18th century with additions of that time. Another large 15th-century house, now divided into three and numbered 86, 87, 88 Bancroft, stands a little to the south. It was much altered in the 19th century, and has now a timber frame filled in different parts with plaster, rough-cast, weather-boards and brickwork. It is L-shaped in plan with a hall of four bays about 12 ft. each and 20 ft. span, facing the street. The solar wing lies to the north and has an archway with a room over. The upper story projects and has a gable at each end with a modern bay-window between them. At the north end of the hall is a panelled canopy of a dais divided into square panels by ogee-moulded ribs with bosses at the junctions which are now lost. There is some 17th-century panelling in the solar, and at the back are some old buildings, probably of the same date as the house. Numbers 89 and 90 at one time apparently formed one house of a similar type, but were very much altered and refronted in the 18th century. Fortmill Lane branches off here to Queen Street. A little way down is the 'Grange,' a 17th-century house much altered in the next century. Beyond Fortmill Lane stands the church. Lower down, on the north-east corner of the market-place, to the south of the church, are the remains of a 15th-century house of the court-yard plan, now used as a dwelling-house and shops. The east wing was rebuilt in the 17th century and altered in the 18th century, but the west wing of the original building remains. The over-hanging gatehouse, with an entrance archway having heavy moulded timbers with curved brackets, still exists. Traces of the north wing have been discovered, but the south wing has been entirely destroyed. Sun Street contains on its eastern side several houses of the 17th century and earlier; they

VIEW IN BANCROFT, HITCHIN

[18] It is now divided into two and numbered 83 and 84.

HITCHIN : OLD HOUSES IN BANCROFT

HITCHIN CHURCH : THE NAVE LOOKING EAST

have, however, been mostly refronted in the 18th century. The more important are the Angel Inn, mentioned in 1632,[19] which is of two stories of timber and plaster and has a tiled roof. It has remains of mediaeval work, although its appearance has been much changed by later alterations. It was originally an L-shaped building facing on to the market-place. It may have had shops on the ground floor facing the street and a hall and small chamber over them. In the 17th century a staircase was added in the angle between the wings and a small addition made at the back. The upper story projects both in front and at the back. An archway of a type usual in old coaching inns leads into the yard, and is supported on 16th-century brackets carved with birds and flowers. The gables at the back have carved barge-boards—the one more elaborately carved is of the 15th century, and the other of the early 17th century. There is a good 17th-century staircase with moulded hand-rail and turned balusters. A little southward is the Sun Inn, which was apparently built in the last few years of the 16th century and is of brick and plastered timber with a tile roof. It was refronted in the 18th century and later much altered. At the back is a courtyard, which is approached by an archway from the street. It was here that the Commissaries' Court was held in 1639,[20] when Joseph Wigg of North Mimms refused to remove his hat upon admonition of the judge, saying he would put off his hat if the judge would lend him a cap; 'he knew where he was : in a place made of wood, stones and other things.' Wigg's example was followed by John Clarke. A new assembly room was built at the 'Sun' in 1770.[21] At this inn, too, the courts of the manor of Portman and Foreign are still held at Michaelmas. Further on, near to Bridge Street, is an old 17th-century brick house with a tile roof. It is rectangular in plan ; the windows on the first floor have wooden mullions and transoms, but those on the ground floor were altered in the 18th century. On the north side is a three-centred arch leading into a yard at the back. On the western side of the market-place there are also many houses of the 17th century or possibly earlier, but here again they have been refronted in the 18th century. In High Street, formerly known as Cock Street, is the Cock Hotel, built of timber with plaster and brick filling of probably the 16th century. It is an L-shaped building with a large yard at the back. It is mentioned in the Hitchin Registers in 1617. In Bucklersbury, which probably takes its name from a house which is referred to in the 17th century,[22] is the George Inn, a two-storied building originally built in the 16th century or possibly earlier, but now much changed owing to frequent alterations. It has in the middle facing the street a high archway leading into the yard, with a high overhanging gable above. The upper story projects. A little further south is the Hart Inn, probably of the last few years of the 16th century. It is of two stories of plastered timber with a tiled roof, and was much altered in the 19th century. It has a projecting upper story and an archway leading into the yard behind, around which are plastered timbered buildings with projecting stories. At the front of this archway is a pair of 17th-century gates.

The houses in Bridge Street are mostly of brick, but there are a few timber and plaster buildings. No. 2 is a small 16th-century house covered with rough-cast and having a tiled roof. Its principal interest is two early 16th-century barge-boards, one with a guilloche pattern and the other with dragons in low relief. On the opposite side Nos. 21 to 23 are interesting old timber and plaster houses with tiled roofs, which may be of about the year 1600. The middle house has a bay window and probably an original door. Nos. 18 and 19 originally formed one 16th-century house of timber and plaster with a tiled roof. On the west side the upper story projects over the river, and on the north over the street. It has a framed archway to the yard behind. At the east end of Bridge Street, looking on to what is called the Triangle, is an interesting timber and plaster house of the 15th century, now much altered and divided into several houses. It is L-shaped in plan with an archway to the yard at the back. The upper story overhangs and had originally an open roof.

Nos. 8 to 11 on the south side of Tilehouse[23] Street were originally one house dating from the early part of the 17th century, but have been much altered. The Three Tuns Inn with the house adjoining it, numbered 11, formed another house of the same date, which has the usual archway leading into a yard. No. 19 is also of the same date and contains some original panelling reset. On the north side is the Coopers' Arms Inn, said to have been the Tilers' Gild Hall. It is built of stone with a tiled roof and dates back to the middle of the 15th century. It was originally of the courtyard type, but only the south and west wings of it now remain. The south wing, which faces on to the street, contains what remains of the hall, which had an open timbered roof, two trusses of which are still in existence. An additional story, however, was made by the insertion of an upper floor which projected into the street, probably in the 17th century. There is an archway from the street to the yard behind.

The old Free School at the west end of Tilehouse Street, now a dwelling-house, was built about 1650,[24] but has been much altered. It is of two stories of plastered timber and brick with a tiled roof.

There are many old and interesting houses in Queen Street, formerly Dead Street and later Back Lane, with arched entrances into the yards behind. Amongst them there may be specially mentioned No. 6, a small 17th-century house of timber and plaster and tiled roof, with an overhanging gabled front. Nos. 103 and 104 were formerly one house, probably the earliest house now remaining in Hitchin. This was built at the end of the 14th or beginning of the 15th century, and has masonry foundations with a plaster and timber superstructure and tiled roof. Originally it had a central hall with a kitchen wing on the north side, which, together with a part of the

---

[19] Recov. R. East. 8 Chas. I.
[20] Cal. S. P. Dom. 1639, pp. 146, 153.
[21] MS. marked Hitchin in Lewis Evans Coll. at Herts. Co. Mus.
[22] Recov. R. 21 Jas. I, rot. 12.

[23] Brick earth is found at Hitchin, and there were probably tile works here in mediaeval times. There were brick works in the early part of the 19th century (MS. marked Hitchin in Lewis Evans Coll.).

[24] In a MS. marked Hitchin in the Lewis Evans Coll. at the Herts. Co. Mus. it is stated that in the wall of the Free School is a date which seems to be T. H. 1641.

A HISTORY OF HERTFORDSHIRE

hall, has been destroyed; and a solar wing of two stories on the south, the outlines of which can still be traced. No early details of the interior remain except parts of two trusses of the hall roof, of the hammer-beam type, 19 ft. span, with moulded wall-plates. The next two houses, which originally formed one house, are of a little later date, being of the 15th century. The hall appears to have been in the upper story which projects over the street. On the overhanging gable above the archway on the south is the date 1729 in the plaster, but the posts supporting the beam of the arch have 15th-century moulded capitals supporting the curved angle brackets.

THE THREE TUNS INN, TILEHOUSE STREET

To the west of Queen Street, near the River Hiz, are the Biggin Almshouses, built in the early part of the 17th century. They consist of four wings built round a small courtyard, on the west side of which is a wooden colonnade forming a cloister. Each wing contains a small set of rooms on each floor. They are of two stories and an attic and are built of timber and plaster and brickwork. They have been much altered at different dates.

There is a Corn Exchange in the town, erected in 1851. The new town hall in Brand Street is dated 1901. This has superseded an older one built in 1840. Among other public buildings may be noticed the Mechanics' Institute and public subscription library adjoining the old town hall. There is a large infirmary called the North Herts and South Beds Infirmary in the Bedford Road, which was erected in 1840. The Home for girls of weak and defective intelligence, in the Triangle, was built in 1893. The Girls' Grammar School, which was built at the cost of £13,000, was opened in July 1908. The Boys' Grammar School is a continuation of the Free School founded by John Mattock in 1650 and removed to new buildings about twenty years ago.

Among the past inhabitants of Hitchin was George Chapman the poet. He is best known as translator of Homer's Iliad and Odyssey, but also wrote other poetry and plays. In *Euthymiae Raptus, or the Tears of Peace*, he alludes to having spent his childhood in the neighbourhood of Hitchin.[25] William Drage, a believer in astrology and witchcraft, and Maurice Johnson, the antiquary, lived here in the 17th century.[26] The 19th century claims Sir Henry Bessemer, the inventor of a new process for making steel, and Robert Bentley, botanist, who was born here. James Hack Tuke, philanthropist, spent a part of his life at Hitchin. Samuel Lucas, a well-known amateur artist, belonged to an old Hitchin family. Good examples of his art are to be seen in the town hall at Hitchin and in the British Museum. Frederick Chapman, publisher and originator of the *Fortnightly Review*, was born in Cock Street in a house said to have belonged to his collateral ancestor George Chapman the poet.

BOROUGH

Hitchin was undoubtedly an important manor and soke before the Conquest, but there is no evidence from the entries in the Domesday Survey that it was a borough. It was probably not till the middle of the 12th century, when the Baliols were lords, that it developed into an inchoate borough.[27] This was the time when so many such market towns arose in consequence of the prosperity of the wool trade, which enabled the townspeople to purchase rights from the nobles and other landowners impoverished by the civil wars. The market at Hitchin was held by prescription, and the right to hold a fair was obtained in 1221.[28] By 1268 we have evidence that the borough was farmed to the burgesses at a rent of 8½ marks.[29] As we find at the

[25] *Dict. Nat. Biog.*
[26] Ibid.
[27] The present church dates from this period and may indicate a rebuilding when the town acquired such borough rights as it had.
[28] Fine R. 6 Hen. III, pt. i, m. 9.
[29] Inq. p.m. 53 Hen. III, no. 43.

same time a distinction between tenants of the borough and those of the manor, we may infer there was then the borough or portmote court as well as the manor or foreign court organized in the same manner as we find them later. A reference to a fulling mill at this date [29a] possibly indicates one source of wealth of the burgesses, but the position of the town on the road to the north may give a more important reason for its prosperity.

Hitchin continued to be called a borough in 1375–6,[30] and it appeared before the justices in eyre as other boroughs by twelve jurors apart from the county in 1248,[31] 1287[32] and 1341.[32] But it was not a fully developed borough, for we find no evidence of burgage rents; it never received a charter of incorporation and never returned a member to Parliament. It was one of those numerous little manorial towns which existed throughout England with varying liberties which bordered upon borough rights.

The town was divided into three wards—namely, Bancroft Ward, Bridge Street Ward and Tilehouse Street Ward—and was governed by a bailiff appointed at the lord's court, and two constables for the town and two for the foreign and two head boroughs for each ward. Besides these there were in 1819 two ale conners, two leather searchers and sealers, one bellman, who was also watchman and town crier.[34]

In 1883 the Crown sold its market rights to the local authorities for £4,000, adding the land on which the market was held as a gift.[35] The market was always celebrated for its corn,[36] and it is said that corn was always free of tolls there.[37]

A fair, as mentioned above, was granted to the lord of Hitchin in 1221. At the beginning of the next century another fair was granted to Robert de Kendale, this fair to be held on the vigil, day and morrow of the Decollation of St. John the Baptist (28–30 August).[38] In 1475 a grant was made to the fraternity or gild here of two fairs, each of three days' duration, with courts of pie powder. These two fairs were held on Wednesday in Easter week and the feast of the Translation of Edward the Confessor (13 October) and the days immediately preceding and following.[39] After the Dissolution they were granted to Ranulph Burgh and Robert Beverley.[40] At the end of the 16th century three fairs were held, in Easter week, on St. Edward's Day, and at Michaelmas.[41] These fairs were leased to John Fitz Acherley with the mills.[42] By 1792 two annual fairs only took place, each lasting one day. The fair days at this time were Easter Tuesday and Whit Tuesday.[43] Fairs are now held on these days and on one day following each. There are also two fairs at Preston held on the first Wednesday in May and on the Wednesday before 29 October.[44]

There is record of a water mill in Hitchin in 1248, which was held by William de Lindlegh,[45] and had been held by William his father. In the 16th century there were two water mills on the demesne lands there.[46] They were called le Shotting Mill and le Porte Mill, and were leased in 1594–5 to John Fitz Acherley for thirty-one years,[47] and other leases were made later.[48] There are still two mills known by these names.[49] Shotting Mill seems to have been known also as Sheekling Mill.[50] At the beginning of the next century there appears to have been another water mill called 'le Malt-milne,' which was granted to Edward Ferrers and Francis Phelipps.[51]

In 1670 a suit arose on account of a windmill belonging to Sir Edward Papworth in Charlton, built some thirteen or fourteen years before, which was said to take away some of the trade from the king's two water mills.[52] This may have been on the site of the mill in Charlton, mentioned as early as 1177,[53] which in 1329 was held by Walter de Nevill.[54] In the 19th century there was a mill called Grove Mill, which was previously known as Burnt Mill.[55]

Hitch Wood, in the south of the parish, was once far more extensive than it is at present. By the end of the 16th century the part of this wood near the town had begun to disappear,[56] but it still extended into Ippollitts, Langley, Minsden and Preston,[57] and its area must have been very considerable, for the woods and underwoods were then granted to the copyholders for the large sum of £266 16s.[58]

MANORS

The manor of HITCHIN was the head of the group of Hertfordshire manors held by Earl Harold, to which William I succeeded after the Conquest. These at the time of the Domesday Survey were farmed out together by the sheriff, and treated for some purposes as one integral manor.[59] The manors which belonged to or 'lay in' the manor of Hitchin were Wymondley, Mendlesdene (Minsden), Welei, Westone, Waldenei (King's Walden), Wavedene (Wandon), Cerletone (Charlton), Deneslai (Temple Dinsley), Offley, Welle (Wellbury in Offley), Wilei, Flesmere, Hexton, Lilley, Flexmere, Leglege [60] (Ley Green in King's Walden [?]), assessed in all at a total of some 37½ hides. Of these manors two were attached to Hitchin by Harold himself. These were Wymondley, which he stole from the nuns of Chatteris, as the shire mote testified,[61] and Hexton.[62] King's Walden, Charlton and Offley were attached after the Conquest by Ilbert Sheriff of Hertfordshire,[63] while Dinsley, Wellbury and Welei were attached by Peter de Valoines, his successor.[64]

Hitchin itself was assessed at 5 hides only, although there was land for thirty-eight ploughs (including the land belonging to the minster).[65] The total value

---

[29a] Inq. p.m. 53 Hen. III, no. 43.
[30] Ibid. 49 Edw. III, no. 75.
[31] Assize R. 318.
[32] Ibid. 325. Hitchin is omitted in the list of township which appeared separately in 1315–16 (ibid. 333).
[33] Ibid. 337.
[34] Seebohm, *Engl. Village Community*, 1c, 445.
[35] *Rep. of Roy. Com. on Markets and Fairs*, xiii (1), 124.
[36] Norden, *Spec. Brit. Pars* (1903), 4.
[37] Seebohm, op. cit. 447.
[38] Chart. R. 11 Edw. II, no. 11.
[39] Cal. Pat. 1467–77, p. 542.

[40] Pat. 2 Edw. VI, pt. iv, m. 27.
[41] Norden, op. cit. 4.
[42] Pat. 37 Eliz. pt. xii, m. 28.
[43] *Rep. on Markets and Fairs*, i, 172.
[44] Ibid.
[45] Assize R. 318, m. 12.
[46] Mins. Accts. 24 Hen. VII–1 Hen. VIII, no. 61.
[47] Pat. 17 Eliz. pt. xii, m. 28.
[48] Land Rev. Misc. Bk. cliii, fol. 16.
[49] *Sess. R.* (Herts. Co. Rec.), ii, 36, 51.
[50] Exch. Dep. East. 22 Chas. II, no. 24.
[51] Pat. 7 Jas. I, pt. xxxiii.
[52] Exch. Dep. East. 22 Chas. II, no. 24.
[53] Pipe R. 23 Hen. II, m. 2.

[54] Chan. Inq. p.m. 3 Edw. III (1st nos.), no. 53.
[55] Seebohm, op. cit. 447, 451.
[56] Norden, op. cit. 19.
[57] Chan. Inq. p.m. (Ser. 2), cclviii, 76.
[58] Pat. 6 Jas. I, pt. xxiii; Seebohm, op. cit. 446.
[59] *V.C.H. Herts.* i, 292, 304b.
[60] Ibid. 301a, 302, 303, 304, 334a, 338a.
[61] Ibid. 301a.
[62] Ibid. 304b.
[63] Ibid. 302b, 303.
[64] Ibid. 303, 304b.
[65] Ibid. 302a.

A HISTORY OF HERTFORDSHIRE

of Hitchin and its appurtenances was £106, whilst the sokes belonging to the manor were worth £40.[66] The services known as 'avera' and 'inward,' rendered by some of these manors, as due from the sokemen of the king, point to Hitchin's having been once ancient demesne.[67] The services, which were carrying services performed with a horse and cart, are distinctive of the two counties of Hertford and Cambridge, and in Hertfordshire the inward (inguard) is peculiar to Hitchin and its sub-manors.[68] Extents of the manor in the 13th and 14th centuries mention the services as owed by the customary tenants of the manor.[69]

According to the legend of the foundation of Waltham Abbey, as related in the 12th-century tract 'De Inventione sanctae Crucis,' Hitchin, or a part of Hitchin,[70] was held with Waltham, co. Essex, in the time of Canute by Tovi 'Pruda,' staller to Canute, a man of great importance, ranking second only to the king. He is said to have granted both Waltham and Hitchin to the church he founded at Waltham for the reception of the Holy Cross.[71] After the death of Tovi, however, his son Adelstan, who succeeded to the lands his father held as staller, forfeited these possessions, which were granted by King Edward the Confessor to Earl Harold.[72] A grant of Waltham was made by Harold to his new foundation there, and confirmed by Edward the Confessor.[73] The charter of confirmation mentions Hitchin as also in the possession of the abbey, but whether it was given by Harold at the same time as Waltham is not clear.[74] No further trace, however, of any connexion with the abbey has been found. It is certain from the Domesday Survey that Earl Harold had held the manor, but in 1086 it was in the hands of William the Conqueror.

In the 13th century it was deposed by the jurors of the hundred that Hitchin was granted by William Rufus to Bernard de Baliol.[75] Nothing, however, is known of this Bernard before the reign of Stephen, and it seems more likely that the grant, if made by William II, was to Guy de Baliol, the founder of the English house, who is said to have received lands from William.[76] Bernard de Baliol was certainly holding before 1153.[77] The Bernard de Baliol, one of the northern barons who raised the siege of Alnwick and took William the Lion prisoner, was apparently his son.[78] The younger Bernard was succeeded by his son Eustace, and Eustace by Hugh, his son.[79] Hugh de Baliol mortgaged the manor to Benedict, a Jew of London, about 1204.[80] It descended to his son John de Baliol, who died in 1268,[81] after which his widow Devorgilda held it in dower.[82] His two elder sons Hugh and Alexander died without issue before 1278, and a younger son John then succeeded to the lands.[83] This John was crowned King of Scotland in 1292. He lost the kingdom in 1296, and his lands were forfeited.

The manor of Hitchin was shortly afterwards granted by Edward I to Roger l'Estrange, formerly justice of the forest for the south of Trent, for the term of his life.[84] In 1306 the reversion of the manor was granted to John of Britanny, the king's nephew, together with the other Baliol lands,[85] but two years later the reversion was granted to Robert Kendale while John of Britanny was still living.[86] Robert Kendale, who was Constable of Dover Castle and Warden of the Cinque Ports,[87] held the manor with his wife Margaret until his death in 1330.[88] His son Edward succeeded to the property on the death of his mother in 1347.[89] Edward Kendale died in January 1372-3,[90] and was succeeded by his eldest son Edward, who, however, only survived his father by about two years, dying in July 1375.[91] Elizabeth his mother and Thomas his brother and heir both died in the following September.[92] Elizabeth widow of Edward, who married Thomas Barre, received dower in one third of two thirds of the manor.[93] Beatrice wife of Robert Turk was her brother's heir,[94] but could not inherit Hitchin, as it was held in tail-male. The two thirds of the property therefore reverted to the Crown and were granted to Alice Perrers, the king's mistress, for her life.[95] She forfeited in 1377 under an Act of the Good Parliament,[96] and in 1380 the manor was granted to Hugh de Segrave for life.[97] In 1382 he further received a grant of an annual payment in compensation for the third still held by Elizabeth widow of Edward Kendale.[98] After the death of Hugh de Segrave the manor was granted in 1387 to Edmund Duke of York,[99] and confirmed to

KENDALE. *Argent bend vert and a label gules.*

BALIOL. *Gules a voided scutcheon argent.*

---

[66] V.C.H. Herts. i, 304b.
[67] Assize R. 325.
[68] V.C.H. Herts. i, 269, 271, 273.
[69] Cal. Doc. of Scotland, i, 2514; Exch. Proc. bdle. 144, no. 133; Chan. Inq. p.m. 1 Ric. II, no. 30.
[70] It is suggested by Mr. Seebohm that 'Hicche,' owned by Tovi, is the 2 hides which in 1086 belonged to the 'monasterium' of the vill, and which formed the Rectory Manor (q.v.).
[71] Cott. MS. Jul. D. vi.
[72] Ibid.
[73] Kemble, *Cod. Dipl.* dcccxiii.
[74] See Huyshe, *Royal Manor of Hitchin,* 8 et seq. [75] Assize R. 323, 325.
[76] See *Dict. Nat. Biog.* s.v. Balliol.
[77] See charter, Dugdale, *Mon.* vii, 820. This charter is witnessed by Eustace son of King Stephen, who died in 1153.

[78] *Dict. Nat. Biog.*
[79] Ibid.
[80] See Pipe R. 6 John, m. 3 d. See also for Hugh Feet of F. Herts. 6 Hen. III; *Red Bk. of Exch.* (Rolls Ser.), 499, 505.
[81] See *Testa de Nevill* (Rec. Com.), 266, 280, 281; Chan. Inq. p.m. 53 Hen. III, no. 43.
[82] *Hund. R.* (Rec. Com.), i, 194; Exch. Proc. bdle. 144, no. 133.
[83] G.E.C. *Peerage,* s.v. Balliol; Fine R. 7 Edw. I, no. 14.
[84] Exch. K.R. Extents, Herts. 396; *Feud. Aids,* ii, 428.
[85] *Cal. Pat.* 1301-7, p. 470.
[86] Ibid. 1307-13, pp. 79, 133, 139. A grant for life was changed into one in tail-male. [87] Ibid. p. 545.
[88] Chan. Inq. p.m. 4 Edw. III, no. 26.

[89] See ibid. 19 Edw. III (2nd nos.), no. 41; 21 Edw. III, pt. i, no. 19; *Abbrev. Rot. Orig.* (Rec. Com.), ii, 187; *Feud. Aids,* ii, 437.
[90] Chan. Inq. p.m. 47 Edw. III (1st nos.), no. 20; Inq. a.q.d. file 340, no. 4.
[91] Chan. Inq. p.m. 49 Edw. III, pt. i, no. 74. [92] Ibid. no. 75.
[93] Ibid. 4 Ric. II, no. 34. This was due to the fact that the elder Elizabeth outlived her son Edward, who consequently never held more than two-thirds of the manor, the other third being his mother's dower. [94] Ibid. 49 Edw. III, no. 75.
[95] Ibid. 1 Ric. II, no. 30.
[96] *Parl. R.* iii, 12b.
[97] *Cal. Pat.* 1377-81, p. 304.
[98] Ibid. 1381-5, p. 156.
[99] Ibid. 1385-9, p. 292; Chart. R. 14 Ric. II, m. 13, no. 8.

HITCHIN : COOPERS' ARMS INN, TILEHOUSE STREET

HITCHIN HUNDRED

him by Henry IV in 1399.[100] The duke died in 1402, his widow Joan surviving until 1434, when the manor descended to Richard Duke of York, grandson of Edmund,[101] who was killed at the battle of Wakefield in 1460. His son Edward Duke of York was crowned King of England in 1461. In the same year he granted Hitchin to his mother Cicely Duchess of York for life.[102] The reversion was granted by Henry VII to his queen Elizabeth in 1491.[103] In 1509 Henry VIII granted the manor to the Princess Katherine of Arragon on his marriage with her,[104] and in 1534 it formed part of the dower of Queen Anne Boleyn.[105] Ralph Sadleir, gentleman of the King's Privy Chamber, was appointed steward and bailiff of the lordship in 1539 in place of William Coffyn deceased.[106] In 1603 James I granted the manor to his queen Anne,[107] and in 1619 it was conveyed by the king to trustees for the use of the Prince of Wales.[108] A Parliamentary survey was taken of it in 1650, as having lately belonged to Queen Henrietta Maria.[109] From the survey it appears that quit-rents were payable to the manor from tenants in Hitchin, Offley, Walden, Preston and Kimpton. The freeholders paid for relief one year's quit-rent, but nothing on alienation; the copyholders paid half a year's quit-rents on alienation and were admitted for a term of forty years, renewable on the payment of another quit-rent, but owed no heriots. The woods on the manor had been granted in 1619 to trustees to the use of the copyholders for a sum of £266 16s. The

EDMUND Duke of York. *The royal arms of EDWARD III with the difference of a label argent with three roundels gules on each pendant.*

RICHARD Duke of York. *FRANCE quartered with ENGLAND differenced with the same label.*

ANNE of Denmark. *Or powdered with hearts gules three leopards azure having golden crowns.*

HENRIETTA MARIA of France. *Azure three fleurs de lis or.*

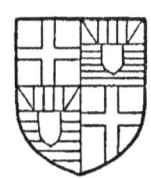

ELIZABETH of York. *Or a cross gules, for DE BURGH, quartered with Barry or and azure a chief or with two piles between two gyrons azure therein and a scutcheon argent over all, for MORTIMER.*

courts baron and leet were kept in one of the stalls in the market-place belonging to the lord of the manor. The common fines, law-day money, head-silver, and tithing silver paid at the Michaelmas leet amounted to £1 15s., the fines, &c., from the courts to £6. In the same year the trustees for the sale of the royal lands conveyed the manor to Samuel Chidley.[110] After the Restoration the queen mother resumed possession.[111] It was held by Catherine, queen of Charles II, and after her death was granted on a lease to Francis Lord Holles for seventy-five years.[112] Leases of the manor continued to be made down to 1843,[113] when the last expired, and Hitchin has since remained in the hands of the Crown.

In the 13th century Devorgilda de Baliol claimed assize of bread and ale, but on what grounds was not known, as this privilege had previously always been in the hands of the king.[114] Free warren was granted to Robert de Kendale and his heirs by Edward II in 1318.[115]

In the survey of 1650 the boundaries of the manor are given as follows: 'The bounds of Hitchin begin at Altonheade, thence to a place called Burford Ray, thence to a water-mill called Hide Mill, thence to a hill called Welberry Hill, thence to a place called Bosrendell, thence to a water-mill called Purwell Mill, thence to a river called Ippolletts Brook, thence to Maiden Croft Lane, thence to a place called Wellhead, thence to Stubborne Bush, thence to Offley Cross, thence to Fiveborrowe Hill, and thence to said Altonheade.'

In the time of Edward the Confessor the manor of *DINSLEY* (Deneslai, xi cent.; Dineslea, Dineslega, xii cent.; Dunsle, Dynesle, Dinglo, xiii cent.; Dyonyse, xvii cent.) was in the possession of Earl Harold, and in 1086 it was held by King William.[116] It was assessed at the time of the Survey at 7 hides. It had been held of Harold by two sokemen as two separate manors, but when it came into King William's

---

[100] Pat. 1 Hen. IV, pt. iv, m. 27.
[101] Chan. Inq. p.m. 12 Hen. VI, no. 43.
[102] Pat. 1 Edw. IV, pt. iv, m. 1. Confirmed by Ric. III in 1485 (ibid. 1 Ric. III, pt. v, m. 14).
[103] Ibid. 7 Hen. VII, m. 8.
[104] L. and P. Hen. VIII, i, 155.
[105] Ibid. vii, 352.
[106] Ibid. xiv (2), g. 780 (42).
[107] Add. MS. 6693, fol. 73 (copy of patent).
[108] Pat. 17 Jas. I, pt. i, no. 4.
[109] Parl. Surv. Herts. no. 22.
[110] Partic. for sale of estates of Chas. I (Augm. Off.), G 9.
[111] See *Cal. S. P. Dom.* 1667–8, p. 89.
[112] Land Rev. Misc. Bks. cliii, fol. 16.
[113] See Clutterbuck, *Hist. and Antiq. of Herts.* iii, 19; Cussans, *Hist. of Herts. Hitchin Hund.* 43.
[114] *Hund. R.* (Rec. Com.), i, 194.
[115] Chart. R. 11 Edw. II, no. 11, m. 4.
[116] *V.C.H. Herts.* i, 303a.

hands he gave it to Ilbert his sheriff for his term of office, and he held the two manors as one.[117] Each of these two manors rendered the service of 2 'averae' and 2 'inwardi.'[118] At the end of this time Ilbert refused to find the customary 'avera' due from the manor, and it was forcibly taken from him by Peter de Valoines, his successor, and Ralph Taillebois, who laid it to the king's manor of Hitchin.[119]

Dinsley was apparently included in the grant of the manor of Hitchin made to Guy or Bernard de Baliol (see above), for in the reign of Stephen Bernard de Baliol granted 15 librates of land at 'Wedelee' (a name used elsewhere for Dinsley), a member of his manor of Hitchin, to the Master and Brothers of the Knights Templars.[120] Other grants of land were made to this order, and together formed the manor of *TEMPLE DINSLEY.* A grant of free warren there was made to them in 1253.[121] They also claimed view of frankpledge, assize of bread and ale and gallows there.[122] In 1309 Ralph de Monchensey and John de Kyreton were appointed to report on the state of the manor[123] preparatory to the suppression of the order, which took place shortly after-

THE KNIGHTS TEMPLARS. *Argent a cross gules and a chief sable.*

THE KNIGHTS HOSPITALLERS. *Gules a cross argent.*

wards.[124] With the other lands of the Templars it passed to the Knights of the Hospital of St. John of Jerusalem, and in 1330 the prior of that order demised it to William Langford for life.[125] The priors held the manor of the lords of the manors of Hitchin, Dinsley Furnival and King's Walden by finding two chaplains annually to celebrate divine service in the chapel of the manor for the souls of the former lords of those manors who had been the feoffors of the Templars.[126] At the suppression of the Hospitallers the manor of Temple Dinsley came to the Crown, and was granted to Sir Ralph Sadleir in March 1542.[127] He settled the manor on his son Edward Sadleir and Edward's wife Anne.[128] Sir Ralph died in 1587, when it descended to Lee son of Edward,[129] the latter having died in 1584. Anne, widow of Edward, who married Ralph Norwich, retained a life interest.[130] Lee died in 1588, and was succeeded by his son and heir Thomas,[131] from whom the manor descended to his eldest surviving son Edwin,[132] who was created a baronet in 1661.[133] He died in 1672. His son Sir Edwin Sadleir sold the manor in 1712 to Benedict Ithell of Chelsea.[134] His son Benedict died without issue in 1758, when the property passed to his sisters Elizabeth and Martha. The former died in 1766 and Martha one year later. Neither left any children, and Martha bequeathed the estate of Temple Dinsley to her steward, Thomas Harwood, who at his death in 1786 left it to a nephew, Joseph Darton.[135] It is now the property of Mr. H. G. Fenwick.

SADLEIR. *Or a lion parted fessewise azure and gules.*

The manor of *MAIDECROFT* (Medcroft, xiii cent.; Maidecroft, xiv cent.) or *DINSLEY FURNIVAL* was another part of the manor of Dinsley which is said in the 13th century to have been granted by William Rufus to Richard de Loveceft. In 1268 it was in the tenure of Thomas de Furnival, who conveyed to his younger brother Gerard de Furnival two parts of the manor.[1] In 1287 Gerard de Furnival son of Gerard de Furnival granted the manor to William Hurst, with remainder in default of issue to Gerard son of William de Eylesford and of Christine Gerard Furnival's daughter, then to Loretta daughter of Gerard de Furnival, wife of John de Useflet.[2] In 1315–16 Gerard son of William de Eylesford[3] recovered the manor against John son of William Hurst.[4] Soon after this the manor came into the hands of the overlord, Robert Kendale, who in March 1317–18 received a grant of free warren in his demesne lands there,[5] and it descended with the manor of Hitchin (q.v.) until the death of Edward Kendale the younger in 1375.[6] It then passed to his sister Beatrice, wife of Robert Turk, as apparently it was not held like Hitchin in tail-male. Beatrice and her husband conveyed the manor in the following year to Sir William Croyser, kt., and Elizabeth his daughter,[7] apparently in confirmation of an earlier grant made by Edward Kendale in 1372.[8] A life interest in the manor was retained by

FURNIVAL. *Argent a bend between six martlets gules.*

---

[117] *V.C.H.* Herts. i, 303*a*.
[118] Ibid.
[119] Ibid.
[120] Dugdale, *Mon. Angl.* vi, 819–20; Addison, *The Knights Templars*, 25.
[121] *Cal. Chart. R.* 1226–57, p. 415.
[122] Assize R. 325.
[123] Pat. 2 Edw. II, pt. i, m. 4 d.
[124] Orig. Mins. Accts. Herts. bdle. 865.
[125] *Cal. Pat.* 1327–30, p. 531.
[126] Dugdale, *Mon.* vii, 819.
[127] *L. and P. Hen. VIII,* xvii, g. 220 (48).
[128] Pat. 13 Eliz. pt. ii, m. 19; Feet of F. Herts. Hil. 13 Eliz. His eldest son was Thomas Sadleir.
[129] Chan. Inq. p.m. (Ser. 2), ccxxxvi, 72.
[130] Com. Pleas D. Enr. Trin. 35 Eliz. m. 2.
[131] Chan. Inq. p.m. (Ser. 2), ccxxxvi, 72; Feet of F. Herts. Trin. 8 Jas. I.
[132] Recov. R. Hil. 1652, rot. 121.
[133] *Cal. S. P. Dom.* 1661–2, p. 84; G.E.C. *Baronetage*.
[134] Close, 11 Anne, pt. v, no. 12.
[135] Cussans, *Hist. Herts. Hitchin Hund.* 49.

[1] See Dugdale, *Baronage*, i, 26; Feet of F. Div. Co. 53 Hen. III, no. 356. The other third part was doubtless held as dower.
[2] Feet of F. Herts. East. 15 Edw. I, no. 198; Wrottesley, *Pedigrees from Plea R.* 84.
[3] Wrottesley, *Pedigrees from Plea R.* 541.
[4] Coram Rege R. no. 60, 7 Edw. II (Agard's MS. Index).
[5] Chart. R. 11 Edw. II, m. 4, no. 11; Inq. p.m. 4 Edw. III, no. 26.
[6] Chan. Inq. p.m. 49 Edw. III, pt. i, no. 74.
[7] Feet of F. Div. Co. 50 Edw. III, no. 150.
[8] Ibid. 46 Edw. III, no. 94.

HITCHIN HUNDRED

HITCHIN

Elizabeth widow of Edward Kendale.[9] In 1379 Sir William Croyser received a grant of free warren.[10]

In 1377 Croyser conveyed the reversion of the manor to Reginald Lord Grey of Ruthyn.[11] In 1391 John Grey and Elizabeth his wife, on whom apparently a settlement had been made by Lord Grey,[12] granted the manor to trustees for conveyance of the reversion after the death of Elizabeth to Sir Thomas Beaufort, kt., who was created Earl of Dorset in 1411 and Duke of Exeter in 1416. He died in 1426, when the manor passed, according to a settlement, to his nephew John Beaufort, created Duke of Somerset

G a x v of Ruthyn. Barry argent and azure with three roundels gules in the chief.

BEAUFORT. *FRANCE and ENGLAND with the difference of a border gobony argent and azure.*

in 1443.[13] The manor descended to his daughter Margaret, wife of Edmund Earl of Richmond, and to her son King Henry VII,[14] and thus became vested in the Crown. In 1524 a lease of the manor was made to Morgan Morice[15] and afterwards to Henry Morice, probably his son.[16]

In 1544 John Cock (Cokke, Cooke) bought the manor of Maidecroft from the king, and with it a wood called Weyndon (Wendon Wood).[17] John Cock by his will of 1553 left the estate to his two sons William and Thomas. A partition was made after 1558, by which William held the capital messuage and some of the land, while Thomas had the residue of the property, including the manorial rights.[18] Thomas conveyed his share of the estate in 1606 to Ralph Radcliffe,[19] who ten years later had a grant of a court leet there.[20] From this date the manor has descended with that of Hitchin Priory (q.v.).

The capital messuage was held by William Cock at his death in 1610, and probably passed to his wife Elizabeth, who survived him, and after her death to her daughter Anne, wife of William Fryer,[21] but this portion of the estate is not further traceable.

In the time of Edward II there was a park at Maidecroft which was visited on one occasion by Isabella his queen and her daughter the Queen of Scotland.[22]

The reputed manor of *CHARLTON alias MOREMEAD* was at the time of the Survey in the possession of King William. Before the Conquest it had been held by two sokemen of Earl Harold, but had been attached by the sheriff Ilbert to Hitchin, in which its soke lay.[23] The history of this manor is scanty,[24] but apparently it came into the possession of the Knights Templars, who received a grant of free warren there in 1269.[25] It was probably held by the Templars[26] and then by the Hospitallers with the manor of Temple Dinsley (q.v.) until the suppression of the latter order. The manor subsequently came to Edward Pulter, who sold it in 1582 to Ralph Radcliffe,[27] from which time it has descended with Hitchin Priory[28] (q.v).

The manor of *MENDLESDEN, MINSDEN,* or *MINSDENBURY* was a member of Hitchin, and passed with that manor from Earl Harold to the Conqueror.[29] In the 12th century Minsden seems to have been held by Guy de Bovencourt, whose heir (unnamed) forfeited his lands in the reign of John. It was then granted to Hugh de Baliol,[30] the lord of the manor of Hitchin. After the forfeiture of John de Baliol (see Hitchin) the manor of Minsden was granted to Robert Kendale, and on the strength of this grant he took possession of Minsden. A suit in Chancery was brought by the king against Edward Kendale, his son (to whom the manor descended), who contended that Minsden was not a separate manor but a hamlet within the manor of Hitchin.[31] The result of the suit seems to have been that the king recovered Minsden, for in 1366 the king's esquire John de Beverle was holding the manor and received a grant of free warren.[32] He held it with his wife Amice until his death in 1380, leaving as heirs his two daughters Anne and Elizabeth.[33] The mother and two daughters appear to have taken one-third of the manor each. Elizabeth married John Dauntesey, who died in January 1404–5.[34] She had died in 1395,[35] leaving a son and heir Walter, then aged twelve, who on reaching his majority received his mother's third, which had been given by the king after John Dauntesey's death to John Cockayne.[36] Anne's husband, William Langford, who survived her, died in 1411. Their heir was their son Robert.[37] Amice married as her second husband Robert Bardolf.[38] Probably Dauntesey sold his share in the manor to Langford, for in 1419 Robert Langford died seised of the whole, and was succeeded by his son Edward.[39] At his death in 1474 his son

---

[9] Anct. D. (P.R.O.), C. 687.
[10] Chart. R. 3 Ric. II, m. 8, no. 23.
[11] Anct. D. (P.R.O.), C. 828. Elizabeth Kendale also attorned the reversion (ibid. C. 2001).
[12] Reginald was the eldest son and heir of Lord Grey.
[13] Chan. Inq. p.m. 5 Hen. VI, no. 56.
[14] Ibid. 22 Hen. VI, no. 19.
[15] *L. and P. Hen. VIII,* iv, g. 213 (16).
[16] Aug. Off. Misc. Bks. ccxxx, fol. 50*b*; *L. and P. Hen. VIII,* xviii (2), g. 107 (5).
[17] Ibid. xix (2), g. 340 (21).
[18] Chan. Inq. p.m. (Ser. 2), cccxxii, 160.
[19] Feet of F. Herts. Trin. 4 Jas. I; Com. Pleas D. Enr. Trin. 4 Jas. I, m. 9.

[20] Pat. 14 Jas. I, pt. xii; *Cal. S. P. Dom.* 1611–18, p. 375.
[21] Chan. Inq. p.m. (Ser. 2), cccxxii, 160.
[22] *Archaeologia,* xxxv, 462.
[23] *V.C.H.* Herts. i, 303*a*.
[24] William son of Gerard de Furnivall was holding land at 'Suckhade' in Charlton in the 13th century. See Harl. Chart. 82 H 27.
[25] Chart. R. 53 Hen. III, m. 3.
[26] See *Cal. Pat.* 1307–13, p. 131.
[27] Cussans, *Hist. Hertz. Hitchin Hund.* 48, who quotes 'Carta orig. penes F. P. Delmé Radcliffe, esq.'
[28] Chan. Inq. p.m. (Ser. 2), dclxxxiv, 25; Recov. R. Mich. 2 Chas. I, rot. 51; Mich. 10 Geo. I, rot. 327; Trin.

35 Geo. III, rot. 382; Hil. 5 & 6 Geo. IV, rot. 22.
[29] *V.C.H.* Herts. i, 302*a*.
[30] *Rot. de Oblatis et Fin.* (Rec. Com.), 212; Pipe R. 6 John, m. 3 d.
[31] Plac. in Canc. no. 52.
[32] Chart. R. 39 & 40 Edw. IV, m. 7, no. 18.
[33] Chan. Inq. p.m. 4 Ric. II, no. 11.
[34] Ibid. 6 Hen. IV, no. 19.
[35] Ibid. 13 Hen. IV, no. 24.
[36] Ibid. The two heiresses each had a third, the remaining third being held by Amice in dower.
[37] Ibid. 13 Hen. IV, no. 32.
[38] Ibid. 4 Hen. V, no. 46.
[39] Ibid. 7 Hen. V, no. 3.

A HISTORY OF HERTFORDSHIRE

Thomas inherited the property[40] and held it for some twenty years. It passed at his death in 1493[41] to his son John, who was afterwards knighted. In 1501–2 he and his wife Katherine sold the property to William Lytton,[42] who died in 1517, leaving as heir his son Robert, aged five years.[43] Robert at his death left three daughters, of whom Ellen wife of John Brockett bought up the shares of the other two.[43a] From this date the manor descended with the manor of Almshoe in Ippollitts (q.v.).

There was a small religious house in this parish called *NEW BIGGING*, belonging to the order of St. Gilbert of Sempringham.[44] This house was founded by Edward de Kendale before 1363, when he obtained licence to divert a grant made by his mother Margaret de Kendale of a rood of land at Orwell, co. Cambridge, and of the advowson of the church there to the warden and chaplains of the chapel of St. Peter within the parish church of Hitchin, for the benefit of the prior and canons of this house.[45] In 1372 two chaplains granted to them, probably on the behalf of Edward de Kendale, certain lands in Willey and Hitchin.[46] The lands of the priory were valued in 1535 at £13 16s.[47] After the Dissolution the priory was granted in 1544 to John Cock, together with a messuage called Barkers Dalles Place in Bancroft Street and nineteen messuages in Hitchin.[48] It apparently descended like their manor of Maidecroft (q.v.), as this is the last mention of it. In the 17th century the manor-house called the Biggin was in the possession of Joseph Kemp, schoolmaster, who in 1654 devised it for charitable purposes (see under Charities). There was also a free chapel at Bigging, of which Robert Turk (lord of the manor of Maidecroft in right of his wife) died seised in 1400.[49]

HITCHIN PRIORY In 1317 the king granted to the Carmelite Friars in frankalmoign a messuage in the parish of Hitchin that they might build a church and house there for their habitation.[50] Other messuages and lands were given to this order by John de Cobham.[51] They built a small convent there which they dedicated to the Blessed Mary. This they held until the dissolution of their house in 1539.[52] In 1546 a survey was made of the priory and its whole estate. The buildings of the priory comprised a mansion house with a frater and dorter over the cloister, a church, the 'old hall,' the prior's lodging, and two little chambers for the brothers, also a kitchen, barn and other premises. There were also other tenements belonging to it in Bridge Street and Bull Street, which were leased out with the convent garden. Except the mansion-house, which had been repaired since the Dissolution, all the buildings were in a miserable state of dilapidation, being 'ruinous both in timber and tile,' and the gardens were like yards or waste places of ground. The church too was defaced, the steeple broken down and decayed by the weather, and all the lead, freestone, glass and bells gone.[53]

This survey was evidently made preparatory to a grant of the site in the same year to Sir Edward Watson, kt.,[54] from whom it passed seven years later to Ralph Radcliffe,[55] who died in 1559, leaving his estates to his eldest son Ralph.[56] He left the property to his nephew Edward, son of his brother Sir Edward Radcliffe, kt.,[57] and died without issue in 1621.[58] In 1660 Edward died also without issue and left as heir his nephew Ralph,[59] who was knighted eight years later.[60] His son Edward succeeded him in 1720, and held the estate until his death in 1727.[61] His three sons, Ralph, Edward, and Arthur, then held it in succession, and after the death of the youngest in 1767 the property was inherited by their nephew John son of John Radcliffe. This John died in 1783, when the priory passed to his eldest sister Penelope, wife of Sir Charles Farnaby, bart., of Kippington near Sevenoaks, who assumed the name of Radcliffe.[62] She died without issue in 1802. Her sister Anne, who married Charles Clarke of Ockley, co. Surrey, had issue John Clarke, who died in 1801 leaving no children, and Anne Millicent, heir to her aunt Penelope; she in 1802 married Emilius Henry Delmé, who on his marriage assumed the name of Radcliffe. His eldest son Henry Delmé Radcliffe having predeceased him, the priory devolved at his

RADCLIFFE of Hitchin. *Argent a crosslet gules between two bends engrailed sable with a label azure.*

DELMÉ. *Or an anchor sable between two lions passant gules.*

RADCLIFFE. *Argent a crosslet gules between three bends engrailed sable a label azure and a quarter sable with a crosslet or thereon.*

death in 1832 upon his second son Frederick H. Peter Radcliffe, captain in the Grenadier Guards, who was

---

[40] Chan. Inq. p.m. 14 Edw. IV, no. 38.
[41] Ibid. (Ser. 2), ix, 67.
[42] Feet of F. Herts. Hil. 17 Hen. VII.
[43] Chan. Inq. p.m. (Ser. 2), xxxiii, 5.
[43a] Ibid. xcv, 199; Feet of F. Herts. Mich. 2 & 3 Eliz.; East. 6 Eliz.
[44] The houses of this order were generally dual, but this seems to have been one of the few for canons only.
[45] *Cal. Pat.* 1343–5, p. 569; 1348–50, p. 9; Pat. 37 Edw. III, pt. i, m. 37.
[46] Inq. a.q.d. file 377, no. 14; see *Cal. Papal Letters*, iv, 349.
[47] *Valor Eccl.* (Rec. Com.), iv, 276.
[48] *L. and P. Hen. VIII*, xix (2), 166 (25); xx (2), g. 496 (44).
[49] Chan. Inq. p.m. 2 Hen. IV, no. 36. The king had obtained the messuage from Adam le Rous of Hitchin.
[50] *Cal. Pat.* 1313–17, p. 662. The king had obtained the messuage from Adam le Rous of Hitchin.
[51] Inq. a.q.d. file 303, no. 12 (25 Edw. III).
[52] Dugdale, *Mon. Angl.* viii, 1571; *L. and P. Hen. VIII*, v, 751.
[53] Rentals and Surv. Herts. portf. 8, no. 29.
[54] Pat. 38 Hen. VIII, pt. iv, m. 40.
[55] Plac. de Banco Hil. 6 & 7 Edw. VI, m. 15.
[56] *V.C.H. Herts. Fam.* 15; Feet of F. Herts. Mich. 17 & 18 Eliz.
[57] Chan. Inq. p.m. (Ser. 2), dclxxxiv, 25.
[58] Ibid.
[59] *V.C.H. Herts. Fam.* 16.
[60] Shaw, *Knights of England*, ii, 243.
[61] Burke, *Landed Gentry*.
[62] Recov. R. Trin. 35 Geo. III, rot. 382.

12

HITCHIN CHURCH: NORTH CHAPEL SCREEN

HITCHIN CHURCH: SOUTH CHAPEL SCREEN

succeeded by his fifth but eldest surviving son Hubert Delmé Radcliffe, J.P. He died in 1878, and his brother Mr. Francis Augustus Delmé Radcliffe is the present owner of Hitchin Priory.[63]

The present house, which stands on the south side of the town, incorporates part of the old house of White Friars. The original structure appears to have been of flint rubble and clunch, with the priory church on the south. No visible detail, however, is earlier than the 15th century, and the remains are confined to a part of the north, or frater, range of the west range. The house as it stands at present was almost wholly built in 1770–1 by John Radcliffe[64] of plastered brick, and stands about the four sides of a courtyard, which represents the old, small, cloister garth. The roofs are covered with tiles and lead. In the original building the church was probably to the south, the frater to the north, the dorter chapter-house to the east of the garth. The walls of the courtyard have been much renewed, but in the north and west wings are many arches, now blocked, of the original cloister arcade, and part of the inner wall, showing the cloister to have been 9 ft. wide. The arches are two-centred and continuously moulded, with double ogees and chamfers, but the tracery is gone; the piers between them are 4 ft. 6 in. wide. One arch remains open, and forms the principal entrance of the house, but three at least are visible inside the wall of the north wing, and two in the west wing, and others are said to be bricked up and plastered. The north cloister is now represented by a loggia with an arcade of the late 17th century, set in place of the bricked-up arcade of the 15th century. The cellarage under the north wing represents that under the frater. The space originally occupied by the frater, on the first floor of this wing, is now divided into several bedrooms. The north elevation was completely altered late in the 17th century. The ground story has an open arcade of five semicircular arches with moulded imposts, and a frieze of rosettes between cable mouldings; the central arch, which is set in a slight projection, has strapwork in the spandrels, with a shield of the Radcliffe arms, the initials R R S, and the date 1679. The windows above the arcade and the moulded cornice, of which all the detail is of plaster, are of the 18th century. The arcade in the courtyard belongs to the same period of reconstruction as the south elevation. The north elevation is of the late 18th century, and is an elaborate Palladian design; the south wing was completely rebuilt about this time, and contains the principal rooms. The east wing, which contains the main staircase, a few rooms and some cellars on the ground level, presents an elevation patched and much repaired, like that of the west wing, which contains the domestic offices, and is much obscured by out-buildings of different dates. There is some early 17th-century panelling in this wing, and in a small north room is a plaster ceiling of the same date, with cable and foliate decoration.

The parish church of ST. MARY[65] CHURCH stands to the north-east of the market-place and the churchyard is bounded on the east by the River Hiz. The church consists of a chancel,[66] nave and aisles, north and south chapels, west tower, north and south porches and charnel. It is built of flint rubble with stone dressings and has been heavily cemented. The tower incorporates some re-used Roman bricks, some 16th or 17th-century brick used in repairs, and also some later brickwork. The roofs of aisles, south porch and tower are of lead, those of nave and chancel are slated.

The general exterior character of the building is that of the 15th century, all the windows being of that date, and the tower, from which a small lead-covered spire rises, aisles and south porch, north and south chapels and chancel having embattled parapets. The aisles, chapels and chancel are buttressed. The fabric, however, ranges from the 12th to the late 15th century.

The nave, and at least the lower stages of the tower, are those of the 12th-century church, which probably consisted of chancel, nave and west tower only. The tower was probably completed about the middle of the 13th century, when the present tower arch was inserted and the stair-turret at the south-east of the tower built. About three-quarters of a century later first the north and then the south aisle was built and the arcades of the nave made. Either at the same time or slightly earlier the chancel was enlarged to about two-thirds of its present length and possibly to its present width. In the following century the chancel was still further enlarged, reaching its present proportions, and the foundation of the 14th-century east wall was made to form the west wall of the charnel, which was constructed at the same time.

The whole church underwent a thorough re-handling during the 15th century; in addition to the enlargement of the chancel and construction of the charnel the north and south chapels were added, and arcades inserted between them and the chancel with a clearstory over. The chancel arch was somewhat clumsily raised to a great height, the clearstory of the nave was added and the north porch built, while new windows were inserted throughout the church, which was largely re-roofed. Lastly, the elaborate south porch was added towards the end of the century. Later work on the church is limited to certain 17th and 19th-century repairs, mostly in brick.

The church is unusually rich in 14th and 15th-century timber and woodwork, which will be described in order of its occurrence.

The chancel has a much-restored 15th-century east window of five lights traceried in the head; the centre light is not crossed by the transoms, of which two divide each pair of side lights.

The north and south sides of the chancel are 15th-century arcades of four bays; the easternmost arch of each arcade is slightly wider in span than the rest and is four-centred of two moulded orders, the inner one springing off carved corbels, the outer one continuous. The rest are two-centred, of two moulded orders, and supported on columns with engaged shafts,

---

[63] V.C.H. Herts. Fam. 15–16; Archaeologia (Soc. of Antiq.), xviii, 447–8.
[64] MS. in Herts. Co. Mus. marked 'Hitchin.'
[65] As late as 1521 the dedication was to St. Andrew.
[66] Dimensions: chancel, 71 ft. 6 in. by 19 ft. 6 in.; north chapel, 22 ft. 6 in. wide; south chapel, 21 ft. wide; nave, 74 ft. 6 in. by 22 ft.; north aisle, 20 ft. wide; south aisle, 19 ft. 6 in. wide; tower, 21 ft. by 20 ft. 6 in.; north porch, 11 ft. 6 in. by 9 ft. 6 in.; south porch, 14 ft. by 11 ft.

with foliate capitals and moulded bases. The clearstory above the arcades is of the same date and has four modern windows on each side. The roof trusses rest on sixteen modern richly foliated corbels with embattled miniature parapets. There are some late 15th-century bench-ends in the chapels. The charnel beneath the east bay of the chancel is reached by a winding stair, now replaced by modern brick steps, and is entered through a moulded four-centred doorway in the west end of its north wall; it has been vaulted with brick in modern times, and has two barred mullioned windows and a third which is now a door on the east.

The chancel arch is an ugly piece of 15th-century are of the 15th century and have undergone considerable repair. They have moulded principals, purlins, wall plates, &c., and there are figures of angels at the foot of the principals, some holding shields. In the north chapel the roof is flat. In the south chapel the roof is ridged, with carved bosses at the intersection of the ridge and the principals, which run to the wall plates. The wall plates here rest directly on the moulded and carved half-octagonal corbels. Both north and south chapels have splendid 15th-century wooden screens inclosing them, in the arches leading to the aisles on the west. That of the north chapel has five two-light openings with elaborate tracery, three to the north and two to the

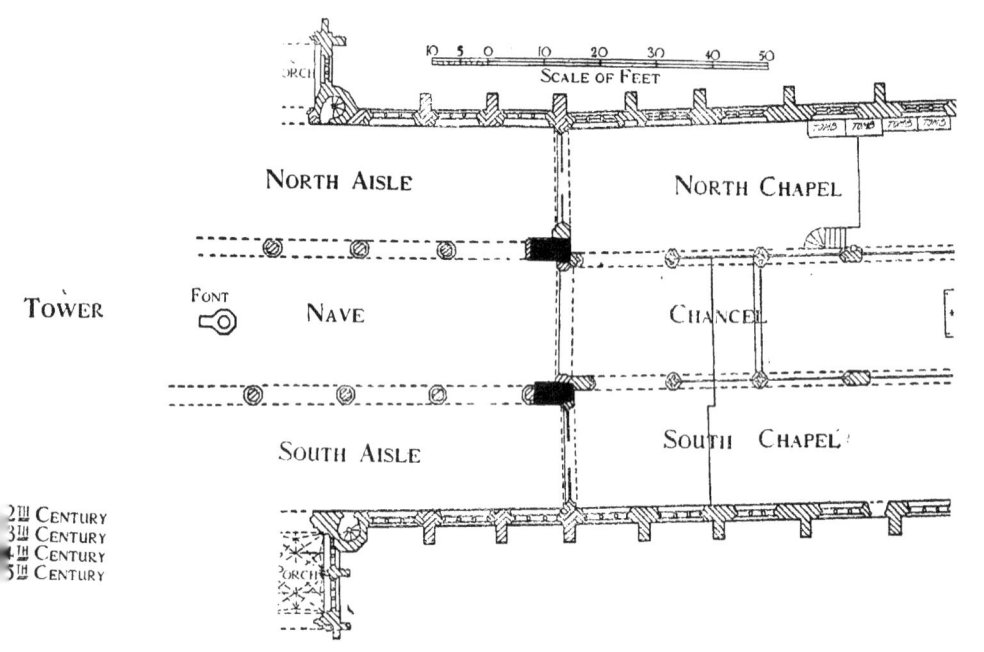

PLAN OF HITCHIN CHURCH

alteration. The original mid-14th-century arch was supported on half-octagonal jambs, simply moulded at their heads. On these has been erected a high four-centred arch with smaller shafted jambs. The outer order of this is continuous and the inner is stopped by the mean capitals of the shafts.

The chapels are separated from the chancel by the remains of 15th-century parclose screens. The north chapel contains the organ; it has an original traceried east window of five lights, and the five windows of three lights in the north wall are also original. A small 17th-century communion table is in the vestry. In the first column of the arcade is a tall moulded niche of the 15th century, with a low projecting bracket. This chapel also contains a 15th-century piscina. The roofs of both the north and south chapels south of a four-centred doorway, equal in width to two of the other compartments. The head of this doorway is continued up into an ogee with rich crockets, to the lowest string of the heavy moulded cornice, which has a Tudor-leaf cresting. On either side of the ogee is tracery similar to that in the remaining compartments, which are separated from one another and from the doorway by slender buttresses with crocketed pinnacles. Between the north shaft of the arch filled by the screen and the northernmost buttress of the screen is an extremely narrow space, with tracery at the head, fitted to the contour of the capital of the shaft. The panels below the middle moulding of the compartments have arches upon them with foliated spandrels, and cusped trefoils within the arches, with foliated points

14

to their main cusps, all within a moulded frame. The two-leaved door of the screen reproduces this panelling in its lower, solid portion, but with two panels in each leaf, and has open lights with tracery above the middle moulding.

The screen of the south chapel is very much richer. It has two openings of two lights each on either side of a central doorway nearly equal in width to two of the openings. In each compartment the two lights are almost round-headed, containing cusped and foliated trefoils, the foliations being three- and four-petalled flowers with berry centres. The lights have a quatrefoil above and are continued into an ogee with florid crockets and a finial, with tracery of two cinquefoiled lights and a quatrefoil on either side. This scheme is bounded above by a very narrow embattled moulding, on which stands an arcade of three traceried two-light arches separated by extremely slender pinnacled and crocketed buttresses, and crowned by double ogee canopies with carved groining, each ogee being continued into a tall pinnacle heavily crocketed, with a third pinnacle of similar pattern between each pair, all reaching to the level of the lowest moulding of the cornice. The solid portion of the screen below the middle moulding consists in each compartment of a panel divided into two by a moulded frame, having in each subsidiary panel an ogee containing a re-cusped trefoil with foliated main cusps. The ogees have small cusps and finials, and there is tracery in the spandrels.

When the double doors in the centre compartment are closed their appearance is almost exactly that of two compartments of the screen. The four-centred head of the opening slightly interrupts the line of the two ogees, and there are two panels, instead of one, in the solid portion of each leaf of the door; while above the embattled moulding the small arcade consists of five traceried lights, instead of six, the centre one being slightly wider than the rest.

The compartments of the screen are separated by slender pinnacled and crocketed buttresses with moulded bases, which run from the ground to the level of the lowest moulding of the cornice. This cornice has a very wide shallow moulding containing a beautiful frieze of twelve angels, with intercrossed wings, issuing from clouds and holding emblems of the Passion, except those on the north and south, which carry shields. Above them is a simple moulding.

There is a small space on the south side between the southernmost buttress of the screen and the shaft of the arch, but this contains no tracery.

In both chapels the arches towards the aisles are of two orders with shafted jambs, and the hood moulds have mask stops.

The arrangement of the windows in the south chapel is like that of the north chapel, except that the east window has only four lights. Towards the east end of the south wall, between the first and second windows, is a small doorway.

The nave is of four bays; the 14th-century two-centred arches with drop mouldings are of two chamfered orders, on octagonal columns with moulded capitals. Over the east respond of the north arcade is a blocked doorway, which formerly led to the rood loft, now destroyed, and over the chancel arch is a window of five lights. The 15th-century clearstory has on each side five windows of three lights. The roof is of 15th-century date, much repaired, and has moulded principals, tie-beams, wall plates, &c. Its wall-pieces rest on moulded corbels sculptured with figures of angels, all of modern workmanship.

The north aisle has four three-light windows with tracery, and one on the west, all of the 15th century, inserted in the 14th-century wall. The north doorway is of the same date as the wall and is of two chamfered orders. It leads to the north porch, which is of two stories, the upper story being reached by a polygonal stair turret which opens into the aisle by a four-centred door. The exterior entrance door of the porch is two centred, of two moulded orders. The lower story has two three-light windows, one on the east and one on the west, and the window in the north wall of the upper story is also of two lights. There are the remains of a stoup in a pointed recess in this porch.

The roof of this aisle, at the western end, is of the 15th century, of the same type as, but plainer than, those already described; but that of the eastern end is a very fine flat roof of 14th-century work; its dimensions tend to show that it was originally the roof of the 14th-century chancel, and was moved here during the general reconstruction of the 15th century.

The south aisle corresponds exactly in all its arrangement to the north aisle, except for a trifling difference in width, and the south door is of 15th-century date, contemporary with the south porch, the upper story of which is approached by an octagonal stair turret at the north-east angle. The doorway to the porch still retains its contemporary door with cusped panelling, but its pointed head has been sawn off and fixed.

The south porch is of two stories. The entrance arch is of two shafted orders, an arch inclosed in a square, with tracery inclosing foliate sculpture in the spandrels. On either side of the entrance is a deep shafted and cusped niche with a pedestal, and below them are cusped panels inclosing shields, one with a merchant's mark and another with a coat of arms. Small shafts with capitals at the same level as that of the entrance, but without bases, meet the frame-moulding of the lower compartments of the scheme. On the east and west sides are traceried three-light windows, having an exterior hood mould with a mask stop at the southern extremity, and dying into a buttress on the northern. The ceiling of the entrance story is elaborately groined, and the interior walls are panelled below the windows. A string-course all round the three sides of the porch marks the level of the upper story, which is plain on the east and west, and lighted by a small three-light window on the south, with identical blind lights below, to the level of the string-course. On either side of these are pairs of niches with shafts and capitals supporting square heads inclosing pointed arches, with foliation in the spandrels. Moulded pedestals stand in the niches on low plinths rising from the sloping upper surface of the string-course. The whole scheme of windows and niches is inclosed in a square frame supported on six slender shafts with capitals and bases resting on similar plinths. Above is another string running round the three sides of the porch, with grotesques at the south-east and south-west angles. Pairs of gabled buttresses at right angles in two stages run up to the level of the upper string, at the south-west and south-east angles. Their upper portions are panelled, the gables are cusped, and they have small sculptured demi-figures in their heads. Identical buttresses stand on the east and west sides of the porch a short distance from the wall of the aisle. The sides of the central crenelle of the battlement on the south side are continued down to the upper string to form a panel with a four-centred head containing sculpture. There is a small shield above, and an iron cross inclosing pierced stone.

Above the buttresses are pinnacles with crockets and finials, and tête-bêche trefoiled panels on the outer faces.

The west tower, which is of two stages, is approached from the nave by an arch of three chamfered orders, with half-octagonal responds, and moulded capitals and bases. On the north side is a much-restored 13th-century lancet window. The upper stage is lighted by two pointed windows in each wall, all much restored with brick in the 17th and again in the 19th century. The west door is of the 13th century and is much decayed. The deep square buttresses, one—to the north—of the same date and four of the 14th century, are built against the remains of 12th-century pilaster buttresses, which were revealed during recent repairs. The stair turret at the south-east angle is also of the 13th century. It is built against the wall, without bonding, and rises above the parapet of the tower. The lower part is lighted by small lancets, and the upper part, which with its parapet has been repaired with 16th or 17th-century brick, has cross-loops.

The fittings of the church include a richly carved twelve-sided font, with defaced figures of saints under elaborate ogee canopies with crockets and finials, resting on sculptured corbels. There are small pinnacled buttresses on high moulded plinths between the figures. The tall cover of 15th-century style is modern.

The pulpit is an early 16th-century structure considerably restored.

The monuments in the chancel include a slab with the indents of a priest and a marginal inscription with roses at the corners, and the brasses of a merchant of the Staple of Calais, 1452, his wife, four sons and six daughters; the inscription containing the date is imperfect; there is one illegible shield, the indents of four others, and of four square plates; a late 15th-century brass of a priest with a brass of a wounded heart, and the indent of another, the indents of two inscriptions and a small plate, which was perhaps a symbol of the Holy Trinity; the brasses of the shrouded figures of a man and his wife, three sons and five daughters; a shield bears a bend in a border engrailed, and there are the indents of an inscription and four roses; a late 15th-century brass of a woman much worn, with the indents of a man and of an inscription; and an early 16th-century brass of a civilian and his wife, with the indents of an inscription and scrolls.

In the north chapel is a 16th-century slab with the indents of an inscription and a shield, re-used in the 18th century as a gravestone. There is also here an early 15th-century Purbeck marble tomb, with quatrefoiled panels in the sides. In the top slab is the indent of a marginal inscription, and a later brass of John Pulter, with a marginal inscription and the date 1485. In the floor is a slab of the 14th century with an incised marginal inscription to Sir Robert de Kendale. This is found not to be a floor-slab, having its edges moulded to a hollow chamfer. An indent of William Pulter, 1549, has a brass inscription and a shield. An altar tomb of c. 1500 is of clunch, with panelled sides, having a slab with a contemporary brass of the shrouded

HITCHIN CHURCH: SOUTH PORCH

HITCHIN CHURCH   THE FONT

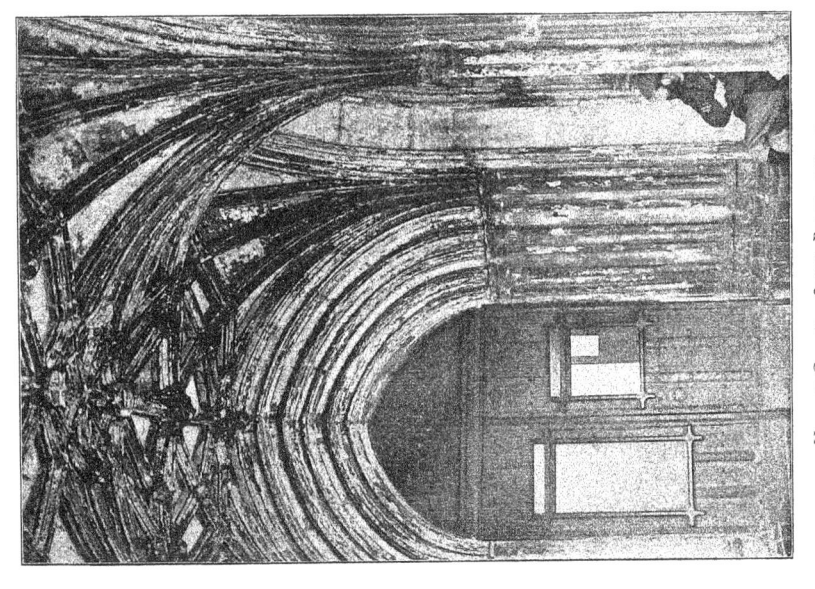

HITCHIN CHURCH   SOUTH PORCH   nter or

HITCHIN HUNDRED

figures of a man and his wife. A late 15th-century altar-tomb has panelled sides with shields inscribed G. A. and T. A., and a slab with the brasses of a civilian and his wife. The mural monuments are those of Edward Docwra, 1610, John Skinner, 1669, and Ralph Skinner, 1697.

The south chapel contains a large 17th-century monument to Ralph Radcliffe, 1559, Ralph Radcliffe, 1621, Sir Edward Radcliffe, 1631, and Edward Radcliffe, 1660, as well as other monuments to members of the same family.

In the floor is the indent with the brass feet remaining of John Pulter, 1421, and his wife Lucia, 1420, with a square plate, worn smooth, a much worn and imperfect inscription, and the indents of two roundels; the half-figure indent of John Parker, 1578, with a square plate and brass inscription; the indents of a civilian and his wife, and inscription brasses of four sons and four daughters of the late 15th century, partly covered by pews; and the brasses of a shrouded woman with four sons and four daughters, with indents of an inscription and seven scrolls, undated.

In the two easternmost window sills of the north aisle are the Purbeck marble effigy of a knight wearing a mail hauberk with a coif, mail chausses and a long surcoat, of mid-13th-century date, and the late 14th-century effigies of a knight and lady, much defaced.

At the west end of the nave are the mid-15th-century brasses of a civilian and his wife, and in the tower the indents of a woman and two men, and of a man and a woman, with an inscription, a scroll, and four roses, of the late 15th century, and much worn.

There is a ring of eight bells, seven of which are by Joseph Eayre of St. Neots, 1762, and the eighth by Edward Arnold of St. Neots, 1784.

The plate includes patens of 1625 and 1634, a salver of 1635, and two cups and two flagons of 1705.

The registers are in eight books. The first book contains baptisms, burials and marriages from 1562 to 1653. The book of the civil register from 1653 does not now exist. The second book contains all entries from 1665 to 1680. On 8 November 1667 William Gibbs, vicar of Hitchin, and nine other persons certified that 'the registry for Christenings, Marriages and Burialls in the Parish of Hitchin . . . through the carelessnes and neglect of former Regesters is wholly lost for the space of seventeen years and upwards last past, from Feb. 1, 1648/9 to Aug. 1, 1665.' The third book contains all entries from 1679 to 1746, and duplicates the second for about a year. The fourth includes baptisms and burials from 1747 to 1800 and marriages from 1747 to 1753. The fifth has baptisms and burials from 1801 to 1812, the sixth, seventh and eighth contain marriages from 1754 to 1776, 1776 to 1811, and 1811–12 respectively.

ADVOWSON   The church of Hitchin is described in the Domesday Survey as the minster (*monasterium*) of Hitchin, and to it belonged as much as 2 hides out of the 5 hides at which Hitchin was assessed. The exact significance of the term minster is not clear, but it would perhaps seem to imply something more than an ordinary parish church, and the very large amount of glebe attached to it is suggestive of this. There is no evidence that there was here an early monastery, but there can be little doubt that ecclesiastically, as well as temporally, Hitchin was the head of a large district. It was the head of a deanery, and, as appears from later evidence, was the mother church of the two Wymondleys, which formed one chapelry, and of the chapelries of Dinsley and Ippollitts.

At the time of the Domesday Survey the church probably belonged, like the manor, to the king.[87] In the 12th century the church was said to have been given to the nuns of Elstow by the Countess Judith, niece of William I, founder of that house, and charters to that effect from the countess, William I and William II were produced by the abbess.[68] The countess's endowment of the monastery, however, took place before 1086, for the lands in Bedfordshire (Elstow, &c.) which she granted to them are said in the Domesday Survey to be held by the nuns of her grant,[69] whereas the church of Hitchin is not mentioned in connexion with Elstow until the time of Henry II, who by charter confirmed the lands granted by the Countess Judith, and granted also the church of St. Andrew of Hitchin.[70] The evidence, therefore, points to the grant by the Countess Judith being fictitious.[71] The abbey held the advowson till the dissolution of this house. Early in the 13th century a vicarage was ordained, to be supported by the altarage of the high altar, 2 acres of land and a suitable house. Out of the stipend the vicar was to pay 13 marks to the monks, but they were to entertain the archdeacon, while the vicar paid the synodals. It was said that two chaplains were necessary for the parish at this date.[71a]

After the Dissolution Henry VIII granted the advowson and rectory of this church with that of Ippollitts (q.v.) to the Master and Fellows of Trinity College, Cambridge,[72] and they have held it ever since.[73]

In 1301 the belfry of the church was in such a bad state as to be dangerous, and the parishioners were ordered to repair it[74]; sentence was then passed against some persons who appropriated some of the goods left to the church and some of the fabric, which hindered the restoration.[75]

In the 15th and 16th centuries many bequests were made to this church. Thomas Pulter[76] and Agnes Lyndesey[77] in 1464, Laurence Bertlott in 1471,[78] left gifts for prayers to be said for their souls. Agnes Lyndesey also gave 3s. 4d. to the great window in the chapel of St. Edmund,[79] and Laurence Bertlott desired that cloth should be hung about his sepulchre in the church.[80] John Pulter in 1487 left 26s. 8d. for repairs and lights before the crucifix. He also made the following bequest: 'I bequeathe to the paynting of the Ile of the north side of the seid paroch church of Hicchen which I did doo to make after the deceese of my fader on whoes soule Jhu doo mercy iiijli to

---

[67] V.C.H. Herts. i, 272, 302a.
[68] Abbrev. Plac. (Rec. Com.), 8.
[69] V.C.H. Beds. i, 353.
[70] Dugdale, Mon. Angl. iii, 413.
[71] In the 13th century William II was the reputed donor (Assize R. 323, m. 46 d.).

[71a] Liber Antiquus Hugonis Wells, 28.
[72] Information from Senior Bursar of Trin. Coll. Camb.
[73] See Inst. Bks. (P.R.O.).
[74] Linc. Epis. Reg. Dalderby, fol. 44 d.

[76] Ibid. fol. 166.
[75] Wills P.C.C. 8 Godyn, 3 Wattys.
[77] Ibid. 6 Godyn.
[78] Ibid. 3 Wattys.
[79] Ibid. 6 Godyn.
[80] Ibid. 3 Wattys.

A HISTORY OF HERTFORDSHIRE

have the sowles of my moder Dame Alice Pulter and Isabel Rych my sister praid for and remembered in the same werke.' He also left various books to the church.[81]

The gild of Our Lady was founded in the church by licence of King Edward IV in 1475.[82] It was to consist of a master, two wardens, brethren and sisters, and was to provide two chaplains to celebrate mass for King Edward IV, Queen Elizabeth and the brethren and sisters of the fraternity. At the same time a grant was made to the brotherhood of two annual fairs of three days' duration each, one to be held on the Wednesday in Easter week and the other on the feast of the Translation of St. Edward the Confessor and the days preceding and following each of these.[83] At the time of its dissolution in the reign of Edward VI the gild apparently found two priests, one to serve the chantry and the other to serve the church in conjunction with the curate.[84] It owned a tenement called le Swanne, five stalls in the market-place, a Brotherhood House and other property, also the profits of the fairs.[85] In 1548 the king granted the gild and Brotherhood House, the Swan and the fairs to Ranulph Burgh and Robert Beverley.[86] The chantry house was granted the next year to Thomas Stevens.[87]

In Minsden are the remains of a chapel which has long been in ruins.[88] The earliest mention of a chapel here is in 1487, when John Pulter left 3s. 4d. to the chapel of St. Nicholas.[89] The only other record is of 1517, when a like sum was left to this chapel.[90] A marriage is said to have been celebrated in it in 1738.[90a]

There was also a chapel at Preston in the manor of Dinsley which is said to have been included in the grant of the church of Hitchin (to which it was appurtenant) to the Abbess and convent of Elstow.[91] After the manor of Dinsley came into the hands of the Templars an agreement was made by them with the Abbess of Elstow by which the nuns were to find a chaplain to hold service in the chapel on Sunday, Wednesday and Thursday, unless it should happen that feast days fell on other days in the week, when these feast days should count among the three days. The Templars were to continue to pay tithes from any lands cultivated by them from which the church of Hitchin or the chapel of Dinsley had been used to receive them. The duty also of finding two chaplains to celebrate mass for the donors of their lands was obligatory on the Templars by their tenure,[92] and afterwards on the Knights Hospitallers. Among the expenses of the latter enumerated shortly before their suppression is that of wax for a light in the chapel and the wages of a chaplain to celebrate divine service daily.[93] The obligation of the Abbess of Elstow seems to have been then commuted for a pension of 14s. 4d.[94] In 1540 John Docwra, farmer of the estate, had to find a chaplain to celebrate in this chapel.[95] After the suppression of the Hospitallers the rectory of Dinsley was granted to Ralph Sadleir with the manor (q.v.).

The church of HOLY SAVIOUR[96] in Radcliffe Road was built in 1865 after the designs of William Butterfield and at the cost of the late Rev. George Gainsford, the incumbent. A district chapelry formed out of the parish of Hitchin was assigned to it. Almshouses in the Radcliffe Road, built in 1870, were made in connexion with this chapelry.

The Roman Catholic chapel of our Lady Immaculate and St. Andrew, a plain building of red brick, was built in 1901.

The first record of Dissent in Hitchin dates from 1666, when 'unlawful meetings' were held in a private house.[97] In 1672 licence was given to Presbyterians to hold their meetings,[98] and under the Toleration Act many places were certified for worship

RUINS OF MINSDEN CHAPEL, HITCHIN

---

[81] Wills P.C.C. 8 Godyn, 3 Milles.
[82] Cal. Pat. 1467–77, p. 542.
[83] Ibid.
[84] Chant. Cert. 20, no. 72; 27, no. 17.
[85] Ibid. For bequests to the gild see the following P.C.C. wills: 46 Milles, 2 Moone, 18 Dogett, 19 Vox, 7 Ayloffe, 13 Maynwaryng, 33 Bodfelde, 31 Hogan.
[86] Pat. 2 Edw. VI, pt. iv, m. 27.
[87] Ibid. 3 Edw. VI, pt. iv, m. 17.

[88] Herts. Gen. and Antiq. ii, 288a–96; V.C.H. Herts. i, 302a.
[89] P.C.C. Will, 3 Milles.
[90] Ibid. 31 Holder.
[90a] North, Ch. Bells of Herts. 200.
[91] Assize R. 323, m. 46 d.
[92] Dugdale, Mon. Angl. vii, 819.
[93] Mins. Accts. bdle. 865, no. 13.
[94] Cf. Misc. Enr. Accts. L.T.R. no. 18, m. 51.

[95] Mins. Accts. 31 & 32 Hen. VIII, no. 114, m. 36 d.
[96] This perhaps took the name from the Gilbertine Priory of St. Saviour which stood near here (Cal. Papal Letters, iv, 349; Index to Lond. Gaz. 1830–83, pp. 825–6).
[97] Sess. R. (Herts. Co. Rec.), i, 183.
[98] Urwick, Nonconformity in Herts. 640; Cal. S. P. Dom. 1672, p. 292.

18

HITCHIN HUNDRED

for various dissenting sects.[99] An Independent chapel was built in Back Street in 1690,[100] which is now represented by one in Queen Street. The Baptists began to meet in Tilehouse Street in 1669,[101] and built a chapel there in 1692,[101a] which was rebuilt in 1838.[102] In the middle of the 19th century the Particular Baptists built Mount Sion Chapel in Park Street[103] and Bethel Chapel in Queen Street.[104] In 1850 a dwelling-house was used by the Baptists,[105] and in 1869 they built a chapel in Walsworth Road.[106] About the same time Salem Chapel was built for this same denomination.[107] There are other modern churches and chapels in the parish.

The first record of Quakers in Hitchin, where they now form an important part of the community, is of 1657. It is said that they then held a firm footing in the town.[108] John Bunyan used to preach in Wain Wood, where there is still a dell known by his name, and a service has been yearly held at this spot in commemoration.[109]

CHARITIES Educational Charities: The Free School founded by John Mattocke and subsidiary endowments,[110] the Girls' Charity School,[111] the Charity School in Back Street.[112]

Elizabeth Ann Lucas's Educational Charity, founded by will proved at London 8 June 1860, consists of £187 14s. 5d. Bank stock and £3,156 12s. 6d. India 3 per cent. stock, held by the official trustees. By a scheme of the High Court (Chancery Division) 8 August 1894 the income, amounting to £112 a year, or thereabouts, is applicable in the advancement of the education of children, in exhibitions and prizes, in providing evening classes, and in subscriptions for the benefit of a public elementary school. See also under the Eleemosynary Charities.

Hailey's Educational Foundation, founded by will of Elizabeth Hailey proved at London 7 January 1864, consists of £878 Great Western Railway 4½ per cent. debenture stock, in the names of trustees, producing £39 10s. a year, which is applicable for the education of children residing in or near Walsworth. See also under Charities for Nonconformists.

In 1894 Robert Curling by a codicil to his will, proved at London 21 March, bequeathed £454 London and North Western Railway 3 per cent. debenture stock (with the official trustees), the dividends amounting to £13 12s. 4d. to be applied in gifts for children attending St. Andrew's School for good conduct.

The Parochial Charities have under a scheme of the Charity Commissioners, 19 June 1908, been consolidated under the title of the United Charities.

I. The almshouse Branch comprises :—

(a) The almshouses, founded by will of John Skynner 4 June 1666, consisting of eight houses in Silver Street, erected on land known as Benn's Mead given in 1670 by Sir Thomas Byde, and endowed with certain lands producing £80 a year or thereabouts.

In 1675 Ralph Skynner gave £82, which was laid out in land known as Benn's Mead. The official trustees also hold £50 consols.

In 1743 Sarah Skynner Byde by deed conveyed to trustees 6 a. 2 r. in Hill Grove Field, the rents to be divided between these almshouses and the almshouses founded by Ralph Skynner. The land is let at £5 a year.

In 1768 Richard Tristram by deed gave land in Ippollitts, the rents to be divided between the same two almshouses. The land was sold in 1904 and the proceeds invested in £221 12s. 2d. consols.

In 1755 John Whitehurst by deed gave land at Hexton, the rents to be divided between the inmates of J. and R. Skynner's Almshouses and the Girls' Charity School. The land has been sold and the proceeds invested in £1,617 5s. consols, of which one moiety, £808 12s. 6d. consols, belongs to the Girls' Charity School.

In 1788 Hannah Wilson by will bequeathed £100 for the poor of Hitchin, now £100 consols, applied for the benefit of the almshouses of J. and R. Skynner.

In 1794 John Davis bequeathed £300 for the augmentation of the same two almshouses, now represented by £450 consols.

In 1802 Dame Penelope Farnaby Radcliffe, by will proved in the P.C.C., 24 July, bequeathed £200 for poor widows, now £235 4s. consols, applied for the benefit of the same almshouses.

In 1824 Elizabeth Whittingstall by will bequeathed £1,000 stock, now £1,000 consols, to be equally divided between John Skynner's, Ralph Skynner's, and Daniel Warner's almshouses.

(b) The almshouses, founded by will of Ralph Skynner 19 May 1696, consist of eight almshouses contiguous to John Skynner's almshouses, and are endowed with 39 acres in Kelshall producing £27 15s. a year.

In 1794 John Pierson by will bequeathed £100, now £133 6s. 8d. consols, for these almshouses.

In 1795 Joseph Margetts Pierson by deed gave £100 consols, the dividends to be applied in repairs.

For other land and stock given for the joint benefit of John and Ralph Skynner's almshouses see above.

(c) The six almshouses near the churchyard known as Daniel Warner's almshouses, originally parish houses, were rebuilt in 1761 by Daniel Warner 'for the warmer and better comfort of the poorer widows or ancient couples of his town.' These almshouses were endowed by the before-mentioned John Pierson with £200 consols, by Joseph Margetts Pierson with £940 consols, and with £333 6s. 8d. consols under the will of Elizabeth Whittingstall (see above).

(d) The scheme further provides that the building known as 'The Biggin' (see Joseph Kemp's Charity below) should, together with two cottages in Tilehouse Street, be used for the residence of almspeople being members of the Church of England. See also Elizabeth Simpson's almshouses under Charities for Nonconformists.

II. The Eleemosynary Branch, &c. :—

In 1591 Simon Warren by will charged two houses in Tilehouse Street with £1 a year.

---

[99] Urwick, *Nonconformity in Herts.* 643–4.
[100] Ibid. 649.
[101] *Baptist Handbook*, 1908.
[101a] Urwick, op. cit. 646.
[102] *Index to Lond. Gaz.* 1830–83, p. 825.
[103] Urwick, op. cit. 855.
[104] Ibid.; *Index to Lond. Gaz.* 1830–83, p. 825.
[105] *Sess. R.* (Herts. Co. Rec.), ii, 460.
[106] *Baptist Handbook*, 1908, p. 70.
[107] Urwick, *Nonconformity in Herts.* 855.
[108] Ibid. 637–8.
[109] Ibid. 641.
[110] See article on Schools, *V.C.H. Herts.* ii, 94.
[111] Ibid. 100.
[112] Ibid. 101.

A HISTORY OF HERTFORDSHIRE

In 1609 Mrs. Elizabeth Radcliffe purchased land for the poor, which now consists of 2 acres at Standhill Common and 2 acres called Cromer's Close, producing £7 a year, and £61 16s. 2d. consols, representing accumulations of income.

In 1613 Thomas Whittamore by will left £20 for the poor, which was laid out in 1619 in the purchase of 2 a. 3 r. 6 p. called Pierwell Field, of which 24 p. was sold to the Great Northern Railway Company, and the proceeds invested in £70 4s. 4d. consols. The land produces £8 13s. 6d. yearly.

In 1625 Edward Radcliffe gave two houses in Tyler's Street for the poor.

In 1635 James Huckle by will devised his house and land in Winkfield, Berks., for the poor. The trust property now consists of three tenements and pasture land in Winkfield producing £55 a year, and £1,237 2s. 11d. consols, representing sale of land in 1867 and accumulations of income.

In 1653 William Guyver by his will gave a perpetual annuity of £4 out of land at Hitchin for putting apprentice a poor boy. This charity also possesses £49 14s. 7d. consols, representing accumulations of income.

Joseph Kemp, M.A., schoolmaster, of Hitchin, by his will dated 17 July 1654, devised his manor-house, commonly called 'The Biggin,' and his copyhold and freehold land in Hitchin for ten disabled women, apprenticing, and other charitable uses. The trust property now consists of 'The Biggin' (directed by the scheme to be used as an almshouse), and 51 acres and eight cottages in Biggin Street, of the annual rental value of £150 or thereabouts, and £959 0s. 6d. consols, arising in part from sale of land and in part from accumulations of income.

In 1660 James Carter by will bequeathed certain leasehold houses in Houndsditch, London, with the rents of which a house and land at Starling's Bridge were purchased. This property was sold in 1870, and the proceeds with accumulations are represented by £285 7s. 6d. consols.

In 1673 William Chambers by his will gave two cottages for the poor, now three cottages in Queen Street, producing £21 yearly.

In 1693 Joseph Kinge by his will left £25 for bread for the poor, which was laid out in 1716 in the purchase of 2 acres at Kelshall now let at £1 10s. a year.

In 1697 Edward Draper by his will devised a perpetual rent-charge of £5 out of a messuage in Angel Street—now Sun Street—20s. thereof to be paid to the minister for a sermon on Easter Monday in commemoration of benefactors of Hitchin, twenty poor to receive 2s. 6d. each and a 6d. loaf, and 20s. for a dinner to the trustees.

In 1705 Ralph Skynner Byde by will charged his lands and tenements within the precinct of Walshoe and Walsworth with an annuity of £5 4s. for the poor in bread.

In 1713 Sir Ralph Radcliffe by will charged his land in Ippollitts with 40s. a year for bread.

In 1716 John Turner charged his messuage in the churchyard with 30s. a year for the poor.

In 1729 William Dawes by will charged land in Great Wymondley with an annuity of £5 for poor housekeepers.

In 1735 Robert Tristram by his will, proved in the court of the archdeaconry of Huntingdon, devised 10s. yearly for the poor, payable out of tenements and land at Great Wymondley.

In 1739 Mrs. Mary Arriss by will charged land at Hitchin with £5 yearly, to be applied as to £4 for poor housekeepers, 10s. to the minister for a sermon on the day of her death—2 September—and 10s. to the trustees. In 1780 Mary Godfrey, testatrix's niece, by deed gave the lands charged to the poor, which consist of 12 acres or thereabouts, let at £10 18s. a year. This charity is also possessed of £493 9s. 8d. consols, arising from sale of land in 1900 and accumulations of income.

In 1780 Elizabeth Ewisdin left £50 for the poor, which was invested in the purchase of 3 r. 13 p. situate in Burbushes, which is let with the property belonging to the preceding charity.

The parish is also in possession of half an acre at the south end of the town let at £3 3s. a year, the donor of which is unknown.

In 1813 John Crabb by his will directed his executors to purchase so much Government annuities as would produce £5 a year for fuel for the poor. The legacy is now represented by £105 consols standing in the names of trustees.

The official trustees also hold £30 17s. 11d. consols arising from accumulations of income of this charity.

In or about 1837 Mrs. Frances Leckie by will left a legacy for the poor, now represented by £217 10s. consols.

Elizabeth Ann Lucas's charity for the poor (see also under Educational Charities) consists of £187 14s. 5d. Bank stock, £3,156 12s. 6d. India 3 per cent. stock, and £185 8s. 2d. consols, producing in the aggregate £117 a year or thereabouts. The several sums of stock, unless otherwise stated, are held by the official trustees.

The scheme for the United Charities provides, inter alia, that a sum of not less than £30 a year out of the income of the charity of Elizabeth Ann Lucas shall be applied in aid of any dispensary, hospital, or institution; that the yearly income of William Guyver's charity, and £20 yearly out of the income of Joseph Kemp's charity, shall be applied in apprenticing; that the residue of the income of Lucas's charity and a yearly sum of £100 shall be provided out of the remaining charities in augmentation of the endowments of the almshouses; and that the remaining income (after satisfying the trusts for ecclesiastical purposes) shall be applied for the benefit of the poor generally, including subscriptions to provident clubs, outfits for children, in maintenance of a reading-room or working-men's club, &c., or in pensions.

The almspeople are entitled to receive not less than 5s. per week.

In 1720 Jacob Marson conveyed a messuage in the market-place to trustees upon trust that the profits should be applied in putting out poor fatherless boys apprentices to freemen of the City of London. The said messuage, which is now a public-house called the 'Rose and Crown,' is let for £40 a year, and there is a sum of £601 18s. 2d. consols with the official trustees producing £15 0s. 8d. a year. The charity is regulated by a scheme of the Charity Commissioners 19 October 1909, whereby the trustees of the United Charities are appointed the trustees. The premiums are to be not less than £10 or more than £25, payable in not less than two portions.

HITCHIN HUNDRED

ICKLEFORD

Ecclesiastical Charities not included in the United Charities:—

In 1696 Ralph Skynner by his will bequeathed £200 in augmentation of the benefice, which sum was invested in a rent-charge of £9 payable out of land in Ickleford.

Oliver Clement by his will (date unknown) gave a rent-charge of £6 13s. 4d. yearly out of houses in the parish of St. Nicholas, London, in augmentation of the vicarage. The annuity is received from the Clothworkers' Company.

William Joyce gave a rent-charge of £2 10s. charged on a house in Cock Street, Hitchin, to the vicar for preaching six sermons annually in the church on the six Sunday mornings next before the feast of St. Michael. (See also under the United Charities.)

In 1901 George Brown Collison by will left £50, the interest to be applied in repair of the churchyard of Hitchin, and the testator expressed a hope that his grave would be maintained in good order. The legacy was invested in £57 14s. 4d. consols with the official trustees, producing £1 8s. 8d. yearly.

Nonconformist Charities: The almshouses in Biggin Lane, founded in 1773 by Elizabeth Simpson for five poor persons being Protestant Dissenters attending the Independent Meeting House in Back Street, and endowed by the founder's will proved in the P.C.C. 3 January 1795, are endowed as follows:—

£448 12s. 1d. consols, Elizabeth Simpson's gift. £300 consols, bequeathed in 1815 by will of Nathaniel Field. £400 17s. 6d. India 3 per cent. stock, derived under the will of Mrs. Elizabeth Harley, proved at London 7 January 1864. £450 stock of the Hitchin and District Gas Company, derived in 1876 under the will of Mary Carter. The trustees also hold a sum of £79 9s. 4d. Bombay, Baroda and Central India Railway stock, producing in the aggregate about £55 a year. In 1908 each of the five inmates received £8 10s. and 1 ton of coal.

The above-mentioned Elizabeth Simpson likewise bequeathed a sum for the minister of the Meeting House in Back Street and £300 for poor members of the congregation. William Crawley likewise by his will dated in 1788 bequeathed £200 for the minister. The three legacies are now represented by £1,115 7s. 6d. consols in the name of the trustees, the annual dividends of which, amounting to £27 7s. 8d., are applied proportionately between the minister and the poor of the congregation.

The trustees of the Meeting House also hold a sum of £407 11s. 2d. India 3 per cent. stock and £80 15s. 10d. stock of the Bombay, Baroda and Central India Railway Company, derived under the will of Mrs. Elizabeth Harley, proved at London 7 January 1864, the annual income of which, amounting to about £15, is applicable for the minister. The same testatrix bequeathed £150 for the Meeting House and school at Walsworth. The legacy is now represented by £173 14s. 3d. India 3 per cent. stock and £34 8s. 8d. stock of the same Indian railway, producing £6 10s. a year or thereabouts. Any part of the income which in any year is not required towards the expenses of a Meeting House at Walsworth is to be applied for the benefit of the school at Walsworth. The same testatrix further bequeathed £350 for pensions for the poor. The legacy was invested in £307 Great Western Railway 4½ per cent. stock, producing £13 16s. 4d. yearly, which is applied in the payment of £1 14s. a quarter to two pensioners.

Hitchin St. Saviour's: The Almshouses and Orphanage was founded by the Rev. George Gainsford, by deed 14 August 1869, whereby 3 roods of land were conveyed to trustees for the purpose of building thereon almshouses and an orphan home for girls. In 1879 the founder transferred to the official trustees a sum of £1,000 consols for the support and maintenance of the institution, which was subsequently augmented by gifts of Francis A. D. Radcliffe, Mrs. A. E. Moreton and Mrs. Burbidge and others. The endowment fund now consists of £1,307 16s. 1d. consols, producing £32 13s. 8d. yearly.

The Orphanage is supported by voluntary contributions, which, with the dividends on the stock, amount to about £300 a year.

ICKLEFORD

Hikleford (xiii cent.); Ikelingford, Ikeleford (xiv cent.); Icklesford (xvi cent.).

Ickleford is a long and narrow parish of 1,036 acres, running northwards from Hitchin, from which parish it is divided by the River Oughton. The average level of the land is only about 180 ft. above the ordnance datum. The parish lies in the valley of the River Hiz, which forms its boundary on the east, parting it from Bedfordshire. The parish is entirely agricultural. In 1905 the arable land was estimated at about 800 acres, permanent grass at about 200 acres, while woodland was only 10 acres.[1] The soil is chalk.

In the middle of the village is a triangular green called the Upper Green, to distinguish it from the Lower Green, which lies at the north end. Around the Upper Green stand, on the south-west the parish church, to the north some cottages and the school, and on the east Pound Farm with a moat supplied with water from the River Hiz. The village extends to the south-west along the Icknield Way and a road leading south to Bearton Green. At the junction of these roads is Ickleford House, the residence of Mr. David Simson. On the road to Bearton Green, about a quarter of a mile from the church, is an old two-storied timber-framed house, on a brick foundation, covered with rough-cast and with a tiled roof. At each end are gabled wings only slightly projecting beyond the central part; one wing has an oriel window, over which is the date 1599. The upper story is overhanging. The village continues northward along the west side of the road, the east side being on low land adjoining the Hiz. The Icknield Way runs through the south of the parish.

Old Ramerick, a moated manor-house, lies 2 miles to the north of the church, and is a two-storied house

---
[1] Statistics from Bd. of Agric.

A HISTORY OF HERTFORDSHIRE

of L-shaped plan. The main block is 18th-century work of brick, the wing is of the 17th century, and is built of clunch with brick quoins. The moat has almost disappeared.

The Bedford branch of the Great Northern railway passes through the parish, but the nearest station is at Hitchin.

Field-names of the 16th century which occur in this parish are Callouse Peece, Whesell Dytch and Hambridge Peece.

MANORS There is no mention of Ickleford in the Domesday Survey. It is evident that it was then included in the manor of Pirton and that the manors which subsequently appear were formed from that manor by subinfeudation.[2]

The manor of ICKLEFORD was held in the 13th century of the lords of Pirton as a quarter of a knight's fee by the family of Foliot.[3] Isabel widow of John Foliot appears in 1285 as holding part of the estate of Thomas de la Sale, a felon.[4] In 1287 John Foliot, then a minor and possibly son of Isabel, claimed view of frankpledge in Ickleford.[5] By 1303 this quarter of a fee was in the hands of John Fitz Simon,[6] and in 1346 Hugh Fitz Simon was holding it with several coparceners. One of these was Simon Francis of London,[7] into whose family the manor seems subsequently to have passed. Ralph Francis (Frauncey's) son of William died seised of the manor in March 1532–3, leaving as heir his son William, aged six years.[8] This William was holding in 1556.[9] In 1585 Richard Francis (of Ticknall, co. Derby), apparently his son,[10] mortgaged the mansion or manor-house of Ickleford, together with certain lands, to Thomas Ansell or Aunsell,[11] and two years later Francis released the manor to Ansell,[12] excepting the manor-house and closes called Conygers, Dovehouse Close, Pennes, the Old Orchard, the New Orchard, Duncroft and Earles Close and a water mill called Newe Mill (probably because Ansell already held these). Ansell died in 1606, leaving three sons, William, Thomas and Edward, between whom, by his will, the estate was divided. Thomas and Alice his wife received the chief part, William, the eldest, having only one messuage, and Edward and his wife Susan a

FRANCIS. *Party bend sinisterwise sable and or a lion countercoloured.*

tenement and the water mill called Westmill.[13] The manor descended in the family of Thomas Ansell,[14] and came to another Thomas Ansell, who was holding in 1714,[15] and apparently to a third Thomas, who suffered a recovery in 1740.[16] His widow Elizabeth was holding in 1763, with reversion to her daughter Mary and her husband Thomas Goostrey,[17] who were in possession in 1776.[18] In that year they conveyed the manor to Charles Loundes and John Dashwood King, probably for a sale to Thomas Whitehurst.[19] He in 1788 sold it to Thomas Cockayne, who died in 1809, leaving a son and heir Thomas.[20] At his death he left an only child Marion Charlotte Emily, who married the Hon. Frederick Dudley Ryder, third son of the first Earl of Harrowby His son, Captain Dudley Ryder, R.N., died in 1898, and the manor was bought by Captain C. J. Fellowes, R.N. After his death it was purchased in December 1910 by Mr. David Simson, who is the present owner.[21]

The manor of RAMERICK (Ranewick, Ramwardwike, Ramardewick, Ramorwyk, xiii cent.; Ranworthewyk, xiv cent.) was also held of the manor of Pirton as a quarter of a knight's fee.[22] The first tenant of whom there is record or tradition is Richard Reincourt, whose daughter Margaret is said to have married Robert Filliot and to have had a son Richard Filliot.[23] Richard Filliot's daughter and heir Margery[24] brought the manor by marriage to her husband Wiscard Ledet.[25] Wiscard's daughter and heir Christine married Henry de Braybrok,[26] by whom she had two sons, Wiscard and John. Wiscard and his son Walter both died before Christine.[27] Walter left two daughters, Alice and Christine, who married two brothers, William and John Latimer.[28] The manor remained with Christine, who held it by subfeoffment from her sister.[29] It descended to her second son John,[30] who took his mother's name of Braybrok and held the property with his wife Joan.[31] Gerard de Braybrok, possibly their son, was assessed for this fee in 1303.[32] In 1333 a grant was made to Gerard de Braybrok, son of the above Gerard,[33] of free warren in his demesne lands of Ramerick,[34] and two years later he (then Sir Gerard) and his wife Isabel settled the estate on themselves for life,[35] with remainder to their son Gerard, with a further

BRAYBROK. *Argent seven voided lozenges gules.*

---

[2] See *Feud. Aids*, ii, 428, 439, 449.
[3] Ibid. 428.
[4] Chan. Inq. p.m. 13 Edw. I, no. 87.
[5] Assize R. 325.
[6] *Feud. Aids*, ii, 428. [7] Ibid. 437.
[8] Chan. Inq. p.m. (Ser. 2), lvii, 4.
[9] See Feet of F. Herts. Hil. 2 & 3 Phil. and Mary.
[10] *Visit. Herts.* (Harl. Soc. xxii), 55.
[11] Com. Pleas D. Enr. Mich. 27 & 28 Eliz. m. 6.
[12] Ibid. Hil. 29 Eliz. m. 8, 42; Feet of F. Div. Co. East. 29 Eliz.; Com. Pleas Recov. R. Mich. 28 & 29 Eliz. rot. 42.
[13] Chan. Inq. p.m. (Ser. 2), ccxcvii, 146.
[14] See Feet of F. Div. Co. Mich. 22 Jas. I; Herts. East. 32 Chas. I.

[15] Recov. R. Trin. 13 Anne, rot. 176.
[16] Ibid. Hil. 14 Geo. II, rot. 166.
[17] See Feet of F. Herts. East. 3 Geo. III.
[18] Ibid. Trin. 16 Geo. III.
[19] See Cussans, *Hist. Herts. Hitchin Hund.* 26.
[20] Ibid.
[21] Inform. from Rev. J. W. Tilt.
[22] See *Feud. Aids*, ii, 428. Alan de Limesi, lord of Pirton, gave a mill at 'Ramordwick' to the Prior and convent of Hertford (Add. Chart. 15476).
[23] Harl. MS. 807, fol. 79.
[24] Ibid.
[25] See Feet of F. Herts. 13 John, no. 124.

[26] He afterwards took the name of Ledet (*Cal. Inq. p.m. Hen. III*, 259). Christine's second husband was Gerard Furnival (Assize R. 323; Chan. Inq. p.m. 8 Edw. I, no. 37).
[27] *Cal. Inq. p.m. Hen. III*, 259, 308.
[28] Chan. Inq. p.m. 8 Edw. I, no. 37; G.E.C. *Complete Peerage*.
[29] Chan. Inq. p.m. 33 Edw. III (1st nos.), no. 31.
[30] Assize R. 325; Harl. MS. 245, fol. 22.
[31] See Harl. Chart. 46 E. 10.
[32] *Feud. Aids*, ii, 428.
[33] Harl. MS. 807, fol. 79.
[34] Chart. R. 7 Edw. III, m. 7, no. 33.
[35] Feet of F. Div. Co. Trin. 9 Edw. III; Harl. Chart. 47 B. 9.

HITCHIN HUNDRED — ICKLEFORD

remainder to their second son Henry.[36] Sir Gerard held till his death in 1359[37] and was succeeded under this settlement by Gerard, his son,[38] who married Eleanor de St. Amand. His only son and heir Gerald died in 1428, leaving by his wife Parnel a daughter Elizabeth,[39] who married first Sir William Beauchamp, kt.[40] (summoned to Parliament as Lord St. Amand from January 1448–9),[41] and secondly Roger Toocotes. Her second husband forfeited the estate early in the reign of Richard III as a rebel, and it was granted to Thomas Meryng, one of the king's servitors,[42] but was restored to Roger Toocotes some seven years later.[43] Elizabeth died in 1491[44] and her husband a year later.[45] The manor was inherited by Richard Beauchamp, kt., Lord St. Amand, son of Elizabeth by her first husband. Richard was attainted in 1483, but restored two years later by Henry VII. He died in June 1508 without legitimate issue,[46] having bequeathed all his estates to his natural son Anthony Wroughton *alias* St. Amand, who conveyed the manor in 1520–1 to St. John's College, Cambridge.[47] This grant caused some trouble between the college and George Brooke, Lord Cobham, who claimed the manor as heir to Richard Beauchamp, being descended from Reginald brother of Sir Gerard Braybrok, who married Eleanor de St. Amand.[48] The master of the college appeared against Brooke in a Star Chamber suit for having in February 1529–30 incited various persons to come with weapons at three o'clock in the morning to break into the manor of Ramerick. According to the master, these brought ladders 6 or 7 ft. high and broke the wall of the house and thus entered it and kept possession, refusing admission to a justice of the peace.[49] Lord Cobham pleaded that he was seised in demesne as of fee of the manor and lived there peaceably until unjustly disseised by the college.[50] A few years later the dispute was brought to a close by the surrender by Lord Cobham to St. John's College of his interest in the manor.[51] In 1617 the college received a grant of court leet and view of frankpledge in Ickleford.[52] The manor has remained in their possession until the present day.

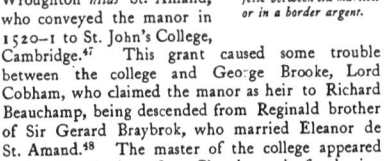

BEAUCHAMP, Lord St. Amand. *Gules a fesse between six martlets or in a border argent.*

ST. JOHN'S COLLEGE, CAMBRIDGE. *The arms of Lady* MARGARET BEAUFORT, *the founder.*

The priory of Wymondley had lands in Ickleford, by whose grant does not appear. A certain Thomas de la Sale, who was imprisoned for felony in the reign of Edward I, held a messuage and 12¾ acres of land of the prior.[53] The monastery also had a mill called Hyde Mill,[54] which at the time of the Dissolution was held by the convent of Elstow, co. Bedford, at a rent of 30s. The mill and the rent were granted by Henry VIII to James Nedeham in February 1542–3.[55] They descended to John Nedeham, who died seised in 1591, leaving a son and heir George.[56]

In 1566 John Brockett and Ellen his wife conveyed an estate, under the name of the manor of Ickleford, to trustees for a settlement.[57] Edward Brockett some years after alienated this to Edmund Knott.[58] A messuage in Ickleford, the residence of Daniel Knott, is mentioned as part of the manor of Ickleford in 1607,[59] and Edmund Knott, yeoman, died seised of a capital messuage there in 1618, leaving a son and heir John.[60]

The parish church of ST. KATHECHURCH RINE, standing in the middle of the village, is of stone, entirely covered with plaster. It consists of a chancel, nave, south aisle and south chapel, north vestry, west tower and south porch.[61]

The earliest part of the church is the nave, dating from the middle of the 12th century. The chancel and west tower were built early in the following century, and the south porch was added about the middle of the 15th century. In 1859 the church was restored and the south aisle, south chapel and north vestry were added.

The chancel windows are all modern except a 13th-century lancet in the north wall. A modern door opens to the north vestry. The piscina, with a broken bowl, is of the 15th century. Above it is some 15th-century tracery, possibly the remnants of a rood screen.

In the north wall of the nave are two windows, one on each side of a blocked 12th-century doorway, which, although it is much decayed and repaired with cement, has a well-preserved cheveron moulding on the rear-arch. The eastern of the two north windows, of the 14th century, is of three cinquefoiled lights with tracery in a square head, and the western, of the 15th century, is of two cinquefoiled lights, also with tracery, in a pointed head. Both are much repaired with cement. At the east end of the wall is a roodloft staircase. A much broken piscina is of the 15th century, probably moved from its original position. The roof is of the 15th century, supported on grotesque stone corbels. The south arcade and

---

[36] Feet of F. Div. Co. Trin. 9 Edw. III; Harl. Chart. 47 B. 9.
[37] Chan. Inq. p.m. 33 Edw. III (1st nos.), no. 31; Add. Chart. 15473; *Feud. Aids*, ii, 437.
[38] Harl. Chart. 46 F. 35; *Feud. Aids*, ii, 449.
[39] Chan. Inq. p.m. 7 Hen. VI, no. 40.
[40] Wrottesley, *Ped. from Plea R.* 345; Feet of F. Div. Co. East. 16 Hen. VI.
[41] G.E.C. *Complete Peerage.*
[42] Pat. 2 Ric. III, pt. iii, m. 1.
[43] Close, 7 Hen. VII, m. 10 d.
[44] Chan. Inq. p.m. (Ser. 2), vii, 49.
[45] Ibid. viii, 96.
[46] G.E.C. *Complete Peerage.*
[47] Salmon, *Hist. of Herts.* 173.
[48] G.E.C. *Peerage.* His father Thomas Lord Brooke had also claimed the manor (Harl. Chart. 46 H. 49).
[49] Star Chamb. Proc. Hen. VIII, bdle. 8, no. 66–7; Harl. Roll C 31.
[50] Star Chamb. Proc. Hen. VIII, viii, no. 66–7; Harl. Roll C 31.
[51] Feet of F. Herts. Hil. 27 Hen. VIII; Harl. Chart. 44 B. 44.
[52] Pat. 15 Jas. I, pt. xviii, no. 12.
[53] Chan. Inq. p.m. 13 Edw. I, no. 87.
[54] Cf. for a field called La Hide, Harl. Chart. 51 B. 45 and 45 F. 62.
[55] L. and P. Hen. VIII, xviii (1), 226 (51).
[56] Chan. Inq. p.m. (Ser. 2), ccxxxii, 63.
[57] Feet of F. Herts. Trin. 8 Eliz.
[58] Ibid. Hil. 15 Eliz.; Pat. 22 Eliz. pt. ix.
[59] Chan. Inq. p.m. (Ser. 2), ccxcvii, 146.
[60] Ibid. ccclxxi, 138.
[61] The dimensions are: chancel, 19 ft. by 14 ft.; nave, 53 ft. by 17 ft.; tower, 10 ft. 6 in. square.

23

A HISTORY OF HERTFORDSHIRE

clearstory of the nave are modern, the latter having three circular lights with roll-ended cusps, surmounted externally by a moulded roll. The modern south aisle has three pairs of pointed lights, with shafted external jambs and drop mouldings with sculptured stops.

In the south wall is a 12th-century doorway with a semicircular arch of three moulded orders, the two shafts on each side having leaf-carved capitals and moulded abaci. The original bases have disappeared, and the doorway has been repaired with cement. This door leads to the south porch, which is embattled, with a central niche over the two-centred entrance arch of two continuous orders. Above the arch is a much decayed string course. To the west of the south door is a 15th-century two-light window with tracery, much repaired with cement. The west tower is of two stages with heavy buttresses, those at the north-west and south-west angles being diagonal. The low pyramidal roof is of lead. The tower arch, which is two-centred, and a small lancet on the south side, are probably original. The west window and the two-light belfry windows are of the 15th century and are repaired with cement.

In the nave is a brass of about 1380 of Thomas Somer and his wife Marjory. The figures are half-length and the inscription is imperfect. There is in the church a 6-in. stone slab measuring 5 ft. by 2 ft. on its upper face and with edges moulded to a large hollow chamfer. An oak chair in the chancel, with a canopy, dates from the end of the 16th or beginning of the 17th century, and is of foreign workmanship.

The bells are five in number : the treble and second are by John Warner & Sons, 1857, the third is by Richard Chandler, 1680, the fourth by Miles Graye, 1650, and the fifth by Thomas Russell of Wootton, 1726.

The plate consists of a cup of 1796, presented by Thomas Cockayne in 1807 and modern paten and flagon, the former made from two old silver patens.

The registers consisted down to 1830 of three books. Since then the first, containing baptisms, burials and marriages from 1653 to 1748, has disappeared ; the second book contains baptisms and burials from 1749 to 1812 and marriages from 1749 to 1753 ; the third book contains marriages from 1756 to 1812.

ADVOWSON The church of Ickleford was a chapel to Pirton[62] (q.v.), and the two livings were held together until divided by order of the Ecclesiastical Commissioners in 1847. The advowson was purchased by Thomas Wilson in 1868.[63] It was conveyed before 1875 to the Rev. T. I. Walton, and now belongs to the Rev. C. A. Walton, his son.

There was also a chapel at Ramerick attached to the church of Pirton in the 13th century,[64] but there seems to be no further trace of it.

ICKLEFORD CHURCH FROM THE SOUTH

---

[62] See Linc. Epis. Reg. Wells, fol. 10 ; Bokingham, fol. 357, and references given under Pirton.

[63] Cussans, *Hist. of Herts. Hitchin Hund.* 31.

[64] Linc. Epis. Reg. Wells, fol. 10 ; Add. Chart. 15470.

HITCHIN HUNDRED

In the 18th century two houses were registered for meetings of Protestant Dissenters, and another was certified in 1824.[65] There is now a Wesleyan chapel in Ickleford.

CHARITIES

In 1657 Edward Ansell by his will gave 40s. a year for the poor charged on 2 acres of land, exchanged under the Ickleford Inclosure Act for a close of 3 acres in Ramerick Farm, now belonging to St. John's College, Cambridge.

In the Parliamentary returns of 1786 it is stated that a donor unknown gave a rent-charge of 20s. to poor widows, which is paid out of West Mill in the parish of Shillington (Beds.).

The annual sum of 60s. is distributed to about thirty recipients.

IPPOLLITTS

Hippolitts, Polettes (xvi cent.); Appolyttes, Epolites (xvii cent.).

The parish of Ippollitts, which is 2,935 acres in extent, lies to the south of Hitchin and has an average height of some 250 ft. above ordnance datum, but it rises on the south-western border to nearly 500 ft. Ippollitts is not mentioned in the Domesday Survey, the earlier settlement having been at Almshoe, where is still the site of a church.[1] When the church of St. Ippollitts was built in the 11th century (see church) it was attached as a chapel to the neighbouring church of Hitchin. The little village and church lie to the east of the Hitchin and Hatfield high road, which runs through the parish north and south. A mile to the west of the village is a small group of houses, which constitute the hamlet known as Gosmore, a name which is found from the 14th century onwards.[2] There is here an old inn built of brick, dating possibly from the end of the 17th century. A little further on is Maydencroft, a two-storied farm-house of the early 17th century, built of brick and timber. It is L-shaped in plan and was originally surrounded by a moat, which has nearly disappeared. The ceiling beams of the hall (which now has a partition dividing it into two rooms) are supported by a pillar dated 1615. The large barn and stable, of timber and brick, are contemporary with the house.

The Wyck, standing about three-quarters of a mile south-east of the church, is a house of 17th-century date, formed out of five two-roomed cottages. It is timber-built, most of the framing being filled with layers of roofing tiles, only the rectangular panels having brick. The upper story is partly in the roof, which is tiled. The walls were raised some feet and underpinned at the end of the last century. Internally some of the roof trusses and also some ceiling-beams of the ground-floor rooms appear to be original, and

THE WYCK, LITTLE ALMSHOE, IPPOLLITTS

old timber has been used for the framing of some fireplaces, but the doors and windows are modern.

Other hamlets in the parish are New England, on the London Road to the north-east; Ashbrook, about a mile to the north-west; and St. Ibbs and Little Almshoe to the south.

Further south still is Almshoebury and the site of the old chapel. It was at the park here that Isabella wife of Edward II and her daughter are said to have hunted on one occasion.[3] A small stream called Ippollitts Brook, rising near Little Almshoe, flows northwards through a pond in the park. It is joined by another stream called Ashbrook, and further on flows into the River Purwell. There are about

[65] Urwick, *Nonconformity in Herts.* 652.
[1] This was probably a small church and manor-house settlement formed at a comparatively late date from Hitchin; cf. the pre-Conquest tenure.
[2] *Abbrev. Rot. Orig.* (Rec. Com.), iii, 310; Pat. 13 Eliz. pt. ii, m. 19; 19 Eliz. pt. v, m. 7; *Sess. R.* (Herts. Co. Rec.), i, 37; Pat. 14 Jas. I, pt. xii, m. 8.
[3] *Arch.* xxxv, 462.

A HISTORY OF HERTFORDSHIRE

1,600 acres of arable land in Ippollitts, 661 of grass and 19 of woodland.[4] The chief wood is Wain Wood, in the south-west of the parish. The main crop grown here is corn, the soil and subsoil being chalk.[5] Ippollitts Common was inclosed under an Act of 1811.[6] Field-names occurring in the 16th century which may be noted are Hermitage and Lampland.[7] The main line of the Great Northern railway runs through the extreme north-east of the parish, but the station is at Hitchin, 2 miles away.

William Lax, a mathematician and astronomer of some note, held the living of Ippollitts and built a small observatory there. He died in 1836.

At the time of the Survey the Bishop MANOR of Bayeux held 1 hide of land in ALMSHOE[8] (Almeshou, xi cent.; Almshoe, Almesby, Almeshobury, xiv cent.; Almyssho, xv cent.; Almeshoebury *alias* Ansibury, xvii cent.; Anstyebury, xix cent.), which before the Conquest had been held by Edmund, a man of Earl Harold. Under the bishop this land was held by Adam Fitz Hubert, brother of Eudo Dapifer.[9] After the bishop's forfeiture it was held of the king in chief, and probably passed from Adam to his brother Eudo Dapifer, and after the latter's death in 1120 to his sister Albreda wife of Peter de Valoines.[10] Through Gunnora, daughter and heir of Robert de Valoines, grandson of Peter de Valoines, the manor came to the Fitz Walter family.[11] They sub-enfeoffed early in the 13th century. The overlordship descended to Robert Fitz Walter, who died without male issue in 1431. Elizabeth his daughter and heir married Sir John Radcliffe, and their son John was summoned to Parliament as Lord Fitz Walter. Robert son of John was created Earl of Sussex in 1529.[12] His great-grandson Robert Earl of Sussex died in 1629 without surviving issue.[13]

Under the Fitz Walters the manor was held in 1241 by Simon Fitz Adam, who settled it on his wife Fyne on their marriage in that year.[14] Simon's heir was his son Sir John Fitz Simon, who was succeeded by his son John. This latter John married Parnel daughter of Henry Graponell[15] and had two sons, Edward his heir and Hugh.[16] At John's death in 1303-4 Parnel retained land in Almshoe as her dower and afterwards married John de Benstede.[17] Edward Fitz Simon apparently died without issue before 1328.[18] Hugh survived his mother and was alive in 1346.[19] Edward son of Hugh succeeded, but died without issue, and the manor passed to his brother Nicholas Fitz Simon,[20] who with his wife Elizabeth granted it in 1398 to John and Ida Cokayn for life,[21] with remainder to Edward Fitz Simon, their son, and his wife Cecilia, who was daughter of John and Ida Cokayn.[22] Elizabeth survived her husband and married John Sapurton, holding a third of the manor in dower. This, however, was quit-claimed in 1400 to John and Ida Cokayn and Cecilia, whose husband Edward was dead,[23] having left two daughters—Elizabeth, who married William Asshe,[24] and Christine wife of John Muslee.[25] They seem to have held one moiety each. Elizabeth and William left an only daughter, Elizabeth[26] wife of Thomas Brockett, who inherited her parents' share of the property,[27] and eventually seems to have become possessed also of Christine's moiety.[28] Thomas Brockett died in 1477[29] and his wife four years later.[30] The manor passed by will to Thomas's brother Edward, who died in 1488, having left a moiety to his wife Elizabeth, with remainder to his eldest son John.[31] John died in 1532, when the manor became the property of his grandson John,[32] subject to the life interest of his uncle Edward Brockett.[33] John (knighted in 1547) died seised of the reversion in 1558,[34] and was succeeded by his son Sir John Brockett, who at his death in 1598 left five daughters—Margaret, Anne, Helen, Mary and Frances—and a grandson John Carleton, son of another daughter Elizabeth, who had died six years previously.[35] The portions of Margaret and Anne were severally conveyed to Helen and her husband, Richard Spencer,[36] who may also have acquired some of the other shares,[37] for their property is called the manor of Almeshoe.

Sir Richard Spencer at his death in 1624 was succeeded by his son John,[38] on whom the property had been settled in tail-male with remainder to his brother Brockett. John, who was made a baronet in 1627, held the manor until his death in 1633, when he left an only child Alice,[39] so that the property

FITZ WALTER. *Or a fesse between two chevrons gules.*

RADCLIFFE. *Argent a bend engrailed sable.*

[4] Statistics from Bd. of Agric. (1905).
[5] *V.C.H. Herts.* i, Geol. Map.
[6] *Blue Bk. Incl. Awards.*
[7] Pat. 19 Eliz. pt. v.
[8] *V.C.H. Herts.* i, 308*b*.
[9] Ibid.; *V.C.H. Northants,* i, 363.
[10] Dugdale, *Baronage,* i, 441; *Monasticon,* iii, 345.
[11] Chan. Inq. p.m. 34 Edw. I, no. 107.
[12] G.E.C. *Complete Peerage.*
[13] Ibid. See Chan. Inq. p.m. (Ser. 2), liv, 5, 29. The overlordship is incorrectly given in Chan. Inq. p.m. 17 Edw. IV, no. 47, and Chan. Inq. p.m. (Ser. 2), iv, 30.
[14] Cussans (*Hist. of Herts. Hitchin Hund.* 113) quoting from MSS. in possession of Sir John Spencer of Offley.
[15] Wrottesley, *Pedigrees from Plea R.* 14.

[16] Chan. Inq. p.m. 32 Edw. I, no. 56.
[17] Ibid. 16 Edw. III, no. 30.
[18] See *Cal. Inq. p.m.* 1–9 *Edw. III,* 129 (Radwell); Feet of F. Div. Co. 5 Edw. III, no. 101.
[19] See *Feud. Aids,* ii, 436 (Radwell).
[20] See Add. MS. 28789; Close, 2 Ric. II, m. 36 d.; Agard, Indexes, vii, fol. 15, no. 27.
[21] Feet of F. Herts. 21 Ric. II, no. 185.
[22] Ibid.
[23] Ibid. 1 Hen. IV, no. 9; 2 Hen. IV, no. 14.
[24] *Visit. Essex* (Harl. Soc. xiii), 100.
[25] See Feet of F. Herts. 11 Hen. IV, no. 84.
[26] *Visit. Essex* (Harl. Soc. xiii), 30.
[27] Feet of F. Herts. 1 Edw. IV, no. 4.
[28] The other half disappears from this date, and Elizabeth's holding is called the manor of Almshoe.
[29] Chan. Inq. p.m. 17 Edw. IV, no. 47.
[30] Ibid. 21 Edw. IV, no. 46.
[31] Ibid. (Ser. 2), iv, 30; Will, P.C.C. 21 Milles. [32] Chan. Inq. p.m. (Ser. 2), liii, 29.
[33] Will, P.C.C. 20 Thower.
[34] Ibid. Noodes 18; Chan. Inq. p.m. (Ser. 2), cxvi, 83.
[35] Ibid. cclvii, 42; cclviii, 76.
[36] Feet of F. Herts. Trin. 41 Eliz.; Recov. R. East. 2 Jas. I, rot. 72.
[37] Frances with her husband Dudley Lord North conveyed her share to Sir Rowland Lytton (Chan. Inq. p.m. [Ser. 2], ccclix, 114).
[38] Chan. Inq. p.m. (Ser. 2), ccccxviii, 95.
[39] Feet of F. Herts. East. 5 Chas. I; Chan. Inq. p.m. (Ser. 2), ccccclxxiv, 4.

Ippollitts Little Almshoe, The Wyck, West Wing

HITCHIN HUNDRED — IPPOLLITTS

passed to Sir Brockett Spencer.[40] The manor passed eventually through Brockett's eldest daughter Elizabeth,

BROCKETT. *Or a cross paty sable.*

SPENCER. *Argent quartered with gules fretty or and a bend sable over all with three fleurs de lis argent thereon.*

In 1616 Ralph Radcliffe, lord of the manor of Hitchin, had a grant of court leet in Ippollitts and Gosmore.[46]

The parish church of ST. HIPPOLYTUS, in the middle of the village, consists of a chancel, nave, north and south aisles, north and south porches and west tower. It is built for the most part of flint with dressings of limestone and clunch. The tower is partly covered with cement, and the south porch is of brick, with a timber south front.[47]

The original church, of the late 11th century, consisted of a chancel and nave, to which north and south aisles were added about 1320, when the chancel was rebuilt. The south aisle was built first and then the north, and the west tower was begun immediately after the completion of the aisles. The 15th-century alterations consisted of the widening of the chancel

IPPOLLITTS CHURCH FROM THE SOUTH-EAST

wife of Sir Humphrey Gore[41] (see Offley), to their only child Elizabeth, who married Sir Henry Penrice.[42] They left an only child, Anna Maria wife of Sir Thomas Salusbury. He died in 1773,[43] leaving the property to his second wife Sarah, who at her death bequeathed the manor to a distant cousin, Sir Robert Salusbury, bart.,[44] who entered into possession in 1804 on the death of Sarah.[45] The manor has descended from this time with the manor of Offley (q.v.). Mr. H. G. Salusbury Hughes is the present owner.

Almshoebury, which is now a farm, is built on the site of the old manor-house.

arch and the erection of the north and south porches. In 1879 practically the whole of the church, with the exception of the tower, was taken down and rebuilt from the foundations, but the old materials were replaced with great care, so that the history of the original building can be followed with ease. In the course of this restoration the north aisle was widened from 6 ft. to 9 ft.

The chancel has a modern window in the east wall, one north and two south windows, all of two lights with tracery. They are of the 14th century and have been much repaired. There is a piscina combined with a credence of the 14th century, and in the

[40] Recov. R. Trin. 10 Chas. I, rot. 47; Com. Pleas D. Enr. Trin. 10 Chas. I, m. 5.
[41] Feet of F. Herts. Trin. 1 Geo. I.
[42] Clutterbuck, *Hist. of Herts.* iii, 97.
[43] Ibid.
[44] G.E.C. *Baronetage.*
[45] Clutterbuck, *Herts.* iii, 94; Cussans, *Hist. of Herts. Hitchin Hund.* 114.
[46] Pat. 14 Jas. I, pt. xii.
[47] Dimensions: chancel, 26 ft. by 13 ft.; nave, 29 ft. by 20 ft.; north aisle, 9 ft. wide; south aisle, 6 ft. wide; tower, 15 ft. 6 in. by 13 ft. 6 in.

north wall are two lockers. The modern screen has a central bay of the 15th century.

The nave has two 14th-century arches on either side, inserted in the earlier wall, about 4 ft. apart. They are of two chamfered orders, of which the inner springs from carved corbel heads, some of them modern. The labels also with their mask stops, and parts of the arches, are modern. A rood-loft door with a four-centred head opens from a stair turret at the former level of the loft. The remains of an original round-headed window built of tufa are visible in the wall above the south arcade.

The north aisle has modern windows, but the north doorway is of the early 14th century, restored, and the rear arch is modern. The doorway opens into the north porch, which is of stone, repaired with cement, and has a pointed entrance arch in a square head, with tracery in the spandrels; on either side of the entrance is a roughly executed niche with a trefoiled head, and a canopied niche of the 15th century is over the centre.

In both the north and the south aisles are piscinae of the 14th century. The east and south windows of the south aisle are of the 14th century; the former is a narrow pointed window of two lights with simple tracery, and the latter a square-headed window of two lights, repaired. The west window is modern. To the west of the south window is the south doorway, dating from about 1320, of moulded clunch, opening into the south porch, which has brick sides and a timber framing. The four-centred entrance arch has two lights on either side, plain open timber-work in the gable and moulded barge-boards. The timber-work is of the 15th century and the brick is a 17th-century repair.

The west tower is entered from the nave by a plain arch with modern abaci. The west window is of the 14th century and has three lights, with tracery; it has been slightly repaired. The second stage of the tower is lighted by loops and the bell-chamber has two-light windows, which have been repaired with cement. There is a stair turret at the north-west. The tower is embattled, with a string-course immediately below the battlements, but is otherwise plain. It has square angle buttresses, and the low pyramidal roof is tiled and surmounted by a tall leaded post.

The font, an octagonal bowl standing on a stem with engaged shafts, is of 14th-century date.

The monuments consist of two brasses, one in the north aisle of Robert Poydres and Alice his wife, 1401, with an incomplete inscription, and the other in the chancel of Alice wife of Ryce Hughes, 1594, a single brass bearing kneeling figures of a man, a woman and children, and an inscription; and of a 14th-century recess in the south aisle with the recumbent effigy of a priest.

The bells are modern.

Among the plate is a silver cup of 1634 and a paten of 1639.

The registers are in three books, the first all entries from 1711 to 1750, the second baptisms and burials from 1750 to 1812 and marriages from 1750 to 1753, and the third marriages from 1754 to 1812.

ADVOWSON   The church of Ippollitts was a chapel to Hitchin, and is found with that church in the possession of the nunnery of Elstow, Bedfordshire, at the time of the Dissolution.[48] Both churches were appropriated by the monastery. After the Dissolution the tithes were granted with the rectory of Hitchin (q.v.) to Trinity College, Cambridge. No mention is made of the advowson, so the church was evidently then served from Hitchin, although later the Institution Books show that separate presentations were made for Ippollitts. In March 1685-6 the benefice was united by the Bishop of Lincoln with that of Great Wymondley, another chapelry of Hitchin, of which the college had the patronage.[49] The joint living is still in the gift of Trinity College, Cambridge.

CHARITIES   In 1612 Thomas Bibsworth by deed conveyed certain lands and cottages in the parish to trustees, the rents and profits to be applied in the relief of the poor. Upon the inclosure of the common lands under the Act of 1811,[50] 2 a. 1 r. 28 p. in Bow Street Common were allotted in lieu of 3 a. in the common fields. The property was sold in 1863 and the proceeds invested in £844 19s. 7d. India 3 per cent. stock with the official trustees, producing £25 7s. yearly. A sum of 4s. yearly is also received by the trustees in respect of a rood of land in a field called Bobwell, Little Wymondley Farm.

In 1623 John Welch by his will gave 6s. 8d. yearly to the vicar and 10s. to the poor, payable out of Red Coats Farm in Great Wymondley.

In 1642 George King by deed gave 40s. yearly out of land at Luton for the poor. The annuity is paid by the owner of Luton Hoo estate.

These charities are administered together; 147 bread and coal tickets of the value of 3s. 9d. each were in 1907 distributed to the poor.

In 1653 William Guyver by his will devised an annuity of £4 for apprenticing a boy or girl. The rent-charge is paid by the owner of St. Ibbs estate and is applied as required.

In 1729 William Dawes by his will gave a yearly sum of £5 out of his property near Hitchin for distribution to the poor on St. Thomas's Day. The annuity, less land tax, is paid out of land called Lower Brook Field, and distributed in money doles.

---

[48] Dugdale, *Mon. Angl.* iii, 416.   [49] Information from the Senior Bursar of Trin. Coll. Camb.   [50] Loc. Act, 51 Geo. III, cap. 192.

Ippollitts Church : The South Porch

Ippollitts Church : The Nave looking East

KIMPTON

Kamitone (xi cent.); Kymitone, Kymbton, Kumynton (xiv cent.); Kympton (xv cent.).

Kimpton is a parish of 3,677 acres, lying on the Bedfordshire border, north of the Ayots and west of Codicote. The northern and southern parts reach a height of 450 ft., but the rest is some 100 ft. lower. The surface is undulating, and the village lies in the lower parts, being built along a road running east and west. The street has several 17th-century houses and cottages which retain many of their ancient features. It is about a mile long, including the hamlet of Kimpton Bottom. There are many hamlets and outlying farms and cottages in the parish. Skegsbury Lane lies to the west, Ansells End to the northwest and Percy Green with Peters Green further to the north-west of the parish.

Bury Farm, the residence of Mr. John Barker, lies to the east of the village; Kimpton Grange, the residence of Mr. C. F. Parr, lies to the west; Lawrence End House, with extensive grounds, the seat of Mr. George Oakley, J.P., lies in the north-west part of the parish. Stoneheaps Farm, lying a little less than a mile to the south-west of the church, is a two-storied house of the L type, of plastered timber and brick, built early in the 17th century. Tallents Farm, Rumeridge, Kimpton Hall and Kimpton Mill Farm are farm-houses in the parish built at about the same date, but they have all undergone much alteration, external as well as internal.

The little River Mimram or Maran flows through the north-east of the parish, and adjoining it are osier beds. The soil is chalk. Nearly the whole of the parish is given up to agriculture, 2,506 acres being under the plough; 682 acres are permanent grass, and some 168 acres are woodland,[1] including Cuckoldscross Wood, Dovehouse Wood, Park Wood and Leggatts Spring.

Some Roman and Celtic coins have been found near Prior's Wood in the south-east.

In the 14th century the hundred court of Hitchin was held at Kimpton.[3]

MANORS. In the time of King Edward Ælveva, mother of Earl Morcar, held *KIMPTON*. In 1086 it was assessed for 4 hides and formed part of the possessions of Odo Bishop of Bayeux, of whom it was held by Ralf de Curbespine.[3] Ralf was of the same family as Gilbert Maminot, Bishop of Lisieux (who was son of Robert de Curbespine), and his lands afterwards descended with the Maminots,[4] of whose Dover-Castleward barony Kimpton was held as two knights' fees.[5] Through Alice sister and heir of Walkelin de Maminot this barony passed to the family of Geoffrey de Say, her husband, and the overlordship then descended with the barony of Say.[6]

Under the Says Kimpton was held by three separate tenants as the manors of Hockinghanger, Parkbury and Leggatts.

HOCKINGHANGER (Hokenhangre, xiv cent.; Hokynanger, xvi cent.). As early as 1235–6 Baldwin de Vere, a member of the Northamptonshire family of Vere, was holding this manor and demanding customs there from a certain William de Bikkeworth.[7] He was succeeded by another Baldwin, probably his son, who died before 1303, when his widow Matilda was assessed for three-quarters of a fee in Kimpton held of William de Say.[8] This descended to John de Vere, probably his son, and his widow Alice was holding in 1346.[9] In 1351 Robert de Vere made a settlement of his land, under the name of the manor of Hockinghanger, on himself and his wife Elizabeth in tail.[10] The manor descended in this family until 1493, when Henry de Vere of Great Addington, co. Northants, died seised, leaving four daughters, Elizabeth, Ann, Constance and Audrey.[11] Elizabeth married John Lord Mordaunt[12]; Ann married Sir Humphrey Browne, kt., of Roding, co. Essex[13]; and Audrey married John Browne, a nephew of Sir Humphrey.[14] These three daughters with their husbands each held one-third of the property. In 1556 Audrey, after her husband's death, conveyed her third to John Lord Mordaunt.[15] These two thirds descended to his son John Lord Mordaunt and to the latter's son Lewis Lord Mordaunt.[16] Sir Humphrey Browne, husband of Ann, died in 1562, leaving the third which had fallen to his wife to his three daughters—Mary, who afterwards married Thomas Wylforde; Christine, later the wife of John Tufton, and Katherine.[17] Mary and Katherine seem to have both conveyed their shares to Christine and John Tufton,[18] who in Hilary Term 1581–2 conveyed this portion to Lewis Lord Mordaunt,[19] who thus acquired the whole.

In 1596 Lord Mordaunt sold the manor to Thomas Hoo of St. Paul's Walden.[20] He was succeeded by

MORDAUNT. *Argent a cheveron between three stars sable.*

---

[1] Statistics from Bd. of Agric. (1905).
[2] Assize R. 340.
[3] *V.C.H. Herts.* i, 310*b*. The tenant is given in Domesday as 'Ralf,' but the descent of the manor with the Maminots shows that he was Ralf de Curbespine; cf. West Fairbourne, Thornham and Waldershare in Kent.
[4] *Possibly* Hugh Maminot (temp. Henry I) was his son.
[5] *Red Bk. of Exch.* (Rolls Ser.), ii, 710, 721, 617. There seems no doubt that the place spelt here Kenintone, Revintone and Kenatune is Kimpton (Kemitone); cf. spelling in *Feud. Aids,* ii, 429.
[6] *Feud. Aids,* ii, 429; Chan. Inq. p.m. (Ser. 2), xxxi, 97.
[7] Close, 19 Hen. III, m. 2 d.
[8] *Feud. Aids,* ii, 429; *Excerpta e Rot. Fin.* (Rec. Com.), ii, 509.
[9] *Feud. Aids,* ii, 438.
[10] Feet of F. Div. Co. 25 Edw. III, no. 67.
[11] Exch. Inq. p.m. (Ser. 2), file 292, no. 1.
[12] *Harl. Soc. Publ.* xix, 41–2.
[13] *Visit. Essex* (Harl. Soc. xiii), 166.
[14] Ibid. The fourth daughter Constance does not appear again.
[15] Feet of F. Herts. Trin. 2 & 3 Phil. and Mary.
[16] Ibid. Hil. 24 Eliz.
[17] Chan. Inq. p.m. (Ser. 2), cxxxv, 75; Recov. R. East. 5 Eliz. rot. 1068. His son George died immediately after his own death.
[18] Recov. R. Trin. 18 Eliz. rot. 1120; Feet of F. Herts. Trin. 18 Eliz. In 1577 John Tufton had licence to alienate his third for the purposes of a settlement (Pat. 20 Eliz. pt. iii, m. 17; Feet of F. Herts. East. 20 Eliz.).
[19] Feet of F. Herts. Hil. 24 Eliz.
[20] Ibid. East. 38 Eliz.

his son William Hoo, on whose death in 1636 the manor descended to his son Thomas.[21] Thomas died in 1650, his son Thomas having predeceased him, and Hockinghanger passed with Hoo in St. Paul's Walden to his daughter Susan wife of Sir Jonathan Keate, bart.[22] It descended to their son, Sir Gilbert Hoo-Keate, who was succeeded by his son Sir Henry Hoo-Keate.[23] He sold the manor in 1732 to Margaret Brand of the parish of St. James's, Westminster, widow of Thomas Brand,[24] from whom it passed successively to her son and grandson, both named Thomas.[25] The son Thomas married in 1771 Gertrude daughter of Henry Roper Lord Teynham, who, on the death of her brother Charles Lord Dacre, became Lady Dacre in her own right. Her son Thomas Brand succeeded his mother as twentieth Lord Dacre, from whom the manor passed in 1851 to his brother Henry Otway, who took the name of Trevor. His two sons Thomas Crosbie William Trevor, Lord Dacre, and Henry Bouverie William Brand, Lord Dacre, created first Viscount Hampden in 1884, successively inherited the estate, and it passed from the latter to his eldest son Henry Robert Brand, second Viscount Hampden and twenty-fourth Lord Dacre, the present lord of the manor.[26]

The manor of *PARKBURY* was held under the Says in the 14th century by the family of Brok as one half and one half of one quarter of a knight's fee.[27] In 1303 Laurence de Brok was assessed for it.[28] He was dead by 1330, when the manor was held by his widow Ellen de Brok for life, with reversion to her son Ralph, and she received a grant of free warren in that year.[29] Before 1346 the manor had passed to Nigel de Loreng, kt.,[30] chamberlain to the Black Prince, who had a large estate at Chalgrave in Bedfordshire.[31] He was in possession in 1384–5, when he conveyed it to trustees.[32] Probably the trustees conveyed to John Fray,[33] who was assessed for the same fee in 1428.[34] In 1436 John Fray and Agnes his wife sold the manor under the name of Parkbury to Richard Hungate and Elizabeth his wife.[35] After Richard's death Elizabeth married John Gunter, and they held it for life with reversion to John Suliard and his wife Agnes daughter and heir of Richard Hungate.[36] Edward Suliard died seised of the manor in 1516, leaving as heir his son William,[37] who died in March 1539–40, having settled the property on his brother Eustace.[38] From Eustace it passed to his son Edward,[39] who in Hilary Term 1579–80 conveyed the property to John Knighton and George his son.[40] John Knighton, of the Inner Temple, died in 1599.[41] His son George must have predeceased his father, for his brother George Knighton of Bayford was his heir.[42] George was knighted in 1603.[43] He settled the property in 1603 on himself and his wife Lady Susan for life, with remainder to their son John, who succeeded in 1613.[44] At John's death in 1635 the manor passed to Knighton Ferrers, son of his sister Anne, who had married Sir John Ferrers of Markyate.[45] His daughter and heir Katherine married Thomas Viscount Fanshawe.[46] In 1665 Basset Cole and his wife Anne[47] sold the property to Sir Jonathan Keate, bart.,[48] after which it descended with Hockinghanger (q.v.).

The manor of *LEGGATTS* was held in 1303 as half a knight's fee and one-eighth of a fee of Lord William de Say by Roger Wyscard.[49] It passed shortly afterwards to the family of Leggatt, from whom it took its name. In 1346 Robert Morlee, a feoffee of John Leggatt, was assessed for it.[50] John's son Edward Leggatt, who was in gaol for felony in 1369,[51] died seised of the manor in 1396.[52] The estate consisted of a messuage and garden, a dove-house, 242½ acres of land, 1 acre of meadow, rents of 42s. 2¾d. and a fishery.[53] His cousin John was his heir.[54] John possibly left co-heiresses, for in 1409 a certain John

Hoo. *Quarterly sable and argent.*

Keate. *Argent three cats passant sable.*

Roper, Lord Dacre. *Six pieces azure and or with three harts' heads or.*

Brand, Viscount Hampden. *Azure two crossed swords argent with their hilts or between three scallops or.*

---

[21] Berry, *Herts. Gen.* 158; Recov. R. East. 13 Chas. I, rot. 5.
[22] Recov. R. Mich. 8 Chas. II, rot. 165; Hil. 12 Chas. II, rot. 3.
[23] See ibid. Trin. 10 Geo. I, rot. 280.
[24] Ibid. 6 Geo. II, rot. 191; Close, 6 Geo. II, pt. xiv, no. 17.
[25] Recov. R. East. 11 Geo. III, rot. 55.
[26] Berry, *Herts. Gen.* 44 et seq.; G.E.C. *Peerage.*
[27] *Feud. Aids,* ii, 429.
[28] Ibid.
[29] Chart. R. 4 Edw. III, pt. i, no. 28.
[30] *Feud. Aids,* ii, 438.
[31] *Dict. Nat. Biog.*
[32] Feet of F. Div. Co. Hil. 8 Ric. II, no. 28.
[33] See Feet of F. Herts. Trin. 10 Hen. IV, no. 74.
[34] *Feud. Aids,* ii, 449.
[35] Feet of F. Herts. Trin. 14 Hen. VI, no. 77.
[36] Close, 37 Hen. VI, m. 31.
[37] Chan. Inq. p.m. (Ser. 2), xxxi, 97.
[38] Ibid. lxiv, 88.
[39] Ibid. lxxxvi, 99.
[40] Feet of F. Herts. Hil. 22 Eliz.
[41] Chan. Inq. p.m. (Ser. 2), cclviii, 77.
[42] Ibid.
[43] Shaw, *Knights of Engl.* ii, 116.
[44] Chan. Inq. p.m. (Ser. 2), cccxliii, 143.
[45] Ibid. ccclxxxvi, 129.
[46] G.E.C. *Peerage,* s.v. Fanshawe; see Feet of F. Div. Co. Hil. 1651.
[47] Chauncy calls the wife Lady Amy Mordaunt, and says she had bought the manor.
[48] Feet of F. Herts. Hil. 16 & 17 Chas. II.
[49] *Feud. Aids,* ii, 429. [50] Ibid. 438.
[51] Chan. Inq. p.m. 43 Edw. III, pt. ii (2nd nos.), no. 3*b*.
[52] Ibid. 20 Ric. II, no. 34.
[53] Ibid. 43 Edw. III, pt. ii (2nd nos.), no. 3*b*.
[54] Ibid. 20 Ric. II, no. 34.

KIMPTON: STONEHEAPS FARM

KIMPTON CHURCH FROM THE SOUTH-WEST

HITCHIN HUNDRED   KIMPTON

Chertsey conveyed a moiety of the manor to John Fray,[55] from whom it passed with Parkbury to Hungate,[56] and the two manors subsequently descended together.

Besides the three manors which formed the holding of the Says in Kimpton there was another manor called *BIBBESWORTH* (Bybesworth, xiv cent.), which was held of the manor of Pirton,[57] from which it was evidently formed by subinfeudation. It gave its name to, or took its name from, a family of Bibbesworth, who held it under the lords of Pirton.[58] In 1277 Walter de Bibbesworth was holding the manor, and received a grant of free warren in January of that year (1276–7).[59] William de Bibbesworth settled it in 1303 on his son Hugh de Bibbesworth and Emma his wife.[60] Later Hugh granted half a hide of his estate to the monastery of St. Albans.[61] He was succeeded by his son John de Bibbesworth,[62] who died in 1361,[63] having previously settled the property on his son Hugh and Amice his wife.[64] In 1402 they settled the manor on their son Edmund.[65] After his death it was held by his widow Goditha,[66] she outliving her son John, who died in 1448,[67] leaving a son Thomas, a minor. Thomas entered into the property on attaining his majority in 1467.[68] He died without issue in 1485, his heirs being his cousins, Joan wife of Thomas Barlee and John Cotys of Hunningham, co. Warwick.[69] The manor of Bibbesworth was assigned to Joan and Thomas Barlee.[70] At his death in 1524 Thomas left a son Robert,[71] who was succeeded by his son Francis.[72]

In 1560 the manor was owned by Richard Barlee,[73] probably son of Francis. Richard died in 1593, leaving as heir a son Thomas,[74] who became a lunatic in 1603, but seems to have held the manor till some four years later, when his heirs are returned as his three sisters, Dorothea Osburn, Anna Lady Dacres and Maria Wiseman.[75] Apparently, however, he had a daughter Grace (perhaps born after this date), the wife of Cressy Tasburgh, who suffered sequestration as a recusant in 1650, but obtained restoration of his lands in 1651.[76] In 1659 Robert Barlee and William Wiseman, probably their trustees, conveyed to Sir Jonathan Keate,[77] and the manor remained with his descendants[78] together with Hockinghanger (q.v.).

LITTLE BIBBESWORTH was another estate formed out of the manor of Pirton. John de Limesi, lord of that manor in the latter part of the 12th century, granted 8 acres in Bibbesworth to Richard de Puteo, who gave them to the monastery of St. Mary, Hertford (to which Ralph de Limesi [see Pirton] had made a grant of tithes and of pannage in his wood there), to the use of the kitchen.[79] In 1291 the priory had lands valued at £2 13s. 8d. in Kimpton.[80] After the Dissolution this estate was granted under the name of the manor of Bibbesworth in February 1537–8 to Anthony Denny and Joan his wife.[81] They conveyed the manor in 1543 to Nicholas Bristowe and his wife Lucy.[82] In the inquisition taken on his death in 1584 the manor is called Little Bibbesworth.[83] He was succeeded by his son Nicholas, who died at Ayot St. Lawrence in 1626.[84] His son, also Nicholas, died in July 1634, and Robert his brother inherited the fee simple of the Bristowe estates.[85] After this time it seems to have descended with the advowson (q.v.).

A reputed manor called *PLUMMERS*[86] was conveyed in 1596 by Thomas Hoo to Edward Sibley,[87] and the next year was acquired from the latter by Thomas Halsey *alias* Chambers.[88] The farm of Plummers is now occupied by Mr. Robert Avery.

Another reputed manor of *LEIGH* or *LYGH* was held by Sir Edward Benstede, kt., at his death in 1518. John Ferrers, his kinsman and heir, succeeded.[89] In 1547 the manor was conveyed by Francis Ferrers to John Brockett and his wife Margaret.[90] Edward Peade was holding it in 1589, when he alienated it to Thomas Cheyne.[91]

The parish church of *ST. PETER CHURCH AND ST. PAUL* stands at the north end of the village. The church consists of a chancel, nave, south chapel, north and south aisles, west tower of three stages with leaded spire, south porch of two stages with an octagonal north-west stair turret, north vestry and organ chamber.[92] It is built of flint rubble with freestone dressings.

The existing nave is probably of the same plan as that of the original 12th-century building, which consisted of an aisleless nave and chancel. About 1200 the north and south aisles were added, and at the same time, or perhaps a little later, the chancel was enlarged to its present size. There are traces of 14th-century alterations in the chancel, but it was not until the 15th century that any further addition was made, when the south chapel was built, the south aisle probably partly rebuilt, the clearstory of the nave was made, and the south porch and west

---

[55] Feet of F. Herts. Trin. 10 Hen. IV, no. 74.
[56] Close, 37 Hen. VI, m. 31.
[57] Chan. Inq. p.m. 35 Edw. III, no. 44; (Ser. 2), ccxli, 107.
[58] See Dugdale, *Mon.* iii, 300, 301.
[59] Chart. R. 5 Edw. I, no. 70.
[60] Feet of F. Herts. 32 Edw. I, no. 386; *Visit. Essex* (Harl. Soc. xiii), 1.
[61] Cott. MSS. Nero, D vii, fol. 92.
[62] Feet of F. Div. Co. Hil. 27 Edw. III, no. 91; *Visit. Essex* (Harl. Soc. xiii), 1.
[63] Chan. Inq. p.m. 35 Edw. III, no. 44.
[64] Feet of F. Div. Co. Hil. 27 Edw. III, no. 496.
[65] *Visit. Essex* (Harl. Soc. xiii), 1; Feet of F. Div. Co. Hil. 3 Hen. IV; Add. Chart. x, 1990.
[66] Chan. Inq. p.m. 5 Edw. IV, no. 22.
[67] Ibid. 27 Hen. VII, no. 35.
[68] Ibid. 7 Edw. IV, no. 59.
[69] Ibid. (Ser. 2), i, 75. Joan was daughter of Thomas Bibbesworth's father's sister Joan, and John Cotys son of another sister Agnes.
[70] Close, 1 Hen. VII, no. 103.
[71] Chan. Inq. p.m. (Ser. 2), xl, 101.
[72] Ibid. lvi, 42; *Visit. Essex* (Harl. Soc. xiii), 1; Court of Wards, cxxix, fol. 207 d.
[73] Feet of F. Div. Co. Mich. 2 Eliz.
[74] Chan. Inq. p.m. (Ser. 2), ccxli, 107.
[75] Ibid. cxxcviii, 72, 82. This is an inq. *de lunatico inquirendo,* not an inq. p.m.
[76] *Cal. Com. for Comp.* 2235.
[77] Close, 6 Geo. II, pt. xiv, no. 17.
[78] See Recov. R. Trin. 10 Geo. I, rot. 280.
[79] Dugdale, *Mon.* iii, 301; Campb. Chart. x, 12.
[80] *Pope Nich. Tax.* (Rec. Com.), 5.
[81] Pat. 29 Hen. VIII, pt. ii, m. 19.
[82] *L. and P. Hen. VIII,* xviii (1), g. 226 (82).
[83] Chan. Inq. p.m. (Ser. 2), ccvi, 12.
[84] Ibid. ccccix, 66.
[85] Ibid. ccccxxiv, 6. See under advowson.
[86] For John Plomer or Plummer, who with his wife Agnes, widow of Richard Nash, held lands in Kimpton in her right about the same date, and from whose family this manor probably took its name, see Chan. Proc. (Ser. 2), bdle. 286, no. 39.
[87] Feet of F. Herts. East. 38 Eliz.
[88] Ibid. Mich. 39 & 40 Eliz.
[89] Chan. Inq. p.m. (Ser. 2), xxxiv, 35.
[90] Feet of F. Herts. Trin. 1 Edw. VI.
[91] Ibid. Mich. 31 & 32 Eliz.
[92] Dimensions: chancel, 36 ft. by 15 ft.; south chapel, 32 ft. by 14 ft. 6 in.; nave, 64 ft. by 18 ft.; north aisle, 12 ft. 6 in. wide; south aisle, 13 ft. 6 in. wide; west tower, 12 ft. 6 in. by 12 ft.; south porch, 9 ft. by 10 ft. 6 in.

A HISTORY OF HERTFORDSHIRE

tower were added. In 1861 the church was rather drastically restored, the north aisle being completely rebuilt, the windows and doors much repaired and altered and the north vestry and organ chamber added.

The chancel has an east window of three lights, in which traces of early 14th-century work remain, but the bulk of it is modern. On either side of it the remains of a 13th-century lancet window are visible with traces of contemporary paintings of figures of angels on the remaining splays. The chapel arcade on the south side is of the 15th century, of three bays with columns of four clustered shafts and moulded arches. Between the chancel and south chapel are parts of a mid-15th-century parclose screen, much repaired, with traceried panels and moulded stiles and cornice. There are six poppy-head bench ends of the 15th century in the chancel, also much restored. The north wall of the chancel is modern.

The south chapel has an east window and three square-headed south windows. The openings are original, but all the tracery is modern, and the south door is much restored. There is here an early 13th-century piscina, which has been reset. The mid-15th-century screen at the west of the chapel has a vaulted canopy. It is much restored throughout.

The nave has arcades of six bays, of the end of the 12th or early years of the 13th century. The arches are two-centred, and of two moulded orders, with drop labels facing the nave. The columns are circular with moulded bases; some of the capitals are scalloped and some foliate. The clearstory windows are three on the north and four on the south. They have two lights, and the westernmost on the south side has a wooden head.

The north aisle is entirely modern. The south aisle, which is much restored, has four three-light windows, of which the jambs and rear arches only are old. The roof of this aisle is of late 15th or early 16th-century date. It has moulded ridges, purlins and wall-plates and cambered trusses resting on corbels carved as angels. The south doorway is of the 15th century and has a continuous moulding, and a label with grotesque stops. It opens to the south porch, of the same date, which is of two stories, and originally had a window opening into the south aisle from the second stage; this is now blocked. The pointed entrance arch is plain and has a label with carved stops. There are square-headed windows on the east and west. The second stage is approached by an octagonal stair turret rising above the porch, at the north-west, at the angle of junction with the aisle, and is lighted by a two-light traceried window with a pointed head. Both the porch and the turret have embattled parapets above string-courses. The west tower is of two stages with strongly projecting buttresses, an embattled parapet and a lead-covered needle spire. At the north-east corner is a projecting stair turret. The tower arch is of the 15th century, and is four-centred, of two moulded orders with flat jambs. The west door is so much restored as to be practically modern, and the same is true of the window above it. The windows of the upper stage of the tower are of two trefoiled lights; they also are much restored.

The earliest monument is an early 15th-century brass in the chancel, with the figure of a woman wearing her hair loose, having no inscription. There are mural monuments to Susannah wife of Sir Jonathan Keate, 1673, to Judith Orlebar, 1690, and to Sir Jonathan Keate, 1700.

There are six bells: the first and third are by Robert Oldfeild, 1636; the second is by John Waylett, 1728; the fourth is by John Saunders, and dates from the middle of the 16th century; the fifth is probably by William Burford, of the middle of the 14th century, and the sixth is by Robert Oldfeild, with the date 1638.

The plate includes a cup of 1635.

The registers are contained in three books, the first containing baptisms and burials from 1559 to 1777 and marriages from 1559 to 1753; the second contains baptisms and burials from 1777 to 1812, and the third marriages from 1777 to 1812.

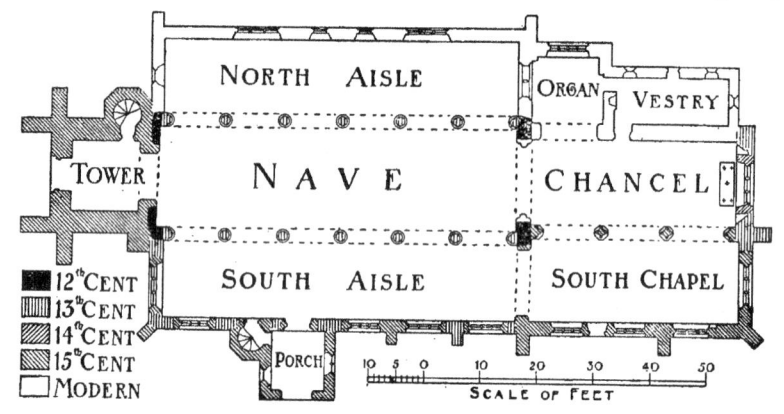

PLAN OF KIMPTON CHURCH

32

Kimpton Church: The Nave looking East

Kimpton Church: The South Aisle looking East

HITCHIN HUNDRED

KING'S WALDEN

ADVOWSON
The advowson of the church of St. Peter and St. Paul of Kimpton was granted, probably by one of the Says, to the priory of Austin Canons of Merton, in Surrey.[93] A vicarage was ordained there previous to 1291,[94] and between 1363 and 1397 the vicar and Prior of Hertford (who had a grant of tithes of pannage from Ralph de Limesi, see above) arranged an allotment of tithes.[95] In February 1542–3 the king granted the advowson to John Williams and Anthony Stringer,[96] who alienated in the same year to Nicholas Bacon and Henry Ashfelde.[97] Nicholas Bacon conveyed the property in 1543 to Nicholas Bristowe,[98] who died in 1584, leaving as heir his son Nicholas.[99] Five years later the advowson was granted to Richard Branthwayte and Roger Bromley,[100] who were possibly acting as trustees or were merely 'fishing grantees.' Nicholas son of the above Nicholas came into possession at his father's death.[101] He was succeeded by his son Nicholas,[102] who held the property until 1634, when he died, leaving to his daughters Elizabeth and Anne a twenty-one years' interest in the estate, which was to revert at the end of that time to their uncle Robert Bristowe.[103] In 1663 Robert Bristowe and his son Nicholas conveyed the advowson to Sir Jonathan Keate, bart.,[104] and it then descended with the manor of Kimpton[105] to Viscount Hampden, the present patron.

In the 15th century Edmund atte Hoo left in his will a bequest to the fabric of the church of Kimpton.[106]

A letter has been preserved, written by the Prior of Merton to the Bishop of Lincoln, asking permission for the construction of a private oratory without a bell-tower. The request was apparently made on behalf of Lady Ellen, formerly wife of Robert de Vere. The chapel was to be used by her household and guests alone, and the chaplain was to make amends to the vicar of the mother church of Kimpton if he gave the sacrament; while the vicar could suspend the celebration if the mother church suffered by it.[107]

The rectory was granted by the king in 1543 to Nicholas Bristowe and Lucy his wife for their lives.[108] In 1567 it was regranted to Nicholas Bristowe, their son, on lease for twenty-one years.[109] A grant to Richard Branthwayte and Roger Bromley in 1589[110] was probably in trust for Richard Spencer,[111] whose son Sir John Spencer of Offley, bart. (so created in 1627), died seised in 1633 under a settlement made by his father.[112] At Sir John's death the rectory passed to his brother Brockett Spencer,[113] and afterwards descended in the family of Salusbury[114] with the manor of St. Ledgers in Offley (q.v.).

There is a Wesleyan chapel in Kimpton.

CHARITIES
William Barford, D.D., Prebendary of Canterbury, Fellow of Eton, and vicar of this parish, by his will proved in the P.C.C. 31 January 1793 bequeathed 20s. yearly for the poor. The legacy is now represented by £33 6s. 8d. consols with the official trustees, and the annual dividends amounting to 16s. 8d. are distributed equally among eight poor persons.

John Bassill by his will, proved in the P.C.C. 1 February 1816, gave £120 stock, the dividends, subject to keeping in repair the testator's vault, to be applied every three years as to one-third for dinner to the resident clergyman, one-third among six poor families, and remaining one-third in prize money for games among young people, first deducting 40s. for a dinner for the church ringers and parish clerk.

The legacy is now represented by £192 0s. 5d. consols with the official trustees, producing £4 16s. yearly.

KING'S WALDEN

King's Walden is a parish 4,392 acres in extent, lying on a spur of the Chilterns at a height of some 450 ft. above the ordnance datum. The surface of the land is slightly undulating, the subsoil chalk,[1] on which corn is largely grown. Arable land covers 2,755 acres, while the grass land extends over only about one-quarter of this area, and the woodland 137 acres.[2] The original settlement seems to have been of the Saxon type, having the church of St. Mary adjoining the manor-house of King's Waldenbury and the village near, the whole being off the road, as is usual in this type of settlement. At a later date the inhabitants migrated to the road, where the market would naturally be held, and eventually deserted the original settlement. Thus the village became established where we find it to-day, nearly a mile from the church and manor-house. It is uncertain when a market was first granted, possibly in the 13th century, when so many grants of market were made, but in 1795 a market was held here on Saturdays.[3] The village consists of two irregular lines of cottages.

Scattered over the parish are many farm-houses and cottages, and there are three small hamlets, Wandon End[4] and Wandou Green on the western and southern borders of the parish, and Ley Green[5] to the north of King's Waldenbury Park. The Inclosure Act is dated 1796–7,[6] and the common was inclosed by an award of 1802.[7]

---

[93] Dugdale, *Mon. Angl.* vi, 245.
[94] *Pope Nich. Tax.* (Rec. Com.), 42.
[95] Linc. Epis. Reg. Bokingham, fol. 338.
[96] *L. and P. Hen. VIII,* xviii (1), 226 (79).
[97] Ibid. xviii (1), g. 226 (87).
[98] Chan. Inq. p.m. (Ser. 2), ccvi, 12; Add. Chart. 1991, 1997.
[99] Chan. Inq. p.m. (Ser. 2), ccvi, 12.
[100] Pat. 31 Eliz. pt. xi, m. 27.
[101] Chan. Inq. p.m. (Ser. 2), cccxlix, 66. [102] Ibid.
[103] Ibid. ccccxxiv, 6.

[104] Recov. R. Mich. 15 Chas. II, rot. 52; Close, 6 Geo. II, pt. xiv, no. 17.
[105] See Inst. Bks. (P.R.O.).
[106] Wills, Archdeaconry of St. Albans, Stonehaven 31.
[107] Cott. MS. Cleop. C vii, 144.
[108] Add. Chart. 1997; *L. and P. Hen. VIII,* xix (1), 644.
[109] Pat. 31 Eliz. pt. xi, m. 27.
[110] Ibid.
[111] Branthwayte and Spencer were connected by marriage; Branthwaite's daughter Margaret married Spencer's nephew Thomas. See G.E.C. *Baronetage,* i, 69; ii, 10.
[112] Chan. Inq. p.m. (Ser. 2), dxii, 4.
[113] Recov. R. Mich. 15 Chas. I, rot. 56.
[114] Ibid. 45 Geo. III, rot. 17.

[1] *V.C.H. Herts.* i, Geol. map.
[2] Statistics from Bd. of Agric. (1905).
[3] *Verulam MSS.* (Hist. MSS. Com.), i, 159.
[4] *V.C.H. Herts.* i, 303*a*.
[5] Ibid. 304*b*.
[6] Local Acts, 1 Geo. I–37 Geo. III.
[7] *Blue Bk. Incl. Awards.*

A HISTORY OF HERTFORDSHIRE

MANORS

From before the time of the Domesday Survey two manors were in existence in King's Walden. Each was estimated at 1 hide, and in the time of Earl Harold both were held of him, one by Leueva, the other by Asgar's widow. At the time of the Survey the former was in the king's hands, the latter was still held by Asgar's widow, of the king.[8] These two manors, both known by the name of King's Walden, existed as separate manors till the middle of the 15th century,[9] when they seem to have become united.

One manor of *KING'S WALDEN*, afterwards called *DUXWORTH*, was granted at an early date to the family of Delamare,[10] who were holding in the neighbouring parish of Offley. Early in the 13th century Robert son of Osbert Delamare[11] held King's Walden by the service of one knight's fee.[12] Robert forfeited his lands in 1224 as an ally of Falkes de Breauté, but they were afterwards restored to his wife Alice for herself and her heirs.[13] Her son John inherited his mother's estate[14] and held it till his death about 1276, leaving as heir his grandson John, a minor,[15] who was assessed for the fee in 1303.[16] It was then extended at a messuage and 60 acres of land, 2 acres of pasture, 2 acres of wood and rents of asize. In this year he alienated it to John de Dokesworth or Duxworth,[17] who settled it in 1316 on himself and his wife Parnel and their heirs.[18] John died in 1338,[19] leaving a son William, who held the manor[20] till his death in 1362, when he was succeeded by his son Elias.[21] He about 1380 alienated King's Walden to John Bixen and Walter Pulter, who enfeoffed John Wylkyn of the same.[22] John Wylkyn was convicted in July 1381 of felony and treason and forfeited his lands, which were granted in fee farm to Hugh Martyn, one of the king's servitors.[23] It would appear that Hugh lost his possessions about 1395 by his outlawry,[24] and they reverted to the Crown. The king made a fresh grant of them to Reginald Lord Cobham of Sterborough, who held a court in 1401.[25] The manor descended to his son Reginald Lord Cobham,[26] who died in 1446. His granddaughter Margaret (daughter of his eldest son Reginald), who succeeded him,[27] died without issue about 1460, and her husband Ralph Earl of Westmorland in 1485. The manor came to Anne daughter of Thomas second son of Reginald Lord Cobham, the wife of Sir Edward Burgh, and it descended to their son Thomas Lord Burgh, who died seised of King's Walden in 1551.[28] His son William Lord Burgh[29] conveyed it in 1576 to Richard Hale.[30] He died in 1621, having settled the property on his second son Richard and his heirs. The estate, however, came eventually to William, the eldest son.[31]

William Hale died in 1633, leaving a son William, whose heir at his death in 1643[32] was his brother Rowland,[33] from whom the manor passed to his son William.[34] It descended in this family to Faggen Hale, who was holding in 1742.[35] He left no issue, so that at his death the property passed to a cousin, William Hale,[36] and from him to his son William, who was holding in 1815.[37] After the death of Charles Cholmondeley Hale in 1884 the property was purchased by Mrs. Hinds, and in 1891 it was bought from her by Mr. Thomas Fenwick Harrison,[38] who is the present lord of the manor and lives at King's Waldenbury.

HALE of King's Walden. *Azure a cheveron or battled on both sides.*

The other manor of *KING'S WALDEN* mentioned in the Survey[39] extended into the hamlet of Wandou End. It was apparently granted at an early date to the family of Valoines, of which barony it was held as one knight's fee.[40] On the death (before November 1220) of Gunnora wife of Robert Fitz Walter, daughter and heir of Robert de Valoines, the manor descended to her daughter Christine, who married, first, William de Mandeville Earl of Essex, and, secondly, Raymund de Burgh, and died without issue in 1233. King's Walden then went to Isabel wife of David Comyn, one of the heirs of Christine.[41] In 1310 it was granted by Edmund Comyn to John de Dokesworth,[42] lord of the other manor of King's Walden (q.v.), and the overlordship remained with his successors in that manor.[43]

This fee, together with other lands held of the Delamares' manor of King's Walden, was held in the first half of the 13th century by John de Nevill.[44] He was succeeded by John de Nevill, who was holding in 1259.[45] He died in 1286, leaving a son John,[45a] who with his wife Denise held the estate[46] till his death in 1313.[47] A windmill and a water mill are mentioned in the extent of the manor at this date. Walter, John's son, succeeded him.[48] He obtained a

---

[8] *V.C.H. Herts.* i, 302*b*.
[9] *Feud. Aids*, ii, 449.
[10] *Testa de Nevill* (Rec. Com.), 266.
[11] *Red Bk. of Exch.* (Rolls Ser.), 499.
[12] *Testa de Nevill*, 279*b*; *Red Bk. of Exch.* 499.
[13] Close, 8 Hen. III, pt. i, m. 20.
[14] *Excerpta e Rot. Fin.* (Rec. Com.), i, 186; *Testa de Nevill*, 266, 272*b*.
[15] Chan. Inq. p.m. 4 Edw. I, file 14, no. 5; file 17, no. 16; Fine R. 4 Edw. I, m. 3.
[16] *Feud. Aids*, ii, 429.
[17] Inq. a.q.d. file 42, no. 8; *Cal. Pat.* 1301–7, p. 118.
[18] Inq. a.q.d. file 113, no. 82; *Cal. Pat.* 1313–17, p. 481; Feet of F. Herts. 10 Edw. II, no. 242.
[19] Chan. Inq. p.m. 11 Edw. III, no. 20.
[20] *Feud. Aids*, ii, 438.
[21] Chan. Inq. p.m. 36 Edw. III, no. 53.
[22] Inq. a.q.d. file 397, no. 3; *Cal. Pat.* 1377–81, pp. 620, 624.
[23] Pat. 5 Ric. II, pt. ii, m. 7.
[24] *Cal. Pat.* 1391–6, pp. 202, 560.
[25] Add. R. 35932.
[26] Close, 10 Hen. IV, m. 32; *Feud. Aids*, ii, 449.
[27] See Feet of F. Div. Co. Hil. 33 Hen. VI, no. 53.
[28] Chan. Inq. p.m. (Ser. 2), xciii, 105.
[29] See Recov. R. Hil. 5 & 6 Edw. VI, rot. 517; Add. R. 35989, 35990, 35993, 35996.
[30] Feet of F. Herts. East. 18 Eliz.; Add. R. 35997.
[31] Chan. Inq. p.m. (Ser. 2), ccclxxxvii, 110; Add. R. 36021.
[32] Chan. Inq. p.m. (Ser. 2), dxxvi, 148.
[33] Ibid. dcxcviii, 65; Add. R. 36055.
[34] Feet of F. Herts. Trin. 8 Anne; Add. R. 36036; Burke, *Landed Gentry.*
[35] Recov. R. Trin. 16 Geo. II, rot. 153.
[36] Ibid. Mich. 11 Geo. III, rot. 185.
[37] Ibid. 55 Geo. III, rot. 243; Burke, *Landed Gentry.*
[38] Information from Mr. T. F. Harrison.
[39] *V.C.H. Herts.* i, 302*b*.
[40] *Testa de Nevill* (Rec. Com.), 271*a*; *Feud. Aids*, ii, 429.
[41] See *Ancestor*, no. xi, 1904.
[42] *Cal. Pat.* 1307–13, p. 223; Feet of F. Herts. 4 Edw. II, file 54.
[43] *Feud. Aids*, ii, 437.
[44] *Testa de Nevill* (Rec. Com.), 271.
[45] Feet of F. Herts. Mich. 43 Hen. III, no. 514.
[45a] Chan. Inq. p.m. 14 Edw. I, no. 9.
[46] See Feet of F. Herts. Mich. 3 Edw. II, no. 47; Add. R. 35925, 35928.
[47] Chan. Inq. p.m. 7 Edw. II, no. 26.
[48] Chart. R. 12 Edw. II, m. 17, no. 72.

34

KIMPTON CHURCH: OLD DESK IN THE CHANCEL

KING'S WALDEN CHURCH: THE NAVE LOOKING EAST

grant of free warren in 1318[49] and died in 1329, leaving as heir his daughter Agnes,[50] who married Thomas Fytlyng.[51] They apparently had no issue. The reversion of the third of the manor held by Katherine widow of Walter de Nevill was granted by them in 1356 to Reginald de Cobham,[52] on whom evidently a settlement of the other two parts was also made, for the manor subsequently descended with Duxworth, and the two manors became amalgamated.

In 1613 a messuage called *WANDE MEADE*, probably situated in the hamlet of Wandon End, was held by Thomas Rudd, who died in that year.[53] His son Thomas, who succeeded him, held it till his death in 1636, when he left a son Thomas, aged four years.[54] This last Thomas was holding in 1657.[55]

Among the possessions of the Crown enumerated in Domesday Book is 'Leglega.'[56] The extent was 1 virgate, and it was held by three sokemen.[57] This estate may possibly be the lands called *LYE*, which in the 15th century were held by the family of Brograve,[58] and the name may survive in Ley Green.

In 1540 there was a *RECTORY MANOR* in this parish attached to the church which had formed part of the possessions of the priory of Old Malton, Yorkshire.[59] There is no previous record of this manor, which had probably been granted to this priory by Walter de Nevill with the advowson of the church.[60] After the Dissolution it was granted in 1550 by the king to Ralph Sadleir,[61] and from that date was held with the advowson of the vicarage (q.v.).

The parish church of *ST. MARY*, CHURCH lying to the west of King's Waldenbury, is faced with flint; the dressings are of stone. The chancel and north vestry are tiled, and the rest of the church is roofed with lead. The nave and tower have embattled parapets. The church consists of a chancel, nave and aisles, south porch, north vestry and west tower.

The original church, dating from the late 11th or early 12th century, probably consisted of a nave and chancel only, now represented by the present walls of the nave, in which the nave arcades were inserted and the aisles added about 1190. The chancel as it now stands probably preserves the plan of that which was built in the 13th century, but has been very much altered. About 1380 the west tower was added, and in the 15th century the clearstory was made and the aisles were partially or wholly rebuilt. The north vestry, of brick, was built early in the 17th century, and the south porch is of the 19th century, when the walls of the whole church were refaced externally and the chancel and aisles were partly rebuilt.

All the windows in the chancel have been renewed. There are a few 15th-century stones in the east window and in the west window of the south wall. Both these windows are of three lights with tracery. There are possibly also a few original stones in the east window of the south wall, which is a lancet. In the chancel is a double piscina of the 13th century. The screen is 15th-century work, with two two-light upper panels with tracery on each side of the central opening. It has a cornice and 'Tudor-flower' cresting. The whole screen is much patched and thickly painted.

The chancel arch is of the early 14th century, and has two chamfered orders and half-octagonal responds, moulded capitals and half-octagonal jambs. The nave arcades are of three bays, of late 12th-century date, with two-centred arches of two chamfered orders. The columns are circular and have capitals of scalloped, trefoil and water-leaf designs. The clearstory has three three-light windows with low two-centred heads on either side, of which the tracery is restored. At the level of the responds of the chancel arch the door to the former rood-loft opens in the east end of the north wall, and is now partly blocked. Two large carved corbels which support the eastern truss of the roof are of the 15th century.

The north aisle has three windows—one at each end and one in the north wall. The last is of three lights and has a four-centred head. The west window is a single trefoiled light. Almost the whole of the exterior stonework and the windows themselves have been renewed. The north door, to the west of the north window, is of the 14th century much restored.

The difference between the height of the bases of the north and south arcades, and the position of the steps from the doorway, indicate that the floor of this aisle has been lowered.

On the east wall, to the north of the east window, is an image bracket, much defaced. On the north wall, at the north-east, is a piscina with a square head. A few 15th-century timbers remain in the roof.

The south aisle extends eastwards beyond the line of the chancel arch and formerly communicated with the chancel by a doorway at the north, which is now blocked. The east window and the south-east window are of three lights, of the 15th century, much restored, and the south-west window, of the same date, and also much restored, has two lights. The south door is also of the 15th century, and has a four-centred arch in a square head with tracery in the spandrels. It is of two moulded orders. At the east end of the aisle, in the north spur wall, is a locker, with a rebate for a door. There is also a late 14th-century piscina, with a cinquefoiled head, in the south wall at the east end. The roof of the aisle is of the 15th century.

The north vestry, of early 17th-century date, has Gothic wooden window frames. It contains a 17th-century oak chest.

The west tower is of three stages, with an embattled parapet and a projecting stair-turret at the south-east corner. It has buttresses, very badly weathered, at the angles, in pairs at the north-west and south-west, and single at the north-east, at the junction with the nave. The tower arch is of the end of the 14th century, and has two chamfered orders. It is two-centred and the jambs are shafted. In the west doorway is an old door. The west window and the four bell-chamber windows are all of

---

[49] Chart. R. 12 Edw. II, m. 17, no. 72.
[50] Chan. Inq. p.m. 3 Edw. III (1st nos.), no. 53.
[51] *Feud. Aids*, ii, 437.
[52] Feet of F. Herts. 23 Edw. III, no. 392; 30 Edw. III, no. 452.
[53] Chan. Inq. p.m. (Ser. 2), ccccxi, 143.
[54] Ibid. dcxxxvi, 98.
[55] Add. Chart. 35508.
[56] *V.C.H. Herts.* i, 304*b*.
[57] Ibid.
[58] Chan. Proc. (Ser. 2), bdle. 155, no. 34.
[59] Mins. Accts. 31 & 32 Hen. VIII, R. 178, m. 9.
[60] Feet of F. Mich. 43 Hen. III, no. 514.
[61] Pat. 4 Edw. VI, pt. iv, m. 21.

two lights, of the late 14th century, with tracery and pointed heads, and all are repaired.

The monuments in the chancel are : a brass, consisting of an inscription only, is to Sybil wife of Robert Barber, 1614, and a mural monument in alabaster, dated 1613, to Timothy Sheppard. In the north aisle are two mural tablets, one to Roland Hale, 1688, and one to Richard Hale, 1689.

The bells are six in number, and of these three—the first, fourth and fifth—by an unknown founder are dated 1627. The second is dated 1629. The third and sixth are by John Warner & Sons.

The plate consists of a silver cup of 1638-9, a modern plated cup, two plated salver-shaped patens, and a tankard of 1736.

The advowson of the church to John, Prior of Malton in Yorkshire.[62] It remained in the possession of the priory of Malton, who appropriated the church, until the Dissolution.[63] In 1550 the king granted the rectory and advowson to Ralph Sadleir,[64] who conveyed them in 1570 to his brother Edward Sadleir and Anne his wife, reserving a life interest.[65] They held till 1582, when they conveyed them to Richard Hale,[66] in whose family they descended with the manor (q.v.) till 1884, when they were purchased by Mrs. Hinds. She sold in 1891 to Mr. Thomas Fenwick Harrison, the present patron.[67]

In 1506 Thomas Pyrden of King's Walden left in his will bequests to the High Rood Light and the Low Rood Light, to Our Lady's Light, St. Thomas's

KING'S WALDEN CHURCH FROM THE NORTH-WEST

The registers are contained in four books, of which the first includes baptisms from 1558 to 1720 and burials and marriages from 1559 to 1721; the second contains baptisms and burials from 1722 to 1781 and marriages from 1722 to 1753; the third contains baptisms and burials from 1782 to 1812 and marriages from 1754 to 1796; the fourth contains marriages from 1796 to 1812.

In the middle of the 13th century *ADVOWSON* Walter de Nevill, then holding the manor of King's Walden, granted

Light and St. Katherine's Light in the parish church.[68]

CHARITIES In 1616 Richard Hale, citizen and grocer of London, by his will charged land known as Holland's Farm at Codicote with an annuity of £5, of which £1 was payable to the vicar for sermons on certain Sundays and £4 to be distributed amongst the neediest inhabitants.

William Smith—as appears from a deed of appointment of trustees dated in 1771—by his will devised

---

[62] Feet of F. Herts. Mich. 43 Hen. III, no. 514.
[63] Mins. Accts. Hen. VIII, R. 178, m. 9; *Valor Eccl.* (Rec. Com.), iv, 277.
[64] Pat. 4 Edw. VI, pt. iv, m. 21.
[65] Ibid. 13 Eliz. pt. ii, m. 19.
[66] Feet of F. Herts. Mich. 25 & 26 Eliz.
[67] Information of Mr. T. F. Harrison.
[68] Wills P.C.C. 8 Adeane.

to trustees 2 a. 2 r. in the parish of Studham in the county of Bedford, the rents thereof to be applied—subject to the payment of 5*s*. to the poor of Studham—for the benefit of the most necessitous and distressed poor of King's Walden. The land is let at £3 a year.

These charities are administered together under the provisions of a scheme of the Charity Commissioners, 2nd September 1898.

In 1910 the sum of £6 7*s*. 6*d*. was distributed in money to forty-six recipients, chiefly widows.

LILLEY

Linlei (xi cent.); Linlea, Linlega, Linlegh, Linlee (xiii cent.); Lynleye, Lyngeleye (xiv cent.); Lylly, Lynley (xv cent.); Lyndley *alias* Lylle (xvi cent.); Lilley (xvii cent.).

Lilley is a small parish of 1,795 acres on the western border of Hertfordshire, adjoining the county of Bedford. The parish lies on the Chilterns on a slightly inclined plane rising from about 400 ft. above the ordnance datum in the south to 602 ft. at Telegraph Hill in the north. There is a small detached portion of Lilley to the south of the main part of the parish and entirely surrounded by the parish of Offley. The land is now, as at the time of the Domesday Survey, chiefly arable, the soil being chalk.[1] In 1905 there were 1,062 acres of arable land, 201 acres of permanent grass, and no woodland,[2] but there are a good many trees scattered about the parish.

The village lies in the south of the parish, and, including a few outlying cottages in the north, extends about a mile along a branch road here called Lilley Street running north-west from the Luton and Hitchin highway to the Icknield Way, which forms part of the parish boundary in the north. The church of St. Peter lies on the west side of the road, and Lilley Park is on the west side of the village. The parish was inclosed by an Act of 1768,[3] but there is still a large open common called Lilley Hoo[4] to the east of the village.

MANOR In the time of Edward the Confessor the manor of LILLEY was held of Earl Harold by Leneva, and a sokeman, a man of Harold's, held 3½ virgates of land in it for which he rendered a carrying service (avera) in Hitchin or 3½*d*. By 1086 Lilley was in the possession of Geoffrey de Bech. We learn also from the Survey that Ilbert as sheriff attached to this manor the manor of Wellbury in Offley.[5] At the beginning of the 13th century the manor was in the tenure of William Malet of Gerardville, who held it until the separation of England and Normandy,[6] when he remained in Normandy. It then escheated to King John, and was granted in 1204 to Matthew de Lilley.[7] A few years later it was in the possession of Pain de Chaworth,[8] having been granted to him to hold at the king's pleasure by the service of one knight.[9] He was still holding it in 1223,[10] but forfeited before 1227, when the manor with all liberties and customs was granted to Richard de Argentein, to be held by him until the king should restore the lands to the heir of William Malet 'of his free will or by a peace,' with the proviso that in that event the king should make to Richard a reasonable exchange in wards or escheats.[11] In 1233 the manor was restored to Pain de Chaworth, with all goods and chattels found by inquisition to have been on the property when Richard entered it.[12]

In or before 1238 the custody of the manor was granted to John Earl of Lincoln, who committed it with the king's consent to his nephews Roger and Geoffrey de Pavilly[13]; but in 1241 Roger, being called upon to prove his claim, instead of evidencing the earl's grant as title, claimed it by hereditary right through his grandmother Theofania, William Malet's sister. She was said to have held the manor by gift from Geoffrey, her brother,[14] and to have been disseised by Pain de Chaworth, whom she had impleaded, the action however having been stopped by her death. On the king's side it was stated that William Malet had been in seisin of the manor after Geoffrey's death, and had forfeited as a Norman, and that Theofania was not his heir because William had left children. The king therefore took the manor as escheat.[15] In 1243 an extent of the manor was taken,[16] and it was granted to Paul de Peyvre,[17] who held it by the service of half a knight's fee.[18] In his time the manor is said to have been withdrawn from the sheriff's tourn and the hundred court.[19]

The manor descended to Paul de Peyvre's son John, and to John son of John, who died in 1316.[20] The manor was held for life by his widow Mary, on whose death in 1333 Nicholas, her grandson (son of Paul son of John), was the heir.[21] Nicholas conveyed it in 1359, two years before his death, to Henry Green,[22] Anne, apparently wife of Nicholas, retaining a third part as dower.[23] Henry Green, chivaler, died in 1369. The manor descended in

CHAWORTH. *Burelly argent and gules with an orle of martlets sable.*

---

[1] *V.C.H. Herts.* i, Geol. Map.
[2] Statistics from Bd. of Agric. (1905).
[3] *Blue Bk. Incl. Awards.*
[4] Exch. Dep. Mich. 5 Geo. II, no. 4.
[5] *V.C.H. Herts.* i, 304*a*, 334*a*.
[6] *Rot. Norman.* 129; Wrottesley, *Pedigrees from the Plea R.* 490.
[7] *Rot. Norman.* 129.
[8] *Red Bk. of Exch.* (Rolls Ser.), 176, 499, 804; Close, 18 John, pt. i, m. 4; *Testa de Nevill* (Rec. Com.), 272*a*, 279*b*.
[9] *Testa de Nevill* (Rec. Com.), 265*b*, 269*b*, 279*b*.
[10] Close, 8 Hen. III, pt. i, m. 19.
[11] *Cal. Chart. R.* 1226–57, pp. 57, 85, 140.
[12] *Cal. Close,* 1231–4, pp. 179, 190–1.
[13] *Cal. Pat.* 1232–47, p. 226.
[14] Wrottesley, *Pedigrees from Plea R.* 490. [15] *Abbrev. Plac.* (Rec. Com.), 114.
[16] *Cal. Pat.* 1232–47, p. 392.
[17] *Cal. Chart. R.* 1226–57, p. 276.
[18] *Hund. R.* (Rec. Com.), i, 188, 194; *Feud. Aids,* ii, 429.
[19] Assize R. 325, m. 29 d.; *Hund. R.* (Rec. Com.), i, 188.
[20] Ibid.; Chan. Inq. p.m. 9 Edw. II, no. 55.
[21] Chan. Inq. p.m. 7 Edw. III, no. 33.
[22] Chan. Inq. a.q.d. file 335, no. 6; Chan. Inq. p.m. 35 Edw. III, pt. ii (1st nos.), no. 42. At this time there was no land in demesne and no manorial site, but there was underwood containing about 10 acres, the whole residue of the manor being in the hands of tenants, some holding in bondage, some at will, and others in fee.
[23] Feet of F. Div. Co. East. 40 Edw. III.

the family of Green[24] to Sir Thomas Green of Boughton and Wood's Norton, co. Northants, who died in 1506, leaving two daughters and co-heirs, Anne, who married Nicholas Lord Vaux of Harrowden,

GREEN of Boughton. *Azure three harts passant or.*

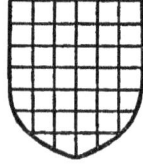

VAUX of Harrowden. *Checky or and gules.*

and Matilda wife of Sir Thomas Parr.[25] In 1512 the manor was settled to the use of Lord Vaux and Anne.[26] In 1523, on the death of Lord Vaux,[27] it passed to their son Thomas Lord Vaux, who conveyed it in 1556 to Thomas Docwra of Temple Dinsley in Hitchin.[28] In 1602 Thomas died, leaving the property to his son Thomas, on whom it had been previously settled.[29] He received a grant of free warren in Lilley, Putteridge, Hockwell and Pirton in 1616.[30] Periam, his son, succeeded him in 1620,[31] and held the manor till his death in 1642.[32] The manor passed to Periam's son Thomas,[33] who settled it in 1710 on his grandson and heir-apparent Sir George Warburton, bart., of Arley, co. Chester (son of his daughter Martha, who married Sir Peter Warburton), on his marriage with Diana daughter of William Lord Alington.[34] Sir George Warburton sold it in February 1729–30 to the Right Hon. Charles Cavendish.[35] In 1738 Lord Charles Cavendish sold it to Sir Benjamin Rawling, kt.[36] Since he left no children, the property was divided at his death in 1775 between his relatives and co-heirs, descendants of his father's sisters

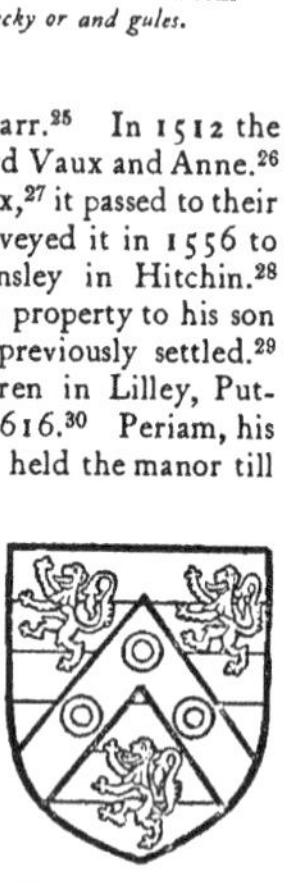

SOWERBY of Putteridge. *Barry sable and gules a cheveron between three lions argent with three rings gules on the cheveron.*

Rebecca Nicholson and Sarah Corney.[37] Thirteen years later these co-heirs sold the whole manor to John Sowerby of Hatton Garden,[38] from whom it has descended to the present owner Captain Thomas George Sowerby,[39] who resides at Putteridge Park.

The parish church of *ST. PETER,* CHURCH which stands in the village, was originally built in the 12th century. It was, however, wholly rebuilt in 1871, a few portions of the old church and some fittings being retained in the new building.

The chancel arch, of tufa, of the 12th century, has been reset in the north wall of the chancel, and there are some 15th-century stones in the south doorway. There is a piscina in the chancel, possibly of the 15th century, with a four-centred head and an octagonal bowl and shelf. It is covered with modern paint. The font, of the 15th century, is octagonal and of clunch. There are mural tablets in the porch to Thomas Docwra, 1602, and to Daniel Houghton, 1672. The pulpit is made up of old oak, with linen panels having traceried heads, brought from St. John's College, Cambridge.

There is a ring of three bells; the treble may be by William Knight of Reading, and is of 1580; the second is by George Chandler, 1703; and the tenor by T. Mears, 1821.

The plate includes a cup of 1689, paten of 1776–7, a pair of cruets and brass almsdish.

The registers are in two books, of which the first contains burials and baptisms from 1711 to 1812 and marriages from 1711 to 1752, and the second marriages from 1754 to 1812.

The earliest record of the advowson *ADVOWSON* of the church of Lilley is in the year 1213, at which date it was in the king's hands, with other property of the Normans,[40] so that it had probably belonged to the Malets. Soon afterwards it was granted to Paul de Peyvre,[41] and descended with the manor (q.v.) until 1730, when Sir George Warburton conveyed it to Lord Charles Cavendish,[42] who sold it the following year to the Master and Fellows of St. John's College, Cambridge, who are the present patrons.[43]

Dwelling-houses were certified for worship for Protestant Dissenters from early in the 17th century.[44] There is now a Wesleyan chapel in Lilley.

There are no endowed charities in this parish.

---

[24] Chan. Inq. p.m. 43 Edw. III, pt. i, no. 48; 15 Ric. II, pt. i, no. 24; *Feud. Aids,* ii, 443; Chan. Inq. p.m. 5 Hen. V, no. 39; *Feud. Aids,* ii, 449; Chan. Inq. p.m. 12 Hen. VI, no. 20; 2 Edw. IV, no. 7; 4 Edw. IV, no. 21; Close, 22 Edw. IV, m. 15.
[25] Chan. Inq. p.m. (Ser. 2), xlii, 97.
[26] Ibid.; Feet of F. Herts. Hil. 7 Hen. VIII.
[27] Chan. Inq. p.m. (Ser. 2), xlii, 97.
[28] Close, 2 & 3 Phil. and Mary, pt. iv, m. 36; Recov. R. Hil. 2 & 3 Phil. and Mary, rot. 427; Feet of F. Herts. East.

2 & 3 Phil. and Mary; Mich. 1 & 2 Eliz.
[29] Chan. Inq. p.m. (Ser. 2), ccclxxxvii, 122.
[30] Pat. 14 Jas. I, pt. xi, no. 7.
[31] Chan. Inq. p.m. (Ser. 2), ccclxxxvii, 122. [32] Ibid. dxxxvii, 97.
[33] Ct. of Wards, Feod. Surv. no. 17; Feet of F. Herts. Trin. 21 Chas. II.
[34] Exch. Dep. Trin. 8 Anne, no. 7; Recov. R. Trin. 9 Anne, rot. 178; Feet of F. Herts. Trin. 9 Anne.
[35] Close, 3 Geo. II, pt. xvi, no. 8. The purchase is made in the name of William Lord Manners and others.

[36] Close, 12 Geo. II, pt. xvii, no. 23.
[37] Clutterbuck, *Hist. and Antiq. of Herts.* iii, 84; Feet of F. Div. Co. Trin. 19 Geo. III; Com. Pleas D. Enr. Trin. 19 Geo. III, m. 167.
[38] Ibid. 28 Geo. III, m. 196.
[39] *V.C.H. Herts. Fam.* 17.
[40] *Rot. Lit. Pat.* (Rec. Com.), ii, 101*b*.
[41] See Assize R. 318, m. 25.
[42] Close, 3 Geo. II, pt. xvi, no. 9.
[43] Title-deeds at St. John's Coll., Camb.; information given by Mr. R. F. Scott, Bursar.
[44] Urwick, *Nonconformity in Herts.* 659.

OFFLEY

Offanleáh, Offanlege (x cent.); Offelei (xi cent.); Offellei, Offelegh (xiii cent.); Offeleg, Doffeleye (xiv cent.); Offeley (xvi cent.).

Offley parish covers 5,569 acres. It lies on the Chilterns, and has an average height of 400 ft. above the ordnance datum, but drops in the east to 224 ft. The Icknield Way separates it on the north from the parish of Pirton. There are two distinct villages, called Great and Little Offley. The latter is about 1¼ miles to the north-west of Great Offley, which is in the centre of the parish. It is on the main road to Hitchin, the nearest town, which lies 3 miles to the east. Wellbury is about 1½ miles to the north of the village.

The church of St. Mary Magdalene and Offley Place lie together off the high road, and they with the houses to the south probably formed the site of the original settlement. The part of the village which has sprung up along the road from Luton to Hitchin is, we may suppose, of a later date. In the village are several timber and plaster cottages with tiled roofs of the 16th and 17th centuries, and also some of brick of the latter date. The Green Man Inn is a 16th-century house of timber covered with rough-cast. It was originally an L-shaped type of house, but has been much altered. Offley Place with its park is the property of Mr. H. G. Salusbury Hughes, J.P. It is a three-storied building of brick. The north wing is of the 17th century, but the remainder of the house was rebuilt about 1770. Great Offley Hall lies to the south and Offley Hoo a little further on.

Westbury Farm, a quarter of a mile from the church, is a plastered timber house, originally of the H type, which seems to have been built in the 16th century. It underwent considerable alteration in the 18th and a wing was added in the 19th century. The hall, with a chamber above, fills the main block; the two wings were occupied by the kitchen and the solar respectively. A 17th-century dove-cote, timber framed with brick nogging, stands near the house.

The house called Little Offley, lying 2 miles to the north-west of the church, is a two-storied brick house of the H type, the main block built early in the 17th century, the wings apparently almost a century later. The date 1695 appears on a rain-water head on the north side. There is a fine carved wooden overmantel in a room on the ground floor. Offley Grange is a mile to the north-east.

The soil is chalk.[1] There are 3,388 acres of ploughland, 1,126 acres of permanent grass, and woods and plantations cover 600 acres.[2] The parish was inclosed by an award under an Act of 1807.[3] The nearest station is at Hitchin, on the Great Northern railway.

MANORS The manor of Offley, afterwards known as *DELAMERS*, was at the time of the Survey of considerable extent, being estimated at 8 hides 8 acres. It had been held before the Conquest by Alestan of Boscumbe; in 1086 it was part of the possessions of William de Ow, and was held under him by William Delamare (de Mara).[4] William de Ow forfeited under Henry I, and the overlordship then seems to have become attached to the manor of Hitchin (q.v.).

The first record of a tenant after 1086 is in 1198, when Geoffrey Delamare was indicted for making a ditch to the injury of the free tenement of Thomas Delamare.[5] Robert son of Osbert Delamare,[6] who held early in the 13th century, forfeited as an ally of Falkes de Breauté in 1224,[7] the king ordered the sheriff to restore Offley to Alice his wife for the maintenance of herself and his heirs.[8] This Robert may be the Robert Delamare who was murdered about 1230.[9] He was apparently succeeded by his son John,[10] who died seised of Offley about 1276, his grandson John, aged sixteen, being his heir.[11] Peter Delamare, son of John (probably the elder John), seems to have been in possession shortly afterwards.[12] He died seised of the manor in 1292, leaving a son and heir Robert.[13] Robert died in 1308. The extent of the manor then included a capital messuage, 620 acres of arable land, 30 acres of wood, but no meadow or pasture.[14] Peter son of Robert received a grant of free warren in 1318.[15] He held the manor until his death in 1349,[16] when it descended to his son Robert, who died in 1382-3.[17] His son Peter, then aged thirteen years, presumably died before his mother Matilda, as he never inherited the property, the manor being held after Matilda's death by her daughter Wilhelmina wife of Sir John Roches.[18] She left two heirs, her daughter Elizabeth, wife of Walter de Beauchamp, and John Benton, son of another daughter Joan.[19]

In 1412 Walter Beauchamp and Elizabeth his wife made a conveyance of the manor of Delamers to John Ludewyk, chaplain, and others[20] either for a settlement or alienation. After this date there is no trace of this manor under the name of Delamers until 1740, but it is perhaps the same as the manor

DELAMARE. *Gules two leopards argent.*

---

[1] *V.C.H. Herts.* i, Geol. Map.
[2] Statistics from Bd. of Agric. (1905).
[3] Private Act, 47 Geo. III, Sess. 2, cap. 25.
[4] *V.C.H. Herts.* i, 328a.
[5] *Rot. Cur. Reg.* (Rec. Com.), i, 157. See also Add. Chart. 35500. This Geoffrey must be the 'G.' son of Amice who gave the advowson (q.v.) to Bradenstoke.
[6] See *Red Bk. of Exch.* (Rolls Ser.), 499.
[7] He was one of the 'familia' of Falkes de Breauté who were excommunicated with him, and who after the rebellion accompanied him to Northampton when he was conducted there by the Archbishop of Canterbury to receive absolution (*Cal. Pat.* 1216-25, p. 461).
[8] *Rot. Lit. Claus.* (Rec. Com.), ii, 3b.
[9] *Cal. Pat.* 1216-25, p. 461.
[10] Anct. D. (P.R.O.), A 6251; *Excerpta e Rot. Fin.* (Rec. Com.), i, 186.
[11] Chan. Inq. p.m. file 17, no. 16 (5 Edw. I).
[12] Add. Chart. 24062, 24065.
[13] Chan. Inq. p.m. 20 Edw. I, no. 39.
[14] Ibid. 2 Edw. II, no. 68.
[15] Chart. R. 12 Edw. II, no. 70.
[16] *Feud. Aids*, ii, 437; Chan. Inq. p.m. 23 Edw. III, pt. ii, no. 143.
[17] Chan. Inq. p.m. 5 Ric. II, no. 40.
[18] Ibid. 6 Hen. IV, no. 3.
[19] Ibid. 12 Hen. IV, no. 38.
[20] Feet of F. Herts. Hil. 13 Hen. IV, no. 98.

A HISTORY OF HERTFORDSHIRE

of WESTBURY *alias* GREAT OFFLEY,[21] which at the beginning of the 15th century seems to have been in the possession of Roger de Sapurton, as his daughter and heir Elizabeth Venour, widow of William Venour,[22] was holding it in 1464,[23] and in 1468–9 settled it on herself and her second husband Robert Worth.[24] Robert died seised in 1502, leaving a son and heir Humphrey, aged sixteen.[25] In 1537 the latter made a conveyance to John Sewster and James Randall, probably in trust for John Bowles,[26] who in 1543 acquired Westbury Wood from George Ackworth,[27] and in the same year died seised of the manor called Westbury *alias* Great Offley.[28] His heir was his grandson Thomas, who conveyed the manor in 1564 to Robert Ivory.[29] William Ivory was holding in 1618,[30] and in 1642 John Ivory.[31] From this date no further record is found of the manor until 1778, when Thomas Hope Byde was holding the manor of Great Offley[32] and at that date suffered a recovery of it.[33] In 1785 it appears he was again dealing with it.[34] Later it was acquired by Dame Sarah Salusbury from John Hope Byde, and descended with the manor of Offley St. Ledgers[35] (q.v.) to Mr. Herbert George Salusbury Hughes, M.A., J.P., the present owner.

The origin of the manor of OFFLEY ST. LEDGERS is somewhat obscure. It was said in the 14th century to be held of the Mortimers of Wigmore,[36] but this overlordship may only have been assumed at a late date. It seems possible that the manor was originally part of the manor of Delamers. A Geoffrey de St. Ledger had some interest in the church, which was appurtenant to the manor of Delamers (see advowson), and William de St. Ledger, probably his son,[37] in confirming the title of the Prior of Bradenstoke to the advowson in 1238, calls himself great-grandson and heir of Amice Delamare.

In 1265 Geoffrey de St. Ledger, possibly brother of the William mentioned above,[38] had a grant of free warren in his demesne lands of Offley.[39] The annals of Dunstable record that in 1267 the steward of the Earl of Gloucester came to Geoffrey's manor at Offley and burnt it,[40] but the reason of this animosity does not appear. In 1301 the grant of free warren was confirmed to his son John and Isabel his wife.[41] John, their son,[42] succeeded them, and left at his death in 1326 a daughter Isabel, aged seven.[43] The extent of the manor at this date included a capital messuage, 320 acres of land, of which 96 lay in severalty and 204 in common, pastures called Le Launde and Sonehull, and 41 acres of wood. Two parts of the manor were taken into the king's hands during the minority of the heir,[44] the other third being dower of the mother. In 1331 the king confirmed a grant by Roger de Mortimer, overlord of the manor, to Richard de St. Ledger, a younger brother of John, of the custody of the manor during his niece Isabel's minority.[45] Isabel married Thomas de Hoo, who held the estate in right of his wife.[46] They settled it in 1342 on their son Thomas, with remainder to his brother William.[47] Thomas the son died before 1377, when Thomas and Isabel granted the manor to William and his wife Isabel.[48] In 1398 John de Hoo, a brother of William, conceded to him all his claim in the estate.[49] William was succeeded by his son Thomas,[50] and he by his son, also Thomas, who married first Elizabeth Wickingham and secondly Eleanor daughter of Leo Welles, kt., on whom he settled the manor in 1445.[51] In 1447 he was created Baron of Hoo and Hastings.[52] He died without male issue in February 1454–5. His brother of the half-blood, Thomas Hoo, succeeded, but died without issue in 1486.

The manor descended to Sir William Boleyn, kt., son of Geoffrey Boleyn and Anne eldest daughter of Lord Hoo and Hastings.[53] His second son and eventual heir Sir Thomas Boleyn, with Elizabeth his wife, daughter of Thomas Howard Duke of Norfolk,[54] sold the property in 1518 to Richard Fermour (Farmer).[55] Fermour forfeited his lands in the next reign under the Statute of Praemunire, but the grant of Offley was confirmed by King Edward VI in 1550,[56] and again by Queen Mary in 1553, to Richard's son John.[57] He conveyed the manor in 1554 to Thomas Spencer and Edward Onley[58] to the use of Sir John Spencer of Althorpe, co. Northants, who died seised of it in 1586.[59] He left it to his fourth son Richard, who was knighted in 1603.[60] Sir Richard and his wife Helen, daughter and co-heir of Sir John Brockett,[61] settled the property on their son John on his marriage

ST. LEDGER. *Azure fretty argent with a chief or.*

---

[21] There must be some continuity in the manors, as Putteridge, which had been held of the Delamares, is said after this date to be held of Westbury.
[22] *Cal. Pat.* 1461–7, p. 512.
[23] Chan. Inq. p.m. 4 Edw. IV, no. 13.
[24] Feet of F. Div. Co. Hil. 8 Edw. IV, no. 65; Chan. Inq. p.m. 14 Edw. IV, no. 14.
[25] Chan. Inq. p.m. (Ser. 2), xvi, 102.
[26] Feet of F. Herts. East. 29 Hen. VIII.
[27] Ibid. 35 Hen. VIII.
[28] Chan. Inq. p.m. (Ser. 2), lxviii, 14.
[29] Recov. R. Mich. 1564, rot. 1541.
[30] Chan. Inq. p.m. (Ser. 2), cclxxxviii, 144; Feet of F. Herts. Mich. 16 Jas. I.
[31] Ct. of Wards, Feod. Surv. no. 17.
[32] This manor is at this date confused with Delamers in Great Wymondley.
[33] Recov. R. Mich. 19 Geo. III, rot. 436.
[34] Ibid. 25 Geo. III, rot. 256; Feet of F. Herts. Trin. 25 Geo. III.
[35] Cussans, *Hist. of Herts. Hitchin Hund.* 100.
[36] *Feud. Aids*, ii, 428; Inq. a.q.d. 20 Edw. II, no. 23; *Feud. Aids*, ii, 437.
[37] See *Cal. Pat.* 1231–4, pp. 149, 296.
[38] Ibid. p. 149.
[39] Chart. R. 49 Hen. III, m. 4.
[40] *Ann. Mon.* (Rolls Ser.), iii, 246.
[41] Chart. R. 30 Edw. I, no. 50; *Cal. Pat.* 1388–92, p. 403.
[42] Add. Chart. 28728.
[43] Chan. Inq. p.m. 20 Edw. II, no. 23.
[44] Exch. L.T.R. Enr. Accts. no. 2.
[45] Pat. 5 Edw. III, pt. i, m. 23
[46] Chan. Inq. p.m. 9 Edw. III, no. 21.
[47] Feet of F. Div. Co. Hil. 16 Edw. III.
[48] Add. Chart. 28724; Feet of F. Herts. 1 Ric. II, no. 2.
[49] Close, 21 Ric. II, pt. ii, m. 18d.; Add. Chart. 28797.
[50] Ibid. 28721; Feet of F. Hil. 6 Hen. V; *Feud. Aids*, ii, 449.
[51] Feet of F. Div. Co. Mich. 24 Hen. VI; L. and P. Hen. VIII, iii (1), 273.
[52] G.E.C. *Peerage*, s.v. Hoo.
[53] Chan. Inq. p.m. (Ser. 2), ii, 5; G.E.C. *Peerage*, loc. cit.
[54] *Visit. Norfolk* (Harl. Soc. xxxii), 52.
[55] Feet of F. Herts. Mich. 10 Hen. VIII.
[56] Pat. 4 Edw. VI, pt. ix, m. 35.
[57] Ibid. 1 Mary, pt. xi, m. 19; *Visit. Shrops.* (Harl. Soc. xxviii), 183.
[58] Feet of F. Herts. Mich. 1 & 2 Phil. and Mary.
[59] Chan. Inq. p.m. (Ser. 2), ccxv, 258; see Recov. R. Mich. 30 & 31 Eliz. rot. 77.
[60] Shaw, *Knights of Engl.* ii, 104.
[61] *Visit. Herts.* (Harl. Soc. xxii), 165.

40

OFFLEY CHURCH FROM THE SOUTH-EAST

OFFLEY CHURCH: THE NAVE LOOKING EAST

with Mary[63] daughter of Sir Henry Anderson, kt. John and Mary succeeded at Sir Richard's death in 1624.[63] John was made a baronet in 1627,[64] and died in 1633,[65] leaving a daughter Alice, then fifteen years old. The manor having been settled in tail-male passed to his brother Sir Brockett Spencer,[66] bart. (so created in 1642). He was succeeded by his son Sir Richard Spencer, and Sir Richard by his son Sir John Spencer, who died without issue in 1699. His uncle and heir Sir John Spencer also died without issue in 1712.[67] The manor then descended to Elizabeth daughter of Sir Humphrey Gore of Gilston, co. Herts., and Elizabeth eldest daughter (and the only one having issue) of Sir Brockett Spencer. She married in 1714 Sir Henry Penrice,[68] judge of the High Court of Admiralty. Their daughter and heir Anna Maria, wife of Sir Thomas Salusbury, succeeded to their estates.[69] She died in 1759. Her husband survived her and died in 1773, leaving the property to his second wife Sarah, with remainder to a distant relative, Sir Robert Salusbury, bart., for life. He entered into possession in 1804 on the death of Sarah. Sir Robert and his son Thomas Robert jointly sold the property in 1806 to the trustees of Sarah's will, and they conveyed it to the Rev. Lynch Salusbury,[70] a younger brother of Sir Robert, who assumed the name of Burroughs. He left an only child Elizabeth Mary, who could not legally inherit, as the property had been left in tail-male by Sarah Salusbury, but acquired the estate by purchase from the heir male Charles thirteenth Marquess of Winchester. Elizabeth Mary married her cousin Sir Thomas Robert Salusbury, second baronet, who died in 1835. Having no children, she adopted as her daughter and heir a cousin Anne Salusbury Steward, who married George Edward Hughes, brother of Thomas Hughes the author, who wrote a biography of George Hughes. Mrs. Hughes entered the manor in 1867 on the death of Dame Elizabeth Mary.[71] The property is now in the hands of Mr. Herbert George Salusbury Hughes, M.A., J.P., who succeeded his father George Edward in 1872,[72] and is the present lord of the manor.

The manor of COCKERNHOE (Qukerno, Cokernhohalle, Cokernho, xiv cent.; Kokernhoo, xv cent.) on the south of the parish is an estate which was held with the manor of Offley by the St. Ledger family. It is mentioned as 'an oxhouse called Qukerno' in an extent of the manor in 1326,[73] but later documents always call it a manor. Its descent is identical with Offley till 1813 (although it is not always separately mentioned), when, according to Cussans, it was sold to Richard Oakley of Hitchin.[74]

The manor of WELLES (Welle, xi cent.; Welbery, xiii cent.; Wellys, xiv cent.) was held at the time of the Survey by a sokeman of King William and was then assessed at 1 hide. In the time of Earl Harold it had belonged to Leneva. It was attached by Ilbert the Sheriff to the manor of Lilley, but after Ilbert was deprived of his office of sheriff Peter de Valoines and Ralf Taillebois took this manor from him and attached it to Hitchin,[75] to which the overlordship henceforth pertained.[76]

The early history of this estate is difficult to trace. It may, perhaps, be the hide in 'Weelberia' which Henry de Tilly granted in 1200 to his brother William.[77] In 1309 the manor was in the possession of William de Goldington and Margaret his wife. They in that year conveyed it to William Tuchet and Ellen de Danarston.[78] William died in February 1327–8, his brother Richard being his heir.[79] Ellen remained seised for life. Shortly afterwards Isabel widow of Richard de Welles brought an action against Ellen de Danarston for a third of the manor which she claimed in dower and of which she recovered seisin.[80] As Ellen called to warranty John son of William de Goldington, possibly the inquisition quoted above, which gives William's brother Richard as his heir, is incorrect. The heir, whether Richard or John, apparently conveyed the manor to Giles de Badelesmere, who died seised in 1338, leaving as heirs his four sisters Margery, Maud, Elizabeth and Margaret.[81] Maud and her husband John de Vere Earl of Oxford took this manor. John de Vere died in January 1359–60[82] and his wife about six years later.[83] Their son Thomas succeeded her.[84] He died in 1371, leaving as heir his son Robert,[85] who held the manor till his attainder in February 1387–8.[86] In 1393 the reversion of this manor, after the death of Maud widow of Thomas, was granted to Thomas Duke of Gloucester,[87] and two years later he granted it to the master, warden and chaplains of the college which he had founded in the church of Pleshey, co. Essex.[88] It remained with the college until its dissolution and was then granted in 1546 to Sir John Gates.[89] He was attainted in the next reign as a follower of the

HUGHES. *Sable a fesse cotised between three lions' heads razed argent.*

---

[62] Or Sarah as in *Visit. of Herts.*
[63] Chan. Inq. p.m. (Ser. 2), ccccxviii, 95.
[64] *Cal. S. P. Dom.* 1627–8, pp. 89, 91.
[65] Chan. Inq. p.m. (Ser. 2), ccccxxxiv, 14.
[66] See Recov. R. Mich. 15 Chas. I, rot. 56. Alice, however, seems to have had some interest in the manor which she probably released to her uncle (Feet of F. Herts. Trin. 12 Anne).
[67] G.E.C. *Baronetage*, ii, 201.
[68] See Feet of F. Herts. Trin. 1 Geo. I.
[69] See Feet of F. Div. Co. Trin. 25 & 26 Geo. II.
[70] G.E.C. *Complete Baronetage.*
[71] Cussans, *Hist. of Herts. Hitchin Hund.* 98.

[72] *V.C.H. Herts. Fam.* 14.
[73] Chan. Inq. p.m. 20 Edw. II, no. 23.
[74] Cussans, *Hist. of Herts. Hitchin Hund.* 99.
[75] *V.C.H. Herts.* i, 303b.
[76] Chan. Inq. p.m. 1 Edw. III (2nd nos.), no. 47; 34 Edw. III, no. 84; 16 Ric. II, pt. ii, no. 34.
[77] Chart. Norman. 2 John, no. 33.
[78] Feet of F. Herts. Mich. 3 Edw. II, no. 32.
[79] Chan. Inq. p.m. 1 Edw. III (2nd nos.), no. 47.
[80] De Banco R. 277, m. 187. If the judgement given in this action was right and Richard de Welles held the manor, William de Goldington must have acquired it from him. For deeds of the family of Welles see Duchy of Lanc. Anct. D. (P.R.O.), A 369, 377.
[81] Chan. Inq. p.m. 12 Edw. III, no. 54a.
[82] Ibid. 34 Edw. III, no. 84.
[83] Ibid. 40 Edw. III (1st nos.), no. 38.
[84] See Feet of F. Div. Co. 45 Edw. III, no. 80.
[85] Chan. Inq. p.m. 45 Edw. III, no. 45.
[86] Ibid. 16 Ric. II, pt. ii, no. 34.
[87] *Cal. Pat.* 1391–6, p. 347.
[88] Ibid. p. 382; Feet of F. Herts. Mich. 18 Ric. II, no. 157; Duchy of Lanc. Misc. x, 57; Duchy of Lanc. Deed L 751.
[89] Pat. 38 Hen. VIII, pt. v; *Harl. Soc. Publ.* xiv, 574.

A HISTORY OF HERTFORDSHIRE

Duke of Northumberland, but a grant of the manor was made to his brother Sir Henry Gates,[90] who with his wife Lucy in 1557 conveyed it to Richard Spicer[91] (*alias* Helder).

About 1569 John Spicer conveyed the manor to William Crawley,[92] and he died seised of it in 1595, having granted the estate to his son Richard and grandson William.[93] From this time no record appears of this manor until 1704, when Henry Bolderne the elder and Anne his wife[94] and Henry Bolderne their son (all holding in Anne's right) levied a fine of it.[95] In 1713 Henry Bolderne the younger seems to have conveyed it to Thomas Ansell.[96] According to Cussans it was acquired later by Samuel Burroughs, whose daughter and heir Sarah married Sir Thomas Salusbury. With St. Ledgers it descended to the Marquess of Winchester, from whom it was bought in 1840 by Ann Burroughs, second wife of the Rev. Lynch Salusbury, and on her death in 1856 came to her sister Maria, wife of James Newbury of Clapham Rise.[97] It was sold in 1872 to Mr. Francis Gosling,[98] and is now the seat of Mrs. Gosling.

The reputed manor known as *HIRSTHALL* or *HALLEBURY* was held in 1625 by Edward House,[99] and in 1658 belonged to John Dermer,[100] in whose family it was still vested in 1698.[101]

A capital messuage called *BULLERS* was in the 15th century in the possession of John Sholfold, who alienated it to the gild of Holy Trinity of Luton.[102] In the reign of Elizabeth it was the subject of a suit in the Court of Requests between Robert Ivory the lessee and Gregory Warren widower of a certain Alice who held it for life.[103] Sir John Spencer acquired this messuage before his death in 1587, and it then descended with the manor of St. Ledgers.

The manor of *PUTTERIDGE* (Potherugge, Poterugg, Pothruge, Pottryggebury, xiv cent.; Podriggebury, xv cent.; Poderiche, xvi cent.) was a mesne manor formed from the manor of Delamers. It was probably the carucate of land in Putteridge which John de Nevill granted in 1240 to Nicholas de Putteridge for life,[104] but nothing is known of the descendants of Nicholas de Putteridge. By 1303 it had passed into the hands of Hugh le Blunt, who held it of Robert Delamare for half a knight's fee.[105] He had a grant of free warren in 1305,[106] and died seised in 1361.[107] In 1346 the manor was held by Nicholas Peyvre,[108] but apparently only during the minority of John son and heir of Hugh le Blunt, since he was in possession in 1363.[109] Thomas le Blunt, who seems to have succeeded John,[110] may perhaps have left heiresses, as in 1391 John Herwe and Christine his wife and John Maps and Joyce his wife conveyed the manor to three feoffees,[111] from whom it was recovered in 1407, after the expiration of a life interest held by Agnes de Havering, by Thomas and Elizabeth Chelrey.[112] After Thomas Chelrey's death Elizabeth married Thomas de la Pole, and died in 1411, leaving as co-heirs her two daughters, Elizabeth wife of John Kyngeston, and Sybil Chelrey, and her granddaughter, Elizabeth Calston.[113] The manor seems to have passed to the latter, who married William Darrell,[114] and joined with him in 1428 in making a settlement of the manor on themselves in tail, with remainder to William's brother John.[115]

On the death of Elizabeth Darrell in 1464[116] it passed to her son George, who died in 1474,[117] when the manor was delivered to Thomas Cardinal Archbishop of Canterbury,[118] apparently during the minority of Edward Darrell, who was only four years old at his father's death.[119] Edward settled the manor on himself and his wife and his heirs in 1503,[120] and in 1520 he sold it to Richard Lyster,[121] the king's solicitor, who conveyed it in 1525 to John Docwra.[122] He was succeeded by his son Thomas Docwra,[123] who in 1556 bought the manor of Lilley (q.v.), since which date the two estates have descended together.

DOCWRA of Putteridge. *Sable a cheveron engrailed argent between three roundels argent with a pale gules on each roundel.*

The first record of the so-called manor of *HOCKWELL* alias *HOCKWELLBURY* (Hokewelle, Hokewellebury, xv cent.) is of the year 1411, at which date the estate was held by Elizabeth widow of Thomas de la Pole,[124] who was then holding the manor of Putteridge. The two manors descended together until 1788, after which Hockwell seems to have been amalgamated with Putteridge.

The parish church of *ST. MARY CHURCH MAGDALENE*, situated about half a mile south-east of the village, is built for the most part of flint and stone. The chancel is faced with Portland stone and the north aisle with cement. The tower is built of brick and the roofs are of lead, except that of the north porch, which is of tiles.

---

[90] Pat. 1 & 2 Phil. and Mary, pt. vi.
[91] Ibid. 3 & 4 Phil. and Mary, pt. iv, m. 20; Feet of F. Herts. Trin. 3 & 4 Phil. and Mary.
[92] Feet of F. Herts. Hil. 12 Eliz. A parcel of the manor, including 300 acres of land, was in 1577 acquired by Richard Spicer, son of the above Richard, from John and Henry Alwey. He died seised in 1611, leaving a son William (Pat. 20 Eliz. pt. viii, m. 23; Chan. Inq. p.m. [Ser. 2], cccxxi, 117).
[93] Chan. Inq. p.m. (Ser. 2), cccvii, 92.
[94] Feet of F. Herts. Trin. 3 Anne.
[95] Ibid.
[96] Recov. R. Trin. 13 Anne, rot. 35, 176.
[97] Cussans, *Hist. of Herts. Hitchin Hund.* 102.
[98] Ibid.
[99] Recov. R. East. 1 Chas. I, rot. 26.
[100] Com. Pleas D. Enr. East. 1658, m. 25.
[101] Feet of F. Herts. Trin. 10 Will. III.
[102] Early Chan. Proc. bdle. 35, no. 74.
[103] Ct. of Req. bdle. 3, no. 288.
[104] Feet of F. Herts. 24 Hen. III, no. 251.
[105] *Feud. Aids,* ii, 428.
[106] *Cal. Chart. R.* 1300-26, p. 59.
[107] Chan. Inq. p.m. file 156, no. 13 (35 Edw. III). The manor is called by the name of 'Huche,' but seems to be this manor.
[108] *Feud. Aids,* ii, 437.
[109] Add. Chart. 24067.
[110] See Morant, *Hist. of Essex,* ii, 48.
[111] It was held in right of Christine and Joyce (Feet of F. Herts, 15 Ric. II, no. 144).
[112] De Banco R. 583, m. 537 d.
[113] Chan. Inq. p.m. 13 Hen. IV, no. 34.
[114] Ibid. 2 Hen. V, no. 52.
[115] Feet of F. Div. Co. Trin. 6 Hen. VI, no. 75. In this year Hugh Blunt was said to be holding the manor (*Feud. Aids,* ii, 449), but this is probably a transcript of an older entry.
[116] Chan. Inq. p.m. 4 Edw. IV, no. 13.
[117] Ibid. 14 Edw. IV, no. 14.
[118] Anct. D. (P.R.O.), C 2872.
[119] Chan. Inq. p.m. 14 Edw. IV, no. 14.
[120] Close, 18 Hen. VII, no. 45.
[121] Feet of F. Herts. Mich. 12 Hen. VIII.
[122] Clutterbuck, *Hist. and Antiq. of Herts.* iii, 86. See Recov. R. East. 35 Eliz. rot. 44.
[123] Clutterbuck, loc. cit.
[124] Chan. Inq. p.m. 13 Hen. IV, no. 34.

OFFLEY CHURCH: THE FONT

The church consists of a chancel, nave and aisles, south porch and west tower.

The nave and aisles belong to the original church of c. 1220, which probably consisted of a chancel, nave and aisles and west tower, and the south porch contains re-used masonry of that date. The windows and doors belong to various dates in the 14th and 15th centuries. In 1777 the chancel was recased, repaired and refitted, and the west tower was entirely rebuilt in the early part of the 19th century. Various minor repairs have also been executed during the 19th century.

The chancel is apsidal in its interior termination but square outside. It is heavily plastered and has a canopy of plaster drapery over the 18th-century east window of one wide pointed light without tracery. Over the apse, which is round-headed, is a plaster moulding carried up to a pointed head inclosing Gothic tracery. The chancel is also lighted by a cupola in the roof. The 18th-century chancel arch is round-headed with niches in the flat jambs and plaster panelling in the soffit of the arch. An ancient stone coffin stands in the chancel.

The nave has arcades of four bays. The arches are of two chamfered orders, with labels running right down to the abaci of the capitals, and with carved stops, some of which are broken off. They are supported by octagonal pillars, which lean outwards considerably, probably owing to the pressure of an earlier roof. The capitals are foliate and the bases are moulded. The 15th-century clearstory has three windows on either side, two of three lights, and one, the westernmost, of two lights, all much restored. The roof has one 15th-century tie, resting on a broken carved corbel of that date, at the eastern end. The north aisle has a modern east window. The three square-headed windows in the north wall are of two lights, of the 15th century, and are much repaired. A small inscription cut on the east jamb of the easternmost of these windows records the consecration, on the feast of St. Sulpicius, of the side altar below the window. In the middle window are some fragments of 14th-century glass. There is no west window. The north door has a two-centred arch of two orders, and was inserted towards the end of the 14th century.

The south aisle has an east window and three south windows, all of two lights. The east window and the western of the two south windows have pointed heads; that at the eastern end of the south wall is square-headed. All have modern tracery, but the inner jambs are probably of the 15th century. At the east end of the south wall is a 15th-century piscina, with a shallow pointed niche over it, in which are two tiles, with the lettering in reverse, probably of the 14th century. The south doorway is also of the 15th century, and has a square head. The roof is of the 15th century. The south porch, of brick covered with cement, has some re-used material of the same date as the nave (c. 1220) in its west window. The entrance arch, which is pointed, is heavily defaced by cement repairs.

The brick tower has a small low spire and an embattled parapet. It is of two stages. The tower arch is plastered.

The font is octagonal, of Totternhoe stone. Each side contains the head of a heavily crocketed ogee with a finial, inclosing tracery of various designs; pinnacles with heavy finials are carved at the angles, and rosettes fill the spaces between them and the finials of the ogees. The bowl rests on a low stem with eight engaged half-octagonal shafts on plinths, with four-leaved flowers between them. The date of the font is the middle of the 14th century. The wooden cover is of the early 17th century.

There is some late 15th-century seating in the nave and aisles westward of the gangway.

On the north wall of the north aisle is a brass of John Samuel, his two wives and one son. Another brass with no inscription is that of a man, his three wives and nine sons; it is plainly by the same engraver as that of John Samuel. On the floor of the aisle are the indents of the brasses in two slabs.

On the west wall of the south aisle is a monument to John Spencer, 1699, with elaborately sculptured figures.

The bells are six: the treble, by Robert Oldfeild, of 1632; the second, of 1618, the fourth of 1619, and the fifth, of 1618, by Thomas Bartlett; while the third is by John Dyer, 1583, and the tenor by John Briant, 1803.

The plate, all presented by Eliza Chamber in 1730, consists of two cups, two patens, flagon and almsdish, of the same date. There is also a large plated shield, bearing the sacred monogram, the origin and purpose of which are unknown.

The registers are contained in six books, the first having all entries from 1653 to 1734, the second baptisms and burials from 1732 to 1812 and marriages from 1732 to 1753, the third, fourth, fifth and sixth marriages from 1754 to 1764, 1764 to 1802, 1802 to 1810, and 1811 to 1812, respectively.

ADVOWSON The advowson of the church of Offley was granted probably about the middle of the 12th century by Amice Delamare and her son Geoffrey (see Delamers Manor) to the church of St. Mary, Bradenstoke, co. Wilts. Geoffrey de St. Ledger (see manor of St. Ledgers) also confirmed the grant before 1207,[125] and in 1237-8 William de St. Ledger, great-grandson of Amice, made a further release of the title to Simon, Prior of Bradenstoke.[126] At the beginning of the 14th century the convent apparently alienated it, for in 1406 it was held by the executors of the will of Robert Braybrook, Bishop of London, who in that year obtained licence to endow with it a chantry in the church of Chalgrave, co. Bedford, for the souls of Robert Braybrook and Sir Nigel Loreng (for whom see Kimpton).[127] Licence was also given for the master and chaplains of the chantry to appropriate the church, maintaining the endowment for the vicarage already made.[128]

At the dissolution of chantries in the reign of Edward VI the advowson came to the Crown, and in 1599 Queen Elizabeth granted it to Henry Best and John Hallywell,[129] probably in trust for Luke Norton, who presented in 1603, 1606, 1608 and 1614. His son Graveley Norton presented in 1661. Luke son of Graveley sold the advowson to

---

[125] *Cal. Rot. Chart.* (Rec. Com.), i, 170.
[126] Feet of F. Herts. 22 Hen. III, no. 241.
[127] *Cal. Pat.* 1405-8, p. 290; *Cal. Papal Letters*, vi, 154.
[128] *Cal. Papal Letters*, vi, 154.
[129] Pat. 42 Eliz. pt. xxiii, m. 28.

A HISTORY OF HERTFORDSHIRE

William Angell, and his son William conveyed it in 1698 to Richard Spicer *alias* Holder, who presented in 1699.[130] Before this date, however, the Spencers (lords of the manor of St. Ledgers) seem to have had or claimed some interest in the advowson,[131] and in 1719 Sir Henry Penrice and his wife Elizabeth (see St. Ledgers) presented. From this date the advowson has descended with the manor of St. Ledgers [132] (q.v.).

The rectory was leased by Queen Elizabeth in 1575 to George Bredyman for twenty-one years.[133] The fee simple was acquired by George Graveley, who died seised in 1600, leaving as heir his daughter Lettice wife of Luke Norton.[134] They held it together [135] till 1630, when Luke died. After Lettice's death it descended to their son Graveley, who married Helen daughter of William Angell of London.[136] Graveley Norton was succeeded by his son Luke, from whom it passed with the advowson to William Angell, and in 1698 to Richard Holder (see above). After this date there is no further descent of the rectory, but conveyances of tithes with the lands to which they were appurtenant are common in the 18th century.[137]

Between 1691 and 1831 there were registered in Offley eight places for Protestant Dissenters, one for Anabaptists and one for Quakers.[138] There is now a Wesleyan chapel in the parish.

CHARITIES — Mrs. Alice Pigott in her lifetime directed that a sum of £20 per annum should be paid out of her estate for augmenting the vicarage of Offley and £10 per annum for apprenticing two boys or girls. This intention was carried into effect by Granado Pigott, her son, who by deed 18 July 1724 charged his share of manor of Symonside in Bishop's Hatfield with the two annuities, which are now paid by the Marquess of Salisbury, and are duly applied.

The Charity School of Dame Sarah Salusbury and the Rev. Lynch Burroughs : Dame Sarah Salusbury, by a codicil to her will dated in 1795, gave £500 for the poor, and by another codicil a further sum of £500, to be at the disposal of the Rev. Lynch Burroughs, then vicar. The school was in 1841 endowed by deed (enrolled) with five cottages and land, producing about £50 a year. It has a further endowment of £2,467 1s. 8d. consols, producing £61 13s. 6d. yearly. The charity is regulated by a scheme of the Court of Chancery, dated 14 June 1858.

PIRTON

The parish of Pirton lies on low ground in the north-west of Hertfordshire at the edge of the Bedfordshire plain. The greater part of it is only about 200 ft. above the ordnance datum, but the ground rises considerably, and in the north-west, where it meets the Chilterns, it has a height of 400 ft. In the south of the parish the little River Oughton takes its rise, and this part of Pirton is known as Oughton's Head (formerly Altonishevyd).[1] The Icknield Way forms part of the southern boundary of the parish. The population is entirely agricultural, the chalk land being particularly adapted for the growth of corn. The arable land covers 1,865 acres, while pasture comprises only 331 acres and woodland 65 acres.[2] An inclosure award was made for the parish in 1814 under an Act of 1811.[9a]

The village lies in the middle of the parish, and is of particular interest, as it was at an early date, possibly before the Conquest, fortified by a ditch. The area inclosed, about 10 acres, was utilized later for a mount and bailey castle, the mount or 'motte' standing about 25 ft. high above the bottom of the surrounding ditch in the north-west corner of the inclosure, and the remainder of the area divided into three baileys, the largest stretching along the north side and including the church and the other two on the south. The ditches are well marked, and there is still at times a good deal of water in parts of them. This castle, unfortunately, has no history. It was probably made in the 12th century, perhaps during the anarchy of Stephen's reign, by Alan or Gerard de Limesi. There is little probability that it was ever defended by masonry walls. On the mount probably stood a timber tower, approached by a steep narrow bridge of timber from the bailey below over the ditch or moat which surrounds it. Timber palisades may have defended the surrounding outer banks of the baileys. We can only conjecture that it was dismantled by Henry II as an adulterine or unlicensed castle, hundreds of which he is said to have destroyed. When the site was abandoned by the Limesis the mount was probably used as a look-out and meeting-place of the villagers, and so came to be called Toot Hill.

The village is now outside this inclosure, principally on the north-west side. At the south end of the village is what remains of the Old Hall, a house of the Docwras, which has been turned into an inn. It is a rectangular two-storied block, 46 ft. by 20 ft.,

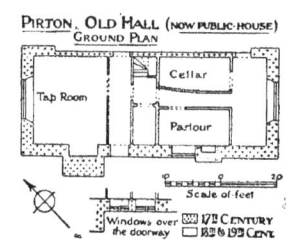

PIRTON. OLD HALL (NOW PUBLIC HOUSE)
GROUND PLAN

---

[130] Inst. Bks. (P.R.O.); Close, 10 Will. III, pt. viii, no. 4 ; Cussans, *Hist. of Herts. Hitchin Hund.* 111. Cussans gives the name of the last patron as Robert Holder.
[131] Chan. Inq. p.m. (Ser. 2), ccclxxiv, 4; Com. Pleas D. Enr. Trin. 10 Chas. I, m. 5.
[132] Inst. Bks. (P.R.O.).
[133] Pat. 17 Eliz. pt. xiii, m. 37.
[134] Chan. Inq. p.m. (Ser. 2), dvii, 47.
[135] Feet of F. Herts. Mich. 43 & 44 Eliz.
[136] Chan. Inq. p.m. (Ser. 2), ccclxv, 38 ; Recov. R. Trin. 14 Chas. I, rot. 49 ; Inst. Bks.
[137] Feet of F. Mich. 13 Geo. I ; 10 Geo. III ; East. 19 Geo. III ; Hil. 21 Geo. III.
[138] Urwick, *Nonconformity in Herts.* 663.
[1] Chan. Inq. p.m. 28 Edw. III, no. 43.
[2] Statistics from Bd. of Agric. (1905).
[2a] Loc. Act, 51 Geo. IV, cap. 96.

PIRTON GRANGE FROM THE SOUTH-WEST

PIRTON: HIGH DOWN FROM THE EAST

having a panel on the west front of the arms of Docwra and the date 1609. There are indications

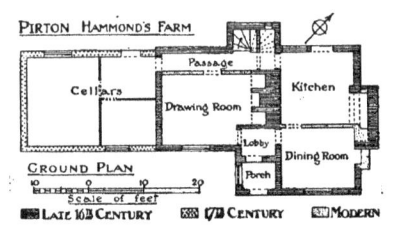

PIRTON HAMMOND'S FARM
GROUND PLAN
Scale of feet
■ LATE 16TH CENTURY ▨ 17TH CENTURY ☐ MODERN

that a wing, only about 12 ft. less than the width of the main block, projected from the back of the house, but this has been entirely removed. The flint and brick walls are plastered, the roof is tiled.

Hammond's Farm lies a quarter of a mile to the north of the church, and takes its name from the family of Hammond. In the 17th century a John Hammond held about 150 acres, and was succeeded by another John Hammond, from whom it has descended to Mr. William Hanscombe.[3] It is a house of the L type, of about 1600, built in two stories, the lower of brick, the upper of timber with tiled roof. The parlour is in the main wing, running east and west; in the south-east wing are the kitchen and offices; the porch with its lobby is in the angle formed by the wings. On the north is a smaller wing containing the staircase. The rooms in the upper story are panelled and have arabesque friezes of early 17th-century work. One of them has a fine chimney-piece. There is a plastered timber 17th-century dove-cote near the house.

[3] Chan. Proc. (Ser. 2), bdle. 92, no. 53.

The Rectory Farm, the residence of Mr. Ernest R. Davis, lies a little more than a quarter of a mile to the west of the church, and was apparently once the manor-house of the rectory manor. It is an early 17th-century timber-framed house of the L type, altered and faced with brick in the 18th and 19th centuries. The main building, running east and west, contains the parlour; from the eastern end of it a wing projects southward, containing the porch, lobby and kitchen. On the north side is a small staircase wing. A moat surrounds the house, and what appear to be traces of an outer moat can be seen on the north-east side. The tithe barn, 135 ft. by 37 ft., seems to be of the 16th century. It is of timber on a foundation of masonry.

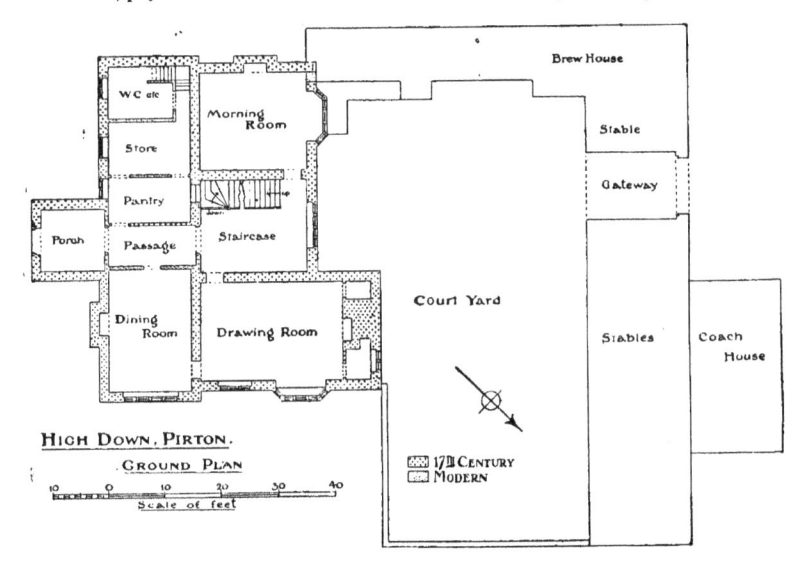

The Grange, the property of Mr. W. Hanscombe, on the western edge of the parish, is a moated

HIGH DOWN, PIRTON.
GROUND PLAN
Scale of feet
▨ 17TH CENTURY ☐ MODERN

timber-framed farm-house of early 17th-century date, but restored and modernized. It seems to have been originally of H type, but has been much altered. The house, which faces eastward, has an L-shaped south wing, whose upper story formerly projected. The kitchen in the north wing has the

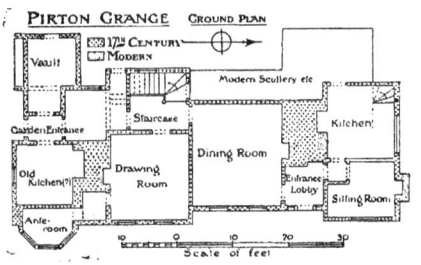

PIRTON GRANGE GROUND PLAN
▨ 17TH CENTURY ☐ MODERN
Scale of feet

45

remains of a large 17th-century fireplace; its chimney corners are now hidden by cupboards. There is an old timber bake-house on the north side of the house, and a contemporary bridge-house of timber and plaster spans the moat.

Pirton Hall, a large red brick house, built in 1879, lies about 2 miles to the north-west of the village; attached to it is a park. It is now the property of Mr. W. Hanscombe.

High Down, the property of Mr. F. A. Delmé Radcliffe, and now occupied by Mrs. Pollard, stands on high ground about three-quarters of a mile south-west of the village. It was apparently the manor-house of the manor of Pirton, and was probably begun about 1599 by Thomas Docwra, lord of the manor, whose arms with the date 1599 appear on the south side of the house. His arms with his name and that of Jane Periam and date 1613 are also over the entrance gateway to the stables. The house is of two stories with basement, and is built of plastered flint and clunch. The main wing forms the south side of a courtyard, and is entered by a gabled porch projecting from its south front and rising the whole height of the house. On the eastern side of the entrance passage is the hall (now the dining-room); on the west are the pantry and some small rooms, with a staircase beyond leading to the floor above. North of the entrance passage is the staircase hall, out of which the morning-room opens to the west and the drawing-room to the east. The drawing-room continuing northward forms the short arm of the L. The kitchens are in the

PANEL WITH ARMS OF SIR THOMAS DOCWRA AT HIGH DOWN

basement under the drawing and the dining rooms. A range of out-buildings forms the western boundary of the courtyard; on the north side are the stables. In the north-east gable of the stables a stone panel has been inserted with a shield of the Docwra arms, the date 1504 and the name of 'Thomas Docwra Miles,' who was prior of the Order of St. John of Jerusalem. The shield has a chief of the arms of the Hospitallers and below is the inscription 'sane boro,' apparently for 'sane baro,' a motto which occurs elsewhere in connection with the Hospitallers, and probably refers to the claim of the priors to be the first barons of England. Near the stables is an old square brick dove-house.

A mill called Oughton Mill or Westmill, which was bequeathed by Thomas Ansell in 1607 to his son Edward,[4] may probably be dated to the 13th century, when a mill formed the subject of dispute between the Prior and convent of Hertford and Wiscard, lord of Ramerick. The mill was said to have been given to the priory by Alan de Limesi.[5] In the 14th century, however, it is found in the tenure of the Oddingselles. It was said in 1353 to be so much out of repair that no one would rent it.[6]

At the time of the Domesday Survey *MANORS PIRTON* was assessed at 10 hides, of which 2 hides were in demesne, and on the manor there were an English knight and three sokemen.

Before the Conquest the manor had been held by Archbishop Stigand. In 1086 it was part of the possessions of Ralph de Limesi, and the estate was held by the family of Limesi in chief as part of their barony of Ulverley[7] until the end of the 12th century. From Ralph it descended to his son Alan de Limesi and from Gerard, son of Alan, to John de Limesi, son of Gerard,[8] after whose death in the reign of Richard I the lands of the Limesi barony were divided between his sisters, Basilia wife of Hugh Oddingselles, or d'Odingseles, and Eleanor wife of David de Lindsey.[9] David had a son David de Lindsey,[10] who left no issue. Gerard his brother succeeded and on his death his property passed to his sister Alice wife of Robert de Pinkney of Weedon Pinkney.[11] The manor remained with the descendants of Hugh Oddingselles, who held it in sub-fee from the Pinkneys. Henry de Pinkney, who died about 1276,[12] was succeeded by his son Robert, and Pirton was held of Robert until his death in 1296–7.[13] His brother Henry, who succeeded, granted the reversion of his estates to the Crown in 1301,[14] from which time Pirton was held of the king in chief. After the division of the manor (see below) the half of William Oddingselles and his descendants was held in socage and owed the rent of a pair of gilt spurs and payment of 2s. 6d. at the view of frank-pledge at Oughton's Head (Altonis Hevyd),[15] and

PINKNEY of Weedon. *Argent a fesse indented gules.*

[4] Chan. Inq. p.m. (Ser. 2), ccxcvii, 146.
[5] Add. Chart. 15470.
[6] Chan. Inq. p.m. 33 Edw. I, no. 74; 27 Edw. III, no. 60.
[7] Ulverley in Solihull, co. Warwick. The place scarcely survives even in name now, but the site of their castle is marked by a moat and banks (Dugdale, *Baronage*, i, 413, and Dugdale, *Warwickshire*, s.v. Solihull).
[8] See Dugdale, *Mon. Angl.* iii, 300; Wrottesley, *Pedigrees from Plea R.* 479.
[9] Wrottesley, *Pedigrees from Plea R.* 479; Dugdale, *Baronage*, i, 413.
[10] See Assize R. 325, m. 29 d.
[11] Dugdale, *Baronage*, i, 76.
[12] *Cal. Pat.* 1272–81, pp. 160, 169.
[13] See Chan. Inq. p.m. 23 Edw. I, no. 130. [14] G.E.C. *Peerage*, s.v. Pinkney.
[15] Chan. Inq. p.m. 15 Edw. II, no. 4; 17 Edw. III (2nd nos.), no. 15.

PIRTON GRANGE; EAST FRONT

PIRTON OLD HALL

the other half was held by Hugh Oddingselles and his descendants by knight service as parcel of the barony of Ulverley.[16]

Basilia and Hugh Oddingselles, the immediate tenants of the manor, left two sons, William and Hugh,[17] who divided the property and so formed two manors. William Oddingselles, who was lord of the manor of Solihull in Warwickshire, took that half which was afterwards known as the manor of PIRTON.[18] Hugh's moiety of the property became the manor of Oddingselles (q.v.).

William Oddingselles died in 1295, leaving as heir his son Edmund,[19] who probably died without issue,

ODDINGSELLES. *Argent a fesse gules with two molets gules in the chief.*

as the manor was divided between two of Edmund's sisters, Ida and Alice.[20] Ida was wife of John de Clinton, first Lord Clinton, Alice was the wife of Thomas de Caunton.[21] Ida was succeeded by her son and then by her grandson, both named John de Clinton.[22] Alice died in 1322 and was succeeded by her son David.[23] David and Joan his wife settled the property on themselves and their heirs with remainder to William de Clinton Earl of Huntingdon, a younger son of John and Ida de Clinton.[24] David died before 1343 and Joan married as her second husband Laurence de Ayot.[25] They held the manor jointly until Joan died in 1354, leaving a daughter Elizabeth,[26] who married a certain Maurice who is called son of John son of Nichol.[27] Elizabeth died without issue in 1364,[28] and the manor passed by the settlement to John de Clinton (nephew and heir of William de Clinton Earl of Huntingdon),[29] to whom William de Caunton, heir of Elizabeth, released all his right. He received an annual pension from the earl of £20 out of the manor for life.[30] Thus both moieties of the manor were united in the hands of John de Clinton. Edward de Clinton son of John de Clinton died seised of the manor in 1399–1400 and was succeeded by his nephew William,[31] who granted the manor to certain feoffees, by whom it was conveyed to Richard Clitheroe. His son Roger died in 1455 and left a daughter Eleanor wife of John Norreys.[32] John survived his wife and died in 1485; his son and heir Edmund was then aged seven. His second wife Isabel afterwards married Henry Marney.[33] In January 1507–8 Edmund Norreys conveyed the manor to Alice Say, widow, and John Lech, her son.[34] According to Chauncy, in the reign of Elizabeth it was in the possession of Samuel Maron of Berkswell, co. Warwick,[35] and was sold by his son Edward in 1611 to Thomas Docwra of Putteridge. But this can scarcely be correct, for the inquisition on Thomas Docwra quotes a settlement made by his father Thomas Docwra on himself (the son), on his marriage with

CLINTON. *Argent six crosslets fitchy sable and a chief azure with two molets or pierced gules therein.*

HAMMONDS FARM, PIRTON, SHOWING PORCH

[16] Chan. Inq. p.m. 20 Edw. III, no. 13.
[17] Arch. xxxviii, 272.
[18] Chan. Inq. p.m. 23 Edw. I, no. 130; Assize R. 323.
[19] Chan. Inq. p.m. 23 Edw. I, no. 130.
[20] Arch. xxxviii, 272. William Oddingselles had four daughters (Cal. Pat. 1313–17, p. 122), of whom Ida was eldest.
[21] Arch. iii, 298.
[22] Nicholas, Historical Peerage.
[23] Chan. Inq. p.m. 15 Edw. II, no. 4.

[24] Cal. Pat. 1343–5, p. 49.
[25] Ibid.; Inq. a.q.d. file 265, no. 11; Feud. Aids, ii, 437.
[26] Chan. Inq. p.m. 28 Edw. III, no. 43.
[27] Abbrev. Rot. Orig. (Rec. Com.), ii, 233; Fine R. 155, m. 3, 14.
[28] Chan. Inq. p.m. 42 Edw. III (1st nos.), no. 21.
[29] Ibid. 28 Edw. III, no. 39.
[30] De Banco R. 433, m. 1.

[31] Chan. Inq. p.m. 1 Hen. IV, pt. i, no. 16; 2 Hen. VI, no. 36.
[32] Ibid. 33 Hen. VI, no. 29; Close, 21 Hen. VI, m. 15.
[33] Exch. Inq. p.m. (Ser. 2), file 29c, no. 4.
[34] Close, 23 Hen. VII, pt. ii, no. 28.
[35] He was the son of Thomas Maron of Hoxton, co. Middlesex, and Alice his wife. The dates will hardly allow of this Alice being identical with Alice Say.

PIRTON GRANGE   EAST PORCH

PIRTON HATCH DOWN, THE PORCH

Jane Periam in 1599.[36] So the manor must have come into the family at an earlier date than that given by Chauncy. Thomas received a grant of free warren at Pirton in 1616.[37] He died in 1620,[38] leaving as heir his son Periam. On the death of Periam in 1642 it descended to his son Thomas,[39] whose only child Martha married Sir Peter Warburton of Arley (co. Ches.). In 1726, after the death of Martha, Thomas Warburton, Sir George Warburton, bart., son of Sir Peter and Martha, and Periam Docwra joined in a conveyance to Ralph Radcliffe.[40] It has since descended in the family of Radcliffe,[41] and is now in the possession of Mr. F. A. Delmé-Radcliffe of the Priory, Hitchin (q.v.).

The manor of ODDINGSELLES (Doddingseles, Odyngseles, xiv cent.), often called also 'half the manor of Pirton,' was that part of the manor of Pirton which on the death of Basilia Oddingselles fell to the share of Hugh her son. Hugh died seised of it in 1304–5, leaving as heir his son John.[42] He and his wife Emma obtained licence in 1316 to grant the manor to Thomas de Wassyngeles for a settlement on them and their heirs.[43] In 1337 John and Emma granted the manor to William Corbet for life, with reversion to their son Thomas.[44] After the death of John, Emma married William Corbet, who died in 1346.[45] She survived until the next year.[46] Her son John Oddingselles succeeded to the manor, and died abroad in 1352, leaving a son John, then aged sixteen.[47] It descended in 1380 to his son Sir John, and in 1404 to Edward son of John[48] (during whose minority the property was entrusted to John Cokayn,[49] his father-in-law), to Edward's son Gerald, and finally to Edward son of Gerald.[50] In 1505 Gerald d'Oddingselles granted the manor to feoffees,[51] who released it to Richard Decons.[52] He sold it shortly afterwards through trustees to Roger Lupton, clerk, Provost of St. Mary's College, Eton.[53] Eton College held the manor till 15 February 1800, when it was purchased by Penelope widow of Sir Charles Farnaby Radcliffe,[54] from whom it has descended to Mr. F. A. Delmé-Radcliffe, the present owner.

RECTORY MANOR The grant by which Ralph de Limesi gave to the priory of St. Mary, Hertford, the church of Pirton (see below) included also 2½ hides of land there and a mill. After the Dissolution this estate

HIGH DOWN, PIRTON: ENTRANCE GATEWAY

was granted in 1538, under the name of Pirton, to Anthony Denny and Joan Champernowne, who were then about to marry.[55] Anthony Denny was succeeded by his son Edward Denny of Waltham Holy Cross.[56] His son Sir Edward Denny, kt., died in February 1600–1,[57] leaving a son and heir Arthur, a minor, whose mother Margaret Lady Denny held one-third of the property in dower.[58] In 1609 Arthur Denny, with his wife Elizabeth and his mother, conveyed the property to Sir John Davies, kt.,[59] and he died seised of the manor and rectory in 1626,

---

[36] See also as to the date of the building of High Down under the description of the parish.
[37] Pat. 14 Jas. I, pt. xi.
[38] Chan. Inq. p.m. (Ser. 2), ccclxxxvii, 122.
[39] Ct. of Wards, Feod. Surv. no. 17; Chan. Inq. p.m. (Ser. 2), dxxxvii, 97.
[40] Recov. R. Mich. 13 Geo. I, rot. 382; Feet of F. Herts. Hil. 13 Geo. I.
[41] Recov. R. Trin. 35 Geo. III, rot. 382; Hil. 5 & 6 Geo. IV, rot. 22.
[42] Chan. Inq. p.m. 33 Edw. I, no. 74.
[43] Cal. Pat. 1313–17, p. 456; Inq. a.q.d. file 113, no. 14; Feet of F. Div. Co. Trin. 9 & 10 Edw. II, no. 135.

[44] Cal. Pat. 1334–8, p. 485; Inq. a.q.d. file 240, no. 2; Feud. Aids, ii, 437.
[45] Chan. Inq. p.m. 20 Edw. III, no. 13; Cal. Close, 1346–9, p. 7.
[46] Inq. p.m. 21 Edw. III, no. 30.
[47] Ibid. 27 Edw. III (1st nos.), no. 60; Abbrev. Rot. Orig. (Rec. Com.), ii, 186, 230.
[48] Chan. Inq. p.m. 5 Hen. IV, no. 19.
[49] Cal. Pat. 1401–5, p. 374.
[50] Pedigree in Dugdale's Warwickshire, p. 343.
[51] Feet of F. Herts. Mich. 21 Hen. VII.
[52] Clutterbuck, Hist. and Antiq. of Herts. iii, 123.

[53] Inq. a.q.d. 7 Hen. VIII, file 301, no. 8; L. and P. Hen. VIII, ii (1), 2146.
[54] Deeds of F. A. Delmé-Radcliffe (quoted by Cussans in Hist. of Herts. Hitchin Hund. 19); see Recov. R. Hil. 5 & 6 Geo. IV, rot. 22.
[55] L. and P. Hen. VIII, xiii (1), 384 (47).
[56] See Com. Pleas D. Enr. East. 1575; Trin. 19 Eliz.
[57] Chan. Inq. p.m. (Ser. 2), cclxv, 69.
[58] Ct. of Wards, Extents and Attachments, 618.
[59] Feet of F. Herts. East. 7 Jas. I.

having settled the manor on his daughter Lucy on her marriage (at the age of ten) with Ferdinand Lord Hastings, son of Henry Earl of Huntingdon.[60] In 1628 the Crown seized this property in payment of debts incurred by Arthur Denny,[61] but it was apparently regranted to Lucy and her husband Ferdinand Lord Hastings, who were in possession in 1634.[62]

Previous to this, however, Sir Archibald Douglas, who had married Eleanor widow of Sir John Davies, had sold the rectory and manor for a term of sixty years to Francis Poulton. In 1642 Lucy Lady Hastings appeared on behalf of her mother to claim the rectory, alleging that Sir Archibald was insane and Eleanor was in prison when he sold the property,[63] and that her mother was in great distress owing to Sir Archibald having appropriated all the profits of this sale, and to the loss of her dower in Ireland, which was in the hands of rebels. Lady Hastings remarked that she was unable to help her mother, as Lord Hastings had lost the greater part of his estate in the Irish Rebellion.[64] The Poultons, however, remained in possession, and the manor was sold in 1656 by William Poulton, son of Francis, to Thomas White,[65] whose executors conveyed it to Anthony Deane, kt., in 1686.[66] Morgan Deane, grandson of Sir Anthony, left the property to his trustees for sale,[67] and in 1736 it was bought by Robert second Lord Raymond,[68] from whom it passed by his father's will to Benesham Filmer, son of Sir Robert Filmer, bart., of East Sutton, co. Kent. He died unmarried in 1763, when it came to his nephew Sir John Filmer, bart.[69] Sir Edmund Filmer, great-grandson of Sir Edmund, brother and ultimate heir of Sir John, sold the manor in 1870 to Messrs. Paine & Brettel of Chertsey, solicitors (since which date most of the tenants have been enfranchised), and the rectory farm and about 415 acres of land to Mr. Daniel Davis of Hexton, farmer. It is now occupied by Mr. E. R. Davis.

FILMER, baronet. *Sable three bars or with three cinquefoils or in the chief.*

The manor of Ramerick in Ickleford extended into this parish, and this part of it is sometimes referred to as the manor of Pirton.[70]

The parish church of CHURCH ST. MARY, standing in the middle of the village, is built of flint rubble with stone dressings. The chancel roof is tiled, and that of the nave is covered with lead.

The church consists of a chancel, central tower, nave and south porch.[71]

The original church, consisting of a chancel, nave and central tower, was built in the 12th century. The chancel was much altered in the 14th century, when a south transept, now demolished, was built on the south side of the tower. New windows were inserted in the nave in the 14th and 15th centuries,[72] and the south doorway was altered about 1380, when the south porch was built. In the 17th century several small alterations were made, notably to the east window, and in 1883 the whole church was restored and the tower rebuilt from the foundations.

DOVE-COTE AT HAMMONDS FARM, PIRTON

The chancel, of which the walls are probably part of the original church, now shows no detail earlier than c. 1330. The east window, which was originally of the 14th century, is now much defaced by 17th-century alterations. The remaining windows are all of the 15th century. One on the north side and one on the south have two lights, cinquefoiled and with tracery. In the south wall there is also a three-light window of three cinque-

---

[60] Chan. Inq. p.m. (Ser. 2), ccccxxxvii, 105.
[61] Pat. 4 Chas. I, pt. xxxii, no. 13.
[62] Com. Pleas D. Enr. Trin. 10 Chas. I, m. 2.
[63] *Hist. MSS. Com. Rep.* v, App. 5, 25, 49.
[64] Ibid. 25.
[65] Recov. R. Mich. 8 Chas. II, rot. 167.

[66] Feet of F. Herts. Mich. 2 Jas. II.
[67] Cussans, *Hist. of Herts. Hitchin Hund.* 20.
[68] See Recov. R. Trin. 13 Geo. II, rot. 346.
[69] Ibid. 24 Geo. III, rot. 45.
[70] See Cal. Pat. 1476–85, p. 478; Chan. Inq. p.m. (Ser. 2), vii, 49; Close, 7 Hen. VII, m. 10a.

[71] Dimensions: chancel, 24 ft. by 18 ft.; central tower, 17 ft. by 16 ft.; nave, 56 ft. by 26 ft.
[72] In 1486 John Dayell (Druall) made a bequest to the work of the church, and the year following another bequest was made by Walter Browne (P.C.C. 1 Milles, 22 Godyn).

50

PIRTON CHURCH FROM THE SOUTH

foiled lights in a square head. A doorway, also on the south side, has a two-centred arch. In the chancel, under the easternmost window on the south side, is a 14th-century double piscina with a central pillar.

The east and west arches of the central tower are semicircular, of about 1130, and several of the stones are ornamented with a diaper pattern. The capitals and abaci are plain, and have been reset and retooled. On the north side is a doorway, of about 1330, with a lancet head and a simple continuous moulding. It now leads to a modern wooden vestry built against the north side of the tower. On the south side is a wide archway, now bricked up, with a low modern two-centred head. This originally opened into a south transept.

The nave is lighted on the north side by two windows, the easternmost of three lights with tracery above, of the 15th century. The lower part of this window is blocked up, the sill being 2 ft. 8 in. below the bottom of the lights. The westernmost window is of two cinquefoiled ogee-headed lights, with a quatrefoil above, and has a high two-centred head. In this window are fragments of 14th-century glass. Between the two windows is visible on the interior side only a 12th-century round-headed window, now blocked. The 14th-century north doorway, to the west of both windows, is blocked, but on the outside its two-centred head and single-splayed jambs are visible, and the door, which is much defaced, is probably contemporary. On this wall are remains of painting, now quite undecipherable, which were discovered in 1883.

The south wall of the nave has two windows similar, and similarly arranged, to those on the north side, but the jambs of the easternmost window are of the 14th century, and the lower part is not blocked, while the lights of the westernmost window are trefoiled, and simple arches instead of ogees. In the easternmost window are fragments of 15th-century glass with the arms of Lindsay. There are between the windows the remains, consisting of the eastern jamb and half the head, of a 12th-century window like that in the north wall. The south doorway, of about 1330, has a two-centred head. The jambs are plain on the interior but moulded on the exterior side. The door is probably contemporary. To the west is the doorway, with a two-centred head, of the stairs to the upper floor of the porch. The west window has three ogee cinquefoiled lights, with tracery above, in a two-centred head. It has been repaired with cement, and is now blocked. The south porch is of two stages, the ceiling of the lower stage having been removed, so that the porch is now open to the roof. There is a stone seat in the west side of the porch ; the east and west windows have been blocked up. There is a small recess over the two-centred entrance arch, and the two-light window of the upper stage above the recess is original, but the dividing mullion is missing.

The upper stage of the tower is reached by a newel in the north-west angle, approached by a door on the outside. The bell chamber is lighted by three two-light traceried windows on the east, north and south, with two-centred heads, and on the west by a square-headed loop. There is a two-light window on the north side of the lower stage. The tower has an embattled parapet and a needle spire. The buttresses at the north-west, south-east and south-west are original, as are those of the nave, but the large diagonal buttress at the north-east angle is modern.

The only monument to be noted is that of Jane wife of Thomas Docwra, 1645, a mural tablet with arms and inscription, on the south wall of the nave.

There is a chest, probably of the 17th century, in the chancel.

The bells are five in number : the treble by John Briant, 1781 ; the second and third by Joseph Eayre of St. Neots, 1763 and 1756 respectively ; the fourth by Thomas Russell of Wootton, 1731 ; and the tenor by Robert Oldfeild, 1634.

The plate includes two cups and two patens of Sheffield plate.

The registers are in four books, the first containing baptisms from 1562 to 1776, burials from 1558 to 1776 and marriages from 1560 to 1753 ; the second baptisms and burials from 1774 to 1812 ; the third marriages from 1754 to 1773 ; and the fourth marriages from 1774 to 1812.

ADVOWSON In the 11th or early 12th century Ralph de Limesi gave the church of Pirton with the tithes of his lands there [73] to the priory of St. Mary, Hertford, which he founded as a cell to St. Albans. A vicarage was ordained before the beginning of the 13th century.[74] The advowson remained with the priory till the Dissolution.[75] It was then granted to Sir Anthony Denny, and descended with the rectory (q.v.) until about the middle of the 17th century. In 1670 presentation was made by the king ; in 1682 by Dorothy, widow of Samuel Howe ; in 1732 by the Bishop of Lincoln ; in 1735 by Isaac Coleman, the late incumbent ; in 1748 by James Colt Ducarel ; in 1773 by Charles Peers ; in 1835 by Susanna Thirlwall ; and in 1847 and 1851 by Ralph Lindsay.[76] In 1870 the advowson was conveyed to the representatives of the late Ralph Lindsay to the Dean and Chapter of Ely,[77] the present owners.

For a very long period before 1851 there had been no resident incumbent. A parsonage-house was then built by Mr. Ralph Lindsay, the rector.

In 1507 Thomas Pyrton left 40s. 'to make an image of the Blessed Mary and a tabernacle to stand in the church there.'[78]

There are a Wesleyan chapel and a Baptist chapel in Pirton at the present time.

CHARITIES In 1641 John Hammond by his will directed that a sum of £100 should be laid out in the purchase of land, the rent thereof to be applied in binding out one apprentice or more to an honest trade. The trust estate consists of two allotments at Punches Cross, containing 6 a. 3 r. 23 p., awarded on the inclosure in 1811 in lieu of land originally purchased.

The testator further devised two cottages, to be occupied by poor families rent free. The charity is regulated by a scheme of the Charity Commissioners, 3 May 1904. A premium of £12 10s. is usually paid, and the cottages, rebuilt by the Hanscombe family, are used as almshouses.

---

[73] Dugdale, *Mon. Angl.* iii, 299, 300 ; *Cal. Rot. Chart.* (Rec. Com.), i, 95.
[74] See Linc. Epis. Reg. Wells, 1209-35.
[75] *Valor Eccl.* (Rec. Com.), iv, 276.
[76] See list of patrons given by Cussans, *Hist. of Herts, Hitchin Hund.* 23-4.
[77] *Lond. Gaz.* 29 Nov. 1870, p. 5404.
[78] P.C.C. Wills, 31 Adeane.

THE HUNDRED OF BROADWATER

CONTAINING THE PARISHES OF

ASTON	HATFIELD OR	TOTTERIDGE
AYOT ST. LAWRENCE	BISHOP'S HATFIELD	WALKERN
AYOT ST. PETER	KNEBWORTH	WATTON-AT-STONE
BALDOCK	LETCHWORTH	WELWYN
BENINGTON	GREAT MUNDEN	WESTON
DATCHWORTH	LITTLE MUNDEN	WILLIAN
DIGSWELL	SACOMBE	GREAT WYMONDLEY
GRAVELEY	STEVENAGE	LITTLE WYMONDLEY

The hundred of Broadwater takes its name from a little hamlet on the boundary line between the parishes of Knebworth and Shephall, at a point about two miles south of Stevenage where the main road from Hertford and a road from Aston join the Great North Road.

At the time of the Domesday Survey Broadwater Hundred included Shephall, which is situated in the centre of the hundred, but was in the 13th century attached to Cashio Hundred as a possession of St. Alban's Abbey; Norton on the northern boundary and Codicote (with Oxewiche) on the west, which were at the same time detached for the like reason; Langley with Minsden, and Almshoe[1] (in Ippollitts), which were afterwards attached to Hitchin Hundred; and part of Tewin, now in Hertford Hundred, which was probably attached to Broadwater because it belonged to the Abbot of Westminster, one of whose principal manors in Hertfordshire was at Stevenage.

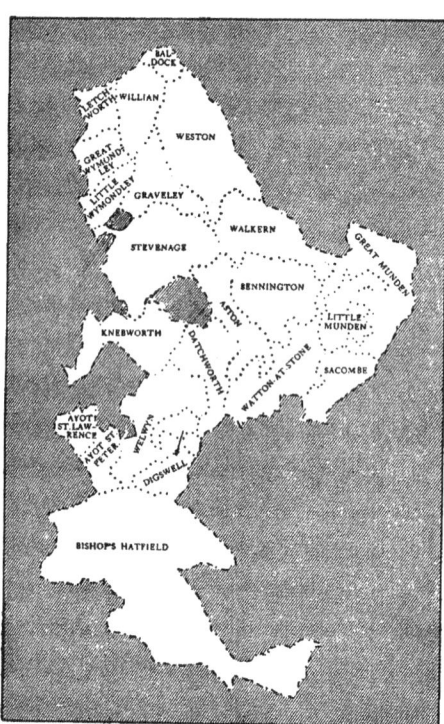

INDEX MAP TO THE HUNDRED OF BROADWATER

Two places now in this hundred are not mentioned in the Domesday Survey: Baldock, which was in the 12th century formed

---

[1] Almshoebury is mentioned as pertaining to Broadwater Hundred as late as 1651 (Parl. Surv. Herts. no. 1).

BROADWATER HUNDRED

out of Weston, and Totteridge, which was a detached part of the parish of Hatfield about twelve miles south of its mother-church.

Two places mentioned in the Domesday Survey have not been identified: Wollenwick (Wlwenewiche),[2] which was probably a portion of Stevenage parish lying between Wymondley and Burleigh, and which is mentioned as late as 1381,[3] and Rodenhanger (Rodehangre, Rodenehangre), which evidently adjoined Norton, with which it was given to St. Alban's Abbey by King Ethelred in 1007.[4]

Broadwater has always been a royal hundred.[5] The hundred court is said to have been sometimes held at Stevenage with the county court, but in the 14th century the sheriff's tourn was held at Broadwater at Easter and Michaelmas.[6] In 1651 the value of the hundred, with profits, perquisites and privileges, was £5 10s. yearly. The total of rents and royalties due to the lord of the hundred amounted to £10 14s.[7] In 1651 payments amounting to 21s. 4d. for frankpledge were due to the lord of the hundred from Welwyn, Knebworth, Bardolfhall (Watton), Little Munden, Letchworth and Wymondley. Rents of assize paid to the sheriff's aid at the same time from various places amounted to £3, and certainty money from freeholders at the sheriff's tourn to 12s. 1d.[8] The waifs, strays, deodands, goods of felons and fugitives, &c., within the hundred belonged to the lord if the bailiff of the hundred seized them first, but if any bailiff belonging to a lord of a manor who had leet within the hundred seized them before the bailiff of the hundred, then that lord in whose leet they were seized commonly had the profit and benefit thereof.[9]

The lords of all the more important manors in the hundred appear to have had right of view of frankpledge.[10] The lords of Aston, Ayot St. Lawrence, Baldock, Benington, Hatfield, Stevenage, Walkern and Weston had also gallows and tumbrel; those of Datchworth, Knebworth, Great Munden and Sacombe had gallows.

[2] See *V.C.H. Herts.* i, 297. [3] Chan. Inq. p.m. 4 Ric. II, no. 110.
[4] *Anecdota Oxoniensia* (Med. and Mod. Ser.), pt. vii, 24, 133.
[5] Assize R. 325; Chauncy, *Hist. of Herts.* 304; Clutterbuck, *Hist. of Herts.* ii, 244.
[6] Chan. Inq. p.m. file 403, no. 38; *Cal. Pat.* 1385–9, p. 68.   [7] Parl. Surv. Herts. no. 1.
[8] Ibid.   [9] Ibid.
[10] Assize R. 325, m. 26 d.; *Rot. Hund.* (Rec. Com.), i, 192; *Plac. de Quo Warr.* (Rec. Com.), 279, 289; Pat. 12 Jas. I, pt. xxii, m. 18; *Cal. Pat.* 1385–9, p. 68; Pat. 5 Edw. VI, pt. iv, m. 27.

ASTON

Easttun, Estone (xi cent.); Aschton, Estona (xiii cent.).

The parish of Aston has an acreage of 2,070 acres, of which 1,007¾ are arable land, 648¾ acres permanent grass and 122¼ acres wood.[1] The height of the parish above the ordnance datum is for the most part from 200 ft. to 300 ft., but rises in the centre to over 300 ft., the highest point (315 ft.) being by the church. The River Beane forms the eastern boundary of the parish and separates it from Benington. A branch road from the Great North Road to Benington passes across the centre of the parish and through the village, where a network of

is the residence of the present lord of the manor, Mr. Vernon A. Malcolmson, and his wife, the Hon. Mrs. Malcolmson. The house is built of brick. Thin 2-in. bricks, rising about 10½ in to every four courses, are used throughout; the north front, however, up to the string over the windows of the ground floor, and parts of the back, are faced with flints, no stone being visible except a built-up arch on the outside, next the hall fireplace. In plan it is a parallelogram, 114 ft. long by 32 ft. wide, running east and west. On the north front is the main entrance, and on the south front are two projecting wings, one near either end and each con-

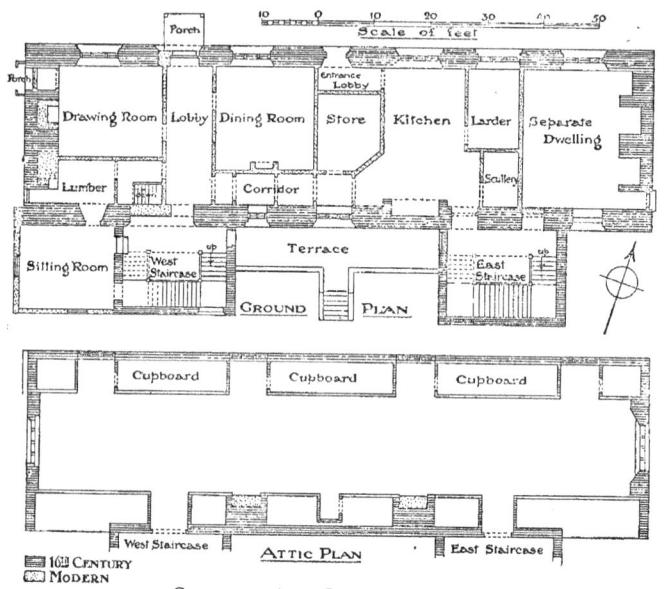

GROUND AND ATTIC PLAN OF ASTON BURY

lanes branch off to north and south. The village lies in the centre of the parish, with the church of St. Mary and the manor-house on the west. In the north of the parish is the hamlet of Aston End. In the south-east is Frogmore Hall, a modern red brick house surrounded by a park, the property of Mr. G. B. Hudson, M.A., D.L., J.P., formerly M.P. for the Hitchin division of Hertfordshire, and now the residence of Major H. F. Low. Aston House, with a small park, is the residence of Mr. F. W. Imbert-Terry, and Barelegh that of Lady Jane van Koughnet.

Aston Bury, the ancient moated manor-house, is supposed to have been built by Sir Philip Boteler about 1540–5. Until recently it has been used as a farm-house, but has now been restored and

[1] Statistics from Bd. of Agric. (1905).

taining a fine oak staircase. All the window openings and angle quoins are of brick. Above the upper floor windows on the north front runs a heavy moulded brick cornice, cut off abruptly without returns at each end of the building. Above the cornice is the long tiled roof, broken by four curved gables, in which are windows which light the attic room. The ends of the main building have curved gables, broken by a pair of chimneys on either side of each gable. One pair of chimneys has been twice rebuilt, once in the 18th century and again recently, this time in exact imitation of the other three, which are fine examples of cut and moulded brickwork, having octagonal moulded bases, circular shafts, richly diapered or twisted, and octagonal capitals at the top. A large attic window occupies the upper part of each gable, and in the west gable are two tiny windows at the first-floor level, lighting the spaces between the projecting chimney breasts inside the rooms and the flank walls. The projecting staircase wings at the back are carried up to the same height as the main walls, and between them are two groups of chimneys similar to those already described, one having three shafts, the other four.

The main entrance is in the centre of the north front, and has a moulded square-headed doorway, with a massive oak moulded door frame, and iron-studded door. The front windows are recessed in moulded brickwork. The ground-floor windows have square brick heads, having a very slight camber; but, as the bricks are not radiated to a centre, the weight seems to be taken by the stout oak window frame and mullions. The upper floor windows have flat arches with properly radiating joints, pointing probably to a somewhat later date.

Internally the building has a ground floor, with basement under, an upper floor and one long apartment in the roof. A chapel which stood at the east end of the building was pulled down many years ago. The hall would measure about 36 ft. by 25 ft., having a large four-centred arched fireplace 8 ft. wide in the centre of the south wall. Beside the fireplace is a doorway leading into the east staircase. East of the hall is another large apartment. The hall and the room to the east take up the eastern half of the building, and the western half contains a panelled room with a large open fireplace and the original kitchen with an old iron-studded door. The doorway near the west end of the north front is modern, and occupies the position of a built-up window; the porch is made up of old woodwork.

The doorway between the hall and the east staircase has a wooden frame with moulded capitals and bases, over which is a four-centred arch with carved spandrels, the carving being of the usual flat 16th-century type. In two of the spandrels, however, are shields of arms ; on the east side are the arms of the Botelers and on the west side are the arms of Drury (Argent on a chief vert a tau cross between two molets or). These arms also appear on a brass in Watton Church. Sir Philip Boteler of Woodhall married Elizabeth daughter of Sir Robert Drury, kt., of Halstead, and, as is shown in the descent of the manor, acquired Aston in 1540 and died in 1545.

The basement cellars are not of much interest; they are only partly below ground and have had windows on both the north and south sides. The massive timbers of the ground floor may be seen, as there is no vaulting or ceiling.

There are a few original partitions on the first floor, into which some 16th-century panelling has been introduced. But the room in the attic story is worthy of notice. It is almost wholly in the roof and is a long apartment running the full length of the building. It measures 108 ft. long by 17 ft. wide. It is lighted at each end by a large mullioned window in the gable, and has besides four windows on the north front set in the curved brick gables before described. These windows are deeply recessed from the room. On the south side of the apartment are two built-up fireplaces with moulded and stopped jambs, the inner moulding being carried over the opening with a flat four-centred arch, the outer moulding running square over it. It is almost identical with the fireplaces at Mackerye End, Hammond's Farm, Pirton, and other old houses in the county. The ceiling of this apartment is of plaster, almost semicircular, and a moulded cornice of oak, presumably the roof purlin, is carried the whole length of each side at the springing level of the arch. Advantage has been taken of the slope of the roof to form a series of cupboards on the south side, entered from the window recesses. Access is gained to the room by short passages from both east and west staircases.

ASTON BURY : ATTIC GALLERY

The two fine oak staircases are the principal internal features of the house, that on the east, which is entered directly from the hall, being the richer of the two. In each case there are straight flights of steps on three sides of the staircase, with landings at the angles, the fourth side having landings at each floor. Both stairs rise from the ground floor to the attics, and the east stair is continued down to the basement.

The parish lies on a subsoil of chalk. There are three chalk-pits in the north of the parish. The nearest railway station is Knebworth, on the Great Northern main line, about three miles to the south-west.

The inclosure award, made in 1858, is in the custody of the clerk of the peace.[2]

MANOR Previous to the Norman Conquest the manor of *ASTON* was held by three of the men of Stigand Archbishop of Canterbury, whose names are not known. After the

[2] *Blue Bk. Incl. Awards*, 63.

A HISTORY OF HERTFORDSHIRE

Conquest it formed part of the demesne lands of Odo Bishop of Bayeux, and was assessed at 10 hides.[3] Odo forfeited in 1088 and Aston remained for some time in the possession of the Crown, until Henry I gave it to his queen Adelaide. After his death Adelaide, who married secondly William de Albini Earl of Arundel in 1138,[4] gave the manor of Aston to the Abbot and monks of St. Mary of Reading for the good of the soul of King Henry her husband.[5] This grant was afterwards confirmed by Henry II,[6] Richard I, John, and Henry III,[7] and the abbey of Reading continued to hold it 'by service of praying for the King, his progenitors and successors'[8] until the Dissolution. After the attainder of Hugh Cooke, the last abbot, all the possessions of the monastery were seized by the king, Nicholas Bristowe being appointed steward in 1540.[9] In the same year the manor of Aston was granted to Sir Philip Boteler of Watton Woodhall, to be held in chief for the tenth part of a knight's fee and rent of 77s. 11d.[10] This Sir Philip had been one of the Knights of the Body to King Henry VIII in 1516,[11] and was Sheriff of Hertfordshire in 1524–6, 1530, 1532 and 1538–40.[12] In 1530 he was one of the commissioners for Hertfordshire to inquire concerning the possessions of Wolsey.[13] In 1537 he was present at the christening of Prince Edward,[14] afterwards Edward VI, and in 1539–40 was among the knights appointed to meet Anne of Cleves,[15] on which occasion he was one of those who 'stood from the park pales upon the heath (Blackheath) to the meeting-place' (at Shooter's Hill).[16] In 1544 his name was enrolled as supplying men for the rearguard in the army against France,[17] and later in the same year he was appointed to levy recruits.[18] He died in 1545.[19] From this date Aston descended in the same manner as Watton Woodhall (q.v.) until 1778, when John Palmer Boteler sold Aston to Sir Thomas Rumbold.[20] The latter died in 1791, and in 1794 the manor was sold by trustees to Paul Bendfield,[21] who in turn sold it to Edmund Darby in 1801.[22] After the death of Edmund Darby in 1831 Aston was sold to Ann Walmsley of Hoddesdon, who left it by will to her great-nephew Donat John

BOTELER of Woodhall. *Gules a fesse checky argent and sable between six crosslets or.*

ASTON BURY FROM THE NORTH-WEST

[3] *V.C.H. Herts.* i, 309a.
[4] G.E.C. *Complete Peerage.*
[5] Dugdale, *Mon.* iv, 29; Add. Chart. 19586; Assize R. 323, m. 51 d.
[6] Add. Chart. 19593.
[7] Assize R. 323, m. 51 d.
[8] *Cal. Close,* 1337–9, p. 5; *L. and P. Hen. VIII,* vii, 1544.
[9] *L. and P. Hen. VIII,* xvi, g. 379 (62).
[10] Ibid. xv, g. 942 (78).
[11] Ibid. ii, 2735.
[12] Ibid. iv, 819, 1795, 2672, 6721; v, 1598 (10); xiii (2), 967; xiv (1), 896; (2), p. 223.
[13] Ibid. iv, 6516.
[14] Ibid. xii (2), 911.
[15] Ibid. xiv (2), p. 201.
[16] Ibid. xv, p. 5.
[17] Ibid. xviii (1), 273, 276.
[18] Ibid. (2), 452.
[19] Chan. Inq. p.m. (Ser. 2), lxxiii, 88.
[20] Clutterbuck, *Hist. of Herts.* ii, 247.
[21] Ibid.
[22] Ibid.

Aston Bury: The North Porch
(Recently removed)

BROADWATER HUNDRED — ASTON

Hoste O'Brien, who was lord of the manor in 1877.[23] His successor, Captain William Edward Freeman O'Brien, sold Aston in 1907 to Mr. Vernon A. Malcolmson and his wife the Hon. Mrs. Malcolmson, granddaughter of the second Earl of Leicester.[24]

In 1287 the Abbot of Reading claimed view of frankpledge and free warren in Aston,[25] but in the reign of Edward I he claimed in addition, in all his Hertfordshire lands, sac and soc, toll and team, infangentheof, utfangentheof, gallows, tumbrel, and chattels of felons and fugitives, also freedom from suit at the hundred court, from paying danegeld, shiregeld and other dues[26]; so doubtless these privileges applied to Aston.

Certain lands in Aston were granted before 1065 by Wulf, 'a certain Dane, a very powerful minister' of King Edward the Confessor, to St. Alban's Abbey.[27] After the Dissolution the lands of St. Alban's Abbey in Aston were granted with the manor of Shephall to George Nodes.[28] In 1570 they were in the possession of Charles Nodes,[29] his nephew,[30] and presumably descended with the manor of Shephall.

In 1564 a messuage in Aston, at the church gate, and a cottage called the Almshouse, with land called Hoobarnetts Croft, Grynsie Croft and Gallowfield, part of the manor of Aston, were granted by Sir John Boteler to John Kent in free socage.[31] The latter died in 1592 and was succeeded by his son Thomas,[32] who died in 1635, leaving a son also named Thomas.[33]

ST. ALBAN'S ABBEY. *Azure a saltire or.*

NODES of Shephall. *Sable a pile argent with three trefoils sable thereon.*

The parish church of *ST. MARY CHURCH THE VIRGIN*,[34] consisting of a chancel, nave, west tower, north aisle, north vestry and south porch, stands on high ground to the west of the village. It is built of flint with stone dressings and the roofs are covered with lead. The tower and nave have embattled parapets. The chancel and nave date from about 1230, and probably represent the whole of the original church. It was not until the end of the 14th or the beginning of the 15th century that the west tower was added. Towards the end of the 15th century new windows were inserted, the church was re-roofed and various repairs were executed. Further alterations took place in the 16th century, and in 1850 the church was restored. Finally, in 1883, restoration again took place, and the north vestry, north aisle and south porch were added.

The chancel has a modern east window of three lights, trefoiled, with tracery above. In the north wall, which is pierced by a wide opening into the modern north vestry, are the jambs and rear arch of a 13th-century lancet window. There is also on this side, at the west, a modern single light with a four-centred head. On the south side are two square-headed 16th-century two-light windows, much restored and repaired with cement; between them is a modern door with a two-centred head. At the south-east end of the wall is a large double piscina with a single drain and divided by a central pillar. The heads are trefoiled, and the date is early in the 13th century.

ASTON CHURCH FROM THE SOUTH-WEST

---

[23] Cussans, *Hist. of Herts. Broadwater Hund.* 194.
[24] Information kindly supplied by Mr. V. A. Malcolmson.
[25] Assize R. 325, m. 26 d.
[26] *Plac. de Quo Warr.* (Rec. Com.), 282–3.
[27] Matt. Paris, *Chron. Maj.* (Rolls Ser.), vi, 32.
[28] L. and P. Hen. VIII, xvii, 220 (96).
[29] Pat. 13 Eliz. pt. xi, m. 29.
[30] *Visit. Herts.* (Harl. Soc. xxii), 80.
[31] Chan. Inq. p.m. (Ser. 2), ccclxxi, 137.
[32] Ibid.
[33] Ibid. dxxii, 17.
[34] Dimensions: chancel, 28 ft. 6 in. by 13 ft. 6 in.; nave, 45 ft. by 22 ft.; tower, 16 ft. 6 in. square.

The roof of the chancel, as also that of the nave, is of the 15th century, low pitched, with moulded trusses, with carved bosses at the intersections of the trusses with the purlins. The screen is a good example of early 16th-century woodwork, with tracery in the heads. The capitals of the chancel arch have been much mutilated to admit of the fitting of the screen, and the arch probably dates from the first years of the 16th century.

In the nave very few original details can be traced; the north arcade is of course contemporary with the building of the aisle in 1883, and the south windows are also modern. The walls, however, are probably of the 13th century. A lofty four-centred arch opens from the nave to the tower, and is original. The west window is also original, and is of three lights, with tracery above, much restored, and repaired with cement. In this window is a little white and gold 15th-century glass. The modern south porch is approached by a two-centred doorway, and has east and west windows of two lights in square heads. Its entrance arch is two-centred with shafted jambs; it is faced with flint and stone in quarries, and has a gable with a stone coping and cross.

The tower is of two stages with diagonal buttresses, and has a 15th-century west door, much repaired. The bell-chamber is lighted by four louvres with two-centred heads.

The communion table is of the 17th century, and the pulpit is octagonal, of panelled oak, of about 1630. There is a brass on the floor of the nave of John Kent and his wife, with an inscription and the date 1592.

The bells number six, and include a second and third by Miles Graye, dated 1629. The fifth is also of 1629, but recast in 1840.

The plate includes a cup, a cover paten and a paten of 1571, and a cup of 1612.

The registers are in two books: (i) baptisms and burials from 1558 to 1812, and marriages from 1558 to 1753; (ii) marriages from 1754 to 1812.

In 1505 Sir John Smith, the parson of Aston, left 26s. 8d. towards the making of a tabernacle for the image of St. Margaret in the church,[35] and in 1524 John Kent left 40s. for the same purpose.[36] An altar of St. Katherine is mentioned, with that of the Blessed Virgin, in 1484.[37]

ADVOWSON The invocation of Aston Church seems to have been changed about the end of the 15th century, for in 1430 and apparently in 1490 it is referred to as St. James,[38] but in 1505 and after as our Lady.[39]

The presentation to the church seems to have always belonged to the lord of the manor. It was confirmed to the monastery of Reading by William Earl of Arundel, Queen Adelaide's husband,[40] and by Henry II[41] and Edward III.[42] The church was never appropriated, and the living is a rectory. The abbey continued to hold the advowson until the Dissolution.[43] In 1540 it was granted together with the manor to Sir Philip Boteler,[44] and followed the same descent until 1801, when it was sold after the death of Paul Bendfield to Alexander Ellice of Bath,[45] who presented to the living in 1804.[46] His son William Ellice[47] presented in 1809.[48] John Corfield made presentation in 1815,[49] and was still patron in 1822[50]; but this was probably only an alienation for a term of years, as the Rev. James Ellice presented in 1829.[51] The latter held the advowson until 1849, when the Rev. George Augustus Oddie became patron,[52] and remained so until 1890. For the next five years the presentation was held by Mr. John Oddie and five others,[53] who were succeeded in 1895 by the Rev. George Venables Oddie, the present patron and incumbent.[54]

A portion of the tithes, granted in 1253 to the abbey of Colchester,[55] is recorded in the Taxation of Pope Nicholas in 1291,[56] and in the assessment for a feudal aid in 1428.[57] In both these entries the portion of Reading is valued at £1, and that of Colchester at £2 6s. 8d.

A terrier of the parsonage made in 1638 states that there was then 'a dwelling house with an orchard, a garden, a courtyard: and an outyeard with 2 barnes, 2 stables, one hayhouse, a Cart house, a Dove coate, 2 smal garners: a woodhouse, a woodyard, a henhouse, with an old outhouse.'[58]

A meeting-place for Protestant Dissenters was certified at Aston at various dates between 1697 and 1834.[59] There is now an undenominational mission-room.

CHARITIES It appears from the parliamentary returns of 1786 that a sum of £80 was given for the poor by a donor unknown. The gift, with accumulations, is now represented by £104 15s. consols with the official trustees. The annual dividends, amounting to £2 12s. 4d., are applied in the distribution of fuel or clothing by the rector and churchwardens.

The official trustees also hold a sum of £65 12s. 4d. consols, arising from the sale of the Calvinistic Baptist chapel at Aston End. The annual dividends, amounting to £1 12s. 8d., are applied towards the support and maintenance of the chapel at Stevenage.

---

[35] P.C.C. 41 Holgrave.
[36] Ibid. 17 Bodfelde.
[37] Wills, Archd. of St. Albans, W 45.
[38] P.C.C. Stoneham 16; Wills, Archd. of St. Albans, W 58 d.
[39] P.C.C. 41 Holgrave; 17 Bodfelde; Bacon, *Liber Regis*.
[40] Add. Chart. 19586.
[41] Ibid. 19593.
[42] *Cal. Close*, 1337–9, p. 5.
[43] See L. and P. Hen. VIII, vi, 1569.
[44] Pat. 32 Hen. VIII, pt. viii, m. 34.
[45] Clutterbuck, op. cit. ii, 248.
[46] Inst. Bks. (P.R.O.).
[47] Clutterbuck, loc. cit.
[48] Inst. Bks. (P.R.O.).
[49] Ibid.
[50] *Clerical Guide*.
[51] Ibid.
[52] *Clergy List*.
[53] Ibid.
[54] Ibid.
[55] *Cal. Chart. R.* 1226–57, p. 424.
[56] *Pope Nich. Tax.* (Rec. Com.), 37a.
[57] *Feud. Aids*, ii, 463.
[58] *Herts. Gen. and Antiq.* ii, 70.
[59] Urwick, *Nonconf. in Herts.* 562-3.

ASTON BURY: OAK GRILL AND STAIRCASE

BROADWATER HUNDRED
AYOT ST. LAWRENCE OR GREAT AYOT

AYOT ST. LAWRENCE OR GREAT AYOT

Aiete (xiii cent.); Ayete (xiv cent.); Eyott (xvi cent.).

The parish of Ayot St. Lawrence has an area of 750 acres, of which about three-fifths are arable, about 200 acres grass, and over 100 acres wood.[1] The greater part of the parish is about 300 ft. above the ordnance datum, but rises to 400 ft. towards the north-west, where the manor-house and park are situated. The new church of St. Lawrence lies on the western side of the park. The little River Mimram or Maran forms the eastern boundary. The subsoil is chalk and gravel, and the surface soil is chalk. There is an old chalk-pit to the south of the village and a disused gravel-pit to the east.

The road from Wheathampstead to Codicote forms the south-eastern boundary of the parish, but the village of Ayot St. Lawrence is situated about a mile to the north, and is reached by three branch roads, of which the central one passes by Hill Farm.

The village lies on the southern side of a winding road, upon which stand the schoolhouse, a timber and plaster house of the 17th century, and the post office, a 16th or 17th-century brick and timber cottage. The rectory, a modern house, contains in a staircase window some 17th-century glass said to have been taken from the old church. The glass is heraldic, and shows shields of France modern quartering England with a label of three points argent; Bristowe; and Bristowe impaling Bibbesworth and Barley quartering possibly Skipwith (Gules three bars or in chief a running greyhound argent). On the opposite side of the road are the ruined church and the grounds of Ayot House, the property of Mrs. A. C. Ames, and now the residence of Mr. Roger Cunliffe, J.P. In the park of Ayot House is the old manor-house, a red brick building, the lower part of which is probably of the 16th century.

The manor of AYOT ST. LAWRENCE MANOR was given by Alwin of Godtone or Gottun, in the time of King Edward the Confessor, to the abbey of Westminster, and was confirmed to the abbey by that king about 1062.[1a] Alwin continued to hold Ayot as sub-tenant of the abbey during Edward's reign, but in 1086 it was held of Westminster by Geoffrey de Mandeville, and assessed at 2½ hides.[2] A portion of 9 acres in Ayot, which had been held by Siward, a man of Alwin of Godtone, was in 1086 held of the king by the reeve of the hundred.[3] The overlordship of Westminster apparently lapsed, for direct possession seems to have been obtained by the Mandevilles, who sub-enfeoffed a tenant before the end of the 13th century. Geoffrey de Mandeville's lands descended through his son William to his grandson Geoffrey de Mandeville, created first Earl of Essex in 1140.[4] The latter died in 1144, and his eldest son Ernulf being outlawed soon after, his earldom and estates were conferred upon his second son Geoffrey, who died childless in 1166. His brother William, who succeeded him, also died without issue in 1189, his nearest heirs being the descendants of his aunt Beatrice, the sister of Geoffrey first Earl of Essex.[5] This Beatrice, who had married William de Say, had two sons William and Geoffrey, the elder of whom predeceased his father, and left two daughters Beatrice and Maud.[6] The earldom of Essex was eventually conferred upon Beatrice's husband Geoffrey Fitz Piers, and was held in turn by their two sons Geoffrey and William, who both took the name of Mandeville and died childless before 1227. Their sister Maud, to whom their title and estates then passed, married Henry de Bohun sixth Earl of Hereford, and Ayot St. Lawrence was held of that earldom until its extinction by the death of Humphrey de Bohun, twelfth earl, in 1373.[7] His lands then passed to his elder daughter Eleanor, wife of Thomas of Woodstock, who was murdered in 1397.[8] Eleanor died in 1399,[9] and the overlordship of Ayot St. Lawrence passed to her sister Mary, the wife of Henry Duke of Lancaster, who in the same year became king as Henry IV,[10] and hence his lands were merged in the Crown. In 1489 Ayot St. Lawrence was said to be held of the king as of the honour of Mandeville, parcel of the duchy of Lancaster, by service of a sparrow-hawk at the feast of St. Peter ad Vincula yearly, or payment of 2s.[11]

MANDEVILLE, Earl of Essex. *Quarterly or and gules.*

BOHUN. *Azure a bend argent between cotises and six lions or.*

The first sub-tenant of the manor to be recorded is William de Ayot, who is mentioned in 1253 as the son of Roger de Ayot,[12] and was certainly lord of the manor in 1257.[13] He held the office of king's steward,[14] and appears among the witnesses of many documents up to the year 1291. In 1303 the manor, consisting of half a knight's fee, was held by his heirs, who were under age,[15] and in 1346 by Lawrence de Ayot[16] and Joan his wife, who in 1347 granted it to Thomas, parson of the church of Ayot, for a settlement.[17] Lawrence died in 1353 and was succeeded by his son William, who was in prison for felony in the Bishop of Winchester's

---

[1] Statistics from Bd. of Agric. (1905).
[1a] Cott. Chart. vi, 2.
[2] *V.C.H. Herts.* i, 313.
[3] Ibid. 343.
[4] Round, *Geoffrey de Mandeville*, 37, 49.
[5] Ibid. 232, 242.
[6] G.E.C. *Complete Peerage.*
[7] Ibid.; *Feud. Aids*, ii, 436; Chan. Inq. p.m. 28 Edw. III, no. 45; 49 Edw. III, no. 28. In 1277–8 it was said to be held of the honour of Boulogne, which is seemingly an error.
[8] G.E.C. *Complete Peerage*; Chan. Inq. p.m. 21 Ric. II, no. 29.
[9] Ibid. Hen. IV, file 11, no. 28.
[10] G.E.C. *Complete Peerage.*
[11] *Cal. Inq. Hen. VII*, i, 215.
[12] *Feet of F. Herts.* 37 Hen. III, no. 425.
[13] *Cal. Chart. R.* 1226–57, p. 474.
[14] Ibid. 1257–1300, p. 496.
[15] *Feud. Aids*, ii, 429.
[16] Ibid. 436.
[17] Feet of F. Div. Co. Hil. 21 Edw. III, no. 8.

A HISTORY OF HERTFORDSHIRE

gaol.[18] He conveyed the manor in 1363 to Richard de Pembrugge.[19] There was also a conveyance to Richard in the same year by William de Wotton and Margaret his wife,[20] but the nature of their interest is not clear. Richard de Pembrugge and his son Henry both died in 1375,[21] and the manor passed to his nephews Richard de Beurlee, son of his sister Amice, and Thomas Barre, son of his sister Hawise. Richard de Beurlee apparently died soon after or quitclaimed his moiety, for in 1383 the whole manor was settled on Thomas Barre and Elizabeth his wife.[22]

Thomas Barre was appointed justice of the peace for Herefordshire in 1384,[23] and surveyor of the king's hay in that county in the same year.[24] At this time he also received a grant for life of 40 marks yearly from the issues of the county, instead of from the Exchequer, from whence it had previously been drawn.[25] In 1397 this was augmented by an allowance of 3 tuns of red wine yearly.[26] He was J.P. for Herefordshire again in 1385[27] and for Hertfordshire in 1401.[28] In 1393 he was appointed with others to deal with Walter Bent 'and other sons of iniquity' for preaching false doctrines in the diocese of Hereford.[29] Early in 1394 he received protection for half a year to go to Ireland on the king's service,[30] which was later extended for another six months, to remain there in the king's company.[31] In 1404 he was exempted for life, on account of his great age, 'from being charged with being sheriff, escheator, collector or other officer of the king, and from all labours in person, provided that he find a competent person to serve the king in his place and to ride with the king when required'[32]; nevertheless he served as justice of the peace for Hertfordshire in 1406 and 1407.[33] He survived his wife and his son Thomas and died in 1420, being succeeded by his grandson John Barre.[34] John's daughter Isabel married first Humphrey Stafford Earl of Devon, who was beheaded in 1469,[35] and upon her father's death in 1482 or 1483[36] Ayot St. Lawrence passed to her and her second husband Thomas Bourchier,[37] who survived her and died in 1491.[38] Isabel died in 1489.

Isabel and Thomas Bourchier had a daughter Isabel, but she predeceased them, and upon the death of Thomas the heirs were declared to be three cousins, viz. Richard Delabere son of Joan sister of John Barre, Thomas Cornwall great-grandson of Elizabeth, a second sister, and Edward Hanmer grandson of Ancret, a third sister of John Barre.[39] These three each received a third part of the manor.[40] In 1505 Edward Hanmer granted his share to Sir William Say, Thomas Cornwall did the same in 1506, and finally in 1508 Richard Delabere released his portion,[41] so that in that year Sir William Say was seised of the whole. From Sir William Say the manor descended to his daughter and co-heir Elizabeth, wife of William Blount, fourth Lord Mountjoy, and to their daughter Gertrude, who married Henry Courtenay Earl of Devon, in 1525 created Marquess of Exeter.[42] Henry Courtenay was attainted for treason and beheaded in 1539, and his wife being attainted in the same year her lands were forfeited to the Crown.[43] In 1543 Ayot St. Lawrence was granted to John Brockett, John Alway and Nicholas Bristowe.[44] Nicholas Bristowe held the manor in 1572 and made his title secure against possible heirs of Sir William Say.[45] He died in 1585,[46] leaving a widow Lucy, and the manor descended successively to his son Nicholas[47] and his grandson Nicholas, the latter inheriting in 1616.[48] In 1661 the manor was held by Robert Bristowe, according to Cussans the brother of a fourth Nicholas.[49] He was succeeded by William Bristowe, his third but eldest surviving son, whose widow was lady of the manor in 1700.[50] She sold it in 1714 to Thomas Lewis,[51] who died in 1718[52]; and five years later his estates were sold by Thomas Lewis and Henry and Margaret Hensleigh to Cornelius Lyde.[53] Rachel, the daughter of Cornelius, with her cousin and husband Lionel Lyde[54] conveyed half the manor and advowson in 1749 to her mother Rachel widow of Cornelius.[55] It perhaps reverted to the daughter Rachel and her husband before 1758, for Lionel Lyde then presented to the church.[56] This Lionel

BRISTOWE of Ayot St. Lawrence. *Ermine a fesse cotised sable with three crescents or thereon.*

---

[18] Chan. Inq. p.m. 28 Edw. III, no. 45.
[19] Feet of F. Div. Co. 37 Edw. III, no. 127.
[20] Ibid. Herts. 37 Edw. III, no. 525.
[21] Chan. Inq. p.m. 49 Edw. III, pt. ii, no. 28.
[22] Feet of F. Herts. 6 Ric. II, no. 56.
[23] Cal. Pat. 1381–5, p. 348.
[24] Ibid. p. 408.
[25] Ibid. p. 477.
[26] Ibid. 1399–1401, p. 107.
[27] Ibid. 1385–9, p. 80.
[28] Ibid. 1399–1401, p. 559.
[29] Ibid. 1391–6, pp. 354–5.
[30] Ibid. p. 472.
[31] Ibid. p. 549.
[32] Ibid. 1401–5, p. 375.
[33] Ibid. 1405–8, p. 492.
[34] Chan. Inq. p.m. 9 Hen. V, no. 63. In 1428 the manor is said to have been held by the 'Lord of Furnevale' (*Feud. Aids*, ii, 448). He was probably the guardian of the heir, then a minor.
[35] G.E.C. *Complete Peerage*.
[36] Chan. Inq. p.m. 22 Edw. IV, no. 39.
[37] Cal. Inq. Hen. VII, i, 215.
[38] Ibid. 682.
[39] Ibid.
[40] Anct. D. (P.R.O.), B 257, 258, 259.
[41] Ibid. B 254, 255, 275.
[42] G.E.C. *Complete Peerage*; L. and P. Hen. VIII, ix, 481.
[43] G.E.C. *Complete Peerage*.
[44] L. and P. Hen. VIII, xviii (1), g. 981 (95). Mr. Round points out that they *bought* the manor for twenty years' purchase, and that Nicholas Bristowe, clerk of the jewel-house, was made steward of Reading Abbey in 1540 (see under Aston). To 'The Monarchs of England' exhibition at the Grafton Gallery (in 1902) there were lent by Mrs. Ames the hat of Henry VIII and the shoes of Anne Boleyn, which, according to the catalogue, were given to Nicholas Bristowe by the king as the title-deeds of Ayot St. Lawrence, and 'have since always gone with the estate.' Mr. Round points out that Anne Boleyn was put to death seven years before Bristowe and his partners acquired the estate, and that the story of the king granting it to him when riding by it with Anne must be wholly false.
[45] Add. Chart. 1994.
[46] Chan. Inq. p.m. (Ser. 2), ccclxiii, 204 (2).
[47] Chan. Decree R. no. 77 (14).
[48] Chan. Inq. p.m. (Ser. 2), ccclxiii, 204 (2).
[49] Cussans, op. cit. *Broadwater Hund.* 236. Nicholas died in 1626, see M.I.
[50] Chauncy, *Hist. of Herts.* 324. There is a fine of 1697 in the name of her daughter Elizabeth and husband Charles Wilson, conveying half the manor to Robert Raworth, but this was probably only a settlement; Feet of F. Herts. Hil. 8 Will. III.
[51] Feet of F. Herts. Trin. 1 Geo. I; Com. Pleas Recov. R. 1 Geo. I, m. 4; Recov. R. Herts. Trin. 13 Anne.
[52] Tombstone at Ayot St. Lawrence.
[53] Feet of F. Herts. Mich. 10 Geo. I; Salmon, *Hist. of Herts.* (1728), 206.
[54] Salmon, op. cit. 253.
[55] Feet of F. Herts. Hil. 23 Geo. II.
[56] Inst. Bks. (P.R.O.).

BROADWATER HUNDRED — AYOT ST. LAWRENCE OR GREAT AYOT

dismantled the old church of Ayot St. Lawrence and built a new one.[57]

Lionel Lyde, who was created a baronet in 1772, died in 1791 and was succeeded by Samuel Lyde, his brother, who presented to the rectory in 1799,[58] after which it passed to his nephew Lionel Poole,[59] who assumed the surname of Lyde. From this Sir Lionel it passed through his sister Anna Maria, the wife of Levi Ames, to their son Lionel,[60] who assumed the surname of Lyde and died unmarried in 1851. He had five brothers, through whom it descended to the youngest George Henry, whose grandson Lionel Neville Frederick also assumed the surname of Lyde. He died in 1883 and Ayot St. Lawrence passed to his brother Lieut.-Col. Gerard Vivian Ames, who died in 1899,[61] leaving a son and heir Lionel Gerard Ames.[62]

AMES. *Argent a bend cotised between two rings sable with a quatrefoil between two roses argent on the bend.*

A fair was granted to William de Ayot in 1257, to be held on the vigil, day and morrow of St. Lawrence[63] (9–11 August). It is mentioned in 1617,[64] but has since been discontinued.

Free warren was also granted to William de Ayot in 1257.[65] A park is mentioned in 1268 when the same William sued Henry, son of Thomas de la Leye, for trespass in it.[66] At the present day it has an area of 200 acres.

In 1274–5 the lord of the manor claimed view of frankpledge, amendment of the assize of bread and ale, and gallows,[67] and in 1277–8 a tumbrel in addition.[68] In 1278–9 he is said to have claimed a trebuchet, the meaning of which is doubtful.[69]

A water mill is mentioned at Ayot St. Lawrence in 1354, when it was said to be in a bad state[70]; it was ruinous in 1375,[71] and probably fell into disuse, as it is not again mentioned.

CHURCHES The old church of ST. LAWRENCE,[72] which stands to the west of the village, is built of flint with stone dressings. It has now fallen into disrepair, having been somewhat unnecessarily superseded in 1779 by the present parish church. It consisted originally of a chancel and nave built probably in the 12th century. Early in the 13th century a north aisle was added, with an arcade of two bays. A century later the nave was partly rebuilt, the chancel was rebuilt from the foundations, and a north chapel was added. At the beginning of the 15th century the north arcade was destroyed, and one of its arches was reset in the west end of the chapel. The aisle was rebuilt a little further to the north, increasing the width of the nave, and a tower was added at the north-west.

The church is now roofless, with the exception of the tower, which retains the flooring of the upper stage, with moulded wall plates. The walls are being torn to pieces by ivy, and the north wall of the chancel is badly out of the perpendicular. The chancel, of which the south and east walls are now almost completely destroyed, has at the south-west the western jambs of an internal wall recess and of a window set in it. The chancel opens into the north chapel by a two-centred chamfered arch of the early 14th century with shafted jambs and moulded abaci, which is now leaning badly.

The chancel arch, now destroyed, was of the same character and date. The shafted jambs remain.

The north chapel has an east window of three lights, and in the north wall are two two-light pointed windows with hollow-moulded jambs; very little of the tracery remains in the heads. The south wall is mainly occupied by the opening of the arch into the chancel already described. On the west the chapel communicates with the north aisle through a 13th-century arch, reset, which was formerly one of the arches of the north arcade. The arch, which is of two moulded orders, is very badly out of true. The responds consist of circular shafts with foliate capitals. A small much defaced figure is inserted in the wall over the north jamb of the arch, and at the north-east of the chapel are a large moulded image bracket and an ogee-headed piscina now blocked. At the north-west is a rough recess, with what appear to be the remains of a flue.

The nave is not separated structurally from the aisle, and the north-western bay is covered by the tower. The windows, two in the south wall and one in the west wall, are all 15th-century insertions, and

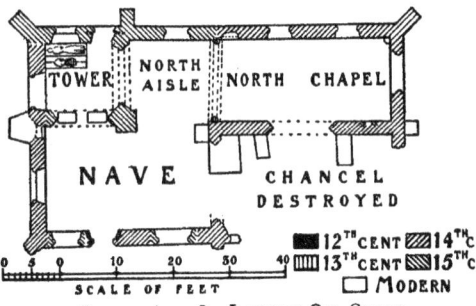

PLAN OF AYOT ST. LAWRENCE OLD CHURCH

very little of their tracery and none of the mullions remain. The south door retains work of the 12th century in the lower part of the internal jambs, but the rest of it is of the 14th century. There is a blocked door at the west end. The aisle has one

---

[57] See below.
[58] Inst. Bks. (P.R.O.).
[59] Clutterbuck, op. cit. ii, 253.
[60] Recov. R. Mich. 2 Will. IV, m. 53. Levi Ames was an alderman of Bristol.
[61] Burke, *Landed Gentry*; Clutterbuck, op. cit. ii, 252.
[62] Walford, *County Families* (1907).
[63] *Cal. Chart. R.* 1226–57, p. 474.
[64] Chan. Inq. p.m. (Ser. 2), ccclxiii, 204 (2).
[65] *Cal. Chart. R.* 1226–57, p. 474.
[66] *Abbrev. Plac.* (Rec. Com.), 163.
[67] *Rot. Hund.* (Rec. Com.), i, 192.
[68] *Assize R.* 323.
[69] Ibid. 324a, m. 25.
[70] Chan. Inq. p.m. 28 Edw. III, no. 45.
[71] Ibid. 49 Edw. III, no. 28.
[72] Dimensions: chancel, 30 ft. 6 in. by 16 ft. 6 in.; north chapel, 30 ft. 6 in. by 14 ft. 6 in.; nave, 29 ft. by 18 ft.; aisle, 14 ft. by 15 ft.; tower, 12 ft. square.

window in the north wall, of the 15th century, with scanty remains of tracery. The tower, which is of three stages and embattled, opens to the aisle on the east and to the nave on the south side by early 15th-century high two-centred arches of three chamfered orders with shafted jambs. On the north are a small door and a two-light window, both of the 15th century, and on the west a window, now blocked, which was apparently the west window of the aisle before its widening; and at the south-west are traces of a stair-turret, which has been destroyed. The windows of the bell chamber are, in common with the rest of the tower, of early 15th-century date, and are much mutilated. They are of two trefoiled lights with a quatrefoil over, in a two-centred head. The tower contains one bell.

The font, which is very much broken, is of early and burials from 1800 to 1812; (iv) marriages from 1756 to 1810.

The modern church of ST. LAWRENCE in Ayot Park was built in 1778 by Sir Lionel Lyde, bart., and consecrated in 1779. It was designed by Nicholas Revett in the classical style, and consists of an apsidal chancel and nave with a gallery at the west end.

ADVOWSON The church of Ayot St. Lawrence is first mentioned in the Taxation made by Pope Nicholas IV in 1291.[73] The advowson is found pertaining to the manor in 1383, when it was conveyed to Thomas Barre,[74] and, from lack of contrary evidence, it may be presumed that it had always passed with the lordship of the manor. After this date the advowson followed the descent of the manor, except in 1429, when the presentation was made by the

Ayot St. Lawrence Old Church from the South-East

15th-century date, and has an octagonal panelled bowl. In the north-west corner of the tower is an altar tomb with panelled sides and the mutilated and defaced remains of the effigies of a knight and lady. The work is of early 15th-century date. In the recess of the blocked window in the tower is a defaced mural monument of 1626 to Nicholas Bristowe, with small kneeling effigies of alabaster.

The plate, now used in the new church, includes a cup of 1659 and a paten of 1696.

The registers are contained in four books: (i) all entries from 1566 to 1720; (ii) baptisms from 1720 to 1799, burials from 1718 to 1799, with a hiatus from 1727 to 1731, and marriages from 1716 to 1754, with a hiatus from 1728 to 1738; (iii) baptisms king.[75] In 1505, when the manor was divided between three heirs, the advowson was held in turn,[76] but the whole came to Sir William Say in 1508.[77] In 1697 presentation was made by George Halsey, who appears with Elizabeth Bristowe, lady of the manor, in a recovery of 1714.[78] Since then it has followed the descent of the manor to the present day, Mr. L. G. Ames being the present patron.

A terrier of 1638 states that the parsonage was surrounded by a close of two acres, with 'one litle Pikle and a spot of ground cald the Orchyarde.' The glebe lands then consisted of 14½ acres besides the churchyard, half an acre lying in Sandridge, and included closes called Hyemares and Kingsland.[79] In 1693 the parsonage-house was said to be 'new

[73] *Pope Nich. Tax.* (Rec. Com.), 37.
[74] Feet of F. Herts. 6 Ric. II, no. 56.
[75] *Cal. Pat.* 1422–9, p. 533.
[76] Anct. D. (P.R.O.), B. 257, 258.
[77] Ibid. B. 254, 255, 275.
[78] Recov. R. Trin. 13 Anne.
[79] *Herts. Gen. and Antiq.* ii, 70.

Ayot St. Lawrence Old Church: Remains of North Chapel and Aisle

Ayot St. Lawrence Old Church: 15th-century Tomb

BROADWATER HUNDRED AYOT ST. PETER

built,' and gardens and orchards lately planted. The half-acre or 3 roods in Sandridge was then known as Penly Park.[80]

CHARITIES — The school, referred to in deeds of 11 May 1837 and 26 March 1872, was erected by Lionel Lyde, and endowed by the Rev. John Olive, who died in 1851, with £1,000 consols, which is now held by the official trustees. The annual dividend, amounting to £25, is applicable in the instruction of children of the Sunday and day school in the doctrines of the Church of England.

AYOT ST. PETER

Little Ayot or Ayot Montfichet, Aiete (xi cent.); Yate, Hayate (xiii cent.); Ayete (xv cent.); Eyott (xvi cent.).

The parish of Ayot St. Peter has an area of 1,093 acres, of which 666 acres are under cultivation, 140¾ are grass and 2¾ wood.[1] The elevation of the parish above the ordnance datum is from 300 ft. to 400 ft., rising to just over 400 ft. about the centre, where the church and rectory are situated. The lowest point is on the north, where the little River Mimram forms the boundary for some distance. The subsoil is chalk and gravel and the surface soil chalk; there are several chalk-pits in the parish. The manor-house, church of St. Peter and the rectory are situated on a branch road, half a mile north-west of the village, which is on the main road at Ayot Green. Ayot Place, now a farm-house, was probably built by Sir George Perient, lord of the manor, as it bears his arms and the date 1615. It is a 17th-century house of timber and plaster (now partly cased with brick) with a tiled roof and is of the L plan, though much repaired in the 19th century. The wing facing north contains the entrance with staircase and living rooms, the wing facing east comprises the hall with a gallery now used as the kitchen. On a frieze in the hall are five shields bearing the arms of Perient, Brockett and Boteler quartering Kilpee and the date 1615 in the middle. There are two chimney stacks with twisted shafts and moulded capitals. Ayot Bury, the seat of Sir Alfred James Reynolds, J.P., is an old house, much altered and enlarged, standing in a small park.

There is a railway station at Ayot, opened in 1877, on the Luton and Hatfield branch of the Great Northern railway. The main road between Hitchin and London passes through Ayot Green, and forms the boundary at the south-east corner of the parish. Large farms in this parish are Linces Farm, Ryefield Farm and Ayot Place Farm.

Place-names occurring in the 16th century are Fyncesfeld or Fincheleyfeld, Smythescroft, Dryvers and Okkelmede.[1a]

There was a great flood in the parish in February 1795, owing to the overflow of the Lea and Mimram.[2]

MANORS — King Edward the Confessor granted the manor of AYOT ST. PETER or AYOT MONTFITCHET to two of his thegns, but after the Conquest it formed part of the lands of Robert Gernon, and was held as 2½ hides by William his man, who is said to have taken it 'by encroachment to the king's wrong, but he called on his lord as warrantor.'[3] The estates of Robert Gernon were granted in the reign of Henry I to William de Montfitchet,[4] in whose family Ayot St. Peter descended in the same manner as Letchworth (q.v.), and came to Richard Montfitchet, who died without issue about 1258. His heirs were his three sisters —Margery, who married Hugh de Bolebek, Avelina the wife of William de Fortibus, last Earl of Albemarle, and Philippa wife of Hugh de Pleys.[5] The manor of Ayot St. Peter fell to the share of Margery and Hugh de Bolebek, and upon the partition between their four daughters[6] to the second, Margery, the wife of Nicholas Corbet, who held the manor in 1277–8.[7] Nicholas died in 1280,[8] and the king took Ayot St. Peter into his hands with the other Corbet lands, but Margery received Ayot back in the following year upon the plea that the Montfitchet lands were her own inheritance.[9] Margery married secondly Ralph Fitz William,[10] and they in 1286 conveyed the manor to Robert Burnell, Bishop of Bath and Wells,[11] a quitclaim having previously being made to him by John de Zelaund,[12] whom they had enfeoffed of the manor.[13] The bishop probably conveyed the manor to Robert de Lacy, for Amice de Lacy his widow was assessed for it in 1303.[14] In 1307 an action was brought by John de Lancaster, the son of Margery Fitz William's eldest sister Philippa, who claimed that Ralph and Margery had exceeded their rights in granting more than half the manor to John de Zelaund,[15] but there is no evidence that he made good his claim to the other half.

Upon the death of Amice or Avice de Lacy[16] the manor was divided between her daughters Joan and Amice. The name of Ayot Montfitchet was kept by the moiety which fell to Amice the second daughter, who married John Poleyn. He is referred to as lord

MONTFITCHET.
Gules three cheverons or.

---

[80] *Herts. Gen. and Antiq.* ii, 71.
[1] Statistics from Bd. of Agric. (1905).
[1a] Add. R. 35325–35330.
[2] Cussans, op. cit. *Broadwater Hund.* 250.
[3] *V.C.H. Herts.* i, 323a.
[4] *V.C.H. Essex,* i, 347.
[5] Close, 52 Hen. III, m. 8.
[6] Wrottesley, *Ped. from the Plea R.* 2.
[7] *Cal. Inq. p.m. Edw. I,* 508; Assize R. 323. The other three daughters of Hugh de Bolebek were Philippa wife of Roger de Lancaster, Alice wife of Walter de Huntercombe and Maud wife of Hugh de la Valle.
[8] *Cal. Inq. p.m. Edw. I,* 508.
[9] Ibid.; *Cal. Close,* 1279–88, p. 88.
[10] *Abbrev. Plac.* (Rec. Com.), 303.
[11] Feet of F. Div. Co. 14 Edw. I, no. 31.
[12] Ibid. 13 Edw. I, no. 14.
[13] Ibid. 10 Edw. I, no. 47; Lansd. Chart. 93.
[14] *Feud. Aids,* ii, 430; Chan. Inq. p.m. 35 Edw. I, no. 25. In the inquisition she is called Advitia (Avice) widow of Robert de Lacy.
[15] *Abbrev. Plac.* (Rec. Com.), 303.
[16] She is also called Matilda in the pedigree given in De Banco R. 4 Hen. VI, m. 124; see Wrottesley, *Ped. from the Plea R.* 328. She married secondly William Baudewyn according to this pedigree.

63

of the manor in 1323.[17] Amice died seised in 1349, when her moiety passed to her son John,[18] who is said to have died without issue.[19] In 1359 it was held by Katharine Poleyn,[20] who was perhaps his widow. It is said to have descended to Rose wife of John Fish as daughter of John son of Michael son of Agnes daughter of Amice Poleyn.[21] Rose Fish granted it for life to Christine Poleyn, who was probably her mother.[22] After the death of Christine William Sakevyle, who had been enfeoffed of the manor, granted it in 1414 to Rose and John Fish her husband,[23] from whom it passed to another John Fish, who died in 1494, his wife Katherine Wotton being attainted and imprisoned at Norwich Castle for the wilful murder of her husband.[24] Ayot Montfitchet was inherited by his brother, presumably the William Fish who died seised of it in 1531. He was succeeded by his son Thomas,[25] who held the manor until his death in 1553.[26] Thomas's son George Fish held Ayot jointly with his mother Elizabeth,[27] who married secondly William Perient, whence it came to her son George Perient,[28] who was holding it in 1614.[29] George Perient's daughter Mary married Nicholas Trott, who in 1623 conveyed the half-manor to William Hale[30] of King's Walden,[31] and in 1624 they both granted it to Michael Grigge,[32] who in 1632 conveyed it to Rowland Hale, son of William.[33] From him it passed to his son William Hale, whose widow Elizabeth was the holder in 1700.[34] It remained in the Hale family until 1832,[35] when it is said to have been sold to Viscount Melbourne, the holder of the Westington moiety (q.v.).

HALE. *Azure a cheveron or battled on both sides.*

The so-called manor of *WESTINGTON* consisted of the moiety of the original manor of Ayot St. Peter which fell to Joan the elder daughter of Amice de Lacy, and took the name of Westington a little later from the family which held it. Joan de Lacy may be identical with Joan the wife of Ralph de Bredon, who in 1332 granted the half-manor to James de Bredon,[36] probably in trust. In 1349 it was held by John de Westwycombe,[37] who was probably the son of Joan.[38] From John it came to his daughter Margaret, the wife of William Westington,[39] who gave his name to this moiety, which extended into the neighbouring parish of Welwyn. Margaret was apparently unjustly disseised by John and Rose Fish, the holders of Ayot St. Peter or Montfitchet, for in 1426 there was a suit between them for its recovery, in which the former was evidently successful in establishing her title.[40] Margaret Westington married secondly Thomas Galyon, and upon her death the manor came to her daughter Margery, who married Thomas Foxlee. Their daughter Elizabeth conveyed it by marriage to Thomas Uvedale, who was seised of it with his son and heir Henry, who predeceased his father in 1469. Thomas died in 1474 and was succeeded by his second son William Uvedale.[41]

By 1487 Westington had come into the possession of Thomas Rogers, probably by purchase, and upon his death in the following year it came to his daughter Elizabeth, the wife of William Essex,[42] who in 1508 conveyed it to Sir William Say.[43] The estates of Sir William Say descended through his daughter Elizabeth to Gertrude Marchioness of Exeter,[44] who was attainted in 1539, when her lands were forfeited to the Crown.[45] In 1546 they were granted to Sir Nicholas Throckmorton,[46] who sold Westington with other manors to Sir John Brockett of Brockett Hall in 1555.[47] He was succeeded by his son and his grandson John, the latter's heirs being five daughters.[48] Helen wife of Sir Richard Spencer is found in possession of a quarter of the manor in 1599,[49] but eventually the whole came to the fifth daughter Mary. She conveyed it in marriage to Sir Thomas Reade, who was holding it in 1615.[50] They had a son Thomas,[51] probably the father of Sir John Reade, who presented to the church in 1686.[52] Sir James Reade, his son, was holding it in 1700,[53] and in 1728 it was in the possession of Sir James's youngest daughter Love, who married Sir Thomas Wymington.[54] The latter died in 1746, and Westington was sold after his death to Sir Matthew Lamb,[55] who in 1768 was succeeded by his son Peniston Lamb, first Viscount Melbourne. His son William Lord Melbourne[56] was the first Prime Minister of Queen Victoria, and succeeded to

LAMB, Viscount Melbourne. *Sable a fesse erminois between three cinqfoils argent with two molets sable on the fesse.*

[17] Inq. a.q.d. 16 Edw. II, no. 100.
[18] Chan. Inq. p.m. 23 Edw. III (2nd nos.), no. 142.
[19] Wrottesley, *Ped. from the Plea R.* 328.
[20] Chan. Inq. p.m. 33 Edw. III (1st nos.), no. 39.
[21] De Banco R. 4 Hen. VI, m. 124.
[22] Ibid.
[23] Ibid.
[24] Cal. Inq. p.m. Hen. VII, i, 459.
[25] Chan. Inq. p.m. (Ser. 2), lxxxii, 15.
[26] M.I. in church of Ayot St. Peter.
[27] Feet of F. Herts. Mich. 6 & 7 Eliz.
[28] *Visit. of Hertf.* (Harl. Soc. xxii), 157; Feet of F. Herts. Hil. 3 Jas. I.
[29] Pat. 12 Jas. I, pt. 22.
[30] Feet of F. Herts. Hil. 21 Jas. I.
[31] *Visit. of Hertf.* (Harl. Soc. xxii), 157.
[32] Ibid. Trin. 22 Jas. I; Add. Chart. 35377, 35378.
[33] *Visit. of Hertf.* (Harl. Soc. xxii), 62; Add. Chart. 35379, 35380; Feet of F. Herts. Trin. 8 Chas. I.
[34] Chauncy, *Hist. of Herts.* (1700), ii, 35.
[35] Salmon, op. cit. 207; Cussans, op. cit. *Broadwater Hund.* 245.
[36] Feet of F. Herts. 6 Edw. III, no. 99.
[37] Chan. Inq. p.m. 23 Edw. III (2nd nos.), no. 142.
[38] See Wrottesley, *Ped. from the Plea R.* 328.
[39] Ibid.
[40] De Banco R. 4 Hen. VI, m. 124.
[41] Chan. Inq. p.m. 14 Edw. IV, no. 26.
[42] Ibid. (Ser. 2), iv, 29.
[43] Feet of F. Herts. East. 23 Hen. VII.
[44] Chan. Inq. p.m. (Ser. 2), li, 50.
[45] Ibid. lxxiii, 93. The manor was claimed by Gertrude's cousin and heir Lady Anne Bourchier, as appears by her inquisition, but she can never have held it, as it was regranted before Gertrude's death (ibid. clvii, 82).
[46] Pat. 38 Hen. VIII, pt. viii, m. 39.
[47] Pat. 1 & 2 Phil. and Mary, pt. i; Feet of F. Herts. East. 1 & 2 Phil. and Mary; Add. Chart. 35327-35330.
[48] *Visit. of Herts.* (Harl. Soc. xxii), 32.
[49] Feet of F. Div. Co. Trin. 41 Eliz.
[50] Pat. 13 Jas. I, pt. xviii.
[51] *Visit. of Herts.* (Harl. Soc. xxii), 162.
[52] Inst. Bks. (P.R.O.).
[53] Chauncy, op. cit. (1700), ii, 35; see Exch. Dep. Trin. 6 Anne, no. 7.
[54] Salmon, op. cit. (1728), 207; Add. Chart. 35375.
[55] Clutterbuck, op. cit. ii, 361. A certain Henrietta, wife of Samuel Masham, apparently had some interest in the manor which she quitclaimed in 1746 to Henry Hoare (Feet of F. Herts. Mich. 20 Geo. II).
[56] G.E.C. *Complete Peerage.*

BROADWATER HUNDRED — BALDOCK

his father's estates in 1828. He acquired from William Hale in 1832 the other moiety of the manor,[57] known as Ayot St. Peter or Ayot Montfitchet, and thus the whole of the original manor was once again united in the same hands. Upon his death in 1848 his estates passed to his brother Frederick James,[58] and from him through his sister Amelia, who married Peter Leopold fifth Earl Cowper, to their son George Augustus in 1853. In 1856 Ayot St. Peter came to Francis Thomas de Grey Cowper, the last earl, who died in 1905.[59] The manor then passed to the younger of his two sisters, Lady Amabel Kerr, who died in 1906, when it came to her husband, Admiral Lord Walter Kerr.[60]

COWPER, Earl Cowper. *Argent three martlets gules and a chief engrailed gules with three rings or therein.*

In 1277–8 Nicholas Corbett owed suit at the county court and aid to the sheriff of 5s. a year.[61] In 1349 this suit was said to be owed every month with the same aid, and suit at the hundred court every three weeks.[62] George Perient obtained a grant of court leet and view of frankpledge twice a year in Ayot Montfitchet in 1614.[63] Nicholas Throckmorton apparently received the same rights in Westington when he obtained that manor in 1546.[64] Free warren was granted to Sir Thomas Reade in Westington in 1615.[65]

Ayot Montfitchet was fined in 1653 for having lacked stocks for a twelvemonth past.[66]

CHURCH The church of *ST. PETER* has been rebuilt more than once. At the latter part of the 17th century considerable alterations were made in the church then existing, and in the middle of the 18th century the church was rebuilt. The church then erected was an octagonal brick building with a detached belfry forming the entrance to the churchyard. This church was rebuilt in a little more appropriate style in 1862. On 10 July 1874 this building was struck by lightning and burnt to the ground. As the church was some distance from the village the new building was erected on its present site. The new church was built from contributions principally from Earl Cowper and Mr. George Robinson of Ayot Bury, from designs by J. P. Seddon. It is a red brick building with Bath stone dressings and a tiled roof, and consists of an apsidal chancel with organ chamber on the south side, nave, north porch and tower.

There are six bells by Warner of London, 1875, the gift of Dr. Jephson of Leamington. The plate includes a silver chalice and paten of the time of Charles I.

The registers are in three books : (i) baptisms and burials 1668 to 1773, marriages 1668 to 1753 ; (ii) baptisms and burials 1773 to 1812 ; (iii) marriages 1754 to 1812.

ADVOWSON The advowson of Ayot St. Peter Church seems to have belonged to the lords of the manor from the earliest times, for it is mentioned as belonging to the lord as early as 1282.[67] When the manor was divided between the daughters of Amice de Lacy the advowson went to the elder branch,[68] but by 1488 it was apparently held alternately, for Thomas Rogers[69] and later Sir William Say[70] were only possessed of half. A short time previous to 1728 the advowson was sold to Ralph Freeman and his heirs,[71] in whose family it descended until Katherine, the daughter of William Freeman, conveyed it in marriage to the Hon. Charles Yorke, whose son Philip became Earl of Hardwicke in 1790[72] and presented to the rectory in 1804.[73] From him it passed to his eldest daughter Anne, the wife of John Earl of Mexborough.[74] Lord Mexborough held the advowson until 1843, after which his widow presented until 1852, when it was sold to the Rev. Edwin Prodgers. On the death of the latter in 1861 the advowson came to his son Edwin Prodgers, who nominated himself to the rectory, but later relinquished Holy Orders.[75] The presentation remained in his hands until 1906, when it was acquired by Miss Wilshere, who is the present patron.

CHARITIES John Henry Peacock, by will, proved in the P.C.C. in December 1849, bequeathed so much stock as would produce £10 a year for education and £10 a year for the poor in clothing, blankets and fuel on Christmas Day. The legacies are represented by £333 6s. 8d. consols and £333 6s. 8d. consols, now producing £8 6s. 8d. for each purpose. The sums of stock are held by the official trustees ; the charity for education is regulated by a scheme of the Board of Education, 4 May 1905.

BALDOCK

Baudac (xii cent.) ; Baldac (xiii cent.) ; Baldoke (xvi cent.). The parish of Baldock has an area of 263 acres, of which 1¾ acres are arable land, 56¼ acres permanent grass, and 4 acres wood.[1] Under the provisions of the Divided Parishes Act, 1876, portions of neighbouring parishes have been added to Baldock for civil purposes at various times.[2] Some small portions of the parish on the west and a part of the ecclesiastical parish of Willian (now included in the civil district of Baldock) were acquired by the First Garden City Pioneer Co., Ltd., in 1903. Baldock is about 200 ft. above the ordnance datum.

---

[57] See above.
[58] G.E.C. *Complete Peerage.*
[59] Burke, *Peerage* (1907).
[60] Information from the Rev. Canon H. Jephson.
[61] Assize R. 323.
[62] Chan. Inq. p.m. 23 Edw. III (2nd nos.), no. 142.
[63] Pat. 12 Jas. I, pt. xxii, no. 18.
[64] Ibid. 38 Hen. VIII, pt. viii, m. 39.
[65] Ibid. 13 Jas. I, pt. xviii.
[66] Add. R. 35380.
[67] Feet of F. Div. Co. 10 Edw. I, no. 47.
[68] Feet of F. Herts. 6 Edw. III, no. 99 ; 7 Hen. V, no. 39 ; Chan. Inq. p.m. 4 Edw. IV, no. 26.
[69] Chan. Inq. p.m. (Ser. 2), iv, 29.
[70] Feet of F. Herts. East. 23 Hen. VII.
[71] Salmon, op. cit. (1728), 207.
[72] G.E.C. *Complete Peerage.*
[73] Inst. Bks. (P.R.O.).
[74] G.E.C. *Complete Peerage.*
[75] Cussans, op. cit. (1877), *Broadwater Hund.* 250.

[1] Statistics from Bd. of Agric. (1905).
[2] Portions of Bygrave, Clothall, Norton, Weston and Willian were added by Loc. Govt. Bd. Order 13027.

The subsoil of the parish is chalk. Baldock station, on the Cambridge branch of the Great Northern railway, is in the extreme north of the parish.

Part of the hamlet of Clothall End is included in the north-east of the parish. Elmwood Manor is a large house surrounded by a park, situated to the south of that end of the town known as Pembroke End, and is the residence of the lord of the manor of Baldock.

BOROUGH BALDOCK At the time of the Domesday Survey was a part of Weston (q.v.) and consequently then belonged to William de Ow.[3] A little before the middle of the 12th century Gilbert de Clare Earl of Pembroke, who died in 1148, granted 10 librates of land from his manor of Weston to the Knights Templars with ample liberties.[4] These 10 librates became the parish of Baldock, and here the Templars, probably about 1199 when they received a grant of market and fair (see below),[5] 'built a certain borough which is called Baldock.' This was a period for the founding and developing of towns with primitive borough rights, and Baldock, being on one of the principal lines of traffic to the north, formed a very eligible site for a market town. It may be noticed that Baldock is not actually on the Roman road which followed the line of Pesthouse Lane to the east, but lies on the main road from Stevenage. This would indicate that the ordinary route here from south to north was along the Stevenage road through the High Street, Baldock, at the northern end of which it turned almost at a right angle down what is now White Horse Street and so into the Roman road. The borough was established at the angle formed by the High Street and White Horse Street, the church of St. Mary being built on the west side of the angle and the market-place apparently extending originally up both streets. Here also the fairs were held.

Besides the two principal streets High Street and White Horse Street, Church Street, Norton Street, and Hitchin Street[6] probably mark mediaeval lines. There are a few interesting houses in these streets.

BALDOCK VILLAGE

In High Street are Wynne's almshouses built in 1621, consisting of a row of six red brick houses with tiled roofs. Each house is of two stories with a mullioned window below and a dormer window above and a porch. There are modern shafts to the three ancient chimney stacks. Above the mullioned windows is the date ANNO DOMINI 1621, and in the middle there is the following inscription on a stone : 'Theis almes howeses are the gieft of Mr. John Wynne cittezen and mercer of London latelye deceased who hath left a yearely stipend to everey poore of either howses to the worldes end September Anno Domini 1620.' On the

[3] *V.C.H. Herts.* i, 327b.
[4] Dugdale, *Mon.* vii, 820.
[5] Chart. R. 1 John, pt. ii, m. 3, no. 3.
[6] There is reference to the following inns and other houses in Baldock : The 'Crown' (1561) (Feet of F. Herts. Mich. 3 & 4 Eliz.) ; 'George' (Chan. Proc. [Ser. 2.], bdle. 282, no. 28) ; the 'Swan' (1557) (Feet of F. Herts. Trin. 3 & 4 Phil. and Mary) ; the 'Tabard' (1537) (L. and P. Hen. VIII, xii [2], 1247) ; Floryes in Brede Street (Early Chan. Proc. bdle. 41, no. 44) ; le Cokestret, 1533 (Add. MS. 36349).

BROADWATER HUNDRED — BALDOCK

south side are the arms of the Merchant Adventurers, and on the north a shield of the Mercers' Company. Southward a little lower down is a modern house with a wing on the south side having an overhanging upper story. In this wing is a gateway with a pair of 15th-century panelled oak gates which are supposed to have belonged to the hospital of St. Mary Magdalene of Clothall, and were placed in their present position in the 19th century. Two houses on the south side of White Horse Street, formerly occupied by the postmaster, are ancient. That on the west has a modern front of brick, but the back is a red brick building of two stories with an attic probably of the middle of the 16th century. The house is rectangular in plan with a central chimney stack. A window of three lights with chamfered brick jambs, mullions and lintel has recently been discovered on the ground floor on the west side of the house. There is an original

Although described as a borough in the charter of William Marshal Earl of Pembroke (1189–1219),[7] Baldock was never anything but a prosperous market town. No evidence of burgage tenure has been found, nor did Baldock ever send members to Parliament. The inhabitants had apparently no separate jurisdiction, but in 1307 there were two bailiffs who were officers of the lord's court.[8] The Gild of Jesus was founded in 1459,[9] and, as appears from wills, all the principal men and women of the town were enrolled among its members. It was of considerable wealth, and after its dissolution its possessions were sold in 1550 for £860,[10] a very large sum for that time. This fraternity probably took over some of the town organizations, as similar gilds did elsewhere.

Like many other towns, Baldock is described in 1550 as a market town much decayed, wherein there

OLD HOUSE, CEMETERY ROAD, BALDOCK

stone fireplace in the attic. The house to the east has been much repaired, but was originally built at the beginning of the 17th century. The back part is of half-timber. There are original fireplaces and a chimney stack. The houses in Church Street and Norton Street are mostly of the 17th century, many of them, including the Bull Inn, with overhanging stories. A house at the corner of Church Street, now divided into cottages, is a timber-framed house of the early part of the 17th century. Carved brackets support the projecting upper story, and in the south front is a large gateway which has apparently been heightened in the 18th century to permit the coaches to pass underneath. It has two original chimney stacks.

were only about 400 'housling people' or communicants.[11] The town evidently regained its prosperity shortly afterwards, judging from the increased number and importance of its fairs.

In 1199 King John granted to the Templars the right of holding a yearly fair at Baldock on St. Matthew's Day and for four days following[12] (21–25 September), and this grant was confirmed in 1227 by Henry III.[13] In 1492 two fairs were granted to the Hospitallers at Baldock, one on the vigil and feast of St. Matthew (20–21 September), and the other on the vigil, feast and morrow of St. James the Apostle[14] (24–26 July). In 1566 there was another alteration, three fairs being granted to Thomas Revett on the feasts of St. James,

[7] Dugdale, *Mon.* vi, 820.
[8] *Cal. Pat.* 1307–13, p. 535.
[9] *L. and P. Hen. VIII*, xvi, g. 578 (28). See Wills, Archdeaconry of St. Albans, Stoneham 115 d.; Wallingford 34 d.;

P.C.C. 30 Blamyr; 35 Holder; 7 Porch; 5 Bennett, &c.
[10] Pat. 4 Edw. VI, pt. iii, m. 7. Grant to John Cock.
[11] Chant. Cert. 20, no. 70; 27, no. 14.

[12] Chart. R. 1 John, pt. ii, m. 3, no. 3.
[13] *Cal. Chart. R.* 1226–57, p. 5.
[14] Pat. 7 Hen. VII, m. 19.

67

A HISTORY OF HERTFORDSHIRE

St. Andrew and St. Matthew [15] (25 July, 30 November and 21 September). Evidently, however, the fair was extended beyond the actual feast of St. Matthew, rightfully or not, for in 1661 Samuel Pepys visited Baldock on 23 September and records that there was a fair held on that day, and adds 'we put in and eat a mouthfull of pork which they made us pay 14*d.* for, which vexed us much.'[16] Two years later he visited the town on September 21, and noted that the fair was 'a great one for cheese and other such commodities.'[17] The fairs seem to have been altered again, as in 1792 there were five fairs every year,[18] horse fairs being held on 7 March, the last Thursday in May, 5 August, 11 December, and a horse and pleasure fair on 2 October. These are still continued.[19] 'In the 14th century the fairs seem to have been the scene of considerable disturbance. In 1312 it is recorded that when Geoffrey de la Lee, the king's custodian, approached the town of Baldock to collect the tolls and other profits of the fair, various persons 'at night assaulted him and his men and servants and took and carried away his goods.'[20] Again in 1343 complaint was made that in Herts. 'there are confederacies of disturbers of the peace, assaulting, mutilating and imprisoning men in fairs and markets and other places, and that they lately coming to Baldock prevented the men and servants of Walter de Mauny from collecting the tolls and other profits of his fair, assaulted them so that their life was despaired of, and wickedly killed William de Myners, the king's serjeant-at-arms, whom the king had sent to keep his peace at the fair and arrest any evil-doer found there.'[21]

A fair was also granted to the 'Leprous Brothers' of St. Mary Magdalene at Baldock in 1226 until the king should come of age. It was held on the vigil and feast of St. Bartholomew[22] (23–24 August). As Henry III declared himself of age in 1227, when he reached his twentieth year, the fair presumably lapsed in that year. There is no evidence of its renewal.

A market at Baldock was granted to the Knights Templars in 1199,[23] and confirmed in 1227 with certain liberties, namely, 'that they shall have three deer and the feet of the deer every year; and they can take them where they wish either in Essex or in Windsor Forest or the view of the Foresters. And all their horses are to be quit from tolls or passage money. And they are not to be disturbed under penalty of £10.'[24] In 1492 the market, to be held on Friday, was confirmed to the Knights Hospitallers.[25] By the grant to Thomas Revett in 1566 the day was altered to Saturday.[26] In 1792 the market was held on Thursday,[27] but before 1888 was changed to Friday.[28] It is not now held.

The Master of the Templars in 1287 claimed in Baldock view of frankpledge and freedom from shire and hundred courts for all pleas. He also claimed to have his own gaol 'from time immemorial,' with gallows, tumbrel, pillory, infangentheof and amendment of the assize of bread and ale.[29] Earl Gilbert, when he gave them land on which to build Baldock, granted them the right of judgement by fire and water and by battle.[30]

It is recorded in 1312 that when Geoffrey de la Lee, custodian of the Templars' lands, 'approached the town to hold a view of Frankpledge there, as was customary, and had attached by Robert Legat and John atte Water, known bailiffs, measures and weights found in the town to examine them at the view, various persons resisted the attachment and forcibly carried off the weights and measures from the bailiffs.'[31]

Baldock is now governed by an urban district council. The chief industries of the town are malting and brewing.

MANOR Gilbert de Clare's grant was confirmed to the Knights Templars at the beginning of the 13th century by William Marshal, Earl of Pembroke, the husband of Gilbert's grand-daughter Isabel.[32] The Templars continued to hold Baldock until the dissolution of their order in 1309, when their lands fell to the Crown.[33] They were first committed to the custody of William Inge,[34] and a few years afterwards to Geoffrey de la Lee, who was custodian in 1312.[35] Shortly afterwards Baldock was acquired with the other lands of the Templars by the Knights Hospitallers. In 1335 the Hospitallers granted the 'Court' of Baldock to John de Blomvill for ten years, and he in 1343 granted it for two years to Walter de Manny.[36] The Hospitallers continued to hold Baldock until 1540,[37] when it again came into the king's hands by the dissolution of their order, and it was granted in 1542 to John Bowles upon his surrender of a lease of twenty-one years from the Hospitallers, dating from 1522.[38] He seems, however, to have immediately conveyed it back to the Crown, for he died in 1543 seised of only a small portion of it.[39] The manor was granted in 1544 to John Allen and others as security for money lent to the king to be repaid in one year.[40] Later in the same year it was granted to Sir John Aleyn, Sir John Champneys, and Ralph Aleyn, aldermen of London.[41] In 1556 Sir John Champneys conveyed Baldock to

THE KNIGHTS TEMPLARS. *Argent a cross gules and a chief sable.*

THE KNIGHTS HOSPITALLERS. *Gules a cross argent.*

---

[15] Pat. 8 Eliz. pt. jv.
[16] *Pepys' Diary* (ed. Wheatley), ii, 107.
[17] Ibid. iii, 285.
[18] *Rep. of Roy. Com. on Markets and Tolls*, i, 170.
[19] Ibid. xiii (2), 232.
[20] *Cal. Pat.* 1307–13, p. 541.
[21] Ibid. 1343–5, p. 179.
[22] Close, 10 Hen. III, m. 19.
[23] Chart. R. 1 John, pt. ii, m. 33; Chauncy (*Hist. of Herts.* 377) says that by a grant of 1 Hen. III it was held on Wednesday.
[24] Chart. R. 11 Hen. III, pt. i, m. 29, no. 226.
[25] Pat. 7 Hen. VII, m. 19.
[26] Ibid. 8 Eliz. pt. iv.
[27] *Rep. on Markets and Tolls*, i, 170.
[28] Ibid. xiii (2), 233.
[29] *Plac. de Quo Warr.* (Rec. Com.), 289.
[30] Dugdale, *Mon.* vii, 820.
[31] *Cal. Pat.* 1307–13, p. 535.
[32] Dugdale, *Mon.* vii, 820.
[33] Ibid. 814.
[34] *Cal. Pat.* 1307–13, p. 131.
[35] Ibid. p. 535.
[36] Chan. Misc. bdle. 62, file 1, no. 7; *Cal. Pat.* 1343–5, p. 179.
[37] Pat. 7 Hen. VII, m. 19; Mins. Accts. 31 & 32 Hen. VIII, no. 114.
[38] *L. and P. Hen. VIII*, xvii, 703.
[39] Chan. Inq. p.m. (Ser. 2), lxviii, 14.
[40] *L. and P. Hen. VIII*, xix (1), 891.
[41] Ibid. (2), g. 166 (44).

68

BALDOCK: VIEW IN HITCHIN STREET

BALDOCK: OLD HOUSE IN WHITE HORSE STREET

Thomas Bowles,[42] grandson and heir of the above-mentioned John Bowles, who sold the manor in 1558 to Thomas Revett.[43] Soon after this Justinian Champneys claimed the manor on the grounds that Thomas Bowles had assured it to him in payment of a debt,[44] but he does not seem to have been successful, for Sir Thomas Revett kept Baldock and it descended about 1583 to his daughter Anne, who married Henry Lord Windsor of Stanwell.[45] Anne sold the manor in 1606 to James Jeve and John Hurst,[46] and in 1614 James conveyed his moiety to John Hurst,[47] who died seised of the whole manor in 1635 and was succeeded by his son John.[48] John Hurst son of the latter died in 1684, his heir being his brother William, who died in 1699.[49] William's son John sold Baldock to Pierce Cleaver, who was lord of the manor in 1700.[50] Pierce gave it to Charles, son of Sir Charles Cleaver, his brother, who held it in 1728,[51] but died young.[52] Pierce Cleaver is then said to have devised it by will to Edward Chester,

CHESTER. *Ermine a chief sable with a griffon passant argent therein.*

MEETKERKE. *Gules two crossed swords or their points downwards.*

son of Robert Chester,[53] and Edward sold the manor in 1755 to Adolphus Meetkerke, whose son Adolphus was possessed of it in 1821.[54] His son Mr. Adolphus Meetkerke of Julians sold Baldock Manor in 1870 to Mr. Thomas Pryor, who died in 1899. It was purchased after his death by Mr. Asplan Beldam, who is the present lord of the manor.[55]

The parish church[56] of ST. MARY CHURCH THE VIRGIN, which stands in the centre of the town, is built of flint rubble with stone dressings. The tower is coated with Roman cement. Pieces of moulding and columns of an earlier building are used in the walls. The roofs of the north chapel and north aisle are of slate, and those of the rest of the church of lead.

The church consists of a chancel, north and south chapels, nave, north and south aisles, west tower, and north and south porches. The whole of the church and the tower have embattled parapets, and the tower is surmounted by a leaden spire on an octagonal drum.

The east end of the chancel is of the 13th century, but the remainder of the chancel, the north chapel, the nave, north and south aisles, west tower, and probably the lower part of the south porch were built about 1330. The south chapel was begun in the last part of the same century and completed in the early 15th century; the clearstory was made in the 15th century, and the parvise was added at the same time, when the church was re-roofed. The north porch was built in the 19th century, when the whole building was repaired, and the north aisle and north chapel were re-roofed. The belfry stage of the tower has been recently restored.

The eastern and earlier portion of the chancel has an east window of five lights, with tracery above in a high two-centred head wholly modern; under this window on the outside is a 14th-century niche with a trefoiled head, having a rebated edge, and the remains of iron hinges. The south window is of three lights with restored tracery. Between it and the south-east corner is a double piscina of the 13th century. The flat head is probably modern. There are traces visible externally on the east and north walls of windows probably dating from the early part of the 13th century. A break in the thickness of the north wall of the chancel marks the junction of the 14th-century work with that of the preceding century, and to the west of this each side of the chancel consists of two bays of an arcade which continues in an unbroken line from the chancel to the nave. These two bays have two-centred arches of two chamfered orders with moulded labels on both sides, and carved heads as stops at the points of junction. They rest on clustered columns of four shafts, with rolls between, and moulded capitals and bases.

The chancel screen, which is in the same line with those of the chapels, is a fine one in carved oak of three bays, and two half bays at the north and south ends. Each complete bay on either side of the central entrance has four lights above solid lower panels with tracery in a lofty two-centred head, the central mullion being much slenderer than those at the sides. The entrance has a low crocketed ogee within the two-centred arch, and the original doors are open, with mullions. The half bays at the sides simply bisect the design of the complete bays. The spandrels are solid and are filled with blind tracery. The cornice is modern. The 15th-century roof of the chancel has moulded wall plates and ties, trusses, with tracery in the spandrels. The wall plates rest on corbels with carved heads.

The north chapel has a modern east window of five lights, containing fragments of coloured glass, probably of early 15th-century date. The two windows, each of three lights, in the north wall, are of the 15th century, with repaired tracery. The outside labels are of the 14th century, re-used. A finely carved string-course of the 14th century runs across the east wall. A small modern porch on the north-

---

[42] Pat. 3 & 4 Phil. and Mary, pt. iv, m. 39.
[43] Ibid. 4 & 5 Phil. and Mary, pt. xi, m. 18; Feet of F. Div. Co. East. 4 & 5 Phil. and Mary.
[44] Chan. Proc. (Ser. 2), bdle. 152, no. 8.
[45] Chan. Inq. p.m. (Ser. 2), ccii, 154; G.E.C. *Complete Peerage*; Chan. Proc. Eliz. Bb 1925.
[46] Feet of F. Herts. Hil. 3 Jas. I.
[47] Ibid. Trin. 12 Jas. I.
[48] Chan. Inq. p.m. (Ser. 2), ccclxxv, 132.
[49] Chauncy, op. cit. 382.   [50] Ibid.
[51] Salmon, op. cit. 178.
[52] *Harl. Soc. Publ.* viii, 66.
[53] This Robert was the son of Robert Chester, first husband of Frances Goffe, who later married Sir Charles Cleaver, brother of Pierce (Berry, *Herts. Gen.* 81).
[54] Clutterbuck, op. cit. ii, 269; see Recov. R. Herts. Hil. 26 Geo. III, rot. 186.
[55] Information kindly supplied by Mr. A. Beldam.
[56] Dimensions: chancel, 50 ft. 6 in. by 22 ft.; north chapel, 36 ft. by 22 ft.; south chapel, 28 ft. by 19 ft.; nave, 71 ft. 6 in. by 22 ft.; north aisle, 72 ft. by 22 ft.; south aisle, 71 ft. 6 in. by 18 ft.; west tower, 16 ft. 6 in. by 16 ft.

west replaces the former rood-loft staircase, but the upper doorway, which is blocked, and part of the lower doorway remain, the latter in the aisle, just outside the screen. At the north-east corner of the chapel is an elaborately carved niche of the 14th century, which must have been moved to its present position in the 15th century, when the wide east window was inserted and the north wall was recessed. On the south side is a 14th-century piscina with an ogee cinquefoiled head and a label with crockets and a foliated finial. No bowl is visible, and a modern slab has been inserted at the back. The screen of the chapel consists of a central doorway with four narrow bays on either side; all have solid lower panels with blind tracery and four-centred cinquefoiled recusped lights, with tracery above carried right up to the line

and resting on plainly moulded corbels. The floor of this chapel seems to have been lowered, and while the lower part of the walls is of the 14th the upper part is of the 15th century. The east window, which is of five lights in a wide four-centred head, and the two south windows of three lights are of the 15th century, but the tracery is modern. Under the south-east window is a double piscina of the 14th century with an ogee trefoiled head, which projects from the wall and has foliated crockets. In range with it, and also beneath the window, are two sedilia with similar heads; the division is repaired with cement, and the western seat is lower than the eastern; all are much mutilated. Over the first pillar on the north side is an early 15th-century carved bracket.

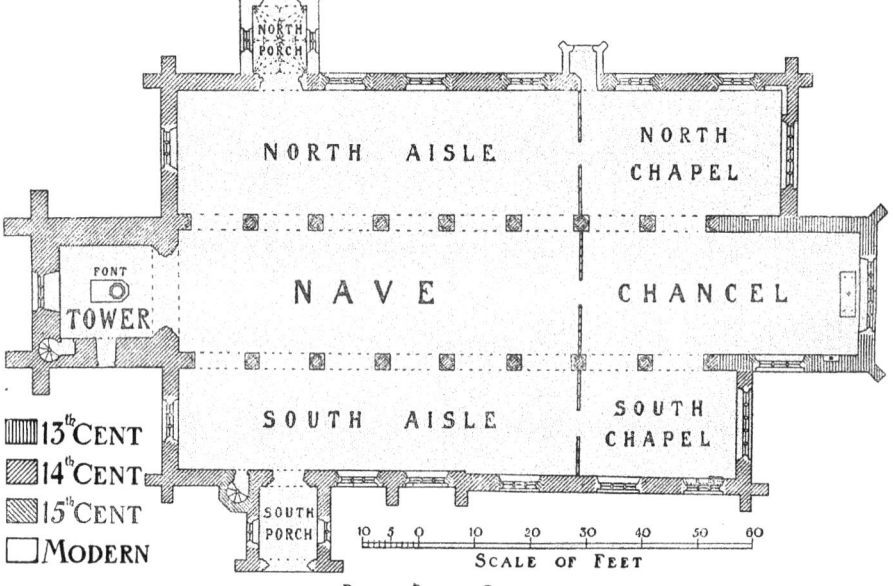

PLAN OF BALDOCK CHURCH

of the cornice. The doors are repaired, and the doorway is cinquefoiled in a four-centred head, with tracery above similar to that in the side bays. It is of the same date as the screen of the chancel and the south chapel. The latter is, however, very much richer, and is designed without a door. It has three bays on either side of the doorway with elaborately cusped ogee lights above traceried panels. Pinnacles are introduced into the tracery, which is in a four-centred head. The screen is elaborately canopied with imitation of vaulting, and immediately below the cresting the cornice is adorned with a beautiful running vine-pattern. The doorway opening is sept-foiled and recusped and has a twisted stem moulding running round the outside, from which the crockets spring. The roof of this chapel is of the 15th century, similar to that of the chancel, but plainer

The communion table in this chapel is of the 17th century.

The nave, of which the arcades are continuous with those of the western portion of the chancel, has six bays of the 14th century, in excellent preservation. They are slightly different from the two bays of the chancel, the two easternmost being rather lower than the rest. The bases, clustered shafts, capitals and moulded labels with mask stops, however, are exactly similar. In the north wall is another rood-loft door, now blocked. The 15th-century clearstory, which runs continuously above the arcades in both nave and chancel, has seven windows on each side with two-centred heads. The roof, also of the 15th century, is precisely like that of the chancel and rests on corbels carved with heads. The easternmost wall plate is close to the westernmost

BROADWATER HUNDRED — BALDOCK

of the chancel roof, between two windows of the clearstory.

The north aisle has three 15th-century windows of three lights with restored tracery, and a modern north door to the west of them, in the north wall. This door opens to the north porch, which is also modern. The west window of three lights has for the most part modern stonework, but a few old stones remain. The south aisle has three 15th-century windows in the south wall and one in the west wall, all of three lights with repaired tracery. The south doorway of the 14th century is to the west of the three windows, and to the west of it is a small 15th-century doorway, formerly leading to the staircase of the parvise. The oak door of this doorway is of the 15th century with a scutcheon for a ring. The south doorway has a two-centred head. It is chamfered internally, and has a fine quadruple suite of mouldings on the exterior side. The south porch has two-light windows on the east and west. The north-west angle stair turret and the floor of the parvise have been removed, and the porch is now open to the roof. A break in the line of the south wall probably indicates the junction with a former transept.

The west tower has a two-centred 14th-century arch of four moulded orders opening to the nave. The west window of three lights is also of the 14th century, with a two-centred rear arch, but the tracery has been much restored in cement, as have the belfry windows also.

The font is of the 13th century, and has an octagonal bowl with beaded edges and a circular stem flanked by octagonal shafts with moulded bases. Near the pulpit is a strong mediaeval iron-bound chest.

In the north chapel is a Purbeck marble coffin lid of the 13th century, with a cross in relief. On the north wall of the chapel is a brass of a man and his wife, of about 1400; the man is dressed as a forester, and the lower part of his figure, and the dog at his feet, together with the inscription, are missing. On the floor is the brass of a man and his wife, of about 1470. On the north wall are two, one with shrouded figures of a man and his wife, of c. 1520, the other an inscription to Margaret Benet, dated 1587.

At the west end of the nave is a brass with a three-quarter figure of a nun of about 1400. The inscription plate is gone and in its place is an inscription to a rector of Baldock of the date 1807. On the floor is also a slab with an indent for a floreated cross. Near the doorway of the north aisle is a slab with an inscription in Gothic capitals, of the 14th century.

In the south aisle are the indents of a man and his two wives, of the 15th century.

Outside the church in the wall of the north aisle is a 14th-century recess with an ogee arch, of which the jambs are restored. Set in the recess is a 14th-century coffin lid with a cross in relief. Also outside in the wall of the south aisle are two recesses, probably of the 15th century, of which the stonework has been renewed.

There is a peal of eight bells: (1), (2), (3), (4), (6) and (7) by Taylor of Loughborough, 1882; (5), with inscription 'Miles Graye made me, 1650'; and (8) 'Laudo Deum verum plebem voco, convoco clerum defunctos ploro nuptus colo festa docoro. Wm. Goodwyn Jam. Manison ch[urch] wards 1711.'

The plate includes a cup and cover paten of 1629.

The registers are in six books: (i) all entries from 1558 to 1709; (ii) baptisms and burials from 1710 to 1792 and marriages from 1710 to 1753; (iii) baptisms and burials from 1793 to 1812; (iv) (v) and (vi) marriages from 1754 to 1788, 1788 to 1804, and 1804 to 1812, respectively.

ADVOWSON The advowson of the church of St. Mary at Baldock belonged to the Knights Templars, who built the church, and it continued in their possession until their suppression in 1309.[57] It was then granted, together with the manor of Baldock, to the Knights Hospitallers, who in 1335 granted the advowson for ten years to John de Blomvill.[58] The latter in 1343 granted it for two years to Walter de Mauny,[59] after which it presumably reverted to the Hospitallers. In 1359 it was claimed by the Crown as parcel of the church of Weston.[60] There seems no reason why the king should have claimed either church at that time, for both belonged to the Hospitallers; however, his claim seems to have been allowed, for the Crown presented to the church in 1383,[61] and apparently continued to do so until after 1822.[62] The patronage was transferred before 1829 to the Lord Chancellor.[63] The latter held it until 1865, when it was transferred to the Bishop of Rochester,[64] who presented until 1877, when it was acquired by the Bishop of St. Albans. Since 1902 the presentation has been in the hands of the bishop and the Marquess of Salisbury alternately.[65]

A terrier of 1638 states that the rectory 'Ioyneth the churchyard against the west end,' and that it included 'Five lower roomes, a bakeing or brewhouse, a hall, two little butteries and a parlour. A loft over the bakehouse, a chamber over the parlour, a studdie and a little loft at the staires head.' The outhouses included a barn and a woodhouse, 'both are thatched and soe is the one side of the bakehouse and the rest is tyled.'[66]

The Fraternity or Gild of Jesus in the church of Baldock was founded, as already stated, in 1459, and the charter confirmed in 1533.[67] At that date it had a master, wardens, brethren and sisters,[68] and found a priest who helped the parson of the church in his duties.[69] At the inquiry of 1548 William Tybie was the brotherhood priest, and he assisted the parson of Baldock in serving his cure.[70] In 1550 it was granted, with the lands belonging, to John Cock.[71]

Modern Dissent is represented in Baldock by the Congregational chapel in Whitehorse Street, built in 1826, the Wesleyan chapel also in Whitehorse Street, the Primitive Methodist chapel in Norton Street, and the Friends' meeting-house in Meeting House Lane, and that of the Plymouth Brethren in Orchard Street. Fox visited Baldock in 1655 and

---

[37] *Cal. Pat.* 1307–13, p. 79.
[58] Chan. Misc. bdle. 62, file 1, no. 7.
[59] Ibid. no. 8.
[60] Ibid.
[61] *Cal. Pat.* 1381–5, p. 311.
[62] Ibid. 1401–5, pp. 345, 486; 1422–9, p. 82; 1436–41, p. 493; 1467–77, p. 440; 1476–85, pp. 54, 465; Inst. Bks. (P.R.O.); Bacon, *Liber Regis*.
[63] *Clerical Guide*.
[64] *Lond. Gaz. Index*, 88.
[65] *Clergy List*.
[66] *Herts. Gen. and Antiq.* ii, 106.
[67] *L. and P. Hen. VIII*, vi, 578 (28).
[68] Ibid.
[69] Chant. Cert. 20, no. 70; 27, no. 14.
[70] Ibid.
[71] Pat. 4 Edw. VI, pt. iii, m. 7.

71

A HISTORY OF HERTFORDSHIRE

there is mention of Quakers here from 1660. Certificates for meeting-places of Protestant Dissenters were granted at various dates between 1689 and 1819.[72]

CHARITIES

Wynne's Almshouses.—In 1617 John Wynne, citizen and mercer of London, by his will bequeathed £1,000 for the purchasing and building of six almshouses for six poor old folk and 40s. a year, to be paid to either of the said poor folk unto the world's end. The devise was carried into effect by a deed of feoffment, bearing date 11 July 1623, made in pursuance of a decree of the Court of Chancery. Augmentations were subsequently made to the revenues both of land and stock.

The trust properties now consist of the almshouses, occupied by twelve widows, and 5 a. 3 r. 14 p. in Weston let at £5 16s. a year, and cottage and premises in Whitehorse Street, Baldock, producing £9 2s. yearly, and £4,050 7s. 9d. consols with the official trustees, producing £101 5s. a year, which includes £1,133 7s. 1d. stock arising from sale of land, and the legacies and gifts following, namely :— £278 16s. 7d. stock, under wills of Grace Mitchell, 1757, and Mary Hill, 1805; £600, will of William Baldock, 1792; £200, Mary Hindley, deed, 1837; £97 19s. 2d., Cornelius Pateman Herbert, will, 1834; £100, Mrs. Mary Cecil Cowell, will, 1830; £108 8s., John Pryor, will proved 1853; £606 4s. 10d., Henricus Octavus Roe, will proved 1854; £100, Lawrence Trustram, will proved 1837; £108 13s. 11d., John Izzard Pryor, will proved 1861; £216 4s. 4d., John Pendred, will proved 1873; £105 2s. 6d., Mrs. Juliana Pryor, will proved 1837; and £395 11s., Emma Pryor, will proved 1885.

This trust also receives £15 a year from the Fifteen Houses Charity in respect of a loan of £300.

The charity estates belonging to the town, called the Fifteen Houses Charity, for the payment of fifteenths and other purposes, originated under deed of feoffment, 30 October 1575, whereby Anthony Fage and James Fage granted to feoffees certain properties upon trust to apply the rents and profits thereof for the support and reparation of the parish church, as also for the bearing and paying of the fifteenths and other taxes of the inhabitants, and also for sustaining the burdens and charges of warriors and soldiers of the inhabitants in or at war for the defence of the kingdom of England. The trust properties now consist of houses and cottages in Baldock, 10 a. of land in Weston, 2 a. 2 r. or thereabouts in Clothall, and 3 r. 16 p. in the parish of Bygrave, producing together about £60 a year, £477 3s. 3d. consols arising from sale of 1 a. 3 r. in Bygrave to the Great Northern railway, and £1,476 7s. 11d. consols arising from sale of 20 a. 2 r. in the parish of Willian, producing £48 16s. 8d. a year. The sums of stock are held by the official trustees, who further hold a sum of £1,000 consols, the dividends of which are being accumulated to replace amount expended on the restoration of the parish church, and a sum of £300 borrowed from Wynne's almshouses charity. The income of this charity is now applied in the repairs and other church expenses.

John Parker of Radwell by deed, 6 January 1604–5, and by his will dated 8 March in the same year, charged his manor of Radwell with an annuity of £10 for the distribution of bread among poor frequenting the church.

In 1797 Miss Jane Brooks by her will, proved in the Archdeaconry Court of Huntingdon 24 January, bequeathed £160 for providing bread in this parish and Hinxworth, and in Biggleswade and Stotfold in the county of Bedford. The legacy was laid out in 7 a. 3 r. 18 p., situate at Stocking Pelham. The share of the rent in 1907 amounted to £1 2s. 3d., which is being accumulated.

Poors Money consists of £2 a year, included in the Fifteen Houses Charity.

In 1692 John Crosse by deed granted an annuity of £3, issuing out of a messuage in Baldock called 'The George,' for the rector, in consideration of the donor taking a certain quantity of ground from the churchyard.

On the inclosure of the parish of Weston in 1798 an allotment of 1 a. 1 r. 37 p. was awarded to the rector.

By the same Act 1 r. 25 p. was awarded for the sexton, who receives £2 11s. 6d. from the Fifteen Houses Charity.

Charities founded by Henricus Octavus Roe.—In 1841 this donor by deed gave £463 15s. consols, the annual dividends, amounting to £11 11s. 8d., to be applied in the distribution of loaves to the poor every Sunday (after divine service) who attend church regularly.

In 1849 the same donor by deed gave £600 consols, the annual dividends, amounting to £15, to be applied in the distribution of bread, fuel, clothing and small sums of money.

The same donor gave £200 consols for the National school.

The several sums of stock are held by the official trustees, who also hold a sum of £1,051 1s. 2d. consols, known as Roe's Almshouse Foundation, producing £26 5s. 4d. yearly, to be distributed half-yearly between two married couples of not less than fifty years of age, poor members of the Established Church, who occupy two almshouses founded by the donor in 1851.

The last-mentioned charity was augmented by £98 17s. 9d. consols (also with the official trustees), producing £2 9s. 4d. yearly, derived under the will of Mrs. Emma Pryor, proved at London 21 September 1885.

Henricus Octavus Roe, likewise by his will, proved in 1854, bequeathed £606 4s. 10d. consols as a further endowment of Wynne's almshouses. See above.

In 1834 Cornelius Pateman Herbert by his will, proved in the P.C.C., bequeathed £97 3s. 4d. consols, the annual dividends, amounting to £2 8s. 4d., to be applied with money usually collected at the sacrament among poor who regularly attend church and lead good lives.

In 1838 William Clarkson by will, proved in the P.C.C., left £102 3s. 3d. consols, the annual dividends of £2 11s. to be applied in the repair of the founder's tomb, £1 to the rector for a sermon on 18 February yearly and 3s. to the singers.

In 1839 Robert Pryor by his will, proved in the P.C.C., bequeathed £213 12s. 4d. consols, producing £5 6s. 8d. yearly, to be applied for the benefit of the poor.

[72] Urwick, Nonconf. in Herts. 568–70.

BALDOCK CHURCH: THE NAVE LOOKING EAST

BALDOCK CHURCH: SOUTH CHAPEL SCREEN

BROADWATER HUNDRED

In 1856 Kitty Cooch by her will, proved in the P.C C., left £47 7s. 4d. consols, the annual dividends, amounting to £1 3s. 8d., to be distributed on St. Thomas's Day in flannel, warm clothing, or fuel to four poor widows who (if able) habitually attend divine service.

In 1870 the Rev. John Smith by his will, proved at London, bequeathed £100 consols, the annual dividends of £2 10s. to be paid to the rector for a sermon to be preached on 26 March each year, for the Sunday following, on certain texts, and a certain Psalm or hymn to be sung, as prescribed in the will.

The several sums of stock are held by the official trustees, who also hold a sum of £193 9s. 5d. consols, arising under the will of Thomas Veasey, the annual dividends, amounting to £4 16s. 8d., to be applied for the benefit of all almshouses existing in the parish.

The National school, comprised in deed 1834, was in 1909 possessed of the following endowments, namely:—£103 7s. 2d. consols, by will of Mrs. Elizabeth Pryor; £100 consols, being a gift by Mrs. Hindley; £22 3s. 7d. consols, under will of Mrs. Emma Pryor; and £60 consols, arising from accumulations of income. Also £200 consols, from a gift of Henricus Octavus Roe, above mentioned. Most of the consols have now been sold out to meet the cost of the recent enlargement of the school.

BENINGTON

Belintone (xi cent); Beninton (xii cent.); Beniton (xiv cent.).

The parish of Benington has an area of 3,060 acres, of which 1,769 acres are arable land, 838¼ acres permanent grass, and 129½ acres wood.[1] The greater part of the parish is over 300 ft. above the ordnance datum, and rises at two points in the north at the upper end of the village, and in the east where Benington Lodge is situated, to over 400 ft. The River Beane forms the western boundary of the parish and the road from Walkern to Watton runs parallel to it. The road from Aston to Benington crosses this, and in the centre of the latter village divides, turning north to meet another branch from the Walkern road, and south towards Hebing End and Whempstead. No railway passes through the parish, the nearest station being Knebworth, 4½ miles south-west. The subsoil is chalk and clay.

There are many chalk-pits in the parish, six of which are still in use, and two gravel-pits in the south-west. The village stands upon a hill, with St. Peter's Church, the manor-house called the Lordship, and the remains of the castle surrounded by a moat standing in a park on the western side of the road. On the south side of the village green is a row of 16th-century timber and plaster and tiled cottages. One of them, known as the Priest's House, has the timber work exposed. The rectory, which stands to the north of the church, is an interesting brick house of two stories with attics. Over the main entrance is the date 1637, which probably indicates the date of building. Towards the end of the 17th century a wing was added at the back and further additions have been made in more recent years. It contains original staircases with square newels and turned balusters and some good 18th-century panelling. Attached to the rooms on the first floor are 'powder closets.'

Beyond the village to the north the road rises to Box Hall, with Cabbage Green a short distance to the east. Along the road turning south-east from the centre of the village is Benington Place, surrounded by a large park, the residence of Mr. Richard Hargreaves, J.P., and south of it the hamlet of Hebing End, in which is Benington House, the residence of Mrs. Parker, widow of the late Rev. James Dunne Parker, LL.D., D.C.L. To the west of Hebing End is Burn's Green, and to the south Cutting Hill. Great Brookfield Common, Lamsden Common, and Leatherfield Common lie in the south of the parish, with Small Hopes Wood and Stocking Spring to the north of the last. Moon Leys Spring is on the south-eastern border. Slipes Farm is situated a little to the west of the Lordship Park.

The inclosure award made in 1858 is in the custody of the rector.[2]

Field-names mentioned in 1638 are Dane Field, Peate Croft, Puckellshedge Field, Great and Little Brooke Field, Lether Field, Popp-hill Field, Baddmeads, Paddocks Penn, Ox Shott Hill, Stocking Corner Shott, Chisill Hill, Beaddales Bush, Langdale Shott, Stowdale and Rowdale Shott.[3]

Nothing is known of the history of CASTLE BENINGTON CASTLE. The earthworks may have been thrown up by Peter de Valognes, when Benington became the head of the Valognes barony.[4] They were in all probability defended in the usual way by a timber tower on top of the mound or 'motte,' which was surrounded by a moat. There was a bailey to the east and within an outer ward on the south the church may have been included.[5] Roger de Valognes, son of Peter, was a partisan of Geoffrey de Mandeville during the period of anarchy in Stephen's reign. He was present with Mandeville at Stephen's celebrated Easter court in 1136, and died in 1141 or 1142. It was this Roger who probably built the masonry works of the castle, upon the earthworks possibly thrown up by his father, for had the earthworks been made in his time they would not have settled sufficiently to carry the masonry walls in Stephen's reign. The keep (*turris*) of the castle was destroyed by Henry II as an adulterine or unlicensed castle in 1177, the charge for the 100 picks used in its demolition being rendered in the Exchequer accounts.[6] The castle, which as a masonry building can only have had an existence for some forty years, was never rebuilt.[7] The ruins, which yet remain above the ground, consist of the bottom courses of the 12th-century keep, destroyed

---

[1] Statistics from Bd. of Agric. (1905).
[2] Blue Bk. Incl. Awards, 63.
[3] Herts. Gen. and Antiq. ii, 108–9.
[4] See Assize R. 323; Plac. de Quo Warr. (Rec. Com.), 290.
[5] For an account of the earthworks of the castle see V.C.H. Herts. ii, 112.
[6] Pipe R. 23 Hen. II, m. 9.
[7] In the extents of the manor in the 14th and 15th centuries there is no reference to the castle, only a capital messuage is returned (Inq. p.m. 17 Edw. II, no. 43; 11 Hen. VI, no. 38; 11 Edw. IV, no. 57).

A HISTORY OF HERTFORDSHIRE

in 1177, rising only to a height of about 2 ft. 6 in. above the ground. It measures about 44 ft. by 41 ft. externally, the walls, which are of flint rubble with ashlar dressings, being from 7 ft. to 8 ft. in thickness with two pilaster buttresses about 4 ft. wide projecting 2 ft. at each angle and one in the middle of each wall. The bailey was surrounded by a curtain wall, fragments of which have been found.

Although the castle was abandoned, the lords of Benington continued to have a residence here probably on the site of the existing house.

BENINGTON MANOR was the head of a Saxon lordship of some importance, which extended apparently into Sacombe, Layston, Ashwell, Hinxworth and Radwell.[8] It was held in the time of Edward the Confessor by Ælmar or Æthelmar, and before him possibly by Ælfric of Benington.[9] William the Conqueror granted the lands of Ælmar to Peter de Valognes, who was sheriff of the county in 1086:[10] Peter de Valognes, as successor to Ælmar, made Benington the head of the Valognes barony, which was sometimes styled later the honour of Benington. Here we find he had 6½ hides in demesne and a park for beasts of the chase, and here either Peter or his son Roger[11] built the castle.[12]

Roger, who probably died in 1141 or 1142,[13] had two sons, Peter, who died about 1158,[14] and whose wife's name was Gundrea,[15] and Robert, who held the barony of Valognes during the reign of Henry II;[16] and who died about 1194.[17] Robert de Valognes was succeeded by Gunnora, his daughter. She married Robert Fitz Walter, but kept the name of Valognes,[18] and died before 1238. The estates next came to Christiana de Valognes, Gunnora's daughter,[19] who married William de Mandeville. Christiana died without issue in 1233,[20] when her estates were divided between three heiresses —Lora, who married Henry de Balliol, Christiana the wife of Peter de Maugne,[21] and Isabel, who married David Comyn.[22] Benington was apportioned to Lora and her husband,[23] who died some time before 1272,[24] and whose son Alexander de Balliol held it in 1278.[25]

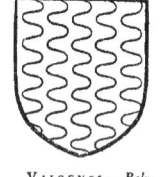

VALOGNES. *Paly wavy argent and gules.*

In 1303 Alexander de Balliol conveyed the manor to John de Benstede and his heirs.[26] This John was king's clerk at the time of the grant, and in 1307 keeper of the wardrobe.[27] In 1309 he was appointed one of the six justices for the Common Bench, and held this appointment until 1320.[28] In 1311 he received leave of absence to go to Rome on the king's business.[29] In 1315 he was again sent abroad with Thomas de Cantebrugge to carry the king's instructions to Almaric de Craön, Seneschal of Gascony, Amaneus Lord of Lebret, and other officials in Gascony and Aquitaine.[30] In 1317 he was appointed one of the two commissioners of array for Hertfordshire.[31] In 1319 he was again sent 'beyond seas,'[32] and died in 1323.[33] His widow Parnel held Benington in dower during her life,[34] outliving their son Edmund, who apparently died about 1338,[35] her own death occurring before April 1342.[36] The custody of John, her grandson, Edmund's son and heir, aged ten, was granted to Walter de Mauny.[37] John died in 1359,[38]

BENSTEDE. *Gules three gimel bars or.*

MOYNE. *Azure a fesse dancetty between six crosslets argent.*

his widow Parnel retaining a third of the manor in dower until her death in 1378.[39] The remainder of the manor passed meanwhile from John's eldest son John, who died in 1376, to his brother Edward,[40] to whom Parnel's portion reverted after her death in 1378.[41] The manor was held at this time as a third of two knights' fees.[42] Edward died in 1432,[43] and Benington was held by his widow Joan during her life, the reversion being settled on their son Edmund.[44] Edmund died in 1439, his heir being his grandson John,[45] to whom the whole manor reverted on the death of Joan in 1449.[46] John's son William, who succeeded his father in 1471, being then a minor,[47]

---

[8] *V.C.H. Herts.* i, 276.
[9] Ibid. 276 n.
[10] Ibid. 336*b*.
[11] Dugdale, *Mon.* iii, 343.
[12] See above.
[13] Round, *Geoffrey de Mandeville*, 172.
[14] *Red Bk. Exch.* (Rolls Ser.), ii, p. cxciv.
[15] Ibid. i, 362.
[16] *Plac. de Quo Warr.* (Rec. Com.), 281.
[17] *Genealogist*, vi, 2.
[18] Ibid.; *Excerpta e Rot. Fin.* (Rec. Com.), i, 317.
[19] Clutterbuck, op. cit. ii, 278, quoting Register Prioratі de Binham (Cott. MSS. Claud. D. xiii, 183); G.E.C. *Complete Peerage.*
[20] *Genealogist*, vi, 2.
[21] See *Excerpta e Rot. Fin.* (Rec. Com.), i, 317.
[22] It was not known whose daughters these heiresses were, and the whole history of the Valognes barony was in much confusion till Mr. Round put it right in the *Ancestor* (no. xi) in 1904. He there showed that the three co-heirs were the daughters of Gunnora's first cousin, Philip de Valognes of Panmure, Chamberlain of Scotland, who died in 1219. He considered Christiana wife of Peter de Maugre to be the youngest. He also showed that Gunnora was not the mother (as stated by Dugdale) of Robert Fitz Walter, so that the two baronies did not descend together.
[23] *Testa de Nevill* (Rec. Com.), 281.
[24] G.E.C. *Complete Peerage.*
[25] *Plac. de Quo Warr.* (Rec. Com.), 281; Assize R. 323, 325; *Feud. Aids*, ii, 430.
[26] *Cal. Pat.* 1301–7, p. 165 (licence for alienation); Chart. R. 32 Edw. I, m. 6 (confirmation of grant).
[27] *Cal. Close*, 1307–13, p. 26.
[28] Ibid. p. 231; 1317–21, p. 508.
[29] Ibid. 1307–13, p. 321.
[30] Ibid. 1313–18, pp. 103, 303, 328.
[31] Ibid. 1317–21, p. 96.
[32] Ibid. p. 317.
[33] Chan. Inq. p.m. 17 Edw. II, no. 43.
[34] *Cal. Close*, 1323–7, p. 296; Chan. Inq. p.m. 16 Edw. III, no. 30.
[35] *Cal. Close*, 1341–3, p. 432.
[36] Ibid.; Chan. Inq. p.m. 16 Edw. III, no. 30.
[37] *Cal. Close*, 1341–3, p. 432.
[38] Chan. Inq. p.m. 33 Edw. III (2nd nos.), no. 110.
[39] Chan. Inq. 2 Ric. II, no. 11; for court held by her see Ct. R. portf. 177, no. 8.
[40] Chan. Inq. p.m. 50 Edw. III (1st nos.), no. 9.
[41] Close, 2 Ric. II, m. 22.
[42] *Feud. Aids*, ii, 443.
[43] Chan. Inq. p.m. 11 Hen. VI, no. 38.
[44] *Cal. Pat.* 1429–36, p. 251; Close, 11 Hen. VI, m. 3.
[45] Chan. Inq. p.m. 17 Hen. VI, no. 43.
[46] Ibid. 27 Hen. VI, no. 27.
[47] Ibid. 11 Edw. IV, no. 57.

BENINGTON CHURCH FROM THE SOUTH-EAST

BENINGTON CHURCH: THE NAVE LOOKING EAST

BROADWATER HUNDRED
BENINGTON

evidently fought on the Yorkist side against Henry VII, for he received a pardon 'for all offences' in 1485.[48] Before this he had sold the reversion of the manor, provided that he died without issue, to Edward IV; but after the change of dynasty he conveyed it to trustees to uses unspecified in his inquisition. In 1485 he died childless and his aunt and heir Ellen succeeded.[49] One Edmund or Edward Benstede, presumably the nearest male heir, claimed the manor, having seized the deed of entail, which was locked in a chest at the time of William's death.[50] Joyce daughter of Sir Edmund Dudley also put in a claim, stating that William Benstede had left the manor to her for life by will, with remainder to Edward Benstede, but the trustees of William Benstede refused to surrender the manor to her.[51] In 1486 Edward Benstede released all his right in the manor to Sir William Say.[52] Next year Ellen Benstede, who was actually in possession, conveyed the manor to Sir William Say,[53] who, on account of William Benstede's sale of the reversion, had to obtain a pardon for acquiring the manor in 1488.[54] In 1486, the year previous to the actual conveyance of the manor, Ellen Benstede and Sir William Say seem to have held alternate courts there,[55] probably because the transaction was in progress.

In 1506 Sir William Say settled Benington on William Blount Lord Mountjoy,[56] the husband of his daughter Elizabeth, but Sir William outlived them, and upon his death in 1530[57] the manor passed to Henry Earl of Essex, the husband of his second daughter Mary. In 1539 it was delivered to their daughter Anne and her husband, Sir William Parr,[58] from whom she was divorced in 1543.[59] In 1553 Sir William Parr Marquess of Northampton was attainted for doing homage to Lady Jane Grey and his lands were forfeited to the Crown[60]; however, as the manor had been settled on him with remainder to his wife, Anne's interests[61] were safeguarded by a grant made to Robert Rochester and Edward Walgrave for a term of forty years.[62] After her death in January 1570–1[63] Benington was granted to Walter Viscount Hereford,[64] who became Earl of Essex in 1572, and was her cousin and nearest heir.[65] Walter died in 1576, bequeathing the manor as a jointure to his wife Lettice,[66] who afterwards married Sir Christopher Blount. She outlived Robert, her son, whose widow Frances married Richard Earl of Clanricarde[67] and seems to have held the manor in dower.[68] She joined with her son Robert Earl of Essex in conveying it to Sir Charles Adelmare or Caesar in 1614.[69] Charles was the third son of Sir Julius Caesar, who took the surname of Caesar from his father Caesare Adelmare, an Italian physician of Treviso, near Venice, who settled in England about 1550.[70] Sir Charles Caesar and his eldest son Julius both died of smallpox in 1642, and the manor passed to the second son Henry,[71] who was succeeded by his son Charles.[72] Charles died in 1694,[73] and his son Charles in 1741,[74] after whose death the manor was sold by trustees to Sir John Chesshyre in 1744. From him it passed to his nephew John Chesshyre,[75] who held it in 1774[76] and was succeeded by his son,[77] also named John, before 1786.[78] In 1826 the last John Chesshyre sold Benington to George Proctor, who was succeeded by his son Leonard in 1840.[79] Leonard was still holding it in 1894, but before 1899 was succeeded by Arthur Procter Pickering, who died in 1902. In 1905 Mr. Arthur F. Bott, the present lord of the manor, acquired it by purchase from Mr. Pickering's successor.[80]

CAESAR. *Gules a chief argent with six roses countercoloured.*

In 1278 Alexander de Balliol claimed in his manor of Benington sac and soc, toll, team and infangentheof, gallows, tumbrel, view of frankpledge, free warren, and amendment of the assize of bread and ale.[81] View of frankpledge in the 15th century was held on the Monday in Pentecost week.[82]

In 1304 John de Benstede was granted a weekly market on Wednesday and a yearly fair on the vigil, feast and morrow of St. Peter and St. Paul.[83] This grant was confirmed by Richard II in 1380,[84] and again by Henry VIII in 1531, the original grant having been lost.[85] The market has long been discontinued. The fair is still held on 10 July, the festival of St. Peter before the alteration of the calendar.[86]

CHURCH

The parish church[87] of ST. PETER, which stands to the west of the village, is built of flint with stone dressings. The nave, which is covered with ivy, is plastered externally.

The chancel and south porch are roofed with tiles and the nave with lead. The tower, which is of two stages, has an embattled parapet and a pyramidal roof.

The present church, which dates from the end of the 13th or the beginning of the 14th century,

---

[48] Cal. Pat. 1476–85, p. 543.
[49] Cal. Inq. p.m. Hen. VII, i, 28.
[50] Early Chan. Proc. bdle. 76, no. 33.
[51] Ibid. no. 124.
[52] Anct. D. (P.R.O.), A 4673. This Edward died childless in 1518 holding lands in Benington of Sir William Say. His heir was John Ferrers (Chan. Inq. p.m. [Ser. 2], xxxiv, 35).
[53] Anct. D. (P.R.O.), B 356.
[54] Pat. 4 Hen. VII, m. 7.
[55] Ct. R. portf. 177, no. 11.
[56] Close, 21 Hen. VII, pt. ii.
[57] Chan. Inq. p.m. (Ser. 2), li, 50.
[58] Ct. of Wards, Misc. Bks. dlxxviii, fol. 372 d.
[59] G.E.C. Complete Peerage. [60] Ibid.
[61] See Chan. Proc. (Ser. 2), bdles. 8, no. 97; 12, no. 45; 22, no. 24; Chan. Decree R. 36, no. 28.

[62] Pat. 3 & 4 Phil. and Mary, pt. xii, m. 42.
[63] G.E.C. Complete Peerage.
[64] Pat. 12 Eliz. pt. iv, m. 18.
[65] Ibid.
[66] W. and L. Inq. p.m. xviii, 39.
[67] G.E.C. Complete Peerage; Feet of F. Herts. East. 37 Eliz.
[68] Feet of F. Div. Co. Mich. 1 Jas. I; Mich. 11 Jas. I; Feet of F. Herts. Mich. 11 Jas. I.
[69] Ibid. Herts. Hil. 11 Jas. I; Recov. R. Hil. 11 Jas. I, rot. 56.
[70] Dict. Nat. Biog.
[71] Chan. Inq. p.m. (Ser. 2), dcclxxiv, 20.
[72] Chauncy, op. cit. 80.
[73] Ibid.
[74] Clutterbuck, op. cit. ii, 286–7.
[75] Ibid.; Dict. Nat. Biog.

[76] Com. Pleas Recov. R. Hil. 14 Geo. III, m. 38.
[77] Clutterbuck, op. cit. ii, 287.
[78] Ibid. 286–7; Recov. R. Trin. 20 Geo. III, rot. 363.
[79] Cussans, op. cit. Broadwater Hund. 128.
[80] Information supplied by Mr. A. F. Bott.
[81] Plac. de Quo Warr. (Rec. Com.), 281; Assize R. 325.
[82] Chan. Inq. p.m. 11 Hen. VI, no. 38.
[83] Chart. R. 33 Edw. I, no. 75.
[84] Pat. 3 Ric. II, pt. ii, m. 32.
[85] L. and P. Hen. VIII, v, g. 559 (29).
[86] Information from Rev. W. Mills.
[87] Dimensions: chancel, 33 ft. by 17 ft. 6 in.; north chapel, 33 ft. by 13 ft. 6 in.; nave, 48 ft. 6 in. by 26 ft.; west tower, 14 ft. square.

originally consisted of a chancel and nave only, built, it would appear from the shields of arms that decorate them, by Sir John de Benstede (ob. 1323). The north chapel and the south porch were added about 1330, apparently by his widow, Parnel Moyne, and early in the 15th century the west tower was built by Edward Benstede (ob. 1432), and an additional arch was inserted beneath his monument below it between the chancel and the north chapel. The raising of the clearstory dates from somewhat later in the 15th century. The modern work upon the fabric consists of the rebuilding in 1889 of the south and east walls of the chancel and the recent restoration of the tower.

The chancel has a modern east window of five lights with tracery in a high two-centred head. In the south wall are three windows. The easternmost has three cinquefoiled lights in a square external head of the 15th century, but mostly of new stonework, only a few old stones remaining. The middle window in the south wall, also of the 15th century, has a four-centred head, and is of three cinquefoiled lights with tracery above. The stonework is all modern. The westernmost window is modern, of three trefoiled lights with 'geometric' tracery. Between the two easternmost windows is a small doorway of the late 13th century, having a slightly ogee-shaped, straight-sided arch moulded externally. The jambs are renewed, but there are a few of the original arch stones remaining.

The north wall of the chancel is pierced by three arches, the two westernmost dating from the erection of the north chapel and the easternmost from about 1430. This last is four-centred, under a square head, with tracery and shields in the spandrels. The soffit and the inner faces of the jambs are panelled, and in the apex of the soffit is carved an angel holding small figures of a knight and a lady, of whose altar-tomb the arch forms the canopy.

The middle and western arches on the north side are of extremely rich 14th-century detail. The middle pier and the responds have engaged shafts with rolls between, and moulded bases and capitals. The arches are of a single order, slightly ogee-shaped and very richly moulded. Both have labels with mask or grotesque stops on the chancel side, that in the centre being the bust of a knight wearing ailettes. The eastern of these two arches has the added enrichment of very closely set and luxuriant crockets on the label, a heavy finial at the apex, and flanking pinnacles, panelled, crocketed and furnished with finials. The gables of the pinnacles are supported by minute mask stops, and that at the east side descends to an independent mask side by side with that at the termination of the label. The two-centred chancel arch was widened and rebuilt early in the 15th century. The responds are cut back to admit a screen. The present screen is modern.

Under the easternmost window of the south wall of the chancel are three sedilia with detached shafts in the jambs. They are of the 13th century, but the two-centred heads and labels date from about 1330. To the east of them is a piscina of the 14th century, with a head similar to, but at a slightly higher level than, those of the sedilia; the sill is modern.

The north chapel has a 15th-century east window of three cinquefoiled lights in a depressed two-centred head. The stonework is original. There are two single-light 14th-century windows, trefoiled, with tracery above in a two-centred head, with labels and mask stops. One is in the north and one in the west wall. There is also a small 15th-century doorway in the north wall, with a four-centred head. It is moulded externally, and has a much mutilated external label with stops.

Behind the organ in this chapel is a communion table of the late 17th century. A piscina of the 14th century in the south end of the east wall has an ogee cinquefoiled head, with a crocketed label, much broken. The sill is also broken and decayed.

The nave is lighted by two two-light windows on either side, of early 14th-century date. They have two-centred heads with tracery, and internal and external labels with carved stops. The clearstory windows, three on each side, are large, of two cinquefoiled lights in a four-centred head. They are of the 15th century, and the stonework is much decayed.

In the north-east corner of the nave, where the window recess is brought down to the ground for half its width, is a doorway to the rood-loft stair, with a four-centred head. At the head of the stair is a similar door facing diagonally to the south-west and opening to the former rood-loft at a high level. The 14th-century north doorway of the nave is blocked and the outer stonework is defaced. The south doorway leading to the south porch is of the late 14th century, and has a pointed arch in a square head. The oak door is of the 15th century. The porch has a similar entrance archway, with shafted jambs and foliated capitals, and in a canopied niche over the archway is a mutilated figure of St. George and the Dragon. On the east and west sides of the porch are windows of two cinquefoiled lights under a square dripstone, and to the east of the inner doorway is a broken stoup. The tower arch opening to the nave is of the 15th century, and has been restored. It is two-centred with chamfered jambs. The windows and doorway of the tower are modern. In the north-west buttress of the tower is a niche with a shield bearing the arms of Benstede and Moyne. The truss roof of the nave is of the 15th century, and rests upon carved mask corbels of that date. At the intersection of some of the beams are bosses bearing the arms of Benstede and Moyne.

In the east jamb of the south-east window of the nave is a bracket carved with angels, roses, a shield with horseshoes impaling a bell. To the west of the same window is another bracket carved with a grotesque figure. There is a plain piscina with a trefoiled head under the window. In the south-east corner of the nave behind the pulpit are the remains of a niche. The canopied head has been broken away, but the carved bracket remains.

The monuments in the chancel include two fine altar tombs below the two eastern arches of the north arcade. That under the middle 14th-century arch is evidently to John de Benstede (d. 1323) and Parnel Moyne, his second wife. It represents the recumbent effigies of a knight and a lady, their heads resting on cushions and their feet upon lions. The knight wears armour of the time of Edward I, and has a long surcoat with a narrow girdle. His legs are crossed below the knee. The lady wears a long head veil and close-fitting dress. The hands of both are broken off at the wrist. In the gable-headed cusped panels, which have shields between them with the

BENINGTON CHURCH : TOMB IN THE CHANCEL

BROADWATER HUNDRED — BENINGTON

arms of Benstede and Moyne, are small figures of 'weepers' all defaced. A much mutilated battlement runs round the edge of the tomb.

The altar tomb under the 15th-century easternmost arch also has recumbent figures of a knight and a lady, possibly Edward de Benstede (d. 1432) and Joan Thornbury his wife, who survived him. The knight, whose feet rest on a lion facing outwards, is clad in plate armour with a finely enriched basinet. The elbow and knee-cops are fluted. He wears plate gauntlets and has a misericorde attached to an enriched baldric on the right side. His head rests on a helm crested with a wolf's head. The sides of the tomb have a series of niches with ogee-shaped crocketed heads with foliated finials and a small battlement around the edge. The niches are all empty.

In the wall between the two arches is a brass, the upper half of a figure of a priest in a cope, probably of the 15th century.

In the nave on the east wall, to the north of the chancel arch, are two brasses, with inscriptions to William Clarke, 1591, and John Clarke, 1604.

The font has a mid-14th-century octagonal bowl of Barnack stone, the alternate sides having engaged shafts resting on carved heads, which have been defaced. The stem is of the 15th century and has panelled sides and base.

There are a few fragments of ancient glass. In the window over the sedilia are three shields: the first is Benstede impaling Or a lion azure with two bends gules over all, for Thornbury; the second is now plain glass; the third is Benstede. In the nave windows are shields of Benstede and Moyne. Part of the seating of the nave consists of 16th-century benches, and there is a chair in the sanctuary of about 1600.

There are eight bells: (1), (2) and (4) by Mears, 1853; (3) by John Briant of Hertford, 1792; (5) by Miles Graye, 1630; (6) by Pack & Chapman, 1777; (7) by an unknown founder, dated 1626; (8) by John Waylett, 1724.

The plate includes a cup and paten of 1639

The registers are in three books: (i) all entries from 1538 to 1722; (ii) baptisms and burials from 1723 to 1812 and marriages from 1725 to 1752; (iii) marriages from 1754 to 1812.

ADVOWSON
A priest is mentioned at Benington in the Domesday Survey,[88] so there was probably a church there before the Conquest. The advowson of the church follows the descent of the manor until the time of Charles Caesar, junior.[89] In 1718 the king presented,[90] in 1719 Charles Caesar, in 1736 Rebecca Knight, widow, and in 1755 Edward Page for one turn,[91] though he still held the advowson in 1817.[92] J. Clarke and others presented in 1822, but the advowson apparently continued to belong to the lord of the manor[93] until John Chesshyre sold it to George Proctor some time before 1836.[94] The latter presented until 1850, after which it was held by the Rev. F. B. Pryor[95] until 1864, after which it passed to the Rev. John Eade Pryor, who continued patron until 1881. Since then it has been in the gift of the trustees of the Rev. William Mills, the present rector.[96]

In 1638 the following closes belonged to and adjoined the rectory: Barne Close, Stable Croft, Washers' Close, Dockcroft, 'the Woode' and 'the litle Spring.'[97]

Various places of meeting for Protestant Dissenters were certified in Benington between 1810 and 1851.[98] There is now a Primitive Methodist chapel in the parish.

CHARITIES
The eleemosynary charities are regulated by scheme of the Charity Commissioners 8 May 1891. They comprise the charities of:—

1. George Clerke, will dated in 1556, being a rent-charge of £2 10s. issuing out of Boxbury Tithe, Walkern, now vested in Mrs. Brand.

2. Hugh Dodd and others, consisting of two closes called Moor's Closes, containing 10 acres, let at £12 a year, purchased with £140 previous to 1681; and £41 16s. 2d. consols, with the official trustees, producing £1 0s. 8d. arising from sale of timber in 1814.

3. Rev. Nathaniel Dodd, a former rector, consisting of 2 acres known as Creedman's Mead, devised by a codicil to will dated in 1661, and let at £4 a year.

4. John Kent, consisting of £20 17s. 4d. consols, with the official trustees, producing 10s. 4d. yearly, representing a legacy by will about 1665.

In 1909 clothing to the value of 2s. 6d. was distributed among ten widows, and the balance in bonuses to depositors of the coal club.

Henry Dixon, by his will dated in 1693, devised certain lands and hereditaments in Benington and Munden in the county of Hertford, and at Enfield in Middlesex and in St. Mildred's, London, to the Drapers' Company, the rents and profits to be applied in apprenticing (among others) poor boys of Benington. A sum of £20 is given annually by the Drapers' Company for an apprenticeship under the terms of his will.

---

[88] V.C.H. Herts. i, 336b.
[89] Pat. 31 Edw. I, m. 8; Chan. Inq. p.m. 17 Edw. II, no. 43; Cal. Close, 1323–7, p. 296; Chan. Inq. p.m. 50 Edw. III (1st nos.), no. 9; 17 Hen. VI, no. 43; 27 Hen. VI, no. 27; Anct. D. (P.R.O.), A 4673; Pat. 12 Eliz. pt. iv, m. 18; Feet of F. Herts. Hil. 11 Jas. I; Recov. R. East. 7 Will. and Mary, rot. 162.
[90] Inst. Bks. (P.R.O.).
[91] Bacon, Liber Regis.
[92] Clerical Guide.
[93] Recov. R. Hil. 14 Geo. III, rot. 327–8; Feet of F. Herts. East. 26 Geo. III; Clerical Guide.
[94] Clerical Guide.
[95] Clergy List.
[96] Information from the Rev. W. Mills.
[97] Herts. Gen. and Antiq. ii, 107–8.
[98] Urwick, Nonconf. in Herts. 573.

DATCHWORTH

Decawrthe (x cent.); Dæccewyrthe, Daceworde (xi cent.); Tachwird, Tacheworth, Thatcheworth (xiii cent.); Dachesworth, Daccheworthe (xiv cent.). The parish of Datchworth has an area of 2,018 acres, of which about three-quarters is arable land, the remainder, with the exception of about 18 acres of wood, being permanent grass.[1] It is long and narrow in shape, sloping upwards from just over 200 ft. in the north to over 400 ft. in the south. The road from Aston to Bramfield winds down the centre of the parish and is crossed in the north of the parish by the main road from Stevenage to Watton; the hamlet of Bragbury End lies at the cross-roads with the house and park of Bragbury, the residence of Mr. Samuel S. Berger, J.P. The park has an extent of about 50 acres and is watered by the River Beane. In the south the central road is crossed by the road from Woolmer Green to Watton, the hamlet of Datchworth Green being situated at this junction.

The village of Datchworth is on the west side of the main road where a lane turns off south-west towards the rectory. The site of the manor-house with the remains of a moat is situated in the angle thus formed and the church of All Saints is a little further south. On the north side of the green is a late 17th-century building of timber and plaster and brick with a tiled roof now divided into two cottages. The initials W ᴬ D and date 1694 are placed in plaster over three gabled windows. Near by on the green is the whipping-post, to which the handcuffs are still attached. About half a mile south of the village is Hoppers Hall, a timber and plaster house with tiled roof of mid-17th-century date. It is gabled and has a small porch. Two of the rooms still have their original fireplaces, over one of which is a painting of a hunting scene, probably of the date of the house. The staircase has turned balusters and square newels with ball heads and is probably original. A little further on is Cherry Tree Farm, a 17th-century brick house plastered, with a tiled roof.

There are several hamlets in the parish. In the south is Painter's Green, where the road forks to Datchworth Green and Hawkin's Hall. In the extreme south of the parish are the hamlets of Bull's Green, where there are the remains of a moat, and Burnham Green, partly in Digswell parish. By the Divided Parishes Act of 1882 Swangley Farm and Cottages in the north-west were attached to Datchworth instead of Knebworth for civil purposes. Oak's Cross, on the road from Stevenage to Watton, marks the north-eastern angle of the parish.

The Great Northern main line touches the parish in the north-west, the nearest station being Knebworth, a mile and a half from Datchworth village.

The subsoil is London Clay in the centre, surrounded by Woolwich and Reading beds, and giving place to chalk in the north, where there are two disused chalk-pits. There are also two small chalk-pits in the south-west and a large gravel-pit west of the village.

Place-names mentioned in the 13th century are Godbyry, Chippeden, Pesecroft, Baronesfeld, and Baronesgrave.[1a] The first three of these survive in the early 18th century as Godbury, Chibden, and Peascroft.[2] Others which occur in the 17th and early 18th centuries are Candell, the Great Lawne, Foldingshott, Cunden Field, Clubden Field, Rockleys, Collewood or Colewood, Datts or Jacks, Lethmore, Feeks Shott Pitle, Shoulder of Mutton Field, Hitchfield, Rush Grounds Field, and Pakesgrove.[3]

MANORS King Edgar, who reigned from 959 to 975, gave land in Datchworth to the church of St. Peter of Westminster,[4] which was confirmed to that abbey by Edward the Confessor as 4 hides and 1 virgate.[5] The abbot himself held 3 hides and 1 virgate[6]; the other hide was held of him by Aluric Blac before the Conquest. With regard to other lands Aluric was the man of Archbishop Stigand, and his successor Lanfranc made this an excuse for seizing Aluric's hide in Datchworth, and was thus in possession of it in 1086.[7] Besides the 4¼ hides in Datchworth originally belonging to Westminster there were 3 virgates, of which previous to the Conquest 2¼ virgates were held by three sokemen of King Edward,[8] and half a virgate by Alstan, a man of Almar of Benington.[9] In 1086 the 2½ virgates were held by two knights of Geoffrey de Bech,[10] and the half virgate by Robert of Peter de Valognes.[11] These portions are not heard of again, so presumably they became absorbed in the manor. The overlordship of Datchworth remained in the hands of the Abbots of Westminster.[12] When the abbey was converted into the seat of a bishop in 1540 Datchworth was confirmed to the see.[13] The bishopric of Westminster was abolished in 1556, but in 1554 Datchworth was granted by the queen to the Bishop of London and his successors to hold in free alms,[14] and an interest in the manor remained to the see as late as 1693, when the manor was still charged with an annual rent of £3 to the bishop.[15]

The earliest recorded sub-tenant is Hugh de Bocland, who was lord of the manor in 1192.[16] His daughter Hawise married William de Lanvaley, and apparently received Datchworth as a marriage portion,[17] for it does not seem to have passed to Hugh's

SEE OF LONDON. *Gules two swords of St. Paul crossed saltirewise.*

---

[1] Statistics from Bd. of Agric. (1905).
[1a] *Abbrev. Plac.* (Rec. Com.), 219.
[2] Close, 6 Geo. I, pt. vii, no. 2.
[3] Ibid. 5 Will. and Mary, pt. vii, no. 23; 6 Geo. I, pt. vii, no. 2.
[4] Dugdale, *Mon.* i, 292.
[5] Ibid. 294; Cott. Chart. vi, 2.
[6] *V.C.H. Herts.* i, 312*b*.
[7] Ibid. 305*a*.
[8] Ibid. 336*a*.
[9] Ibid. 336*a*.
[10] Ibid. 333*a*.
[11] Ibid. 333*a*.
[12] Feet of F. Herts. 4 Ric. I, no. 1; Feud. Aids, ii, 436; Chan. Inq. p.m. 20 Edw. IV, no. 77.
[13] Dugdale, *Mon.* i, 280; *L. and P. Hen. VIII*, xvi, g. 503 (33).
[14] Pat. 1 Mary, pt. iv, m. 16.
[15] Close, 5 Will. and Mary, pt. vii, no. 23.
[16] Feet of F. Herts. 4 Ric. I, no. 1.
[17] *Cart. Mon. St. John Bapt. de Colchester* (Roxburghe Club), 202; *Excerpta e Rot. Fin.* (Rec. Com.), i, 246.

DATCHWORTH: WHIPPING-POST ON THE GREEN

DATCHWORTH CHURCH: THE NAVE LOOKING EAST

son William de Bocland. In 1215 the manor was granted to Nicholas de Joland, and is described as having belonged to Geoffrey de Bocland,[18] who was perhaps a predecessor of Hugh. In 1217, however, the custody of the lands of William de Lanvaley was granted to Robert Delamare and Thomas de Winton.[19] This suggests that William had forfeited; eventually, however, Datchworth returned to the Lanvaleys and descended to Hawise's granddaughter Hawise, who married John de Burgh,[20] son of the famous Hubert de Burgh.[21] John and Hawise de Burgh conveyed the manor in 1240 to Gilbert de Wanton, for the rent of a pair of gilt spurs or 6d. at Easter.[22] Gilbert de Wauton was succeeded before 1287 by his son John de Wanton,[23] but by 1302 Datchworth had passed into the hands of William de Melksop,[24] and in 1346 was held by Henry Melksop.[25] Some time after this it was acquired by John de la Lee, from whom it passed upon his death in 1370 to his son Walter de la Lee,[26] who held it in 1376.[27] Walter's heirs were his two sisters, Margery the wife of Robert Newport and Joan wife of John Barley.[28] These two sisters in 1406 conveyed their moieties to John Coke,[29] who was succeeded by Thomas Coke after 1410[30] and before 1428.[31] Who were the heirs of Thomas Coke is not recorded, but it seems as if the manor was divided between two daughters. One of these may have been Joan the wife of John Shawarden, who died in 1479 seised of half the manor of Datchworth.[32] She left a son John, to whom her moiety descended, and who died in 1555. By his will the rent of the half-manor was to be used to raise portions for his daughters Ellen and Susan and his younger sons Thomas and Laurence.[33] The moiety descended to his eldest son John Shawarden, who in 1572–3 sold it to Richard Foster.[34]

The history of the other moiety of Datchworth after the death of Thomas Coke is more obscure. In 1533 a portion, which from subsequent evidence would appear to be a half, was conveyed by Robert and Alice Darkenoll to John Covert and others and the heirs of John.[35] In 1559 the moiety was held by Richard Covert,[36] presumably the son of John, and was later purchased from him by Thomas Johnson.[37] By his will of 1569 Thomas Johnson bequeathed his lands to his wife Grace for life with remainder to Margaret wife of Thomas Appowell, who seems most probably to have been his niece. The half-manor passed to Margaret and Thomas, but a few years later was claimed by Richard Fuller, nephew of Grace Johnson, on the ground that Thomas Johnson had promised to convey it to him failing his own issue.[38] His claim, however, was not allowed, and in 1571 the moiety was conveyed by Thomas and Margaret Appowell to Richard Foster,[39] who a year or two later became possessed of the other moiety. Thus Datchworth was again united in the same hands. Richard Foster was succeeded before 1614 by Thomas Foster,[40] who in 1620 conveyed the manor to John Gamon.[41] Datchworth remained in the Gamon family[42] until 1693, when it was sold by Richard and Mary Gamon to William Wallis.[43] In 1719 it was purchased from the latter by Edward Harrison,[44] upon whose death in 1732 the manor passed to his daughter Audrey, who married Charles third Viscount Townshend.[45] She survived her husband and died in 1788. Her will provided that part of the Datchworth estate should go to her grandson John Townshend, but the manor was to be sold to provide an annuity for her granddaughter Anne Wilson.[46] Anne and her husband Richard Wilson seem, however, to have kept the manor,[47] for they were in possession of it in 1791,[48] and sold it about ten years later to Samuel Smith of Watton Woodhall,[49] with which manor it has since descended.

In 1275 it was found that the Abbot of Westminster had been holding view of frankpledge illegally in Datchworth for the past forty years and had neglected to attend the sheriff's tourn, for which offence he was fined.[50] Apparently, however, he continued to hold it, sometimes as appurtenant to his main manor of Stevenage.[51]

Free warren was granted by Henry III to Gilbert de Wauton in 1253,[52] and there is a reference to free fishery in the manor in 1719.[53]

The reputed manor of *HAWKIN'S HALL* or *HAWKYNS* first appears in 1564, when it was in the possession of the younger branch of the Bardolf family, who held the manor of Crowborough in Watton-at-Stone until 1564. Hawkin's Hall seems to have extended into Watton parish, so it probably joined their lands there. In 1564 Edmund Bardolf settled the manor of Hawkin's Hall on Elizabeth Bardolf, widow, presumably his mother, for her life, with annual rents to be paid to Edward, Ralph, and Richard Bardolf, with remainder to himself and his heirs.[54] Lands in Tewin and elsewhere were conveyed with the manor.[55] In 1591 the estate was

---

[18] Close, 17 John, m. 5.
[19] Cal. Pat. 1216–25, p. 98.
[20] Excerpta e Rot. Fin. (Rec. Com.), i, 269.
[21] Burke, Dormant and Extinct Peerages.
[22] Feet of F. Herts. 24 Hen. III, no. 289. The mesne overlordship of the Burghs seems to have soon fallen into abeyance, for it is not mentioned after 1303 (Feud. Aids, ii, 429), when the manor was said to be held of Robert Fitz Walter in right of his wife, the granddaughter of John de Burgh.
[23] Assize R. 325.
[24] Chart. R. 30 Edw. I, no. 17; Feud. Aids, ii, 429.
[25] Feud. Aids, ii, 436.
[26] Chan. Inq. p.m. 44 Edw. III (1st nos.), no. 37.
[27] Close, 50 Edw. III, pt. ii, m. 13 d.
[28] Feet of F. Herts. 8 Hen. IV, no. 45; Morant, Essex, ii, 625. It is stated here that there was a third sister, Alice, wife of Thomas Morewell, but she does not appear in this descent.
[29] Feet of F. Herts. 8 Hen. IV, no. 45.
[30] Ibid. 12 Hen. IV, no. 88.
[31] Feud. Aids, ii, 448.
[32] Chan. Inq. p.m. 20 Edw. IV, no. 77.
[33] Ibid. (Ser. 2), cv, 36.
[34] Feet of F. Herts. East. 15 Eliz.; Recov. R. Hil. 1572, rot. 443.
[35] Feet of F. Div. Co. Mich. 25 Hen. VIII.
[36] Recov. R. Trin. 1559, rot. 124.
[37] Chan. Proc. (Ser. 2), bdle. 6, no. 11.
[38] Ibid.
[39] Recov. R. Trin. 13 Eliz. rot. 848; Feet of F. Herts. Trin. 13 Eliz.
[40] Feet of F. Herts. Trin. 12 Jas. I.
[41] Ibid. Mich. 18 Jas. I.
[42] Recov. R. Mich. 22 Chas. I, rot. 100; Feet of F. Herts. Trin. 24 Chas. II; East. 2 Jas. II.
[43] Ibid. Mich. 5 Will. and Mary; Close, 5 Will. and Mary, pt. vii, no. 23.
[44] Ibid. 6 Geo. I, pt. vii, no. 2.
[45] G.E.C. Complete Peerage.
[46] P.C.C. 160 Calvert.
[47] Salmon, op. cit. 215, says that Richard Wilson bought it of the Townshend trustees.
[48] Recov. R. East. 31 Geo. III, rot. 160.
[49] Clutterbuck, op. cit. ii, 315.
[50] Hund. R. (Rec. Com.), i, 192.
[51] Ct. R. portf. 178, no. 47, 53, 62.
[52] Pat. 37 & 38 Hen. III, pt. ii, no. 77, m. 12; Assize R. 325.
[53] Close, 6 Geo. I, pt. vii, no. 2.
[54] Feet of F. Herts. Mich. 6 & 7 Eliz.
[55] Ibid.

sold by Francis and John Symonde and John and Elizabeth Clerke to Edward Fitz John.[56] In 1657 it was in the possession of Ralph Pennyfather,[57] who in 1673 sold it to Edmund Knight.[58] After this date there is no further record of the manor.

Hawkin's Hall, now a farm-house, is situated a little east of Datchworth Green on the road to Watton.

BRAGBURY (Bragborrowes, Brackberrie, xvii cent.) was owned at the end of the 16th century by Thomas Michell, son of John Michell, who held it of the manor of Friars in Standon in socage by fealty. He settled it in 1602 on his son Thomas, who was about to marry Martha Bussye, and who succeeded his father in 1610.[59] Bragbury is now in the possession of Mr. Samuel S. Berger, J.P.

The parish church of ALL SAINTS[60] CHURCH consists of a chancel, nave, north aisle, north vestry, west tower and south porch. It is built of flint rubble with stone dressings, and the roofs are tiled. The whole building is plastered externally. The nave is probably of the 12th century. Late in the 13th century the north aisle was added, and the lower part of the tower dates from the 14th century. The chancel arch is of late 15th-century date, but the rest of the chancel was wholly remodelled at the end of the 16th or beginning of the 17th century, and none of the original work can now be traced. The south porch is probably of the same date as the alteration of the chancel. The top stage of the tower was rebuilt in 1875 when the church was restored ; the north vestry is modern.

The chancel has an east window, and two in the south wall, of about 1600. The east window has a four-centred head which has been blocked, and the three cinquefoiled lights in a square top are modern. The two south windows are of two lights. On the north a modern two-centred doorway leads to the vestry. The roof, of the late 16th or early 17th century, is of the collar beam type, with plaster.

The nave has a north arcade of four bays, which is now much out of the perpendicular, and a truss has been thrown across the aisle, against it, with a buttress outside the aisle wall to support it. The arches are two-centred, of two hollow-chamfered orders, and rest on octagonal columns with moulded capitals and bases. The responds have modern detached shafts of Purbeck marble with crudely foliated capitals, which support the inner order only, the outer hollow chamfer descending without interruption to the ground. In the south wall are two windows, one on each side of the south door. That on the east, of about 1360, is two-centred within, but externally shows two cinquefoiled lights in a square head. That on the west is also of two cinquefoiled lights much repaired. The heads are wholly modern, but the jambs are old.

The south doorway is modern, with detached shafts on the outside. The 17th-century south porch has a four-centred entrance arch and four narrow blocked loops, two in the east and two in the west wall.

The roof of the nave is of the 15th century and is plastered.

DATCHWORTH CHURCH FROM THE SOUTH-EAST

The north aisle has a 15th-century window of two cinquefoiled lights in a square head at the eastern end of the north wall. The jambs only are old. The east and west windows and the western of the two in the north wall are modern, of two lights, with rear arches of the late 14th century. Over the east window of the aisle are the remains of three small niches.

The tower arch is lofty, and, in common with the whole of the lower stage of the tower, is of about 1380. The west doorway is blocked and the

---

[56] Feet of F. Herts. Hil. 34 Eliz.
[57] Recov. R. East. 1657, rot. 144.
[58] Feet of F. Herts. Mich. 25 Chas. II.
[59] Chan. Inq. p.m. (Ser. 2), cccxxvii, 107.
[60] Dimensions : chancel, 23 ft. by 14 ft. nave, 38 ft. by 19 ft. ; north aisle, 39 ft. by 10 ft. 6 in. ; tower, 11 ft. by 10 ft. 6 in.

BROADWATER HUNDRED

tracery in the west window is modern. The upper stage of the tower and the tiled octagonal spire with dormers is modern. The windows of the upper stage are of two cinquefoiled lights, with a quatrefoil over, in a two-centred head.

A recess under the south-east window of the nave, with a chamfered two-centred arch of the 14th century, contains a stone slab with a floreated cross. There is a brass in the chancel to William Paine, with a symbolical device. The date is about 1600.

The font, standing at the south entrance, has an octagonal bowl with trefoiled panelled sides and an embattled edge, on a moulded octagonal stem and base. A chair in the chancel and an oak chest with three locks in the vestry are of the 17th century, to which century also the poor box may probably be referred.

A bequest to the altar of St. Dunstan occurs in 1512.[61]

There are six bells, of which the last four are by Anthony Chandler, with the date 1673.

The plate includes a cup and cover paten of 1569.

The registers are in four books : (i) all entries 1570 to 1700; (ii) baptisms and burials 1710 to 1783 and marriages 1710 to 1753; (iii) baptisms and burials 1784 to 1812; (iv) marriages 1754 to 1812.

ADVOWSON The advowson of the church of All Saints (or All Hallows) at Datchworth belonged to the lords of that manor at an early date. In 1192 the Abbot of Westminster made an agreement with Hugh de Bocland, then lord of the manor, that he should pay 20s. to the abbot on each institution.[62] In 1240, however, John de Burgh, who was lord of Datchworth and Walkern, granted the manor of Datchworth to Gilbert de Wauton, but kept the advowson of that parish with his manor of Walkern.[63] From that date Datchworth advowson followed the same descent as the manor of Walkern[64] until 1725, when William Capell, third Earl of Essex, sold it to the Rev. William Hawtayne.[65] The latter a few months later sold it to William Greaves, fellow of Clare College, Cambridge,[66] and he shortly afterwards conveyed it to his college,[67] in whose hands it has since remained.[68]

A terrier of the reign of Charles I gives a very detailed description of the rectory-house and lands. The house is described as being covered with tiles, the chiefest part of the building whereof is 62 ft. longe north and south and is 18 ft. broade east and west, which is devided into two stories conteyning 10 roomes, whereof 5 are upon the ground viz. one little lodgeing chamber, one seller, one hall, one parlor, one buttery. And 5 roomes over these, viz. one chamber over the seller and little chamber, one chamber over the hall with a closet or studye belongeing to it, and one chamber over the parlor, with a studye over it over ye buttery. One other part or parcell of the said dwelling house adjoyning unto the forenamed part and is 35 ft. longe east and west and 14 ft. broad, which containeth 4 roomes, viz. one kitchen and a brewhouse on the ground and 2 chambers and boarded over the kitchen.

There was also near by another 'parcell of buildinge' covered with thatch, 44 ft. by 15 ft., with 'three severall roomes upon the ground, and one roome at the west end hath a chamber boarded over it.' Another similar structure but smaller contained three rooms, and there was also a great barn 94 ft. long, with six bays, and a small barn 34 ft. long. These buildings were surrounded by a garden, an orchard, and various yards. The glebe lands then extended over about 15 acres.[69]

Places of meeting for Protestant Dissenters were certified in Datchworth from 1719 to 1809.[70] There is now a Baptist chapel at Datchworth Green.

CHARITIES In 1685 Richard and Mary Gamon granted an annuity of 40s. charged upon an estate called Datchworth Bury Farm, for the use of the poor, to be distributed at Christmas.

In 1881 Mrs. Elizabeth Bunting by her will, proved at London 30 November, bequeathed £500, which was invested in £500 11s. consols, the annual dividends, amounting to £12 10s., to be applied in support of the Sunday school and day school held in the National schoolroom.

In 1899 the Rev. John Wardale, the rector, by deed gave the sum of £22 London, Brighton and South Coast Railway 5 per cent. stock, the annual dividends of £1 2s. to be paid to the parish clerk for the winding up of the church clock.

The sums of stock are held by the official trustees.

DIGSWELL

Dicheleswell (xi cent.); Digeneswell, Dikneswell (xiii cent.); Digoneswell (xiv cent.); Dikkeswell, Dixwell (xvi cent.); Diggeswell (xvii cent.).

The parish of Digswell has an area of 1,673 acres, of which 746¼ acres are arable land, 465¾ acres permanent grass, and 18¼ acres wood.[1] The land reaches an elevation of over 400 ft. in the south, where the rectory and Sherrard's Park Wood are situated, but is lower in the north, sloping down to the River Mimram, which crosses the parish in that part. The northern part of the parish is divided from the southern by an irregular strip of the parish of Welwyn. It lies at an altitude of from 300 ft. to 400 ft. The larger part of it has been developed by a syndicate, and is now covered with houses; its western boundary takes in a small portion of the hamlet of Burnham Green. A detached portion of Welwyn parish was added to Digswell for ratable purposes under the Divided Parishes Act of 1882.

The village of Digswell is situated in the valley of the Mimram, in an open space surrounded by the park, the church and manor-house, the seat of Mr. Alfred Dyke Acland, lying at the south-western end. From these a long avenue called the 'Monk's

---

[61] P.C.C. 10 Fetiplace.
[62] Feet of F. Herts. 4 Ric. I, no. 1.
[63] Ibid. Mich. 24 Hen. III, no. 289.
[64] Feet of F. Herts. 8 Edw. II, no. 167; Cal. Pat. 1313–17, p. 274; Chan. Inq. p.m. 3 Ric. II, no. 47; 4 Hen. V, no. 49; 5 Hen. VI, no. 52; 21 Hen. VI, no. 38;
Cal. Pat. 1476–85, p. 33; Feet of F. Herts. East. 21 Hen. VII; Trin. 42 Eliz.; Chan. Inq. p.m. (Ser. 2), xxx, 25; (Ser. 2), cccxcvi, 148; Feet of F. Div. Co. Mich. 3 Chas. I; Cal. Com. for Comp. iii, 1932; Inst. Bks. (P.R.O.); Bacon, Liber Regis.
[65] Close, 12 Geo. I, pt. iv, no. 5.
[66] Ibid. pt. vi, no. 2.
[67] Cussans, op. cit. Broadwater Hund. 197.
[68] Bacon, Liber Regis; Inst. Bks. (P.R.O.); Clergy List (1908).
[69] Herts. Gen. and Antiq. ii, 251–3.
[70] Urwick, Nonconf. in Herts. 570.
[1] Statistics from Bd. of Agric. (1905).

A HISTORY OF HERTFORDSHIRE

Walk' leads to the rectory and Sherrard's Park Wood. In the east of the parish, on the main road from Welwyn to Hertford, is the hamlet of Digswell Water, now recognized as the village of Digswell, though some way from the church. It was probably here that the market was held. The Great Northern railway passes through the parish, crossing the valley of the Mimram by a viaduct. The nearest station is Welwyn, half a mile north-east. The subsoil is chalk in the north, and London Clay and Reading and Woolwich beds in the south. There are two disused chalk-pits in Digswell Park, another near Digswell Lodge Farm, and a fourth in the north-east. A large gravel-pit is still worked south of Digswell Water, and there are several disused ones further down the road.

The following place-names occur in the middle of the 17th century: the Malmes, Dockclose, the Scrubbs, Cowmead, Henley hill, Conduck hill, Tylekill field, Piggott hill, Estoll hill, and Hatches wood.[1a]

Before the Conquest DIGSWELL MANOR formed part of the lands of Asgar the Staller, and was subsequently granted to Geoffrey de Mandeville, being then assessed at 2 hides.[2] One hide, which had been held by Topi, a man of Almar, presumably Ælmar of Benington, was in 1086 in the possession of Peter de Valognes.[3] This hide, which was held by a certain Roger, probably became absorbed in the manor, as it is not heard of again; half the multure of the two mills at Digswell belonged to this estate in 1086.[4]

The lands of Geoffrey de Mandeville descended to his grandson Geoffrey, first Earl of Essex,[5] and remaining with the holders of that earldom[6] came to Maud the heiress of the Mandevilles, who married Henry de Bohun Earl of Hereford and died in 1236.[7] The Earls of Hereford and Essex continued to hold Digswell[8] until their lands were divided between the daughters of Eleanor, daughter and co-heir of Henry de Bohun, and King Henry V, who represented her sister Mary.[9] Digswell thus came into the possession of the Crown, and was thenceforward held of the king, of the duchy of Lancaster, as of his manor of Hertford by fealty and the rent of 6d. or one pound of pepper, to be paid yearly at Christmas.[10]

In the time of Edward the Confessor and in 1086 the sub-tenant of Digswell was Torchil[11]; he was one of the Domesday jurors for Broadwater Hundred,[12] but nothing is known of his descendants. Between 1167 and 1189 the manor was granted by William de Mandeville to William son of Benedict of London,[13] who seems to have been also known as William de St. Michael.[14] In 1223 Laurence de St. Michael, son and heir of William de St. Michael, did homage for lands in Nottingham,[15] and in 1248 this Laurence is called son of William son of Benedict.[16] Laurence died some time previous to 1268, for in that year his widow Ada complained that malefactors had lately come to her manor of Digswell and taken her goods and chattels to the value of 100 marks and more.[17] The manor passed before 1274 to another Laurence de St. Michael,[18] presumably her son, who died about 1283, leaving a son Laurence[19] and a widow Margaret.[20] This Laurence obtained a licence in 1285 to stop a path through his wood of Slirigge, leading from Digswell to Bishop's Hatfield (where he held the manor of Ludwick), on condition that he made another path on the east side of the wood.[21] In 1291–2 he closed a path running through the middle of 'Chirchegrave,' and made another which, he averred, would be much more useful.[22]

The manor was shortly afterwards acquired by William de Melksop, who received a grant of free warren in his lands in Digswell in 1301–2.[23] These lands were probably not the manor, for the latter was not conveyed to him by Laurence de St. Michael until 1305.[24] This William had been assessor for a subsidy in Surrey in 1297[25]; in 1298 he was appointed attorney for two years to Stephen, Prior of Holy Trinity, London.[26] In 1300 he and John de la Leye were commissioned to survey the obstructions in the river leading from Ware to the Thames.[27] In 1304 William de Melksop was keeper of the manor of Clopton, formerly part of the possessions of Edmund Earl of Cornwall,[28] and about the same time he bought from the executors of the same Edmund the custody of the lands of Hamo de Gatton, which in 1305 he sold to John de Northwode.[29] In 1313 and again in 1315 he received licence to go 'beyond seas' with Aymer de Valence.[30] He died about 1317, having been for some time previous to his death farmer of the king's castle and manor of Hertford, where he had executed extensive repairs.[31] He had a son William,[32] who in 1318 received a pardon for killing William de Ponton at a tournament at Luton.[33] Henry de Melksop is mentioned as of Digswell in 1323,[34] but apparently the manor was alienated soon afterwards, for by 1346[35] it had come into the possession of William de Ludwick,[36] from

---

[1a] *Herts. Gen. and Antiq.* ii, 296; Close, 1656, pt. xxxv, no. 40.
[2] *V.C.H. Herts.* i, 330.
[3] Ibid. 336.
[4] Ibid.
[5] G.E.C. *Complete Peerage.*
[6] Ibid.; Duchy of Lanc. Misc. Bks. xxv, 15 d.
[7] G.E.C. *Complete Peerage.* For details of this descent see Ayot St. Lawrence.
[8] Chan. Inq. p.m. 30 Edw. I, no. 58.
[9] G.E.C. *Complete Peerage.*
[10] Chan. Inq. p.m. 14 Edw. IV, no. 29; (Ser. 2), lxiii, 61; lxxiii, 89; cclxxxviii, 145; Duchy of Lanc. Decrees, file 28.
[11] *V.C.H. Herts.* i, 330.
[12] Cott. MSS. Tib. A. vi, fol. 38.
[13] Duchy of Lanc. Misc. Bks. xxv, 15 d.
[14] The change in name was possibly to distinguish him from a William son of Benedict, presumably his brother, who was surety for the relief of Laurence son of William de St. Michael after the latter's death (*Excerpta e Rot. Fin.* [Rec. Com.], i, 100).
[15] Ibid. ii, 41.
[16] Ibid. ii, 41. The father is here called Benedict son of William, but this seems to be an error for William son of Benedict.
[17] *Abbrev. Plac.* (Rec. Com.), 171.
[18] *Hund. R.* (Rec. Com.), i, 188; Assize R. 323, m. 40 d.
[19] Chan. Inq. p.m. 11 Edw. I, no. 13.
[20] *Cal. Pat.* 1288–96, p. 117.
[21] Ibid. 1281–92, p. 214.
[22] Chan. Inq. p.m. 20 Edw. I, no. 151.
[23] Chart. R. 30 Edw. I, no. 17.
[24] Feet of F. Herts. 33 Edw. I, no. 396.
[25] *Cal. Pat.* 1292–1301, p. 298.
[26] Ibid. p. 341.
[27] Ibid. p. 547.
[28] Ibid. 1301–7, p. 240.
[29] Ibid. p. 339.
[30] Ibid. 1307–13, p. 581; 1313–17, p. 282.
[31] *Cal. Close,* 1313–18, p. 515.
[32] Ibid. p. 616.
[33] *Cal. Pat.* 1317–21, p. 124.
[34] Ibid. 1321–4, p. 383.
[35] *Feud. Aids,* ii, 437.
[36] He is said to have succeeded John de Bakewell in this fee, and John de Bakewell was assessed for it in 1303 (ibid. 430). But at this date the manor seems to have been in the possession of Laurence de St. Michael (see above). There is, however, some uncertainty as to the date at which William de Melksop obtained it, and the quitclaim by Laurence de St. Michael in 1305 may have relation to some previous transactions of which we have no record.

Digswell Church from the North-East

BROADWATER HUNDRED — DIGSWELL

whom it passed to his son John de Ludwick before 1377.[37] In 1414 it was conveyed by Ludwick's feoffees to John Perient,[38] who according to the monument to him in the church died in the following year. He was succeeded by his son John, from whom it passed in 1432 to his son John,[39] who died in 1442.[40] He was succeeded by Edmund Perient, who died in 1474, when Digswell came to his son Thomas.[41] In 1539 Thomas Perient the younger succeeded,[42] and died in 1545, leaving four daughters, Mary the wife of Affabell or Amphabell Rowlett, Dorothy, Anne, and Elizabeth.[43] Digswell came to Mary, the eldest daughter, whose first husband died in 1546,[44] and who married secondly George Horsey, and held the manor until her death in 1551.[45] It was then divided between her sisters Dorothy, who had married George Burgoyne, and Anne the wife of Anthony Carleton[46]; Elizabeth had presumably died in the mean time. In 1552 Anne and Anthony Carleton conveyed their moiety back to George Horsey,[47] who had just married Anne Sadler,[48] and in 1557 he acquired the second half from George and Dorothy Burgoyne.[49] Ralph Horsey succeeded his father[50] before 1591,[51] and in 1599 conveyed Digswell to John Sedley and Nicholas Hyde.[52] John Sedley died in 1605 seised of half the manor, which passed to his brother William.[53] Apparently the moiety held by Nicholas Hyde also came to him, for in 1656 he sold the whole manor to Humphrey Shallcross.[54] The latter died in 1665,[55] and was succeeded by his son Francis Shallcross,[56] and his grandson Francis Boteler Shallcross in 1681.[57] The last-named died without issue in 1693,[58] and Digswell passed to his uncle Henry Shallcross,[59] who died in 1696.[60] Henry's son Thomas is mentioned as lord of the manor in 1728[61] and 1729,[62] and William Shallcross in 1757.[63] He was succeeded by another Thomas Shallcross, who died in 1770[64] and left Digswell

PERIENT. *Gules three crescents argent.*

SHALLCROSS. *Gules a saltire between four rings or.*

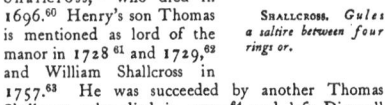

to Richard Willis, the husband of his niece.[65] Elizabeth Willis, their daughter, sold the manor in 1786 to Henry Cowper.[66] The latter occupied the position of guardian to the young Earl Cowper,[67] and the sale was in reality to his ward, for the earl was in possession of the manor in 1821.[68] Digswell remained in the possession of the Earls Cowper until the death in 1905 of the seventh and last earl, whose trustees are at present lords of the manor.

The manor of Digswell possessed two mills as early as 1086, at which time a half mill was held by Roger of Peter de Valognes.[69] Two mills, together with a carucate of land, were the subject of a fine in 1233 between Simon Fitz Simon and Henry Sifriwast,[70] to one of whom they had doubtless been leased by the lord of the manor. They are mentioned as late as 1786,[71] but only one exists now.

Laurence de St. Michael in 1274 had free warren on one side of the river, and claimed it on the other side.[72] He also claimed at the same time view of frankpledge, gallows, and amendment of the assize of bread and ale.[73] William de Melksop received a fresh grant of free warren in 1301–2.[74] In 1278 Laurence de St. Michael claimed by charter of Henry III a weekly market on Thursdays and a fair every year for ten days.[75] Neither now survives. They probably died out owing to decrease in the population, caused presumably by the Black Death, for in 1428 Digswell only possessed six householders.[76]

The parish church of *ST. JOHN*[77] is CHURCH covered with cement outside and plastered inside, and consists of a chancel, nave, north chapel and north aisle, north-west tower, and south porch.

The original church, probably consisting of a chancel and nave, was built in the 12th century, and to that date the present chancel and nave may probably be referred. The north aisle was built about 1300, with a chantry chapel added at its east end a quarter of a century later, but the arcade no longer exists.

In the first decade of the 16th century the present north chapel was built, replacing the smaller chantry, for the erection of which John Perient left £200 at his death in 1324 for the souls of himself, his wife and parents, and John Ludwick and John Derham.[78] At the same period the north-west tower was added to the west of the aisle, its north and west walls being continuous with those of the aisle and nave. The south porch seems to belong to the end of the 17th or the beginning of the 18th century. The church

---

[37] See manor of Ludwick in Hatfield; Chan. Inq. p.m. 21 Ric. II, no. 29.
[38] Close, 1 Hen. V, m. 6 d. (see also ibid. 4 Hen. IV, m. 11 d.); *Feud. Aids*, ii, 449.
[39] Chan. Inq. p.m. 10 Hen. VI, no. 1.
[40] Gibbons, *Early Linc. Wills*, 170; monumental inscription.
[41] Chan. Inq. p.m. 14 Edw. IV, no. 29; Ct. R. portf. 72, no. 893.
[42] Chan. Inq. p.m. (Ser. 2), lxiii, 61.
[43] Ibid. lxxiii, 89.
[44] P.C.C. 22 Alen; *Herts. Gen. and Antiq.* ii, 128.
[45] Feet of F. Herts. Hil. 4 Edw. VI; Chan. Inq. p.m. (Ser. 2), xciii, 104.
[46] Ibid.
[47] Feet of F. Herts. Mich. 6 Edw. VI.
[48] *Visit. of Herts.* (Harl. Soc. xxii), 114.

[49] Feet of F. Herts. Trin. 3 & 4 Phil. and Mary.
[50] *Visit. of Herts.* (Harl. Soc. xxii), 114.
[51] Feet of F. Herts. Trin. 33 Eliz.
[52] Ibid. East. 41 Eliz.
[53] Chan. Inq. p.m. (Ser. 2), cclxxxviii, 145; Recov. R. Hil. 1655, rot. 55.
[54] Close, 1656, pt. xxxv, no. 40.
[55] Monum. Inscr.
[56] Ibid.
[57] Ibid.
[58] Chauncy, op. cit. 316.
[59] Ibid.
[60] Monum. Inscr.
[61] Salmon, op. cit. 208.
[62] Inst. Bks. (P.R.O.).
[63] Ibid.
[64] Monum. Inscr.
[65] Clutterbuck, op. cit. ii, 323.

[66] Feet of F. Herts. Hil. 26 Geo. III.
[67] Sess. R. (Herts. Co. Rec.), ii, 167.
[68] Clutterbuck, op. cit. ii, 320.
[69] *V.C.H. Herts.* i, 336.
[70] Feet of F. Herts. 17 Hen. III, no. 164.
[71] Ibid. Hil. 26 Geo. III.
[72] *Hund. R.* (Rec. Com.), i, 192.
[73] Ibid.; *Plac. de Quo Warr.* (Rec. Com.), 287; Assize R. 32.
[74] Chart. R. 30 Edw. I, no. 17.
[75] Assize R. 323, m. 40 d.
[76] *Feud. Aids*, ii, 454.
[77] Dimensions: chancel, 22 ft. by 20 ft.; nave, 31 ft. by 22 ft.; north chapel, 21 ft. 6 in. by 9 ft. 6 in.; north aisle, 25 ft. by 7 ft. 6 in.; tower, 7 ft. 6 in. square.
[78] P.C.C. 15 Luffenam.

A HISTORY OF HERTFORDSHIRE

was extensively altered in 1811, and was restored in 1874.

The chancel has a modern east window of three lights in a two-centred head. On the north side is

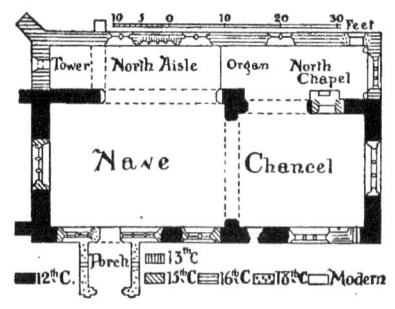

PLAN OF DIGSWELL CHURCH

an arch of about 1200 opening into the north chapel. The face towards the chancel is modern. The arch is two-centred of a single chamfered order; to the east of it is a deep recess with a four-centred head, of the 15th century, which may have been originally open on both sides. In the south wall at the east is a modern three-light window with a square head. At the west end of this wall is a lofty segmental-headed window, probably of the 13th century, now blocked. To the east of the easternmost window in the south wall is a double piscina of the 13th century with two high two-centred chamfered heads and a central shaft, of which the base is old.

Between the chancel and the chapel is a screen of the early 16th century, of which the lower part has been destroyed. A similar screen, formerly the rood screen, with the lower part also destroyed, divides the chapel from the aisle. The north chapel has two early 16th-century windows, that in the east wall having three trefoiled lights in a four-centred head, and the north window two cinquefoiled lights in a square head. At the northeast corner is a small door with a two-centred head, leading to the churchyard. On each side of the east window is a stone bracket, moulded and carved with shields of Perient, three crescents quartering a cross paty. It is possible that these may have been originally in John Perient's chantry. The roof of the chapel is low pitched, of panelled oak, and dates from the early 16th-century remodelling.

The nave walls are probably of the 12th century, but there is no detail of an earlier date than the 15th century. There were three windows in the south wall, but the middle one of three lights is blocked by the east wall of the porch; the other two contain some 15th-century stones and are of two cinquefoiled lights with tracery above in a two-centred head. The west window is of three lights with tracery above in a two-centred head. The roof has 15th-century tie-beams. The south door opens to the cemented and embattled porch, which has a small light in the east and west walls.

The north aisle opens to the nave by a single modern arch, which replaces the original arcade of two bays. In the north wall are two two-light cinquefoiled windows of the same date as those of the chapel, and obviously inserted when the chapel was rebuilt. Between them is a remarkable recess with a richly moulded two-centred arch, containing tracery of the end of the 13th century. The lower part of the recess is destroyed, but the tracery is intact and consists of four high trefoiled heads, supported on three corbels with the heads of a priest, a woman and a bishop, and having above them two trefoils surmounted by a quatrefoil, the space in the middle being filled by the dove, the symbol of the Holy Ghost. The lower part of the label of the arch, with returns, is modern.

The north-west tower has a north wall of the same thickness as that of the nave. It is open only to the aisle by a four-centred plastered arch. The oak doors in this arch, of early 16th-century work, were probably originally those of the rood screen. They have traceried and moulded panels and a four-centred cusped and foliated head. The west window of the tower is of a single light, of the 16th century. It is unglazed and closed by a door. The four bell-chamber windows are also of the 16th century, of two cinquefoiled lights under a square head.

In the chapel are mural monuments to William Sedley, 1658, Eliza Shallcross, 1677, and Francis Shallcross, 1681, and some 17th-century floor-slabs

DIGSWELL CHURCH : NORTH AISLE, SHOWING RECESS WITH TRACERY

BROADWATER HUNDRED — GRAVELEY

to members of the Shallcross family. There is in the chancel a brass of John Perient, standard-bearer to Richard II, Henry IV, and Henry V, and his wife Joan Risain, who died in 1415. The figures are 5 ft. long. The man is in armour, and the arms and part of the inscription remain. Another brass of a knight in armour, with two symbols of the Evangelists, is most probably that of his son John Perient, who died in 1432. On the same slab is an inscription to Thomas Robynson and his wife, 1495. A brass of Thomas Hoore, 1495, his wife, four sons and eight daughters, has an inscription and four shields with a double-headed eagle, the arms of Hoore, the Mercers' Company and a defaced coat. There are also in the chancel brasses of William Robert, auditor of the Bishop of Winchester, 14— (the date has not been filled in), his wife, 1484, and two sons; the figures are shrouded and there are two shields and an inscription: of John Perient, a small, undated inscription; of Robert Battyl, 1552, his wife, four sons and six daughters; and of two daughters of Sir Alexander Cave, 1637.

The bells are three in number, the first and second by Robert Oldfeild, 1605.

The plate includes an engraved cup of 1563, a paten of 1673 and a flagon of 1672.

The registers are in three books: (i) all entries from 1538 to 1731; (ii) baptisms and burials from 1731 to 1812 and marriages from 1731 to 1753; (iii) marriages from 1758 to 1812. Book i has been recovered since the return of 1830.

ADVOWSON The church was given to the abbey of Walden, in Essex, by Geoffrey de Mandeville, first Earl of Essex, the founder of that monastery [79] and lord of the manor of Digswell. The grant was confirmed by Alice de Vere,[80] said to have been the sister or half-sister of William de Mandeville, the third earl.[81] Geoffrey Fitz Piers, who was Earl of Essex from 1199 to 1213,[82] laid claim to the advowson, and litigation arose between him and the Abbot of Walden. It was decided that the earl and his son Geoffrey should present to the church during their lives, and that after their decease it should return to the abbot for ever.[83] The advowson then remained to Walden Abbey until the surrender of the abbot in 1538.[84] The church was never appropriated, and the living was always a rectory. In 1538 the abbey, at the earnest suit of Thomas Audley, then Lord Chancellor,[85] was granted to him with all its possessions,[86] among which, however, Digswell advowson is not mentioned.[87] Although there is no record of any grant,[88] the advowson seems to have been acquired by the lords of the manor, for John Sedley was seised of half of it at his death in 1605.[89] After that date it descended with the manor until 1786,[90] when it was sold by Elizabeth Willis to Jane Pearce,[91] who left it by will to her nephew the Rev. Nathaniel May,[92] the patron in 1811.[93] In that year, however, he sold it to Joshua Watson, to hold in trust for the use of his brother the Rev. John James Watson and his heirs.[94] In 1829 the advowson was sold by Dr. Watson to S. Everard,[95] who again sold it late in 1836 to William Willoughby Prescott.[96] The latter died in the same year, leaving it by will to his fourth son, the Rev. George Edward Prescott, who was patron and incumbent until 1888.[97] His trustees held the presentation from that date until 1900, when it was acquired by Miss Wilshere[98] of the Frythe, Welwyn, who is the present patron.

In 1638 the parsonage of Digswell was said to be 'sufficient and commodious for habitation.' Adjoining there was 'one large nue barne thatched and bourded on the outside, of length five bayes, also one hay barne and stable nue built conteining both fower bayes covered with tiles being all under one roofe.' The glebe lands amounted to 40 acres.[99]

CHARITIES The parliamentary returns of 1786 mention certain tenements and land held by the parish under a gift of Thomas Shallcross and of a donor unknown, situated respectively at Burnham Green and at Harmer Green. Questions arose, however, as to the title of the parish to the property at Burnham Green, but three small tenements at Harmer Green were inhabited by three poor families rent free.

GRAVELEY

Gravelai (xi cent.); Gravele (xiv cent.).

The parish of Graveley has an area of 1,837 acres, of which 581¾ are arable land, 297¾ acres permanent grass and 85¼ acres wood.[1] The elevation of the parish is greatest in the east, where it attains a height of over 460 ft. It slopes down towards the west, but the level of the entire parish is over 300 ft., with the exception of a small portion in the extreme south-west.

The village of Graveley is on the west side of the parish and is situated between Stevenage and Baldock on the Great North Road, which forms a part of the western boundary of the parish. The church of St. Mary lies a little way off the high road on the east side, and just to the west of it is Graveley Hall, a 17th-century house refaced with brick, but having its original chimney stacks. A little to the south of the church is Graveley Bury, a 17th-century farm-house with pargeted walls and tiled roof. The village has

---

[79] Dugdale, *Mon.* iv, 133; Harl. MS. 3697, fol. 1.
[80] Ibid. fol. 21 d.
[81] G.E.C. *Complete Peerage.*
[82] Ibid.
[83] Duchy of Lanc. D. Box A, no. 11.
[84] L. and P. Hen. *VIII*, xiii (1), 575.
[85] *Dict. Nat. Biog.*
[86] L. and P. Hen. *VIII*, xiii (1), 575.
[87] Nor is it mentioned in the inquisition taken at his death (Chan. Inq. p.m. [Ser. 2], lxx, 3).
[88] In the survey of the property of the abbey taken in 1535 Digswell is not mentioned (*Valor Eccl.* [Rec. Com.], vi). Hence it may have already been alienated.
[89] Ibid. cclxxxviii, 145.
[90] Bacon, *Liber Regis.*
[91] Com. Pleas D. Enr. Hil. 52 Geo. III, m. 72; P.C.C. 57 Kenyon.
[92] Com. Pleas D. Enr. 52 Geo. III, m. 72.
[93] Inst. Bks. (P.R.O.).
[94] Com. Pleas D. Enr. Hil. 52 Geo.III, m. 72.
[95] *Clerical Guide*; Cussans, op. cit. Broadwater Hund. 263.
[96] Cussans, loc. cit.; *Clerical Guide.*
[97] *Clergy List.*
[98] Ibid.
[99] *Herts. Gen. and Antiq.* ii, 296.
[1] Statistics from Bd. of Agric. (1905).

A HISTORY OF HERTFORDSHIRE

at some time migrated to the main road. About a mile east is the hamlet of Chesfield with its ruined church or chapel of St. Etheldreda, adjoining which is Chesfield Manor House, now a farm-house. The existing building is only a portion of the old house which has been considerably modernized. What is left dates from the beginning of the 17th century. The house consists of what was apparently the old hall, having a projection at the back or north side containing the staircase and a long wing, in which are the kitchen offices, projecting northwards and connected now to the main block at one corner only. The hall has been subdivided into a drawing room and dining room, each having a modern fireplace, the old fireplace on the north side of the hall having been built up, though the original chimney still exists. The dining room contains some old moulded panelling. The old entrance door has disappeared, but it was with moulded mullions and frame of oak, the casements being glazed with the old diamond panes in lead. It is the only original window left in the building.

Chesfield Park, the seat of Mr. Charles Poyntz Stewart, J.P., was erected towards the end of the 17th century. It is a plain building, with very little architectural pretension. The front is of brickwork, with painted stone or cement moulded architraves round the windows. The house has recently been considerably added to at the back. The park lies partly in this parish and partly in that of Stevenage.

In the extreme east of the parish is the hamlet of Botany Bay.

Corey's Mill is situated on the south-western boundary of the parish.

The subsoil, like that of the surrounding country, is chalk, with a surface soil of gravel and clay. There are some old chalk-pits in the neighbourhood of Chesfield Church, and others, still in use, to the west of that village. There is a gravel-pit beside the road in the south of the parish and a disused one to the north of Graveley village. No railway passes through the parish; the nearest station is Stevenage, a mile and a half south.

Place-names mentioned in the early 17th century are 'la Holt,' Rainehill and Annicks.[1a]

MANORS The manor of *GRAVELEY* was held in the time of King Edward by Swen, one of Earl Harold's men, and was granted by William the Conqueror to Goisbert of Beauvais. At this time it was assessed at 2 hides. Half a hide, formerly held by two men of Godwin of Bendfield, was held in 1086 by William of Robert Gernon.[2]

The manor of Goisbert of Beauvais seems to have been granted with Great Wymondley (q.v.) to

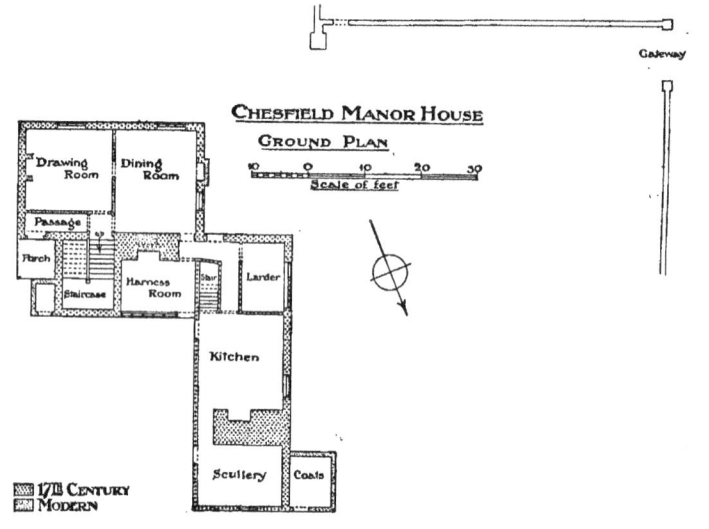

probably on the south side, as the old boundary walls and gate piers still remain on that side of the house. On the north side of the old hall a modern passage has been formed giving access to the staircase and to the present entrance door. The stair is the original one and is of the type known as 'dog-legged,' having two straight flights without a wall between them. The stair is all of oak, with square newels finished with moulded tops, the balusters are of the usual pattern, 3 in. square at top and bottom, the centre part being turned and moulded. The main block consists of two stories and attics, but there is very little of interest internally. Externally, the chief feature is the brick chimney stack at the back, which consists of a row of three square chimney shafts set diagonally on a heavy mass of brickwork, all of a plain character. The bricks are 2¼ in. thick, rising about 11 in. to four courses, but much of the work has been refaced. The south and west of the kitchen wing are of brick, but the other two sides are timber-framed and plastered. In the west wall is a long low window of five lights,

[1a] Chan. Inq. p.m. (Ser. 2), cccxxii, 162; *Herts. Gen. and Antiq.* iii, 56.
[2] *V.C.H. Herts.* i, 335, 308, 323.

86

BROADWATER HUNDRED — GRAVELEY

Reginald de Argentein early in the 12th century. The estate of Robert Gernon in Little Wymondley was held in the 13th century by the Argenteins, so it is probable that here the two estates of 1086 became amalgamated. The overlordship of this manor, therefore, follows the descent of Great Wymondley.[3]

The early sub-tenants of the manor under the lords of Great Wymondley are obscure. Early in the reign of Richard I and in 1198 there is mention of William de Graveley,[4] and in the latter year of John de Graveley and Beatrice his wife,[5] who were ultimately succeeded (if they held the manor) by Robert de Graveley, who died about 1311.[6] Robert's wife Beatrice outlived him by many years,[7] and also survived their son John, who was seised of the manor and died without issue before 1321.[8] In that year Pagana de Merdele sued Beatrice for the manor on the ground that John's heir was his aunt Alice, the mother of Pagana. Beatrice stated in defence that John had quitclaimed all his right in the manor to her and her husband and her heirs.[9] The result of the suit is not recorded. Beatrice died about 1337.[10] In the same year Thomas Fitz Eustace conveyed the manor to John de Blomvile,[11] lord of the manor of Chesfield. He died in the same year,[12] and was succeeded by his son John, and he after 1351 by his son, also John de Blomvile,[13] after whose death the manor came into the possession of John Barrington[14] and Margaret his wife, who is said to have been the daughter and heir of John de Blomvile the third.[15] After the death of her husband Margaret granted Graveley to Edmund Barrington,[16] who held it in 1428.[17] He was succeeded by Thomas Barrington, who died in 1472, when the manor passed to his son Humphrey,[18] as Edmund, his eldest son, had died without issue. Nicholas Barrington, the next holder, died in 1505 and was succeeded by his son of the same name.[19] Nicholas the younger died in 1515, and the manor passed to his son John,[20] who was succeeded by Thomas Barrington. Thomas alienated the manor in 1565–6 to Thomas Bedell, who conveyed it a few months later to William Clarke.[21] He was succeeded by his son William,[22] whose daughter Elizabeth married George Throckmorton, who held the manor in right of his wife and died in 1696.[23] His son John succeeded him,[24] and sold the manor in 1704 to Edward Lawndy of Baldock.[25] The latter is said to have bequeathed it to his grandson, Edward Sparhawke, who held it in 1728,[26] and died without issue in 1741.[27] The manor passed to his nephews Lawndy and Edward Sparhawke,[28] who, however, both died without issue, and their lands passed in 1778[29] to William Parkins, son of their sister Katherine, who held Graveley in 1821.[30] Both William and his brother and heir Edward Parkins died without issue, and the manor was divided between Captain Obert, son of their sister Margaret, and Richard Lack, son of their younger sister Catherine. In 1858 Richard Lack sold his moiety to Lieut.-Col. Robert Hindley Wilkinson, who married Caroline sister of Captain Obert.[31] Lieut.-Col. Wilkinson died in 1888, and his widow continued to hold the manor until December 1894, the other moiety also having come to her. She was succeeded by her daughter Caroline Elizabeth, wife of Mr. Charles Poyntz-Stewart, M.A., J.P., who is the present lord of the manor in right of his wife.[32]

WILKINSON. *Gules a fesse vair between three unicorns passant argent.*

CHESFIELD or *CHISFIELD* (Chevesfeld, xiii cent.; Chenesfeld, Chiffield, Chelsfeld, xiv cent.; Chenyfeld, xvi cent.).

This manor may be identified by its subsequent history with the holdings of Peter de Valognes in 1086. Two hides and 1½ virgates in Graveley which formed a manor before the Conquest had been held by Ælmar or Æthelmar of Benington. Another virgate had been held by Alestan of Boscombe, and belonged to Weston; half a virgate had been held by Lepsi, a sokeman of King Edward, and 8 acres and a toft lying in Stevenage by the Abbot of Westminster, by gift of King Edward. In 1086 the 'manorial' portion was held by Godfrey of Peter de Valognes the sheriff.[33] The virgate and a half was held by Peter de Valognes of William de Ow, and the 8 acres and a toft, apparently reclaimed from Westminster, were in the hands of Roger, Peter's bailiff.[34] Probably Peter de Valognes also acquired the 1½ hides 10 acres which Adam Fitz Hubert held of the Bishop of Bayeux in 1086,[35] through his marriage with Albreda, sister of Eudo Dapifer, brother and heir of Adam Fitz Hubert. The manor thus formed was held of Benington Manor as of the barony of Valognes,[36] and the overlordship follows the descent of Benington.

In the 13th century the manor of Chesfield was held of the barony of Valognes by the family of La Haye. The first of them mentioned in connexion

---

[3] *Feud. Aids*, ii, 429, 436, 443, 448; Chan. Inq. p.m. 12 Edw. II, no. 43.
[4] *Rot. Cur. Reg.* (Pipe R. Soc. xiv), 27.
[5] *Feet of F.* (Pipe R. Soc. xxiv), 53; *Rot. Cur. Reg.* (Rec. Com.), i, 175; *Feet of F.* (Pipe R. Soc. xxiv), 45.
[6] Harl. Chart. 51 D. 26; Harl. MS. 5836, fol. 147.
[7] *Cal. Close*, 1307–13, p. 317.
[8] De Banco R. Mich. 15 Edw. II, m. 18.
[9] Ibid.
[10] *Cal. Close*, 1337–9, p. 18.
[11] Feet of F. Herts. Trin. 11 Edw. III, no. 184.
[12] *Cal. Close*, 1337–9, p. 263.
[13] Feet of F. Herts. 25 Edw. III, no. 387.
[14] Close, 2 Ric. II, m. 35 d.
[15] Cussans, op. cit. *Broadwater Hund.* 64.
[16] Close, 6 Ric. II, pt. i, m. 15 d.
[17] *Feud. Aids*, ii, 448.
[18] Chan. Inq. p.m. 14 Edw. IV, no. 35.
[19] Ibid. 24 Hen. VII, no. 72, 74.
[20] Harl. MS. 756, fol. 381; Chan. Inq. p.m. (Ser. 2), xxx, 147.
[21] Feet of F. Herts. East. 7 Eliz.; Mich. 8 & 9 Eliz.
[22] *Visit. of Herts.* (Harl. Soc. xxii), 42; Recov. R. Mich. 18 Jas. I, rot. 73.
[23] Chauncy, op. cit. 368.
[24] Ibid.
[25] Feet of F. Herts. Hil. 2 Anne.
[26] Salmon, op. cit. 186.
[27] Clutterbuck, op. cit. 230.
[28] Recov. R. Hil. 2 Geo. III, rot. 30.
[29] Clutterbuck, op. cit. ii, 3, quoting monumental inscription.
[30] Ibid. 330.
[31] Cussans, op. cit. *Broadwater Hund.* 64–5.
[32] Burke, *Landed Gentry* (1907). Information kindly supplied by Mr. C. Poyntz-Stewart.
[33] *V.C.H. Herts.* i, 336.
[34] Ibid. 327.
[35] Ibid. 308.
[36] *Testa de Nevill* (Rec. Com.), 271; *Feud. Aids*, ii, 430; Chan. Inq. p.m. 17 Edw. II, no. 43.

A HISTORY OF HERTFORDSHIRE

with Graveley are Ralph and Robert de la Haye, who held one fee there early in the 13th century.[37] Robert de la Haye is again mentioned in 1232 and 1248,[35] but some time between the latter date and 1255 the manor seems to have been acquired by John de Blomvile and Joan his wife.[39] John de Blomvile, apparently their son, held it in 1303,[40] and died in 1337.[41] Immediately before his death he became lord of the manor of Graveley,[42] which passed to his son, and Chesfield has descended with that manor until the present day.[43]

A windmill in Chesfield was leased to the lord of the manor of Great Wymondley in 1318.[44] In 1328 the site is described as land where there was lately a mill.[45] There is now a windmill on Jack's Hill in the north of the parish.

This manor of *GRAVELEY HALL* was formed from the lands in Graveley which belonged to Sopwell Nunnery, St. Albans. It is unfortunately impossible to ascertain from what donor the nunnery received them, and hence the overlordship is unknown. In 1528 the Prioress of Sopwell leased them to Agnes Gascoigne for a term of twenty years,[46] and in 1538 the king renewed the lease for twenty-one years to Agnes Gascoigne, widow, and John Graveley. The reversion and rent were granted later in the same year to James Needham of Wymondley Priory,[47] who in 1541 obtained a licence to alienate them to John Graveley and his heirs.[48] John Graveley was succeeded by his son Thomas, who bought up other lands in Graveley from John Brockett and John Graveley of Hitchin,[49] and thus consolidated his estate. He died in 1583 and bequeathed his lands in Graveley to his wife for the education of his four children, with remainder to Francis, his eldest son.[50] Francis became lord of the manor, but died in 1584, and was followed successively by his brothers Thomas,[51] who died unmarried in 1587,[52] and Rowland, his youngest brother, who lived until 1610. Rowland Graveley's eldest son John died on the day after his father, so that the reversion of the manor after the death of Rowland Graveley's widow, the life-tenant, passed to the second son Thomas, a minor in wardship of his mother Anne.[53] Thomas Graveley and Winifred his wife sold the manor in 1627 to Richard Nixon,[54] and he in 1637 to Eustace Needham.[55] Graveley Hall thus returned to the family of its early owners and seems to have remained in that family. Almost a hundred years later the Needham co-heirs were holding the manor,[56] after which it seems to have followed the descent of Wymondley Priory Manor.[57]

Sir Henry Holmes or Helmes, the occupier during the ownership of Richard Nixon,[58] was granted court leet and view of frankpledge there in 1616.[59]

GRAVELEY of Graveley. *Sable a cross pointed argent with a molet argent in the quarter.*

CHESFIELD MANOR HOUSE FROM THE NORTH-EAST

---

[37] *Testa de Nevill* (Rec. Com.), 271; Cur. Reg. R. 110, m. 6.
[38] Maitland, *Bracton's Note Bk.* ii, 671; Feet of F. Herts. 32 Hen. III, no. 362; Harl. Chart. 51 D. 26; Harl. MS. 5836, fol. 147.
[39] Feet of F. Herts. 39 Hen. III, no. 469; Harl. Chart. 46 E. 28.
[40] *Feud. Aids,* ii, 430.
[41] *Cal. Close,* 1337–9, p. 18.
[42] Feet of F. Herts. Trin. 11 Edw. III, no. 184.
[43] Close, 2 Ric. II, m. 35 d.; Chan. Inq. p.m. 14 Edw. IV, no. 35; (Ser. 2), xxx, 147; Chan. Proc. (Ser. 2), bdle. 22, no. 58; Feet of F. Herts. East. 7 Eliz.; Recov. R. Hil. 2 Geo. III, rot. 30.
[44] Chan. Inq. p.m. 12 Edw. II, no. 43.
[45] Ibid. 49 Edw. III, pt. ii, no. 17.
[46] Dugdale, *Mon.* iii, 364.
[47] *L. and P. Hen. VIII,* xiii (1), g. 887 (13).   [48] Ibid. xvi, g. 780 (6).
[49] Com. Pleas D. Enr. Mich. 6 & 7 Eliz.; Hil. 7 Eliz. m. 6.
[50] Chan. Inq. p.m. (Ser. 2), ccv, 192.
[51] Ibid. ccvi, 42.
[52] Ibid. ccxvi, 104.
[53] Ibid. cccxii, 162.
[54] Feet of F. Herts. Mich. 3 Chas. I.
[55] Com. Pleas D. Enr. Hil. 12 Chas. I.
[56] Feet of F. Herts. East. 13 Geo. I; Mich. 2 Geo. II.
[57] Ibid. Mich. 7 Geo. II; Recov. R. East. 10 Geo. III, rot. 311.
[58] Com. Pleas D. Enr. Hil. 12 Chas. I.
[59] Pat. 14 Jas. I, pt. xxv, no. 21.

BROADWATER HUNDRED — GRAVELEY

CHURCHES The parish church of ST. MARY is built of flint rubble with stone dressings; the chancel is roofed with tiles and the nave with lead. The church consists of a chancel, nave, north aisle, north vestry, west tower and south porch.[60]

The nave is the oldest part of the present structure and probably dates from the 12th century. In the 13th century the chancel was either enlarged or wholly rebuilt. The west tower was added about 1480, and the south porch probably in the 18th century. The north aisle and north vestry date from 1887, when the church was restored throughout.

The original 13th-century roll-moulded east windows of the chancel are replaced by a window of about 1500 of three cinquefoiled lights; but the interior jambs with part of the arch are still visible on either side of the existing window. In the north wall are two windows, probably of the 13th century, with a modern window between them. The doorway in the north wall is of the 12th century, moved to its present position from the north wall when the north aisle was built. In the south wall the easternmost window is a plain single light of the 13th century, and the westernmost is of about 1500 of three cinquefoiled lights in a low two-centred head. Between them a doorway and window above it, both blocked and only visible internally, are of the 13th century. The piscina in the south-east corner is of the 13th century; it is double and has two detached shafts and a central pillar with moulded bases and capitals supporting two richly moulded half-arches and an intersecting arch, all semicircular. It is surrounded by a square moulded setting. The drains are very deep; the eastern is eight-foiled and the western a quatrefoil. All the work is original and in excellent condition.

The chancel arch is of the late 15th century, of two orders, the inner order supported on half-octagonal pilasters with moulded capitals extending round the three complete faces only. A 15th-century oak rood screen stands in the archway with plain lower panels and three open bays of two cinquefoiled lights with tracery above on either side of the four-centred entrance, which has open tracery in the spandrels and no doors. The cornice has an embattled cresting, and the foot of the cross remains over the doorway.

The nave has a window of about 1330 in the south wall with two cinquefoiled lights and a quatrefoil in a two-centred head, and a 15th-century two-light window, with similar tracery in a four-centred head. Between them is the south doorway leading to the south porch. The roof of the nave is low-pitched, of 15th-century date, but most of the carving is modern. At the north-east, beside the chancel arch, is a tall shallow niche of the 15th century, with a two-centred arch in a moulded rectangular frame. The north arcade with the north aisle is modern, but a 14th-century window has been reset in the north wall.

The west tower, of two stages with an embattled parapet, has a late 15th-century arch towards the nave. The west doorway is of the same date. The west window has modern stonework, and the two-light windows of the bell chamber are repaired with cement.

GRAVELEY CHURCH FROM THE SOUTH-EAST

The font, of limestone, is octagonal, of the 15th century. The pulpit is modern. A piece of wood tracery of the 14th century is worked into the reading desk.

In the nave is a floor slab with an incised marginal inscription, '..... Elienora conjux virgo simulata (Xpus meus?) ora quod sit beatis sociata,' which probably refers to a vow of celibacy in wedlock.[60a] In the slab are also the indents of brass shields and an inscription plate.

The bells, of which there are six, include a third of 1605 by Robert Oldfeild and a fifth of 1589 by John Dyer.

The plate belonging to the church of St. Mary, Graveley, is modern, and consists of a cup and paten and a small plated flagon.

The registers are in four books: (i) baptisms from 1555 to 1748, burials from 1551 to 1751 and

[60] Dimensions: chancel, 31 ft. by 16 ft.; nave, 30 ft. by 19 ft.; west tower, 11 ft. by 10 ft.

[60a] Referred to by Salmon (1728) and Cussans, op. cit.

marriages from 1555 to 1750; (ii) baptisms from 1749 to 1812, burials from 1751 to 1812 and marriages from 1751 to 1753; (iii) and (iv) marriages from 1754 to 1812 and from 1792 to 1812 respectively.

The ruined church of ST. ETHELDREDA[61] at Chesfield stands on rising ground about a mile to the east of the village. It consists of a chancel, nave and south-east chapel, and is built of flint roughly plastered, with stone dressings. The whole building dates from the middle of the 14th century. The side walls are about 14 ft. high, and the west walls of the nave and chapel are gabled. There are no roofs, and the east end of the south wall has entirely disappeared, while the east wall can only be traced by the foundations. The condition of the remains is very bad, the walls being heavily covered with ivy, the buttresses defaced, and the floor overgrown with grass and weeds.

The chancel and nave form a continuous rectangular building. At the west end of the north wall is a doorway with chamfered jambs and a two-centred head. A scroll moulded label with return ends is partly broken away, and the rear arch is missing. To the east of the doorway is a two-light window opening, of which only the sill and the west jamb remain. Near the east end a large break in the wall probably indicates the position of a third window. In the south wall is a doorway with a two-centred chamfered arch of two orders, with only one piece of label remaining; and to the east of it, at the angle formed by the south wall and the west wall of the chapel, is a two-light window, of which only the west jamb and the sill, much thrust out of position, remain.

In the west wall is a traceried window of two trefoiled lights, of which only the jambs and head remain at all complete; the sill is partly broken away, and the mullion and most of the tracery are gone.

Only the west wall and part of the south wall of the chapel remain. In the former is a doorway of the same detail as those in the nave, with its north jamb broken away. In the south wall is a single cinquefoiled light of the 14th century very much defaced. In the chancel is a hole containing a stone coffin. There are traces of colour on the internal plaster of the walls.

ADVOWSON In 1225 the advowson of Graveley was the subject of a dispute between John, Ralph and Adam, the sons of William Fitz Simon,[62] formerly patron. Adam Fitz Simon appears to have obtained it.[63] This family were lords of the manor of Symondshyde in Hatfield (q.v.), with which the advowson of Graveley descended[64] until 1818, when Sir Thomas Salusbury sold it to John Green of Great Amwell.[65] From John Green it descended to his grandson the Rev. George Dewe Green, after whose death in 1871[66] it passed to the Rev. G. Dunn,[67] who held it until 1880.[68] From this date until 1899 it was in the hands of the trustees of the Rev. J. Pardoe.[69] In that year it came into the possession of the Rev. George Clennell Rivett-Carnac, from whom it passed in 1900 to Mrs. M. F. Chesshyre-Walker,[70] and in 1902 to the Rev. Roland E. Chesshyre-Walker,[71] who is the present patron and incumbent.

The church or chapel of Chesfield is first mentioned in 1232, when the advowson belonged to the patron of the church of Graveley.[72] It seems to have usually had a separate incumbent from Graveley, though occasionally the same parson served both.[73] Early in the 13th century a certain Thomas, who held both livings, seems to have alienated the advowson collusively to the lord of the manor of Chesfield,[74] and in consequence of this the lords claimed half of it throughout that century. This first occurred in 1232, when Robert de la Haye claimed it against Adam Fitz William.[75] In 1248 he again claimed it against Simon Fitz Adam, and was worsted.[76] John de Blomvile did the same in 1255,[77] but finally in 1331 Parnel widow of John de Benstede, lady of the manor of Benington, of which Chesfield was held, confirmed the advowson to Hugh Fitz Simon.[78] From this time it continued to be held with the manors of Symondshyde in Hatfield and Almshoe in Ippollitts in the same manner as Graveley advowson. There was evidently considerable rivalry between the two incumbents, and on one occasion it attained such proportions that John Smyth, the parson of Graveley, killed Robert Schorthale, the parson of Chesfield, for which offence he obtained a pardon in 1384.[79] The two churches were united in the 15th century; Salmon gives the date as 1445.[80] That of Chesfield was dismantled in 1750, under a licence from the Bishop of Lincoln. The two churchyards were still in use in 1686. The glebe lands then consisted of about 68 acres.[81]

A dwelling-house in Graveley was registered in 1799 as a meeting-place for Protestant Dissenters.[82] There is a Wesleyan chapel in the parish.

CHARITIES In 1626 Edmund Jordane by his will charged an acre of land in Graveley Bottom with 4s. a year for the poor, payable at the feast of St. John the Baptist.

---

[61] Chancel and nave 50 ft. by 18 ft. 6 in.
[62] Maitland, *Bracton's Note Bk.* ii, 543.
[63] Cur. Reg. R. 110, m. 6.
[64] Feet of F. Div. Co. Mich. 5 Edw. III, no. 101; Chan. Inq. p.m. (Ser. 2), iv, 30; Recov. R. East. 17 Hen. VIII, rot. 410; Feet of F. Div. Co. Trin. 41 Eliz.; Inst. Bks. (P.R.O.).
[65] Cussans, op. cit. *Broadwater Hund.* 69.
[66] Ibid.
[67] Clergy List.
[68] Ibid.
[69] Ibid.
[70] Ibid.
[71] Ibid.
[72] Cur. Reg. R. 110, m. 6.
[73] Ibid.
[74] Ibid.
[75] Ibid.
[76] Feet of F. Herts. 32 Hen. III, no. 362.
[77] Ibid. Hil. 39 Hen. III, no. 469.
[78] Ibid. Div. Co. 5 Edw. III, no. 101.
[79] Cal. Pat. 1381–5, p. 444.
[80] Salmon, op. cit. 186.
[81] Herts. Gen. and Antiq. iii, 57.
[82] Urwick, *Nonconf. in Herts.* 581.

GRAVELEY CHURCH : THE CHANCEL

GRAVELEY : RUINS OF CHESFIELD CHURCH

marriages from 1555 to 1750; (ii) baptisms from 1749 to 1812, burials from 1751 to 1812 and marriages from 1751 to 1753; (iii) and (iv) marriages from 1754 to 1812 and from 1792 to 1812 respectively.

The ruined church of ST. ETHELDREDA[61] at Chesfield stands on rising ground about a mile to the east of the village. It consists of a chancel, nave and south-east chapel, and is built of flint roughly plastered, with stone dressings. The whole building dates from the middle of the 14th century. The side walls are about 14 ft. high, and the west walls of the nave and chapel are gabled. There are no roofs, and the east end of the south wall has entirely disappeared, while the east wall can only be traced by the foundations. The condition of the remains is very bad, the walls being heavily covered with ivy, the buttresses defaced, and the floor overgrown with grass and weeds.

The chancel and nave form a continuous rectangular building. At the west end of the north wall is a doorway with chamfered jambs and a two-centred head. A scroll moulded label with return ends is partly broken away, and the rear arch is missing. To the east of the doorway is a two-light window opening, of which only the sill and the west jamb remain. Near the east end a large break in the wall probably indicates the position of a third window. In the south wall is a doorway with a two-centred chamfered arch of two orders, with only one piece of label remaining; and to the east of it, at the angle formed by the south wall and the west wall of the chapel, is a two-light window, of which only the west jamb and the sill, much thrust out of position, remain.

In the west wall is a traceried window of two trefoiled lights, of which only the jambs and head remain at all complete; the sill is partly broken away, and the mullion and most of the tracery are gone.

Only the west wall and part of the south wall of the chapel remain. In the former is a doorway of the same detail as those in the nave, with its north jamb broken away. In the south wall is a single cinquefoiled light of the 14th century very much defaced. In the chancel is a hole containing a stone coffin. There are traces of colour on the internal plaster of the walls.

ADVOWSON
In 1225 the advowson of Graveley was the subject of a dispute between John, Ralph and Adam, the sons of William Fitz Simon,[62] formerly patron. Adam Fitz Simon appears to have obtained it.[63] This family were lords of the manor of Symondshyde in Hatfield (q.v.), with which the advowson of Graveley descended[64] until 1818, when Sir Thomas Salusbury sold it to John Green of Great Amwell.[65] From John Green it descended to his grandson the Rev. George Dewe Green, after whose death in 1871[66] it passed to the Rev. G. Dunn,[67] who held it until 1880.[68] From this date until 1899 it was in the hands of the trustees of the Rev. J. Pardoe.[69] In that year it came into the possession of the Rev. George Clennell Rivett-Carnac, from whom it passed in 1900 to Mrs. M. F. Chesshyre-Walker,[70] and in 1902 to the Rev. Roland E. Chesshyre-Walker,[71] who is the present patron and incumbent.

The church or chapel of Chesfield is first mentioned in 1232, when the advowson belonged to the patron of the church of Graveley.[72] It seems to have usually had a separate incumbent from Graveley, though occasionally the same parson served both.[73] Early in the 13th century a certain Thomas, who held both livings, seems to have alienated the advowson collusively to the lord of the manor of Chesfield,[74] and in consequence of this the lords claimed half of it throughout that century. This first occurred in 1232, when Robert de la Haye claimed it against Adam Fitz William.[75] In 1248 he again claimed it against Simon Fitz Adam, and was worsted.[76] John de Blomvile did the same in 1255,[77] but finally in 1331 Parnel widow of John de Benstede, lady of the manor of Benington, of which Chesfield was held, confirmed the advowson to Hugh Fitz Simon.[78] From this time it continued to be held with the manors of Symondshyde in Hatfield and Almshoe in Ippollitts in the same manner as Graveley advowson. There was evidently considerable rivalry between the two incumbents, and on one occasion it attained such proportions that John Smyth, the parson of Graveley, killed Robert Schorthale, the parson of Chesfield, for which offence he obtained a pardon in 1384.[79] The two churches were united in the 15th century; Salmon gives the date as 1445.[80] That of Chesfield was dismantled in 1750, under a licence from the Bishop of Lincoln. The two churchyards were still in use in 1686. The glebe lands then consisted of about 68 acres.[81]

A dwelling-house in Graveley was registered in 1799 as a meeting-place for Protestant Dissenters.[82] There is a Wesleyan chapel in the parish.

CHARITIES
In 1626 Edmund Jordane by his will charged an acre of land in Graveley Bottom with 4s. a year for the poor, payable at the feast of St. John the Baptist.

---

[61] Chancel and nave 50 ft. by 18 ft. 6 in.
[62] Maitland, *Bracton's Note Bk.* ii, 543.
[63] Cur. Reg. R. 110, m. 6.
[64] Feet of F. Div. Co. Mich. 5 Edw. III, no. 101; Chan. Inq. p.m. (Ser. 2), iv, 30; Recov. R. East. 17 Hen. VIII, rot. 410; Feet of F. Div. Co. Trin. 41 Eliz.; Inst. Bks. (P.R.O.).
[65] Cussans, op. cit. *Broadwater Hund.* 69.
[66] Ibid.
[67] *Clergy List.*
[68] Ibid.
[69] Ibid.
[70] Ibid.
[71] Ibid.
[72] Cur. Reg. R. 110, m. 6.
[73] Ibid.
[74] Ibid.
[75] Ibid.
[76] Feet of F. Herts. 32 Hen. III, no. 362.
[77] Ibid. Hil. 39 Hen. III, no. 469.
[78] Ibid. Div. Co. 5 Edw. III, no. 101.
[79] *Cal. Pat.* 1381-5, p. 444.
[80] Salmon, op. cit. 186.
[81] *Herts. Gen. and Antiq.* iii, 57.
[82] Urwick, *Nonconf. in Herts.* 581.

GRAVELEY CHURCH : THE CHANCEL

GRAVELEY : RUINS OF CHESFIELD CHURCH

HATFIELD OR BISHOP'S HATFIELD

Haetfeld (x cent.) ; Hetfelle (xi cent.) ; Hatfeud (xiv cent.) ; Cecil Hatfield (xvii cent.).

The parish of Hatfield has an area of 12,884 acres, of which 3,895½ acres are arable land, 4,941¾ permanent grass and 1,668¾ wood.[1] From the great extent of the parish and from documentary evidences it is clear that Hatfield was originally forest land, of which Hatfield Park is the survival. The greater part of the parish lies at an elevation of between 200 ft. and 300 ft., but rises to 300 ft. in the north, at Handside and Brockett Park. South-east of Hatfield Park, which lies in the centre of the parish, the ground rises considerably, the highest points, 419 ft., being south and east of Woodhill. The River Lea enters the parish at Brockett Park, crosses it diagonally from east to west, passes through the north of the Home Park, and forms a portion of the parish boundary in the direction of Holwell. The Great North Road runs through the centre of the parish, and is crossed by the main road from St. Albans to Hertford.

The town of Hatfield is situated a short distance south of the cross roads. The church of St. Etheldreda lies a little way off the main road, and adjoining it are the remains of old Hatfield House, now used as stables. Between the church and the main road is Fore Street, formerly the principal part of the town, where the market was held. There are here several interesting houses, notably one of the 17th century of timber and plaster with an overhanging story and tiled roof, now converted into two shops, and some late 18th and early 19th-century red brick houses, including the old Salisbury Arms. Park Street branches off to the north, and in it is the Eight Bells Inn, an early 17th-century plastered timber house of one story, with an attic having dormer windows. The town has now extended northward of Fore Street along the main road and around the railway station in the direction of the road to St. Albans.

Facing the station yard immediately outside the park gates of Hatfield House is a bronze statue of Robert third Marquess of Salisbury, designed by Sir George J. Frampton, and erected by subscription by the Marquess's Hertfordshire friends and neighbours in 1906.

The Great Northern railway has a station at Hatfield, which is also a junction for the branch lines to St. Albans, Luton, Dunstable and Hertford.

In the extreme north of the parish are the hamlet of Handside, Brockett Hall and Park, with Lemsford at its southern extremity. These, with Cromer Hyde, now form the ecclesiastical parish of Lemsford. Brockett Hall was rebuilt by Sir Matthew Lamb in the middle of the 18th century from designs by James Paine. It is a brick house surrounded by a park of 500 acres, in which is a lake. The Prince Regent frequently stayed with the first Lord Melbourne at Brockett, and in 1841 Queen Victoria visited Lord Melbourne there, writing to the King of the Belgians on 3 August in that year that her 'visit to Brockett naturally interested us very much for our excellent Lord Melbourne's sake. The park and grounds are beautiful.' Lord Melbourne died at Brockett in 1848. Lord Palmerston resided for some years at Brockett and died there in 1865. It is now the property of Admiral Lord Walter Kerr, but has been occupied for many years by Lord Mountstephen, who has on several occasions entertained royalty.

The little village of Stanborough lies on the North Road a little further south. To the west are the village of Cromer Hyde, Symondshyde Farm, with Symondshyde Great Wood, and Astwick Manor. To the east is the village of Hatfield Hyde, with Woodhall Farm, Ludwick Hall and Holwell Manor, and Camfield Place (for which see Essendon), the residence of Mr. Frederick Vavasour McConnell. A little distance west of the town of Hatfield are New Town, where is the union workhouse, and Roe Green. Pope's Farm is on the west side of Hatfield Park, and Bush Hall (the residence of Mr. A. L. Stride, J.P.) on the north. Beyond the parks the parish extends to the east in a long narrow strip. Here are situated Woodside, Lower Woodside, Woodhill, the property of Canon Jones, and also Woodside Place, the residence of Sir William S. Church, M.D., and Warrenwood, the residence of Captain Butler. In the extreme east is the village of Newgate Street, with the manor of Tolmers, the residence of Mr. J. H. Johnson, and Ponsbourne Park, the house of which, erected about 1761 and added to later, is now the property of Col. Edward Hildred Carlile, M.P., J.P.

In this part of the parish there are several old claypits and a gravel-pit which is still worked. There is also a large gravel-pit north of the Home Park. In the north-east of the parish are a number of old chalk-pits. The greater part of the parish lies on a subsoil of chalk, but south-east of the town there is a belt of Woolwich and Reading beds, and beyond that a stretch of London Clay.

In the reign of King Edgar *HAT-MANORS FIELD* was in the possession of 'a certain powerful man' named Oedmaer, whose daughter Æthelflaed was King Edgar's wife.[2] Oedmaer and his wife Ælalde demised the 40 hides of Hatfield to the king, probably for the purposes of a benefaction, and in order that, by passing through the king's hands, it might become 'bocland.' Edgar transferred it to the monks of Ely, being under a promise to endow that abbey, the large quantity of wood it contained making it specially valuable for building purposes. During Edgar's lifetime the monastery enjoyed it without disturbance, but after his death in 975 their claim was disputed. An alderman or earl named Ægelwin and his brothers declared that their father Æthelstan had exchanged his patrimony in Devonshire for the 40 hides of Hatfield, but that King Edgar had by violence deprived him of both lands, ignoring the exchange he had made with him, and that therefore the title of the monks of Ely to Hatfield was invalid. The brothers prevailed, and the monks were obliged to buy back Hatfield, giving them in payment for it 30 hides in Hemingford and land elsewhere, after which their title was made secure.[3]

---

[1] Statistics from Bd. of Agric. (1905).   [2] Freeman, *Old Engl. Hist.* 178.   [3] *Liber Eliensis* (Impensis Soc.), i, 115.

A HISTORY OF HERTFORDSHIRE

The grant of Edgar to the church of Ely was confirmed by Ethelred and Edward the Confessor.[4] In the Great Survey of 1086, and in the *Inquisitio Eliensis* taken about the same time, Hatfield was still assessed at 40 hides, of which half was demesne land and a large proportion forest.[5] It continued in the possession of the abbots until 1109,[6] when it was transferred to the Bishops of Ely.

HATFIELD HOUSE. The Bishops of Ely, from an early date, had a house at Hatfield, which they frequently visited,[7] and at which they often entertained royal visitors. King John passed through Hatfield in March 1211,[8] and Edward I spent a few days there in February 1303.[9] Edward II visited it in July 1309,[10] and Edward III was six times there, including the Christmas of 1336.[11] In 1514, probably on the nomination of Henry VIII, Hannibal Zenzano, the king's farrier, was made lessee of the manor and keeper of the parks,[12] and from this time the king seems to have made use of Hatfield House almost as if it belonged to him, although it did not really come into his possession until 1538. In 1517 Lady Frances Brandon, daughter of the Duke of Suffolk and mother of Lady Jane Grey, was born and christened there.[13] Henry VIII visited it in November 1522,[14] the same month in 1524,[15] and August 1525.[16] In June 1528 he removed to Hatfield from Hertford 'because of the sweat.' The Marquess of Exeter and his wife were ill and the master of the horse 'complained of his head; nevertheless,' says Hennerage, 'the King is merry and takes no conceit.'[17] Princess Mary resided at Hatfield with a household suitable to her state as Princess Royal until Henry's divorce from Katherine of Aragon in 1533. In December of that year her household was diminished, and the infant Princess Elizabeth was also conveyed there.[18] A little later Mary's household was entirely dissolved and she remained at Hatfield as a mere lady-in-waiting to the infant Elizabeth.[19] In March 1534, when the young Elizabeth was removed from Hatfield to Hunsdon, Mary refused to accompany her, but she was put by force by a certain gentleman into a litter with the queen's aunt and thus compelled to make court to Elizabeth. She afterwards made a public protest.[20]

In 1538 the manor of Hatfield was conveyed by Thomas Bishop of Ely to Henry VIII, in exchange for the site of the dissolved monastery of Ickleton, the possessions of the dissolved priory of Swaffham Bulbeck, a single parish, and various lands in Essex.[21]

The Princess Elizabeth and the young Edward seem to have passed much of their childhood at

SEE OF ELY. *Gules three crowns or.*

Hatfield, and Elizabeth, although removed from there at the death of her father, had returned there by 1548, when she received the ambitious attentions of Thomas Seymour Lord Sudeley.

In 1549 Edward VI granted the manor of Hatfield to John Earl of Warwick,[22] but Princess Elizabeth had become so attached to it that she petitioned against its loss, in consequence of which the Earl of Warwick returned it to the king in 1550,[23] and with the consent of the Privy Council it was conveyed to Elizabeth herself, who gave other lands in exchange for the Earl of Warwick.[24]

At the accession of Queen Mary Elizabeth left Hatfield, but in 1555 was permitted to return there under the supervision of Sir Thomas Pope, and devoted herself to study. There Elizabeth refused proposals of marriage from Philibert Duke of Savoy and Prince Eric, son of Gustavus Vasa of Sweden. She was there in November 1558 when the news of Mary's death was brought to her; this news she received, according to tradition, seated under an oak tree in the park, which still exists. Her first three councils were held at the house before she quitted it for London. Hatfield was still maintained as a royal palace and Elizabeth paid frequent visits to it. After her death in 1603 it was granted in dower to Anne of Denmark, the queen of James I.[25] James, however, in the same year visited the Earl of Salisbury at his manor of Theobalds, and was so pleased with it that he entered into negotiations with the earl for the exchange of that manor with Hatfield.[26] The transfer was effected in 1607, Robert Earl of Salisbury receiving the grant of the lordship and manor of Hatfield, with the three parks, and all appurtenances, to hold in socage.[27] In 1611 he obtained a licence, for himself and his heirs, to alienate lands and tenements in Hatfield 'notwithstanding the statute of Quia Emptores terrarum, or any other statutes.'[28] As soon as he had entered upon possession of Hatfield Lord Salisbury appears to have set about pulling down half the old palace and building the present house.[29] (For description of both see below.)

CECIL, Marquess of Salisbury. *Barry of ten pieces argent and azure six scutcheons sable with a lion argent on each with the difference of a crescent.*

Immediately after Lord Salisbury had settled at Hatfield he initiated a scheme for the relief of the poor there by means of the establishment of a weaving industry, and in December 1608 he made an agreement with one Walter Morrall, by which Morrall was to teach his art to fifty persons to be chosen by the earl in the parish of Hatfield.[30-32]

---

[4] Cart. Antiq. B 12.
[5] *V.C.H. Herts.* i, 311b; *Inquisitio Eliensis* (ed. Hamilton), 125.
[6] Dugdale, *Mon.* i, 462.
[7] P. F. Robinson, *Vetruvius Britannicus*, 3 et seq.
[8] 'Itin. of King John,' *Rot. Lit. Pat.* (Rec. Com.).
[9] *Cal. Pat.* 1301–7, pp. 116–17.
[10] Ibid. 1307–13, pp. 175–6.
[11] Ibid. 1330–4, p. 250; 1334–8, pp. 86, 345; 379; 1338–40, p. 69; 1348–50, p. 225.

[12] Mins. Accts. bdle. 6, no. 4.
[13] *St. Albans Arch. Soc.* 1901–2, 338.
[14] Ibid. iii, 2694.
[15] Ibid. iv, 546.
[16] Ibid. 1676.
[17] Ibid. 4429.
[18] Ibid. vi, 1528.
[19] Ibid. vii, 38.
[20] Ibid. 393.
[21] D. of purchase and exchange, 148; L. and P. Hen. VIII, xiii (2), 904; Pat. 30 Hen. VIII, pt. iii, no. 30.
[22] D. of purchase and exchange, 96.

[23] Ibid. 98.
[24] *Acts of P.C.* 1550–2, p. 52.
[25] Pat. 1 Jas. I, pt. xx, m. 5.
[26] See under Theobalds; *Cal. S. P. Dom.* 1603–10, p. 354.
[27] Pat. 5 Jas. I, pt. xix, m. 29.
[28] *Cal. S. P. Dom.* 1611–18, p. 104.
[29] *St. Albans and Herts. Archit. and Arch. Soc. Trans.* i (4), 348–9.
[30-32] *Cal. S. P. Dom.* 1603–10, p. 478; *St. Albans and Herts. Archit. and Arch. Soc. Trans.* i (4), 350.

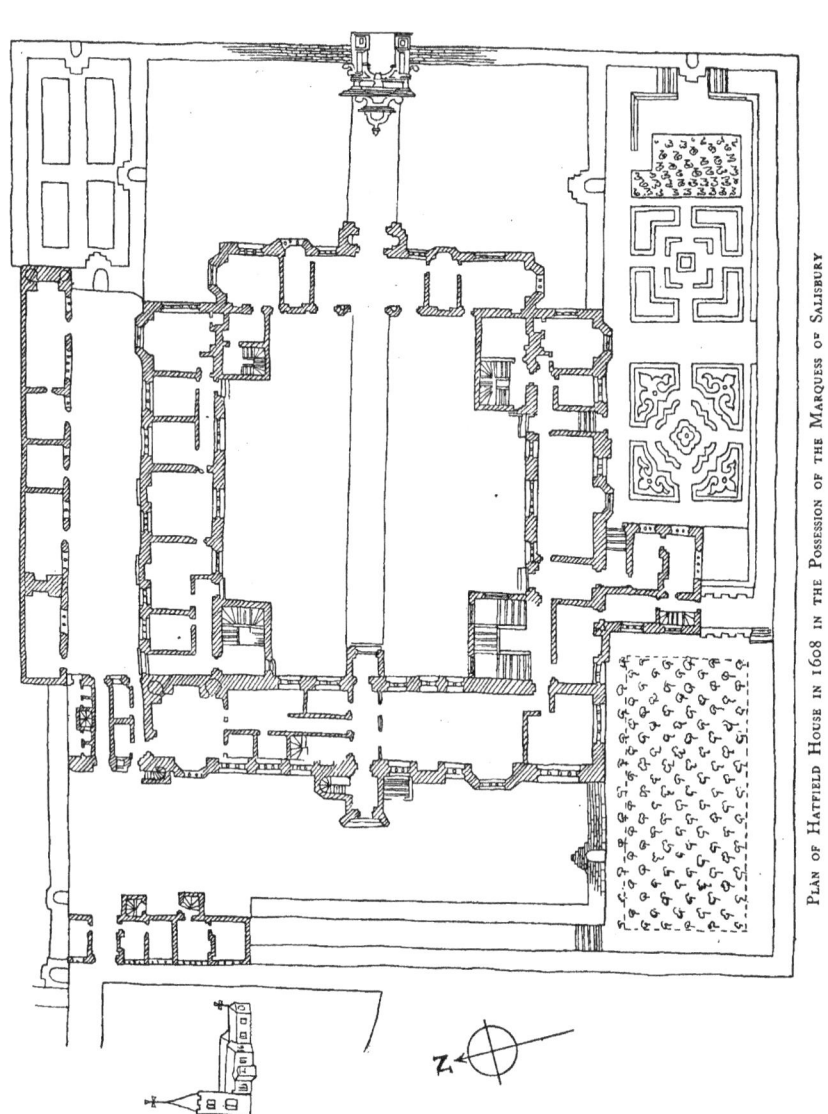

PLAN OF HATFIELD HOUSE IN 1608 IN THE POSSESSION OF THE MARQUESS OF SALISBURY

(*Adapted from the Inventory of the Historical Monuments of Hertfordshire with the permission of the Royal Commission and the consent of the Controller of His Majesty's Stationery Office.*)

BROADWATER HUNDRED

HATFIELD OR BISHOP'S HATFIELD

Robert Earl of Salisbury died in 1612, and was succeeded by his son William, who took the side of the Parliament in the Civil War, and subsequently sat in Cromwell's Lower House, though he had received a 'marquessate' by vote.[33] Charles I, while in the custody of the army, was at Hatfield House at the end of June 1647.[34] The Earl of Salisbury was, however, reconciled to the king at the Restoration, and was appointed high steward of St. Albans in 1663.[35] He died at Hatfield in December 1668, leaving as his heir his grandson James, the son of his younger son Charles Viscount Cranborne and Diana daughter and co-heir of James Earl of Dirletoun.[36] The third Earl of Salisbury died in 1683 and was succeeded by his son and namesake, who became a Roman Catholic and was made high steward of Hertford by James II in 1688.[37] In the following year he was impeached, but was discharged after two years' imprisonment. He died in 1713,[38] leaving as his heir his son James, who died in 1728 and was succeeded by his son of the same name, the sixth earl.

With the seventh earl, a fifth James who succeeded his father in 1780,[39] began a revival of the political traditions of the family. He had been M.P. for Great Bedwyn for six years (1774–80) and was elected for Launceston, when his father's death transferred him to the House of Lords[40]; in the same year he was made treasurer of the household and a privy councillor. He was Lord-Lieutenant of Hertfordshire from 1771 to 1823,[41] and from 1773 to 1815 Colonel of the county Militia. In this double capacity he entertained King George III on the occasion of a great review in June 1800.[42] 'Their Majesties in a post-chaise and four, and their Royal Highnesses the Princess Augusta, the Princess Elizabeth and the Princess Mary in a post-coach and four, attended by the Countess of Harrington, arrived at Hatfield at ten minutes before nine' in the morning on 13 June and 'breakfasted in the summer dining-room.' The review was held immediately after breakfast, and 'His Majesty and Their Royal Highnesses passed the highest encomiums on the appearance of the troops.'[43] Afterwards they 'walked on the lawn, and saw the different corps march into the square where the tables were laid for their reception' and 'then adjourned to the library and waited there until dinner was ready; when "The Roast Beef of Old England" was played as they passed through the gallery.'[44]

The seventh Earl of Salisbury was created Marquess 24 August 1789 and four years later was elected K.G.[45] He married in 1773 Mary Emilia Hill, daughter of the Earl of Downshire, a sportswoman whose fame is still remembered.[46] She played a conspicuous part in the meetings of the Archery Society[47] and was for many years Master of the Hatfield Hounds, only resigning when, at the age of seventy-eight, she found it wiser to go through gates than to jump them[48]; it is recorded of her that even then she considered herself well able to hunt with the harriers. She survived her husband and perished in the great fire which burned the west wing of Hatfield in 1835.[49] James Brownlow William second Marquess of Salisbury, who had taken by royal licence the surname of Gascoyne before that of Cecil, on his marriage to Miss Frances Mary Gascoyne of Childwall Hall, Lancashire, in 1821,[50] succeeded his father in 1823.[51] He had already been in Parliament ten years, as a member for Weymouth from 1813 to 1817 and for Hertford from 1817 to 1823.[52] From 1818 to 1827 he was a commissioner for Indian affairs and was elected K.G. in April 1842.[53] He was visited at Hatfield in 1846 by the Queen and Prince Consort, in honour of whose visit he placed new entrance gates of elaborate French metal work to the park.[54] He was Lord Privy Seal in 1852 and President of the Council 1858–9.[55] He died in April 1868 and was buried at Hatfield.[56]

Robert Arthur Talbot, his younger but eldest surviving son, succeeded him as third marquess. He had already achieved some political distinction, having been M.P. for Stamford in four Parliaments (1853–68) and Secretary of State for India 1866–7,[57] an office which he resumed on the return of the Conservatives to power in 1874. He was ambassador in 1876 to the Conference at Constantinople and joint ambassador to the Congress at Berlin in 1878; on his return from this mission he received the order of the Garter. In this year also he entered on that distinguished administration of the Foreign Office which will always remain his chief title to fame. In 1885 he became Prime Minister, continuing as Foreign Secretary until 1886, when he became First Lord of the Treasury. In the following year, however, he resumed his work at the Foreign Office, where he remained until the Conservatives lost power in 1892; and on the return of his party in 1895 he again became Prime Minister and Foreign Secretary, continuing in both offices until 1900, when he gave up the latter for the less arduous duties of Lord Privy Seal. During this period Hatfield became the scene of 'great official garden parties with their strange congeries of Eastern statesmen, Indian chiefs and Negro kings; warriors and diplomatists; the great world of London; the little world of the country; Tory members whom it was a duty to invite and Radical members who were delighted to be asked.'[58] One of the most important of these took place in July 1887, when Queen Victoria and many distinguished foreign visitors, who had come to England for her Jubilee, were present.[59] The weather on this occasion was beautiful, but the Hatfield garden parties were not always fortunate in this respect, for the first visit of the Prince and Princess of Wales and the Crown Prince and Princess of Germany in 1885 [59a] and that of the Shah of Persia in 1889 were overshadowed by 'sullen and menacing' or 'positively weeping skies.'[59b]

---

[33] V.C.H. Hertfordshire Families, 114.
[4] Cal. S. P. Dom. 1645–7, p. 564.
[35] V.C.H. Hertfordshire Families, 115.
[36] Ibid. 117.
[37] Ibid. 120.
[38] Ibid.
[39] Ibid. 121.
[40] Ibid.
[41] Ibid.
[42] Lewis Evans Collection of Pamphlets, 3 B. Tickets granting admission to Hatfield Park during the review were issued by Lord Salisbury (ibid.), a precedent which was followed by his grandson in favour of the Hatfield school children and their elders on the occasion of Queen Victoria's visit in her first Jubilee year (Daily Telegraph, 14 July 1887).
[43] Lewis Evans Collection, ut supra.
[44] Ibid.
[45] V.C.H. Hertfordshire Families, 121.
[46] Ibid.
[47] Home Cos. Mag. ii, 13.
[48] V.C.H. Hertfordshire Families, 112.
[49] Ibid.
[50] Ibid. 122.
[51] Ibid.
[52] Ibid.
[53] Ibid.
[54] Daily Telegraph, 9 July 1889.
[55] V.C.H. Hertfordshire Families, loc. cit.
[56] Ibid.
[57] Ibid. 123.
[58] The Times, 24 Aug. 1903.
[59] Daily Telegraph, 14 July 1887.
[59a] The Graphic, 25 July 1885.
[59b] Daily Telegraph, 9 July 1889.

A HISTORY OF HERTFORDSHIRE

The last of these great garden parties was held in the coronation year of King Edward VII, in which year Lord Salisbury resigned. He died 22 August 1903,

CECIL, Marquess of Salisbury

and was succeeded by his son James Edward Hubert, the present marquess.

HATFIELD HOUSE ARCHITECTURAL DESCRIPTION

In 1292 the house at Hatfield, already clearly of some size, was being enlarged, the Bishop of Ely then being given permission to divert a pathway from the churchyard to a field called Osmundescroft to enlarge his courtyard.[60] This fixes the site of the enlargement as being the same as that of the present stables, which themselves constitute the only remains of the palace in the form in which it was rebuilt by John de Morton, Bishop of Ely, about 1480. Nothing of earlier date than these stables now remains, but of the palace of which they formed the western wing a complete plan survives, made only a few years before the demolition of the palace. This plan, which is in the possession of the present Marquess of Salisbury, shows an imposing building of quadrangular form, with stair towers in the internal angles of the central court and a principal entrance in the centre of the outer eastern face. The great hall, solar, kitchen and butteries were in the west wing, now surviving. The state apartments were probably in the south wing. It was a building not only of some size, but also of considerable elaborateness, for Morton was a great builder, and when he became Archbishop of Canterbury in 1486 did much building in Canterbury; Maidstone, Lambeth and Croydon, besides rebuilding Wisbech Castle.

In 1538 in a survey of the building, then in the tenancy of Hannibal Zenzano, the king's master of the horse, the palace is described as 'a very goodly and stately manor place . . . constructed alle of

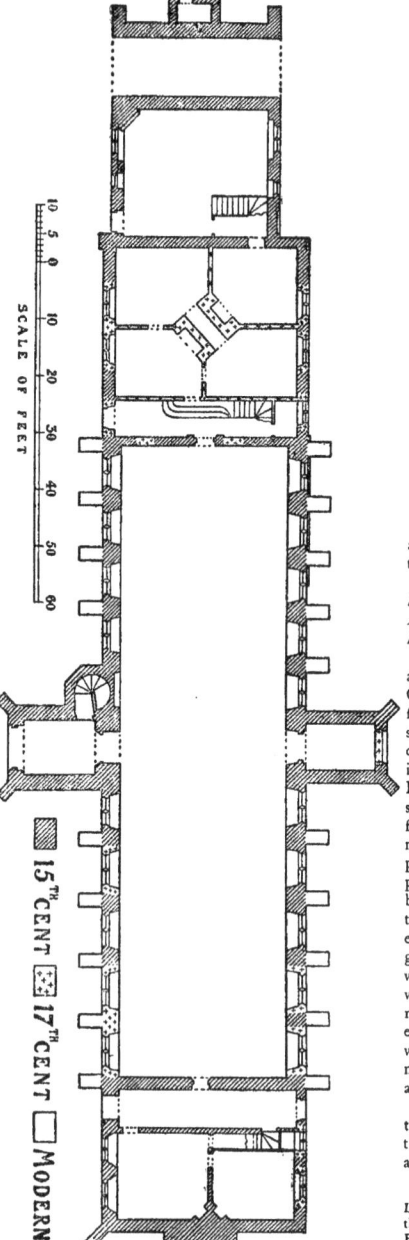

PLAN OF HALL OF THE OLD PALACE, HATFIELD[60a]

[60] Inq. p.m. 20 Edw. I, no. 69. In 1342-7 Bp. Bek of Lincoln granted licence to consecrate an altar in the chapel of the manor of Bishop's Hatfield (Linc. Epis. Reg. Mem. Bp. Bek, no. 7).
[60a] Adapted by permission from plan in *Rep. of Roy. Com. on Hist. Monum. of Herts.*

BROADWATER HUNDRED — HATFIELD OR BISHOP'S HATFIELD

brykke, having in the same very stately lodgynges with romes and offices to the same very necessary and expedient, albeit in some places it ys oute of reparaciones.'

There can be no doubt, however, that the necessary 'reparaciones' were made for its royal occupancy, and that when James I handed it over to the Earl of Salisbury it was in good repair. This, however, did not save it from destruction. The fashion of architecture had changed with the great national changes entailed in the coming of the Tudors and the passing of mediaeval life and thought, and accordingly Hatfield Palace gave place to Hatfield House.

The remnant of the old palace consists of one long range, facing east and west, and a gate-house to the north-west. Both are of brick, and the former is roofed with tiles. The position of the destroyed north, south and east wings can be traced in the sunk garden, between the present forecourt and the remaining old west wing. The roof of this west wing, which is of open timber construction, runs in one range over the hall and the great chamber over the kitchen and butteries, but the divisions of the latter have been removed, and between the solar and the kitchen the building is open from floor to roof and is fitted as stables. The kitchen has been divided into harness rooms and a laundry, but at the other end the solar remains, though the rooms beneath it have been subdivided by partitions.

The eastern exterior has suffered much from restoration and alteration. Its two extremities, which were originally interior to the north and south wings, were refaced in the 17th century, when those wings were destroyed. The windows are practically new, and the buttresses, nine in number on this, as on the west, side, are 19th-century additions. The central projecting porch, which forms a small tower of three stages, still retains its original doorway, which is moulded and has a four-centred head, but it is disused, and the floors of the stages have been removed.

The west side is in somewhat better condition, but here also the windows are completely restored, and the elevation of the hall is denuded of the projecting bays of a window and a fireplace shown in the old plan. Straight joints in the wall indicate their exact position. The central porch forms a tower, as on the east side, but here it is more massive. It has thicker walls, bold angle buttresses and a four-centred doorway of two moulded orders. The tower is of three stages and is decorated with patterns of black bricks, a brick corbel-table, and a plain parapet carried on a small arcade of semicircular arches, above which rise octagonal chimney-shafts from the fireplaces in each stage. The rooms are in good preservation and are lighted by small brick window openings with four-centred heads under square labels. In the north-east angle, formed by the tower and the wall of the wing, is a newel-turret showing three sides of an octagon.

The north and south ends of the west side are both gabled. The gable at the kitchen end appears to have been rebuilt, and all the windows are either modern or restored, but at the south, or solar, end little modification has taken place. The gable here is stepped and coped and terminates in a twisted chimney shaft. The ground floor door and windows appear to be a medley of old material reset and altogether new work. The first floor windows are original, though restored, the middle one being a three-light window with pointed heads under a four-centred main head having two orders and a label, all in moulded brick. This window is flanked by single lights like those of the porch.

The south end wall of the wing is blind. The north end has a stepped gable, and is marked by the small extension through which runs the archway, formerly to the kitchen court. This arch is four-centred, of two moulded orders, and the windows are like those of the rest of the building. The roof ridge is rather lower than that of the main building.

Internally the chief feature of the building is the continuous open timber roof of eleven bays, without variation of detail, which covers that portion of the wing formerly occupied by the hall and great upper chamber. The trusses rest on carved stone corbels, probably early 19th-century imitations of the originals, and have moulded arched braces and short cambered collars, with cross-trussing above them. The wall-plates and purlins are moulded, and from them rise short nearly vertical struts to each rafter. Between the trusses are ogee-shaped wind-braces, rising from immediately above the meeting level of the small struts with the rafters.

The gate-house, standing at the north-west of the west front, indicates the position of the north-west angle of the old west forecourt. It now faces into the High Street, and is a rectangular building of brick with an archway running through it near the north end. The porter's small room is to the north of this archway, but to the south of the entrance the gate-house has been converted into two cottages, which have undergone much repair. On the east side is a long shallow projection containing stairs and offices. A few original windows still exist. They are of two pointed lights, in moulded brick, but many, particularly on the west side, have 17th-century wooden casement frames ; some are modern. On the inner side the entrance archway was altered from a four-centred to a three-centred form. On the east side the wood lintel is original. It is cambered, and has carved angle brackets, so that the actual opening is four-centred. Over the archway is a room on the walls of which is a late 16th-century tempera painting, representing a lion hunt.

The present house stands on the west side of the park on a gentle eminence close to the church and to the east of the previous house. It is built of red brick with stone dressings, and the roofs are partly of lead and partly tiled. It is a particularly fine and complete example of early 17th-century domestic architecture, and its proportions, rather those of a palace than a country house, afford scope for the successful use of comparatively severe detail and symmetrical massing to achieve a dignity only toned to homeliness by the warm colouring of the material. Constant care has been exercised to preserve the character of the building, which, as originally erected, presented the same homogeneous aspect as at present. It was begun by the Earl of Salisbury immediately after the exchange of Theobalds with King James I had been effected (see above), and was completed in 1611. Although it has since undergone frequent repairs and some internal alterations, and although in 1835 the west wing from the chapel wall to the south end was completely gutted by fire, the general appearance of the building remains unaltered, and in many cases old material has been re-used in repairs, making it a matter of extreme difficulty to distinguish between old and new. In 1846 the cloister was glazed, and from 1868 to 1869 considerable interior alterations were made in the third stage. The forecourt on the north front was enlarged in the latter year, and the modern walls which surround it are pierced in imitation of the parapet of the house. The present gardens are apparently modern. The great hall was redecorated, and its ceiling painted, in 1878.

Though the design as it now stands is sufficiently imposing, it is not so magnificent as it was originally intended to be. A much more ambitious scheme was originally projected, and the State Papers Domestic of James I contain many detailed references to the saving of expense by the curtailing of ornament. The Earl of Salisbury does not appear to have employed an architect, and probably the design was largely his own. Thomas Wilson, his servant, seems to have made the plans; this Wilson was afterwards knighted and made Keeper of the State Papers. He had the assistance at Hatfield of William Basill, Surveyor of the King's Works. A very large part of the responsibility appears, from the correspondence in the State Papers Domestic, to have fallen on the shoulders of Robert Lemming, who was clerk of the works and who was entrusted with the actual designing of much of the detail. The joiners' work and wainscoting and the designing of the chimney-pieces were in the hands of one Jenever, a Dutchman living in London. Hoocker of St. Martin's Lane, who made the turners' work, would seem from his name to have been of the same nationality. A French engineer devised an elaborate system of water supply, and French gardeners laid out and maintained the gardens.

The house consists of a north main wing with east and west wings projecting southwards and inclosing a courtyard, and may be described as E shaped, the serif of the E being represented only by the very slight projection of the central south entrance. Its principal interior features are the great hall, in the north wing, with its screen and gallery, the grand staircase immediately to the east of the hall, and the long gallery on the first floor of the north wing and running the whole length of its south side. Below it the cloisters now form a second inclosed gallery on the ground floor.

The north wing is exactly regular, having a central entrance porch of three stages, of slight projection on the north or exterior face, which opens to the screens. The doorway is of stone, much restored, and has a semicircular head; it is flanked by pairs of stone columns with a complete Doric order, and above it a curvilinear pierced cresting of stone. The screens continue through the building to the cloisters, into which they open exactly opposite the central entrance on the courtyard side. On either side of the north entrance are three windows of three lights, those to the east being the windows of the hall. Flanking them to east and west are two bay windows, the eastern being the last window of the hall and the western that of the steward's room. The east and west extremities of the north face are the plain butts of the east and west wings, each with a central projecting bay with lights of four stories, containing stairs, and a six-light window carried up to the full height next the central portion of the north side. The east and west wings are irregular in plan on both their sides, but almost exactly correspond to one another. On the east face the summer drawing room, occupying the north-east angle, has two bay windows, one of three and the other of five sides, this latter being answered by a flat six-light window in the west wing and constituting almost the only external difference between the two wings. The yew room, with a single oriel, balances the northern of the two drawing room windows. The face of the wing is then set back somewhat, and in the recess rises the oriel of the morning room. The study, with an external door in its out-set north wall, has a square projecting window in the east face, and at the corner of the room beyond it to the south stands a turret rising above the parapet—one of four finishing the southern extremities of the east and west wings. In the west wing the upper part of the kitchen answers the drawing room of the east wing, the maple room corresponds to the yew room and the chapel to the morning room. On each inner face of these wings is a central doorway from the courtyard, with flat pilasters supporting a complete Doric order over an archway, flanked on either side by a bay window rising to the full height of the first two stages. Above this the third stage is set back behind a flat cornice and is crested with a pierced parapet concealing the roof and stopped at the ends by the third stage of the north-east and north-west blocks and by the angle turrets at the south.

The most ornate portion of the exterior is the south face of the centre wing. It is of two principal stages of stone with an open parapet, and behind it a third stage, set back with four stepped and curved gables, masking the stacks of the north side of the wing and connected by a second pierced parapet. These gables are set in pairs on either side of the third stage of the central compartment containing the principal south entrance-porch. This third stage is blind and forms a screen for the display of the full achievement of the Earl of Salisbury. Behind this screen rises a wooden clock-tower of three stages, the first two with pairs of columns at the angles on each face supporting an entablature; the lowest order is Doric, with arches between. In the second stage is the clock face, between Ionic columns, and above the second entablature the third stage rises, from a square balustrade with figures at the angles, in the form of an octagonal rusticated arcade surmounted by a cornice and cupola with a vane.

The ground stage of the south front is occupied wholly by the arcade of the cloister and the central porch, the whole consisting of nine bays. The arcade has semicircular arches, four on each side of the porch, forming part of a Doric arcade, with flat pilasters enriched with arabesques and fluted,[60a] between the responds, and elaborate carving in the spandrels. The metopes of the frieze are set with ox-skulls alternating with carbuncles. Above the

---

[60a] These were originally projected to have had columns in front of them (S. P. Dom. Jas. I, xlv, 69). 'If front of gallery be built with pilasters as it is begun, and leave out the columns, he may deduct £120.' Many other modifications of the original design are to be traced in the same place, and in ibid. c. 84, where estimates of reduction of expenses are set out in full. See article by W. Page in the *Trans. St. Albans and Herts. Arch. Soc.* 1901–2, i (4) (new ser.), 334, in which the correspondence regarding the building of the house is printed.

	Ash	Ash
ime Room	Room	Dressing
		Room

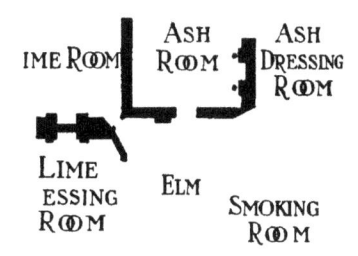

Lime
essing   Elm
Room   Smoking
                 Room

Chapel

Maple Room

Upper Part
of
Kitchen

ajesty's Stationery Office)

A HISTORY OF HERTFORDSHIRE

material has been re-used in repairs, making it a matter of extreme difficulty to distinguish between old and new. In 1846 the cloister was glazed, and from 1868 to 1869 considerable interior alterations were made in the third stage. The forecourt on the north front was enlarged in the latter year, and the modern walls which surround it are pierced in imitation of the parapet of the house. The present gardens are apparently modern. The great hall was redecorated, and its ceiling painted, in 1878.

Though the design as it now stands is sufficiently imposing, it is not so magnificent as it was originally intended to be. A much more ambitious scheme was originally projected, and the State Papers Domestic of James I contain many detailed references to the saving of expense by the curtailing of ornament. The Earl of Salisbury does not appear to have employed an architect, and probably the design was largely his own. Thomas Wilson, his servant, seems to have made the plans; this Wilson was afterwards knighted and made Keeper of the State Papers. He had the assistance at Hatfield of William Basill, Surveyor of the King's Works. A very large part of the responsibility appears, from the correspondence in the State Papers Domestic, to have fallen on the shoulders of Robert Lemming, who was clerk of the works and who was entrusted with the actual designing of much of the detail. The joiners' work and wainscoting and the designing of the chimney-pieces were in the hands of one Jenever, a Dutchman living in London. Hoocker of St. Martin's Lane, who made the turners' work, would seem from his name to have been of the same nationality. A French engineer devised an elaborate system of water supply, and French gardeners laid out and maintained the gardens.

The house consists of a north main wing with east and west wings projecting southwards and inclosing a courtyard, and may be described as E shaped, the serif of the E being represented only by the very slight projection of the central south entrance. Its principal interior features are the great hall, in the north wing, with its screen and gallery, the grand staircase immediately to the east of the hall, and the long gallery on the first floor of the north wing and running the whole length of its south side. Below it the cloisters now form a second inclosed gallery on the ground floor.

The north wing is exactly regular, having a central entrance porch of three stages, of slight projection on the north or exterior face, which opens to the screens. The doorway is of stone, much restored, and has a semicircular head; it is flanked by pairs of stone columns with a complete Doric order, and above it a curvilinear pierced cresting of stone. The screens continue through the building to the cloisters, into which they open exactly opposite the central entrance on the courtyard side. On either side of the north entrance are three windows of three lights, those to the east being the windows of the hall. Flanking them to east and west are two bay windows, the eastern being the last window of the hall and the western that of the steward's room. The east and west extremities of the north face are the plain butts of the east and west wings, each with a central projecting bay with lights of four stories, containing stairs, and a six-light window carried up to the full height next the central portion of the north side. The east and west wings are irregular in plan on both their sides, but almost exactly correspond to one another. On the east face the summer drawing room, occupying the north-east angle, has two bay windows, one of three and the other of five sides, this latter being answered by a flat six-light window in the west wing and constituting almost the only external difference between the two wings. The yew room, with a single oriel, balances the northern of the two drawing room windows. The face of the wing is then set back somewhat, and in the recess rises the oriel of the morning room. The study, with an external door in its out-set north wall, has a square projecting window in the east face, and at the corner of the room beyond it to the south stands a turret rising above the parapet—one of four finishing the southern extremities of the east and west wings. In the west wing the upper part of the kitchen answers the drawing room of the east wing, the maple room corresponds to the yew room and the chapel to the morning room. On each inner face of these wings is a central doorway from the courtyard, with flat pilasters supporting a complete Doric order over an archway, flanked on either side by a bay window rising to the full height of the first two stages. Above this the third stage is set back behind a flat cornice and is crested with a pierced parapet concealing the roof and stopped at the ends by the third stage of the north-east and north-west blocks and by the angle turrets at the south.

The most ornate portion of the exterior is the south face of the centre wing. It is of two principal stages of stone with an open parapet, and behind it a third stage, set back with four stepped and curved gables, masking the stacks of the north side of the wing and connected by a second pierced parapet. These gables are set in pairs on either side of the third stage of the central compartment containing the principal south entrance-porch. This third stage is blind and forms a screen for the display of the full achievement of the Earl of Salisbury. Behind this screen rises a wooden clock-tower of three stages, the first two with pairs of columns at the angles on each face supporting an entablature; the lowest order is Doric, with arches between. In the second stage is the clock face, between Ionic columns, and above the second entablature the third stage rises, from a square balustrade with figures at the angles, in the form of an octagonal rusticated arcade surmounted by a cornice and cupola with a vane.

The ground stage of the south front is occupied wholly by the arcade of the cloister and the central porch, the whole consisting of nine bays. The arcade has semicircular arches, four on each side of the porch, forming part of a Doric arcade, with flat pilasters enriched with arabesques and fluted,[60a] between the responds, and elaborate carving in the spandrels. The metopes of the frieze are set with ox-skulls alternating with carbuncles. Above the

---

[60a] These were originally projected to have had columns in front of them (S. P. Dom. Jas. I, xlv, 69). 'If front of gallery be built with pilasters as it is begun, and leave out the columns, he may deduct £120.' Many other modifications of the original design are to be traced in the same place, and in ibid. c. 84, where estimates of reduction of expenses are set out in full. See article by W. Page in the *Trans. St. Albans and Herts. Arch. Soc.* 1901–2, i (4) (new ser.), 334, in which the correspondence regarding the building of the house is printed.

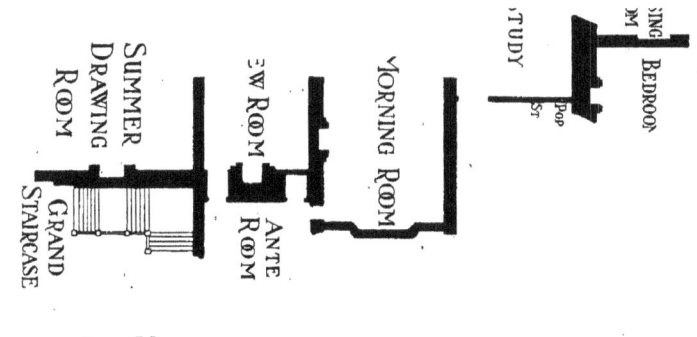

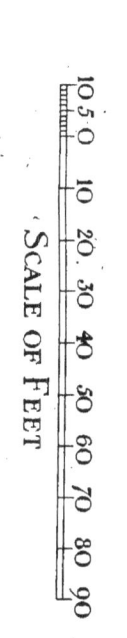

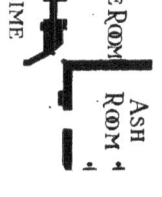

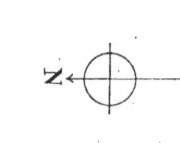

BEDROOM
'SING
ROOM
STUDY
St Pop
MORNING ROOM
NEW ROOM
ANTE ROOM
SUMMER DRAWING ROOM
GRAND STAIRCASE
MARBLE HALL

N ←

SCALE OF FEET
10 5 0 10 20 30 40 50 60 70 80 90

UPPER PART OF KITCHEN

TIME ROOM
ASH ROOM
LIME

BROADWATER HUNDRED — HATFIELD OR BISHOP'S HATFIELD

frieze a deep cornice, mitred and broken out over the pilasters, forms the basis of the second stage (the exterior of the long gallery), which has eight rectangular windows of two lights with a transom, four on each side of the central bay, and separated by flat Ionic pilasters on flat plinths to the sill level, the plinths being sculptured with trophies of arms, including both classical and later forms, even firearms. The continuous frieze is of flowers, fruit and grotesques. Above the cornice of this stage is the openwork parapet, the strapwork piercing being interrupted above the pilasters of the lower stages and at midway intervals between those points by flat balusters, from which, above the coping, rise figures.

The central bay, containing the porch, resembles the rest, but projects some 5 ft. from the wall face. On either side of the entrance archway are pairs of round Doric columns, over which the entablature breaks out. Similarly on the first stage pairs of Ionic columns flank the central three-light rectangular window with two transoms of the long gallery, and the Cecil achievement in the third stage (mentioned above) has on either side of it a pair of slender coupled Corinthian columns, with a frieze like that of the second stage. Above the cornice of this stage is a solid parapet with the date 1611 in large raised figures, and on it above the coupled columns are four lions carrying shields. The centre of the parapet is surmounted by the Cecil crest in open stonework.

The screens, entered from the north porch, have on the west side a stone arcading of three Doric bays, either wholly modern or much restored. On the south a doorway with pilasters and a pediment opens to the cloister, and has over it the Cecil arms and quarterings in painted wood, with the date 1575, possibly brought from Theobalds. On the east side is the oak screen of the hall in five bays. On the screens side the posts form a plain Doric arcade, the arches filled with large moulded panels and pierced lunettes. The frieze is of pierced strapwork, which appears to be modern. The central bay contains the doorway to the hall. On the side facing the hall this screen is elaborately carved and decorated. The posts are carved as grotesque caryatides, and the panels, four in each bay, are filled with large oval cartouches and scroll-work. The lunettes above are carved as shells, and above them are bold carved brackets with grotesque work and heads supporting the upper stage, which overhangs and may originally have been an open balcony. It is divided into five bays by flat carved pilasters rising from breaks in the cornice above the brackets, with blind-pierced designs between in the side bays, and in the centre two panels containing scrolled cartouches of the Cecil arms with quarterings. Above these panels, and divided by grotesque pilasters with heads below the capitals, is an arcade with carved spandrels and flatly ornamented panels, obviously a later addition, in the four side bays, while the centre bay contains two small arched sight-holes with carved spandrels between, and over them a panel with two putti supporting the Cecil crest and an earl's coronet of the Caroline form, which must therefore necessarily be of later date than the original building.[60b] It is set in an arch like that of the rest of this arcade. The sight-holes open into the ante-room of the winter dining room on the first floor. At the east end of the hall is a gallery of similar design to that of the screen, supported on grotesque brackets. The coved soffit is plastered, and was painted in 1878. The front forms an open arcade of twelve bays, with grotesque pilasters and a cornice and a balustrade of pierced strapwork. In the centre at the top is an achievement of the Cecil arms. The screen and the gallery have both undergone much restoration, but the constructional parts, with their decoration, are all original. The panelling of the hall, divided into bays by Doric pilasters, is either modern or very much restored. The fireplace and mantel on the south are modern. The south wall above the panelling is covered with 17th-century tapestry.

Below the gallery are two doorways with round heads and square stone architraves; one of them has one of the few original doors in the house; it has small oblong and oval panels and moulded styles and rails.

The hall ceiling is plastered and decorated with bands of ornament in low relief, these bands inclosing flat panels, which were filled with paintings in 1878; the ceiling is coved, and is divided into four bays by moulded principals with pendants, and decorated with scroll work. These descend to carved lions holding shields, and resting on the moulded wall-plate. The lunette spaces inclosed in the line of the coved ceiling at each end of the hall have a low-relief filling of flat arabesques. There was no dais in the original construction of the floor, which is in squares of black and white marble. Among the furniture are two long tables of early 17th-century date,[61] with pierced square baluster legs.

The cloister, entered from the south end of the screens, is altered in character by the filling of the arcade with pierced stonework containing glazing, of a monotonous honeycomb pattern, converting it from an exterior to an interior feature. It is now paved with squares of black and white marble, and has on the north wall four 17th-century panels of tapestry, and on both sides are stands of armour, mostly of the late 16th century, but a good deal restored, and including some pieces of doubtful antiquity. At each end of the cloister three steps lead up to the wings. The ceiling is modern, plastered with an arabesque design in low relief.

The grand staircase, at the east end of the hall, is of open newel construction, and has quarter-landings at every six steps. The moulded balusters are square-raked, are berm-shaped with Ionic capitals in the place of heads, and have between them arches with carved spandrels, and the balusters and newels are carved in high relief with trophies and grotesque designs. The newels rise to some height above the moulded rail in herm shape, and are surmounted by nude amorini holding various objects, and lions supporting shields. The soffits and string are ornamented with strapwork and pendants. Against the wall is a similar balustrade with newels and figures, and on the first landing is a pair of carved dog-gates.

[60b] S. P. Dom. Jas. I, lxiii, 88 (1). 17 May 1611: 'The hall is fully joined with tables and forms fitting to it, the lower part of the screen is set up and finished by the carpenters and carvers, and the upper part of the screen is framed and carved and is now fitting up.' This cannot refer to the filling of the upper arcade as at present, but may quite well refer to the arcade *minus* its filling.

[61] See note 60b above.

A HISTORY OF HERTFORDSHIRE

At the foot of this stair is the doorway to the summer drawing room, with the original stone architrave and semicircular head. The moulded abaci and stopped jambs are semi-classical in type. The summer drawing room retains its original panelling, which is elaborately mitred, and divided into bays by fluted Doric pilasters, supporting a heavy cornice and a frieze of a small order of Ionic pilasters. The panels contain inlaid and 'planted' arabesque work. The mantelpiece is a marble copy of the oak original, which is now in King James's bedroom. The ceiling is either completely restored or modern.

In the morning room is a large mantelpiece of 17th-century date, of various coloured marbles with caryatides and herms on either side, and some carvings of figure subjects in high relief brought from elsewhere. The remaining five rooms in the wing are modern, but have mantelpieces made up of pieces of 16th and 17th-century carving, probably Dutch. The Poplar staircase is modern.

In the west wing the Adam and Eve staircase, which takes its name from a picture hanging on its wall, is either wholly remodelled or so restored as to present scarcely any original feature. It has turned balusters and a moulded rail. At the head of the stairs is a doorway leading to the west ante-room of the long gallery, with two wooden Corinthian columns attached to pilasters on either side, of early 18th-century work. The walls of the staircase are panelled with made-up old material. In the chapel the bay window on to the court forms the sanctuary, and is glazed with 17th-century glass with Biblical subjects; this glass seems to be of French, Flemish and Dutch workmanship.[61a] It was certainly made expressly for these windows. The walls are covered to the soffit of the gallery with panelling, original but much restored; the front of the gallery has a carved arcade with closed panels below; the openings are round-headed, the pilasters between them are carved, and the cornice is moulded. The ceiling is coved, and is set with carved grotesque brackets of late 16th-century date, which were brought from Hoddesdon, where they formed part of the old Market House. The ceiling and gallery have been painted in modern times. The old seating[61b] has been replaced by modern, and the west screen is also modern. The floor is paved with marble.[62]

The long gallery, running the whole length of the north wing above the cloister, has its walls covered with panelling divided into bays by fluted Ionic pilasters. For these pilasters square columns are substituted at either end, where the gallery opens to the ante-rooms. The cornice has a considerable projection, and is much enriched, and above it is a small Corinthian order with detached columns and a dentil cornice. The upper part of the panelling in the bays of the lower arcade consists of rusticated arcading, with arabesque decoration, all worked in thin applied planking. The panels of the upper order and the lower part of the bays of the lower order are filled with extremely elaborate mitred and moulded panels, of the fitted L and square type. This panelling is of the original design, and contains a large proportion of original material, though it is said to have been entirely renewed early in the 19th century. The ceiling is original though much restored, and is flat, richly decorated with pendants and a flat arabesque pattern.[62a] The mantelpieces are not original. The ante-rooms at each end, and that of the winter dining-room, have modern decoration copied from that of the gallery. The door on the north side of the west ante-room of the gallery opens on to the Adam and Eve staircase through the Corinthian portico described with the staircase.

In the library, which also opens off this ante-room, is no decoration of original date except the mantel piece, which is of large size in black and white marble. It is of two orders, Doric and Ionic, with detached circular columns. In a central panel is a mosaic portrait of Sir Robert Cecil, 1608.

The summer dining room is lined with panelling, either modern or wholly re-worked, and contains a large marble mantelpiece with figures in high relief and an achievement of the Cecil arms. This mantelpiece is made up of portions of two 17th-century mantelpieces.

King James's bedroom, facing outwards in the middle of the east wing, contains the original oak mantelpiece which was formerly in the summer drawing room. This has square baluster columns, moulded and enriched with carving, supporting a heavy mantelshelf. Above this are three small Ionic columns, and between them moulded panels containing arabesques surmounted by a deep cornice with elaborate enrichment. There is some late 17th-century furniture in this room. It is completely covered with yellow damask, which is glued to the woodwork. The Wellington room, on the opposite side of the same wing, contains some 17th-century tapestry panels.

King James's drawing room, which occupies the whole of the north-east angle of the first stage, contains a massive original mantelpiece of black, white and veined marble. The lower part has in the angles black fluted Doric columns, with architrave and metope. Above is the shelf, supported where it projects in the centre by a fluted bracket flanked by modillions. The upper portion consists of four black Corinthian columns on pilasters with scrolled cartouches, forming part of an order with a heavy modillioned cornice, above which are panels, those at the sides containing circles inclosing profiles in low relief in black marble, and the central one a rectangular black slab. The two side bays between the columns have panels of veined marble, and the central bay contains a semi-domed niche, in which stands a statue of King James I, painted to represent bronze. The ceiling of this room has elaborate arabesques

---

[61a] S. P. Dom. Jas. I, lvjii, 9. 'Montague Jenings . . . intreats him to tell Mr. Bowle that he will bring a just mould of the light of the chapel windows according to the proportion concluded of between them, at his next return to London.'
[61b] Ibid. lxv, 3. '1 July 1611. The Chappell. The closett chimney peece and hanginges chaires and stooles sutable readie (wanteth good andirons). The chappell, the frise and pulpit to be don uppon Thursdaie.'
[62] Ibid. lxiii, 88 (1). '17 May 1611. The chapel is now a-paving by the mason.'
[62a] Ibid. '17 May 1611. The frett ceiling in the gallery will be fully finished with the whitening of it on Tuesday, the gallery will then be ready for the joinery work which is framed at London.' '1 July 1611. The Gallerie. The chimney peeces of plain wainscott sett uppe. The south side wilbe wainscotted but not the frise, by Thursdaie. Both the ends wainscotted but to be hanged. The returne to be hanged for the tyme and the prospect in the haule over the skreene to be meuved up this daie. The north side to be hanged.'

98

WALNUT ROOM   WALNUT DRESSING ROOM

BEACONSFIELD ROOM

Y

BRARY

At the foot of this stair is the doorway to the summer drawing room, with the original stone architrave and semicircular head. The moulded abaci and stopped jambs are semi-classical in type. The summer drawing room retains its original panelling, which is elaborately mitred, and divided into bays by fluted Doric pilasters, supporting a heavy cornice and a frieze of a small order of Ionic pilasters. The panels contain inlaid and 'planted' arabesque work. The mantelpiece is a marble copy of the oak original, which is now in King James's bedroom. The ceiling is either completely restored or modern.

In the morning room is a large mantelpiece of 17th-century date, of various coloured marbles with caryatides and herms on either side, and some carvings of figure subjects in high relief brought from elsewhere. The remaining five rooms in the wing are modern, but have mantelpieces made up of pieces of 16th and 17th-century carving, probably Dutch. The Poplar staircase is modern.

In the west wing the Adam and Eve staircase, which takes its name from a picture hanging on its wall, is either wholly remodelled or so restored as to present scarcely any original feature. It has turned balusters and a moulded rail. At the head of the stairs is a doorway leading to the west ante-room of the long gallery, with two wooden Corinthian columns attached to pilasters on either side, of early 18th-century work. The walls of the staircase are panelled with made-up old material. In the chapel the bay window on to the court forms the sanctuary, and is glazed with 17th-century glass with Biblical subjects; this glass seems to be of French, Flemish and Dutch workmanship.[61a] It was certainly made expressly for these windows. The walls are covered to the soffit of the gallery with panelling, original but much restored; the front of the gallery has a carved arcade with closed panels below; the openings are round-headed, the pilasters between them are carved, and the cornice is moulded. The ceiling is coved, and is set with carved grotesque brackets of late 16th-century date, which were brought here from Hoddesdon, where they formed part of the old Market House. The ceiling and gallery have been painted in modern times. The old seating[61b] has been replaced by modern, and the west screen is also modern. The floor is paved with marble.[62]

The long gallery, running the whole length of the north wing above the cloister, has its walls covered with panelling divided into bays by fluted Ionic pilasters. For these pilasters square columns are substituted at either end, where the gallery opens to the ante-rooms. The cornice has a considerable projection, and is much enriched, and above it is a small Corinthian order with detached columns and a dentil cornice. The upper part of the panelling in the bays of the lower arcade consists of rusticated arcading, with arabesque decoration, all worked in thin applied planking. The panels of the upper order and the lower part of the bays of the lower order are filled with extremely elaborate mitred and moulded panels, of the fitted L and square type. This panelling is of the original design, and contains a large proportion of original material, though it is said to have been entirely renewed early in the 19th century. The ceiling is original though much restored, and is flat, richly decorated with pendants and a flat arabesque pattern.[63a] The mantelpieces are not original. The ante-rooms at each end, and that of the winter dining-room, have modern decoration copied from that of the gallery. The door on the north side of the west ante-room of the gallery opens on to the Adam and Eve staircase through the Corinthian portico described with the staircase.

In the library, which also opens off this ante-room, is no decoration of original date except the mantel piece, which is of large size in black and white marble. It is of two orders, Doric and Ionic, with detached circular columns. In a central panel is a mosaic portrait of Sir Robert Cecil, 1608.

The summer dining room is lined with panelling, either modern or wholly re-worked, and contains a large marble mantelpiece with figures in high relief and an achievement of the Cecil arms. This mantelpiece is made up of portions of two 17th-century mantelpieces.

King James's bedroom, facing outwards in the middle of the east wing, contains the original oak mantelpiece which was formerly in the summer drawing room. This has square baluster columns, moulded and enriched with carving, supporting a heavy mantelshelf. Above this are three small Ionic columns, and between them moulded panels containing arabesques surmounted by a deep cornice with elaborate enrichment. There is some late 17th-century furniture in this room. It is completely covered with yellow damask, which is glued to the woodwork. The Wellington room, on the opposite side of the same wing, contains some 17th-century tapestry panels.

King James's drawing room, which occupies the whole of the north-east angle of the first stage, contains a massive original mantelpiece of black, white and veined marble. The lower part has in the angles black fluted Doric columns, with architrave and metope. Above is the shelf, supported where it projects in the centre by a fluted bracket flanked by modillions. The upper portion consists of four black Corinthian columns on pilasters with scrolled cartouches, forming part of an order with a heavy modillioned cornice, above which are panels, those at the sides containing circles inclosing profiles in low relief in black marble, and the central one a rectangular black slab. The two side bays between the columns have panels of veined marble, and the central bay contains a semi-domed niche, in which stands a statue of King James I, painted to represent bronze. The ceiling of this room has elaborate arabesques

---

[61a] S. P. Dom. Jas. I, lviii, 9. 'Montague Jenings . . . intreats him to tell Mr. Bowle that he will bring a just mould of the light of the chapel windows according to the proportion concluded of between them, at his next return to London.'
[61b] Ibid. lxv, 3. '1 July 1611. The Chappell. The closett chimney peece and hanginges chaires and stooles sutable readie (wanteth good andirons). The chappell, the frise and pulpit to be don uppon Thursdaie.'
[62] Ibid. lxiii, 88 (1). '17 May 1611. The chapel is now a-paving by the mason.'
[63a] Ibid. '17 May 1611. The frett ceiling in the gallery will be fully finished with the whitening of it on Tuesday, the gallery will then be ready for the joinery work which is framed at London.' '1 July 1611. The Gallerie. The chimney peeces of plain wainscott sett uppe. The south side wilbe wainscotted but not the frise, by Thursdaie. Both the ends wainscotted but to be hanged. The retorne to be hanged for the tyme and the prospect in the haule over the skreene to be meuved up this daie. The north side to be hanged.'

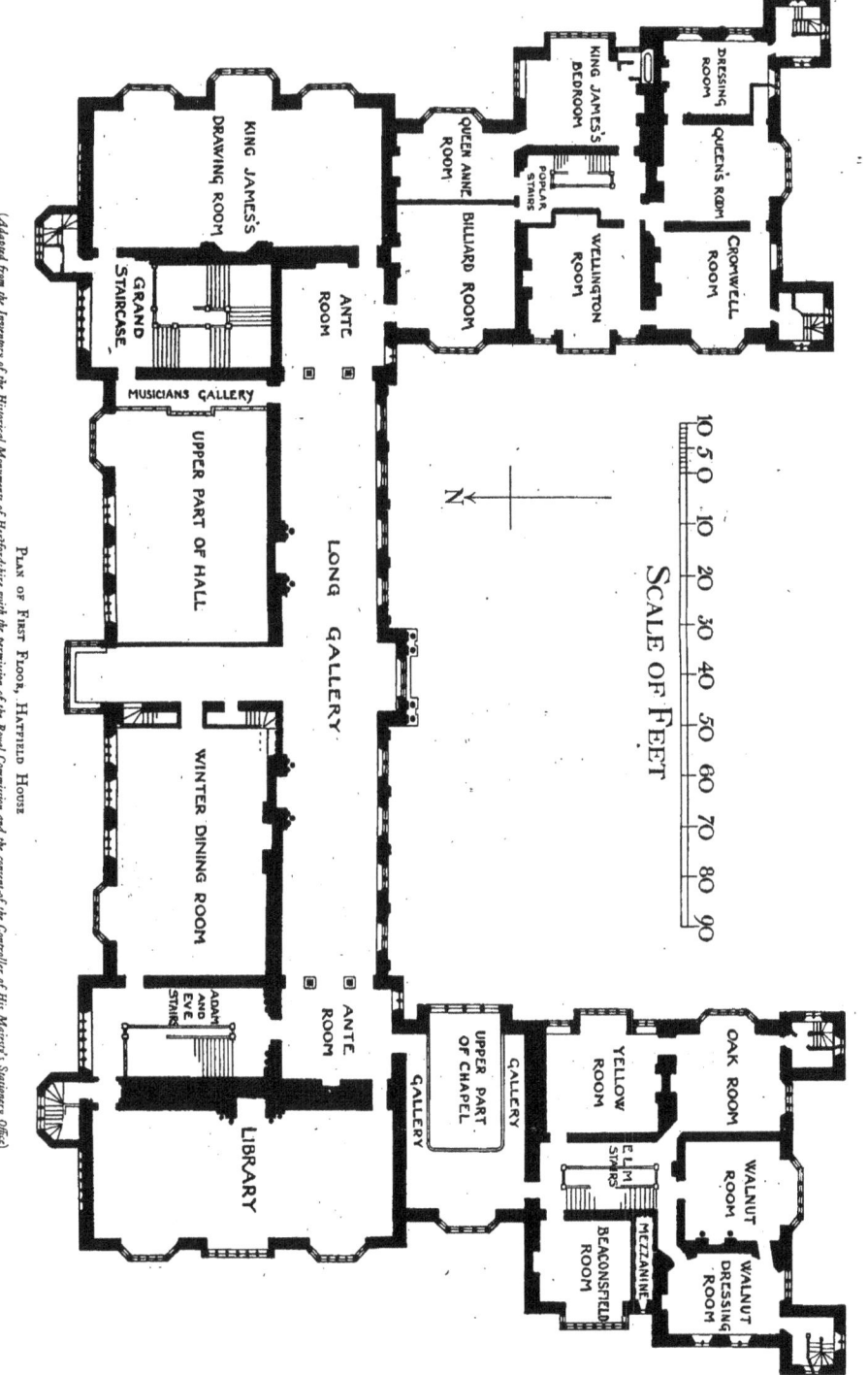

PLAN OF FIRST FLOOR, HATFIELD HOUSE
(Adapted from the Inventory of the Historical Monuments of Hertfordshire with the permission of the Royal Commission and the consent of the Controller of His Majesty's Stationery Office)

and pendants, which are modern. The walls, of which the lower part is panelled, are covered with portraits.

The Abbots of Ely claimed in Hatfield the comprehensive franchises granted to them by successive royal charters. These included exemption from suit at the shire and hundred courts, and freedom for the abbot's men from toll throughout England.[67b]
In 1251 a grant of free warren was obtained from Henry III.[63] In 1534 the freedom of the bishop's men from tolls in all markets and fairs in England was again claimed and confirmed.[64] A fair was granted to the Bishop of Ely in Hatfield in 1226. It was to be held annually for four days, on the vigil and feast of St. John the Baptist and two days following (23–6 June).[65] In 1318 the date was changed to the vigil and feast of St. Etheldreda the Virgin and two days following[66] (16–19 October). In 1466 it was restricted to three days, the vigil, feast and morrow of St. Etheldreda.[67] In 1538 the fairs were held on the feasts of St. Luke the Evangelist (18 October) and St. George (23 April),[68] but there is no charter recording the alteration until the manor was granted to the Earl of Warwick in 1550. The right to hold a court of pie powder is mentioned in this grant.[69] The two fairs are still held; that on 18 October is for toys.[70]

The right of holding a weekly market on Thursday was granted to the bishop in 1226.[71] The day was altered to Tuesday in 1318,[72] and to Wednesday in 1466,[73] but before 1538 was changed back to Thursday,[74] and was confirmed on that day in 1550.[75] A market was held in 1792, but was discontinued before 1888.[76]

Hatfield possessed four mills in 1086,[77] of which three survive, all on the River Lea: Lemsford Mills at the southern extremity of Brockett Park, Cecil Mill at the north-eastern corner of the Home Park, and the third, which gives its name to Mill Green, a little north of the park. In 1277 the bishop had two mills 'under one roof.'[78]

The free fishery of the bishop in the River Lea extended in 1277 from Hatfield Mills, which would probably be Cecil Mill, to the bridge of Stanberue (Stanborough), and from there to the mill of Simon Fitz Adam (Lemsford Mill), where the latter had joint rights of fishery with the bishop. Beyond this the bishop's right extended to Stonenbrig[79] (later Stoken Bridge).[80] The same extent of fishery is mentioned in 1538.[81]

In 1391 the Bishop of Lincoln granted to the Bishop of Ely licence to confirm, elect and celebrate orders, prove wills and consecrate oil in his manor of Hatfield.[82]

In the account of the manor of Hatfield given in the Domesday Survey there is no mention of parks, but the domain is said to possess woods sufficient to feed 2,000 swine,[83] which indicates a large area of forest. In fact, the manor was given to the monks of Ely by King Edgar in order that they might have wood for their building.[84] In the 13th century at least two parks had already been inclosed. The Great Park, or Hatfield Wood, had an area of about 1,000 acres, and provided pasture for the horses and cattle and pannage for the swine of the tenants in chief of the bishop, all of whom had rights of common and 'woderight' in it in 1277.[85] In 1538 all freeholders and copyholders holding within 'Bukamwykehide' had rights of common feeding in it. Lanes and highways passing through it were common to all inhabitants of the lordship indifferently.[86] It was in the custody of a bailiff in the 14th century,[87] who later became keeper or master of the game. This office was held in 1538 and later by Sir Anthony Denny, the king's servant.[88] At this time the Great Park contained 10,000 oaks and beeches, valued at 8d. each.[89] It seems to have extended over the south-eastern projection of the parish, which lies between Essendon and Northaw, and probably stretched from Woodside eastward to the hamlet of Newgate Street, for in the reign of Henry VIII a house was purchased there to form one of its lodges.[90] At this time it had a circuit of 7 miles, and extended from 'a place called Fisshes Grove to Hansmeregate.' There were within it eighteen deer of antlers and sixty-two raskells.[91] The breed of deer kept there was evidently a good one, for in 1621 the king requested the Earl of Salisbury to spare him a brace of bucks from his park to bestow on the men of Northaw, his own stock of deer being 'much wasted.'[92]

The Middle Park had an extent of 350 acres, and in 1277 was stated to be the private property of the lord of the manor, the tenants having no rights in it.[93] In 1538 it contained 2,000 oaks and beeches. The pasture was scant but sufficient for the deer, of which there were seventy-three raskells and seven deer of antlers. At that date it is recorded that the little lodge was not thoroughly repaired,[94] and about this time payments are recorded for building a new house there, with a frame-house and new kitchen.[95]

It was probably this park which in 1252 was the scene of an outrage by William de Valence, afterwards lord of the manor of Gacelyns. It is recounted by Matthew Paris that William came from his castle of Hertford and violently and against the decree of the king entered the park of the Bishop of Ely near his manor of Hatfield and hunted therein without the licence of anyone, and afterwards he went to the bishop's house, and because they would

[67b] *Plac. de Quo Warr.* (Rec. Com.), 279.
[63] Assize R. 325; Charter quoted in Dugdale, *Mon.* i, 486.
[64] Anct. D. (P.R.O.), B 3764.
[65] Close, 10 Hen. III, m. 17.
[66] Chart. R. 12 Edw. II, m. 16, no. 58.
[67] Ibid. 5–7 Edw. IV, no. 12.
[68] Land Rev. Misc. Bks. ccxvi.
[69] Pat. 4 Edw. VI, pt. viii, m. 8.
[70] *Rep. on Markets and Tolls*, i, 170.
[71] Close, 10 Hen. III, m. 17.
[72] Chart. R. 12 Edw. II, m. 16, no. 58.
[73] Ibid. 5–7 Edw. IV, no. 12.

[74] Land Rev. Misc. Bks. ccxvi.
[75] Pat. 4 Edw. VI, pt. viii, m. 8.
[76] *Rep. on Markets and Tolls*, i, 170.
[77] *V.C.H. Herts.* i, 311b.
[78] Cott. MSS. Claud. cxi.
[79] Ibid.
[80] Land Rev. Misc. Bks. ccxvi.
[81] Ibid.
[82] Linc. Epis. Reg. Mem. Bp. Buckingham, fol. 376.
[83] *V.C.H. Herts.* i, 311b.
[84] *Liber Eliensis* (Impensis Soc.), i, 115.

[85] Cott. MSS. Claud. C xi.
[86] Land Rev. Misc. Bks. ccxvi.
[87] Feet of F. Herts. 17 Edw. II, no. 384.
[88] *L. and P. Hen. VIII*, xvii, 692.
[89] Rentals and Surv. R. Herts. 276.
[90] Land Rev. Misc. Bks. xvi (6).
[91] Ibid. ccxvi; Exch. Spec. Com. Eliz. no. 1026.
[92] *Cal. S. P. Dom.* 1619–23, p. 278.
[93] Cott. MSS. Claud. C xi.
[94] Land Rev. Misc. Bks. ccxvi; Rentals and Surv. R. Herts. 276.
[95] Land Rev. Misc. Bks. xvi (6).

A HISTORY OF HERTFORDSHIRE

not give him any drink but ale he broke down the door of the buttery, making a great tumult, swearing and using evil language. He drew out the taps from the casks, spilling a great quantity of choice wine, and when he had drunk enough distributed the same amongst his grooms, as if it had been water or common ale. Having drunk their fill they departed with ribald laughter and derision. When these things were related to the bishop, he said with a serene countenance, 'Ut quid necesse fuit rapere et praedari, quae satis civiliter sponte et abundanter postulantibus distribuuntur ? Maledicti igitur tot in uno regno reges, sed tiranni.'[96]

The Innings Park, a little park of 100 acres, seems to be of later origin than the two former, as it is not mentioned in the register of 1277. There was, however, at that date a grove of oaks of 5 acres,[97] which was perhaps the nucleus of the 10 acres of great oaks included in the Innings Park in the time of Henry VIII.[98] This park lay near the manor-house on the north-east, and in 1538 contained five deer of antlers and thirty-five raskells. There were then 8 acres of great timber in two places, which could not be spared for the shadowing of the deer. There was also 'a warren of coneys conveniently stored with game, and most part of the game black.' The pasture was then said to be very bare and mossy, and scarcely enough to feed the deer,[99] and in 1578 it was found to be so much overgrown with moss that the deer 'had been corrupted and wanted sufficient feeding whereby many had died.' It was recommended that, in order to remedy this, portions of the park should from time to time be inclosed, ploughed and sown with corn, and afterwards thrown open again. But the queen's hunting was not to be impaired nor her walks in the said park, 'wherein she took great pleasure.'[100] Either the proposed remedy was successful or the Cecils found some other means of providing pasture, for deer were not only kept as late as 1735, but seem to have been in a flourishing condition, as the Earl of Salisbury sent a supply of red deer from his own woods to Windsor Forest in that year.[1]

Hatfield Park was improved by the first Earl of Salisbury after the manor of Hatfield had been granted to him by James I in exchange for Theobalds. He apparently formed it from part of the Great Wood, for he was designated in a local epitaph

'Not Robin Goodfellow, nor Robin Hood,
But Robin the encloser of Hatfield Wood.'[2]

In 1611 the cottagers consented to the 'improvement' of Hatfield Wood.[3] In a letter[4] of George Garrard describing a house party at Hatfield in July 1636 we read of Lord Salisbury killing a deer in his woods, but Lord Cottington, who had attracted attention on his arrival by 'his white beaver with a studded hatband,' was at first less fortunate. When a bow was placed in his hands he bungled and shot thrice before he killed, all the ladies standing by.[5]

The Hatfield parks no longer retain the old names. Hatfield Park, which surrounds the house and is of the greatest extent, is very finely timbered, and includes Coombe Wood. This wood is mentioned in the Survey of 1538 as having an extent of 21 acres, and as having been replenished with oak, hornbeam, sallow and hazel,[6] but is not said to be within a park. North of this is the Home Park, much more thickly wooded, at the edge of which stands the oak under which Queen Elizabeth is said to have been seated when she received the news of her accession. This was the Innings Park and includes the warren, which is separated from it by the River Lea, in this part artificially widened. On either side of the water is a vineyard, which was planted by the first earl,[7] who, like his father,[8] took a keen interest in plant cultivation. This vineyard was considered by John Evelyn, who saw it in 1643, 'the most considerable rarity next to the house.'[9] This was an expert's enthusiasm; his fellow diarist Pepys, who visited Hatfield in 1659, was more delighted by 'the gardens, such as I never saw in all my life; nor so good flowers, nor so great goosburys, as big as nutmegs.'[10] Probably 'Mr. Looker my Lord's gardener' would have found Evelyn a more interesting if less lively visitor; he certainly seems to have been a safer one, for Pepys' second visit is thus recorded : 'At Hatfield we bayted and walked into the great house; and I would fain have stolen a pretty dog that followed me, but could not, which troubled me.'[11]

South of the main park, and extending from it to the Great North Road, is a large wood, traversed by many paths. This is the old 'Middle Park,' which was later called 'Miller's Park,'[12] and so became 'Millward's,' by which name it is known at the present day.

The manor of ASTWICK (Alswyk, Halewyk, xiii cent.; Alstwyk, xvi cent.) was held of the Bishop of Ely as of his manor of Hatfield by military service,[13] and afterwards by the Earls of Salisbury when Hatfield came into their possession. The lords of the manor had the right of feeding their pigs in the Great Park of Hatfield, belonging to the Bishop of Ely,[14] as tenants in chief of the bishop. Together with the manor of Woodhall it was assessed at one knight's fee, and was held from an early date by the family of Bassingburn. The first actual mention of the manor occurs in 1274,[15] but as early as 1198 a John de Bassingburn held Woodhall,[16] so it is possible that he held Astwick also at that date. In 1274 John de Bassingburn and Agnes his wife made a

---

[96] Matt. Paris, *Chron. Majora* (Rolls Ser.), v, 344.
[97] Cott. MSS. Claud. C xi.
[98] Rentals and Surv. R. Herts. 276.
[99] Land Rev. Misc. Bks. ccxvi.
[100] Exch. Spec. Com. Eliz. no. 1026.
[1] *Cal. Treas. Bks.* 1725–38, p. 112.
[2] G.E.C. *Complete Peerage.*
[3] *Cal. S. P. Dom.* 1611–18, p. 32.
[4] Ibid. 1636–7, p. 75.
[5] Ibid.
[6] Land Rev. Misc. Bks. ccxvi.
[7] Brayley, *Beauties of Engl. and Wales,* vii, 279.

[8] Lord Burghley had made John Gerarde superintendent of his gardens in the Strand and at Theobalds, and to him Gerarde dedicated his 'Herball' in 1597. It is not clear if Gerarde was ever at Hatfield, though he lived until 1612; he is described as Herbarist to the king in 1605, in which year he granted to Lord Salisbury his interest in a garden near Somerset House (*Cal. S. P. Dom.* 1603–10, p. 141).
[9] *Diary and Correspondence of John Evelyn* (ed. Bray), i, 39. Evelyn records on the same date the appearance of 'what amazed us exceedingly . . . a shining cloud in the air in shape resembling a sword, the point reaching to the north; it was as bright as the moon, the rest of the sky being very serene. It began about eleven at night and vanished not until above one.'
[10] *Pepys' Diary* (ed. Wheatley), ii, 69.
[11] Ibid. 77.
[12] P. F. Robinson, *Vetruvius Brittanicus,* 16.
[13] Cott. MSS. Claud. C xi.
[14] Ibid.
[15] Feet of F. Herts. 2 Edw. I, no. 27.
[16] Ibid. 9 Ric. I, no. 21.

100

Hatfield House South Façade

BROADWATER HUNDRED

HATFIELD OR BISHOP'S HATFIELD

settlement of the manor on themselves.[17] John died in 1276.[18] In 1277 his lands were held by Albreda de Bassingburn.[19] She was succeeded by Stephen de Bassingburn,[20] whose son John received a grant of free warren in 1300[21] and was holding in 1303.[22] He was followed by his son Stephen before 1333, Joan his widow keeping a third of Astwick as dower.[23] Stephen was still holding the manor in 1347[24] and was followed by Thomas de Bassingburn, who was Sheriff of Hertfordshire in 1370.[25] In 1428 Edward Tyrell was returned as holding the half fee of John de Bassingburn[26] (who succeeded his father Thomas before 1397),[27] but he was possibly a feoffee, for the inquisition taken at his death in 1442 states that he held no lands in Hertfordshire.[28] In 1493 the manor was held by Thomas Bassingburn, and according to Clutterbuck had been held by his father John.[29] Thomas married Katherine, the sister of Sir William Say, and in the year mentioned settled the manors of Astwick and Woodhall to her use for life, with remainder to himself and his heirs, Thomas Earl of Surrey being the trustee.[30] After her death Astwick came to her son John Bassingburn,[31] who some years before this had 'entered into her house and wounded her contrary to right, and attacked her servants,' denying his father's settlement and claiming the manor by right of a fine levied to him by his father.[32] He died in 1535, leaving as his heirs two daughters, Katharine the wife of Nicholas Hare and Anne wife of Thomas Gawdy.[33] The manor of Astwick was apportioned to Katharine Hare, who held it with her mother Etheldreda Bassingburn.[34] Nicholas and Katharine Hare both died in 1557. The manor was held by their eldest son Michael Hare[35] in 1607.[36] He died without issue, and in 1614 it was conveyed by trustees to Ralph Thrale.[37] He and Mary his wife, together with a certain William Grimwyne and his wife Elizabeth, joined in 1625 in a conveyance to William Deyes.[38] In 1656 it was held by John Deyes,[39] from whom it came to Sir Henry Tulse,[40] who is said to have married Deyes's daughter.[41] Sir Henry was Sheriff of London and Middlesex in 1673,[42] Lord Mayor of London in 1684 and Lieutenant of the City in 1690.[43] He had a daughter and heir Elizabeth, who brought his lands in marriage to Sir Richard Onslow, created Lord Onslow in 1716.[44] In 1712 he sold Astwick to Sidney Lord Godolphin,[45] whose son and heir Francis married Henrietta, eldest daughter and co-heir of John Churchill, first Duke of Marlborough. Astwick passed with the other Marlborough lands to her nephew Charles, third Earl of Sunderland, who became in 1733 Duke of Marlborough.[46] He was succeeded in 1758 by his son George, who died in 1817.[47] George, the fifth duke, sold Astwick in 1819 to John Lloyd,[48] from whom it passed to his son John, who died in 1875, then to the latter's son John Lloyd of Abbey Gate, St. Albans.[49] The manor now belongs to Mr. John Lloyd, J.P.

LLOYD. *Vert a cheveron between three wolves' heads rased argent.*

BROCKETT HALL, WATERSHIPS or DURANTSHIDE was held of the manor of Hatfield for the service of half a knight's fee.[50] It seems to have been formed by the union in the same hands of several tenements. In 1234–5 Adam Fitz William held rent in 'Watershepe' from Robert and Alice de Cranemere, to whom he paid 1d. rent.[51] In 1413 John Mortimer held Waterships of Philip Asshe and John and Christine Muslee (heirs of the Fitz Simons of Symondshyde and Almshoe),[52] and in that year granted it to the Bishop of Winchester and others, apparently to the use of his wife Eleanor.[53] In 1277 Simon Fitz Adam (see Almshoe) held Durantshide of the Bishop of Ely for a rent of 60s.,[54] and in 1477 Thomas Brockett held both Waterships and Durantshide[55]; so we may conclude that the latter descended in the same manner as Symondshyde in the interval. The term 'manor' does not actually occur until 1532.[56] After 1477 Brockett Hall continued in the family from which it took its name until the death of Sir John Brockett in 1598.[57] His heirs were his five daughters and a grandson, the child of his sixth daughter.[58] Ultimately the whole came to the fifth daughter Mary and her husband Sir Thomas Reade before 1637.[59] The manor since that date has followed

BROCKETT. *Or a cross paty sable.*

READE. *Gules a saltire between four sheaves or.*

[17] Feet of F. Herts. 2 Edw. I, no. 27.
[18] Clutterbuck, op. cit. ii, 344, quoting Plac. Hil. 5 Edw. I, rot. 40.
[19] Cott. MSS. Claud. C xi.
[20] *Abbrev. Plac.* (Rec. Com.), 270.
[21] Chart. R. 28 Edw. I, m. 10.
[22] *Feud. Aids*, ii, 428; *Cal. Pat.* 1307–13, p. 472.
[23] Feet of F. Div. Co. 7 Edw. III.
[24] De Banco R. 350, m. 3 d.
[25] P.R.O. *List of Sheriffs*, 43.
[26] *Feud. Aids*, ii, 449.
[27] See Hoddesdon.
[28] Chan. Inq. p.m. 21 Hen. VI, no. 58.
[29] Clutterbuck, op. cit. ii, 344.
[30] Close, 9 Hen. VII, no. 34–6.
[31] Ct. of Req. bdle. 13, no. 84; Recov. R. Hil. 17 Hen. VIII, rot. 347.
[32] Ct. of Req. bdle. 13, no. 84.
[33] Chan. Inq. p.m. (Ser. 2), lxii, 64.
[34] Feet of F. Herts. Mich. 28 Hen. VIII.
[35] *Dict. Nat. Biog.*
[36] Cussans, op. cit. *Broadwater Hund.* 271.
[37] Feet of F. Herts. Mich. 12 Jas. I.
[38] Recov. R. East. 1 Chas. I, m. 2.
[39] Ibid. Trin. 1656, rot. 164.
[40] Feet of F. Div. Co. Mich. 28 Chas. II.
[41] Cussans, loc. cit.
[42] *Cal. S. P. Dom.* 1673–5, p. 410.
[43] Ibid. 1689–90, p. 502.
[44] G.E.C. *Complete Peerage.* Salmon, op. cit. 212, states that Sarah Duchess of Marlborough, Henrietta's mother, was holding Astwick in 1721.
[45] G.E.C. *Complete Peerage.*
[46] Ibid.
[47] Clutterbuck, op. cit. ii, 353.
[48] Cussans, loc. cit.
[49] Chan. Inq. p.m. 17 Edw. IV, no. 47; (Ser. 2), cclvii, 42.
[50] Feet of F. Herts. 19 Hen. III, no. 218.
[51] See Almshoe in Ippollitts, Hitchin Hundred.
[52] Chan. Inq. p.m. 2 Hen. VI, no. 14.
[53] Cott. MSS. Claud. C xi.
[54] Chan. Inq. p.m. 17 Edw. IV, no. 47.
[55] Ibid. (Ser. 2), liii, 29.
[56] Ibid. cclvii, 42.
[57] See Feet of F. Midd. and Herts. Trin. 10 Jas. I; Div. Co. Trin. 41 Eliz.; Recov. R. East. 11 Jas. I, rot. 30.
[58] Feet of F. Div. Co. Mich. 13 Chas. I.

101

A HISTORY OF HERTFORDSHIRE

the same descent as that of Westingtons (in Ayot St. Peter, q.v.). Brockett Hall passed on the death of the seventh and last Lord Cowper to his sister Lady Amabel Kerr, and at her death to her husband, the late Admiral Lord Walter Kerr.

Sir Thomas Reade obtained a grant of free warren in 1615.[60]

The manor of BLOUNTS is first mentioned, together with the manor of Hornbeamgate, in 1370, when it was granted by John de Louth to Nicholas and Robert his uncles.[61] It descended with the latter manor, and with it was granted by Robert Louth to Nicholas Britte and Nicholas Leventhorpe in 1468.[62] These were apparently trustees for Sir John Say, who was in possession in 1468.[63] After this there is no further record of the manor.[64]

CHEWELLS (Chivalls, xvi and xvii cent.) was a small reputed manor situated in Cromerhyde and held of the manor of Hatfield.[65] It is not called a manor until the 15th century,[66] but is first mentioned in the reign of Henry III, when Nigel son of Richard de Chewell held land in this district.[67] In the register of 1277 Nigel de Chewell is entered as holding two parts of a fee.[68] Shortly afterwards it came into the possession of John de Queye or Coye, who held it in 1303 [69] and in 1317–18 conveyed it to John Benstede,[70] lord of the manor of Benington, who died seised of it in 1324.[71] From this date Chewells follows the descent of the manor of Benington until the end of the 15th century.[72] Sir John Benstede possessed it at his death in 1471, but his son and heir William evidently sold it, for he died in 1485 seised of Benington only. In the reign of Henry VIII the owner was named Blake,[73] but by 1555 it had been acquired by John Brockett [74] of Brockett Hall and Symondshyde, and continued in his family, following the same descent as Symondshyde[75] (q.v.) and presumably becoming merged in it. The only trace of it now remaining is Benstead's Wood, which lies a little south of the village of Cromerhyde.

CROMERHYDE (Creymore Hyde, xvi cent.) is situated between the estates of Symondshyde and Brockett Hall. There is no early mention of the manor ; it first appears in the possession of Sir John Brockett,[76] lord of both the above manors, who probably acquired it as a connecting link between his two estates. After this date Cromerhyde followed the descent of the manor of Symondshyde [77] (q.v.).

The manor of GACELYNS (Gastlyn, Gasselyns) was held partly of the manor of Hatfield and partly of the manor of Bayford,[78] and took its name from Geoffrey Gacelin, who held land in Hatfield in 1255.[79] In 1268 Geoffrey Gacelin and his wife Joan conveyed it as a messuage and 2 carucates of land to William de Valence Earl of Pembroke,[80] from whom it passed to his son Aylmer de Valence.[81] The latter died in 1323 without issue seised of 'a tenement called Gacelines,' his three heirs being John de Hastings, son of his sister Isabel,[82] and Elizabeth Comyn and Joan, wife of the Earl of Atholl, daughters of his sister Joan.[83] Gacelyns, under the name of the manor of Bishop's Hatfield, was apportioned to Joan and David de Strathbolgi,[84] the latter of whom died in 1327.[85] His son and heir David complained in 1332 that the portion of the lands of Aylmer de Valence assigned to his parents had not been delivered, and procured an order for their proper delivery.[86] The manor was shortly after granted for a fixed rent of £6, and at the death of this David in 1335 was in the occupation of Ralph de Blithe, a citizen of London.[87] The rent remained in the king's hands owing to the minority of David's heir, and was granted to Adam de Walton.[88] Next year, however, the £6 rent from these lands was granted as dower to Katherine, widow of David de Strathbolgi, who gave it back to the king in exchange for lands in Northumberland.[89] Robert de Blithe possibly alienated the manor to Sir Simon de Lek of Cottam, co. Nottingham, for in 1377 he enfeoffed of it William Batesford, Richard Halle, Roger Assheburnham and Edmund del Clay, who released their right to Walter Frost and others.[90] In 1387 Walter Frost with other feoffees conveyed the manor to Solomon Fresthorp.[91] This may possibly have been in trust for Walter Marewe, or Fresthorp may have alienated to Marewe, for in 1429 John Marewe son and heir of Walter remitted his right in the manor to John and Elizabeth Kirkeby.[92] In 1432–3 John Kirkeby granted back rents in the manor to John Marewe.[93] Kirkeby, however, seems to have held the manor (through feoffees) at the time of his death in 1441.[94] He left a daughter Alice, aged four. In 1447–8 a certain Richard Clynt and his wife Elena, whose connexion with the manor is not clear, conveyed it to John Fortescue,[95] who about five years later obtained a release from Elizabeth wife of John London, daughter and heir of John Marewe.[96] This is the last record of the manor, and it perhaps became absorbed in the Ponsbourne estate.

The park of Gacelyns is first mentioned in 1300, when Aylmer de Valence complained that while he

---

[60] Pat. 13 Jas. I, pt. xviii.
[61] Anct. D. (P.R.O.), B 4213.
[62] Feet of F. Herts. 6 Edw. IV, no. 14.
[63] Rentals and Surv. R. Herts. 269. For transactions between Britte and Leventhorpe and Sir John Say see Anct. D. (P.R.O.), B 1443.
[64] It is a curious coincidence that there was a manor of Blounts which descended in the Leventhorpe family. There seems no doubt, however, that this manor was in Sawbridgeworth (Braughing Hundred) and that in the case of Blounts in Hatfield Leventhorpe was not buying for himself.
[65] Chan. Inq. p.m. 17 Edw. II, no. 43 ; Rentals and Surv. R. Herts. 276 ; Cott. MSS. Claud. C xi.
[66] Chan. Inq. p.m. 11 Edw. IV, no. 57.
[67] Harl. Chart. 54 C. 30.
[68] Cott. MSS. Claud. C xi.

[69] Feud. Aids, ii, 428.
[70] Feet of F. Herts. 11 Edw. II, no. 270.
[71] Chan. Inq. p.m. 17 Edw. II, no. 43.
[72] Ibid. 11 Hen. VI, no. 38 ; 11 Edw. IV, no. 57 ; Add. R. (B.M.), 28767.
[73] Rentals and Surv. R. Herts. 276.
[74] Feet of F. Herts. East. 1 & 2 Phil. and Mary.
[75] Chan. Inq. p.m. (Ser. 2), cclvii, 42 ; Recov. R. Trin. 10 Chas. I, rot. 47 ; East. 3 Anne, rot. 31.
[76] Feet of F. Herts. Hil. 26 Eliz.
[77] Chan. Inq. p.m. (Ser. 2), cclvii, 42 ; Recov. R. Trin. 10 Chas. I, rot. 47 ; East. 3 Anne, rot. 31 ; Mich. 43 Geo. III, rot. 17.
[78] Chan. Inq. p.m. 17 Edw. II, no. 75 ; 1 Edw. III, no. 85.
[79] Feet of F. Herts. Hil. 39 Hen. III, no. 458.

[80] Ibid. Trin. 52 Hen. III, no. 599.
[81] G.E.C. Complete Peerage. [82] Ibid.
[83] Chan. Inq. p.m. 17 Edw. II, no. 75.
[84] Cal. Close, 1323–7, p. 446.
[85] Chan. Inq. p.m. 1 Edw. III, no. 85.
[86] Cal. Close, 1330–3, p. 456.
[87] Chan. Inq. p.m. 11 Edw. III (1st nos.), no. 46.
[88] Cal. Pat. 1334–8, p. 258.
[89] Cal. Close, 1337–9, pp. 27, 166. She held no lands in Herts. at her death.
[90] Close, 51 Edw. III, m. 14.
[91] Ibid. 11 Ric. II, pt. i, m. 17 d.
[92] Ibid. 7 Hen. VI, m. 6.
[93] Ibid. 11 Hen. VI, m. 5.
[94] Chan. Inq. p.m. 22 Hen. VI, no. 26.
[95] Feet of F. Herts. 26 Hen. VI, no. 140.
[96] Ibid. 31 Hen. VI, no. 162.

Hatfield House: West end of Long Gallery

BROADWATER HUNDRED

HATFIELD OR BISHOP'S HATFIELD

was in Scotland on the king's service certain persons broke into his park at Hatfield, hunted therein and carried away deer.[1] Apparently he failed to obtain immediate justice, for in 1312 he again advanced his complaint of this offence,[2] and in 1313 was at length awarded damages.[3] In 1323 the extent of the park was 60 acres, the wood being valued at 8s. a year.[4] Free warren was granted to Aylmer de Valence in his demesne lands at Hatfield in 1309.[5]

The name of *LITTLE HOLEWELL* was given to certain tenements in Holewell or Holwell which first appear in the possession of Aylmer de Valence, when they were valued at 23s. 1½d.[6] They were held of the manor of Symondshyde.[6a] Little Holewell passed in the same manner as Gacelyns to Joan and David de Strathbolgi, the latter of whom died seised of it in 1327, holding it of Hugh Fitz Simon of Symondshyde.[7] It is still mentioned in connexion with Gacelyns in 1336[8] and 1377,[9] but disappears after this date.

HANDSIDE (Haneshyde, xiii cent.) is now represented by a hamlet in the extreme north of the parish. It was held of the Bishop of Ely by service of a quarter of a knight's fee.[10] It seems to have had its origin in the lands held by John Polayn in Hatfield in 1324.[11] John son and heir of John Polayn also held lands in this parish previous to 1351.[12] Both were lords of the manor of Ayot Montfitchet (Ayot St. Peter, q.v.), which manor passed at the death of the second John to the Fish family. The 'manor of Handside' first appears in the possession of a member of the Fish family in the reign of Henry VIII.[13] A little later it was held by Thomas Fish.[14] Elizabeth widow of Thomas Fish married secondly William Perient, and continued to hold Handside.[15] Some time between 1558 and 1579 Edward Brockett brought an action against her, stating that Edward and George, the sons of Thomas Fish, had granted him the reversion of the manor after her death, and protesting because he had heard that she and her husband intended to cut down the wood on the estate, which was valued at 1,000 marks.[16] Edward Brockett died seised of Handside in 1599, his heir being his son John.[17] After this there is no further mention of the manor; probably it became absorbed in the Brockett estates.

HERONS was a small reputed manor situated in Cromerhyde, and seems to have been held of Symondshyde.[18] Its origin is uncertain, but as early as the reign of Henry III one Simon le Heron held land in this district. At this time 4 acres of land granted to Nigel de Chewell are described as lying 'between the land of Simon le Heyrun and the way which leads across Croymer,'[19] which proves that Simon's land lay in a locality corresponding with the later manor of Herons. In 1293 Geoffrey le Heron received damages from John de Bassingburn and others because they had broken down 10 ft. of his hedge.[20] In 1315–16 there was a conveyance from Simon Heron to John Bensted of the reversion of a messuage, 240 acres of arable land, rent of money and rent of three clove gillyflowers, one goose, two fowls and five sheep and rights of pasture in Hatfield,[21] these tenements being probably coincident with the manor. This John de Benstede died in 1359 seised of land in Hatfield called Chewells, some of which was held of the Bishop of Ely and the rest of Hugh Fitz Simon[22] (of Symondshyde). As Chewells was held of the bishop only, and Herons at a later date is said to be held of Symondshyde, it seems as if 'the rest' here was synonymous with Herons. Edward Benstede was certainly possessed of it at his death in 1432,[23] so it is probable that it followed the descent of the manor of Benington from an earlier date. After this it is not again separated from Chewells.

POPES or *HOLBEACHES* (Holbeches, Holbeckes, Holbaches) was held of the manor of Hatfield by fealty and free socage.[23a] In 1330 John de Hotham, Bishop of Ely, granted to Robert de Holbeaches and Emma his wife in tail-male a messuage and lands in Hatfield for the rent of one rose yearly at the Nativity of St. John Baptist.[24] Emma, after the death of Robert de Holbeaches, married John Molyn, the king's envoy, and in 1351 granted these same lands to John de Berland of Prittlewell to hold during her life.[25] In the reign of Edward III the manor is said to have been held by William Stalworth,[26] from whom it descended successively to his son John and his grandson William, the latter of whom left two daughters, Elizabeth and Jane, between whom the manor was divided. Elizabeth is said to have married Richard Hall, and her moiety to have descended to two granddaughters, Elizabeth the wife of Laurence Woodhall, who had a son Fulk, and Alice, who married John (James?) ap Jenkyn. Jane, the second daughter of William Stalworth, is said to have married Charles Blount, and her moiety to have come to her daughter Margaret, who married Thomas Woodhall.[27]

In 1542 Thomas Woodhall and Margaret his wife conveyed the 'manor of Popes Park,' which was presumably the name given to their moiety, to Fulk Woodhall,[28] who thus became possessed of three-quarters of the original manor, which he held in 1545.[29] In 1529 James ap Jenkyns and Alice his wife sold a quarter of the manor of Popes to Roger Belamy.[30] This quarter came to William Belamy, son and heir of Richard Belamy, in 1538,[31] who sold it in 1548 to William Tooke,[32] auditor-general of the Court of Wards and Liveries.

Chauncy says that Fulk Woodhall afterwards joined with William Belamy in a conveyance to William

---

[1] Cal. Pat. 1292–1301, p. 352.
[2] Ibid. 1307–13, p. 542.
[3] Ibid. p. 575.
[4] Chan. Inq. p.m. 17 Edw. II, no. 75.
[5] Chart. R. 2 Edw. II, no. 23.
[6] Chan. Inq. p.m. 17 Edw. II, no. 75; Cal. Close, 1323–7, p. 446.
[6a] Chan. Inq. p.m. 1 Edw. III, no. 85.
[7] Ibid.
[8] Cal. Pat. 1334–8, p. 258.
[9] Close, 51 Edw. III, m. 14.
[10] Rentals and Surv. R. 276.
[11] Feet of F. Herts. Trin. 17 Edw. II, no. 384.
[12] Add. Chart. 1988.
[13] Rentals and Surv. R. 276.
[14] Chan. Proc. (Ser. 2), bdle. 8, no. 30.
[15] Ibid.
[16] Ibid.
[17] Chan. Inq. p.m. (Ser. 2), dvii, 48.
[18] Ibid. 11 Hen. VI, no. 38.
[19] Harl. Chart. 54 C. 30.
[20] Assize R. 1298, m. 71.
[21] Feet of F. Herts. 9 Edw. II, no. 229.
[22] Chan. Inq. p.m. 33 Edw. III (2nd nos.), no. 110.
[23] Ibid. 11 Hen. VI, no. 38.
[23a] Ibid. (Ser. 2), cccxviii, 163.
[24] Feet of F. Herts. 4 Edw. III, no. 57.
[25] Cal. Close, 1349–54, p. 360.
[26] Chauncy, op. cit. 310.
[27] Ibid. 310–11. The pedigree is so far unsupported by documentary evidence, but if authentic explains the existing documents which follow.
[28] Feet of F. Div. Co. Mich. 34 Hen. VIII.
[29] Ibid. Herts. Mich. 37 Hen. VIII.
[30] Ibid. East. 21 Hen. VIII.
[31] Ct. of Wards Misc. Bks. dlxxviii, fol. 330.
[32] Plac. de Banco, Trin. 2 Edw. VI, m. 6 d.; Feet of F. Herts. Trin. 2 Edw. VI.

A HISTORY OF HERTFORDSHIRE

Tooke,[33] who appears in possession of the manor in 1548.[34] His son Walter died seised of it in 1609,[35] and was succeeded by his son Ralph, who died unmarried in 1635.[36] George, his brother, inherited the manor,[37] but died also without heirs, and the manor came to his brother Thomas. Thomas Tooke sold Holbeaches in 1664 to Stephen Ewer and Joshua Lomax,[38] who sold it in the following year to Thomas Shatterden,[39] who possessed it as late as 1696.[40] Before 1705 it came into the possession of Vice-Admiral Sir David Mitchell,[41] who died there in 1710,[42] leaving the manor to his nephew David Cooke, who took the surname of Mitchell.[43] The latter was succeeded by his son David Mitchell,[44] who sold Holbeaches in 1744 to William Hulls.[45] Thence it passed to Rebecca Assheton, daughter of William Hulls,[46] and to her son William Assheton,[47] who in 1817 sold it to James Marquess of Salisbury,[48] and it thus became united to Hatfield.

The manor-house was burnt down in January 1745–6, and a farm-house now occupies the site.

The manor of HOLWELL alias HOLWELL GRAY was held of the Bishop of Ely in chief for half a fee,[49] and later of the Earls of Salisbury as of the manor of Hatfield,[50] but a mesne lordship vested in the Peyvre family (of Willian) is mentioned in the 14th century.[51]

The first sub-tenant mentioned is John de Grey, who held the manor in 1265, for in that year his manor-house there was broken into.[52] He was succeeded by his son Reginald,[53] who held the half fee in 1303.[54] His son John succeeded him in 1308.[55] In 1309 he complained 'that certain men entered his manor at Holwell, broke into the houses thereof, carried away his goods, felled trees in his wood of Frythewood, and with nets snared rabbits in his free warren.'[56] John de Grey died about 1324.[57] He had settled Holwell on his second son Roger,[58] and the latter obtained a release of the manor from his elder brother Henry in 1328.[59] He was succeeded by his son Sir Reginald Grey of Ruthyn. Reginald died in 1388[60]; his widow Eleanor continued to hold the manor until her death in 1396.[61] Holwell then passed to their son

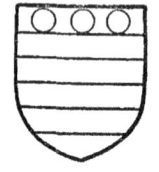

GREY of Ruthyn. *Barry argent and azure with three roundels gules in the chief.*

Reginald.[62] Early in the next century it came into the possession of John Perient, who held it in 1428,[63] and who also held the manors of Digswell and Ludwick. From this date Holwell followed the descent of Ludwick Manor until 1642,[64] when it was held by Frances Weld,[65] but it does not seem to have passed with Ludwick to the Shallcross family, and it is lost sight of until the beginning of the next century.

Some time previous to 1728 Thomas Goddard inherited Holwell from his mother and mortgaged it to Charles Clarke.[66] Thomas died intestate, and Charles Clarke entered as mortgagee and was in possession in the year mentioned.[67] In 1743 William Clarke and Mary his wife and Anna Clarke, widow, sold the manor to John Edwards.[68] Later it was held by Sir Thomas Cave and Sarah his wife,[69] and passed from them to their daughter Sarah, the wife of Henry Otway, who possessed it as late as 1794.[70] After this there is no further record of the manor.

HORNBEAMGATE (Hermebemgate, xiv cent.) was a small manor held from an early date by the family of Louth or de Luda. This family held land in Hatfield early in the 14th century,[71] when Roger de Louth and Joan his wife were living. In 1366 Roger, possibly son of the first-named Roger, and Margery de Louth are mentioned. They possessed a messuage and curtilage in 'Herinbenegatestrat,' which may possibly be the same as Hornbeamgate.[72]

The first actual mention of the manor of Hornbeamgate is in 1370, when John son and heir of Roger de Louth granted it to Nicholas and Robert, his uncles.[73] Nicholas died some time before 1392,[74] and the manor apparently continued to descend in the Louth family. John son of Roger was still living in 1372[75]; another Robert de Louth appears in 1420.[76] In 1466 Robert Louth and Edith his wife conveyed the manor of Hornbeamgate to Nicholas Leventhorpe and Nicholas Britte,[77] apparently in trust for Sir John Say, who was in possession in 1468.[78] There seems to be no further trace of it.

The manor of LUDWICK (Lodewyk, xiv and xv cent.) was held successively by the Bishops of Ely, the king and the Earls of Salisbury[79] as of the manor of Hatfield. It seems to have belonged early in the 13th century to a family of the name of Ludwick. The first mentioned is Roger de Ludwick, whose name occurs in a document of 1220.[80] William de Ludwick is mentioned in 1248[81] and Adam de

---

[33] Chauncy, op. cit. 310–11.
[34] Chant. Cert. 27, no. 5; see also Inq. quoted in next note.
[35] Chan. Inq. p.m. (Ser. 2), cccxviii, 163.
[36] Ibid. ccccixxx, 103.
[37] Dict. Nat. Biog.
[38] Feet of F. Herts. Trin. 16 Chas. II.
[39] Close, 17 Chas. II, pt. iv, m. 26.
[40] Feet of F. Herts. East. 4 Will. and Mary; Mich. 8 Will. III.
[41] Ibid. East. 4 Anne.
[42] Dict. Nat. Biog.
[43] Salmon, op. cit. 212.
[44] Recov. R. Mich. 11 Geo. II, rot. 328; Clutterbuck, op. cit. ii, 352.
[45] Recov. R. Trin. 17 & 18 Geo. II, rot. 296.
[46] Clutterbuck, op. cit. ii, 352.
[47] Recov. R. Mich. 53 Geo. III, rot. 265.
[48] Cussans, op. cit. *Broadwater Hund.* 272.
[49] Cott. MSS. Claud. C xi; Anct.

Extents, no. 78 (1); Chan. Inq. p.m. 1 Edw. II, no. 54.
[50] Ibid. (Ser. 2), cccii, 132.
[51] Feud. Aids, ii, 428; Chan. Inq. p.m. 12 Ric. II, no. 23.
[52] Abbrev. Plac. (Rec. Com.), 158.
[53] Wrottesley, Ped. from the Plea R. 14.
[54] Feud. Aids, ii, 428.
[55] Chan. Inq. p.m. 1 Edw. II, no. 54.
[56] Cal. Pat. 1307–13, p. 170.
[57] Chan. Inq. p.m. 17 Edw. II, no. 74; Anct. Extents, no. 78 (1).
[58] Feet of F. Herts. 5 Edw. II, no. 101.
[59] Cal. Close, 1327–30, p. 399.
[60] Chan. Inq. p.m. 12 Ric. II, no. 23.
[61] Close, 19 Ric. II, m. 4; Chan. Inq. p.m. 19 Ric. II, no. 30.
[62] Ibid.
[63] Feud. Aids, ii, 449.
[64] Chan. Inq. p.m. 14 Edw. IV, no. 29; (Ser. 2), lxiii, 61; lxxiii, 89; Recov. R. Hil. 1566, rot. 643; Trin. 1573, rot. 633;

Feet of F. Herts. East. 30 Eliz.; Ct. of Wards, Feod. Surv. 17.
[65] Recov. R. Trin. 18 Chas. I, rot. 47.
[66] Salmon, op. cit. 213.
[67] Ibid.
[68] Feet of F. Herts. Hil. 17 Geo. II.
[69] Clutterbuck, op. cit. ii, 359.
[70] Recov. R. Hil. 34 Geo. III.
[71] Chan. Inq. p.m. 4 Edw. III, no. 94.
[72] Anct. D. (P.R.O.), B 4098.
[73] Ibid. B 4213.
[74] Chan. Inq. p.m. 16 Ric. II, pt. i, no. 71.
[75] Anct. D. (P.R.O.), B 4215.
[76] Ibid. D 894.
[77] Feet of F. Herts. Trin. 6 Edw. IV, no. 14.
[78] Rentals and Surv. R. 269.
[79] Chan. Inq. p.m. 14 Edw. IV, no. 29; (Ser. 2), lxxiii, 89; Feod. Surv. Ct. of Wards, 17.
[80] Cal. Pat. 1216–25, p. 263.
[81] Assize R. 318, m. 5.

104

BROADWATER HUNDRED

Ludwick in 1284.[82] In 1294 John de Ludwick conveyed 'the manor of Ludewyk' to William de Melksop,[83] who held the manor of Digswell. After the death of William de Melksop, however, the manor apparently returned to the Ludwicks, as the family seems to have been settled at Hatfield throughout the 14th century. In 1316 William de Ludwick went 'beyond seas' on the king's service with Aylmer de Valence,[84] and in 1332 accompanied his neighbour Hugh Fitz Simon on a pilgrimage to Santiago.[85] In 1342 there is an order for the arrest of William de Ludwick and his brother John,[86] upon what charge is not stated. He seems, however, to have been a somewhat turbulent neighbour, for in 1348 Stephen de Bassingburn of Woodhall complained that William and his sons John and Thomas 'broke his close and house in Bishop's Hatfield, entered his free warren, carried away his goods and hares, rabbits, pheasants and partridges from the warren, and assaulted his servant.'[87] John de Ludwick succeeded his father at some date before 1377, and in that year, and for many years up to 1406, was justice of the peace for Hertfordshire.[88] In 1413 John Ludwick and Alice his wife held Ludwick with John Deram, Philip Thornbury and Nicholas Rys,[89] and in 1413–14 it was released to John Peryan or Perient of Digswell.[90] In 1421–2 John Bassingburn and Alice Countess of Oxford and John Mortimer her husband released to him some interest which they had in the estate.[91] Ludwick descended in the Perient family in the same manner as Digswell[92] until it came to Thomas Perient, who died in 1545.[93] His heirs were four daughters, but his brother John, being the nearest male heir, held Ludwick[94] until his death without male issue, when this manor was apportioned to Anne the third daughter of Thomas Perient and the wife of Anthony Carleton,[95] who held it in 1566,[96] and sold it before 1569 to Edward Denton.[97] Edward and Joyce Denton conveyed it in 1575 to John Lacy.[98] The latter sold Ludwick in 1588 to Humphrey Weld,[99] who died possessed of it in 1610 and was succeeded by his son John.[100] In 1622 it came to his son Humphrey, a minor,[1] who held the reversion of the manor after the death of his mother Frances, who survived until after 1642.[2] Some time before 1716 Ludwick came into the possession of Thomas Shallcross,[3] who held it then, and in 1720 sold it to Jeremy Hale of King's Walden,[4] who held it in 1728,[5] and in whose family Ludwick descended[6] until 1819,

HATFIELD OR BISHOP'S HATFIELD

when William Hale gave it to the Earl of Salisbury in exchange for Quickswood in the same county,[7] and it thus became united to the main manor.

William de Melksop obtained a grant of free warren in this manor in 1301–2.[8]

PONSBOURNE (Pomelesborne, Ponnysbourne, xvi cent.) was held of the manor of Hatfield.[9] There is no early mention of it by name, but as members of the family called Ponsbourne held lands in Hatfield in the 13th and 14th centuries it seems likely that they were the early possessors. The first of these to be mentioned is William de Ponsbourne in 1281.[10] The name of John de Ponsbourne occurs in 1293,[11] and of Robert the son of William de Ponsbourne in 1308.[12] In 1346 the heir of Robert de Ponsbourne is mentioned,[13] after which there is no further record of the family, but in 1441 John Kirkeby died seised of lands formerly of Robert Ponsbourne.[14] It probably was acquired with Gacelyns by Sir John Fortescue, the chief justice. He forfeited in 1462, when Lord Wenlock was granted his lands.[15] John Fortescue, who ultimately succeeded, was sheriff in 1481 and 1485; he died in 1499–1500 and was succeeded by his son John.[16] This John Fortescue died seised of the manor of Ponsbourne in 1517.[17] His son and heir Henry Fortescue next held it. He leased Ponsbourne to Sir William Cavendish for eighty years and sold the reversion in 1538 to Sir Thomas Seymour, Lord Admiral of England, who conveyed it to the Crown in exchange for other lands.[18] In 1553 Ponsbourne was granted by Edward VI to Sir John Cock,[19] who died in 1558 and was succeeded by his son Henry.[20] In 1622 the manor was held by Sir Edmund Lucy, the husband of Elizabeth daughter of Henry Cock.[21] He conveyed it in that year to Edward Sheldon, who in 1630 sold Ponsbourne to Sir John Ferrers,[22] who died seised of the manor and disparked park called Ponsbourne Park in 1640.[23] Sir John's eldest son Knighton Ferrers predeceased him, leaving a widow Katharine and an infant daughter of the same name.[24] In 1649 Ponsbourne was in the possession of Thomas Viscount Fanshawe of Dromore and Katharine his wife, the daughter and heir of Knighton Ferrers,[25] who in 1655 conveyed the manor to Stephen Ewer.[26] In 1660 Stephen Ewer repaired the chapel at Ponsbourne,[27] and in 1672 obtained a licence as a Presbyterian, presumably to hold services in his house.[28] In 1674 he sold the manor to John Woollaston,[29]

---

[82] Assize R. 1256, m. 49.
[83] Feet of F. Herts. 22 Edw. I, no. 306.
[84] Cal. Pat. 1313–17, p. 573.
[85] Ibid. 1330–4, p. 136.
[86] Ibid. 1340–3, p. 442.
[87] Ibid. 1348–50, p. 248.
[88] Ibid. 1377–81, p. 38; 1405–8, p. 492.
[89] Close, 14 Hen. IV, m. 11.
[90] Ibid. 1 Hen. V, m. 6.
[91] Ibid. 9 Hen. V, m. 24.
[92] Feet of F. Herts. 23 Hen. VI, no. 122; Chan. Inq. p.m. 14 Edw. IV, no. 29; (Ser. 2), lxiii, no. 61.
[93] Ibid. lxxiii, no. 89.
[94] Recov. R. Mich. 4 Edw. VI, rot. 546.
[95] Visit. of Herts. (Harl. Soc. xxii), 157.
[96] Feet of F. Herts. Trin. 3 Eliz.; Recov. R. Hil. 1566, rot. 643.
[97] Feet of F. Herts. Trin. 11 Eliz.; see Recov. R. Trin. 1572, rot. 427.
[98] Feet of F. Herts. Mich. 17 & 18 Eliz.
[99] Ibid. East. 30 Eliz.
[100] Chan. Inq. p.m. (Ser. 2), cccxxii, 173.
[1] Ibid. ccccii, 132; Feod. Surv. Ct. of Wards, no. 17.
[2] Com. Pleas D. Enr. Trin. 15 Chas. I, m. 7; Recov. R. Trin. 15 Chas. I, rot. 60; Trin. 18 Chas. I, rot. 47.
[3] Ibid. 2 Geo. I, rot. 15.
[4] Ibid. Mich. 7 Geo. I, rot. 13; Close, 7 Geo. I, pt. xi.
[5] Salmon, op. cit. 213.
[6] Recov. R. Mich. 11 Geo. III, rot. 185; Hil. 55 Geo. III, rot. 248.
[7] Cussans, op. cit. Broadwater Hund. 273.
[8] Chart. R. 30 Edw. I, no. 17.
[9] Chan. Inq. p.m. (Ser. 2), xxxiii, 126.
[10] Assize R. 1256, m. 7.
[11] Cal. Close, 1288–96, p. 318.
[12] Ibid. 1307–13, p. 54; Chan. Inq. p.m. 1 Edw. III, no. 85.
[13] Cal. Close, 1346–9, p. 142.
[14] Chan. Inq. p.m. 22 Hen. VI, no. 26.
[15] Cal. Pat. 1461–7, 192.
[16] Chan. Inq. p.m. (Ser. 2), xv, 3.
[17] Ibid. xxxiii, 126.
[18] Feet of F. Herts. 29 Hen. VIII, no. 3; Aug. Off. Proc. xxvii, fol. 65.
[19] Pat. 7 Edw. VI, pt. v.
[20] Chan. Inq. p.m. (Ser. 2), iii, 82.
[21] Feet of F. Herts. Trin. 20 Jas. I; Cussans, op. cit. Broadwater Hund. 270.
[22] Feet of F. Herts. Mich. 6 Chas. I.
[23] Chan. Inq. p.m. (Ser. 2), ccccxciv, 61.
[24] Harl. MS. 411, p. 146; Chan. Inq. p.m. (Ser. 2), ccccxciv, 59.
[25] G.E.C. Complete Peerage; Feet of F. Div. Co. Hil. 1649.
[26] Recov. R. East. 1655, rot. 192.
[27] Sessions R. (Hertford Co. Rec.), i, 134.
[28] Cal. S. P. Dom. 1672, p. 402.
[29] Feet of F. Herts. Mich. 26 Chas. II.

A HISTORY OF HERTFORDSHIRE

who sold it again to Paris Slaughter, whose son Paris succeeded in 1693.[30] His daughter and heir married a Mr. Clarke, whose son William Clarke[31] sold Ponsbourne to Samuel Strode, who was lord of the manor in 1728.[32] He was succeeded by his son William, who died in 1756, and by his grandson William, who in 1761 conveyed the manor to Lawrence Sullivan.[33] From Lawrence it passed to his son Stephen, who sold it in 1811 or 1812 to William Busk,[34] from whom it was purchased in 1819 by his brother Jacob Hans Busk. In 1836 the manor was again sold to Mr. Wynn Ellis, who disposed of it in 1875 to Mr. James William Carlile.[35] The latter is the present lord of the manor, and resides at Ponsbourne Park. Ponsbourne Manor House is the residence of Colonel Sir E. Hildred Carlile, M.P. for Mid-Herts.

CARLILE. *Or a cross paty gules and a chief gules with a saltire or therein.*

The manor of SYMONDSHYDE was held of the manor of Hatfield for the service of half a knight's fee and suit of court every three weeks.[36] In the *Inquisitio Eliensis*, compiled about 1086, Adam is stated to hold 2 hides of the abbot, which may represent Symondshyde.[37] Adam is the only tenant mentioned as holding as much as 2 hides, which was the quantity held by the Fitz Simons in 1277.[38] Moreover, Adam Fitz Hubert was the Domesday holder of Almshoe, and this manor and Symondshyde appear later in the hands of the same sub-tenants, the Fitz Simons. At the beginning of the 13th century William Fitz Simon was holding half a knight's fee in Hatfield, and in 1237 Adam Fitz William was a party to a conveyance of land there.[39] The manor then follows the same descent[40] as Almshoe (Hitchin Hundred) until 1805, when Symondshyde was sold by Sir Robert Salusbury to John Fordham.[41] John Fordham was succeeded by his son John Edward Fordham, who in 1852 sold the manor to the Marquess of Salisbury,[42] after which it became merged in the main manor of Hatfield.

TOLMERS or NEWGATE STREET was held of the Bishop of Ely and later of the Crown.[43] Its early history is very obscure; the name Tolmers suggests that it was formerly in the possession of a family of that name. In the register of the lands of Ely, compiled in 1277, a certain Walter de Tolymer was entered as holding land of the bishop in Hatfield, together with the right as a tenant in chief of pasturing his cattle in the Great Park of Hatfield belonging to the bishop.[44] In 1308 John the son of William Tolymer released the lands in Hatfield which he had acquired from his brother William to John le Hayward.[45] These lands were probably the manor of Tolmers, but there is no record of their descent for two centuries following. The first actual mention of the manor of Tolmers occurs in 1516, when Edmund Chyvall and Alice his wife, in whose right he held the manor, conveyed it to William Tattorn.[46] Thirteen years later Sir William Say, the holder of many Hertfordshire manors, died seised of it.[47] Tolmers then descended with the manor of Benington[48] (q.v.), and in 1566 the reversion was granted to Robert Earl of Leicester.[49] He died without heirs in 1588, and his lands reverted to the Crown.[50] In 1608 Tolmers was granted to Sir Henry Goodere or Goodyer, to be held of the king as of his manor of East Greenwich by fealty and free socage.[51] Sir Henry was perpetually in straits for want of money, and was much given to composing flattering poems, perhaps with a view to bettering his fortunes. In 1619 he wrote an ode to the Marquess and Marchioness of Buckingham on the occasion of their marriage,[52] and in 1623, when Prince Charles made his journey to Spain in search of a bride, he addressed poems to him both on his departure and his return.[53] In 1626 he petitioned to be admitted a Gentleman Usher of the Queen's Privy Chamber, saying that he 'desired only meat, drink and lodging, with some dignity, in that place where he had spent most of his time and estate.'[54] It is not recorded whether he was successful, but he died in the following year, and his son-in-law Francis Nethersole was granted £1,000 in consideration of his own and his father-in-law's services.[55] He left four daughters, Lucy the wife of Francis Nethersole, Elizabeth, Mary and Anne,[56] but the manor passed to another Sir Henry Goodere and Etheldreda his wife,[57] who was succeeded by his son Francis before 1638.[58] In 1649 Francis Goodere sold Tolmers to Robert Shiers of the Inner Temple[59]; he was succeeded by his son George Shiers,[60] who is said to have died in 1685, and devised his estates to charitable uses.[61]

In 1714 Hugh Shortridge, S.T.P., was lord of the manor.[62] In 1715 he conveyed Tolmers to Sir Francis Vincent and other trustees to hold to his own use for life, with remainder to the trustees to carry out his charitable bequests, among which was an annual payment of £220 to Exeter College,

---

[30] Chauncy, op. cit. 310.
[31] Feet of F. Herts. Trin. 9 Anne.
[32] Salmon, op. cit. 212.
[33] Clutterbuck, op. cit. ii, 348.
[34] Ibid.; Feet of F. Herts. Mich. 52 Geo. III.
[35] *Dict. Nat. Biog.*; Cussans, op. cit. *Broadwater Hund.* 270.
[36] Chan. Inq. p.m. 32 Edw. I, no. 56; Feud. Aids, ii, 428; Chan. Inq. p.m. 17 Edw. IV, no. 47; (Ser. 2), iv, 30; liii, 29.
[37] *Inquisitio Eliensis* (ed. Hamilton), 125.
[38] Cott. MSS. Claud. C xi.
[39] Feet of F. Herts. 21 Hen. III, no. 228.
[40] Feud. Aids, ii, 428; Feet of F. Div. Co. 5 Edw. III, no. 101; Add. R. 28799; Feud. Aids, ii, 450; Feet of F. Herts.

16 Hen. VI, no. 88; 15 Edw. IV, no. 42; Chan. Inq. p.m. 21 Edw. IV, no. 46; (Ser. 2), cxvi, no. 83; Feet of F. Div. Co. Trin. 41 Eliz.; 10 Jas. I; Recov. R. East. 11 Jas. I, rot. 30; Chan. Inq. p.m. (Ser. 2), ccclxxiv, 4; Recov. R. Trin. 10 Chas. I, rot. 47; East. 3 Anne, rot. 31; Feet of F. Herts. Trin. 12 Anne; Recov. R. Mich. 4 Geo. III, rot. 17.
[41] Clutterbuck, op. cit. ii, 357.
[42] Cussans, op. cit. *Broadwater Hund.* 275.
[43] Chan. Inq. p.m. (Ser. 2), li, 50; Pat. 5 Jas. I, pt. xviii.
[44] Cott. MSS. Claud. C xi.
[45] Close, 1 Edw. II, m. 9 d.
[46] Feet of F. Herts. Trin. 8 Hen. VIII.
[47] Chan. Inq. p.m. (Ser. 2), li, 50.

[48] Feet of F. Herts. Hil. 33 Hen. VIII.
[49] Pat. 8 Eliz. pt. vii, m. 26.
[50] G.E.C. *Complete Peerage*.
[51] Pat. 5 Jas. I, pt. xviii.
[52] *Cal. S. P. Dom.* 1619–23, p. 556.
[53] Ibid. p. 585; 1623–5, p. 105.
[54] Ibid. 1625–6, p. 403.
[55] Ibid. 1627–8, p. 432.
[56] Chan. Inq. p.m. (Ser. 2), ccccxliv, 93.
[57] Feet of F. Herts. Mich. 3 Chas. I.
[58] Ibid. 14. Chas. I; *Visit. of Herts.* (Harl. Soc. xxii), 58.
[59] Close, 1649, pt. xlvi, m. 22.
[60] Feet of F. Herts. East. 35 Chas. II.
[61] Cussans, op. cit. *Dacorum Hund.* 292. This may be a confusion with the next owner.
[62] Recov. R. Mich. 1 Geo. I, rot. 64.

106

HATFIELD CHURCH: THE CHANCEL AND BROCKETT CHAPEL

HATFIELD CHURCH: SALISBURY CHAPEL

BROADWATER HUNDRED

HATFIELD OR BISHOP'S HATFIELD

Oxford.[63] In 1802 Sir William Geary and others, who seem to have been the trustees succeeding Sir Francis Vincent and the others, sold Tolmers to Garnet Terry.[64] In 1827 it was sold by Margaret wife of Charles Mousley, who may have been the daughter of Garnet Terry, to Charles John Dimsdale.[65] He sold it in 1834 to Samuel Mills, who died in 1847,[66] and was succeeded by his son Thomas Mills,[67] from whom it passed to his brother John Remington Mills, who was lord of the manor in 1877.[68] He died in 1879,[69] and his eldest son John Remington Mills having predeceased him in 1865, his estates passed to his two granddaughters, who were co-heiresses.[70] One of them was lady of the manor in 1880. It now belongs to Mr. J. Henry Johnson.

WOODHALL was held of the manor of Hatfield for the service of one knight's fee.[71] The earliest mention of the manor occurs in 1198, when it was held by John de Bassingburn and Albreda his wife, and leased to Hamelin de Andeville and Alice for her life.[72] Albreda was still living in 1248.[73] Woodhall descended in the Bassingburn family in the same way as the manor of Astwick [74] until the death of John Bassingburn in 1535, when Woodhall passed under a settlement to Thomas Gawdy, the son of Anne, second daughter of John Bassingburn.[75] In 1564 Thomas Gawdy and Honor his wife conveyed the manor to Sir John Boteler of Watton Woodhall.[76] Sir John's eldest son Philip sold Hatfield Woodhall to his brother Henry, who died in 1609 seised of it jointly with his son John.[77] Sir John Boteler the younger died in 1637,[78] and his two elder sons Henry and Philip having died without issue the manor came to his third son William, an idiot,[79] who died in 1665. His next heirs were his five sisters, two of whose husbands, Francis Lord Dunmore and Endymion Porter, had been his guardians. The manor, however, was held in tail-male, so that it passed to Francis son of Ralph Boteler, the third of Sir John Boteler's eight half-brothers.[80] Francis Boteler died in 1690 and was succeeded by his daughter Juliana, the wife of Francis Shallcross.[81] She died in 1726 and Woodhall passed by will to her sister Isabel, the wife of Charles Hutchinson,[82] who died in 1728. Their son Julius Hutchinson succeeded[83] and was followed by his son Thomas, who died in 1774.[84] Woodhall then passed to his nephew, the Rev. Julius Hutchinson, son of his brother Norton,[85] and in 1792 was sold to the Earl of Salisbury, and thus became merged in the manor of Hatfield.[86]

Free warren was granted to the lord of the manor in 1300.[87]

The parish church of ST. ETHELDREDA,[88] standing on high ground on the east side of the town, is built for the most part of flint rubble with stone dressings. The roofs are tiled and the tall spire is shingled. It consists of a chancel, north and south chapels, north and south transepts with western chapels, nave, west tower of four stages with angle buttresses, embattled parapet and tall spire and north and south wooden porches.

The original church of the early 13th century appears to have been cruciform with a central tower, of which evidence remains in the thickened east wall of the nave and the north wall on the north side. The chancel and transepts appear to have formed part of this church, and the north wall of the nave probably stands on the foundations of the nave wall of the 13th century. Late in the same century the small chapels on the west side of the transepts were built and a south chapel was added; this chapel was widened late in the 15th century. In the 15th century also the nave was widened to the south, when the central tower was destroyed and the present west tower built. The north chapel, known as the Salisbury chapel, was added about 1600–10. In the 19th century the walls of the nave were rebuilt, the porches were added, and all the window tracery and most of the external stonework were renewed.

The chancel has a two-centred east window of three lights with tracery above. The shafted inner jambs with foliated capitals are of the 13th century. The north arcade, built about 1610, is of three bays of semicircular arches on Roman Doric columns. The soffits are richly decorated and the arches have modillion-shaped keystones. On the south side are a two-light window and an arcade of two bays of the 15th century. The central pillar and responds are of clustered shafts with ogee rolls between, and there are angels bearing shields in the capitals on the north and south sides. The middle shield on the central pier has the arms of Fortescue, Azure a bend engrailed argent cotised or on the bend in chief a molet sable. The two-centred chancel arch is modern, and has detached shafts with capitals carved with lilies and a label with mask stops. Under the south-east window is a piscina of the 13th century, with a modern arch.

An iron screen of the 18th century separates the chancel from the north chapel, which has three three-light windows—one at the east and two in the north wall—all of about 1610. On the west two modern arches, supported on responds and a central pillar, open to the north transept. The walls of the chapel are richly decorated with modern coloured mosaics and marble work, and the panelled and painted roof is also modern.

The south chapel has an east window of five lights and two south windows of four lights each, probably of the late 15th century, all with much restored tracery, and a small south doorway under the westernmost of the two south windows. The windows and

---

[63] Com. Pleas D. Enr. Hil. 43 Geo. III, m. 183.
[64] Ibid.
[65] Feet of F. Herts. East. 8 Geo. IV.
[66] Cussans, loc. cit.
[67] Ibid.
[68] Ibid.
[69] Burke, *Landed Gentry* (1882).
[70] Ibid.
[71] Rentals and Surv. R. 276; Chan. Inq. p.m. (Ser. 2), lxii, 64; cccviii, 113.
[72] Feet of F. Herts. 9 Ric. I, no. 21
[73] Assize R. 318, m. 5.
[74] *Abbrev. Plac.* (Rec. Com.), 270; Feet of F. Div. Co. 7 Edw. III; Close, 9 Hen. VII, no. 36; Feet of F. Herts. East. 14 Hen. VII; East. 20 Hen. VII; Recov. R. Hil. 17 Hen. VIII, rot. 347.
[75] Chan. Inq. p.m. (Ser. 2), lxii, 64.
[76] Feet of F. Herts. Hil. 6 Eliz.
[77] Chan. Inq. p.m. (Ser. 2), cccviii, 113.
[78] Ibid. dxxix, 56.
[79] Ibid. ccclxxxi, 150.
[80] Ibid. dxl, 90.
[81] Chauncy, op. cit. 309.
[82] Salmon, op. cit. 211.
[83] Recov. R. Trin. 2 & 3 Geo. II.
[84] Cussans, op. cit. *Broadwater Hund.* 270.
[85] Ibid.
[86] Ibid.
[87] Chart. R. 28 Edw. I, m. 10.
[88] Dimensions: chancel, 40 ft. by 26 ft. 6 in.; north chapel, 40 ft. by 21 ft.; south chapel, 25 ft. by 17 ft.; nave, 100 ft. by 29 ft.; north transept, 24 ft. by 15 ft. 6 in.; south transept, 21 ft. by 15 ft. 6 in.; tower, 16 ft. square.

doors all have four-centred heads. The two-centred arch at the west end, opening into the south transept, is of the 13th century, of three continuous chamfered orders, and immediately to the south of it is a plain narrow doorway of the 15th century, also leading to the south transept, which was inserted when the chapel was widened.

In the east wall of the chapel are two brackets, each carved with an angel bearing a shield, one on each side of the east window. The roof retains much of its late 15th-century woodwork.

The nave, of which the axial line is about 6 ft. south of that of the chancel, has a 13th-century arch at the north-east and south-east, opening into the chapels west of the transepts. Both bases and capitals of the arch on the south side are modern, but on the north side the bases are old. The responds are half-octagonal, and the arches are two-centred, of three chamfered orders. There are three two-centred modern windows of three lights, with tracery of three quatrefoils, in the north and in the south walls. The north door, which is much repaired, is of the 15th century, and the south doorway is modern. To the north of the chancel arch is a moulded piscina of the late 14th century. In the roof are six small modern dormer lights.

The north transept has a north window of four trefoiled lights with tracery above; it is possibly of the 15th century, but has been wholly restored. Below it is a doorway with a two-centred head. In the west wall is a 15th-century doorway leading to the vestry, which is modern, with a two-light window in the north wall and an exterior doorway and another two-light window in the west wall. To the south of the doorway from the transept is a semi-arch or flying buttress of the 13th century.

The chapel, which opens to the transept through the semi-arch, has a modern west window of two lights.

The south transept retains older detail than any other part of the church. In the east wall is a lancet window of the 13th century, now blocked, and to the north of it is a large trefoiled recess of the same period. Both are set high in the wall, and the latter is cut into on the north side by the arch leading to the south chapel. The archway which opens to the chapel west of the transept is a fine example of the work of about 1240, and shows traces of having been rebuilt in the position it now occupies. The arch is of two orders, deeply moulded with richly undercut rolls and hollows. The two innermost rolls have fillets and the rest are plain. The responds have their engaged round shafts with dog-tooth ornament

HATFIELD CHURCH FROM THE SOUTH

between them, which has been much restored. The capitals are foliated and the bases are modern.

The south window of the transept is wholly renewed, and is of four trefoiled lights with geometrical tracery in a two-centred head. The chapel has modern south and west windows, both of two trefoiled lights with a quatrefoil over, in a two-centred head.

The roof of the south transept is largely of late 15th-century date, and is ornamented with modern colour; the wall plates rest on modern foliated corbels.

The lofty tower arch is of about 1440, and is of three weakly moulded orders. It is two-centred and has a label with return stops. The west doorway has a two-centred arch in a square head, with tracery in the spandrels. Both it and the window above it are original work of the 15th century. At the southwest angle of the tower a door gives access to a turret

PLAN OF HATFIELD CHURCH

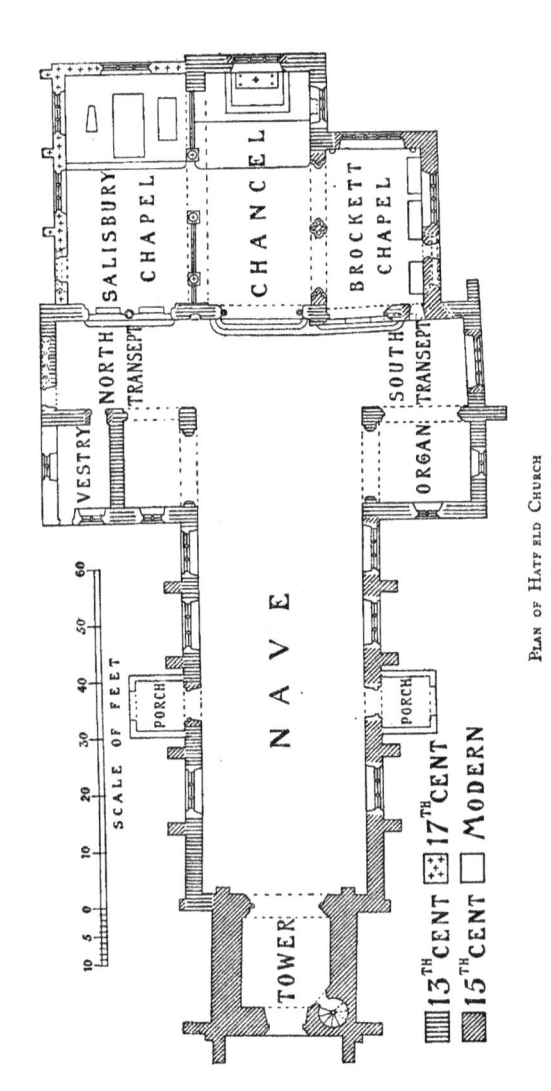

stairway leading to the upper stages of the tower, built in the thickness of the wall, and not projecting externally. This turret rises very slightly above the parapet of the tower. The top stage of the tower is lighted by four windows of two cinquefoiled lights, with a quatrefoil in a two-centred head. They are arranged in pairs on the north and south sides.

The oldest monument in the church is now in the north chapel, and consists of a small coffin-lid with the figure in low relief of a knight in armour of about 1160. The body is almost wholly covered by a large heater shield.

Also in the north chapel, to the south of the coffin-lid, is the large and elaborate marble altar tomb with the effigy of Robert first Earl of Salisbury, the founder of the chapel, who died in 1612. The altar slab, with the recumbent effigy of the earl wearing an armet with the visor open and the collar of the Garter, and holding a staff in his right hand, is supported by four finely-sculptured kneeling figures holding a sword, vases, broken columns and a skull. Beneath the slab, and between the four figures, is the representation of a skeleton.

Immediately to the south of this tomb is one with a life-size recumbent effigy, of about 1560, said to be that of Sir Richard Kyrle.

A brass in the chancel commemorates Fulk Onslow, 1602, and his wife, with a shield of arms and an inscription. There is another brass with inscription to Fulk Onslow in the tower.

In the south chapel is a large monument between the south windows to Dame Elizabeth Saunders, 1612, and Dame Agnes Saunders, 1588. It consists of an altar-tomb with marble panelled sides, with the effigies of the two ladies, half-recumbent, with their heads to the west, lying, one on the tomb itself and the other behind it raised upon a step. Behind them a recess is formed by a semicircular arch resting on modillions, with Renaissance foliation in the flat spandrels. This recess contains the inscription on a rectangular slab. On the cresting of the cornice are two shields and a lozenge in the centre. The left-hand shield bears Moore : Argent a fesse dancetty gobony gules and sable between three molets sable. The right-hand shield has the arms of Saunders : Party cheveronwise sable and argent three elephants' heads razed and counter-coloured, and on the lozenge is Moore impaling Barry ermine and gules, for Hussey. There is also in the south chapel a tomb of John Brockett, 1598, with shields of Brockett impaling and quartering other coats.

In the tower is an iron-bound chest dated 1692.

There are eight bells : 1, 2, 3, 4, 5 and 7 by John Briant of Hertford, 1786; 6 by Thomas Mears, London, 1841 ; and 8 with the names of Charles Pratchell and William Woodards, churchwardens.

The plate consists of a silver gilt chalice, paten, flagon and almsdish, each inscribed 'The parish church of Bishop's Hatfield in ye county of Hertford 1685,' two other silver chalices and patens, and another silver flagon.

The registers are in eight books : (i) baptisms 1653 to 1713, burials 1653 to 1690, marriages 1653 to 1740 ; (ii) burials 1678 to 1713 ; (iii) burials 1695 to 1750 ; (iv) baptisms 1713 to 1782, marriages 1741 to 1753 ; (v) baptisms 1783 to 1812 ; (vi) burials 1751 to 1812 ; (vii) marriages 1754 to 1772 ; (viii) 1772 to 1812.

The chantry at the altar of St. Anne in the parish church of Hatfield was founded in 1330 by Roger de Louth, 'for the good estate of himself and his wife Joan in life, for their souls after death, and for the souls of Thomas de Louth, late treasurer of the Church of St. Mary, Lincoln, John Hayward and Katharine his wife.'[89] He gave ten messuages, 40 acres of land and 10s. rent in Hatfield to the Prior and convent of Wymondley for a chaplain to celebrate daily service.[90] In 1392 John de Wendelyngburgh and others, apparently trustees of Nicholas de Louth, added two messuages, 33 acres of land, 2 acres of meadow and 2 acres of wood for the benefit of the soul of Nicholas de Louth[91] (or Luda). The advowson was held by the Louth family.

In the report made to Edward VI in 1548 the revenue from the tenements was reckoned at £9 8s. 8d. James Shawe, the incumbent, was 'an impotent man of the age of seventy years.'[92] After its suppression the lands were granted in the same year to Ralph Burgh and Robert Beverley.[93]

A chapel connected with the lords of the manor of Ponsbourne existed in the parish church of Hatfield, and was situated next to that of the Blessed Mary of Ludwick.[94] In 1518 John Fortescue left provision for 'an honest clerk' to celebrate mass there annually for the souls of himself and his ancestors.[95] In 1660 the 'Chapel of Ponsbourne' adjoining the church was repaired by Stephen Ewer, who had refused to pay the assessment for the repair of the parish church unless his own chapel was also repaired.[96]

The image of the Blessed Mary of Ludwick in Hatfield Church is mentioned in 1470,[97] also the images of the Blessed Mary of Pity (de Pete),[98] St. Anne, St. Etheldreda and the Holy Trinity.[99]

There are references in the 16th century to a Gild or Fraternity of St. John the Baptist. In 1510 a bequest was made to it by John Lowen[100] and others, in 1514 by Nicholas Lanam,[1] and in 1520 by William Clarke.[2] In 1538 a tenement in Woodside yielding a yearly rent of 4s. belonged to 'a brotherhood,'[3] and in 1545 a Fraternity is entered as paying 6d. towards a subsidy.[4] After this it disappears.

Lemsford, in the north of the parish, was formed into a separate ecclesiastical parish in 1858,[5] and the church of ST. JOHN, LEMSFORD, was erected in that year by the Dowager Countess Cowper of Brockett Hall and her children as a memorial to her husband, the sixth earl.

The church of ST. MARY, NEWGATE STREET, was built in 1847 by Thomas Mills of Tolmers. The living is a perpetual curacy.

ST. MARK'S chapel of ease at Woodhill was built in 1852 by the Marquess of Salisbury.

---

[89] *Cal. Pat.* 1330–4, p. 15.
[90] Ibid. ; Chan. Inq. p.m. 4 Edw. III, no. 94.
[91] *Cal. Pat.* 1391–6, p. 177 ; Chan. Inq. p.m. 16 Ric. II, pt. i, no. 71.
[92] Chant. Cert. 27, no. 5.
[93] Pat. 2 Edw. VI, pt. iv, m. 27.
[94] Chan. Inq. p.m. (Ser. 2), xxxiii, 126.
[95] Ibid.
[96] *Sessions* R. (Herts. Co. Rec.), i, 134–5.
[97] Will, P.C.C. 1 Wattys.
[98] Ibid. 34 Vox.
[99] Ibid. 1 Wattys.
[100] Ibid. 36 Bennett.
[1] Ibid. 5 Holder.
[2] Wills, Archd. of St. Albans, 152a.
[3] Land Rev. Misc. Bks. ccxvi.
[4] *Herts. Gen. and Antiq.* i, 324.
[5] *Lond. Gaz. Index*, 996.

BROADWATER HUNDRED — KNEBWORTH

The chapel of ease at Hatfield Hyde was erected in 1882, also by the Marquess of Salisbury.

ADVOWSON The advowson of the church of St. Etheldreda at Hatfield [6] belonged from the earliest times to the Abbots and Bishops of Ely,[7] and remained in their hands until it was conveyed with the manor to King Henry VIII in 1538.[8] The church was never appropriated, and the living has always been a rectory. It remained in the hands of the sovereign until 1549, when it was granted to the Earl of Warwick.[9] It must have been conveyed with the manor to Elizabeth, for she granted it in free socage to Thomas Poyner and William Wolriche in 1563,[10] from whom it is said to have been purchased in the same year by Richard Onslow.[11] About 1570 the latter gave the rectory as a lay estate to his brother, for his own and his wife's life.[12] Richard Onslow was Speaker of the House of Commons and Solicitor-General in 1566.[13] In 1574 the advowson was held by Fulk Onslow,[14] and in 1604 by Edward Onslow,[15] who in that year conveyed it to Goddard Pemberton.[16] The latter is said to have sold it to the Earl of Salisbury in 1607 [17]; it was certainly in the hands of the second earl,[18] and has remained in the possession of the same family since.[19] In 1534 a survey of the parsonage was made by command of Thomas Cromwell for purposes of repair. It then consisted of a hall and parlour with chambers over, an entry between the hall and kitchen, a kitchen, bake-house, malt-house, oat barn, ox-house, sheep-house, cart-house and hen-house,[20] so it must have been a considerable establishment.

In 1307 the parson of Hatfield was granted free warren in the lands belonging to the church.[21]

In 1538 there was a church-house called the 'common church-house,' which was used for bridal feasts, and was let at other times to provide funds for its maintenance.[22]

The advowson of St. John's, Lemsford, belongs to Countess Cowper, that of St. Mary, Newgate Street, to Mr. Joseph Trueman Mills of Leighton Buzzard.

Various meeting-places for Protestant Dissenters were certified in Hatfield from 1694 onwards.[22a] There is a Union chapel in Park Street, built in 1823, and a Wesleyan chapel. The Roman Catholic Church of the Blessed Sacrament was completed in 1910.

CHARITIES In 1678 Sir Francis Boteler and Dame Elizabeth Boteler his wife by deed conveyed to trustees a messuage and farm called Clarke's Farm, situate at Ludwick in this parish, the rents and profits thereof to be applied for such purposes as the said Dame Elizabeth Boteler should direct. The said Dame Elizabeth by her will, dated in 1681, directed that the objects of the bounty should be five widows, four to be chosen from the inhabitants of Bishop's Hatfield and one an inhabitant of the parish of Tewin. The trust property now consists of £2,397 4s. 1d. consols held by the official trustees, arising from sales of land and accumulations of income, and producing £59 18s. 4d. yearly.

In 1667 Thomas Tooke by deed charged his manor of Wormley with an annuity of £3 to be distributed on St. Thomas's Day to the six poorest and most aged men and women, and in 1720 Mrs. Julia Shallcross by a codicil to her will directed £9 a year to be paid out of her estate of Hatfield Woodhall to three widows of the parish for ever. It appears that the payment of these charges is now in abeyance.

Edward Smith's charity, being an annual charge of £2, is received (less tax) from the agent of Earl Cowper, the owner of Place Farm, which lies in the parishes of Wheathampstead [23] and Sandridge.

In 1733 Ann Countess of Salisbury by deed gave a fee-farm rent of £50 (subject to deduction of £10 for land tax) towards clothing and teaching twenty girls. The fee-farm rent is understood to be vested in the Corporation of Southampton, and is duly paid.

In 1807 Mrs. Mary Ross by her will, proved in the P.C.C. 12 March, charged certain land and hereditaments at Bather Dell with an annuity of £3 to be applied on St. Thomas's Day in clothing for six old and poor widows.

KNEBWORTH

Chenepeworde (xi cent.); Cnebbeworth, Knebbeswrth (xiii cent.); Knybbeworth (xiv cent.); Knecbworth, Knebeworth.

The parish of Knebworth has an area of 2,677 acres. The north-eastern part is over 400 ft. above the ordnance datum, and rises to a height of 461 ft. From this point the ground slopes downwards to the south and more gradually to the east; south of the village it rises again to 426 ft. The greater part of the parish is arable land, which covers 1,284 acres; 661¾ acres are permanent grass and 277 acres are wood.[1] The main road from Hitchin to London passes through the centre of the parish. A road turns off from it to the west and forks, one branch going north to St. Paul's Walden and the other south past Three Houses. Another road turns east from the Hitchin road, runs along the south of Knebworth Park and turns north, forming its eastern border. The village is situated on this road on the opposite side from the park.

Knebworth House is a building of two stories, and the whole of the external detail is of a florid late Gothic type, executed in stucco during the early part of the 19th century. The original 16th-century house inclosed a courtyard, but in 1811 the north, south and east sides were pulled down, and the west

---

[6] P.C.C. 1 Wattys; 36 Bennett.
[7] Cal. Pat. 1225–32, p. 234; Cott. MSS. Claud. C xi.
[8] Close, 30 Hen. VIII, pt. i, no. 61.
[9] Deeds of purchase and exchange, 96.
[10] Pat. 5 Eliz. pt. ii, m. 30.
[11] Clutterbuck, op. cit. ii, 362.
[12] Hist. MSS. Com. Rep. xiv, App. ix, 473.
[13] Ibid.
[14] Feet of F. Herts. East. 16 Eliz.
[15] Ibid. Trin. 2 Jas. I.
[16] Ibid.
[17] Clutterbuck, op. cit. ii, 362.
[18] Recov. R. Mich. 20 Jas. I, rot. 90.
[19] Inst. Bks. (P.R.O.).
[20] L. and P. Hen. VIII, vii, 1551.
[21] Chart. R. 35 Edw. I, no. 11, m. 5.
[22] Land Rev. Misc. Bks. ccxvi.
[22a] Urwick, op. cit. 586–7.
[23] See under Wheathampstead, V.C.H. Herts. ii, 313.
[1] Statistics from Bd. of Agric. (1905).

A HISTORY OF HERTFORDSHIRE

wing which remained was altered and added to and completely renewed externally. From plans [1a] and sketches of the old building prior to its demolition it would appear that the house must have been altered during the 17th and perhaps 18th century, but the entrance gateway in the centre of the east side of the courtyard, now partly incorporated in the West Lodge referred to below, appears to have been untouched, and was the last portion to be pulled down. The old plan of the west wing, as it existed before 1811, can still be traced in the present building, though no detail of the 16th century now remains except a plain tablet fixed in the entrance porch, which bears the arms of Sir Rowland Lytton and the date 1563. In the centre of the east front was the porch entering directly into the screens, on the right was the hall, which still remains, and on the west side of the hall was the library, now occupied by a modern stair, and at the north-west corner was the main staircase, now the library; this portion of the building was probably a later addition to the 16th-century house. At the north end of the hall was the dining parlour, now a modernized drawing room. The south end of the wing was occupied by the domestic offices, but all that portion facing the west has been formed into a long picture gallery; a back staircase at the south-east angle still retains its old position, but the stair is modern. A modern south wing has been added. The hall, which is of the same extent as formerly, and which is carried up

[1a] 'Excursion from Camerton to London and thence into Herts.' Add. MS. 33641, fol. 202; *Gent. Mag.* Nov. 1790.

GROUND PLAN OF KNEBWORTH HOUSE IN 1805

two stories, underwent considerable alterations during the 17th century. It has a coved ceiling with moulded oak principals, ribs and cornice and carved brackets. The spaces between the timbers are plastered. It was probably put up under the original open-timber roof early in the 17th century. The screen belongs to the same period, and behind it, over the screens, is the musicians' gallery. The oak screen is in three bays with semicircular arched openings. The central opening, which is the entrance, is flanked by caryatides formed of demi-human figures on tapering pedestals, the panels of which are carved. The spandrels of the arches are filled with pierced ornament. Above the arches is a bold entablature with moulded cornice and carved frieze and brackets, surmounted by the oak front to the gallery, which is carved with an open arabesque pattern. Each side arch is partly filled with solid panelling surmounted by a broken pediment with moulded cornice; in each panel is a cartouche containing arms of the Lytton and allied families.

The other three sides of the hall are covered with deal panelling, the design of which is attributed to Inigo Jones, and which may date from about 1650. The north end is an elaborate design with detached fluted Corinthian columns dividing the end of the hall into three bays, with an enriched entablature with moulded cornice; this is broken over the middle bay by a round-arched pediment with moulded cornice and panelled soffit; in the side bays are doors opening into the drawing room, formerly the dining parlour of the old house. The east and west sides of the hall are panelled in a more simple manner, with fluted Corinthian pilasters as divisions; in the centre of the west side is a plain fireplace with a large picture panel over, surmounted by a moulded cornice and pediment. The whole of the woodwork, both oak and deal, has been recently scraped and cleaned and left in its natural colour. The hall is lighted by windows in the east wall only. The drawing room has been completely modernized. There is a quantity of old panelling, chiefly of the 17th century, in some of the rooms on the upper floor, most of which appears to have been brought from elsewhere.

Part of the original gateway of the old house, which was pulled down in 1811, was incorporated in the West Lodge of the park on the Hitchin road, and the fact is recorded on a tablet, dated 1816, on the walls. The lodge is in two parts, connected by the old arches which span the drive. Two old windows and a turret doorway have also been reset in the walls of the lodge, which have been partly built with old thin bricks at the back. All the old work, which is of clunch, belongs to about the

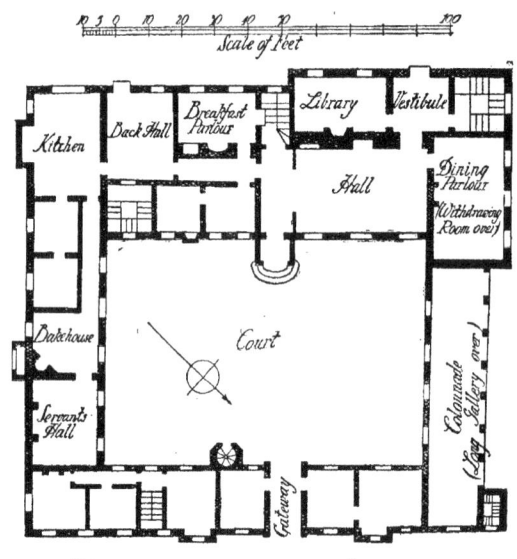

· 112 ·

middle of the 16th century. The two four-centred arches which span the drive are of two double-ogee continuously moulded orders, a good deal restored and with cement panelled bases. The windows are of two lights with four-centred arches under square moulded labels; the jambs and mullions are moulded. The turret doorway has a moulded four-centred arch with carved spandrels under a square head; one spandrel is carved with foliage, the other with a tun or barrel and vine leaves and fruit. The ornamental iron gates under the eastern arch and the fencing to the windows next the park are of 18th-century work.

From the centre of the village a road runs eastward to Deard's End, where there is an interesting late 16th-century farm-house of timber and brick nogging and a tiled roof. The church of St. Mary is a gravel-pit at Deard's End and another near Three Houses. There is a railway station on the Great Northern main line, situated in the extreme east of the parish near Deard's End.

The inclosure award was made in 1819, the authorizing Act being passed in 1810.[2]

In 1882 a portion of the parish on the east, including Swangley's Farm, was transferred to Datchworth.[3]

Place-names mentioned in 1638 are Courtfield, Blackhouse Ground, Coxe, Black Pitt, Neze Field, Blackwell Field and Wellfield.[4]

MANORS
The manor of *KNEBWORTH* was held in the time of Edward the Confessor by Aschil, a thegn of the king. In 1086 it formed part of the lands of Eudo Dapifer,

KNEBWORTH HOUSE: WEST LODGE ARCHES FROM THE WEST

is situated in the park which surrounds Knebworth House, and lies a short distance north-west from the village. Rustling End is a hamlet in the north-west of the parish, with Crouch Green about half a mile south. Little Rustling End Farm is a 17th-century timber and brick and timber and plaster house. Part of the hamlet of Broadwater lies on the north-eastern boundary of the parish. There are two tumuli in Graffridge Wood, somewhat damaged.

The subsoil of the parish is chalk. There are chalk-pits beside the railway and disused ones in Knebworth Park and west of Rustling End. There son of Hubert de Ryes, and was assessed at 8¼ hides.[5] About the middle of the 12th century the 'honour of Eudo Dapifer' was in the hands of Warine Fitz Gerold.[6] This honour evidently included Knebworth, for it is found in the possession of Margery or Margaret daughter and heir of Warine son of Warine Fitz Gerold, who married Baldwin de Redvers Earl of Devon, after whose death in 1216[7] she received Knebworth in dower.[8] She married secondly Falkes de Breauté, who held the manor in right of his wife, but was banished in 1224, when his lands were taken into the king's

[2] *Blue Bk. Incl. Awards*, 63–4.
[3] *Divided Parishes Act*, 1882.
[4] *Herts. Gen. and Antiq.* iii, 185.
[5] *V.C.H. Herts.* i, 328*b*.

[6] *Black Bk. Exch.* (ed. Hearne), i, 237–9; *Red Bk. Exch.* (Rolls Ser.), i, 38.
[7] G.E.C. *Complete Peerage*. Henry, brother of the elder Warine, held the honour in 1166. The younger Warine was chamberlain early in the 13th century (*Red Bk. of Exch.* i, 94, 175, 356; ii, 461).
[8] *Abbrev. Plac.* (Rec. Com.), 160.

A HISTORY OF HERTFORDSHIRE

hands.[9] Certain timber which Falkes had felled at Knebworth was then granted by the king to William Earl Marshal for building purposes.[10] The manor was restored to Margaret, being part of her own inheritance. Baldwin, Earl of Devon, her son, died in February 1244–5, and his son Baldwin in 1262,[11] leaving no issue. In 1267 there was a process concerning Knebworth between Margaret his widow and her sister-in-law Isabel, the wife of William de Fortibus Earl of Albemarle and heir of Baldwin.[12] Isabel died without surviving issue in 1293,[13] whereupon the descendants of Warine Fitz Gerold became extinct. The overlordship of Knebworth then passed to the descendants of Henry Fitz Gerold, brother of Warine. Henry's daughter and heir Alice, wife of Robert Lisle, had two sons, Robert and Gerard.[14] Robert Lisle, the grandson of the elder son Robert, therefore became heir of the Fitz Gerold property in 1293.[15] He was summoned to Parliament as Lord Lisle of Rougemont from 1311.[16] He was succeeded by his son John,[17] of whom Knebworth was held in 1346.[18] He died in 1356, and was succeeded by his son Robert Lord Lisle,[19] who probably died without issue about 1399,[20] when Knebworth presumably passed to Thomas Lord Berkeley, husband of Margaret, a descendant of Gerald Lisle, younger son of Alice Fitz Gerold and Robert Lisle.[21] The overlordship of Knebworth would thus pass through Elizabeth daughter of Thomas Lord Berkeley and wife of Richard Earl of Warwick to her daughter Margaret Countess of Shrewsbury, whose son John Talbot was created Lord and Baron of Lisle and died in 1453. His granddaughter and heir Elizabeth Talbot married Sir Edward Grey, who was also created Lord Lisle,[22] and Knebworth was held of him in 1482.[23] His son John died in 1504 without male heirs, when the overlordship escheated to the Crown, for in 1517 and after it was held of the king as of the duchy of Lancaster, of the fee of Lisle, by knight's service and suit of court of the duchy at Walbrook.[24]

LISLE. *Gules a leopard argent with a crown or.*

GREY, Lord Lisle. *Barry argent and azure with three roundels gules in the chief and a label argent.*

The sub-tenant of Knebworth in 1086 was Humphrey d'Ansleville[25] or Andevill, whose immediate heir is not known. Thomas de Andevill held lands of Eudo Dapifer's fief in 1166,[26] and Richard son of Thomas de Andevill seems to have been lord of the manor of Knebworth in 1214.[27] This Richard held the lands in Cambridgeshire which belonged to Humphrey d'Ansleville in 1086, and so was apparently his descendant.[28] In 1214–15 Richard settled the advowson of the church on Hamelin de Andevill.[29] In 1215 20 librates of land in Knebworth, 'which were of Hamon de Ablevill,' were granted to Hugh of Bath, clerk, to hold as long as the king pleased.[30] This was possibly owing to a forfeiture, for Richard de Andevill was holding Knebworth before 1224, and received seisin of it again in that year, with corn and timber, &c., for a payment of £50, after the king had taken it into his hands at the banishment of Falkes de Breauté.[31] The successor of this Richard is not known, and Knebworth next appears in 1292 in the possession of Robert de Hoo,[32] who seems to have held the Andevill lands in Cambridgeshire as well. He was still holding Knebworth in 1303,[33] but died before 1316, when his widow Beatrice conveyed the manor to Richard and Joan de Perers, who were to pay her 50 marks annually during her life, and afterwards a rose at Midsummer to her heirs. Failing the heirs of Richard and Joan de Perers, the manor was to return to Beatrice de Hoo and her heirs.[34] Richard and Joan, who appears to have been Beatrice's daughter,[35] had a son Richard, who died before 1346, leaving a son Edmund, who enfeoffed Walter de Mauny and his heirs of the manor and family without issue.[36] In 1346 Knebworth was said to be held by Walter de Mauny and Thomas de Hoo[37] (grandson of Robert and Beatrice),[38] who possibly had a life interest. The heirs of Edmund de Perers were his three sisters, Isabel, Margaret wife of John de la Ryvers, and Joan,[39] and in 1348 they confirmed Knebworth to Walter de Mauny,[40] who died seised of it in 1372.[41] After his death it seems to have been acquired by Guy de Bryan, who in 1388 conveyed it to Thomas Beauchamp Earl of Warwick.[42] The latter forfeited his lands in 1397, about which time Knebworth was conveyed by his brother Sir William Beauchamp[43] and others to Richard Forster, who held it jointly with Thomas Thorneburgh, John Onyng and John Shordich.[44] In 1398 an action was brought against Richard Forster by William de Hoo, who stated that he was son of Thomas grandson of Beatrice de Hoo, and claimed the manor by the terms of the fine of 1316 (see above), by which Beatrice had conveyed Knebworth to Richard and Joan de Perers, with reversion on failure of their heirs. Edmund de Perers and his three sisters, the grandchildren of Richard and Joan,

---

[9] Fine R. 8 Hen. III, m. 2.
[10] Rot. Lit. Claus. (Rec. Com.), i, 611b.
[11] G.E.C. Complete Peerage.
[12] Ibid.; Abbrev. Plac. (Rec. Com.), 160.
[13] G.E.C. Complete Peerage. [14] Ibid.
[15] Chan. Inq. p.m. 3 Edw. II, no. 60.
[16] G.E.C. Complete Peerage.
[17] Ibid. [18] Feud. Aids, ii, 437.
[19] G.E.C. Complete Peerage; Chan. Inq. p.m. 42 Edw. III (2nd nos.), no. 53; 46 Edw. III (1st nos.), no. 38.
[20] See G.E.C. Complete Peerage.
[21] Ibid. [22] Ibid.
[23] Chan. Inq. p.m. 22 Edw. IV, no. 39.
[24] Ibid. (Ser. 2), xxxiii, 5; Ct. of Wards, Feod. Surv. bdle. 17.
[25] V.C.H. Herts. i, 328b.
[26] Red Bk. Exch. (Rolls Ser.), i, 355.
[27] Feet of F. Herts. 16 John, no. 131.
[28] Testa de Nevill (Rec. Com.), 273.
[29] Feet of F. Herts. 16 John, no. 131.
[30] Rot. Lit. Claus. (Rec. Com.), i, 242b.
[31] Fine R. 8 Hen. III, m. 2.
[32] Chart. R. 20 Edw. I, no. 34.
[33] Feud. Aids, iii, 430.
[34] Feet of F. Herts. 9 Edw. II, no. 221.
[35] De Banco R. East. 21 Edw. II, m. 279.
[36] Ibid.
[37] Feud. Aids, ii, 437.
[38] Wrottesley, Ped. from the Plea R. 212–13.
[39] De Banco R. East. 21 Ric. II, m. 279.
[40] Feet of F. Herts. 22 Edw. III, no. 350; De Banco R. 355, m. 299.
[41] Chan. Inq. p.m. 46 Edw. III (1st nos.), no. 38.
[42] Feet of F. Herts. 12 Ric. II, no. 105. Guy was an executor of this earl's father, who died in 1369 (Dugdale, Baronage, i, 234). [43] Ibid. 238.
[44] De Banco R. 21 Ric. II, m. 279.

Knebworth House from the South

had all died childless. William de Hoo was their cousin and heir, but he also claimed that their father had had two sisters, Margaret and Rose, and that Margaret's grandson Richard Fitz Herbert, or Twycrosse, and Rose's great-grandson Walter Touneford should have been the rightful heirs, but were also dead without issue, and that the line being extinct the manor reverted to him. Richard Forster denied the existence of Rose de Peters and the descent of Richard Fitz Herbert, and apparently based his claim on the various conveyances of the manor since the death of Walter de Mauny. Judgement was given for Richard Forster,[45] and William de Hoo finally surrendered his claim to him in 1401–2.[46] In 1407 Richard conveyed Knebworth to Robert Brome,[47] who released it to William Askham and others in 1411–12,[48] apparently for the purpose of a conveyance to John Hotoft, who was in possession of the manor soon afterwards. In 1426 a claim to the manor was made by William Beleverge, who also declared himself to be a descendant of Beatrice de Hoo, and based his claim on the fine of 1316. The pedigree he gave claimed that Beatrice had had a son James, whose daughter Margaret had a son William Beleverge, whose son Stephen was the father of the claimant. The descent, however, seems to have been entirely spurious, and his claim was unsuccessful.[49]

John Hotoft was holding Knebworth in 1428,[50] and in 1430–1 received a release of all right in the manor from William Perers.[51] In 1440 he settled it on himself for life, with remainder to his daughter Idonia, wife of Sir John Barre, and her heirs.[52] Sir John Barre died in 1483, and was succeeded by his daughter Isabel, widow of Humphrey Stafford Earl of Devon, who married secondly Thomas Bourghchier.[53] Isabel and Thomas settled Knebworth on themselves in the same year,[54] and again in 1491,[55] and afterwards sold the reversion to Robert Lytton,[56] to whose son William Lytton two-thirds of the manor came upon Thomas Bourghchier's death in 1492,[57] one-third being claimed by Anne, Thomas's second wife, who survived him and was living in 1519.[58] William Lytton died in 1517, leaving an infant son Robert, the custody of whom was granted to Sir Richard Weston,[59] then a knight of the body to King Henry VIII.[60] In 1518 Sir Richard was made a Knight of the Bath, and next year was one of the 'sad and ancient knights put into the king's privy chamber.'[61] In 1520 he accompanied the king to the Field of the Cloth of Gold, and in the following year sat on the jury which condemned Edward Stafford, third Duke of Buckingham. In 1525 he was made Treasurer of Calais and in 1528 Under-Treasurer of England.[62] In 1533–4 his

LYTTON of Knebworth. *Ermine a chief indented azure with three crowns or therein.*

KNEBWORTH HOUSE: WEST LODGE

---

[45] De Banco R. 21 Ric. II, m. 279. Close, 3 Hen. IV, pt. i, m. 6.
[46] Feet of F. Herts. 9 Hen. IV, no. 62.
[47] Close, 13 Hen. IV, m. 41, 31, 30.
[48] Wrottesley, *Ped. from the Plea R.* 329.
[49] Feud. Aids, ii, 449.
[50] Close, 9 Hen. VI, m. 10.
[51] Feet of F. Herts. Trin. 18 Hen. VI, no. 101.
[52] Chan. Inq. p.m. 22 Edw. IV, no. 39.
[53] Feet of F. Div. Co. Mich. 1 Ric. III, no. 1.
[54] Ibid. Herts. Hil. 6 Hen. VII.
[55] Chan. Inq. p.m. (Ser. 2), xxxiii, 5.
[56] Ibid. vii, 3.
[57] L. and P. Hen. VIII, iii, 154.
[58] Ct. of Wards, Bks. of Liveries, liv, fol. 87a.
[59] Dict. Nat. Biog.
[60] Ibid. quoting Hall's Chronicle.
[61] Dict. Nat. Biog.

A HISTORY OF HERTFORDSHIRE

connexion with Knebworth ceased, for in that year Robert Lytton came of age and received his inheritance.[63] Upon Robert's death without male heirs Knebworth passed by will to his brother Rowland,[64] whose son Rowland inherited it in 1582.[65] William Lytton, son of the second Rowland, succeeded to Knebworth at his father's death in 1615,[66] and held it until 1660, when he was succeeded by his son, another Rowland.[67] William son of Sir Rowland Lytton inherited the manor in 1674, and died in 1705 without issue, when Knebworth passed to Lytton Strode, grandson of William's sister Judith and son of George Strode and Mary Robinson.[68] He assumed the surname of Lytton, which was also taken by his cousin William Robinson, who succeeded him in 1710, but had no Lytton descent. John Robinson-Lytton inherited the manor from his father in 1732, but died without issue in 1762, when his nephew Richard Warburton succeeded and took the name of Lytton. His daughter Elizabeth Barbara Warburton-Lytton married William

hoc virtutis opus

LYTTON, Earl of Lytton

Earle Bulwer, and upon inheriting Knebworth in 1810 assumed the surname of Lytton in addition. She died in 1843, leaving Knebworth to her third son Edward George, the famous novelist, who became Lord Lytton of Knebworth in 1866 and died in 1873. His son Edward Robert was created Earl of Lytton, and was succeeded in 1891 by his third but eldest surviving son Victor Alexander George Robert Lytton, second earl, who is the present lord of the manor.[69]

The great park of Knebworth is mentioned in 1472.[70] There is still a deer park of 156 acres, which is finely wooded and surrounds the house. A fair was granted to Robert de Hoo in 1292, to be held annually on the vigil, day and morrow of the Decollation of St. John the Baptist[71] (28–30 August). It was confirmed in 1547,[72] but was discontinued before the end of the 18th century. Free warren was granted and confirmed at the same time as the fair and was also confirmed to Richard de Perers in 1317[73] and to William Lytton in 1616.[74]

A mill is mentioned in Knebworth in 1086[75] and in 1611,[76] but does not appear to exist now. In 1274–5 the lord of the manor held view of frankpledge, gallows and the assize of bread and ale; he paid 17*s.* 4*d.* yearly to the sheriff's tourn.[77] Court leet was granted to William Lytton in 1616.[78]

The manor of *THREHOUS* (Trehus, le Trehouse, Treyhouse) is first mentioned in 1303.[79] It seems to have been a part of the manor of Knebworth and was perhaps the two messuages, 160 acres of land and 100 acres of wood which were excepted in the fine of 1316, settling Knebworth on Richard and Joan de Perers.[80] This estate was conveyed by William de Beauchamp to Richard Forster and others, but owing to its omission from the fine could not be claimed by William de Hoo in 1398.[81] It followed the same descent as the manor of Knebworth,[82] and presumably became eventually merged in it. The manor of Threhous is last mentioned separately in 1616.[83] It lay in the western part of the parish, and the locality is still marked by a tenement called Three Houses.

The parish church of *ST. MARY CHURCH AND ST. THOMAS OF CANTERBURY*[84] stands to the north-east of Knebworth House in the park. It is built of flint rubble, with clunch dressings and the roofs are tiled. It consists of a chancel and nave, north chapel, west tower, south porch and north vestry.

The nave was built about the middle of the 12th century and the chancel is probably of the same date. The west tower dates from about 1420, the north chapel from a century later, and the south porch from about 1600. The nave was re-roofed in the 15th century and the north chapel was rebuilt about 1700. In the 19th century the chancel was almost entirely rebuilt and the north vestry was added.

The chancel, which is almost wholly modern, still has in the north wall a blocked window with an edgeroll moulding of about 1150, and below it is an arched recess of the early 16th century. To the west of the recess and of the same date is the arch which opens into the north chapel. It has been much repaired and has half-octagonal responds supporting the inner order. The round chancel arch, of about 1150, has engaged shafts with rudely scalloped capitals. On the south side of the chancel under the easternmost window is a 14th-century piscina, with an ogee

---

[63] Ct. of Ward Bks. clxxiii, fol. 73.
[64] Chan. Inq. p.m. (Ser. 2), xcv, 99. Robert had three daughters, Ellen, Elizabeth and Anne.
[65] Ibid. cxcix, 89; Ct. of Wards, Feod. Surv. bdle. 17; Recov. R. Trin. 30 Eliz. rot. 21; Hil. 9 Jas. I, rot. 99.
[66] Chan. Inq. p.m. (Ser. 2), ccclix, 114; Recov. R. Hil. 6 Chas. I, rot. 53.
[67] *Visit. of Herts.* (Harl. Soc. xxii), 73.
[68] *V.C.H. Herts. Families,* where a detailed descent is given.

[69] Ibid.
[70] Harl. Roll, H 13.
[71] Chart. R. 20 Edw. I, m. 5, no. 34.
[72] Pat. 1 Edw. VI, pt. ii, m. 47.
[73] Chart. R. 10 Edw. II, no. 28, m. 13.
[74] Pat. 14 Jas. I, pt. xvii, no. 9.
[75] *V.C.H. Herts.* i, 328*b*.
[76] Recov. R. Hil. 9 Jas. I, rot. 99.
[77] *Rot. Hund.* (Rec. Com.), i, 192.
[78] Pat. 14 Jas. I, pt. xvii, no. 9.
[79] *Feud. Aids,* ii, 430, 437.

[80] De Banco R. East. 21 Ric. II, m. 279.
[81] Ibid.
[82] Close, 13 Hen. IV, m. 41; Feet of F. Herts. 18 Hen. VI, no. 101; Hil. 6 Hen. VII; Chan. Inq. p.m. (Ser. 2), vii, 3; xxxiii, 5; xcv, 99.
[83] Pat. 14 Jas. I, pt. xvii, no. 9.
[84] Dimensions: chancel, 27 ft. 6 in. by 13 ft. 6 in.; north chapel, 27 ft. 6 in. by 12 ft.; nave, 57 ft. 6 in. by 20 ft.; tower, 12 ft. square.

116

KNEBWORTH HOUSE: WEST LODGE: 16TH-CENTURY WINDOW

KNEBWORTH CHURCH: THE CHANCEL ARCH

cinquefoiled head. The sill is modern. The chancel roof has an oak-panelled wagon ceiling.

The north chapel has two square-headed windows, at the east and north, of about 1700, with wooden frames. An elaborate ironwork screen of the same date, set in the arch on the south side, separates the chapel from the chancel. The flat plaster ceiling is of about the same date also.

The nave is approached from the north chapel by a square-headed skew doorway emerging at the north-east corner of the nave. Beside it, in the north wall, is a single-light window with modern tracery. Immediately above this window is the upper doorway of the rood-loft stair, and the blocked lower doorway with a moulded two-centred arch is visible to the west of the window. To the west of this is a much repaired two-centred arch, which now leads to a vestry, and west of this is a wide single-light window, a modern insertion, which probably marks the position of an earlier two-light window.

On the south side are a modern single-light window, a square-headed window of three lights with much restored tracery of about 1350, and a two-light window of the 15th century, which is also much restored. To the west of these is the south doorway, of about 1380. It has a two-centred arch, much repaired, leading to the south porch, which is heavily covered with ivy and shows only traces of the original windows. The entrance archway is four-centred and coated with cement. To the west of the south doorway is a window of about 1500, from which the central mullion is gone.

The tower arch, of about 1420, is of two moulded orders with engaged shafts. The tracery of the west window is modern, but the window itself is original with grotesque heads on the stops of the labels. The west doorway has a two-centred arch in a square head. There are shields in the spandrels, one of which bears the arms of Hotoft : Sable three dragons' heads erect and razed argent.

On the north and south sides of the second stage are narrow loops, and in the bell chamber are four windows of two cinquefoiled lights with a quatrefoil over.

The nave is seated throughout with a complete set of 15th-century oak seats, moulded and having rich tracery in the end panels. At the north-east is a high pew with pinnacles at the corners and a pierced cresting. The pulpit is of richly carved 16th-century Flemish panelling, made up in the 18th century. One of the panels is dated 1567. There is similar panelling on the east wall of the nave behind the pulpit.

The font is octagonal, of limestone and plainly moulded. It dates from about 1480.

KNEBWORTH CHURCH FROM THE SOUTH-EAST

In the chancel is a brass of Simon Bache, 1414, a priest in eucharistic vestments, with figures of saints on his cope, and an inscription ; under the archway between the chancel and the chapel and partly covered by the iron grille another, to John Hotoft, of about 1470, with an inscription on six strips of brass, and three shields of arms. The brass is said to have been on an altar tomb and is not now on its original slab. On the chancel wall is a slab to Judith Lytton, wife of Nicholas Strode, 1662 ; and a floor slab is to John Ham, *clericus*, 1684.

The monuments in the chapel are mostly to various members of the Lytton family. There are a brass of Rowland Lytton and his two wives, 1582, with arms and an inscription ; a monument, 1601, to Anna the wife of Rowland Lytton, with arms ; a tomb of Sir William Lytton, 1704–5, with a recumbent marble figure under an elaborate canopy with the arms and quarterings of Lytton. There are floor

A HISTORY OF HERTFORDSHIRE

slabs to Judith the wife of Rowland Lytton, 1659; to Sir William Lytton, 1660; Sir Rowland Lytton, 1674; Judith (Lytton) wife of Sir Thomas Barrington, 1657, with arms, and to the son of Giles Strangways, 1646. In the nave, on the west splay of the north window, is a defaced inscription, said to be to John de Hall, rector, with the date of birth, 1395.

There are five bells: (1) by John Waylett, 1716; (2) and (3) by Edward Hall, 1730 and 1732; (4) dated 1697; and (5) by J. Briant, 1812.

The plate includes a 17th-century cup, with the date erased, and a paten of 1668.

The registers are contained in four books: (i) all entries 1606 to 1702; (ii) baptisms and burials 1703 to 1812, marriages 1703 to 1753; (iii) baptisms and burials 1709 to 1812, marriages 1709 to 1753; (iv) marriages 1754 to 1812.

ADVOWSON The advowson of the church has always belonged to the lord of the manor. In 1214–15 it was granted by Richard de Andevill to Hamelin de Andevill and his heirs[65] (see manor). The Earl of Lytton is the present patron.

A terrier of 1638 describes the parsonage as 'contayning a hall, two parlours, a kitchin, a larder and buttery below stayres and seaven severall roomes above stayres.' There were also 'a milke house and bolting house, a barne contayning five bayes, a garner, a stable, an hayhouse, a carthouse, a little stable, hogscoate and hennhouse; a garden and oarchard.' The glebe lands consisted of 51 acres, with a cottage 'tyled contayning three rooms below and one above.'[66]

There seems to be no record of early Dissent in Knebworth, but a Congregational chapel was erected in 1887.

CHARITIES In 1811 William Johnson by his will bequeathed £100 consols, the annual dividends, amounting to £2 10s., to be distributed among eight poor housekeepers, with a preference to those attending divine worship. The stock is held by the official trustees.

In 1836 Mrs. Elizabeth Barbara Bulwer Lytton erected five almshouses on the Codicote road for old and deserving people of the parish, supported by the Earl of Lytton.

LETCHWORTH

The parish of Letchworth, containing about 888 acres of land, lies between Walsworth and Willian; its northern boundary is formed by the Icknield Way, the southern by the main road between Great Wymondley and Baldock. The detached part of the parish surrounding Burleigh Farm, 8 miles south of the town of Letchworth, was transferred to Knebworth by a Local Government Board Order of 1907. By the same order Norton and Willian were amalgamated with Letchworth for civil purposes, but by a further order of 1908 the latter was made a civil parish.

The town of Letchworth stands on the borders of Bedfordshire. It has a station on the Hitchin and Cambridge branch of the Great Northern railway.

The grounds of Letchworth Hall, now an hotel belonging to the Garden City, adjoin the churchyard on the south side. It is said to have been built by Sir William Lytton about the year 1620, on the site of an earlier house, and all the old parts of the existing building are Jacobean in character. In plan it resembles the letter T, the hall and some rooms to the southward forming the vertical portion, while a wing on the west containing the dining room, &c., and another on the east, occupied by the kitchen offices, form the upper part of the T. A large block of buildings was erected on the north side by the Rev. John Alington before 1846. He also built some detached stables to the south of this block. The old part of the building is of thin 2-in. bricks. Some blocks of clunch and flint in a small disused porch at the extreme south end may be a portion of the former building. The eaves of the central hall are low, but rooms are formed in the roof, lighted by dormer windows at the back, and on the front by a window in a brick gable which seems to be a much later addition or a rebuilding. The principal entrance is by a porch, with a room over, on the east side of the hall. This porch has a low entrance of brick with a flat three-centred arch. Each of the gables has a brick coping, with an octagonal terminal at the apex, but the top of the finial at the apex has disappeared. All the roofs are tiled. At the back or west side of the hall is a boldly projecting chimney, with offsets above the roof, and finished on the top with two square detached shafts set diagonally. All the older windows have oak mullions, but many of the others are more modern in construction. On the south wall of the west wing are three stone panels; the central one, which has been rebuilt into a modern bay window, bears a shield with the following arms: Quarterly of 4: (1) Ermine a chief indented with three crowns therein, for Lytton; (2) Three boars' heads, for Booth; (3) A fesse between six acorns with three oak leaves on the fesse for Ogden; (4) Ermine a cross with five escallops thereon. The shield on the right bears the arms of Lytton impaling St. John. The panel on the right is carved with two birds holding a ring between them, with the inscription above: 'Sic nos junxit amor.' Beyond the porch is a passage running the full width of the hall, under what was, until Alington's time, the musicians' gallery, now built up and thrown into a bedroom. A small modern stair at the end of the passage no doubt occupies the position of the old gallery stair. Some old balusters and newels have been re-used on this stair. The oak screen next the hall is a very fine and highly enriched piece of work of the time of James I. It is in a perfect condition, though one section of it has been moved about 2 ft. forward to give more room for the stair behind, and the upper part has been removed. There are two openings in the centre, each about 4 ft. wide, with flat arches over, the openings being separated by a circular column with Doric capital. The remainder of the screen is filled in with diagonal

[65] Feet of F. Herts. 16 John, no. 131. [66] *Herts. Gen. and Antiq.* iii, 184–5.

KNEBWORTH CHURCH: THE PULPIT

BROADWATER HUNDRED   LETCHWORTH

panelling. The spandrels of the arches and the mouldings are carved. Above is the cornice which formerly supported the front of the gallery. It projects about 2 ft. On the frieze is a row of small squares and circles alternating, with leaves carved in them. There are carved consoles at intervals along the cornice. On the small brackets carrying the outer ends of the arches thistles are carved. The hall is a large apartment 47 ft. by 21 ft. It has windows on each side and is flat ceiled with plaster. There is a large fireplace 6 ft. wide with splayed three-centred arch on the west side near the screen. Over the fireplace a carved stone shield has been inserted, bearing

crowned by a cornice. All the work is elaborately carved. The upper floor of the main building, including over the hall, is subdivided into a number of rooms, most of them small, and containing little of interest. There is a fine fireplace, however, over that in the dining room, but owing to the formation of new rooms it is now in a passage. The lower part is of clunch, having a four-centred arch with mouldings similar to that in the dining room; on either side are half female figures undraped, on carved pedestals, supporting the projecting portion of the entablature, which has a moulded cornice, with dentil enrichment, moulded architrave, and carved frieze

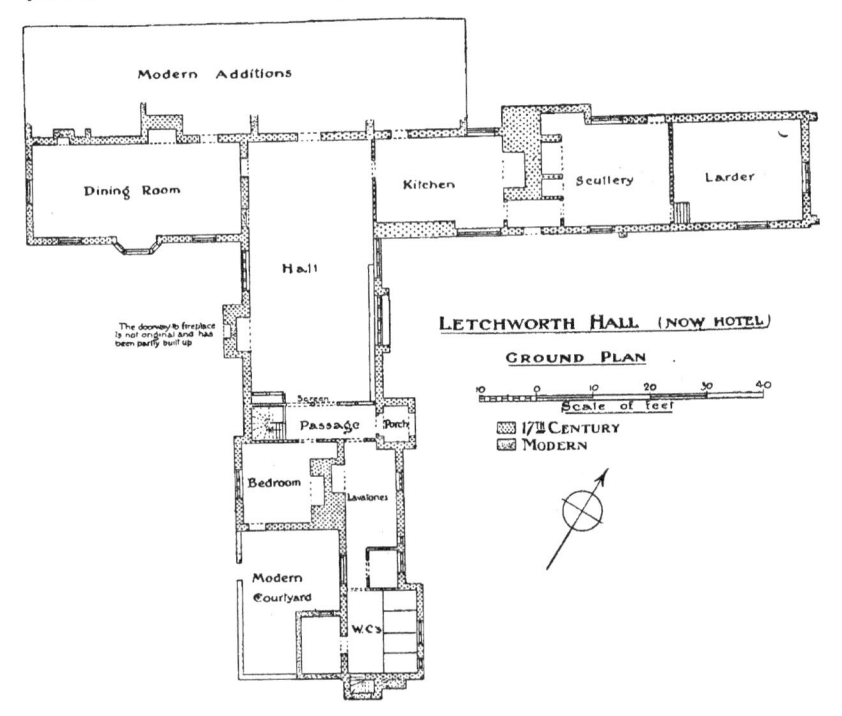

[Ground plan of Letchworth Hall (now Hotel), showing Modern Additions, Dining Room, Kitchen, Scullery, Larder, Hall, Screen, Passage, Porch, Bedroom, Lavatories, Modern Courtyard, W.Cs. Scale of feet. 17th Century and Modern indicated.]

the arms of Alington, which are Sable a bend engrailed between six billets argent. On the other side there is a brick seat along part of the wall, which, however, appears to be modern. The floor is paved with modern bricks. At the north end of the hall is the modern entrance to the additions of last century. The dining room, about 37 ft. by 16 ft., extends to the west of the hall. The old doorway, now built up, still remains. A modern doorway has been opened into the dining room, which contains a good stone fireplace and carved oak chimneypiece. The fireplace is of the usual early 17th-century type with four-centred arch with the outer moulding carried square above it. The overmantel is carried up to the ceiling, and is divided into two panelled compartments flanked by human demi-figures and

with consoles at intervals. All this work appears to be Jacobean, but above it is a large panel reaching to the ceiling containing four figures in high relief, representing the Judgment of Paris, which is probably of late 17th-century date. It is executed in plaster and the figures are only slightly draped. Paris stands in the centre offering the apple to Venus, who has a Cupid clinging to her knees; beside her are Juno with a peacock at her feet and Minerva with a helmet.

North of the church is a timber-framed house now divided into cottages; it is of early 17th-century date with a projecting porch. The post-office is a house of the same age and style of construction, now L-shaped, a south wing having apparently been removed.

Little Rustling End Farm, a mile and a half west of Knebworth Church and now in that parish, is a rectangular two-storied timber-framed house of the 17th century. The construction, with brick filling below and plaster above, is only seen at the back of the house, the front being cemented. The kitchen has an open timber-roof supported by a beam. At the back of the house is a small staircase wing.

The Garden City Pioneer Company are now the sole landowners in Letchworth parish, which is being laid out by them for residential and business purposes; it is said that over 9 miles of new roads have been made.

The soil is sandy loam, in some parts clay with beds of sand and gravel; the subsoil is chalk.

LETCHWORTH HALL: PART OF STAIR

MANORS LETCHWORTH (HANCHETS or MONTFITCHETS).—Before the Norman Conquest Letchworth was held by Godwin of Souberie (Soulbury), a thegn of King Edward the Confessor. In 1086 it formed part of the domain of Robert Gernon, and was assessed at 10 hides.[1] Robert Gernon's estates were acquired early in the reign of Henry I by William de Montfitchet,[2] who with his wife Rohais seems to have been holding Letchworth at the beginning of the 12th century.[3] His son William[4] succeeded him before 1135 and married Margaret[5] the daughter of Gilbert Fitz Richard de Clare.[6] His wife outlived him and was still holding some of the Montfitchet lands in 1185.[7] The rest of William's lands seem to have passed about 1167 to his son Gilbert,[8] whose wife's name was Avelina.[9] Gilbert was succeeded by his son Richard about 1190,[10] whose son, also named Richard,[11] was one of the confederate barons of 1215 who demanded the Charter of Liberties from King John.[12] He was among those excommunicated by Pope Innocent III in 1216,[13] and was taken prisoner by Henry III at Lincoln in 1217.[14] In 1244 he was one of the barons' deputies chosen to consider the king's demand for a subsidy.[15] He appears in connexion with Letchworth in 1240.[16] He died without issue about 1258,[17] his heirs being his three sisters: Margery wife of Hugh de Bolbek, Aveline wife of William de Fortibus Earl of Albemarle, and Philippa wife of Hugh de Pleyz.[18] The third of his inheritance, including the portion held by his widow Joyce in dower until 1274, was assigned to the children of Margery de Bolbek, the eldest sister, and was divided between her daughters Philippa de Lancaster, Margery Corbett and Maud de la Val,[19] Letchworth being apportioned to the second daughter Margery and her husband Nicholas Corbett.[20] Margery afterwards married Ralph Fitz William.[21] She is known to have conveyed her lands in Ayot St. Peter to Robert Burnell, Bishop of Bath and Wells and chancellor of Edward I, and as Philip Burnell, Robert's nephew and heir,[22] died seised of Letchworth in 1294,[23] it seems probable that Margery conveyed Letchworth also to Philip's uncle. In 1295 Letchworth was assigned to Philip's widow Maud in dower,[24] and passed after her death to her son Edward, who died childless in 1315, and

[1] V.C.H. Herts. i, 323b.
[2] V.C.H. Essex, i, 347.
[3] Dugdale, Mon. ii, 229. [4] Ibid.
[5] Ibid. v, 586-7.
[6] S. Grimaldi, Rot. de Dominabus, 45.
[7] Ibid.
[8] Dugdale, Mon. v, 586-7; Red Bk. Exch. (Rolls Ser.), i, 349, 38.
[9] Dugdale, Mon. iv, 231.
[10] Ibid.; Red Bk. Exch. (Rolls Ser.), ii, 730.
[11] Dugdale, Mon. iv, 231.
[12] Matt. Paris, Chron. Majora (Rolls Ser.), ii, 585.
[13] Ibid. 644.
[14] Ibid. iii, 22.
[15] Ibid. iv, 362.
[16] Feet of F. Herts. 24 Hen. III, o. 283.
[17] Banks, Dormant and Extinct Peerages, i, 140.
[18] Close, 52 Hen. III, m. 8; G.E.C. Complete Peerage; Wrottesley, Ped. from the Plea R. 2.
[19] Close, 52 Hen. III, m. 8. Alice de Huntercombe, a fourth daughter, had presumably died between 1268 and 1274.
[20] Cal. Close, 1272-9, p. 82.
[21] Abbrev. Plac. (Rec. Com.), 303.
[22] Dict. Nat. Biog.
[23] Chan. Inq. p.m. 22 Edw. I, no. 45.
[24] Cal. Close, 1288-96, p. 463.

BROADWATER HUNDRED — LETCHWORTH

subsequently to his sister Maud, the wife of John Handlo.[25] Nicholas son of Maud and John assumed the surname of Burnell; he was holding Letchworth in 1346[26] and died in 1382, when he was succeeded by his son Hugh.[27] Hugh Burnell died in 1420 seised of the Montfitchet lands on the Essex border,[28] which may have included Letchworth, though it is not mentioned by name. His heirs were his three granddaughters Joyce Erdington (who died childless), Katherine Ratcliffe and Margaret Hungerford.[29] Edmund Hungerford, husband of Margaret, was seised of the Montfitchet lands in Essex, but the overlordship of Letchworth cannot be definitely traced any further.

Very little is known of the early sub-tenants of Letchworth. In 1086 William of Letchworth, a Norman and one of the Domesday jurors for Broadwater Hundred,[30] held the manor of Robert Gernon.[31]

holding it as late as 1314[37]; in 1346 it was held by another Richard Montfitchet.[38] Edmund Barrington was assessed for it in 1428,[39] but it is not clear whether he acquired it from the Montfitchets. About the middle of the 15th century it came into the possession of Thomas Hanchet of Bedford, who was holding it in 1474.[40] He was succeeded by William Hanchet, who died seised of it in 1515, leaving a son Andrew.[41] Andrew, however, died in the following year and his lands passed to his brother John, an infant of two.[42] Letchworth had been settled to the use of

SNAGGE of Letchworth. *Argent three pheons sable.*

LETCHWORTH HALL: WEST FRONT

Later the sub-tenancy seems to have been acquired by a younger branch of the Montfitchet family. In 1274, when Margery and Nicholas Corbett acquired the manor, the sub-tenant was a John Muschet,[32] whose name is probably a corrupt form of Montfitchet.[33] In 1295 Letchworth is said to have been held of Maud Burnell by 'the heirs of Richard de Montfitchet,'[34] and a Richard de Montfitchet claimed the advowson in 1302.[35] In 1303 Custancia Montfitchet was assessed for the fee,[36] and seems to have been

John's mother Margery for her life.[43] John attained his majority in 1535,[44] and together with Bridget his wife sold Letchworth in 1547 to Thomas Snagge.[45] Thomas was succeeded at Letchworth by his second son Robert Snagge,[46] who was lord of the manor in 1574.[47] His brother and successor William Snagge[48] died before 1596, leaving a widow Margaret, who by that time had married William Walford, and a son William.[49] William Snagge, jun., soon after conveyed the manor to Sir Rowland Lytton

---

[25] G.E.C. *Complete Peerage*; *Feud. Aids*, ii, 430.
[26] *Feud. Aids*, ii, 436. The name of Burnell is here ascribed to John as well as Nicholas.
[27] G.E.C. *Complete Peerage*.
[28] Chan. Inq. p.m. 8 Hen. V, no. 116.
[29] G.E.C. *Complete Peerage*.
[30] *V.C.H. Herts.* i, 265.
[31] Ibid. 323*b*.
[32] *Cal. Close*, 1272–9, p. 82.

[33] Cf. the spelling in *Feud. Aids*, ii, 930.
[34] *Cal. Close*, 1288–96, p. 463.
[35] *Abbrev. Plac.* (Rec. Com.), 246.
[36] *Feud. Aids*, ii, 430.
[37] She was then assessed for property in Letchworth (Lay Subs. R. bdle. 120, no. 9).
[38] *Feud. Aids*, ii, 436.
[39] Ibid. 448. See also Montfitchets in Wallington.
[40] Chan. Inq. p.m. 14 Edw. IV, no. 35.

[41] Ibid. (Ser. 2), xxxi, 57.
[42] Exch. Inq. p.m. (Ser. 2), file 301, no. 6; *L. and P. Hen. VIII*, iv, g. 297 (21).
[43] Ct. of Wards, Misc. Bks. dlxxviii, fol. 272 *d*.
[44] Ibid.
[45] Feet of F. Herts. Mich. 1 Edw. VI.
[46] *Visit. of Herts.* (Harl. Soc. xxii), 22.
[47] Recov. R. Mich. 1574, rot. 1304.
[48] *Visit. of Herts.* (Harl. Soc. xxii), 22.
[49] Chan. Proc. (Ser. 2), bdle. 291, no. 5.

of Knebworth,[50] who died seised of it in 1615.[51] Letchworth then followed the descent of Knebworth Manor[52] until 1811,[53] but a few years later it was sold to John Williamson of Baldock, who possessed it in 1821.[54] He died in 1830 and left Letchworth to his grandson the Rev. John Alington, son of his daughter Sarah, who died in 1863.[55] The manor then passed successively to John Alington's second but eldest surviving son William, who died childless in 1874, and to his youngest son the Rev. Julius Alington of Little Barford.[56] The latter possessed Letchworth until 1903, when the First Garden City Pioneer Company acquired the whole parish by purchase.[57]

William Lytton was granted court leet and free warren in Letchworth in 1616.[58]

Half a fee in Letchworth was held by the Knights Templars in the 13th century, and 120 acres in addition were granted to them by Richard de Montfitchet for a term of fifty years.[59] Nothing more is known of the descent of this half fee.

NEVELLS or *NEVILLS* was a small manor which was held of the manor of Letchworth.[60] It is not called a manor until 1324. In 1198 John de Nevill claimed 4 virgates of land in Letchworth as his inheritance from Alban his grandfather, who was seised of it.[61] A John de Nevill appears again in 1247-8,[62] and in 1324 Walter de Nevill, son of this or another John, conveyed the reversion of the manor, which another Walter de Nevill held for life, to John de Blomvile,[63] lord of the manor of Chesfield in Graveley. Following the descent of this manor[64] (q.v.) it passed to the Barringtons,[65] and remained in that family until it came to John son of Nicholas Barrington[66] in 1515. In 1524 the wardship of John Barrington was granted to Henry Earl of Essex,[67] but John seems to have attained his majority in the following year.[68] Soon after this the Barringtons must have conveyed Nevells to the Snagge family, who acquired Letchworth in 1547, for in 1596 William Snagge and his mother conveyed Nevells to Sir Rowland Lytton.[69] Sir Rowland died in 1615 seised of the reversion of the 'capital messuage called Nevill' after the death of Margaret Walford (William Snagge's mother), and was possessed of the residue of the manor.[70] He already held Letchworth, and from that date Nevells and Letchworth followed the same descent and were presumably amalgamated.

BURLEIGH or *BURLEY* (Borneleye, Boureleghe, xiii cent. ; Borleye, xiv cent. ; Burlee, xv cent.) is now represented by Burleigh Farm in a detached portion of Letchworth parish between Stevenage and Knebworth, situated about 8 miles south of Letchworth. In the 14th century it appears held with Wollenwich as a quarter of a knight's fee, so it is possible that in 1086 it was included in the half hide and half virgate in Wollenwich (Wlwenewiche) held of Robert Gernon by the William who held Letchworth.[71] The overlordship of Burleigh appears in the same hands as that of Letchworth (q.v.), passing from the Montfitchets (the successors of Robert Gernon) to the Burnells. Philip Burnell died seised of a quarter fee in Burleigh in 1294,[72] and in 1303 a quarter fee in Burleigh and Wollenwich was held of the heirs of Philip Burnell by Laurence de Brok.[73]

The family of Brok had probably been holding the fee in sub-tenancy for some time previous to this, for a Laurence de Brok, who died about 1275, appears as grantee in conveyances of land in Wollenwich.[74] He had a son Hugh, who was the father of the Laurence of 1303.[75] This Laurence[76] was holding Burleigh in 1294,[77] and died before 1330, leaving a widow Ellen,[78] after whose death his lands passed to their son Ralph.[79] Ralph's heirs, who were holding Burleigh in 1346,[80] were his three daughters, Joan, who died childless, Ellen and Agnes.[81] There is no evidence to show which of the two latter inherited Burleigh, but Agnes is known to have had a daughter Joan and a granddaughter Katrine, whose daughter was named Cecily.[82] Possibly the Thomas Vinter who was holding the property in 1428[83] was the husband of Katrine or Cecily, in which case Burleigh would have descended to one of Cecily's granddaughters, Joan Alington, Elizabeth Taillard and Margaret Langley, who claimed some of the Brok lands in 1468.[84] Early in the 16th century Burleigh came into the hands of Ralph Praunces, son of William Fraunces, from whom he perhaps inherited it. Ralph died seised of it in 1533, leaving an infant son William, who was placed in the wardship of Sir Henry Sacheverell.[85] In 1557 William Praunces and Elizabeth his wife conveyed the property to John Godfrey or Cowper.[86] The latter died in 1565, leaving Burleigh to his younger son Francis, then under age.[87] The latter died in 1631, leaving 'Burley Ground and the Hault' to be divided between his three sons Edward, William and John,[88] after which all records of the estate cease, but it seems to

---

[50] Feet of F. Herts. Trin. 39 Eliz.
[51] Chan. Inq. p.m. (Ser. 2), ccclix, 114.
[52] Recov. R. Hil. 6 Chas. I, rot. 53 ; Chauncy, op. cit. 385 ; Salmon, op. cit. 176 ; Recov. R. Trin. 21 Geo. II, rot. 273.
[53] Ibid. Hil. 51 Geo. III, rot. 41.
[54] Ibid.
[55] Clutterbuck, op. cit. ii, 385.
[56] Burke, *Landed Gentry.*
[57] Ibid.
[58] *Prospectus First Garden City Co., Ltd.*
[59] Pat. 14 Jas. I, pt. xvii.
[60] Assize R. 323, m. 40 d.
[61] Chan. Inq. p.m. 14 Edw. IV, no. 35 ; (Ser. 2), lxxx, 13 ; *L. and P. Hen. VIII,* iv, 297 (21).
[62] *Rot. Cur. Reg.* (Rec. Com.), i, 166.
[63] Assize R. 318, m. 17.
[64] Feet of F. Herts. East. 17 Edw. II, no. 375.
[65] Feet of F. 25 Edw. III, no. 387.
[66] Ibid. 12 Ric. II, no. 103 ; *Feud. Aids,* ii, 448 ; Chan. Inq. p.m. 14 Edw. IV, no. 35.
[67] Ibid. (Ser. 2), lxxx, 13.
[68] *L. and P. Hen. VIII,* iv, 297 (21).
[69] Ct. of Wards, Misc. Bks. cxxix, fol. 36.
[70] Feet of F. Herts. Mich. 38 & 39 Eliz.
[71] Chan. Inq. p.m. (Ser. 2), ccclix, 114.
[72] *V.C.H. Herts.* i, 323. There were also 1½ virgates in Wiwenewiche held by a certain Roger of Peter de Valognes (ibid. 336*b*).
[73] Chan. Inq. p.m. 22 Edw. I, no. 45.
[74] *Feud. Aids,* ii, 430.
[75] See Add. Chart. 15467 and Harl. Chart. 45 B. 1.
[76] See Brooks in Stevenage. This seems to be the last mention of Wollenwich in connexion with this holding, so that the Wollenwich held by Robert Gernon in 1086 is probably coincident with the later Burleigh. There was, however, other land at Wollenwich attached to the Argenteins' manor of Wymondley (see Chan. Inq. p.m. 4 Ric. II, no. 110). The name seems to be now lost.
[77] See Add. Chart. 977.
[78] Chan. Inq. p.m. 22 Edw. I, no. 45 d.
[79] Chart. R. 4 Edw. III, m. 14, no. 28.
[80] Wrottesley, *Ped. from the Plea R.* 428.
[81] *Feud. Aids,* ii, 436.
[82] Wrottesley, *Ped. from the Plea R.* 428.
[83] Ibid.
[84] *Feud. Aids,* ii, 448.
[85] Wrottesley, *Ped. from the Plea R.* 428.
[86] Chan. Inq. p.m. (Ser. 2), lvii, 4.
[87] Feet of F. Herts. Trin. 3 & 4 Phil. and Mary.
[88] Chan. Inq. p.m. (Ser. 2), cli, 57 ; Chan. Proc. (Ser. 2), bdle. 210, no. 25.
[89] Chan. Inq. p.m. (Ser. 2), ccclxiv, 50.

LETCHWORTH HALL. PART OF SCREEN IN HALL.

LETCHWORTH HALL. FIREPLACE ON FIRST FLOOR.

A HISTORY OF HERTFORDSHIRE

of Knebworth,[50] who died seised of it in 1615.[51] Letchworth then followed the descent of Knebworth Manor[52] until 1811,[53] but a few years later it was sold to John Williamson of Baldock, who possessed it in 1821.[54] He died in 1830 and left Letchworth to his grandson the Rev. John Alington, son of his daughter Sarah, who died in 1863.[55] The manor then passed successively to John Alington's second but eldest surviving son William, who died childless in 1874, and to his youngest son the Rev. Julius Alington of Little Barford.[56] The latter possessed Letchworth until 1903, when the First Garden City Pioneer Company acquired the whole parish by purchase.[57]

William Lytton was granted court leet and free warren in Letchworth in 1616.[58]

Half a fee in Letchworth was held by the Knights Templars in the 13th century, and 120 acres in addition were granted to them by Richard de Montfitchet for a term of fifty years.[59] Nothing more is known of the descent of this half fee.

NEVELLS or *NEVILLS* was a small manor which was held of the manor of Letchworth.[60] It is not called a manor until 1324. In 1198 John de Nevill claimed 4 virgates of land in Letchworth as his inheritance from Alban his grandfather, who was seised of it.[61] A John de Nevill appears again in 1247–8,[62] and in 1324 Walter de Nevill, son of this or another John, conveyed the reversion of the manor, which another Walter de Nevill held for life, to John de Blomvile,[63] lord of the manor of Chesfield in Graveley. Following the descent of this manor[64] (q.v.) it passed to the Barringtons,[65] and remained in that family until it came to John son of Nicholas Barrington[66] in 1515. In 1524 the wardship of John Barrington was granted to Henry Earl of Essex,[67] but John seems to have attained his majority in the following year.[68] Soon after this the Barringtons must have conveyed Nevells to the Snagge family, who acquired Letchworth in 1547, for in 1596 William Snagge and his mother conveyed Nevells to Sir Rowland Lytton.[69] Sir Rowland died in 1615 seised of the reversion of the 'capital messuage called Nevill' after the death of Margaret Walford (William Snagge's mother), and was possessed of the residue of the manor.[70] He already held Letchworth, and from that date Nevells and Letchworth followed the same descent and were presumably amalgamated.

BURLEIGH or *BURLEY* (Borneleye, Boureleghe, xiii cent.; Borleye, xiv cent.; Burlee, xv cent.) is now represented by Burleigh Farm in a detached portion of Letchworth parish between Stevenage and Knebworth, situated about 8 miles south of Letchworth. In the 14th century it appears held with Wollenwich as a quarter of a knight's fee, so it is possible that in 1086 it was included in the half hide and half virgate in Wollenwich (Wlwenewiche) held of Robert Gernon by the William who held Letchworth.[71] The overlordship of Burleigh appears in the same hands as that of Letchworth (q.v.), passing from the Montfitchets (the successors of Robert Gernon) to the Burnells. Philip Burnell died seised of a quarter fee in Burleigh in 1294,[72] and in 1303 a quarter fee in Burleigh and Wollenwich was held of the heirs of Philip Burnell by Laurence de Brok.[73]

The family of Brok had probably been holding the fee in sub-tenancy for some time previous to this, for a Laurence de Brok, who died about 1275, appears as grantee in conveyances of land in Wollenwich.[74] He had a son Hugh, who was the father of the Laurence of 1303.[75] This Laurence[76] was holding Burleigh in 1294,[77] and died before 1330, leaving a widow Ellen,[78] after whose death his lands passed to their son Ralph.[79] Ralph's heirs, who were holding Burleigh in 1346,[80] were his three daughters, Joan, who died childless, Ellen and Agnes.[81] There is no evidence to show which of the two latter inherited Burleigh, but Agnes is known to have had a daughter Joan and a granddaughter Katrine, whose daughter was named Cecily.[82] Possibly the Thomas Vinter who was holding the property in 1428[83] was the husband of Katrine or Cecily, in which case Burleigh would have descended to one of Cecily's granddaughters, Joan Alington, Elizabeth Taillard and Margaret Langley, who claimed some of the Brok lands in 1468.[84] Early in the 16th century Burleigh came into the hands of Ralph Fraunces, son of William Praunces, from whom he perhaps inherited it. Ralph died seised of it in 1533, leaving an infant son William, who was placed in the wardship of Sir Henry Sacheverell.[85] In 1557 William Praunces and Elizabeth his wife conveyed the property to John Godfrey or Cowper.[86] The latter died in 1565, leaving Burleigh to his younger son Francis, then under age.[87] The latter died in 1631, leaving 'Burley Ground and the Hault' to be divided between his three sons Edward, William and John,[88] after which all records of the estate cease, but it seems to

---

[50] Feet of F. Herts. Trin. 39 Eliz.
[51] Chan. Inq. p.m. (Ser. 2), ccclix, 114.
[52] Recov. R. Hil. 6 Chas. I, rot. 53; Chauncy, op. cit. 385; Salmon, op. cit. 176; Recov. R. Trin. 21 Geo. II, rot. 273.
[53] Ibid. Hil. 51 Geo. III, rot. 41.
[54] Clutterbuck, op. cit. ii, 385.
[55] Burke, *Landed Gentry*.
[56] Ibid.
[57] *Prospectus First Garden City Co., Ltd.*
[58] Pat. 14 Jas. I, pt. xvii.
[59] Assize R. 323, m. 40 d.
[60] Chan. Inq. p.m. 14 Edw. IV, no. 35; (Ser. 2), lxxx, 13; *L. and P. Hen. VIII*, iv, 297 (21).
[61] *Rot. Cur. Reg.* (Rec. Com.), i, 166.
[62] Assize R. 318, m. 17.
[63] Feet of F. Herts. East. 17 Edw. II, no. 375.
[64] Feet of F. 25 Edw. III, no. 387.
[65] Ibid. 12 Ric. II, no. 103; *Feud. Aids*, ii, 448; Chan. Inq. p.m. 14 Edw. IV, no. 35.
[66] Ibid. (Ser. 2), lxxx, 13.
[67] *L. and P. Hen. VIII*, iv, 297 (21).
[68] Ct. of Wards, Misc. Bks. cxxix, fol. 36.
[69] Feet of F. Herts. Mich. 38 & 39 Eliz.
[70] Chan. Inq. p.m. (Ser. 2), ccclix, 114.
[71] *V.C.H. Herts.* i, 323. There were also 1½ virgates in Wlwenewiche held by a certain Roger de Peter de Valognes (ibid. 336*b*).
[72] Chan. Inq. p.m. 22 Edw. I, no. 65.
[73] *Feud. Aids*, ii, 430.
[74] See Add. Chart. 15467 and Harl. Chart. 45 B. 1.
[75] See Brooks in Stevenage. This seems to be the last mention of Wollenwich in connexion with this holding, so that the Wollenwich held by Robert Gernon in 1086 is probably coincident with the later Burleigh. There was, however, other land at Wollenwich attached to the Argentines' manor of Wymondley (see Chan. Inq. p.m. 4 Ric. II, no. 110). The name seems to be now lost.
[76] See Add. Chart. 977.
[77] Chan. Inq. p.m. 22 Edw. I, no. 45 d.
[78] Chart. R. 4 Edw. III, m. 14, no. 28.
[79] Wrottesley, *Ped. from the Plea R.* 428.
[80] *Feud. Aids*, ii, 436.
[81] Wrottesley, *Ped. from the Plea R.* 428.
[82] Ibid.
[83] *Feud. Aids*, ii, 448.
[84] Wrottesley, *Ped. from the Plea R.* 428.
[85] Chan. Inq. p.m. (Ser. 2), lvii, 4.
[86] Feet of F. Herts. Trin. 3 & 4 Phil. and Mary.
[87] Chan. Inq. p.m. (Ser. 2), cli, 57; Chan. Proc. (Ser. 2), bdle. 210, no. 25.
[88] Chan. Inq. p.m. (Ser. 2), ccclxiv, 50.

LETCHWORTH HALL. PART OF SCREEN IN HALL

LETCHWORTH HALL. FIREPLACE ON FIRST FLOOR

have subsequently come into the possession of the Lyttons of Knebworth,[89] whose estates it adjoined.

CHURCH The parish church, the dedication of which is unknown, stands to the north of Letchworth Hall and about half a mile to the south of the village. It is built of flint rubble with freestone dressings, and the roof is tiled. It consists of a chancel and nave, with a south porch, and has a bellcote at the west end.[90] The original church of the 12th century is represented by the nave, while the chancel of the 13th century appears to have been rebuilt, as it leans to the south. In the 15th century the south porch was added and the church was re-roofed. About 1500 windows were inserted in the nave, and the bellcote appears to date from about the same time, though it has been altered externally. The church was repaired in the 19th century.

The east wall of the chancel appears to have been rebuilt in the 16th or early in the 17th century, and the east window of three lights under a square head is of that date. In the north wall is a 13th-century lancet window, and there is a low-side window of about 1350 in the west end of the north wall. In the south wall are similar windows and a 14th-century doorway, which has been blocked and can only be seen on the outside. The chancel arch has very coarse mouldings, and appears to have been rebuilt in the 16th century. The roof is plastered, but the 15th-century trusses and wind-braces are visible. The nave has two single-light windows in the north wall, of about 1500, with tracery in four-centred heads. The easternmost of these contains 15th-century glass, with a shield of Montfitchet: Gules three cheverons or and a label azure. There is also in this wall a blocked doorway, apparently of 14th-century date. At the north-east angle a thickening of the wall probably indicates the position of the rood-loft stair, of which the foundations have recently been discovered. At the same angle is an early 15th-century niche for an image. The head is partly buried in the north wall, and the south jamb has been cut back. The windows in the south wall are modern, of two lights, in 13th-century style. The west window, of two cinquefoiled lights, is of about 1500, and contains some fragments of mediaeval glass. The ceiling of the nave is plastered, but the beams and wall cornices of the 15th-century roof are still in position. The south doorway, of two moulded orders, with a four-centred head, is of the same date, and on the door is some ironwork of the 13th century. The south porch has a two-centred entrance arch of two moulded orders, with shields in the spandrels; the western shield is carved with lozenges, the other is illegible. There is the base of a stoup in the north-east corner. The bellcote, which is cemented externally, has north and south windows with two-centred heads, and is supported on a four-centred wooden arch, now painted, which spans the nave at the west end. Its roof is pyramidal and tiled. It contains a bell, probably of the 14th century, by an unknown founder, with the inscription ' Ave Maria Dracia (sic) Plena.'

The bowl of the font is probably of the 14th century, and there are some 15th-century benches with broken ends in the nave. A remarkable monument on the sill of the north-east window of the nave is a miniature recumbent effigy (2 ft. 2 in. long by 1 ft. wide) in chain armour and a long surcoat, holding a heart in his hands. The figure is of about 1300 and is much defaced. In the chancel is a brass of a priest in eucharistic vestments, with an inscription and the date 1475. In the nave is a brass with the half-length figures of a man and his wife, with a fragmentary inscription which records the name of the wife, Isabelle; the man is said to be William Overbury, and the date is about 1470.

The plate includes a cup and cover paten of late 16th-century style, but without hall-marks.

The registers are in four volumes: (i) 1695 to 1748; (ii) baptisms 1749 to 1806, marriages 1749 to 1754, burials 1749 to 1804; (iii) baptisms and burials 1807 to 1812; (iv) marriages 1754 to 1805.

ADVOWSON There is mention of a priest at Letchworth in 1086.[91] The church of Letchworth was granted, with all appurtenances and 12 acres of land in the parish, to the monastery of St. Albans by William de Montfitchet and Rohais his wife and William their son at the beginning of the 12th century.[92] The living was not appropriated and is still a rectory. About 1297 John de Ulseby, rector of Letchworth, was deprived of his living for his connexion with Cardinal James Colonna, who was excommunicated by Boniface VIII for his opposition to that pope's election.[93] The Abbot of St. Albans then presented Robert de Donnebrugge, but the Bishop of Lincoln refused to institute him; in 1301, however, Pope Boniface VIII sent a mandate to his successor commanding the institution.[94] In 1302 and in 1320 the king presented by reason of the voidance of St. Albans[95]; on the first occasion Richard Montfitchet claimed the right, but his claim was not allowed.[96] The advowson remained to the monastery of St. Albans until its surrender at the end of 1539,[97] after which it was presumably held for a while by the Crown. Some time before 1610 it was granted to Sir Henry Cock, who died possessed of it in that year, and was succeeded by his grandson Henry Lucy, son of his elder daughter Frances and Edmund Lucy.[98] Soon after this the advowson was acquired by the Lytton family, William Lytton presenting in 1676,[99] and after this it followed the descent of the manor until 1903, when it was sold to Mr. Walter Plimpton, Mr. Henry William Hill and Major Gilbert E. W. Malet, who form a syndicate.[100]

In 1544, after the dissolution of St. Albans Abbey, a pension of 13s. from Letchworth rectory was granted to George Nodes[1] of Shephall, and apparently remained in his family, for in 1643 a George Nodes died possessed of 'rent from the rectory of Letchworth,' leaving a son Charles.[2]

In 1638 the parsonage contained 'one hall, one pallor, one kichin, two buttries, one milkhouse, one

---

[89] Information kindly supplied by Mr. E. B. Lindsell.
[90] Dimensions: chancel, 19 ft. by 14 ft.; nave, 32 ft. by 16 ft. 6 in.
[91] V.C.H. Herts. i, 323b.
[92] Dugdale, Mon. ii, 229, 232.
[93] Biog. Universelle, viii, 654.
[94] Cal. Papal Letters, i, 597.
[95] Cal. Pat. 1301–7, p. 40; 1317–21, p. 446.
[96] Abbrev. Plac. (Rec. Com.), 246.
[97] Dugdale, Mon. ii, 207.
[98] Chan. Inq. p.m. (Ser. 2), cccxvi, 29.
[99] Inst. Bks. (P.R.O.).
[100] Information kindly supplied by Mr. E. B. Lindsell.
[1] L. and P. Hen. VIII, xix (1), 278 (2).
[2] Chan. Inq. p.m. (Ser. 2), dcclxxi, 91.

A HISTORY OF HERTFORDSHIRE

larder, five chambers with a study.' The glebe lands then consisted of about 45 acres.[3]

The mission church of ST. MICHAEL in Norton Way was built before 1910.

A Roman Catholic church dedicated in honour of St. Hugh was built in Pixmore Way in 1908; the Presbytery adjoins it. There is a meeting of the Society of Friends at Howgills, Sollershott; the Wesleyan Methodists hold services in the Pixmore Institute, and the Salvation Army in the Co-operative Hall. There is also a Free Church in Norton Way, which was built in 1905 and enlarged in 1907.

A chapel existed at Burleigh at the beginning of the 13th century, and is mentioned in 1218 as attached to the church of Letchworth, and therefore as belonging to St. Alban's Abbey.[4] In 1311 licence was given to the Broks, lords of Burleigh, for a chantry in the chapel of Burleigh,[5] and the whole seems to have been subsequently known as Brook's Chapel or Burleigh's Chapel. It seems to have soon decayed, for in 1548 it possessed no plate, ornaments, goods or chattels beyond the tithes of the land attached. The incumbent was then William ap Rise.[6] Upon its dissolution the site and lands pertaining were granted in 1553 to John and William Dodington and their heirs,[7] but seem to have come not long after into the possession of John Godfrey or Cowper, who held the manor of Burleigh (q.v.) and died in 1565. He held the 'tithe called Brokes Chappell or Burleyes Chappell' of the queen as of her manor of East Greenwich in socage,[8] and left it to his younger son Francis, who died in 1631 seised of 'Burley Ground, le Hault, and Brooks Chappell,' which he had settled on his younger sons William and John.[9]

There are no endowed charities. The children attend the school at Willian.

GREAT MUNDEN

Mundene (xi cent.); Mundun, Mundon (xiii cent.).

The parish of Great Munden has an area of 3,758 acres, of which 1,895¾ acres are arable land, 927½ permanent grass and 97 wood.[1] The elevation of the parish is for the most part well over 300 ft., and in the north-west and along the eastern border of the parish it is over 400 ft. The village of Great Munden lies on the road which branches off westwards from Ermine Street at Puckeridge; the road from Little Munden to Westmill crosses it in the centre of the village, and passes through the hamlet of Nasty to the north of it. The church of St. Nicholas, with Munden Bury adjoining, is at the west end of the village, and the rectory about three-quarters of a mile further along the road to the south. The old rectory, with the remains of a moat, is about the same distance due west of the village. In 1606 it is described as a house consisting of eleven bays built of timber and covered all (excepting one bay) with tile, 'five bayes being chambred over and boorded, these five bayes being contrived into two heights or stories and the whole building disposed into 17 roomes vizt. the halle, buttrey, parlour, three bedchambers below and six chambers above (the dayrie having a cornloft over it boorded), kitchin and three other roomes adioyning.' There was also a dove-house within the moat and a bridge with a gate of timber and boards over the moat. The glebe lands consisted of about 53 acres.[2]

Near the old rectory is an early 17th-century cottage, with weather-boarded timber framing and thatched roof. Brockholds Farm, with the remains of a moat, is on the eastern boundary of the parish, a short distance north-east of Levens Green. There are remains of homestead moats also at Mill Farm and Rush Green. Rowney Priory, with the site of the small house for Benedictine nuns, founded in 1164 by Conan Duke of Britanny, is in the extreme south. The present house is modern, but there is a wall within it about 3 ft. 6 in. thick, faced with flint, which may have been a part of the priory. In the grounds a stone coffin and a stone mortar with two handles have been found. Potter's Green is a little to the north. About a mile and a half south of the village is High Trees Farm, an early 17th-century timber and plaster house of two stories with later additions. It still retains its original brick chimney stacks. Within, the hall is now divided into two rooms, the south end being cut off by an oak panelled screen. Much original oak panelling, an oak staircase and an old kitchen fireplace still remain.

The nearest station is Braughing, 2¾ miles east, on the Buntingford branch of the Great Eastern railway.

The parish lies on a subsoil of chalk, and there are chalk-pits in use west of the old parsonage and west of Levens Green.

The inclosure award was made in 1852, with an amendment in 1858. Both are in the custody of the clerk of the peace.[3]

In 1888 a detached portion of Little Munden was added to this parish.[4]

MANORS In the time of King Edmund *GREAT MUNDEN* or *MUNDEN FURNIVALL* belonged to one Ethelgifu, who by her will of 944–6 demised it to one Elfwold for his lifetime.[5] Immediately before the Norman Conquest it was held by Eddeva the Fair.[6] William the Conqueror gave it to Count Alan of Britanny, in whose time it was assessed at 7 hides and half a virgate.[7] The overlordship of Munden Furnivall remained in the hands of the subsequent holders of the honour and earldom of Richmond.[8]

The earliest sub-tenant recorded is Gerard de Furnivall, who died in Jerusalem at the beginning of the reign of Henry III. The manor came into the king's hands by his death, presumably owing to the minority of the heir, and was granted, saving the dower of Gerard's widow, to Lady Nichola de Haye,

---

[3] *Herts. Gen. and Antiq.* iii, 185–7.
[4] Dugdale, *Mon.* ii, 232.
[5] Linc. Epis. Reg. Mem. Bp. Dalderby, fol. 243 d.
[6] Chant. Cert. 20, no. 64; 27, no. 9.
[7] Pat. 6 Edw. VI, pt. v, m. 10.

[8] Chan. Inq. p.m (Ser. 2), cli, 57.
[9] Ibid. ccclxiv, 50.
[1] Statistics from Bd. of Agric. (1905).
[2] *Herts. Gen. and Antiq.* iii, 297–9.
[3] *Blue Bk. Incl. Awards,* 64.
[4] Local Govt. Bd. Order 22217.

[5] Thorpe, *Dipl. Angl. Aevo Sax.* 497; Matt. Paris, *Chron. Majora* (Rolls Ser.), vi, 13.
[6] *V.C.H. Herts.* i, 319*b*.   [7] Ibid.
[8] Assize R. 318, m. 22 d.; Chan. Inq. p.m. 9 Edw. III, no. 7; (Ser. 2), li, 50.

124

LETCHWORTH HALL FROM THE EAST

LETCHWORTH CHURCH FROM THE NORTH

who had been an ardent supporter of King John against the barons, 'for her support in our castle of Lincoln, for as long as it pleases us.'[9] Later in the same reign Munden was again in the possession of the Furnivalls, and in 1242 Christiana, widow of another Gerard de Furnivall, was granted the custody of his heir.[10] Christiana's son Gerard lived until almost the end of the century, dying some time between 1290 and 1302.[11] He had two daughters, Christiana de Aylesford and Lora or

FURNIVALL. *Argent a bend between six martlets gules.*

had the title of Lord Furnivall and was descended from Thomas de Furnivall, brother of Gerard de Furnivall and uncle of Lora and Christiana.[15] In 1461 it was held by John Talbot, Earl of Shrewsbury and Lord Furnivall,[16] who had married the heiress of the Furnivalls, and the manor continued to be held of his heirs, in socage, for the rent of a pair of gloves.[17]

In 1285 Gerard de Furnivall had created a further sub-tenancy by conveying the manor to John de Kirkeby, Bishop of Ely, for the yearly rent of a pair of gilt spurs or 6*d*.[18] John died in 1290, and was succeeded by his brother William de Kirkeby,[19] who lived until 1302. At this time a third of the manor was in the hands of Mathania, the second wife of John de Cobham,[20] but the remainder passed on the division of William's inheritance between his sisters

GREAT MUNDEN : OLD FARM

Loretta, widow of John de Ulvesflete,[12] the manor of Munden Furnivall being apportioned to the younger.[13] Both Lora and Christiana had descendants, Gerard de Ulvesflete descendant of the former, and John de Aylesford, a minor, descendant of the latter, both being alive about 1362.[14] During the hundred years following, however, both lines apparently died out, for by 1461 this mesne lordship of Great Munden had passed to another branch of the family, who

to Margaret, wife of Walter de Osevill,[21] with the reversion of Mathania's third and the third held in dower by Christine de Kirkeby, William's widow.[22] In 1304 Walter and Margaret de Osevill settled Munden Furnivall upon their sons John and Henry and the heirs of Henry.[23] Henry de Osevill died before 1334,[24] when his widow Alice held one third and his brother John, who survived him until 1335, held the other two thirds.[25] Eventually the whole

[9] Close, 3 Hen. III, m. 9 ; Dugdale, *Baronage*, i, 598.
[10] *Cal. Chart. R.* 1226–57, p. 265.
[11] *Rot. Hund.* (Rec. Com.), i, 188 ; *Cal. Pat.* 1281–92, p. 94 ; Chan. Inq. p.m. 18 Edw. I, no. 37 ; 30 Edw. I, no. 31.
[12] Wrottesley, *Ped. from the Plea R.* 84.
[13] Chan. Inq. p.m. 30 Edw. I, no. 31.

[14] Wrottesley, *Ped. from the Plea R.* 84.
[15] G.E.C. *Complete Peerage.*
[16] Chan. Inq. p.m. 1 Edw. IV, no. 28.
[17] Ibid. 18 Edw. IV, no. 45.
[18] Feet of F. Herts. 13 Edw. I, no. 157.
[19] Chan. Inq. p.m. 18 Edw. I, no. 37.
[20] Ibid. 30 Edw. I, no. 31. This was apparently a right of dower.

[21] *Abbrev. Rot. Orig.* (Rec. Com.), ii, 123.
[22] Feet of F. Herts. 32 Edw. I, no. 388.
[23] Ibid. ; Wrottesley, *Ped. from the Plea R.* 14, 399.
[24] *Cal. Pat.* 1330–4, p. 578.
[25] Chan. Inq. p.m. 9 Edw. III, no. 7.

A HISTORY OF HERTFORDSHIRE

came to John son of Henry de Osevill. Cecily his daughter and heiress married Guy de Boys,[26] who was holding the manor in right of his wife in 1350.[27] He died before 1370, in which year Cecily was holding it alone.[28] After her death Munden Furnivall seems to have been held by John and Agnes Durham,[29] who conveyed it in 1389 to Margaret, daughter of Cecily and Guy de Boys, and her husband Robert Dykeswell.[30] Margaret married secondly Henry Hayward,[31] and thirdly, before 1419, Walter Pejon or Pegeon.[32] She was succeeded by Thomas Hayward or Howard, her son by her second husband.[33] Thomas died shortly before 1447, when the manor of Great Munden was conveyed by trustees to Sir John Fray, chief baron of the Exchequer.[34] He also made himself secure against the claims of various heirs of Thomas Howard.[35] In 1460, however, he was obliged to sue Simon Rode and Joan his wife for illegal entry by force into the manor. Joan claimed that she was the heir of Mabel Grimbaud, one of the sisters of Walter de Osevill, upon whom the manor had been entailed failing the heirs of Henry de Osevill.[36] The claim was not successful, for Sir John Fray died seised of Great Munden in the following year.[37] His widow Agnes, who married secondly Sir John Say, held the manor until her death in 1478, when it passed by grant of the trustees to her second daughter Margaret, the wife of John Leynham or Plomer.[38] Some years later Munden Furnivall came into the possession of Sir William Say (son of Sir John Say by an earlier wife), who had married Margaret Lynham's elder sister Elizabeth, then the widow of Sir Thomas Waldegrave. Though he is said to have acquired it by purchase,[39] it is thus possible that it came to him by failure of Margaret's heirs. He died seised of it in 1529,[40] and it descended in the same manner as his other lands (v. s. Benington) in Hertfordshire until it came to the Crown upon the death of Lady Anne Parr.[41]

In 1572 the manor was leased by the Crown to William Lord Burghley for a term of thirty-one years from 1595,[42] which lease was renewed to Sir Robert Cecil in 1600 for twenty-one years.[43] The latter died in 1612, bequeathing the lease of Great Munden to William, Earl of Cranbourne, with remainder to James Lord Stanley and his wife and Robert Stanley, his brother.[44] It reverted to the Crown on the expiration of the lease, and is said to have been granted to Charles Prince of Wales in 1620, but the grant does not seem to be extant.[45] In 1628 it was granted to Edward Ditchfield and others,[46] and is said to have been sold later to Edward Arris.[47] Thomas Arris, his son,[48] sold the manor in 1700 to Robert Hadsley,[49] whose son Robert sold it to Sir John Jennings in 1723.[60]

In 1789 it was purchased from his son George Jennings by William Baker of Bayfordbury,[51] in whose family it descended[52] until it was purchased by Messrs. Paine, Brettell & Porter, solicitors, in 1900.

The park of Great Munden is first mentioned in 1283, when Gerard de Furnivall complained that certain persons had repeatedly broken his park at Munden Furnivall, hunted therein and carried away deer.[53] In 1302 the park is described as having an area of 40 acres[54]; later it seems to have been called Fludgate Park, and was leased with the manor to the Cecils under that name.[55] This name occurs again in 1723 and also the form Flutgate Park,[56] which does not occur elsewhere. It seems to have been subsequently disparked.

BAKER of Bayfordbury. *Party ermine and gules a greyhound running between two bars invecked with two quatrefoils in the chief and another in the foot all countercoloured.*

In 1275 Gerard de Furnivall is said to have appropriated free warren to himself in Munden where he ought not to have had it[57]; in 1295, however, William de Kirkeby received a grant of free warren in due form.[58] The grant was renewed in 1320 to John and Henry de Osevill and their heirs.[59] In 1397 one John Potter was fined 20d. because he 'dug the land of the lord in the free warren of the lord and put nets in the warren and took there conies and carried them away to the damage of the lord.'[60] The warren is mentioned again in 1723.[61]

In 1275 the lord of the manor of Munden Furnivall possessed view of frankpledge, gallows and amendment of the assize of bread and ale.[62] John de Kirkeby, Bishop of Ely, claimed there in 1287 pillory, tumbrel, infangentheof and outfangentheof in addition.[63] His brother held view of frankpledge at Whitsuntide and courts every three weeks.[64] View of frankpledge is mentioned in connexion with the manor in a deed of 1723.[65] False imprisonment in the stocks was complained of against the bailiff of Sir William Say early in the reign of Henry VIII.[66] The lord also possessed the liberty of a pinfold for sheep.[67] There was a mill in Great Munden in 1086.[68] A windmill is mentioned in 1290[69] and after.[70] There is still a windmill in the south of the parish, a little to the east of the road from Little Munden.

---

[26] Wrottesley, *Ped. from the Plea R.* 399.
[27] Ct. R. portf. 178, no. 7.
[28] Ibid. no. 8.
[29] Ibid. no. 10; Early Chan. Proc. bdle. 5, no. 109.
[30] Close, 12 Ric. II, m. 16 d.
[31] *Cal. Pat.* 1422–9, p. 250.
[32] Ibid.; Chan. Inq. p.m. 7 Hen. V, no. 19; 4 Hen. IV, no. 6.
[33] Wrottesley, *Ped. from the Plea R.* 399.
[34] Anct. D. (P.R.O.), D 465.
[35] Feet of F. Herts. 26 Hen. VI, no. 137, 138.
[36] Wrottesley, *Ped. from the Plea R.* 399.
[37] Chan. Inq. p.m. 1 Edw. IV, no. 28.
[38] Ibid. 18 Edw. IV, no. 45.
[39] Cussans, op. cit. *Broadwater Hund.* 140.

[40] Chan. Inq. p.m. (Ser. 2), li, 50.
[41] Ct. of Wards, Misc. Bks. 578, fol. 372a; Feet of F. Herts. Hil. 33 Hen. VIII; Pat. 3 & 4 Phil. and Mary, pt. xii.
[42] Ibid. 15 Eliz. pt. i.
[43] *Cal. S. P. Dom.* 1598–1601, p. 380.
[44] P.C.C. 49 Fenner.
[45] Chauncy, op. cit. 341.
[46] Pat. 4 Chas. I, pt. xxxv, B, m. 16.
[47] Chauncy, loc. cit.
[48] Ibid.
[49] Feet of F. Herts. Mich. 12 Will. III.
[50] Close, 10 Geo. I, pt. xi, no. 21.
[51] Feet of F. Herts. Mich. 29 Geo. III.
[52] Clutterbuck, op. cit. ii, 392; Cussans, op. cit. *Broadwater Hund.* 140.
[53] *Cal. Pat.* 1281–92, p. 94.
[54] Chan. Inq. p.m. 30 Edw. I, no. 31.

[55] Pat. 15 Eliz. pt. i; 7 Jas. I, pt. iii.
[56] Close, 10 Geo. I, pt. xi, no. 21.
[57] *Rot. Hund.* (Rec. Com.), i, 188.
[58] Chart. R. 24 Edw. I, no. 23, m. 3.
[59] Ibid. 13 Edw. II, no. 16.
[60] Ct. R. portf. 178, no. 11.
[61] Close, 10 Geo. I, pt. xi, no. 21.
[62] *Rot. Hund.* (Rec. Com.), i, 193.
[63] Assize R. 325, m. 26 d.
[64] Close, 10 Geo. I, pt. ii, no. 21.
[65] Star Chamb. Proc. Hen. VIII, bdle. 28, no. 108.
[66] Pat. 15 Eliz. pt. i; Close, 10 Geo. I, pt. xi, no. 21.
[67] *V.C.H. Herts.* i, 319b.
[68] Chan. Inq. p.m. 18 Edw. I, no. 37.
[69] Ibid. 30 Edw. I, no. 31.

GREAT MUNDEN

BROKHOLES or *BROCKHOLDS* was a small manor, held of the manor of Great Munden[71]; in 1550 it was said to be held in socage for a rent of 36s. It owed suit of court to Great Munden.[72] A Geoffrey de Brokhole occurs in a Watton fine of 1258–9,[73] but the earliest to be mentioned in Great Munden is the Geoffrey de Brokhole who in 1327 represented Hertfordshire in Parliament.[74] In 1338 one Thomas de Burnham was summoned to answer an indictment 'that he took Alice, wife of Geoffrey de Brokhole, and her goods at Munden Furnivall and carried them away.'[75] Geoffrey seems to have been succeeded by another Geoffrey Brokhole, who was Sheriff of Essex and Herts. in 1385, and is mentioned in 1397.[76] His widow Ellen died in 1419, leaving as her heirs a daughter Joan, widow of Thomas Aspall, and a grandson John Sumpter, son of her second daughter Mary,[77] between whom the manor was divided.

John Sumpter's moiety passed at his death in 1420 to his sisters Christine and Ellen,[78] of whom the elder died without issue.[79] Ellen, who thus became possessed of the half-manor, married James Bellewe or Bellers,[80] and later, about 1439, Ralph Holt,[81] in whose family the moiety descended.

Joan, the widow of Thomas Aspall, to whom the other half was apportioned, married Robert Armeburgh,[82] and lived until 1443. Robert survived her and continued to hold the half-manor, with remainder to John Palmer, Joan sister of John Palmer, and Philip Thornbury.[83] Before 1452 it had come to Philip Thornbury, for in that year he and Reginald Armeburgh made an arrangement with Ralph Holt, to whom they owed £100,[84] which seems to have been the final step in the transfer of the estate to the latter. Ralph Holt thus became possessed of the whole manor, which descended in his family until 1543, when Thomas Holt conveyed it to John Gardiner.[85] John died in 1550, leaving a son Thomas,[86] after which Brokholes descended in the Gardiner family until 1742,[87] when it was sold by John Gardiner to Francis Welles.[88] Eventually it seems to have become merged in the main manor. The moated farm-house called Brockholds probably represents the manor-house.

GARNONS or *HENRY-AT-DANES*, of which no trace now remains, probably took its name from the family who originally held it, for a John Garnon appears in a list of the tenants of Great Munden manor in 1346.[89] In 1417 there is mention of Henry atte Dane in Great Munden,[90] who seems to have been succeeded by Robert atte Dane.[91] In 1473 Garnons was merely called a tenement; it was then in the possession of John Humberston.[92] In 1526 John Humberston, perhaps the son of the last-named John, conveyed Garnons, then called a manor, to William Hamond and others.[93] Sixty years later another William Hamond was holding it,[94] and sold it about 1600 or later to Sir John Watts.[95] The latter died seised of it in 1616, leaving a son John,[96] and it apparently remained in his family, for in 1665 Garnons was held by Richard Watts,[97] who had married Catherine Werden.[98] His daughter Katharine, to whom the manor descended, married Charles first Earl of Dunmore,[99] who in 1709 conveyed it to Sir John Werden, his wife's uncle.[100] Sir John's heir was his son John, who died without male heirs in 1758.[1] In that year Garnons was sold by William and Caroline Louisa Kerr to Francis Fryer,[2] which suggests that it had either been previously sold to the Kerrs or that they were Sir John Werden's executors. Next year Francis Fryer sold it to Robert Ireland,[3] who died soon after, leaving a widow Anne and three sons, the eldest of whom was William Ireland, upon whom Garnons was settled after the death of his mother.[4] After this settlement in 1786 there is no further record of Garnons.

In 1551 the buildings and lands of the dissolved priory of *ROWNEY* were granted to Thomas Bill,[5] who is said to have devised them to his daughter Margaret and her husband Michael Harris,[6] but if so they cannot have held them long, for before 1566 they had been acquired by Richard Smythe.[7] In that year he sold the chapel and lands for £20 to John Ruse, who sold them for £25 to Cyrus Ruse. In 1569 the last-named complained that Richard Smythe refused to give up the documents connected with the lands. Richard Smythe replied that the bargain had never been completed, and that Cyrus had entered into the premises and destroyed his grass.[8]

Later Rowney is said to have been sold to John Fleming.[9] In 1641 Thomas and Richard Fleming brought a suit against Henry Birchenhead, 'by whose unconscionable practices they had been deprived of the chantry house in Rowney and other property.'[10] In the following year, however, Thomas Fleming sold Rowney to Henry Birchenhead,[11] in whose family it descended for a while. It is said to have been conveyed to Thomas Jenner, whose daughter Anne married Francis Browne,[12] who possessed it in 1700.[13] Their son Thomas Browne is said to have devised it to Charles and Robert Jenner, of whom the latter conveyed the whole to Thomas Marlborough, whose second daughter Elizabeth possessed it in 1821. She was married to James Cecil Graves of Baldock, and

---

[71] Chan. Inq. p.m. 7 Hen. V, no. 19; 4 Hen. VI, no. 6; 22 Hen. VI, no. 28; (Ser. 2), xciii, 107.
[72] Ct. R. portf. 178, no. 11.
[73] Feet of F. Herts. 43 Hen. III, no. 502.
[74] Salmon, op. cit. 359.
[75] Cal. Pat. 1338–40, p. 84.
[76] Ct. R. portf. 178, no. 11.
[77] Chan. Inq. p.m. 7 Hen. V, no. 19.
[78] Ibid. 4 Hen. VI, no. 6.
[79] Morant, *Hist. of Essex*, ii, 536.
[80] Feet of F. Div. Co. Trin. 15 Hen. VI.
[81] Early Chan. Proc. bdle. 9, no. 356.
[82] Morant, loc. cit.; Feet of F. Div. Co. 22 Hen. VI, no. 13.
[83] Chan. Inq. p.m. 22 Hen. VI, no. 28.
[84] Close, 31 Hen. VI, m. 4 d.

[85] Feet of F. Herts. Mich. 35 Hen. VIII.
[86] Chan. Inq. p.m. (Ser. 2), xciii, 107.
[87] Chan. Proc. (Ser. 2), bdle. 74, no. 6; Feet of F. Herts. Mich. 33 Chas. II; Mich. 4 Geo. I.
[88] Ibid. East. 15 Geo. II.
[89] Rental and Surv. Herts. R. 280.
[90] Ct. R. portf. 178, no. 14.
[91] Ibid.
[92] Ibid. no. 288.
[93] Feet of F. Herts. East. 18 Hen. VIII.
[94] Ibid. Mich. 28 & 29 Eliz.
[95] Chan. Inq. p.m. (Ser. 2), ccclvi, 135.
[96] Ibid.
[97] Feet of F. Herts. Trin. 17 Chas. II.
[98] *Douglas' Scots Peerage* (ed. Paul), iii, 384–5.
[99] Ibid.

[100] Ibid.; Feet of F. Herts. Trin. 8 Anne.
[1] Burke, *Extinct Baronetage*.
[2] Feet of F. Herts. Mich. 32 Geo. II.
[3] Ibid. Hil. 32 Geo. II.
[4] Close, 26 Geo. III, pt. xxii, no. 9; Feet of F. Herts. Hil. 26 Geo III; Recov. R. Hil. 26 Geo. III, rot. 354.
[5] Pat. 5 Edw. VI, pt. vi.
[6] Clutterbuck, op. cit. ii, 393. They held the rectorial tithes in 1581 and as late as 1596.
[7] Chan. Proc. (Ser. 2), bdle. 149, no. 48.
[8] Ibid.
[9] Clutterbuck, op. cit. ii, 393.
[10] *Hist. MSS. Com. Rep.* iv, App. i, 212.
[11] Close, 18 Chas. I, pt. xx, no. 17.
[12] Clutterbuck, op. cit. ii, 393.
[13] Chauncy, op. cit. 342

had a daughter Mary.[14] The subsequent owners are not known. Michael William Balfe, the Irish composer, is said to have resided at Rowney for a while, and to have died there in 1870.[15] It is now the residence of Mr. James Henry Dugdale, J.P.

The parish church of ST. NICHOLAS CHURCH lies to the west of the village, and consists of a chancel, nave, south aisle, south porch and west tower.[16] It is built of flint rubble with stone dressings ; pudding-stone occurs in the foundations. The tower is plastered and the roofs are tiled.

The nave and chancel were built in the 12th century and the south aisle in the middle of the 14th century. The tower dates from the latter part of the 15th century, and at the same time, or it may be in the first years of the 16th century, the chancel arch was widened southwards. The porch is modern, and the repairs of the 19th century include considerable restoration of the south arcade.

The east window of the chancel is modern, of three lights, with flowing tracery in a pointed head. In the north wall is a narrow single-light window of original 12th-century date, having a round head and widely splayed jambs. It is much repaired externally with cement. In the south wall is a 14th-century doorway with a pointed head, almost wholly restored, and to the west of it a two-light square-headed window of the 15th century. The wagon roof is modern. The chancel arch is four-centred and flat, and is supported on the north side by the respond of the original 12th-century arch, which dates from about 1120 and has circular angle-shafts on the east and west sides and a rudely voluted capital with a square abacus and a moulded base. On the south side the chancel arch dies into the south wall of the chancel, and thus is considerably southward of the axis of the chancel and nave.

In the north wall of the nave are three three-light 15th-century windows ; the first has a four-centred head, the second is similar but with tracery, and the third has a segmental head. All are much repaired. Between the two easternmost windows is an image niche of the 15th century with an ogee crocketed head, and retaining traces of decoration in blue, red and gold. The north doorway, which is now blocked, stands between the two westernmost windows, and is of the 12th century, with a round head. Externally it has a large edge-roll supported by engaged shafts with cushion capitals enriched with incised ornament. The abaci are splayed and the bases moulded. The nave arcade is modern, with a few old stones. The west respond is of the first half of the 14th century. At the west end is a 14th-century door opening into the tower. The roof of the nave is of the late 15th century supported on carved corbels. The east window of the south aisle is original ; it is of three lights with flowing tracery. Beneath it stands a stone reredos discovered during repairs in 1865 ; it consists of a central trefoil-headed panel, with a smaller one on either side. The head of the central panel has been cut down, destroying the proportions of the design. A piscina of the 14th century is in the south wall at the east end, with an ogee trefoiled head. Occupying nearly the whole length of the south wall between the piscina and the south doorway are two moulded ogee-headed recesses of about 1350. Above them is a three-light window with a four-centred head, and there is a similar one to the west of the south door ; all but the jambs of these windows is modern.

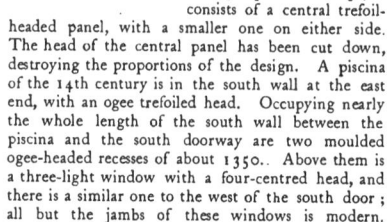

GREAT MUNDEN CHURCH FROM THE SOUTH-EAST

---

[14] Clutterbuck, op. cit. ii, 393.
[15] Cussans, op. cit. Broadwater Hund. 142.
[16] Dimensions : chancel, 22 ft. 8 in. by 18 ft. 7 in. ; nave, 44 ft. 9 in. by 21 ft. 9 in. ; south aisle, 46 ft. 5 in. by 11 ft. 3 in. ; south porch, 7 ft. 6 in. by 7 ft. ; and tower, 11 ft. 6 in. square.

BROADWATER HUNDRED

LITTLE MUNDEN

The south door, which is two-centred of two moulded orders, is original. The west window, which is much restored, also dates from the middle of the 14th century.

The tower is of three receding stages, and is surmounted by an embattled parapet and a small needle spire. The string below the parapet has grotesque gargoyles, much defaced, at the angles. The west window appears to be modern. There is an original single light on the south side of the second stage. In the north face of the bell-chamber is a two-light window with a quatrefoil in the head. The windows in the west and south faces are similar but much decayed.

There is an early 17th-century oak pulpit of hexagonal shape, carved with two stages of arcading and enriched with strap ornament. The base is modern. In the chancel are early 16th-century stalls and bench ends, some of them carved with the initials R. K.

In the churchyard is the octagonal base of an old churchyard cross.

Of the six bells, the treble is by John Warner & Sons, 1882; the second, inscribed 'Jesus be our spede,' 1621, with a shield inclosing an arrow between the letters R.O.; the third, 'Praise the Lord,' 1621; the fourth, 'God save the King,' 1621; the fifth, 'Sonoro sono meo sono deo,' 1621, all by Robert Oldfeild; and the sixth, by John Warner & Sons, 1881.

The plate includes a cup of 1696.

The registers are contained in four books: (i) all entries 1558 to 1682; (ii) baptisms 1678 to 1787, burials 1678 to 1787, marriages 1687 to 1753; (iii) baptisms 1788 to 1812, burials 1788 to 1812; (iv) marriages 1788 to 1812.

ADVOWSON The advowson of the church was from the earliest times in the possession of the lords of the manor.

In 1285 it was conveyed with the manor to John de Kirkeby,[17] and followed the descent of the manor until it came to the Crown at the death of Lady Anne Parr.[18] In 1604 it was granted for one turn to Thomas Nicholson,[19] and in 1688 to John and George Churchill and Thomas Docwray.[20] With the exception of these two cases the Crown has presented down to the present date.[21]

In 1581 and as late as 1596 the tithes of sheaves, grain and hay were held by Michael and Margaret Harris.[22] A hundred years later it appeared that only a few of the lands paid tithe, and that some had been commuted for money.[23] In 1723 and 1789 some of them at any rate were held by the lord of the manor.[24]

A certificate for a meeting-place of Protestant Dissenters in Great Munden was taken out in 1700.[25] There is now a Gospel Hall at Levens Green.

CHARITIES In the parliamentary returns of 1786 it is stated that a donor unknown gave a rent-charge of £5 4s. to twelve poor persons. The annuity was redeemed in 1904 by the transfer to the official trustees of £208 consols, the dividends of which are applied in pursuance of a scheme 19 May 1905 for aged and deserving poor resident in the parish, with a preference for widows.

In the same returns it is also stated that a donor unknown gave land for bread for the poor, in respect of which the parish is in possession of 13 a. 1 r. 34 p., producing about £11 a year, which is applied in the distribution of sheets and towels to about fifty cottagers.

In 1902 Anne Dawson, by will proved at London 14 June, left £160 15s. consols, the annual dividends, amounting to £4 0s. 4d., to be applied for the benefit of poor widows at Christmas. The stock is held by the official trustees.

LITTLE MUNDEN

Mundane (xi cent.).

The parish of Little Munden has an area of 1,774 acres, of which nearly three quarters are arable land, 400 or 500 acres being permanent grass, and over 100 acres wood.[1] The elevation of the parish is for the most part over 300 ft., except a diagonal strip from north-west to south-east where a slight depression is caused by the Old Bourne, at the south-eastern end of which is situated the hamlet of Dane End. Little Munden Church and School, with the Lordship Farm and one or two cottages, are situated half-way between Dane End and Green End, of which the latter is about half a mile north-west of the church. The road from Watton to Great Munden passes across the parish; at Dane End it is joined by the road from Sacombe, and further on roads turn off eastwards to Potter's Green and Levens Green in Great Munden, and northwards to Haultwick, a hamlet in the north of Little Munden parish. Libury Hall, now a German Industrial Home, is situated in a north-eastern projection of the parish. The rectory is some distance west of Dane End. The parish lies on a subsoil of chalk; there is a chalk-pit near Lordship's Farm, and a disused one in the west of the parish. The nearest station is Standon, 4 miles east, on the Buntingford branch of the Great Eastern railway.

The inclosure award was combined with that of Great Munden.[1a]

The following field-names occur in the 14th century: Newelond, Attresfeld, Wykefeld, Brache, Wydiwellefeld and Dymaunfeld[2]; and in the 15th century Cumbes Wood, Lynleyze, Hapsele, Pondfeld, Reyneres Croft, Chosescroft, Cuttedenestrate, Crowedenefeld and Velawesfeld.[3]

MANORS Previous to the Norman Conquest *LITTLE MUNDEN* or *MUNDEN FREVILL* was held by Lewin, a man of Earl Harold. Before 1086 it was granted to Walter the Fleming, and was then assessed at 5 hides and

---

[17] Feet of F. Herts. 13 Edw. I, no. 157.
[18] See references under manor.
[19] *Cal. S. P. Dom.* 1603–10, p. 131.
[20] Inst. Bks. (P.R.O.).
[21] Ibid.; *Cal. S. P. Dom.* 1660–1, p. 67; 1661–2, p. 630; 1675–6, p. 429; Bacon, *Liber Regis*; *Clergy List* (1908).
[22] Feet of F. Herts. Mich. 23 & 24 Eliz.; Div. Co. East. 38 Eliz.
[23] Exch. Dep. Herts. Hil. 33 & 34 Chas. II, no. 1.

[24] Close, 10 Geo. I, pt. ii, no. 21; Feet of F. Herts. Mich. 29 Geo. III.
[25] Urwick, op. cit. 598.
[1] Statistics from Bd. of Agric. (1905).
[1a] *Blue Bk. Incl. Awards*, 64.
[2] *Cal. Pat.* 1338–40, p. 154.
[3] Auct. D. (P.R.O.), D 109, 110.

A HISTORY OF HERTFORDSHIRE

1 virgate.[4] The descendants of Walter the Fleming held the manor of Wahull or Odell in Bedfordshire, from which they took their name.[5] The overlordship of Little Munden remained in this family.[6] In 1304 it was held for the service of a knight's fee and 6s. paid to the warden of Rockingham Castle; in 1385 the payment was 10s.[7]

The manor was granted by the Wahulls to the family of Scales, though at what date is not known. William de Scales was lord of the manor in 1181,[8] and is mentioned again in 1189.[9] He was succeeded by his son Richard de Scales before 1208.[10] Richard died about 1231, leaving a daughter Lucy, whose wardship was purchased for 200 marks by Baldwin de Frevill, who afterwards married her.[11] From this family the manor took its name of Munden Frevill. Baldwin was succeeded before 1278 by Richard de Frevill,[12] whose son John inherited the manor in 1299.[13] John de Frevill died in 1312, leaving a son John,[14] who died before 1377. In that year his widow Ellen sold the manor to Philip Wyndok and William and Joan Hosell,[15] who in 1379-80 conveyed it to Sir John Thornbury.[16] Sir John died about 1396, having settled the manor on his son Philip,[17] and left a widow Nanerina. Philip settled Little Munden on himself and his wife Margaret.[18] In 1404 he went to sea on the king's service 'in the company of the king's brother Thomas Beaufort, admiral towards the north and east, on the safe-custody of the sea.'[19] In 1448 one Richard Whitwik was 'witholden to serve Sir Philip Thornbury and dame Margret his wife in the offices of lardyner, catour and cook,' during their lives. He was to receive 20s. yearly with clothing, and a tenement at Pottersgrene called 'Bathis,' for which he was to yield them yearly a 'roseflour' and suit of court. He was also to have reasonable fuel in the east park, 'except for bakyng or brewyng to chepe.'[20]

Sir Philip Thornbury died about 1457,[21] leaving a daughter Margaret, who was married to Nicholas Appleyard.[22] The manor was settled on Margaret's daughter Elizabeth, wife of William Bastard, with remainder to Thomas and John, sons of Richard Thornbury.[23] In 1481 Elizabeth Bastard released the manor to trustees,[24] and in 1486 John Thornbury did the same,[25] apparently for the purpose of a conveyance to Sir William Say, into whose possession Little Munden came. He died seised of it in 1529,[26] after which it descended to his heirs in the same

THORNBURY. *Party fessewise or and argent a lion azure with two bends gules athwart him.*

LORDSHIP FARM, LITTLE MUNDEN

---

[4] *V.C.H. Herts.* i, 328*b*.
[5] G.E.C. *Complete Peerage.*
[6] Chan. Inq. p.m. 27 Edw. I, no. 16; 32 Edw. I, no. 45; 6 Edw. II, no. 54; Close, 6 Edw. II, m. 22; Chan. Inq. p.m. (Ser. 2), li, 50.
[7] Chan. Inq. p.m. 8 Ric. II, no. 144.
[8] Pipe R. 27 Hen. II, m. 7.
[9] Ibid.
[10] *Rot. de Oblat. et Fin.* (Rec. Com.), 426.
[11] Banks, *Dormant and Extinct Peerages,* ii, 477.
[12] Assize R. 323.
[13] Chan. Inq. p.m. 27 Edw. I, no. 16.
[14] Ibid. 6 Edw. II, no. 54.
[15] Anct. D. (P.R.O.), B 2572, 2575.
[16] Ibid. B 2576.
[17] Ibid. B 2574.
[18] Ibid. B 2567, 2569, 2570, 2571.
[19] *Cal. Pat.* 1401-5, p. 394.
[20] Anct. D. (P.R.O.), D 1172.
[21] Will, P.C.C. 11 Stokton.
[22] Feet of F. Herts. 35 Hen. VI, no. 181.
[23] Ibid.
[24] Anct. D. (P.R.O.), A 5236.
[25] Ibid. D 439 and 795. In the last of these documents Philip Thornbury is called the grandfather of John. This probably should be great-uncle, as there is no record that Philip had a son.
[26] Chan. Inq. p.m. (Ser. 2), li, 50.

BROADWATER HUNDRED — LITTLE MUNDEN

manner as Benington[37] (q.v.), and came with that manor to the Crown. It was leased to Thomas Crompton in 1594–5 for twenty-one years.[38] In 1602 Thomas Crompton conveyed his lease to Michael Woodcock,[29] who is said to have settled it upon his son Michael on his marriage with Dorothy Woodhall.[30] He was holding it in 1606,[31] but sold it in 1607 to Peter Vaulore,[32] who conveyed it in 1614 to his son-in-law Sir Charles Caesar and his daughter Anne.[33] The title, however, was defective, probably because only the twenty-one years' lease of the manor had been sold by Thomas Crompton, which term would run out about this time. Finally the manor was bought by Edmund Woodhall, brother of Dorothy Woodcock.[34] He died seised of it in 1639, leaving two sons Edmund and John.[35] Edmund died without issue, and in 1675 Little Munden was held by his brother Robert Thornton Heysham,[40] and his grandson of the same name,[41] who in 1816 sold the manor to Nathaniel Snell Chauncy.[42] In 1844 the latter conveyed it to his brother Charles, from whom it passed upon his death in 1866 to his daughter Elizabeth and her husband Henry Edward Surtees.[43] It was acquired about 1895 by Mrs. Edwin Prodgers, the present owner.

Previous to 1385 the tenants of Little Munden did suit at the sheriff's tourn held at Broadwater at Easter and Michaelmas; in that year, however, view of frankpledge was granted to John de Thornbury,[44] for which he was to pay 20s. yearly.[45] This grant was confirmed in 1439,[46] and the view is mentioned as late as 1816.[47]

LIBURY (Stuterehela, Sutreshela, xi cent.; Leighbury, Lyebery, xv cent.).—Before the Conquest and

Little Munden Church from the North-East

John,[36] from whom it passed to his youngest sister Mary Thornton. She had two daughters Mary and Jane, who possessed the manor in 1700,[37] and who both in succession married Robert Heysham. Robert and Jane had a son Robert,[38] who died unmarried in 1734, bequeathing Little Munden to his kinsman Giles Thornton on condition of his assuming the name of Heysham.[39] He was succeeded by his son at the time of the Domesday Survey Stuterehele, as Libury was then called, was a large estate of almost 10 hides, but was very much divided up in ownership. In the time of King Edward Lewin held about 2½ hides[48]; two sokemen held of him 1 hide 1 virgate 10 acres, rendering an avera (a carrying service) or 5¼d. yearly to the king's sheriff[49]; Torchil held of him 1 hide and half a virgate, and Walter 11 acres.[50]

[37] Pat. 29 Eliz. pt. vii.
[28] Ibid. 37 Eliz. pt. x.
[29] Feet of F. Herts. Hil. 44 Eliz.
[30] Cussans, op. cit. *Broadwater Hund.* 149.
[31] Hertf. Gen. and Antiq. iii, 60.
[32] Feet of F. Herts. Trin. 5 Jas. I.
[33] Ibid. East. 12 Jas. I.
[34] Cussans, op. cit. *Broadwater Hund.* 149.
[35] Chan. Inq. p.m. (Ser. 2), cccclxx, 75.

[36] Recov. R. Trin. 27 Chas. II, rot. 160. [37] Chauncy, op. cit. 330.
[38] Cussans, loc. cit.
[39] Will, P.C.C. 148 Ockham.
[40] Ibid.
[41] Clutterbuck, op. cit. ii, 397; Recov. R. Trin. 8 Geo. II, rot. 50; Mich. 31 Geo. III, rot. 21.
[42] Feet of F. Herts. East. 56 Geo. III.
[43] Cussans, op. cit. *Broadwater Hund.* 150.

[44] Chan. Inq. p.m. Ric. II, file 403, no. 38; *Cal. Pat.* 1385–9, p. 68.
[45] Chart. R. 9 & 10 Ric. II, m. 14, no. 20.
[46] *Cal. Pat.* 1436–41, p. 350.
[47] Feet of F. Herts. East. 56 Geo. III.
[48] Half a hide was also held by a man of Lewin Scoua, who was probably the same.
[49] *V.C.H. Herts.* i, 309a.
[50] Ibid. 328b.

131

A HISTORY OF HERTFORDSHIRE

1 virgate.[4] The descendants of Walter the Fleming held the manor of Wahull or Odell in Bedfordshire, from which they took their name.[5] The overlordship of Little Munden remained in this family.[6] In 1304 it was held for the service of a knight's fee and 6s. paid to the warden of Rockingham Castle; in 1385 the payment was 10s.[7]

The manor was granted by the Wahulls to the family of Scales, though at what date is not known. William de Scales was lord of the manor in 1181,[8] and is mentioned again in 1189.[9] He was succeeded by his son Richard de Scales before 1208.[10] Richard died about 1231, leaving a daughter Lucy, whose wardship was purchased for 200 marks by Baldwin de Frevill, who afterwards married her.[11] From this family the manor took its name of Munden Frevill. Baldwin was succeeded before 1278 by Richard de Frevill,[12] whose son John inherited the manor in 1299.[13] John de Frevill died in 1312, leaving a son John,[14] who died before 1377. In that year his widow Ellen sold the manor to Philip Wyndok and William and Joan Hosell,[15] who in 1379–80 conveyed it to Sir John Thornbury.[16] Sir John died about 1396, having settled the manor on his son Philip,[17] and left a widow Nanerina. Philip settled Little Munden on himself and his wife Margaret.[18] In 1404 he went to sea on the king's service 'in the company of the king's brother Thomas Beaufort, admiral towards the north and east, on the safe-custody of the sea.'[19] In 1448 one Richard Whitwik was 'witholden to serve Sir Philip Thornbury and dame Margret his wife in the offices of lardyner, catour and cook,' during their lives. He was to receive 20s. yearly with clothing, and a tenement at Pottersgrene called 'Bathis,' for which he was to yield them yearly a 'roseflour' and suit of court. He was also to have reasonable fuel in the east park, 'except for bakyng or brewyng to chepe.'[20] Sir Philip Thornbury died about 1457,[21] leaving a daughter Margaret, who was married to Nicholas Appleyard.[22] The manor was settled on Margaret's daughter Elizabeth, wife of William Bastard, with remainder to Thomas and John, sons of Richard Thornbury.[23] In 1481 Elizabeth Bastard released the manor to trustees,[24] and in 1486 John Thornbury did the same,[25] apparently for the purpose of a conveyance to Sir William Say, into whose possession Little Munden came. He died seised of it in 1529,[26] after which it descended to his heirs in the same

THORNBURY. *Party fessewise or and argent a lion azure with two bends gules athwart him.*

LORDSHIP FARM, LITTLE MUNDEN

---

[4] *V.C.H. Herts.* i, 328b.
[5] G.E.C. *Complete Peerage.*
[6] Chan. Inq. p.m. 27 Edw. I, no. 16; 32 Edw. I, no. 45; 6 Edw. II, no. 54; Close, 6 Edw. II, m. 22; Chan. Inq. p.m. (Ser. 2), li, 50.
[7] Chan. Inq. p.m. 8 Ric. II, no. 144.
[8] *Pipe R.* 27 Hen. II, m. 7.
[9] Ibid.
[10] *Rot. de Oblat, et Fin.* (Rec. Com.), 426.
[11] Banks, *Dormant and Extinct Peerages,* ii, 477.
[12] Assize R. 323.
[13] Chan. Inq. p.m. 27 Edw. I, no. 16.
[14] Ibid. 6 Edw. II, no. 54.
[15] Anct. D. (P.R.O.), B 2572, 2575.
[16] Ibid. B 2576.
[17] Ibid. B 2574.
[18] Ibid. B 2567, 2569, 2570, 2571.
[19] *Cal. Pat.* 1401–5, p. 394.
[20] Anct. D. (P.R.O.), D 1172.
[21] Will, P.C.C. 11 Stokton.
[22] Feet of F. Herts. 35 Hen. VI, no. 181.
[23] Ibid.
[24] Anct. D. (P.R.O.), A 5236.
[25] Ibid. D 439 and 795. In the last of these documents Philip Thornbury is called the grandfather of John. This probably should be great-uncle, as there is no record that Philip had a son.
[26] Chan. Inq. p.m. (Ser. 2), li, 50.

BROADWATER HUNDRED — LITTLE MUNDEN

manner as Benington[37] (q.v.), and came with that manor to the Crown. It was leased to Thomas Crompton in 1594–5 for twenty-one years.[28] In 1602 Thomas Crompton conveyed his lease to Michael Woodcock,[29] who is said to have settled it upon his son Michael on his marriage with Dorothy Woodhall.[30] He was holding it in 1606,[31] but sold it in 1607 to Peter Vaulore,[32] who conveyed it in 1614 to his son-in-law Sir Charles Caesar and his daughter Anne.[33] The title, however, was defective, probably because only the twenty-one years' lease of the manor had been sold by Thomas Crompton, which term would run out about this time. Finally the manor was bought by Edmund Woodhall, brother of Dorothy Woodcock.[34] He died seised of it in 1639, leaving two sons Edmund and John.[35] Edmund died without issue, and in 1675 Little Munden was held by his brother

Robert Thornton Heysham,[40] and his grandson of the same name,[41] who in 1816 sold the manor to Nathaniel Snell Channcy.[42] In 1844 the latter conveyed it to his brother Charles, from whom it passed upon his death in 1866 to his daughter Elizabeth and her husband Henry Edward Surtees.[43] It was acquired about 1895 by Mrs. Edwin Prodgers, the present owner.

Previous to 1385 the tenants of Little Munden did suit at the sheriff's tourn held at Broadwater at Easter and Michaelmas; in that year, however, view of frankpledge was granted to John de Thornbury,[44] for which he was to pay 20s. yearly.[45] This grant was confirmed in 1439,[46] and the view is mentioned as late as 1816.[47]

LIBURY (Stuterehela, Sutreshela, xi cent.; Leighbury, Lyebery, xv cent.).—Before the Conquest and

LITTLE MUNDEN CHURCH FROM THE NORTH-EAST

John,[36] from whom it passed to his youngest sister Mary Thornton. She had two daughters Mary and Jane, who possessed the manor in 1700,[37] and who both in succession married Robert Heysham. Robert and Jane had a son Robert,[38] who died unmarried in 1734, bequeathing Little Munden to his kinsman Giles Thornton on condition of his assuming the name of Heysham.[39] He was succeeded by his son

at the time of the Domesday Survey Stuterehele, as Libury was then called, was a large estate of almost 10 hides, but was very much divided up in ownership. In the time of King Edward Lewin held about 2½ hides[48]; two sokemen held of him 1 hide 1 virgate 10 acres, rendering an avera (a carrying service) or 5¼d. yearly to the king's sheriff[49]; Torchil held of him 1 hide and half a virgate, and Walter 11 acres.[70]

[37] Pat. 29 Eliz. pt. vii.
[28] Ibid. 37 Eliz. pt. x.
[29] Feet of F. Herts. Hil. 44 Eliz.
[30] Cussans, op. cit. *Broadwater Hund.* 149.
[31] *Herts. Gen. and Antiq.* iii, 60.
[32] Feet of F. Herts. Trin. 5 Jas. I.
[33] Ibid. East. 12 Jas. I.
[34] Cussans, op. cit. *Broadwater Hund.* 149.
[35] Chan. Inq. p.m. (Ser. 2), ccclxx, 75.

[36] Recov. R. Trin. 27 Chas. II, rot. 160.   [37] Chauncy, op. cit. 330.
[38] Cussans, loc. cit.
[39] Will, P.C.C. 148 Ockham.
[40] Ibid.
[41] Clutterbuck, op. cit. ii, 397; Recov. R. Trin. 8 Geo. II, rot. 50; Mich. 31 Geo. III, rot. 21.
[42] Feet of F. Herts. East. 56 Geo. III.
[43] Cussans, op. cit. *Broadwater Hund.* 150.

[44] Chan. Inq. p.m. Ric. II, file 403, no. 38; Cal. Pat. 1385–9, p. 68.
[45] Chart. R. 9 & 10 Ric. II, m. 14, no. 20.
[46] Cal. Pat. 1436–41, p. 350.
[47] Feet of F. Herts. East. 56 Geo. III.
[48] Half a hide was also held by a man of Lewin Scoua, who was probably the same.
[49] V.C.H. Herts. i, 309a.
[50] Ibid. 328b.

131

A HISTORY OF HERTFORDSHIRE

Asgar the staller had 2 hides, which were held by Almar, rendering 2 averae or 8*d*. to the king's sheriff.[51] Elmer of Benington possessed 1 hide 3½ virgates, of which Leueron held a hide, Alwin 3 virgates, paying ¾ avera or 3*d*. to the sheriff, and 'a certain woman' held half a virgate.[52] Archbishop Stigand had 1 hide 3 virgates 22 acres, three of his men holding all of it save 13 acres,[53] 11 of which were held by Alward[54] and 2 acres by 'an Englishman' in mortgage.[55] There were also 25 acres held by a sokeman of King Edward, who rendered ¼ avera or 1*d*.[56]

By 1086 the land had entirely changed hands with the exception of the Englishman's 2 acres, which he continued to hold of Lanfranc, Stigand's successor.[57] Three virgates were held by Derman, and belonged to his manor of Watton.[58] Peter de Valognes had obtained all Elmer of Benington's land,[59] and had taken in addition the 25 acres of the sokeman of King Edward on the ground that he had not discharged the king's geld, but the men of the shire moot testified that the land was free of geld.[60] This part of Libury doubtless became absorbed in Peter's manor of Benington. Walter the Fleming was in possession of 1 hide ½ virgate and 11 acres, formerly held of Lewin by Torchil and Walter.[61] The rest of Lewin's land had been acquired by the Bishop of Bayeux, and was held of him by Peter.[62] The bishop also had the half hide of Lewin Scona and the whole of Stigand's land,[63] with the exception of the 2 acres already mentioned; he also had the 2 hides of Asgar the staller, which were held of him by Turstin[64]; his holding therefore amounted to 5¾ hides. The fee of Walter the Fleming is the only one which can be traced. His descendants took the name of Wahull or Odell from their chief manor in Bedfordshire, and the overlordship of the manor of Libury remained in their hands.[65] In 1304 it was held for a quarter fee of Thomas de Wahull and paid 18*d*. to Rockingham Castle (Northants).

John de Grey was the subtenant of the manor under the Wahulls in 1243,[66] and was still holding it in 1265.[67] He was the second son of Henry Grey of Grays Thurrock, Essex, and was some time Steward of Gascony and Governor of the castles of Northampton, Shrewsbury, Dover and Hereford.[68] He was succeeded by his son Reginald,[69] who became Lord Grey de Wilton about 1295.[70] From this date the manor of Libury descended in the family of Grey of Wilton[71] until it came to John Grey of Wilton, who in 1496 sold it to Richard Hill.[72] Richard settled the manor to the use of his wife Elizabeth for her life, with reversion to Ralph Latham. Elizabeth married secondly Anthony Poyntz, and in 1506 leased the manor to Ralph for a yearly rent of £75.[73] Ralph Latham died about 1520, leaving Libury to his son William and Elizabeth his wife, after the death of his mother.[74] By 1580 it had come to another William Latham and Susan his wife, who in that year sold it to Richard Brokeman.[75] The latter conveyed it in 1582 to Rowland Beresford,[76] who died seised of it in 1605, leaving a son Rowland,[77] who inherited the manor.[78] In 1608, however, he sold Libury to Robert Spence,[79] from whom it passed to his son Robert in 1618,[80] who was still holding it in 1648.[81] He is said to have had two sons—William, who died without issue, and John,[82] who with Edith his wife was holding it in 1682[83] and whose son John was lord of the manor in 1700[84] and as late as 1713.[85] The son of the latter, Charles, was holding Libury in 1779,[86] and was succeeded by his daughter Graciana Spence before 1821.[87] Graciana died in 1858, her nearest heirs being Henry Lowry Jearrad and Harriet Lister. A partition of the property was made in 1864, when Libury was apportioned to the former.[88] Mr. Jearrad was still holding it in 1899, after which it was acquired by Baron Schröder, Baron Bruno Schröder and Mr. C. A. Bingel. It has been converted into a German Industrial and Farm Colony to provide work and shelter for German-speaking unemployed and destitute, under the management of these three trustees.

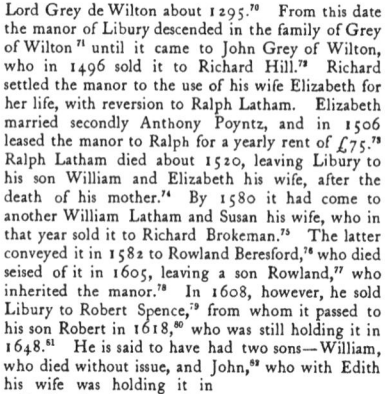

SPENCE. *Sable a fesse battled argent.*

The manor of Libury possessed two mills in 1086.[89] Mills are mentioned in 1608,[90] but do not appear to belong to it now, the estate having been much reduced.

John de Grey received a grant of free warren in 1243.[91] In 1370 the lord of the manor held a court every three weeks and view of frankpledge.[92]

The manor of GIFFORDS is first heard of in 1473, when it was held by Ralph Ashley.[93] In the 16th century (or perhaps in the late 15th century) 'certain lands and tenements in Much and Little Munden called Giffords' were held by William

WAHULL. *Or three crescents gules.*

---

[51] *V.C.H. Herts.* i, 309*b*.
[52] Ibid. 337*a*.
[53] Ibid. 309*a*.
[54] Ibid. 309*b*.
[55] Ibid. 305*a*.
[56] Ibid. 337*a*.
[57] Ibid. 305*a*.
[58] Ibid. 342*b*.
[59] Ibid. 337*a*.
[60] Ibid.
[61] Ibid. 328*b*.
[62] Ibid. 309*a*.
[63] Ibid. 309*a* and *b*.
[64] Ibid. 309*b*.
[65] Chan. Inq. p.m. 32 Edw. I, no. 45; 16 Edw. III (1st nos.), no. 45; 44 Edw. III (1st nos.), no. 30.
[66] *Cal. Pat.* 1232–47, p. 371.
[67] *Abbrev. Plac.* (Rec. Com.), 158.
[68] G.E.C. *Complete Peerage.*
[69] Ibid.; *Rot. Hund.* (Rec. Com.), i, 188.
[70] G.E.C. *Complete Peerage.*
[71] Ibid.; Chan. Inq. p.m. 16 Edw. III (1st nos.), no. 45; 44 Edw. III (1st nos.), no. 30.
[72] Close, 12 Hen. VII, no. 31; Feet of F. Herts. Hil. 12 Hen. VII.
[73] Com. Pleas D. Enr. East. 21 Hen. VII, m. 11.
[74] Will, P.C.C. 32 Ayloffe.
[75] Feet of F. Herts. Trin. 22 Eliz.
[76] Ibid. Hil. 24 Eliz.
[77] Chan. Inq. p.m. (Ser. 2), ccxcviii, 8.
[78] Feet of F. Herts. Mich. 6 Jas. I; Hil. 5 Jas. I.
[79] Close, 6 Jas. I, pt. v, no. 26.
[80] Chan. Inq. p.m. (Ser. 2), ccclxxx, 109.
[81] Feet of F. Div. Co. Hil. 23 Chas. I.
[82] Chauncy, op. cit. 340.
[83] Feet of F. Div. Co. Trin. 34 Chas. II.
[84] Chauncy, loc. cit.
[85] Recov. R. Mich. 12 Anne, rot. 74.
[86] Ibid. Hil. 19 Geo. III, rot. 25; Clutterbuck, op. cit. ii, 407.
[87] Clutterbuck, loc. cit.
[88] Cussans, op. cit. *Broadwater Hund.* 151.
[89] *V.C.H. Herts.* i, 309*a* and *b*.
[90] Close, 6 Jas. I, pt. v, no. 26.
[91] *Cal. Pat.* 1232–47, p. 371.
[92] Chan. Inq. p.m. 44 Edw. III (1st nos.), no. 30.
[93] Rentals and Surv. R. Herts. 288.

132

BROADWATER HUNDRED LITTLE MUNDEN

Andrewe.[94] It was probably no more than a freehold held of the manor of Great Munden.[95] Andrewe's possession of the estate was disputed by Thomas Ashley, and it was decided by arbitrators that William Andrewe should keep it for life upon payment of £8, with remainder to Thomas Ashley and his heirs. After the death of William a fresh suit took place, Giffords being claimed by George Carleton, who stated that he had purchased Thomas Ashley's interest in the estate, and was therefore the rightful owner, but that John Andrewe, William's son, and John Lane would not allow him possession. John Andrewe denied Thomas Ashley's title to Giffords, and said that the arbitrators decided that it was to remain to William and his heirs. He also said that the deeds connected with the matter had been stolen by William's wife Anne and delivered to John Lane, who claimed the estate by just conveyance.[96] The result of the suit is not recorded, and Giffords had passed by 1580 into the possession of Matthew Lowe, who apparently held it in right of his wife Anne.[97] It was then called a manor. Soon after it came into the hands of William Kinge, who sold it to his brother-in-law Robert Brisco.[98] Robert died seised of it in 1616, holding it of the king in free socage as of the manor of Great Munden, by fealty and free rent of 10s. yearly. He left it by will to his wife Ellen, after whose death it presumably passed to his nephew and heir Edward Brisco.[99] In the following century it had passed into the hands of the Spence family,[100] lords of the manor of Libury, in which manor it presumably became merged.

Two parks are mentioned in Little Munden in 1299.[1] One of them, however, seems to have been disparked before the 15th century, for in 1480 and again in 1594 only 'Munden Park' is mentioned.[2] It does not now remain, unless Lordship's Wood is a survival of it.

CHURCH The church of *ALL SAINTS*, standing on high ground about the centre of the parish, is built of flint rubble with stone dressings and the roofs are tiled. It consists of a chancel, north chapel, nave and north aisle, south-west tower, north and south porches and south vestry.[3]

Although the original 11th-century church has been almost wholly obscured by later alterations and additions, it seems certain that in the latter half of that century it consisted of a chancel, nave and north aisle, with an arcade of three bays. The 14th-century alterations consisted of building the western portion of the present north chapel about 1340, and about 1360 replacing the two eastern bays of the nave arcade by those now in existence; at the same time the aisle may have been widened. In the 15th century the north chapel was extended eastwards to

LITTLE MUNDEN: OLD COTTAGE AT DANE END

its present size, new windows were inserted almost throughout the church, a rood turret was built, and the aisle was probably rebuilt and towards the end of the century the west tower was built. In the 19th century the church was restored, the western arch of the nave was replaced by a two-centred arch and the south vestry and north and south porches were added.

[94] Ct. of Req. bdle. 3, no. 335.
[95] Chan. Inq. p.m. (Ser. 2), ccclix, 133.
[96] Ct. of Req. bdle. 3, no. 335.
[97] Feet of F. Herts. Mich. 22 & 23 Eliz.; Trin. 24 Eliz.
[98] Chan. Inq. p.m. (Ser. 2), ccclix, 133.
[99] Ibid.
[100] Recov. R. Herts. Hil. 19 Geo. III, rot. 25.
[1] Chan. Inq. p.m. 27 Edw. I, no. 16.
[2] Anct. D. (P.R.O.) B 2562; Pat. 37 Eliz. pt. x.
[3] Dimensions: chancel, 21 ft. 6 in. by 16 ft. 6 in.; north chapel, 21 ft. 6 in. by 12 ft. 6 in.; nave, 41 ft. by 21 ft. 6 in.; north aisle, 10 ft. wide; west tower, 11 ft. square.

A HISTORY OF HERTFORDSHIRE

The east window of the chancel is of three cinquefoiled lights with tracery above in a two-centred head, and has been almost entirely restored. In the south wall is a similar window of two trefoiled lights which has been wholly restored. In the north wall are two arches, the easternmost being of the early 15th century. It is four-centred, and has a panelled soffit and a carved figure of an angel holding a shield in the apex; an ogee label, with a finial and crockets, piercing a square outer label, surmounts it, and in the spandrels of the outer label are shields, while a rose fills the space above the apex of the arch. This arch forms a canopy for a tomb to be described below.

The westernmost arch is two-centred, of about 1340, and is of two moulded orders with shafted jambs. In the south wall is a doorway of the 12th century, but almost wholly restored. It was formerly external, but now leads into the modern vestry. To the east of the window in the south wall is a piscina of the late 14th century with a trefoiled head. The chancel arch is 15th-century work, and is of two moulded orders with shafted jambs and a label with return ends. The openings of the windows of the north chapel are of the 15th century, but the windows are otherwise modern. Of the low two-centred arch leading to the aisle only the north jamb is original. It is filled by a screen of the late 15th century, of three bays, with open upper panels with tracery and solid lower panels. The roof of the chapel is an early 16th-century king-post roof, much repaired. The nave has a north arcade of three bays, of which the two eastern arches are of about 1360, of two chamfered orders and supported on an octagonal column and half-octagonal responds, of which the western abuts on a jamb of the 11th century, one of the two of that date which support a modern two-centred arch, the third of the arcade. These jambs have abaci roughly cable-moulded, and the eastern is set in pink mortar, which does not appear elsewhere in the church. In the easternmost respond of the arcade are three niches, those at the side higher than that in the centre and trefoiled, while the centre one is cinquefoiled; all three have crocketed labels and small pinnacles at the sides. In that on the north side is a portion of a small female figure. On the north side of the western pier of the arcade is a small bracket. The rood-loft door pierces the north wall at the eastern end, its sill being at the level of the abacus of the eastern respond. In the south wall at the eastern end is a window of three lights, of the 15th century, with modern tracery. The rear arch is original and is ogeed at the head. The south doorway is of the 14th century, and is of two continuously moulded orders, unrestored. The south porch is modern. At the west end of the nave a two-centred archway opens into the west tower, which is of three stages, with an embattled parapet and a small leaded spire. The west doorway, with a pointed arch in a square head and tracery in the spandrels, the west window above, and the four bell-chamber lights are all of the late 15th century, the date of the tower itself. The vaulting of the ground stage is modern. The north aisle has at the north-east angle a newel stair to the rood-loft, approached by a 15th-century doorway with a four-centred head and continuously moulded, and opening at the upper end by a plain splayed four-centred archway. The two three-light windows in the north wall are of the late 15th century, with cinquefoiled heads, and are very much restored. A two-light window in the west wall is probably a little earlier, but is also restored. The north doorway is of the 15th century, and has a four-centred head continuously moulded with the jambs. The north porch is modern.

The tomb under the eastern arch in the north wall of the chancel is that of a knight and his lady, with recumbent effigies on an altar tomb with panelled sides, of about 1440. The knight is in full plate armour, with a finely carved girdle and collar, and wears a rich and heavy orle on his uncovered head, which rests on his great helm. His feet rest on a lion. The lady, whose arms are broken away, wears a square headdress. The tomb is probably that of Philip Thornbury, who died about 1457. Under the western arch of the same wall is another altar tomb of the late 14th century, probably that of Sir John Thornbury, who died about 1396. It has large shields in square quatrefoiled panels, alternating with niches containing small figures. One of the shields bears the arms of Thornbury. The effigies are those of a knight and lady. The former wears plate armour with a pointed basinet and a camail. The head rests on the great helm and the feet on a lion, while the head of the lady, who wears a honeycombed headdress, is supported by figures, now broken away, and her feet rest on a lap-dog. The figures are in very bad condition, the arms of both being gone, and many names being scratched upon them, but there are traces of gilding on the effigy of the knight. In the north wall of the north chapel is a tomb-recess of the 15th century.

There are six bells: (1) by Miles Graye, 1629; (2) a mid-15th-century bell, inscribed 'Sancte Petre

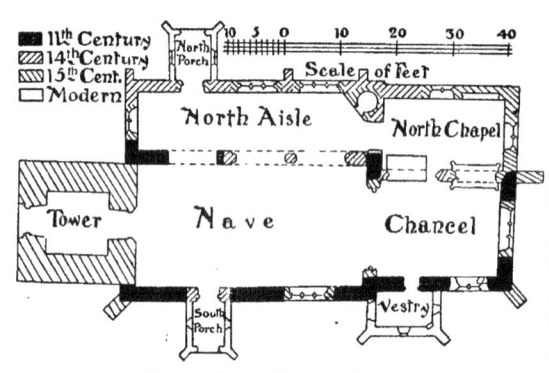

PLAN OF LITTLE MUNDEN CHURCH

134

LITTLE MUNDEN CHURCH: TOMBS IN THE CHANCEL

Clement Dungan, Jeremiah Dungan, James Carrell, John Morris, Thomas Dungan, John Clark, David Griffith, Christopher Day, Nathaniel West, William Gregory and Samuel Selers. The Dungans were sons of Reverend Thomas Dungan, who emigrated from Rhode Island, and organized the Baptist church at Cold Spring, near Bristol, 1684. Joseph Dungan, grandson of the Reverend Thomas, died August 25, 1785, in his 78th year, and was buried at Southampton. We find no further mention of Thomas Cutler, but William, who was an early settler there, died in 1714. They were probably brothers of John Cutler, who made the re-survey of the county, 1702-3. James Carter died, 1714. John Morris bought five hundred and eighty-two acres of James Plumley, 1698, which lay in the upper part of the township, between the Street road and county line, and a considerable part, if not all, north of the Middle road. When the re-survey was made, 1702, Thomas Harding was one of the largest land owners in the township, his acres numbering six hundred and eighteen. Joseph Tomlinson was there early, and died, 1723. April 20, 1705, four hundred and seventeen acres were surveyed by warrant to Thomas Callowhill, the father-in-law of William Penn, situated in the upper part of the township, and bounded by the Street road and Warminster line. It covered the site of Davisville. John, Thomas, and Richard Penn inherited this tract from their grandfather, Callowhill, and January 20, 1734, they conveyed one hundred and forty-nine acres by patent to Stephen Watts. The land of John Morris bounded this tract on the southwest.

On Holme's map is laid off, in about the middle of the township, a plat one mile square, similar to that in Newtown and Wrightstown. As in those townships it was, no doubt, intended for a park, or town plat, and to have been divided among the land owners in the township outside of it, in the proportion of one to ten. But as we have not met with it in any of the Southampton conveyances, it probably had no other existence than on the map.

At an early day, and following the English Friends, there was a considerable influx of Hollanders into the township, and the large and influential families of Krewson, Vanartsdalen, Vandeventer, Hogeland, Barcalow, Vanhorne, Lefferts, Vansant and Vandeveer descend from this sturdy stock. Other families, which started out with but one Holland ancestor, have become of almost pure blood by intermarriage. The descendants of Dutch parentage in this and adjoining townships have thus become very numerous, but both the spelling of the names, and their pronunciation, have been considerably changed since their ancestors settled in the township.

Derrick Krewson[6] was a land-holder, if not a settler, in Southampton as early as 1684, for the 11th of September, 1717, he paid to James Steele, receiver of the Proprietary quit-rents, £9. 11s. 4d. for thirty-three years' interest due on five hundred and eighty acres of land in this township. In March, 1756, Henry Krewson paid sixteen years' quit-rent to E. Physic on two hundred and thirty acres in Southampton.[7] The will of Derrick Krewson was executed January 4, 1729, but the time of his death is not known. He probably came from Long Island, the starting point of most of the Hollanders who settled in Bucks county.[8]

6 Original spelling Kræsen.

7 Down to 1756 the Proprietary quit-rents were paid at Pennsbury, but we do not know how much later.

8 Helena Temple, Churchville, who died. February, 1884, would have been one hundred years old had she lived to June 10. She was of Low Dutch stock, daughter of

BROADWATER HUNDRED   LITTLE MUNDEN

ora pro nobis' and maker's mark D. I. (John Danyell); (3) by J. Briant, 1816; (4) a mid-15th-century bell, with inscription 'Sit nomen Domini benedictum' and the royal arms, which is probably also by John Danyell; (5) by Warner & Sons, 1859; and (6) modern.

The plate consists of a silver chalice and a silver paten; there is also a flagon.

The registers begin in 1680, and are contained in two books: (i) baptisms 1610 to 1812, burials 1680 to 1812, marriages 1680 to 1753; (ii) marriages 1754 to 1812.

ADVOWSON The advowson of the church belonged to the lords of the manor[4] until about 1818, when it was sold to Francis Riddel Reynolds, who presented in 1819.[5] He sold it about 1830 to the Rev. C. Jollands,[6] who continued to hold it until 1867, when it was acquired by Lieut.-Col. Loyd.[7] The latter died about 1891, when the advowson passed to his wife, who held it until 1900.[8] It continued in the hands of her trustees for the next two years, after which it came into the possession of Mr. Llewellyn Loyd, the present patron.[9]

Early in the 13th century a vicarage seems to have been endowed, for upon the presentation of Andrew de Scales by William de Scales, which must have occurred shortly before 1209, a vicarage was reserved to William de Standon. This vicarage consisted of 1 acre of land, the tithes of the whole parish, and of the vill of Haultwick.[10] This arrangement seems to have been only temporary.

In 1335 William de Munden had licence for an oratory in his manor in the parish of Munden Frevill.[11]

Meeting-places for Protestant Dissenters in Little Munden were registered from 1709 onwards. In 1809 a chapel was registered,[12] but there is now no Nonconformist place of worship in the parish.

CHARITIES This parish was in possession of detached pieces of land and cottages which were supposed to have been derived under a devise by will of Ralph Fordham, dated in 1591. The land and two cottages were sold in 1886, and the proceeds invested in £399 5s. consols with the official trustees, producing £9 19s. 4d. yearly.

In the parliamentary returns of 1786 it is stated that donations amounting to £60, being the gifts of Thomas Hall, 1643, John Kent, 1665, and others, were made for bread to the poor. These gifts are now represented by £69 9s. 4d. consols with the official trustees, producing £1 14s. 8d. yearly.

In 1883 George Pooley by his will, proved at London 29 June, bequeathed £1,000, the income to be applied towards the maintenance and support of the poor under the title of 'The George and Mary Ann Pooley Trust.' The legacy was invested in £984 0s. 2d. consols with the official trustees, producing £24 12s. yearly. The income of these charities was in 1908 applied mainly in bonuses to members of coal and clothing clubs, interest on children's bank, and in temporary relief in money.

In 1906 Joseph Singleton by will, proved 25 June, left a legacy, represented by £269 12s. 8d. consols with the official trustees, the annual dividends, amounting to £6 14s. 8d., to be applied in bread (or in such way as minister approves) for poor of sixty years of age and upwards on 1 January yearly.

LITTLE MUNDEN CHURCH: THE NAVE LOOKING NORTH-EAST

[4] See refs. under manor; Inst. Bks. (P.R.O.); Bacon, *Liber Regis.*
[5] *Clerical Guide.*
[6] Ibid.
[7] *Clergy List.*
[8] Ibid.
[9] Ibid.
[10] *Rot. Hug. Wells* (Cant. and York Soc.), i, 94.
[11] Linc. Epis. Reg. Burghersh.
[12] Urwick, op. cit. 600.

135

A HISTORY OF HERTFORDSHIRE

SACOMBE

Suevecampe, Sevechampe, Stuochampe (xi cent.); Savecampe, Sawecampe, Sevechaumpe (xiii cent.); Savecampe (xiv cent.); Savecome, Sawcompe (xv cent.).

The parish of Sacombe has an area of 1,534 acres, of which 405½ acres are arable land, 683½ acres permanent grass, and 123½ acres wood.[1] The general elevation of the parish is a little over 200 ft., sinking to below 200 ft. along the banks of a small stream which runs through the centre of the parish into the River Beane. In the north-west Sacombe Hill rises to over 300 ft., and in the north-east at Sacombe Green the land reaches a height of 362 ft. In the west the parish takes in a large portion of Woodhall Park, and the River Beane flowing out of this passes through the south of Sacombe parish for a short distance. The road from Benington to Ware runs through the parish from north-west to south-east, having Woodhall Park on its western side. About the centre of the parish a branch road turns off from it and runs north-east to Little Munden, passing through Sacombe Pound. A road turns east from Sacombe Pound, leading up the hill to the hamlet of Sacombe Green and branching off to Sacombe Church, rectory, and school, which compose all the village that there is. Sacombe House, surrounded by a park of 150 acres, lies south-east from the church. It was rebuilt by Mr. George Caswall early in the 19th century, and was recently the scene of a destructive fire. Burr's Green is a hamlet in the south of the parish. The subsoil of the parish is chalk in the west and north and Woolwich and Reading Beds in the east. There is a chalk-pit beside the road to Sacombe Green, a disused one north of Woodhall Park, and another disused one, with an old kiln, on the west side of Sacombe Park. The nearest stations are Hertford, 4 miles south, and Ware, the same distance south-east, both on a branch line of the Great Eastern railway.

The inclosure award was made in 1852, and is in the custody of the clerk of the peace.[2]

Place-names which occur in the parish are Reddinges, Blindman's Hill, Crossefield, Great Emdell Field, Emden Spring, Charden, and Mobsden.

In the time of Edward the Confessor MANOR there were two manors in Sacombe. The larger, held by Ælmer of Benington, was assessed at 4 hides. Besides the manor there were 1 hide and 1 virgate held by four of Ælmer's sokemen, and 5 virgates held by a certain woman under Anschil of Ware, one of which was mortgaged to Ælmer. The other manor, consisting of 1 hide 3 virgates, was held by Lewin, a thegn of King Harold. Both these manors were granted by William the Conqueror to Peter de Valognes, who held them as one manor assessed at 8¾ hides,[3] the assessment having seemingly increased half a hide. Half a virgate held by Aluric Blac of Stigand, and in 1086 by Anschil of Stigand's successor,[4] and another half-virgate held in 1086 and before by a sokeman of the king[5] were probably absorbed in the manor of Sacombe.

The manor, held of the king in chief by knight service, passed to the descendants of Peter de Valognes in the same way as his chief manor of Benington (q.v.) until the death of Christiane de Valognes and her husband William de Mandeville. The Valognes' estates were then divided between the three heirs: Lora, the wife of Henry de Balliol, Christiane, wife of Peter de Maune, and Isabel, who was married to David Comyn. Sacombe was apportioned to Isabel, the youngest, and passed upon her death, about 1253, to her son William Comyn.[6] William died about 1283,[7] and his son John being a minor, custody of two thirds of the manor was granted to Matthew de Columbars, and shortly after, at the request of the latter, to John de Gisorz, citizen of London, for four years.[8] In 1284 the remaining third was confirmed to William Comyn's widow Eufemia in dower, on her taking an oath not to marry again without the king's licence.[9] She broke her oath, however, and the king took the third part of the manor back into his hands before her death, which occurred about 1289.[10] Her son John Comyn came of age in 1286-7,[11] and probably held the manor, but he died soon after and Sacombe passed to Edmund Comyn, said to have been his brother,[12] who died seised of it about 1314.[13] The latter left two infant daughters and a widow Mary, who held a third of the manor in dower.[14] She afterwards forfeited it.[15] Sacombe was eventually divided between the two daughters, the elder of whom, Eufemia, was holding it in 1320 (then aged fourteen years), at which time she was the wife of William de la Beche.[16] The moiety was settled in 1330 on William and Eufemia for their lives and the heirs of Eufemia.[17] William died in 1333, leaving a son John.[18] Eufemia continued to hold the moiety, and in 1334 received licence to have an oratory in her house at Sacombe.[19] She married secondly John de Walkefare, who died abroad in 1345, leaving a son John.[20] Apparently, however, both these sons died young, for upon Eufemia's death in 1361 her lands passed to her daughter Elizabeth, the wife of Roger de Elmerugge (Elmbridge).[21]

Eufemia's sister Mary Comyn, who received the other moiety of Sacombe Manor, was married by licence of the king to Edmund de Pakenham while

---

[1] Statistics from Bd. of Agric. (1905).
[2] *Blue Bk. Incl. Awards*, 63.
[3] *V.C.H. Herts.* i, 337*a*.
[4] Ibid. 305*b*.
[5] Ibid. 343*b*.
[6] Chan. Inq. p.m. 37 Hen. III, no. 45; *Plac. de Quo Warr.* (Rec. Com.), 281.
[7] Chan. Inq. p.m. 11 Edw. I, no. 49.
[8] *Cal. Pat.* 1281-92, p. 60; Assize R. 325.
[9] *Cal. Close*, 1279-88, p. 265.
[10] Chan. Inq. p.m. 17 Edw. I, no. 13.
[11] Ibid. 15 Edw. I, no. 71.
[12] Clutterbuck, op. cit. ii, 422.
[13] Chan. Inq. p.m. 8 Edw. II, no. 18.
[14] *Cal. Close*, 1313-18, p. 121.
[15] Chan. Inq. p.m. 7 Edw. III (1st nos.), no. 34.
[16] Ibid. 14 Edw. II, no. 25.
[17] Ibid. 4 Edw. III (2nd nos.), no. 32;
[18] Chan. Inq. p.m. 7 Edw. III (1st nos.), no. 83.
[19] *Cal. Pat.* 1330-4, p. 33; Feet of F. Div. Co. Trin. 5 Edw. III, no. 83.
[20] *Cal. Close*, 1333-7, p. 75; Linc. Epis. Reg. Burghersh.
[21] Chan. Inq. p.m. 19 Edw. III, no. 24; *Cal. Close*, 1346-9, p. 9.
[22] Chan. Inq. p.m. 35 Edw. III (1st nos.), no. 43.

she was still under age. He died in 1351,[22] leaving a son Thomas. Mary conveyed her moiety of the manor to her sister Eufemia in 1355,[23] so that the whole manor came to Eufemia's daughter Elizabeth and Roger de Elmerugge in 1361.[24] Roger died in 1375,[25] and in the next year Elizabeth sold Sacombe to John de Holt and Alice his wife.[26] Sir John Holt was involved on the king's side in the rebellion of 1387, when the royal army under Robert Duke of Ireland was defeated. He was among the five judges sentenced by Parliament to be hanged, but, the sentence being remitted, he with the rest was banished to Ireland and his estates forfeited.[27] Sacombe thus came into the king's hands in 1388.[28] Upon Sir John Holt's death, however, in 1419, or perhaps before, it was restored to his son Hugh.[29] Hugh Holt died in 1420 and Sacombe passed to his brother Richard,[30] who sold it in the same year to Robert Babthorpe.[31] The manor-house at that time contained a hall, 'five chambers high and low, and a house for the making of tiles.'[32] Robert Babthorpe died in 1436, and the manor came to his son Ralph.[33] From Ralph Babthorpe it passed to his son Robert in 1455,[34] and to Robert's son Ralph in 1466.[35] Ralph died in 1490, leaving a daughter Isabel, who was married to Sir John Hastings,[36] and died in 1495.[37] Her heir was her 'kinswoman' Isabel Plompton, daughter of Robert Babthorpe, who seems most probably to have been her first cousin, but was possibly her aunt.[38] This Isabel was married to William Plompton, and was holding the manor as his widow in 1547.[39] She died in 1552,[40] and Sacombe passed to her grandson William Plompton, who in 1593 conveyed the manor to Sir Philip Boteler of Watton Woodhall.[41] At Sir Philip's death in 1607 Sacombe came to his widow Jane,[42] and after her death to his grandson Robert Boteler,[43] from whom it passed in 1623 to his daughter Jane,[44] who married John, afterwards Lord Belasyse of Worlaby.[45] The latter is said to have sold Sacombe, owing to pecuniary embarrassment, to Sir John Gore,[46] who seems to have been in possession of it in 1669.[47] In 1688 it was purchased from him with the manor of Temple Chelsin by Sir Thomas Rolt,[48] formerly president of the East India Company and Governor of Bombay, from whom it passed to his son Edward[49] in 1710.[50] Edward Rolt, who was M.P. for Chippen-

ham, was succeeded by his son Thomas, who was holding the manor in 1728[51] and died in 1754, leaving a son Thomas, of the 1st Guards, who was killed in action in 1758, when Sacombe seems to have come to his youngest sister Mary Constantia Rolt,[52] who married Timothy Caswall of the Guards,

ROLT. *Argent a bend sable with three dolphins argent thereon having golden crowns.*

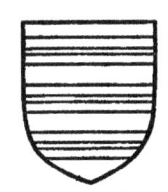

CASWALL. *Argent three gimel bars sable.*

M.P. for Brackley. He was a personal friend of Pitt, who used to visit him at Sacombe, and was there with Dundas, his Home Secretary, at the critical time when Lord Gower, ambassador in Paris, fleeing from the French Revolution, hastened to them (2 September 1792), before proceeding to the king.[52a] The bust of Pitt presented to Mr. Caswall is now in possession of his great-great-grandson, Mr. J. H. Round, LL.D. He died in 1802 and was succeeded by his son George Caswall,[53] after whose death in 1825[54] the manor was sold to Samuel Smith of Watton Woodhall,[55] with which manor it has since descended.

In 1275 the lord of Sacombe was said to have view of frankpledge, gallows and assize of bread and ale.[56] In 1278 William Comyn claimed in his manor of Sacombe all liberties formerly pertaining to the Valognes' lands, viz. soc and sac, toll, team and infangentheof by charter of Henry I, and view of frankpledge, tumbrel and amendment of the assize of bread and ale 'of ancient custom.'[57] In 1287 gallows and free warren were claimed in addition.[58] In 1361 court leet was held at Whitsuntide.[59] Free fishery in the River Benwith (Beane) was said to pertain to the manor in 1590,[60] 1609[61] and 1688.[62] Sacombe possessed a water mill in 1086,[63] which is

[22] Chan. Inq. p.m. 25 Edw. III (1st nos.), no. 36; *Cal. Close*, 1349–54, p. 449.
[23] Feet of F. Herts. 29 Edw. III, no. 442; Chan. Inq. p.m. 29 Edw. III (2nd nos.), no. 43.
[24] Chan. Inq. 35 Edw. III (1st nos.), no. 43; *Abbrev. Rot. Orig.* (Rec. Com.), ii, 263; Feet of F. Div. Co. 36 Edw. III, no. 99.
[25] Chan. Inq. p.m. 49 Edw. III (1st nos.), no. 43.
[26] Feet of F. Herts. 50 Edw. III, no. 669; *Abbrev. Rot. Orig.* (Rec. Com.), ii, 347.
[27] Cussans, op. cit. *Broadwater Hund.* 159; *Cal. Pat.* 1385–9, p. 548.
[28] See *Cal. Pat.* 1388–92, p. 80.
[29] Chan. Inq. p.m. 6 Hen. V, no. 43.
[30] Ibid. 8 Hen. V, no. 103.
[31] *Cal. Pat.* 1422–9, p. 65; Chan. Inq. p.m. 15 Hen. VI, no. 2.
[32] Chan. Inq. p.m. 15 Hen. VI, no. 2.
[33] Ibid. no. 60.
[34] Ibid. 33 Hen. VI, no. 40.
[35] Ibid. 6 Edw. IV, no. 37.
[36] Ibid. (Ser. 2), vi, 47.

[37] Ibid. lxxix, 277.
[38] Ralph Babthorpe, father of Isabel Hastings, was twenty-two at his father's (Robert's) death in 1466, at which time Isabel Plompton was three, thus making rather a large difference in age if she was his sister. It, therefore, seems more probable that her father Robert was Ralph's younger brother, who might have married at sixteen or seventeen.
[39] Recov. R. Herts. Hil. 1 Edw. VI, rot. 157.
[40] Chan. Inq. p.m. (Ser. 2), xcvi, 8.
[41] Feet of F. Herts. Hil. 35 Eliz.
[42] Ibid. Mich. 10 Jas. I.
[43] Chan. Inq. p.m. (Ser. 2), ccxcvii, 149.
[44] Ibid. ccccii, 144; Ct. of Wards, Feod. Surv. 17; Privy Seal Docket Bk. xi; Recov. R. Herts. East. 14 Chas. I, rot. 5.
[45] G.E.C. *Complete Peerage.*
[46] Chauncy, op. cit. 336.
[47] Harl. MS. 5801, fol. 36.
[48] Close, 4 Jas. II, pt. v, no. 10. Sir John Gore wished to have the bargain rescinded, but the House of Lords decided

against him (*Hist. MSS. Com. Rep.* vi, App. 353–4).
[49] *Genealogist*, Jan. 1901, p. 148.
[50] Mon. Inscr.
[51] Salmon, op. cit. 225; see also Recov. R. Herts. Mich. 29 Geo. II, rot. 47.
[52] Ibid. East. 32 Geo. II, rot. 361. His elder sister Cecilia lived until 1761, but apparently did not inherit, as Mary was in possession in 1759.
[52a] *Hist. MSS. Com. Rep.* v, App. 307, 309.
[53] Clutterbuck, op. cit. ii, 426; Recov. R. Herts. Mich. 43 Geo. III, rot. 7.
[54] Mon. Inscr.
[55] Cussans, op. cit. *Broadwater Hund.* 160. [56] *Rot. Hund.* (Rec. Com.), i, 192.
[57] *Plac. de Quo Warr.* (Rec. Com.), 281.
[58] Assize R. 325.
[59] Chan. Inq. p.m. 35 Edw. III (1st nos.), no. 43.
[60] Pat. 33 Eliz. pt. i.
[61] Chan. Inq. p.m. (Ser. 2), cccix, 164.
[62] Close, 4 Jas. II, pt. v, no. 10.
[63] *V.C.H. Herts.* i, 337a.

A HISTORY OF HERTFORDSHIRE

frequently mentioned in connexion with the manor,[64] and was presumably situated on the River Beane at Mill End.

In the 13th century the Knights Templars held some lands in Sacombe, Rocelin, master of the order, receiving a grant of free warren there in 1253.[65] A reminiscence of their holding is found, perhaps, in 1698, when Sir Thomas Holt, lord of the manor, was presented for not keeping the 'Temple pound' in order.[66]

There was a hide in Sacombe held before the Conquest by three sokemen, two of them men of Anschil of Ware and the third a man of Aluric Blac. This land in 1086 belonged to Hardwin de Scales,[67] and was perhaps later annexed to Little Munden.

Half a virgate held in 1086 by Derman, and formerly belonging to Alwin Horne,[68] would naturally become absorbed in Derman's neighbouring manor of Watton.

All the doors and windows of the chancel and nave are modern. They have two-centred heads, the east and west windows being of three and the north and south windows of two lights with 'decorated' tracery. The responds of the chancel arch are of the 14th century with wave mouldings on both sides. The sub-arches are also original.

In the chancel is a piscina with a modern recess, with a cinquefoiled ogee head and a sexfoiled bowl, probably of the 14th century.

In the chancel are brasses of Eleanor Dodington, 1537, and John Dodington, her husband, 1544, which consist of inscriptions only. On the north wall of the chancel is a monument to the Rev. John Meriton, vicar, who died in 1669; and on the west wall of the vestry is a reset tablet to Sir Thomas Rolt, 'Agent of Persia and President of India,' 1710, and his wife, 1716. There is also in the vestry a 17th-century hour-glass stand of iron.

There are three bells, of which the first is by John

SACOMBE CHURCH FROM THE SOUTH-EAST

CHURCH The church of *ST. CATHERINE* stands on high ground in the middle of the parish. The walls are faced with flint and the roofs are tiled.[69] The church consists of a chancel, nave, north vestry and south tower. The original plan of the 14th-century church was the same as that of the present building, and the chancel and nave are of that date. The tower was rebuilt in 1855–6, and the north vestry was added at the same time, when the whole church was restored, faced with flint and re-roofed. A great part of the stonework of this church was brought from the demolished church of Thundridge.

Waylett, dated 1722, and the third by James Bartlett, 1683.

The plate includes a cup of 1688 and a flagon of 1715.

The registers begin in 1726 and are contained in four books: (i) baptisms 1726 to 1773, burials 1726 to 1773, marriages 1726 to 1754; (ii) baptisms 1773 to 1812; (iii) burials 1773 to 1812; (iv) marriages 1754 to 1811.

ADVOWSON In 1086 there was a clerk among the tenants of the manor,[70] so that there was probably then a church there. The advowson has always belonged to the

[64] Chan. Inq. p.m. 37 Hen. III, no. 45; 11 Edw. I, no. 49; 8 Edw. II, no. 18; 7 Edw. III (1st nos.), no. 34; 8 Hen. V, no. 103; (Ser. 2), cccix, 164.
[65] *Cal. Chart. R.* 1226–57, p. 415.
[66] *Sess. R.* (Herts. Co. Rec.), i, 431.
[67] *V.C.H. Herts.* i, 338*b*.
[68] Ibid. 342*b*.
[69] Dimensions: chancel, 24 ft. 6 in. by 16 ft.; nave, 43 ft. 6 in. by 21 ft. 3 in.; tower, 11 ft. square.
[70] *V.C.H. Herts.* i, 337*a*.

138

BROADWATER HUNDRED

STEVENAGE

lord of the manor.[71] The church is now generally known as the church of St. Catherine, but the earlier invocation seems to have been St. Mary.[72] In 1638 the rectory possessed two barns, a yard, orchard and garden adjoining the house, and about 15 acres of glebe.[73]

In 1819 a dwelling-house was registered for Protestant Dissenters under the Toleration Act.[74]

CHARITIES The charity of Rev. John Meriton, a former vicar, for apprenticing, now consists of £260 6s. 7d. consols, and £251 15s. 7d. Natal 3½ per cent. stock with the official trustees, arising respectively from the sale in 1906 of land purchased in 1699 with £100 given by the donor and from accumulations of income, and producing £15 6s. 4d. in annual dividends. The charity is regulated by schemes of the Charity Commissioners, 1881 and 1910.

By an order of 9 March 1905 made under the Board of Education Act the stock arising from accumulations of income and all net income not applied within the year for apprenticing under clause 23 of the principal scheme constitute the Meriton educational foundation.

The Parish Clerk's land consists of 3 r. 26 p. of the annual letting value of 5s.

STEVENAGE

Stithenaece, Stigenace (xi cent.); Stitenache, Styvenach, Stiveneth (xiii cent.); Stivenhatch, Stevenach (xiv to xvi cent.).

The parish of Stevenage has an area of 4,545 acres, of which 3,200¼ acres are arable land, 916 acres permanent grass and 325⅛ acres wood.[1]

The parish is for the most part a little over 300 ft. above the ordnance datum, a slight depression in the south being the only part below this level. In the north-east the ground rises to 470 ft., and reaches an altitude of just over 400 ft. in two isolated points on the western border of the parish. The Great North Road runs through the centre of the parish. About three-quarters of a mile south of Stevenage, lying beside the road, are six tumuli, known as the Six Hills, which point to the antiquity of this road. The Great North Road forms the main street of the town. At the northern end of the town it forks, one branch going slightly westwards to Hitchin and the other northwards to Graveley and Baldock. At the same point Julian's Road turns west to Fisher's Green. The church of the Holy Trinity is situated at the south end of the High Street; a road running behind it in a north-easterly direction leads to the older church of St. Nicholas and passes on to Chesfield Park, a branch road from it turning east up Almond's Hill to the hamlet of Pin Green. From the church of St. Nicholas a road runs west into the Baldock Road, passing the Bury, the Rectory and Woodfield, the residence of Rear-Admiral Sir Thomas Butler Fellowes, K.C.B., J.P.

Stevenage Bury adjoins the north side of the churchyard. For a long time it was used as a farm-house, but is now occupied as a private residence by Mr. Algernon Gipps. It has undergone considerable alterations at different times, and a porch and ground-floor extension has been added to the front. The old part of the building is timber framed, covered with plaster externally, the plasterwork still showing traces of flush panels filled with curved basketwork pattern. There are two short wings flanking the back and a small projecting staircase between them. So far as can be traced now, the old entrance faced the super-structure of the chimney, a small lobby being formed as at other old early 17th-century houses in the county, the hall, now the dining-room, being in the centre of the building to the left of the entrance and the drawing-room or parlour in the wing to the right. The kitchen offices occupy the other wing. There is a built-up window, with oak mullions, in a room over the drawing room, but all the other windows are modern. In a cellar under the kitchen parts of the walls are of flint and parts of thin bricks. Adjoining the house is a square timber-framed building of two stories, with a tiled pyramidal roof, which may at one time have been a dove-house.

Part of Chesfield Park, the residence of Mr. Poyntz-Stewart, is included in the north of the parish. The hamlet of Fisher's Green lies in the north-west, with Symond's Green about three-quarters of a mile south. Broomin Green is a short distance west of the south end of the town, with Norton Green still further south. Almost opposite Broomin Green, on the other side of the Great North Road, is Bedwell Plash. In the extreme east of the parish is Chells, with Chells Green on the borders of Walkern parish. The old manor-house is now used as a farm-house and has been much restored, but the fabric of the building dates from the early 17th century. It is a timber-framed house resting on brick foundations, and in plan resembles the letter H. The principal front, which extends to about 62 ft., faces the south-west and is flanked by steep gables overhanging at the level of the first floor and again at the eaves. The wings extend out at the back of the house. The roof is tiled and the walls are now plastered externally, and all the chimneys, doors and windows are comparatively modern. The entrance doorway on the south-west side now opens into the drawing room, which has lately been extended, but it formerly opened into the hall, which occupied the whole of the central part of the building and which had a large fireplace at the end. This fireplace has recently been transformed into an inglenook and the old arch removed. The hall, now the dining room, has been further reduced by forming a passage-way at the back of the house. The old back-doorway to the courtyard still remains with its old plank door, but both are quite plain. As this doorway faces the wide mass of brickwork inclosing the hall fireplace, it would not enter the hall direct, but would have the usual small lobby. At the back of the hall fireplace is a very narrow stair, evidently original, leading to the upper floor. This is lighted by a very small window in the front. Access is gained to

---

[71] See references given under manor. Also *Rot. Hug. Wells* (Cant. and York Soc.), i, 66; Inst. Bks. (P.R.O.); Bacon, *Liber Regis*; *Clergy List* (1907).
[72] See *East Herts. Arch. Soc. Trans.* i, 86. It is so called in the early 13th century (*Rot. Hug. Wells*, i, 66).
[73] *Herts. Gen. and Antiq.* iii, 334.
[74] Urwick, op. cit. 602.
[1] Statistics from Bd. of Agric. (1905).

139

this stair both from the hall and from the north-west wing, and there is no indication of any larger stair having existed, though a modern one has been placed in the other wing beside a modern entrance. The kitchen still retains its old fireplace, but it is quite plain. On the side of the upper room next the courtyard are the remains of an old three-light window having moulded oak mullions. This window is now blocked up. Most of the rooms on the upper floor still retain their original wide oak flooring.

Pin Green lies rather more than a mile west from Chells. Sishes, near Pin Green, is the residence of Mr. Julius Bertram. Whitney Wood, on the Hitchin road, is the residence of Mrs. Barclay. In Whomerley Wood are slight remains of a homestead moat.

names of streets such as 'Pilgryms,'[2] and a little later 'Lycchenstret,' 'Baldokstret,'[3] 'Laschmerstret,' and 'Pavylane,'[4] which indicates a town of some size. It is clear from the number of presentments relating to innkeepers on the manor rolls[5] that by the beginning of the 15th century it had become the resort of travellers on the Great North Road. Possibly on account of this prosperity and the increasing size of the town we find that about 1405 a number of London tradesmen purchased, probably as building speculations, small plots of land here. Richard Foster of London[6] had a messuage and 6 acres of land; John Sylam, citizen and pewterer of London, had 4 acres 'built upon'; William Rendre of London had land in Churchfield called 'Pyedelacre'; William Waldern, citizen and grocer, John Hamond, citizen

STEVENAGE BURY : BACK VIEW

Stevenage is a good example of the development of the Teutonic type of settlement which is so frequently met with in Hertfordshire. The old church of St. Nicholas and the 'Bury,' with a few cottages lying about half a mile off the Great North Road, evidently formed the site of the original Saxon village, consisting of an agricultural community which desired to be in the midst of its territories. Probably before the Conquest, but at all events before the grant of a market and fair in 1281, a settlement on the road-side was established, where at the fork of the road was the natural position for the market. The road-side settlement seems to have prospered, and by the end of the 14th century we have the

and barber, William Marchford, citizen and mercer, Edward Grymston, citizen and vintner, and others, all of London, purchased small freeholds.[7] There is, however, no evidence that Stevenage was ever anything more than a manorial market town, though the gild of the Holy Trinity, established probably in the early part of the 15th century with a gildhall or brotherhood house, may have had some powers in the management of the affairs of the town. Early in the 16th century we can tell from the evidence of architectural remains that the road-side town extended from the point where the Great North Road forks, or a little northward, to the old workhouse, an interesting timber and plaster building,

[2] Ct. R. (Gen. Ser.), portf. 178, no. 54.
[3] Ibid. no. 56.
[4] Ibid. no. 57.
[5] Ibid.
[6] Ibid. no. 55.
[7] Ibid. no. 56.

Stevenage Bury : Front View

Stevenage : Chells Farm from the South

originally a dwelling-house, which stands opposite the modern church of Holy Trinity.

Although a great part of the town was burnt in a fire which occurred on 10 July 1807,[8] there still remain many interesting specimens of 17th-century timber and plaster houses with tiled roofs, principally in the High Street. The grammar school, the history of which will be found elsewhere,[9] stands at the north end of the bowling green. It was enlarged and considerably altered in 1905, but there survives a small rectangular building consisting of one room, probably of the foundation of 1561. It was originally of timber and brick, but is now largely refaced with brick. On the east side of the High Street opposite the green is a 17th-century timber and brick house refronted, with an original chimney stack; a little southward are a 17th-century inn and cottages.

Towards the south end of the street is a two-storied gabled shop, the upper story of which is covered with basket-work pargeting in panels. The Castle Inn, with the cottage adjoining, originally formed one building, probably of the latter part of the 16th century. They have basket-work pargeting in the upper story and gables. On the west side of the street are several other instances of the use of basket-work pargeting in 17th-century houses; many of them, however, are now refaced in front with brick. The inns called the 'White Lion' and the 'Red Lion' have timber coach entrances, but much of the old 17th-century timber and plaster work has been renewed in brick. In the yard of the latter are the remains of a 16th-century building with a projecting upper story. South of the 'Red Lion' is a 17th-century house, partly used as a shop. It has a gable at each end and a dormer window between; the upper part is of pargeted timber and the lower of brick, plastered. It has an octagonal brick shaft on a moulded base.

The main line of the Great Northern railway runs through the parish parallel to the Great North Road.

The subsoil of the parish is chalk, and there are many chalk-pits in various parts.

The inclosure award was made in 1854, and is in the custody of the clerk of the peace.[10]

MANORS The manor of *STEVENAGE* was granted to the abbey of St. Peter at Westminster by Edward the Confessor about 1062,[11] and was entered among the possessions of the abbot in 1086, when it was assessed at 8 hides.[12] Stevenage Manor remained in the hands of the Abbots of Westminster[13] until January 1539–40, when the monastery and its possessions were surrendered to the Crown.[14] At the end of 1540, however, the bishopric of Westminster was created and endowed with the lands which had belonged to the monastery,[15] and Stevenage pertained to the bishopric[16] until its surrender to Edward VI in 1550,[17] when this manor was presumably given to Bishop Ridley of London, together with the greater part of the Westminster lands.[18] It was confirmed to the bishopric of London by Mary in 1554,[19] and then remained in the

CHELLS FARM FROM THE NORTH

Lewis Evans Coll. (Herts. Co. Mus.), MS. marked Hitchin.
[9] *V.C.H. Herts.* ii, 69–71.
[10] *Blue Bk. Incl. Awards,* 64.
[11] Cott. MS. vi, 2.

[12] *V.C.H. Herts.* i, 312*b*.
[13] Assize R. 323, m. 51 d.; Mins. Accts. 31–2 Hen. VIII, no. 113.
[14] Dugdale, *Mon.* i, 280.
[15] Ibid.

[16] *L. and P. Hen. VIII,* xvi, g. 503 (33); Ct. R. (Gen. Ser.), portf. 178, no. 62.   [17] D. of Purch. and Exch. 189.
[18] Dugdale, *Mon.* i, 281.
[19] Pat. 1 Mary, pt. iv, m. 16.

possession of the Bishops of London [20] until the Commonwealth. Upon the sale of lands pertaining to bishoprics it was bought in 1649 by Thomas Ayres.[21] The latter was still holding it in 1657–9.[22] At the Restoration Stevenage was restored to the bishopric of London, and remained in the possession of that see until 1868, when it was transferred to the Ecclesiastical Commissioners,[23] who are the present lords of the manor.

A fair was granted to the Abbot of Westminster at Stevenage in 1281, to be held on the vigil, feast, and morrow of St. John the Baptist[24] (23–25 June), and was confirmed by Henry VI in 1448.[25] In 1624 the Bishop of London

WESTMINSTER ABBEY. *Gules St. Peter's keys or with St. Edward's ring or in the chief.*

A warren is mentioned as belonging to the lord of the manor in 1393, when John Wheler and others were accused of hunting in it and taking partridges and pheasants.[35] It is mentioned again in 1408, when William Rendre of London was granted the 'custody and profit of the warren for hunting and chasing hares and rabbits.'[36]

In 1287 the Abbot of Westminster claimed in Stevenage view of frankpledge, return of writs, amendment of the assize of bread and ale, infangentheof, utfangentheof, gallows, tumbrel and pillory.[37] The view of frankpledge extended into the tithings of Holwell, Cadewell, Watton, Datchworth, Tewin and Stevenage.[38] In the 13th century and early 14th century the abbot held five courts yearly for Stevenage and its dependencies — two in the autumn, two in early spring, and one in summer. In 1271–2 the profits amounted to 43s. 3d., and in 1320–1 to 69s. 2d.[39] From the middle of the 14th century four yearly courts seem to have been usual. These

MAIN ROAD, STEVENAGE, SHOWING 17TH-CENTURY HOUSE

was granted three fairs, to be held on Ascension Day, St. Swithun's Day (15 July), and on the Friday following.[26] In 1792 fairs were held for nine days before Easter, nine days before Whit Sunday, and on the first Friday in September.[27] In 1821 the September fair was held on the 22nd of that month,[28] and it is now held on the 22nd and 23rd.[29]

A market was granted to the abbot in 1281, to be held on Mondays,[30] and was confirmed in 1448.[31] In 1624 the day was altered to Friday,[32] on which day it was held as late as 1792.[33] In 1821 it is said to have been held on Wednesday,[34] but it has since been discontinued.

were at first held at the feasts of St. Andrew (30 November), St. Denis (9 October), St. Matthew (21 September), and at Pentecost, but a little later the first two were changed to St. Lucy (13 December) and the Annunciation (25 March). At the end of the 14th or beginning of the 15th century the number of courts varied, one being held at the feast of the Conception (8 December). The average value of the courts in the 14th century seems to have been about £3, but it dropped during the next century, the profits in 1499–1500 only amounting to 28s. 7d.[40]

In 1409 it was presented at the view of frankpledge that the lord was bound to have within his liberty a

[20] *Cal. S. P Dom.* 1623–5, p. 6.
[21] Add. MS. 9049, p. 15 ; Close, 1649, pt. xlvi, no. 41.
[22] Ct. R. (Gen. Ser.), portf. 178, no. 64.
[23] Cussans, op. cit. *Broadwater Hund.* 88.
[24] Chart. R. 9 Edw. I, m. 7, no. 45.
[25] Pat. 26 Hen. VI, pt. i, m. 10.
[26] Ibid. 22 Jas. I, pt. xvii.

[27] *Rep. of Roy. Com. on Markets and Tolls,* i, 171. [28] Clutterbuck, op. cit. ii, 440.
[29] *Rep. on Markets and Tolls,* xiii (2).
[30] *Cal. Chart. R.* 1257–1300, p. 252.
[31] Pat. 26 Hen. VI, pt. i, m. 10.
[32] Ibid. 22 Jas. I, pt. xvii.
[33] Chauncy, op. cit.; *Rep. on Markets and Tolls,* i, 171.

[34] Clutterbuck, op. cit. ii, 440.
[35] Ct. R. portf. 178, no. 54.
[36] Ibid. no. 56.
[37] Assize R. 325, m. 26 d.
[38] Ct. R. portf. 178, no. 56.
[39] Doc. at Westm. Herts. no. 26340–4.
[40] Ibid. 26366–82 ; Ct. R. portf. 178, no. 48–60.

STEVENAGE : MAIN ROAD

STEVENAGE : OLD HOUSE NOW GAS COMPANY'S OFFICES

pillory and a cucking-stool and that they were not there to the damage of the community. The bailiff was therefore ordered to supply them.[41] In 1542 it was ordered that the stocks should be amended and 'le kucking-stole and le pillarye' newly made.[42]

In 1310 the king had a prison at Stevenage within the liberty of the Abbot of Westminster. In that year an order was issued for the justices of gaol delivery to release from the prison one Andrew Baron 'and to lead him back to the church of Stevenage whither he had fled for sanctuary for larceny, certain malefactors having withdrawn him from the church and taken him to the said prison.'[43]

The manor of *HALFHIDE*, of which the overlordship is not known, first appears in 1408–9, when it was held by John Chertsey of Broxbourne, who in that year released his right in it to William Skrene,[44] probably for the purpose of a settlement. Edmund Chertsey, son or grandson of John Chertsey,[45] died before 1475, leaving a son William[46]; Eleanor his widow, however, conveyed the manor to John Northwood and others, probably trustees in a sale, in 1478–9.[47] In the first half of the next century Halfhide came into the possession of Matthew Ward and Alice his wife, who in 1553 conveyed it to John Lord Mordaunt.[48] The latter was succeeded in 1561 by his son John, whose son and heir Lewis inherited Halfhide with the rest of his father's estates in 1571,[49] and sold the manor in 1601 to Rowland Lytton and Sir Henry Wallop.[50] Sir Henry Wallop conveyed his moiety to Rowland Lytton in 1610,[51] and it descended in his family in the same way as the manor of Knebworth.[52]

Free warren in Halfhide was granted to William Lytton in 1616[53] and is mentioned with free fishery in 1811. The present farm-house called Halfhide lies in the neighbouring parish of Shephall.

The manor of *HOMELEYS* probably took its name from the family of Ivo de Homeley (Homlie), who held land in Stevenage in 1275, 140 acres of which were then held of him by Laurence de Brok.[54] It appears to have been held of the Abbot of Westminster of the manor of Stevenage.[55] In 1305 Robert de Depedene, who was holding the manor in right of his wife Isabel, conveyed it to William de Chilterne.[56] In the reign of Edward III it seems to have been held by Alice Homeley, whose predecessor had been Robert de Sutton.[57] Probably it was among the possessions of John Chertsey of Broxbourne at the beginning of the 15th century, for his successor Edmund Chertsey gave Homeleys to Thomas Skrene, with remainder in tail to William Skrene, brother of Thomas, with remainder to the heirs of Edmund Chertsey.[58] Upon the death of Thomas Skrene without issue in 1466 the manor passed to John Skrene, grandson of his brother William.[59] John died in 1474 without heirs, whereupon Homeleys reverted to William son and heir of Edmund Chertsey.[60] After this date Homeleys followed the same descent as the manor of Halfhide.[61]

Free warren in Homeleys was granted to William Lytton in 1616.[62]

The manor or tenement of *BROMESEND* was held of the Abbot of Westminster of his manor of Stevenage for rent and suit of court.[63] It seems to have taken its name from the family of Brome, who appear in Stevenage in the 14th century. Roger atte Brome held a messuage and half virgate in the reign of Edward II, and was living in 1325,[64] after which he was succeeded by Robert atte Brome, who held it in the time of Edward III. Anabill Brome, who had held 2 acres in Chalkdellfeld before Robert's time,[65] was doubtless one of the same family. In the 15th century Bromesend came into the possession of the Chertseys, and was given by Edmund Chertsey to Thomas Skrene,[66] together with the manor of Homeleys, with which it subsequently descended.[67]

Free warren in Bromesend was granted to William Lytton in 1616.[68]

CHELLS.—In the reign of Edward the Confessor a hide and a half in 'Escelveia,' which had once belonged to Welwyn, were held by Alwin, with the exception of 10 acres and a toft which belonged to Alwin Dode, a man of Aluric the Little.[69] Half a hide in 'Scelva' was held by Aluric, a man of Aluric of Benington,[70] and a half virgate belonged to Aluric Busch, who at that time was one of Swen's men and of King Edward's soke.[71] By 1086 Alwin's hide and a half had come into the hands of Peter de Valognes, of whom they were held by Godfrey.[72] The half hide was held of Robert Gernon by the William who held Letchworth and other lands,[73] while the half virgate had been retained by Aluric Busch, but was held of Geoffrey de Bech.[74] The Scelva or Escelveia of these holdings has been identified with Chells (Chelse, xv and xvi cent.), a manor in this parish.[75] The overlordship of Chells, however, does not seem to have been held by the descendants of any of these three, for in 1295 the manor was held for a sixth of a fee of Roger le Strange.[76] This Roger, who was the son of Hamon le Strange, married Maud widow of Roger Mowbray and coheiress of William de Beauchamp,[77] so that this fee may have been previously held by any of the three families of Le Strange, Mowbray, or Beauchamp.

---

[41] Ct. R. portf. 178, no. 55.
[42] Ibid. no. 62.
[43] Cal. Close, 1307–13, p. 292.
[44] Close, 10 Hen. IV, m. 31.
[45] Ibid. 9 Hen. VI, m. 3, 4; Feet of F. Herts. 6 Hen. V, no. 38.
[46] Chan. Inq. p.m. 14 Edw. IV, no. 42.
[47] Close, 18 Edw. IV, m. 14.
[48] Recov. R. East. 7 Edw. VI, rot. 100; Feet of F. Herts. Trin. 7 Edw. VI.
[49] G.E.C. Complete Peerage.
[50] Feet of F. Herts. Hil. 43 Eliz.
[51] Ibid. 7 Jas. I.
[52] Chan. Inq. p.m. (Ser. 2), ccclix, 114; Feet of F. Div. Co. Trin. 13 Chas. II; Recov. R. Hil. 51 Geo. III, rot. 41; Cussans, op. cit. Broadwater Hund. 90.
[53] Pat. 14 Jas. I, pt. xvii, no. 9.
[54] Chan. Inq. p.m. 3 Edw. I, no. 10.
[55] Doc. at Westm. Herts. Stevenage, no. 26386.
[56] Feet of F. Herts. 34 Edw. I, no. 412.
[57] Doc. at Westm. Herts. Stevenage, no. 26386.
[58] Chan. Inq. p.m. 14 Edw. IV, no. 42; 6 Edw. IV, no. 25.   [59] Ibid.
[60] Chan. Inq. 14 Edw. IV, no. 42.
[61] Recov. R. East. 7 Edw. VI, rot. 100; Mich. 2 Eliz. rot. 710; Mich. 42 Eliz. rot. 55; Feet of F. Herts. Hil. 43 Eliz.; Chan. Inq. p.m. (Ser. 2), ccclix, 114; Feet of F. Div. Co. Trin. 13 Chas. II; Recov. R. Hil. 51 Geo. III, rot. 41.
[62] Pat. 14 Jas. I, pt xvii, no. 9.
[63] Doc. at Westm. Herts. Stevenage, no. 26386.
[64] Ibid.; Cal. Pat. 1324–7, p. 91.
[65] Doc. at Westm. Herts. Stevenage, no. 26386.
[66] Chan. Inq. p.m. 14 Edw. IV, no. 42.
[67] Recov. R. East. 7 Edw. VI, rot. 100; Mich. 2 Eliz. rot. 710; Mich. 42 Eliz. rot. 55; Feet of F. Herts. Hil. 43 Eliz.; Hil. 7 Jas. I; Chan. Inq. p.m. (Ser. 2), ccclix.
[68] Pat. 14 Jas. I, pt. xvii, no. 9.
[69] V.C.H. Herts. i, 336b.
[70] Ibid. 323b.
[71] Ibid. 333a.
[72] Ibid. 336b.
[73] Ibid. 323b.
[74] Ibid. 333a.
[75] Ibid. 297.
[76] Chan. Inq. p.m. 24 Edw. I, no. 66.
[77] G.E.C. Complete Peerage.

A HISTORY OF HERTFORDSHIRE

It seems probable, however, that Roger le Strange held it in right of his wife Maud, for upon his death without children in 1311 [78] it evidently passed to Roger de Mowbray son of Maud by her first husband, since Chells was held in 1359 of John de Mowbray, great-grandson of Maud.[79] The tenure does not therefore confirm the identification of Chells with the Scelva of 1086.

Under Roger Le Strange the manor appears in the tenure of the family of Pateshull. The earliest known member of the family is Simon de Pateshull, chief justice of the Common Pleas, who died about 1217,[80] and had a son John.[81] The first, however, who is known to have held Chells is Simon de Pateshull, son of this John,[82] a well-known judge, who died seised of the manor about 1295, and was succeeded by his son John.[83] John's son [84] and successor William de Pateshull died in 1359, leaving as his heirs his three sisters : Sibyl wife of Roger de Beauchamp, Alice wife of Thomas Wake and Catherine wife of Robert de Todenham ; and also Roger son of a fourth sister Maud and her husband Walter de Fauconberg.[85] Chelis was assigned to Alice and Thomas Wake, who in 1373 conveyed it to their son Thomas and his wife Maud.[86] Maud survived her husband and held the manor until her death in 1425, when it passed to her grandson Thomas Wake.[87] There is then a gap in the records of the manor. This Thomas is known to have died in 1458 and to have been succeeded by his son Thomas.[88] It was perhaps the latter who conveyed Chells to John Norreys, who died seised of it in 1521.[89] John Norreys was also lord of the manor of Boxbury, which manor his son and successor John Norreys sold to Philip Boteler in 1526.[90] Probably Chells was conveyed to the Botelers about the same time, for it was settled by Sir Philip on his son John,[91] and appears in his possession in 1562.[92] After that date it follows the same descent as the manor of Boxbury [93] in Walkern, with which it has henceforward associated.

The manor of BROOKS (Brokes, Brokys) took its name from the family of Brok, who held land in Stevenage in the 13th century. Laurence de Brok, son of Adam de Brok,[94] died about 1275 seised of considerable possessions in Stevenage, of which 300 acres with a capital messuage were held of the Abbot of St. Albans, 200 acres with a windmill of the Abbot of Westminster, 140 acres of Ivo de Homeley and 100 acres of Robert de Graveley.[95] Some or all of these portions were probably known as 'Brooks,' for the manor is mentioned by that name in a deed of the same year by which it was conveyed to Laurence's son and heir Hugh.[96] Hugh de Brok was succeeded before 1294 by his son, another Laurence,[97] whose widow Ellen was holding his lands in 1330, with reversion to her son Ralph.[98] Ralph's heirs, who succeeded before 1346,[99] were his three daughters Joan, Ellen and Agnes, the eldest of whom died without issue. His lands were therefore divided between Ellen and Agnes. Agnes had a daughter Joan,[100] who was perhaps identical with Joan the wife of Robert Corbet, who was holding Brooks with her husband in 1400.[1] There is no further record of the manor until towards the end of the 15th century, by which time it had come into the possession of Edmund Node.[2] His wife Joan survived him, and enfeoffed her second son William to the use of herself and her heirs, with the condition that he made an estate to his elder brother, who was also called William. He, however, refused to do this, and between 1493 and 1500 his mother brought a suit against him to compel him to give up the manor.[3] William Node was holding Brooks in 1521,[4] and seems to have been succeeded by another William, who in 1564 sold the manor to Robert Ivory.[5] The latter conveyed it in the same year to John Bagshawe.[6] In 1608 it was purchased from Edmund Bagshawe, probably the son of John, by William Field,[7] who in 1614 sold it in his turn to Ralph Radcliffe of Hitchin Priory [8] (q.v.). Brooks has since descended in the Radcliffe family,[9] and is now in the possession of Mr. Francis A. Delmé-Radcliffe, J.P.

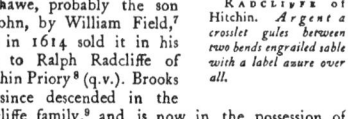

Ellen widow of Laurence de Brok was granted free warren in her lands in Stevenage in 1330.[10]

CANNIX, CANWYKES, or BROXBOURNES, was named from its early tenants, and was held of the manor of Stevenage by military service.[11] It seems to have been identical with the messuage and virgate held of the Abbot of Westminster in 1315 by John de Broxbourne.[12] His son Richard held the

PATESHULL. *Argent a fesse wavy between three crescents sable.*

RADCLIFFE of Hitchin. *Argent a crosslet gules between two bends engrailed sable with a label azure over all.*

---

[78] G.E.C. *Complete Peerage.*
[79] Ibid. ; Chan. Inq. p.m. 33 Edw. III (1st nos.), no. 40.
[80] *Dict. Nat. Biog.*
[81] Wrottesley, *Ped. from the Plea R.* 74.
[82] Ibid.
[83] Chan. Inq. p.m. 24 Edw. I, no. 66.
[84] Wrottesley, *Ped. from the Plea R.* 74.
[85] Chan. Inq. p.m. 33 Edw. III (1st nos.), no. 40.
[86] Feet of F. Div. Co. 47 Edw. III, no. 100.
[87] Chan. Inq. p.m. 3 Hen. VI, no. 20.
[88] Ibid. 37 Hen. VI, no. 19.
[89] Ibid. (Ser. 2), xxxviii, 34.
[90] Feet of F. Herts. East. 18 Hen. VIII.
[91] Chan. Inq. p.m. (Ser. 2), clxxiii, 72.
[92] Feet of F. Herts. East. 4 Eliz.
[93] Chan. Inq. p.m. (Ser. 2), ccccii, no. 144 ; Privy Seal Docket Bk. xi ; *Cal. S. P. Dom.* 1637–8, p. 19 ; Feet of F. Herts. Mich. 33 Chas. II ; Recov. R. Mich. 1 Geo. II, rot. 22 ; Mich. 11 Geo. III, rot. 185 ; Hil. 55 Geo. III, rot. 248.
[94] *Excerpta e Rot. Fin.* (Rec. Com.), ii, 516.
[95] Chan. Inq. p.m. 3 Edw. I, no. 10.
[96] Harl. Chart. 46 F. 45.
[97] Add. Chart. 977 ; Harl. Chart. 46 G. 3.
[98] Wrottesley, *Ped. from the Plea R.* 428 ; Chart. R. 4 Edw. III, m. 14, no. 28.   [99] *Feud. Aids*, ii, 436.
[100] Wrottesley, *Ped. from the Plea R.* 428.
[1] Feet of F. Herts. Trin. 1 Hen. IV, no. 1.
[2] Early Chan. Proc. bdle. 216, no. 19.
[3] Ibid.
[4] Chan. Inq. p.m. (Ser. 2), xxxvi, 76.
[5] Feet of F. Herts. East. 6 Eliz. ; Recov. R. East. 6 Eliz. rot. 153.
[6] Close, 7 Eliz. pt. xviii, m. 2.
[7] Ibid. 6 Jas. I, pt. xxiv, no. 7.
[8] Ibid. 12 Jas. I, pt. xxiv, no. 29.
[9] Chan. Inq. p.m. Misc. dxviii, 25 ; Recov. R. Mich. 13 Chas. I, rot. 83 ; 10 Geo. I, rot. 327.
[10] Chart. R. 4 Edw. III, m. 14, no. 28.
[11] Mins. Accts. 1 & 2 Hen. VIII, no. 20.
[12] MSS. quoted by Clutterbuck, op. cit. ii, App. p. 14 ; Linc. Epis. Reg. Burghersh.

144

STEVENAGE CHURCH FROM THE NORTH-EAST

STEVENAGE CHURCH: THE NAVE LOOKING EAST

property during the reign of Edward III. It is then described as being at 'Srewentenwode.' The same Richard also held a third of a fee in 'Kechenbrech' which had formerly belonged to Laurence de Brok, and for which he paid 24s.[13] Nothing more is heard of the estate until about 1509, when William Canwyke paid a relief of 40s. for certain land in Stevenage called 'Broxborne' which he had received from Petronilla his mother.[14] In 1510 Samuel and Clemence Canwyke sold the 'manor' to William Lytton of Knebworth, who died seised of it in 1517.[15] At the death of his son Robert Lytton in 1550 it was divided among his three daughters, Ellen the wife of John Brockett, Elizabeth wife of Thomas Lyttel, and Anne, who married John Burlace.[16] It seems to have been divided later among the five daughters of Ellen and John Brockett, for a fifth of Cannix was held in 1599 and 1623 by Sir Richard Spencer and Helen daughter of Ellen and John Brockett,[17] and in 1604 another fifth appears in the possession of Alexander Cave and Anne, another daughter.[18] Eventually, however, the whole returned to the male line of the Lyttons and descended in the same manner as Knebworth[19] (q.v.). It is mentioned in 1811,[20] after which its identity was probably lost among the other lands held by the Lyttons in Stevenage. Cannocks Wood in the southwest of the parish perhaps preserves its name.

In 1308 John de Broxbourn obtained a licence for an oratory in his 'manor of Stevenage,'[21] probably at Cannix.

The parish church of ST. NICHOLAS consists of a chancel, nave, north and south aisles, and north and south chapels in line with the aisles, west tower, north vestry, south transept and south porch.[22] It is probably built of flint, but the walls are covered with cement. The flat roofs are covered with lead, and the tower has a tall octagonal leaded spire. The tower, nave and chancel and aisles have embattled parapets.

The earliest portion of the existing church is the tower, which was built in the first half of the 12th century, and appears to have formed the tower and west porch combined of the original church, which probably consisted of a chancel, nave and tower. Early in the 13th century it is probable that the whole church except the tower was rebuilt and aisles added. The present nave is of this date. The chancel now standing was built about 1330, and the aisles were widened to their present dimensions at the same time. A doorway in the east wall of the tower above the low-pitched roof seems to indicate that the roof of the 14th century was of a pitch high enough to inclose it. The present roof with the clearstory is of the 15th century, when the nave arcades were rebuilt from the capitals upwards, the pillars with their bases being of the earlier date. The bell chamber of the tower was also added or rebuilt in the 15th century. The south porch, if not actually modern, has been wholly restored, and the south transept is modern.

The chancel has a modern east window of four lights with tracery in 15th-century style. In the north wall is a window of the 14th century, now blocked up, with three lights under a square head. The inner jambs have an edge-roll and the low rear arch is two-centred with an internal hood mould. The south window is like it, but is open and has been repaired externally with cement.

The arcades between the chancel and the north and south chapels are of two bays and are of the 14th century. The middle pillar on each side is octagonal, but, while the responds of the north arcade are semi-octagonal, those of the south arcade are semicircular. The bases and capitals of both pillars and all the responds are moulded. The two-centred arches are of two chamfered orders.

In the chancel is a piscina now cemented over which may be old ; against the east wall behind the altar is the upper part of a 15th-century traceried screen, painted over, of which the lower part stands at the entrance to the chancel. The three sedilia on the south side, of cement, are modern. There is no chancel arch.

The north chapel has an east window of four lights with tracery of the 14th century. It has an inner edge-roll like those in the chancel, and has been much repaired with cement. The north wall has two 14th-century windows of two lights with pointed heads and labels, and a third window which is modern but a copy of the other two. The first window is blocked externally, but the tracery is visible inside. The second is altogether blocked, only the outline being visible externally. The south chapel has an east window and two south windows like those in the north chapel and of the same date. Those in the south wall differ from the rest in having their inner jambs and arches moulded with an undercut edge-roll and in having moulded labels ; they are repaired with cement externally. Between the two windows is a pointed doorway also of the 14th century. There is a piscina in this chapel, probably contemporary, which has a cinquefoiled head and a trefoiled basin.

The nave has north and south arcades of four bays, with octagonal pillars and moulded bases of the 13th century, but the capitals and pointed arches of two hollow-chamfered orders were inserted early in the 15th century. The bases, and the labels of the western bays, are mutilated, the latter for the fitting of a gallery. The clearstory of the 15th century has square-headed windows from which the tracery is gone.

The north aisle has three windows in the north wall, the easternmost being of four lights in a square head. It is probably a 15th-century insertion, but the tracery is modern ; the second is a two-light window, with tracery in a pointed head, and is probably of the 14th century, but here again the tracery is modern.

---

[13] Doc. at Westm. Herts. Stevenage, no. 26386.
[14] Mins. Accts. 1 & 2 Hen. VIII, no. 20.
[15] Chan. Inq. p.m. (Ser. 2), xxxiii, 5.
[16] Feet of F. Herts. East. 1 & 2 Phil. and Mary; Mich. 4 & 5 Phil. and Mary; Mich. 2 & 3 Eliz.; East. 7 Eliz.

[17] Ibid. Trin. 41 Eliz.; Recov. R. Trin. 21 Jas. I, rot. 55.
[18] Ibid. East. 2 Jas. I, rot. 72 ; Visit. of Herts. (Harl. Soc. xxii), 32.
[19] Chauncy, op. cit. 358.
[20] Recov. R. Hil. 51 Geo. III, rot. 41.

[21] Linc. Epis. Reg. Mem. Bp. Dalderby, 117.
[22] Dimensions : chancel, 39 ft. by 17 ft.; north chapel, 25 ft. by 13 ft.; south chapel, 25 ft. by 12 ft.; nave, 43 ft. by 16 ft.; north aisle, 13 ft. 6 in. wide ; south aisle, 12 ft. 6 in. wide ; west tower, 16 ft. by 15 ft.

A HISTORY OF HERTFORDSHIRE

The third is similar, of the 14th century, and is repaired externally. Close to the west extremity of the wall is a doorway of 14th-century date, restored. The west window is modern.

The south aisle has a modern archway in the south, opening into the transept, and west of it a 14th-century window of two lights, like those in the south chapel; near the west wall is a pointed doorway of the 14th century, which has been repaired; the west window is modern.

The west tower opens to the nave by a 12th-century arch with shafted jambs on the west side, roughly carved capitals, and a semicircular head with an edge-roll. The east side of the arch is plain. The tower is of two stages without external division. It is of the 12th century, but the diagonal angle buttresses were added probably in the 15th century. It has an embattled parapet and a leaded spire. The west doorway is of the 12th century, but has been much has been repaired. At the feet of the principal cross-ribs of the chancel roof are carved angels; the other parts of the church have wood corbels, some of them carved.

The font is of early 13th-century date, and has a square bowl, carved with foliage, and standing on a circular stem with small round detached angle-shafts having moulded bases and capitals.

There are three stalls in the chancel, and three in the tower, with carved misericordes, dating from the end of the 14th or the beginning of the 15th century.

In the chancel is a brass of Stephen Hellard, rector, of about 1500, with the figure of the priest in a cope, and an inscription. The date is not filled in, but he died in 1506. In the north aisle are the indents of a man and his two wives, with their sons and daughters, and of an inscription, of mid-15th-century type; and in the nave is a slab with the indent of a floreated cross, apparently of the 14th century.

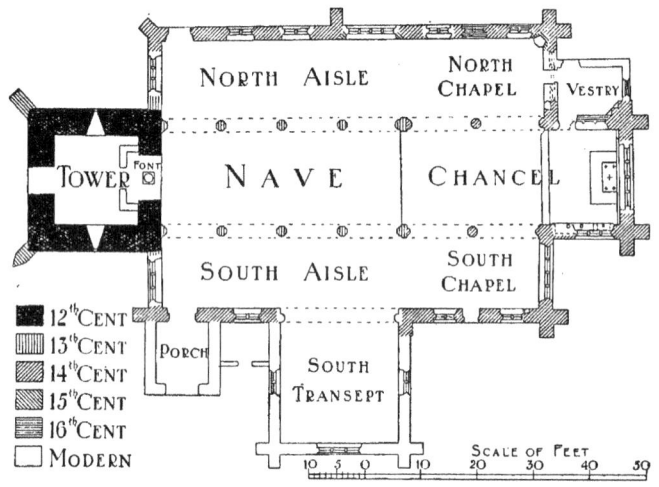

PLAN OF STEVENAGE CHURCH

repaired with cement. The jambs have shafts with rude bases, capitals and abaci. The arch, which is semicircular, is of two orders, the outer having an edge-roll. The north and south walls have small round-headed windows of original date, high up, and above the tower arch is a round-headed doorway which formerly gave access to the 12th-century roof. Over this again is a pointed doorway, which from its position would seem to have opened to the 14th-century roof, but is now outside, above the present roof. On each side of this doorway is a small circular opening in the bell-chamber wall. The three remaining sides at this level have repaired 15th-century windows of two lights in a pointed head.

No date can be assigned to the south porch, owing to its complete restoration.

The roofs of the chancel and nave are of the 15th century, of a low pitch, with traceried trusses. The lean-to roofs of the nave and aisles, which are of the same date, are nearly flat; that of the north aisle

In the north aisle is a (formerly) recumbent effigy of a lady. Her hands are raised in prayer, and an angel and a priest support her elbows. The date appears to be late 13th or early 14th century. The effigy is much mutilated, the part below the knees being wanting, and the fragment is now set upright, to the east of the north door. In the chancel is a mural monument to William Pratt, 1629.

There are six bells: the treble by John Briant, 1797, the second dated 1670, by an unknown founder, and the remainder by John Briant, dated 1783, 1795, 1783, and 1783 respectively. The fifth bell has been recast.

The plate consists of a silver cup and cover paten of 1634 and a paten and flagon of 1683.

The registers, beginning in 1564, are contained in seven books, as follows: (i) baptisms 1542 to 1599, burials 1545 to 1598, marriages 1539 to 1598; (ii) baptisms 1565 to 1649; (iii) baptisms 1653 to 1726, burials 1653 to 1726, marriages 1661 to 1726; (iv)

146

STEVENAGE CHURCH : THE FONT

BROADWATER HUNDRED — STEVENAGE

baptisms 1726 to 1761, burials 1726 to 1755, marriages 1726 to 1753; (v) baptisms 1762 to 1812, burials 1756 to 1812; (vi) marriages 1754 to 1765; (vii) marriages 1766 to 1812.

ADVOWSON The advowson of the church belonged to the Abbot of Westminster. In the 13th century the incumbent paid a pension of 50s. to the abbey.[23] The church belonged subsequently to the Bishop of Westminster until the surrender of that bishopric to Edward VI in 1550.[24] In that year the advowson and rectory were granted by the king to Sir William Herbert, K.G.,[25] who was created Earl of Pembroke in 1551 and died in March 1569–70.[26] His son Henry sold the advowson in 1575 to Edward Wilson,[27] who is said to have conveyed it in the same year to Thomas Clerke. Thomas had a son John,[28] to whom he conveyed the advowson in 1589,[29] John having previously obtained a release of the same from Edward and William Clerke,[30] perhaps his brothers. He died in 1595, leaving four sons, of whom Thomas was the eldest.[31] The advowson is said to have been subsequently acquired by the families of Smith and Chester.[32] In 1664 presentation was made by Francis Flexmere and Allan Read, merchant tailors,[33] and in 1678 by James Goulston,[34] who perhaps obtained it for one turn from Stafford Leventhorpe, who owned the rectory about that time.[35] Thomas Duckett presented in 1689,[36] about which time the advowson and rectory came into the hands of Joseph Bentham, D.D., who presented in 1719.[37] The latter sold the advowson in 1720 to Charles Baron,[38] who presented with George Whorton and Jacob Jefferey in 1723,[39] and is said to have sold the rectory and advowson to Nicholas Cholwell in 1724.[40] The latter presented in 1725, with Rowland Ingram, in 1733.[41] Ann Ingram, widow, presented in 1737,[42] probably for one turn, after which Nicholas Cholwell the younger is said to have sold the rectory and advowson in 1761 to William Baker,[43] who possessed the advowson in 1762,[44] and whose son was holding it in 1821.[45] His grandson William Robert Baker sold it in 1869 to John Allen,[46] who held it until 1899, when it was acquired by the Rev. Canon Allen. It was transferred to the Bishop of St. Albans in 1906.[47]

A fraternity of the Holy Trinity in the church of St. Nicholas at Stevenage is mentioned in 1446.[48] Bequests were also made to it in 1483 and 1497.[49] In 1558 the Brotherhood House with 6 acres of ground belonging was granted to Sir George Howard.[50] There was a light to the Virgin in the church mentioned in 1512.[51]

The church of the *HOLY TRINITY*, which was erected in 1861, is served from that of St. Nicholas.

Meeting-places for Protestant Dissenters in Stevenage were certified from 1698. In 1814 a chapel was opened in connexion with the Academy at Wymondley[52] (q.v.). At the present time there are in the parish chapels of the Wesleyans, Baptists and Strict Baptists.

CHARITIES Educational Charities.—For the grammar school, endowed by will of the Rev. Thomas Alleyn, 1558, and the English or Pettits School, founded in 1562, see article on 'Schools.'[53]

The National school, comprised in deed, 1834, is endowed with £106 7s. 8d. consols, by will of Miss Charlotte Amelia Hinde Whittington, proved in 1867; £21 10s. 4d. consols, by will of Miss Susanna Smyth, proved in 1867; and £321 5s. 9d. consols, by will of George Smyth, proved in 1868.

The several sums of stock are held by the official trustees, producing in the aggregate £11 4s. 4d. yearly.

The Consolidated Charities are regulated by a scheme of the Charity Commissioners, 26 March 1909, as varied by scheme of 26 April 1910. They comprise the charities of—

1. The almshouses founded by Stephen Hellard, priest and rector, by deed, 20 November, 17 Henry VII (1501), whereby certain lands and a newly-built messuage, to be called 'All Christian Souls' House,' were conveyed to the uses of donor's last will, bearing date 20 December 1501. The trust property now consists of eight almshouses in Back Lane and 13 a. 3 r. 13 p. of land with messuage let at £14 a year.

2. George Clerke, will, 1556, being a rent-charge of £2 10s. issuing out of Boxbury Tithe, parish of Walkern.

3. Robert Gynne, by will, 1604, consisting of a rent-charge of £1 issuing out of Ditchmore Mead, another rent-charge of £1 10s. out of Maidenhead in Stevenage, £13 14s. 8d. consols, and the right of the poor to receive 10 bushels of good grain (commonly called Misleyne or Maslin) charged on Fisher's Green Farm.

4. John Elmer, will, 1622, formerly consisting of a messuage or inn in Ware, called the 'Black Swan,' which has been sold, the share of Stevenage being represented by £414 7s. 3d. consols.

5. Edward Swallow, will, 1629, being a rent-charge of £1 issuing out of land at Cottered.

6. Rev. Richard Cholwell, a former rector, by deed, 1773, formerly a poor-house, now occupied by the premises of the Stevenage Gas Company at a rental of £18 a year.

7. Miss Charlotte Amelia Hinde Whittington, for poor, by will proved 1867, trust fund, £319 3s. consols.

8. Susanna Smyth, for poor, by will proved 1868, trust fund, £162 3s. 3d. consols; and

---

[23] *Rot. Hug. Wells* (Cant. and York Soc.), i, 21.
[24] *Cal. Pat.* 1330–4, pp. 106, 486; Dugdale, *Mon.* i, 281.
[25] Pat. 4 Edw. VI, pt. ix, m. 41.
[26] G.E.C. *Complete Peerage*.
[27] Clutterbuck, op. cit. ii, 441, quoting evidences of William Baker.
[28] Chan. Inq. p.m. (Ser. 2), ccxliii, 83.
[29] Feet of F. Herts. Hil. 31 Eliz.
[30] Pat. 27 Eliz. pt. xvii, m. 38.
[31] Chan. Inq. p.m. (Ser. 2), ccxliii, 83.
[32] Clutterbuck, op. cit. ii, 441.
[33] Inst. Bks. (P.R.O.).
[34] Ibid.
[35] Exch. Depos. 24 & 25 Chas. II, Hil. no. 2.
[36] Inst. Bks. (P.R.O.).
[37] Clutterbuck, op. cit. ii, 441; Exch. Depos. 5 Anne, East. no. 8; Bacon, *Liber Regis*.
[38] Clutterbuck, loc. cit. quoting evidences of William Baker.
[39] Inst. Bks. (P.R.O.).
[40] Clutterbuck, op. cit. ii, 442.
[41] Inst. Bks. (P.R.O.).
[42] Ibid.
[43] Clutterbuck, loc. cit.
[44] Feet of F. Herts. Trin. 2 Geo. III.
[45] Clutterbuck, loc. cit.
[46] Cussans, op. cit. *Broadwater Hund.* 98.
[47] *Clergy Lists*; information kindly supplied by Rev. W. Jowitt.
[48] Archd. of St. Albans Wills, Stoneham, 50a.
[49] Ibid. 44; P.C.C. 15 Horne.
[50] Pat. 5 & 6 Phil. and Mary, pt. iii.
[51] Archd. of St. Albans Wills, Wallingford, 119.
[52] Urwick, op. cit. 605–6.
[53] *V.C.H. Herts.* ii, 69 et seq.

147

9. George Smyth, for poor, by will proved 1871, trust fund, £762 18s. 10d. consols.

The several sums of stock, amounting in the aggregate to £1,672 7s. consols, are held by the official trustees, producing an annual income of £41 16s.

The scheme provides that the full number of almspeople shall be eight in number and that every almsperson shall be in receipt of a properly secured income of not less than 5s. a week, either from the charities or other sources, a yearly sum of not more than £58 10s. out of the net income of the charities to be applied for this purpose. The residue of the income is directed to be applied for the benefit of the poor generally, including donations to a dispensary, hospital, &c., or any provident club; also in contributions towards the provision of nurses, and also to the extent of £10 a year in the distribution of articles in kind and in medical aid in sickness.

Charity of Rev. Thomas Alleyn for four poor men.[54]—The sum of £5 6s. 8d. is received from Trinity College, Cambridge, and duly applied.

In 1668 the Rev. Thomas Chapman by his will devised certain messuages and lands in Stevenage, subject to the payment of £8 per annum, to buy cloth and bread for the poor of this parish, Ashwell, St. Paul's Warden and Norton. The property charged has been sold, and, being difficult of identification, the payments have ceased to be made.

'The Eadon Fund' consists of £113 9s. 6d. Tasmanian Government 3 per cent. inscribed stock, arising under the will of Elinor Maria Frederica Eadon, proved at London 4 January 1902. The stock is held by the official trustees, and the annual dividend, amounting to £3 8s., is in pursuance of a scheme, 30 November 1909, applicable in apprenticing a boy who is a baptized member of the Church of England, the income to accumulate until sufficient for the purpose.

TOTTERIDGE

Taterugg, Titerege (xiii and xiv cent.); Tateryche, Thariges, Taregh (xv and xvi cent.); Tatteridge (xvii cent.).

The parish of Totteridge is entirely separate from the rest of the hundred, and lies about 10 miles south of Hatfield. It was till 1892 a detached chapelry of Hatfield parish, being an outlying part of the possessions of the Bishops of Ely, lords of the manor of Hatfield. It adjoins the parish of Arkley on the north, and on the south, east and west is surrounded by the neighbouring parishes of Middlesex. The Dollis Brook forms the eastern boundary.

The parish has an area of 1,603 acres, of which 20 acres are arable land, 1,424½ acres permanent grass and 2 acres wood.[1] The subsoil is London Clay.

The land attains a height of 400 ft. in the centre of the parish, from which it falls towards the north and south to a little under 300 ft., and in the east, towards the Dollis Brook, to about 230 ft. The road from Whetstone to Mill Hill runs through the parish from east to west along the central ridge, and the long and straggling village of Totteridge follows its course. At the eastern end is Totteridge Green, which runs south from the road, towards Laurel Farm. A short distance further up the hill westwards is the church of St. Andrew, on the north side of the road, and Copped Hall, with an extensive park, on the opposite side. Near the hall is a 17th-century timber barn with a tiled roof, and a similar barn is near the church. Further west along the village street are the Grange, the property of Sir Charles Nicholson, and Totteridge Park, on the site of the old manor-house, the residence of Mr. A. Barratt. Poynter's Hall (formerly when in the possession of the Paget family called Poynter's Grove) is the residence of Mrs. Harmsworth; the old house called the Priory that of Miss Foss.

Richard Baxter, the Nonconformist divine and author, lived for a time at Totteridge after his discharge from prison in the reign of Charles II. Rachel Lady Russell also had a house in this parish where she sometimes resided after the execution of Lord Russell.

The nearest railway station is that of Totteridge and Whetstone, a short distance beyond the eastern boundary of the parish, on the High Barnet branch of the Great Northern railway.

MANORS TOTTERIDGE is not mentioned in the Domesday Survey. The first record of it seems to be in 1248, when Hugh Bishop of Ely received licence 'that during any vacancy of the see four chaplains appointed by the said bishop to celebrate mass daily for the souls of the king and queen, his ancestors and successors, and for the souls of the bishop, his predecessors and successors, shall receive yearly from the issues of the manors of Totteridge and Brumford, which the said bishop bought for that purpose, 20 marks by the hands of the keepers of the said manors, 10 marks at Michaelmas at the Exchequer of Ely and 10 marks at Lady Day.'[2] It seems probable that the bishop had bought out the under-tenant and that the manor had always been an outlying member of Hatfield, for as parochially Totteridge was a chapelry of Hatfield there must have been some ancient connexion between the two places, and in 1277 it was returned as 'accustomed to return half a knight's fee in the manor of Hatfield.'[3] In the second half of the 13th century the manor seems to have been held by Laurence de Brok for life, for in 1275 Matilda widow of Laurence claimed a third of the manor in dower from Bishop Hugh and had it duly delivered.[4] Possibly Laurence de Brok was the tenant who sold the manor to the Bishop of Ely.

The Bishops of Ely continued to hold the manor [5] until 1561, being allowed to keep it when the manor of Hatfield was sold to the king in 1538.[6] In 1561, however, Totteridge was acquired by Queen Elizabeth in exchange for a pension to the bishop.[7] Before

---

[54] See *V.C.H. Herts.* ii, 69.
[1] Statistics from Bd. of Agric. (1905).
[2] *Cal. Chart. R.* 1226–57, p. 329.
[3] Clutterbuck, op. cit. ii, App. 15,
quoting Inq. of 1277; *Feud. Aids*, ii, 423.
[4] De Banco R. 11, m. 70 d.
[5] *Feud. Aids*, ii, 444, 449.

[6] *L. and P. Hen. VIII*, xiii (2), 904.
[7] Gibbons, *Ely Epis. Records*, 12; Pat. 4 Eliz. pt. i, m. 12.

148

BROADWATER HUNDRED — TOTTERIDGE

this a lease of the manor had been granted by the Bishop of Ely to John Brockett, who sold it some time later to Richard Peacock for £1,100.[8] In 1579–80 Elizabeth granted the court leet and view of frankpledge and the profits of the manor to John Moore for twenty-one years,[9] and in 1590 she granted the manor to John Cage, to hold for one-twentieth of a knight's fee, of the honour of Hampton Court.[10] About 1603 John Cage and Richard Peacock had a prolonged lawsuit for the possession of the manor.[11] John and Katherine Cage and Richard their son and heir released their right in 1607,[12] apparently in favour of the Peacocks, for it seems to have descended to another Richard Peacock, who married Rechard Grigge, who was holding the manor in 1678[13] and died before 1689.[14] Rechard had fourteen children, and, surviving her husband and all her sons, sold Totteridge in that year to Sir Francis Pemberton and Isaac Foxcroft.[15] They apparently conveyed it to Sir Paul Whichcote, who was lord of the manor in 1700.[16] The latter sold Totteridge in 1720–1 to James Duke of Chandos,[17] from whom it passed to his son Henry in 1744.[18] Henry Duke of Chandos conveyed it in 1748 to Sir William Lee, Lord Chief Justice of the King's Bench,[19] who was succeeded by his son William,[20] and before 1786 by his grandson, also Sir William Lee, who took the additional surname of Antonie.[21] Sir William Lee Antonie died in 1815, when Totteridge passed to his nephew John, the son of his sister Harriet and John Fiott. This John, who was a scientist and collector of antiquities, assumed the surname of Lee, and was holding the manor in 1821.[22] Upon his death without children in 1866 Totteridge was inherited by his brother the Rev. Nicholas Piott, who also took the name of Lee.[23] Sir Samuel Boulton, bart., is the present lord of the manor.[24]

Free warren was granted to the Bishop of Ely at Totteridge in 1250–1.[25] About 1580 the office of keeper of the pheasants and partridges was surrendered by Augustine Sparks and was granted to John Pratt, with a fee of 4d. a day and £1 6s. 8d. for a yearly livery coat.[26] In 1611 the reversion of this office was granted in survivorship to Alban Coxe and John his son.[27]

A new windmill is mentioned at Totteridge in 1277.[28]

Totteridge seems to have had courts of its own separate from the manor of Hatfield,[29] although view of frankpledge is not mentioned in connexion with it until 1580, when court leet and view of frankpledge were granted by Elizabeth to John Moore for twenty-one years, for a rent of 3s. 4d.[30] The rights of the Bishops of Ely in Hatfield probably extended to Totteridge as a member of that manor.[31]

A capital messuage, held of the manor of Totteridge by knight's service, was purchased from the trustees of John Cage at the beginning of the 17th century by Hugh Hare and his brother John, who were jointly seised of it.[32] John Hare died in 1613, leaving his house in Totteridge to his honest bailiff Richard Hare and his wife for their lives,[33] after which it seems to have passed to his son Hugh, who in 1625 was created Lord Coleraine.[34] The latter died and was buried at Totteridge in 1667, and was succeeded by his son Henry, second Lord Coleraine, who died in 1708. At the death of Henry Hare, grandson of the second baron, in 1749 the peerage became extinct.[35] The house is said to have been afterwards the residence of Sir Robert Atkyns, K.B., Lord Chief Baron of the Exchequer, but it was pulled down shortly before 1821 and another house built on its site by John Fiott,[36] lord of the manor of Totteridge.

HARE, Lord Coleraine. *Gules two bars and a chief indented or.*

COPPED HALL in this parish is perhaps identical with a capital messuage held in the 16th century by one John Copwood, who died seised of it in 1543, leaving a daughter Sophia.[37] It seems to have passed soon afterwards into the possession of the family of Clyffe. Richard Clyffe held a 'manor or capital messuage' in Totteridge at his death in 1566, leaving it to his illegitimate son William Clyffe or Smyth, with remainder to Richard's brother Geoffrey and his son Richard.[38] In the following century it was held by Edward Clyffe, who died about 1635, leaving two sons, William, on whom the property was settled, and Edward.[39] Copped Hall was for some time owned by William Manning, father of Henry Edward, Cardinal Manning, who was born there in 1808.[40] Since 1875 it has been occupied by Sir Samuel Bagster Boulton, bart., A.I.C.E., F.R.G.S., J.P., D.L., who has enlarged the house.

SERLESFIELD, which is mentioned in 1277,[41] was in the 16th century in the tenure of Richard Snowe, who between 1544 and 1549 conveyed 'land called Serlys' to William Blakewell and Margaret his wife.[42] It appears at the same time in connexion with 'Beauchampfeld' or 'Beauchampsted,' which was also conveyed by Snowe to William Blakewell.[43] By 1689 Serlys, then called Searles, had become united with

---

[8] Chan. Proc. (Ser. 2), bdle. 228, no. 2.
[9] Pat. 22 Eliz. pt. vii.
[10] Ibid. 32 Eliz. pt. vii, m. 21.
[11] Lansd. MS. 161, fol. 145.
[12] Feet of F. Herts. Hil. 4 Jas. I.
[13] Recov. R. Hil. 30 & 31 Chas. II, rot. 121.
[14] Chauncy, op. cit. 305.
[15] Close, 1 Will. and Mary, pt. vi, no. 21; Feet of F. Herts. East. 1 Will. and Mary.
[16] Chauncy, loc. cit.
[17] Feet of F. Herts. Hil. 7 Geo. I; Add. MS. 9434, p. 58.
[18] G.E.C. *Complete Peerage*; Recov. R. East. 19 Geo. II, rot. 229.
[19] Add. MS. 9434, p. 58.
[20] Ibid.
[21] Ibid.; Recov. R. Trin. 26 Geo. III, rot. 257.
[22] Clutterbuck, op. cit. ii, 449.
[23] *Dict. Nat. Biog.*
[24] Information from Rev. E. A. Smith.
[25] Chart. R. 35 Hen. III, m. 2.
[26] *Cal. S. P. Dom.* 1580–1625, p. 18.
[27] Ibid. 1611–18, p. 57.
[28] Clutterbuck, op. cit. ii, App. 16.
[29] Mins. Accts. bdle. 1132, no. 10.
[30] Pat. 22 Eliz. pt. vii.
[31] Assize R. 325, m. 26 d.
[32] Chan. Inq. p.m. (Ser. 2), cccxliii, 181.
[33] Will, P.C.C. 66 Capel.
[34] G.E.C. *Complete Peerage*. His son Nicholas had presumably died in the mean time.
[34] Ibid.
[36] Clutterbuck, op. cit, ii, 454.
[37] Ibid. cxlvi, 62.
[38] Ibid. dxxii, 50.
[40] *Dict. Nat. Biog.*
[41] Clutterbuck, op. cit. ii, App. 15–16.
[42] Com. Pleas D. Enr. Mich. 36 Hen. VIII, m. 22 d.; East. 37 Hen. VIII, m. 16; East. 1 Edw. VI, m. 5, 6 d.; East. 3 Edw. VI, m. 13.
[43] Ibid.

149

the main manor.[44] A close or croft called 'Dyngleys' was conveyed by John Snowe, perhaps the son of Richard, to the Blakewells in 1555.[45]

'Gladwyns lands,' apparently freeholds of the manor, were in the possession of William Gladwyn, husbandman, in the 15th century.[46] After the death of his son John there was an action in Chancery in 1481–2 between John's widow and executrix Juliana and Joan wife of John Osborne and Agnes Gladwyn, the two daughters of John Gladwyn,[47] to whom the lands probably descended. In 1548 the estate was conveyed by William Copwood to William and Margaret Blakewell.[48]

CHURCH The parish church of ST. ANDREW, which stands on a hill in the middle of the village, consists of a chancel with apsidal termination, north vestries, south organ chamber, nave, and west porch. The material is red brick. The present church dates wholly from the 18th and 19th centuries, but is on the old site, and in the churchyard is a yew tree 27 ft. in circumference. A church is known to have existed here at least from the end of the 13th century.

In 1702 a wooden tower and spire were built to the then existing church, which from an engraving of 1730 would appear to have been not older than the preceding century, and to have had wooden casement windows. In 1790 the present nave was built. The west porch was added in 1845, when the parapets were removed. In 1869 the east wall was taken down and the present chancel built, and at the same time the spire was removed, the smaller vestry and the organ chamber were built, stone windows were inserted, an open timber roof was erected over the nave, and a west gallery was demolished. The larger north vestry was built in 1897.

On the north wall of the nave is a monument from the old church to Dorothy Taylor, 1673, and Susanna Turner, 1672, daughters of Richard Turner.

The pulpit, of early 17th-century workmanship, was brought here from Hatfield parish church.

There are two bells in the gable which are inaccessible. One is by John Waylett, 1727, and the other by Samuel Newton, 1707.

The plate includes a silver gilt cup of 1599; there is also a cup of 1876 and a flagon of 1867, besides two patens of recent date.

The registers, beginning in 1570, are in five books as follows : (i) all entries 1570 to 1720 ; (ii) all entries 1723 to 1746[49] ; (iii) baptisms and burials 1746 to 1812 and marriages 1746 to 1753 ; (iv) marriages 1747 to 1753 ; (v) marriages 1754 to 1789.[50]

ADVOWSON The church of St. Andrew at Totteridge has changed its invocation since the 16th century,[51] when it was dedicated in honour of St. Etheldreda or Audrey, an invocation evidently borrowed from Ely.[52] It is suggested that St. Andrew is a corruption of St. Audrey.[53]

Totteridge remained a chapelry of Hatfield, from which it is about 8 miles distant, until 1892, a curate being appointed by the rector of Hatfield[54] (q.v.). In 1892 it was made a vicarage in the gift of the same rector.[55]

In 1650 the commissioners recommended that it should be made a separate parish.[55a]

In 1638 and 1693 the curate's house at Totteridge had pertaining to it 'one orchard garden with a litell Backside contayning by estimacon 2 roods,' and 7½ acres of pasture land.[55b]

In 1307 the parson of Hatfield obtained a grant of free warren in the demesne lands of his church in Totteridge.[56]

In 1471 John Sugden, rector of Hatfield, left a torch to the chapel of Totteridge.[57]

Various meeting-places for Protestant Dissenters were certified in Totteridge from 1823. In 1827 a chapel was built, which was still in existence in 1884,[58] but there is now no Nonconformist place of worship in Totteridge.

CHARITIES The following trusts for the direct benefit of the poor are regulated by a scheme of the Charity Commissioners, namely, the charities of—

William Sheppey, founded by will, 1808, trust fund, £2,105 5s. 3d. consols.

Sukey Richardson, will, 1828, trust fund, £48 3s. 7d. consols.

Martha Barrett, being an annual sum of £1 13s. 4d. received from the Haberdashers' Company, London.

William Campion, will, 1720, being an annual sum of £2 payable out of copyhold lands at Tottenham Court.

Waste Lands Charity, being £66 13s. 4d. consols, set aside in 1799 by William Manning in consideration of permission to inclose certain land.

William Manning, being £100 consols, established in 1810 in commemoration of fiftieth anniversary of King George III.

Volunteer Corps, £36 3s. 9d. consols, representing balance in hand on dissolution of corps in 1810.

Sir Alexander Maitland, consisting of £73 11s. 4d. consols, representing a legacy received in 1820.

Louisa Arrowsmith for poor, trust fund, £89 13s. 7d. consols.

The several sums of stock are held by the official trustees, producing £62 19s. 8d. in annual dividends, which with the income of Barrett's ar¹ Campion's charities are applied in the distribution of fuel.

In 1789 Mrs. Elizabeth Williams by her will bequeathed £400, the interest to be applied—subject to keeping in repair her husband's tomb—towards the support of her Sunday school. The legacy is now represented by £539 8s. 1d. consols with the official trustees, producing £13 9s. 8d. yearly, who also hold a further sum of £234 4s. consols, producing £5 17s. yearly, known as the Louisa Arrowsmith's Education charity.

---

[44] Close, 1 Will. and Mary, pt. vi, no. 21.
[45] Ibid. Mich. 2 & 3 Phil. and Mary.
[46] Early Chan. Proc. bdle. 62, no. 291.
[47] Ibid.
[48] Com. Pleas D. Enr. Trin. 2 Edw. VI, m. 4 d.
[49] An entry states 'no Registers kept from 1720 to 1723 in Mr. Charles Ogbald's time' (Midd. and Herts. N. and Q. iv, 136).
[50] There should be a Book vi, marriages 1790 to 1812 (ibid.).
[51] Bacon, Liber Regis.
[52] P.C.C. 8 Cromwell ; 19 and 22 Horne.
[53] Salmon, op. cit. 59.
[54] Feud. Aids, ii, 457 ; Pat. 5 Eliz. pt. ii, m. 30 ; Feet of F. East. 16 Eliz. ; Bacon, Liber Regis.
[55] Clergy List, 1912.
[55a] Urwick, op. cit. 607.
[55b] Herts. Gen. and Antiq. iii, 57, 59.
[56] Chart. R. 35 Edw. I, m. 5, no. 11.
[57] P.C.C. 1 Wattys.
[58] Urwick, op. cit. 610–11.

WALKERN

Walchra (xi cent.); Walkre, Waukre, Wauker (xiii cent.).

The parish of Walkern has an area of 2,992 acres, of which 1,727½ acres are arable land, 686¾ acres permanent grass, and 138 acres woods and plantations.[1] Nearly all the western half is over 300 ft. in height; the valley of the little River Beane causes a slight depression down the centre of the parish, but the land rises again in the east, and at three points, Walkern Hall, Bassus Green, and Walkern Park, reaches a height of over 400 ft.

The village lies off the main road in the valley of the Beane on the road to Watton. It is fairly large and somewhat straggling, the church, rectory and school, and Walkern Place, a 17th-century farm-house of timber and plaster, refaced in the 18th century, lying at the north end. There are several 17th-century cottages in the village, and the White Lion Inn, although much altered, is probably of that date. At the south end of the village are the mill on the River Beane and the early 17th-century farm-house called Rook's Nest. It is chiefly built of the narrow 2-inch red bricks, and is of two stories and attics. It is L-shaped on plan, though a long brew-house projects northward from the kitchen wing. The main building faces east, and has the usual two-storied gabled porch nearly in the centre of the front. At the back is a boldly projecting staircase carried well above the eaves of the main building and finished with a gable. A long kitchen wing facing the south projects from the main building. The main building is divided internally into two nearly equal parts by the massive substructure of the central chimney, the drawing-room or old parlour being on the right of the entrance, and the hall, now the dining room, on the left. In both these rooms the old fireplaces have been built up and modern grates substituted. A south entrance door formerly existed from the dining room. The staircase opens directly into the dining room, and the arrangement of the stair is very similar to that at Queen Hoo Hall, Tewin, and is an intermediate stage between the newel and the open stair; but in this instance the stair winds round three sides only of the timber-framed newel, which is 2 ft. 3 in. wide, and is lined up to the first floor level with old oak panelling. The panels are moulded, and inside each is a lozenge-shaped inner panel. This is the only old panelling left in the house. At the landing above are some flat-moulded balusters, cut out of 3 in. by 1½ in. oak. The kitchen has an old fireplace 9 ft. 6 in. wide, with a plain lintel, which is partly occupied by a modern range. There is a small parlour between the kitchen entrance and the dining room. The whole of the kitchen wing is formed of timber framing, the timbers being placed close together and filled in between with thin bricks. The chimney over the main building has a group of four square shafts set diagonally on a massive square base; the chimney over the kitchen wing is of wide brickwork, with a plain sunk panel in its width. The roofs are tiled. All the windows on the east front have moulded mullions and transoms formed in cement, and over each is a brick dripstone with returned ends. All the windows on the south front have been modernized. They formerly had oak mullions and diamond-shaped lead lights.

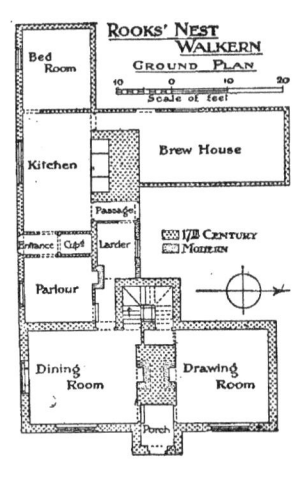

Bridgefoot Farm, an interesting and picturesque timber-framed house, stands a little to the south-west of the church, and was probably erected about the beginning of the 17th century. It has been very little altered externally, and internally the old arrangement of the plan is still quite clear, though a few partitions have been added and the rooms modernized. The plan is L-shaped and the principal entrance is on the north side, and formerly opened directly into the common living room or hall, but this has been subdivided into a sitting-room, dairy and passage to the kitchen at the back. The beams over the hall are 17 in. wide, and the soffits are carved with a flat geometrical ornament consisting of alternate rows of four circles and four rectangular figures all connected together by fillets. There is no other carved work in the house. The old wide square-headed fireplace of the hall still remains in the sitting room, but a modern grate has been inserted and the sides filled with cupboards. To the right of the hall is the old parlour, with a wide slightly projecting bay window, which is carried up to the floor above and finished with a gable, very similar to those at Wymondley Hall and Egerton House, Great Berkhampstead. Between the parlour and the north front is a small outhouse, evidently part of the original plan. Beyond the hall, and forming the wing of the building, is the kitchen, which still retains its old fireplace, 10 ft. 6 in. in width, although it is partly occupied by a modern range. The old seats have given way to cupboards, but the small niches for flagons still remain, as at Upp Hall, Braughing. A small gabled staircase occupies the angle of the L between the old hall and

ROOKS' NEST WALKERN GROUND PLAN

[1] Statistics from Bd. of Agric. (1905).

the kitchen, but the stair itself is very plain. All the external walls are timber-framed, lathed and plastered on the outside, the plaster being ornamented with the usual large flush panels filled with some roughly scratched pattern. The roofs are steep and covered with tiles, and all terminate in plain gables. There is an overhanging upper story on the east side. Some of the windows retain their oak mullions and transoms. The two old chimneys are groups of plain shafts of bricks 2 in. in thickness.

Three roads branching to the east run into the road to Ardeley, on the east side of which is Walkern Bury, now a modern farm-house. Adjoining it on the south is a small castle of the mount and bailey type, thrown up possibly by Hamo de St. Clare in the reign of Stephen.[2] Hamo was, we know, an adherent of the turbulent Geoffrey de Mandeville, and was with him at Stephen's celebrated Easter Court in

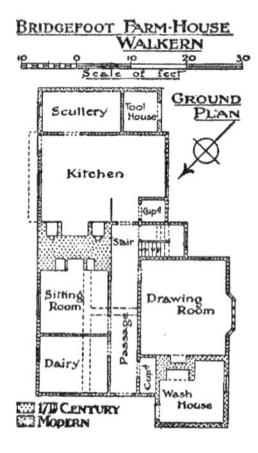

1136. Although the castle stands fairly high, being about 400 ft. above the ordnance datum, it does not seem to have commanded any large extent of country, and would appear to have been built at Walkern as a manorial stronghold, because that was the head of the St. Clare barony in Hertfordshire. It never apparently had any masonry works, the earthworks being defended by a wooden keep on the mound and timber stockades on the outer defences. The castle was probably destroyed, with numerous other adulterine or unlicensed castles, in the reign of Henry II.

At Clay End a road branches off still further east to Walkern Park, the residence of Mrs. Cotton Browne. Boxbury Farm and Box Wood are in the west of the parish. The parish lies on a subsoil of chalk; there are many chalk-pits and gravel-pits, especially between Walkern and the Ardeley road.

In 1403 a commission was granted to John Couper of Walkern, John Matmakere of Watton, Thomas Barbour and William Templier of Walkern 'to search for certain treasure of no small amount, which the King understands to be hidden in a pit in the field of Walkern called "Marlepitte," and to bring it when found before the King and Council with all speed.'[3]

The nearest railway station is Stevenage, on the Great Northern main line, 5 miles west. The inclosure award is dated 1850, and is in the custody of the clerk of the peace.[4]

Place-names that occur in Walkern are Tristrammes Grove, Cheney Hall and Tonecrofts.

MANORS WALKERN was held by Alwin Horne, one of the king's thegns. After the Conquest it was granted to Derman, a thegn of William the Conqueror, at which period it was assessed at 10 hides.[5] Derman was succeeded in the manor of Walkern, as in Watton, by his brother Leofstan,[6] but the two manors did not continue in the same hands. It seems probable that Walkern was the 'manor of Derman, which Leofstan his brother held,' given by William Rufus to Eudo Dapifer, for he seems to have possessed the tithes of Walkern, and the manor appears to have been subsequently held by his successor Hamo de St. Clare,[7] who gave the mill of Walkern to the church of St. Mary for the souls of King Henry and Queen Maud and Eudo Dapifer.[8] The manor passed from him and his wife Gunnora to their son Hubert de St. Clare,[9] who was living in the reign of Stephen, and who died in 1155.[10] Hubert's daughter and heir Gunnora married William de Lanvaley,[11] whose son William married Hawise daughter of Hugh de Bocland,[12] and was one of the barons appointed to impose the observance of Magna Charta. Hawise survived William and died before 1233,[13] her son William de Lanvaley[14] having apparently predeceased her, for his daughter Hawise, the wife of John de Burgh,[15] seems to have succeeded her grandmother.[16] John de Burgh's son John predeceased his father about 1278, when John de Burgh, senior, was said to be holding the manor by courtesy as of the barony of Lanvaley, of the heirs of John his son.[17] In 1281 John granted to Ralph de Hauville, for his service and for 100 marks, 14 acres of the demesne land 'lying between the croft that belonged to Warin de Waukre and the Greneweye and the Heldeburweye, together with Richard de Boxe, Ralph de Boxe, William de Boxe, William Aumfrey, Godahuge, Stephen de Boxe, Geoffrey son of Adam, Mila atte Holm, Isabella Ruald, Basilia Wlmer, John son of the beadle, and Walter de Boxe, formerly John's bondmen, with all their issue, chattels and tenements held by them of John in Walkern, rendering therefor two barbed arrows fledged with peacock feathers yearly at Midsummer.'[18] John de Burgh died shortly afterwards, leaving as his heirs his two granddaughters Hawise widow of Robert

[2] See *V.C.H. Herts.* ii, 118.
[3] *Cal. Pat.* 1401–5, p. 201.
[4] *Blue Bk. Incl. Awards,* 64.
[5] *V.C.H. Herts.* i, 342a.
[6] *Cart. Mon. St. John Bapt. de Colcestr.* (Roxburghe Club), i, 28.
[7] *V.C.H. Herts.* i, 286 n.
[8] *Cart. Mon. St. John Bapt. de Colcestr.* (Roxburghe Club), i, 156.

[9] Wrottesley, *Ped. from the Plea R.* 486.
[10] Information from Mr. J. H. Round.
[11] Ibid.; *Cart. Mon. St. John Bapt. de Colcestr.* (Roxburghe Club), i, 147.
[12] Ibid. 200, 202.
[13] *Excerpta e Rot. Fin.* (Rec. Com.), i, 246.
[14] *Cart. Mon. St. John Bapt. de Colcestr.*

(Roxburghe Club), i, 201; *Rot. de Oblat. et Fin.* (Rec. Com.), 372.
[15] Burke, *Dorm. and Extinct Peerages.*
[16] *Excerpta e Rot. Fin.* (Rec. Com.), i, 269; Assize R. 323.
[17] Burke, *Dorm. and Extinct Peerages*; Assize R. 323; Feet of F. Div. Co. 7 Edw. I, no. 12.
[18] *Cal. Close,* 1279–88, pp. 128–9.

Rook's Nest, Walkern : East Front

Old Cottage, Walkern

A HISTORY OF HERTFORDSHIRE

Grelle, and Devorgill the wife of Robert Fitz Walter, and Walkern was assigned to the latter in 1282.[19] In 1294 Robert Fitz Walter went to Gascony on the king's service and let the manor to farm in the mean time to Reginald de Silverle.[20] Devorgill died in 1284. In 1313 a purparty of her lands was assigned to her daughter and co-heir Christine,[21] who granted her reversion of this moiety to her father,[22] then holding the manor for life 'by the courtesy of England' of the inheritance of his wife.[23] Two years later Robert Fitz Walter granted the reversion of the manor after the death of a life-tenant, John Bensted, to John Lord Marshal,[24] of Hingham, co. Norfolk.[25] Upon his death without issue in 1316–17 it passed to his sister Hawise, the wife of Robert, second Lord Morley.[26] Robert died in 1360,[27] leaving a son William, the third lord, who in 1379 was succeeded by his son Thomas, fourth Lord Morley,[28] his widow Cecilia holding a third of the manor in dower until her death in 1386.[29] The fourth lord, who was Marshal of Ireland and a Knight of the Garter, died in 1416, being succeeded by his grandson Thomas.[30] Anne widow of Thomas, fourth Lord Morley, married secondly Sir Hugh Hastings, and held the whole manor until her death in 1426.[31] Thomas, fifth Lord Morley, was succeeded in 1435 by his son Robert,[32] who died in 1442, leaving an only daughter Eleanor, at that time only forty-two weeks old.[33] She subsequently married William Lovel, who was thereupon summoned as Lord Morley. They both died within a month of each other in 1476.[34] The custody of their son Henry during his minority, together with his marriage, was granted to Richard, Bishop of Salisbury, and Peter Courteney.[35] He died without issue in 1489, his lands passing to his sister Alice,[36] who married first William Parker, and secondly Sir Edward Howard,[37] afterwards Lord High Admiral. Shortly after 1506[38] Alice and Sir Edward Howard sold the manor of Walkern to Sir William Capell, Lord Mayor of London, who died seised of it in 1515,[39] and whose descendant Arthur Lord Capell of Hadham was created Earl of Essex after the Restoration.[40] Walkern has descended in this family,[41] and is now held by the seventh earl.

MORLEY, Lord Morley. *Argent a lion sable crowned or.*

CAPELL, Earl of Essex

Walkern Park is first mentioned in 1360.[42] In 1373 John Basset was keeper.[43] His name perhaps and that of his family survives in Bassus Green, called by Cussans Bassett's Green.[44] In 1379 the park had an area of 398 acres,[45] and in 1435 the 'agistment' was stated to be worth 26s. 8d. beyond the sustentation of the wild animals.[46] John Hotoft was keeper in 1427 and John Humberston in 1428.[47] It is now of the extent of 30 acres and surrounds Walkern Hall.

Walkern Mill was given to the church of St. Mary of Walkern by Hamo de St. Clare in the reign of Henry I[48] (see above). In 1313 a water mill was pertaining to the manor,[49] and in 1360 a windmill is mentioned.[50] There is still a water mill.

View of frankpledge, amendment of the assize of bread and ale, gallows, tumbrel, infangentheof and free warren were claimed by Robert Fitz Walter in 1287.[51] In 1360 the court leet was held on Tuesday in Whitsun week.[52]

The manor of *BOXBURY* or *BOXE* in Walkern and Stevenage was assessed in the 11th century at

---

[19] *Cal. Close*, 1279–88, p. 186; *Feud. Aids*, ii, 430.
[20] *Cal. Pat.* 1292–1301, p. 85.
[21] *Cal. Close*, 1307–13, p. 523; Chan. Inq. p.m. 6 Edw. II, no. 58.
[22] *Cal. Pat.* 1307–13, p. 528. Christine is referred to as Devorgill's co-heir and as being of full age, which implies that there was another daughter then under age. As there is no record of any transaction between Robert Fitz Walter and the latter and yet he seems to have had the reversion of the whole manor, it seems probable that she died whilst still a minor.
[23] *Cal. Close*, 1307–13, p. 523.
[24] Inq. a.q.d. file 106, no. 4; Feet of F. Herts. 8 Edw. II, no. 167; *Cal. Pat.* 1313–17, p. 274.
[25] G.E.C. *Complete Peerage.*
[26] Ibid.
[27] Chan. Inq. p.m. 34 Edw. III (1st nos.), no. 81.
[28] Ibid. 2 Ric. II, no. 34.
[29] Ibid. 10 Ric. II, no. 27.
[30] Chan. Inq. p.m. 4 Hen. V, no. 49. The manor is said to be held as parcel of the barony of Rye. This barony came to the Morleys by inheritance from the Marshals, and to them through the marriage of John Marshal, ancestor of John Lord Marshal, with Aliva daughter of Hubert de Rye (G.E.C. *Peerage*, s.v. Marshal).
[31] Chan. Inq. p.m. 5 Hen. VI, no. 52; *Cal. Pat.* 1422–9, p. 391.
[32] Chan. Inq. p.m. 14 Hen. VI, no. 20.
[33] Ibid. 21 Hen. VI, no. 38.
[34] Ibid. 16 Edw. IV, no. 73; *Cal. Pat.* 1467–77, p. 603.
[35] Ibid. 1476–85, p. 48.
[36] Chan. Inq. p.m. (Ser. 2), v, 48.
[37] Feet of F. Herts. Hil. 21 Hen. VII.
[38] Ibid. East. 21 Hen. VII.
[39] Chan. Inq. p.m. (Ser. 2), xxx, 25.
[40] V.C.H. *Herts. Families*, 96.
[41] Feet of F. Trin. 42 Eliz.; Chan. Inq. p.m. (Ser. 2), cccxcvi, 148; ccclxv, 54; Feet of F. Div. Co. Hil. 3 Will. and Mary; Mich. 5 Geo. I.
[42] Chan. Inq. p.m. 34 Edw. III (1st nos.), no. 81.
[43] Ibid. 47 Edw. III (2nd nos.), no. 27.
[44] Cussans, op. cit. *Broadwater Hund.* 73.
[45] Chan. Inq. p.m. 2 Ric. II, no. 34.
[46] Ibid. 14 Hen. VI, no. 20.
[47] Ibid.
[48] *Cart. Mon. St. John Bapt. de Colcestr.* (Roxburghe Club), i, 156.
[49] Chan. Inq. p.m. 6 Edw. II, no. 58.
[50] Ibid. 34 Edw. III (1st nos.), no. 81.
[51] Assize R. 325, m. 26 d.
[52] Chan. Inq. p.m. 34 Edw. III (1st nos.), no. 81.

WALKERN : BRIDGEFOOT FARM FROM THE SOUTH-WEST

WALKERN CHURCH : THE NAVE LOOKING EAST

BROADWATER HUNDRED — WALKERN

5 hides. In the time of Edward the Confessor 2 hides and 3 virgates were held by Alward, a man of Alestan of Boscombe,[53] and half a hide by Samar, a man of Alnod.[54] A hide and 3 virgates also in Boxe belonged to Benington.[55] By 1086 Alward's 2¾ hides had been acquired by William de Ow, and were held of him by Peter de Valognes,[56] who had gained possession of the Benington portion,[57] and Samar's half-hide was held by Osbern of the Bishop of Bayeux.[58] These holdings may have become amalgamated, for the only manor of which later there is any evidence descended in the family of Valognes with their principal manor of Benington.[59] It was held as half a knight's fee.

The first sub-tenant of Boxbury to be mentioned is William de Boxe, who held one knight's fee in Hertfordshire of Robert de Valognes in 1166.[60] Almaric de Boxe was holding land in Walkern in 1200,[61] and his son William sued Richard de Boxe for a tenement in Stevenage in 1229.[62] Richard de Boxe obtained a grant of free warren in his demesne lands of Boxe in 1253.[63] He appears to have been succeeded by a John le Sarmonner or Summoner (see Boxe's manor of Hoddesdon in Hertford Hundred). The heirs of this John were assessed for Boxe in 1303.[64] These heirs seem to have been Thomas de Langton and Richard de St. Edmund (probably sons of his daughters).[65] Richard de St. Edmund apparently left an heiress Margery, who married Ralph de Foxton (see Hoddesdon), and in 1346 Margery de Foxton, with John de Broxbourne, Thomas Ty and John de Blomvile, was assessed for the half-fee in Boxe.[66]

After this date the history of this manor is for a long time obscure. It reappears as the manor of Boxbury in 1521, in which year John Norreys died seised of the manor, which was settled on himself and his wife Katherine.[67] His son John, who succeeded him, sold Boxbury in 1526 to Philip Boteler,[68] in whose family it descended in the same manner as Watton Woodhall [69] (q.v.) until the death of Robert Boteler in 1622.[70] Boxbury then came to his daughter Jane, who married John Lord Belasyse [71] and sold the manor some time after 1638 to Sir John Gore of Sacombe.[72] The latter conveyed it in 1681 to Thomas Ashby,[73] who was still holding it in 1727.[74] Subsequently it came into the possession of William Hale of King's Walden, who was lord of the manor in 1771,[75] and in whose family it descended.[76]

Christiana de Valognes and her descendants claimed in Boxe the same privileges which they held in their main manor of Benington [77] (q.v.).

LANGTONS, a manor of which scanty records remain, was probably that part of Boxe which descended to the second heir of John le Sarmonner, Thomas de Langton (cf. Langtons in Hoddesdon). Later it came into the same hands as Boxbury. John Norreys died seised of it in 1521,[78] and it apparently came with that manor to Philip Boteler in 1526, for Sir John Boteler was holding it in 1562.[79] It probably became merged with Boxbury.

The church of ST. MARY THE CHURCH VIRGIN stands to the north-east of the village on the east bank of the River Beane. It is built of flint rubble with dressings of Barnack stone and clunch, and consists of a chancel, nave and aisles, west tower, south porch and modern north and south chapels.[80]

The original church consisted probably of a chancel and nave. The former has been wholly rebuilt, and the earliest part of the existing church is the nave,

ROOK'S NEST, WALKERN, FROM THE SOUTH-WEST

which dates from the 11th century and is probably part of the pre-Conquest church, as the walls are only 2 ft. 3 in. thick, and over the position of the former south door is a piece of sculpture of pre-Conquest date described in detail below. The south aisle was added early in the 12th century. In the following century the chancel was rebuilt and the north aisle added. The tower was built in the middle of the 14th century. In the early part of the 15th century the south porch was added, and at the end of the same century new windows were inserted in both aisles, while early in the 16th century the clearstory was built. The north and south chapels were added

---

[53] V.C.H. Herts. i, 327b.
[54] Ibid. 309a.   [55] Ibid. 336b.
[56] Ibid. 327b.
[57] Ibid. 336b.
[58] Ibid. 309a.
[59] Red Bk. Exch. (Rolls Ser.), i, 361; Plac. de Quo Warr. (Rec. Com.), 281; Feud. Aids, ii, 430, 436; Chan. Inq. p.m. (Ser. 2), xxxviii, 34.
[60] Red Bk. Exch. (Rolls Ser.), i, 361.
[61] Rot. Cur. Reg. (Rec. Com.), ii, 275.
[62] Cal. Pat. 1225–32, p. 309.
[63] Cal. Chart. R. 1226–57, p. 416.
[64] Feud. Aids, ii, 430.
[65] Cf. ibid. 430, 433.
[66] Ibid. 436.
[67] Chan. Inq. p.m. (Ser. 2), xxxviii, 34.
[68] Feet of F. Herts. East. 18 Hen. VIII.
[69] Ibid. East. 4 Eliz.
[70] Chan. Inq. p.m. (Ser. 2), cccii, 141.
[71] Privy Seal Docket Bk. xi.
[72] Recov. R. East. 14 Chas. I, rot. 5.
[73] Feet of F. Herts. Mich. 33 Chas. II.
[74] Recov. R. Mich. 1 Geo. II, rot. 22.
[75] Ibid. Mich. 11 Geo. III, rot. 185.
[76] Ibid. Hil. 55 Geo. III, rot. 248; Cussans, op. cit. Broadwater Hund. 89.
[77] Plac. de Quo Warr. (Rec. Com.), 281.
[78] Chan. Inq. p.m. (Ser. 2), xxxviii, 34.
[79] Feet of F. Herts. East. 4 Eliz.
[80] Dimensions: chancel, 29 ft. 6 in. by 16 ft. 6 in.; nave, 37 ft. 6 in. by 20 ft. 6 in.; north aisle, 7 ft. wide; south aisle, 9 ft. 6 in. wide; west tower, 11 ft. square; south porch, 11 ft. by 8 ft.

155

A HISTORY OF HERTFORDSHIRE

and the chancel was completely restored during the 19th century. Thus the church as a whole presents a complete series of examples of architecture from the earliest to the latest of the English styles.

The east windows of the chancel are three modern lancets. The arches opening into the chapels are also modern. In the north wall is a modern single lancet, and in the south wall is a 13th-century piscina with shafted jambs, and to the west of it three sedilia of the same date separated by detached shafts. Both the piscina and sedilia are much restored.

The material of the two-centred chancel arch is of 13th-century date, but it has been rebuilt late in the 14th century. The nave has a north arcade of the 13th century of three bays, with two-centred arches of two chamfered orders. The columns, with their moulded capitals and bases, are octagonal. The bases are much mutilated. At the east and west ends the inner orders rest on corbels on the faces of the responds. The easternmost capital was either recut or inserted in the 15th century. The south arcade is of the 12th century, and is of two bays with semi-circular arches of one square order. The abaci are plain with one exception, which is cable-moulded. The clearstory windows, three on each side, do not correspond with the bays of the arcades. They are each of two four-centred lights with a dropped two-centred rear arch and square external head.

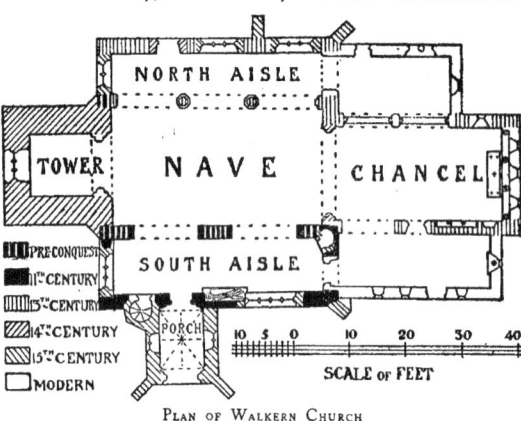

The north aisle has two windows of three lights in the north wall and a similar window of two lights in the west wall. All are of late 15th-century date and are much restored. The pointed north doorway, which is to the west of both the north windows, is of late 14th-century date, and is of two continuously moulded orders. The south aisle has in its east wall a modern doorway to the south chapel, and in the south wall is a late 15th-century four-light window in a four-centred head. The entrance to the rood stair is from a splay in the north-east angle of the south aisle by a doorway some height from the ground. The stair is intact, and the upper doorway to the rood loft is visible from the interior of the stair, but is quite hidden by plaster on the nave side. In the west wall of the south aisle is a window of three lights similar to that in the south wall, and traces are visible in the wall above the modern doorway in the east wall of another window of like date and detail. The south doorway is of the 12th century, and has been much restored. It has a semicircular head and shafted external jambs, the outer order being continuous. The south porch is of two stages, of early 15th-century date, and has an entrance archway with a two-centred head, the inner order supported on semi-octagonal responds and the outer continuous. The ground stage has a two-light window with a quatrefoil in a pointed head in the east and west walls. The vaulting is on the original springers, but is modern. The upper stage is approached by a stair from the aisle, its lower doorway opening to the west of the south door. The stair turret projects externally in the angle of the aisle and porch as one side and a half of an octagon. The upper stage of the porch has one two-light window in a square head in the south wall. Immediately above the doorway to the parvise stair in the aisle is one jamb and part of the rear arch of a semicircular-headed 12th-century window.

In a wide recess with a dropped two-centred head and simple continuous moulding is a fine recumbent effigy in Purbeck marble of about 1220, possibly that of William de Lanvaley, who married Hawise de Bocland. The legs are crossed and the hands are clasped on the hilt of a great sword. The figure is clad in a fine mail hauberk, with a coif and chausses without knee-cops. The long surcoat is parted above the knees, and on the left arm is a long kite-shaped shield reaching from the shoulder to below the knee. The left leg is broken, but the fragment is undamaged. The figure wears a flat-topped helm with a wide eye-slit and perforations.

On the south side of the south wall of the nave, rather westward of the middle and above the arcade, and so now included in the south aisle, are the remains of a rood of very early date, about 4 ft. 6 in. high, carved in chalk. It probably indicates the position of the original south doorway of the nave, over which it stood, and affords additional evidence of the pre-Conquest date assigned to the nave.

The west tower is of three stages with an embattled parapet and spire. The tower arch is original work of the 14th century. The west window is also of the 14th century, and has net tracery in a pointed head. The bell-chamber has single-light windows of the 15th century. On the plinths of the tower are several consecration crosses worked in scappled flints and chalk.

The roofs of the nave and aisles are 15th-century work, almost entirely plain. The font is of the late 14th century and is made of clunch, octagonal in shape and roughly moulded. It has plain sides and angle shafts.

PLAN OF WALKERN CHURCH

WALKERN CHURCH: TOMB IN SOUTH AISLE

BROADWATER HUNDRED — WALKERN

In the chancel are the brasses of William Chapman, 1621, and his wife, 1636, with an inscription. On the north side of the nave is a brass of the late 15th century of a civilian and his wife, with a shield of arms of Humberstone; at the west end is a brass of Edward Humberstone, 1583, and his wife, which is said to be a palimpsest; it has an inscription. In the north aisle is an inscription only to William Bramfeilde, 1596; in the vestry a brass, with an imperfect inscription, to John Humberstone, 1590, and an inscription to Rychard Humberstone, 1581, which is a palimpsest on an inscription to John Lovekyn, 1370.

Besides these brasses and the 13th-century monument described above there are two 17th-century mural monuments, the one in the south wall of the chancel to Daniel Gorsuch and his wife, 1638, a classical composition with kneeling figures, and the other on the south side of the nave to Giles Humberstone, 1627, and his wife, having kneeling figures, arms and an inscription.

The small oak pulpit is of the early 16th century. It is octagonal, with plain panelled sides.

The chancel screen of five bays is of the 15th century. The upper panels of the side bays are open and traceried, and the lower are close. The centre is occupied by the doorway.

There are five bells, the first being dated 1626, by an unknown founder; the second is by Thomas Mears, 1833; and the third, fourth and fifth of 1713, by John Waylett.

The plate consists of a silver chalice and paten and almsdish, the gift of Benjamin Heath, rector, 1782.

The registers begin in 1680, and are contained in one book: baptisms 1680 to 1812, burials 1680 to 1812, marriages 1680 to 1812.[81]

Boxe is said to have anciently been a parish possessing a church. In 1700 the foundations of the church are said to have been visible in a field called the Church-yard, near Boxe Wood.[82] There is no mention of Boxe Church in the *Taxation of Pope Nicholas* or the *Valor Ecclesiasticus* of Henry VIII, but it is worthy of note that at an early date the tithes of Boxbury were in different hands from those of Walkern.

ADVOWSON A certain Hamo, brother of Robert de Villiers, possibly a lord of the manor, gave two parts of the tithes of Walkern and a bordar with 2 acres to the monastery of St. John at Colchester.[83]

William de Lanvaley, the second husband of Hawise de Bocland, gave the church to the monastery of St. John the Baptist at Colchester,[84] and in 1204 the abbot and monks were 'canonically instituted and inducted' as rectors, saving the vicarage of Geoffrey de Bocland for his life, on condition that he paid them 1 mark yearly.[85] No more is heard of the vicarage, so that probably after the death of Geoffrey de Bocland the monastery either served the church by one of their own monks or put in a stipendiary. The living was a rectory at the Dissolution.[86]

In 1546 the advowson was granted to Sir Philip Hobby and his heirs.[87] After this the descent lacks documentary evidence for more than a century. It is said to have come into the possession of John Cock of Broxbourne, whose son Henry Cock conveyed it in 1560 to Henry Willan of Kelshall, who sold it in 1564 to George Brende of London. In 1587 George Brende sold it to Edward Horne, then rector, who conveyed it in 1604 to Conant Prowse, and in 1609 the latter sold it to Agnes Wardley, widow. Five months later she conveyed it to William Humberstone of Digswell, who sold it before 1632 to Daniel Gorsuch. It was afterwards purchased by Andrew Gardiner, who conveyed it in 1669 to the Rev. Samuel Gardiner,[88] who presented in 1686.[89] It was purchased from him in 1702 by King's College, Cambridge,[90] the present patrons.[91]

The tithes of Boxbury belonged to St. Alban's Abbey before the Dissolution, and were leased in 1518 to William and Alice Day for forty years from July 1531. William and Alice sold their interests in 1519 to John Norreys, after whose death they were to come

WALKERN CHURCH FROM THE SOUTH-WEST

---

[81] This book has all the entries written, no new marriage register of the form prescribed by Hardwicke's Act of 1753 having been obtained (*Midd. and Herts. N. and Q.* iv, 137).
[82] Chauncy, *Hist. of Herts.* 370.
[83] *Cal. Chart. R.* 1226–57, p. 424.
[84] *Cart. Mon. St. John Bapt. de Colcestr.* (Roxburghe Club), i, 200.
[85] Ibid. 126.
[86] *Valor Eccl.* (Rec. Com.) iv, 278. A grant of the rectory in 1545 to Sir Robert Tyrwhitt at the price of one year's purchase may have lasted until the time when the advowson was disposed of (Partic. for Grants, Augm. Off. 38 Hen. VIII, no. 576).
[87] Pat. 38 Hen. VIII, pt. xiii, m. 7; *Cal. D. of Purch. and Exch.* 395.
[88] Cussans, op. cit. *Broadwater Hund.* 83.
[89] Inst. Bks. (P.R.O.).
[90] Close, 1 Anne, pt. ix, no. 5.
[91] See Inst. Bks. (P.R.O.).

157

A HISTORY OF HERTFORDSHIRE

to Robert Hocknell. The latter complained that two years after this George Clarke of Walkern purchased the tithes and took them by force while Hocknell was away in France, and continued to do so.[92] Hocknell's suit appears to have been successful, for he is mentioned as holding them later.[93] The abbey leased them in 1539 to John Rotherham,[94] but Henry VIII granted them in 1544 to Richard Bowle, barber-surgeon, and John Howe, grocer, of London.[95] In the 17th century the tithes seem to have been paid partly to Walkern and partly to Stevenage, presumably according to the parish in which the lands lay. In 1671 the tithes of Boxwood, held by John or Thomas Harvey, were paid to Walkern,[96] and in 1728 tithes from part of Boxbury, owned by Thomas Adams, were paid to Stevenage.[97] Mary Adams was holding this land in 1748.[98] In 1783 tithes in the manor of Boxbury were conveyed by Rose and Mary Nicolls to Richard Down.[99]

Meeting-places of Protestant Dissenters in Walkern were certified from 1699. A Congregational chapel was built in 1810,[100] which still exists, and there is also a Baptist and a Wesleyan chapel in the parish.

CHARITIES

The charities subsisting in this parish have by a scheme of the Charity Commissioners, 8 March 1907, been consolidated and placed under the administration of one body of trustees. They comprise the charities of :—

An unknown donor No. 1, mentioned in the Parliamentary returns of 1786, consisting of 3 a. 1 r. 31 p., known as Cadcroft Field, and 1 a. known as Brockwell Shot, in Walkern, of the annual rental value of £6.

Unknown donor No. 2, consisting of 1 a. 2 r. 20 p. in Yardley, let at £3 a year, known as Leycroft, comprised in deed of 24 January 1707.

Unknown donor No. 3, being a rent-charge of 6s. 8d. for the poor, vested in the rector of Walkern; and the charity of John Izard Pryor, being £108 11s. consols, with the official trustees, derived from will proved at London 13 July 1861, producing £2 14s. yearly.

The scheme provides that the yearly income of the charities shall be applied for the benefit of the poor in such way as the trustees may consider most conducive to the formation of provident habits, including donations to any dispensary, infirmary, provident club, provision of nurses, &c., or in distribution of articles in kind.

WATTON AT-STONE

Wodtone, Wattune (xi cent.).

The parish of Watton has an area of 3,585 acres, of which 1,912¼ acres are arable land and 670 acres permanent grass.[1] It attains a height of over 300 ft. in the north, slopes downwards towards the south, but rises again to 300 ft. in the south-west. The River Beane flows through the parish from the north-west, and through Woodhall Park, where it is artificially widened.

The church stands a little to the west of the road from Stevenage to Hertford, but the village lies along the road. There are in this part one or two late 16th-century houses, notably a timber and plaster house in the middle of the village on the north side of the road, now much repaired, but still retaining an oak door frame and some original beams. On the south side of the road are some 17th-century timber and plaster cottages with overhanging upper stories, one of which is thatched.

Watton Place, Low a farm-house, stands beside the main road at the north end of the village. It consists of a main building of two stories and a low kitchen wing, forming an L-shaped plan. The front part of the main building, above the ground floor, is timber-framed, and overhangs the wall below, the upper part being divided into three equal gables. All the other walls are of brickwork, the old bricks being two inches thick. The building has been much altered both outside and inside, so that not many features of architectural interest remain. It was probably erected towards the close of the 16th century. There are some good brick chimneys on the main building consisting of a row of three shafts, a fourth, which was no doubt formerly there, having disappeared. The front shaft is circular with a large moulded twist, the capital consisting of triangular projections corbelled out; the second shaft is octagonal with moulded capital; the third is missing; the fourth is circular, with a moulded octagonal capital: the upper part of the shaft is covered with raised mouldings forming a honeycomb pattern, the lower part is twisted. The interior of the house has been so much altered that it is not possible to trace the original plan. Most of the work appears to be of the 18th century or later. A part of the old cellar still exists under the main building. It is approached from a doorway outside. Immediately opposite the door and only a few feet from it, over the stair, is a small shallow niche with arched head, and in the cellar itself are a number of similar niches in the walls. These are about 14 in. wide by 1 ft. 4 in. high, and 7 in. deep, and have four-centred arches of brick plastered. There are thirteen or fourteen of these niches, all about 2 ft. 8 in. from the floor. There is besides a large square-headed aumbry 2 ft. wide and 1 ft. 9 in. deep, with an oak frame round the opening and oak lining inside. The door has disappeared. These niches are very similar in shape and size to those in the cellars at Wymondley Bury and Delamere.

Broom Hall is a late 16th-century farm-house in the north-west of the parish. It is a rectangular building of brick in two stories, and with a small porch. The windows of the first floor have brick mullions.

At Watton Green, and a little south of the Green, and at Well Wood, are homestead moats, and in Chapel Wood there are some defensive earthworks.

Bardolphs, the ancient manor, with Bardolphspark Wood, is situated east of the village, a short distance north of Woodhall Park, which is in the south-east of

---

[92] Ct. of Req. bdle. 12, no. 67.
[93] L. and P. Hen. VIII, xix (1), 10 5 (25).
[94] Convent. Leases, Herts. 16.
[95] L. and P. Hen. VIII, xix (1), 1035 (25).
[96] Exch. Dep. 23 Chas. II, East. no. 24.
[97] Salmon, Hist. of Herts. 192.
[98] Recov. R. Mich. 22 Geo. II, rot. 168.
[99] Feet of F. Herts. Hil. 23 Geo. III.
[100] Urwick, op. cit. 615–16.
[1] Statistics from Bd. of Agric. (1905).

158

BROADWATER HUNDRED WATTON-AT-STONE

the parish. The hamlet of Whempstead lies in the north-east, about half-way between Watton and Little Munden. Watkins Hall, in the south of the parish, has been rebuilt, but an old beam over the entrance bears the inscription 'Watton Hall *alias* Watkins Hall I.M. 1636.'

The parish lies on a subsoil of chalk. There is a chalk-pit south of Watkins Hall, and two now disused north of the village. No railway passes through the parish, the nearest station being Knebworth, 3½ miles to the west.

Watton was anciently Crown land, *MANORS* and was of the extent of about 10 hides. Of these, 4½ hides were granted to the abbey of Westminster by King Edgar,[1a] and confirmed to that monastery by Edward the Confessor[2] (*vide infra*). During the reign of the latter the remaining 5 hides, which apparently formed the manor of

days in Scotland, or 13*s*. 4*d*. rent and 2*s*. a year payable at the two sheriffs' tourns in the hundred of Broadwater.[6] In the 15th century it was held for a quarter of a knight's fee[7]; it continued to be held of the king in chief by fealty and rent.[8]

Of the two sub-tenants of Watton in 1086, Alward apparently died without heirs, for the whole manor was held by the descendants of Derman. Derman's heir was his brother Leofstan,[9] whose son Ailwin or Elwyn was the father of Henry, first Mayor of London[10] and lord of the manor of Watton.[11] Henry is first mentioned in 1164–5,[12]

AGUILLON. *Gules a fleur de lis argent.*

WATTON PLACE: FRONT VIEW

WATTON, were held by Alwin Horne, one of the king's thegns.[3] In 1086 it was held of the king by two thegns named Derman and Alward.[4] The service by which the manor was subsequently held was the petty serjeanty of sending one foot-soldier equipped with bow and arrows to the army of the king in Wales for forty days.[5] In 1394 the service is said to be for fifteen

and died in 1212.[13] His nearest heir was a granddaughter, the daughter of his eldest son, who was first married to Ralph le Parmenter and afterwards (5 October 1212) to William Aguillon,[14] whose son[15] Robert became lord of the manor before 1248.[16] Robert Aguillon died about 1286, leaving as his heir his daughter Isabel, who was betrothed to

---

[1a] Dugdale, *Mon.* i, 292.
[2] Cott. Chart. vi, 2.
[3] *V.C.H. Herts.* i, 342.
[4] Ibid.
[5] *Red Bk. Exch.* (Rolls Ser.), ii, 507; *Testa de Nevill* (Rec. Com.), 266, 270; Assize R. 323; Chan. Inq. p.m. 14 Edw. I, no. 16, m. 13; 32 Edw. I, no. 64; 17 Edw. II, no. 39.
[6] Fine R. 18 Ric. II; Chan. Inq. p.m. 18 Ric. II, no. 7.
[7] Chan. Inq. p.m. 4 Hen. IV, no. 39; *Feud. Aids,* ii, 443.

[5] Chan. Inq. p.m. 25 Hen. VI, no. 29; 3 Edw. IV, no. 30; Harl. MS. 756, fol. 19; Pat. 13 Hen. VIII, pt. i
[9] *V.C.H. Herts.* i, 286 n.
[10] *Pipe R.* 11 *Hen. II* (Pipe R. Soc.), 18. He and his brother Alan then gave 20 marks on succeeding to Elwyn's lands. Mr. Round, who has devoted much attention to the first Mayor of London, points out that these lands were probably at Watton, but that 1164–5 is late for the death of a Domesday tenant's nephew, though not actually impossible.

Mr. Round's paper on 'The first Mayor of London' will be found in the *Antiquary,* xv (1887).
[11] *Red Bk. Exch.* (Rolls Ser.), ii, 507; *Testa de Nevill* (Rec. Com.), 270; *Liber Albus* (Rolls Ser.), i, 21, 319.
[12] *Pipe R.* 11 *Hen. II* (Pipe R. Soc.), 18.
[13] *Dict. Nat. Biog.*
[14] Round, *The King's Serjeants,* 245–6.
[15] Wrottesley, *Ped. from the Plea R.* 549.
[16] *Cal. Chart. R.* 1226–57, p. 329; Assize R. 318, m. 2.

159

A HISTORY OF HERTFORDSHIRE

Hugh Bardolf.[17] The manor was granted to Margaret, Robert Aguillon's widow, until the regular assignment of dower was made by the king,[18] but in 1287 it was held by Hugh Bardolf in right of his wife.[19] He was warden of Arundel Castle in 1272,[20] and, having been summoned to Parliament as Lord Bardolf from 1299 to 1302, died in 1304.[21] Isabel having quit-claimed her right in the manor upon her husband's death, it was re-granted to her for life, with reversion to her son William,[22] but in 1318 it was entailed on Thomas Bardolf, the elder son.[23] Isabel died about 1324,[24] and Thomas, who had succeeded as second Lord Bardolf in 1304, became lord of the manor. He died in 1329,[25] and his widow Agnes held Watton in dower until her death,[26] which occurred in 1357,[27] when she was succeeded by her son John, third Lord Bardolf of Wormegay.[28] William, fourth Lord Bardolf, son of John, became lord of the manor in 1363.[29] He granted Watton to Robert Bardolf for life, in exchange for the manor of Stow Bardolph in Norfolk,[30] and died in January 1385–6.[31] Upon the death of Robert Bardolf in 1394 the manor reverted to Thomas, fifth Lord Bardolf, son and heir of William, the fourth lord,[32] after the death in 1403 [33] of his mother Agnes, to whom it had been granted in dower by Richard II. Thomas, the fifth lord, joined Northumberland's rebellion in 1405, and died of wounds received at the battle of Bramham Moor in 1408,[34] leaving two daughters, Anne, who married, first, William Clifford, and secondly Reginald Cobham, and Joan the wife of Sir William Phelip.[35] The manor was divided between the two sisters. Sir William Phelip, who was a Knight of the Garter, and was in 1437 created Lord Bardolf, had served at the battle of Agincourt in 1415, being afterwards made Captain of Harfleur. Later he occupied the post of Treasurer of the Household to Henry V, and that of Privy Councillor and Chamberlain to Henry VI.[36] He died in 1441,[37] his wife Joan surviving until 1447, when the half-manor of Watton passed to her grandson William, second but eldest surviving son of her daughter Elizabeth and John Viscount Beaumont.[38] William Viscount Beaumont and Lord Bardolf married Joan daughter of Humphrey Duke of Buckingham, from whom he was divorced before 1477,[39] but who

BARDOLF, Lord Bardolf. *Azure three cinqfoils or.*

survived him. Upon the death of Anne Cobham, his great-aunt, in 1454 he became possessed of the whole of Watton Manor, her moiety passing to him as the next heir,[40] but he was at-tainted after the battle of Towton Field in 1461 [41] and his lands forfeited. Watton was granted in the following year to his wife Joan, with Thomas Archbishop of Can-terbury and George Bishop of Exeter as trustees, and with remainder to William Beau-mont,[42] who was still under attainder. Joan was still living in the reign of Richard III,[43] but in 1467 the manor was granted to Roger Ree, one of the ushers of the king's chamber, for his good services to the king's father.[44] Roger died in 1476,[45] leaving a son and heir William. William Viscount Beaumont was, however, restored to his honours in 1470. He was again attainted in 1471,[46] but was finally restored in 1485. He lost his reason in 1487, and was placed under the custody of John Earl of Oxford [47] until his death in 1507, when he was seised of the manor of Watton.[48] His nearest heir should have been Francis Lord Lovell, son of his sister Joan, but he was under attainder; the remaining heirs were John Norreis, son of his niece Frideswide, and Bryan Stapleton, son of his niece Joan.[49] The Crown, however, seems to have taken possession of the manor owing to Lord Lovell's attainder,[50] and it was granted in 1509 to John Earl of Oxford,[51] who had married Elizabeth widow of William Beaumont, to whom it was confirmed for life by Act of Parliament after her husband's death.[52] The reversion of the manor was granted in 1521 to Sir Wistan Brown, Knight of the Body,[53] and Watton, or Bardolf Hall as it was now called, came to his son John,[54] and from him descended to his son and heir George Brown in 1550.[55] In that year, probably for assurance of title, Edward VI granted the manor to Sir Thomas Darcy, Lord Darcy of Chich; George Brown seems to have remained in possession, for in 1552 he conveyed the manor to Matthias Bradbury.[56] In 1576 Thomas Bradbury sold the manor of Bardolfs to Philip Boteler,[57] after which it followed the descent of Watton Woodhall Manor until 1801, when it was sold, after the bankruptcy of Paul Bendfield, to Edward Lord Ellenborough, Lord Chief Justice of the King's Bench. The latter

BEAUMONT. *Azure powdered with fleurs de lis or and a lion or.*

---

[17] Chan. Inq. p.m. 14 Edw. I, no. 16, m. 13.
[18] Cal. Close, 1279–88, p. 385.
[19] Assize R. 325.
[20] Excerpta e Rot. Fin. (Rec. Com.), ii, 575.
[21] Chan. Inq. p.m. 32 Edw. I, no. 64.
[22] Chart. R. 33 Edw. I, no. 77, m. 12.
[23] Cal. Pat. 1317–21, p. 135; Inq. a.q.d. file 134, no. 7. This gave rise to confusion in later inquisitions, which state that Thomas was the son of William; but that Thomas was the son of Hugh is supported by Wrottesley, *Ped. from the Plea R.* 103, 352.
[24] Chan. Inq. p.m. 17 Edw. II, no. 39.
[25] Ibid. 3 Edw. III, no. 66.
[26] Cal. Close, 1330–3, p. 8; Abbrev. Rot. Orig. (Rec. Com.), ii, 44.
[27] G.E.C. Peerage.
[28] Abbrev. Rot. Orig. (Rec. Com.), ii, 170.
[29] Chan. Inq. p.m. 45 Edw. III (1st nos.), no. 7.
[30] Cal. Pat. 1377–81, p. 207.
[31] Chan. Inq. p.m. 13 Ric. II, no. 6.
[32] Ibid. 18 Ric. II, no. 7.
[33] Ibid. 4 Hen. IV, no. 39.
[34] G.E.C. Complete Peerage.
[35] Chan. Inq. p.m. 9 Hen. IV, no. 31.
[36] G.E.C. Complete Peerage.
[37] Chan. Inq. p.m. 19 Hen. VI, no. 30.
[38] Ibid. 25 Hen. VI, no. 29, 30.
[39] G.E.C. Complete Peerage.
[40] Chan. Inq. p.m. 32 Hen. VI, no. 26.
[41] Ibid. 3 Edw. IV, no. 30; G.E.C. Complete Peerage.
[42] Cal. Pat. 1461–7, p. 179.
[43] G.E.C. Peerage.
[44] Cal. Pat. 1467–77, p. 22. A grant was made to him in lieu of this one in 1475 during Lord Beaumont's second attainder (ibid. pp. 530–1).
[45] Chan. Inq. p.m. 15 Edw. IV, no. 33.
[46] G.E.C. Complete Peerage. [47] Ibid.
[48] Chan. Inq. p.m. (Ser. 2), xxiv, 62.
[49] Ibid.; Harl. MS. 756, fol. 19.
[50] L. and P. Hen. VIII, iii (1), 1379 (26).
[51] Chan. Inq. p.m. (Ser. 2), xciii, 80.
[52] Pat. 13 Hen. VIII, pt. i, m. 20.
[53] Ibid.
[54] Ibid. 5 Edw. VI, pt. iv, m. 27.
[55] Ibid.; Chan. Inq. p.m. (Ser. 2), xciii, 80.
[56] Feet of F. Herts. Mich. 6 Edw. VI.
[57] Ibid. Trin. 18 Eliz.

conveyed it in 1813 to Samuel Smith, lord of the manor of Woodhall, with which manor it has since been united.[58]

The manor of Watton possessed a mill in 1086,[59] which in 1324 was valued at 13s. 4d.[60] It is mentioned in a conveyance in 1651,[61] and is still working.

Robert Aguillon obtained a grant of free warren in 1248.[62] The right to hold a fair yearly on the vigil, feast and morrow of the Nativity of the Blessed Virgin (7–9 September) was granted to Robert Aguillon in 1248.[63]

King Edgar gave 4½ hides in Watton to the abbey of Westminster,[64] which grant was confirmed by Edward the Confessor.[65] Of this land, which is reckoned in the Domesday Book as 5 hides, 1 hide was held by the abbot himself[66]; 2 hides were held of the abbot by Aluric Blac, together with half a hide held by Almar, a man of Aluric (which was perhaps the added half-hide)[67]; and 1½ hides were held by Goduin of the abbot.[68] Before 1086 this Westminster estate had become broken up. The hide held by the abbot remained in his possession,[69] and was afterwards united to the manor of Stevenage,[70] the chief manor of the Abbot of Westminster in Hertfordshire. Goduin's 1½ hides should have reverted to the abbey after his death, but his widow put herself by force under Eddeva the Fair, who was in possession of the land 'on the day when King Edward was living and died.' It was granted by William the Conqueror to Count Alan,[71] who was also lord of Great Munden, and hence seems to have become permanently attached to that manor.[72] Aluric Blac, although he held his land in Watton of the Abbot of Westminster, was at the same time the man of Archbishop Stigand, and hence it happened, as in Datchworth, that Archbishop Lanfranc annexed his 2½ hides in Watton and was holding them in 1086, with Anschitil de Ros as tenant under him.[73]

It seems impossible to trace any connexion between these holdings and the manor of *WOODHALL*. This seems to have been held of the lords of the neighbouring manor of Benington[74] (q.v.). In 1278 Alexander de Balliol, lord of Benington, claimed liberties in his manor of Watton.[75]

In the 12th century the sub-tenants of the manor appear to have been a family of Watton. There was a Ralph de Watton, whose son Robert succeeded, and settled his 'vill of Wattun' on his wife Katherine in dower, some time before 1158.[76] 'Selidus' de Watton is mentioned in 1166[77] and Gilbert de Watton in 1207,[78] both of whom were perhaps sub-tenants. After this the manor passed to John de Tuwe or Teu, who was holding it in 1248, and was in that year accused of obstructing a way in Watton by making a ditch where the road was accustomed to be.[79] He was succeeded before 1303

WATTON PLACE : BACK VIEW

[58] Chan. Inq. p.m. (Ser. 2), ccxcvii, 149; ccccii, 144; Ct. of Wards, Feod. Surv. 17; Close, 1 Anne, pt. ix, no. 8; Recov. R. Mich. 1 Anne, rot. 120; Hil. 15 Geo. III, rot. 387; Mich. 20 Geo. III, rot. 487. [59] *V.C.H. Herts.* i, 342.
[60] Chan. Inq. p.m. 17 Edw. II, no. 39; see ibid. 14 Edw. I, no. 16; 3 Edw. III, no. 66.
[61] Recov. R. East. 1651, no. 66.
[62] *Cal. Chart. R.* 1226–57, p. 329.
[63] Ibid.
[64] Dugdale, *Mon.* i, 292.
[65] Ibid. 294; Cott. Chart. vi, 2.
[66] *V.C.H. Herts.* i, 313.
[67] Ibid. 305a. [68] Ibid. 319.
[69] Ibid. 313.
[70] Ct. R. portf. 120, no. 53.
[71] *V.C.H. Herts.* i, 319.
[72] Ct. R. portf. 178, no. 8, 9, 10, 17.
[73] *V.C.H. Herts.* i, 305a.
[74] *Feud. Aids,* ii, 429, 436; Chan. Inq. p.m. 18 Edw. II, no. 62; *Cal. Close,* 1323–7, p. 296; Chan. Inq. p.m. 8 Hen. V, no. 78; 13 Hen. VI, no. 11; 31 Hen. VI, no. 27; (Ser. 2), ccxcvii, 149; ccccii, 144; *V.C.H. Herts.* i, 305.
[75] *Plac. de Quo Warr.* (Rec. Com.), 281.
[76] Doc. at Westminster, press 17, shelf 4, box 85, no. 4737. Peter and Robert de Valognes (see Benington) are witnesses to this document, which points to the 'vill' mentioned being the manor later known as Woodhall. It is not dated, but this Peter de Valognes died about 1158 and was succeeded by his brother Robert.
[77] Pipe R. 12 Hen. II (Pipe R. Soc.), 127.
[78] *Abbrev. Plac.* (Rec. Com.), 56.
[79] Assize R. 318, m. 2; *Testa de Nevill* (Rec. Com.), 271. Mr. Round states that John de Tuwe was holding as early as 1236.

A HISTORY OF HERTFORDSHIRE

by Mabel de Tuwe,[80] probably his daughter. In 1308 she conveyed the reversion of the manor to Philip de Peletot,[81] who was still holding it in 1346,[82] and died in 1361.[83] Philip is said to have had a daughter Katherine, who married, first, Ralph le Boteler (by whom she had a son Philip), and secondly Edmund Bardolf.[84] Edmund Bardolf and his wife Katherine were holding Woodhall in 1372,[85] when the manor was claimed by Elizabeth Peletot, as daughter of Adomar, son of Philip de Peletot,[86] but there seems to have been a defect in her title, as the manor passed to Philip Boteler, the son of Katherine. In 1382 Philip received an exemption for life from being put on juries, &c., and from being made mayor, sheriff, escheator, or other minister of the king against his will.[87] He died in 1420, and his eldest son Edward dying a few weeks after, Woodhall came to his second son Philip,[88] who came of age in 1435.[89] Philip died in 1453, and his widow Elizabeth immediately married Laurence Cheyney and held the manor with him until her death, when it came to her son John Boteler.[90] John was succeeded by Philip Boteler, presumably his son, in 1514,[91] who in turn was succeeded by his son John in 1545.[92] From John's son, Sir Philip, Woodhall passed in 1607 to his grandson Robert Boteler, son of an intervening Philip who died during his father's lifetime.[93] Robert died in 1622, leaving a daughter Jane and a brother Sir John.[94] John Boteler succeeded,[95] and the lord of the manor in 1700 was Philip Boteler,[96] his son. The last-named Philip died in 1712 without issue, and his estates passed to John Boteler, the son of his great-uncle John.[97] From John Boteler Woodhall came to his grandson John Palmer Boteler,[98] who sold it to Sir Thomas Rumbold. After the death of the latter Woodhall was purchased in 1793 by Paul Bendfield, after whose bankruptcy it was sold, and acquired in 1801 by Samuel Smith,[99] who died in 1834.[100] His great-grandson Mr. Abel Henry Smith is the present lord of the manor.

BOTELER of Woodhall. *Gules a fesse checky argent and sable between six crosslets or.*

SMITH of Woodhall. *Or a cheveron cotised between three demi-griffons sable.*

CROWBOROUGH (Croubery, Crobberewe, xiii cent.; Crobbergh, Crowbergh, Crebborogh, xv cent.; Crowbury, xvii cent.) was held of the lords of the manor of Benington for the service of a quarter of a knight's fee. Alexander de Balliol claimed liberties there as at Woodhall in 1278.[1] In 1266 the sub-tenant of Crowborough was Alice de Rivers, who in that year settled it on herself for life, with remainder to her daughter Christine.[2] In 1270 Christine de Rivers conveyed the remainder of the manor after her death to Robert de Graveley,[3] who had a grant of free warren in 1292[4] and was holding it in 1303.[5] He died before 1311, his lands passing to his widow Beatrice de Graveley,[6] who in 1329 conveyed Crowborough to Thomas Bardolf,[7] who seems to have joined it to his manor of Watton and paid Beatrice an annuity of 66s. 8d.[8] He was succeeded by his son John Bardolf, who in 1340 granted the manor of Crowborough to his brother Edmund for life.[9] Edmund was still holding it in 1346,[10] but after his death it reverted to the heirs of John Bardolf, being held by his son William.[11] After the death of Agnes, widow of William Bardolf, in 1403[12] Crowborough passed to a younger branch of the family; probably William Bardolf settled it on a younger son, for in 1384–5 he had granted it to trustees, from whom his widow Agnes held it in dower.[13] In 1405 it was held by another William Bardolf,[14] and in 1428 by Edmund Bardolf.[15] Edmund Bardolf, apparently grandson and successor of the latter,[16] died about 1472, bequeathing to his wife Margery 'certain rooms at his manor of Crowborough where she can bake bread and brew ale.' He left a son Henry and a grandson George, the son of Henry.[17] In 1562 Edmund Bardolf, perhaps a son or grandson of the last-named George, conveyed the manor to Sir John Boteler[18] of Watton Woodhall, after which date Crowborough followed the descent of that manor.[19] In 1702 Philip Boteler exchanged the site of Crowborough Hall (which is still marked by the moats near Watton Green) for the old rectory-house [20] (see advowson). Apparently, however, the manor was kept by Philip Boteler, for it appears in the Boteler family as late as 1780.[21] It apparently passed later to Mrs. Abel Smith (see advowson).

WATTON HALL, or *WATKIN'S HALL*, is an estate which first appears about 1540. The first recorded owner is Thomas Munden, whose

---

[80] Feud. Aids, ii, 429.
[81] Feet of F. Herts. 1 Edw. II, no. 10.
[82] Feud. Aids, ii, 436.
[83] Monum. Inscr.
[84] Clutterbuck, Hist. of Herts. ii, 473.
[85] Wrottesley, Ped. from the Plea R. 107.
[86] Ibid. [87] Cal. Pat. 1381–5, p. 149.
[88] Chan. Inq. p.m. 8 Hen. V, no. 78.
[89] Ibid. 14 Hen. VI, no. 49; 13 Hen. VI, no. 11. The Feud. Aids of 1438 (ii, 448) give John Cheyney as the holder of Woodhall. Doubtless he was guardian during Philip's minority.
[90] Chan. Inq. p.m. 31 Hen. VI, no. 27.
[91] Monum. Inscr.
[92] Chan. Inq. p.m. (Ser. 2), lxxiii, 88.
[93] Ibid. ccxcvii, 149.
[94] Ibid. ccccii, 144.
[95] Chan. Proc. Eliz. Bb 5, no. 11; Recov. R. Hil. 21 Jas. I, rot. 19; Cal.

S. P. Dom. 1631–3, p. 78; Recov. R. Mich. 16 Chas. II, rot. 56.
[96] Chauncy, Hist. of Herts. 332.
[97] Salmon, Hist. of Herts. 218.
[98] Recov. R. Mich. 20 Geo. III, rot. 487.
[99] Clutterbuck, Hist. of Herts. ii, 475.
[100] Cussans, Hist. of Herts. Broadwater Hund. 181.
[1] Plac. de Quo Warr. (Rec. Com.), 281; Ct. R. portf. 177, no. 8–11; Chan. Inq. p.m. 4 Hen. IV, no. 39. The Feud. Aids of 1303 and 1346 (ii, 429 and 436) give Hugo and John de Bibbesworth as the overlords. As this family belonged to Kimpton it would seem that this is an error.
[2] Feet of F. Herts. 50 Hen. III, no. 582, 584. [3] Ibid. 54 Hen. III, no. 627.
[4] Cal. Chart. R. 1257–1300, p. 421.
[5] Feud. Aids, ii, 429.

[6] Cal. Close, 1307–13, p. 317.
[7] Feet of F. Herts. 3 Edw. III, no. 31.
[8] Chan. Inq. p.m. 3 Edw. III, no. 66.
[9] Cal. Pat. 1340–3, p. 17.
[10] Feud. Aids, ii, 436.
[11] Close, 8 Ric. II, m. 32 d.
[12] Chan. Inq. p.m. 4 Hen. IV, no. 39.
[13] Ibid.; Close, 8 Ric. II, m. 32 d.
[14] Cal. Pat. 1405–8, p. 89.
[15] Feud. Aids, ii, 448.
[16] Early Chan. Proc. bdle. 41, no. 27.
[17] Will, P.C.C. 6 Wattys.
[18] Feet of F. Herts. Mich. 4 & 5 Eliz.
[19] Chan. Inq. p.m. (Ser. 2), ccxcvii, 149; ccccii, 144; Com. Pleas D. Enr. Mich. 15 Chas. I, m. 8; Recov. R. Mich. 1 Anne, rot. 120.
[20] Priv. Act, 4 & 5 Anne, cap. 5.
[21] Recov. R. Hil. 15 Geo. III, rot. 387; Mich. 20 Geo. III, rot. 487.

daughter and heir Elizabeth married Robert Burgoyn.[22] The latter is mentioned in 1540,[23] and was holding Watton Hall, with his wife Elizabeth, in 1543.[24] In 1547, his son and heir Robert being a minor, the custody of his lands was granted to Lord Rich.[25] In 1615 the 'manor' was held by Robert's son, Roger Burgoyn,[25] who was succeeded before 1626 by his son John Burgoyn.[27] John was living in 1634, and had three sons,[28] but by 1636 from a date and initials I.M. on an old beam inserted in the present house it would appear to have passed to the Miles family, as it was in the possession of John Miles in 1719.[29] From John Miles it went to William Miles before 1731.[30] In 1788 it was held by Samuel Rogers and Jane his wife.[31] It is now a farm-house.

A water mill [32] and free fishery [33] are mentioned as pertaining to this estate.

The church of ST. ANDREW AND CHURCH ST. MARY stands on rising ground to the south-west of the village, and is built of flint rubble with stone dressings. It consists of a chancel, north chapel, nave, north and south aisles and porches and a west tower, all of a 15th-century rebuilding. In 1851 the church was restored throughout by the late Mr. Abel Smith.[31]

The original church was entirely obliterated by the 15th-century rebuilding. The east window of the chancel and the two windows in the south wall are each of three lights with tracery in a two-centred head, but very few of the stones are old. A door between them is modern, as are also the chancel arch and the arcade of three bays opening to the modern north chapel. Below the eastern of the two south windows is a 15th-century piscina, in one range with three sedilia of the 15th century, with cinquefoiled canopies and cusped spandrels. All are much restored.

The nave arcades are of the 13th century and are of four bays with two-centred arches of two moulded orders, supported on piers of four shafts separated by hollows and having moulded capitals and bases. The two arcades are almost exactly alike in detail. At the north-east and south-east angles are stair turrets to the roof, which also served as rood-stairs ; only that on the south side is accessible from the nave. Above on each side are the doors opening from the stairs to the rood loft. The turrets are carried up beyond the nave parapet in an octagonal form, and that on the south is embattled, while the northern one is plain.

The clearstory has on each side four much restored two-light windows of the 15th century. The north aisle has a modern arch at the east end opening into the north chapel, in the north wall three three-light traceried windows, and in the west wall a two-light window, all much restored. The north door and another small door to the east of it are both modern. The north porch, of two stages, is of the 15th century, but all the detail is renewed, and the straight stair and the parvise are also modern. The south aisle has an east window of three lights, and the remaining windows are like those of the north aisle. The south doorway, with a two-centred arch of two wave-moulded orders, is of the 15th century. The south porch was wholly rebuilt in the 19th century.

The west tower opens to the nave by a 15th-century arch of three moulded orders. The tower is of three stages with an embattled parapet ; it has a stair turret at the south-west and two square buttresses at each angle. The turret is carried up above the parapet and is itself embattled. At the foot are an interior and an exterior doorway, both with four-centred heads. The west doorway and the three-light window above it are so much restored as to be almost wholly modern. The bell-chamber windows, which are of two lights, are also much restored.

There is a brass in the chancel of a priest in a quire cope of mid-15th-century date. In the north chapel is a brass of a knight in armour under an ogee-shaped canopy, with a marginal inscription '+ icy gist Philip Peletoot chevaler qe morust le XIIII | jour de Aust lan de | Grace mill CCCLXJ | .' Above the canopy are two shields, the dexter paly and a chief indented. The other shield is plain, a modern restoration. The upper part of the figure and the inscription were restored in 1851. Also in the north chapel are the following brasses : a knight in armour, said to be John Boteler, who died in 1514, with five shields of arms ; Boteler quartering Kilpeck (twice), and Boteler impaling Tyrrel, Acton and (?) Belknap, his three wives ; a civilian of late 15th-century date ; and one to Richard Boteler of Stapleford, 1614, with Anna his wife, daughter of John Mynne of Hertingfordbury, 1619, and their only daughter Elizabeth wife of Rowland Graveley of Graveley, 1600. This brass has an inscription and two shields of Boteler and Graveley. A third shield of Mynne is lost.

At the east end of the nave is a much mutilated brass of a lady with the lower part of the figure missing ; there are indents of her husband, sons and daughters, and two brass shields, the one of Drury, and the other Kilpeck quartering Boteler. The fragment of the inscription reads '. . . . Knyght, late Lorde of Wodhall whyche deceassed th . . . .'

In the north aisle is a brass with the headless figure of a civilian of the late 15th century, and the indents of two figures and of a marginal inscription.

In the south aisle is a brass of a lady with a shield of Bardolf. This is only a portion of the brass of Sir Edmund Bardolf (1438) and Edmund Bardolf his kinsman and Joan wife of Edmund.

In the chapel are also a monumental slab with a marginal inscription in French to Sir Robert de Graveley of 14th-century date, and an alabaster slab, 8 ft. 2 in. long, incised and inlaid with figures of Sir John Boteler of Woodhall, in armour (the date of his death not filled in), his two wives, Elizabeth, who died in 1471, and Constance, who died in 14—, his eight children, and an inscription and three shields of the arms of Boteler, Kilpeck, and Downhall. In the chancel is a floor slab to John Saywell, rector, died 1693, and in the north aisle is a 14th-century floor slab to Roger de Larebi.

---

[22] Visit. Beds. (Harl. Soc. xix), 87–8.
[23] L. and P. Hen. VIII, xvi, 86 ; xvii, 13.
[24] Feet of F. Herts. East. 35 Hen. VIII.
[25] Pat. 1 Edw. VI, pt. i, m. 29.
[26] Feet of F. Herts. Trin. 13 Jas. I.
[27] Recov. R. Mich. 2 Chas. I, rot. 98.
[28] Visit. Beds. (Harl. Soc. xix), 87–8.
[29] Feet of F. Herts. Hil. 5 Geo. I.
[30] Recov. R. Hil. 4 Geo. II, rot. 290.
[31] Ibid. Trin. 28 Geo. III, rot. 147.
[32] Feet of F. Herts. East. 35 Hen. VIII.
[33] Recov. R. Mich. 2 Chas. I, rot. 98.
[34] The internal dimensions are : chancel, 38 ft. 6 in. by 22 ft. 6 in. ; nave, 54 ft. 6 in. by 22 ft. ; aisles, 9 ft. wide ; and tower, 14 ft. by 13 ft.

A HISTORY OF HERTFORDSHIRE

There are a few important monuments of more recent date. In the chancel chapel is one to Sir Thomas Rumbold, formerly Governor of Fort St. George, who for his eminent services under the East India Company was created a baronet. He died 11 November 1791. There are also tablets to his two sons Thomas Henry and Anwaer Henry Rumbold; to their mother Joanna, daughter of Bishop Law of Carlisle; and to Captain William Richard Rumbold, who carried the Pondicherry dispatches and the colours of the fortress to the king. He died 14 June 1786.

In the manor chapel are many monuments to the Smiths of Woodhall with their arms. In the south aisle is the monument of Philip Boteler, only son of Sir John Boteler, kt., who died 7 May 1712, aged thirty-one, and of his cousin and heir John Boteler of Woodhall, who died 17 July 1774, aged ninety. Above is a shield of Boteler impaling Ettrick, Argent a lion and a chief gules, for Philip Boteler and his wife Elizabeth Crane Ettrick, who died childless.

In the chapel is preserved a large iron-bound chest of late 16th or early 17th-century date.

The bells are six in number, the treble being by J. Briant, 1785; the second by George Chandler, 1682; the third by the same maker and of the same date was recast by Bowell in 1907; the fourth by J. Briant, 1785; the fifth by C. & J. Mears, 1852; and the sixth by Thomas Mears, 1841.

The plate consists of two chalices and two patens of 1855 and a flagon of 1860.

The registers date from 1560 and are contained in four books: (i) baptisms, burials, and marriages from 1560 to 1737; (ii) baptisms and burials from 1737 to 1812, marriages from 1737 to 1753; (iii) marriages from 1754 to 1806; (iv) marriages from 1807 to 1812.

ADVOWSON The advowson is first mentioned in 1304, when it was in the hands of Mabel de Tuwe,[35] who in 1308 conveyed it with the manor of Woodhall to Philip de Peletot.[36] The living is a rectory. It continued to descend with the manor of Watton Woodhall until the 19th century.[37] After the death of Paul Bendfield in 1801 it was sold separately from the manor to Alexander Ellice,[38] who presented in 1804.[39] His son William Ellice presented in 1809,[40] and John Corfield for one turn in 1814,[41] after which the advowson was acquired by Abel Smith,[42] lord of the manor of Woodhall, and has since remained with the manor. In 1702 the parsonage and certain of the glebe lands were exchanged with Philip Boteler for Crowborough Hall and the premises and lands pertaining. The old house lay east of the River Beane. The glebe still forms part of the Woodhall Park estate and is called the Springs or the Rector's Springs. The new site, which adjoined the church-yard, was more convenient, as before, 'when the waters are out and overflow the banks of the river there, which runs between the parsonage and the church aforesaid, the minister cannot pass over the same to go to the church.'[43] The second rectory, which stood about 100 yards north-west of the church, was pulled down about the middle of the 19th century and a new rectory built close by. This house, which is called by the old name of Crowbury (Crowborough), was bought in 1898 by the trustees of the Woodhall estate, and is now the residence of Mrs. Abel Smith. The present rectory was built with part of the proceeds of the sale.[43a]

In 1423 the advowson was in the king's gift by reason of the minority of Sir Philip Boteler's heir,[44] and again in 1635-6.[45] Dr. Halsey, the incumbent by this presentation, in 1638 brought a suit against Sir John Boteler, concerning which the king wrote to the Master of the Court of Wards: 'We were informed that the church suffered much by the indirect courses held by the Botelers, patrons, in obtaining leases of the parsonage house, glebe and tithes, at an undervalue of the incumbents whom they presented, and therefore we resolved to redeem the church from that pressure, and when the church became void determined to bestow the same on Dr. Halsey divers months before our presentation passed. This being the case you are first to preserve the rules and orders of your Court for our better service, and next if you still find that such indirect courses have been held by patrons, if any advantage has thereby happened to us, you are not to remit it.'[46]

In 1644-5 the inhabitants of Watton petitioned Sir John Boteler not to bestow the living on the curate, 'who is not a quiet and peaceable man, and who will neither bury or christen or administer the Sacrament.' Sir John was, however, at that time imprisoned at Peterhouse for malignancy.[47] In 1734 Hamond Cross presented for one turn,[48] and in 1781 John Stockwell.[49] Edward Bickersteth, who was instituted by Mr. Abel Smith in 1830, was the compiler of the *Christian Psalmody*, on the basis of which his son, the Rev. E. H. Bickersteth, formed the collection of hymns known as the *Hymnal Companion*.

There was a church house connected with the church of Watton, of which mention is made in 1504, when a chamber in it was provided by Sir John Boteler for a priest.[50]

Whempstead Chantry or Free Chapel, dedicated in honour of the Blessed Mary, was founded by Henry Mayor of London late in the 12th or early in the 13th century. He endowed it with a carucate of land of the value of 40s. yearly.[51] There are references to a chapel in the parish of Watton in the episcopal registers during the 13th and 14th centuries, the incumbent of which was called a warden, who also served the parish church. In 1261 this chapel was said to be without cure of souls.[51a] Sir Robert Aguillon by his will (? 1286) left a tenterground in London to the chapel in his fief of Watton,

---

[35] Linc. Epis. Reg. Mem. Bp. Dalderby, fol. 235 d.
[36] Feet of F. Herts. East. 1 Edw. II, no. 10.
[37] Close, 14 Ric. II, m. 8 d.; Chan. Inq. p.m. 13 Hen. VI, no. 11; (Ser. 2), lxxiii, 88; Recov. R. Hil. 21 Jas. I, rot. 19; Mich. 1 Anne, rot. 120; Hil. 15 Geo. III, rot. 387; Mich. 20 Geo. III, rot. 487; *Clergy List*, 1908.
[38] Cussans, *Hist. of Herts. Broadwater Hund.* p. 187.
[39] Inst. Bks. (P.R.O.).
[40] Ibid.
[41] Ibid.
[42] Ibid.
[43] Priv. Act, 4 & 5 Anne, cap. 5.
[43a] Information from Mr. A. H. Smith.
[44] *Cal. Pat.* 1422-9, p. 160.
[45] *Cal. S. P. Dom.* 1635-6, p. 252 (2).
[46] Ibid. 1638-9, p. 60.
[47] *Hist. MSS. Com. Rep.* vi, App. viii, 43a.
[48] Bacon, *Liber Regis*; Inst. Bks. (P.R.O.).
[49] Ibid.
[50] Will, P.C.C. 17 Holgrave.
[51] *Rot. Hund.* (Rec. Com.), i, 192.
[51a] Linc. Epis. Reg. Buckingham Mem. pt. i and ii; ibid. Gravesend.

WATTON CHURCH FROM THE NORTH-EAST

WATTON CHURCH: THE NAVE LOOKING EAST

in relief of the poor.[52] It is uncertain if reference was made to this chapel in the licence, dated 1390, to build a chapel in a place called 'la Lowe,' in the parish of Watton, to the honour of the Blessed Virgin. The advowson of the chantry remained vested in the lords of the manor of Bardolf[52a] until the forfeiture of that manor by William Viscount Beaumont in 1461, when it escheated to the Crown.[53] In 1521 it was granted, together with the reversion of the manor, to Sir Wistan Brown.[54] The chapel was, however, allowed to fall into disuse by Sir Wistan's son and successor. The last incumbent, one Goldingham, a layman, died about 1547, 'after whose decease John Brown being patron of the said chapel did enter and the profit thereof took and enjoyed to his own use, and between Michaelmas and Hollomas hath felled and sold ten acres of wood.' By the time of the survey of 1548 the chantry was 'utterlie decayed,' and was farmed out with its lands and appurtenances to Joan Curtes, a widow, for the rent of £4 8s. 4d.[55] Upon the dissolution of the chantry in the same year the site and lands, including the woods of 'Bushey Layes and Comes wood,' were granted to William Twisden and John Brown and their heirs.[56] In 1584 Whempstead, still called the 'free chapel,' was conveyed by Edward Walgrave to John Harvey,[57] who died seised of it in 1606.[58] He left a widow Clemence, who enjoyed the profits during her lifetime, after which Whempstead came to William Harvey, his second son, upon whom it was entailed.[59] William died in 1621, leaving it to his third son William, with remainder in equal division to his four remaining children.[60] William Harvey the younger died without issue in 1626,[61] and his estates were in consequence divided between his brothers John and Thomas Harvey and his sisters Mary Storer and Elizabeth Harvey. Thomas Harvey and William Storer conveyed their fourths to Sir John Boteler.[62]

A capital messuage called Whempstead appears in 1592 in the possession of John Scroggs, who died seised of it in that year. He left a son Edward.[63]

A portion of the estate belonging to Whempstead Chapel, called Olivers, was apparently kept by the Botelers after the dissolution of the chantry and did not go with the rest of the lands.[64] It presumably became absorbed in the manor of Watton.

A portion of the buildings formerly belonging to the chantry was remaining in 1877,[65] but has since been pulled down. Near the site is Lowfield Grove (see the name La Lowe above) and adjoining this was a field called Lowfield.[66]

Meeting-places for Protestant Dissenters were registered in Watton from 1697. In 1820 a Wesleyan chapel was certified,[67] and there is at the present time a Wesleyan chapel in the parish.

CHARITIES

The Free School, founded in 1662 by Maurice Thompson and Sir William Thompson, kt., and augmented by will of Abraham Crosland, 1703 (see article on Schools).[68]

This foundation is now regulated by scheme of the Board of Education, 30 April 1906.

The endowments now consist of 8 a. 3 r. 22 p. of the annual rental value of £11 10s. and £688 5s. 10d. consols, invested in 1857 with the official trustees and producing £17 4s. yearly.

The scheme includes appointment of trustees, and provides for the application of the income in prizes for boys and girls at or leaving public elementary schools, a payment of not more than £5 a year in provision of books for a school library, and for exhibitions at a secondary school, and in the maintenance of bursaries, also for the instruction of children in the theory and practice of gardening.

In 1867 Lady Susan Smith erected almshouses for the use of three aged widows and as many widowers, which were supported by Mr. Abel Smith.

WELWYN

Welge (xi cent.); Wyluwes, Welewes, Weluen (xiv cent.).

The parish of Welwyn has an area of 3,064 acres, of which 1,028 acres are arable land, 1,160 acres permanent grass and 613½ acres wood.[1] It is divided into two by the River Mimram or Maran, which flows through it from north-west to south-east. The height of the parish above the ordnance datum is from 200 ft. to 250 ft. in the centre, where the village is situated; to the north, east and south-west of the village are three hills occupied by the estates of Danesbury, Lockleys, and the Frythe. The highest ground is on the south-west, where an altitude of over 400 ft. is reached. The most northern part of the parish, near Knebworth station, is called the Gun.

The town of Welwyn is situated on the Great North Road, 4½ miles north of Hatfield. At the north of the village the road divides, one branch running north-west through Codicote to Hitchin, and the other north-east to Stevenage. The church of St. Mary is situated at the north end of the town. At the south-east of the churchyard is a 17th-century two-storied building, probably originally the church house, afterwards used as the poor-house and now as the police station. It is partly of timber and plaster, with an overhanging upper story. Under the projection of this story is the large parish fire-hook formerly used for tearing off the thatch of cottages in case of fire. The houses in the town are for the most part of brick of the 18th and 19th centuries. The settlement here is early, as a rich burial of the late Celtic period has

---

[52] Information from Mr. J. H. Round.
[52a] Chan. Inq. p.m. 13 Ric. II, no. 6; Fine R. 18 Ric. II; Chan. Inq. p.m. 4 Hen. IV, no. 39.
[53] Cal. Pat. 1461–7, p. 223; 1467–77, p. 176.
[54] Pat. 13 Hen. VIII, pt. i, m. 20.
[55] Chant. Cert. 17, no. 8.
[56] Pat. 2 Edw. VI, pt. iv.

[57] Feet of F. Herts. East. 26 Eliz.
[58] Chan. Inq. p.m. (Ser. 2), cccvii, 82.
[59] Ibid. ccclxxxvii, 113. [60] Ibid.
[61] Ibid. dccxlvii, 135.
[62] Com. Pleas D. Enr. East. 8 Chas. I, m. 11; Trin. 12 Chas. I, m. 3.
[63] Chan. Inq. p.m. (Ser. 2), ccl, 69; ccclvii, 10.
[64] Ibid. ccccii, 144; Ct. of Wards

Feod. Surv. 17; Chan. Inq. p.m. (Ser. 2), ccxcvii, 149.
[65] Cussans, Hist. of Herts. Broadwater Hund. 186.
[66] Information from Mr. Abel Smith.
[67] Urwick, op. cit. 620–1.
[68] V.C.H. Herts. ii, 100.
[1] Information from Bd. of Agric. (1905).

been discovered near to Lockleys and a Roman villa in the garden of the rectory.

Danesbury is the property of Colonel A. M. Blake, C.B., D.L., J.P., and is situated in a park of about 200 acres. Lockleys is an 18th-century red brick house with a park, the property and residence of Mrs. Neall. The Frythe, a modern brick gabled house with extensive grounds, is the residence of the Misses Wilshere. Sherrard's House, to the south of the Frythe, is the residence of Mr. Robert D. Balfour. In the north of the parish is the hamlet of Woolmer Green, with Mardleybury to the east and Mardley Heath to the west. Welch's Farm lies about a mile south. Harmer Green is situated in an eastern extension of the parish, and part of Burnham Green is included in a detached part of Welwyn parish about a mile north-east.

There was a chalybeate spring in the parish, referred to by Camden as being in the corner of the old rectory garden.[2] An attempt was made in the 18th century under the auspices of Dr. Young to make Welwyn a watering-place. Assembly rooms were built, which enjoyed a short vogue, and which still survive as tenements.[2a] The spring has been covered over, the garden having been converted into a timber-yard, but is believed still to exist.[3]

The main line of the Great Northern railway runs through the parish; the railway station is situated rather more than a mile to the south-east of the town.

In 1882 a detached portion of the parish was transferred to Digswell for civil purposes.[4] The subsoil of the parish is chalk, except for a small district in the east, where it gives way to Woolwich and Reading Beds. There are a number of chalk-pits in the north of the parish and some gravel-pits in the centre. The inclosure award was made in 1819, the Authorizing Act being dated 1810. Both are in the custody of the clerk of the peace.[5]

In the time of Edward the Confessor MANORS WELWYN was held of the king in frankalmoign by the priest of the vill, and belonged to the church of Welwyn.[6] The same man held it in 1086 'in alms' of King William, when it was assessed at 1 hide. It was stated at that time that William Blach, a man of the Bishop of Bayeux, occupied 12 acres to the king's injury.[7] The manor of Welwyn has been held ever since by the rector of the parish.[8] The rector becomes lord of the manor upon his institution to the living.[9] In 1275 the parson claimed view of frankpledge, gallows, and amendment of the assize of bread and ale.[10] Manorial courts are still occasionally held.

A water mill pertained to the manor in 1461,
and in 1469 Thomas Dene of Ayot Montfitchet broke and entered it to the rector's damage.[11] In 1471 Thomas Payn the miller was fined for obstructing the course of the mill-stream and causing it to overflow the king's highway.[12] In 1463 John Porter, chaplain, and Thomas son of William Fyssh of Welwyn were presented as 'common fishers' for taking fish on the banks of the river and carrying them away without licence. In the following year the same chaplain was presented for making an 'unjust footpath' through Diggesmede.[13] In 1475 various people in the manor were fined for playing at dice and cards.[14]

In addition to this rectory manor there were others in Welwyn of which the early history is obscure. Mr. Round points out that in 1235–6 Geoffrey de Beauchamp held half a fee in 'Welewe' of Robert 'de Hirbeygin' (of Cainhoe) and that in 1346 both the quarter fees in Welwyn (one of which was Lockleys) are entered as held 'de baronie de Kaynho.' This holding he takes back to 1183, when 'Robert de Albeneio' gave 2½ marks that Baldwin 'Wach' might be summoned to warrant his wife 'de terra de Welewe.'[14a]

The manor of *LOCKLEYS* (Lockele, Lokkelebery, Lokley) was held in 1303 as a quarter fee of Agnes de Valence,[15] daughter of William and sister of Aylmer de Valence, Earl of Pembroke, to whom the overlordship came at her death about 1309.[16] After Aylmer's death in 1324,[17] Lockleys was granted in dower to his widow Mary, who obtained possession in 1325.[18] Aylmer's heirs were his nephew John de Hastings and his two nieces Elizabeth Talbot and Joan the wife of David de Strathbolgi.[19] Lockleys was assigned to Joan and David,[20] but it so happened that neither they nor their heirs obtained possession, for Mary de Valence lived until 1377, while David de Strathbolgi, grandson and heir of David and Joan, died without male issue in 1375.[21] The overlordship is found later vested in John of Gaunt, Duke of Lancaster, of whom Lockleys was held as of his manor of Hertingfordbury.[22] He was succeeded in 1399 by his son Henry, who in the same year became king as Henry IV,[23] and the overlordship of Lockleys with his other possessions thus came to the Crown, and the manor was subsequently held of the king.[24]

The first sub-tenant of Lockleys to be mentioned is Adam de Mandeville, who was connected with Welwyn in 1288,[25] and certainly held the quarter fee in 1303[26] and in 1325.[27] He seems to have been succeeded by William de Mandeville, whose son William conveyed the manor in 1340 to Sir Walter de Crek and his brother Master John de Crek, with

---

[2] Camden, *Brit.* (ed. Gough), i, 343.
[2a] Information from Rev. A. C. Headlam, D.D. References to the assembly rooms occur in Lord Chesterfield's letters.
[3] Information supplied by the Rev. P. M. Wathen.
[4] Divided Parishes Act, 1882.
[5] *Blue Bk. Incl. Awards*, 63.
[6] *V.C.H. Herts.* i, 343a.
[7] Ibid.
[8] Court Rolls from Edward I to the present day in the possession of Mr. A. C. Davidson, steward of the manor; *Abbrev. Plac.* (Rec. Com.), 45. It seems possible that some of the other estates mentioned in 1086 (*V.C.H. Herts.* i, 311b, 324a, 327b, 333a) became attached to it, as it is otherwise difficult to account for them.
[9] Information supplied by Mr. A. C. Davidson.
[10] *Rot. Hund.* (Rec. Com.), i, 192.
[11] Ct. R. *penes* Mr. A. C. Davidson.
[12] Ibid.
[13] Ibid.
[14] Ibid.
[14a] *Pipe R.* 27 Hen. II (Pipe R. Soc.), 125.
[15] *Feud. Aids*, ii, 429. In the 13th century Christiana de Mandeville, daughter of Gunnora de Valognes, and Robert Fitz Walter held certain fees in the honour of Valognes in 'Lockeley,' but this seems probably not to have been Lockleys in Welwyn (*Testa de Nevill* [Rec. Com.], 271b).
[16] Chan. Inq. p.m. 3 Edw. II, no. 37.
[17] G.E.C. *Complete Peerage*.
[18] *Cal. Close*, 1323–7, p. 267.
[19] G.E.C. *Complete Peerage*.
[20] Chan. Inq. p.m. 14 Ric. II, no. 139b.
[21] G.E.C. *Complete Peerage*. In 1346 Lockleys is said in *Feud. Aids*, ii, 436, to have been held of the barony of Cainhoe, but this is evidently a confusion with another quarter fee in Welwyn (see above).
[22] Duchy of Lanc. Misc. Bks. xiii, fol. 90 d.; Chan. Inq. p.m. 14 Ric. II, no. 51.
[23] G.E.C. *Complete Peerage*.
[24] Chan. Inq. p.m. (Ser. 2), lxiii, 61; lxxiii, 89.
[25] *Cal. Close*, 1279–88, p. 548.
[26] *Feud. Aids*, ii, 429.
[27] *Cal. Close*, 1323–7, p. 267.

BROADWATER HUNDRED
WELWYN

remainder to the heirs of Waker.[28] Sir Walter was holding it in 1346,[29] after which it passed to John Haggeford, son of Walter de Crek's sister Joan and Walter de Haggeford, who held in tail-male.[30] At this time the capital messuage was ruined and worth nothing and the land in a poor state.[31] John Haggeford died childless in 1373,[32] and the manor was granted by Edward III to his 'kinsman' and heir Edmund de Vauncy, who was the illegitimate son of Edmund de Vauncy, husband of Joan daughter of William de Crek, brother of Walter and John.[33] As he was a minor the custody of his lands was granted in 1374 to Robert de Bolthorp,[34] and later to John Pusy, who died before 1387, when he and his executors were charged with having committed waste in the manor and having diminished the buildings, woods and men thereon.[35] Edmund died in 1390 and was succeeded by his half-sister Joan daughter of Edmund de Vauncy the elder and wife of Thomas Prior.[36] Joan seems to have married secondly John Hore of Cambridge, who together with his wife conveyed Lockleys in 1415 to John Perient[37] of Digswell, in whose family it descended[38] in the same manner as Digswell (q.v.).

Upon the death of Thomas Perient in 1545[39] Lockleys was divided between his second and third daughters, Dorothy the wife of George Burgoyne, and Anne, who married Anthony Carleton.[40] In 1557 George and Dorothy Burgoyne conveyed their moiety of the manor to William Perient,[41] Dorothy's uncle,[42] who acquired the other half from Anthony and Anne Carleton in 1559,[43] and thus became possessed of the whole manor. William Perient sold Lockleys in 1564 to Henry Walter,[44] who in 1566 conveyed it to George Horsey,[45] husband of Mary Perient, the elder sister of Dorothy and Anne.[46] George Horsey died in 1587, and was succeeded by his son Ralph,[47] from whom the manor apparently passed to his brother Jasper Horsey,[48] for he, together with his wife and son Eustace Needham, conveyed Lockleys in 1624 to Edward Wingate.[49] The latter was succeeded by his son Edward before 1675,[50] whose son Ralph

WINGATE of Lockleys. *Sable a bend ermine cotised or between six martlets or.*

Wingate[51] was lord of the manor in 1698,[52] and sold it in 1715 to Edward Searle.[53]

Elizabeth daughter and heir of Edward Searle married Charles Gardiner, whose son Charles[54] was lord of the manor in 1815,[55] but sold it soon after to Sir George Shee, bart., who possessed it in 1821.[56] Sir George died in 1825,[57] his widow holding Lockleys until her death in 1838, when the manor passed to her daughter Letitia the wife of Robert Dering.[58] Their son Mr. George Edward Dering succeeded his father in 1859[59] and died in 1911, when he was succeeded by his daughter Mrs. Neall, who is now lady of the manor.

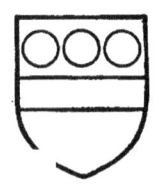

DERING. *Argent a fesse azure with three roundels gules in the chief.*

In the time of Edward the Confessor **MARDLEY** or **MARDLEYBURY** (Merdelai, xi cent.; Mardeleye, xiii to xiv cent.; Magdaleynbury, Mawdleynbury, xvi to xix cent.) was held by Alward, who was still holding it in 1086 of Robert Gernon. It was then assessed at 1 hide.[60] Robert Gernon also held the neighbouring manor of Ayot St. Peter, and the overlordship of Mardley presumably followed the descent of that manor[61] (q.v.).

The mesne overlordship belonged to the sub-tenants of Ayot St. Peter, Mardley being held of them for the service of 20s. and suit of court twice a year.[62] It seems to have followed the descent of the moiety of Ayot St. Peter known as Ayot Montfitchet.[63] Early in the 14th century lands forming part of the manor were held of the Abbot of Reading and of Henry Melksop of Datchworth.[64]

Alward de Mardley, sub-tenant of the manor in 1086,[65] was one of the Domesday inquisitors for Broadwater Hundred.[66] There is no record of his family and no further mention of a sub-tenant until 1288, when the manor was held by Philip de Mardley, perhaps a descendant of Alward. In that year Philip released his right in his lands in Welwyn to Robert Burnell,[67] lord of Ayot St. Peter. Philip had a daughter Pagana de Mardley,[68] but probably the manor did not come to her, for it was held soon afterwards by Adam de Twynham. He died seised of it about 1307.[69] His son Walter being a minor, the custody of his lands was granted to

---

[28] *Cal. Close*, 1339–41, p. 487.
[29] *Feud. Aids*, ii, 436.
[30] Chan. Inq. p.m. 13 Ric. II, no. 29.
[31] Ibid. 48 Edw. III (1st nos.), no. 34.
[32] Ibid.
[33] Ibid. 13 Ric. II, no. 6.
[34] Duchy of Lanc. Misc. Bks. xiii, fol. 90 d. [35] *Cal. Pat.* 1385–9, p. 320.
[36] Chan. Inq. p.m. 14 Ric. II, no. 51.
[37] Feet of F. Herts. Trin. 3 Hen. V, no. 18.
[38] Chan. Inq. p.m. (Ser. 2), lxiii, 61.
[39] Ibid. lxxiii, 89.
[40] Ibid.; *Visit. Herts.* (Harl. Soc. xxii), 157.
[41] Feet of F. Herts. Trin. 2 & 3 Phil. and Mary.
[42] Cussans, *Hist. of Herts. Broadwater Hund.* 253.
[43] Feet of F. Herts. East. 1 Eliz.
[44] Ibid. Trin. 6 Eliz.; Pat. 7 Eliz. pt. ii.
[45] Pat. 8 Eliz. pt. iv, m. 17; Feet of F. Herts. Hil. 9 Eliz.
[46] *Visit. Herts.* (Harl. Soc. xxii), 157.
[47] Ibid. 114; Com. Pleas D. Enr. Mich. 33 & 34 Eliz.
[48] *Visit. Herts.* (Harl. Soc. xxii), 114.
[49] Feet of F. Herts. Hil. 21 Jas. I.
[50] *Visit. Herts.* (Harl. Soc. xxii), 105;
Feet of F. Herts. East. 27 Chas. II.
[51] Salmon, *Hist. of Herts.* 204.
[52] Feet of F. Herts. Mich. 10 Will. III.
[53] Ibid. Mich. 2 Geo. I.
[54] Clutterbuck, *Hist. of Herts.* ii, 497.
[55] Feet of F. Herts. Hil. 55 Geo. III.
[56] Clutterbuck, *Hist. of Herts.* ii, 497.
[57] G.E.C. *Complete Baronetage.*
[58] Burke, *Landed Gentry.*
[59] Cussans, *Hist. of Herts. Broadwater Hund.* 210.
[60] *V.C.H. Herts.* i, 323a.
[61] See *Cal. Close*, 1279–88, p. 548; *Abbrev. Plac.* (Rec. Com.), 214.
[62] Chan. Inq. p.m. 35 Edw. I, no. 25; Chan. Inq. a.q.d. 16 Edw. II, no. 100. A manor of 'Welwys' or Welwyn appears among the possessions of the 1428 (Feet of F. Herts. 7 Hen. V, no. 39; De Banco R. Trin. 4 Hen. VI, m. 124).
[63] Inq. a.q.d. 16 Edw. II, no. 100; Chan. Inq. p.m. 2 Edw. III (2nd nos.), no. 23; 12 Edw. III (2nd nos.), no. 54*a*; 23 Edw. III (2nd nos.), no. 142; 33 Edw. III (1st nos.), no. 39.
[64] Ibid. 35 Edw. I, no. 25; 16 Edw. II, no. 100; 2 Edw. III (2nd nos.), no. 23.
[65] *V.C.H. Herts.* i, 323a.
[66] Cott. MS. Tib. A. vi, fol. 38.
[67] *Abbrev. Plac.* (Rec. Com.), 214; *Cal. Close*, 1279–88, p. 548.
[68] De Banco R. Mich. 15 Edw. II, m. 18.
[69] Chan. Inq. p.m. 35 Edw. I, no. 25.

167

A HISTORY OF HERTFORDSHIRE

William Bacon, king's yeoman, in 1308.[70] In 1316 Walter de Twynham granted to Roger de Luda or Louth one robe at the price of £1, to be paid yearly from the manor.[71] In 1318 he conveyed Mardley to Adam de Eglesfeld, who, however, died twelve weeks later and was succeeded by his brother John. John de Eglesfeld confirmed Walter's grant to Roger de Louth, and afterwards sold the manor to John de Sandale, who increased Roger's payment to 40s. John de Sandale was succeeded about 1320 by his kinsman and heir John de Sandale, who immediately conveyed Mardley to Bartholomew de Badlesmere.[72] Bartholomew was attainted for rebellion and hanged in 1322, but his widow Margaret, after having been imprisoned for a time in the Tower, was released and dower assigned to her.[73] This grant apparently included part of Mardley, for in 1332 Beatrice widow of John de Eglesfeld claimed from Margaret one third of the manor in dower.[74] The result of the claim is not recorded, nor is there evidence to show whether Beatrice had been holding the third since the death of her husband. Giles de Badlesmere, son of Bartholomew, obtained a reversal of his father's attainder in 1329 and livery of his lands in 1333[75]; he, however, died without issue in 1338, at which time the 40s. granted to Roger de Luda was still charged on the manor.[76] Giles's widow Elizabeth, who married secondly Hugh le Despenser, and thirdly, after 1349, Guy de Bryen, held Mardley until her death in 1359.[77] The manor was then assigned to Margaret youngest sister of Giles de Badlesmere and her husband John,[78] second Lord Tiptoft. Her eldest son John died in 1359. His heir was his brother Robert,[79] whose widow Margaret, after his death in 1372, held a third of Mardley in dower, and married secondly John Cheyney.[80] In 1374 John and Margaret Cheyney granted their third of the manor to Geoffrey Sightere,[81] but who was holding the remaining two-thirds at that time does not appear. Robert Tiptoft left three daughters—Margaret the wife of Roger Lord Scrope, Millicent wife of Stephen Scrope, and Elizabeth, who married Philip le Despenser,[82] but, as Mardley does not appear in the possession of either of these or of their descendants, it seems probable that there was a sale.

No further tenant is recorded until the second half

BADLESMERE. *Argent a fesse between two gimel bars gules.*

of the 15th century, when Mardley was held by one William Toppesfeld, who left it by will to his wife Jane for life (according to her own testimony), the reversion to be settled by her upon one of their children. Jane settled it upon her younger son Ralph, but the manor was claimed about 1470–3 by William Toppesfeld, her grandson, son of her elder son Thomas.[83] Complaint had been made shortly before by Ralph's two daughters and heirs, Margaret Bernard and Jane Toppesfeld, that this cousin William had 'by subtle means' entered the said manor.[84] Eventually, either as a result of this claim or upon the death of Margaret and Jane, the manor came to William Toppesfeld, for it was held by his daughter Elizabeth, who married Richard Garneys of Mendlesham.[85] Richard and Elizabeth conveyed Mardley in 1507 to Sir William Say,[86] among whose heirs it descended in the same manner as Westington in Ayot St. Peter[87] (q.v.), was forfeited to the Crown in 1539, and was granted together with the above manor to Sir Nicholas Throckmorton in 1546.[88] The latter sold Mardley, or Magdalenybury as it was then called, to Thomas Nicholls, a mercer of London, in 1555,[89] who sold it in the following year to John Forster.[90] John died seised of Mardley in 1558 and was succeeded, after the death of his widow Margery, by their son Humphrey,[91] who in 1563 conveyed the manor to Jasper and Antonia Warren.[92] The latter sold it in 1567 to John and Joan Spencer.[93] John Spencer settled Mardley on his wife Joan for her life, with remainder to their youngest son Henry Spencer, to whom it came upon Joan's death in 1599, although his elder brothers Robert and William seem to have retained portions of the estate.[94] Presumably Henry died without issue, for in 1616–17 his eldest brother Robert Spencer was seised of the 'liberty' of Mardley,[95] and his son Robert held parcels of the manor in 1632–3.[96] John Spencer was lord of the manor in 1697–8,[97] almost immediately after which it seems to have been sold to Sir William Lytton of Knebworth, who possessed it in 1700.[98] Mardleybury has since descended with the manor of Knebworth,[99] Lord Lytton being the present lord of the manor.

View of frankpledge is mentioned as pertaining to the manor in 1614.[100] William Lytton obtained a grant of free warren there in 1616.[1]

The FRYTHE formed part of the possessions of Holywell Priory, Shoreditch, and it therefore seems probable that it was given to that monastery, together with the advowson of Welwyn Church, by Gunnora daughter of Robert de Valognes.

In 1523 William Wilshere (Wiltshire) obtained a sixty years' lease from Holywell Priory of the Frythe, and

---

[70] Pat. 1 Edw. II, pt. ii, m. 19.
[71] Chan. Inq. a.q.d. 16 Edw. II, no. 100.
[72] Ibid.
[73] G.E.C. *Complete Peerage.*
[74] De Banco R. 292, m. 276 d.
[75] G.E.C. *Complete Peerage.*
[76] Chan. Inq. p.m. 2 Edw. III (2nd nos.), no. 23.
[77] *Cal. Close,* 1337–9, pp. 498–9; Clutterbuck, *Hist. of Herts.* ii, 494.
[78] *Cal. Close,* 1341–3, p. 147.
[79] G.E.C. *Complete Peerage*; Chan. Inq. p.m. 33 Edw. III (1st nos.), no. 39.
[80] G.E.C. *Complete Peerage.*
[81] Feet of F. Herts. 48 Edw. III, no. 656.
[82] G.E.C. *Complete Peerage.*

[83] Early Chan. Proc. bdle. 49, no. 23.
[84] Ibid. bdle. 32, no. 177.
[85] Burke, *Commoners,* iv, 564.
[86] Feet of F. Herts. Mich. 23 Hen. VII.
[87] Chan. Inq. p.m. (Ser. 2), lxxiii, 93.
[88] Pat. 38 Hen. VIII, pt. viii, m. 39.
[89] Ibid. 1 & 2 Phil. and Mary, pt. i; Feet of F. Herts. East. 1 & 2 Phil. and Mary.
[90] Feet of F. Herts. Hil. 2 & 3 Phil. and Mary; Pat. 2 & 3 Phil. and Mary, pt. i; De Banco R. East. 2 & 3 Phil. and Mary.
[91] Chan. Inq. p.m. (Ser. 2), cxviii, 64.
[92] Feet of F. Herts. Trin..5 Eliz.; Pat. 5 Eliz. pt. v.
[93] Ibid. 9 Eliz. pt. iv, m. 31; Feet of

F. Herts. Trin. 12 Eliz. The manor appears in the Inquisition of Lady Anne Bourchier in 1570, heir of Gertrude Courteney (one of the heirs of Sir William Say), who forfeited it in 1539; but there is no other indication that she ever held it (Chan. Inq. p.m. [Ser. 2], clvii, 88).
[94] Ibid. cccxlviii, 151.
[95] Fine R. 14 Jas. I, pt. ii, no. 24.
[96] Ibid. 8 Chas. I, pt. ii, no. 18.
[97] Pipe R. 9 Will. III.
[98] Chauncy, *Hist. of Herts.* 30.
[99] Recov. R. Trin. 21 Geo. II, rot 273; Hil. 51 Geo. III, rot. 41.
[100] Chan. Inq. p.m. (Ser. 2), cccxlviii, 151.
[1] Pat. 14 Jas. I, pt. xvii.

WELWYN CHURCH FROM THE SOUTH

WELWYN CHURCH : INTERIOR LOOKING SOUTH-EAST

BROADWATER HUNDRED — WELWYN

a messuage called the Boarshead.[2] After the dissolution of Holywell in 1539[3] these two tenements, with 50½ acres of land, were granted in March 1539-40 to Sir John Gostwick and Joan his wife.[4] Sir John died in April 1545, and at his inquisition in October 1546 it was stated that Wilshere had collected the profits of the estate during the interval,[5] so that it seems probable that he had remained as occupier of the Frythe. Sir John Gostwick's heir was his son William, who, however, died almost immediately after his father, his lands passing to his uncle William, Sir John's brother.[6] William Gostwick the elder sold the Frythe in 1546 to William Wilshere,[7] who alienated it to his son Thomas in 1549[8] and died in 1558.[9] From Thomas Wilshere, who died in 1570,[10] the Frythe descended to his son Thomas, who was a minor at his father's death,[11] and whose son John Wilshere inherited the estate in March 1620-1.[12] This John granted the Frythe to his eldest son John, who, however, predeceased him[13]; Thomas Wilshere the second son therefore succeeded his father at his death in February 1646-7.[14] Thomas died in 1666 or 1667, and his eldest son Thomas shortly afterwards, when the Frythe came to the second son John, who was succeeded by his only surviving son William in 1721. William Wilshere,

GOSTWICK. *Argent a bend cotised gules between six Cornish choughs.*

WILSHERE of the Frythe.

son of the last William, inherited the property in 1786, and his son, also named William, in 1798.

This third William died in 1824, having settled the Frythe in tail-male upon the children of his youngest brother Thomas Wilshere. William the eldest son succeeded his uncle, but died unmarried in 1867, when the Frythe came to his brother Charles Willes Wilshere, who died in 1906, leaving three daughters,[15] the eldest of whom, Miss Edith Elizabeth Marie Wilshere, inherited this estate. The Frythe is now the residence of the three Misses Wilshere.

The farm of *WELCHES* was held in the first half of the 15th century by Richard Welch (Walsh), whose son and heir Edward Welch conveyed it in 1454-5 to John Fortescue, chief justice, to the use of John Barry and his heirs.[16] In the following century it came into the possession of John Warde, citizen and grocer of London, who with his wife Mary and his son William conveyed it in 1596 to Edward Fitz John,[17] who died seised of it in 1610, holding it of the king as of the honour of Richmond. He settled the reversion of Welches in 1602 on his nephew Edward Pennyfather, to whom it came at his uncle's death.[18] Welch's Farm is now the property of Col. A. M. Blake.

The parish church of *ST. MARY CHURCHES* stands to the north of the village, and is built partly of flint rubble and partly of modern brick, with stone dressings. It consists of a chancel, nave, north and south aisles, north organ chamber, south chapel, south porch, and south-west tower. Of these, the north aisle, organ chamber, chapel, and tower are modern. The plan of the nave is probably that of a 12th-century nave, and the chancel dates from a late 13th-century enlargement. The south aisle, which was probably built about the same time as the chancel, was rebuilt, probably in the 15th century when the south porch was added. In 1663[19] a heavy storm did great damage, destroying the tower, which had stood on the north side of the church, and laying open that side and the vestry; the whole building was at this time tied and strengthened at a cost of about £2,000. In 1910 considerable alterations were carried out and the tower was rebuilt.[19a]

There is hardly any original detail left in the chancel, the only old work being a blocked lancet in the north wall, of late 13th-century date; the high, pointed chancel arch, which is of two chamfered orders, with octagonal responds, and moulded capitals; and a much restored double piscina with ogee-shaped trefoiled heads, and a thin jamb between the two bowls, which are set eastward of the centres of the recesses. The sedilia are modern, and the rest of the south side is taken up by a modern arcade of two bays opening to the south chapel. The east window is of three grouped lancets, and there is a wide single light in the north wall, and also a door to the vestry. All these are modern.

The south arcade of the nave is of four bays of late 13th-century work, much restored. The arches are pointed and of two chamfered orders, resting on octagonal columns with plain moulded bell-capitals. The bases are modern. The north arcade, which is

---

[2] Aug. Off. Convent. Leases, Midd. 37.
[3] Dugdale, *Mon.* iv, 392.
[4] *L. and P. Hen. VIII,* xv, g. 436 (9).
[5] Chan. Inq. p.m. (Ser. 2), lxxiii, 95.
[6] *V.C.H. Herts. Families,* 245.
[7] Pat. 37 Hen. VIII, pt. vi, m. 12.
[8] *V.C.H. Herts. Families,* 245.
[9] Will, P.C.C. 47 Welles.
[10] Chan. Inq. p.m (Ser. 2), clv, 157.
[11] Ibid.
[12] Ibid. dclv, 97.
[13] Ibid. dcxxxiv, 46.
[14] *V.C.H. Herts. Families,* 245-51.
[15] Ibid.
[16] Close, 33 Hen. VI, m. 15, 21.
[17] Feet of F. Herts. Trin. 38 Eliz.
[18] Chan. Inq. p.m. (Ser. 2), dcxlv, 51.
[19] *Sess. R.* (Herts. Co. Rec.), i, 158.
[19a] By Mr. Charles Blomfield, R.I.B.A., at the sole cost of the Misses Wilshere, of the Frythe.

modern, repeats the design formerly in brick and cement, but rebuilt in 1910, when the gallery was removed. This arcade, with the north aisle and gallery, dates from the early part of the 19th century. The west window has original jambs and arch, but the filling is modern. The south aisle has been much altered at various times, and the south wall, which was formerly very irregular externally, was wholly rebuilt in 1910. The windows and door are modern. In the south wall is a much restored piscina with a modern head, and on either side of the modern archway at the east, opening into the south chapel, are image brackets with carved heads of late 13th-century date. The south porch, which was of late 15th-century date, with a plain two-centred archway of two chamfered orders, was replaced by the present structure in 1910.

Till 1910 there stood in the arch opening to the organ chamber an oak screen of good 15th-century work, of three bays with a central doorway. The heads of the compartments are ogee-shaped and the upper portions are elaborately traceried. It is now restored to its original position under the chancel arch.

There is one bell, by Joseph Eayre, 1760, inscribed 'Prosperity to the Established Church, and no encouragement to Enthusiasm.'[19b]

The plate consists of a flagon of 1750, a cup of 1666, and a paten of 1678.

The registers date from 1558, and are contained in six books: (i) baptisms from 1559 to 1703, burials from 1558 to 1703, marriages from 1559 to 1701; (ii) baptisms from 1704 to 1779, burials from 1704 to 1783, marriages from 1704 to 1741; (iib) baptisms from 1780 to 1783[20]; (iii) baptisms from 1780 to 1812, burials from 1784 to 1812; (iv) marriages from 1754 to 1781; (v) marriages from 1781 to 1812.

The church of ST. MICHAEL AND ALL ANGELS at Woolmer Green was built in 1900, and is served from the parish church.

ADVOWSON The advowson seems to have early belonged to the family of Valognes, for it appears in the possession of Robert Fitz Walter, husband of Gunnora de Valognes, in 1198.[21] In 1235 it was granted by Gunnora to the convent of Holywell, Middlesex,[22] and confirmed to it by Pope Clement in 1238.[23] The living was not appropriated, but the rector was to pay 5 marks of silver annually to the convent.[24] The right of the Prioress of Holywell to the advowson was also confirmed in 1240 by the three Valognes heiresses and their husbands.[25] It remained in the possession of Holywell Priory until the Dissolution,[26] and was granted in 1540 to John Gostwick.[27] John Gostwick died seised of the advowson in 1545,[28] and his son William sold it in 1549 to William Wilshere,[29] in whose family it descended in the same manner as the Frythe[30] until Thomas Wilshere sold it in 1616 to All Souls College, Oxford,[31] in whose possession it has since remained.[32]

The site of the rectory has been changed, the old building having been cut up into cottages and the garden converted into a timber-yard.[33] Dr. Young, the author of 'Night Thoughts,' was for some time rector of Welwyn and lived at the house named Guessens.[34] He was buried at Welwyn in 1765.

Places of worship for Protestant Dissenters at Welwyn were registered under the Toleration Act at various dates from 1691.[35] In 1834 Ebenezer Chapel was certified. At the present time there is a Wesleyan chapel and a chapel of Lady Huntingdon's Connexion in the parish.

CHARITIES The Educational Foundation of the Rev. Edward Young, LL.D., a former rector, was founded by deed 15 April 1760 (enrolled), whereby the donor transferred a sum of £1,500 Old South Sea Annuities to trustees to be applied towards the maintenance of a charity school—subsequently combined with the National school—and for clothing and apprenticing the scholars.

By an order of the Charity Commissioners 24 November 1905 it was directed that the residuary rents and profits of the endowment should be applied for such other charitable uses and purposes, being educational and including instruction in the principles and duties of the Christian religion as laid down in the catechism of the Church of England, as the trustees should judge to be most for the real benefit and utility of the poor inhabitants.

The endowment now consists of £1,918 17s. 2d. consols with the official trustees, who also hold a further sum of £180 consols representing a legacy by the will of Daniel Spurgeon, dated 1807, in augmentation of Dr. Young's charity, producing £52 9s. 4d. annually.

The remaining charities in the parish are regulated by a scheme of the Charity Commissioners of 5 November 1909 under the title of the United Charities. They comprise the charities of:—

Anthony Charleton, founded by will dated in 1568, now consisting of a house used as a police station, let at £12 a year.

John Bexfield, founded by deed 1570, trust fund, £1,729 2s. 2d. consols arising from sale in 1865 of allotment in the parish of Caddington, producing yearly £43 4s. 4d.

— Denny, will dated 1707, trust fund, £835 11s. 7d. consols, arising from sale in 1872 of old workhouse building, producing yearly £20 17s. 8d.

Thomas Kentish, will in or about 1712, being a rent-charge of 10s. issuing out of a farm known as Cisaferns in Welwyn and Codicote.

Josias Berners, mentioned in the table of benefactions as founded by will (date not mentioned), consisting of a rent-charge of £5 issuing out of Wormley Bury estate in Cheshunt and applicable in apprenticing.

Unknown donors' charities, mentioned in the table of benefactions as consisting of a rent-charge of £1

[19b] 'Enthusiasm' was the technical name of Wesleyanism at this date.
[20] Only the first few pages of book iib have been used.
[21] Rot. Cur. Reg. (Rec. Com.), i, 165.
[22] Cal. Chart. R. 1226-57, p. 201.
[23] Harl. Chart. 43 A. 37.
[24] Ibid.
[25] Feet of F. Herts. 25 Hen. III, no. 295.
[26] Dugdale, Mon. iv, 394.
[27] L. and P. Hen. VIII, xv, g. 436 (9).
[28] Chan. Inq. p.m. (Ser. 2), lxxiii, 95.
[29] V.C.H. Herts. Families, 245.
[30] Chan. Inq. p.m. (Ser. 2), clv, 157.
[31] Clutterbuck, Hist. of Herts. ii, 497; Inst. Bks. (P.R.O.).
[32] Inst. Bks. (P.R.O.); Bacon, Liber Regis, 518; Clergy List, 1912.
[33] Information from the Rev. P. M. Wathen.
[34] Information from the Rev. A. C. Headlam, D.D.
[35] Urwick, Nonconf. in Herts. 625.

BROADWATER HUNDRED — WESTON

and another of 8s. for the poor, which were redeemed in 1878 and 1879 by the transfer to the official trustees of £47 5s. consols, producing £1 3s. 4d. yearly.

Daniel Spurgeon, for bread, will dated in 1807, trust fund, £195 5s. 8d. consols, yearly income £4 17s. 8d.

The several sums of stock are held by the official trustees.

It is provided by the scheme that the yearly income of Josias Berners' charity should be applied primarily in putting out as apprentices deserving poor boys bona fide resident in the ancient parish at a premium of not less than £10 or more than £20, the income to be accumulated for the purpose. The yearly income of the remaining charities to be applied in such way as the trustees thereby appointed may consider most conducive to the formation of provident habits, including donations to any dispensary, hospital or convalescent home, or to a provident club or society. Also contributions towards the provision of nurses or in the distribution of articles in kind.

WESTON

Westone (xi cent.).

The parish of Weston has an area of 4,539 acres. Almost the whole of it lies considerably over 400 ft. above the ordnance datum, and in the centre of the village the ground reaches a height of 484 ft. The land slopes down along the north-west border of the parish and in the extreme south; there is also a depression in the east. There are 3,201½ acres of arable land in the parish, 967 acres of permanent grass and 218½ acres of wood.[1]

The road from Baldock to Walkern forms the eastern boundary of the parish and the Great North Road part of the western boundary. The village of Weston is situated in the highest part of the parish, on the road from Stevenage to Clothall, which crosses the centre of the parish. Two roads turn westwards from the village to join the Great North Road, the most southerly passing Lannock Farm. Another road runs east from the village, and after passing the church of the Holy Trinity runs in a southerly direction through Hall's Green towards Howell's Farm and Dane End. The manor-house and park, the residence of Mr. M. R. Pryor, lie at the south end of the village. There was possibly a Toothill or meeting-place in the village, as reference is found to a presentment of the vicar for not scouring his ditch lying in 'le Cherchelane next Totehyll' in 1528[2] and in 1611 to a little way called 'Tottylle Lane.'[3] The hamlet of Warren's Green is situated in the south of the parish, with Hall's Green about half a mile east.

The subsoil is chalk, and there are many chalk-pits in various parts of the parish. There are two disused gravel-pits near Lannock Farm and some old clay-pits north-west of the village. There is a cave in a field near Welbury Farm, in the north of the parish. The nearest railway station is Baldock, 3 miles north-west, on the Cambridge branch of the Great Northern railway.

The inclosure award was made in 1801, the Authorizing Act being granted in 1797.[4]

In 1881 a portion of the parish in the north was transferred to Baldock.[5]

The following place-names occur in court rolls: Doddeswyke, Irelonde Green, Kittes atte Dane (later Kyttysdane), Heryngsdelle, Horells, Marches (xiv–xv cent.); 'le Vyneyerde' (1485 and 1531); Bernewyksvaley, Hykksgravefeld, Vecchecroft, Hoggescroft, Redyngcroft, Notislane, Parkestrete, Danecroft, Daneway, Whitemansfeld, Rolls Lane, Dame Hawes-grene, le Freerstokyng, le Jubitt Hyll, Warymede, Fleggys pitell, Dernewelleland, Sewell Cross (xvi cent.); Cumberloes or Round Pightell, Brendwick, Rolles Croft, Fontley Field and Fontley Pound (xvii cent.).

In the 17th century there was a tile kiln in the possession of the Humberstone family, possibly near to the existing Tilekiln Wood and Tilekiln Farm, in the south of the parish.[6]

MANORS WESTON was held by Alestan de Boscumbe, a thegn of King Edward, but by 1086 formed part of the lands of William de Ow, at which time it was assessed at 10 hides.[7] After the forfeiture of William de Ow his lands were granted by Henry I to Walter son of Richard de Clare,[8] who is known to have held lands in Hertfordshire in 1130.[9] At his death his estates passed to his nephew Gilbert de Clare,[10] who was created first Earl of Pembroke by King Stephen and died in 1148.[11] His son Richard Strongbow[12] inherited the manor of Weston,[13] which was held by his widow Eva, daughter of Dermot King of Leinster, after his death in 1176.[14] She was still living in 1185, when she was referred to as 'Countess of Ireland,'[15] her marriage being in the gift of the king. Her daughter and heir Isabel married William Marshal Earl of Pembroke, whose lands passed to his eldest son William in 1219.[16] The latter held Weston and died in 1231,[17] the manor remaining for life to his widow Eleanor, sister of Henry III, who, notwithstanding her vow of chastity, married secondly Simon de Montfort, Earl of Leicester.[18] She lived until 1275.[19]

MARSHAL, Earl of Pembroke. *Party or and vert a lion gules.*

---

[1] Statistics from Bd. of Agric. (1905).
[2] Add. MS. 36346.
[3] Ibid. 36372.
[4] *Blue Bk. Incl. Awards*, 64; *Private Acts of Parl. Inner Temple Cal.*
[5] Divided Parishes Act (1876).
[6] *Herts. Gen. and Antiq.* ii, 50, 99.
[7] *V.C.H. Herts.* i, 327b.
[8] *Genealogist* (new ser.), xviii, 167.
[9] *Pipe R.* 30–31 Hen. I.
[10] *Genealogist*, Jan. 1902.
[11] G.E.C. *Complete Peerage.*
[12] *Pipe R.* 16 Her. II (Pipe R. Soc.), 105; 17 Hen. II, 119.
[13] Ibid.
[14] Ibid. 23 Hen. II, 149; G.E.C. *Complete Peerage.*
[15] S. Grimaldi, *Rot. de Dominabus*, 35.
[16] G.E.C. *Complete Peerage.*
[17] Ibid.; *Cal. Close*, 1227–31, p. 489.
[18] Chan. Inq. p.m. 40 Edw. III (2nd nos.), no. 53.
[19] The inquisition above quoted is wrong in stating that it was Alice who married Simon de Montfort. Alice de Bethune was the first wife of William Marshal and died before 1219 (G.E.C. *Complete Peerage*).

171

A HISTORY OF HERTFORDSHIRE

In the mean time the estates of the earldom of Pembroke had passed through the hands of William's four brothers, and in 1245 were divided among his five sisters and their heirs. The office of Marshal of England was inherited by the eldest sister Maud wife of Hugh le Bigod Earl of Norfolk, and descended to her son Roger, and in 1270 to her great-nephew Roger le Bigod.[20] At the death of the Countess of Pembroke the manor of Weston was assigned by the king to this Roger le Bigod, who in 1279 made an agreement with the king by which the reversion was to fall to the Crown if he died without issue.[21] The manor thus came into the king's hands in 1306,[22] and was granted in 1312, together with the earldom of Norfolk and the marshalship, to Thomas of Brotherton, fifth son of Edward I.[23] Weston was delivered to his widow Mary in dower in 1338,[24] and at her death in 1362[25] was assigned to her eldest daughter Margaret, then the wife of Sir Walter de Mauny.[26] From her it passed to her grandson Thomas Mowbray Duke of Norfolk,[27] whose son Thomas inherited it in 1399.[28] The latter was involved in the Scrope conspiracy and was beheaded in 1405,[29] when Weston was granted to John Cornwall for life.[30] In 1406 it was granted to the queen consort.[31] However, as there had been no trial or attainder of Thomas Mowbray, the manor was recovered in dower by his widow Constance, who married secondly Sir John Grey,[32] and held the manor until her death in 1437, when it passed to Thomas's brother and heir John Mowbray Duke of Norfolk.[33]

Weston descended to John Mowbray's son John Duke of Norfolk, who died in 1461,[34] and to John, son of the latter, a minor at his father's death.[35] Weston was settled upon his wife Elizabeth as part of her jointure, and she was allowed to hold it during her husband's minority.[36] John left an only daughter and heir Anne, aged four at her father's death in 1476.[37] She was married soon after to Richard Duke of York, the younger of the two sons of Edward IV, but she died in 1480, her boy husband being murdered in 1483.[38] Anne's heirs were her cousins John Lord Howard (son of Margaret sister of Anne's great-grandfather) and William, second Lord Berkeley, of the creation of 1421, called 'the Wast all,' son of Isabel, her great-grandfather's other sister. Upon Anne's marriage with Richard Duke of York Lord Berkeley released his right to the reversion of half her estates to King Edward IV and his male issue, in exchange for the discharge of his debts to the amount of £34,000. The king's male issue, however, became extinct by the murder of his two sons in the Tower in 1483, and Richard III conferred the moiety of Anne's estates, including Weston, on Lord Berkeley, together with the title of Earl Marshal.[39] He died without issue in 1491-2 and Weston lapsed to the Crown.[40]

In 1519 Henry VIII granted the manor to Sir William Fitz William for the lives of himself, his wife Elizabeth and their eldest son,[41] but in 1531 Sir William surrendered it again in payment of a debt to the king.[42] In the following year, when Anne Boleyn was created Marchioness of Pembroke, Weston was granted to her together with that dignity.[43] She became queen in the same year, but was executed in 1536. Weston was then conferred on Queen Jane Seymour,[44] who, however, died in the following year.[45] The manor then seems to have remained in the king's hands[46] until it was granted to Queen Katharine Parr in 1544.[47] After the death of Henry VIII, Edward VI granted the reversion of Weston after Katharine's death[48] to Sir William Herbert,[49] who had been a gentleman of the Privy Chamber to Henry VIII, and was created Earl of Pembroke in 1551.[50] At the accession of Mary in 1553 it was discovered by an inquisition that as William Lord Berkeley, who died in 1491-2, had settled the reversion of the manor on Henry VII and his heirs male, with remainder to heirs of William, the manor now rightly belonged to that heir, viz. Henry Lord Berkeley, grandson of William's brother Maurice,[51] the male heirs of Henry VII being extinct with Edward VI. Henry Lord Berkeley had special livery of his lands, although under age, in 1554.[52]

In 1572 Henry Berkeley sold the manor to George Burgoyne,[53] whose son Thomas succeeded him in 1588[54] and sold Weston in 1593 to Sir John Puckering,[55] who died seised of it about 1596.[56] Sir John's son Thomas Puckering was holding the manor in

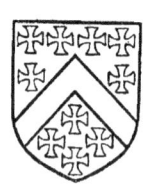

BERKELEY. *Gules a cheveron between ten crosses formy argent.*

---

[20] G.E.C. *Complete Peerage.*
[21] *Cal. Close,* 1272-9, pp. 535, 569; Feet of F. Div. Co. 7 Edw. I, no. 11.
[22] Chan. Inq. p.m. 35 Edw. I, no. 46.
[23] G.E.C. *Complete Peerage;* Chan. Inq. p.m. 5 Edw. III, no. 46.
[24] *Cal. Close,* 1337-9, p. 582.
[25] Chan. Inq. p.m. 36 Edw. III, pt. ii (1st nos.), no. 9.
[26] *Abbrev. Rot. Orig.* (Rec. Com.), ii, 271; Chan. Inq. p.m. 46 Edw. III (1st nos.), no. 38.
[27] Ibid. 1 Hen. IV, no. 71.   [28] Ibid.
[29] G.E.C. *Complete Peerage;* Chan. Inq. p.m. 8 Hen. IV, no. 76.
[30] *Cal. Pat.* 1405-8, p. 68.
[31] Ibid. p. 115.
[32] Chan. Inq. p.m. 2 Hen. VI, no. 27.
[33] Ibid. 16 Hen. VI, no. 60; Close, 22 Hen. VI, m. 16.
[34] Chan. Inq. p.m. 1 Edw. IV, no. 46.
[35] Ibid.
[36] *Cal. Pat.* 1461-7, p. 212.
[37] Chan. Inq. p.m. 17 Edw. IV, no. 58.
[38] G.E.C. *Complete Peerage.* Her mother Elizabeth Duchess of Norfolk had settled Weston on herself for life in 1477 (Feet of F. Div. Co. Hil. 16 Edw. IV, no. 117; Close, 16 Edw. IV, m. 10).
[39] G.E.C. *Complete Peerage;* Feet of F. Div. Co. Hil. 5 Hen. VII.
[40] William Lord Berkeley had a brother Maurice, but he disinherited him (G.E.C. *Complete Peerage; L. and P. Hen. VIII,* ii, 621, 3568; Add. R. 36162, 36171).
[41] *L. and P. Hen. VIII,* iii (1), p. 209.
[42] Ibid. v, p. 219.
[43] Ibid. g. 1499 (23), p. 634.
[44] Ibid. xii (1), p. 608; Add. R. 36202, 36205.
[45] *L. and P. Hen. VIII,* xii (2), pp. 974-5.
[46] Ibid. xvi, g. 878 (56); Add. R. 36206-7.
[47] *L. and P. Hen. VIII,* xix (1), g. 141 (65); Add. R. 36214. Both Anne Boleyn and Katharine Howard were great-granddaughters of John Howard, who was co-heir of the Norfolk estates with William Lord Berkeley.
[48] Add. R. 36217.
[49] Pat. 1 Edw. VI, pt. vii, m. 38. In 1549 John Cock held the manorial court there (Add. R. 36218). He was possibly a lessee or steward of the manor. See also note 52.
[50] G.E.C. *Complete Peerage.*
[51] Chan. Inq. p.m. (Ser. 2), ci, 108.
[52] G.E.C. *Complete Peerage;* see Add. R. 36230-7. A licence for William Earl of Pembroke to alienate Weston to Henry Cock of Broxbourne in 1557 is not altogether easy to explain (Pat. 4 & 5 Phil. and Mary, pt. ii, m. 25). Perhaps the Earl of Pembroke had refused to surrender his title, or this may be a formal quitclaim in trust for Lord Berkeley.
[53] Recov. R. Mich. 14 Eliz. rot. 159; Feet of F. Herts. Trin. 14 Eliz.
[54] Harl. MS. 757, fol. 268.
[55] Feet of F. Herts. Mich. 35 & 36 Eliz.
[56] Chan. Inq. p.m. (Ser. 2), ccxlvi, 125.

172

BROADWATER HUNDRED — WESTON

1638.[57] He was succeeded before 1652 by his nephew Henry Puckering or Newton, son of his sister Catherine Newton,[58] who seems to have sold the manor in 1654 to Sir John Hale.[59] The latter left an only daughter and heir Rose, who married Sir John Austen.[60] Their son Sir Robert Austen, bart., sold Weston in 1703 to Robert Heysham,[61] lord of the manor of Little Munden (q.v.), in whose family Weston descended[62] until 1852, when it was sold to Samuel Adams, who in the next year sold it to Robert Pryor,[63] whose son Mr. Marlborough Robert Pryor is the present owner.

PRYOR. *Argent three bars wavy azure and a chief gules with a saltire argent therein charged with a ring gules.*

Weston possessed a mill in 1086.[64] In 1201 Jurdan the miller was fined for 'filling up the millpond,'[65] probably so that it overflowed its banks, but it seems to have been later disused in favour of a windmill, which is first mentioned in 1275.[66] There is still a windmill in the parish situated on Lannock Hill.

The park of Weston is first mentioned in 1231, when Ranulf Briton claimed therefrom fifteen deer and five stags which he stated that Earl William Marshal had given him before he died and which had not been delivered.[67] In 1306 and later it is referred to as 'a park called Yppegrave.'[68] Two parks are mentioned in 1366, but not again.[69] In 1384 Margaret Countess of Norfolk granted the custody of her park, warren and game to her butler John Ethom, with 'clothing' of the suit of her esquires, or 13s. 4d. yearly in lieu thereof, and 100s. yearly rent from the issues of the manor.[70] This grant was confirmed to John Ethom in 1399[71] at Margaret's death. In 1405, Weston being in the king's hands by reason of the insurrection of the Earl Marshal, the office of parker was granted during good behaviour to the king's esquire Robert Scot.[72] In 1437 the park was stated to be worth nothing beyond the profit of the deer.[73] John Duke of Norfolk granted the custody of the park 'with the custody of the coneys in it' to the king's esquire Laurence Fairclough; the office was confirmed to him in 1476 after the duke's death, by which time Fairclough had become one of the marshals of the king's hall.[74] In 1515, when the park was again in the king's hands, John Sharpe and James Druel were appointed keepers of it in survivorship in place of Ralph Pudsey.[75] It seems to have been disparked before 1541, for in that year a messuage called the Lodge and certain lands 'parcel of the late park of the manor of Weston' were leased to Edmund Kympton.[76] The park is not again referred to, but Weston Wood with a warren is mentioned in 1557[77] and the wood in 1703.[78] There is now a park surrounding the manor-house.

View of frankpledge was claimed in the manor of Weston in 1287.[79] The rolls for the court and leet held there in 1397 and later are extant.[80] In 1287 Roger le Bigod claimed, in addition to frankpledge, amendment of the assize of bread and ale, tumbrel, gallows, infangentheof and free warren.[81]

The manor of *WESTON ARGENTEIN* was held of the manor of Weston for the service of half a knight's fee.[82] It is first referred to as a manor in 1381.[83] In 1205–6 Roger son of Nicholas conveyed 2 carucates of land in Weston to Richard de Argentein,[84] which land was doubtless the manor of Weston Argentein. Richard was lord of Great Wymondley, and Weston Argentein descended with that manor[85] until William Alington and Elizabeth his wife, heiress of the Argenteins, conveyed their manor in Weston to Peter Paule and others, apparently trustees, in 1440.[86] These feoffees conveyed the manor to others in 1452,[87] from whom it seems to have come to Laurence Harreys, who held it in 1489,[88] and afterwards to Thomas Harreys and Agnes his wife, who sold it in 1514 to Sir William Say.[89] The latter died seised of it in 1529,[90] and afterwards it came to the Crown in the same manner as his other lands[91] (see Benington). In 1556 it was leased for forty years to Sir Robert Rochester and Edward Walgrave.[92] At the end of that term it reverted to the Crown and was granted to Edward Vaughan and Thomas Ellys, probably in trust for Sir John Puckering, as he died seised of it in 1596.[93] John Puckering was lord of the manor of Weston, with which Weston Argentein descended from that date,[94]

---

[57] Feet of F. Div. Co. Hil. 13 Chas. I; see also Chan. Inq. p.m. (Ser. 2), ccccviii, 118; Add. R. 36290.
[58] *Visit. of Herts.* (Harl. Soc. xxii), 160; Recov. R. Mich. 1652, rot. 228.
[59] Ibid. Trin. 1654, rot. 144.
[60] Chauncy, op. cit. 374.
[61] Close, 2 Anne, pt. viii, no. 21.
[62] Recov. R. Trin. 8 Geo. II, rot. 50; Feet of F. Div. Co. Mich. 25 Geo. III; Recov. R. Mich. 31 Geo. III, rot. 21; Feet of F. Herts. Hil. 45 Geo. III; Mich. 3 & 4 Will. IV.
[63] Cussans, op. cit. *Broadwater Hund.* 41. [64] *V.C.H. Herts.* i, 327b.
[65] *Abbrev. Plac.* (Rec. Com.), 33.
[66] Chan. Inq. p.m. 40 Edw. III (2nd nos.), no. 53; 35 Edw. I, no. 46.
[67] *Cal. Close*, 1227–31, p. 489.
[68] Chan. Inq. p.m. 35 Edw. I, no. 46; Feet of F. Herts. 8 Edw. II, no. 190.
[69] Chan. Inq. p.m. 40 Edw. III (2nd nos.), no. 53.
[70] *Cal. Pat.* 1381–5, p. 482.
[71] Ibid. 1399–1401, p. 77.
[72] Ibid. 1405–8, p. 24.

[73] Chan. Inq. p.m. 16 Hen. VI, no. 60.
[74] *Cal. Pat.* 1467–77, p. 599.
[75] *L. and P. Hen. VIII*, ii, 621.
[76] Ibid. xvi, g. 878 (56).
[77] Pat. 4 & 5 Phil. and Mary, pt. xi, m. 25.
[78] Close, 2 Anne, pt. viii, no. 21.
[79] Assize R. 325, m. 26 d.
[80] Add. R. 36086. There are a great number of Court Rolls of this manor extant, both in the British Museum and in the possession of the lord of the manor.
[81] Assize R. 325, m. 26 d.
[82] Feet of F. Div. Co. 7 John, no. 38; *Feud. Aids*, ii, 430; Chan. Inq. p.m. 12 Edw. II, no. 43; 2 Hen. VI, no. 27; 6 Hen. VI, no. 53; (Ser. 2), li, 50. It is said (*Feud. Aids*, ii, 437) to be held of the Earl of Hertford, but this is obviously an error (cf. the former entry).
[83] Chan. Inq. p.m. 4 Ric. II, no. 110.
[84] Feet of F. Div. Co. 7 John, no. 38.
[85] *Feud. Aids*, ii, 430, 437, 449; Chan. Inq. p.m. 12 Edw. II, no. 43; *Abbrev. Rot. Orig.* (Rec. Com.), i, 243; *Cal. Pat.* 1327–30, p. 2; Chan. Inq. p.m. 4 Ric. II,

no. 110; Feet of F. Div. Co. Mich. 5 Ric. II, no. 57; Chan. Inq. p.m. 6 Hen. V, no. 13; 2 Hen. VI, no. 27; 6 Hen. VI, no. 53.
[86] Feet of F. Herts. Mich. 19 Hen. VI, no. 104; Close, 19 Hen. VI, m. 36, 38.
[87] Ibid. 30 Hen. VI, m. 18.
[88] Add. R. 36138.
[89] Feet of F. Herts. East. 6 Hen. VIII.
[90] Chan. Inq. p.m. (Ser. 2), li, 50.
[91] Ct. of Wards, Misc. Bks. dlxxviii, fol. 372a; Feet of F. Herts. Hil. 33 Hen. VIII.
[92] Pat. 3 & 4 Phil. and Mary, pt. xii, m. 42.
[93] Chan. Inq. p.m. (Ser. 2), ccxlvi, 125.
[94] Feet of F. Div. Co. Hil. 13 Chas. I; Recov. R. Mich. 1652, rot. 228; Trin. 1654, rot. 144; 4 Will. and Mary, rot. 185; 11 Will. III, rot. 211; Close, 2 Anne, pt. vii, no. 14; pt. viii, no. 21; Recov. R. Trin. 8 Geo. II, rot. 50; Mich. 31 Geo. III, rot. 21; Feet of F. Div. Co. Mich. 25 Geo. III; Herts. Hil. 45 Geo. III; 50 Geo. III; Mich. 3 & 4 Will. IV.

A HISTORY OF HERTFORDSHIRE

and passed with it into the hands of Mr. Robert Pryor in 1857, his son Mr. M. R. Pryor being the present lord.[95]

Court rolls are not extant for Weston Argentein until a late date. The existing rolls show that court baron was held there in 1489[96] and court leet in 1536.[97]

The manor of LANNOCK (Langenache, xiii cent.; Langenoke, xiv cent.; Langnock), which originally formed part of the manor of Weston, was given to the Knights Templars by Gilbert de Clare, first Earl of Pembroke, who died in 1148,[98] and was confirmed to them by William Marshal, husband of Gilbert's granddaughter and heir Isabel.[99] It remained in the possession of the Templars until the suppression of their order in 1309,[100] after which it was granted with the other lands of the Templars to the Knights Hospitallers.[1]

In 1353 the Prior of the Hospitallers seems to have been embroiled with Mary widow of Thomas of Brotherton Earl of Norfolk (who was lady of the manor of Weston), for she came with a number of others and 'broke his close and house, drove away 40 horses, 30 oxen, 12 bullocks, 10 cows and 800 sheep of his, worth £300, carried away his goods, impounded without reasonable cause ten other of his horses, kept them impounded so long that two of the ten, worth 100s., died, and so threatened his men and servants deputed to preserve his liberties and till his lands and make his other profits there, that they dared not stay there for this, whereby he lost their service and the profit of the manor.'[2]

About 1540 Lannock came into the king's hands owing to the dissolution of the Hospitallers,[3] and remained in his possession until 1544,[4] when it was granted to Sir Michael Dormer.[5]

Sir Michael Dormer is said to have died in 1545[6]; John and William Dormer were holding the manor in 1552,[7] and Katrine Dormer, widow of one of them, was lady of the manor in 1560.[8] Soon afterwards it came into the possession of George Burgoyne of Quickswood,[9] who in 1577-8 alienated it to his second son George.[10] After his father's death George joined with his mother Dorothy and his younger brother Ralph in 1590 in conveying Lannock to James Spurling.[11] The next year they made a similar conveyance to Arthur Aty.[12] The nature of these transactions is not clear; possibly Spurling and Aty were mortgagees. In 1594 Spurling and Burgoyne both appear as deforciants in a fine levied of the manor.[13] Ultimately James Spurling acquired it, for he held courts there from 1600 to 1619.[14] In 1621 James Spurling sold Lannock to William Hale of King's Walden,[15] who died seised of it in 1633, when it passed to his son William,[16] who died without issue in 1641.[17] His sister Dionisia, wife of Sir Thomas Williamson, then held Lannock for a while,[18] but in 1683 shortly before her death it was in the possession of her nephew William Hale, son of her brother Rowland.[19] This William, who was M.P. for Hertfordshire, was succeeded by his son Richard in 1688, who, however, died in the following year, leaving a son William under age.[20] The latter died in 1717, leaving two sons.[21] The elder, William, died without issue in 1741 and was succeeded by his brother Faggen Hale,[22] after whose death the manor passed to his second cousin William, son of Bernard Hale and nephew of Paggen's grandfather Richard Hale.[23] William's son William inherited Lannock in 1793[24] and was followed by his son, a third William, in 1829.[25] Charles Cholmeley Hale, son of the last named, succeeded his father and was lord of the manor in 1877.[26] In 1896 Lannock was acquired from the trustees of Mr. C. C. Hale by Mr. M. R. Pryor, lord of the manor of Weston, and has thus become united with that manor.[27] It is now a farm.

View of frankpledge and manorial courts were held at Lannock in 1476 and later.[28] They seem to have been held yearly at Easter in the 15th century and later at Whitsuntide. Court Rolls are extant up to 1685.[29]

Free warren was appurtenant to Lannock Manor in 1480, when one William Munde, a labourer, entered the warren and took rabbits with ferrets and nets without licence.[30]

The manor of NEWBERRY (Le Neuebery, xiv cent.), which lay partly in Weston and partly in Graveley, was held of the lords of the manor of Weston for the service of half a knight's fee.[31] In 1522 it is said to have been held of Sir William Say as of his manor of Weston Argentein,[32] but this was perhaps the result of a confusion with the manor of Chesfield, which was held by the lord of Newberry of Sir William Say.

It was apparently the manor of Newberry which was granted at an early date to Hubert de St. Clare, son of Hamo de St. Clare (see Walkern), and which in 1185 was held by his young widow Clementia,

---

[95] Information kindly supplied by Mr. M. R. Pryor.
[96] Add. R. 36138.
[97] Ibid. 36199.
[98] G.E.C. Complete Peerage.
[99] Dugdale, Mon. vii, 820.
[100] Ibid. 814; Cal. Pat. 1307-13, p. 131.
[1] Add. R. 36329-33, 36347, 36350.
[2] Cal. Pat. 1350-4, p. 512.
[3] Dugdale, Mon. vii, 799-800.
[4] Add. R. 36354-6. The farm of the manor had been granted in 1511 to John Boiler for a term of seventy years and passed to his son Laurence before 1560 (Mins. Accts. 31 & 32 Hen. VIII, no. 114; Chan. Proc. [Ser. 2], bdle. 30, no. 18).
[5] L. and P. Hen. VIII, xix (2), g. 166 (51).
[6] Clutterbuck, op. cit. i, 494.
[7] Feet of F. Herts. Mich. 6 Edw. VI.
[8] Add. R. 36360.
[9] Chan. Proc. (Ser. 2) bdle. 30, no. 18.
[10] Feet of F. Herts. Hil. 20 Eliz.; Pat. 20 Eliz. pt. viii, m. 21; Visit. of Cambs. (Harl. Soc. xli), 26.
[11] Pat. 32 Eliz. pt. xxii, m. 35; Feet of F. Herts. Mich. 32 & 33 Eliz.; Recov. R. Mich. 32 Eliz. rot. 11.
[12] Pat. 33 Eliz. pt. vi, m. 28; Feet of F. Herts. Mich. 33 & 34 Eliz.
[13] Ibid. East. 36 Eliz. In 1591-2 there was a grant of the manor to William Typper and Robert Dawe. These were the well-known fishing grantees (Pat. 34 Eliz. pt. vii, B).
[14] Add. R. 36372, 36375-83.
[15] Feet of F. Herts. Trin. 19 Jas. I.
[16] Chan. Inq. p.m. (Ser. 2), ccclxxvi, 148.
[17] Berry, Herts. Gen. 34.
[18] Add. R. 36397.
[19] Ibid.; Recov. R. Hil. 35 & 36 Chas. II, rot. 79; Berry, op. cit. 35.
[20] Berry, op. cit. 35; Chauncy, op. cit. 374; Recov. R. Trin. 8 Anne, rot. 198.
[21] Salmon, op. cit. 183.
[22] Berry, op. cit. 37; Recov. R. Trin. 16 Geo. II, rot. 153.
[23] Berry, op. cit. 38; Recov. R. Mich. 11 Geo. III, rot. 185.
[24] Ibid. Hil. 55 Geo. III, rot. 248; Clutterbuck, op. cit. ii, 518; Berry, op. cit. 38.
[25] Berry, op. cit. 38.
[26] Cussans, op. cit. Broadwater Hund. 43.
[27] Information kindly supplied by Mr. M. R. Pryor.
[28] Add. Chart. 36125-7, 36329-42, 36346-56, 36360; Mins. Accts. 31 & 32 Hen. VIII, no. 114.
[29] Add. Chart. 36372-83, 36397-8.
[30] Ibid. 36326.
[31] Feud. Aids, ii, 430, 448; Chan. Inq. p.m. 2 Edw. II, no. 80.
[32] Ibid. (Ser. 2), lxxx, 13.

174

WESTON CHURCH: CAPITAL OF IMPOST OF SOUTH-EAST PIER OF TOWER

WESTON CHURCH FROM THE SOUTH

under the guardianship of the king.[33] Her grandson William son of William de Lanvaley held this half fee,[34] after which it descended to John de Burgh,[35] husband of Hawise de Lanvaley, and to Robert Fitz Walter,[36] husband of Devorgill de Burgh, in the same manner as Walkern (q.v.). After this the mesne overlordship seems to have died out.

William de Lanvaley the second, who died before 1233, granted 'all his lands in Weston' to Eustace de Rochester,[37] apparently identical with Eustace de Merk of Newsells, from whom the property passed to William de Rochester, son of his nephew Ralph (see Royston), who sub-enfeoffed Henry de Rochester.[38] William died about 1248, leaving Peter de Rochester his brother and heir.[39]

At the end of the 13th century the sub-tenant of Newberry was Robert Walerand, who died in 1272,[40] the manor being assigned in dower to his widow Matilda.[41] As Robert and Matilda had no children their nearest heirs were their nephews Robert and John Walerand.[42] Robert was apparently the elder and died unmarried before March 1308 ; John, who married Isabel, died in 1308 [43] soon after his brother. Both of them were idiots.[44] The heirs of John Walerand were Alan de Plokenet, grandson of his aunt Alice de Odworthe ; John son of Alice de Odworthe ; Alice daughter of his second aunt Cecilia de Everingham ; Bevis de Knovile, son of Cecilia's daughter Joan; Matilda widow of Richard le Bret and Cecilia wife of Peter de Heluin, daughters of Cecilia daughter of Cecilia de Everingham.[45] There is nothing to show to which of these heirs Newberry was apportioned ; probably it was eventually sold, as in 1346 it was in the possession of John de Blomvile,[46] lord of the manor of Graveley, with which manor it descended until the end of the 16th century.[47] It was sold with Graveley to Thomas Bedell in 1565, but it is not clear whether the whole estate passed with that manor to William Clarke in the following year, but the portion of it lying in Graveley parish evidently did so.

It appears at this date or after to have been divided. That part of it which lay in the parish of Weston was acquired by Thomas Puckering, lord of the manor of Weston, before 1620,[48] and followed the descent of that manor,[49] eventually becoming absorbed in it.[50] It is mentioned separately as late as 1810.[51] There is still a wood known as Newberry Grove in the south of the parish.

The portion of Newberry lying in Graveley parish seems to have continued in the possession of the lords of that manor [52] until 1877,[53] after which it presumably became absorbed in that manor or in Weston.

The reputed manor of *HOWELLS* or *HAWVYLES* is mentioned in 1543 as being held of the manor of Weston by fealty, suit of court and rent.[54] John Bowles, who died seised of it in that year, left a grandson Thomas Bowles, son of his son Richard, who was a boy of thirteen.[55] The manor consequently fell into the king's hands and an annuity from it, with the wardship and marriage of the heir, were granted to John Sewester, Attorney of the Court of Wards.[56] In 1609 it appears in the possession of George Kympton, who died in that year, leaving a son and heir George,[57] after which there is no further mention of it. Howell's Farm and Wood still survive, and are situated in the south-east of the parish.

The tenement known as *FAIRCLOUGH HALL*, *FAIRCLOTH HALL*, and now as *HALLS GREEN FARM*, is about a mile to the south-east of the village. It is a 17th-century building of timber and plaster with a tiled roof and a central chimney stack. It takes its name from a family of Fairclough who resided here certainly as early as 1461 and probably before. A Sir Ralph Fairclough is mentioned as the father or grandfather of the possessor in that year,[58] and at the same date Laurence Fairclough and Elizabeth his wife settled their possessions in Weston on themselves for life with remainder to their son John for life, and afterwards to his brother Ralph and his heirs.[59] Laurence and Elizabeth were still living in 1469, when Ralph's son Laurence is mentioned.[60] Ralph is again mentioned in 1497.[61] Fairclough Hall descended in the family without a break to Thomas Fairclough, who was living in 1634,[62] soon after which his son John sold Fairclough Hall to William Hale,[63] lord of the manor of Weston, in which it presumably became absorbed.

The parish church of the *HOLY CHURCH TRINITY* stands to the south-east of the village on high ground, and is built of flint and coursed ironstone rubble ; the quoins and dressings generally are of oolite and clunch. The roof is slated. The church consists of a chancel, nave with clearstory, north transept, central tower, south aisle and south porch and vestry.[64]

The original cruciform church of the 12th century is now represented by the north transept, central tower and nave, and there are traces of a north chapel to the east of the transept. The south aisle, south porch and clearstory were added in the 15th century, and new windows were inserted. The original south transept was at the same time rebuilt so as to incorporate it in the aisle as its easternmost

---

[33] S. Grimaldi, *Rot. de Dominabus*, 35.
[34] Harl. Chart. 52 I. 37.
[35] *Cal. Close*, 1339–41, p. 36 ; *Cal. Inq. Hen. III*, 38. [36] *Feud. Aids*, ii, 430.
[37] Harl. Chart. 52 I. 37.
[38] *Cal. Inq. Hen. III*, 38.
[39] Ibid. See Newsells in Barkway, Edwinstree Hundred.
[40] Chan. Inq. p.m. 1 Edw. I, no. 6.
[41] *Cal. Close*, 1272–9, p. 67.
[42] Ibid. ; 1307–13, p. 293.
[43] Chan. Inq. p.m. 2 Edw. II, no. 80.
[44] *Feud. Aids*, ii, 430.
[45] Chan. Inq. p.m. 2 Edw. II, no. 80.
[46] *Feud. Aids*, ii, 436.
[47] Chan. Inq. p.m. (Ser. 2), xxx, 147 ; lxxx, 23 ; Ct. of Wards, Bks. clxxix, fol. 36 ; Feet of F. Herts. East. 7 Eliz.
[48] Com. Pleas D. Enr. Hil. 17 Jas. I, m. 9.

[49] Feet of F. Div. Co. Hil. 13 Chas. I ; Recov. R. Mich. 1652, rot. 228 ; Trin. 1654, rot. 144 ; 4 Will. and Mary, rot. 185 ; 11 Will. III, rot. 211 ; Close, 2 Anne, pt. vii, no. 14 ; pt. viii, no. 21 ; Recov. R. Trin. 8 Geo. II, rot. 50 ; Mich. 31 Geo. III, rot. 21 ; Feet of F. Herts. Hil. 45 Geo. III.
[50] Information kindly supplied by Mr. M. R. Pryor.
[51] Feet of F. Herts. Hil. 50 Geo. III.
[52] Recov. R. Hil. 2 Geo. III, rot. 30.
[53] Cussans, op. cit. *Broadwater Hund.* 44.
[54] Chan. Inq. p.m. (Ser. 2), lxviii, 14 ; cccviii, 118.
[55] Ibid. lxviii, 14.
[56] *L. and P. Hen. VIII*, xviii (2), g. 449 (67).

[57] Chan. Inq. p.m. (Ser. 2), cccviii, 118.
[58] *Visit. of Herts.* (Harl. Soc. xxii), 52. Chauncy (*Hist. of Herts.* 375) gives both the father and grandfather of Laurence as Ralph, also Richard as father of the elder Ralph and Laurence as his grand-father.
[59] Add. R. 36100.
[60] Ibid. 36108.
[61] Ibid. 36141.
[62] *Visit. of Herts.* (Harl. Soc. xxii), 52–3.
[63] Chauncy, op. cit. 375.
[64] Dimensions : chancel, 32 ft. by 17 ft. 6 in. ; tower, 13 ft. 6 in. square ; north transept, 14 ft. by 12 ft. 6 in. ; nave, 44 ft. 6 in. by 21 ft. 6 in. ; south aisle, east bay, 14 ft. 6 in. wide, remainder 12 ft. wide ; south porch, 12 ft. by 10 ft.

A HISTORY OF HERTFORDSHIRE

bay. The modern work includes the rebuilding of the chancel early in the 19th century and the upper portion of the central tower in 1867, besides extensive and somewhat drastic restoration between this date and 1880, when the vestry was added.

The modern chancel is of red brick, coated with stucco, a treatment also applied to the north transept. The crossing arches of the tower are semicircular and unmoulded, and rest on abaci of unusual type, deeply moulded and divided into upper and lower portions.

In the north transept a blocked and partly destroyed semicircular arch in the east wall indicates the position of an opening to the destroyed north chapel. In the north and west walls are small single round-headed lights of the 12th century with deep internal splays. The character of the south transept has been much disguised by the 15th-century altera-

portion (14 ft. 6 in. wide) is 1 ft. 6 in. wider than the later portion. In the aisle is a piscina of the 15th century, with a plain pointed head.

The south doorway is original, of the same date as the windows, and the south porch, also of the 15th century, has an entrance archway of two moulded orders with shafted jambs.

The nave roof is of the 15th century, and rests on original grotesque corbels.

The font is of the 15th century also, and is octagonal. The sides of the bowl, which is moulded, have quatrefoiled panels, and the stem is also moulded and panelled.

On the chancel wall is a small mural monument to John Fairclough, 1630, with shields.

In the nave is a small carved chest of 17th-century date.

WESTON CHURCH, INTERIOR LOOKING EAST

tions, and it will be described as part of the south aisle. The nave has two windows in the north wall, both of the 15th century, the eastern of two and the western of three lights with tracery. Between them is a blocked north door of similar date. The south arcade, of three bays, has two-centred arches of two hollow-chamfered orders with hollows between, supported on octagonal columns with moulded capitals and bases; all are of 15th-century date, though much recut, scraped and otherwise defaced. Above the arcade are four square openings, probably the original clearstory windows. At present, however, owing to the raising of the aisle roof, they are internal, and probably tracery has been removed from them.

The south aisle, which includes the south transept, has an east window of three traceried lights and three two-light south windows, all of the 15th century, and very like those of the nave. The transept

There are five bells: the treble by John Waylett, 1716; the second and third by Miles Graye, 1634; the fourth by Warner & Sons, 1867; and the tenor by R. Chandler, 1682.

The plate consists of a cup of 1638, a large paten of 1661, a small paten, undated (no hall-mark), a modern cup and a modern plated flagon.

The registers, beginning in 1539, are included in four books: (i) baptisms 1539 to 1759, burials 1539 to 1760, marriages 1539 to 1753; (ii) baptisms 1761 to 1794, burials 1761 to 1794; (iii) baptisms 1795 to 1812, burials 1795 to 1812; (iv) marriages 1754 to 1812.

ADVOWSON The church of the Holy Trinity at Weston was given to the Knights Templars by Gilbert de Clare Earl of Pembroke at some date previous to 1148 and was confirmed to them by William Marshal Earl of

BROADWATER HUNDRED

Pembroke, one of his successors.[65] The living was appropriated and a vicar appointed, the vicarage to consist of small tithes and offerings from the soil of Weston, with a suitable manse, and the vicar to pay synodals.[66] The rectory and advowson follow the descent of the manor of Lannock[67] (q.v.), except that the rectory and advowson were acquired from James Spurling before 1616 by Richard Hale,[68] father of the William Hale who purchased Lannock from the former in 1621. It was bought from the executors of Charles Cholmeley Hale in 1885 by Thomas Pryor of Baldock, who in 1889 sold it to Mr. Marlborough Robert Pryor, the present patron.[69]

In 1481 the inhabitants of Weston complained that their vicar John Hawthorn was ' a common player, and daily played le Penyprykke[70] and Bowles'; he was duly warned to amend his ways under penalty of a fine of 12d.[71]

Certificates were granted for meeting-places of Protestant Dissenters in Weston from 1696. In 1723 the congregation were described as Quakers. A chapel was registered in 1802.[72] At the present time there are a Wesleyan chapel and a Catholic Apostolic church in the parish.

In 1841 Henricus Octavus Roe *CHARITIES* erected an almshouse known as the Church Almshouses for widows or married couples and endowed the same with £519 15s. 7d. consols, producing £12 19s. 8d. a year.

The same donor likewise gave £463 15s. consols, the annual dividends, amounting to £11 11s. 8d., to be applied in the distribution of sixteen loaves every Sunday after divine service to sixteen poor married men most constant in attendance at church.

The same donor also endowed the National school with £200 consols, producing £5 a year.

In 1839 Robert Pryor by his will, proved in the P.C.C. 16 April, left a legacy for the poor, now represented by £106 15s. 8d. consols, producing £2 13s. 4d. yearly.

The several sums of stock are held by the official trustees, the dividends of which are applied in accordance with the respective trusts.

WILLIAN

Wilie (xi cent.); Wilya, Wylye (xiii cent.); Wylien (xiv cent.); Wickley (xvii cent.).—The parish of Willian has an area of 1,864 acres, of which 1,372½ acres are arable land, 308¾ acres permanent grass, and 19¾ woodland.[1] The greater part of the parish stands over 300 ft. above ordnance datum, but slopes down slightly on the north and in the south-west, where the village and manor-house are situated. It is bounded on the north by the Icknield Way, and for some distance on the west by the main north road. The road between Hitchin and Baldock passes through the northern part of the parish, and this and another road parallel to it form the main streets of the village. The village pond is on the north side of the main road, opposite the Fox Inn ; a little further along is a 16th-century thatched and timbered cottage, known as the Old Vicarage. It is of two stories, the upper of which projects at the back. The church and rectory stand on a hill rising on the south side of the road, with the schools just below them. Punch-arden Hall, the residence of Mr. Ivor Tuckett, M.D., lies at the north end of the village opposite the church. It is a 17th-century house of timber and plaster, the front of which was refaced with brick in the 18th century. It is an L-shaped building with a central chimney stack of brick with octagonal shafts and moulded capitals and bases. On the ground floor there is an original fireplace, the grate of which bears the arms of the Merchant Taylors' Company.

The subsoil is chalk and boulder clay. There is a chalk-pit on the south-east, close to the boundary road, a disused one further south, and a sand-pit just north of the village. There is no railway station in the parish, the nearest being Letchworth, a mile and a half away. Farms in the parish are Norman's Farm and Pixmore. The part of the parish lying north of the road which forms the village street and runs on to Baldock, comprising more than half of the whole, was acquired by the First Garden City Co. in 1903. A portion of the parish was annexed to Baldock for civil purposes in 1881.[1a]

The manor of *WILLIAN* was held *MANORS* in the time of Edward the Confessor by Lewric, a house-carl of Earl Lewin. Half a hide also was held by a sokeman, Elmar of Benington, and a half a hide all but 10 acres of Godwin of Letchworth (Godwin of Souberie) by a certain widow. By 1086 the whole had come into the possession of Geoffrey de Bech, and was assessed at 5½ hides.[2]

Nothing is known of the descendants of Geoffrey de Bech. At the beginning of the 13th century the manor was held by William Malet de Graville,[3] who, it is said, was son of Matthew de Graville, son of William de Rue.[4] William Malet, being a Norman, lost his English lands upon the separation of Normandy, and in 1204 Willian was granted in farm to Matthew de Lilley.[5] In 1216 King John granted the manor to Pain de Chaworth or Chaurces,[6] and he was still holding in 1223.[7] In 1227, however, Pain apparently

---

[65] Dugdale, *Mon.* vii, 820 ; Chan. Inq. p.m. 35 Edw. I, no. 46.
[66] *Liber Antiquus Hug. Wells*, 28.
[67] Feet of F. Herts. East. 40 Eliz. ; Recov. R. Trin. 44 Eliz. rot. 93.
[68] Chan. Inq. p.m. (Ser. 2), ccclxxxvii, 110 ; Inst. Bks. (P.R.O.) ; Bacon, *Liber Regis* ; *Clergy List*.
[69] Information kindly supplied by Mr. M. R. Pryor.
[70] 'Penny-Pricke consisted in throwing with a piece of iron at pence, which were placed on pieces of stick called holes. It was a common game in the 15th century, and is reproved by a religious writer of that period' (J. Strutt, *Sports and Pastimes*, 312).
[71] Add. Chart. 36326.
[72] Urwick, *Nonconf. in Herts.* 626-7.
[1] Statistics from Bd. of Agric. (1905).
[1a] Divided Parishes Act.
[2] *V.C.H. Herts.* i, 333.
[3] Wrottesley, *Ped. from the Plea R.* 490.
[4] Cur. Reg. R. 120, m. 14 ; see *Red Bk. of Exch.* (Rolls Ser.), ii, 731. A Robert Malet is later referred to as having held Willian (Assize R. 325, m. 18 ; *Abbrev. Rot. Orig.* [Rec. Com.], i, 12). The name is probably an error for William. Mr. Round points out that a Mathew de Graville (Gerardi villa) was holding a knight's fee *in capite* in Hertfordshire in 1166 (*Red Bk. Exch.* [Rolls Ser.], i, 362), and that this may have been William Malet's father.
[5] *Rot. Norman.* 129.
[6] Close, 18 John, pt. i, m. 4. Possibly this is a confirmation (see *Red Bk. of Exch.* [Rolls Ser.], ii, 804).
[7] Close, 8 Hen. III, m. 19.

A HISTORY OF HERTFORDSHIRE

forfeited,[8] and the manor was held by Richard de Argentein[9] until 1232, when it was returned to Pain.[10] About 1237 it was committed by the king to John Earl of Lincoln 'during pleasure' and granted by him in 1238 to his nephew Thomas de Pavilly.[11] In 1241, however, the king brought a suit against him and disputed his title to the lands.[12] Thomas claimed to be great-nephew and heir of William Malet the Norman through his grandmother Theofania, sister of William, who was said to have had the manor granted to her by Geoffrey Malet, younger brother of William. Theofania was said to have sued Pain de Chaworth for the manor, but to have died before the suit was settled. Thomas de Pavilly's claim, however, broke down on the ground that it was William the elder brother of Geoffrey who held the manor, and that he was a Norman and had moreover left children. The king therefore took the manor into his own hands.[13]

In 1243 Willian was granted to Paul Peyvre and heirs 'until the land of England and Normandy be one,' in which event Paul was to have a reasonable exchange. £10 from lands in Willian, which the king had given to Hugh de Botyun his yeoman for life, were excepted from the grant.[14] Probably this portion was identical with the 10 librates of land granted to Paul in 1249-50.[15] In 1272 the manor was held by John Peyvre, grandson of Paul, a minor in the custody of Queen Eleanor.[16] John died in 1316 and was succeeded by his son Paul,[17] who granted Willian in 1321 to his brother John and Margaret his wife for their lives.[18] Margaret outlived her husband and married secondly John Mallore, who was holding the manor in right of his wife in 1346.[19] At Margaret's death in 1348 it passed to her nephew Nicholas Peyvre, son of Paul.[20] Nicholas died in 1361 and was succeeded by his son Thomas,[21] his widow Avice, who married secondly William de Clopton, keeping a third of the manor in dower.[22] Thomas settled Willian on himself and his wife Margaret in tail in 1375-80[23] and died in 1429, when the manor passed to his grandson John Broughton, son of his only daughter Mary.[24] Robert Broughton, grandson of John, inherited it in 1489[25] and was succeeded by his son John in 1506,[26] who granted the manor to Edward Cornwall and Elizabeth his wife for their lives, with reversion to the heirs of John Broughton. The latter died in 1518, leaving a son[27] and two daughters. The son John, who was aged six at his father's death, died about 1529.

Willian was then divided between his two sisters Anne and Katherine.[28] Katherine, who was the first wife of Thomas Lord Howard of Effingham, died without male issue in 1535,[29] when her moiety of the manor apparently reverted to her sister Anne, who had married Sir Thomas Cheney, K.G., Lord Warden of the Cinque Ports,[30] for the whole manor came to their son Henry Cheney, afterwards Lord Cheney of Toddington.[31] Henry Cheney and his wife Joan conveyed Willian in 1563 to William Totnam,[32] who in the following year received a pardon for acquiring it without licence.[33] Towards the end of 1564 he sold it to Edward Wilson,[34] who granted it to his son Edward in 1574.[35] Edward Wilson, junior, settled the manor upon his second wife Joan Grey, who afterwards married Edward Lacon,[36] and after whose death in 1624[37] it passed to Edward Wilson, son of Edward Wilson, junior, by his first wife.[38] Ralph Wilson, son of the third Edward, died in 1637 during his father's lifetime, leaving two young sons,[39] Edward, who died in 1639,[40] and Thomas, who died in 1656.[41] After the death of the latter the manor seems to have been divided, for another Thomas Wilson appears in possession of a moiety of Willian in 1672.[42] After this the manor is said to have been divided between three sisters, Frances, Elizabeth and Mary Adams, daughters and co-heiresses of Mary Adams, widow, one of whom must have died soon after, for Mary was holding a moiety in 1728. The second sister is said to have sold her moiety to Richard Way, who sold it to Sir John Dimsdale, from whom it passed to his nephew John Dimsdale, the possessor in 1728.[43] John left it to his cousin Thomas, who acquired the other half of the manor by purchase in 1767 from Elizabeth Marshall, to whom Mary Adams had left it by will.[44] Thomas Dimsdale inoculated the Empress Catherine and various Russian princes for the smallpox and was created a Baron of the Russian Empire in 1769. He died in 1800.[45] Willian continued in the Dimsdale family until 1867, when it was sold to Charles Frederick Hancock,[46] from whom

DIMSDALE. *Argent a fesse dancetty azure between three molets sable with three bezants on the fesse and an augmentation of a scutcheon or with an eagle's wing sable thereon.*

---

[8] See *Abbrev. Plac.* (Rec. Com.), 114: 'Pagan de Chahurz was disseised for war.'
[9] *Cal. Chart. R.* 1226-57, pp. 57, 85, 140.
[10] *Cal. Close*, 1231-4, pp. 190-1.
[11] *Cal. Pat.* 1232-47, p. 226.
[12] Wrottesley, *Ped. from the Plea R.* 490.
[13] *Abbrev. Plac.* (Rec. Com.), 114.
[14] *Cal. Chart. R.* 1226-57, p. 276.
[15] *Abbrev. Rot. Orig.* (Rec. Com.), i, 12.
[16] *Abbrev. Plac.* (Rec. Com.), 180; Assize R. 325, m. 18; *Feud. Aids*, ii, 430.
[17] Chan. Inq. p.m. 9 Edw. II, no. 55.
[18] *Cal. Pat.* 1317-21, p. 579; Chan. Inq. p.m. 7 Edw. III, no. 33.
[19] Feet of F. Herts. 18 Edw. III, no. 296; *Feud. Aids*, ii, 436.
[20] Chan. Inq. p.m. 7 Edw. III, no. 33; 23 Edw. III, pt. ii (1st nos.), no. 41.

[21] Ibid. 35 Edw. III, pt. i (1st nos.), no. 42.
[22] Feet of F. Div. Co. East. 40 Edw. III, no. 22.
[23] *Abbrev. Rot. Orig.* (Rec. Com.), ii, 341; Chan. Inq. p.m. 49 Edw. III, pt. ii (2nd nos.), no. 27; Pat. 4 Ric. II, pt. i, m. 41; *Cal. Pat.* 1377-81, p. 521.
[24] Chan. Inq. p.m. 8 Hen. VI, no. 21.
[25] Ibid. (Ser. 2), v, 131.
[26] Ibid. 23 Hen. VII, no. 67.
[27] Ibid. (Ser. 2), xxxiv, 110.
[28] Ct. of Wards, Misc. Bks. dlxxviii, fol. 178 d., 187 d.
[29] G.E.C. *Complete Peerage*.
[30] Ibid.
[31] Ibid.
[32] Feet of F. Div. Co. East. 5 Eliz.; Recov. R. Hil. 5 Eliz. no. 157.
[33] Pat. 6 Eliz. pt. iii.

[34] Feet of F. Herts. Mich. 6 & 7 Eliz.
[35] Chan. Inq. p.m. (Ser. 2), cxcix, 88; Pat. 27 Eliz. pt. viii, m. 39.
[36] Chan. Decree R. no. 57; Chan. Inq. p.m. (Ser. 2), ccxcviii, 80.
[37] Monum. Inscr.
[38] *Visit. of Herts.* (Harl. Soc. xxii), 105; Feet of F. Herts. Mich. 22 Jas. I.
[39] Chan. Inq. p.m. (Ser. 2), ccclxxxi, 199; Ct. of Wards, Feod. Surv. 17.
[40] Chan. Inq. p.m. (Ser. 2), ccccxc, 65.
[41] Monum. Inscr.
[42] Recov. R. Trin. 24 Chas. II, rot. 128.
[43] Salmon, op. cit. 177.
[44] Clutterbuck, op. cit. ii, 530.
[45] Berry, *Herts. Gen.* 212; see Recov. R. Mich. 13 Geo. III, rot. 12.
[46] Cussans, op. cit. *Broadwater Hund.* 28.

178

it passed to his son Col. Mortimer Hancock. In 1901 the manor came to Capt. Mortimer Fawson Hancock,[47] who in 1903 sold a large part of his estate to the Garden City Pioneer Company Limited.[48] Captain Hancock holds the remainder of the property.

BRAYS or *BRAIES* Manor, of which no trace now remains, belonged to Bigging Priory at Hitchin, and was leased by that house to Richard Yerdeley in 1521, together with a messuage called le Poundehouse.[49] After the Dissolution it was granted with 'le Poundhouse' to John Cock in 1545.[50] By 1564 Brayes had come into the possession of James Needham of Wymondley Priory and was conveyed by him in that year to Thomas Rivett[51] of Baldock, from whom it descended about 1583 to his daughter and co-heiress Anne Lady Windsor,[52] who held it in 1606.[53] For almost a century there is no further record of the manor, but before 1692 it was acquired by Richard Way, patron of Willian rectory. In that year he conveyed it to Knightley Holled, clerk,[54] who held it in 1730.[55] In 1746 it was the subject of a fine between various members of the Priest family,[56] after which no more is heard of it.

Two and a half hides in 'Wilga' were held before the Conquest by Alestan of Boscumbe, and in 1086 by William de Ow. They belonged to the neighbouring manor of Weston.[57] In the time of Edward the Confessor 1 hide of this land was held of Alestan de Boscumbe by Alviet, and in 1086 this hide and another were held of William de Ow by William de Mare. Later the tithes of 'Wilia' were given to the monastery of St. Albans by Thurstan, brother of William de Mare, and 'Robert de Mare gave his tithe likewise.'[58] In 1086 (as Mr. Round points out) there were also 1½ hides in 'Welga' held by Robert de Pontcardon (Punchardon) of Robert Gernon.[59] It seems possible that there has been some confusion between 'Wilga' and 'Wilei' (Welwyn and Willian) here, and that both these holdings lay in Willian. Certainly the estate afterwards known as *PUNCHARDEN* was in this parish. The Punchardon family appear to have been tenants of some importance in Willian in the 13th century. Gilbert de Tany gave a virgate and a half in Willian to St. Albans[60] about the time of Stephen or Henry II; this grant was confirmed by Gilbert's son Walter,[61] and by Ralph de Punchardon,[62] probably his overlord. Roger de Punchardon was holding land in Willian in 1202.[63] In 1247–8 Richard de Punchardon called himself 'lord of Wylye,'[64] and a Wygan Delamere appears as owing him homage. During the abbacy of Roger de Norton, who was Abbot of St. Albans from 1263 to 1301,[65] William son of Geoffrey Punchardon quitclaimed his right in a tenement in Willian to St. Albans.[66] After this the history of the estate is lost until a 'capital messuage called Puncherdownes,' with lands belonging, appears in 1625 in the possession of Edward Wilson, lord of the manor of Willian.[57] He settled it on his son Ralph Wilson, who held it during the lifetime of his father. Ralph died in 1637 and Punchardens passed to his son Edward[58] who died in 1639. His brother and heir Thomas[59] succeeded his grandfather as lord of the manor of Willian, and Puncharden presumably continued with that manor.

The parish church of *ALL SAINTS*,[59a] *CHURCH* standing to the south of the village, is built of flint, mixed in places with freestone, and consists of a chancel, nave, west tower and south porch. The chancel and nave date from the earlier part of the 12th century. About 1430 the west tower was added, outside the west wall of the nave; this wall was then taken down and the nave lengthened about 4 ft. to join the tower, the east diagonal buttresses of the tower being built against the quoins of the nave. A south porch was added in the 15th century, and the chancel was remodelled and probably lengthened in the early part of the 19th century.

In the east wall of the chancel is reset a 15th-century window of three lights containing 17th-century glass with heraldic panels. In the south wall are a doorway with a 12th-century rear-arch and modern external stonework and a late 14th-century two-light window with a square head. The chancel arch is of about 1430 and is of two moulded orders with shafted jambs. On the outside of the south wall of the chancel is a 14th-century tomb recess, very much repaired with cement.

The north wall of the nave has two windows, the easternmost being of the 15th century, of two lights with tracery over, in a dropped two-centred head. The westernmost is modern, and cuts into the arch of the blocked north doorway. There is only one window in the south wall, of the 15th century, and of similar type to that in the north wall, but of three lights. The south doorway, which is of 14th-century character, has been almost wholly restored in cement.

The tower arch is of similar character to the chancel arch and is also of about 1430. The west tower, into which it opens, is of two stages, with diagonal buttresses, and has a stair turret on the north-east and an embattled parapet. The west doorway has a pointed arch inclosed in a square head, with shields in the spandrels, one bearing the instruments of the Passion and the other a bend in an engrailed border. There is an oak lintel which is possibly old. Above the door is a window of three cinquefoiled lights with tracery in a two-centred head. In each face of the belfry stage is a two-light window, with cinquefoiled lights and a quatrefoil over in a two-centred head and a label with grotesque stops. Below the parapet is a

---

[47] Walford, *County Families* (1907).
[48] *Prospectus, First Garden City Ltd.*
[49] Mins. Accts. 32 & 33 Hen. VIII, no. 71.
[50] *L. and P. Hen. VIII,* xx (2), g. 496 (44).
[51] Feet of F. Herts. Hil. 6 Eliz.
[52] Chan. Inq. p.m. (Ser. 2), ccii, 154; G.E.C. *Complete Peerage.*
[53] Recov. R. Mich. 4 Jas. I, rot. 10.
[54] Feet of F. Herts. Trin. 4 Will. and Mary.
[55] Recov. R. East. 3 Geo. II, rot. 129.
[56] Feet of F. Herts. Mich. 20 Geo. II.
[57] *V.C.H. Herts.* i, 327*b*. This holding may be the manor of Lockleys in Welwyn, which in 1303 was held of the heir of the Earl of Pembroke (cf. Weston).
[58] Dugdale, *Mon.* ii, 220.
[59] *V.C.H. Herts.* i, 327*b*.
[60] Cott. MS. Otho, D iii, fol. 167.
[61] Ibid.
[62] Ibid.; Dugdale, *Mon.* ii, 229.
[63] Feet of F. Herts. 4 John, no. 38.
[64] Assize R. 318, m. 4.
[65] Dugdale, *Mon.* ii, 194.
[66] Cott. MS. Otho, D iii, fol. 167.
[67] Ct. of Wards, Feod. Surv. 17.
[68] Chan. Inq. p.m. (Ser. 2), ccclxxxi, 199.
[69] Ibid. ccccxc, 65.
[69a] Dimensions: chancel, 26 ft. 6 in. by 13 ft. 6 in.; nave, 38 ft. by 18 ft. 6 in.; tower, 11 ft. 6 in. square.

A HISTORY OF HERTFORDSHIRE

string with grotesques at the angles and in the centre of each face of the tower. The stair-turret rises above the parapet and is also embattled. The south porch is old, probably of the 15th century, and has a dropped two-centred entrance archway of two orders.

The walls of the nave externally show the uncut small flints, in wide-jointed courses, of 12th-century work. Some of the courses are set in herring-bone pattern, and mixed with the flint are some large blocks of freestone, one of them being a piece of 12th-century moulding re-used in the 15th century when the walls were raised. The masonry of the tower is also small, and has been much faced with cement.

There are the remains, in the chancel archway, of a rood screen of the 15th century, which has been restored with plaster. It is of three bays, the centre being the entrance way, with a four-centred arch, and the side bays similar but traceried. The central doors have been removed to the porch. Set against the south chancel wall are the remains of another similar screen restored with plaster. The stalls in the chancel are good work of the late 15th century, with carved standards, one being an elephant's head, and one the head of St. John the Baptist in a charger.

On the north wall of the chancel is a brass of Richard Golden, 1446, with the figure of a priest in eucharistic vestments; the inscription is broken. On the same wall is a mural monument of Edward Lacon of Willey in Shropshire, 1625, and Joan his wife, 1624, with kneeling figures of the man in armour, his wife and three children. Below is a Latin inscription and above is the shield of Lacon, Quarterly (1) and (6) : Quarterly fessewise indented ermine and [azure], for Lacon ; (2) Three cheverons in a border engrailed ; (3) A ragged cross ; (4) A bend cotised, for Harley ; (5) Three buckles, for Remevill.

On the south wall of the chancel is a large mural monument, with busts and inscription below, of Thomas Wilson, 1656, and Lucia his wife. Above is a shield of the arms : Sable a leaping wolf or and in the chief three stars or ; with the crest of a demi-wolf or. On the same wall are monuments to John Chapman, vicar of the parish, 1624, and his wife Anne, 1633, and to Matthew Thorley, 1634 ; the former having small kneeling figures in a circular head niche and the latter being simply a tablet.

In the east window are three pieces of heraldic glass which are said to be 17th-century work. These are shields of the arms of Chester impaling Berry of Toddington, Cheney of Sherland quartered with Shottesbroke, and Engayne impaling an unknown coat. The shield of Cheney is surrounded by a garter and appears to refer to John Lord Cheney, who died in 1496.

On the chancel floor are slabs to Richard Way, vicar, 1673, and to Alice his wife; 1662.

There are three bells ; the treble by Joseph Eayre, 1760, and the second and third by Miles Graye, 1662.

The plate consists of a cup and cover paten of 1718 and a pewter flagon.

The registers begin in 1558 and are contained in three books : (i) all entries 1687 to 1738 ; (ii) baptisms 1739 to 1812, burials 1739 to 1812, marriages 1739 to 1751; (iii) marriages 1754 to 1812.

WILLIAN CHURCH FROM THE SOUTH-EAST

WILLIAN CHURCH: CHANCEL SCREEN

BROADWATER HUNDRED

GREAT OR MUCH WYMONDLEY

ADVOWSON The advowson belonged to the lord of the manor, and is first mentioned in 1239, when Thomas and Roger de Pavilly established their claim to it against the Prior of Envermeu,[70] on the ground that their grandfather Matthew de Graville presented to the church. The prior stated that William de Rue, father of Matthew, gave the church of Willian to Envermeu, but the claim was not allowed.[71] Paul Peyvre held it in 1247–8,[72] and in the time of his grandson John the king presented owing to his minority. On this occasion the Prior of Bec Hellouin, to which Envermeu was a cell, is mentioned as having contested the king's claim to the advowson.[73] At the Taxation by Pope Nicholas in 1291 the church was valued at £13 6s. 8d., in addition to a portion of 26s. 8d. belonging to the Prior of St. Neots[74]; this payment was evidently long retained by that priory, for as late as 1428 the same sum was paid to it.[75] The advowson continued in the Peyvre family until about 1384,[76] in which year Nigel Loring received a pardon for acquiring it from Thomas Peyvre,[77] his son-in-law. In the year following, Nigel Loring granted it to Robert Braybrook, Bishop of London, and others,[78] who in 1394, or a little before, conveyed it to the king.[79] In that year Richard II gave it to the Prioress and convent of Dartford, on condition that they should appropriate it to the use and profit of the Friars Preachers at Langley.[80] The grant was confirmed in 1399,[81] 1424,[82] and 1466,[83] and the advowson remained in the possession of the Friars until the Dissolution. The rectory was appropriated by the nuns of Dartford and a vicarage ordained between 1399 and 1405.[84] In 1544 the rectory and advowson of the vicarage of Willian were granted by Henry VIII to Thomas Calton, a goldsmith of London, and Margaret his wife.[85] Margaret survived her husband, and she and William their eldest son settled them in 1570 on George and Henry the younger sons, with the remainder to William and his son Thomas. Margaret died in 1571.[86] Henry Calton was in possession of his moiety in 1583,[87] and by 1589 had apparently become sole heir, for in that year he conveyed the whole rectory and advowson to John Phillips.[88] Elizabeth widow of John Phillips held them until her death in 1614, when they came to her granddaughter Elizabeth Johnson.[89] At this date the rectory consisted only of an annual rent of 20 marks issuing from the vicarage. After this there is some obscurity in the descent. Richard Way presented in 1673[90] and died in that year,[91] so that the Richard Way who presented in 1676[92] must have been his heir. In 1725 presentation was made by Stephen Ashby, and in 1739 by Anne Rooke,[93] widow of John Rooke, who died in 1755.[94] According to Clutterbuck the advowson had been sold previous to this to Henry Kingsley, whose granddaughter Elizabeth married William Pym.[95] Their son Francis Pym presented to the vicarage in 1792, 1804 and 1816,[96] and the rectory and advowson continued in the Pym family until 1893, when they were acquired by Mr. Joseph Chalmers-Hunt. They are now in the possession of the Rev. Leonard Chalmers Chalmers-Hunt, M.A.

A dwelling-house was certified as a meeting-place of Protestant Dissenters in Willian in 1714.[97]

CHARITIES In a terrier, dated in 1788, it is stated that 'there are two acres of inclosed pasture given by the late Rev. Mr. Ward, vicar, and by John Izard, to be fed by cows of the poor people of Willian.' The land is let at £2 2s. a year, which is distributed in money.

In 1880 James Smyth, by his will, proved at London 28 February, left £400, now represented by £413 8s. 3d. India 3 per cent. stock, the annual dividends, amounting to £12 8s., to be distributed in meat and coal at Christmas. The stock is held by the official trustees.

GREAT OR MUCH WYMONDLEY

Wimundeslai (xi cent.); Wilmundele (xiv and xv cent.); Wimley.

The parish of Great Wymondley has an area of 1,490 acres, of which 1,397¾ acres are arable land, 348¾ acres permanent grass and 92 acres wood.[1] Two portions of the parish are detached. The first portion, lying a mile south of Great Wymondley proper and separated from it by Little Wymondley, contains the hamlet of Titmore Green, which lies between Redcoats Green and Todd's Green, each of which gives its name to a few cottages. The second detached portion lies still further south, on the borders of Stevenage parish, and has no houses within its area, but contains part of Lucas's Wood. The elevation of the parish in the east is between 300 ft. and 400 ft., but it slopes downwards towards the River Purwell on the western boundary. This river turns the mill of the same name which was leased by the lord of the manor of Great Wymondley from Hitchin.[2] Near to the mill the foundations of a Roman house were found in 1884. A little distance from the boundary, in a meadow beside the road from Hitchin, are the 'Nine Springs' from which rises a brook flowing into the Purwell.

[70] The Priory of St. Lawrence of Envermeu in Seine Inférieure.
[71] Cur. Reg. R. 120, m. 14. According to the descent given under the manor Matthew de Graville would have been great-grandfather of Thomas and Roger de Pavilly. [72] Assize R. Herts. 318.
[73] Ibid. 1220, m. 2.
[74] *Pope Nich. Tax.* (Rec. Com.), 33.
[75] *Feud. Aids*, ii, 463.
[76] Chan. Inq. p.m. 9 Edw. II, no. 55; *Cal. Pat.* 1317–21, p. 579; *Abbrev. Rot. Orig.* (Rec. Com.), ii, 341; Pat. 4 Ric. II, pt. i, m. 41.
[77] Pat. 7 Ric. II, pt. ii, m. 5.
[78] *Cal. Pat.* 1385–9, p. 64.
[79] Ibid. 1391–6, p. 373.
[80] Ibid.
[81] Ibid. 1399–1401, p. 59.
[82] Ibid. 1422–9, p. 264.
[83] Ibid. 1461–7, p. 556.
[84] Linc. Epis. Reg. Mem. Bp. Beaumont, fol. 31 d.
[85] *L. and P. Hen. VIII*, xix (2), g. 527, (8). Under this grant a fee of 24s. is annually paid to the Crown by the owner of the impropriate rectory. Information from Rev. L. C. Chalmers-Hunt.
[86] Chan. Inq. p.m. (Ser. 2), clx, 9.
[87] Feet of F. Div. Co. East. 25 Eliz.
[88] Ibid. Mich. 31 & 32 Eliz.
[89] Chan. Inq. p.m. (Ser. 2), cccxlvii, 6.
[90] Inst. Bks. (P.R.O.).
[91] M.I.
[92] Inst. Bks. (P.R.O.).
[93] Ibid.; Bacon, *Liber Regis*.
[94] M.I.
[95] Clutterbuck, op. cit. (1821), ii, 532.
[96] Inst. Bks. (P.R.O.).
[97] Urwick, op. cit. 629.
[1] Statistics from Bd. of Agric. (1905).
[2] Chan. Inq. p.m. 12 Edw. II, no. 43.

181

A HISTORY OF HERTFORDSHIRE

In the southern part of the parish, where the roads from Hitchin to Graveley and from Little Wymondley to Willian cross, lies the village, at the east end of which is the church. In the village are the former Green Man Inn, a picturesque little thatched house, and one or two late 16th-century or early 17th-century timber and plaster cottages. On the east side of the road from Willian to Little Wymondley are three ponds. Adjoining the churchyard on the east side are the remains of a mount and bailey type of castle. Like the other smaller castles of Hertfordshire it was probably only in use for a short time, and was defended merely by a timber keep on the mount and stockades around the bailey. There is no evidence of any masonry works. It may have been thrown up by John de Argentein, an adherent of King Stephen, in the time of the anarchy as a manorial stronghold, Wymondley being the head of the Argentein barony in Herts. It was probably destroyed as an adulterine or unlicensed castle in the reign of Henry II. Adjoining are indications of Roman occupation.[3]

The Manor Farm is a 16th-century three-gabled and plastered house situated at the left-hand corner where the road from Hitchin enters the village. There is a tradition that James I once slept there. It has a fine yew hedge of great age penetrated by arches. The house is a rectangular building, with a central porch, the inner doorway to which has the original oak frame and door. There are also one or two original fireplaces in the house.

Delamere House, now a farm-house, the residence of Mr. Hailey, stands a little south of the village. Only the central part of the old building remains, flanked on either side by modern additions. No part of it appears to be earlier than the end of the 16th or beginning of the 17th century. It measures about 44 ft. in length by 33 ft. in width. The south or garden front is built of red brick 2 in. thick, and the building consists of two stories and attics. All the windows have mullions, and the lower have transoms as well. There is a modern doorway in the centre, not apparently part of the original design. Over the first floor windows is a brick moulded cornice with dentil course running the whole length of the building, above which are two brick gables, the upper parts of which are semicircular, and resemble those at Rawdon House, Hoddesdon, a building erected in 1622. The north front seems to have been built at a somewhat later period, but probably before the middle of the 17th century. There are two gables on this front also, of different sizes, both being straight and steep, the smaller having kneelers at its springing. The windows, which are placed irregularly, have all stone mullions, the upper having a small moulded cornice over them. The entrance doorway has splayed stone jambs and lintel, and a small fanlight over. The oak door is original and is studded with iron nails. This entrance adjoins the old main stair, which is an unusual position, but the plan may have been governed by the arrangement of the previous building. Under the stair is an old built-up doorway with a four-centred arch, which gave access to the cellars which were under the old west wing, now destroyed. A part of the original wall still exists in the modern cellar, in which is a little shallow niche about 9 in. wide, with arched head. Similar niches exist in the old cellars at Watton Place and Little Wymondley Bury. The drawing room is panelled with old oak up to the ceiling, and has a good oak chimney-piece. The lower part of this, together with the fireplace, is modern, but the upper part has two arched panels, with the nail-head ornament, the panels being flanked and separated by Ionic columns which support the projecting entablature. The architrave and cornice are moulded and the frieze is carved with a flat pattern, which is carried round the frieze of the room. The arrangement is very similar to the panelling at Turner's Hall, Harpenden, and Hammond's Farm, Pirton.

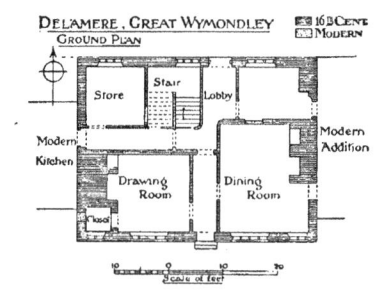

The brickwork of the chimney is of considerable thickness, and affords space for a small closet between the chimney breast and the outer south wall. This closet is lighted by a large window in the south wall, and there is a small bricked-up window in the west wall, which seems to show that the west wing did not project southwards, although old foundations have been dug up to the south.

In an old house, now pulled down, in the hamlet of Redcoats Green resided James Lucas, the 'hermit of Hertfordshire.' His mother's death in 1849, by which he inherited the family estate at Redcoats Green, seems to have greatly accentuated his eccentricities. He barricaded his house and henceforth lived in the kitchen, where he slept on a bed of cinders and clothed himself in a blanket. He protected himself by an iron grille from unwelcome visitors, but was fond of children, to whom he would give sweets. He died of apoplexy in 1874, having hoarded a considerable sum of money in his living room.[4]

The inclosure award, dated 1814, is in the custody of the clerk of the peace. The Authorizing Act was passed in 1811.[5]

The subsoil of the parish is chalk, with a thick deposit of boulder clay above it. On the surface clay is mixed with gravel, penetrated by occasional bosses of chalk. There is an old chalk-pit near the Purwell. The chief crops are wheat, barley and oats alternating with clover, sainfoin, turnips, mangolds and beans.

MANOR In the time of King Edward the Confessor 8 hides in *GREAT WYMONDLEY* were held by the church of St. Mary of Chatteris, Cambs., but three years before King

DELAMERE, GREAT WYMONDLEY
GROUND PLAN
16 B CENT
MODERN

[Floor plan showing: Store, Stair, Lobby, Modern Kitchen, Modern Addition, Drawing Room, Dining Room. Scale of feet.]

---

[3] Mr. F. Seebohm thinks that the inclosure with the site of the Roman occupation represents a Roman holding of about 25 jugera (*Engl. Village Communities*, 431).
[4] *Dict. Nat. Biog.*
[5] *Blue Bk. Incl. Awards.*

182

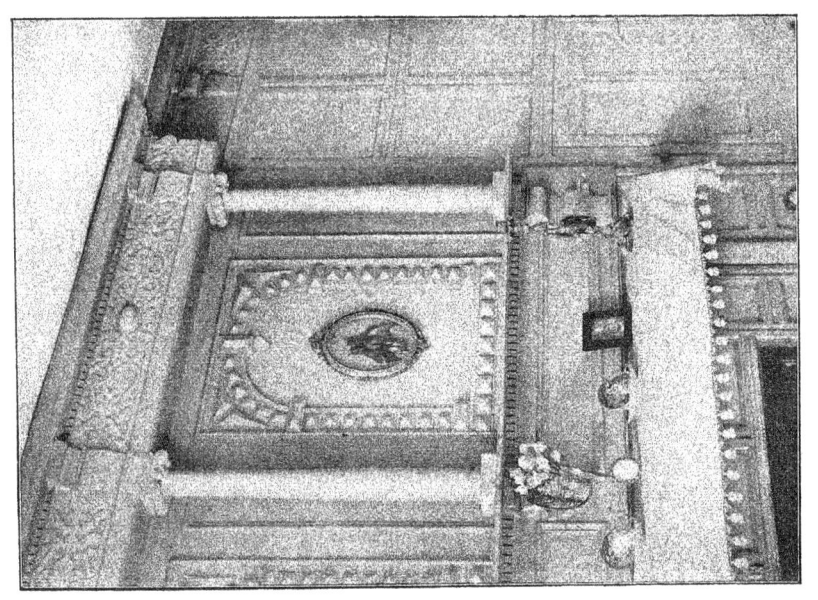

GREAT WYMONDLEY DELAMERE, DRAWING-ROOM CHIMNEY-PIECE

GREAT WYMONDLEY CHURCH, SOUTH DOORWAY

BROADWATER HUNDRED   GREAT OR MUCH WYMONDLEY

Edward's death, i.e. about 1063, the manor was taken away from that church by Earl Harold, afterwards king, and attached by him to his neighbouring manor of Hitchin.[6] Three and a-quarter hides, probably in this parish also,[7] were held before the Conquest by Swen, one of Earl Harold's men.[8] In 1086 King William held the 8 hides,[9] while the other 3¼ hides had been granted to Goisbert de Beauvais.[10]

William I or William Rufus gave the whole estate as an escheat to Reginald de Argentein, as appears from the evidence of his grandson.[11]

The manor was held of the king in chief by grand serjeanty for the service of rendering the king a silver-gilt cup at his coronation feast.[12] This service was performed by the lords of the manor until the coronation of George IV. Since that date the state banquet has been dispensed with, and the lords of the manor have been exempt from this service.

The manor was confirmed to John, son of Reginald de Argentein, by King Stephen,[13] and he was still living in 1166.[14] Reginald de Argentein, presumably the son of John, since he was grandson of the elder Reginald,[15] is mentioned in 1194,[16] and was Sheriff of Hertfordshire in 1196.[17] He was succeeded by Richard de Argentein, who seems to have forfeited, for in 1203 he received a pardon at the petition of the Earl of Albemarle from King John, and had his patrimony restored.[18] Part of it he delivered to Isabel de Argentein in dower in the same year.[19] In 1224 Richard de Argentein was Sheriff of Hertfordshire and Essex,[20] and in 1225 and 1226 custodian of Hertford Castle.[21] He was also the founder of Little Wymondley Priory,[22] and in 1228 is spoken of as 'a noble and one strenuous in arms' who had already been on a pilgrimage to the Holy Land.[23] He returned there later as a Crusader and was killed in an engagement in 1246.[24] His son and successor Giles[25] was engaged in the war against Prince Llewellyn during his father's lifetime, and in 1231 was taken prisoner by the Welsh.[26] Reginald de Argentein, son of Giles, inherited Wymondley in 1283,[27] and was still holding in 1303.[28] His son John, who succeeded in 1307,[29] died about 1318, leaving an infant son John, aged six months,[30] and a widow Agnes, who received Great Wymondley in dower.[31] She afterwards married John Maltravers, who forfeited his lands in 1327,[32] probably being involved in Mortimer's rebellion, but afterwards received them back. At some time, possibly between these two marriages, Agnes was the wife of John de Nerford.[33] In 1331 Great Wymondley was restored to her by the king,[34] and in 1346 John de Maltravers was holding it in her name.[35] Agnes died in 1375, when Wymondley passed to John de Argentein, her son by her first husband,[36] who performed his office of cupbearer at the coronation of Richard II.[37] In 1381 he obtained a licence to entail the manor on his son William and his wife Isabel,[38] but upon the death of John it was claimed in 1383 by his daughter Matilda and her husband Ivo Fitz Warin, and his grandson Baldwin St. George, son of another daughter Elizabeth.[39] These made complaint 'that whereas the said John [de Argentein] delivered certain muniments concerning his lands in a chest under lock and seal to the Prior of [Little] Wylmondesle for safe custody, certain evildoers seized the prior at Neumarkethethe as he was coming to Hallesworth, co. Suffolk to celebrate the obsequies of the said John, patron of his priory, forced him to send for the deeds and deliver them to one William Dargentein and afterwards assaulted the said Ivo and Margaret wife of the said John and their friends at Hallesworth, so that they could not do what was honorably due in oblations, etc., for his decent burial.'[40] This strange tale seems to support the statement of Cussans that William was an illegitimate son. William, however, on the strength of the settlement of 1381, made good his claim, and the manor was delivered to him.[41] In 1400 he obtained a confirmation of Stephen's charter to his ancestor John de Argentein.[42] He died in 1419, leaving an infant grandson John[43] and a widow Margaret, who held a third of the manor in dower until her death in 1427.[44] The young John died in 1420, leaving as his heirs his two sisters Elizabeth and Joan,[45] between whom the manor was divided. Joan, who had married Robert Alington, died childless in 1429, and her moiety passed to her sister Elizabeth, wife of William Alington,[46] who thus became possessed of the whole manor. William Alington, who held Wymondley in right of his wife, died in 1460, leaving a son John,[47] who held it until 1480, when he was succeeded by his son William Alington.[48] The

ARGENTEIN. *Gules three covered cups argent.*

---

[6] *V.C.H. Herts.* i, 301.
[7] The holdings in Great and Little Wymondley are difficult to distinguish, as they are both called Wymondley.
[8] *V.C.H. Herts.* i, 335*b*.
[9] Ibid. 301.   [10] Ibid. 335*b*.
[11] *Rot. Cur. Reg.* (Rec. Com.), i, 391–2.
[12] Ibid. 162; *Testa de Nevill* (Rec. Com.), 270; Assize R. 318, 323, 325; *Cal. Pat.* 1381–5, p. 20; *Cal. S. P. Dom.* 1660–1, p. 585; Coron. Rolls; Round, *The King's Serjeants.*
[13] *Cal. Pat.* 1399–1401, p. 293.
[14] *Pipe R.* 5 *Hen. II* (Pipe R. Soc.), 6; *Red Bk. of Exch.* (Rolls Ser.), i, 332.
[15] *Abbrev. Plac.* (Rec. Com.), 8.
[16] *Rot. Cur. Reg.* (Rec. Com.), 106, 162.
[17] *V.C.H. Herts. Families,* 281.
[18] *Rot. Lit. Pat.* (Rec. Com.), 25.
[19] *Feet of F. Div. Co.* 5 John, no. 35.
[20] *V.C.H. Herts. Families,* 281.

[21] *Rot. Lit. Claus.* (Rec. Com.), ii, 88, 139.
[22] Dugdale, *Mon.* vi, 555.
[23] Matt. Paris, *Chron. Maj.* (Rolls Ser.), iii, 164.
[24] Ibid. iv, 587; Chan. Inq. p.m. 31 Hen. III, no. 16.
[25] Assize R. 318, 323; *Excerpta e Rot. Fin.* (Rec. Com.), ii, 5.
[26] Matt. Paris, *Chron. Maj.* (Rolls Ser.), iii, 203.
[27] G.E.C. *Complete Peerage;* *Abbrev. Rot. Orig.* (Rec. Com.), i, 43; Assize R. 325.   [28] *Feud. Aids,* ii, 429.
[29] G.E.C. *Complete Peerage.*
[30] Chan. Inq. p.m. 12 Edw. II, no. 43.
[31] *Cal. Close,* 1318–23, p. 50.
[32] Exch. Enr. Accts. (L.T.R.), no. 2.
[33] *Cal. Pat.* 1330–4, p. 84.
[34] Ibid.; *Abbrev. Rot. Orig.* (Rec. Com.), ii, 52.

[35] *Feud. Aids,* ii, 436.
[36] Chan. Inq. p.m. 49 Edw. III, pt. ii, no. 17.
[37] Close, 1 Ric. II, m. 45.
[38] *Cal. Pat.* 1381–5, p. 20; Chan. Inq. p.m. 4 Ric. II, no. 110.
[39] John de Argentein also had a third and eldest daughter Joan, whose daughter Margaret wife of Robert de Bokenham was a third heir (Close, 7 Ric. II, m. 5 d.).
[40] *Cal. Pat.* 1381–5, p. 260.
[41] Close, 7 Ric. II, m. 5 d.; Coron. Roll, Hen. IV.
[42] *Cal. Pat.* 1399–1401, p. 293; *Feud. Aids,* ii, 443.
[43] Chan. Inq. p.m. 6 Hen. V, no. 13.
[44] Ibid. 6 Hen. VI, no. 53.
[45] Ibid. 2 Hen. VI, no. 2.
[46] Ibid. 7 Hen. VI, no. 8.
[47] Ibid. 38 & 39 Hen. VI, no. 42.
[48] Ibid. 20 Edw. IV, no. 58.

183

A HISTORY OF HERTFORDSHIRE

latter was killed at the battle of Bosworth Field in 1485, his son Giles, who was only two years old, succeeding him.[49] Giles Alington held Wymondley until 1521,[50] after which it was held by his widow Mary in dower until her death in 1540,[51] when it passed to their son Giles.[52] Sir Giles outlived his son Robert and his grandson Giles and was succeeded in 1586 by his great-grandson, also named Giles, then aged fourteen.[53] At the coronation of James I both Giles Alington and his mother Margaret Elrington claimed the service.[54] From the younger Giles the manor descended in 1638 to his son William, on whom he had settled it in 1631 on the occasion of the latter's marriage with Elizabeth Tollemache.[55] In 1642 William was created first Lord Alington of Killard in Ireland and died in 1648.[56] His son Giles held Wymondley until 1659,[57] when he died a minor and unmarried, and his brother William succeeded.[58] He inherited the Irish title, and in 1682 was also created Lord Alington of Wymondley.[59] He died in 1684, leaving an infant son Giles, for whom his mother Diana (Verney) claimed the service at the coronations of James II and William and Mary. As she was a woman, however, the service was performed in 1685 by Giles's uncle Hildebrand Alington, and in 1689 by John Jacob, stated to be the nearest relation.[60]

Upon the death of Giles Lord Alington without issue in 1691 the barony of Alington of Wymondley became extinct, while the Irish title passed to Hildebrand Alington, uncle of Giles and brother of William Alington.[61] Hildebrand claimed the English estates also, but Wymondley was sold upon a decree passed in Chancery to Elizabeth Hamilton or Hamblenton, widow,[62] daughter of John Lord Colepeper, who claimed to perform the service at the coronation of Anne and was allowed, William Hamilton her son executing the office.[63] Hildebrand, Lord Alington, bought back Wymondley from Mrs. Hamilton in 1704,[64] but died childless in 1722–3,[65] leaving the manor by will to his three nieces, daughters of William Alington and sisters of Giles.[66] These three ladies were Juliana Viscountess Howe, Diana wife of Sir George Warburton and Catherine wife of Sir Nathaniel Napier; at the coronation of George II the service was claimed by Juliana Howe, Sir Richard Grosvenor, husband of Diana's daughter Diana,[67] and Nathaniel Napier, widower of Catherine.[68] It seems to have been performed by Sir Richard, to whom Diana Warburton had conveyed her third of the manor upon his marriage, and to whom the other two thirds subsequently came. He died childless in 1732, and his brother and heir Thomas in the following year.[69] The next brother, Sir Robert Grosvenor, who thus inherited the estates,[70] is said to have acquired Wymondley from Sir Richard in 1730,[71] two years before he would otherwise have obtained it. His son Sir Richard Grosvenor, who succeeded him in 1755,[72] sold the manor in 1767 to the Hon. Mordaunt Cracherode,[73] from whom it descended in 1773 to his son Clayton Mordaunt Cracherode, the well-known collector of books and prints.[74] He is said to have been of such a retiring disposition that his dread lest he should at any time be called upon to undertake the service of cupbearer embittered his whole life.[75] Upon his death in 1799 his lands passed to his sister Anne,[76] who left Wymondley by will to Shute Barrington, Bishop of Durham, in trust for sale.[77] The latter sold the manor in 1806 to William Wilshere of the Frythe, Welwyn, who performed his service at the coronation of George IV,[78] the last occasion upon which it has been necessary. William Wilshere was succeeded in 1824 by his nephew William Wilshere, who died in 1867.[79] Charles Willes Wilshere, brother and heir of the latter,[80] lived until 1906, and was survived by three daughters, the eldest of whom, Miss Edith Marie Wilshere, is the present lady of the manor.

ALINGTON. *Argent a bend engrailed between six billets sable.*

GROSVENOR. *Azure a garb or.*

Sac and soc, toll, team and infangentheof were granted to John de Argentein by King Stephen, and confirmed to William de Argentein in 1400.[81] In 1278 Giles de Argentein claimed view of frankpledge and amendment of the assize of bread and ale.[82]

The manor of *DELAMERE* (Lammers, xv cent.; Delamers, xvii cent.), now Delamere House, was held of Great Wymondley,[83] and evidently took its name from the family of Delamare; John Delamare is mentioned as living in Great Wymondley in 1308.[84] The manor is first mentioned in 1487, when John Pulter died seised of it.[85] He was succeeded by his son William, who held it by service of 40s. yearly, and it remained in the Pulter family. In 1600 Edward Pulter, whose father Edward held it before him,[86] settled it on his son Litton, on the

---

[49] Chan. Inq. p.m. (Ser. 2), i, 34.
[50] Feet of F. Trin. 8 Hen. VIII; L. and P. Hen. VIII, ii, 2875; Chan. Inq. p.m. (Ser. 2), xxxvi, 16.
[51] Ct. of Wards, Misc. Bks. dlxxviii, fol. 426 d.
[52] L. and P. Hen. VIII, xvi, 1056 (54).
[53] Chan. Inq. p.m. (Ser. 2), ccxi, 163. Coron. Roll, Jas. I; Cal. S. P. Dom. 1603–10, p. 24.
[54] Chan. Inq. p.m. (Ser. 2), ccccxci, 90.
[55] G.E.C. Complete Peerage.
[56] Ibid.; Feet of F. Div. Co. Mich. 1656.
[57] G.E.C. Complete Peerage; Coron. Roll, Chas. II; Cal. S. P. Dom. 1660–1, p. 585.

[58] G.E.C. Complete Peerage; Recov. R. East. 24 Chas. II, rot. 8.
[59] Coron. Rolls, Jas. II and Will. and Mary.
[60] G.E.C. Complete Peerage.
[61] Chauncy, op. cit. ii, 115; Feet of F. Div. Co. Mich. 10 Will. III.
[62] Coron. Rolls, Anne and Geo. I.
[63] Ibid. Geo. I.
[64] G.E.C. Complete Peerage.
[65] Salmon, op. cit. 188.
[66] G.E.C. Complete Baronetage.
[67] Coron. Roll, Geo. II.
[68] G.E.C. Complete Baronetage.
[69] Feet of F. Div. Co. Trin. 26 & 27 Geo. II.
[70] Cussans, op. cit. Broadwater Hund. 52.

[71] G.E.C. Complete Baronetage.
[72] Coron. Roll, Geo. IV; Com. Pleas D. Enr. Mich. 8 Geo. III, m. 114.
[73] Dict. Nat. Biog.
[74] Ibid.
[75] Ibid.; Coron. Roll, Geo. IV.
[76] Will, P.C.C. 603 Kenyon.
[77] Coron. Roll, Geo. IV.
[78] V.C.H. Herts. Families, 250.
[79] Ibid. 251.
[80] Cal. Pat. 1399–1401, p. 293.
[81] Assize R. 323, 325.
[82] Chan. Inq. p.m. (Ser. 2), iii, 74; Ct. of Wards, Feod. Surv. 17.
[83] Cal. Pat. 1307–13, p. 87.
[84] Chan. Inq. p.m. (Ser. 2), iii, 74.
[85] Visit. of Herts. (Harl. Soc. xxii), 116.

184

GREAT WYMONDLEY CHURCH FROM THE NORTH-EAST

BROADWATER HUNDRED

GREAT or MUCH WYMONDLEY

occasion of his marriage with Penelope Capell.[87] Litton Pulter died in 1608 and his father in 1629, after whose death the manor descended to Litton's son Arthur.[88] The next evidence of this manor is a recovery suffered in 1740 by Pulter Forester,[89] suggesting that an heiress of the Pulters conveyed the manor to the Forester family. In 1779 it was conveyed by Benjamin Palmer and Sarah his wife to Clayton Mordaunt Cracherode,[90] lord of the manor of Wymondley, and probably it became merged in that manor.

The parish church of *ST. MARY, CHURCH* which stands at the east end of the village, is built of flint with stone dressings. The nave walls are of wide jointed courses of uncut pebbles, with a few Roman tiles interspersed. The chancel is tiled and the nave roof is of lead.[90a]

The church consists of a chancel, nave, west tower, north vestry and south porch. The first two are of the 12th century, the west tower was built in the 15th century and the vestry and porch are modern. In 1883-4 the building was restored throughout and the stonework to a great extent renewed. Windows were inserted in the 13th, 14th and 15th centuries.

The chancel is apsidal, with a 14th-century east window of three lights, with tracery in a square head. In the north wall a 13th-century lancet has been set in the jambs and rear-arch of a 12th-century window. In the south wall are a 13th-century lancet and a low-side window probably also of the 13th century. All these windows have undergone modern repair. The early 12th-century chancel arch is in good preservation. It is semicircular, and rests on engaged shafts with voluted capitals and scalloped bases. In the chancel is a 13th-century piscina with angle shafts and a modern square head. The sill is also modern, and the capitals of the shafts are restored. There is an aumbry in the south-west corner of the chancel, recessed in the east jamb for a door. The nave is lighted on the north by a two-light window of the 14th century, with a quatrefoil in a two-centred head, very much repaired, and by two late 15th-century three-light windows, which have been repaired and their cusps cut away. The north doorway, possibly retaining remnants of 14th-century work, now opens to the vestry. The south doorway is of about 1120, but has been greatly repaired. It has a round arch with an edge roll and star ornament on the tympanum. The jambs are of two orders, with abaci, on which the star ornament is repeated on each face. The shafts of the outer order have capitals carved with human faces and inverted cushion bases.

On the north side of the chancel arch is a low squint of the 15th century into the chancel. Above it is a corbel, probably originally under the rood-

DELAMERE, GREAT WYMONDLEY : SOUTH FRONT

---

[87] Chan. Inq. p.m. (Ser. 2), cccci, 94.
[88] Ibid. ; Ct. of Wards, Feod. Surv. 17.
[89] Recov. R. 12 & 14 Geo. II, rot. 238.

[90] Feet of F. Herts. East. 19 Geo. III ; Com. Pleas D. Enr. Trin. 19 Geo. III, m. 17.

[90a] Dimensions: chancel, 20 ft. by 16 ft.; nave, 45 ft. by 19 ft. 6 in. ; tower, 11 ft. square.

BROADWATER HUNDRED — GREAT or MUCH WYMONDLEY

occasion of his marriage with Penelope Capell.[87] Litton Pulter died in 1608 and his father in 1629, after whose death the manor descended to Litton's son Arthur.[88] The next evidence of this manor is a recovery suffered in 1740 by Pulter Forester,[89] suggesting that an heiress of the Pulters conveyed the manor to the Forester family. In 1779 it was conveyed by Benjamin Palmer and Sarah his wife to Clayton Mordaunt Cracherode,[90] lord of the manor of Wymondley, and probably it became merged in that manor.

CHURCH The parish church of ST. MARY, which stands at the east end of the village, is built of flint with stone dressings. The nave walls are of wide jointed courses of uncut pebbles, with a few Roman tiles been set in the jambs and rear-arch of a 12th-century window. In the south wall are a 13th-century lancet and a low-side window probably also of the 13th century. All these windows have undergone modern repair. The early 12th-century chancel arch is in good preservation. It is semicircular, and rests on engaged shafts with voluted capitals and scalloped bases. In the chancel is a 13th-century piscina with angle shafts and a modern square head. The sill is also modern, and the capitals of the shafts are restored. There is an aumbry in the south-west corner of the chancel, recessed in the east jamb for a door. The nave is lighted on the north by a two-light window of the 14th century, with a quatrefoil in a two-centred head, very much repaired, and by two late 15th-century three-light windows, which have been

DELAMERE, GREAT WYMONDLEY : SOUTH FRONT

interspersed. The chancel is tiled and the nave roof is of lead.[90a]

The church consists of a chancel, nave, west tower, north vestry and south porch. The first two are of the 12th century, the west tower was built in the 15th century and the vestry and porch are modern. In 1883-4 the building was restored throughout and the stonework to a great extent renewed. Windows were inserted in the 13th, 14th and 15th centuries.

The chancel is apsidal, with a 14th-century east window of three lights, with tracery in a square head. In the north wall a 13th-century lancet has repaired and their cusps cut away. The north doorway, possibly retaining remnants of 14th-century work, now opens to the vestry. The south doorway is of about 1120, but has been greatly repaired. It has a round arch with an edge roll and star ornament on the tympanum. The jambs are of two orders, with abaci, on which the star ornament is repeated on each face. The shafts of the outer order have capitals carved with human faces and inverted cushion bases.

On the north side of the chancel arch is a low squint of the 15th century into the chancel. Above it is a corbel, probably originally under the rood-

---

[87] Chan. Inq. p.m. (Ser. 2), cccci, 94.
[88] Ibid. ; Ct. of Wards, Feod. Surv. 17.
[89] Recov. R. 13 & 14 Geo. II, rot. 238.

[90] Feet of F. Herts. East. 19 Geo. III ; Com. Pleas D. Enr. Trin. 19 Geo. III, m. 17.

[90a] Dimensions: chancel, 20 ft. by 16 ft.; nave, 45 ft. by 19 ft. 6 in. ; tower, 11 ft. square.

loft, the stairs to which remain on the north-east in the thickness of the wall. The upper and lower doorways are also still in existence, but their stonework has been entirely renewed. The nave roof is of the 15th century and rests on large grotesque corbels.

The tower arch is four-centred and of two moulded orders, the inner resting upon the shafts of the jambs and the outer continuous. The work is of late 15th-century type.

The tower is of three stages, marked externally by strings, and has diagonal buttresses. The parapet is embattled and the roof is pyramidal and tiled. The west doorway is two-centred, of two moulded orders, and has been greatly repaired. The west window above it is old, but the tracery is wholly modern. In the belfry stage there is a window of two lights in each face; all of these are much repaired. The string below the parapet has a gargoyle in the middle of each face, and at the north-west corner the stair-turret rises above the parapet.

In the north-east corner of the nave is an image niche with a trefoiled head. The font, which is octagonal and quite plain, is of the late 15th or early 16th century. At the west end of the nave are several late 15th or early 16th-century benches, repaired.

In the nave, at the north-east, is a floor slab, inscribed 'Henry Barnewell 1638.' On the outside of the south wall is an imperfect incised sundial.

There are six bells, of which the third is by Joseph Eayre, 1760, and the fifth by John Dyer, 1595. The remainder are by Mears & Stainbank, 1908.

The plate is modern.

The registers begin in 1561, and are contained in three books: (i) all entries 1561 to 1690; (ii) baptisms 1710 to 1812, burials 1710 to 1812, marriages 1710 to 1755; (iii) marriages 1755 to 1811.

ADVOWSON
The church of Great Wymondley seems to have been originally a chapel to Hitchin.[91] In 1199 it was the subject of a suit between Reginald de Argentein and the Abbess of Elstow.[92] The abbess maintained that Judith niece of William the Conqueror, who founded the abbey of Elstow, gave to the nuns the vill of Hitchin with its church and the chapel of Wymondley pertaining to it, and she produced the charter and confirmations by William I and Henry I and II, also the testimonials of the archdeacon and the bishop who dedicated the church, and of Henry the king. Reginald on the other hand said that the church of Wymondley had never pertained to that of Hitchin, and that in the time of William I a certain Alfled made presentation to that church, and that afterwards it was given to his grandfather Reginald together with the manor, and therefore he now claimed the advowson, as two presentments had already been made by his family. In 1208–9 Richard de Argentein, the son of Reginald, acknowledged the right of the Abbess of Elstow to the advowson on condition that she would 'receive him into all benefits and prayers which were made in the church of Elstow.'[93] About this time Elstow appropriated the church, and a vicarage was ordained by Hugh Wells, Bishop of Lincoln, whose episcopacy lasted from 1209 to 1235.[94] Elstow kept the church until the Dissolution, after which the tithes were included in the grant of Hitchin rectory to Trinity College, Cambridge, by Henry VIII. The church was evidently built as a chapel to Hitchin and the advowson is not mentioned in the grant.[95] The few presentations of which there are record were made by Trinity College except in 1663 and 1675, when the Bishop of Lincoln presented by lapse.[96] The benefice was united with that of St. Ippollits by an instrument dated 15 March 1685,[97] and the vicar resides in the latter parish.

Meeting-places for Protestant Dissenters in Great Wymondley were registered at various dates from 1776 to 1814.[98]

CHARITIES
In 1623 John Welch by will charged his estate of Redcoats in this parish with an annuity of £4, of which £1 10s. was payable to the vicar and £2 to the poor for bread and 10s. to Little Wymondley.

In 1735 Robert Tristram by his will devised 10s. a year for bread for the poor of this parish.

In 1821 James Lucas by deed gave £150 consols, the annual dividends, amounting to £3 15s., to be applied as to two-thirds for the relief and assistance of the poor of this parish and one-third for the poor of Little Wymondley.

The charities are duly applied.

LITTLE WYMONDLEY

This parish has an area of 1,006 acres, of which 599 acres are arable land, 226½ acres permanent grass and 6½ acres wood.[1] Two portions of the parish are detached. One of very small area lies west of Redcoats Green and the other is situated south of Titmore Green and contains a few cottages which are called Lower Titmore Green. The parish slopes downward in a south-westerly direction from an elevation of nearly 400 ft. The Great Northern railway passes through the village, but the nearest stations are Stevenage, 2 miles south-east, and Hitchin, 2½ miles north-west. The village lies on the road from Hitchin to Stevenage. Near its centre a road branches off northwards to Great Wymondley, passing the site of the former priory. The Great North Road runs along the north-east boundary of the parish. The subsoil is chalk with a layer of boulder clay; the surface soil is clay and gravel with occasional chalk. There is a chalk-pit south of the village and a gravel-pit in a field east of the vicarage. The village has many old and picturesque cottages. The Buck's Head Inn is an early 17th-century timber and plaster house, with

[91] See *Pope Nich. Tax.* (Rec. Com.), 36.
[92] *Abbrev. Plac.* (Rec. Com.), 8; *Rot. Cur. Reg.* (Rec. Com.), i, 391–2.
[93] *Feet of F. John*, no. 120. The Alfled who is mentioned as an early patron was lord of Little Wymondley before the Conquest. It was perhaps he who granted Great Wymondley to St. Mary of Chatteris, with a reservation of the advowson.
[94] *Liber Antiquus* (ed. Gibbons), 28.
[95] Information kindly supplied by the Bursar of Trinity Coll.
[96] Inst. Bks. (P.R.O.).
[97] Information kindly supplied by the Bursar of Trinity Coll.
[98] Urwick, op. cit. 631.
[1] Statistics from Bd. of Agric. (1905).

BUCK'S HEAD INN, LITTLE WYMONDLEY

LITTLE WYMONDLEY BURY FROM THE EAST

an overhanging gable at each end, and the 'Plume of Feathers' is an old red brick house on the opposite side of the road.

Wymondley Hall, now a farm-house, the residence of Mr. M. H. Foster, is a picturesque many-gabled building, standing close to the railway where it crosses the main road to Hitchin. There is nothing of architectural interest inside the building, and modern subdivisions of the rooms have destroyed all traces of the original plan. The house appears to have been erected during the early part of the 17th century, and is built of thin 2-in. bricks, with a good deal of timber-framed work covered with plaster on the upper story. The principal front, which faces west, has six gables, the two northernmost, however, being modern additions. Of the two middle gables, one has a bay window its whole height, the other having merely a slightly projecting oriel on the upper story with an entrance porch under. The south gable has a projecting upper story, timber framed and plastered, below which is a bay window, and up in the gable is an oriel window finished with a small gable under the main gable. The corresponding large gable at the north end has a projecting bay continued up the two stories and finished with a similar small gable. All the roofs are tiled. The entrance door and frame are original. The frame is moulded and square-headed, the mouldings having ornamental stops outside. Many of the features of this front, such as the moulded door frame and the subsidiary gables over the oriels and bays immediately underneath the main gables, bear a close resemblance to those on the front of Egerton House, Berkhampstead. The back of the house is chiefly remarkable for the picturesque disposition of the chimneys. There are two stacks of chimneys separated by a small projecting gable.

The Priory farm-house, the property of Col. Heathcote of Shephallbury and residence of Mrs. Charles Sworder, stands about half a mile north of the church on the site of part of the old Priory buildings, some parts of which are incorporated in the present house. Chauncy, writing about the year 1700, mentions the cloisters and chapel which existed in his time, but these have now almost disappeared. The plan of the house is not on the usual lines, due to the positions of the old walls; indeed, it seems that the builder of the dwelling-house merely surrounded a part of the aisleless nave of the priory church with an external wall. The old thick 13th-century walling has been a good deal cut about in order to afford passages to the different apartments, and some arches which are said to exist in the wall next the drawing room and pantry, probably part of the arcade of the north wall of the cloister, have been built up. The only arch now remaining is a portion of one of the south windows of the church over a doorway to the bedroom above the drawing room, and it appears to be in its original position. The opening is 4 ft. 8 in. wide, and has a pointed arch of 13th-century date, with arch mould consisting of two rolls with a deep hollow between, resting on a detached shaft with moulded capital. It is of soft limestone or clunch, and a portion of one side is hidden by a later wall. The oldest portion of the external wall is at the back or east side of the house. It is built mainly of clunch, and in the wall is a doorway, now built up, with splayed four-centred arch. This wall may belong to the latter part of the 16th century. All the rest of the external walling is of brick, a good deal of it refaced in modern times, but the older parts, chiefly on the north side, are faced with the original thin bricks rising about 9½ in. to four courses. On the north side are three equal gables, the windows still retaining their old oak mullions and transoms. Elsewhere the windows have been modernized. The old chimneys consist of square shafts of brick set diagonally, and probably belong to the early part of the 17th century. The west front has been much modernized. Internally many of the rooms are lined with oak moulded panelling of early 17th-century date, and there is a small plain old stair in the north-east

LITTLE WYMONDLEY HALL : ENTRANCE DOORWAY

LITTLE WYMONDLEY HALL FROM THE SOUTH-WEST

LITTLE WYMONDLEY PRIORY FROM THE NORTH-WEST

BROADWATER HUNDRED — LITTLE WYMONDLEY

corner of the building. The old front entrance door is now used in the doorway to the store adjoining the pantry. To the east of the house is the old garden, which still retains part of the old brick inclosure wall, at one point in which is a small niche with circular arched head of stone. There are traces of coloured ornament in the niche. South of the house is a large tithe barn of nine bays, with weather-boarded sides and tiled roof. It measures externally about 102 ft. by 39 ft. The remains of a moat are still visible, partly surrounding the house, garden and barn. Beyond the moat, to the south-east of the house, is the old orchard completely encircled by a grove of very old box trees, about 20 ft. in height. To the north-west of the house is the old dove-house, now converted into a cottage. In a field some few hundred yards north-east of the house are the remains of the old conduit head, from which water was brought to turn the spit in the kitchen, being used for that purpose until the middle of the 19th century. The conduit head is a small shallow basin sunk below the floor of a small building, some of the old floor tiles being still in their places. The walls of the building have lately been partly rebuilt, but, as no record of the old building could be found, the new work was copied from another old building elsewhere. The old stone doorway with its four-centred arch still remains.

Wymondley Bury, the residence of Mr. Henry Parkes, stands in a moated inclosure adjoining the south side of the church, a little to the south-east of the village. The moat contains water on the north-west and north-east sides of the house, but has been filled up on the other sides. The principal, or north-east, front of the house is approached by a modern bridge over the moat. The present house, which is probably only a portion of the late 16th-century house, is L-shaped, and has been much added to in the 17th century and modernized both outside and inside. All the brick facing, except to the chimneys, and all the windows have been renewed. The principal entrance still retains the old door of two thicknesses of oak planks fastened with iron studs. The dining room, to the right of the entrance, has a very interesting fireplace. The old moulded oak beam over the ingle-nook is 13 ft. 4 in. in length, and the depth of the opening is 5 ft., but its width has now been much reduced by inserting new oak jambs moulded to match the lintel. This room was probably the hall of the old manor-house. Beside the dining room is a small room used as a study, below which is an old cellar, in the walls of which are eight or nine small niches with arched heads formed in brickwork. They are placed from 3 ft. 6 in. to 4 ft. above the floor, and are from 9 in. to 11 in. wide and 9 in. in depth. Their average height is about 12 in. They were probably used to hold wine flasks. None of them appear to have had a door. There is a very similar series of niches in the cellar at Watton Place. Close to the house on the north is the old brick dove-house which still contains some 300 nests. A little to the south-east of the house stands a fine Spanish chestnut evidently of great age but still flourishing. Gilpin refers to it in his 'Forest Scenery' about the year 1789. The main trunk is badly split, rendering any measurements misleading.

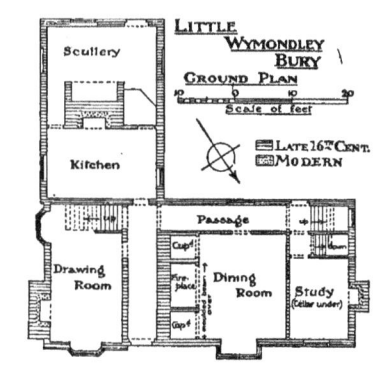

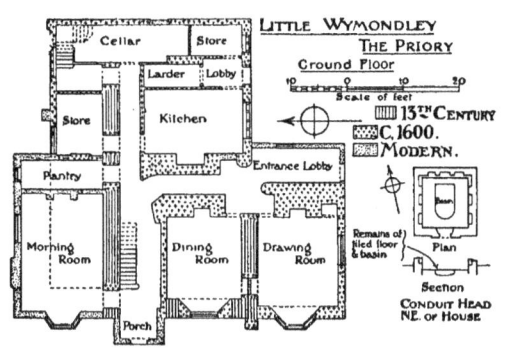

The old manor-house of Great and Little Wymondley was probably on the same site,[1a] but no trace of it now remains. It is described as 'a hall with chambers, chapels and rooms annexed,' and was called 'Somerhalle.'[2]

Wymondley House, a square modern residence, is now the residence of Mr. James W. Courtenay. From 1799 to 1832 it was used as an academy for training young men for the Nonconformist ministry. This had been founded by Dr. Doddridge at Northampton about 1738, and in 1832 was removed to London.

The inclosure award is included in that of Great Wymondley.

Before the Norman Conquest *LITTLE MANORS WYMONDLEY* (Wymundeslai) was held by one Alflet of Robert Fitz Wimarc.[3] After the Conquest it was divided between two owners, 1 hide being held in 1086 by William of Robert Gernon,[4] and a hide and a quarter by

---

[1a] Chan. Inq. p.m. 2 Hen. VI, no. 27.   [2] Ibid. 6 Hen. VI, no. 53.   [3] *V.C.H. Herts.* i, 309, 323.   [4] Ibid. 323*b*.

189

A HISTORY OF HERTFORDSHIRE

Adam Fitz Hubert of the Bishop of Bayeux.[5] The lands of Adam Fitz Hubert, brother of Eudo Dapifer, went in other Hertfordshire cases to the Valognes family, but there is nothing to show what happened to them here. The Gernon lands forming the manor of Little Wymondley came to the Montfitchet family (see Letchworth), and were divided about 1258 between the three sisters and heirs of Richard de Montfitchet, to the second of whom, Aveline, Little Wymondley was apportioned. This Aveline married William de Fortibus Earl of Albemarle,[6] who was starved to death in the Levant in 1241, and who was succeeded by his son William. The latter died in 1256 and his two children died during the lifetime of their mother.[7] The earldom of Albemarle being thus extinct, Little Wymondley was thenceforward held of the king in chief of the honour of Albemarle for 20*s*. rent yearly to be rendered at the ward of Craven Castle.[8] By 1419 the service was reduced to 6*s*. 8*d*.[9]

with the reversion of all the lands belonging to the priory, was granted to James Needham, 'accountant, surveyor-general and clerk of the king's works,'[12] to be held of the king in chief by the service of a tenth part of a knight's fee.[13] James obtained a licence to entail the manor on his son John,[14] who succeeded his father in 1545.[15] George Needham, son of John, settled the manor on his son Eustace on his marriage in 1615, and in 1623 it was settled on George the son of Eustace.

NEEDHAM. *Argent a bend engrailed azure between two harts' heads caboshed sable.*

George Needham the first died in 1626.[16] George the younger died in 1669 and was succeeded by another George,[17] his son, who

LITTLE WYMONDLEY PRIORY : NORTH FRONT

Before the end of the 13th century the manor of Little Wymondley was held in sub-tenancy by the Argentein family ; it is first mentioned in the possession of that family upon the delivery of the lands of Giles to his son and heir Reginald in 1282–3.[10] From that date it has followed the same descent as the manor of Great Wymondley (q.v.).

WYMONDLEY PRIORY was founded during the reign of Henry III by Richard de Argentein, lord of the manor of Great Wymondley, some time previous to 1218.[11] It was suppressed in 1537 and the site,

died without male issue in 1725.[18] His heirs were his daughters, Barbara, who married John Sherwin, and Martha the wife of Thomas Browne,[19] the eminent land surveyor, who for a while resided at his wife's manor in Little Wymondley. In 1733 the manor was sold to Samuel Vanderplank,[20] from whom it is said to have descended,[21] through his daughter Anna, who married Gilbert Joddrell, to Anna Joddrell,[22] the wife of Christopher Clitherow of Essendon, who sold it in 1806 to Samuel Heathcote. In 1812 it came by the will of the latter to his grandson

---

[5] *V.C.H. Herts.* i, 309*a*.
[6] G.E.C. *Complete Peerage* ; *Testa de Nevill* (Rec. Com.), 280.
[7] G.E.C. *Complete Peerage*.
[8] Chan. Inq. p.m. 12 Edw. II, no. 43 ; 49 Edw. III (2nd nos.), no. 17 ; *Cal. Pat.* 1381–5, p. 20.
[9] Chan. Inq. p.m. 6 Hen. V, no. 13 ; 7 Hen. VI, no. 8 ; 38 & 29 Hen. VI, no. 42 ; 20 Edw. IV, no. 58.
[10] *Abbrev. Rot. Orig.* (Rec. Com.), i, 43.
[11] Dugdale, *Mon.* vi, 555.
[12] *Dict. Nat. Biog.*
[13] *L. and P. Hen. VIII*, xiii, p. 589 ; Aug. Off. Dec. ii, R. 57.
[14] *L. and P. Hen. VIII*, xvi, 780.
[15] Chan. Inq. p.m. (Ser. 2), vii, 112.
[16] Ibid. cccxxx, 161.
[17] Recov. R. Trin. 5 Will. and Mary, rot. 91 ; Trin. 8 Anne, rot. 94.
[18] Salmon, op. cit. (1728), 189.
[19] *Dict. Nat. Biog.*
[20] Feet of F. Herts. Mich. 7 Geo. II.
[21] Cussans, op. cit. *Broadwater Hund.* 59.
[22] Recov. R. East. 10 Geo. III, rot. 311.

190

LITTLE WYMONDLEY CHURCH FROM THE NORTH-WEST

LITTLE WYMONDLEY PRIORY BARN

Samuel Heathcote Unwin, who took the additional surname of Heathcote,[23] and died in 1862. The manor descended to his son Col. Unwin Unwin-Heathcote,[24] who is the present holder.

The capital messuage called *WYMONDLEY BURY*, which belonged in the 16th century to Wymondley Priory (q.v.), was sold after the dissolution of that house by an indenture of 1544 to John Pigott and Margaret Grainger, whom he was about to marry.[25] John Pigott died in 1558, but the messuage remained in the possession of his widow, who married John Palmer. Upon her death in 1581 it passed to her son Maurice Pigott.[26] The latter was succeeded by Thomas Pigott, who in 1609 settled the estate upon himself and Elizabeth his wife for their lives, with remainder to his daughter Elizabeth and her husband. Thomas died in 1611, his heirs being his daughters, Rebecca wife of Henry Bull of Hertford and Elizabeth wife of Beckingham Butler, upon whom it was settled.[27] Beckingham Butler became lord of the manor of Tewin (q.v.) in 1620, and Wymondley Bury descended with that manor until at least 1746,[28] when it was held by Edmund Bull.

The parish church of *ST. MARY CHURCH* stands by itself on rising ground about a quarter of a mile from the village, and is built of flint rubble cemented over, with stone dressings and a tiled roof. It consists of a chancel, nave, north aisle, north vestry, south porch and west tower.[28a]

The chancel, nave and tower are of the 15th century, probably late, but the restoration in the 19th century, when the chancel was lengthened and the aisle, vestry and porch were added, has obscured the history of the building.

The east and north windows of the chancel and the chancel arch are modern. In the south wall are two single lights, probably of the 15th century, but greatly repaired with cement. The western of the two is set low in the wall. In the east wall is reset a 15th-century piscina.

The nave has a modern north arcade. On the south side the wall is thickened towards the east by nearly a foot, probably for the rood-stair, as one of the doors to the rood-loft was discovered during a repair. In the south wall are two windows, possibly of the 15th century, but much defaced with cement. That near the east is of two lights and the other of a single light. Between them is the south doorway, also of the 15th century; it is two-centred and of two wave-moulded orders. The modern porch is of brick. The tower arch is of 15th-century date. It is two-centred, of two chamfered orders, and has shafted jambs with clumsy capitals. The tower, of two receding stages, has a brick parapet, probably modern. The west window is of two lights with tracery in a four-centred head, and is much repaired with cement; the belfry stage windows, in the north and west faces, are of two lights in a square head and are in very bad condition.

On the north wall of the chancel is a brass, consisting of an inscription to James Needham, who came into the county in 1536, and his son, with arms. The plate was set up in 1605 by the grandson of the former and son of the latter to record his erection of a monument to them.

There are three bells: the first bears the inscription 'Prosperity to the Church of England, and no encouragement to Enthusiasm,' 1760 ; the second is by John Dyer and dated 1595; the third is without marks.

The plate for the church of Little Wymondley is modern and consists only of a silver communion cup, a silver paten and a flagon.

The registers begin in 1577, and are contained in three books, of which the first and second are fragmentary : (i) baptisms 1577 to 1727, burials 1628 to 1629, marriages 1629[29]; (ii) baptisms 1750 to 1812, burials 1750 to 1812, marriages 1750 to 1753 ; (iii) marriages 1756 to 1811.

ADVOWSON It is uncertain at what date Little Wymondley became a parish. There is no evidence of a church in 1086, and the living is not mentioned in the *Taxatio* of 1291. In 1218, however, the master of the hospital of Little Wymondley was inducted into the church,[30] and a vicarage was ordained before 1235.[31] After the Dissolution in 1537 the rectory was granted to James Needham.[32] After this the rectory follows the descent of the Priory manor, and presumably the lords of this manor presented to the church, but the advowson seems to be only once mentioned among the records of the manor.[33] The living is now a vicarage in the gift of Colonel Heathcote, who holds the Priory manor. There appears to have been a chantry chapel attached to the manor-house of Little Wymondley,[34] the advowson of which always belonged to the lord of that manor and Great Wymondley. It is not heard of after 1485, and had disappeared before the survey taken by Edward VI.

CHARITIES The annual sum of 10s. is received from the parish of Great Wymondley and applied in the distribution of bread in respect of the charity of John Welch.

The sum of £1 5s., being one-third of the dividends on £150 consols, is also received from the parish of Great Wymondley in respect of the charity of James Lucas.

In 1668 Thomas Chapman by his will charged a cottage and yard in Stevenage with 5s. a year for the poor, to be distributed in bread on St. Andrew's Day.

---

[23] Clutterbuck, op. cit. ii, 550.
[24] Cussans, loc. cit.
[25] Chan. Inq. p.m. (Ser. 2), cccxviii, 153. [26] Ibid. cxciii, 54.
[27] Ibid. cccxviii, 153.
[28] Feet of F. Div. Co. Trin. 3 Jas. II ; Herts. Hil. 7 Will. III ; Will, P.C.C. 149 Price ; Feet of F. Div. Co. Trin. 19 & 20 Geo. II.

[28a] Dimensions : chancel, 31 ft. by 14 ft. 6 in. ; nave, 31 ft. by 18 ft. 6 in. ; tower, 9 ft. square.
[29] This book has only two marriages.
[30] Dugdale, *Mon.* vi, 1555 n.
[31] *Liber Antiquus* (ed. Gibbons), 28.
[32] *L. and P. Hen. VIII*, xiii (1), 887 (13) ; Aug. Off. Dec. ii, 57. The 'parsonage of Great Wymondley' here is evidently an error for the parsonage of Little Wymondley.
[33] Feet of F. Herts. Mich. 17 & 18 Eliz. There are no institutions to this church in the Inst. Bks. (P.R.O.).
[34] Chan. Inq. p.m. 4 Ric. II, no. 110 ; 2 Hen. VI, no. 27 ; 6 Hen. VI, no. 53 ; 38 & 39 Hen. VI, no. 42 ; (Ser. 2), i, 34.

THE HUNDRED OF ODSEY

CONTAINING THE PARISHES[1] OF

ARDELEY	CALDECOTE	KELSHALL	RUSHDEN
ASHWELL	CLOTHALL	RADWELL	SANDON
BROADFIELD	COTTERED	REED	THERFIELD
BYGRAVE	HINXWORTH	ROYSTON	WALLINGTON

The area of jurisdiction of this hundred extended over a large portion of the 'champaign country,' which forms the distinctive feature of the Hertfordshire chalk hills. The two great roads from London to the north roughly form its boundaries east and west, and its northern limit is the border between Hertfordshire and the counties of Bedford and Cambridge, following in part the line of the Icknield Way.

The parishes of Hinxworth, Ashwell, Caldecote, Bygrave and Radwell form with Newnham a tongue of land projecting northwards between the counties of Bedford and Cambridge. In 1086 Newnham was within the hundred of Odsey[2]; but the Abbots of St. Albans, who were lords of the manor, had transferred the suit of their tenants to Cashio Hundred before 1286.[3] Since this time Newnham has formed a detached portion of Cashio Hundred within the hundred of Odsey.[4] With this exception there has been little change in the geographical extent of the hundred since the time of the Domesday Survey.[5] It is probable that the Survey records under Odsey Hundred the assessment of Offley, now in Hitchin Hundred, merely through the omission of a sub-heading.[6] The holding of Count Alan in Anstey was placed under the heading 'Odsey Hundred' in 1086,[7] but the lands of Harduin de Scales there are mentioned under Edwinstree Hundred,[8] in which Anstey was included in the 13th and following centuries.[9] The Survey also includes under Odsey Hundred the unidentified lands of Ralf de Limesy at

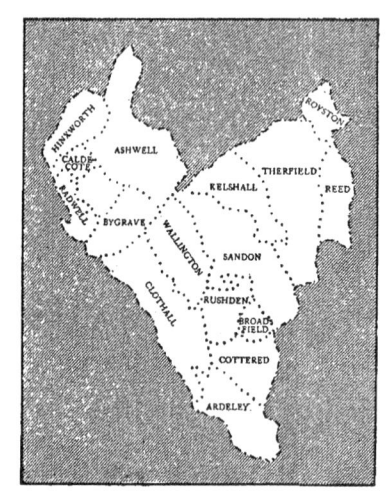

INDEX MAP TO THE HUNDRED OF ODSEY

---

[1] This list represents the extent of the hundred in 1831 (*Pop. Ret.* 1831).
[2] *V.C.H. Herts.* i, 315*b*.   [3] Assize R. 325, m. 34 d.   [4] *V.C.H. Herts.* ii, 320.
[5] Ibid. i, 301 et seq.   [6] Ibid. 328; cf. foot-note.   [7] Ibid. 321*a*.   [8] Ibid. 340*b*.
Hund. R. (Rec. Com.), i, 193; *Feud. Aids,* ii, 431, 439, 453.

192

ODSEY HUNDRED

'Hainstone.'[10] Royston, not specifically mentioned in 1086, was only partly in Therfield; the nucleus of the town lay within the parish of Barkway in Edwinstree Hundred, or across the Cambridgeshire borders in Arningford Hundred.[11]

The inclusion of certain manors within ecclesiastical liberties greatly reduced the royal jurisdiction in this hundred. Before 1278 the tenants of the Abbot of Westminster at Ashwell, of the Bishop of Ely at Kelshall, of the Dean and Chapter of St. Paul's at Ardeley and Sandon, of the Abbot of Ramsey at Therfield, and those of the Prior of Royston and the Knights Templars had withdrawn their suit and aid from the hundred in accordance with royal charters granted to their respective lords.[12] In 1275 it was stated that Caldecote had not rendered aid since the siege of Bedford Castle (June 1224).[13] The men of West Reed in Therfield had also withdrawn from the sheriffs' tourns; the aid due from the holding formerly of Theobald 'de Mora' in Wallington had been withheld for sixteen years by the bailiff of the honour of Richmond; and Richard de Ewell had withdrawn the aid for 'Blayneham' in Ashwell.[14] Nevertheless, the farm of the hundred had recently increased from 100s. to £12.[15]

Odsey Hundred was vested in the Crown until the beginning of the 17th century, and was farmed out together with the neighbouring hundred of Edwinstree.[16] Thus about 1314 Edmund de Ayete received a grant of the bailiwick of these two hundreds during the king's pleasure.[17] In March 1612–13 the hundred was alienated to William Whitmore, esquire, and Jonas Verdon, gentleman, and to their heirs in perpetuity.[18] They sold within a few days to Sir Julius Adelmare, otherwise Caesar, kt., then chancellor and under-treasurer of the Exchequer.[19] He granted the hundred in 1633 to his son Sir John Adelmare, otherwise Caesar, kt., whose son John sold it in March 1662–3 to Arthur Earl of Essex.[20] The hundred has thenceforward remained with the successive Earls of Essex.[21]

The meeting-place for the hundred court is unknown. The name Odsey survives in Odsey Grange and manor in the parish of Guilden Morden, co. Cambs. The Grange now lies without the county boundary, but in the first half of the 16th century the lands of the manor extended into Hertfordshire, and Speed's map of the county published in 1611 shows Odsey Grange within the county boundary and in the hundred of Odsey.[22] The Grange was the property of the Abbot of Warden,[23] who withdrew from the hundred of Odsey the suit and service of his lands and tenements in that hundred.[24]

---

[10] *V.C.H. Herts.* i, 325.
[11] See the account of Royston; cf. *Pop. Ret.* 1831; *Parl. Papers*, 1895, iv, 543.
[12] *Hund. R.* (Rec. Com.), i, 193; *Plac. de Quo Warr.* (Rec. Com.), 276, 291.
[13] *Hund. R.* loc. cit.; cf. *V.C.H. Beds.* ii, 28.
[14] *Hund. R.* loc. cit. [15] Assize R. 323, m. 45.
[16] *Hund. R.* loc. cit.; cf. *Cal. Pat.* 1321–4, p. 61.
[17] *Abbrev. Rot. Orig.* (Rec. Com.), i, 202. [18] Pat. 10 Jas. I, pt. xxi, no. 7.
[19] Chart. *penes* Earl of Essex quoted by Chauncy, *Hist. Antiq. of Herts.* 28.
[20] Ibid.; cf. Recov. R. East. 15 Chas. II, m. 135.
[21] Chauncy, loc. cit.; Recov. R. East. 39 Geo. III, m. 33; Cussans, *Hist. of Herts. Odsey Hund.* 5.
[22] *L. and P. Hen. VIII*, xviii (2), g. 327 (19); Speed, *Theatre of Great Britain* (ed. 1676), 39.
[23] Dugdale, *Mon.* v, 375.
[24] *Plac. de Quo Warr.* (Rec. Com.), 276.

ARDELEY

Erdelei or Erdele (xi–xiii cent.) ; Erdele or Ardley (xiv cent.) ; Yerdley (xv–xvi cent.) ; Yardley (xvi cent. to about 1850).

The parish of Ardeley was included in Odsey Hundred until 14 October 1843, when it was transferred to Edwinstree Hundred.[1] It consists of scattered hamlets lying on the southern slope of the chalk hills of north-east Hertfordshire, at about an equal distance from Stevenage station on the main line of the Great Northern railway and the terminus of Buntingford on a branch line of the Great Eastern railway. The River Beane flows through the northern part of the parish, and the numerous lanes connecting the outlying parts of the parish[2] are carried across it and its tributaries by means of fords. It is recorded that the water did great damage to the roads early in the last century.[3]

The village of Ardeley lies on the western edge of the hill overlooking the village of Walkern and the valley of the River Beane. It consists of the church and the vicarage (a rectangular plastered house built in 1685,[4] having a carved wooden fireplace on the ground floor) and a few cottages around the farm known as Church End. The manor-house called Ardeley Bury, the residence of Col. Hans C. M. Woods, R.A., is situated a little to the west.

North of Ardeley Bury the village street of Cromer lies on the road from Walkern to Rushden. It has its own church and a hall, now converted into two cottages, and is surrounded by its own common arable fields. To the south is Cromer Farm, a timber and plaster house on a brick base, built towards the end of the 16th or early in the 17th century. It is L-shaped in plan and has two original chimney stacks. In the hall is an iron fireback bearing the date 1630, a pheon, an earl's coronet and the letters R.L. The outbuildings are probably original. Another timber and plaster house in the middle of Cromer Street, now divided into two cottages, is of about the same date. On the higher ground north-east of Cromer is a windmill probably on the site of the ancient manorial mill of Ardeley Bury, which was built on land acquired by exchange from the lords of Cromer.[5] Luffenhall Street is a hamlet also surrounded by unin-closed common fields and is partly in Clothall parish.

Wood End, a considerable hamlet in the timbered district in the south of the parish, contains the modern church of St. Alban, a Congregational chapel[6] and several farm-houses, including Lite's Farm, possibly the old manor-house.[7] Two of the farm-houses are of timber and plaster and apparently date from the 17th century. The manor-house of Moor Hall, now converted into a farm, is about a mile north of Wood End. At Gardner's is a homestead moat surround-ing farm-buildings near the road from Great Munden to Rushden which here forms the boundary between Ardeley and Cottered and further north passes through the hamlet of Hare Street.

These considerable farms and houses in a purely agricultural district doubtless represent the tenements of the well-to-do yeomen freeholders, who 'dealt much in the making of malt.'[8] Chief among these were the Halfhide family, members of which lived at Gardner's End,[9] Moor Green[10] and Wood End,[11] and the Shotbolt family which occupied the tenement called 'Cowherds' or 'Cowards,' afterwards called 'The Place.'[12] By 1700, however, the prosperity of these families had much diminished.[13]

In addition to barley, wheat and beans are the chief crops grown. Of 2,424 acres, rather more than half is arable land. The permanent grass covers 660 acres.[13a] Some of the grass-land consists of open greens such as Parker's Green, Munches Green and Moor Green, and in the 17th and preceding centuries the inhabitants depastured cattle along the roadside and on the 'balks' dividing the holdings in the common fields.[14] The woodland (about 80 acres) is chiefly about Ardeley Bury and in the south of the parish. In 1649 seven 'groves' appertained to Ardeley Manor ; among these were Deereloves, Rooks, Cockshott, and Great Sprosewell.[15]

The public elementary school dates from 1834, and was enlarged in 1845.[16]

MANORS

The manor of *ARDELEY* was held in 1086 by the canons of St. Paul's, London. It had belonged to the church before the Conquest,[17] and possibly the tradition that the canons acquired it of the gift of King Athelstan (924–40 A.D.) is correct, although the charter re-cording the gift must be rejected as a forgery.[18]

Apparently the manor included the whole parish in 1086, and the canons owned also 2 hides in the hamlet of Luffenhall, which lies partly in Clothall, partly in Ardeley.[19] In 1086 Ardeley was assessed at 6 hides, of which 3 were in the demesne.[20] In the time of Henry I the manor was assessed at 7 hides, but only 6 of these were accounted for ; 2 hides were in the demesne, 1 hide having evidently been alienated to tenants since the time of the Domesday Survey.[21]

The manor was allotted for the maintenance of the keeper of the brew-house of St. Paul's.[22] The manor-house and demesne lands were let on lease as early as the 12th century. The rent due from Osbert of Ardeley, to whom a lease for life was granted

---

[1] Hardy, *Sess. R.* (Herts. Co. Rec.), ii, 427.
[2] The Court Rolls (D. and C. of St. Paul's, B Boxes 57 and 58) record many of the names of these lanes, some of which survive. They were Bedwill Lane, Hony Lane, Porte Oke Lane, Quynton Lane and Chesilpette Lane.
[3] *Sess. R.* (Herts. Co. Rec.), i, 264.
[4] Chauncy, *Hist. Antiq. of Herts.* 64.
[5] *Dom. of St. Paul's* (Camd. Soc.), 21 ; but the mill was accounted parcel of Cromer Manor in 1576 (Ct. R. St. Paul's, B Box 57).

[6] The trust deed is enrolled on Close, 1864, pt. lxvii, no. 11.
[7] In 1674 the homage of Ardeley Manor returned that there was 'a house and land called Lights and a cottage to the left of the highway leading to the church' (Ct. R. of D. and C. of St. Paul's W.C. 1).
[8] Chauncy, op. cit. 65.
[9] Add. R. (B.M.), 27169.
[10] Ibid. 27170.
[11] Ibid. 27171 ; Chan. Proc. (Ser. 2), bdles. 211, no. 83 ; 462, no. 11.
[12] See Chauncy, op. cit. 62. See below under 'Cromer.'
[13] Chauncy, loc. cit.

[13a] Statistics from Bd. of Agric. (1905).
[14] Add. R. 27169–72.
[15] Close, 1649, pt. l, no. 15.
[16] Cf. Trust D. Enr. on Close, 1837, pt. clxxxi, no. 13 ; 1846, pt. cxviii, no. 11.
[17] *V.C.H. Herts.* i, 316b.
[18] It is printed in Kemble's *Cod. Dipl.* 1127, and Dugdale's *Hist. of St. Paul's* (ed. 1818), 3 ; see the account of Sandon.
[19] *V.C.H. Herts.* i, 317a. [20] Ibid.
[21] *Dom. of St. Paul's* (Camd. Soc.), 140.
[22] *Cal. Pat.* 1313–17, p. 81 ; *Dom. of St. Paul's* (Camd. Soc.), 160.

ODSEY HUNDRED   ARDELEY

in 1141, was paid four times a year,[23] on the ninth, twenty-sixth, fortieth and forty-sixth Sundays after the feast of St. Faith.[24] The rent paid to the brew-house at each term was 64 quarters of wheat, 12 quarters of barley, 64 quarters of oats and a money rent of 42s. At the same time there were due to the chamberlain, besides a fixed sum from the church, £11 12s. 4d. from the manor for wages, wood and alms[25] and 40s. towards the obit of John Malemeyns.[26] The 12th-century lessee received in addition to the farm-stock and three barns filled with wheat, oats, barley and hay, a good hall (doubtless on the site of Ardeley Bury) with 'cloisters' (*trisana*) and a chamber leading out of the hall, courtyard, granary and kitchen, stables and a place for storing hay. In the hall were four small butts, three cups, 'lead above the oven,' a bench, a cupboard and two tables.[27]

DEAN AND CHAPTER OF ST. PAUL'S. *Gules the crossed swords of St. Paul with a D in the chief or.*

In 1222 the farmer of the manor was Theobald Archdeacon of Essex,[28] and it became customary for the lessee to be one of the canons of St. Paul's[29] and to farm the courts as well as the demesne lands.[30]

Sir Henry Chauncy, writing in 1700, stated that the manor-house and demesne lands (only) had been held for above 200 years by his ancestors, who had had several leases for lives from the dean and chapter.[31] In 1610 Henry Chauncy of Ardeley, gentleman, evidently the writer's grandfather,[32] sublet 'the Owld House' with various lands and tenements, including the great barn called 'Powles Barn,' to one John Wright of Ardeley, yeoman.[33] Chauncy then had a lease for three lives, which was renewed to his son Henry Chauncy in 1634.[34]

CHAUNCY. *Gules a cross paty argent and a chief or with a lion passant azure therein.*

In 1649 the Parliamentary trustees for the lands of deans and chapters sold the manor to Montague Lane of London, esquire, Peter Burrough of Clement's Inn, gentleman, and Edward Head of Ardeley, yeoman.[35] At the Restoration the dean and chapter recovered their lands,[36] and continued to take the profits of Ardeley until 1808, when the manor-house and demesne lands were sold to John Spurrier, auctioneer.[37]

The manorial rights were not included in the sale, but are now vested in the Ecclesiastical Commissioners. Ardeley Bury and the demesne lands were sold by John Spurrier to Sir David Baird, K.B., 19 January 1810. He conveyed them in the subsequent year to Commissary-General John Murray. At his death in 1834 his estate descended to his daughter Susannah Catherine Saunders Murray, wife of Major Adolphus Cottin, who assumed the name of Murray.[38] She resided at Ardeley Bury and died 21 April 1860.[39] Her son and heir Adolphus William Murray bequeathed the property to Philip Longmore of the Castle, Hertford, his solicitor. Shortly after his death, which occurred in 1879, the estate was purchased by Mr. J. J. Scott, father of the late Major J. T. Scott,[40] in whose trustees it is now vested.

At Ardeley, as in their other manors, the Dean and Chapter of St. Paul's exercised many liberties and privileges. In 1287 the tenant of their manor claimed assize of bread and ale, free warren and gallows.[41] They held view of frankpledge for the whole parish as late as 1638.[42] King Edward II exempted their tenants at Ardeley from supplying corn to the royal purveyors.[43] A grant of free warren in Ardeley was made by the same king in February 1315–16.[44] The lords of the manor were entitled to fines arising from pleas before the barons of the Exchequer, the judges of both benches, the judges on assize, and all 'Greenwax' fines.[45]

In Chauncy's time Ardeley Bury stood in the midst of an ancient park, then disparked, and was surrounded by a moat.[46] It may therefore have occupied the site of the ancient hall let to Osbert of Ardeley in 1141,[47] for in 1222 the manor-house was surrounded by a park of 60 acres.[48] The present house was built in the latter part of the 16th century, but was much altered and modernized by John Murray in 1820.[49] It is a red-brick house L-shaped in plan with three towers in the front. The hall has some original panelling reaching to about 6 ft. 6 in. from the floor, and there is panelling in some other rooms. The deep moat, with an inner rampart, which surrounded the house, is now dry.

Within the parish three small manors were held of the main manor of Ardeley, in which they were probably included at the time of the Domesday Survey.

CROMER HALL (Crawmere, xiii cent.; Cromarhall, xvi cent.) originated in 'assart' land reclaimed from the wood or waste of Ardeley Manor.[50] It is evidently identical with a 'place' next Ardeley Park, which Ralph son of William of Cromer held of the main manor in 1222 by service of rendering three

---

[23] *Dom. of St. Paul's* (Camd. Soc.), 135.
[24] Ibid. 154–7.
[25] Ibid. Introd. p. xlvii.
[26] Ibid. 162.
[27] Ibid. 136; the lease to Master Aubrey, also in the 12th century, adds 'one handmill, a high ladder, winnowing-fans, baskets,' &c. (137).
[28] Ibid. 21.
[29] MSS. of D. and C. of St. Paul's, A Boxes 26–40, nos. 424, 425, &c.; cf. no. 1411, 1412, and A Box 52, no. 1.
[30] See the court rolls, ibid. B Boxes 57, 58.
[31] Chauncy, *Hist. Antiq. of Herts.* 53; courts were held in the name of the dean and chapter, 1630–8.
[32] Cf. Chauncy's pedigree of the family, loc. cit.
[33] Chan. Proc. (Ser. 2), bdle. 304, no. 45.
[34] Close, 1649, pt. 1, no. 15.
[35] Ibid.
[36] Cf. *V.C.H. Lond.* i, 418.
[37] Clutterbuck, *Hist. and Antiq. of Herts.* iii, 600.
[38] Cussans, *Hist. of Herts. Odsey Hund.* 88.
[39] *Gent. Mag.* 1860, i, 641. She had married secondly Sir Robert Murray, bart. (Cussans, loc. cit.).
[40] Cussans, loc. cit.; information kindly supplied by Messrs. Sworder & Longmore.
[41] *Plac. de Quo Warr.* (Rec. Com.), 290.
[42] Add. R. (B.M.), 27169–73.
[43] *Cal. Pat.* 1313–17, pp. 81, 103, 190; 1321–4, pp. 52, 221.
[44] *Cal. Chart. R.* 1300–26, p. 305.
[45] Close, 1649, pt. 1, no. 15.
[46] Chauncy, *Hist. Antiq. of Herts.* 53.
[47] See above.
[48] *Dom. of St. Paul's* (Camd. Soc.), 21.
[49] Clutterbuck, loc. cit. It is not quite clear whether Chauncy the historian of Hertfordshire lived at Ardeley Bury or at Lite's.
[50] *Dom. of St. Paul's* (Camd. Soc.), 24.

capons yearly.[51] Ralph son of William also held 3 acres of the demesne,[52] which he had in exchange for land given for the site of the manorial windmill,[53] and half a virgate held in villeinage 'for Robert, servant of Nicholas the Archdeacon.'[54] From Ralph the manor apparently descended to Roger of Cromer and to his daughter Sabina, who married Ralph son of Roger of Westover (Westoouer), for they surrendered 122 acres in Ardeley, Cromer and Luffenhall to the lord of Ardeley in 1258–9.[55]

The history of the manor during the following two centuries is obscure. Chauncy[56] identifies Cromer with the 'manor' in Ardeley held in 1278 by Roger de la Lee, together with a warren which had been made by Philip Lovell[57]; but it seems more probable that Roger's manor was Lite's.[58] Possibly the later tenants again took their name from their holding, for John of Cromer was living in Ardeley in 1290–1,[59] and in 1322–3 Alice of Cromer paid towards a subsidy in Ardeley.[60]

In 1526 Hugh Brabham with his wife Margaret, in whose right he was evidently holding, sold the manor of Cromer to Thomas Catesby and others for £100.[61] This Thomas appears to have been the younger son of Sir Humphrey Catesby, kt., of Northamptonshire.[62] His heir was his elder brother Anthony Catesby of Whiston, co. Northants,[63] who in 1540 sold Cromer Hall to George Clerke of Benington, yeoman.[64]

In 1550 the homage presented George Clerke for cutting down trees in the highway at Cromer.[65] He transferred the manor in 1557 to his son Thomas Clerke of Stevenage,[66] whose title was disputed by John Austen, citizen and haberdasher of London, who called himself great-grandson of William Austen and his wife Katherine, who was daughter of Sir John Clerke, kt.[67] Thomas Clerke retained the manor until his death about 1597, when his next heir was his son William.[68] Thomas and William Clerke and Beatrice Clerke, widow, dismembered the manor,[69] a process already begun by the alienation of the windmill in 1576.[70] The manorial rights with a messuage, possibly the hall, were purchased by Matthew Scrivener of Walkern and his wife Grace.[71] Cromer Hall was ultimately acquired by John Shotbolt.[72] Courts having ceased to be held, 'some of the copyholders took up their lands in Ardeley Manor, some ceased to perform any of the customary dues.'[73]

The family of Shotbolt had long resided in Ardeley, where they held a tenement called Cowards. In 1618 John and Philip Shotbolt granted an annuity of £400 out of their 'capital messuage and demesnes' in Ardeley (? Cromer Hall) to Lady Elizabeth Griffin,[74] who is also said to have purchased Cowards through the agency of Thomas Taylor.[75] Lady Elizabeth Griffin, 'uneasie in this place,'[76] perhaps owing to the difficulty she experienced in obtaining her annuity from Cromer Hall, surrendered her copyhold tenements (Cowards, &c.) to Sir Edward Baesh, kt., and his wife Mary and to Edward Adkyns in 1637.[77] In 1619 Lady Elizabeth had sought to enter upon the capital messuage and demesnes of Cromer Hall, since John Shotbolt had failed to pay the annuity due to her; but she was 'defeated' in consequence of a conveyance made to Mary Shotbolt, mother of John.[78] Shortly afterwards the house was acquired (probably by purchase) by William Halfhide, who in 1630 conveyed it to his son John Halfhide,[79] whose family had long resided at Ardeley.[80]

Cromer Hall is a late 16th-century house, now divided into two cottages. It is of two stories constructed of timber and plaster on a brick base. It still retains the oak ceiling beams, some oak doors, and the original staircase.

LITE'S MANOR (Leightes, xvi–xviii cent.; Lights, xvii–xix cent.) is possibly identical with the manor of Ardeley which Roger de la Lee held in 1278. Philip Lovell had made there a warren which Roger held with the manor.[81] It may be that 'Little Lye Grove,' near the site of Lite's, is identical with this warren.

Towards the end of the 13th century Lite's was held by Richard de Harwedune, who was succeeded by his daughter Maud. About 1322 she conveyed the manor to Theobald de Bridebrook.[82] Theobald's name does not occur among the inhabitants who paid to a subsidy in 1322–3, but there was then living at Ardeley a 'Robert Lithe.'[83]

In 1414 John Morris of Ardeley sold the manor of Lite's to John Hotoft and others. They transferred their rights to John Bardolf and his wife Joan, who afterwards married Robert Carleton.[84] How long it

---

[51] *Dom. of St. Paul's* (Camd. Soc.), 24.
[52] Ibid. 22.
[53] Ibid. 21.
[54] Ibid. 27.
[55] MSS. of D. and C. of St. Paul's, A Boxes 26–40, no. 422.
[56] Op. cit. 54.
[57] Assize R. 323.
[58] See below; it is also difficult to identify the messuage, toft and 16 acres of land to which Geoffrey Ede maintained his claim against Joan and Alice daughters of John Ede in 1328 (De Banco R. 268, m. 30; 272, m. 11; 274, m. 5); probably it was one of the freehold tenements.
[59] Lay Subs. R. bdle. 120, no. 2; he is styled John 'de Caumere,' evidently an error for 'Craumere.'
[60] Ibid. no. 11.
[61] Feet of F. Herts. Trin. 18 Hen. VIII.
[62] Chan. Inq. p.m. (Ser. 2), lii, 99; Will, P.C.C. 23 Holgrave.
[63] Ibid.; no confirmatory evidence of Chauncy's statement that Cromer was held by William Catesby, the counsellor of Richard III, has been found.
[64] Com. Pleas D. Enr. Trin. 32 Hen. VIII, m. 3.
[65] MSS. of D. and C. of St. Paul's, B Box 57.
[66] Ibid.
[67] Chan. Proc. (Ser. 2), bdle. 203, no. 17. Chauncy inserts a generation between Thomas and George Clerke, but Thomas calls himself *son* of George in the Chancery proceedings, and is so styled in the court rolls of Ardeley.
[68] MSS. of D. and C. of St. Paul's, B Box 58.
[69] Ibid.
[70] Ibid. B Box 57.
[71] Feet of F. Herts. Mich. 44 & 45 Eliz.; cf. ibid. Mich. 38 & 39 Eliz.; MSS. of D. and C. of St. Paul's, B Box 58.
[72] Feet of F. Herts. Mich. 16 Jas. I. He acquired 20¼ acres of the demesne lands about 1597 (D. and C. of St. Paul's, B Box 58).
[73] Chauncy, op. cit. 55.
[74] Chan. Proc. (Ser. 2), bdle. 353, no. 18; cf. Feet of F. Herts. Mich. 16 Jas. I.
[75] Chauncy, op. cit. 62.
[76] Ibid.
[77] Add. R. (B.M.) 27173. Sir Edward Baesh bequeathed the house called Cowards or The Place to Philadelphia wife of Justinian Sherborne, in whose time it was partly demolished. William Peirson, goldsmith of London, purchased the remainder and bequeathed it to Robert Markham, who made additions to the house (Chauncy, loc. cit.).
[78] Chan. Proc. (Ser. 2), bdle. 353, no. 18.
[79] Add. R. (B.M.) 27169.
[80] Lay Subs. R. bdle. 120, no. 115; see above.
[81] Assize R. 323.
[82] Title-deeds quoted by Chauncy, op. cit. 55.
[83] Lay Subs. R. bdle. 120, no. 11.
[84] Title-deeds quoted by Chauncy, loc. cit.

Ardeley Church: The Nave looking East

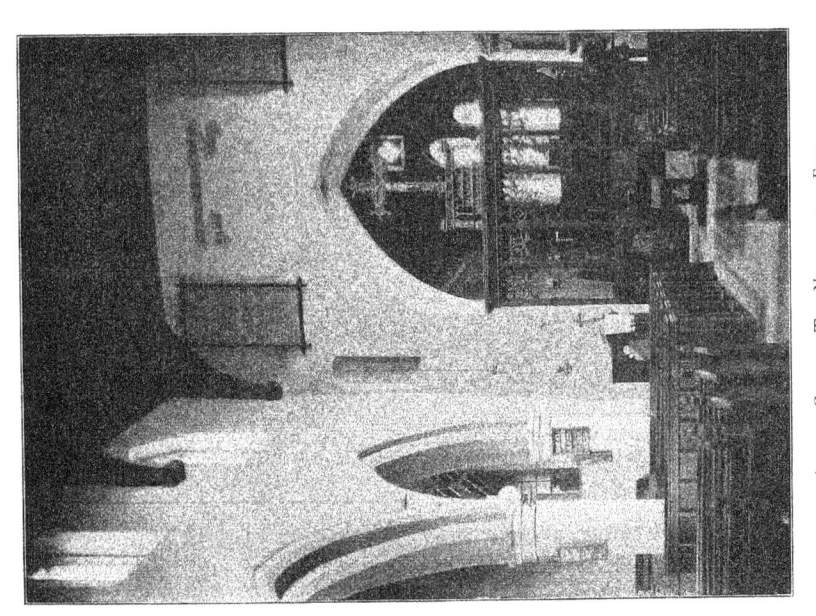

Ardeley Church: The Roof of the Nave

remained in this family is unknown.[85] In 1558 William Fanne suffered a recovery of certain lands and tenements in Ardeley.[86] These may have been identical with Lite's, which was sold by William Fanne to George and Joan Brewster in about 1563.[87] Joan survived her husband, and was succeeded by his sister's son, Toby Middleton, gentleman.[88] About 1621 a settlement of the manor was made [89] whereby Toby Middleton was to hold it for life and at his death it was to pass to Henry Chauncy and his heirs. Henry Chauncy having died in 1631 before Toby Middleton,[90] the estate passed to his son Henry Channey of Ardeley Bury, who was succeeded in 1681 by Sir Henry Channey, the historian of Hertfordshire.[91] His grandson and heir, also named Henry, mortgaged the estate to John Hawkins, and Chauncy's bequest of the manor to 'the infant Japhet Crook' was set aside in favour of Thomas Hawkins. He died in 1742, having bequeathed it to his niece Katherine, wife of William Woolball of Walthamstow.[92] Their daughter and heir Katherine carried the estate in marriage to Sir Hanson Berney, bart., of Kirby Bedon, co. Norfolk.[93] In 1789 their son and heir Sir John Berney, bart., conveyed it to trustees, from whom it was purchased by John Spurrier. He sold it in 1808 to John Simon Harcourt.[94] The latter's only son George Simon Harcourt succeeded to the estate,[95] and sold it to Commissary-General Murray, the owner of Ardeley Bury.[96] The two estates have thus been amalgamated.

MOOR HALL was also held of the main manor of Ardeley.[97] The early tenants were called after their holding. In 1284 John 'de la More' was the wealthiest inhabitant of Ardeley, if the farmer of Ardeley Bury be excepted.[98] It is said that a John 'de la More' conveyed Moor Hall to John Munden about 1317, and that Munden shortly afterwards conveyed to John de Wylye, parson, of Walton-on-Thames, probably for a settlement.[99] In 1324 Robert of Munden, clerk, possessed a 'little manor' (*manerettum*) of Moor Hall in Ardeley, which he had leased for life to John 'de la Forde' of Edmonton and his wife Maud.[100] The site of the manor subsequently came into the hands of Edward Kendale.[1] John de Wylye is said to have conveyed the manor to Kendale and his wife Elizabeth,[2] but she had dower only in it after his death,[3] and his right heir was his son Edward Kendale,[4] possibly by a former wife.[5]

The subsequent history of Moor Hall is uncertain. Beatrice, sister of Edward Kendale the younger, married Robert Turk.[6] Their grandchild, Joan Wallis, married Nicholas Morley. Apparently Moor Hall descended to the Morleys in the same way as the manor of Wakeley.[7] The manor of Moor Hall had been acquired by Thomas Morley, gentleman, before June 1559, when the homage returned that he was recently dead and that his heir failed to appear.[8] This heir was his son William,[9] who sold the manor in 1568 to Edward Halfhide of Aspenden.[10] In 1572 Halfhide conveyed it to William Gurney, otherwise Gornell,[11] probably in trust, for the latter transferred his rights in 1595 to Mary wife of George Shurley and daughter and heir of Edward Halfhide.[12]

From George Shurley the manor was purchased in 1598 by Richard Saltonstall, alderman and goldsmith of London.[13] He settled it on his son Peter upon the latter's marriage with Anne daughter of Edmund Waller.[14] In 1605 Peter Saltonstall sold it to Robert Spence, citizen and fishmonger of London and Master of the Levant Company of merchants.[15] Spence bequeathed it to his wife Audrey,[16] who died seised of it about 1635, and was succeeded by Robert Spence of Balcombe, co. Sussex, her son and heir.[17] In 1648 Robert Spence settled it upon his son and heir-apparent William Spence of Lincoln's Inn, upon the latter's marriage with Mary daughter of Samuel Short. William Spence having died about 1678 without male issue, the manor descended to his brother John Spence, also of Lincoln's Inn.[18] He was succeeded by his son John Spence,[19] whose second son Luke Spence inherited the estate.[20] He died at Malling, co. Sussex, in July 1800, at the age of

SPENCE. *Sable a fess battled argent.*

---

[85] A John 'Calton' was living in Ardeley about 1523 (Lay Subs. R. bdle. 120, no. 115); Henry Bardolf had a house at Munches Green in 1637 (Add. R. [B.M.], 27172).
[86] Recov. R. East. 4 & 5 Philip and Mary, m. 547.
[87] Title-deeds quoted by Chauncy, loc. cit.
[88] Ibid.; cf. MSS. of D. and C. of St. Paul's, B Boxes 59–60.
[89] Feet of F. Herts. Mich. 19 Jas. I; cf. Chauncy, loc. cit.
[90] Chauncy, loc. cit.; cf. Add. R. (B.M.), 27171.
[91] Chauncy, loc. cit.; cf. MSS. of D. and C. of St. Paul's, W.C. 1.
[92] Notes of Thomas Tipping of Ardeley, quoted by Cussans, *Hist. of Herts. Odsey Hund.* 89; cf. Recov. R. East. 2 Geo. I, m. 71; Feet of F. Herts. Hil. 4 Geo. I; Recov. R. Hil. 4 Geo. I, m. 18.
[93] Clutterbuck, *Hist. and Antiq. of Herts.* iii, 603; cf. Feet of F. Div. Co. Mich. 31 Geo. II.
[94] Clutterbuck, loc. cit. In 1810 Hanson Berney, heir-apparent to Sir John, was dealing with the manor (Recov. R. Hil. 50 Geo. III, m. 218); he probably surrendered his rights in favour of Harcourt.
[95] Clutterbuck, op. cit. iii, 604; Recov. R. East. 9 Geo. IV, m. 283.
[96] Cussans, loc. cit.
[97] Ct. R. D. and C. of St. Paul's, B Box 58, &c.
[98] Lay Subs. R. bdle. 120, no. 2.
[99] Chauncy, op. cit. 53, quoting title-deeds.
[100] *Cal. Close,* 1323–7, p. 178.
[1] Chan. Inq. p.m. 47 Edw. III (1st nos.), no. 20. [2] Chauncy, loc. cit.
[3] Chan. Inq. p.m. 49 Edw. III (1st nos.), no. 74.
[4] Ibid. 47 Edw. III (1st nos.), no. 20.
[5] Elizabeth lived to a great age and died in 1420. Her first husband was Ralph Camoys; Edward Kendale was her second husband, and she survived a third, Thomas Barre. Her heir was her grandson John, son of her son Thomas Barre (Chan. Inq. p.m. 9 Hen. V, no. 47). It is therefore possible that she had no children by Edward Kendale, unless Edward Kendale the younger was her son and died s.p. before her.
[6] *V.C.H. Herts.* ii, 156.
[7] See the account of Aspenden.
[8] MSS. of D. and C. of St. Paul's, B 57.
[9] Title-deeds quoted by Chauncy, loc. cit.
[10] Recov. R. Mich. 1568, m. 1014; MSS. of D. and C. of St. Paul's, B Box 57.
[11] MSS. of D. and C. of St. Paul's, B Box 57.
[12] Ibid. 58; Feet of F. Herts. Hil. 37 Eliz.
[13] Feet of F. Herts. East. 40 Eliz.
[14] Ibid. Hil. 42 Eliz.; title-deeds quoted by Chauncy, op. cit. 54.
[15] MSS. of D. and C. of St. Paul's, B Boxes 59–60.
[16] Chan. Inq. p.m. (Ser. 2), ccclxxx, 109.
[17] Add. R. (B.M.), 27171.
[18] Title-deeds quoted by Chauncy, loc. cit.; Ct. R. D. and C. of St. Paul's, W.C. 1.
[19] Ct. R. D. and C. of St. Paul's, loc. cit.; cf. Recov. R. Mich. 12 Anne, m. 74.
[20] Clutterbuck, op. cit. iii, 601; cf. Recov. R. Hil. 19 Geo. III, m. 25.

eighty-five, having acted as magistrate for that county for more than sixty years,[21] and was succeeded by his grandson Henry Hume Spence. Moor Hall subsequently came into the possession of Lord Salisbury, and was purchased by the present owner, Miss G. Cotton Browne, whose father, the late Rev. J. G. Cotton Browne, had acquired certain land in the parish.[31a]

CHURCHES The church of ST. LAWRENCE, which stands on high ground to the west of the village, is built of flint rubble, mostly covered with rough-cast, with stone dressings, and roofed with tiles and with lead. It consists of a chancel, nave, aisles, west tower, north porch and north vestry.[22]

In the 13th century the church probably consisted of a chancel and nave only. The nave, the oldest portion of the church now remaining, was in existence early in the 13th century, when the old chancel was rebuilt and a north aisle added. The south aisle was not built till a century later, when the present chancel arch appears to have been built, and the west tower in about the fourth decade of the 14th century. During the 15th century the clearstory was added, the north porch was built,[22a] the north windows of the north aisle were inserted, and those of the south aisle altered externally; both aisles were partly rebuilt, the windows of the bell chamber inserted, and the embattled parapets of the tower and north aisle added. The church was also re-roofed and was seated with the existing pews. In the 19th century the chancel was almost entirely rebuilt and the north vestry was added.

The chancel has two of the original early 13th-century lancets rebuilt into the north and south walls. The east window is modern. At the north-east is a 13th-century tomb recess with shafted jambs and dog-tooth ornament, which may have been used as an Easter sepulchre, and at the south-east is a piscina of the same date, also with shafted jambs and dog-tooth ornament. The chancel arch, which is apparently of the 14th century, is plain, of two chamfered orders. It may have been altered when the south arcade of the nave was built. The rood-loft was approached by a staircase at the north-east of the nave, of which some remains exist, but the upper door is blocked.

The nave, of three bays, has on the north side an arcade of the early 13th century, consisting of two-centred arches on octagonal columns with plain bell capitals. The south arcade is similar, but more massive, and is a century later in date. None of the detail of the original nave now exists, but the walling over the arcades is a survival from the first fabric, dating from before the 13th century. The rather late 15th-century clearstory consists of three two-light windows on each side.

The walls and north door of the north aisle are of 13th-century date. The east and west windows are either original or not much later, but the two north windows are of the late 15th century, and contain fragments of 15th-century glass, some of which occupy their original positions. The south aisle largely escaped the 15th-century alteration, for though the windows are externally of that date the openings are of the same date as the erection of the aisle, the 14th century. The south door is modern.

The tower arch has shafted jambs, and both it and the west window are of the late 14th century. The font is octagonal and the workmanship is rough, dating probably from the early 15th century, while the cover is of the early 17th century.

The roof of both nave and aisles is a good example of 15th-century woodwork. The principals are moulded, and there are carved bosses at their intersections. At the feet of the principals are carved figures of angels playing upon various musical instruments, and the nave principals have brackets containing tracery. One of the beams at the east end of the nave bears traces of decoration in colour, and the eastern half of the first bay of the roof is panelled to form a canopy over the rood. The open seating, with ends adorned with poppy heads, is of the same date.

There are three ancient brasses in the church. The oldest, in the chancel floor, is fragmentary. It consists of the lower part of a woman's figure, with an inscription to John Clerke and his wife; the date is about 1430. On the chancel wall is a brass of Philip Metcalf, vicar of the parish, dated 1515, and on the south jamb of the chancel arch is another of Thomas Shotbolt, his wife, four sons, and two daughters.

In the nave is a mural monument, with a bust, of Mary Markham, 1673.

Of the six bells in the tower the first is by Pack & Chapman, of 1771; the second by James Bartlett, 1685; the third and sixth are mediaeval, but of uncertain date, inscribed 'Vocor Maria' and 'Sit Nomen Domini Benedictum' respectively; the fourth is by John Dier, 1587, and the fifth, probably by Robert Oldfeild, 1613.

The plate includes two patens of 1678 and 1690.

The registers are contained in four books: (i) baptisms, burials and marriages from 1546 to 1701; (ii) baptisms, burials and marriages from 1702 to 1753; (iii) baptisms and burials from 1754 to 1812; (iv) marriages from 1754 to 1812.

The chapel of ST. ALBAN, Wood End, was built in 1853, largely, it is said, of the stones picked up in the fields by the children of the parish.[23]

The chapel of ST. JOSEPH, Cromer, was built in 1890.

ADVOWSON The right of presentation has always belonged to the Dean and Chapter of St. Paul's.[24] In March 1290 a vicarage was ordained,[25] and the church was then assessed at £12.[26]

From 1690 onwards meeting-places were certified for Protestant Dissenters in Ardeley. The chapel at Wood End was built in 1820, as a preaching station for students at Wymondley Academy, and was rebuilt in 1855.[27]

---

[21] *Gent. Mag.* lxx, 6.
[31a] Information from Miss Cotton Browne.
[22] Dimensions: chancel, 31 ft. by 15 ft.; nave, 39 ft. by 21 ft.; north and south aisles, 10 ft. wide; tower, 10 ft. square.
[22a] In 1508 J. Halfhide left 10s. towards the porch (P.C.C. 11 Bennett).
[23] Cussans, *Hist. of Herts. Odsey Hund.* 94.
[24] Linc. Epis. Reg. Grosteste, roll 8, records the institution of William of Lichfield, canon of St. Paul's, about 1241; cf. Liber A. Pilosus (D. and C. of St. Paul's), fol. 23, 30, 66; Inst. Bks. (P.R.O.).
[25] Linc. Epis. Reg. Sutton, fol. 85; Liber A. Pilosus (St. Paul's), fol. 66.
[26] *Pope Nich. Tax.* (Rec. Com.), 37, 51b.
[27] Urwick, *Nonconf. in Herts.* 769–70.

ARDELEY CHURCH FROM THE NORTH

ASHWELL: OLD HOUSE NEAR CHURCH

ODSEY HUNDRED

ASHWELL

CHARITIES

The Ardeley charity estates are regulated by a scheme of the high court of Chancery, 2 March 1836, as varied by schemes of the Charity Commissioners dated respectively in 1887 and 1897. They comprise:—

1. A piece of copyhold land called Plaistowe's or Town Close, containing 1 a. 2 r. 6 p., granted by the lords of the manor of Ardeley Bury in 1630.

2. The Poor's Acre, copyhold of the said manor, granted in 1630.

3. Pearson's gift, being a close called 'The Ainage,' containing 3 a. 3 r. 14 p., the rents and profits to be applied in bread to the poor, one half on the first Sunday in January and the remainder on the first Sunday in February.

4. Robert Austin's gift, founded by deed 1647, and consisting of a piece of land called Churchfield, containing 1 a. 1 r. 33 p.

5. Edward Hoad's gift, founded by will 1655, under which the testator gave £20 to be laid out in land, the interest to be applied in apprenticing poor children. The endowment consists of a piece of land now called the Apprentice Land, containing 2 a. 2 r.

6. Henry Chauncy's gift, founded by will 8 February 1680, and consisting of two small cottages containing two rooms each called 'Reedings' with garden of 16 poles, and the Pightle containing 1 a. 2 r.

7. The Town Stock arising from subscriptions made in 1807 and consisting of £69 6s. 11d. consols in the name of the official trustees, producing £1 14s. 8d. yearly.

The income arising from Pearson's gift shall be applied in bread in accordance with the will of the donor.

The rents from the Apprentice Land shall accumulate until there is sufficient money to place a poor child out as apprentice to some trade or business.

The 'Reedings' shall be used for poor people to live in rent free, and two loads of fuel, to be provided out of the rent of the Pightle, shall be delivered at the 'Reedings' at Michaelmas and Christmas.

From the income arising from the remaining property a sum of £5 yearly shall be applied towards the support of the master or mistress of a school, and the residue for the general benefit of the poor.

The gross income from the estates in 1907 was £15 9s. 8d.

ASHWELL

Aescwelle, Eswell, Assewell, Asshewell.

The parish of Ashwell has an area of about 4,108 acres. The ground slopes down towards the north, the height in the south varying from 200 ft. to 300 ft. (with Claybush Hill attaining 328 ft.) and in the north from 100 ft. to 200 ft. above the ordnance datum. The northern portion lies between the River Rhee or Cam—which has its source in springs in Ashwell village and flowing north-west and then north forms the north-western boundary of the parish—and a small stream which flows northward and forms the eastern boundary, ultimately joining the Rhee at the junction of the three counties. On the south-west the parish is bounded by another tributary of the Rhee, and on the south-east, for about three-quarters of a mile, by the Icknield Way. Shire Balk divides Ashwell from Cambridgeshire on the north-east.

The soil consists entirely of chalk, except where the Rhee enters the Gault formation along the western boundary, and there are some chalk-pits at the junction of the lower with the higher level. There are in the parish 3,692 acres of arable land, 398 of permanent grass and 20 of woods and plantations.[1] The extensive common fields called Ashwell Fields covered the southern part of the parish.

An inclosure award was made in 1862.[2] The Cambridge branch of the Great Northern railway crosses the parish in the extreme south-east, but Ashwell station is over the Cambridgeshire border, about 2 miles from the village.

Arbury Banks, about three-quarters of a mile south-west of the village, is a prehistoric camp of the hill-fort type, now nearly obliterated. Within the parish of Ashwell a copper coin of Cunobeline has been found, also a barbed flint arrow. Roman coins, pottery and glass have been found in the neighbourhood. There is a tumulus at Highley Hill, and at Mobs Hole near Guilden Morden, Love's Farm, Bluegates Farm and Westbury Farm are homestead moats.

The village of Ashwell is situated rather more than a mile from the Icknield Way. The ancient road called Ashwell Street enters the parish from Steeple Morden on the east. This if continued in a straight line would skirt the village on the north, but the present continuation of it called Ashwell Street Way makes a bend and passes the village on the south and then ends. Branching off from the Icknield Way a little beyond the eastern boundary of the parish is a road running north through Steeple Morden, and from this a road branches westward, runs through Ashwell, where it is called Station Road, skirts the village on the north, then as Northfield Road runs parallel with the Rhee until within about 250 yards of the Cambridgeshire border, where it turns sharply north-west and crosses the river into Bedfordshire at Whitegate Bridge. Two other roads connect the village with Newnham to the south-west and Hinxworth to the north-west. It was probably the means of communication afforded by the neighbourhood of the Icknield Way and of Ashwell Street (which may have originally joined the Roman Stane Street further to the west) that made Ashwell a place of some importance in the 11th century. The Domesday Survey records the presence of fourteen burgesses, the borough dues—which fell to the Abbot of Westminster—amounting to 49s. 4d. a year.[3] Evidence of this small prescriptive borough exists in occasional references to burgage tenure in

---

[1] Statistics from Bd. of Agric. (1905).   [2] Under Loc. Act, 20 Vict. cap. 5.   [3] *V.C.H. Herts.* i, 313a.

A HISTORY OF HERTFORDSHIRE

the 14th and 15th centuries,[4] but there is no sign of separate borough presentments or of a corporate body. A frequently recurring entry is that of payments 'for whate-silver' from the burgages.[5] The gild of St. John the Baptist may have had some share in the government of the town. The Brotherhood House stood in the High Street of Ashwell (see under gild). The town was divided into five wards in the 15th century, the name of one ward being 'Dokelake' Ward, and another High Street Ward.[6] The name Chepyng Street occurs in the 16th century.[7]

In 1295 the Abbot of Westminster claimed the right to hold a market by virtue of the original grant of the manor by Edward the Confessor,[8] and it is probable that the market dates back to that period. The first mention of it is in 1211, when it is recorded that 'the Abbot of Westminster rendered account of 2 palfreys that the market of Ashwell may return to Sunday from Saturday.'[9] In 1575 Queen Elizabeth granted to the Bishop of London the right to hold a market weekly on Mondays.[10] It had lapsed before 1792.[10a] The distance from a main road evidently made it impossible to maintain successfully a market at Ashwell in later times. But a thriving manufacture of malt was carried on in the 17th century. In 1637 the inhabitants of Hinxworth complained that they were not taxed in fair comparison with Ashwell, 'which has many rich maltsters and three times as much land and as good as Hinxworth.'[11]

Fairs were claimed by the Abbot of Westminster in 1295,[12] by virtue of a grant of Henry III, which is, however, not extant. Three fairs yearly were granted to the Bishop of London by Queen Elizabeth,[13] but afterwards there appears to have been only one fair, which was abolished by law in 1872.[14]

The High Street of the village runs in a north-easterly direction parallel with Ashwell Street Way. It contains some old houses, notably a cottage formerly the British Queen Inn, which was originally built in the 15th century, but was much altered in the 17th century. It is a timber-framed house with a thatched roof. On the north side is a stone window partially destroyed and in the kitchen is a moulded oak beam. There are three or four 17th-century houses of red brick or timber and plaster in this street, one bearing the date 1681 and the figure of a dolphin in the plaster. At right angles to it is Mill Street, which runs past St. Mary's Church to the corn mill. This is probably the water mill mentioned in early extents of the manor. Close by the mill is a brewery, and there is another to the south-west of the village. Brewing is the chief industry besides agriculture.

Ashwell Bury, the residence of Mr. J. W. Attwood, is situated just beyond the church. Elbrook House, to the north of the village, is the residence of Mr. E. S. Fordham. At Ashwell End, about half a mile north-west of the church, is a 17th-century farm-house of two stories. It is of timber plastered and decorated with combed pargeting.

Ralph Cudworth, divine and author, was vicar of Ashwell 1662 to 1688.[14a]

MANORS ASHWELL, originally part of the demesne of the Crown, was granted by Edward the Confessor in his first charter to the abbey of St. Peter, Westminster, dated December 1066.[15] The Domesday Survey records that of the 6 hides at which Ashwell was assessed the abbot himself held two and a half in demesne, the manor at this date being evidently a large one, with land for twelve plough-teams and meadow sufficient for six. Peter de Valognes held half a hide and Geoffrey de Mandeville 1 virgate of the abbot.[16] There is nothing particularly worthy of note concerning this manor during the period of nearly 500 years during which it was held by the Abbots of Westminster. The abbots possessed here, as in their other manors, the privileges of free warren,[17] view of frankpledge, assize of bread and ale, pleas of *namii vetiti*, and exemption from sheriff's tourn and from scot, geld, aid and toll.[18]

VIEW IN ASHWELL VILLAGE

---

[4] Mins. Accts. at Westm.
[5] Mins. Accts. P.R.O. bdle. 862, no. 8, 12.
[6] Will of William Freeman, P.C.C. 12 Stokton; Will of John Bill, ibid. 29 Blamyr.
[7] Com. Pleas D. Enr. Mich. 36 Hen. VIII, m. 17.
[8] *Plac. de Quo Warr.* (Rec. Com.), 288.
[9] Pipe R. 13 John, m. 6 d.
[10] Pat. 17 Eliz. pt. i, m. 1.
[10a] *Rep. Com. on Market Rights and Tolls*, 170.
[11] *Cal. S. P. Dom.* 1636–7, p. 405.
[12] *Plac. de Quo Warr.* (Rec. Com.), 288.
[13] Pat. 17 Eliz. pt. i, m. 1.
[14] *Lond. Gaz.* 28 June 1872, p. 2976.
[14a] Urwick, op. cit. 779; *Dict. Nat. Biog.*
[15] Cott. Chart. vi, 2.
[16] *V.C.H. Herts.* i, 313a. These tenements held by Peter de Valognes and Geoffrey de Mandeville must not be confused with their independent holdings in the same parish (see below).
[17] Assize R. 225.
[18] *Hund. R.* (Rec. Com.), i, 193; *Plac. de Quo Warr.* (Rec. Com.), 275, 288.

On 16 January 1539–40 Abbot Boston and twenty-four monks surrendered the abbey of Westminster to Henry VIII.[19] Eleven months later that king erected the short-lived bishopric of Westminster, turning the abbey into a cathedral, and in January 1540–1 Ashwell was included in the endowment of the new bishop,[20] Thomas Thirlby, formerly Dean of the King's Chapel. But on 29 March 1550 Thirlby resigned the bishopric of Westminster into the hands of Edward VI, who dissolved it, translating Thirlby to Norwich.[21] Ashwell Manor was granted a fortnight later by the king to his nominee Nicholas Ridley, Bishop of London,[22] on his installation as successor to Bishop Bonner. The accession of Queen Mary brought about the deprivation of Ridley and the reinstatement of Bonner (5 August 1553) and in March 1554 a new grant of the manor of Ashwell was made to Bishop Bonner and his successors in the see of London.[23] At the time of the appropriation of the bishops' lands by Parliament during the great Civil War Ashwell was taken from Bishop Juxon and a complete survey of the manor was made by order of the trustees for the bishopric in June 1647. It was then reported that the demesne lands, consisting of 30 acres, were held on lease by Jeremiah Whitacre, and that there was a lime kiln on the demesne lands valued at £30 per annum. Court leet and court baron were at this time held at the parsonage.[24] On 19 March 1648–9 the trustees sold the manor to Thomas Challoner of Steeple Claydon, Bucks., for £416 9s. 2d.[25] When the bishops were reinstated at the Restoration Ashwell was restored to the see of London, and so remained until 1868, when, in accordance with the Ecclesiastical Commissioners Act of 1860, the voidance of the see on the translation of the Rev. Archibald Campbell Tait, D.D., Bishop of London, to the see of Canterbury in 1868 was taken as the opportunity for transferring the lands of the bishopric to the Ecclesiastical Commissioners.[26] The latter continue to be lords of this manor.

WESTMINSTER ABBEY. *Gules the crossed keys of St. Peter with the ring of St. Edward in the chief all or.*

SEE OF LONDON. *Gules the crossed swords of St. Paul.*

Two mills were appurtenant to the abbot's manor of Ashwell in 1086, one held by him in demesne and one held of him by Peter de Valognes.[27] The Ministers' Accounts of the 13th and 14th centuries contain frequent references to a water mill and a horse mill (or windmill) in Ashwell and the necessity for their repair.[28] In 1198 we hear of a man and a woman being 'drowned in the pool of the mill of Ashwell.'[29]

THE 'ROSE AND CROWN,' ASHWELL HIGH STREET

[19] Dugdale, *Mon.* i, 280, 329.
[20] *L. and P. Hen. VIII,* xvi, g. 503 (33).
[21] *Dict. Nat. Biog.*
[22] Pat. 4 Edw. VI, pt. iv, m. 16.
[23] Ibid. 1 Mary, pt. iv, m. 19.
[24] Add. MS. 37682, fol. 21.
[25] Close, 1649, pt. xlvi, m. 36 ; Add. MS. 9049, fol. 12.
[26] Stat. 23 & 24 Vict. cap. 124.
[27] *V.C.H. Herts.* i, 313*a*.
[28] Mins. Accts. at Westm.
[29] *Rot. Cur. Reg.* (Rec. Com.), i, 159.

A HISTORY OF HERTFORDSHIRE

In 1086 Peter de Valognes held '2 hides as 1 manor' in Ashwell, these having been part of the possessions of the Anglo-Saxon thegn Athelmar of Benington.[30] In the reign of Henry II (1154–89) Robert de Valognes, grandson of Peter, held '14 librates of land' here, which descended to his daughter Gunnora, the wife successively of Durant de Ostelli and Robert Fitz Walter.[31] Christina daughter of Robert and Gunnora married William de Mandeville Earl of Essex, and possibly Ashwell was settled on her, for she granted 'all her men in the vill of Ashwell' to the priory of Walden in Essex.[32] On her death without issue in 1233 the overlordship apparently passed to her brother Walter Fitz Walter, for his grandson Robert Fitz Walter died seised of one fee in Ashwell in 1328,[33] and his grandson Walter Fitz Walter died seised in 1386.[34] No further trace of Walden Priory in connexion with Ashwell has been found, and it seems reasonable to identify this holding with the manor of *ASHWELL*, which, in 1345, was settled upon Henry Gernet and Joan his wife.[35] She and her husband held lands in this parish (perhaps the same holding as that afterwards termed a manor) in 1338.[36] Under the settlement Henry and Joan were to hold for life with reversion to John Darcy le Fitz and his wife Margery, to Thomas de Charnels and his wife Maud, and to Margaret sister of Maud, successively, Margery, Maud and Margaret being daughters of Henry and Joan. Henry Gernet died the same year.[37] It was specially reported that he held his lands jointly with Joan his wife not of the king in chief, but 'of others,' probably the Fitz Walters.[38] Joan survived her husband,[39] and in 1345 received a quitclaim of the manor from Thomas de la Haye and Elizabeth his wife, who were possibly holding it in dower.[40] The tenement (or part of it) subsequently descended to Thomas Brydd, possibly heir of one of the daughters, who in 1428 was holding 'a quarter of a knight's fee in Ashwell, which Henry Gernet formerly held.'[41]

The county historians are unanimous in identifying this manor (which is not again heard of as Ashwell Manor) with a manor of *DIGSWELL* in this parish,[42] though the descents they give after this date vary considerably, Cussans (alone) maintaining that it was held by the family of Bill in Ashwell in the 16th and 17th centuries.[43] The latter theory is supported by the will of John Bill in 1557, whereby he leaves his 'manor of Dixwell *alias* Diggewell with a tenement called Wattes, and land in Glitton and Ashwell' to his son James.[44] A few years later there was a complaint over unlawful entry into a messuage 'in Mill Street in Ashwell,' which the father of the complainant (Thomas Rooke) had held 'of James Bill, by copy of court roll of his manor of Dykeswell.'[45] When Chauncy was writing in 1700 there was a manor of Digswell in Ashwell parish, owned by Samuel Gatward, and said to have been acquired by him from Sir William Whitmore, bart.[46] According to Clutterbuck he sold it in 1716 to Christopher Anstey, and it descended to his son Christopher,[47] who in 1805 suffered a recovery of this manor.[48] He sold it, according to Clutterbuck's descent, to William Heath in 1808, and after the death of the latter it became the property of Richard Westrope of Ashwell.[49] Since that date the manor has disappeared.

In 1086 Theobald held half a hide in Ashwell of Harduin de Scales, which may be identified as *WESTBURY*.[50] Harduin is said subsequently to have divided his lands between his two sons Richard and Hugh, the latter's son Hugh being in possession of three knights' fees in several places in Hertfordshire, including Ashwell, at the close of the 12th century.[51] Beyond this date the tenure of the Scales family is not traceable.

In 1198 the nuns of Holywell (Middlesex) impleaded Fulk son of Theobald (possibly son of the Theobald of 1086) for a rent of 1 mark in Ashwell which had been granted to them by charter of the said Theobald.[52] There is no trace of a grant of land in Ashwell to the nunnery, but it has been suggested that the 'virgate of land in Hinxworth of the gift of Theobald son of Fulk' confirmed to the nuns by Richard I in 1195[53] really lay in the neighbouring parish of Ashwell.[54] There is no subsequent trace of property held by the Holywell nuns in Hinxworth, whereas there were possessed of a manor of Westbury in Ashwell at the Dissolution, at which time it war held on lease by one John Bailey.[55] The nunnery also held tithes in Ashwell from at least the reign of Richard II,[56] the value of such tithes amounting at the Dissolution to £2.[57]

The subsequent descent of this manor is very difficult to trace. Setting aside the references to the manor of Westbury Nernewtes (of which the descent is given below) there is no record of it until 1606, when James I granted 'a messuage called le Westbury' to Thomas Norwood,[58] who was already possessed of the manor of Westbury Nernewtes. In 1664 a conveyance of Westbury was made to Elizabeth Sone, widow, by Thomas Bromfield, Laurence Marsh and a number of persons who were evidently co-heirs.[59] In 1678 a settlement was made by Richard Hutchinson,[60] in whose family it remained[61] until at

---

[30] *V.C.H. Herts.* i, 337b, 276.
[31] *Red Bk. Exch.* (Rolls Ser.), 78, 94, 97, 175; *Abbrev. Plac.* (Rec. Com.), 29.
[32] Harl. MS. 3697 (Chartul. of Walden), fol. 27.
[33] Chan. Inq. p.m. 2 Edw. III, pt. i, no. 59.
[34] Ibid. 10 Ric. II, no. 15.
[35] Feet of F. Herts. East. 19 Edw. III, no. 304.
[36] Ibid. Div. Co. East. 12 Edw. III.
[37] Chan. Inq. p.m. 19 Edw. III, no. 36.
[38] *Cal. Close,* 1346–9, p. 28.
[39] See *Cal. Pat.* 1345–8, p. 111.
[40] Feet of F. Div. Co. 19 Edw. III, no. 355.
[41] *Feud. Aids,* ii, 447.
[42] Direct evidence of such a connexion is completely lacking.

[43] Cussans, *Hist. of Herts. Braughing Hund.* 26.
[44] Will, P.C.C. 28 Mellershe.
[45] Chan. Proc. (Ser. 2), bdle. 23, no. 33. There seems no reason to connect this manor with the manor of Digswell in South Herts, which was never held by the Bills.
[46] Chauncy, *Hist. Antiq. of Herts.* 35.
[47] Clutterbuck, *Hist. and Antiq. of Herts.* iii, 485. Salmon, however, says that it descended to Samuel the son of the above-mentioned Samuel Gatward (*Hist. of Herts.* [1728], 344).
[48] Recov. R. Mich. 46 Geo. III, rot. 388.
[49] Clutterbuck, loc. cit.
[50] *V.C.H. Herts.* i, 339b.
[51] *Abbrev. Plac.* (Rec. Com.), 9).

[52] Ibid. 8.
[53] Dugdale, *Mon.* iv, 393; *Abbrev. Plac.* (Rec. Com.), 37. The nunnery was founded in 1127.
[54] Salmon, *Hist. of Herts.* 344. Probably also they acquired lands from the holders of Westbury Nernewtes, for in later times this estate is said to be held of Westbury Nernewtes (ibid.).
[55] Misc. Bks. (Ld. Rev. Rec.), cclxii, fol. 60 d.
[56] Mins. Accts. at Westm.
[57] Rentals and Surv. bdle. 11, no. 35.
[58] Pat. 4 Jas. I, pt. xiii.
[59] Feet of F. Div. Co. Trin. 16 Chas. II.
[60] Ibid. Hil. 29 & 30 Chas. II.
[61] Recov. R. East. 1 Anne, rot. 83; 1 Geo. I, rot. 189.

ASHWELL: HOUSE IN THE MAIN STREET (*Dated* 1681)

ASHWELL

least 1728, when Salmon writes that 'the western part of this manor (Westbury) is a farm of Sir Richard Hutchinson's, which holds of Sir George Humble,'[62] the Humbles, as hereafter shown, being at this date owners of Westbury Nernewtes. Subsequently it passed to the Leheups. William Leheup was holding in 1779[63] and Michael Peter Leheup in 1809.[64] Westbury Farm still remains a property quite separate from the manor of Westbury Nernewtes (see below). It is situated on the west of the village. Westbury Farm has a homestead moat.

The Buckinghamshire family of Nernewt (Nernuyt) held land in Ashwell in the 14th century which was probably originally part of the Abbot of Westminster's manor.[65] This land became the manor of *WESTBURY NERNEWTES*. In 1340 Sir John Nernewt of Burnham and Fleet Marston, Bucks., settled 'two thirds of one messuage, two mills, 40 acres of land, 10 acres of meadow and 18 marks' rent in Ashwell and Hinxworth' upon his son and heir John,[66] whose daughter Elizabeth, wife of John Hertishorne, inherited the property.[67] John Hertishorne (together with two others, presumably his feoffees) was holding 'half a fee in Ashwell which John Nernewt lately held there' in 1428.[68] The Nernewt property is said to have passed by female line to the Harveys, and on the death of Sir George Harvey (before 1520) to have been purchased by the Lees.[69] This descent is doubtful, but the Lees did acquire possession of Westbury Nernewtes. In 1540–1 a conveyance by Richard Heigham and his wife Mary, Thomas Colt and Thomas Lysley was made to Anthony Lee, kt., of a moiety of the Buckinghamshire manors and of the manor of Westbury in Ashwell.[70] After this the connexion with Buckinghamshire ceases. In 1557 this manor (henceforward invariably called Westbury Nernewtes) was conveyed by William Hawtrey and Agnes his wife to Thomas Norwood,[71] son and heir of William Norwood of Ashwell. Thomas was succeeded at Westbury Nernewtes by his son Nicholas, and Nicholas by his nephew Tirringham Norwood, who in 1611 sold this manor to Edward Waller *alias* Warren.[72] Channcy says that Edward Waller conveyed it to Andrew Laut, citizen of London, whose son Andrew Laut (of Thorpe Underwood, Northamptonshire) was lord of the manor at the date

NERNEWT. *Gules a lion argent in a border gobony argent and sable.*

of writing (1700).[73] The marriage of Sarah daughter and co-heir of Andrew Laut to Sir John Humble brought Westbury Nernewtes to the Humbles.[74] Elizabeth Humble, daughter-in-law of Sir John, who survived both her husband and her only son, bequeathed this property by her will of 1758 (proved in March 1770–1) to her brother the Hon. Charles Vane,[75] from whom it passed in 1789 to John Pennell, and on the latter's death in 1813 to his daughter Margaret, the wife of Bernard Geary Snow of Highgate. On the latter's death the manor went to his widow for life, and after her death was divided among his children by Margaret Pennell and by a former wife. Henrietta, a daughter of the former marriage, died unmarried, leaving her share of the property to her betrothed, the Rev. J. B. Smith. Anna María, a daughter of the Pennell marriage, married Mr. Edward King Fordham of Ashwell Bury, who bought up all the shares of the manor (including Smith's) excepting that of the Rev. John Pennell Snow, an elder brother of Anna María. This latter share (one-sixth) was bequeathed by Mr. Snow to Rupert Donald Fordham, who sold it to Mr. Edward Snow Fordham, who had already (in 1889) inherited the remaining five-sixths of the manor from his father and is the present lord of the manor. The tenants are, however, nearly all enfranchised and the manorial rights have lapsed.[76]

FORDHAM. *Barry wavy or and azure a chief gules with two crossed arrows therein between two castles all argent.*

In 1441 John Kirkeby died seised of 'a messuage, 140 acres of land, 8 acres of meadow, 2 acres of pasture and 50s. rent in Ashwell and Hinxworth,' 'a parcel of land in Ashwell called Quarrepette,' and 'a tenement, an acre of land and a croft called Chalgravecroft' in the same parish, all held of the Abbot of Westminster's manor of Ashwell.[77] He left a daughter and heir Alice. This estate may be identified with the manor of *KIRKEBIES* or *KIRBYS* in this parish, which in 1489 was settled upon Elizabeth Mervyn, widow of Thomas Mervyn, and her heirs.[78] She appears to have married subsequently John Clerke, and by 1530 to have been a second time a widow, for in that year Elizabeth Clerke sold the manor to Richard Copcot of Pyrton.[79] He sold it in 1533 to John Bowles, who sold it in 1540 to James Randall.[80] By 1546 it had passed to Anthony Randall, the kinsman and heir of James,[81] who in 1548 conveyed this

---

[63] Salmon, op. cit. 344. Salmon adds, 'The Farmer and his neighbours call it Nunwick.'
[63] Recov. R. Trin. 19 Geo. III, rot. 238.
[64] Ibid. Mich. 50 Geo. III, rot. 393.
[65] See Salmon (loc. cit.), who gives the tenure.
[66] Feet of F. Div. Co. Trin. 14 Edw. III, no. 280. William brother of John, sen., was apparently holding the other third for life.
[67] See Lipscomb, *Hist. of Bucks.* i, 327.
[68] *Feud. Aids*, ii, 447.
[69] Lipscomb, op. cit. i, 327.
[70] Feet of F. Div. Co. Hil. 32 Hen. VIII.

[71] Ibid. Herts. Mich. 4 & 5 Phil. and Mary. It was presumably to this Thomas that a grant was made by James I in 1606 of 'le Westbury' (see above).
[72] Com. Pleas D. Enr. Mich. 9 Jas. I, m. 13.
[73] Chauncy, *Hist. and Antiq. of Herts.* 35.
[74] Salmon (loc. cit.), writing in 1728, says that George, a minor, had then succeeded his father Sir John. Clutterbuck (*Hist. and Antiq. of Herts.* iii, 484) gives Sir William Humble as the son and heir of Sir John, and in this he is supported by the pedigree in Burke, *Extinct Baronetcies*.
[75] Clutterbuck, loc. cit.

[76] Information supplied by Mr. Fordham of Elbrook House.
[77] Chan. Inq. p.m. 22 Hen. VI, file 115, no. 26. Cussans (*Hist. of Herts. Odsey Hund.* 32) considers this early holding of the Kirkebys to be identical with a manor of Gasselyns held by John Kirkby, but the inquisition shows the latter manor to have been in the parish of Hatfield.
[78] Feet of F. Herts. Mich. 5 Hen. VII.
[79] Ct. of Req. bdle. 17, no. 117.
[80] Feet of F. Herts. Mich. 25 Hen. VIII; Ct. of Req. bdle. 17, no. 117.
[81] Feet of F. Herts. Mich. 38 Hen. VIII.

A HISTORY OF HERTFORDSHIRE

manor to Robert Leete and Christopher Browne.[82] Possibly the latter were trustees for St. John's College, Cambridge; at all events, it was in the hands of that body in 1565, when it was leased by the college to 'Alice Browne, late the wife of Andrewes,' for twenty-one years.[83] The estate is henceforward found continuously in the possession of the college and leased out by them. Kirkby's Manor Farm is situated in the north of the parish. The Northfield Road passes close by it and connects it with the village.

A few traces exist of a manor of STANES alias WAFRIES in this parish. Possibly its origin is to be found in the tenure of John de Stanes, who in 1303 held one quarter of a knight's fee in Ashwell of William Fitz Ralph[84] (for whose family see Broadfield Manor). The earliest mention of a manor extant is in 1567, when William Bourne and his wife Margaret conveyed it to John Burgoyne.[85] In the conveyance it is called Stanes alias Wafries, though it is not until forty years later that it is found held by an owner of the name of Waferer.[86] In 1570 Thomas Ward was apparently in possession.[87] In January 1609–10 Arden Waferer, who had been a member of the Inner Temple and a recusant,[88] died seised of this manor, having already by his will bequeathed it to his wife Elizabeth for her life, with reversion to his son James, then a minor. It was at this date said to be held of the Bishop of London's manor of Ashwell by fealty, suit of court and a rent of 12s. 10d.[89] In 1636 it was held by Edward Greene[90] and in 1703 by Samuel Gatward,[91] who acquired a considerable amount of land in this parish about this date. It then descended with Digswell (q.v.). The last trace of the manor to be found is in 1805, when a recovery of it was suffered by Christopher Anstey.[92]

Two small manors and estates in this parish, invariably found together, were those of SONWELL and OTWAYS. The earliest notice of them is in 1508, when they were held by Elizabeth Orrell, widow.[93] In 1528 James Orrell of Ashwell is mentioned in connexion with Sonwell,[94] and in 1563 Thomas Orrell, called of Walsoken, co. Norfolk, sold both estates to Ralph Dixon of Doddington, Isle of Ely.[95] After this date the property followed the same descent as Westbury. It was acquired by Elizabeth Sone in 1664,[96] and passed to the Hutchinsons and Leheups. The last mention of it is in 1829, when it was held by Michael Peter Leheup.

A manor of SUNINGS appears in 1585 held by Thomas Meade,[97] but it is not found again.

The church of ST. MARY has a CHURCH chancel 50 ft. 6 in. long by 19 ft. 6 in. wide, nave 89 ft. 8 in. by 24 ft., with north aisle 89 ft. 8 in. by 13 ft. 8 in., and south aisle 90 ft. 6 in. by 13 ft. 6 in.; there is a west tower 16 ft. square and a north and south porch. There was formerly a vestry or chapel on the north side of the chancel. All dimensions are taken internally. The church is built of flint rubble and clunch, the tower being faced with clunch.

The nave is the earliest portion of the church, the first four bays from the east, together with the clearstory and chancel arch, belong to the middle of the 14th century; the chancel, west tower and western bay of the nave, together with the side aisles, were constructed some thirty years later. The south porch was built about 1420 and the north porch about the middle of the 15th century. During the 19th century new roofs were put on the nave and chancel and the chancel was repaired.

The east window is of five lights, and the three windows on the south side of the chancel and the two on the north are of three lights each. All the tracery is of a late 14th-century type, and much of it has been renewed. On the north side are two blocked 14th-century doorways, one partly under a window; the other, to the east, was the entrance to the chapel probably of the Holy Trinity,[98] piscina of which still exists on the outer wall. On the south wall is a triple sedilia and piscina, each under an ogee cinquefoiled arch with crocketed labels and finials, dating from about 1380. There are small plain recessed niches on the eastern jambs of two of the side windows, on north and south respectively, one having a small carved bracket at its base.

The lofty chancel arch is of two moulded orders supported upon engaged shafts with moulded capitals and bases, all of 14th-century work. The built-up doorways to the rood loft are visible, but there is no trace of a rood stair.

The nave consists of five bays. The eastern four (c. 1350) have piers of clustered shafts with moulded capitals and bases, the latter somewhat mutilated. The arches are of two moulded orders, with labels in nave and aisles. The details of the western bay differ a little from the others and the span is wider, and they abut on solid walling covered with lofty traceried panels, which form eastern buttresses to the tower. There are six windows to each side of the clearstory. The two westernmost windows on each side belong to the later 14th century, the two middle ones on the

---

[82] Feet of F. Herts. Hil. 2 Edw. VI.
[83] Baker, Hist. of St. John's Coll. Camb. 393, being an extract from the 'Thick Black Book' of the college. For similar extracts see pp. 401, 420, 424, 425, 435, 442, 450, 455.
[84] Feud. Aids, ii, 432. A John de Stanes received a life-grant of lands in this parish in 1275 (Feet of F. Div. Co. Mich. 3 & 4 Edw. I, no. 37).
[85] Feet of F. Herts. Mich. 9 & 10 Eliz.
[86] But the Waferers held the neighbouring manor of Hinxworth in the 15th and 16th centuries.
[87] Recov. R. Mich. 12 & 13 Eliz. (1570), rot. 613.
[88] Cal. of Inner Temple Rec. pp. l, lii, &c.
[89] Chan. Inq. p.m. (Ser. 2), cccxxxv, 26.
[90] Feet of F. Div. Co. Hil. 11 Chas. I.
[91] Ibid. Herts. Hil. 1 Anne.

[92] Recov. R. Mich. 46 Geo. III, rot. 388.
[93] Feet of F. Herts. Trin. 23 Hen. VII. In the 14th century there was a family called Otway (Otewy) living in Ashwell (Cal. Pat. 1334–8, p. 284; 1340–3, p 483).
[94] Star Chamb. Proc. Hen. VIII, bdle. 17, no. 332.
[95] Feet of F. Herts. Trin. 5 Eliz.; Com. Pleas D. Enr. Trin. 5 Eliz.; Recov. R. Trin. 5 Eliz. rot. 339.
[96] Feet of F. Div. Co. Trin. 16 Chas. II.
[97] Chan. Inq. p.m. (Ser. 2), ccvi, 39.
[98] In 1458 William Freeman of Ashwell directed that his body should be buried in the chapel of the Holy Trinity in the parish church of Ashwell and desired that the chapel should be paved with 'Flaunders tile.' He also left 40s. to the fabric of the body of the church, 131. 4d. to the rood light and £18 to a chaplain to pray for his soul for three years at the altar of the Holy Trinity (P.C.C. Wills 12 Stokton). In 1505 William Sewster, mercer of London, desired that his body should be buried in the chapel on the north side of Ashwell Church and directed that 'a stone of marble to be laid on me my name in brass to be written on it with these words: "Here lyeth William Sewster of Glitton in the parisshe of Asshwell gent sometime mercer of London the which died, " &c.' He left land in Hinxworth for an obit for himself, his father Nicholas and his mother, and for the repair of the church, especially of the chapel where his body should lie (ibid. 39 Holgrave).

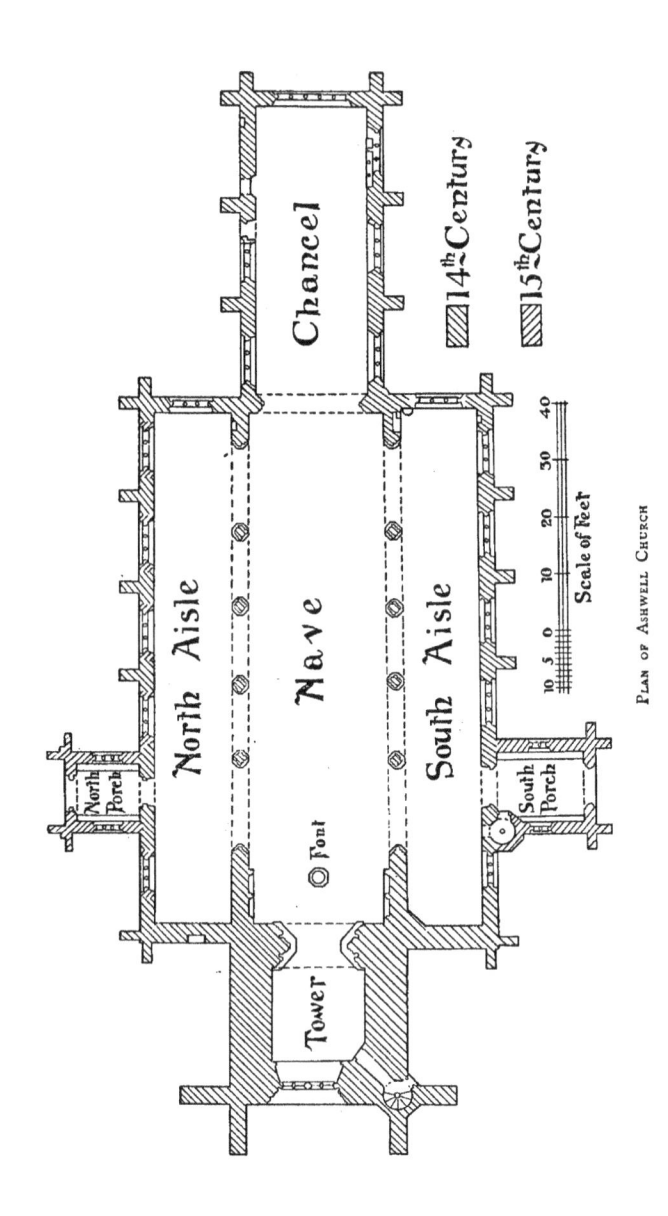

PLAN OF ASHWELL CHURCH

north side to the middle of the century, the others being alterations of the 16th century.

There is a three-light window of the 14th century with flowing tracery at the east end of the north aisle, the five windows on the north being of three lights, of 15th-century date; the tracery of these windows is much decayed. The north doorway belongs to the latter part of the 14th century. The north porch is a good type of 15th-century work with traceried windows, unglazed, under four-centred moulded arches. The outer doorway is set under a square head, the inner moulded order forming the arch. Holes, evidently for a bar, have been roughly cut in the mouldings of the jamb outside the position the door occupied. There is a mutilated 14th-century piscina at the east end of the aisle and a fragment of a stone bracket, indicating that there was an altar here and possibly a chantry.[99]

The south aisle has an east window of three traceried lights corresponding to those in the chancel. The five windows in the south wall were raised in the 15th century, and decayed remains of the tracery of that period still remain. The south doorway belongs to the 14th century, and immediately to the west of it is a blocked doorway to the parvise stair. The roof of the aisle appears to be the original one. The south porch has a parvise over it, the entrance to the turret stair, which projects on the western angle outside, is now from the porch itself. There is a modern stone vault to the porch, and a late flat roof over the parvise has taken the place of the original steep sloping roof, the front gable now standing unsupported. The porch has unglazed windows with iron stanchions. At the east end of the south aisle are traces of a reredos of an altar; on the south side is a 14th-century piscina, above which is a lofty niche of, probably, 15th-century date, which apparently held the image of our Lady.[100] On the north side is a recess or aumbry, which may have been formed from the partly built-up doorway to the rood stair, which was on the south side.[1] On the east wall is a defaced bracket for an image, with remains of carving, and above it can be seen traces of a distemper painting behind the coats of whitewash, which probably represents the figure of our Lady, to whom the chapel was dedicated.[2]

The west tower is a very striking feature of the church, and is unusually high, rising, with its spire, to a height of about 176 ft. Ashwell and Northchurch towers are the only two in the county which are completely encased with stonework externally. The walls are about 8 ft. thick at the base. The tower is of four diminishing stages, with massive buttresses stopping under the fourth stage. Access to the tower is by a turret stair at the south-west angle as far as the top of the first stage, and thence through a passage-way in the wall to another turret stair at the south-east angle. The stair has a rounded handrail cut out of the solid stone wall. The first stage, inside the church, was formerly covered with a sexpartite vault of stone, but only the wall ribs and corbels now remain. The tower arch is of three subdivided moulded orders, resting on shafts with moulded capitals and bases, of about 1360–70. On the west side the arch above the capitals has been much mutilated, no doubt to obtain support for a gallery which has been removed. The west window, which is not central in the tower, has four lights, but the tracery has been much mutilated and repaired with cement. On each face of the second stage of the tower is a long narrow single light, above which is a wide band of square cusped panels set diagonally The third or belfry stage has on each face two lofty arched openings, each of two lights with traceried heads, but much decayed and hidden behind wood lattices. Underneath the openings are arched and cusped panels. The topmost stage is pierced on each side by a two-light window with traceried head. The tower was formerly finished with battlements of which only the corner portions remain. Owing to the soft nature of the clunch the whole of the face work of the tower is in a very decayed condition. The tower is surmounted by a timber spire on an octagonal drum, very similar to that at Baldock, the whole being covered with lead. The following inscription is in raised letters on the leadwork:

THO[S] EVERARD | LAID ME HERE | HE SAID TO L(AST) | AN HVNDRED | YEAR | 1714.

There are oak traceried and carved 15th-century screens at the west ends of the aisles, removed from the Lady chapel in the south aisle[3]; there are also some traceried panels of the same period, probably the lower part of the old chancel screen, now made up into a screen behind the organist's stool; two old carved finials are fixed on the modern end posts. The pulpit is of oak, panelled and carved and dated 1627. In the south aisle is an oak chest of early 17th-century work, and beside the south door is an alms box on a narrow oak pedestal which may belong to the same century. The communion table is also of the 17th century. The north and south doors are original and have plain old iron hinges. The font is modern, but the steps appear to be original. There are fragments of 15th-century glass in some of the clearstory windows, and some of later date in the north aisle.

At the east end of the north aisle stands a 15th-century tomb, with panelled tracery, much defaced, it bears no inscription; on the floor of the nave is a brass inscription to John Sell, 1618, and in the chancel are three slabs with indents of the 15th century, and a part of another lies at the south door. On the east wall of the nave is a mural tablet to Ralph Baldwyn, 1689, with his arms.

On the north wall of the tower, internally, the following 14th-century inscription has been roughly scratched. The beginnings of the second and third lines are imperfect:

'xlix
pestilecia q[i]nz
M. C. T. X penta miserāda ferox violēta
. . . supest plebs pessima testis 'in fine q̇[e] vēt' valid'
. oc anno Maurus in orbe tonat MCCC lxi.'

This has been translated by Mr. C. Johnson, M.A.,[4] as '1000, three times 100, five times 10, pitiable,

---

[99] This may have been the altar and chantry of the Virgin; see under advowson.
[100] See will of John Bill (1503) quoted in Cussans' *Hist. of Herts. Odsey Hund.* 26. An indulgence was granted probably for building this chantry by Bishop Burghersh (1320–40); see his register (Memo. fol. 109 d.).
[1] The remains of the circular wall inclosing the stair may be seen outside.
[2] Will of John Bill, as above.
[3] Cussans, op. cit. *Odsey Hund.* 35.
[4] See a paper by Mr. C. Johnson in *Trans. St. Albans and Herts. Arch. Soc.* 1899–1900, p. 277.

Ashwell Church from the South-east

Ashwell Church: The Nave looking South-west

ODSEY HUNDRED — ASHWELL

savage and violent. A wicked populace survives to witness [to the shocking plague].' These lines with their glosses refer to the Black Death of 1350. The third line alludes to the great storm on St. Maur's Day (15 Jan.), 1361, mentioned in the 'Eulogium Historiarum.'[4a] It may be that this great wind destroyed the newly-erected tower and two western bays of the nave, which had to be rebuilt; the present western bay, which is wider than the others, and the panelled buttresses to the tower occupy the same space as two of the earlier eastern bays. Underneath the inscription is a roughly incised drawing of a large church with double transepts, and a lofty central tower and spire.[5]

1686 to 1754; (ii) burials 1678 to 1728 and 1735 to 1783; (iii) baptisms 1783 to 1801; (iv) burials 1783 to 1801; (v) baptisms and burials 1802 to 1812; (vi) marriages 1754 to 1801; (vii) marriages 1802 to 1812.

ADVOWSON The record of a priest among the tenants of the Abbot of Westminster in 1086 implies the existence of a church there at that date.[6] In 1223 Honorius III appropriated the church of Ashwell to the Abbot and convent of Westminster,[7] and in 1241 Bishop Grosteste of Lincoln (in whose diocese Ashwell was situated) ordained a vicarage there, endowing the vicar with the court and house next the churchyard.[8]

ASHWELL: LYCH-GATE TO CHURCHYARD

There is an open timber lych-gate, with tiled roof, at the south-western entrance to the churchyard. It appears to be of 15th-century work.

There are six bells in the tower: the treble by John Briant, 1791; the second by Charles Newman, 1694; the third and fourth by John Briant, 1817; the fifth by Robert Taylor, St. Neots, 1808; and the tenor by John Briant, 1789.

The communion plate includes an engraved cup of 1568 and paten of 1632.

The registers are in seven books: (i) baptisms from 1686 to 1785, burials 1729 to 1735, marriages

In 1239 a dispute arose between the Bishop of Lincoln and the Abbot of Westminster as to the appropriation, Grosteste making provision of the church to a certain clerk of his diocese.[9] Peace was only secured by the intervention of King Henry III, who decided that while the church of Ashwell should remain in the possession of the abbey the right of presentation should be reserved to the bishop.[10] Matthew Paris remarks that 'by this the Abbey of Westminster gained great honour, and the Abbot an increase of 300 marks a year.'[11] It would seem, however, that a later composition must have taken place by which the

---

[4a] Op. cit. (Rolls Ser.), iii, 2.
[5] Neither Old St. Paul's Cath. nor Westminster. It has the tower of St. Paul's and the transept of Westminster.
[6] *V.C.H. Herts.* i, 313a.
[7] Cott. MSS. Faust. A iii; *Cal. Papal Letters*, i, 181.
[8] Cott. MSS. Faust. A iii.
[9] *Cal. Papal Letters*, i, 181; Matth. Paris, *Chron. Maj.* (Rolls Ser.), iv, 151.
[10] Matth. Paris, op. cit. iv, 154.
[11] Cf. Dugdale, *Mon.* i, 271.

207

abbots recovered the right of presentation, for by the year 1334 the patronage had clearly come to them.[12] The dissolution of Westminster Abbey brought the advowson and rectory of Ashwell into the king's hands, and they were granted by him to the first Bishop of Westminster in 1541,[13] a pension from the vicarage being granted the following year to the dean and chapter.[14] Subsequently the advowson was granted with the manor, first to Bishop Ridley and secondly to Bishop Bonner.[15] In 1556 the vicarage pension was granted to the reinstated Abbot of Westminster —all that remained to the abbey of the manor and advowson of Ashwell. It is interesting to note that Laud's appointment of Herbert Palmer, the Puritan divine, to this benefice in 1632 was brought forward by him at his trial as evidence of his impartial patronage.[16] The survey of Ashwell taken by the Parliamentary Commissioners in 1647 describes the parsonage of Ashwell as 'consisting of a hall, a kitchen, 2 butteries, a brew-house, a malt-house, tiled, with five chambers over them, 3 great barns, 2 stables thatched, a granary, a garden, an orchard, a great yard; the whole containing about 4 acres.'[17] The sale of the manor by the trustees for the sale of church lands in 1648 makes special exception of the advowson, though one of the trustees himself obtained leave to buy the parsonage-house and the glebe land.[18] In 1662 the Bishop of London once more presented to the living,[19] and the patronage remained with his successors until 1852, when it was transferred to the Bishop of Rochester,[20] in whose diocese Ashwell had already been placed in 1846.[21] In 1877, however, Hertfordshire was placed in the new diocese of St. Albans, all patronage of the Bishop of Rochester in that diocese being transferred to the Bishop of St. Albans.[22] In 1867 this benefice was declared a rectory.[23]

In 1306 Thomas de Staunton and Simon le Bakestere founded a chantry in Ashwell Church, dedicated to the Blessed Virgin,[24] for the support of which Thomas granted 12 acres and Simon 1 acre of land in the parish.[25] In 1351 William de Risseby, the king's yeoman, founded a similar chantry, which he endowed with land of the annual value of 15s. and with 5s. rent,[26] and in 1401 John Sennesterre made a bequest to maintain a chantry priest in the church.[27] In 1450 is the record of the induction of a chaplain into apparently the first of these chantries, the collation being in the hands of the abbot's treasurer.[28] The foundation in 1476 of a chantry for the founders of the gild of St. John the Baptist is mentioned below. At the Dissolution only one chantry is mentioned, value 100s. per annum.[29] The advowson was included in the grant to the Bishop of Westminster in 1541.[30] In the reign of Elizabeth the chantry estate was in the possession of Nicholas West,[31] who settled it upon his son and heir William West by indenture of 1572. Nicholas West died seised of this chantry (described as 'the late chantrey') with appurtenant lands, rents and services in 1586.[32]

On 26 August 1476 licence was granted to George Duke of Clarence (brother of the king), Thomas Bishop of Lincoln, the chancellor, and others, to found 'a fraternity or gild of four wardens and other persons wishing to be of the fraternity, to be called the fraternity or gild of St. John the Baptist within the church of St. Mary Ashwell.' The members, who were to include both brethren and sisters, were to elect their wardens annually, and to act as a corporate body in the acquisition of lands, &c. Licence was also given to them to found a chantry in Ashwell Church for the souls of the king's father, of the present king and queen after their deaths, and of the founders and members of the gild.[33] A fraternity of St. John the Baptist had existed before this, for in 1457 one William Freeman of Ashwell, merchant, left 6s. 8d. by will 'to the fraternity of St. John the Baptist.'[34] Similar bequests follow throughout the reigns of Henry VII and Henry VIII.[35] In 1574 Andrew Bill and Elizabeth his wife surrendered to Nicholas West and Joan his wife and William West their son and heir 'a house or tenement called le Guyldehowse or St. John's House or le Brotherheadhowse' in Ashwell, situate 'in the High Street of Ashwell,' and 'a barn and a close of pasture containing 1 acre, pertaining to the said house.'[36] There was also a fraternity of St. George in Ashwell.[37]

Licence for a Presbyterian meeting-place at Ashwell was taken out in 1672, and meeting-places for Protestant Dissenters were certified from 1692. The Congregational chapel, dating from about 1767, was burnt down in 1850 and rebuilt.[38]

CHARITIES

The following charities are regulated by a scheme of the Charity Commissioners dated 25 May 1897:

1. Lawrence Williams's, founded by will dated 10 September 1582, consisting of a yearly payment of £3 by the Fishmongers' Company, of which a yearly sum of 2s. is applicable for the sexton and of 6s. for the reparation of the church.

2. John Sell's, by will 24 May 1618, consisting of 1 a. 3 r. 10 p. of land in Ashwell.

3. Thomas Chapman's, by will dated 8 March 1668, now consisting of £120 consols with the official trustees, producing £3 yearly, representing redemption of rent-charge.

4. Thomas Plomer's, by will dated 2 August 1701, under which testator gave £80 to purchase land, 5s. yearly out of the income to be paid to the parish clerk.

5. The poor's land comprised in indenture of 6 September 1718 and indentures of lease and release 20 and 21 April 1722. The endowment of this

---

[12] *Cal. Pat.* 1330–4, p. 492.
[13] *L. and P. Hen. VIII*, xvi, g. 503 (33).
[14] Ibid. xvii, g. 714 (5).
[15] See under manor.
[16] *Dict. Nat. Biog.*
[17] Add. MS. 37682, fol. 21. Nevertheless an incumbent wrote of Ashwell in 1675: 'It is of small advantage, so that I could easily quit it' (*Cal. S. P. Dom.* 1675–6, p. 42).
[18] Add. MS. 17682, fol. 26–30; Close, 1651, pt. xxvi, no. 48.
[19] Inst. Bks. P.R.O.
[20] *Lond. Gaz.* 4 June 1852, p. 1578.
[21] Ibid. 8 Aug. 1845, p. 2541.
[22] Ibid. 4 May 1877, p. 2933.
[23] Ibid. 29 Nov. 1867, p. 6524.
[24] *Cal. Pat.* 1301–7, p. 483.
[25] Inq. a.q.d. file 65, no. 4.
[26] *Cal. Pat.* 1350–4, p. 184.
[27] Court of Husting wills.
[28] Doc. at Westm. 26302. It is called the chantry of the Blessed Virgin Mary. Possibly the chantries had been amalgamated.
[29] *Valor Eccl.* (Rec. Com.), iv, 278.
[30] *L. and P. Hen. VIII*, xvi, g. 503 (33). See manor of Ashwell.
[31] Pat. 1 Eliz. pt. x.
[32] Chan. Inq. p.m. (Ser. 2), ccxi, 173.
[33] *Cal. Pat.* 1467–77, p. 597.
[34] Will P.C.C. 12 Stokton.
[35] Wills P.C.C. 29 Blamyr; 39 Holgrave; 35 Bennett; 23 Holder; Anct. D. (P.R.O.), C477.
[36] Ct. R. P.R.O. (Gen. Ser.), bdle. 176, no. 139.
[37] Will P.C.C. 12 Stokton.
[38] Urwick, op. cit. 780–1.

ODSEY HUNDRED

BROADFIELD

charity together with the charities of John Sell and Thomas Plomer consists of 32 a. 2 r. 7 p. of land in Mob's Hole in Ashwell North Fields, producing £32 10s. yearly.

The income of these charities after deduction of the fixed payments mentioned above is applicable for the general benefit of the poor.

In 1886 Miss Anne Heath Westrope, by her will proved at London 28 July, bequeathed £100 to the rector for the time being, represented by £100 5s. consols, the annual dividends, amounting to £2 10s., to be distributed among the poor, especially the afflicted poor, without regard to sect or denomination.

The same testatrix bequeathed £100 to the minister and deacons of the Independent Chapel upon the same trusts. This legacy is represented by £100 5s. consols, and the charity is regulated by a scheme of the Charity Commissioners dated 14 July 1905, which also regulates the trust estate of the Congregational Chapel comprised in deeds 1829, 1864 and 1875.

In 1891 Mrs. Mary Hitch Westrope, by her will proved at London 1 April, left a legacy, now represented by £187 19s. 9d. consols, the annual dividends amounting to £4 14s. to be distributed among the afflicted poor, especially widows, without regard to sect or denomination.

The Moss Cottage Homes were founded by George Moss by indenture 10 July 1905 and endowed by him with £2,000 London and North Western Railway 3 per cent. Perpetual Debenture Stock. The endowment was increased in 1907 to £2,800 London and North Western Railway stock by augmentation of Mrs. Frederika Emily Bowman, producing £84 a year. The Homes consist of six cottages for six aged and infirm persons, and the inmates, who receive 5s. weekly, may be either married couples (each married couple counting as one inmate), single women or widows.

The several sums of stock above mentioned are held by the official trustees.

The school was founded by the will of Henry Colborn dated 1 August 1655.[39] The Educational Charity was founded by deed of grant dated 22 March 1842 made by Michael Edward Rogers, Charles Stubbs Tinling and Mary Susanna his wife, and consists of a sum of £306 10s. 3d. consols with the official trustees, producing £7 13s. yearly, purchased with £300 produced by sale of the old school site, &c. The charity is regulated by a scheme of the Charity Commissioners dated 6 August 1878. The endowment was augmented in 1878 by a donation of £50 by Edward King Fordham. This was invested in £51 18s. 9d. consols with the official trustees, producing £1 6s. yearly.

BROADFIELD

Bradefella (xi cent.); Bradefeld (xii cent.); Bradfeld (xiv cent.).

Broadfield is a small parish containing 374 acres. As its name would possibly imply, it is comprised within field boundaries, and was probably originally a part of Rushden, of which parish it was said to have been a chapelry in the 16th century.[1] About two-thirds of the parish are arable land and the remainder permanent grass. There are now only three small woods in the centre of the parish, called Great Wood, Middle Wood and Chapel Wood, and a small copse in the south called Foxholes. In the 17th century, however, the woodland was probably more extensive, as Chauncy describes Broadfield as situated on a hill in woods.[2] The soil is generally heavy, with a subsoil of chalk. A spring which rises a mile to the north of Broadfield Hall is said to have had at one time powers of petrifaction.[3] The parish lies on the high chalk land, reaching an altitude in the south-east of 465 ft. above the ordnance datum, but falls to a little over 400 ft. in the west.

The nearest railway station is in Buntingford on the Great Eastern railway, about 3 miles to the east. The small village lies a little north of the road from Cottered to Throcking, with which it is connected by a branch road. Until the beginning of the 19th century this road went no further than Broadfield, but turned south again and joined the Cottered-Buntingford road.[4] It is probably largely due to this limited communication that the village has consistently diminished in size and importance. Even during the last century the population has fallen from thirty-one to seven, and consists of little more than Broadfield Hall, the manor-house, now the residence of Mr. T. H. Whitehead. Chapel Wood, supposed to mark the site of the church which fell into ruins in the 16th century, lies a little to the north of the hall.

Broadfield Hall stands about a mile to the north of the village of Cottered. Portions of a moat which originally surrounded the site still exist as ornamental water. The house was built about the year 1689, and existed until the middle of the 19th century, when it was allowed to fall into ruins. In 1882 it was practically rebuilt on a smaller scale, and portions of the old house still remain incorporated with the new work. In the east wall is one of the old windows with stone mullions and transoms, and part of the north side is old and has a large brick niche with semicircular head set in the brickwork. Some of the old cellars still exist and have round vaults of brick. On the modern front door is a fine iron knocker of late 17th-century work, said to have come from Cottered Lordship. It represents two dolphins with entwined tails, holding a human head between them in their jaws. The old staircase and an old chimneypiece from the old hall are now at Coles Park, Westmill.[4a] The original entrance door is of oak and is richly covered with moulded panels. The top part of the door has a semicircular panel with fluted and moulded spokes radiating from the centre. There is a good lion's head knocker and a drop handle on a shaped plate. Both on the rails and in the panels are a number of iron studs.

The brick stables, which stand immediately behind the hall, are of the early part of the 18th century. Some of the old oak stalls still remain in the stable

---

[39] See article on Schools, *V.C.H. Herts.* ii, 99.
[1] Norden, *Description of Herts.* (ed. 1903), 15.
[2] Chauncy, *Hist. and Antiq. of Herts.* 71.

[3] *East Herts. Arch. Soc. Trans.* iii, 170.
[4] Ibid. 168.
[4a] Ibid. 172.

A HISTORY OF HERTFORDSHIRE

and in the yard behind is an 18th-century square dove-house of brick, now used as a granary.

The fact that the hall stood empty for nearly thirty years during the 19th century[5] evidently tended to lessen the prosperity of the village.

Foxholes Farm, a name which occurs as early as 1591,[6] lies in the south of the parish. Although much repaired, the house appears to date from the beginning of the 18th century.

MANOR In the time of Edward the Confessor Broadfield was divided between the Archbishop of Canterbury and Queen Edith.[7] The lands of the former, assessed at 2½ hides, were held of him by Ledmaer, Ansgot and two brothers.[8] Queen Edith's lands, assessed at half a hide, were held of her by Goda.[9] By 1086 the three holdings of the archbishop had passed to three separate overlords, Sigar de Cioches,[10] Hardwin de Scales[11] and Robert Bishop of Chester,[12] the last holding a virgate only. Earl Roger de Montgomery had obtained possession of the lands of Queen Edith.[13] It is probable that the lands of Roger de Montgomery formed the estate in Rushden which was given by his daughter Sybil to the Knights Hospitallers.[14] Sigar de Cioches held also the manor of Rushden (q.v.), and probably his lands in Broadfield were attached to that manor.

In 1086 Hardwin de Scales had obtained possession of the chief holding in Broadfield, viz. a hide and one-fourth of a virgate, and this appears subsequently as the manor of BROADFIELD. The overlordship of the manor remained with the Scales family,[15] and descended to Sir John de Scales, who died seised of the manor in 1388.[16] It was apparently attached to his manor of Throcking (q.v.), for this in 1486 was in the hands of Robert Hyde, of whom Broadfield at that date was said to be held.[17]

Of the tenants in demesne it appears that in 1086 Theobald was holding this manor under Hardwin de Scales.[18] He seems to have had a son Fulk, who had two sons Theobald and William.[19] About 1159 Theobald was holding Broadfield, and with the consent of his brother William leased it to the abbey of Warden (co. Beds.).[20] The latter Theobald had a son Fulk, who had succeeded to his lands by 1198-9, when he disputed his father's gifts to the nuns of Holywell.[21] On the death of Fulk, Broadfield descended to his son Ralph, who levied a fine of the advowson in 1222.[22] Ralph had a son of the same name, who appears to have forfeited about 1266, when the king granted Broadfield to Maud his wife for the maintenance of herself and her children.[23] Ralph was still living in 1283.[24] His lands were held by William Fitz Ralph in 1303,[25] from whom they probably descended to his son William (see Aspenden). In 1356 Margaret and Sybil, daughters and heirs of William, are mentioned.[25a] But a William Fitz Ralph was holding Aspenden in 1383, when he granted it to his son William.[26] The manor of Broadfield apparently also remained with the heirs male, for on the death without issue of a William Fitz Ralph (probably the last mentioned) before 1428 it went to his co-heirs, John Hughessene of Ashwell and John Clerk, senior, of Ardeley.[27] These both quit-claimed their right to John and Thomas Clerk, who apparently conveyed it to Richard Whapled, vicar of Steeple Morden, and John Suttrey, for they in 1449 granted the manor to John Dunstable and Margaret his wife, Ralph Grey and Henry Wells.[28] Margaret Dunstable died seised of the manor in 1486.[29] Henry Wells survived the other feoffees, and on his death it passed to his cousin and next heir John Fayrewayre. He conveyed it to Henry Snow of London and Magdalen his wife.[30] It descended to their son John Snow, whose daughters and co-heirs Elizabeth and Dorothy[31] conveyed it in 1537-8 to Edward Brockett.[32]

In 1571 Edward Brockett settled the manor on himself with remainder to Ellen his wife for life with remainder to John Brockett of Brockett Hall and Ellen his wife.[33] On Edward Brockett's death his executors conveyed the manor to his widow Ellen and her kinsman Richard Bardolf. In 1580 John Brockett, who had been knighted in 1577, and his wife Ellen, released their interest in the manor to Edward Pulter[34] of Great Wymondley,[35] and in 1592 Ellen Brockett and Richard Bardolf conveyed their interest.[36] Edward Pulter held the manor until 1600, when he settled it on his son Litton Pulter in consideration of his marriage with Penelope daughter of Sir Arthur Capell, kt.[37] Litton Pulter died in 1608, in his father's lifetime, leaving a son Arthur, then aged four years.[38] Arthur Pulter held a prominent position in the county, acting as justice of the peace, a captain in the militia, and high sheriff for Hertfordshire, but at the outbreak of the Civil War he resigned all these offices, led a retired life, and at the instigation of his wife Lady Helen Ley, daughter of James Earl of Marl-

PULTER. *Argent two bends sable with a Cornish chough in the cantle.*

---

[5] *East Herts. Arch. Soc. Trans.* iii, 170; Cussans, *Hist. of Herts. Hund. of Odsey,* 178.
[6] Com. Pleas D. Enr. Mich. 33 & 34 Eliz. m. 1.
[7] *V.C.H. Herts.* i, 311, 322, 339, 342.
[8] Ibid. 311, 339, 342.
[9] Ibid. 322.   [10] Ibid. 342.
[11] Ibid. 339.   [12] Ibid. 311.
[13] Ibid. 322.
[14] See land of the Knights Hospitallers in Rushden.
[15] *Abbrev. Plac.* (Rec. Com.), 99; *Feud. Aids,* ii, 433; *Cal. Inq. p.m.* (Rec. Com.), iii, 93. See manor of Challers, Reed, for Scales pedigree.
[16] *Cal. Inq. p.m.* (Rec. Com.), iii, 93.
[17] Chan. Inq. p.m. (Ser. 2), xxiii, 65.
[18] *V.C.H. Herts.* i, 339.
[19] Dugdale, *Mon.* iv, 393; v, 372.
[20] Ibid. v, 372. Although no term of years is mentioned in the charter, the form in which the date is given implies a lease, as does the subsequent history of the manor.
[21] *Abbrev. Plac.* (Rec. Com.), 8.
[22] Feet of F. Herts. 6 Hen. III, no. 45.
[23] *Cal. Pat.* 1258-66, p. 526.
[24] De Banco R. 55, m. 101.
[25] *Feud. Aids,* ii, 433.
[25a] *Cal. Pat.* 1354-8, p. 647; J. Harvey Bloom, *Cartae Antiquae of Lord Willoughby de Broke,* ii, 7.
[26] Anct. D. (P.R.O.), B 154. He was witness to a deed in 1361 (J. Harvey Bloom, *Cartae Antiquae of Lord Willoughby de Broke,* ii, 8).
[27] Close, 6 Hen. VI, m. 14.
[28] Chauncy, *Hist. and Antiq. of Herts* 71 et seq.
[29] Chan. Inq. p.m. (Ser. 2), xxiii, 65.
[30] Chauncy, loc. cit.
[31] Ibid.; see Close, 30 Hen. VIII, pt. vi, no. 5.
[32] Chauncy, loc. cit.; Close, 30 Hen. VIII, pt. vi, no. 5.
[33] Chauncy, loc. cit.; see Feet of F. Herts. Hil. 14 Eliz.; Recov. R. Mich. 14 Eliz. rot. 513.
[34] Feet of F. Herts. Hil. 22 Eliz.
[35] The Pulters had the manor of Delamere in that parish.
[36] Chauncy, loc. cit.
[37] Feet of F. Div. Co. Mich. 42 & 43 Eliz.; see Chan. Inq. p.m. (Ser. 2), cccv, 111.
[38] Chan. Inq. p.m. (Ser. 2), cccv, 111.

Broadfield : Old Oak Entrance Door from Broadfield Hall

ODSEY HUNDRED

borough, began rebuilding Broadfield Hall. But at the time of his death in 1689 the building was still unfinished.[39] He had a large family, but all his children died during their father's lifetime. His sons had no children, but his daughter Margaret, who married John Forrester, citizen of London, left one son James, who succeeded his grandfather.[40] James Forrester married Martha daughter of Sir Henry Chauncy, kt., and died in 1696, when his young son Pulter became lord of the manor.[41] Pulter Forrester appears to have been concerned with the fashionable bands of rioters who called themselves the 'Mohocks' and the 'Hawkubites,' and rendered the streets of London dangerous for the ordinary traveller. In 1711 he was one of the sureties for Lord Hinchinbrooke's appearance at the quarter sessions to answer for assaulting the watchman and causing a riot in Essex Street in the early hours of the morning.[42] Pulter Forrester married Agnes daughter of William Harvey of Chigwell, Essex, and died in 1753.[43] His son William succeeded him.[44] He had no children, and on his death he left the manor of Broadfield to his wife's niece, Millicent daughter of Wrightson Mundy of Markeaton Park, co. Derby, with remainder to her eldest son on condition that he should take the name of Forrester.[45] She married Richard French, captain in the Royal Horse Guards, and on her death the manor passed to her eldest son Richard Forrester French of Abbot's Hill, co. Derby.[46] He suffered a recovery in 1793,[47] and continued to hold until his death in 1843.[48] He left no children, and in 1852 his executors sold the manor of Broadfield to Mr. Robert Bird Wilkins, timber merchant, of Ware.[49] He died in 1868, and the manor passed to his son Robert Usborn Wilkins,[50] who devised it to Mr. Nathan Humphrey. He died in 1906,[51] leaving the manor to his two daughters, Mrs. H. W. Smith of Ware and Mrs.

BYGRAVE

H. E. Dudley of Stansted, co. Essex, who now hold the manor.[52]

The land which Robert Bishop of Chester held in Broadfield in 1086 consisted of 1 virgate.[53] There is no record to show how this land descended, but it appears that like the other lands which Robert held in this county it passed to the Somerys.[54] It is probable that this land was appurtenant to the manor of Bygrave (q.v.), for in the reign of Edward I John de Wengham, Precentor of St. Paul's, who held a lease of that manor from the Somerys, also held a park in Broadfield, which in 1297 was broken into.[55] John de Wengham's holding in Broadfield was described as a quarter of a knight's fee in 1303.[56] In 1346 it had descended to his nephew Master Thomas de Wengham,[57] but after this date there is no further record of it.

CHURCH AND ADVOWSON Broadfield Church was a chapel of ease,[58] apparently dependent on the church of Rushden. In 1222 William Basset, lord of the manor of Rushden, quitclaimed all right in the church of Broadfield to Ralph son of Fulk, lord of Broadfield.[59] The advowson has always passed with the manor.[60] It is not known at what date the church fell into disuse, but as no inventory was made for it in 1553 it seems that by this date the church was no longer used for religious services. The rectory was valued at 10s. only in 1535.[61] The advowson was still included in the sale of the manor until the year 1580.[62] Norden, in his description of Hertfordshire in 1598, states that Broadfield had once had a chapel of ease which at that time was decayed.[63] The site of the church is supposed to have been in Chapel Wood in the centre of the parish, and certain irregularities in the ground may point to the former existence of a building here.[64] By the 18th century Broadfield had become ecclesiastically attached to Cottered,[65] and still remains so.

There are no endowed charities.

BYGRAVE

Biggrafan (x cent.); Bigrave (xi–xvii cent.).

The small compact parish of Bygrave, containing 1,793 acres, lies below the northern slope of the Hertfordshire chalk hills in the angle formed by the Icknield Way and the North Road through Barnet, which meet in the adjacent town of Baldock. On the north and east the boundary is formed by a road known as the Green Lane. The ecclesiastical parish was amalgamated with Baldock in 1901,[1] but Bygrave is still a distinct civil parish.

This parish is still uninclosed, and forms perhaps one of the most interesting examples in this country of a concentric mediaeval village of the Teutonic type of settlement. Although the lands were now all held by two or three farmers and the village community has been lost, the mediaeval arrangements are still clearly marked. The village is in the middle of the parish on high land. Like other early Teutonic settlements in this country it lies off the main road, about a mile and a half from the Roman road to the west and half a mile from the Icknield Way on the south. It is approached by roads or drifts uninclosed by hedges across the open fields from both these main roads, and by an inclosed road from Ashwell. The church stands in the highest part of the village, 314 ft. above the ordnance datum. Adjoining the churchyard on the south side is the site of the old fortified manor-house,[2] surrounded by a series of moats which, from indications

---

[39] Chauncy, loc. cit.
[40] Ibid.
[41] Ibid.
[42] *Hist. MSS. Com. Rep.* xv, App. ii, 346.
[43] Clutterbuck, *Hist. and Antiq. of Herts.* iii, 516.
[44] See Recov. R. Hil. 27 Geo. II, rot. 219.
[45] Clutterbuck, loc. cit.
[46] Ibid.
[47] Recov. R. Trin. 33 Geo. III, rot. 174.

[48] Cussans, *Hist. of Herts. Odsey Hund.* 174.
[49] Ibid.
[50] Ibid.
[51] *East Herts. Arch. Soc. Trans.* iii, 168.
[52] Information supplied by Mr. T. H. Whitehead of Broadfield Hall.
[53] *V.C.H. Herts.* i, 311.
[54] See Bygrave and North Mimms. Elias de Somery appears as witness to a lease of the manor of Broadfield in the reign of Henry II (Dugdale, *Mon.* v, 369).
[55] *Cal. Pat.* 1292–1301, p. 316.
[56] *Feud. Aids,* ii, 433.

[57] Exch. Q.R. Misc. Bks. no. 3.
[58] Norden, *Description of Herts.* (ed. 1903), 15.
[59] Feet of F. Herts. 6 Hen. III, no. 45.
[60] See under manor.
[61] *Valor Eccl.* (Rec. Com.), iv, 278.
[62] Feet of F. Herts. Hil. 22 Eliz.
[63] Norden, loc. cit.
[64] *East Herts. Arch. Soc. Trans.* iii, 168.
[65] Bacon, *Liber Regis,* 513.
[1] Under Loc. Act, 60–1 Vict. cap. 228.
[2] Styled the 'Palace' in the Ordnance Survey of 1896.

211

on the ground, may have at one time inclosed the church. The modern rectory-house stands on the east of the church. The village lies to the north-west of the church along a broad street, which was evidently the market-place for the market which was established here by the Somerys in the 13th century. The attempt to make Bygrave a market town in competition with Baldock, then a new town on the more important site at the cross roads, was renewed by the Thornburys two centuries later. Along the village street are a few cottages and a house now called the Manor House, occupied as a farm by Mr. C. E. E. Cook.

The village is immediately surrounded by its inclosed pasture lands, which extend west and south-west to the road running south-westward to Baldock. The name 'Ploughed Warren' applied to certain arable land immediately east of a part of this road suggests that it was originally grass land also, which would make the pasture land more compact. On the eastern side of the pasture surrounding the village near the rectory is 'Park Wood,' which possibly marks the site of the inclosed lands attached to the Thornburys' house.

Beyond the pasture land are the great common fields which occupy not far short of 1,000 acres undivided by hedge or fence. They stretch in every direction upon the slopes which surround the village, and consist of open arable land broken into irregular strips of uneven size. There are two outlying farms in addition to the Manor Farm, and the occupiers of these, with other landowners, hold strips scattered over the whole area of the field. Parallel strips lie together in 'furlongs,' such as 'Miller's Furlong,' shown on the plan. This and other 'furlongs' generally abut on one of the broad field-paths. Where there is no road the plough is turned on transverse strips known as 'headlands.' In consequence the owner of the 'headland' must wait until the adjacent land is ploughed before ploughing his own. Sometimes the strips, and more often the furlongs, are divided by narrow grass banks known as 'balks.' Here and there, especially in the neighbourhood of the village, bushes growing on the balks have formed small hedges ; but for the most part a single furrow is all that divides the strip of one occupier from that of his neighbour. The cottagers, as such, appear now to have no common rights over the open fields ; but each occupier of arable land grazes his cattle over the whole field after harvest is gathered, the lord of the manor also having a right of sheep-walk for one month in May and October. This right is let with one of the farms, but it is not exercised, for the other occupiers purchase exemption.[3]

Bygrave has always possessed a very small population. There are now about thirty-one houses, and the population has increased between 1891 and 1901 from 99 to 148.[4] In 1428 the whole parish was said to contain only seven inhabitant householders.[5] The recent increase is due to the eastward extension of the town of Baldock around the station on the Cambridge branch of the Great Northern railway, which skirts the southern boundary of Bygrave, running parallel with the Icknield Way.

Near Baldock a small portion of the parish lies to the west of the North Road. It consists of some rough pasture, water-cress beds and rush-grown waste, and is traversed by the River Ivel. There can be little doubt that this extension over the Roman road, which would otherwise be the obvious boundary of the parish, was made by the early settlers with the object of obtaining the water-power from the Ivel to drive the manorial mill which certainly existed down to the 17th century. The pathway from the village which comes into the Roman road near to Blackhorse Farm or Blackhorse Mill is still known as Miller's Way. It was probably on this land to the west of the Roman high road in the neighbourhood of Baldock that there existed a glover's pit and 'Currier's' pasture early in the 17th century.[6] A part of Bygrave civil parish was annexed to Baldock in 1881.[7]

MANOR Athelstan Atheling (born about 986), son of Ethelred the Unready, took *BYGRAVE* from a certain 'Leofmere,' but restored it by his will.[8] In the time of Edward the Confessor 'Lemar' (the same name as Leofmere)[9] held it. He was a man of Archbishop Stigand, but could alienate his land without the archbishop's licence. In 1086, however, Robert (de Limesey), the recently consecrated Bishop of Chester and Lichfield, held the manor in demesne. There were also two sokemen there holding 3 virgates which they had been unable to alienate in the Confessor's time without the leave of the archbishop.[10] Robert de Limesey probably held the manor as his personal property, as he did North Mimms.[11] Like that manor it became attached at an early date to the honour of Gloucester.[12] It is possible that Limesey died without heirs, and that his lands were granted to the Earls of Gloucester. Bygrave was held of the honour by Miles de Somery as three knights' fees and a half in 1201.[13] In later records the service due for Bygrave is variously stated as two knights' fees,[14] one fee,[15] and half a fee.[16] The honour was vested in the Crown by the marriage of Anne, heiress of the Despensers, with Richard III, and in 1678 a rent of one-tenth was still reserved to the Crown.[17]

It seems possible that Miles de Somery had been preceded by Elias de Somery.[18] Miles de Somery evidently made sub-enfeoffment of the manor to another member of his family before his death, which occurred before 1229,[19] for in 1220 Hugh de Somery conveyed Bygrave to John de Somery in consideration of an annuity of 16 marks.[20] Upon the death of Stephen, son and ultimate heir of Miles de Somery, the service from Bygrave was assigned to his widow

---

[3] Slater, *Engl. Peasantry and Encl. of Com. Fields*, 45. [4] *Pop. Ret.* 1901.
[5] *Feud. Aids*, ii, 454.
[6] Com. Pleas D. Enr. Mich. 1651, m. 26.
[7] Loc. Act, 43–4 Vict. cap. 58.
[8] Kemble, *Cod. Dipl.* 722.
[9] It is interesting to note that the name survived in Clothall in the 13th century, when 'Goling son of Lemmar' held land in Upcroft (Exch. Transcr. of Charters 15, m. 2).

[10] *V.C.H. Herts.* i, 311*b*.
[11] Ibid. ii, 252.
[12] *Testa de Nevill* (Rec. Com.), 280.
[13] *Rot. Canc.* 3 *John* (Rec. Com.), 56.
[14] *Testa de Nevill* (Rec. Com.), 280 ; Feet of F. Div. Co. 4 Hen. III, 13 ; but this includes land at 'Fennes,' co. Kent.
[15] *Feud. Aids*, ii, 447.
[16] Ibid. 433 ; Misc. Bks. Exch. K.R. iii, fol. 118 d.
[17] Misc. Bks. (Duchy of Lanc.), lxxii, fol. 58.

[18] See the account of Monks' Lands below.
[19] *Excerpta e Rot. Fin.* (Rec. Com.), i, 182 ; see *V.C.H. Herts.* ii, 252. In 1212 North Mimms alone is stated to have been held of the honour of Gloucester by Miles de Somery (*Red Bk. of Exch.* [Rolls Ser.], 506). The sub-enfeoffment may therefore have taken place before that date.
[20] Feet of F. Div. Co. 4 Hen. III, no. 13 ; Pipe R. 4 Hen. III, m. 7 d.

MAP OF BYGRAVE PARISH

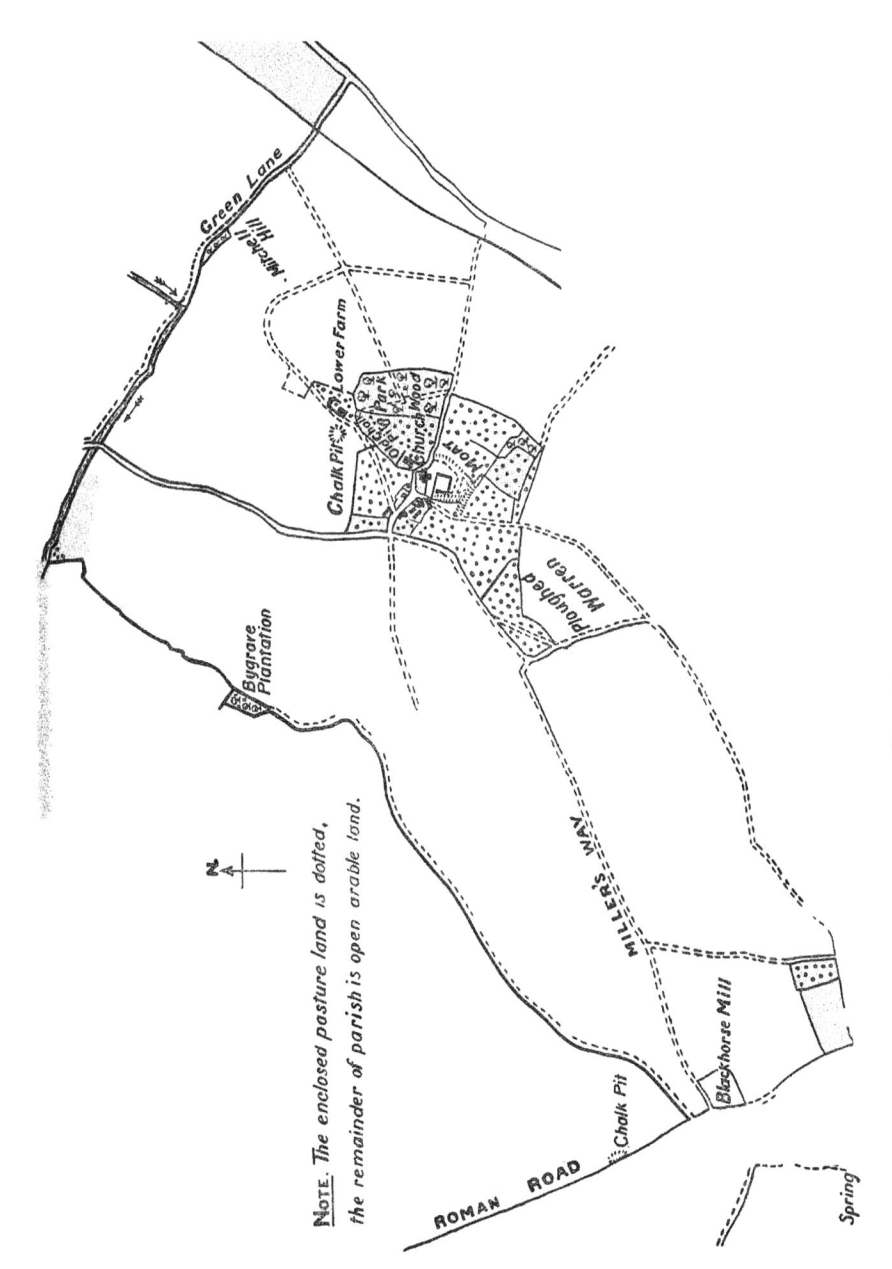

A HISTORY OF HERTFORDSHIRE

Joan in dower,[21] and it afterwards passed to Richard de Bachesworth,[22] one of the sons of Maud, sister and co-heir of Stephen de Somery.[23] No later trace of the mesne lordship has been found.

John de Somery was succeeded as tenant of the manor by Adam de Somery, who had a grant of a market, fair and free warren on 20 October 1256.[24] His widow Margery claimed dower in Bygrave in 1272.[25] His heir appears to have been another Adam de Somery, who gave a life interest in the manor to Master John de Wengham, Precentor of St. Paul's.[26]

In 1287 the manor was again alienated from the direct line of the Somery family. Adam de Somery granted his reversionary rights upon the death of John de Wengham to John son of John de Somery, reserving only to himself and his own son John two mills, 4 acres of meadow and 100s. rent.[27] John son of Adam was in 1312 charged with breaking the park of the Earl of Pembroke at Bishop's Hatfield.[28] It is not clear whether it was this John de Somery or the actual lord of the manor (John son of John) who as 'John de Somery of Bygrave' received pardon in October 1313 for adherence to the party of Thomas of Lancaster and complicity in the murder of Piers Gaveston.[29]

OMERY. *Quarterly or and azure a bend gules.*

The manor was held in 1327 by Sir Richard de Somery, kt., possibly the heir of John son of John. He then settled it upon himself and his wife Elizabeth.[30] According to the statement of Richard de Somery, Robert de Prestbury, the king's yeoman,[31] and others of his ill-wishers came to his manor and carried off goods and chattels, horses, oxen, sheep and pigs to the value of £200. This they did under the pretext that he was an ally of Robert de Baldock the chancellor, who in 1326 suffered imprisonment for his support of the Despensers. Somery maintained that he had even suffered grievous wrong at the hands of Baldock, and prayed the king to compensate him from the profits of Orwell Manor (co. Cambs.), the custody of which had been given to the same 'Master' Robert [? de Baldock].[32]

Richard de Somery was succeeded by his son John, to whom a certain Geoffrey Somery surrendered all right in the manor on 8 June 1349.[33] In 1357 John de Somery settled the manor upon himself and his wife Margery (or Margaret) for life with remainder to their son John in tail-male and remainder in default of heirs male to their daughter Elizabeth.[34] Margery de Somery seems to have survived her husband and her son and to have taken a second and a third husband, Sir John Maynard, kt.,[35] and Thomas Paynell.[36] The daughter Elizabeth married Sir William de Elington, kt.[37] In 1379 Sir Alexander de Walden, kt., and his wife Elizabeth (probably Elizabeth Somery)[38] made a settlement of the manor upon themselves and their heirs with contingent remainder to the right heirs of Elizabeth.[39] Four years later they sold Bygrave to Sir John Thornbury,[40] the 'king's knight,'[41] and one of his justices of the peace in Hertfordshire.[42]

In 1386 Thornbury had licence to crenellate his two houses within the manor of Bygrave.[43] He served as commissioner of array in the county in 1392, when it was feared that the expiration of the truce with France might be followed by invasion.[44] He was succeeded before 1428 by Sir Philip Thornbury, kt.,[45] who in 1435 obtained confirmation of the liberties formerly granted to Adam de Somery.[46] In 1457 Thornbury settled the manor upon himself for life with remainder to his daughter Margaret and her husband Nicholas Appleyard; after their death it was to pass to their son John in tail-male with contingent remainder to the heirs male of Margaret.[47]

John Bensted, heir of Edward Bensted (who had apparently held the manor in trust for either John or Philip Thornbury),[48] surrendered all claim in it to Nicholas and Margaret Appleyard in 1458.[49] Roger, son of a Nicholas Appleyard, inherited the manor from his father and died seised of it in 1528, leaving an infant son John.[50] In 1550 this John Appleyard with his wife Elizabeth conveyed the manor to Hugh Stukeley, gent., of London,[51] evidently agent in a sale to Laurence Warren and his wife Joan.[52] The latter survived her husband, who died 4 August 1556.[53] Their son William Warren apparently took the name of 'Bygrave,' for in the visitation of 1586 'Jane' (for 'Juliana') Needham is said to have married William 'Warren *alias* Bygrave.'[54] He settled an annuity out of the manor upon her, and died 3 February 1588-9, leaving a young son William.[55] The latter entered upon the manor about 1602.[56] During his long minority his debts had accumulated and he was

---

[21] *Cal. Inq. p.m. Edw.* I, 448.
[22] *Feud. Aids,* ii, 433.
[23] See the account of North Mimms, *V.C.H. Herts.* ii, 252.
[24] Confirmed 1435; *Cal. Pat.* 1429-36, p. 461. [25] Cur. Reg. R. 208 A, m. 9.
[26] *Plac. de Quo Warr.* (Rec. Com.), 278; Assize R. 325, m. 17 et seq.; upon one occasion he is called 'de Wautham' (*Plac. de Quo Warr.* 291); Feet of F. Herts. 15 Edw. I, no. 197.
[27] Feet of F. Herts. loc. cit.
[28] *Cal. Pat.* 1307-13, p. 542. He had in 1287 warranted to John de Wengham the liberties of which his father Adam de Somery died seised in Bygrave (Assize R. 325, fol. 17 et seq.).
[29] *Cal. Pat.* 1313-17, p. 24.
[30] Feet of F. Herts. 1 Edw. III, no. 1; De Banco R. 269, m. 12 d. (East. 1 Edw. III).

[31] *Cal. Pat.* 1327-30, *passim.*
[32] *Parl. R.* ii, 389*b*; the petition was referred to the common law.
[33] *Cal. Close,* 1349-54, p. 84.
[34] Feet of F. Herts. 31 Edw. III, no. 459.
[35] Ibid. 46 Edw. III, no. 640.
[36] Ibid. Div. Co. 1 Ric. II, no. 6.
[37] Wrottesley, *Ped. from Plea R.* 108.
[38] Her first husband was dead in 1378 (Feet of F. Div. Co. 1 Ric. II, no. 6, 9).
[39] Ibid. 2 Ric. II, no. 18.
[40] Ibid. Herts. 6 Ric. II, no. 52.
[41] *Cal. Pat.* 1385-9, p. 535.
[42] Ibid. 1388-92, p. 137.
[43] Ibid. 1385-9, p. 235.
[44] Ibid. 1391-6, pp. 68, 92.
[45] *Feud. Aids,* ii, 447.
[46] *Cal. Pat.* 1429-36, p. 461.
[47] Feet of F. Herts. 35 Hen. VI, no. 181; there were contingent remainders to Thomas son of Richard Thornbury, John brother of Thomas and to Richard Thornbury in tail-male; then to the heirs of Margaret, then to Thomas Eston, kinsman of Philip, and to the right heirs of Philip.
[48] Sir Edward Bensted and others presented a rector to the church in 1415 (Cussans, *Hist. of Herts. Odsey Hund.* 54).
[49] Close, 37 Hen. VI, m. 34.
[50] Chan. Inq. p.m. (Ser. 2), xlix, 37.
[51] Ibid. cix, 30; Recov. R. Hil. 4 Edw. VI, m. 155.
[52] Feet of F. Herts. Mich. 4 Edw. VI.
[53] Chan. Inq. p.m. (Ser. 2), cix, 80.
[54] *Herts. Visit.* (Harl. Soc. xxii), 77.
[55] Chan. Inq. p.m. (Ser. 2), ccxxi, 113.
[56] Ct. of Wards, Misc. Bks. dcxviii: Extents and Attachments.

214

further burdened with the maintenance of his brothers and sisters. In order to make fitting provision for them he sold Bygrave Manor about 1613 to William Whettell of Thetford and Sir John Heveningham, kt.,[57] of Ketteringham, Norfolk, endeavouring to raise the price by hints that the estate was desired in high quarters. Warren had apparently resided at Bygrave, only moving to London after its sale; but to Whettell the value of the estate was diminished by its distance from his own home, yet he refused to accept Warren's offer to retain the 'mansion house dovehouse buildings gardens and orchards' on a ten years' lease.[58] Whettell seems to have transferred all his rights to Sir John Heveningham, for whom he may possibly have acted from the beginning.[59]

WARREN. *Checky or and azure a quarter gules with a lion argent therein.*

In November 1627 Sir John Heveningham was imprisoned with Sir Thomas Darnel and others, by special command of the king, for refusing to contribute to a forced loan.[60] This case was among the immediate causes of parliamentary assertion of the liberty of the subject in the Petition of Right. Released in January 1627–8, Sir John Heveningham settled Bygrave on his eldest son William in the following March.[61]

Upon Sir John's death in 1633 the estate passed to William Heveningham, who took sides with the Parliament at the outbreak of the Civil War. He was a member of the court nominated to try the king, and was present 22, 23 and 27 January 1649, when sentence was confirmed, but he refused to sign the death-warrant.[62] In 1651 he sold Bygrave to Francis Cleaver, citizen and draper of London,[63] who already resided in the parish.[64] He transferred the estate to his son Charles Cleaver,[65] who was knighted at Whitehall 7 June 1660.[66] It was, however, seized by the Crown with the other lands of William Heveningham the regicide, owing to some flaw in the conveyance to Francis Cleaver.[67] Sir Charles petitioned for its restoration 4 June 1663, and received a grant from the Crown six years later.[68] About 1682 he sold the

CECIL, Marquess of Salisbury. *Barry of ten pieces argent and azure six scutcheons sable with a lion argent in each differenced with a crescent.*

manor at the (then) large price of £13,000 to James third Earl of Salisbury, who thus consolidated his estate in the neighbourhood of 'Quicksett Hill.'[69] Bygrave has since remained with the direct descendants of the earl.[70]

There was probably a mansion or manor-house at Bygrave at an early date. Possibly it was at the house of Master John de Wengham that Edward I stopped on his way to St. Albans in January 1299 and April 1302.[71] It has been shown that a John de Somery was resident at Bygrave in 1313.[72] In 1386, as already stated, Sir John Thornbury seems to have had two houses at Bygrave.[73] The mansion house in which William Warren lived[74] was probably the capital messuage sold with the manor and with Bygrave Farm to Francis Cleaver in 1651.[75] Manorial works still exist at Bygrave House and at the adjacent site of the so-called 'Palace.'

The lords of Bygrave had court baron, but the Crown held the view of frankpledge by the sheriff, who either received 5s. or at his departure 'partook with the lord of whatever stood on the table.'[76]

The market granted to Adam de Somery in 1256 was held on Mondays. The fair lasted three days, beginning on the eve of the feast of St. Margaret.[77] The date of the fair had been changed by 1880; it was then held on Easter Monday.[78] It is now extinct. In 1286 John de Wengham claimed amendment of assize of bread and ale. He likewise made good the right of the lord to infangtheof and gallows, and asserted a claim to pillory and tumbrel.[79]

Free warren was also granted to Adam de Somery in 1256, and with the market and fair was confirmed to Sir Philip Thornbury in 1435, and the right of free warren is recited in later records relating to the manor.[80] John de Wengham twice complained of persons who fished in his stews at Bygrave.[81] Free fishing is mentioned as pertaining to the manor in 1658.[82]

In 1086 there was one water mill at Bygrave,[83] possibly on the River Ivel, near Baldock. Two mills were reserved by Adam de Somery in granting the manor to John son of John de Somery in 1287,[84] but a water mill belonged to the manor at the death of Laurence Warren.[85] It was excepted from the sale to Sir John Heveningham.[86] No mill exists at present.

MONKS' LANDS, an estate comprising a house and 500 acres of land (measuring 16 ft. to the perch),[87] with a roadway from the land, was acquired by Adam the Cellarer of St. Albans from William 'de Wedona' at an unknown date. The estate is at the same time enumerated among the lands acquired by Adam the Cellarer from Elias de Somery. It is therefore possible that William de Wedona held the land of Elias as

---

[57] Feet of F. Herts. Trin. 11 Jas. I; Trin. 14 Jas. I.
[58] Chan. Proc. (Ser. 2), bdle. 327, no. 5.
[59] Chan. Inq. p.m. (Ser. 2), dxv, 68.
[60] Cobbett, *State Trials*, iii, 1.
[61] Chan. Inq. p.m. (Ser. 2), dxv, 68.
[62] *Dict. Nat. Biog.*
[63] Le Neve, *Knights* (Harl. Soc.), 66.
[64] Com. Pleas D. Enr. Mich. 1651, m. 26.
[65] Recov. R. East. 1658, m. 200; Com. Pleas D. Enr. East. 1658, m. 10.
[66] Le Neve, loc. cit.
[67] The Attorney-General stated that the deed of purchase had not been enrolled, but the enrolment is given above.
[68] *Cal. S. P. Dom.* 1663–4, pp. 163, 167; Orig. R. 13 Chas. II, pt. ii, m. 13.
[69] Feet of F. Herts. Mich. 19 Chas. II; Hil. 28 & 29 Chas. II; Recov. R. Hil. 28 & 29 Chas. II, m. 47; *Buccleuch MSS.* (Hist. MSS. Com.), i, 338.
[70] See the account of Hatfield.
[71] *Cal. Close,* 1296–1302, p. 229; *Cal. Pat.* 1301–7, p. 27.
[72] See above.
[73] *Cal. Pat.* 1385–9, p. 235.
[74] See above.
[75] Com. Pleas D. Enr. Mich. 1651, m. 26.
[76] *Plac. de Quo Warr.* (Rec. Com.), 278.
[77] *Cal. Pat.* 1429–36, p. 461.
[78] Cussans, op. cit. *Odsey Hund.* 52.
[79] *Plac. de Quo Warr.* (Rec. Com.), 278, 291; Assize R. 325.
[80] e.g. Recov. R. East. 1658, m. 200.
[81] *Cal. Pat.* 1291–1301, pp. 158, 219, 472.
[82] Recov. R. East. 1658, m. 200.
[83] *V.C.H. Herts.* i, 311.
[84] Feet of F. Herts. 15 Edw. I, no. 197.
[85] Chan. Inq. p.m. (Ser. 2), cix, 80.
[86] See Com. Pleas D. Enr. Mich. 1651, m. 26.
[87] Misc. Bks. (Aug. Off.), cclxxii, fol. 33.

A HISTORY OF HERTFORDSHIRE

lord of the manor. Henry II confirmed this gift between the years 1174 and 1182, and the profits were assigned to the use of the monks' kitchen.[88] As early as 1291 the estate was let out to farm.[89] The yearly rent was then £6 9s. 4d. By 1526 the house was demolished and the lands let to Roger Appleyard, the lord of the manor, on a twenty-one years' lease.[90]

The abbey surrendered to the Crown 5 December 1539.[91] In February 1543 50 acres of meadow and pasture called Monks' Lands were granted to Sir John Williams and Sir Edward North, treasurer of the Court of Augmentations.[92] Six months later (26 August 1543) the toft with lands called Monks' Lands was granted to Thomas Godwin.[93] Both had been leased to John Bowles. The toft and garden commonly called Monks' Lands subsequently came into the possession of Nathaniel Disborrow, son of John Disborrow of Eltisley, co. Cambs., who sold them to William Whettell. The estate was thus united to the manor of Bygrave.[94]

CHURCH The church, of unknown dedication,[95] consists of a chancel 25 ft. 6 in. by 14 ft. 6 in., nave 31 ft. by 20 ft. 6 in., and south porch 6 ft. by 5 ft. All dimensions are

St. Albans Abbey. *Azure a saltire or.*

taken internally. The church is cemented on the outside, the dressings being of stone and the roofs tiled.

The nave is the earliest part of the church, and belongs to the 12th century, the chancel to the latter part of the 14th century, and the west turret to the 15th century, when the windows were altered and the rood stair was built.

The east window is transomed and has three cinquefoiled lights, traceried in the head. In the north wall is a small 14th-century door, and beside it a low-side window of one cinquefoiled light; the only other window is of two cinquefoiled lights set under a square head. In the south wall are two windows, one a window of two lights similar to that on the north side, the other of three cinquefoiled lights under a four-centred arch. On the south side of the chancel is a 14th-century moulded and arched piscina, and on the north side is an arched niche for a tomb. The chancel arch is of two moulded orders, with engaged shafts under.

The nave has a window in each of its north, south and west walls consisting of two cinquefoiled lights under square heads. The doorway to the rood stair is set in a splay on the north side of the chancel arch; the stair and openings to the rood loft still remain. The north doorway has been blocked; the south doorway is of the 12th century, but is much restored. The arched head is slightly pointed and has the roll moulding. There are shafts in the jambs with scalloped heads, but the whole has been much restored. The south porch is of 18th-century work.

There is a small semi-octagonal turret against the west wall on the south side of the west window which gives access to the bell.

The font belongs to the 15th century; it is octagonal, standing on a square base. The sides of the basin have rectangular panels, carved with the instruments of the Passion; round the stem are angels holding shields. The wooden cover is a bastard Gothic of perhaps the 18th century.

The rood screen is of the 15th century, the upper part having open tracery work, the lower closed panels being traceried. There is a carving of the royal arms on the cornice of the screen of late 17th-century work. The communion table and rails also belong to the 17th century.

There are some traceried panels of the 15th century incorporated with the modern pulpit, and

BYGRAVE CHURCH FROM THE NORTH-WEST

---

[88] Dugdale, *Mon.* ii, 229, cf. p. 233.
[89] *Pope Nich. Tax.* (Rec. Com.), 51b.
[90] Misc. Bks. (Aug. Off.), cclxxii, fol. 33.
[91] Dugdale, op. cit. ii, 249.
[92] *L. and P. Hen. VIII*, xviii (1), p. 132; xix (1), 368 (vii).
[93] Ibid. xviii (2), g. 107 (50).
[94] Com. Pleas D. Enr. Mich. 1651, m. 26.
[95] It is to be noted that the fair was held on the feast of St. Margaret.

216

ODSEY HUNDRED

fixed to the pulpit is a 17th-century wrought-iron hour-glass stand. There are some 15th-century bench ends with poppy heads in the church and some plain old seating. Some fragments of 15th-century glass still exist in the nave windows, and in the churchyard by the west wall of the church is an old stone coffin without a lid.

The bell is dated 1718, but has no maker's mark. The communion plate is a modern set presented by the rector, the Rev. J. H. Carnegie, in 1873.

The surviving registers are in two books : (i) baptisms from 1802 to 1805, burials 1805 to 1808 ; (ii) marriages 1765 to 1808. The earlier books were accidentally destroyed by fire.

ADVOWSON The church was given to the monks of St. Albans by William de Wedona and assigned with Monks' Lands to the use of the kitchen.[96] The assignment was confirmed by the pope in 1218.[97] No appropriation took place,[98] however, and in 1220 it was John de Somery, lord of the manor, who presented a rector.[99]

The right of John de Somery to the advowson is not clear, but the successive lords of the manor subsequently presented when the church became void, and the patronage of the church continued with them until 1901, when the parish was united to that of Baldock.[100]

The case of an early rector of Bygrave shows the lawless condition of the country. John Legat, rector, it was presented in 1381, went to the house of John de Walden, probably a relative of Sir Alexander de Walden, for a time lord of the manor, and with his chaplain William Huberd and others beat and killed John de Walden and threw his body into the highway.[101]

In 1608 George Coke, brother of Sir John Coke, 'using but his purse and labours,' became rector of Bygrave.[102] While parson there he purchased a little land at Baldock ' upon twenty-six years' frugality '[103]; but Archbishop Laud blamed him for leaving the parsonage 'stark nought and unfit for any man's habitation '[104] when he was consecrated Bishop of Bristol 10 February 1632–3.

Another notable incumbent was John Savage, the historian, who held the living from 1701 to 1708, when he resigned it for the more valuable benefice of Clothall.[105]

There are no schools or endowed charities at Bygrave.

CALDECOTE

Caldecota (xi cent.) ; Caldecote and Chaldecote (xiv cent.) ; Calcott or Caldecott (xvi–xvii cent.).

The parish of Caldecote, which is only 325 acres in extent, forms part of the plain in the north-west of the county. The highest part of the parish is in the south, where the land is some 190 ft. above the ordnance datum, but from here the ground has a gradual slope downwards to the north-west to a level of 157 ft. near the bed of the Cat Ditch, a small stream which forms part of the south-western boundary of the parish. The low ground about this stream is probably that referred to in a charter of 1671 as 'Caldecott Marish.'[1] The manor-house with a few farm buildings lies in the south-west of the parish near the church. These are the only buildings of importance in the parish. Nor does the village appear ever to have been of much greater extent, for in 1428 it was said that Caldecote paid no subsidy because there were less than ten householders,[2] and in the 17th century the population was formed of six families.[3] But, small though this village probably was in the 14th century, it took its share in the peasant revolt and aided in extorting a charter of liberties from the Abbot and convent of St. Albans.[4] There are no main roads within the parish, but the Great North Road running at a distance of about three-quarters of a mile from the village gives easy communication with the station of Baldock on the Cambridge branch of the Great Northern railway. The soil is of a chalky nature, and lies on a subsoil of chalk. The inhabitants are occupied in agriculture, the greater part of the land being arable. There are about 35 acres of grass land and some 4 acres of woodland.[4a] In the 14th century it appears that the manorial lands were cultivated on the two-field system.[5] A 14th-century place-name is 'Eldefeldbrade.'[6]

In 1274–5 it was said that the vill of Caldecote had been accustomed to pay 4s. yearly to the sheriff, but that this payment ceased[7] about the time of the siege of the castle of Bedford (June 1224), though by what warrant was unknown.

MANOR Before the Conquest Caldecote was held by Lemar, a man of Archbishop Stigand, and he had the power to sell. In 1086, at the time of the Domesday Survey, it was part of the Hertfordshire estate owned by Ralph de Limesi, who held the manor in demesne.[9] From Ralph it presumably descended to Alan his son and heir, who was succeeded by his son Gerard. This Gerard owed scutage for lands in Hertfordshire about 1160.[10] His heir was his elder son John.[11] The heirs of John de Limesi were his sisters Basilia wife of Hugh Oddingselles and Eleanor wife of David Lindsay.[12] In 1213 the former had livery of a moiety of the Limesi inheritance in Hertfordshire and elsewhere.[13] Apparently the manor of Caldecote

---

[96] Dugdale, *Mon.* ii, 229.
[97] Ibid. 233.
[98] *Pope Nich. Tax.* (Rec. Com.), 37.
[99] See the list of patrons given by Cussans, *Hist. of Herts. Odsey Hund.* 53.
[100] Under Loc. Act, 60–1 Vict. cap. 228.
[101] Assize R. 337, m. 4 d.
[102] *Hist. MSS. Com. Rep.* xii, App. ii, 133–4.
[103] Ibid. App. ii, 146.
[104] Ibid. 198. [105] *Dict. Nat. Biog.*

[1] Add. Chart. 35409.
[2] *Feud. Aids*, ii, 454, 458.
[3] *Herts. Gen. and Antiq.* i, 22.
[4] Walsingham, *Gesta Abbat.* (Rolls Ser.), iii, 330.
[4a] Statistics from Bd. of Agric. (1905).
[5] Walsingham, op. cit. iii, 94–5.
[6] Lansd. MS. 404, fol. 46.
[7] i.e. it was probably appropriated by the lord of the manor.
[8] *Hund. R.* (Rec. Com.), i, 194.
[9] *V.C.H. Herts.* i, 325*b*.

[10] *Red Bk. of Exch.* (Rolls Ser.), 29, 693.
[11] Dugdale, *Mon.* iii, 300–1 ; Stacey Grimaldi, *Rot. de Dominabus*, 27.
[12] *Excerpta e Rot. Fin.* (Rec. Com.), i, 81, 323 ; *Rot. de Oblatis et Fin.* (Rec. Com.), 507 ; cf. the account of Pirton. The younger brother Alan (Dugdale, loc. cit.) evidently died without issue before John.
[13] *Rot. de Oblatis et Fin.* (Rec. Com.), 507.

217

was included in the lands assigned to Oddingselles in right of his wife.[14] A sub-enfeoffment was made probably before 1215,[15] the overlordship descending after Hugh's death about 1305[16] to his son John Oddingselles.[17] The latter remained in possession of the overlordship until 1328,[18] when, under the style of 'Sir John de Odyngselles lord of Long Igington' (Itchington, co. Warw.), he surrendered to the Abbot of St. Albans, then actual tenant of the manor, all his rights except scutage.[19] No further record of this service has been found.

Gerard Furnivall was apparently tenant of the manor under the Oddingselles in 1287.[20] His grandfather Gerard Furnivall had presented to Caldecote Church in 1239,[21] and was probably at that time lord also of the manor. Gerard Furnivall, the grandson, conveyed the manor to William Hurst in 1287,[22] reserving to himself the service of 1*d*.[23] This rent of 1*d*. descended to his daughter Loretta and her husband John of Ousefleet (Usflete).[24] Apparently it was intended that Hurst should convey to the priory of Bushmead, co. Beds., for he had already obtained the necessary licence to alienate in 1283.[25] It was intended to endow two canons at Bushmead to pray for the souls of 'Sir' Gerard, his son and his wife, and for Walter Hurst, brother of William, and others.[26] The priory had owned 4*s*. rent in Caldecote in 1236.[27]

FURNIVALL. *Argent a bend between six martlets gules.*

Apparently the intended alienation of the manor by Hurst to Bushmead Priory did not take effect. The priors had no interest in the manor in 1291,[28] and in 1303 it was still held by William Hurst.[29] His widow Alice gave full seisin of this estate in 1317 to Thomas of Chedworth and Robert his brother.[30] Yearly rents of corn were reserved to Alice Hurst, John Hurst (possibly her son), and to John's sisters Christiana and Joan.[31]

Chedworth and his brother appear to have conveyed the manor to Adam of Newnham,[32] chaplain, probably an agent for its conveyance to Abbot Hugh and the convent of St. Albans.[33] This conveyance took place about 1321[34] with the licence of John Oddingselles, the overlord.[35] Royal licence also was given for the acquisition of this manor by St. Albans, in part fulfilment of a permit to acquire lands and rents to the value of £100 a year.[36] From this date the manor was retained by the monastery of St. Albans until the Dissolution.[37]

The Prior of Bushmead brought his claim to the manor against the abbot in 1341, asserting that he had been unjustly dispossessed by William Hurst.[38] Before the plea was terminated the prior made a formal surrender of his claim to the abbot.[39] At this time Adam of Newnham was tenant for life, holding a lease under the abbot.[40]

In 1356 the escheator seized the manor into the king's hands, laying claim to the profits during the last three vacancies of the abbey.[41] The abbot, however, 'lacked not the heart to defend his right,' and upon inquisition[42] it was found that the corrodies due to Alice Hurst, John Hurst and his sisters had exceeded the profits of the manor, which was therefore restored to the abbot.[43]

After the dissolution of the monastery in 1539 the king held the manor for a short time, and in 1540 granted it to Ralph Rowlatt the elder to hold in as full a manner as Richard Bourman (Boreman), the last of the abbots, had held it.[44] Rowlatt dying in March 1542-3 left as heir his son Sir Ralph,[45] who entered the estate and held courts in July 1544.[46] Early in the year 1557 Sir Ralph granted the manor to John Sapcote, John Dowman and Jane his wife.[47] This conveyance appears to have been on behalf of the Dowmans, and the manor remained with that family until 1593-4, when James Dowman and Jane his wife, Edward Dowman and Mary his wife conveyed it to James Spurling, gent.[48] The latter sold to William Plomer of Gray's Inn and George Cockayne, and in 1597 Plomer again sold to John Spurling for £1,200.[49] John Spurling died seised of it in September 1603.[50] By his will he directed that the manor should be sold to pay his debts, the residue of the price to be

---

[14] In 1222 the custody of the lands of David Lindsay which belonged to the inheritance of John de Limesi in Hertfordshire and elsewhere was granted to the King of the Scots (*Excerpta e Rot. Fin.* [Rec. Com.], i, 81), but no record has been found of any connexion between Lindsay or his heirs (the Pinkeney family) and Caldecote Manor (cf. the account of Pirton). [15] See below.
[16] Roberts, *Cal. Gen.* ii, 690.
[17] Ibid.; Add. Chart. 19960.
[18] Walsingham, *Gesta Abbat.* (Rolls Ser.), ii, 121; iii, 93; Lansd. MS. 404, fol. 46; Add. Chart. 19959; *Cal. Pat.* 1317-21, p. 563; *Hist. MSS. Com. Rep.* viii, App. i, 2*a*.
[19] Add. Chart. 19960.
[20] Feet of F. Herts. 15 Edw. I, no. 208.
[21] Linc. Epis. Reg. quoted by Cussans, *Hist. of Herts. Odsey Hund.* 20. Cussans also includes John de Redewill, 1215, in his list of patrons; it is possible that in this, as well as in other cases, the presentation was to Caldecote, co. Cambs.
[22] Feet of F. Herts. 15 Edw. I, 208; Add. Chart. 19958.

[23] Feet of F. Herts. 15 Edw. I, no. 208.
[24] Inq. a.q.d. file 145, no. 10. This mesne lordship continued for a time with the Furnivalls, but is later lost sight of (*Feud. Aids*, ii, 432).
[25] *Cal. Pat.* 1281-92, p. 71. The licence styles the estate to be alienated 'one carucate of land in Caldecote and the advowson of the church.'
[26] Stevens, *App. to Mon.* ii, 97.
[27] Dugdale, *Mon.* vi, 283.
[28] *Pope Nich. Tax.* (Rec. Com.), *passim*.
[29] *Feud. Aids*, ii, 432.
[30] Cott. MS. Otho, D iii, fol. 140 et seq.
[31] Chan. Inq. p.m. 30 Edw. III (2nd nos.), no. 63; Walsingham, *Gesta Abbat.* (Rolls Ser.), iii, 94.
[32] Otherwise called Adam Flaun of Newnham (Walsingham, op. cit. ii, 330).
[33] Inq. a.q.d. file 145, no. 10.
[34] Chan. Inq. p.m. 30 Edw. III (2nd nos.), no. 63.
[35] *Cal. Pat.* 19959.
[36] *Cal. Pat.* 1317-21, p. 563; *Hist. MSS. Com. Rep.* viii, App. i, 2*a*.
[37] *L. and P. Hen. VIII*, xv, g. 733 (42).

[38] Walsingham, loc. cit.
[39] Ibid. 332; cf. Stevens, *App. to Mon.* ii, 97.
[40] Walsingham, op. cit. ii, 331.
[41] Ibid. iii, 92-3.
[42] Chan. Inq. p.m. 30 Edw. III (2nd nos.), no. 63.
[43] Walsingham, *Gesta Abbat.* (Rolls Ser.), iii, 92-5.
[44] *L. and P. Hen. VIII*, xv, g. 733 (42).
[45] *Herts. Gen. and Antiq.* ii, 87; Harl. MS. 757.
[46] Ct. R. portf. 177, no. 2, 5.
[47] Pat. 3 & 4 Phil. and Mary, pt. iv, m. 24; Feet of F. Herts. Hil. 3 & 4 Phil. and Mary.
[48] Feet of F. Herts. Hil. 36 Eliz.
[49] Com. Pleas D. Enr. Mich. 39 Eliz. m. 3; Add. Chart. (B.M.), 35403, 35405; Inq. p.m. (Ser. 2), cclxxxv, 127. There was a reversionary lease for twenty-one years to Henry Spurling and others contingent upon the death of Jane Turpyn, widow.
[50] Chan. Inq. p.m. (Ser. 2), cclxxxv, 127.

218

ODSEY HUNDRED — CALDECOTE

divided among his five daughters.[51] His son and heir Philip entered upon the estate,[52] and in June 1604 he and his mother Anne sold the manor to Richard Hale of Mincing Lane, citizen and grocer of London,[53] and lord of the manor of King's Walden. Richard Hale died in 1621, having settled Caldecote on his second son Richard.[54] It apparently descended to the latter's son Robert Hale of Newnham,[55] since a Robert Hale presented to the church in 1666.[56] In 1672 Robert Hale the elder and his son Robert conveyed the manor to Sir John Hale, kt., of Stagenhoe,[57] and in that year an agreement was made between William Hale of King's Walden and Sir John Hale of Stagenhoe,

HALE. *Azure a cheveron or barbed on both sides.*

under the tower, 33 ft. by 14 ft., tower erected over the west end of the nave, and south porch 9 ft. 6 in. by 7 ft. All dimensions are taken internally.

The walls are of flint rubble covered with cement, with stone dressings ; the low-pitched roof is lead-covered.

The whole of the building belongs to the middle of the 15th century, with later repairs.

The chancel is of the same width as the nave, and there is no chancel arch ; the old screen was demolished before the middle of the 19th century.[62] The east window is of three cinquefoiled lights, traceried and transomed. In the north wall is a two-light window under a square head, and there is a similar window in the south wall ; there is also in the south wall a single-light low-side window.

In the south wall of the nave is a three-light traceried and transomed window, and on the north side is a similar window which has lost its tracery, and has had two mullions and a transom substituted,

CALDECOTE CHURCH FROM THE NORTH-WEST

whereby it was settled upon the latter for life with remainder to his grandson John, second son of Sir John Austen, bart., of Bexley.[58] Sir John Austen presented to the church in 1680,[59] but in 1685 he transferred the manor to William Hale of King's Walden.[60] It subsequently descended in this family until after 1873. It was held by Mr. Wickham Inskip in 1906, and Mr. William Dawe is now owner.

In 1356–7 there was on the estate a capital messuage,[61] possibly on the site of the present farm, where there are traces of a homestead moat.

The church of ST. MARY MAGDA-CHURCH LENE consists of a chancel 17 ft. by 14 ft., nave, inclusive of western bay

all covered with cement. The south doorway has an arch of two moulded orders and moulded jambs without capitals ; the north doorway has been much renewed. The south porch has a moulded arch under a square head ; the jambs are semi-octagonal with moulded capitals, but partly made up with cement ; there is a two-light window on either side of the porch. In the north-east corner is a 15th-century stoup under a lofty and richly crocketed canopy, with a broken basin supported on a stem decorated with quatrefoiled panels. The whole is about 8 ft. 9 in. in height, but much defaced.

The west tower is carried over the western bay of the nave by three arches ; on the east by an arch of

[51] Chan. Inq. p.m. (Ser. 2), cclxxxv, 127.
[52] Add. Chart. 35405, 35407.
[53] Ibid. 35403, 35404.
[54] Chan. Inq. p.m. (Ser. 2), ccclxxxvii, 110.
[55] *Visit. of Herts* (Harl. Soc.), 61; cf. V.C.H. Herts. ii, 355.
[56] Inst. Bks. (P.R.O.).
[57] Add. Chart. 35412 ; Recov. R. Hil. 23 & 24 Chas. II, m. 63.
[58] Add. Chart. 35411.
[59] Inst. Bks. (P.R.O.).
[60] Add. Chart. 35413 ; Feet of F. Herts. Hil. 1 Jas. II.
[61] Walsingham, *Gesta Abbat.* (Rolls Ser.), iii, 94.
[62] Cussans, op. cit. *Odsey Hund.* 18.

A HISTORY OF HERTFORDSHIRE

two moulded orders, the outer order being continuous down the jambs, the inner having a shafted jamb with moulded capitals and bases; on the north and south by arches of two chamfered orders, well within the lines of the nave walls, dying on the wall under the eastern side of the tower; and by the west wall of the nave, which carries the west side of the tower. The spaces thus formed between the tower and the north and south walls of the nave are covered with lean-to tiled roofs, the battlements on the walls of the chancel and nave being stopped and returned against the east angles of the tower. A similar form of construction may be found at the neighbouring church of Newnham, but not elsewhere in the county.

The tower is of one stage above the roof, and has no spire; the parapet is plain. On each side of the upper or belfry stage of the tower and in the west wall of the nave is a two-light window with a quatrefoiled head, all repaired with cement.

The font is octagonal, of 15th-century date. The sides of the basin are decorated with traceried panels. Underneath are shields facing the four cardinal points; that on the east bears a saltire, that on the north a cross, that on the west the instruments of the Passion, and that on the south three crowns.

There are some plain 15th-century benches in the nave.

In the east window are some remains of 15th-century decorative glass, and in the south nave window is part of a kneeling figure in a blue gown and the name William Makeley.

There is a tablet on the south wall of the nave to Francis Squire, 1732, and a floor slab to James Flint, 1763.

There is one bell, dated 1630, by Robert Oldfeild. The communion plate includes an engraved cup of 1569 and a paten of 1638.

There is a transcript of parish registers from October 1609 to 1725,[63] but the existing registers date only from 1726. Book (i) contains baptisms, burials and marriages from 1726 to 1807; (ii) baptisms and burials from 1808 to 1812. This last book was designed for marriages also, but none were solemnized in this parish during that period.[64]

ADVOWSON

In 1086 the nine villeins of Caldecote with one priest had a plough and a half.[65] The advowson was probably attached to the manor from the first. The patron in 1239 was Gerard de Furnivall,[66] grandfather of the Gerard who held the manor in 1287.[67] Thenceforward the advowson descended with the manor. The present patron is Mr. Wickham Inskip.

No appropriation seems to have taken place while the Abbots of St. Albans were patrons of the living. A terrier of 1638 states that 'the custome for milch cows is fourepence a piece for ghest cows twopence for lambes whose number amounts not to a tyth fourepence a piece and for weaneling calves but half-pence.' Other dues to the parsonage were 'the goring of two calves in the common and the custome of paying two-pence for every plowe.'[68] In 1657 the living of Caldecote was worth £40 annually, and that of the adjoining parish of Newnham only £17.[69] As there were only thirty-three families in all in the two parishes, the churches were only three-quarters of a mile apart and none of the houses at a great distance from either, it was thought advisable to unite the two livings. The sale of the advowsons by Robert Hale probably prevented the execution of this plan. The present rector holds both livings, and since 1894 service has been held in either church alternately. The rector lives at Newnham, and the old rectory-house at Caldecote, which is near the church, is now converted into a cottage. It dates from the end of the 16th century, but little remains of the original work except the moulded beams.

The church terrier of 1638 mentions a 'parsonage howse and yearde,' a barn, a stable, and other out-houses, and a 'plott of ground being in all by estimation about the quantitie of three roodes of grounde lying on the north side of the church and compassed about on every side with high wayes save only on the west side lyeth the cottage ground in ye tenure of William Starre.'[70] He was apparently the churchwarden whose 'mark' is subscribed to this terrier.[71]

There are no endowed charities.

CLOTHALL

Cladhele (xi cent.); Clahall or Clohall (xiii cent.); Clothale (xiv cent.).

The parish of Clothall lies on the summit and slopes of the chalk hills to the south-east of the town of Baldock. It is a district of scattered farms and homesteads. The church, with the rectory and schools, lies to the south-east of the main road from Buntingford to Baldock in a commanding but somewhat isolated position on the eastern slope of Hickman's Hill. A branch of the main road here turns the summit of the hill at a height of about 492 ft. above sea level, descending abruptly northwards. Between Baldock and Clothall Church lies Clothall Field, containing about 600 acres, a 'common-field' of open arable land famous for its barley, and divided into irregular strips by 'balks,' or narrow banks of grass, sometimes grown with bushes.[1] The strips are still divided among the three chief landowners: the rector, the Marquess of Salisbury and Miss Cotton Browne.[2] On the hill-side the scarped terraces, or 'lynches,' form a distinctive feature of the parish. The high ridges between these terraces have the appearance of artificial defences, but are in reality due to the custom of turning the

---

[63] *Herts. Gen. and Antiq.* iii, 32.
[64] *Midd. and Herts. N. and Q.* iii, 62.
[65] *V.C.H. Herts.* i, 325*b*.
[66] *Epis. Reg.* quoted by Cussans, *Hist. of Herts. Odsey Hund.* 20.
[67] See the account of Great Munden. The list of patrons given by Cussans includes John de Redewell, 1215. It is not clear whether he presented to Caldecote in Herts. or to Caldecote in Cambs. To the latter belong the presentations in 1262 and 1268 included in Cussans' list (cf. Chan. Inq. p.m. file 45, no. 9 [Edw. II]; *Testa de Nevill* [Rec. Com.], 354, 356).
[68] *Herts. Gen. and Antiq.* ii, 226.
[69] *V.C.H. Herts.* ii, 357.
[70] *Hertz. Gen. and Antiq.* ii, 224.
[71] Ibid.
[1] Cf. the open field at Bygrave.
[2] Inform. kindly supplied by the Rev. A. R. Buckland.

CALDECOTE CHURCH: 15TH-CENTURY STOUP IN SOUTH PORCH

ODSEY HUNDRED   CLOTHALL

sod down-hill in ploughing. Groups of parallel strips lie together in 'furlongs.' In the 13th century 'Greneweyhull' was the lord's furlong; other furlongs were 'Hepingborow' and 'Smelinke.'[3] The lord of the manor had right of foldage.[4] The villagers no longer claim any rights in the open fields. An attempt to inclose in 1885 was frustrated by lack of unanimity among the landowners.[5]

Westfield, the second common field, lies south-east of the church. In 1609 there were at least two other open fields, 'Piebushfield' and 'Sheldonfield,'[6] the former near Kipple Field in Luffenhall.[7] The arable land south and east of the church is for the most part inclosed; in fact, the inconvenience of scattered holdings in the common fields was already experienced by the middle of the 13th century, when a certain William Pasket apparently endeavoured to consolidate an estate by buying up 23 acres in ten parcels in addition to bondmen, houses, crofts of pasture and other lands.[8] Especially about Kingswood Farm are the lands inclosed; in a 15th-century lease of the farm it was agreed that the owner should do all 'reparacions as of dyking and closing.'[9] In 1547 the owner of Kingswood had also 27 acres in the common field called Sheldonfield and 38 acres in Westfield, and these were held in twenty-one separate strips.[10]

The most notable of the scattered homesteads is Quickswood, which lies to the north-east of the church near the site of the former residence of the Earls of Salisbury.[11] The old house was demolished about 1790, but the brick foundations of the house and cellars exist immediately to the west of the present farm-house. The cock-pit may still be seen in a field to the north of the old house. Near Quickswood on the borders of Wallington is Spital Wood, evidently at one time the property of the hospital of St. Mary Magdalene.[12] Farther south a larger wood shelters Clothallbury, which appears to be on the site of the house called 'Clothall', held by George Kympton at the beginning of the 17th century.[13] The existing farm-house is said to have portions of the out-houses of the old 'bury' incorporated with it, though it shows very little signs of antiquity, but a few hundred yards to the south-east are traces of an extensive mansion apparently of considerable antiquity. Within the well-defined inclosure are several old pollard oaks, one of which measures 18 ft. in circumference 5 ft. from the ground. The inclosure has been moated.

South of the church is Hooksgreen Farm with a few cottages and the 'Barley Mow' public-house opposite the ancient site of Hook's manor-house. These lie near a moated site which tradition asserts was that of Clothall Hospital. Another such site to the south-east, upon Burnt House Lane, is that of the 'Tabard,' a 16th-century inn, which with the adjacent meadow called Fidler's Mead and other land (probably including the neighbouring field called Chapels) belonged to the gild of Baldock.[14]

Kingswood Bury is a farm in the occupation of Mr. Edward White in the south-east of the parish. Beyond it the ground slopes downwards to the hamlet of Luffenhall, built in a single street and lying partly in Clothall, partly in Ardeley. Around it lie three small open fields, known as Luffenhall, Newell and Swamstey Commons. Over these the farmers have the right of 'shackage' or grazing after harvest; but the farmers generally come to a mutual agreement about their rights of sheep-walk,[15] and the greater part of the Luffenhall land is inclosed. The hamlet is well watered by the River Beane and its tributaries.

The hospital of St. Mary Magdalene was founded by Sir Hugh de Clothall, kt., probably the Hugh de Clothall who was lord of the manor in 1217.[16] It was at first a house for lepers, known as the 'Hospital without Baldock.'[17] In 1226 a two-days' fair upon the feast of St. Bartholomew was granted to the hospital until the king (Henry III) should be of age.[18] In 1275 the brethren had licence to inclose a highway 588 ft. long from their close to Clothall Church.[19] The original building was in an unsafe place, more than a mile from the town, and suffered much from raids and burnings by robbers.[20] About 1308 it was therefore removed to a more secure spot at 'Brade,'[21] but the brethren were bound to continue the services at the old chapel. Tradition locates its second site within the moat near Hook's Green, but the name 'High Brade' was applied in 1839 to a field on the main road, further south, between Luffenhall Common and Westfield.[22] The advowson of the hospital belonged to the lords of the manor, and the lords of Botteles and Hauvills evidently presented jointly.[23] When suppressed in 1547 the chapel was said to be more than a mile from the church, and there were many people dwelling about it.[24] It was then simply a chantry chapel.

MANORS In 1086 Clothall consisted of a main manor and several small holdings. Osbern held the main manor of Bishop Odo. Leuiet held a virgate which may have been the nucleus of the lands known as Mundens.[25] The manor of William de Ow, in the neighbouring parish of Weston, extended into Clothall, where a certain William (lord also of Hinxworth) held half a virgate and 3 acres of him.[26] Luffenhall was already a separate hamlet, part of which was held by Osbern, while the Dean and Chapter of St. Paul's held the manor of Luffenhall,[27] and Theobald, tenant under Hardwin Scales, had a holding which included half

---

[3] Exch. Transcr. of Chart. xv.
[4] *Cal. Close,* 1360–4, p. 387.
[5] See Slater, *Engl. Peasantry and Encl. of Com. Fields,* 43–4.
[6] Add. MS. 33582, fol. 5 d., 8 d.
[7] Tithe apportionment, 1839.
[8] Exch. Transcr. of Chart. xv, *passim.*
[9] Add. Chart. (B.M.), 35421.
[10] Close, 5 Edw. VI, pt. iv, no. 26.
[11] See below.
[12] See below.
[13] Chan. Inq. p.m. (Ser. 2), cccviii, 118.
[14] Misc. Bks. (Aug. Off.), lxviii, fol. 270 d.; Com. Pleas D. Enr. East.

1 Eliz. m. 11; cf. tithe apportionment.
[15] Slater, op. cit. 45; inform. kindly supplied by the Rev. A. R. Buckland.
[16] There is no direct proof that this Hugh was the founder, but the priests were to celebrate daily for his soul and those of his parents (Harl. Chart. 112 A 3).
[17] Harl. Chart. 112 A 3.
[18] *Rot. Lit. Claus.* (Rec. Com.), ii, 107.
[19] *Cal. Pat.* 1272–81, p. 85; Inq. a.q.d. file 4, no. 7.
[20] Harl. Chart. 112 A 3; Linc. Epis. Reg. Dalderby, fol. 239.

[21] See an interesting article on the hospital by H. C. Andrew, *East Herts. Arch. Soc. Trans.* iv (1), 86.
[22] Tithe apportionment 1839; the name 'Brode,' however, seems to have been somewhat general; it was also applied to a field near Baldock abutting on the Icknield Way and on 'Bradstreet' (Harl. Chart. 112 F 14).
[23] Clutterbuck, *Hist. and Antiq.* of Herts. iii, 506.
[24] Chant. Cert. Herts. 20, no. 65.
[25] See below.
[26] *V.C.H. Herts.* i, 328a.
[27] See below.

221

A HISTORY OF HERTFORDSHIRE

a hide in Luffenhall and a virgate all but 3 acres in Clothall.[28]

The main manor of CLOTHALL was held in the time of Edward the Confessor by Alnod Grud, a man of Archbishop Stigand's, and he could sell it without the archbishop's licence. After the Conquest it was acquired by Odo of Bayeux, of whom Osbern, tenant of a considerable fief in Hertfordshire, held it. Osbern's holding included 7 hides and 3½ virgates.[29] In the time of King Edward three sokemen of the king held 2 hides and 3 virgates, paying 11d. to the sheriff as commutation for 'avera,' or cartage; but after the king's death (and presumably before that of Stigand, whose men they became) their land was attached to the manor.[30] Two other sokemen of the archbishop held half a virgate which they retained in 1086. It also seems probable that the land which Osbern held of Odo of Bayeux in the hamlet of Luffenhall was added in the course of time to the manor of Clothall. This holding consisted of 2½ hides; 1½ hides had been held by two men of Archbishop Stigand, while the remaining hide had been held by a man of Almar de Benington, who had formerly rendered 'avera' as the king's sokeman.[31]

Odo of Bayeux forfeited Clothall with all his other English possessions in 1088, when he led the Norman rebellion against William Rufus. Many of his lands were subsequently held by service of castle guard at Dover; some of these were assigned to the *custodia*, or castle-guard barony, of Port,[32] and among them was Clothall. The barony was held by the family of Port of Basing,[33] and in 1166 John de Port returned the name of Robert de Clothall (*Clahalde*) among the knights who owed him service.[34] This Robert had apparently succeeded to the holding of Osbern.

The holding of Robert was stated to be one knight's fee,[35] but early in the next century the tenant of Clothall owed the service of two fees to the Port barony.[36] It was rendered three times yearly,[37] covering altogether twenty-four weeks.[38] During the 16th century the manor was still said to be held of the king as of the 'honour of Dover,'[39] but the re-grant to Thomas Chalmer and Edward Cason, kt., in 1604 stipulated that it should be held in socage and not by knight's service of the manor of East Greenwich.[40]

The overlordship passed from John de Port to his son Adam de Port,[41] and probably from him to his son William 'de St. John.' It remained in the male line of the St. John family until 1337.[42] It was then assigned in dower to Mirabel widow of Hugh de St. John, who had married Thomas de Aspall.[43] It afterwards formed part of the share of Margaret wife of John de St. Philibert, eldest daughter and co-heir of Hugh de St. John, after the death of her young brother Edmund.[44] Her heir was her sister Isabel wife of Luke Poynings,[45] but the mesne lordship was probably allowed to lapse, for late returns record only the service due to the Crown at Dover Castle.

In the 12th and 13th centuries the immediate tenants of the manor took their surname from Clothall. It is possible that one of these was a certain Laurence called 'Laurence Scot of Clothall,' for 13th-century charters refer to service due to the 'heir of Laurence Scot lord of Clothall.'[46] Robert de Clothall held the manor in 1166.[47] Richard de Clothall, who was living in 1200, was tenant of the manor in 1211–12.[48] During the disturbances of 1215 and 1216 his lands were in the hands of the king, who granted them to Eustace 'de Campo Remigii.'[49] The overlord, however, had the custody of Clothall, possibly during the minority of Richard's heir.[50] This seems to have been his son Hugh de Clothall,[51] who probably founded the hospital of St. Mary Magdalene.[52] In 1217 Hugh was restored to all the lands of which he had been dispossessed at the beginning of the war,[53] evidently in consequence of the grant to Eustace. At the same time he delivered to the Sheriff of Hertfordshire for the king certain chirographs and charters of the Jews.[54] He may possibly be identical with Hugh de Clothall (Clahull), who died seised of lands in Ireland before 1246.[55] At Clothall he was succeeded by his brother Simon de Clothall,[56] who died before 1248,[57] leaving three daughters and co-heirs, Emecine, Muriel and Maud.[58] During their minority Robert de St. John, the overlord, granted the manor to John de Gisors for fourteen years. He subsequently sold the marriage of Emecine for 40 marks to Geoffrey de Hauvill, the king's falconer and bailiff of Rockingham Forest.[59] Geoffrey and Emecine in contravention of an agreement made with the overlord entered upon the manor before the lease to John de Gisors had expired. The tenant brought a plea into the King's Court charging Geoffrey and Emecine with ejecting him by force, 'with habergeons, bows and arrows,' and with carrying off his corn and goods. It was finally agreed that John de Gisors should retain two-thirds of the manor (possibly the shares of Emecine's younger sisters) till the end of his term, while Geoffrey and Emecine paid the compensation estimated by Richard de Havering and William Pasket.[60]

In 1271 Maud wife of Richard de Bottele and youngest daughter of Simon de Clothall surrendered one-third of 32s. 5d. rent and of the advowson to Geoffrey and Emecine.[61] It is said that this Maud died childless, and that her portion of the inheritance

---

[28] *V.C.H. Herts.* i, 338*b*.
[29] Ibid. 309*b*.
[30] Cf. ibid. 267–70.
[31] Ibid. 309*b*.
[32] *Red Bk. of Exch.* (Rolls Ser.), 618.
[33] Cf. *V.C.H. Hants*, iv, 115–16.
[34] *Red Bk. of Exch.* (Rolls Ser.), 208.
[35] The same service is given in the time of Adam de Port (*Testa de Nevill* [Rec. Com.], 270, 280).
[36] *Red Bk. of Exch.* (Rolls Ser.), 618, 721.
[37] Ibid. 706.
[38] Memo. R. (Exch. L.T.R.), Trin. 44 Edw. III, 'Recorda,' m. 1.
[39] Chan. Inq. p.m. (Ser. 2), xlv, 23.
[40] Pat. 2 Jas. I, pt. xix, m. 21.
[41] *Testa de Nevill* (Rec. Com.), 270, 280.
[42] *Feud. Aids*, ii, 433; Chan. Inq. p.m. 3 Edw. III, no. 67; 11 Edw. III, no. 49. For the pedigree see *Gen.* (new ser.), xvi, 1, and *V.C.H. Hants*, iv, 115–16.
[43] *Cal. Close*, 1337–9, p. 20.
[44] Ibid. 1349–54, p. 70.
[45] *V.C.H. Hants*, iv, 115–16.
[46] Exch. Transcr. of Chart. xv, m. 1 d.; Harl. Chart. 111 D 24.
[47] *Red Bk. of Exch.* (Rolls Ser.), 208.
[48] Ibid. 618; *Rot. Cur. Reg.* (Rec. Com.), ii, 275.
[49] *Rot. Lit. Claus.* (Rec. Com.), i, 251.
[50] *Testa de Nevill* (Rec. Com.), 270, 280.
[51] Exch. Transcr. of Chart. xv, m. 1.
[52] See above.
[53] *Rot. Lit. Claus.* (Rec. Com.), i, 324.
[54] Ibid. 323.
[55] *Cal. Pat.* 1232–47, p. 487. There were, however, others besides the lords of the manor who took the name of Clothall (cf. Exch. Transcr. of Chart. xv, *passim*).
[56] Exch. Transcr. of Chart. xv, m. 1; *Red Bk. of Exch.* (Rolls Ser.), 706.
[57] Cur. Reg. R. 161, m. 3.
[58] De Banco R. 578, m. 231.
[59] *Cal. Pat.* 1301–7, p. 227.
[60] Cur. Reg. R. 161, m. 3.
[61] Feet of F. Div. Co. 55 & 56 Hen. III, no. 488.

was so divided between her two sisters that Muriel had the greater part of the manor.[62] It is doubtless due to this fact that Muriel's purparty in Clothall was known from the 15th century onwards as 'the manor of *BOTTELES*.' Apparently she married first Roger Scales,[63] and afterwards John Poley,[64] who was holding this moiety of the manor in 1303.[65] It is said that she had a son Laurence,[66] possibly that Laurence 'de Bottle' who held land in Clothall about 1317.[67] In February 1361–2 Henry 'son of John Bottele of Clothall' conveyed certain rents with manorial rights and one-third of the common fold of Clothall and one-third of the advowson of the church to Sir John de la Lee, kt., and Joan his wife.[68] These appear to have been identical with Botteles Manor. This Henry was said (in 1405) to have been son of Laurence son of Muriel Poley.[69] It seems possible that he was grandson of Laurence, and that the descendants of Muriel took the name of Bottele from their estate at Clothall.

Sir John ' atte Lee,' kt., died seised of the manor in 1369, leaving a son and heir Walter,[70] afterwards knighted. Sir Walter was burdened with debt,[71] and after his death his trustees transferred all his rights in Clothall to three brothers, Matthew and Henry Rede and Thomas Blount.[72] By 1405 these three had also acquired the manor of Hauvills (see below). Henry Rede died about 1421 and Matthew before that date.[73] Hauvills and Botteles were settled upon Margaret wife of John Mitchell,[74] for whom they had possibly been holding in trust. Her husband was returned as the tenant of a knight's fee (Hauvills) in Clothall in 1428,[75] and in February 1444–5 he died seised of both Hauvills and Botteles.[76] Margaret survived till about 1455.[77] Of her three daughters, Cecily wife of William Sydney, who died in her mother's lifetime, had two grandchildren, Elizabeth and Anne, aged respectively seven and six in 1465. Another daughter Elizabeth wife of John Wode died 26 March 1463–4, and the third, Joan, married first William Druell and afterwards John Brunne.[78]

Hauvills and Botteles passed to the descendants of Joan Druell. In 1485 William Druell (possibly the son of William and Joan) died seised of them.[79] He was succeeded by his son John, who died childless in 1495, his mother Anne (then wife of George Alyson)[80] being still alive.[81] His brother and heir Richard Druell came of age in 1503.[82] The Clothall estate descended at his death in 1525 to his daughter Anne, who married first Robert Warner[83] and secondly Thomas Perient of Digswell.[84] Two of her daughters, Mary then wife of George Horsey and Anne wife of Anthony Carleton, conveyed their shares in Clothall in the spring of 1550 to George Burgoyne,[85] who had married a third daughter, Dorothy.[86] In 1572 settlement of two-thirds of the manors was made on George and Dorothy Burgoyne with successive remainders in tail-male to their sons Thomas, George and others. George Burgoyne died in 1588,[87] but his widow apparently continued to reside at Clothall, with her younger son George,[88] upon whom the remaining third of the manors was settled.[89] During his mother's life the elder son Thomas Burgoyne of Weston raised £2,000 on his reversionary rights in the two-thirds of the estate acquired by his father.[90] In February 1602 Dorothy Burgoyne presented to the rectory.[91] Probably she died soon afterwards, for in 1603 Peter Pierson and William Plomer and others were dealing with the estate,[92] and in 1604 her first cousin George Perient of Little Ayot and others surrendered to the Crown ' the manor of Clothall and manors of Hauvills, Botteles, Hooks and Brickfields formerly the possessions of Simon of Clothall and late of George Burgoyne and Dorothy his wife.'[93] The surrender seems to have been intended to procure a change in the tenure.[94] In 1604 the estate was re-granted to Sir Thomas Challoner, kt., and Edward Cason,[95] agents in a conveyance to Nicholas Trott,[96] son-in-law to George Perient.[97] Trott sold to William second Earl of Salisbury in June 1617,[98] and the estate has remained with his direct descendants until the present day.

The moiety of the main manor which descended to Geoffrey and Emecine de Hauvill after the death of Simon de Clothall afterwards took the name of *HAUVILLS*.[99] Geoffrey de Hauvill died about

BURGOYNE. *Gules a cheveron or between three talbots argent with a battled chief argent and three martlets azure therein.*

---

[62] De Banco R. 578, m. 231.
[63] Feet of F. Herts. 56 Hen. III, no. 638.   [64] De Banco R. 578, m. 231.
[65] *Feud. Aids*, ii, 433.
[66] De Banco R. 578, m. 231.
[67] Lay Subs. R. bdle. 120, no. 10.
[68] *Cal. Close*, 1360–4, p. 387. It is noteworthy that the manor of Hooks was, at a later date, said to be held of John Botles (Chan. Inq. p.m. [Ser. 2]. xlv, 23).
[69] De Banco R. 578, m. 231. It is to be noted that Laurence ' de Bottele' was coroner of Hertfordshire till 1327, when he was disqualified by infirmity and age (*Cal. Close*, 1327–30, p. 16).
[70] Chan. Inq. p.m. 44 Edw. III, no. 37. In 1357 Thomas Hauvill, lord of the second moiety of Clothall, released all reversionary rights in this moiety to Sir John (Assize R. 339).
[71] Close, 50 Edw. III, pt. ii, m. 8 d., 9, 12, 13 d.
[72] De Banco R. 578, m. 231.
[73] Sharpe, *Cal. of Wills in Ct. of Husting*, ii, 424.

[74] The manor was settled on her heirs (Inq. p.m. 33 Hen. VI, no. 31).
[75] *Feud. Aids*, ii, 447.
[76] Chan. Inq. p.m. 23 Hen. VI, no. 15.
[77] Ibid. 33 Hen. VI, no. 31.
[78] Ibid. 4 Edw. IV, no. 25.
[79] Chan. Inq. p.m. (Ser. 2), i, 134.
[80] H. C. Andrew, ' Hospital of St. Mary Magdalene,' *East Herts. Arch. Soc. Trans.* iv (1), 92.
[81] Chan. Inq. p.m. (Ser. 2), xi, 12.
[82] Ibid. xvi, 119–20.
[83] Ibid. xlv, 23. His second daughter Joan, who was fourteen years younger, does not seem to have inherited and possibly died s.p. In 1546 Anne was styled heir, not co-heir, of Richard Druell (Feet of F. Herts. East. 38 Hen. VIII).
[84] *Visit. of Herts.* (Harl. Soc. xxii), 157.
[85] Feet of F. Herts. Hil. 3 Edw. VI.
[86] *Visit. of Herts.* loc. cit.
[87] Chan. Inq. p.m. (Ser. 2), cciii, 85.
[88] Chan. Proc. Eliz. Bb iii, 40. Evidently misled by an erroneous reading of these proceedings, Mr. Andrew asserts that this Dorothy was wife of the younger George (*East Herts. Arch. Soc. Trans.* iv [1], 95).
[89] Close, 36 Eliz. pt. x, m. 2.
[90] Ibid. The money was to be repaid to John Goodman of Cumberlow in the church porch of Clothall; cf. Feet of F. Herts. Mich. 29 & 30 Eliz.; Mich. 33 & 34 Eliz.; Hil. 35 Eliz.; Hil. and East. 38 Eliz.; Recov. R. Trin. 39 Eliz. m. 6. Dorothy Burgoyne suffered recovery of the remaining third in 1588 (Recov. R. Hil. 30 Eliz. m. 66).
[91] Cussans, *Hist. of Herts. Odsey Hund.* 72.
[92] Feet of F. Herts. East. 1 Jas. I.
[93] Close, 2 Jas. I, pt. xxxi.
[94] See above.
[95] *Pat.* 2 Jas. I, pt. xix, m. 20.
[96] Close, 9 Jas. I, pt xxxiv, no. 13; cf. Feet of F. Herts. Hil. 10 Jas. I.
[97] *Herts. Visit.* (Harl. Soc. xxii), 157.
[98] Hatfield MSS. quoted by Clutterbuck, op. cit. iii, 503.
[99] The name has first been found in 1445 (Chan. Inq. p.m. 23 Hen. VI, 15).

1302,[100] and was succeeded by his son John,[1] who also held his father's office in Rockingham Forest.[2] It is said that Richard Monchesney and his wife Joan acquired a life interest in Hauvills in accordance with a settlement made by Geoffrey de Hauvill, and that a certain Reginald de Hauvill succeeded under the same settlement.[3] Certainly Richard Monchesney was assessed for a sixteenth in Clothall in 1316–18,[4] and he had grant of free warren in Clothall in 1333.[5] Joan widow of John (possibly an error for Richard) Monchesney was holding this moiety of Clothall in 1349.[6] She seems to have been succeeded by Reginald de Hauvill,[7] and his son Thomas witnessed the conveyance of Botteles to John atte Lee in 1362.[8] Reginald de Hauvill had a brother Ralph of Baldock, whose widow Beatrice claimed dower in certain small parcels of land in Clothall in 1356[9]; but it does not appear that Ralph had any right in the manor, although his title to it was asserted later.[10]

The earlier settlement on Richard Monchesney evidently brought upon Thomas de Hauvill dissensions with the Monchesney family, for he was charged with entering the manor of Walter Monchesney[11] at Clothall and carrying away £280. At the same time he was accused of imprisoning the king's bailiff at Southwark for thirty-seven weeks and committing various other enormities.[12] The heirs of Thomas were his sisters Emecine and Anne. Anne's son Robert sold his moiety of Hauvills to Matthew and Henry Rede and Thomas Blount, who also acquired Botteles. The second moiety descended to Emecine's granddaughter Katherine wife of John Piers.[13] In 1395–6 John and Katherine conveyed their share in the manor to John and Anne Burwell,[14] from whom it was acquired by Matthew and Henry Rede and Thomas Blount.[15] It was thus re-united with Botteles and the rest of Hauvills.

The reputed manor of BRICKFIELDS (Brettevyle, xv cent.; Brytvyles or Britfield, xvi cent.) was held of the manor of Hooks[16] (q.v.). During the 14th century it was held by the Bretteville family. In 1300 Hugh Bretteville of Hertford gave to his son William, upon his marriage with Eleanor daughter of William Bretun, his tenement in Clothall with villeins, homage, wards, reliefs and escheats.[17] William son of Hugh Bretteville was possessed of land in Clothall in 1318,[18] and in 1333 William and Eleanor Bretteville granted their 'manor of Clothall' to Hugh Bretteville and his wife Joan in tail with remainder to John brother of Hugh.[19] A William Bretteville and his wife Joan conveyed the manor to William Pekke and William Goldington in 1443.[20] It ultimately came into the possession of Richard Druell, who held it with Hauvills and Botteles at his death in 1525.[21] Its subsequent descent is identical with that of the main manor (q.v.).

HOOKS (Hokeslond, xv cent.; Howkes, xvi cent.) was apparently held of the manor of Botteles.[22] It was presumably held by Robert Hook, citizen and grocer of London, about 1408, when he presented a rector to the church.[23] He would therefore appear to have acquired the one-third of the advowson which was subsequently attached to the 'manor' of Hooks between 1405, when Matthew and Henry Rede and Thomas Blount were possessed of the entire advowson, and 1408.[24] Robert Hook again presented a rector in 1421,[25] but between that date and 1445 'a moiety of the manor of Clothall called Hokeslonds' was granted to John Mitchell, lord of Hauvills and Botteles, by a certain William Aston.[26] 'Hokesmanoir' was settled on Elizabeth daughter of Margaret Mitchell. Her heirs were her sister Joan and nieces Elizabeth and Anne.[27] The subsequent history of Hooks is identical with that of the main manor.

The site of the 'manor-house' lies on the way from Clothall to Cumberlow, nearly opposite Hook's Green Farm.[28]

KINGSWOOD BURY (Kingeswode, xii–xiii cent.; Kingswoodbery, xv–xvi cent.) was held of the Abbot of Westminster as of his neighbouring manor of Ashwell.[29]

A separate tenement of this name existed in 1198, when seisin of it was recovered by Robert son of Osbert,[30] who seems to have been succeeded by Julianne de Kingswood.[31] Robert de Kingswood owed service in Clothall about the middle of the 13th century; and there is reason to suppose that Kingswood was identical with the wood called 'Socage' in Clothall Park, for which Simon de Clothall owed two pounds of pepper to Adam de Hippegrave.[32]

The Kingswood family held land in Clothall during the first half of the 14th century.[33] The 'manor' of Kingswood Bury came later to John and Joan Venour and was divided among their daughters and co-heirs. Margery Venour, one of these, surrendered her third share in the manor to Peter Paul and his wife Alice in 1422.[34] Alice Paul seems to have held another third in her own right.[35] Peter Paul was in possession

---

[100] He was pardoned for taking a stag in the king's forest 28 May 1302 (Cal. Pat. 1301–7, p. 227). His son held Clothall in 1303 (Feud. Aids, ii, 433).
[1] Lay Subs. R. bdle. 120, no. 8.
[2] Cal. Pat. 1301–7, p. 323; see Cal. Gen. ii, 707. [3] De Banco R. 578, m. 231.
[4] Lay Subs. R. bdle. 120, no. 10, 11.
[5] Chart. R. 7 Edw. III, no. 23. In 1329 an inquisition on the knights' fees held of John de St. John returns the tenant as 'Amice' de Hauvill (Chan. Inq. p.m. Edw. III, file 19, no. 1). It is possible that this refers to Emecine wife of Geoffrey, for in such returns the name given is often that of a former tenant.
[6] Cal. Close, 1349–54, p. 70.
[7] De Banco R. 578, m. 231. A Reginald Hauvill was also assessed for the sixteenth of 1317–18 (Lay Subs. R. bdle. 120, no. 11).
[8] Cal. Close, 1360–4, p. 387; cf. De Banco R. 578, m. 231.
[9] De Banco R. 348, m. 435 d.; 349, m. 171 d.
[10] Ibid. 578, m. 231, by James Billingford and his wife Aubrey, who failed to make good their claim to it.
[11] This may refer to part of Wallington Manor (q.v.), which continued in Clothall.
[12] Assize R. 339. The roll is undated; apparently the presentments were made in or after 1362.
[13] De Banco R. 578, m. 231.
[14] Feet of F. Herts. 19 Ric. II, no. 169.
[15] De Banco R. 578, m. 231.
[16] Chan. Inq. p.m. (Ser. 2), xlv, 23.
[17] Harl. Chart. 111 D 57.
[18] Lay Subs. R. bdle. 120, no. 11; cf. Cal. Close, 1318–23, p. 382.
[19] Feet of F. Herts. 7 Edw. III, no. 153.
[20] Ibid. 22 Hen. VI, no. 116.
[21] Chan. Inq. p.m. (Ser. 2), xlv, 23.
[22] Ibid.
[23] Epis. Reg. quoted by Clutterbuck, Hist. and Antiq. of Herts. iii, 504.
[24] Chan. Inq. p.m. 33 Hen. VI, no. 31; De Banco R. 578, m. 231.
[25] Epis. Reg. quoted by Clutterbuck, loc. cit.
[26] Chan. Inq. p.m. 23 Hen. VI, no. 15; cf. 33 Hen. VI, no. 31.
[27] Ibid. 4 Edw. IV, no. 25.
[28] See Andrew, 'Hospital of St. Mary Magdalene,' East Herts. Arch. Soc. Trans. iv (1), 89.
[29] Chan. Inq. p.m. (Ser. 2), x, 70; xxxix, 88; De Banco R. 349, m. 279.
[30] Rot. Cur. Reg. (Rec. Com.), i, 177.
[31] Ibid. ii, 233.
[32] Exch. Transcr. of Chart. xv, m. 1 d.
[33] Lay Subs. R. bdle. 120, no. 11; De Banco R. 349, m. 279.
[34] Close, 10 Hen. V, m. [8?].
[35] Feet of F. Herts. 1 Hen. VI, no. 2; cf. ibid. no. 14.

ODSEY HUNDRED

of the whole manor by 1437.[36] In accordance with settlements made in 1445 and 1466[37] it descended to his son Richard Paul of Baldock, who in 1477 let it to John Sturgeon for twelve years in return for £50 and a gown of cloth.[38] In 1484 Richard Paul conveyed the manor (probably in trust) to John Sturgeon and others.[39] In 1485 Thomas Nudegate, son of Richard's sister Alice, surrendered his right in the manor to Sturgeon.[40] The latter sold to Richard Sheldon, who was succeeded in 1494 by his son Richard.[41] Richard Sheldon the younger settled this manor on himself and his wife Alice with remainder to his nephew Richard Barington. He died in 1518, but his wife survived.[42] It is not clear whether Barington inherited the manor. Some, at least, of the manorial lands had been leased to Edmund Kympton of Weston.[43] In 1546 Peter Hering and his wife Joan conveyed the manor to Thomas Matthew and others,[44] evidently trustees in a sale to George Lucy, to whom Edmund Kympton released his rights in 1551.[45]

George Lucy was succeeded by his son Sir Edmund Lucy, kt., of Broxbourne before 1580,[46] and in 1610 Sir Edmund entailed the manors of Kingswood Bury and Mundens upon his son Henry and the latter's wife Anne Sheldon.[47] Sir Edmund died in 1630, and his son Henry inherited the estate,[48] which was retained by his widow after his death. In 1656 she joined with her eldest son, Edward Lucy, in a sale to Rowland Hale of King's Walden for the benefit of his son William Hale of Gray's Inn, who was about to marry Mary Elwes.[49] The manor remained thenceforward in the family of Hale[50] until 1888, when it was purchased by the Marquess of Salisbury, in whose family it still remains.

In 1552 the site of the manor is described as 'motted rounde abowte with an orcheyard gardeyn and a cow-yard adjoyning to the same motte.'[51]

LUFFENHALL was granted with Ardeley to the Dean and Chapter of St. Paul's.[52] It has since continued to be a member of Ardeley Manor in this hundred (q.v.).

MUNDENS was a reputed manor near Kingswood Bury, its lands lying on the side of Burnt House Lane opposite the place called 'Chapels.'[53] Some of these may be identical with the virgate held by Osgot, one of Eddeva's men, before the Conquest, and afterwards attached to Munden in Broadwater Hundred. In 1086 this virgate was held of Count Alan by Leuiet.[54]

The earliest known reference to the 'manor' of Mundens in Clothall dates from 1466, when it was entailed upon the heirs of Peter Paul and his wife Alice.[55] It has subsequently remained in the possession of the successive lords of Kingswood Bury (q.v.).

QUICKSWOOD or QUICKSETT was the residence of George Burgoyne in 1554.[56] It may therefore be the site of either of his manors, Hauvills or Botteles. The site of the former house is near that of the present farm. Nicholas Trott resided at Quickswood,[57] and for many years after the acquisition of Clothall Manor by the Earl of Salisbury Quickswood was an occasional residence of the Cecil family.[58] It was occupied by the earl in 1620,[59] and in 1632 he caused the annual sermon provided by St. John's College, Cambridge, to be preached at Clothall instead of Cheshunt.[60] In 1647 the earl's bailiff was obliged to quarter four Parliamentarian soldiers at Quickswood.[61] The house was razed to the ground by James Cecil, the seventh earl, about 1790.[62]

The church of ST. MARY THE VIRGIN stands on rising ground to the north-east of the village, and is built of flint rubble with stone dressings; the roofs are of lead. It consists of chancel 27 ft. by 16 ft. 6 in., nave 36 ft. 6 in. by 19 ft., south chapel 18 ft. by 10 ft. 6 in., and south tower, the lower stage of which forms the porch. All the measurements are taken internally. A north vestry was added in the 19th century. The present church appears to have been erected c. 1350–70 on the foundations of the older one or the older stones re-used, as some of the lower stones are of shelly oolite, the rest of the stonework being of clunch. The south chapel, tower and chancel may have been built a little later in the 14th century.[63] All the windows of the chancel were of modern stonework, and the chancel arch has been cemented. The roof is modern. In the south wall is a trefoil-headed piscina of late 14th-century work, and in the north wall is a square locker with rebated edge; there is a blocked doorway on the south side. On the north wall of the nave are two windows having two cinquefoiled lights; one is of 15th-century date, the other being a modern copy; the west window of two cinquefoiled lights also belongs to the 15th century. All the old tracery has been repaired with cement. In the south wall is a 14th-century arch opening into the south chapel. The arch is of two splayed orders, the jambs of semi-octagonal piers separated by filleted bowtels, and with moulded capitals and bases. The south doorway is of the 14th century, and retains the original plank door, with ornamental iron hinges. The name 'John Warrin' is painted in black letter on the inside. The south chapel has an east window with 15th-century tracery of three lights, the jambs being of earlier date.

---

[36] Close, 15 Hen. VI, m. 10.
[37] Add. Chart. (B.M.), 35417–19.
[38] Ibid. 35421.
[39] Feet of F. Herts. 2 Ric. III, no. 8; cf. Add. Chart. (B.M.), 35422.
[40] Add. Chart. 35423–4; cf. Feet of F. Herts. 22 Edw. IV, no. 65, a quitclaim from Naverina wife of William Foljambe two years before the conveyance from Paul.
[41] Chan. Inq. p.m. (Ser. 2), x, 70.
[42] Ibid. xxxix, 88.
[43] Close, 5 Edw. VI, pt. iv, no. 26.
[44] Feet of F. Herts. Hil. 37 Hen. VIII.
[45] Ibid. Mich. 5 Edw. VI.
[46] Recov. R. East. 22 Eliz. m. 105.
[47] Add. Chart. 35429–30; cf. ibid. 35431.
[48] Chan. Inq. p.m (Ser. 2), ccclxvi, 58; cccclxxxi, 186.
[49] Add. Chart. 35432–3; Recov. R. East. 1656, m. 107.
[50] Add. Chart. 35416; Feet of F. Herts. Hil. 10 Anne; see the account of King's Walden.   [51] Add. MS. 33582, fol. 4.
[52] MSS. of D. and C. of St. Paul's, W.D. xvi, fol. 80, &c.
[53] Add. MS. 33582, fol. 5.
[54] V.C.H. Herts. i, 319b.
[55] Add. Chart. 35419. In 1362 Henry Bottele had rent from lands 'sometime Mundenes' in Clothall (Cal. Close, 1360–4, p. 387).   [56] Acts of P.C. 1554–6, p. 106.
[57] Visit. of Herts. (Harl. Soc. xxii), 157.
[58] Buccleuch MSS. (Hist. MSS. Com.), i, 338.
[59] Cal. S. P. Dom. 1619–23, p. 113.
[60] Andrew, 'Quickswood,' East Herts. Arch. Soc. Trans. iv (1), 96.
[61] Hist. MSS. Com. Rep. vi, App. i, 170a.
[62] Cussans, Hist. of Herts. Odsey Hund. 64. See above.
[63] Richard Druell (d. 1525) bequeathed 3s. 4d. to the sepulchre light in the church of Clothall (P.C.C. Wills, 7 Porch). In 1526 Grace Druell directed that her body should be buried in the chapel of St. James within the parish church of our Lady of Clothall, leaving 26s. 8d. for the repair of the chapel and all her bee-hives for the maintenance of the lights (ibid. 14 Porch). The south chapel is probably the chapel of St. James here referred to.

A HISTORY OF HERTFORDSHIRE

In the south wall is a two-light window with flowing tracery of the 14th century, the inner sill being carried down to form a seat, and beside it is a single-light window of the same date. There is a cinquefoil-headed piscina in the south wall, and just above it and in the north wall opposite are two small stone brackets, with sockets in their tops, probably for lights; there is a small square locker in the north wall.

The tower is of two stages with a tiled pyramidal roof. The lower stage forms the south porch, which has a moulded arched entrance, the mouldings dying on the splayed jambs. There is a single-light cusped opening on each face of the tower at the belfry stage. There are a few old timbers in the nave roof. The font is of the 12th century. It is of Purbeck marble, and has a square basin carried upon a large central shaft, with a smaller shaft at each angle; the bases are moulded and rest on a square plinth. On each face of the basin are four shallow round-headed panels. The 17th-century cover is of wood.

In the east window is some old glass; the head of a female saint is probably of late 14th-century work; a number of quarries painted with birds and a border with 'Maria' monogram repeated may belong to the next century. In the south-west window of the chapel are some heraldic fragments.

There are some 15th-century bench ends with poppy heads at the west end of the church, much defaced. In the chapel are fragments of a slab with foliated cross and remains of a marginal inscription in Lombardic characters, probably of mid-14th-century date.

In the chancel are several brasses: a priest in cope, without inscription, of the early 16th century; a priest in eucharistic vestments, the arms missing, to John Vynter, rector of the parish, who died in 1404; a priest in eucharistic vestments, holding chalice and wafer, with the symbol of the Trinity above, to John Wryght, rector of the parish, 1519; to Anne Bramfield, 1578; to William Lucas, rector of the parish, 1602. Fixed to the wall of the chapel is an inscription to Thomas Dalyson, rector of the parish, who died in 1541; this probably belongs to the brass in the chancel.

There are two bells in the tower: the treble is inscribed 'CALIT ME JOANNES +' with mark of Richard Wymbish, 14th century; the tenor 'I.H.S. ✠ T . W ✠ S.' by an unknown 16th-century founder.

The communion plate includes an engraved cup and cover paten, 1571, and a paten of 1693 presented by Rev. W. Neale, M.A., rector in 1755.

The registers are in two books: (i) baptisms and burials from 1717 to 1812 and marriages 1717 to 1753; (ii) marriages from 1754 to 1812.

There is a bishop's transcript for the year commencing Michaelmas 1588.

ADVOWSON The earliest known record of Clothall Church is the presentation of a rector in 1237 by Simon de Clothall, lord of the manor.[64] Maud de Bottele, one of his three daughters, surrendered her share in the advowson to her sister Emecine de Hauvill in 1271,[65] and at the same time it was agreed that Muriel Scales, the third daughter, and her heirs should present for one turn and Emecine and her heirs for the two following turns.[66] This arrangement held good until 1404, when James Billingford and his wife Aubrey presented a certain John Hogges, under colour of their acquisition of the rights of John son of Richard kinsman of Ralph brother and heir of Reginald de Hauvill. Matthew and Henry Rede and Thomas Blount, who had acquired the manors of Hauvills and Botteles (q.v.), brought a plea against Billingford in 1405, and judgement was given in their favour.[67]

It has been seen that one-third of the advowson subsequently descended with the manor of Hooks (q.v.). The whole advowson was re-united when John Mitchell acquired that manor, and has since been retained by the successive lords of the main manor.

A meeting-place for Protestant Dissenters in Clothall was certified in 1720.[68]

CHARITIES The official trustees hold a sum of £131 6s. 2d. consols, which is regarded as representing the investment of £60, stated in the Parliamentary returns of 1786 to have been given to the poor by Dr. James Sibbald and others, and of a legacy of £50 by will of James Smyth, proved in the P.C.C. 20 September 1810. The annual dividends, amounting to £3 5s. 8d., are distributed in bread at Christmas-time.

COTTERED

Choldrei (xi cent.); Keldreia (xii cent.); Codreye, Coudray, Coddram, Coddred, Codreth (xiii cent.); Cotrede (xvi cent.).

The parish of Cottered contains 1,832 acres. Of this about two-thirds consist of arable land and one-quarter of permanent grass.[1] The only piece of woodland in the parish is Drinkwater Wood, which lies to the south-east. The soil is generally heavy on a subsoil of chalk. The River Beane flows through the parish, the western districts of which are liable to floods. In the north-east the land rises as high as 493 ft. above the ordnance datum.

The Roman road known as Stane Street passed through Hare Street, a hamlet on the borders of Cottered and Ardeley, its course being apparently marked by Back Lane, which forms the south-western boundary of Cottered. There is a record of this road in Cottered in 1346, when the 'King's Highway called Stanestrat' is referred to as a boundary.[2]

Cottered lies 3 miles west of Buntingford, in which town is its nearest railway station on the Great Eastern railway, and 6 miles east of the market town of Baldock.

The main road which connects these two towns passes through Cottered. Other roads connect it with Throcking and Ardeley.

---

[64] Linc. Epis. Reg. Grosteste, R. 8, m. 1.
[65] Feet of F. Herts. 56 Hen. III, no. 488.
[66] Ibid. 638.
[67] De Banco R. 578, m. 231.
[68] Urwick, op. cit. 787.

[1] Statistics from Bd. of Agric. (1905).
[2] J. Harvey Bloom, *Cartae Antiquae of Lord Willoughby de Broke*, 6.

226

CLOTHALL CHURCH FROM THE SOUTH-EAST

COTTERED CHURCH FROM THE SOUTH

The village of Cottered lies about three-quarters of a mile north of the Roman road above referred to, around and within a triangle formed by the junction of the roads from Buntingford, Ardeley and Cumberlow Green. The church stands at the south angle of the triangle in a fairly large churchyard [a] with the Lordship to the south-east of it and Cheynes, the manor-house of Cheyney Cottered, to the south-west. The village is mainly along the road a little to the north of the church. The 18th-century almshouses known as the Town Houses, the village school built in 1829, the rectory and a Congregational mission chapel stand in this road.

The Lordship, now a farm-house, is a timber-framed building, occupied by Mr. Tucker. It stands in a moated inclosure, the moat being fairly perfect and filled with water on the south and east sides of the house, but filled in on the north and west. The house apparently dates from about the middle of the 15th century, and contains several interesting features of an early date. It is roughly T-shaped on plan, and the entrance porch of two stories is placed in an angle of the cross which only projects 4 ft. on the north or entrance front. It is not now easy to determine the original plan, owing to alterations and later subdivisions of the apartments.

The entrance door is evidently part of the original house. It is of oak, and has four panels the full height

THE LORDSHIP, COTTERED.
GROUND PLAN

of the door with pointed arched heads filled with cusping. The moulding is a simple cavetto. On the door is an excellently designed late 17th-century iron knocker. It seems probable that the present kitchen, and perhaps a small room and lobby to the west of the kitchen, formed the old hall, the existing passage occupying the place of the 'screens.'

COTTERED : THE TOWN HOUSES

To the left of the entrance is now a sitting room with oak panelling of the Jacobean period, which apparently formed part of the original kitchen, as the brew-house adjoins it and appears to have entered off it at one time, and the fireplace and oven are back to back. There is a Jacobean chimney-piece in the sitting room, with an overmantel divided into two parts by flat fluted pilasters, having projecting carved frieze and cornice above. The frieze between the pilasters is fluted. Each panel has two circular-headed arches, round which are bands of a richly carved interlacing pattern. Between the arches is a moulded spindle or drop carried down about three-fourths the height of the panels. The fireplace is modern.

The upper floor contains a good deal of plain Jacobean panelling, and some of the doors retain the old iron hinges of the period. A few months ago some of this panelling was temporarily taken down for repairs, and it was found that the partitions had been previously lined with boarding, much of which still remains, and was decorated with painted work.

There are large attics in the roof, but these are not now used, as there is very little flooring on the joists and there are no windows. There were no doubt dormer windows at one time, as there are several octagonal shafts of oak with perpendicular moulded bases and embattled capitals, over which are curved struts supporting the main roof timbers. These form part of the original structure, and occupy a similar position to the portion of the shaft still remaining in the roof at Little Wymondley Bury.

Externally the house is plastered, and at one time was ornamented with flush panels filled with the usual basketwork and other patterns, but only a little of the

[a] In 1657 there were houses in the churchyard which were afterwards pulled down (*East Herts. Arch. Soc. Trans.* iii, 230).

227

old work remains on the brew-house. The two old chimney stacks are built with thin 2 in. bricks. That over the present kitchen fireplace is a massive projecting chimney with offsets at intervals, but its appearance is marred by the modern scullery and chimney. The old wide fireplace in the kitchen still remains with its seats in the ingle-nook. The chimney over the present sitting room and brew-house has two square shafts set diagonally. The roofs are steep and tile-covered. The moat averages about 24 ft. in width and appears to have inclosed a space measuring about 184 ft. from east to west by about 64 ft. from north to south.

Broom Farm is a 16th-century timber and brick house, to which a brick front was added about 1700, in the hamlet of Hare Street. It is L-shaped in plan and has many original details inside the house. Near to it is a large 17th-century barn of timber on a brick base.

From the village a road runs south, passing Cripplegate, Little Osbournes and Meeting House Cottages; it then forms a loop, passes the Warren, Flanders Green and Brook-end and rejoins the main road further east. Both Cripplegate and Brook-end are described among the lands which were purchased in accordance with Robert Page's will in 1553.[4] The Osbournes are referred to in a will of 1577.[5] In 1762 the farm called the Warren was included in a settlement of the manor,[6] and is mentioned in the will of Edmund Swallow of 1629.[7] Meeting-places for Protestant Dissenters in Cottered were certified from 1691. There was a chapel in 1810, the minister of which was the Rev. T. B. Browne. On his death in 1823 the services were discontinued for a time.[8] The chapel is now served from Buntingford. Dissent has always had a strong hold in Cottered. The rector of Cottered is said to have been one of the ministers who were turned out of their livings in 1662. Many of his parishioners sympathized with him and many belonged to the Society of Friends.[9] In this movement William Joyce, a carpenter, and the Extons were the leaders. John Exton in 1710 gave a piece of land on the Lordship estate to the Friends for a burial-ground.[10]

Among those who have held the living of Cottered may be mentioned the Rev. Anthony Trollope, who was grandfather of the authors Anthony Trollope and Thomas Adolphus Trollope. He was incumbent of Cottered for forty-four years and died in 1806.[11]

MANORS In the reign of Edward the Confessor Cottered formed part of the demesne lands of St. Peter of Winchester.[12] The Norman Conquest did not disturb this tenure, and in 1086 the manor of Cottered was held by Bishop Walkelin of Winchester.[13] On his death in 1098 [14] it appears to have been detached from the bishopric and to have become part of the honour of Boulogne. Queen Maud, daughter of Count Eustace of Boulogne and wife of King Stephen, is said to have granted half a virgate of land in Cottered to Reimer de Wivellelme, to hold of the Knights Templars.[15] Her son William de Blois granted the honour of Ongar to Richard de Lucie,[16] and apparently part of his lands in Cottered were granted at the same time, and became the manor of COTTERED.[17] Maud, the daughter and heiress of Richard de Lucie, married Richard de Rivers in the reign of John,[18] and the overlordship of Cottered descended with this family, and was held in 1303 by John Lord Rivers.[19] He died about 1311 and was succeeded by his son John Lord Rivers. His son Edmund left a daughter and heiress,[20] and it is probable that on his death the overlordship of Cottered passed to the king, for in 1461 the manor was said to be held of the king as of his duchy of Lancaster,[21] and subsequently of the king in chief.[22]

RIVERS, Lord Rivers. *Or a lion azure.*

In the reign of Henry II Jordan Chamberlain was apparently holding this manor in sub-tenancy, for he made a grant of the advowson during that period.[23] He was succeeded by his son Martin Chamberlain, who in 1258 disputed the grant of the advowson.[24] The records of this family are few, but by 1303 the manor had come into the possession of John Chamberlain, who was holding a quarter of a knight's fee in Cottered of John de Rivers.[25] This descended to Sir William Chamberlain, kt., and from him passed to his daughter Cecily, who married Andrew de Bures of Suffolk.[26] Cecily died before 1367, in which year her husband Andrew de Bures was holding the manor of Cottered for life, the reversion belonging to Katherine the wife of William Phelip and Ellen wife of John Owdyn, sisters of Sir William Chamberlain.[27] As they are also described as kinswomen and heirs of Andrew's son William [28] it seems probable that Andrew and Cecily had an only son William who died before his father. Andrew de Bures died in January 1368–9.[29] Katherine died in 1371, leaving a son Brian, aged twelve.[30] He apparently died young, as there is no further trace of him in Cottered. Ellen appears also to have died before 1372, for in that year Katherine

BURES. *Ermine a chief indented sable with two lions or therein.*

---

[4] Cussans, *Hist. of Herts. Odsey Hund.* 184.
[5] Ibid.
[6] Close, 6 Geo. III, pt. vi, no. 8.
[7] Cussans, op. cit. *Odsey Hund.* 184.
[8] Urwick, *Nonconformity in Herts.* 791.
[9] Ibid. 788, 790.
[10] *East Herts. Arch. Soc. Trans.* iii, 158, 230.
[11] Cussans, op. cit. *Odsey Hund.* 178.
[12] *V.C.H. Herts.* i, 305*b*.
[13] Ibid.
[14] *Dict. Nat. Biog.*
[15] Chauncy, *Hist. and Antiq. of Herts.* 66.
[16] Morant, *Essex*, i, 127.
[17] See also advowson.
[18] G.E.C. *Complete Peerage*, s.v. Rivers.
[19] *Feud. Aids*, ii, 433; G.E.C. loc. cit.
[20] G.E.C. loc. cit.
[21] Chan. Inq. p.m. 1 Edw. IV, no. 28.
[22] Ibid. 18 Edw. IV, file 546, no. 45; Cal. Inq. p.m. Hen. VII, i, 102.
[23] Cur. Reg. R. 160, m. 25; Dugdale, *Mon.* v, 456.
[24] Cur. Reg. R. 160, m. 25.
[25] *Feud. Aids*, ii, 433.
[26] De Banco R. 427, m. 1.
[27] See Chan. Inq. p.m. 49 Edw. III, pt. ii, no. 40.
[28] De Banco R. 427, m. 1; Feet of F. Div. Co. East. 41 Edw. III, no. 33.
[29] Chan. Inq. p.m. 49 Edw. III, pt. ii, no. 40.
[30] Ibid.

ODSEY HUNDRED
COTTERED

wife of Edmund Gessyng, presumably her daughter, levied a fine of the manor.[31]

In 1387 Katherine, then the wife of Philip Bluet, joined with her husband and a certain Margaret and John Radeswell in selling the reversion of the manor after the death of John Owdyn to Andrew de Bures, son and heir of an Andrew de Bures of Suffolk.[32] Andrew de Bures was holding Cottered in 1400,[33] but shortly afterwards seems to have conveyed it to John Fray, who was holding it in 1428.[34] Fray became chief baron of the Exchequer, and held the manor until his death in 1461,[35] when it passed by his will to his wife Lady Agnes Fray. Some accounts of the manor between the years 1462 and 1467 show that the lord of the manor received yearly for rents and customs £23 6s., fifteen capons, £4 for the farm of the water mill, one pair of gloves and one needle and thread, whilst the perquisites of the court included two capons.[36] Lady Agnes Fray died in 1478.[37] The reversion of Cottered had been settled on their daughter Agnes with remainder to their youngest daughter Katherine.[38] Agnes died without issue, and the manor passed to Katherine wife of Humphrey Stafford,[39] who held it until her death in 1482.[40] She was succeeded by her son Humphrey, aged eight,[41] who was knighted and held the manor of Cottered until his death in 1545.[42] His son Humphrey Stafford inherited his lands,[43] and in February 1546-7 was knighted by Edward VI after his coronation.[44] In 1574 Sir Humphrey Stafford died and the manor of Cottered passed to his brother John Stafford,[45] who sold it in 1581 to Edward Pulter.[46] At this time there was a windmill in Cottered, the lease of which was not included in the sale of the manor. Edward Pulter bought the neighbouring manor of Broadfield (q.v.), and from this date the two estates have descended together. In 1624-5 his grandson Arthur Pulter sold the site of this manor to Toby Cocks and Edward Hamond.[47]

STAFFORD. *Or a cheveron gules and a border engrailed sable.*

COTTERED: THE LORDSHIP FROM THE NORTH-WEST

The manor of *CHEYNEY-COTTERED* (Cottered, xiii cent. ; Cheines Place, Cheyneys, xv cent.) formed part of the honour of Boulogne, but its lands extended into Ardeley, Aspenden, Wakeley Throcking, Rushden and Broadfield, and parcels of the manor were held of various overlords.[48]

The lands forming this manor were apparently reserved by William de Blois when he granted the manor of Cottered to Richard de Lucie (see above), and remained part of the honour of Boulogne until it

---

[31] Feet of F. Herts. 46 Edw. III, no. 630.
[32] Ibid. 11 Ric. II, no. 97.
[33] Chan. Inq. p.m. 2 Hen. IV, no. 36.
[34] *Feud. Aids,* ii, 447.
[35] Chan. Inq. p.m. 1 Edw. IV, no. 28.
[36] Mins. Accts. bdle. 849, no. 10.
[37] Chan. Inq. p.m. 18 Edw. IV, file 546, no. 45.
[38] Early Chan. Proc. bdle. 71, no. 40.

[39] Ibid. ; Chan. Inq. p.m. 18 Edw. IV, file 546, no. 45.
[40] Chan. Inq. p.m. (Ser. 2), ii, 72.
[41] Ibid. ; see Feet of F. Herts. Trin. 6 Hen. VIII.
[42] Chan. Inq. p.m. (Ser. 2), lxxii, 86 (i).
[43] Ibid.
[44] Shaw, *Knights of England,* ii, 60.
[45] Chan. Inq. p.m. (Ser. 2), clxxiii, 74.
[46] Feet of F. Herts. Mich. 23 & 24

Eliz. ; Com. Pleas D. Enr. Mich. 23 & 24 Eliz. m. 1 ; Recov. R. East. 25 Eliz. rot. 147.
[47] Feet of F. Herts. Hil. 22 Jas. I.
[48] *Red Bk. of Exch.* (Rolls Ser.), ii, 582 ; *Testa de Nevill* (Rec. Com.), 274b ; Com. Pleas D. Enr. Trin. 1 Mary, m. 11 ; Chan. Inq. p.m. 19 Edw. III, no. 49 ; 2 Hen. IV, no. 52 ; 8 Hen. V, no. 46 ; 9 Hen. VI, no. 42.

A HISTORY OF HERTFORDSHIRE

came into the king's hands.[49] William de Ken received a grant of £6 rent there at the beginning of the 13th century.[50] He died before 1224 and his lands descended to his son William.[51] In the same year they were granted to Fulk de Montgomery for his maintenance in the king's service.[52] He held them until 1236, when they were restored to William de Ken.[53] In February 1243-4 he granted 10 marks rent in Cottered, apparently the extent of the manor, to Walter de Ken. These rents were taken into the king's hands among the lands of the Normans in March of the same year.[54] In 1248 the king granted all William de Ken's lands in Hertfordshire and Cambridgeshire, including Cottered, to William Chesney,[55] who received a grant of free warren in his demesne lands of Cottered and other lands of his possession in 1258.[56] He died in 1274 and was succeeded by his son Nicholas Chesney,[57] whose holding in Cottered was described as a quarter of a knight's fee in 1303.[58] He died in 1326 and was succeeded by his son William,[59] who died in 1345, when his lands descended to his son Edmund,[60] who made proof of age in March 1346-7.[61] In 1374 Edmund Chesney, kt., settled the manor of Cottered on the heirs of his body with contingent remainder in tail to his brother Sir Ralph Chesney.[62] Sir Edmund appears to have died without issue before 1383, for the manor had passed to Sir Ralph by that year.[63] In 1400 Sir Ralph died and was succeeded by his son William,[64] who held Cottered until his death in 1420,[65] when his lands passed to his son and heir Edmund, aged eighteen.[66] The manor of Cottered was settled on Edmund and his wife Alice in tail.[67] Edmund de Chesney died in 1430, his wife Alice surviving him. He left three daughters and co-heirs, Elizabeth, aged six, Anne, aged three, and Cecilia, aged one.[68] Cecilia died the same year as her

CHEYNEY. *Gules a fesse indented of four points argent with four scallops sable thereon.*

WILLOUGHBY. *Or fretty azure.*

father.[69] Elizabeth married Sir John Colyshull, kt., of Benamy, co. Devon,[70] but had no children,[71] and Anne became sole heir. She married Sir John Willoughby, kt.,[72] grandson of Lord Willoughby de Eresby,[73] and had one son, Sir Robert Willoughby.[74] He was a staunch supporter of Henry VII and took a prominent part in the battle of Bosworth Field. He was rewarded by being created Lord Willoughby de Broke in 1491, taking his title from one of the manors he had inherited from his grandfather, Sir Edmund Chesney.[75] In 1502 he was succeeded by his son Robert, Lord Willoughby de Broke, who held the manor of Cottered[76] until his death in 1521.[77] Edward, his only son by his first wife Elizabeth daughter and co-heir of Richard Lord Beauchamp, had died during his father's lifetime, leaving three daughters, Elizabeth, Anne and Blanche.[78] He had two sons by Dorothy, his second wife, of whom Henry was aged twelve at his father's death, but they died within a few weeks of one another, and the barony fell into abeyance.[79] His three granddaughters then became his sole heirs. Anne died while still a child, Blanche married Sir Francis Dawtrey, but had no children, and on her death Elizabeth, the eldest sister, became one of the richest heiresses in England. She married Fulk Greville, second son of her guardian, Sir Edward Greville of Milcote, co. Warwick.[80] In March 1541-2 Sir Anthony Willoughby, kt., of Gorley quitclaimed to Fulk Greville and Elizabeth his wife and her heirs all right in the manor of Cottered.[81] Fulk Greville died in 1559 and Elizabeth in the following year. Their lands Passed to their son Sir Fulk Greville,[82] and in 1606 to his son Sir Fulk Greville.[83] He in January 1620-1 was created Baron Brooke of Beauchamp's Court.[84] In 1628 Lord Brooke was stabbed by a man named Heywood, who considered that his services had been insufficiently rewarded.[85] He left no children, and the manor of Cottered passed to his only sister Margaret the wife of Sir Richard Verney of Compton Murdock, co. Warwick.[86] She held it until her death in 1631, when it descended to her son Sir Greville Verney, aged forty.[87] He died in 1642 and his son Greville in 1648. His lands were inherited by his posthumous and only child, Greville Verney, who held them until his death in 1668. William Verney, his son, died in France in 1683, at the age of fifteen, and his lands reverted to his great-uncle, Richard Verney. The barony of Willoughby

GREVILLE. *Sable a cross engrailed and a border engrailed or with five roundels sable on the cross.*

---

[49] See *Red Bk. of Exch.* (Rolls Ser.), ii, 582.
[50] Ibid. 582, 804.
[51] *Excerpta e Rot. Fin.* (Rec. Com.), i, 110.
[52] *Rot. Lit. Claus.* (Rec. Com.), ii, 7.
[53] *Cal. Close*, 1234-7, p. 386.
[54] *Cal. Inq. p.m. Hen. III*, 21.
[55] *Cal. Chart. R.* 1226-57, p. 331.
[56] Ibid. 1257-1300, p. 8.
[57] J. Harvey Bloom, *Cartae Antiquae of Lord Willoughby de Broke*, pt. iv, preface.
[58] *Feud. Aids*, ii, 433.
[59] *Cal. Inq. p.m.* 10-20 Edw. II, 475.
[60] Chan. Inq. p.m. 19 Edw. III, no. 49.
[61] *Cal. Close*, 1349-54, p. 257.
[62] Chan. Inq. p.m. 48 Edw. III (2nd nos.), no. 20; see *Abbrev. Rot. Orig.* (Rec. Com.), ii, 334.
[63] J. Harvey Bloom, op. cit. ii, 10.
[64] Chan. Inq. p.m. 2 Hen. IV, no. 52.
[65] Ibid.; see *Feud. Aids*, ii, 444.
[66] Chan. Inq. p.m. 8 Hen. V, no. 46.
[67] Ibid. 9 Hen. VI, no. 42.
[68] Ibid
[69] Ibid. no. 53.
[70] Wrottesley, *Ped. from Plea R.* 472.
[71] See Chan. Inq. p.m. 1 Ric. III, no. 42.
[72] Wrottesley, loc. cit.
[73] G.E.C. *Complete Peerage*.
[74] Ibid.
[75] Ibid.
[76] See Feet of F. Herts. Trin. 8 Hen. VIII.
[77] G.E.C. op. cit.
[78] Ibid.; Chan. Inq. p.m. (Ser. 2), xlii, 98.
[79] Ibid.; Chauncy, *Hist. and Antiq. of Herts.* 68.
[80] G.E.C. op. cit
[81] Com. Pleas D. Enr. East. 34 Hen. VIII, m. 5.
[82] G.E.C. *Complete Peerage*.
[83] Ibid.; Harl. MS. 758, fol. 112*b*.
[84] G.E.C. op. cit.
[85] Chauncy, op. cit. 67.
[86] W. and L. Inq. p.m. xlix, 213.
[87] Chan. Inq. p.m. (Ser. 2), ccclxxiv, 55.

COTTERED THE LORDSHIP: ENTRANCE FRONT

COTTERED THE LORDSHIP: JACOBEAN CHIMNEY-PIECE IN THE DINING-ROOM

ODSEY HUNDRED — COTTERED

de Broke, which had been in abeyance since 1521, was allowed to Richard Verney in 1696 by the decision of the House of Lords,[67a] and the manor descended with the Lords Willoughby de Broke until it was sold to Mr. Newbolt, who sold it to Mrs. Campe, from whom it was bought by Mr. Herbert Goode, the present owner.[88]

The church of ST. JOHN THE BAPTIST consists of chancel 35 ft. 6 in. by 16 ft., north vestry 13 ft. by 12 ft. 6 in., north chapel 22 ft. 6 in. by 13 ft., nave 60 ft. by 25 ft., south porch 11 ft. 6 in. by 10 ft. 6 in., and west tower 12 ft. 6 in. by 12 ft., all dimensions taken internally. The walls are of flint rubble covered with cement and the dressings are of stone; the north wall of the vestry is of brick. The roofs are tiled and leaded. There are large blocks of flint conglomerate, or 'pudding stones,' used as foundations under the western angles of the tower.

The chancel, nave, with south porch and west tower, were built about 1350; the north chapel and the roof and windows of the nave belong to the 15th and the north vestry to the 16th century.

The east window is modern. On the north side of the chancel is an arcade of two arches of 15th-century work, opening into the north chapel. The arches and jambs are of two continuously moulded orders; much of the work has been renewed. In the south wall are two early 16th-century windows with square heads, one of which is inserted in an earlier opening, partly blocked. The south doorway is blocked, and above it is a small quatrefoil light of modern stonework, the jambs of which, internally, are old. In the south wall is a small plain pointed piscina, and adjoining it a sedile, 4 ft. 7 in. wide, under a moulded arch. Both are of the 14th century. The chancel arch, c. 1350, is of two moulded orders, whose separate shafts have moulded capitals and bases. The jambs have been forced out of the perpendicular.

The vestry has one window in the east wall, of two cusped lights under a square head, of 16th-century date, with the original iron stanchions; the door is original. In the north wall of the chapel are two windows, each of three cinquefoiled lights with tracery, under a four-centred arch; the tracery is modern. The 15th-century doorway has a modern arch. There is an opening with a modern arch between the chapel and the nave; its sill is 6 ft. 4 in. above the floor; it is probably 14th-century work. There is a 15th-century piscina in the south wall.

The two eastern windows in the north wall of the nave are each of three lights and are very lofty; they have a transom over cusped lights midway up, and traceried head under a four-centred arch; the two opposite windows in the south wall are similar. The westernmost windows in the north and south walls are similar in detail, but are of two lights only, with cusped arches under square heads. All the windows are of 15th-century work, a good deal repaired. Some fragments of 15th-century glass remain in the heads of the north windows. At the north-east angle of the nave, externally, is an octagonal turret containing the stair to the rood loft, which is continued up to the roof. The upper and lower entrances, which are both in the north wall of the nave, are blocked, only the arch of the doorway remaining in the case of the latter. The north nave doorway is blocked and much defaced; on the outer side the original door still remains *in situ*. The south doorway is of two moulded orders with the original 15th-century door; both doorways are of c. 1350. At the east end of the south wall is a 14th-century piscina.

There is an early 16th-century two-light window, under a square head, on either side of the south porch; the entrance doorway is coated with cement. There are remains of a stoup in the porch.

The west tower is of three stages, with an embattled parapet, and a slight, lofty spire covered with lead. The tower arch is of three chamfered orders, the innermost stopping on jambs with moulded capitals and bases, and the two outer continuous; the stonework has been restored. The west doorway is modern, but the window over it is of c. 1350; it is of two lights and has been repaired with cement. On each face of the tower, at the belfry stage, was a two-light trefoiled opening, the tracery of which is almost gone.

The roof over the nave is of 15th-century date, with moulded principals and purlins. Many of the corbels and carved bosses are missing. Parts of the chancel roof and the beams over the north chapel belong to the same period.

The font, which dates from about 1700, is of grey Derbyshire marble and has a moulded circular basin, decorated with scallops, resting on a circular moulded stem.

On the north wall of the nave is a large distemper painting of St. Christopher, now very indistinct.

There is a late 16th-century chest in the vestry. In the chapel is a brass inscription (partly broken) to [Litton] Pulter, 1608, in the porch are some slabs with indents for brasses, and on the chapel floor are several inscribed slabs of the 17th century to members of the Pulter family. In the vestry is a 17th-century table.

There are five bells: the treble by John Briant, 1793; the second by Thomas Mears, 1841; the third by Lester & Pack, 1759; the fourth and tenor by Miles Graye, 1651 and 1650.

The communion plate includes cup and cover paten, 1711.

The registers are in five books: (i) baptisms from 1563 to 1684, burials 1558 to 1686, marriages 1558 to 1684; (ii) baptisms and burials from 1688 to 1772, marriages 1691 to 1772; (iii) baptisms and burials from 1773 to 1791; (iv) baptisms and burials from 1792 to 1812; (v) marriages from 1773 to 1812.

ADVOWSON The advowson of the church of Cottered was held in the reign of Henry II by Jordan Chamberlain, lord of the manor of Cottered, and he gave it in the same reign to the abbey of Westwood in Lesnes, in the parish of Erith, co. Kent, which was founded by Richard de Lucie in 1178.[89] In 1258 Martin Chamberlain, son of Jordan, claimed to present, and brought a suit against the abbot, but judgement was given for the latter.[89a] The advowson remained with the abbey until the 15th century, when the abbot granted it to John Fray, lord of the manor

---

[67a] G.E.C. *Complete Peerage*.
[88] Inform. supplied by Mrs. A. B. Hobart-Hampden.
[89] Dugdale, *Mon.* v, 456.
[89a] Cur. Reg. R. 160, m. 25.

A HISTORY OF HERTFORDSHIRE

of Cottered, who died seised of it in 1461.[90] It remained attached to the manor until the end of the 18th century,[91] when Richard French Forrester appears to have granted it for life to the Misses Harriet and Anna Jones, who presented in 1806,[92] and held the patronage as late as 1822.[93] By 1835 it had reverted to Richard French Forrester,[94] but in 1841 H. Brown presented,[95] from whom it passed to the Rev. W. Brown,[96] who presented himself to the church of Cottered in 1854.[97] In 1861 the advowson was in the hands of the Rev. John I. Manby, who presented himself.[98] The Rev. Aaron Manby presented himself in 1870,[99] and he held the advowson until 1885, when it was held by the trustees of the rector, the Rev. T. Izod,[100] who left the advowson by will to his nephew, the Rev. Henry Izod Rogers,[101] who had been appointed rector of Cottered in 1895.[102] He held it until 1908, when it was acquired by Mrs. A. B. Hobart-Hampden, the wife of the present rector, who continues to hold it.[103]

CHARITIES In 1492 Robert Page by his will gave £20 to be invested in land, the rents to be received by the church greaves, part thereof to be applied to superstitious uses, other part thereof in payment of two whole tasks of the town of Cottered, and the residue 5s. to be spent in charitable uses and meritorious deeds. Since the inclosure of the common fields in 1805 the property has consisted of about 34 acres of land and several cottages, producing about £50 yearly; 5s. yearly is distributed in cash to widows and the residue is applied in upkeep of the church. A tenement called the Town House, belonging to this charity, contiguous to the churchyard, was pulled down by Dr. Chauncy, rector 1723–62, who erected a new building at a short distance from the original site. In 1819 this was used by the parish as a poor-house, and still retains the name of the Town House.[104]

In 1714 Joseph Edmonds by his will gave £5, the interest to be applied to poor who usually receive the sacrament and resort to the parish church. A sum of 4s. yearly is distributed to poor widows in respect of this bequest.

In 1577 Philip Antwissell by his will gave 20s. yearly to the poor out of his lands called Osbourne's, at Michaelmas and Lady Day.

In 1629 Edmund Swallow by his will gave 20s. yearly, out of a farm called the Warren Farm, to the poor.

In the *Parliamentary Returns* of 1786 it is stated that George Roberts gave a rent-charge of £1 to the poor. This sum is paid out of Coles Green Farm.

The income from these three last-mentioned charities is distributed as follows: £2 10s. in bread to about fifty or sixty persons and 10s. in cash to widows and widowers.

In 1689 Arthur Pulter by his will gave £40 for apprenticing children. The endowment now consists of a sum of £43 1s. consols, producing £1 1s. 4d. yearly. The income is accumulated and applied as required in apprenticing.

In 1768 Anne Chauncy by her will gave £200, the interest to be expended in firing for the poor at Christmas, and £100, the interest to be spent in material for gowns for six poor women, the same women only to receive the benefaction once in three years. These sums were invested in £337 1s. 6d. consols, producing £8 8s. 4d. yearly.

In 1888 John Riggs Miller by deed gave £100, the interest to be applied in coals to the poor. This sum was invested in £103 4s. 6d. consols, producing £2 11s. 4d. yearly.

The several sums of stock are held by the official trustees, and the dividends are duly applied.

The school.—Henry Aldwin Soames by deed dated 24 June 1825 (enrolled in Chancery 17 October following) conveyed to himself and others a clear yearly rent-charge of £40 issuing out of a messuage at the corner of Bow Lane, Cheapside, to be applied in the education of children of poor cottagers. The annuity was applied towards the salaries of the schoolmaster and schoolmistress of the school, which was erected by the donor in 1829 on the village green.

HINXWORTH

Haingesteworde, Hainsteworde, Hamsteworde (xi cent.); Hingslewurd (xii cent.); Hengsteworth, Hyngstrigge, Heynceworth (xiii cent.); Hangteworth, Hynxworth (xiv cent.); Hyggextworth, Hyngxtworth (xv cent.); Henxworth (xvi cent.).

The parish of Hinxworth is in the extreme north of the county on the borders of Cambridgeshire and Bedfordshire. It lies low, the ground nowhere rising more than 172 ft. above the ordnance datum. An ancient track called the Ridgeway crosses the low land on the east of the parish, running parallel with the River Rhee, which forms the north-east boundary. The area is 1,463 acres, of which nearly three-quarters are arable land, and the remainder, except for some 8 acres of woodland, pasture.[1] The soil is loam and blue clay, the subsoil varies. The chief crops are wheat, barley and turnips. Coprolites have been dug in the parish and are still to be found. An Act authorizing the inclosure of the common fields was passed in 1802 and the award was made in 1806.[1a]

The nearest railway station is Baldock, 5 miles to the south, on the Hitchin and Cambridge branch of the Great Northern railway.

The Roman road through Hertfordshire, known further east as Stane Street, skirts the parish on the west and forms its south-west boundary. Not far from this road, on the borders of Hinxworth and

---

[90] Chan. Inq. p.m. 1 Edw. IV, no. 28.
[91] Clutterbuck, *Hist. and Antiq. of Herts.* iii, 519; see Inst. Bks. (P.R.O.), 1662, 1681, 1723, 1762.
[92] Inst. Bks. (P.R.O.), 1806.
[93] *Clergy List.*
[94] Ibid.
[95] Ibid.
[96] Ibid.
[97] Cussans, *Hist. of Herts. Odsey Hund.* 182.
[98] Ibid.
[99] Ibid.
[100] *Clergy List.*
[101] Inform. supplied by Mrs. A. Hobart-Hampden.
[102] *Clergy List.*
[103] Inform. supplied by Mrs. A. Hobart-Hampden.
[104] *Char. Com. Rep.* xxix, 451.
[1] Statistics from Bd. of Agric. (1905).
[1a] *Blue Bk. Incl. Awards*, 64.

HINXWORTH

Caldecote, Roman remains were discovered about 1720 by some workmen who were digging there for gravel with which to repair the road. These included several human bodies, urns and paterae and other objects, and a Danish or Dutch coin.[2] In 1810 a further find of great interest was made in the parish of two rare Greek coins or medals, one of Mithridates King of Pontus, and the other of Perseus King of Macedonia, both very well preserved.[2a] Near the River Rhee in the north of the parish and not far from the camp at Arbury Banks or Harboro, and near the Ridgeway, a hoard of more than 500 Roman coins was discovered. Near them were found other Roman remains.[2b]

The village of Hinxworth lies a little more than a mile to the east of the Roman road, with which it is connected by roads leading north-west and south-west, the former being continued on to Ashwell. The church[3] and rectory stand on the south-east of the angle formed by the road to Ashwell and that leading south-west to the Roman road, and the small village lies a little to the north-west of the church. At the beginning of the 18th century it had only thirty-five houses, of which three were alms-houses.[4]

Hinxworth Place, the manor-house, the residence of Mrs. Sale, stands about half a mile south of the village.[5] It consists of a rectangular block, measuring externally about 55 ft. by 38 ft., at the south end of which is a portion of a wing. The main block is faced externally with soft limestone, or clunch, and, judging from the characteristic features of the doorways and windows, a great part of the main walls must have been erected towards the close of the 15th century. The south wing appears to belong to the 16th century.

Beside the principal doorway is a small two-light window with arched and cusped heads, and square hood moulding over. This window is recessed from the face of the wall, and the sill is carried down so as to form a seat outside. The details of this window are almost identical with those of the low-side window in the south nave wall of the parish church. The principal entrance opens directly into the old hall, a room measuring about 21 ft. by 20 ft., now used as a kitchen. To the south of this is a smaller apartment used as a dining room, off which a passage has been cut to give access to the south wing from the kitchen. Between the kitchen and the dining room are two wide fireplaces placed back to back. Sixty years ago there were no partitions between the kitchen and the dining room, so that they formed practically one large room with the fireplaces in the centre. Each room is lighted by a large four-light early 17th-century window, with moulded stone transoms and mullions and a small cornice over. In the kitchen is a long narrow Jacobean oak table with heavy moulded legs. Extending the whole length of the main building on the west side is a low one-story building, the north end of which is a later addition built of old material. It is covered by the roof of the main building, which is continued down so as to form a lean-to roof. There are three doorways in the separating wall, all having splayed jambs and four-centred arches. There is a similar external doorway on the west side, and another now built up at the north end. There are two three-light windows, one four-light and one single-light window, with stone-moulded mullions and cusped-pointed arch-heads, similar to the window on the east front, and all late 15th-century work. This part of the house has been divided into scullery, larder and stores. The modern passage by the dining room leads to the south wing, the lower part of which is of brick, the upper story being of timber, overhanging 18 in. on the south and west fronts. It was originally one large room, with a four-centred stone doorway at the east end, similar to that from the dining room, but now there is a small lobby between the outer door and the old parlour. There is a built-up external doorway in the south wall, and a large five-light window, with moulded stone mullions

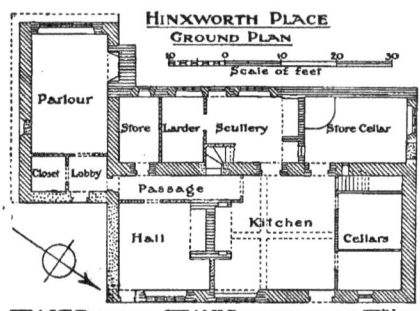

HINXWORTH PLACE GROUND PLAN

Scale of feet

Parlour | Store | Larder | Scullery | Store Cellar
Closet | Lobby | Passage
Hall | Kitchen | Cellars

■ 15TH CENTURY. ▨ 16TH CENTURY & LATER. ▦ MOD.

and transoms, in the west wall. In this window are three interesting shields with the arms of former owners, one bearing the date 1570. The colour is on the surface of the glass only, or as it is called 'flashed,' such as was usual at that period, the older glass being stained right through. There is a good stone fireplace in the parlour, the details of which have a more classic feeling than the 17th-century work in the main building. The fireplace has moulded jambs and straight lintel, the mouldings being late Gothic in character. On either side is a short three-quarter-round column with rude Ionic volutes, above which is a long rectangular fluted and panelled pilaster, supporting a moulded stone cornice or mantel shelf. Over the fireplace and under the cornice is a frieze with four plain sunk panels. There is a large room over the parlour, open to the roof, which is plastered internally, the only timber showing being

---

[2] Brayley, *Beauties of Engl. and Wales*, vii, 176; Salmon, *Hist. of Herts.* 339; Camden, *Brit.* (ed. Gough, 1789), i, 342.
[2a] Lewis, *Topog. Dict. of Engl.* ii, 520.
[2b] Cussans, op. cit. *Odsey Hund.* 316.

[3] In the 16th century there were many fine trees in the churchyard which the farmer of the parsonage was charged with having cut down (Star Chamb. Proc. Edw. VI, bdle. 5, no. 81).
[4] Chauncy, *Hist. and Antiq. of Herts.* 53.
[5] Cussans, *Hist. of Herts. Odsey Hund.*

10, states that the house was probably on the site of a cell of the Cistercian Convent of Pipewell, Northants, but there seems to be no evidence of such a cell having existed. Hinxworth Place is said to be identical with the manor-house of Pulters Manor (ex inform. Mrs. Sale).

a massive oak moulded tie-beam, with a considerable camber, a tree with a natural bend having evidently been utilized for the purpose. The upper floor in the main building contains some four-centred doorways of stone, in several of which the original iron studded door remains, and in the north bedroom is a stone fireplace of the usual early 17th-century type, with moulded four-centred arch inclosed by a square moulding above, and with the usual ornamental stops to the mouldings.

There is no trace of any main stair having existed, access to the upper floor being by two narrow wooden ones. All the chimneys are of brick, and are plain modern rebuildings. The roofs are tiled. Preserved in the house are two large iron spring man-traps, and the original notice to beware of them may still be seen on one of the barns.

Bury End, which is situated nearly opposite the church, at the point where the Ridgeway joins the village street, is of interest, as it is partly surrounded by a fragment of a homestead moat.[6]

There is a Wesleyan chapel in Hinxworth, which lies on the south side of the village. Its site was purchased in 1831 for £7 by public subscription among the Methodists.[7] The village school was built in 1876. It stands on the north side of the village street west of the church.

Among those who have held the living of Hinxworth may be noted the Rev. Percival Stockdale (1736–1811), who in 1756 accepted a commission in the army and was attached to the expedition sent by Admiral Byng to relieve the garrison of Minorca. He was ordained deacon in 1759, and coming to London became intimate with Johnson, Garrick, Goldsmith and other literary men. In 1779 he made a complaint, probably groundless, that the agreement to bring out the lives of the English poets had been originally entrusted to him. In 1780 he was presented by Sir Adam Gordon to the rectory of Hinxworth.[8]

MANORS HINXWORTH [9] In the time of Edward the Confessor was divided between Ethelmer of Benington and his tenants, the sokemen of the king, the archbishop and others. After the Conquest it was held by three tenants in chief, William de Ow,[10] Hardwin de Scales,[11] and Peter de Valognes.[12] Peter de Valognes's holding was a berewick of his holding at Ashwell, and the overlordship descended with his manor there (q.v.) until the death without issue of Christine de Mandeville Countess of Essex in 1233. Her lands in Ashwell seem to have reverted to Robert Fitz Walter, her brother, but the overlordship of her lands in Hinxworth appears to have remained with Maud, her husband's sister and heir, whose son Humphrey de Bohun was created Earl of Essex,[13] for in 1345 Humphrey de Bohun appears as overlord of a manor of Hinxworth which was held of him by Henry Gernet and Joan his wife.[14] These were the tenants also of Ashwell, with which manor Hinxworth had descended in sub-tenancy until this date, after which there is no further trace of it as a separate property.

HINXWORTH PLACE: PRINCIPAL ENTRANCE DOORWAY

Hardwin de Scales's lands were divided between his sons Richard and Hugh. Their descendants were still holding part of a knight's fee in Hinxworth in 1207–8 when William grandson of Richard de Scales claimed possession of the holding against Hugh grandson of Hugh. The suit was decided in favour of Hugh.[15] No further record of the Scales in Hinxworth appears. Theobald was tenant of this fee in 1086, and his descendants the Fitz Ralphs appear subsequently as holding a third of a fee. In 1303 this was held of William Fitz Ralph by Henry de' Aula.[16] It descended to William de Aula, from whom it passed to William Zerde, who was holding it in 1428.[17] After this date the fee can be no further traced.

The land of William de Ow in Hinxworth (held under him in 1086 by two knights) was apparently granted with other estates by Henry I to Walter son of Richard de Clare,[18] on whose death they passed to his nephew Gilbert de Clare,[19] who was created Earl of Pembroke in 1138.[20] He was succeeded by his

---

[6] *Hist. Monum. Com. Rep. Herts.* 116.
[7] Close, 2 Will. IV, pt. lxxv, no. 9.
[8] *Dict. Nat. Biog.*
[9] *V.C.H. Herts.* i, 276, 328*a*, 338*a*, 339*a*.
[10] Ibid. 328*a*.
[11] Ibid. 339*a*.
[12] Ibid. 338*a*.
[13] G.E.C. *Complete Peerage*, s.v. Essex.
[14] Chan. Inq. p.m. 19 Edw. III, no. 36. The Gernets held land in Hinxworth as early as 1323 (*Cal. Close*, 1327–30, p. 574).
[15] *Abbrev. Plac.* (Rec. Com.), 99.
[16] *Feud. Aids*, ii, 432. For descent of Fitz Ralphs see manor of Broadfield.
[17] *Feud. Aids*, ii, 474.
[18] *Gen.* (new ser.), xviii, 167.
[19] Ibid.
[20] G.E.C. *Complete Peerage*, s.v. Pembroke.

234

son Richard de Clare,[21] who died in 1176, when his estates passed to his daughter Isabel.[22] She married Sir William Marshal, created Earl of Pembroke,[23] and with her husband was holding land in Hinxworth in 1196.[24] William Marshal died in 1219,[25] and his estates passed in rapid succession through the hands of his five sons, all of whom died without issue.[26] On the death of the youngest, Anselm Marshal,[27] in 1245, their lands were divided among his five sisters and co-heirs.[28] The eldest of these,

MARSHAL. *Party or and vert a lion gules.*

BIGOD. *Or a cross gules.*

Maud, married Hugh le Bigod Earl of Norfolk,[29] and her grandson Roger[30] claimed view of frankpledge and assize of bread and ale in Hinxworth in 1277–8.[31] He died in 1306[32] holding a quarter of a fee in Hinxworth.[33] In consequence of his having rebelled against the king his estates reverted to the Crown.[34] His land in Hinxworth was amongst the estates which the king granted in dower to his widow Alice.[35] In 1312 Thomas Plantagenet, fifth son of Edward I, was created Earl of Norfolk, and he received all the lands of the late earl.[36] He died in 1338 and his lands were divided between his two daughters and co-heirs.[37] The elder of these, Margaret, married Lord Segrave.[38] The younger, Alice, married Edward de Montague, and, with the consent of her sister Margaret and her husband, certain estates, including the fifth part of a fee which her father had held in Hinxworth, were assigned to her.[39] Her daughter Joan married William Ufford Earl of Suffolk.[40] She had no children and died in 1375.[41] Her husband died in 1382 seised of a fifth of a knight's fee in Hinxworth.[42] The second sister and co-heir of Anselm Marshal, Isabel, married Gilbert de Clare Earl of Gloucester and Hertford,[43] who was assessed for half

CLARE. *Or three cheverons gules.*

a fee in Hinxworth in 1303,[44] and who died seised of it in 1314.[45] A third sister and co-heir of Anselm Marshal[46] who had rights in Hinxworth was Joan wife of Warin de Munchensy. Her title passed to her daughter Joan wife of William de Valence, created Earl of Pembroke.[47] Their son Aymer de Valence inherited a quarter of a knight's fee in Hinxworth, which he had alienated in 1303.[48] After this date the different holdings cannot be distinguished except by their under-tenants, who are numerous and not easy to trace, for the land seems to have been much divided up as it was before the Conquest.

VALENCE. *Burelly argent and azure an orle of martlets gules.*

Under William Marshal a hide of land was held in 1196 by Eustace son of Airic Longi of Weston, and was in that year granted by him to Richard de Milkley.[49] In 1278 Robert de Milkley was summoned to show by what warrant he held view of frankpledge in Hinxworth,[50] but he withdrew his claim in favour of the overlord Roger Bigod. In 1287, however, he was said to hold this and other liberties in Hinxworth of the said Roger.[51] This fee is returned in 1306 (on the death of Roger Bigod) as held by Walter le Band,[52] and Thomas le Baud was holding it in 1428.[53]

Another holding was that which in the 13th century was in the tenure of a family named Stopham. Ralph de Stopham and Milisent his wife claimed view of frankpledge and assize of bread and ale in Hinxworth in 1286–7.[54] This holding, described as a quarter of a knight's fee, was in the hands of Isabel de Stopham in 1303.[55] In 1428 it had become the property of Thomas Bryd, then a minor.[56] A Roger Brian also held lands and rents in Hinxworth in 1292,[57] in which year he granted 2 acres of land and 100s. rent to a chaplain in the chapel of St. John the Baptist at Buntingford, retaining other land there. This land, described as a quarter of a knight's fee, he was still holding in 1303.[58]

At the end of the 15th century these different holdings seem to have been amalgamated in the manor of *HINXWORTH* or *WATTONBURY*, which was then owned by Richard Waferer, who leased it in 1471–2 to John Ward, alderman of London.[59] It descended to Thomas Waferer of Sundridge, co. Kent, who in 1521 sold it to John Bowles of Wallington, co. Herts.[60] John Bowles died in 1543,[61] and the manor passed to his grandson Thomas Bowles,[62] who

---

[21] G.E.C. *Complete Peerage,* s.v. Pembroke.
[22] Ibid. [23] Ibid.
[24] Feet of F. Herts. file 1, no. 2 (7 Ric. I); see also Pipe R. 22 Hen. II (Pipe R. Soc.), 6.
[25] G.E.C. loc. cit.
[26] Ibid. [27] Ibid. [28] Ibid. [29] Ibid.
[30] G.E.C. *Complete Peerage,* s.v. Norfolk.
[31] *Plac. de Quo Warr.* (Rec. Com.), 290.
[32] G.E.C. loc. cit.
[33] Chan. Inq. p.m. 35 Edw. I, no. 46.
[34] G.E.C. loc. cit.
[35] *Cal. Close,* 1302–7, p. 511.
[36] G.E.C. loc. cit.
[37] Ibid.
[38] Ibid.
[39] *Cal. Close,* 1339–41, p. 39.
[40] G.E.C. *Complete Peerage,* s.v. Suffolk.
[41] Ibid.
[42] Chan. Inq. p.m. 5 Ric. II, no. 57.
[43] G.E.C. *Complete Peerage,* s.v. Pembroke.
[44] *Feud. Aids,* ii, 432.
[45] Chan. Inq. p.m. 8 Edw. II, no. 68.
[46] G.E.C. *Complete Peerage,* s.v. Pembroke.
[47] *Feud. Aids,* ii, 432; G.E.C. *Complete Peerage.*
[48] *Feud. Aids,* ii, 432.
[49] Feet of F. Herts. 7 Ric. I, file 100, no. 2.
[50] *Plac. de Quo Warr.* (Rec. Com.), 290. [51] Assize R. 325.
[52] Chan. Inq. p.m. 35 Edw. I, no. 46.
[53] *Feud. Aids,* ii, 447. See Milkley in Standon. [54] Assize R. 325.
[55] *Feud. Aids,* ii, 432.
[56] Ibid. 447.
[57] Inq. a.q.d. file 18, no. 13 (20 Edw. I); *Cal. Pat.* 1281–92, p. 486.
[58] *Feud. Aids,* ii, 432.
[59] Early Chan. Proc. bdle. 233, no. 80.
[60] Com. Pleas D. Enr. Hil. 13 Hen. VIII; Feet of F. Herts. Hil. 13 Hen. VIII.
[61] Chan. Inq. p.m. (Ser. 2), lxviii, 14.
[62] Ibid.

A HISTORY OF HERTFORDSHIRE

in 1556 sold it to William Hyde.[63] It was sold by William Hyde before 1571 to Jasper Smyth and Elizabeth his wife, for in that year they conveyed it to Thomas Norwood.[64] Thomas Norwood died in February 1587-8 and left the manor to Thomas Norwood, third son of his son John Norwood.[65] He in 1613-14 sold it to Thomas Draner of Hoxton, co. Middlesex.[66] Thomas Draner held the manor till his death in 1632. Having no children he left it by will to his cousin William Boteler for life with remainder in tail-male to his great-nephew Francis Halton (a younger son of Sir Roger Halton, son of Joan, Thomas Draner's sister)[67] with contingent remainder successively to his great-nephews Draner and Henry Massingberd,[68] the sons of Frances daughter of Joan, who had married Thomas Massingberd of Bratoft, co. Lincs.[69] Thomas Draner's nearest heir was his great-great-niece Elizabeth Halton,[70] then aged nine, who in 1665 with her second husband James Moseley[71] quitclaimed all right in the manor of Hinxworth.[72] William Boteler and Francis Halton, the first and second devisees, seem to have died without children, for the manor came to Sir Draner Massingberd, knighted in 1660-1,[73] and was held after his death by his widow.[74] On her death it descended to her son[75] Burrell Massingberd, who was holding the manor in 1705.[76] In 1709 he sold it to Sussex Sell of Hinxworth,[77] who with his wife Sarah sold it in 1711 to John Izard[78] of Baldock, draper.[79] By the will of John Izard dated 25 April 1713 and proved in August 1714, Hinxworth was left to his wife Ellen for life with remainder to his son Robert.[80] Robert Izard married Grace Cox in 1719 and had a daughter Grace who was seised of the manor on his death. In 1744 she married Thomas Daniel of Devizes, co. Wilts., but died childless a year later, when she left the manor to her husband.[81] John Izard (elder brother of Robert) quitclaimed all right in the manor to Thomas Daniel in 1754,[82] and the latter continued to hold it until 1766, when he sold it to Robert Thurgood of Baldock.[83] Sarah, daughter of the latter, married Thomas Clutterbuck,[84] and by her father's will dated 26 March 1774[85] inherited the manor of Hinxworth. On her death in 1788,[86] by the terms of the will,[87] it descended to her son Robert Clutterbuck, the historian. He died in 1831 and was succeeded by his son Robert,[88] who died in 1879.[89] The manor was bought of his trustees by Mr. John Sale in 1881. He died in 1894, and the manor is now held by his trustees.

The manor of *CANTLOWBURY* (Cantilbury, Cantlebury, Cantlobury, xvi cent.) is not mentioned by name before 1521-2.[90] It probably took its name from the family of Cantlow or Cantelupe, who had land in Hinxworth as early as 1176, when Walter de Cantelupe held property there.[91] It seems probable that their lands in Hinxworth were not inconsiderable, for they owned the advowson of Hinxworth Church,[92] which continued with their descendants until 1346.[93] In spite of this no further record can be found of what land they held. The manor of Cantlowbury was held in 1522 by Thomas Waferer,[94] who also held the manor of Hinxworthbury *alias* Wattonbury (q.v.). From this date the two manors descend together.[95] The manor-house of Cantlowbury was for some time held by a family of the name of Harvey, but was pulled down about 1865.[95a]

The priory of Newnham in Bedfordshire held lands in Hinxworth in the 13th century, and in 1278 the prior was summoned to show by what warrant he held view of frankpledge and assize of bread and ale there. The prior, however, withdrew all claim to these liberties.[96] His lands and rents in Hinxworth were valued in 1291 at £1 10s.,[97] and described as a quarter of a knight's fee in 1303.[98] These lands remained with the priory until the 16th century,[99] and it is probable that on its dissolution by Henry VIII[100] they became absorbed in the manor of Hinxworth.

The reputed manor of *PULTERS* (Polters, xviii cent. ; Potters, xix cent.) seems to be first mentioned by name in the year 1782. Chauncy says that it was held in the reign of Edward IV by a family of the name of Pulter, who held it of the king for a yearly rent of 10s. 8d.[1] From them he says it was sold to John Ward, son of Richard Ward of Holden, co. York., who was Lord Mayor of London for one month in 1484.[2] The Wards appear to have been connected with Hinxworth as early as 1453, for Simon Ward, who died in that year, was buried in Hinxworth Church.[2] John Ward, who placed a window in Hinxworth Church, certainly held land in Hinxworth, for Chauncy says he gave cow commons to maintain the church in repair, the people of Hinxworth being taxed according to the number of cows they had on the common.[4] But there seems to be no direct proof that his lands were the manor of Pulters. Chauncy says that after the death of John Ward in 1487 his lands in Hinxworth were conveyed to John Lambard, master of the Mercers' Company and alderman of London.[5] John Lambert

---

[63] Feet of F. Div. Co. Mich. 3 & 4 Phil. and Mary.
[64] Feet of F. Herts. East. 13 Eliz.
[65] Chan. Inq. p.m. (Ser. 2), ccxvii, 117.
[66] Feet of F. Herts. Hil. 11 Jas. I.
[67] *Lincs. Pedigrees* (Harl. Soc.), ii, 657, 446.
[68] Chan. Inq. p.m. (Ser. 2), ccclxxiii, 34.
[69] *Lincs. Pedigrees* (Harl. Soc.), ii, 657, 446.
[70] Ibid.
[71] Ibid. 446.
[72] Feet of F. Herts. Mich. 17 Chas. II.
[73] *Lincs. Pedigrees* (Harl. Soc.), ii, 657.
[74] Chauncy, op. cit. 31.
[75] *Lincs. Pedigrees* (Harl. Soc.), ii, 660.
[76] Recov. R. Hil. 4 Anne, rot. 86.
[77] Clutterbuck, *Hist. and Antiq. of Herts.* iii, 526.
[78] Feet of F. Herts. Hil. 9 Anne.

[79] P.C.C. 161 Aston.
[80] Ibid.
[81] Clutterbuck, op. cit. iii, 524.
[82] Feet of F. Div. Co. Trin. 27 & 28 Geo. II.
[83] Clutterbuck, loc. cit.
[84] Ibid.
[85] Ibid. ; P.C.C. 74 Alexander.
[86] Clutterbuck, loc. cit.
[87] P.C.C. 74 Alexander.
[88] Cussans, op. cit. *Odsey Hund.* 9.
[89] Ibid. 140.
[90] Com. Pleas D. Enr. Hil. 13 Hen. VIII.
[91] *Pipe R.* 22 Hen. II (Pipe R. Soc.), 6 ; 23 *Hen. II* (Pipe R. Soc.), 150 ; Pipe R. 7 Ric. I, m. 6.
[92] Cussans, loc. cit.
[93] *Vide* advowson.
[94] Com. Pleas D. Enr. Hil. 13 Hen. VIII.

[95] Feet of F. Div. Co. Mich. 3 & 4 Phil. and Mary ; Herts. Mich. 3 & 4 Phil. and Mary ; Div. Co. Trin. 27 & 28 Geo. II ; Recov. R. East. 9 Geo. IV, rot. 12.
[95a] Cussans, op. cit. *Odsey Hund.* 10 et seq.
[96] *Plac. de Quo Warr.* (Rec. Com.), 290.
[97] *Pope Nich. Tax.* (Rec. Com.), 51*b*.
[98] *Feud. Aids*, ii, 432.
[99] Ibid. 447 ; *Valor Eccl.* (Rec. Com.), iv, 187.
[100] Dugdale, *Mon. Angl.* vi, 372.
[1] Chauncy, op. cit. 32.
[2] Ibid. ; Kingsford, *Chron. of London*, 193.
[3] Chauncy, loc. cit.
[4] Ibid.
[5] Ibid.

Hinxworth Place from the North-east

Hinxworth Place from the South-west

or Lambard was holding lands in Hinxworth of the manor of Hinxworth at the end of the 15th century,[6] but there is nothing to show that they represent the manor of Pulters. In the 16th century this holding had descended to Thomas Lambert, and included a capital messuage.[7] Channey says Thomas Lambert was charged in Exchequer for this manor by the name of Pulters with a yearly rent of 10s. 8d.[8]

According to some proceedings in the court of Chancery Thomas Lambert fell into financial difficulties. It appears that Andrew Gray of the Inner Temple promised to give him introductions which would lead to an advantageous marriage,[9] and in return Thomas Lambert granted him a lease of his lands in Hinxworth on very favourable terms.[10] He eventually mortgaged his property to Gray.[11] As a natural consequence he brought a suit against Gray[12] in which he said he had never received the introduc-

latter was divided between the daughters of the first Viscount Bayning. Pulters was then sold to Edward Pecke,[17] from whom it descended to his son William Pecke,[18] whose son Edward Pecke was holding the manor in 1700.[19] It passed finally with the advowson to Richard Holden.[20] On his death it descended to his son Robert Holden,[21] and in 1782 was held by the latter's two daughters, Elizabeth wife of Richard Webb and Charlotte wife of Sir Adam Gordon.[22] It finally became the exclusive property of Elizabeth,[23] and she with her husband Richard Webb, her son Richard Holden Webb, and his wife Frances[24] sold it in 1801 to Henricus Octavus Roe,[25] apparently in trust for Robert Clutterbuck,[26] who held the manor of Hinxworth. In 1828 Robert Clutterbuck suffered a recovery of Pulters,[27] after which date it became merged in the manor of Hinxworth.

HINXWORTH PLACE: PART OF SOUTH-WEST FRONT

tions nor been enabled to make a good marriage.[13] The lands, however, were probably retained by Gray,[14] who died in 1614 and whose monument is in the parish church. From him they appear to have passed to Andrew Bayning,[15] who held, besides the advowson of Hinxworth, four messuages, two dove-houses, four gardens and four orchards, 489 acres of land and 10s. rent in Hinxworth, Caldecote and Ashwell.[16] These descended with the advowson (q.v.) until the

CHURCH The church of ST. NICHOLAS consists of chancel 20 ft. by 16 ft., nave 42 ft. 6 in. by 20 ft., west tower 10 ft. 6 in. square, and south porch 12 ft. by 10 ft., all dimensions taken internally. The walls are of flint with stone dressings and the low-pitched roofs are covered with lead.

The general walling of nave and west tower, the north and south doorways and the windows adjoining

[6] Early Chan. Proc. bdle. 233, no. 80.
[7] Chan. Proc. (Ser. 2), bdle. 110, no. 54.
[8] Chauncy, loc. cit. He gives as reference Cur. Augment., but it is insufficient for the document to be traced.
[9] Chan. Proc. (Ser. 2), bdle. 110, no. 54.
[10] Ibid.
[11] Ibid.; see also bdle. 114, no. 57.
[12] Ibid. bdle. 110, no. 54.
[13] Ibid.
[14] Clutterbuck, op. cit. iii, 526.
[15] Ibid.
[16] Chan. Inq. p.m. (Ser. 2), ccclxxx, 127.
[17] Clutterbuck, op. cit. iii, 526; see Feet of F. Div. Co. Mich. 16 Chas. II.
[18] Clutterbuck, loc. cit.
[19] Chauncy, op. cit. 31.
[20] Clutterbuck, loc. cit.
[21] Ibid.
[22] See Feet of F. Div. Co. Mich. 22 Geo. III.
[23] Clutterbuck, loc. cit.
[24] Ibid.
[25] Feet of F. Herts. Trin. 41 Geo. III.
[26] Clutterbuck, loc. cit.
[27] Recov. R. East. 9 Geo. IV, rot. 12.

them on the west, belong to the middle of the 14th century ; the west window of the tower and the north, south and west belfry openings were inserted later in the century [28.9] ; the east belfry opening may be original. About 1440 the chancel arch was pulled down and built about 2 ft. further east, and the two large nave windows with their niches and the low-side window were inserted, and the upper passage to the rood-loft roughly formed eastward towards the new chancel arch. The clearstory was raised about the close of the 15th century and the south porch was erected, and the chancel arch recut to fit it under the new low-pitched roof, the former roof having been high-pitched, as shown by the marks on the east face of the tower. The chancel was rebuilt of brick about the beginning of the 18th century. In 1887 the

the north and south walls of the nave shows the old position of the chancel arch. In the north wall of the nave is a large 15th-century three-light window with tracery in the head under a four-centred arch ; in the east jamb is a canopied niche with carved crockets and finials and cusped pedestal. In the south wall is a similar window, and to the east of it is a low-side window of two cinquefoiled lights under a square head, of the same date as the larger windows ; in the south-east angle of the nave is a canopied niche very similar to that on the north side ; both niches have traces of colour. The north door is of 14th-century date, of two hollow-chamfered orders, but the label has been cut off. The south doorway is similar to the north. Both doorways retain their original oak doors, with plain iron hinges ; the south

HINXWORTH CHURCH FROM THE SOUTH-EAST

church was restored, a new roof put over the nave, and stone windows inserted in the chancel. The nave and tower walls are embattled.

At the north-east angle of the nave externally the 14th-century external angle of the nave wall may be seen ; the recess adjoining it, which is corbelled over above, shows the 15th-century extension of the nave eastward. At the north-east part of the nave internally is the entrance doorway to the rood-loft stair, which projects on the outer face of the wall ; it is of 14th-century work, but the original upper doorway is blocked, and a rough passage tunnelled through the wall eastward to reach the 15th-century chancel arch ; some 14th-century moulded stones have been used in its construction ; the rough state of

[28.9] In 1364-5 Nicholas de Hyngestworth (Hinxworth) left 20s. for the repair of the belfry (Court of Husting Will).

doorway has deep sockets in the jambs for the oak bar. The floor of the nave is about 2 ft. lower than the ground outside. To the west of the north doorway is a 14th-century two-light window, cusped and under a square head. The label has the wave moulding. The opposite window in the south wall of the nave was a similar two-light window, but one light has been blocked by the south porch, and the remaining light widened by the insertion of a keystone in the apex of the arch. The nave roof is modern, but contains four figures of monks holding shields, from the old roof ; three of the shields are plain, the fourth is barred.

The south porch is of late 15th-century work ; on the west side is a three-light window, with trefoiled cusps, under a four-centred head : a similar window on the east side has been blocked. The entrance

238

doorway has a moulded four-centred arch under a square head.

The tower arch, c. 1350, is of two splayed orders, with semi-octagonal jambs and moulded capitals and bases; the west window is an insertion of the latter part of the century, and is of two cusped lights with a large cusped opening in the head; it has been repaired with cement. Underneath the window a rough doorway has been cut in comparatively recent times. The tower, which has no stairway, is of two stages, with embattled top, with moulded string-course under, at the angles of which are carvings, that at the south-west representing a soldier's head armed with basinet and camail of the 14th century. In the north, south and west faces of the belfry stage are two-light cusped openings, similar in character to the west window and of late 14th-century work. On the east face is a small trefoil-headed opening, above the apex of the old steep roof, which is probably original.

The font is modern, but the remains of the old one, consisting of a circular basin with a plain square top, lie in the garden of the Glebe Farm. It appears to be of the late 12th century. The communion table is of Italian workmanship, with claw feet on balls and a marble top. The pulpit is of plain panelled oak of the 18th century.

In the porch is a portion of a stone coffin lid, with the lower part of a cross, and the ends of scrolls, probably of late 13th or early 14th-century work.

On the north wall of the chancel is a brass of a man and his wife; the inscription has gone, but is given by Chauncy as being the figures of Simon Ward, 1453, and his wife, 1481; the slab from which this brass was taken lies at the north doorway. On the chancel floor is a brass of a man with his wife and children, one of whom is a priest. According to Chauncy this brass represents John Lambert, citizen and mercer of London, who died in 1487. There are some shields; one bears the arms of the Mercers' Company, another a merchant's mark; these are of brass, but there are three of lead, one of which bears a saltire; the other two bear a fesse between three defaced animals, probably lambs, as a punning coat of Lambert. There is a brass inscription to 'Andrewe Grey,' who died in 1614.

There are six bells: the treble by Mears & Stainbank, 1908; second by J. Briant, 1820; third and fourth by Miles Graye, 1651; fifth and tenor by J. Briant, 1825 and 1820 respectively.

The communion plate consists of cup and paten, 1762, and two pewter plates.

The registers are in two books: (i) baptisms and burials 1739 to 1812; (ii) marriages 1754 to 1812.

HINXWORTH

ADVOWSON The advowson of the church was held in the 13th century by the Cantlowes. William de Cantlowe presented in 1218 and 1236[30]; he died in 1238-9[31] and was succeeded by his son William, who died in 1250-1.[32] He was succeeded by his son, also named William, who died in 1253-4.[33] During the minority of the latter's heir George[34] the right of presentation was exercised by the king in 1273.[35] George was still living in May 1273,[36] but died some time before February 1274,[37] and his lands were divided between his two sisters, Millicent, who married first John de Montalt and secondly Eudo la Zouch of Harringworth, and Joan, who married John de Hastings.[38] The advowson of Hinxworth was inherited by the elder sister Millicent, who as Millicent de Montalt presented in 1293 and 1295.[39] It descended to her son by her second marriage, William la Zouch,[40] who presented in 1303.[41] He in 1344 alienated the advowson to the Abbot and convent of Pipewell, co. Northants,[42] perhaps on account of their poverty, for in 1322 the monks had been so poor that they had been obliged to leave their abbey for a time.[43] The advowson was held by the Abbot and convent of Pipewell (who do not seem to have appropriated the church) until their dissolution in 1538-9,[44] after which in 1545 the advowson of the rectory was granted to Anthony Forster.[45] From Forster it passed to John Brockett, who in February 1561-2 granted the next presentation to John Adams, but on his presenting refused to admit his nominee.[46] Brockett probably conveyed to Andrew Bayning[47] of Mark Lane, London, who died seised in 1610 and left it to his brother Paul Bayning for life with remainder to his son Paul Bayning the younger.[48] Paul Bayning died in 1616,[49] and the advowson passed to his son Paul,[50] who married Anne daughter of Sir Henry Glenham (afterwards Viscountess Dorchester),[51] and who in March 1627-8 was created Viscount Bayning of Sudbury.[52] He died in 1629 and his son Paul being a minor[53] the king presented in 1636.[54] The Viscountess Dorchester, however, opposed the king's right to present,[55] and in consequence the Bishop of Lincoln refused to admit the king's nominee, Dr. Andrew Clare.[56] A three years' lawsuit followed,[57] during the course of which Paul Viscount Bayning died in 1638,[58] and the king as guardian of his two daughters and co-heirs Anne and Penelope, who were minors, appointed Robert Cheslen on the resignation of Dr. Clare.[59] The Viscountess Dorchester died in February 1638-9[60] before the close of the suit, but in 1639 judgement was given in her favour,[61] and the Bishop of Lincoln being suspended at that date, a writ was addressed to Archbishop Laud to admit her

---

[30] Cussans, op. cit. *Odsey Hund.* 14.
[31] Dugdale, *Baronage*, i, 732.
[32] Ibid.
[33] Ibid.
[34] Ibid.
[35] Cussans, loc. cit.; *Cal. Pat.* 1272-81, p. 5 (styled son of Nicholas instead of son of William).
[36] *Cal. Pat.* 1272-81, p. 9.
[37] Ibid. p. 43.
[38] Dugdale, *Baronage*, i, 732.
[39] Cussans, loc. cit.
[40] G.E.C. *Complete Peerage*, s.v. Zouch of Haryngworth.
[41] Cussans, loc. cit.

[42] *Cal. Pat.* 1343-5, pp. 198, 243; Feet of F. Herts. East. 20 Edw. III, no. 317.
[43] Dugdale, *Mon. Angl.* v, 433.
[44] Ibid.
[45] Pat. 37 Hen. VIII, pt. iv, m. 9.
[46] Ct. of Req. bdle. 30, no. 14.
[47] Chan. Inq. p.m. (Ser. 2), ccclxxx, 127.
[48] Ibid.
[49] Chan. Inq. p.m. (Ser. 2), ccclviii, 158.
[50] Ibid.
[51] G.E.C. *Complete Peerage*, s.v. Bayning and Dorchester.

[52] Ibid. s.v. Bayning; Chan. Inq. p.m. (Ser. 2), ccclviii, 158.
[53] Ibid.
[54] *Cal. S. P. Dom.* 1635-6, p. 430.
[55] *Hist. MSS. Com. Rep.* xii, App. ii, 120; *Cal. S. P. Dom.* 1640-1, p. 459.
[56] *Hist. MSS. Com. Rep.* xii, App. ii, 120.
[57] *Cal. S. P. Dom.* 1640-1, p. 459.
[58] G.E.C. *Complete Peerage*, s.v. Bayning; Harl. MS. 760, fol. 162*b*.
[59] *Cal. S. P. Dom.* 1638-9, p. 163.
[60] G.E.C. *Complete Peerage*, s.v. Bayning.
[61] *Cal. S. P. Dom.* 1640-1, p. 459.

nominee, Daniel Falkner.[62] The archbishop at first refused to admit Falkner on the ground that he must take care of the king's title,[63] but admitted him finally. This reluctance was one of the matters brought against him in his trial in February 1640–1.[64] Anne and Penelope Bayning both died without issue, Penelope in 1657, Anne in 1659.[65] Anne's husband, the Earl of Oxford,[66] presented in 1660.[67] The advowson then reverted to the heirs of Paul first Viscount Bayning, and was divided among the descendants of his four daughters, Cecily, Anne, Mary and Elizabeth.[68] Cecily married Henry Pierrepont Marquess of Dorchester,[69] and their daughter Anne married in 1658 John Manners, styled Lord Roos, from whom she was divorced in 1666,[70] and married secondly John Tildesley. In 1674 she was holding an eighth part of the advowson.[70a] William Pierrepont, evidently her heir, suffered a recovery of it in 1703.[71] The second daughter Anne married Henry Murray,[72] whilst the third daughter Mary seems to be represented in 1661 by Arthur Gorges and Mary his wife.[73] They sold all right in the advowson to Edward Pecke in 1664.[74] Mary the daughter and co-heir of Anne and Henry Murray married Sir Roger Bradshaigh, bart.,[75] and her son Sir Roger Bradshaigh in 1697 conveyed to his father-in-law Sir John Guise[76] his mother's share in the advowson of Hinxworth.[77] The fourth and youngest daughter of Paul Viscount Bayning, Elizabeth, married Francis Lennard Lord Dacre,[78] and her son Thomas Lennard, who was created Earl of Sussex in 1674,[79] suffered a recovery of it in 1704.[80] The whole of the advowson seems to have been acquired by Richard Holden (see Pulters), who presented in 1727.[81] On his death it descended to his son Robert, who presented in 1739 and 1777.[82] Robert Holden left two daughters and co-heirs, Charlotte and Elizabeth ; Charlotte married the Rev. Sir Adam Gordon and sold her share in the advowson to the Rev. Thomas Whitehurst in 1785.[83] Elizabeth married Richard Webb[84] and sold her share in the advowson also to the Rev. Thomas Whitehurst in 1787.[85] Thomas Whitehurst held the whole of the advowson till 1791, when he sold it to William Parkins,[86] possibly in trust for Richard Parkins, who presented in 1795.[87] In 1797 Robert Albion Cox presented.[88] By 1822 the advowson had come into the hands of John Lafont,[89] the rector of Hinxworth, who held it till his death, which took place between 1840 and 1844. It was held by his trustees until 1892, when it came into the possession of the Bishop of St. Albans, in whom it is still vested.

Meeting-places for Protestant Dissenters in Hinxworth were registered in 1763 and 1823.[90]

In 1797 Jane Brooks, by her will proved in the Archdeaconry Court of Huntingdon 24 January, gave £160, the interest to be distributed equally among the poor of Hinxworth, Baldock, Biggleswade, and Stotfold. The property now consists of 7 a. 3 r. 18 p. of land at Stocking Pelham, in the county of Hertford, and the churchwardens receive one-quarter of the rent, amounting to £1 2s., which is distributed in bread on Good Friday and at Christmas.

CHARITIES

The Wesleyan Methodist chapel comprised in deed of 1831 is regulated by a scheme of the Charity Commissioners of 1882.

KELSHALL

Chelesele (x, xi cent.) ; Kelshulle, Kelshille (xiii cent.).

The parish of Kelshall, containing about 4,703 acres, lies on the chalk hills. On its eastern side the land rises as high as 519 ft. above the ordnance datum, but falls to 300 ft. in the west. The Icknield Way forms the parish and county boundary on the north-west, and near to it on Gallows Hill is a tumulus. The soil is chiefly clay or chalk and gravel. The parish is mainly agricultural, the chief crops being wheat, oats and roots, and only a small proportion of the land is laid down to pasture. There are only a few acres of woodland, and these are principally in the south of the parish where Philpotts Wood marks the site of the manor of Woodhall alias Philpotts (q.v.). The common lands were inclosed by Act of Parliament passed in 1795, the award being dated 1797.[1]

The village lies about 2 miles to the south of the Icknield Way, with which it is connected by roads leading north, joining in the village and thence going to Therfield and the Ermine Street at Buckland. The main part of the village lies along the road to Buckland and the church occupies a commanding position in the highest part of it. Several small ponds lie on the east of the church, and from the formation of the ground it appears probable that there was once a moat here.[2] On the small green in the middle of the village is the stone base of a village cross, which was found in 1906, and set up here on a brick base. It has been very much worn by the weather, but enough remains to show that it probably

---

[62] Cal. S. P. Dom. 1640–1, p. 459.
[63] Ibid.
[64] Ibid.
[65] G.E.C. Complete Peerage, s.v. Bayning.
[66] Ibid.
[67] Inst. Bks. (P.R.O.).
[68] Chan. Inq. p.m. (Ser. 2), ccccviii, 158.
[69] G.E.C. Complete Peerage, s.v. Dorchester.
[70] Ibid. s.v. Rutland.
[70a] Feet of F. Herts. Mich. 26 Chas. II.
[71] Recov. R. East. 2 Anne, rot. 39.

[72] G.E.C. Complete Peerage, s.v. Bayning.
[73] Feet of F. Div. Co. Hil. 13 & 14 Chas. II.
[74] Ibid. Mich. 16 Chas. II.
[75] G.E.C. Complete Baronetage, iv, 110.
[76] Ibid.
[77] Feet of F. Div. Co. Trin. 9 Will. III.
[78] G.E.C. Complete Peerage, s.v. Dacre ; see Feet of F. Div. Co. Trin. 4 Will. and Mary.
[79] G.E.C. Complete Peerage, s.v. Dacre.
[80] Recov. R. Trin. 3 Anne, rot. 36.

[81] Inst. Bks. (P.R.O.).
[82] Ibid.
[83] Com. Pleas D. Enr. Trin. 25 Geo. III, m. 3.
[84] Ibid.
[85] Feet of F. Herts. Hil. 27 Geo. III.
[86] Ibid. East. 31 Geo. III.
[87] Inst. Bks. (P.R.O.).
[88] Ibid.
[89] Clutterbuck, op. cit. iii, 527.
[90] Urwick, op. cit. 794.
[1] Blue Bk. Incl. Awards.
[2] East Herts. Arch. Soc. Trans. iii, 14.

HINXWORTH PLACE   HERALDIC GLASS WINDOW IN DRAWING-ROOM

KELSHALL CHURCH: THE NAVE LOOKING WEST

ODSEY HUNDRED

KELSHALL

belongs to the 14th century. The lower half is square, and supports an octagonal shaft, with ogee stops, which has a socket for a cross. It is surrounded by iron railings, and is under the charge of the Hertfordshire County Council.

Kelshall has always been off the lines of communication and therefore dependent upon Royston. When James I had a hunting lodge at Royston the inhabitants of the surrounding villages, including Kelshall, were compelled to cultivate their lands to suit the king's pleasure. They were forbidden to plough their fields in narrow ridges, their swine had to be ringed that they should not root holes to the danger of the king or prince when hunting or hawking, and they had to take down any high boundaries between their lands, that the king might always have an easy passage whenever he wished.[3]

In 1768 Richard Hassell, lord of the manor of Kelshall, complained that his letters even from the neighbourhood were sent him via London, so that they took two days and cost 6d., whereas they might have come direct to Royston for a penny.[4] The nearest railway station is at Ashwell, 3 miles to the north, though Royston is the nearest town.

Several notable men have been incumbents of Kelshall. Among them may be mentioned the Rev. John Watson, who, with a success that suggests the policy of the Vicar of Bray, was known and rewarded as a Reformer under Edward VI, received preferment from Mary and was made Bishop of Winchester by Elizabeth. He was appointed rector of Kelshall in 1554 and held it as a pluralist.[5] The Rev. Joseph Beaumont, D.D., Master of Peterhouse and a poet, held the rectory from 1643 but was non-resident.[6] The Rev. George Henry Law, D.D., who became successively Bishop of Chester and of Bath and Wells, was rector of Kelshall for eleven years.[7] His son Henry Law was born there in 1797. He also entered the Church and was one of the leaders of the Evangelical party.[8]

The manor of *KELSHALL* was held MANORS before the Conquest by the Abbot and monks of Ely,[9] and is said to have been given them in the year 1000 by Ethelflaeda wife of Duke Ethelstan.[10] They were confirmed in their possession by a charter of Edward the Confessor, which confirmed the grants of his father and grandfather.[11] The Abbots of Ely retained possession of the manor after the Conquest,[12] and when a bishopric was erected at Ely in 1108–9[13] Kelshall became part of the possessions of that see.[14] In 1251 Hugh Bishop of Ely received a grant of free warren in his lands in Kelshall.[15] Return of writs, pleas *de namio verito*, gallows and assize of bread and ale were also claimed by the bishops.[16] In 1285–6 there was a mill attached to the manor.[17]

Kelshall remained with the bishopric till 1600,[18] when Martin Heaton, then Bishop of Ely, alienated it with several other manors to the queen.[19] It was then held by the Crown for nine years.[20] In 1609 James I granted it to George Salter[21] in trust for Ralph Freeman, and the latter sold it in 1628 to James Willymot.[22] He held the manor till his death in 1662,[23] when it passed to his son James Willymot, who was Sheriff of Herts in 1683.[24] He sold it to John Poynter in 1695,[25] at whose death in 1718[26] the manor descended to his son Samuel,[27] who held it till his death in 1747.[28] It then passed to his sister Sarah,[29] who married Richard Hassall in 1754.[30] When Richard Hassall died the manor was sold to John Kenrick of Blechingley, Surrey.[31] On his death in 1799 it passed to his brother the Rev. Matthew Kenrick, rector of Blechingley,[32] who died in 1803,[33] when his property went by will to his brother the Rev. Jarvis Kenrick, rector of Chilham, Kent.[34] From him it descended to his son William Kenrick.[35] After his death Kelshall was held by Mrs. Kenrick until about 1899, when it passed to Colonel Byrne. Mr. John Inns, the present lord of the manor, purchased the property from Colonel Byrne a few years ago.

The manor of *WOODHALL* alias *PHILPOTTS* was held of the Bishops of Ely as of their manor of Kelshall.[36]

The earliest reference to the manor seems to be in 1430–1, when it was held by John Philpott and Matilda his wife.[37] It received its second name from this family, with whom it remained until the beginning of the 17th century. John Philpott died in 1436,[38] and the manor passed to his son John, at that date aged five.[39] This John was knighted and died in 1502, when his son Peter succeeded him.[40] Peter also received the honour of knighthood, and died in 1540.[41] In 1543 his son Thomas was seised of the manor, and was declared to have

SEE OF ELY. *Gules three crowns or.*

PHILPOTT. *Sable a bend ermine.*

---

[3] Cal. S. P. Dom. 1611–18, p. 488.
[4] Sess. R. (Herts. Co. Rec.), ii, 111.
[5] Dict. Nat. Biog.
[6] Ibid.   [7] Ibid.
[8] Ibid.
[9] V.C.H. Herts. i, 312a.
[10] Bentham, *Hist. of Conventual Church of Ely*; Cussans, op. cit. 131; *Liber Eliensis* (ed. D. T. Stewart), ii, cap. 64, 83.
[11] Kemble, *Codex Dipl.* iv, 246.
[12] V.C.H. Herts. i, 312a.
[13] Dugdale, *Mon. Angl.* i, 462.
[14] Ibid.
[15] Cal. Chart. R. 1226–57, p. 367; Cart. Antiq. II, 51.
[16] Hund. R. (Rec. Com.), i, 188.

[17] Mins. Accts. bdle. 1132, no. 9.
[18] Ibid. no. 9, 10, 11, 13; Assize R. 325; Add. MS. 6165, pp. 232, 506; *Feud. Aids*, ii, 446.
[19] Close, 42 Eliz. pt. cxxx; Add. MS. 5847, p.137; Dugdale, *Mon. Angl.* i, 466.
[20] Ld. Rev. Ct. R. bdle. 30, no. 1.
[21] Pat. 7 Jas. I, pt. xxxvii.
[22] Feet of F. Herts. Mich. 4 Chas. I.
[23] Clutterbuck, op. cit. iii, 533.
[24] Ibid. ; Berry, *Herts. Geneal.*
[25] Com. Pleas D. Enr. Mich. 7 Will. III, m. 7.
[26] Clutterbuck, op. cit. iii, 536.
[27] See Feet of F. Herts. Trin. 13 & 14 Geo. II.

[28] Cussans, op. cit. *Odsey Hund.* 131 et seq.
[29] Ibid.
[30] Clutterbuck, op. cit. 533; Cussans, loc. cit.
[31] Ibid.   [32] Ibid.   [33] Ibid.
[34] P.C.C. 712 Marriott.
[35] Clutterbuck, op. cit. 533; Cussans, loc. cit.
[36] Chan. Inq. p.m. 15 Hen. VI, no. 11; (Ser. 2), xvii, 44.
[37] Feet of F. Div. Co. Hil. 9 Hen. VI.
[38] Chan. Inq. p.m. 15 Hen. VI, no. 11.
[39] Ibid.
[40] Ibid. (Ser. 2), xvii, 44.
[41] Ibid. lxiv, 152.

A HISTORY OF HERTFORDSHIRE

been a lunatic since 1534.[42] In 1607 Sir George Philpott, kt., made a settlement of the manor.[43] He died in 1622 and was succeeded by his son Sir John Philpott.[44]

The Philpotts had remained adherents of the old religion, and in consequence of heavy fines for recusancy found themselves involved in money difficulties.[45] In 1625 Sir John Philpott, in order to pay the legacies left in his father's will and also his own debts, demised the manor of Woodhall with various other estates for the term of sixteen years to three of his creditors, John Lord St. John, Sir Thomas Stukely and Sir Richard Tichborne.[46] John Lord St. John released all his estate in these manors to his co-feoffees, and in 1627 the king confirmed the grant to Sir Thomas Stukely and Sir Richard Tichborne for the term of sixteen years.[47] The feoffees appear to have conveyed their right in Woodhall to James Willymot, who held a court there in 1635.[48] Henry Philpott was holding in 1650,[49] but apparently he also released his right to the Willymots, and the manor was given by James Willymot to his younger son Thomas.[50] He married Rachel the daughter of Dr. Pindar, and the manor was settled on her.[51] Afterwards it was bought from the Willymot family by Hale Wortham, who died in 1778 and was succeeded by his son Hale Wortham.[52] He died without any direct heir and the manor passed to his brother James.[53] From him it descended to his eldest son Biscoe Hill Wortham, who sold it to John Phillips of Royston.[54] John Phillips died in 1871[55] and was succeeded by his son Mr. John Phillips, the present lord.[56]

The manor of *HORWELLBURY* (Ordwelle, xi cent.; Orewell, xii cent.; Horewell, xiii cent.) was held before the Conquest by three men of Archbishop Stigand.[57] In 1086 half a hide was held of the Bishop of Bayeux by Osbern,[58] while a larger holding of nearly one and a half hides had been acquired by Hardwin de Scales, under whom a certain Wisgar held.[59] No further record exists of the holding of the Bishop of Bayeux, but the lands of Hardwin de Scales were divided between his two sons Richard and Hugh and were held by their descendants until the beginning of the 13th century.[60] In 1195–6 William, grandson of Richard, claimed (*inter alia*) three knights' fees in Horwellbury and other places against Hugh grandson of Hugh. Judgement was given for Hugh.[61] The Scales do not appear again in Horwellbury, but possibly before this date they had subinfeudated it to the Fitz Ralphs, who were holding of them elsewhere, for in 1303 Horwellbury was said to be held of William Fitz Ralph.[62] In the 16th century, when the overlordships given in inquisitions are unreliable, Horwellbury was said to be held of the king[63] except a small portion called Kymberleyn's, which was held of the queen as of her manor of Popshall.[64]

In 1229 John de Bassingburn, who was holding half a knight's fee in Kelshall of the Bishop of Ely,[65] claimed customs and services there from a certain Ralph Marshal.[66] In 1282 a grant of the manor in subinfeudation was made by William le Moine of Raveley to another Ralph Marshal, clerk, and Nichola his wife.[67] On Ralph's death it passed to his brother Robert.[68] An attempt was made in 1291 by a certain John Deynill to gain possession of the manor. He disseised Robert and claimed that Ralph Marshal had been his villein.[69] But Robert successfully maintained that Ralph had been a free man and held the manor of William le Moine, and he recovered seisin of the manor.[70]

In 1303 Hugh Barry was holding the manor of William Fitz Ralph.[71] Soon after this the manor passed to Edmund Barry, who granted it to John Barry, probably his son, and Elizabeth his wife. From them it descended to their son Edmund Barry.[72] He had two daughters, Agnes and Alice,[73] and on the marriage of the elder of these, Agnes, with William Paston in 1420 the manor of Horwellbury was settled on them and their heirs.[74] Her sister Alice and her husband Thomas Bardolf[75] renounced all right to the manor in 1436.[76]

William Paston in 1444 left the manor by will to his wife Agnes with remainder to their heirs.[77] At the same time he directed that all lands not mentioned in his will (except Sweynthorpe) should go to his two younger sons William and Clement.[78] John Paston, however, his eldest son and heir, did not carry out these directions, but took possession of all the lands.[79] Agnes Paston held Horwellbury during her life,[80] but on her death she left it by will dated 1466 to her two younger sons in recompense for the lands their brother had withheld from them.[81] Her son

PASTON. *Argent six fleurs de lis azure and a chief indented or.*

---

[42] Chan. Inq. p.m. (Ser. 2), lxv, 84.
[43] Feet of F. Div. Co. Hil. 4 Jas. I.
[44] Chan. Inq. p.m. (Ser. 2), ccccli, 129.
[45] Pat. 3 Chas. I, pt. iv, no. 1.
[46] Ibid.; Feet of F. Div. Co. Hil. 1 Chas. I.
[47] Pat. 3 Chas. I, pt. iv, no. 1.
[48] Add. R. 33006.
[49] Recov. R. Mich. 1650, rot. 44.
[50] Clutterbuck, op. cit. 534; Cussans, op. cit. 132; Feet of F. Herts. Hil. 1 Anne.
[51] Chauncy, op. cit. 84; Clutterbuck, op. cit. 534; Cussans, op. cit. *Odsey Hund*. 132.
[52] Clutterbuck and Cussans, loc. cit.
[53] Cussans, op. cit. *Odsey Hund*. 131.
[54] Ibid.
[55] Ibid.
[56] Information given by Mr. John Phillips of Royston, co. Herts.
[57] *V.C.H. Herts.* i, 310a, 339a.
[58] Ibid. 310a.
[59] Ibid. 339a.
[60] *Abbrev. Plac.* (Rec. Com.), 99.
[61] Ibid.
[62] *Feud. Aids*, ii, 433. See manor of Broadfield for descent of Fitz Ralphs.
[63] Chan. Inq. p.m. (Ser. 2), xxv, 96; lxviii, 14.
[64] This portion took its name from the family of Kimberley, one of whom, William Kimberley, and afterwards his heir Thomas Kimberley, held the manor for a short time on lease or in mortgage at the end of the 14th century (De Banco R. 572, m. 110).
[65] *Red Bk. of Exch.* ii, 526.
[66] *Cal. Close*, 1227–31, p. 226. Albreda Bassingburn in 1240 granted a carucate of land in Kelshall to Alexander de Bassingburn to be held of herself and her heirs; Feet of F. Div. Co. Trin. 24 Hen. III, no. 161.
[67] Feet of F. Herts. 10 Edw. I, no. 145; see Assize R. 1291, m. 4 d.
[68] Assize R. 1291, m. 4 d.
[69] Ibid.
[70] Ibid.
[71] *Feud. Aids*, ii, 433.
[72] De Banco R. 572, m. 110.
[73] Wrottesley, *Ped. from the Plea R.* 366.
[74] *Paston Letters* (ed. Gairdner), i, 11.
[75] Wrottesley, *Ped. from the Plea R.* 366.
[76] Feet of F. Div. Co. East. 14 Hen. VI; William Paston's name is wrongly given in *Feud. Aids*, ii, 447, as John.
[77] *Paston Letters* (ed. Gairdner), iii, 459.
[78] Ibid. ii, 287.
[79] Ibid.
[80] Ibid. i, 87, 247–8, 255.
[81] Ibid. ii, 287.

242

ODSEY HUNDRED   KELSHALL

John Paston died the same year and was succeeded by his son Sir John Paston.[82] In spite of his grandmother's will, Sir John endeavoured on the death of Agnes to take possession of Horwellbury,[83] and on his death in 1479 his brother and heir John Paston renewed the attempt to enter on the manor.[84] But his uncle William Paston had leased the manor to John King, who refused to recognize the right of the elder branch of the family.[85] John Paston never acknowledged his uncle's claim to the manor and drew up long lists of complaints against him.[86] But he had no supporters among the tenants of Horwellbury,[87] and finally William Paston sold the manor to Thomas Bradbury, Mayor of London in 1507.[88]

Before his death in January 1509–10 Thomas Bradbury left it to his widow Joan Bradbury with remainder to his nephew and heir William Bradbury.[89] Joan at once bought the reversion of the manor from her nephew,[90] but must soon after have sold it, for in 1536 it was held by John Bowles,[91] who died in 1543[92] and left it to his grandson and heir Thomas Bowles, then aged thirteen.[93] The manor again changed hands within a short time and in 1577 was held by Edward Hammond, who died in February 1579–80. He settled Horwellbury on his son Alexander Hammond,[94] who held the manor[95] till his death in 1604,[96] when it passed to his son John Hammond. No further trace is found of the Hammonds in Horwellbury, and in 1695 the manor was held by James Willymot,[97] owner of the manor of Kelshall (q.v.), and from this date the two manors descend together.

The house called Orwellbury lies north of the church and to the north-east of the road from Kelshall to Sandon. In 1797, when the Kelshall allotment award was made, there were three fields in this district which were called Great Horwell, Mead Horwell and Horwell Pightle, which adjoined a piece of common land called Horwell Green.[98]

The church of *ST. FAITH* consists CHURCH of a chancel 29 ft. by 18 ft., nave 42 ft. by 18 ft., north and south aisles 43 ft. by 9 ft., south porch 12 ft. by 10 ft., and west tower 12 ft. square; all dimensions taken internally.

The walls are of flint with stone dressings. The whole of the church belongs to the 15th century, but was thoroughly repaired, all but the tower, in 1870, most of the external stonework being replaced and the church re-roofed. The tower was restored in 1911 and a lych-gate was added in the previous year.

KELSHALL CHURCH FROM THE SOUTH-WEST

In the chancel is an east window of three lights, and in each side wall are two windows, and a doorway in the south wall, all modern. There is a carved bracket for an image on either side of the east window, a good deal damaged. The chancel arch is of two moulded orders, with moulded responds, of the 15th century. The nave has north and south arcades of four bays with moulded arches and piers with engaged shafts, which have moulded capitals and bases. The two-light windows in the clearstory are modern, as is also the roof. In the north-east angle is the stair to the rood-loft; the lower doorway is blocked, but the upper one remains.

---

[82] *Paston Letters* (ed. Gairdner), ii, 290.
[83] Ibid. iii, 267, 275.
[84] Ibid. 263.   [85] Ibid. 275.
[86] Ibid. 267, 311.   [87] Ibid. 315.
[88] Feet of F. Herts. Mich. 22 Hen. VII; Add. Chart. 27442.
[89] Add. Chart. 27442; Chan. Inq. p.m. (Ser. 2), xxv, 96.
[90] Add. Chart. 27442.
[91] Chan. Inq. p.m. (Ser. 2), lxviii, 14.
[92] Ibid.
[93] Ibid.
[94] Ibid. clxxxix, 88.
[95] See Recov. R. East. 1583, rot. 61.
[96] Chan. Inq. p.m. (Ser. 2), cclxxxiv, 96.
[97] Com. Pleas D. Enr. Mich. 7 Will. III, m. 7.
[98] *Home Cos. Mag.* x, 317.

A HISTORY OF HERTFORDSHIRE

In the east wall of the north aisle is a three-light window with a traceried head; there are two windows in the north wall and one in the west wall, each of two lights with tracery above, all of late 15th-century work, with repaired stonework. The north doorway has a double ogee moulding with label and defaced stops. At the east end are two damaged carved stone brackets. There are some fragments of 15th-century glass in one of the windows in the north wall. In the north-west angle of the aisle is a tall locker, circular on plan internally, with a diameter of 2 ft. 5 in.; the recess has a pointed arched head, and is about 12 ft. in height; it has a rebate for door, and the iron hooks for the hinges remain; it was probably used to hold the processional cross and staves. The roof of the aisle is modern, but a few old timbers remain.

There is a three-light window in the east wall of the south aisle, and two of two lights in the south wall, all of modern stonework. A 15th-century piscina, somewhat mutilated, remains at the east end of the aisle. The south doorway, of 15th-century date, has a moulded arch under a square head, with traceried spandrels. The door is the original one of oak, but has been restored. The west window of the aisle is of two lights with a traceried head; it is of 15th-century work repaired.

The entrance doorway to the south porch and the side windows are modern; it has a parvise over it, approached by a turret stair in the north-west angle outside, the door being in the south aisle.

The west tower is of three stages, finished with an embattled parapet. The tower arch is of three moulded orders, with moulded capitals and bases to the jambs. The west window is of two cinquefoiled lights, with a six-foiled opening in its head. The second stage is pierced by single lights in the west and south; the bell-chamber has, on each side, a two-light opening with traceried head, much broken and decayed.

The lower part of the rood screen remains *in situ*; the panels are cusped, with carved spandrels, and retain their original paintings; two of them have kings, with their names, Edmund and Edward, on scrolls, the other two being bishops, unnamed. All the other fittings are modern.

In the churchyard, south of the church, is the base of an octagonal stone cross of the 15th century. Mr. F. J. Fordham gave a small piece of land for an addition to the churchyard on the west side.

There are five bells: the treble by R. Catlin, 1748 (recast in 1860); the second by Miles Graye, 1642; the third by John Briant, 1790 (recast in 1860); the fourth and tenor by Miles Graye, 1642.

The communion plate consists of paten, 1685, and modern chalice and paten.

The registers are in three books: (i) and (ii) baptisms and burials 1538 to 1812, marriages 1538 to 1687, 1691 to 1753; (iii) marriages 1754 to 1812.

ADVOWSON The patronage of the church was originally attached to the manor of Kelshall,[99] and remained so until 1600, when the Bishop of Ely surrendered the manor to the queen,[100] but retained the advowson in his own hands.[101] It continued to be part of the possessions of the see of Ely until 1852,[102] when it was transferred to the Bishop of Oxford,[103] who in 1855 conveyed it to the Crown,[104] in whom it is at present vested.

In 1779 a meeting-place for Protestant Dissenters was certified in Kelshall.[105]

CHARITIES The Poor's Land consists of a field called Town Closes of about 8 acres, and 8 a. 1 r. of land let in allotments, together producing £12 5s. yearly. In 1908 1s. 6d. per head was distributed to each labourer and his wife and all in family under sixteen years of age, and 2s. 6d. a head to five aged and infirm widows.

There is also a close of 2 a. 1 r. 5 p., called the Clerk's Close, the rent of which is payable to the parish clerk, he paying land tax rates and tithe-charge.

RADWELL

Radewelle (xi cent.); Redewell (xv cent.); Radiwell (xvi cent.).

The parish of Radwell lies in the extreme north-west of the county on the borders of Bedfordshire. It is very small, containing only about 743 acres, of which the greater part is arable land and about one-ninth permanent grass. There are only 3½ acres of woodland.[1] The chief crops are wheat, barley, beans and turnips. The parish is on the chalk hills, but lies comparatively low, rising nowhere more than 263 ft. above the ordnance datum. The River Ivel flows through the south-west of the parish and forms part of its western boundary, dividing it from Norton. Radwell lies 2 miles north-west of Baldock, at which town is its nearest railway station. The road to Biggleswade, after passing through Baldock, runs northward through Radwell and forms part of the western boundary of the parish, which here coincides with the boundary between Hertfordshire and Bedfordshire. On the east the Cat Ditch forms part of the boundary.

The village lies in the south-west of the parish between the road to Biggleswade and the River Ivel, and along a lane which runs westward from the main road to the river. On the north side of this lane are the church and rectory; a little to the west are the corn mill and mill pond, probably occupying the site of the mill mentioned in the Domesday Survey.

Radwell House, the manor-house, and Bury Farm are on the south side of the lane. These buildings form the greater part of the village, which has always been very small, the population in 1428 being only seven inhabitants.[1a] In 1656 the people of Radwell petitioned that they might be assisted in the repairing of the Great North Road, which was then in great decay, as the soil was so poor that the winter devoured

---

[99] *Cal. Pat.* 1422–9, p. 235.
[100] Close, 42 Eliz. pt. cxxx.
[101] Add. MS. 5847, p. 137.
[102] Inst. Bks. (P.R.O.).
[103] Cussans, op. cit. *Odsey Hund.* 138.
[104] *Ind. to Lond. Gaz.* 915.
[105] Urwick, op. cit. 798.
[1] Statistics from Bd. of Agric. (1905).
[1a] *Feud. Aids*, ii, 454, 458.

244

Kelshall Church: Locker in North-west angle of North Aisle

whatever they were able to lay on in the summer, and the parish was so small that it had only two teams.[2]

The Ridgway is a 16th-century place-name.

MANORS
In the reign of Edward the Confessor and in the early days after the Conquest there were two manors in Radwell.[3] The larger of these was assessed at 4 hides and had a mill attached worth 8s.[4] It was held before the Conquest by Alnoda, a man of Archbishop Stigand.[5] In 1086 it had become part of the extensive lands of the Bishop of Bayeux and was held of him by Adam son of Hubert de Rye.[6] On Adam's death his lands passed to his brother Eudo Dapifer.[7] He died in 1120,[8] when Radwell apparently passed to his sister Albreda, the wife of Peter de Valognes,[9] and then became amalgamated with the other manor of Radwell. The smaller manor in Radwell was assessed in 1086 at only 2 hides [10] and had a mill worth 6s. 8d.[11] In the reign of Edward the Confessor it was held by Ethelmaer of Benington.[12] Ethelmaer's brother held half a hide of it under him.[13] By 1086 Radwell had passed with Ethelmaer's other estates to Peter de Valognes and was held of him by Roger.[14]

Peter de Valognes having acquired the other manor (see above) the two became the manor of RADWELL. On the death of Peter de Valognes his lands descended to his son Roger de Valognes.[15] He had a son Peter, who appears to have died without issue and to have been succeeded by his brother Robert.[16] This Robert left an only daughter Gunnora, who married Robert Fitz Walter.[17] In the struggle between King John and the barons Robert Fitz Walter was one of the leaders of the latter party,[18] and when Louis of France arrived in England he joined with William de Mandeville Earl of Essex in subjugating Essex and Suffolk.[19] He had by Gunnora [20] a daughter Christine, who married William de Mandeville Earl of Essex,[21] and as Christine Countess of Mandeville held of the gift of her father of the honour of Valognes four fees, including Radwell.[22] She died without issue, and Radwell seems to have passed to her step-brother Walter Fitz Walter, who died in 1257.[23] He was succeeded by his son Robert,[24] who on his death in 1325 was succeeded by his son also named Robert.[25] This Robert died in 1328 holding fees in Radwell and elsewhere,[26] which descended to his son John. John held till his death in 1361,[27] when his lands passed to his son Walter Fitz Walter. In 1386 Walter Fitz Walter died seised with his wife Philippa of the fee in Radwell.[28] He left a son and heir Walter.[29] Before this date the Fitz Walters had enfeoffed a sub-tenant in Radwell,[30] and this is the last of the family whose rights of overlordship are recorded. Walter, grandson of the younger Walter Fitz Walter, died in 1431, leaving a daughter Elizabeth, aged only eighteen months.[31] It is possible that during her minority the claim of the Fitz Walters to the overlordship of Radwell Manor was allowed to lapse, for in 1438 it was said to be held of John Barre, who held land in Radwell,[32] as of his manor of Ayot,[33] and in 1543 it was said to be held of the king in chief,[34] but by this date tenures had become uncertain.

The earliest known sub-tenant in the manor of Radwell is Simon Fitz Adam de Hatfield, to whom Henry III granted free warren in his demesne lands of Radwell and elsewhere in 1254.[35] John Fitz Simon, his grandson,[36] presented to the church of Radwell in 1304.[37] He died in that year, and his son Edward was his heir.[38] Edward died without issue before 1328, when these lands had passed to his brother Hugh Fitz Simon,[39] who was still holding in 1346, at which date the fee was held under him by John Mallore and Margaret his wife.[40] He settled the manor of Radwell on his son Edward Fitz Simon, kt., his wife Nichola and their heirs.[41] Edward died without children,[42] and the manor was inherited by his brother Nicholas,[43] subject to the life interest of his brother's widow Nichola.[44] In 1398 he with Elizabeth his wife granted it to John and Ida Cokayn for life with remainder to Edward Fitz Simon, their son, and Cecilia his wife, daughter of John and Ida.[45] Edward died before 1400,[46] and Radwell appears finally to have come to Christine, one of his two daughters and co-heiresses,[47] for in 1428 it was held by her husband John Muslee.[48] Shortly afterwards in 1433 the manor was conveyed by trustees to John Fray, chief baron of the Exchequer, and Agnes his wife, on whom it was settled for life and a year beyond, with remainder to trustees.[49] In 1438 John Fray obtained licence to alienate Radwell in mortmain to the Abbot and convent of St. Albans, receiving from it for life an annual rent of 20 marks.[50]

The manor remained with the abbey until its dissolution in 1538,[51] and was granted in 1540 to Ralph Rowlett.[52] He held it till his death in March 1543-4, when it passed to his son Ralph Rowlett.[53] In 1548-9 Ralph Rowlett the younger settled Radwell on himself

---

[2] Sess. R. (Herts. Co. Rec.), i, 118.
[3] V.C.H. Herts. i, 310a, 338a.
[4] Ibid. 310a.
[5] Ibid.
[6] Ibid.; V.C.H. Northants, i, 363.
[7] V.C.H. Northants, i, 363.
[8] Round, Studies in Peerage and Family Hist. 163.
[9] Dugdale, Baronage, i, 441; Dugdale, Mon. Angl. iii, 345; iv, 608.
[10] V.C.H. Herts. i, 338a.
[11] Ibid.
[12] Ibid.
[13] Ibid.
[14] Ibid. 338a, 276.
[15] Dugdale, Baronage, i, 441.
[16] Ibid.
[17] Ibid. 218.
[18] Ibid.; G.E.C. Complete Peerage, s.v. Fitz Walter.
[19] Dugdale, Baronage, i, 218.
[20] His heir Walter was not the son of Gunnora.
[21] Dugdale, Baronage, i, 218.
[22] Testa de Nevill (Rec. Com.), 271b.
[23] Dugdale, Baronage, i, 218; G.E.C. Complete Peerage, s.v. Fitz Walter.
[24] Ibid.
[25] Ibid.
[26] Cal. Inq. p.m. 1–9 Edw. III, 129.
[27] G.E.C. loc. cit.
[28] Cal. Inq. p.m. (Rec. Com.), iii, 82.
[29] G.E.C. Complete Peerage, loc. cit.
[30] See below.
[31] G.E.C. loc. cit.
[32] Cal. Inq. p.m. Hen. VII, i, 215.
[33] Cal. Pat. 1436–41, p. 243; Arund. MS. 34, fol. 15.
[34] Chan. Inq. p.m. (Ser. 2), lxviii, 40.
[35] Cal. Pat. 1247–58, p. 388.
[36] See Chan. Inq. p.m. 32 Edw. I, no. 56.
[37] Cussans, op. cit. Odsey Hund. 59.
[38] Chan. Inq. p.m. 32 Edw. I, no. 56.
[39] Cal. Inq. p.m. 1–9 Edw. III, 129.
[40] Feud. Aids, ii, 436.
[41] Add. MS. 28789.
[42] Ibid.
[43] Ibid.
[44] Close, 1 Ric. II, m. 10 d.; Feet of F. Herts. 13 Ric. II, no. 139.
[45] Feet of F. Herts. 21 Ric. II, no. 185.
[46] Ibid. 1 Hen. IV, no. 9; 2 Hen. IV, no. 14.
[47] See Feet of F. Herts. 11 Hen. IV, no. 84.
[48] Feud. Aids, ii, 448; Feet of F. Herts. 11 Hen. IV, no. 84.
[49] Feet of F. Herts. Mich. 12 Hen. VI, no. 66.
[50] Cal. Pat. 1436–41, p. 243; Inq. a.q.d. file 448, no. 22 (17 Hen. VI); Arund. MS. 34, fol. 15; Dugdale, Mon. Angl. ii, 244.
[51] Dugdale, Mon. Angl. ii, 207.
[52] L. and P. Hen. VIII, xv, 733 (42).
[53] Chan. Inq. p.m. (Ser. 2), lxviii, 40.

A HISTORY OF HERTFORDSHIRE

and his wife Dorothy, with remainder to his sister Joan, who was the wife of Thomas Skipwith.[54] Ralph

ROWLETT. *Gules a cheveron between couple closes argent with three lions gules on the cheveron.*

SKIPWITH. *Argent three bars gules and a greyhound sable with a golden collar running in the chief.*

and Dorothy continued to hold the manor as late as 1556,[55] soon after which Dorothy must have died, for in 1558 Sir Ralph Rowlett settled the manor on himself and his wife Margaret, one of the daughters of Sir Anthony Cooke, kt.[56] In February 1562–3 Sir Ralph leased the manor to William Plomer for seventy years.[57] Sir Ralph died in 1571, and as he left no children he bequeathed the manor to William Skipwith, the son and heir of his sister Joan, to hold with remainder to his brothers Ralph, Edward and Henry Skipwith.[58] In 1577 William Skipwith and Edward and Henry Skipwith received licence to alienate the manor, including one mill and view of frankpledge,[59] for settlement on William and his heirs, William Skipwith promising to settle lands of equal value on his brothers if he should die without children.[60] This bond, on the death of Ralph Skipwith, came into the hands of John Cheyney, who refused to give it up.[61] William Skipwith brought a suit against him, and declared that he had settled lands on his brothers according to the bond and to the will of Sir Ralph Rowlett.[62] In January 1577–8 William Skipwith sold the manor to Sir Rowland Hayward, kt.[63] He sold it in 1580 to John Parker and Katherine his wife, and their son John Parker.[64] John Parker died in March 1595–6,[65] and his son John in March 1604–5.[66] He was succeeded by his uncle William Parker (son of John Parker of Baldock), brother to John Parker the father,[67] who sold Radwell in 1607 to William Plomer,[68] then lessee of the manor (see above).

PYM. *Sable a fess between three owls or with three crosslets sable on the fess.*

William Plomer died in March 1625–6, and was succeeded by his son William, then aged thirty.[69] From him the manor passed to Sir Robert Berkeley of East Barnet, a lawyer who was imprisoned in the Tower for his loyalty to the Stuarts.[70] His brother John Berkeley resided at Radwell House.[71] In 1650 Sir Robert sold the manor to Thomas Cole, citizen and merchant tailor, of London.[72] The sale included a water corn mill, all water-courses, flood-gates and dams on the manor, the liberty of a swan-mark, or of keeping swans in or near Radwell, court leet and court baron. Thomas Cole continued to hold the manor until 1677, when he sold it to Robert Bell.[73] Radwell remained in this family until 1720–1, when Robert Bell and his son Richard were empowered to sell it by a Private Act of Parliament.[74] It was purchased by William Pym of Nortonbury.[75]

In 1723 a suit was brought against Pym by Robert and Richard Bell, farmers of the tithes of Radwell, and it was then stated that no courts had been held in Radwell for many years, and that during the time

RADWELL CHURCH FROM THE SOUTH-EAST

---

[54] Feet of F. Herts. Hil. 2 Edw. VI.
[55] Recov. R. Hil. 1554 ; Trin. 1556.
[56] Pat. 4 & 5 Phil. and Mary, pt. xv, m. 2 ; Recov. R. East. 1558, rot. 619.
[57] Chan. Inq. p.m. (Ser. 2), ccxciii, 22 ; see Com. Pleas D. Enr. East. 17 Eliz.
[58] Chan. Inq. p.m. (Ser. 2), ccvi, 3.
[59] Pat. 19 Eliz. pt. xi, m. 17 ; Feet of F. Herts. Mich. 19 & 20 Eliz.
[60] Ct. of Req. bdle. 89, no. 47.
[61] Ibid.
[62] Ibid. ; see also Chan. Proc. (Ser. 2), bdle. 250, no. 21.
[63] Pat. 20 Eliz. pt. iii, m. 30 ; Feet of F. Herts. East. 20 Eliz.
[64] Chan. Inq. p.m. (Ser. 2), ccxciii, 22.
[65] Ibid. [66] Ibid. [67] Ibid.
[68] Feet of F. Herts. Trin. 5 Jas. I.
[69] Chan. Inq. p.m. (Ser. 2), ccccxxxiv, 84.
[70] Chauncy, op. cit. 43 ; Close, 1650, pt. lxvii, no. 17.
[71] Close, 1650, pt. lxvii, no. 17.
[72] Ibid.
[73] Feet of F. Herts. Mich. 29 Chas. II.
[74] Priv. Act, 7 Geo. I, cap. 31.
[75] Cussans, op. cit. *Odsey Hund.* 55.

246

ODSEY HUNDRED

when Thomas Cole was owner of the manor some of the tenants had been summoned to a court at Rushden.[76] William Pym held Radwell until his death in 1788, when his lands descended to his son Francis Pym.[77] Francis Pym died in 1833 and was succeeded by his son also Francis Pym.[78] He died in February 1861, and his son Francis only lived to enjoy his inheritance for a few months; as he was killed in a railway accident in April of that same year. His son Francis Pym, a minor, succeeded him.[79] He was holding the manor in 1871,[80] and afterwards sold it to Mr. J. Remington Mills, from whom it descended to Mr. J. Truman Mills, and later to Mr. John Layton Mills, the present lord of the manor.

CHURCH
The church of *ALL SAINTS* consists of chancel 20 ft. by 13 ft. 6 in., north vestry 14 ft. by 7 ft., nave 35 ft. by 16 ft. 6 in., and south porch 8 ft. 6 in. by 8 ft. The walls are of flint rubble covered with cement, the roofs are tiled.

The chancel arch is the only structural feature in the church which shows detail of an earlier date than the 15th century, and it is mid-14th-century work; the walling may belong to that or an earlier period, but all early detail has been lost in the repairs of the 15th century. The vestry and south porch were added in 1882, when the whole building was re-roofed and thoroughly repaired.

The chancel has a three-light east window of about 1500, a single modern light in the south wall, and a modern vestry doorway in the north. The chancel arch, of about 1340, is of two wave-moulded orders on octagonal piers with moulded capitals and bases.

There is a two-light window in each of the north, south and west walls of the nave, all of modern stonework; the western bay of the nave is divided off by a wall containing an arch, coarsely moulded, and probably of early 16th-century work. The arch is surmounted on its eastern side by the royal arms carved in stone. There is a small bell-cote over the west end, which appears to be chiefly modern work. The south doorway belongs to the latter part of the 14th century.

The font is of stone, roughly worked; on the sides are shields of a late type. It is probably of 15th-century date, although the form of the font itself belongs to an earlier period.

The communion rails, with moulded balusters and rail, a carved oak chest in the nave, and a pair of high-backed chairs are early 17th-century work.

In the chancel is a brass of William Wheteaker, his wife and son Thomas, a priest in eucharistic vestments, who died in 1487; another of Elizabeth wife of John Parker, who died in 1602. In the nave, near the pulpit, is the brass of John Bele, who died in 1516, with two wives and two children.

On the north wall of the chancel is a small monument to John Parker, who died in 1595, his wife Mary, who died in 1574, and their son John, all kneeling effigies. A large alabaster monument against the south wall is to Mary Plomer, who died in 1605, with effigies of a woman with six sons, four daughters and a chrisom child. On the same wall is a small mural monument to Ann Plomer, who died in 1625. On the south nave wall is a small marble and alabaster monument to Sir William Plomer, who died in 1625.

There are two bells, undated.

The communion plate includes an incised cup, 1574, paten, 1796, and two 18th-century plated cups and patens.

The registers are contained in four books: (i) parchment, all entries 1590 to 1699; (ii) and (iii) baptisms and burials 1700 to 1812, marriages 1700 to 1753; (iv) marriages 1754 to 1812.

ADVOWSON
The church of All Saints, Radwell, has always been in the gift of the lord of the manor,[81] the earliest recorded presentation occurring in 1304.[82] When Francis Pym sold the manor of Radwell (q.v.) he retained the advowson in his own hands and still holds it.

There are apparently no endowed charities.

REED

Rode (x cent.); Retth, Rete (xi cent.); Rede (xii cent); Rud, Roed, Ruth (xiii cent.); Estrede (xiv cent).

The parish of Reed is a long, narrow piece of land containing about 1,477 acres. By far the greater portion of the parish consists of arable land, but woods exist, mostly in the south part, where Reed Wood, the largest in the parish, is situated. Reed lies high, the ground rising to as much as 500 ft. above the ordnance datum. It is near the summit of the chalk range, from which the waters on the north join with the Cam and run into Lynn Deeps, while those on the south run into the Lea and the Thames. The chief crops are wheat, barley, beans and roots. The commons of Reed were inclosed in 1808.[1]

The village of Reed lies almost midway between Royston and Buntingford (at which two towns are its nearest railway stations), and a little to the east of the Roman road, known as Ermine Street, which connects these towns and forms the western boundary of the parish. There is a reference to this road as Arning Street in 1251.[2] A road runs east through Reed from Ermine Street to Barkway. Running south from this is a road which forms the main street of the village, then turns sharply west and south and joins Ermine Street. At the angle thus formed stands Reed Hall, the manor-house, close to which is the church of St. Mary. The manor-house of Queenbury stands east of the road a little further north. There is a Congregational chapel near Queenbury and brickworks further north. On a road running parallel with this road are situated the church mission-room

---

[76] Exch. Dep. East. 9 Geo. I, no. 7.
[77] Burke, *Landed Gentry* (1906); see Inst. Bks. (P.R.O.).
[78] Burke, *Landed Gentry* (1906).
[79] Ibid.
[80] Cussans, loc. cit.
[81] See references under manor and Inst. Bks. (P.R.O.).
[82] Cussans, op. cit. *Odsey Hund.* 59.
[1] Com. Pleas D. Enr. Trin. 10 Geo. IV, m. 23.
[2] *Cal. Chart. R.* 1226–57, p. 360.

and Wisbridge Farm, to the north-east of these are North Farm and a smithy, whilst other scattered parts of the village lie at Fiddler's Green and Billingsgate.

The most distinctive feature of Reed is the number of homestead moats about it. Two of the more important of these lie near Reed Hall, one inclosing a rectangular space of 1¼ acres and the other a space of half an acre. Both are nearly dry. At Queenbury a moat runs round three sides of the house and gardens, inclosing altogether a piece of land about 400 ft. square. There appear to have been two inclosures here originally. At Fiddler's Green is a dry fosse which forms a square. A moat at Gannock Green incloses a piece of land 200 ft. by 300 ft., and at Bushwood a moat incloses a rectangular piece of land containing over half an acre. There were also probably other moats whose position can now only be traced by ponds. Such a pond lies west of Reed Hall. It is large and irregularly shaped, and there seem to be traces that it was once connected with the two moats which adjoin the house and also with the moats at Queenbury. Connecting fosses also appear to have run from Queenbury to the moat at Fiddler's Green. The two ponds which lie near Goodfellows, a house standing south-east of Reed Green, also probably mark the site of an old moat.[3]

There are several greens in the parish: Fiddler's Green to the east of Queenbury, Gannock Green in the south, and Reed Green, which lies north of Queenbury.

Among those who have been rectors of Reed may be mentioned Andrew Willet (1562–1621), a theologian and Biblical critic of some note. He was also a famous preacher, and his learning was so great that he was called a walking library. He held the living of Reed from 1613 to 1615.[4]

The manor of CHALLERS (Deschalers, xv cent.), known also as the manor of REED or EAST REED, was formed from several of a number of holdings which existed in Reed in the reign of Edward the Confessor. The most important of these holdings was that of Siret, a man of Earl Harold, consisting of 4 hides a virgate and a half.[5] Two other holdings of 1 hide and 1 virgate were in the hands of Sinod, a man of St. Mary Charteris.[6] One hide was held by Eddeva the Maiden of Archbishop Stigand,[7] and two of her men, Lening, a priest, and Turbern, each held a hide.[8] Of these in 1086 Hardwin de Scales had obtained all the land of Siret and 1 hide of the land of Sinod, which together made his manor.[9] He also held of Count Alan the land which had belonged to Leuing, the priest.[10] Eudo Fitz Hubert had obtained the remaining virgate of Sinod,[11] and the land of Eddeva the Maiden was held by Osbern of the Bishop of Bayeux,[12] and that of her man Turbern was held by Alward of Count Alan.[13] Of these smaller holdings no further trace is to be found, and it is probable that at an early date they became absorbed in the manor held by Hardwin de Scales. But it is perhaps due to the varied origin of this manor that, while it was always held of the king in chief[14] by barony,[15] certain portions of it were held of other overlords. Thirty acres called 'Gannok'[16] were held of the Dean and Chapter of St. Paul's in the 14th century.[17] Other land was held of the Earl of Hertford in 1364,[18] and part was held of John de Lancaster as of his manor of Barkway in 1342.[19] Challers was probably the head of the Scales' holding in Hertfordshire, for here they had a little castle, consisting merely of a moated mound, the remains of which still exist. This accounts for the fact that the manor was held by barony.

On the death of Hardwin de Scales his lands were divided between his two sons Richard and Hugh.[20] Reed evidently fell to the share of Hugh, and from him descended to his son Henry,[21] for in the reign of Henry II the abbey of Coggeshall held land in Reed of the fee of Henry de Scales.[22] On the death of Henry, his son Hugh succeeded to his lands in Reed, but in 1195 William de Scales, grandson of the above-mentioned Richard de Scales, brought a suit against him claiming various lands of his inheritance, including those in Reed.[23] The case was adjourned in 1199 for so long as Henry son of Hugh should be in the service of the king beyond the sea.[24] But later it was adjudged that Richard was not seised of the lands which Hugh held at the time of the death of Henry II, and judgement was given in favour of Hugh.[25] On Hugh's death his lands descended to his son Henry, who made a pilgrimage to Jerusalem and died there, leaving no children.[26] His brother Geoffrey was his heir, and did homage for his lands in 1221.[27]

In 1258 Geoffrey de Scales found himself too old and infirm to perform in person the services due to the king for his lands, and at the instance of Queen Eleanor Henry III granted that his son Geoffrey de Scales should do service in his stead in the king's armies and expeditions. In consideration of this Geoffrey de Scales granted his son his lands in Reed and Wyddial on condition that he should perform these duties and also attend the courts of the justices in eyre and of the sheriff.[28] In 1260 Henry III granted Geoffrey de Scales free warren in his lands in Reed and elsewhere.[29] Geoffrey de Scales, the father, and his son Geoffrey both died before 1267, and the

SCALES. *Gules six scallops or.*

---

[3] *East Herts. Arch. Soc. Trans.* ii, 266–8.
[4] *Dict. Nat. Biog.*
[5] *V.C.H. Herts.* i, 339*a.*
[6] *Ibid.* 339*a,* 329*a.*
[7] *Ibid.* 310*a.*
[8] *Ibid.* 319.
[9] *Ibid.* 339*a.*
[10] *Ibid.* 319. See manor of Chamberlains.
[11] *Ibid.* 329*a.*
[12] *Ibid.* 310*a.*
[13] *Ibid.* 319.
[14] *Abbrev. Rot. Orig.* (Rec. Com.), i, 25; *Cal. Pat.* 1340–3, p. 384; Chan. Inq. p.m. 29 Edw. III (2nd nos.), no. 4; 38 Edw. III, no. 10; 11 Ric. II, no. 15.
[15] *Feud. Aids,* ii, 433, 434.
[16] Chan. Inq. p.m. 38 Edw. III, no. 10.
[17] *Ibid.*
[18] *Ibid.* 16 Edw. III (2nd nos.), no. 41; Inq. a.q.d. file 317, no. 4; Chan. Inq. p.m. 38 Edw. III, no. 10.
[19] Chan. Inq. p.m. 16 Edw. III (2nd nos.), no. 41.
[20] *Abbrev. Plac.* (Rec. Com.), 99.
[21] Dugdale, *Baronage,* i, 616.
[22] *Cal. Pat.* 1388–92, p. 79.
[23] *Abbrev. Plac.* (Rec. Com.), 99.
[24] *Rot. Cur. Reg.* (Rec. Com.), i, 410.
[25] *Abbrev. Plac.* (Rec. Com.), 99.
[26] *Excerpta e Rot. Fin.* (Rec. Com.), i, 69.
[27] *Ibid.*
[28] *Cal. Pat.* 1247–58, p. 626.
[29] *Ibid.* 1258–66, p. 117.

custody of Thomas, son of the younger Geoffrey and a minor, was granted to his mother Eleanor, and the tenants of his lands were allowed quittance of suit at the hundred and county court during the minority of the heir.[30] In 1268 Thomas de Scales brought a suit against Ralph de Chamberlain for deforcing him of his lands in Reed while he adhered to the king against Simon de Montfort.[31] As Thomas was only five years old at this date[32] the suit must have been brought by his guardian, and the statement that he adhered to the king must refer rather to his family than to himself. Eleanor de Scales continued to hold in custody for her son until 1283.[33] Thomas then came of age and wished to assume possession of his lands, but his mother and her second husband, Robert Angot, opposed this on the ground that he was not yet twenty-one and that as he had been born at Boulogne he could not be admitted to proof of age.[34] An inquisition was held by which it was determined that he had reached his majority,[35] and the following year his mother and her husband acknowledged him and restored him his lands.[36] They obtained a grant of Reed, however, for the term of their lives.[37] It had reverted to Thomas de Scales by 1303,[38] and he continued to hold it till his death in 1341.[39] It then comprised a capital messuage worth nothing beyond repairs, 100 acres of land, of which 70 acres were sown before his death, 1 acre of meadow and 4 of pasture. There were four customary tenants.

Thomas de Scales's heir was his son, also Thomas, aged forty-two. He immediately granted the manor, with the exception of 30 acres of wood, to John de Scales for life.[40] In 1356–7 Thomas de Scales settled the reversion of the manor on himself and his wife Amice with remainder to his son Thomas in tail and contingent remainder to another son John.[41] Thomas de Scales died in 1364, and his son Thomas must have died before him, as his heir then was his grandson John the son of Thomas.[42] John died in 1388, and Reed descended to his son Thomas,[43] who held it until his death in February 1442–3.[44] His son John, aged twenty, succeeded him,[45] and was the last of this name to hold the manor, which had been in the possession of his ancestors for 400 years and by this date was called after them the manor of Deschallers or Challers. He died in 1467, leaving three daughters, Alice the wife of John More of More, co. Oxford, Margaret de Scales, and Anne the wife of John Harecourt.[46] The manor of Challers became the possession of Anne.[47] On the death of her first husband she married Giles Wellesborne, who also predeceased her.[48] Both her husbands suffered from financial embarrassment, as appears from the marriage settlement she made on her daughter and heir Margery with Humphrey Wellisburne in January 1493–4.[49] By this, in consideration of this marriage and of the fact that Humphrey had paid several of her debts and of the debts of her two husbands, she granted him the yearly issues of the manor, receiving only for the maintenance of herself and her maid 20 marks a year if she made her home with Humphrey or 40 marks if she lived elsewhere.[50] Margery seems to have had another suitor, John Rushton, who alleged a contract between them which Anne refused to acknowledge. In the event of John Rushton taking any step to annul the marriage of Humphrey and Margery, Challers was to go by her settlement to Humphrey for life with reversion to the heirs of Sir John de Scales, kt., other than the said Margery.[51] Anne died in March 1493–4, when Margery, her heiress, was aged eighteen.[52]

Humphrey Wellisburne died in 1516, and by his will left his wife all his lands in Great Wycombe for life and £40. In return for this, and in accordance with a promise she had made him, Margery Wellisburne in 1516 conveyed the manors of Reed and Wyddial to trustees to be settled to her use for life with remainder to her son Arthur Wellisburne and his heirs, or failing such heirs to her sons Ardewyn, Jasper and Henry Wellisburne and their heirs in succession.[53] Margery married as her second husband Thomas Cheyne, and in 1522 she sold the manor of Reed to Robert Dormer,[54] to whom Arthur Wellisburne also conveyed his rights in the manor.[55] Robert Dormer held the manor until 1530, when he received licence to alienate it to John Bowles.[56] In 1543 John Bowles died and his grandson Thomas inherited his estates.[57] Thomas Bowles was only thirteen, and his wardship and marriage with an annuity of £20 out of his estates were granted to John Sewester, attorney of the Court of Wards.[58] In 1557 Thomas sold Challers to William Hyde of Throcking,[59] who held it till 1567–8, when he sold it to Robert Bell of the Middle Temple and Dorothy his wife.[60] Sir Robert Bell, kt., chief baron of the Exchequer, died in 1576 seised of the manors of Chamberlains and Challers, with fisheries, free warren, court leet and view of frankpledge.[61] His eldest son and heir Edmund Bell of Beaupre, aged fifteen, succeeded to the property in Norfolk[62] which Dorothy Bell née Beaupre had brought her husband in marriage.[63] The property in Reed had been settled in 1573 on the second son Robert Bell with remainder to his father Sir Robert Bell and his heirs.[64] Robert Bell was captain of a company in the Netherlands and died leaving no children.[65] The manor of Challers appears to have reverted to his mother, who took for her second husband Sir John Peyton, Lieutenant of the Tower of London, by whom she had a son

[30] Close, 51 Hen. III, m. 6.
[31] *Abbrev. Plac.* (Rec. Com.), 177.
[32] See Coram Rege R. 88, m. 1 (Hil. 13 Edw. I).
[33] Assize R. 323; see Fine R. 4 Edw. I, m. 28; *Cal. Inq. p.m. Edw. I*, 45.
[34] Coram Rege R. 88, m. 1 (Hil. 13 Edw. I). [35] *Cal. Inq. p.m. Edw. I*, 309.
[36] *Abbrev. Plac.* (Rec. Com.), 206; Coram Rege R. 88, m. 1 (Hil. 13 Edw. I).
[37] Assize R. 325.
[38] *Feud. Aids*, ii, 432, 433.
[39] Chan. Inq. p.m. Edw. III, file 64, no. 20.
[40] *Cal. Pat.* 1340–3, p. 384; Inq. a.q.d. file 261, no. 17.

[41] Feet of F. Herts. 30 Edw. III, no. 447; Inq. a.q.d. file 317, no. 4.
[42] Chan. Inq. p.m. 38 Edw. III, no. 10; 6 Ric. II, no. 31.
[43] Ibid. 11 Ric. II, no. 15.
[44] Ibid. 21 Hen. VI, no. 20.
[45] Ibid.
[46] Ibid. Edw. IV, file 24, no. 28.
[47] *Cal. Inq. p.m. Hen. VII*, 426–7.
[48] Ibid. [49] Ibid.
[50] Ibid.
[51] Ibid.
[52] Ibid.
[53] Close, 7 Hen. VIII, no. 41.
[54] Ibid. 14 Hen. VIII, no 24; Feet of F. Herts. Mich. 14 Hen. VIII.

[55] Close, 14 Hen. VIII, no. 25.
[56] *L. and P. Hen. VIII*, iv, g. 6751 (28).
[57] Chan. Inq. p.m. (Ser. 2), lxviii, 14.
[58] *L. and P. Hen. VIII*, xviii (2), g. 449 (67).
[59] Pat. 3 & 4 Phil. and Mary, pt. iv, m. 16; Recov. R. East. 3 & 4 Phil. and Mary, rot. 560.
[60] Pat. 10 Eliz. pt. iv, m. 6.
[61] Chan. Inq. p.m. (Ser. 2), clxxxii, 28.
[62] Ibid.
[63] *Visit. of Norf.* (Harl. Soc. xxxii), 34.
[64] Chan. Inq. p.m. (Ser. 2), clxxxii, 28.
[65] *Visit. of Norf.* (Harl. Soc. xxxii), 34.

A HISTORY OF HERTFORDSHIRE

John Peyton.[66] In 1612 Sir John Peyton, sen., and Sir John Peyton, jun., and his wife Alice sold the manor of Chaliers to Sir Julius Adelmare *alias* Caesar, kt.[67]

Sir Julius was the son of an Italian named Caesar Adelmare, who came to England in 1550 and was court physician successively to Queen Mary and Queen Elizabeth.[68] In 1596 Sir Julius was made master of the hospital of St. Katharine,[69] and is said to have held a lease of the manor of Queenbury.[70] He was appointed chancellor of the Exchequer in 1606.[71] He married twice, and in 1625 he settled Reed on John,[72] the eldest son by his second marriage.[73] John Caesar was knighted in 1617, and married Anne the daughter of William Hungate.[74] In 1636 his father died and he came into possession of his property in Reed.[75] This he continued to hold[76] until 1668, when with his wife Anne he sold it to William Newland.[77] On the death of William it descended to Thomas Newland, who presented to the church in 1718.[78] In 1722 Thomas Newland and Mary his wife sold their property in Reed, which at this date appears for the first time as one manor styled Challers Chamberlains *alias* Chamberlains Challers (see below for Chamberlains), to John Manley and Kendrick Edesbury for ninety-nine years during their lives and the life of Isaac Manley of Dublin and of their son George Newland.[79]

Reed soon after came into the hands of Sir John Jennings, kt., commander-in-chief in the Mediterranean in 1711, who presented to the church in 1727.[80] Sir John died in 1743,[81] and the manor descended to his son George Jennings,[82] who married Mary the daughter of Michael Bourke, tenth Earl of Clanricarde.[83] He had a daughter Hester Elizabeth, who married John Peachey, the only son and heir of Sir James Peachey, bart.[84] In 1787 George Jennings settled the manor on John Peachey and Hester Elizabeth,[85] and on the death of George Jennings in 1790 it descended to his daughter and her husband.[86] In 1794 Sir James Peachey was created Lord Selsey, and on his death in 1808 his son succeeded to the title.[87] He held Reed[88] till his death in 1816,[89] when it passed to his son Henry John Peachey, third Lord Selsey, who died in 1838, leaving no children.[90] His sister the Hon. Caroline Mary Peachey inherited his estates[91] She married the Rev. Leveson Vernon-Harcourt, but

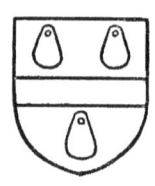

CAESAR. *Gules a chief argent with six roses countercoloured.*

JENNINGS. *Argent a fesse gules between three plummets sable.*

PEACHEY. *Azure a lion ermine with a forked tail and a quarter argent with a pierced molet gules therein.*

had no children.[92] On her death in 1871, according to the will of her mother Hester Elizabeth Jennings, Reed passed to the Rt. Hon. Hugh Henry Rose, first Lord Strathnairn of Strathnairn and Jhansi, who was descended through his mother from Philip Jennings of Dudleston Hall, co. Salop, the father of Sir John Jennings before mentioned.[93] He had gained his titles for his services in India.[94] He died unmarried in Paris in 1886,[95] and Reed passed to his brother Sir William Rose, who only survived him one month. It then descended to Admiral the Hon. George H. Douglas, the son of his sister the Countess of Morton, who subsequently sold his lands in Reed to Mr. Edward Pigg of Chipping, but all manorial rights appear by this date to have lapsed.[96]

The manor of *CHAMBERLAINS* possibly represents that hide of land which before the Conquest was held by Lening, a priest, one of Eddeva's men.[97] In 1086 this land had come into the possession of Hardwin de Scales, but was held by him of Count Alan of Britanny apart from his other and more important lands in Reed.[98] It remained with the descendants of Hardwin de Scales until the reign of Henry III.[99] At that time, while they adhered to the king in his struggle with Simon de Montfort, Ralph le Chamberlain seized some of their land by force.[100] A suit was brought against him in 1268 for its recovery by Thomas de Scales,[1] but it is probable that Ralph kept possession, for in 1346 his descendant Ralph le Chamberlain was holding land in Reed of Thomas de Scales by service of half a knight's fee.[2] It is from this family that the manor takes its name. Ralph le Chamberlain died in 1346, and his lands descended to his son Ralph, aged twenty.[3] Nothing further is heard of the Chamberlains in Reed, but

---

[66] *Visit. of Norf.* (Harl. Soc. xxxii), 34.
[67] Feet of F. Herts. Trin. 10 Jas. I; see Feet of F. Div. Co. Mich. 10 Jas. I.
[68] Lodge, *Life of Sir Julius Caesar*, 20.
[69] Ibid.
[70] Clutterbuck, *Hist. and Antiq. of Herts.* iii, 556.
[71] Lodge, op. cit. 22.
[72] Feet of F. Div. Co. East. 1 Chas. I; Recov. R. East. 1 Chas. I, rot. 36.
[73] Lodge, op. cit. 21.
[74] Ibid. 53, 54.
[75] Chan. Inq. p.m. (Ser. 2), cccclxxxiv, 159.
[76] Recov. R. East. 1649, rot. 46; Feet of F. Herts. Trin. 16 Chas. II.
[77] Feet of F. Herts. Trin. 20 Chas. II; see Feet of F. Herts. East. 35 Chas. II.
[78] Inst. Bks. (P.R.O.).
[79] Feet of F. Herts. East. 8 Geo. I.
[80] Inst. Bks. (P.R.O.).
[81] *Dict. Nat. Biog.*
[82] See Feet of F. Herts. Trin. 27 Geo. III; Inst. Bks. (P.R.O.).
[83] G.E.C. *Complete Peerage*, s.v. Selsey.
[84] Ibid.
[85] Feet of F. Herts. Trin. 27 Geo. III.
[86] See Inst. Bks. (P.R.O.); Clutterbuck, *Hist. and Antiq. of Herts.* iii, 554.
[87] G.E.C. *Complete Peerage*, s.v. Selsey.
[88] See Inst. Bks. (P.R.O.).
[89] G.E.C. loc. cit.
[90] Ibid.
[91] Cussans, *Hist. of Herts. Odsey Hund.* 141.
[92] Ibid.
[93] Ibid.
[94] G.E.C. *Complete Peerage*, s.v. Strathnairn.
[95] Ibid.
[96] Inform. from Captain Geo. Sholto Douglas.
[97] *V.C.H. Herts.* i, 319.
[98] Ibid.
[99] *Abbrev. Plac.* (Rec. Com.), 177.
[100] Ibid.
[1] Ibid.
[2] *Cal. Close*, 1346-9, pp. 109, 110. Henry le Chamberlain, who held the manor of Nuthampstead for a short time from 1315, may have been of the same family (see *Cal. Pat.* 1313-17, pp. 283-4).
[3] Chan. Inq. p.m. 20 Edw. III, no. 3.

250

ODSEY HUNDRED

REED

their lands may have come into the possession of Adam Esmond or Edmond, who was imprisoned for debt in 1373, at which date he held 3 acres of meadow, 34 acres of pasture and 3 acres of wood in Reed,[4] for in 1405 John Edmond was holding the manor of Chamberlains[5] first mentioned by that name. He conveyed it in that year to feoffees,[6] apparently in trust for John Walsingham,[7] for the latter granted it during the reign of Henry IV to John Grey and Joan his wife,[9] and Margaret Walsingham, widow, released all right in the manor in 1430.[9] On the death of John Grey Chamberlains descended to his son Ralph Grey, kt.,[10] who presented to the church in 1450.[11] He died in 1464, when the manor passed to his son Ralph, aged at that date twenty-four.[12]

Shortly after this Chamberlains came into the possession of John Horne, who presented to the church in 1477.[13] He must have died soon after, for John Shukburgh, husband of his daughter Clemency, presented in her right in 1479. John Shukburgh predeceased his wife, and she took to live with her son Thomas with his wife and three children.[14] Leaving them in her house at Reed, she went to London, where she married Thomas Staunton, 'contrarie to the will and mynde' of her son, who refused to allow Staunton to enter the house at Reed and assaulted his servants.[15] In consequence he was arrested, but escaped with the help of his friends and tried to break into the house.[16] Clemency and her husband brought a suit against her son in 1493,[17] but in February 1494–5 she joined with her husband and son in making a settlement of the manor.[18] By 1511 Chamberlains had descended to John Shukburgh,[19] who sold it in 1519 to Robert Dormer.[20] In 1522 Robert Dormer purchased the manor of Challers (q.v.), and from this date the two manors have descended together.

The manor of *QUEENBURY* (Querenebury, Quinbury, xvi cent.) was held in the time of Edward the Confessor by Aelfward, a man of Earl Harold. By 1086 it had become part of the possessions of Count Eustace of Boulogne, and was held of him by Robert Fitz Rozelin.[21] Queenbury always remained part of the honour of Boulogne.[22] From Robert Fitz Rozelin it passed, as did other fees held in this county by Robert, to the Trikets, who were possibly his descendants.[23] It was held by Hugh Triket,[24] who was living in the reign of Henry II, and descended to Simon Triket, who was holding it in 1210.[25] The Trikets do not again appear in Reed. Apparently a sub-feoffment of the manor had already been made to John Fitz Bernard,[26] and from him it descended to Walter Fitz Bernard.[27] In the reign of Henry III he sold it to Queen Eleanor.[28] In 1255 Eleanor had caused the dissolution of the hospital of St. Katharine outside the Tower of London, which had been founded by Queen Matilda, wife of Stephen, and the patronage of which was vested in the Queens of England.[29] She refounded it in 1273, and bestowed on it, among other estates, all her lands in Reed to be held in frankalmoign without power of alienation,[30] a grant which was declared to be to the king's loss.[31] It is to this circumstance that the manor of Queenbury appears to owe its name. In 1278 the hospital claimed in Reed view of frankpledge, gallows, and assize of bread and ale.[32] In 1287 it claimed these liberties and also tumbril.[33] At the time of the Dissolution the manor was farmed out for £7 6s. 8d.[34] It is probable that Henry VIII intended to dissolve the hospital, but that it was saved by Anne Boleyn, to whom as Queen of England it belonged.[35] Queenbury remained with the hospital of St. Katharine, which for many years leased it for a term of three lives to the lords of the manor of Challers.[36] The Hon. Mrs. Vernon-Harcourt, who died in 1871,[37] left the remainder of her lease to her god-daughter the Hon. Caroline Mary Frances Jervis.[38] About the year 1900 the hospital of St. Katharine sold Queenbury,[39] which passed through several hands before it was purchased about 1909 by Mr. Thomas E. Brandt, the present owner.[40]

St. Katharine's Hospital. *Party fessewise gules and azure with a sword lying fessewise in the chief and a broken Katharine wheel or in the foot.*

The tithes of the manor of Queenbury, together with certain lands called the demesne lands of Mynchey Porcyn, were held by the priory of St. Leonard of Stratford-at-Bow.[41] These lands were valued at £2 in 1535.[42] After the dissolution of the priory of St. Leonard they were granted in 1539 to Ralph Sadleir.[43] He restored them to the Crown in exchange for other lands in 1547–8,[44] and they then came into the possession of Richard Chambers, who died in 1549, and left them to his son Robert, aged eleven.[45] Robert Chambers received a quitclaim from a certain Robert Johnson and his wife

---

[4] Chan. Inq. p.m. 47 Edw. III (1st nos.), no. 49.
[5] Close, 10 Hen. IV, m. 32.
[6] Ibid.
[7] See Chan. Inq. p.m. 5 Edw. IV, no. 27b.
[8] Ibid.
[9] Close, 8 Hen. VI, m. 4.
[10] Chan. Inq. p.m. 5 Edw. IV, no. 27b.
[11] Clutterbuck, *Hist. and Antiq. of Herts.* iii, 555.
[12] Chan. Inq. p.m. 5 Edw. IV, no. 27b.
[13] Clutterbuck, loc. cit.; see Star Chamb. Proc. Hen. VII, no. 59.
[14] Star Chamb. Proc. Hen. VII, no. 59.
[15] Ibid.
[16] Ibid.
[17] Ibid.; see Star Chamb. Proc. Hen. VIII, bdle. 20, no. 129.
[18] Feet of F. Herts. Hil. 10 Hen. VII.
[19] Clutterbuck, *Hist. and Antiq. of Herts.* iii, 555.
[20] Close, 11 Hen. VIII, no. 2; Feet of F. Herts. Trin. 11 Hen. VIII.
[21] *V.C.H. Herts.* i, 321a, 282.
[22] *Liber Niger Scacc.* (ed. T. Hearne), i, 389, 390; *Red. Bk. of Exch.* (Rolls Ser.), ii, 501, 581; *Testa de Nevill* (Rec. Com.), 270, 274; *Hund. R.* (Rec. Com.), i, 88.
[23] See manors of Corneybury in Wyddial and Barkesdon Green in Aspenden.
[24] *Liber Niger Scacc.* loc. cit.; *Red Bk. of Exch.* loc. cit.
[25] *Red Bk. of Exch.* loc. cit.
[26] See *Liber Niger Scacc.* loc. cit.; *Testa de Nevill* (Rec. Com.), 270.
[27] See *Red Bk. of Exch.* ii, 581; *Testa de Nevill* (Rec. Com.), 274.
[28] *Hund. R.* (Rec. Com.), i, 88 seq.
[29] Dugdale, *Mon.* vii, 694.
[30] Ibid.; *Cal. Chart. R.* 1257–1300, p. 409.
[31] *Hund. R.* (Rec. Com.), i, 88 seq.
[32] Assize R. 323.
[33] Ibid. 325.
[34] *Valor Eccl.* (Rec. Com.), i, 386.
[35] Dugdale, *Mon.* vii, 694.
[36] Cussans, *Hist. of Herts. Odsey Hund.* 143; see Feet of F. Herts. East. 8 Geo. I; East. 47 Geo. III.
[37] Cussans, loc. cit.
[38] Ibid.
[39] Inform. from the Rev. Severne Majendie of St. Katharine's Hospital.
[40] Inform. from Mr. Thomas Brandt of Queenbury.
[41] Chan. Inq. p.m. (Ser. 2), lxxxviii, 88; Ct. of Req. bdle. 135, no. 1; Dugdale, *Mon.* iv, 119.
[42] Dugdale, loc. cit.
[43] *L. and P. Hen. VIII*, xiv (1), 403 (44).
[44] Dugdale, loc. cit.
[45] Chan. Inq. p.m. (Ser. 2), lxxxviii, 75.

251

A HISTORY OF HERTFORDSHIRE

Audrey (possibly lessees) in 1562.[46] In 1573, Francis Ridall, rector of East Reed, claimed all tithes in East Reed except those from certain freeholds and demesne lands of the manor of Queenbury, and he brought a suit against Robert Chambers and his tenant John Cannon, who refused to pay tithes from the copyhold land of that manor.[47] Robert Chambers claimed that these tithes never had belonged to the rector of East Reed.[48] Mynchey Porcyn and the tithes of Queenbury came later into the possession of Richard Turner, who in 1597 demised the close called Mynchens to Thomas Turner for eighty years with reversion to John Turner.[49] John Turner died in 1602, and Thomas Turner, aged sixty, was his brother and heir.[50] Richard Turner died in 1604, at which date he was seised of the tithes and the close.[51] It appears, however, that in lieu of tithes the rectors of Reed had the right to half an acre of wheat and half an acre of barley in Queenbury. This, before 1722, had been commuted for a payment of 40s. chargeable on an acre of land called Parson's Acre.[51a]

Certain lands in Reed, appandant to the manor of Sandon, were held by the Dean and Chapter of St. Paul's in the 10th century, and the latter were confirmed in their possession by King Athelstan in 939.[52]

PLAN OF REED CHURCH

SCALE OF FEET

TOWER | NAVE | CHANCEL
PORCH

▓ 11th CENT ░ 15th CENT
▓ 14th CENT ☐ MODERN

These lands are not recorded in the Domesday Survey in 1086, but they remained attached to the manor of Sandon (q.v.), which was subsequently called Gannocks Manor. In the 14th century the lands in Reed were also called Gannocks,[53] and were described as 30 acres of land held of the Dean and Chapter of St. Paul's.[54] No record of these lands occurs after this time, but there still exist in the south of the parish a grove and green which bear the name of Gannocks.

The church of ST. MARY consists of chancel 21 ft. 6 in. by 17 ft., nave 34 ft. by 19 ft., south porch and west tower 10 ft. 6 in. by 10 ft.; all dimensions taken internally. The walls are of flint with stone dressings, the roofs are tiled.

The nave appears to belong to a pre-Conquest period, probably about the middle of the 11th century; part of the chancel dates from about 1350; the west tower is early 15th-century work; the east wall of the chancel, the chancel arch and the south porch were rebuilt in the 19th century, when other repairs were made.

The large five-light east window of the chancel is modern, but parts of the reticulated tracery belonged to the 14th-century window. In the north wall is a window of two trefoiled lights with a quatrefoil in the head, of about 1350 date; the two-light window in the south wall is modern; the chancel arch also is modern.

In the north wall of the nave are two windows, each of two cinquefoiled lights under a square head, and of 15th-century date; they have been much repaired; between them is a blocked north doorway, which has a semicircular head, rudely moulded, and with a plain tympanum; the jambs have engaged shafts with roughly voluted capitals under a heavy splayed abacus; the bases are much decayed. The doorway appears to date from the beginning of the 12th century. The doorway itself is of Barnack stone, but the inner arch is of clunch. There are two modern two-light windows in the south wall of the nave, and the doorway between them is of late 14th-century work, with arch and jambs of two orders continuously moulded; the label has foliated stops. In the east jamb of the doorway outside are remains of a stoup. In the north-east corner of the nave are remains of the stair to the roodloft. Each of the four angles of the nave externally is formed of long-and-short work of Barnack stone. The western angles have two splayed base-courses, one 2 ft. above the other; the lower one has the base-course on the angle quoin only, all the rest, which presumably was carried round the nave, has disappeared; the upper base-course has also disappeared round the church, but is carried round the west tower.[55] The quoin stones are flush with the flint walling.

The pointed tower arch is of two splayed orders, and in the north jamb is an ogee-headed shallow niche, about 3 ft. from the ground. The west tower is of three stages, with an embattled parapet, except on the east, which is plain. The west window is of two trefoiled lights, with much of the stonework restored. Under the window there has been at one time a rough opening, now blocked. The second stage is pierced on the south side with a narrow single light; the belfry has a single pointed light on each face, much worn.

The font is modern, but the remains of the 15th-century one formerly in the garden of Reed Hall, are now in Barkway Church; the bowl is octagonal, and underneath are carved flowers and shields and some emblems of the Passion; some fragments of tracery are also at Reed Hall.

The communion table is of early 17th-century work and has turned and moulded legs.

There are no memorials in the church.

---

[46] Feet of F. Herts. Hil. 4 Eliz.
[47] Ct. of Req. bdle. 135, no. 1.
[48] Ibid.
[49] Chan. Inq. p.m. (Ser. 2), cclxvii, 55.
[50] Ibid.; Ct. of Wards, Misc. Bks. Extents and Attachments, dcxviii.
[51] Chan. Inq. p.m. (Ser. 2), cccix, 103.
[51a] Note in parish register book communicated by Rev. W. T. Stubbs.
[52] Birch, Cart. Sax. ii, 451.
[53] Chan. Inq. p.m. 38 Edw. III, no. 10.
[54] Ibid. 16 Edw. III (2nd nos.), no. 41; 29 Edw. III (2nd nos.), no. 4.
[55] It is possible that the double base-course of the quoins, the upper of which is carried round the 15th-century tower, together with its disappearance from the nave walls, may be due to a later re-building of the nave walls, re-using the old quoin stones. The clunch inner arch of the north door may give colour to this.

252

REED CHURCH FROM THE NORTH-EAST

ROYSTON CHURCH: 14TH-CENTURY EFFIGY IN CHANCEL

ODSEY HUNDRED

ROYSTON

There are three bells : the treble and second are unmarked, and the tenor, by Robert Oldfeild, is inscribed 'God save the King,' and dated 1614. The communion plate consists of paten, 1806, small cup, 1804, and another paten, 1863. The registers are as follows : (i) baptisms and burials from 1539 to 1768, marriages 1540 to 1752 ; (iii) marriages 1755 to 1807. In 1830 there was a book (ii) baptisms and burials 1768 to 1812, but this has since disappeared.

The living of the church of Reed is a rectory. The advowson was originally held by the Scales family, who were lords of the manor of Challers. Henry de Scales and Hugh his son granted it in the reign of Henry II to the Cluniac convent of Lewes, together with an annual pension.[56] This pension was still chargeable on the church in 1428,[57] but it is probable that at some time while the convent of Lewes was in the king's hands during the wars with France the advowson was acquired by the lord of Chamberlains, or that the convent itself alienated it, for in 1405 John Edmond, lord of the manor of Chamberlains, held the advowson,[58] and from this date it descended until lately with that manor (q.v.). When Admiral the Hon. George H. Douglas sold his lands in Reed he retained the advowson, and it is held at the present time by his son, Captain George Sholto Douglas. The parish of Reed was united to that of Barkway in 1800.

ADVOWSON

CHARITIES In 1602 Richard Turner by his will gave 20s. a year to the poor. This sum is paid out of the close called 'Barton's' and is distributed in bread.

ROYSTON

Crux Roys,[1] Crux Roaesie, Rhosiae, Roais, Roeis, Roheise or Roihes (xii cent.) ; Crux Roesia or Roys (xiii cent.) [2] ; Crux Roesea [3] or Roesia and Roiston [4] (xiv cent.).

Royston lies upon the northern slopes of the Hertfordshire Chalk Downs, which almost surround the town. Royston Heath (in Therfield parish) is noted as the recreation ground of the town. The heath has given its name to the 'Royston Crow.'[5] It was a favourite hunting-place of James I,[6] was the site of the Royston races[7] and prize-fights,[8] and may have been the spot intended for tournaments at Royston forbidden by the king in 1234 and 1331.[9]

The town itself, on the north-eastern edge of the heath, is built about the intersection of Ermine Street, which runs northward from London to York, with the Icknield Way running almost due east and west. The town is divided for Parliamentary purposes by the Icknield Way, which here forms the boundary between Cambridgeshire and Hertfordshire. The same division existed for administrative purposes until September 1897, when the whole of Royston was included in the administrative county of Hertford.[10]

Royston was accounted a distinct 'vill' for the assessment of subsidies in 1307,[11] but it lay within five ecclesiastical parishes, viz. Barkway, Reed and Therfield, co. Herts., Melbourn and Kneesworth, co. Cambs.,[12] until 1540, when an Act of Parliament constituted it a separate ecclesiastical parish.[13] For administrative purposes the Cambridgeshire and Hertfordshire portions of the town were united under one vestry in 1781.[14] Under the Local Government Act of 1894 [15] there were set up within the township separate councils for the two parts of Royston (ecclesiastical) parish and for the several parishes of Therfield, Barkway, Bassingbourn, Kneesworth and Melbourn.[16] Finally, in 1897, the whole township was converted

---

[56] Cott. MS. Vesp. F xv, fol. 310.
[57] *Feud. Aids*, ii, 461.
[58] Close, 10 Hen. IV, m. 32.
[1] The earliest form of the name yet found. It occurs in the charter of Ralph of Rochester (1163–84) and is applied to a district and not a cross, for Ralph mentions his men and tenants 'in Cruce Roys' (Harl. MS. 7041, fol. 7). The nominative form is found in the bull of Lucius III (see below) and in Lay Subs. R. bdle. 120, no. 8.
[2] 'Cruceroye' occurs once in 1269 (Hunter, *Rot. Selecti*, 242).
[3] 'Villa de Cruce Roesia,' 'villa de Cruce Roesea' (*Cal. Pat.* 1317–21, p. 371; 1330–4, p. 138).
[4] The earliest instance of 'Roiston' has been found in a plea of 1327 (Plac. de Banco, East. 1 Edw. III, m. 22). Camden says that the town is 'not very ancient as having risen since the Norman Conquest, for in those days there was a famous lady named Roysia (by some supposed to have been the Countess of Norfolk) who erected a cross upon the roadside in this place from thence for many years called Royse's cross . . . and by degrees it came to be a town which instead of Royse's Cross took the name of Royston' (*Britannia* [ed. Gough], i, 318). Following this statement, which is apparently a mere conjecture, antiquaries have put forward many 'ladies candidates for giving the name' (Salmon, *Hist. of Herts.* 355). Among them are Rose wife of Richard de Clare (Camden, loc. cit.); Rose wife of Eudo Dapifer, within whose fee of Newsells the priory of Royston was founded later ; Rose widow of Geoffrey de Mandeville and wife of Payn de Beauchamp. Stukeley imagined the last-named Rose going over the heathland from her manor of Newsells to her oratory at Royston (*Palaeographia Britannica*, no. 1, Origines Roystonianae). She, however, did not hold the manor of Newsells, which belonged to the honour of Boulogne and was held by the family of Merk and Rochester. The supposition may have arisen from the fact that the manor of Nuthamstead next Newsells was parcel of the Mandeville fief. For a summary of these suggestions see Beldam, *Origin and Uses of the Royston Cave*, 6–10. It is clear that the name was originally 'Rose's Cross' and that it referred to a wayside cross erected by a certain Rose, but her identity remains uncertain. The most probable conjecture is that she was Rose wife of Eudo Dapifer.
[5] *V.C.H. Herts.* i, 204.
[6] See below.
[7] *V.C.H. Herts.* i, 366 ; they existed in 1605 (Rutland MSS. [Hist. MSS. Com.], iv, 454, 455).
[8] *V.C.H. Herts.* i, 370.
[9] *Cal. Pat.* 1232–47, p. 70 ; 1330–4, p. 139.
[10] A. Kingston, *Hist. of Royston*, 192.
[11] Lay Subs. R. bdle. 120, no. 8.
[12] Stat. 32 Hen. VIII, cap. 44 ; cf. Exch. Dep. Mich. 25 Geo. II, no. 3.
[13] Stat. 32 Hen. VIII, cap. 44. The following were reported to be the parish bounds in 1607 : 'from Roiston Townesende towards Walden to the place where the gallowes did lately stande, from thence over the heath to the nether end of the Granges called the Priory Granges or Roiston Granges to London Waie, from thence overthwart the lands to Reede Balke, from thence overthwart the footpath to the south end of the close late of Mychaell Chambers gent. deceased, and from thence along by the closes ends to the lymekill, and from thence to the utter parte of the Cardinall Hatt Closes to London Highwaie going from thence untill they come to Salter's Mare going to the end of it and from thence Retourne to the eight-acre close ende and soe to Walden Waie' (Exch. Dep. East. 5 Jas. I, no. 16).
[14] A. Kingston, *Fragments of Two Centuries*, 34. There were, however, separate overseers and churchwardens.
[15] Stat. 56 & 57 Vict. cap. 73.
[16] Kingston, *Hist. of Royston*, 192.

253

A HISTORY OF HERTFORDSHIRE

into a single urban district lying entirely within the county of Hertford.[17]

The intersection of the roads in the centre of the town is still called 'the Cross.' In the garden of the town hall in Melbourn Street is preserved a large boulder of Red Millstone Grit, weighing approximately two tons, supposed to be the base of a cross removed from the cross roads. It has a square socket on its upper surface, probably for a cross.[18] Beside it are two fragments of a stone coffin-lid with a cross on the face removed from 'Chapel Field' in Kneesworth Street. Under the old butter market, which stood in the middle of the Icknield Way, now the west end of Melbourn Street, a little south-east of the Cross, a cave hollowed out of the chalk was discovered in 1742.[19] It was then partly filled with earth. Dr. William Stukeley, Secretary of the Society of Antiquaries, conjectured that the cave was the oratory of the 'Lady Rose,' wife of Geoffrey de Mandeville.[20] His romance was rudely destroyed by the Rev. Charles Parkin, who maintained that the excavation was of Saxon origin.[21] A heated argument followed,[22] but the origin and use of the cave remain uncertain. In mediaeval times it was evidently used for religious purposes, and the fact that a hermit lived at Royston about 1506 has led to the supposition that it became a hermitage.[23] It may be identical with the 'Hermitage' in the parish of Barkway acquired by Sir Robert Chester after its suppression.[23a] The cave is a large dome-shaped hole, about 28 ft. deep and 17 ft. in diameter at the bottom, cut out of the solid chalk. It is ventilated by a small grating in the pavement above. In 1790 the present passage was cut to the cave through the chalk. The walls of the cave are rudely sculptured with figures in low relief, among which are figures of St. Christopher, St. Katherine, the Cross of St. Helena, the Holy Family, Conversion of St. Paul, and many others. There appears to have been an upper story to the cave at one period, the walls having been cut back to receive the timbers. The figures were probably carved in the 13th or 14th century. It seems probable that the cave was filled in during the 16th century when the lord of the manor 'buylded up in the myddest of Icknell Streate . . . a fayer House or Crosse . . . for a clockhowse and a Pryson Howse.'[24]

It would seem probable that the market-place, around which the early town would naturally be formed, originally occupied the widened part of Ermine Street to the north and south of the point where the Icknield Way crosses it. As in other towns, this market-place seems to have become at an early date covered by permanent stalls and then by shops till these buildings divided it into two streets and became known as early as the 16th century as Middle Row. The western street in its southern part was called later Dead Street and afterwards Back Street.[25] The present market-place is on sloping ground east of the High Street and south of the church and site of the priory.

In 1189 Richard I granted to the priory the right to hold a market at Royston and to have a fair there throughout Whitsun week and a market on the fourth day of each week with court of pie-powder and all the customs of the fair of Dunstable.[26] Another fair to be held on the eve and day of the translation of St. Nicholas (May 8–9) was granted to the hospital of St. Nicholas on 2 January 1212–13,[27] and was probably held in the Cambridgeshire portion of the town, where the hospital was situated.[28] In 1236 it was converted into a three days' fair on the eve, day and morrow of the same feast.[29] It probably became extinct with the hospital, which had ceased to exist before 1359.[30] In 1242 Henry III granted to the Prior of Royston another fair to be held on the vigil and feast of St. Thomas the Martyr (July 6–7), the patron saint of his house.[31]

From the first the situation of the town on the cross-roads in the midst of the barley-growing country must have caused the markets and fairs to prosper. In 1291 they were valued at £9 13s. 4d.[32] In 1223 and 1226 the maximum price of wine was fixed at a higher rate in Royston than elsewhere, owing to the distance of the town from the coast.[33] The prior made good his right to the market and to the fairs at Whitsuntide and the feast of St. Thomas in 1278.[34] The prior had been involved in disputes with the Abbot of Westminster and the Master of the Knights Templars, who claimed exemption from toll in all English markets. In 1247–8 the abbot pleaded the charters of Edward the Confessor and William I against the claims of the prior.[35] The dispute with the Templars, who owned property in Royston,[36] began in 1199 and was still continuing in 1200.[37] In 1254 the Master of the Templars impleaded the prior for imprisoning and beating certain of his men who had come to the market on the Templars' business.[38] The markets and fairs were frequently disturbed during the 13th and 14th centuries.[39] In May 1537, shortly after the dissolution of the priory, the market, fairs, court of pie-powder with the stallage and piccage and the profits of the windmill of the late priory were leased to Richard Cromwell (afterwards knighted) for twenty-one years.[40] Much of the market-place was, however,

---

[17] Kingston, *Hist. of Royston*, 192.
[18] Ibid. 203; cf. Beldam, *The Origin and Uses of Royston Cave* (ed. 1858), 7.
[19] Dr. Stukeley describes its discovery and the excavation of the loose earth which filled it (*Origines Roystonianae*, pt. i, 5).
[20] Ibid.
[21] C. Parkin, *Answer to Dr. Stukeley's Origines Roystonianae* (ed. 1744).
[22] *Origines Roystonianae*, pt. ii. Mr. J. Y. Akerman in 1834 noted its similarity to a Roman sepulchral vault (*Archaeologia*, xxxiv, 27; Beldam, *Origin and Uses of the Royston Cave*, 17 et seq.).
[23] Beldam, op. cit. 48.
[23a] See under Barkway.

[24] Survey in 1610 printed by Kingston, *Hist. of Royston*, 117.
[25] Mins. Accts. Hen. VIII, no. 1606. There were twenty-five shops in Bochery Row and Smithy Row (Kingston, *Hist. of Royston*, 116 et seq.).
[26] Cart. Antiq. R. 6, printed by Dugdale, *Mon.* vi, 405; cf. Memo. R. (Exch. L.T.R.), Hil. 12 Hen. VI, 'Records,' m. 18.
[27] *Cal. Rot. Chart.* (Rec. Com.), 189*b*, 192*b*.   [28] See below.
[29] *Cal. Chart. R.* 1226–57, p. 218.
[30] Chan. Inq. p.m. 33 Edw. III (1st nos.), no. 44.
[31] *Cal. Chart. R.* 1226–57, p. 268.
[32] Pope Nich. Tax. (Rec. Com.), 14*b*.

[33] *Rot. Lit. Claus.* (Rec. Com.), i, 568; ii, 149.
[34] *Plac. de Quo Warr.* (Rec. Com.), 283.
[35] Assize R. 318, m. 5 d.
[36] Attached to Shingay preceptory (*L. and P. Hen. VIII*, xv, 613 [1]).
[37] *Rot. Cur. Reg.* (Rec. Com.), i, 229; ii, 82, 143, 217, 218. This plea concerned 'liberties,' probably the exemption from toll claimed by both parties. Salmon (*Hist. of Herts.* 356) states that the prior was obliged to restore 37s. taken from the Templars as stallage.
[38] *Abbrev. Plac.* (Rec. Com.), 137.
[39] Misc. Chan. Inq. file 53, no. 4; see below.
[40] *L. and P. Hen. VIII*, xiii (1), p. 584.

254

ODSEY HUNDRED — ROYSTON

occupied by about fifty shops held on lease by various owners.[41] Sir Richard Cromwell transferred his interest in the market to Edward Annesby.[42] Nevertheless in 1540 a grant was made to Robert Chester of all the possessions of the priory 'with two fairs, one lasting throughout Whitsun week, the other on 7 July and the two days following, and a market on every Wednesday at Royston.'[43] The claims of Annesby and Chester were considered by the Court of Augmentations between 1540 and 1544, and apparently the decision was in favour of the lord of the manor. The profits of the fair and market have since remained with the successive lords.

The great corn market of Royston is frequently noticed in the writings of 17th-century travellers, one of whom describes Royston as a 'dry town good for the utterance of cattell barley and malt.'[44] The Corn Exchange was built by the lord of the manor in 1829.[45] The present market-house on the hill was built about 1836. A 'tolbooth' had existed in 1341 and contained the stocks.[46] It may have been at the cross-ways near the site of the Clock House, where the stocks stood until they were removed to the Market Hill.[47] Before 1792 fairs on Ash Wednesday, Wednesday in Easter week and the first Wednesday after 10 October had been added to those granted to the priory,[48] and these still existed in 1888,[49] but the Whitsun fair is now extinct, the July fair, sometimes called Becket's fair, has almost disappeared, and the October fair alone is of any importance.[50]

At the apex of the present triangular market is Fish Hill, facing the county court erected in 1849.[51] On this hill a schoolhouse was built by contributions from gentlemen of the town and neighbourhood about 1716.[52] It was afterwards given to the use of the parish.[53] Henry Andrews, astronomer, calculator to the Board of Longitude and to Moore's Almanack, taught in this school in 1767.[54] The infants' schools date from 1827; Board and National schools were established about 1840.[55]

In High Street are a few 17th-century cottages built of timber and plaster with modern fronts, and opposite the Bull Hotel is a 15th-century timber and plaster house on brick foundations with a projecting upper story supported on brackets and bow windows on the ground floor. A way called John Street was opened into the High Street from Fish Hill after a disastrous fire which occurred in 1841.[56] At the north-east corner of John Street the present Congregational chapel was built soon after the fire[57] to replace the old Meeting House which had existed in Middle Row, Kneesworth Street, since 1706.[58] The Congregationalists had met in the house of John Wheeler in 1672,[59] and their meetings possibly originated in the lectures given on market days by Nathaniel Ball, the ejected minister of Barley (1660–2).[60] The Baptist chapel near Barkway Street was built in 1896.[61]

The High Street and Back Street contain numerous inns, some of which date from posting days. The 'Red Lion' on the east side of the High Street, now no longer an inn, was the chief of these. In rooms at the back of it was held the famous Royston Club, partly political, partly convivial, which was in existence before 1689 and broke up about the middle of the 18th century.[62] The 'Bull' at the top of the High Street has existed since 1520.[63] Petty sessions were held there, and it was under protest that the magistrates moved to the new county court in 1850.[64] The end house of Middle Row on the west side of the High Street near the Cross was the Tabard Inn,[65] where in 1539 a servant of the Bishop of Durham spoke openly against the dissolution of monasteries before the 'good man' of the inn.[66] At least eleven such inns in the town then gave accommodation to the travellers who passed through on the way from London to the north.[67] For the spiritual 'relief of poor people coming and going through the town' Richard Argentine, Sheriff of Cambridgeshire in 1224, founded the chapel of St. John and St. James on the south side of Baldock Street.[68] It was evidently identical with the hospital of St. James existing in 1251,[69] and there was added to it the chantry of St. Nicholas, once a separate chapel in the Cambridgeshire portion of the town.[70] The chapel of St. John and St. James was suppressed in 1547,[71] and the site let in succession to Edward Chester in January 1565–6, to John Hall and to John Moore.[72] Hall, acting in trust for Edward Chester, who was serving in the Netherlands, obtained a confirmation of title against Sir Giles Alington, kt., heir to the patrons and founders, who asserted his right to the 'chapel lands.'[73] In 1607 a grant in fee simple of the late chapel or hospital and its possessions was

---

[41] Mins. Accts. Hen. VIII, no. 1606.
[42] Ct. of Aug. Proc. i, 55.
[43] L. and P. Hen. VIII, xvi, 379 (60).
[44] Ely Episcopal Records (ed. Gibbon), 152; Hist. MSS. Com. Rep. xiii, App. ii, 274 (Baskerville); Ogilby, Britannia, 10.
[45] Kingston, Hist. of Royston, 202.
[46] Assize R. 337, m. 4.
[47] They were afterwards set up on Fish Hill for Hertfordshire, and in Kneesworth Street for Cambridgeshire (Kingston, Hist. of Royston, 200–1).
[48] Rep. on Markets and Tolls (1888), i, 170.
[49] Ibid.
[50] Kingston, Hist. of Royston, 257.
[51] Ibid. 202; Herts. Co. Rec. Sess. R. ii, 461.
[52] Salmon, Hist. of Herts. (ed. 1728), 358.
[53] Kingston, Hist. of Royston, 181.
[54] Ibid. 212; Dict. Nat. Biog.
[55] Ibid.; cf. Close, 1840, pt. clxviii, no. 12; pt. clxxv, no. 21; 4 Will. IV, pt. l, no. 4; 1861, pt. cxxv, no. 1.
[56] Kingston, Hist. of Royston, 200.
[57] Ibid. 155; Close, 1841, pt. cxci, no. 10.
[58] Kingston, Hist. of Royston, 153–5; the 'covenant' of the members was made in 1705, five years after the first organization of the meeting.
[59] Cal. S. P. Dom. 1672, p. 379.
[60] Urwick, Nonconformity in Herts. 811. It has recently been proved that the Puritan controversialist Cartwright was a native of Royston (Kingston, Hist. of Royston, 204).
[61] Kingston, Hist. of Royston, 157. The Anabaptist, Edward Wightman, prosecuted in consequence of a petition which he presented to James I at Royston, 1611, was the last person burnt for heresy in England (Dict. Nat. Biog.).
[62] Gent. Mag. l, 474; liii, 813.
[63] Kingston, Hist. of Royston, 198.
[64] Hardy, Sess. R. (Herts. Co. Rec.), ii, 461.
[65] Beldam, 'Royston Court House' (Arch. xl, 137).
[66] L. and P. Hen. VIII, xiv (2), p. 281.
[67] Mins. Accts. Hen. VIII, no. 1606. They were the 'Lamb,' 'Crane,' 'Swan,' 'Dolphin,' 'Sarsonesbedd,' 'Greyhound,' 'White Hart,' 'Bell,' 'George,' 'Crown,' and the 'Tabard' with its 'garden called Babiarde.' For a further account of the inns see Kingston, Hist. of Royston, 198–200.
[68] Chant. Cert. Herts. 20, no. 62; Beldam, 'Royston Court House' (Arch. xl, 137).
[69] Cal. Pat. 1247–58, p. 92; the double invocation has been found first in 1363 after the transfer of the chantry of St. Nicholas (Linc. Epis. Reg. Inst. Bk. Bokingham; cf. Cal. Pat. 1377–81, p. 55).
[70] Cal. Close, 1354–60, p. 587.
[71] Chant. Cert. 20, no. 62.
[72] Pat. 18 Eliz. pt. xiv, m. 29; 22 Eliz. pt. vii.
[73] Ct. of Req. bdle. 78, no. 72; cf. Feet of F. Herts. East. 2 & 3 Phil. and Mary.

made to Sir Roger Aston, kt., one of the gentlemen of the Bedchamber, and to John Grymesditch.[74] The chapel was 'new made into a fair dwelling house' shortly before 1610, and was then in the occupation of Francis Hall.[75] On the opposite (north) side of Baldock Street a house and yard formed part of the endowment of the chapel.[76] West of it the 'Gables' represents the 'Cardynall's Hat' of 1610, and east of it was another inn, the 'Half Moon,' next the corner house of Back Street.[77]

For a short distance north of the Cross, Back Street and Kneesworth Street are still divided by 'Middle Row.' The whole of this neighbourhood is associated with the house and lodgings occupied by James I and Charles I and their court. A building in Kneesworth Street is all that remains of the eastern part of the 'King's Lodgings,' the rest having been demolished probably early in the 18th century. The building is rectangular and measures, roughly, about 53 ft. by 19 ft.; the front is on the east side facing the garden, the back facing the street. It consists of two stories with attics and a cellar under the south part. At either end on each story is an apartment, and between them is a square staircase with a newel stair, the old octagonal oak post of which still remains but without its finial at the top. The south room on the ground story has an old fireplace with a wooden lintel, partly built up, above which are remains of a 17th-century painted ornament; in the south wall is a wide niche with blocked hatchway to the adjoining buttery, now demolished. Some chamfered beams still remain in some of the rooms. The south room on the upper story has an old brick fireplace with four-centred arch with splayed edge and stops, all cemented; it is surrounded with 18th-century wooden jambs and lintel, bolection moulded. In the north room are remains of a coloured stencilled pattern, about 6 in. wide, under the small plaster cornice, and as vertical bands dividing the walls into panels; it is of 17th-century work. Externally the street front has two large plain projecting chimneys, mostly rebuilt, only the lower parts being of the old thin bricks. The entrance doorway and windows are modern. The east or garden front was entirely rebuilt early in the 18th century, and has moulded brick cornice and plain flanking pilasters. The whole building was repaired in 1910 and a wing added on the north. The roof is tiled. A timber-built house with projecting upper story and tiled roof in Kneesworth Street, to the south of the palace, evidently formed part of the palace out-buildings.[77a] It belongs to the 16th century, and retains its old wooden door frame and open roof with moulded trusses. The interior has been considerably altered. To the north of the palace are some remains of the brick walls of the old stables.

OLD HOUSES, HIGH STREET, ROYSTON

---

[74] Pat. 5 Jas. I, pt. xvii, m. 16.
[75] Survey printed by Kingston, *Hist. of Royston*, 116. Among its endowments was the house called Copthall in Bassingbourn, which was let in 1547 to 'one Dixe,' and granted after the suppression of the hospital to Thomas Wendye (Aug. Off. Misc. Bks. lxvii, fol. 625; Pat. 2 Edw. VI, pt. ii).
[76] Survey printed by Kingston, *Hist. of Royston*, 116.
[77] Ibid.
[77a] It is probably identical with the 'Greyhound,' converted into a guard-chamber, or with the Prince's Buttery (see below).

ODSEY HUNDRED

In 1652 the whole of the Lodgings, which then projected westwards into the park, so commanding a view of the road north and south, is described as 'all of brick well-tiled double-built, in length 78 ft., breadth 43 ft., height from eaves to ground 24 ft., thickness of walls 24 inches.' Below stairs were six lodging-chambers well-floored and well-matted ; above stairs six rooms, including the presence and privy chambers, with wainscot shuttings to all windows.[78] James I passed through Royston on Friday, 29 April 1603, on his way to London in the month following his accession and was entertained by Robert Chester at the Priory.[79] Attracted by the opportunities afforded by Royston for his favourite sport of hunting, James I hired Chester's house for one year,[80] probably the first of his reign, and began in 1604 to convert the 'Cock' and the 'Greyhound' into a house for himself.[81] Simon Basill was responsible for the 'finishing' of the King's Lodgings in 1607. During this year partitions were set up 'in the pages' chamber at the presence door,' many new doors were put in and the king's garden was made. Many repairs, including the rebuilding of a fallen chimney, the replacing of a timber chimney, setting up a stone mantel in the chamber of the Duke of Lennox and the repair of the wine-cellar door, 'being broken all to pieces,' are evidence of the decayed state of the buildings purchased by the king.[82]

Apparently the King's Lodgings described above were on the site of the 'Cock.'[83] The tiled-timber buildings called the 'Greyhound' were not rebuilt, but were converted as they stood into a guard-chamber and other officers' lodgings.[84] Between these and the King's House stood the Prince's Buttery, an old building partly tiled, partly thatched.[85] The 'Greyhound' was a freehold tenement of Royston Manor occupied by John Newport in 1539.[86] In its stables in 1537 Robert Dalyvell, saddler, prophesied the death of Henry VIII and the extinction of English nobles before Midsummer's Day, 1538.[87] James purchased the inn from the Earl of Lincoln,[88] who may have acted for him in acquiring it. South of the 'Greyhound' was the house of Judith Wilson in 1610[89] with a malt-house attached.[90] In 1628 Thomas Wilson let a part of this house to the king as a privy kitchen.[91] Beyond this were the pantry and waiting offices of Prince Charles. The corner house at the Cross was called the 'Howletts' and was held by the occupier of the 'Greyhound' in 1539.[92] Under James I it was converted into the Prince's Lodgings,

described in 1652 as a brick and timber building 117 ft. by 18 ft., three stories high with three rooms below stairs and four above.[93] At the rear of the 'Greyhound' or guard-house were the king's butteries.[94] The King's Privy Garden lay behind his lodgings and to the north of it was the Great Garden with the porter's lodge facing on Kneesworth Street.[95] This lodge was built on land formerly demesne of the manor let to John Gott and abutted on Gray's Close.[96] In the course of time the royal buildings were extended. Larders, pantries, bake-houses, the wardrobe and the lodgings for the keeper of the house were established in the 'Swan,' a double row of two-storied timber buildings at the rear of the Prince's Lodgings,[97] with a gateway at each end, the southern one opening into Melbourn Street.[98] The grounds of the 'Swan,' at the back of the king's buildings, contained his cock-pit, 'with substantial tile-covered roof,' and a large close between the gardens and the lane formerly called Field Lane, now Dog-Kennel Lane. Buildings were added for visitors, partly in the gardens, partly in the close, and a garden for them was inclosed from the latter. At the north end of the king's property, where Dog-Kennel Lane bends round into Kneesworth Street, was the dog-house, and next it lodgings for servants were built on a garden formerly belonging to the 'Talbot.' Between these and the Great Garden were the Duke of Hamilton's stables for hunting-horses.[99] The dog-house and the stables, with 'Little Mcadow Plotts,' had been known as 'John Almonde's Barnyard,' which James purchased from Edward Smith, one of the yeomen of the chamber.[100] East of the royal buildings and beyond Dog-Kennel Lane lay the old pasture paled in. A portion of this is still called the Park.

The equerries were lodged in Middle Row, opposite Wilson's house. The coach-houses formed a large block on the west side of Kneesworth Street opposite the King's Lodgings. North of them James had his bowling-green or 'Paradise.'[1]

James spent nearly £4,000 on his house at Royston between 1603 and 1611[2]; and in 1610 the Hertfordshire magistrates complained of the inconvenience of carting 500 loads of building material to Royston in the harvest season.[3] The king was frequently at Royston. In 1617 he was so 'exceedingly well pleased with the air of these parts' that his courtiers suspected he would 'have a more Royston life than ever he had.'[4] He caused the game to be preserved

---

[78] Parl. Surv. Cambs. 4.
[79] Nichols, *Progresses of Jas. I*, i, 105 ; Beldam, op. cit. 121.
[80] *Cal. S. P. Dom.* 1628–9, p. 31.
[81] The keeper of the house was appointed 12 Nov. 1604, and money had been allotted to its repair 27 Sept. 1604 (*Cal. S. P. Dom.* 1603–10, pp. 153, 174 ; Survey of 1610 quoted by Kingston, *Hist. of Royston*, 116).
[82] Declared Accts. Pipe Off. R. 3369.
[83] According to the survey of 1610 the king held 'one fayre Howse sometime two several tenements namely ye Greyhound & ye Cock late in the Tenure of Simon Swynbourn Gent.' James Palmer gave a part at least of the site of the king's house, and received in exchange the manor of Spaldwick, co. Hunts., and part of Wingham Manor in Kent (*Hist. MSS. Com. Rep.* xii, App. i, 184). Possibly his property was that acquired by Andrew Palmer in 1585 (Feet of F. Herts. Trin. 27 Eliz.).
[84] Parl. Surv. Cambs. 4.
[85] Ibid.
[86] Mins. Accts. Hen. VIII, no. 1606.
[87] *L. and P. Hen. VIII*, xii (2), 74, 80.
[88] Exch. Dep. Trin. 18 Chas. II, no. 5; *Cal. S. P. Dom.* 1603–10, p. 532.
[89] Survey quoted by Kingston, op. cit. 116.
[90] Parl. Surv. Cambs. 4.
[91] *Cal. S. P. Dom.* 1628–9, p. 406 ; cf. Chan. Proc. Eliz. Ww. viii, 23 for Wilson's house.
[92] Mins. Accts. Hen. VIII, no. 1606.
[93] Parl. Surv. Cambs. 4.
[94] Ibid.
[95] Beldam, loc. cit.
[96] Survey quoted by Kingston, loc. cit.
[97] From which they were separated by the house of John Issard, now the Cave estate.
[98] Parl. Surv. Cambs. 4.
[99] Parl. Surv. ; cf. the plan printed in *Arch.* xl, 136.
[100] Exch. Dep. Trin. 18 Chas. II, no. 5.
[1] A croft called 'Parrydyne' with a toft and a barn in Back Street was held by Robert Bell in 1539 (Mins. Accts. Hen. VIII, no. 1606). For the account of the buildings see Parl. Surv. Cambs. 4 ; Exch. Dep. Trin. 18 Chas. II, no. 5 ; Survey of 1610 printed by Kingston, *Hist. of Royston*, 115–18 ; plan drawn up by Beldam, *Arch.* xl, 136.
[2] Beldam, 'Royston Court House,' *Arch.* xl, 123.
[3] *Cal. S. P. Dom.* 1603–10, p. 625.
[4] *Buccleuch MSS.* (Hist. MSS. Com.), i, 203.

A HISTORY OF HERTFORDSHIRE

within a radius of 16 miles,[5] appointing numerous keepers to guard against poachers and 'persons of base condition'[6] and also against the scholars of Cambridge.[7] He appointed also a master of the harriers, three principal huntsmen and four huntsmen in liveries, issued proclamations against the 'audacious and irregular persons' who failed in 'forbearance of their own delight for our desport,'[8] and even called upon the farmers to take down the high bounds between their lands[9] and upon neighbouring gentry to diswarren their preserves.[10] Regular posts were organized from London.[11] The postmaster, there Haggar, seems to have abused his office by taking more horses than was necessary from poor countrymen.[12] Another effect of the king's residence at Royston was the extraordinary care bestowed upon the roads, which were cut up by great malt-waggons drawn by teams of horses.[13] At a later date the roads were endangered by highway robbers.[14]

Matters of state were occasionally forced upon the king at Royston. The people of the neighbouring parishes petitioned James, when in the hunting-field on 6 November 1604, to encourage faithful pastors.[15] Shortly before this the country people made use of the king's special hound 'Jowler' to bear a petition that he would leave Royston, as their provision was spent and they were unable to entertain him any longer.[16] With a 'small train of forty persons' James set out in January 1612–13 for Royston, where he was joined by Prince Charles and the Elector Palatine, and there he signed the agreement for the dower of the Princess Elizabeth.[17] It was at Royston that the king parted with his favourite, Somerset,[18] in 1615, and while staying there in October 1618 he caused Raleigh to be executed under the sentence passed against him in 1603.[19] In March 1619 he lay there dangerously ill[20] and left the town in a 'Neapolitan portative chair,'[21] 24 April.[21] In October 1623, after the return of Prince Charles and Buckingham from their fruitless journey to Spain, James received them on the stairs at Royston, 'when they fell on their knees and all wept together.'[22] James dubbed his last knight, Sir Richard Bettenson, at Royston 28 February 1624–5, a month before his death.[23]

Charles I visited the Court House less frequently than his father, but occasionally stayed there on the way to or from Newmarket.[24] On his journey to York in 1642 he stayed at Royston from 5 to 7 March, while continuing negotiations with Parliament respecting the militia.[25] In April 1646 M. Montreuil met the Chancellor of Scotland and others here, and made definite arrangements for the king's reception by the Scottish army.[26] Apparently the king himself passed through Royston on his way to Newark a few weeks later.[27] He returned thither as a prisoner of the Parliamentary army in June 1647.[28] The main body of the army, under the command of Fairfax, Ireton and Cromwell, had preceded the king and was at Royston 10 June, advancing thence to St. Albans.[29] The townspeople do not appear to have been enthusiastic supporters of the royal cause,[30] but the 'murthering of their king' roused them to assault a recruiting party from General Ireton's foot which visited Royston fair in 1649,[31] and in 1651 Thomas Coke confessed that he employed one Major Hall there to urge the people to join with the king if there were occasion. He was aided by Charles Baxton, an innkeeper, and Thomas Turner, both of Royston.[32] In 1649 the Court House was seized by the Parliament with the other possessions of the Crown, but Philip (Herbert) Earl of Pembroke put in a claim to the lands and buildings formerly belonging to the 'Swan', with the east part of the new lodgings for visitors, the cock-pit and the dog-house, and also 'that part of the king's lodgings that jutteth out on the east part thereof, being three bays of brick building 50 ft. by 22 ft., containing the king's bedchamber, drawing-room,' &c., with the king's privy garden.[33] The earl had purchased the 'Swan' in 1621[34] from Sir William Russell, kt., treasurer of the Royal Navy, and John Bedell, a merchant of London.

At the death of Charles the buildings, except only the king's and prince's lodgings, were much out of repair, but the commissioners who surveyed them recommended that they should be turned into tenements rather than demolished, and their suggestion seems to have been carried out.[35] The whole of the Court House seems to have come into the possession of Lewis and William Awdley during the Protectorate.[36] After the Restoration Edward Chester, lord of the manor, and others laid claim to some part of the buildings.[37] The King's House, however, was

---

[5] *Cal. S. P. Dom.* 1619–23, p. 460.
[6] Ibid. 1623–5, p. 105.
[7] Ibid. 107.
[8] Beldam, 'Royston Court House,' *Arch.* xl, 128–9.
[9] *Cal. S. P. Dom.* 1611–18, p. 488.
[10] Ibid. 1619–23, p. 500.
[11] A horseman was ordered to be ready to carry letters in 1536 (*Hist. MSS. Com. Rep.* xiv, App. viii, 35).
[12] *Cal. S. P. Dom.* 1637–8, pp. 269, 390; cf. *Hist. MSS. Com. Rep.* xii, App. ii, 180. As many as 200 horses were commandeered in two days.
[13] *Cal. S. P. Dom.* 1619–23, pp. 383, 495; 1631–3, pp. 66, 404, 409; 1633–4, pp. 232, 477, 478. The cuttings through the hills on the London and Newmarket roads were made about 1835 (Kingston, *Hist. of Royston*, 179).
[14] The mail was robbed Oct. 1669 half a mile out of the town (*Cal. S. P. Dom.* 1668–9, p. 525; cf. Kingston, *Fragments of Two Centuries*, 14).
[15] The petition is printed by Kingston, *Hist. of Royston*, 106; cf. *Cal. S. P. Dom.* 1580–1625, p. 449. It was one among

many 'millenary' petitions (Fuller, *Church Hist.* v, 311), and is to be distinguished from the famous Millenary Petition presented 4 Apr. 1604 (ibid. 305–9).
[16] Nichols, *Progresses of Jas. I*, i, 464–5.
[17] *Cal. S. P. Dom.* 1611–18, pp. 162, 171–2; cf. Beldam, op. cit. 131.
[18] Nichols, op. cit. iii, 105.
[19] Ibid. 493; *Cal. S. P. Dom.* 1611–18, p. 586.
[20] Ibid. 1619–23, pp. 28, 35.
[21] Ibid. 39.
[22] *Cal. S. P. Dom.* 1623–5, p. 93. The marriage treaty with Henrietta Maria was ratified not at Royston as stated by Beldam (op. cit. 132), but at Cambridge 12 Dec. 1624 (*Cal. S. P. Dom.* 1623–5, pp. 405, 411).
[23] Nichols, *Progresses of Jas. I*, iv, 1028.
[24] *Cal. S. P. Dom.* 1633–4, pp. 259, 504; 1625–49, p. 510; 1636–7, p. 66.
[25] *Hist. MSS. Com. Rep.* xiv, App. viii, 35, 200; xii, App. ii, 98; *Cal. S. P. Dom.* 1641–3, pp. 293, 463; he was accompanied by Prince Charles, and also by the Elector Palatine, who deserted him

at York (ibid. 289; Clarendon, *Hist. of the Rebellion*, vii, 413).
[26] *Cal. of Clarendon S. P.* i, 311–12.
[27] Kingston, *Herts. during the Civil War*, 62.
[28] *Cal. S. P. Dom.* 1645–7, pp. 564, 592; cf. *V.C.H. Herts.* ii, 33.
[29] *Hist. MSS. Com. Rep.* vi, App. 182*b*, 184*b*.
[30] Kingston, *Hist. of Royston*, 140.
[31] '*A bloody fight in Hertfordshire*,' King's Pamphlets, E 565 (73); '*The man in the moon discovering a world of knavery under the sunne*,' King's Pamphlets, quoted by Kingston, *Hist. of Royston*, 140–2.
[32] *Hist. MSS. Com. Rep.* xiii, App. i, 581. A regiment of Parliamentary troops passed through the town on its way to take part in the Worcester campaign 23 Aug. 1651 (*Cal. S. P. Dom.* 1651, p. 359).
[33] Parl. Surv. Cambs. no. 4, 5.
[34] Close, 19 Jas. I, pt. i, no. 1.
[35] Parl. Surv. Cambs. 4.
[36] Exch. Dep. Trin. 18 Chas. II, no. 5.
[37] Ibid.

258

Royston Cave: Sculptured Figures on Wall below Cornice

Royston Cave: Sculptured Figures on Wall below Cornice

occupied by lessees of the Crown for about a century and a-half. In 1731 it was occupied by John Buxton, attorney. The lessee in 1753 was John Minchin. In 1812 it was purchased by John Stamford, carpenter, whose son John bequeathed it in succession to his nephews John Whyatt and Samuel Luke of New Zealand.[38] The Crown rights had all been sold by 1866.[39]

Just north of the site of the king's Dog House is Chapel Field,[40] recently proved to be the site of an ancient burial-ground.[41] Here apparently stood the hospital and chantry chapel of St. Nicholas, which was founded for lepers early in the 13th century[42] on land held of Wendy Manor, co. Cambs., by the service of maintaining a lamp in Wendy Church. It consisted of a chapel and lodgings for the lepers.[43] Its founder, Ralph son of Ralph son of Fulk,[44] gave the advowson of the hospital to Giles Argentine, lord of Melbourn Manor,[45] in which parish the chapel was apparently situated.

The Congregational chapel in Kneesworth Street originated in the secession of the 'New Meeting' from the 'Old Meeting' in 1791.[46] The building, erected in 1792, has since been altered and enlarged.[47] There was a considerable Quaker community in Royston from 1655 onwards.[48] Tombstones still mark the site of their meeting-place at the back of the houses on the east side of Kneesworth Street.[49]

The town has spread northwards in the direction of the station on the Cambridge branch of the Great Northern railway, opened in 1850.[50] In this neighbourhood is the Wesleyan chapel, erected in 1887.[51] Here are also the nurseries of Mr. J. C. Pigg, a corn mill and large maltings. Eastwards at some distance from the Cross along Melbourn Street is the town hall built in 1855 as a Mechanics' Institute.[52] Westwards the town extends to the union workhouse, built in 1835. The poorhouse for Royston formerly stood near the Warren, south of the market-place.

The position of the town on the borders of two counties made it the scene of much crime and disorder, which the Prior of Royston, who had considerable jurisdiction within the town, failed to check. Robert of Bures and others carried off the goods of the prior himself in 1314.[53] Cases of assault at Royston were frequent during the 13th and 14th centuries.[54] Breaches of the Statute of Northampton were daily committed, and the offenders escaped arrest by the king's officers by fleeing from one county to another, while their number and confederacy made them too strong for the bailiffs of the prior,[55] whose liberty extended into both counties.[56] The ringleaders of the 'Murdrisours de Croysroys'[57] were Richard 'Howessone' the Marshal, of Royston, and John his son.[58] In 1337 a separate commission of the peace was formed for the town of Royston.[59] Three years later Warin of Bassingbourn, the Sheriff of Cambridgeshire, entering the town armed, seized and carried off Simon Bakoun 'sitting in the stocks in the Tolbothe.' An affray followed in which the sheriff's bailiff wounded 'Simon le Irenmonger' of Royston. The prior seems to have tried to preserve his liberties by buying off the sheriff,[60] who was, nevertheless, included in a new commission of the peace for Royston in 1341,[61] and appointed to attach Richard the Marshal in 1342.[62] The commission was renewed from time to time.[63] In 1437 the Crown released to the priory the goods of felons and fugitives in Royston and the prior at the same time received the royal pardon for the escape of prisoners.[64]

The town has suffered much by fire. It is said to have been burnt in 1324.[65] A great fire broke out in 1405 on the feast of the Translation of St. Martin.[66] Another serious fire occurred 22 March 1734.[67] Royston appears to have been visited by Henry III,[68] Edward I,[69] Edward III[70] and Richard II.[71] Richard Duke of York and the Earls of Warwick and Salisbury sent from here, 20 May 1455, their manifesto demanding the dismissal of Somerset.[72]

In the summer of 1553 John Cooke, carpenter, and other Royston men made 'commocion at Royston' and were bidden as well 'to leave of their assemblies as having just occasion against any man to come up and give information to the Council.'[73]

---

[38] Cussans, *Hist. of Herts. Odsey Hund.* 103; cf. Clutterbuck, *Hist. and Antiq. of Herts.* iii, 563.
[39] Beldam, 'Royston Court House,' *Arch.* xl, 134. [40] Parl. Surv. Cambs. 4.
[41] Kingston, *Hist. of Royston*, 46–7; the remains of a stone slab discovered here are preserved in the town hall gardens. Some Saxon relics are said to have been found.
[42] Before Jan. 1212–13, when a fair was granted, see above.
[43] *Cal. Close*, 1354–60, p. 587.
[44] For an account of this family see the history of Broadfield.
[45] *Cal. Inq. p.m. Edw. I*, 275.
[46] Urwick, *Nonconformity in Herts.* 814. The first minister was the Rev. Thomas Towne, whose son Joseph distinguished himself as an anatomical modeller (*Dict. Nat. Biog.*).
[47] Kingston, *Hist. of Royston*, 155.
[48] Ibid. 151–3.
[49] Kingston, *Fragments of Two Centuries*, 126; Urwick gives a list of six places certified for Protestant Dissenters 1691–1833 (op. cit. 813).
[50] Kingston, *Hist. of Royston*, 182. It was possibly in this part of the town that lay the tenements which formed part of the endowment of the Savoy Hospital (Pat. 7 Edw. VI, pt. xiii, m. 11).
[51] Kingston, *Hist. of Royston*, 157.
[52] Ibid. 182.
[53] *Cal. Pat.* 1313–17, p. 229.
[54] *Cal. Close*, 1272–9, pp. 171, 189; 1296–1302, p. 451; Cur. Reg. R. 189, m. 6; *Cal. Pat.* 1272–9, p. 339; 1317–21, pp. 371, 540, 545; Chan. Criminal Inq. Edw. I, file 9, no. 10; Agarde's Cal. to Coram Rege R. 21 Edw. III, m. 173 d.
[55] *Cal. Pat.* 1334–8, p. 576.
[56] *Feud. Aids*, i, 156; the demesnes of the manor extend into Cambridgeshire, see the description of the king's palace above.
[57] Druce MSS. quoted by Kingston, *Hist. of Royston*, 30.
[58] *Cal. Pat.* 1340–3, p. 555; 1354–6, pp. 341, 647; cf. *Cal. Close*, 1343–6, p. 362; 1346–9, pp. 413, 596. John 'le Mareschal' was a chaplain and was aided by 'William le Chircheclerk' of Royston (Plac. de Banco 269, m. 22). On several occasions the plaintiff is Hugh 'le Mareschal,' possibly Richard's own father (Plac. de Banco, 169, m. 18 d.; 270, m. 53; *Cal. Pat.* 1334–8, p. 282).
[59] *Cal. Pat.* 1334–8, p. 576.
[60] Assize R. 337, m. 4, 9 d.
[61] *Cal. Pat.* 1340–3, p. 217.
[62] Ibid. p. 555. The prior fined with the Crown in 1264 to have the goods of 'John son of Richard Mareschall the elder' an outlaw for felony (*Abbrev. Rot. Orig.* [Rec. Com.], ii, 283).
[63] *Cal. Pat.* 1377–81, pp. 205, 361, 575.
[64] Memo. R. (Exch. L.T.R.), Hil. 12 Hen. VI, 'Recorda,' m. 17. The prior had a 'gaol' in Royston in 1233 (*Cal. Close*, 1231–4, p. 539).
[65] Kingston, *Hist. of Royston*, 37.
[66] Thomas of Walsingham, *Ypodigma Neustriae* (Rolls Ser.), 417.
[67] Hardy, *Sess. R.* (Herts. Co. Rec.), ii, 71.
[68] *Cal. Pat.* 1232–47, pp. 139, 224, 279; 1247–58, pp. 91, 666; *Cal. Close*, 1234–7, p. 250.
[69] *Cal. Close*, 1272–9, p. 161; 1288–96, p. 228; 1302–7, pp. 21, 22, 78, 80; *Cal. Pat.* 1281–92, p. 486; 1272–81, p. 468; 1292–1301, pp. 175, 182, 215.
[70] *Cal. Pat.* 1340–3, p. 129; *Cal. Close*, 1333–7, p. 345; 1341–3, p. 9.
[71] *Cal. Pat.* 1381–5, p. 310.
[72] *Parl. R.* v, 280; cf. *V.C.H. Herts.* ii, 18.
[73] *Acts of P.C.* 1552–4, pp. 310, 313. These assemblies may have been political or religious (cf. *V.C.H. Herts.* ii, 23).

A HISTORY OF HERTFORDSHIRE

The priory to the south of Melbourn Street was founded within the manor of Newsells in Barkway parish.[74] Eustace de Merk, kt., lord of Newsells, built a chapel for three chaplains on the site of the present priory.[75] His nephew Ralph of Rochester established a house of Austin canons on the same spot.[76] It was dedicated in honour of St. John the Baptist and St. Thomas the Martyr. Ralph of Rochester erected the buildings and gave the land on which they stood, the soil of the inclosed precinct, the green space (probably heathland) extending from the priory gate to 'Holewey' and 'Cawden,' 140 acres of arable land in 'Eldefeld,' rights of pasture over all the rest of Eldefeld and the homage and service of his men and tenants there and in Royston.[77] The endowment took place within the lifetime of Eustace, between 1163 and 1184.[78] William of Rochester, the founder's son, added 40 acres more in 'Eldefield,' extending from the path from Barley to Royston, next the canons' mill.[79] The Popes Lucius III and Celestine III confirmed their possessions to the canons.[80] Richard I granted them extensive liberties within their lands.[81] Successive priors obtained confirmatory charters from Henry III,[82] Edward III,[83] Richard II,[84] Henry IV,[85] Henry V,[86] Henry VI[87] and Edward IV.[88] The house now known as the Priory was possibly part of the house erected on the site of the priory after the Dissolution. There is some 17th-century brickwork on the south-west side.

MANOR The charter of Ralph of Rochester proves that the greater part of Royston originally lay within the manor of Newsells in Barkway. The latter was held in 1086 by Eudo Fitz Hubert.[89] It was attached later to the honour of Boulogne,[90] of which it was held by Eustace de Merk and subsequently by his nephew Ralph of Rochester.[91] Ralph endowed the Priors of Royston with manorial rights over the lands which he granted to them.[92]

The manor of ROYSTON thus formed was retained by the priors until the dissolution of their house,[93] which took place in 1536.[94] The priory buildings, the demesne lands and the scattered lands in 'Elfeld Clepitsholte Redfeld Tharfeld Milbournefeld and Newsells' were leased to Robert Chester before Michaelmas 1537. The market rights were let for twenty-one years to Richard Cromwell, who acted also as steward of the manor,[95] and was probably the person by whose 'importunate labours' Dr. Wendy, physician to the Earl of Northumberland, was prevented from obtaining a lease of the demesnes and market rights.[96] Robert Chester had a new lease of the priory 20 May 1539,[97] and in 1540 he received a grant in fee of the house and site of the priory, the lordship and manor of Royston and all the lands of the late prior in the counties of Hertfordshire and Cambridgeshire.[98] He was gentleman usher of the chamber to Henry VIII and in July 1544 left Royston with twenty-five archers, who formed the king's bodyguard when he left Calais for the siege of Boulogne.[99] In 1551 Chester (who was knighted about this date)[100] entertained Mary of Guise at Royston on her return to Scotland from France.[1] In 1565 he served as Sheriff of Essex and Hertfordshire.[2] In November 1564 there took place at Royston a double marriage between Sir Robert Chester, then a widower, and Lady Magdalene, widow of Sir Jaques Granada, kt., and between Sir Robert's son and heir Edward and Katherine daughter of the Lady Magdalene by her former husband.[3] At the same time Royston was settled upon Edward and Katherine in tail-male.[4] Sir Robert Chester died 25 November 1574.[5] Shortly afterwards Edward Chester, 'getting greate credytt in respect of his good service' in the Low Countries, received an annuity from the Estates of 400 marks to himself and his eldest son for life. He died 25 November 1577 beyond the seas, having transported a band of volunteers to the Netherlands at his own cost.[6] His son and heir Robert was then aged twelve.[7] He had livery of Royston Manor about 1586,[8] and was engaged in continual litigation in respect of the annuity due to his grandmother Lady Magdalene, the extent of the possessions of the late priory and the market rights of Royston.[9] He was

CHESTER. *Ermine a chief sable with a griffon passant argent therein.*

---

[74] Harl. MS. 7041, fol. 7; Assize R. 323, m. 45.
[75] Baker (Harl. MS. 7041, fol. 7) transcribes the charter of Ralph of Rochester from the original. The word 'Senseles' is evidently a clerical error for 'Neuseles' (cf. Assize R. 323, m. 45).
[76] Harl. MS. 7041, fol. 7.
[77] Ibid. The exact wording is of interest, since it shows the extent of the manor which Ralph carved out of his fee of Newsells for the canons. It is as follows:—'dedi . . . et . . . confirmavi locum ipsum in quo prefatam ecclesiam construxi cum toto solo existente in precinctu quem dictis Canonicis meis feci ibidem sub murali clausura totam etiam viridem placeam que est de feodo meo de [N]euseles ante januam et frontem muri ibidem usque in Holewey et Cawden centum similiter et quadraginta acras terre arabilis in le Eldefelde a predicto precinctu et viridi placea continue jacentes juxta Hikenild usque Salteresdoune et pasturam ad centum oves per sexies viginti numeratas pascendas extra eandem terram viz. in le Eldefeld per totam terram meam cum omnibus homagiis et servitiis omnium hominum et tenentium meorum ibidem et in Cruce Roys' . . .
[78] The charter is witnessed by Gilbert Bishop of London (1163–87). The confirmatory bull of Lucius III is dated 8 Kal. May 1184. In all probability the foundation took place before 1179 (see the account of the church).
[79] Harl. MS. 7041, fol. 7b.
[80] Cott. MS. Aug. ii, 124, 130.
[81] Cart. Antiq. R. 6; Dugdale, *Mon.* vi, 405 (see below).
[82] Cal. Chart. R. 1226–57, p. 360; Chart. R. 56 Hen. III, no. 5.
[83] Chart. R. 18 Edw. III, no. 2.
[84] Cal. Pat. 1377–81, p. 181.
[85] Ibid. 1399–1401, p. 198.
[86] Ibid. 1413–16, p. 136.
[87] Ibid. 1422–9, p. 427.
[88] Ibid. 1467–77, p. 423.
[89] V.C.H. Herts. i, 329.
[90] Cart. Mon. S. Johannis de Colecestria (Roxburghe Club), i, 47; cf. Red Bk. of Exch. (Rolls Ser.), 502.

[91] Red Bk. of Exch. (Rolls Ser.), 502; Harl. MS. 7041, fol. 7.
[92] Harl. MS. 7041, fol. 7.
[93] Mins. Accts. Hen. VIII, no. 1606.
[94] L. and P. Hen. VIII, xii (1), 571.
[95] Mins. Accts. Hen. VIII, no. 1606–15, 1632, 1633.
[96] L. and P. Hen. VIII, xii (1), 1057, 1211.
[97] Ibid. xiv (1), p. 606.
[98] Ibid. xvi, 379 (60).
[99] Ibid. xix (2), 424, 524 (8).
[100] Shaw, *Knights of Engl.* ii, 65.
[1] Acts of P.C. 1550–2, p. 406.
[2] List of Sheriffs (P.R.O.), 45.
[3] Chan. Inq. p.m. (Ser. 2), clxx, 51.
[4] Ibid.
[5] Ibid.
[6] Ct. of Req. bdle. 60, no. 51; Chan. Inq. p.m. (Ser. 2), clxxxvi, 8.
[7] Chan. Inq. p.m. (Ser. 2), clxxxvi, 8.
[8] Ct. of Wards, Misc. Bk. dcxviii.
[9] Ct. of Req. bdle. 60, no. 51; Exch. Dep. East. 5 Jas. I, no. 16; Aug. Off. Proc. i, 55.

260

ROYSTON CHURCH   THE SOUTH ARCADE

ROYSTON CHURCH   THE PULPIT

ROYSTON

knighted in 1603 by James I,[10] whom he had entertained upon his first journey to London from Edinburgh.[11]

Sir Robert Chester resided at Cockenhatch in Barkway,[12] and died in 1640, having settled Royston Manor upon his son Edward, who married Katherine daughter of John Stone of London.[13] The manor evidently passed to their second son John.[14] His son Edward was Sheriff of Hertfordshire in 1675 and died in his year of office.[15] He was succeeded by his son Robert,[16] whose son Edward Chester[17] sold the manor in 1759 to Thomas Plumer Byde of Ware Park.[18]

Royston was purchased in 1770 by Thomas Brand and bequeathed by him to his grandson Thomas (Brand) Lord Dacre.[19] His heir was his brother Henry Otway (Trevor) Lord Dacre, whose second son Sir Henry-Bouverie-William Brand was created Viscount Hampden. His grandson Thomas Walter,

BRAND, Viscount Hampden

Viscount Hampden, is the present lord of the manor.[70]

The Priors of Royston claimed by prescription view of frankpledge, gallows, tumbril and amendment of the assize of bread and ale.[21] Under the charter of Richard I they had within their manor of Royston soc, sac, tol, tem, infangthef, utfangthef, hamsac, grithbriche, bloodwite, murder, forestall, flemaniswite, ordeal and orest.[22] They and their men were quit of scot, geld and aids, shires, hundreds, &c.[23] Their jurisdiction was therefore very extensive; but their failure to enforce order in the 13th and 14th centuries has been seen. Confirmation of their liberties was made in February 1271-2,[24] and in 1278 their claims were again acknowledged.[25]

A court leet for certain of the tenants of the honour of Clare in Cambridgeshire was held at Royston,[26] but Richard de Clare Earl of Gloucester and patron of Royston Priory had only one tenant in the town at his death in 1262.[27] The courts were held throughout the 15th century[28] and descended to Edward IV as grandson of Anne wife of the Earl of Cambridge and direct descendant of Elizabeth de Burgh, one of the three sisters and co-heirs of Gilbert de Clare Earl of Gloucester, slain at Bannockburn in 1314.[29] Edward assigned the court at Royston to his mother Cicely in dower.[30] It was apparently extinct by the beginning of the 17th century.[31]

The church of ST. JOHN THE CHURCH BAPTIST[32] consists of chancel 34 ft. 6 in. by 22 ft., north vestry and organ chamber, nave 70 ft. 6 in. by 22 ft., north aisle 58 ft. by 14 ft. 6 in., south aisle 86 ft. by 13 ft. 6 in., west tower 20 ft. 6 in. from north to south and 14 ft. from east to west; all internal dimensions. The walls are of clunch and rubble, with modern flint facing and stone dressings. The present church consists mainly of the chancel and quire of the monastic church, with later additions. In 1600 the justices of the peace certified that the church was 'utterly ruinated and fallen downe to the ground,' whereupon the Privy Council gave licence for collections to be made for its rebuilding.[33]

The history of the church is a little difficult to trace owing to the alterations and re-use of old materials after the dissolution of the monastery, but the original church appears to have consisted of a chancel which was lighted by the triple lancets, parts of which remain in the north and south walls, the chancel arch being at the second pier west of the modern chancel arch,[33a] and a quire of probably two bays, of which those on the south side still remain. The quire screen may have stood at the west of these two bays, the remains of a turret stair[33b] having been discovered in the south wall opposite that point. Another bay, perhaps similar to the others, or of

---

[10] Shaw, *Knights of Engl.* ii, 123.
[11] Nichols, *Progresses of Jas. I,* i, 105.
[12] *Herts. Visit.* (Harl. Soc. xxii), 40.
[13] Chan. Inq. p.m. (Ser. 2), ccccxci, 65; cf. Feet of F. Div. Co. Mich. 13 Jas. I.
[14] Chauncy, *Hist. Antiq. of Herts.* 91. The elder son Robert mentioned in the visitation of 1634 probably died before his grandfather (cf. Chan. Inq. p.m. [Ser. 2], ccccxciv, 65).
[15] *List of Sheriffs* (P.R.O.), 64.
[16] Chauncy, loc. cit.; cf. Feet of F. Div. Co. Mich. 12 Will. III; Recov. R. Mich. 9 Anne, m. 171.
[17] For the pedigree see Exch. Dep. Mich. 25 Geo. II, no. 3; cf. Feet of F. Div. Co. Mich. 4 Geo. II.
[18] Feet of F. Div. Co. Trin. 32-3 Geo. II; Clutterbuck, *Hist. and Antiq. of Herts.* iii, 561.

[19] Clutterbuck, loc. cit.; cf. Recov. R. Trin. 25 Geo. III, m. 354.
[20] Cf. the account of Hoo.
[21] *Plac. de Quo Warr.* (Rec. Com.), 100.
[22] Dugdale, *Mon.* vi, 405; some of the readings have been corrected by Inq. a.q.d. file 3, no. 31, and *Plac. de Quo Warr.* (Rec. Com.), 283.
[23] *Plac. de Quo Warr.* (Rec. Com.), 100.
[24] Inq. a.q.d. file 3, no. 31; *Cal. Chart. R.* 1257-1300, p. 180.
[25] *Plac. de Quo Warr.* (Rec. Com.), 283.
[26] *Cal. Inq. p.m. Hen. III,* 160; Chan. Inq. p.m. 35 Edw. I, no. 47; Mins. Accts. (Gen. Ser.), bdles. 1110, no. 2, 24; 1111, no. 2, 16, 24; 1112, no. 1; Ct. R. (G·n. Ser.), portf. 155, no. 2, 73; 213, no. 57.
[27] *Cal. Inq. p.m. Hen. III,* 160.
[28] Ct. R. quoted above.
[29] G.E.C. *Peerage,* viii, 214-15.
[30] *Cal. Pat.* 1461-7, p. 131; it is here called a court of the 'honour of Gloucester'; cf. Feet of F. Mixed Co. Mich. 3 Hen. VIII.
[31] It is omitted from the Survey of the honour in Cambridgeshire in 1650 (Duchy of Lanc. Parl. Surv. 1), and was evidently extinct when Gibbons described the town in the reign of James I (*Ely Epis. Rec.* [ed. Gibbons], 152).
[32] The monastery was dedicated to St. John the Baptist and St. Thomas of Canterbury; by the Act (32 Hen. VIII, cap. 44) constituting the vicarage the name of St. Thomas was omitted.
[33] *Acts of P.C.* 1599-1600, p. 304; *Hist. MSS. Com. Rep.* x, App. iv, 484.
[33a] The bases of the chancel piers were discovered then.
[33b] It is not certain that the stair led to the gallery, it may have been connected with the monastic buildings.

261

A HISTORY OF HERTFORDSHIRE

solid walling, was interposed between the quire screen and the central tower. There is evidence that a central tower, with at least a south transept, existed, the present tower being in almost the same position as the old one.

The lower part of the old clunch wall of the south nave aisle still exists, and is continued eastwards with only one break as far as the west wall of the present south aisle in a line with the east face of the present tower. The break is a projecting impost which probably carried the arch between the south aisle and the transept, and if so it marks the western face of the old tower, and the dimensions show that it was square, not oblong as at present. In the rebuilding of the tower the west face appears to have been built about 7 ft. east of the old one, the other sides remaining as before.

arches beneath them. The windows have moulded arches enriched with the dog-tooth ornament; the jambs have clustered shafts and moulded capitals and bases. The north arcade consists of four plain pointed arches, the wall above being only 1 ft. 6 in. thick. The imposts and two of the supporting piers are octagonal with moulded capitals, probably modern; the central pier, which is of 14th-century character and is of greater diameter than the others, is composed of four large half-round shafts separated by smaller ones; it has a moulded capital similar to the others, which is probably modern. The north arcade appears to have been rebuilt during the 17th century, the middle pier being all that remained of the old arcade. The south arcade is of five arches. The eastern arch and central pier are modern; the second arch is of three hollow-chamfered orders with moulded labels of 14th-century character; the next two arches apparently formed the original quire and retain their old responds with a little plain walling at either end. The arches consist of three hollow chamfers with moulded labels, the jambs of large clustered shafts separated by acutely pointed rolls; the capitals and bases are moulded. The date of this arcade is c. 1250–60. There is a piece of wall about 6 ft. in length, including the imposts, between this arcade of two arches and the westernmost arch of the nave, and the western end of the wall has been roughly thinned down to make it fit the imposts and arch of the westernmost opening, which is only 8 ft. wide. The imposts are of the same section as the old central

ROYSTON : HOUSE IN THE CHURCHYARD

The chancel, vestry and organ chamber were built in 1891, and at the same time the south aisle was lengthened eastwards about 27 ft. In the chancel wall has been reset the sill of a 13th-century piscina with octofoil basin.

The nave, which consists of the chancel and quire of the old church, was built c. 1250. At the east end are the remains of the triple lancet windows in the north and south walls. In the north wall the eastern window alone remains, the bases and capitals of which have been restored. In the south wall are portions of three arches with some of the capitals; these are partly built up and the lower portions have been cut away to allow of the insertion of arcade

262

PLAN OF ROYSTON CHURCH

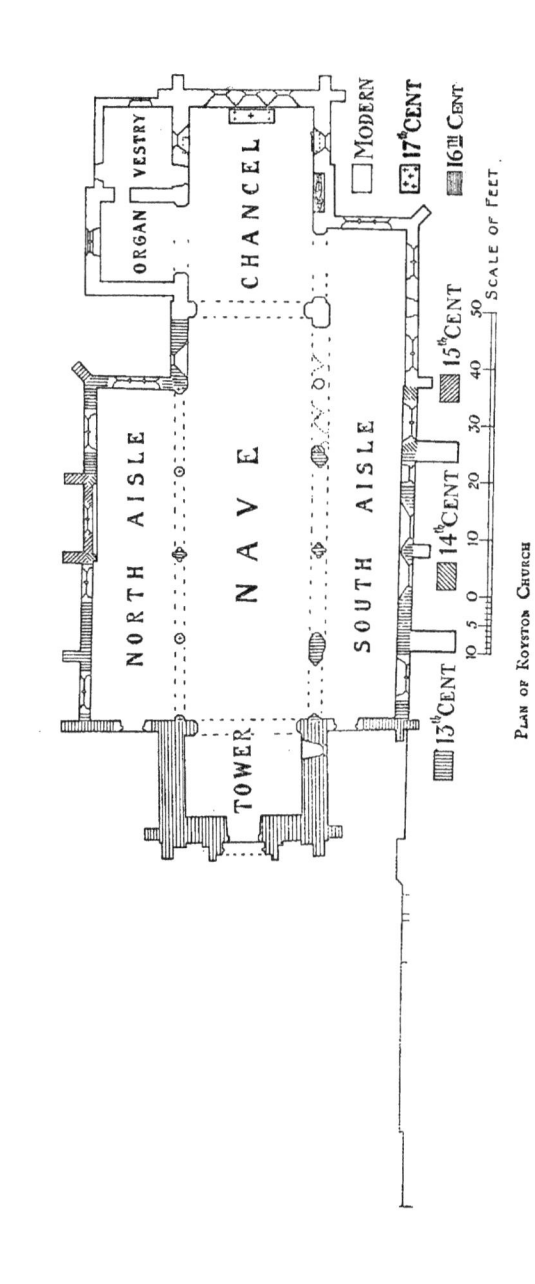

pier in the north arcade and look as if they had been detached piers before they were inserted in their present position.[34] The moulded capitals of these imposts are of the same section as those of the adjoining two bays, but the arch moulding is of an earlier period, probably about 1240. There can be little doubt but that this arch was inserted when the tower was rebuilt about 1600 of old materials. The clearstory window above the arch was probably also inserted at that period or later. There are two small clearstory lights on the north side.

The roof of the nave has moulded trusses and carved bosses and is probably of early 16th-century work.[35]

The stonework of the three-light window in the east wall of the north aisle and of the four two-light windows in the north wall is modern; the second window from the east is inserted in a partially blocked archway which opened into a former chapel; the arch is of two orders, the inner one a hollow chamfer, the outer one moulded with undercut rolls; the jambs have clustered shafts with rolls between, like the central pier in the north arcade, and the capitals are moulded. It appears to be of 14th-century work, but has been restored. There is a break back of 8 in. in the north wall adjoining this arch. The west doorway is modern. Parts of the aisle roof are of 15th-century timbers re-used. In one of the windows are some fragments of 15th-century painted glass. All the windows in the south aisle are of modern stonework, and the west door is modern; a doorway in the south wall is blocked. The roof is a plain one of 15th-century date.

The tower is in three stages with crocketed pinnacles at the angles. It has been refaced with flint, and all the stonework of the west door, belfry windows and battlements is modern. The wide tower arch has been rebuilt with 14th-century materials, the section of the mouldings corresponding with that of the second arch from the east in the south arcade; the responds, which are semi-octagonal, and the moulded capitals are of 16th-century date; the arch has been roughly built. It is clear that the whole tower was rebuilt in the 16th century,[36] old materials being re-used as before suggested, that the tower was square originally and rested on large piers, but no trace of them is now visible. At the eastern end of the old south nave wall the upper part of an arched recess appears above the ground: it was probably a tomb. Adjoining it on the east is the head of another recess about 3 ft. wide, possibly a piscina.

The old font has recently been placed in the churchyard, after being for many years in private hands; it has a plain octagonal bowl of the 13th century and a 15th-century stem with a plain arched recess in each face.

A fine 15th-century oak panelled and carved door, until lately in the west doorway, is now in the belfry; it appears to have been the original door of the church, but has been considerably damaged.

The tower walls on the ground floor have been lined with 17th-century oak panelling taken from old pews.

The pulpit has a stone base composed of parts of an old panelled tomb, the pulpit itself, as well as two reading desks, being made up from a fine 15th-century oak screen which was discovered during the 19th century; it is said to have fitted the second arch from the east in the south nave arcade.

Two badly damaged images of alabaster were found during restoration and are now in the chancel; one is of the Virgin and Child: the figure of the Virgin is headless and in the left hand of the Child is a bird; the other is the figure of a bishop with head and pastoral staff broken away. They are of the 15th century.[37]

Under a modern recess in the south wall of the chancel is the recumbent effigy of a knight, in alabaster, of the 14th century, clad in plate armour with a surcoat.

On a stone slab now beneath the communion table is a long brass cross on stepped base; it is incised with a Bleeding Heart and the other four Wounds of the Passion, and is probably of 15th-century date. In the nave is a brass with figures of a man and his wife, with indent of a second wife; there is no inscription, but it dates from about 1500; another brass has a half figure of a priest in hood and tippet, under a cusped and crocketed canopy, to William Tahram, rector of Therfield, 1462. On the east wall of the north aisle are three brass inscriptions: to William Chamber, who died in 1546; to Robert White, Prior of Royston, who died 1534; the third bears a verse in English, but neither name nor date; it probably dates from about 1500.

There are six bells: four by Thomas Lester, 1739, and two recast by John Taylor, 1901.

The communion plate consists of a cup of 1621, an elaborately chased paten of 1629, another paten of 1718, a modern flagon and a plated chalice.

The registers are in three books: (i) baptisms from 1662 to 1812, burials 1662 to 1678, marriages 1662 to 1754; (ii) burials 1678 to 1812; (iii) marriages 1754 to 1812.

ADVOWSON

The canons at Royston built a chapel with a burial-place attached possibly between 1164 and 1179.[38] The lack of a separate parish church for so considerable a town was thus 'little prejudicial' to the inhabitants while the priory existed. Soon after its dissolution they bought the priory church 'to their great charges.' By Act of Parliament the town, which had formerly been in five different parishes, was in 1540 constituted a distinct parish within the diocese of London.[39] The vicar was to have tithes, offerings and oblations

---

[34] The western pier of the 13th-century arcade of two arches has the same look of having been a detached pier, and it seems possible that a third arch completed the arcade to the central tower, the space left just allowing for it.

[35] In 1524 William Lee of Radwell left £10 towards finishing the chancel roof (P.C.C. Wills 24 Porch).

[36] In 1511 Thomas Chamber of Royston left 20 marks to the work upon condition that the 'stepull' be built in two years (P.C.C. Wills 1 Fetiplace).

[37] There were in the priory church altars of Our Lady of Pity, referred to in the will of William Marshall of Royston in 1507 (P.C.C. Wills 29 Adeane), and an image of the Trinity, mentioned in the will of Henry Deggon in 1508 (ibid. 4 Bennett), and of Henry Bedale in 1517 (ibid. 33 Ayloff), and an image of the Virgin under a tabernacle, mentioned in the will of John Crespede in 1500 (ibid. 13 Moone). There was in the priory, whether in the church is not stated, a chapel of the Rood (ibid.) and Mordon chapel (ibid. 16 Bennett).

[38] Cart. S. Johannis de Colecestria (Roxburghe Club), ii, 513. The date is limited by the approximate dates of the rule of Abbot Walter of Colchester.

[39] Stat. 32 Hen. VIII, cap. 45.

ODSEY HUNDRED

except tithe of corn, hay, wool, lambs and calves, which were reserved to the incumbents of the five original parishes.[40] The king was patron, the advowson being attached to the priory manor, then in his hands. The advowson is not specifically mentioned in the grant of the manor to Robert Chester,[41] but it evidently passed under it. It continued in the possession of the successive lords until 1891, when it was transferred to the bishop of the diocese.[42]

There were several devotional gilds in Royston. We have reference to the brotherhood of Jesus,[43] the gild of St. Laurence[44] and the Rood gild.[45]

A chantry for the soul of Richard de Stamford, clerk of the Exchequer, was founded about 1290 and endowed by him with certain houses in Fleet Street, London.[46]

CHARITIES — In the Parliamentary Returns of 1786 it is stated that — Chester gave a rent-charge of £5 4s. per annum for bread to the poor. This sum is paid out of the manor of Royston and is distributed in bread by the vicar and churchwardens.

In 1609 Robert Warden left a yearly sum of £2 12s. out of a tenement in St. Peter Cornhill, London, to be distributed in bread every Sunday to the poor. The property charged with this payment now belongs to the Merchant Taylors' Company, and the annuity is regularly received from them and distributed in bread.

In 1687 Sir Thomas Foot, by his will proved 17 November, gave an assignment of £42 of Exchequer annuities for the benefit of the poor of certain parishes, including the parish of Royston. The endowment of the charity for Royston has come to be represented by £56 4s. 6d. £2 10s. per cent. annuities, producing £1 8s. yearly, which is distributed in bread to the poor every week.

The charity of William Lee, founded by will dated 8 October 1527, is regulated by a scheme of the Charity Commission dated 30 June 1893. The property consists of two shops and dwelling-houses in Royston, producing £55 yearly; a barn and yard in Royston producing £8 yearly; and a sum of £598 4s. India 3 per cent. stock with the official trustees, representing accumulations of income and producing £17 18s. 8d. yearly. The net income is applied in accordance with the scheme in subscriptions to Herts. Convalescent Home, Royston Nursing Association, Addenbrooke's Hospital and Royston Cottage Hospital; in assistance to invalids in hospitals, and in exhibitions to children from public elementary schools.

In 1689 Joseph Wortham by his will gave 30s. yearly out of his messuage in Royston to the poor, 20s. thereof to be distributed in bread at Candlemas to poor widowers and widows of Royston, and 10s. to widowers and widows of Barley. The sum of 26s. out of the Falcon Inn, Royston, is received yearly in respect of this gift and distributed in bread.

In 1851 Lester Brand by his will gave a sum of money now represented by £434 15s. 9d. consols with the official trustees, producing £10 17s. 4d. yearly, which is applied in the purchase of coal and blankets for the poor.

In 1834 Mrs. Mary Barfield, by her will proved in the P.C.C. on 26 November, bequeathed part of her residuary personal estate for the maintenance and support of the almshouses situate at Bassingbourn and founded by her in 1833 for poor widows of sixty years and upwards inhabitants of Royston. The endowment consists of £4,022 4s. 4d. India 3 per cent. stock in the name of the official trustees, and producing £120 13s. 4d. yearly. The almshouses are now eight in number, and each inmate receives 5s. weekly and one ton of coal yearly.

The charity of Mrs. Sarah Ellen Pyne, for the general purposes of Royston Cottage Hospital, founded by will proved at London 13 June 1899, is regulated by a scheme of the Court of Chancery dated 24 March 1903. The endowment consists of a sum of £5,420 1s. 2d. consols with the official trustees, producing £135 10s. yearly.

The same testatrix by her will also founded a charity for the benefit of Royston Nursing Association. This charity is regulated by the scheme above mentioned. The endowment consists of a sum of £542 consols with the official trustees, producing £13 11s. yearly, which is applied towards the salary of a district nurse.

The same scheme also directed that a sum of consols equivalent at the price of the day to £1,000 sterling should out of the residuary estate of Mrs. Sarah Ellen Pyne be applied in providing a site for, and building, a mission room for the parish of Royston.

RUSHDEN

Risendene (xi cent.); Ressenden, Ryshenden, Russenden (xiii and xiv cent.); Rissheden, Russhenden (xiv cent.); Risden (xvii cent.).

Rushden is a small parish with an area of only 1,508 acres, of which about two-thirds are arable land, a quarter permanent grass and a fifteenth woodland.[1] Friars Wood, of some considerable size, is in the north-east of the parish and Bachelors Wood to the north of Southend Green. The parish lies on the chalk downs, which here reach a height of 500 ft. in the north-east, sloping down to about 350 ft. in the south.

Evidence of early settlement on the chalk lands of this district is furnished by the discovery of about forty implements of the Bronze Age at Cumberlow Green, which is the most important find of this period in Hertfordshire.[1a]

The village of Rushden is very small. It is situated a little off the road connecting Baldock and Buntingford, and lies about midway between these two towns, in which are its nearest railway stations. An old road, called in Rushden (of which it forms the western boundary) Shaw Green Lane, intersects this road near Cumberlow Green, and after passing through

---

[40] Stat. 32 Hen. VIII, cap. 44.
[41] L. and P. Hen. VIII, xvi, 379 (60).
[42] Kingston, Hist. of Royston, 190.
[43] P.C.C. Will 1 Fetiplace; cf. 13 Moone.
[44] P.C.C. Will 1 Fetiplace.
[45] Ibid. 5 Maynwaring.
[46] Memo. R. (Exch. L.T.R.), Mich. 18 & 19 Edw. I 'Communia,' m. 6 d.

[1] Statistics from Bd. of Agric. (1905).
[1a] Rep. of Royal Com. on Hist. Monum. of Herts.

Rushden and Wallington joins the road known as the Icknield Way. Another road which branches off from this at Cumberlow Green and joins it again near Redhill passes through the Mill End. The church of St. Mary stands a little to the east of it, with the school close by. The vicarage is half a mile to the east at Southend Green. To the south of the church in the main part of the village called Church End is a plastered timber building of the 16th or 17th century, formerly used as a post office. It has a tiled roof and one overhanging gable. It bears the date 1730, but this probably only refers to the plaster. Near it stands the old Rose and Crown Inn, which dates from the end of the 16th century. It also has a tiled roof and is built of plastered timber which is decorated with combed work. In addition to these there are some 17th-century thatched cottages and farm buildings. The village smithy is at Mill End.

The parish of Rushden includes several small hamlets. Shaw Green, on Shaw Green Lane, is a mile to the north-west of the village, Mill End is half a mile to the west, Southend Green half a mile to the east, connected with the village by a road, Offley Green a mile to the north-east between Julians and Friar's Wood, whilst Cumberlow Green is situated on the main road at the point where it enters the parish one mile to the south-west of the village.

MANORS The manor of RUSHDEN was held before the Conquest by two sokemen, 'men' of Archbishop Stigand.[2] In 1086 it was assessed at 5 hides and was held by Sigar de Cioches.[3] The lands of the Cioches family lay for the most part in Northamptonshire and were known as the honour of Chokes.[4] These lands descended to Anselm de Cioches, who forfeited under Henry I, and in 1130–1 paid 170 marks of silver, five war-horses and three palfreys for the restoration of his lands.[5] He was succeeded by his son Robert de Cioches or Chokes.[6] Robert was the last in the direct line to hold this honour, which on his death passed to William de Bethune, advocate of Arras, brother of Baldwin de Bethune Earl of Aumâle, who in 1200 paid £100 to have seisin of the lands in England[7] which had belonged to Robert de Cioches and which he claimed as great-nephew of Anselm father of Robert.[8] In 1203 Baldwin was granted the lands and possessions of his brother William in England.[9] Baldwin died in 1212,[10] and William de Bethune must have died shortly after, as in 1214 his son Robert was allowed full seisin of his lands.[11] Robert was succeeded by his brother Daniel in 1217,[12] and the latter before 1223 by Robert de Bethune, advocate of Arras,[13] presumably his son. Robert granted the honour of Chokes to Robert Count of Gisnes, who became the advocate of Bethune.[14] He was holding 3 hides of land in Rushden when he died.[15] After this the overlordship of Rushden appears to have lapsed. In 1461 the manor was said to be held of George Hyde in socage,[16] but this was possibly an error, as seventeen years later it was said to be held of the king in chief.[17]

The first sub-tenant in the manor of Rushden of whom there is any trace is William Basset, who held it at the beginning of the 13th century.[18] In 1239 a William Basset, probably his son (see advowson), was holding a carucate of land in Rushden of Thomas de Breauté.[19] This William paid £6 yearly for the lands which he held in Rushden of the honour of Chokes.[20] In 1272 Peter Basset was evidently lord of the manor,[21] but before 1310 he had been succeeded by Robert Basset,[21a] of whom there is mention in 1313, 1353, and 1384.[22]

With La More in Sandon (q.v.) Rushden came soon after to the Bealknaps and in 1390 was in the king's hands by the forfeiture of Sir Robert Bealknap. It was granted with other lands to Juliane, wife of Robert, for the support of Robert, then in exile-in Ireland, and of Juliane and her children.[23] Hamon son of Robert was holding the manor in 1419 and sold it in that year to John Fray and Agnes his wife.[24] John Fray held it until his death in 1461,[25] when by his will it remained with his widow Agnes for life, with reversion to their daughter Agnes and her heirs, with contingent remainder to their youngest daughter Katherine and their other daughters in succession.[26] Agnes Fray died in 1478,[27] their daughter Agnes died without issue,[28] and Rushden passed to Katherine, then wife of Humphrey Stafford.[29] In 1482 Katherine died,[30] her husband only surviving her for four years,[31] and Rushden descended to her young son Humphrey, aged eight.[32] He was knighted before 1531,[33] and died in 1545, his son Humphrey, aged forty, being his heir.[34] This Humphrey (of Kirby Hall, co. Northants) was knighted in February 1546–7 at the coronation of Edward VI.[35] He held the manor[36] until 1574, when he sold it with a wood called Westhay to Robert Newport of Sandon (co. Herts.).[37] Robert Newport died in 1583,[38] and Rushden passed to Edward Newport,[39] apparently his son.[40] He with his wife Anne sold it in 1604 to John and William Rowley.[41] By 1615 it had come

---

[2] V.C.H. Herts. i, 342a.
[3] Ibid.
[4] Baker, Hist. of Northants, ii, 272.
[5] Ibid.
[6] Red Bk. of Exch. (Rolls Ser.), i, 334.
[7] Rot. de Oblatis et Fin. (Rec. Com.), 59; Rot. Lit. Pat. (Rec. Com.), i, 7.
[8] See Baker, Hist. of Northants, ii, 272.
[9] Liberate R. (Rec. Com.), 41.
[10] Dugdale, Baronage, i, 63.
[11] Rot. Lit. Claus. (Rec. Com.), i, 208b, 324. [12] Ibid. 328, 329.
[13] Ibid. 574b.
[14] See Chan. Inq. p.m. 31 Hen. III, no. 44; Testa de Nevill (Rec. Com.), 270, 26, 30.
[15] Misc. Chan. Inq. file 18, no. 10 (incert. annis Hen. III).
[16] Chan. Inq. p.m. 1 Edw. IV, no. 28 (file 2).
[17] Ibid. 18 Edw. IV, no. 45 (file 546).
[18] Testa de Nevill (Rec. Com.), 270.
[19] Feet of F. Herts. Mich. 24 Hen. III, no. 290.
[20] Misc. Chan. Inq. p.m. file 18, no. 10; Testa de Nevill (Rec. Com.), 270.
[21] See De Banco R. 55, m. 101 (an action concerning suit of court owed to him at Rushden).
[21a] Confirmation of the advowson to the priory of Dunstable by Robert Basset, MS. in Lincoln Cath. Muniment Room D, ii, 86, i.
[22] Cal. Pat. 1313–17, p. 62; 1350–4, p. 386; Feet of F. Herts. 7 Ric. II, no. 61.
[23] Cal. Pat. 1388–92, p. 231.
[24] Feet of F. Herts. 7 Hen. V, no. 40.
[25] Chan. Inq. p.m. 1 Edw. IV, no. 28 (file 2); see Inq. a.q.d. file 448, no. 18, 22.
[26] Early Chan. Proc. bdle. 71, no. 40.
[27] Cal. Inq. p.m. (Rec. Com.), iv, 390.
[28] Early Chan. Proc. bdle. 71, no. 40.
[29] Ibid.; Chan. Inq. p.m. 18 Edw. IV, no. 45 (file 67).
[30] Cal. Inq. p.m. Hen. VII, 102.
[31] Ibid. 100.
[32] Ibid.
[33] Feet of F. Div. Co. Hil. 23 Hen. VIII.
[34] Chan. Inq. p.m. (Ser. 2), lxxii, 86 (1).
[35] Shaw, Knights of Engl. ii, 60.
[36] Feet of F. Herts. Hil. 4 Edw. VI; Div. Co. East. 5 Eliz.
[37] Close, 16 Eliz. pt. xii.
[38] Chan. Inq. p.m. (Ser. 2), cc, 52.
[39] Pat. 28 Eliz. pt. xi, m. 17.
[40] The name of the heir is illegible in the inquisition.
[41] Feet of F. Herts. Trin. 2 Jas. I.

ODSEY HUNDRED
RUSHDEN

into the possession of John Goodman (whose family had held land in Rushden for some time previously),[42] who with John Goodman, junior, and Grace his wife then conveyed it to Sir William Smyth.[43]

From Goodman the manor seems to have passed to Sir Thomas Stanley, kt., of Leytonstone (co. Essex).[44] His wife was Mary Hammond, sister to William Hammond and cousin to Richard Lovelace the poet. Stanley held in 1648, when he settled the manor on his son Thomas Stanley,[45] who is known as a poet and as the author of the *Lives of the Philosophers*,[46] on the occasion of his marriage with Dorothy daughter of Sir James Enyon, bart., of Floore (co. Northants).[47] Thomas Stanley died in 1678,[47a] and his widow Dorothy Stanley and his son Thomas sold the manor the following year to Joseph Edmonds[48] of Cumberlow Green, son of Simon Edmonds, alderman of London.[49] On the death of Joseph Edmonds Rushden descended to his daughter and heiress Anne, who married Sir Cleave More, bart., in or before 1689.[50] She died in 1720,[51] and Rushden was inherited by her son Sir Joseph Edmonds More,[52] who continued to hold it with his wife until 1729, when it was bought by John Spence[53] in trust with other lands under the terms of the will of Luke Hodges, merchant of London, who had married John's daughter Mary Spence in 1692.[54] This was proved in 1715 by his widow,[55] who subsequently married Benjamin Avery, LL.D.[56] On her death in 1737[57] these lands passed by settlement to the sons of Dorothy Mole, cousin of Luke Hodges. The two eldest sons must have died without children, for in 1779 Rushden had descended to Christopher Hodges, formerly Mole, late of the Inner Temple, only son and heir of Christopher Mole, late of the East India House, deceased,[58] third son of Dorothy Mole.[59] In this year Christopher Hodges sold it to Adolphus Meetkerke the younger of Julians.[60] He died in 1784,[61] and his son Adolphus Meetkerke died in 1841.[62] He was succeeded by a son of the same name, who on his death in 1879 left two daughters.[63] The elder of these, Mary Florence, married in 1878 Frederick Morehouse Metcalfe of Inglethorpe Hall (co. Norfolk), who died in 1893.[64] Mrs. Metcalfe inherited her father's estates in Rushden, and is the present owner of the manor, residing at Julians.[65]

BRADFIELD GRANGE alias FRYERS GRANGE[66] originally formed part of the manor of Broadfield, but there seems no doubt that it lay in Rushden.[67] In the days of Edward the Confessor Broadfield was divided between the men of the Archbishop of Canterbury and Queen Edith.[68] In 1086 one of these holdings, a hide and a quarter of a virgate, had passed into the possession of Hardwin de Scales and was held of him by Theobald.[69] In 1150 Theobald, probably grandson of the former Theobald, with consent of his brother William, granted 30 acres of land in Broadfield (i.e. in the manor of Broadfield) to Warden Abbey (co. Beds.).[70] This estate, according to a later confirmation of the grant, included the grange of Bradfield and a wood named Fildenwode.[71] In 1291 the abbot was assessed at £1 19s. 8¼d. for his lands in Rushden.[72] These remained with the abbey until its dissolution.[73] In 1543 they were granted as 'Bradfield Grange in the parish of Rushden' to Richard Andrewes of Hailes (co. Gloucester),[74] who in the same year alienated the Grange to John Newport, who for many years had held a lease of it under the abbey of Warden.[75]

John Newport died in 1552 and his lands passed to his son and heir Robert, aged thirty.[76] Robert acquired the manor of Rushden (q.v.), and on his death in 1583 Edward Newport inherited his lands.[77] In 1603 Edward Newport alienated Bradfield Grange to John and William Rowley,[78] who sold it to John Stone of co. Hunts.,[79] son of William Stone of Segenhoe (co. Beds.). After this there seems no trace of it as a separate property. The situation of Bradfield or Fryers Grange is marked by a large wood called Friars Wood in the north-east of the parish, which has Friars Farm on its north side.

JULIANS was a capital messuage or farm which Richard and William, sons of John Stone, bought in 1603 from Edward Newport, who had acquired it in 1586 by purchase from William Wilson of Walkern.[80] Richard Stone was knighted, and in 1651, with Elizabeth his wife and John Stone, was holding land in Rushden.[81] On his death his heir was his son Thomas Stone, who died in 1696.[82] He left no son, and his elder daughter and co-heir Penelope inherited Julians.[83] She married in 1699 Adolphus Meetkerke, who was descended from Sir Adolphus Meetkerke, President of the High Court of Flanders in the latter half of the 16th century.[84] He was an adherent of the Reformed religion and took part in an endeavour to surrender Leyden to the Earl of

WARDEN ABBEY. *Azure a crozier between three warden pears or.*

---

[42] See manor of Cumberlow Green.
[43] Feet of F. Herts. Mich. 13 Jas. I
[44] Notes of Fines Div. Co. East. 24 Chas. I; *Visit. of Essex* (Harl. Soc. xiii), 493.
[45] Notes of Fines Div. Co. East. 24 Chas. I.
[46] *Dict. Nat. Biog.*
[47] Baker, *Hist. of Northants*, i, 153.
[47a] *Dict. Nat. Biog.*
[48] Recov. R. Trin. 31 Chas. II, rot. 131.
[49] G.E.C. *Complete Baronetage*, iv, 71; see *Visit. of Lond.* (Harl. Soc. xv), 246.
[50] G.E.C. loc. cit.
[51] Ibid.
[52] Feet of F. Herts. Mich. 8 Geo. I.
[53] Recov. R. Trin. 3 Geo. II, rot. 126.
[54] P.C.C. 90 Fagg; see Close, 19 Geo. III, pt. xx, no. 3.
[55] Ibid.   [56] P.C.C. 27 Brodreff.
[57] Ibid.
[58] Close, 19 Geo. III, pt. xx, no. 3.
[59] P.C.C. 90 Fagg.
[60] Close, 19 Geo. III, pt. xx, no. 3.
[61] Burke, *Landed Gentry* (1906).
[62] Ibid.
[63] Ibid.
[64] Ibid.
[65] Ibid.
[66] Harl. MS. 758, fol. 28; Pat. 1 Jas. I, pt. xi.
[67] *L. and P. Hen. VIII*, xviii (1), 981 (56).
[68] *V.C.H. Herts.* i, 339, 342, 322, 311.
[69] Ibid. 339.
[70] Dugdale, *Mon.* v, 372. For the family of Theobald see manor of Broadfield.
[71] Ibid.
[72] *Pope Nich. Tax.* (Rec. Com.), 51b.
[73] See *Valor Eccl.* (Rec. Com.), iv, 193.
[74] *L. and P. Hen. VIII*, xviii (1), g. 981 (56).
[75] Ibid. (2), g. 107 (56, ix).
[76] Chan. Inq. p.m. (Ser. 2), c, 48.
[77] Ibid. cc, 52. (The date is uncertain, as the inquisition is very much decayed.)
[78] Pat. 1 Jas. I, pt. xi.
[79] Chauncy, *Hist. and Antiq. of Herts.* 74.
[80] Com. Pleas D. Enr. East. 1 Jas. I, m. 22.
[81] Feet of F. Div. Co. Mich. 1651.
[82] Cussans, *Hist. of Herts. Odsey Hund.* 164 seq.
[83] Ibid.
[84] Ibid.

A HISTORY OF HERTFORDSHIRE

Essex.[85] The plot failed and he was obliged to take refuge in England. Later he was appointed ambassador to England by the United States of Holland, and he died in London in 1591.[86] His two eldest sons were killed fighting in the Netherlands, but his fourth son Edward, who was only a year old at the time of his father's death, settled in England, and, taking holy orders, was for many years Professor of Hebrew at Christ Church, Oxford.[87] His grandson, who married the heiress to Julians, died in 1732,[88] and Penelope died in 1746,[89] when Julians descended to their son Adolphus Meetkerke,[90] who purchased the manor of Rushden in 1779, and from this date Julians has descended with that manor (q.v.).

MEETKERKE. *Gules two swords or crosses saltirewise with the hilts upwards.*

The mansion-house of Julians is situated about half a mile north of the church. It was erected by William Stone about 1610. The house was entirely recased about the beginning of the 18th century, but the old walls appear to have been left standing, so that the general arrangement of the house is very little changed. The present front is cemented and is very plain. The doorway is in the middle, entering into the hall. The staircase opens directly off the hall, and probably at one time formed a back projection, but considerable additions have been made to the house. The stair is a very good example of the Queen Anne period, with delicately twisted and fluted balusters and carved ends to the steps. The details are very similar to the stair at the Great House, Cheshunt, which belongs to the same period, though the arrangement of the returned ends of the steps is somewhat different. There are wide folding doors at the foot of the stair, to shut it off from the hall when desired. To the right of the hall on entering is the drawing-room—no doubt the old parlour, and to the left is the kitchen wing, which still contains a little 17th-century panelling and an oak chimneypiece. The site of the old Bury can be traced in the park, immediately to the north of the church.

The descent of the manor of CUMBERLOW GREEN (Comerlowe Green, Cumbarlo Green, xvi cent.) is very difficult to trace. It appears to have been called the manor of Broadfield in 1346, when it was held by Walter de Mauny,[91] and from him it afterwards took the name of Maunseys.[92] He does not appear to have held it long, and it may probably be identified with the manor of Broadfield which in February 1361–2 was in the hands of John de Ellerton, King's Serjeant-at-Arms, to whom Edward III granted free warren.[93] In 1376 Sir Walter Lee, kt., quitclaimed all right in the manor of Cumberlow to Richard de Ravensere and others,[94] probably in trust for the lord of the manor of Broadfield, for in 1428 Walter de Manny's holding had come to John Clerk, to whom the manor of Broadfield belonged.[95] It descended with that manor (q.v.) until 1486, when, on the death of Margaret Dunstable, they became separated and Maunseys in Cumberlow descended to her son and heir Thomas Hatfield,[96] who sold it in 1492, as the manor of Broadfield in Cumberlow Green, to Thomas Oxenbrigge.[97] He must have sold it to John Fortescue, who died seised of the manor of Cumberlow Green in 1517, when it descended to his son Henry.[98] Henry Fortescue was holding lands in Cumberlow in 1537–8,[98a] but he conveyed the manor to William Goodman,[99] who was holding it in 1574.[100] On his death it descended to his son John, to whom Francis Fortescue quitclaimed all right in the manor in 1577.[1] John Goodman, who built a house at Cumberlow Green,[2] was holding the manor in 1601.[3] He shortly afterwards acquired the manor of Rushden (q.v.), and from this date the two manors have descended together. Cumberlow Green lies in the south-west of the parish, on the borders of Clothall, into which parish the manor extended and in which the manor-house was situated.[4]

The Knights Hospitallers held certain lands in Rushden which were attached to their preceptory of Shingay in Cambridgeshire.[5] This manor of Shingay was given them by Sybil de Raynes, daughter of Roger de Montgomery, in 1140,[6] and it is probable that the land attached to it in Rushden represents the half hide which Earl Roger held in Broadfield in 1086,[7] for there is no further trace of this holding in Broadfield and the boundaries of the manorial holdings do not seem to correspond with the present boundaries of the parishes.[8] In 1198 the Knights Hospitallers were holding land in Rushden and were fined for receiving a fugitive, Ralph Rusticus, there.[9] They continued to hold these lands[10] until the dissolution of the order, after which the preceptory of Shingay with all its appurtenances in Rushden and elsewhere was granted by Henry VIII to Sir Richard Long in tail-male in 1540.[11] There is no further record of the Rushden estate after this date. Shingay survived as the name of a wood, which is marked on the tithe map of 1845.[12]

The Knights Templars also seem to have had a small holding in Rushden, attached to their manor of Temple Dinsley, in 1309, the year of the suppression of their order, when a report was ordered to be made on all their lands in Hertfordshire.[13] After the grant

---

[85] Cussans, *Hist. of Herts. Odsey Hund.* 164 seq.
[86] Ibid.
[87] Ibid.
[88] Burke, *Landed Gentry.*
[89] Ibid.
[90] Ibid.
[91] Chan. Inq. p.m. 20 Edw. III (1st nos.), no. 51.
[92] Ibid. (Ser. 2), xxiii, 65.
[93] Chart. R. 34 & 35 Edw. III, m. 2, no. 6.
[94] Close, 50 Edw. III, pt. ii, m. 9, 12, 13.
[95] *Feud. Aids*, ii, 447.
[96] Chan. Inq. p.m. (Ser. 2), xxiii, 65.
[97] Close, 7 Hen. VII, pt. i, no. 9, 10.
[98] Chan. Inq. p.m. (Ser. 2), xxxiii, no. 126.
[98a] Feet of F. Herts. Hil. 29 Hen. VIII.
[99] Chauncy, *Hist. Antiq. of Herts.* 50.
[100] Feet of F. Herts. Mich. 16 & 17 Eliz.
[1] Ibid. Mich. 19 & 20 Eliz.
[2] Close, 19 Geo. III, pt. xx, no. 3.
[3] Feet of F. Herts. East. 43 Eliz.
[4] See Close, 19 Geo. III, pt. xx, no. 3; information from Rev. J. Mearns.
[5] L. and P. Hen. VIII, xv, 613 (1).
[6] Dugdale, *Mon.* vi, 808, 834.
[7] V.C.H. Herts. i, 322.
[8] Cf. Bradfield Grange.
[9] *Rot. Cur. Reg.* (Rec. Com.), i, 159, 168.
[10] See Cal. Pat. 1327–30, p. 531.
[11] L. and P. Hen. VIII, xv, 613 (1).
[12] Information from Rev. J. Mearns.
[13] Cal. Pat. 1307–13, p. 131.

ODSEY HUNDRED

of the Templars' lands to the Knights Hospitallers [14] this estate probably became amalgamated with the Hospitallers' other holding in Rushden.

The church of ST. MARY THE CHURCH VIRGIN consists of chancel 28 ft. by 14 ft., nave 43 ft. by 20 ft., south porch, west tower 11 ft. by 10 ft. 6 in., all dimensions taken internally. The walls are of flint rubble covered with cement, the dressings are of stone; the chancel is built of brick and the roof slated, the nave roof being covered with lead.

The nave dates from about 1340–50; the chancel is modern, although built on the old foundations, parts of which are visible on the south side. The chancel arch is of 15th-century date; the west tower of about 1400.

In the original 14th-century plinth visible on the south side of the chancel are the jambs of an old doorway. The four-light window in the east wall of the chancel and the two windows of two lights in each of the north and south walls, together with the doorway in the south, are all modern. In the south wall a late 14th-century piscina has been reset; the head is cinquefoiled and the plain projecting sill is made up with cement. The 15th-century chancel arch is of two moulded orders, the inner one supported on responds with capitals but no bases, the mouldings stopping on a plain splay. The jambs have been repaired. In the north wall of the nave is a late 15th-century window of three cinquefoiled lights under a four-centred arch, a good deal repaired; a late 14th-century doorway has been blocked: it has an arch of two orders. In the south wall are two windows of two cinquefoiled lights with transom and traceried heads under four-centred arches; they are of late 15th-century work much repaired. The mid-14th-century south doorway is of three moulded orders, with moulded capitals and splayed bases; the capital on the east side is enriched with leaf ornament, the other being plain. The south porch is modern. At the south-east angle of the nave are the remains of the stair to the rood loft, constructed in the thickness of the wall. In the east wall, north of the chancel arch, is a large niche with cinquefoiled four-centred arch under a square head; above is a frieze filled with square panels cusped and traceried; portions of the flanking buttresses and the sill have been cut away. It is of 15th-century work. On the north wall of the nave, opposite the south door, are traces of paintings.

The west tower is of three stages with an embattled parapet. The tower arch is of three splayed orders with responds and moulded capitals, the bases are modern. The west window is of two trefoiled lights with a sixfoiled opening in the centre and is of late 14th-century date. The second stage is pierced on the south face only by a narrow loop-light; the belfry lights are single with trefoiled heads and are much decayed.

The low-pitched roof over the nave has been much restored, but some of the old timbers still remain; the marks of the original high-pitched roof are visible on the east face of the tower.

The octagonal font belongs to the middle of the 15th century; the sides of the basin are decorated with cusped and foliated panels; the base mouldings have been repaired with cement; the cover is of 17th-century work.

The communion table is of the early part of the 17th century and has plain turned legs. All the other fittings are modern.

On the south nave wall is a mural monument, with arms, to Sir Adolphus Meetkerke, who died in 1591.

There are five bells cast from four old ones in 1787 by john Briant of Hertford.

[14] See Dugdale, *Mon.* vi, 789; Addison, *Knights Templars*, 299.

RUSHDEN CHURCH FROM THE SOUTH-EAST

A HISTORY OF HERTFORDSHIRE

The communion plate consists of cup, paten and flagon, 1714, and another paten, 1847.

The registers are in four books : (i) baptisms from 1607 to 1668, burials 1607 to 1668, marriages 1607 to 1669; (ii) baptisms and burials from 1673 to 1770, marriages 1673 to 1753; (iii) baptisms and burials from 1700 to 1812, marriages 1700 to 1748; (iv) marriages from 1792 to 1812. It will be seen that book iii is largely a repetition of book ii. A book containing marriages (1754-92) was accidentally burnt in 1792.

ADVOWSON The patronage of the church of St. Mary the Virgin was originally vested in the lord of the manor, the earliest recorded presentation being made by William Basset in 1220.[15] Soon after he granted the church to the Prior and convent of Dunstable.[16] On the living falling vacant in 1241, however, William Basset, probably his son, disputed the presentation, but the prior succeeded in securing the living to his own nominee. In 1272 a similar dispute took place between the prior and Peter Basset, who presented his brother John. This ended in a composition made between them by which Basset quit-claimed all right to the prior.[17] In 1310 the Prior and convent of Dunstable received a confirmation of the church from Robert Basset, and in the same year obtained licence to appropriate the church,[18] which in 1310 they alienated in mortmain to the Chapter of Lincoln.[19] To this alienation Robert Basset gave his consent.[20] The advowson of Rushden remained with the Dean and Chapter of Lincoln until 1908,[21] when an exchange was made by which the Dean and Chapter of Lincoln became patrons of South Reston, co. Lincoln, and the Chancellor of the Duchy of Lancaster became patron of Rushden.[22]

The living was formally declared a vicarage in 1336. A terrier of 1709 shows that besides the small tithes the vicar had half the tithes of hay and the tithe of wood excepting Shingay Wood, which was tithe free.[23]

CHARITIES In 1815 William Love by his will gave £180 3 per cent. consols, the dividends thereon to be applied towards providing a master or mistress of the Sunday or any other school for the instruction of poor children and for purchasing books and other necessaries for the use of the school. This stock was sold in 1819, and with the proceeds and from part of the residue of the personal estate a sum of £233 6s. 8d. consols was purchased.

The dividends, amounting to £5 16s. 8d., are paid to the mistress of the Sunday school.

SANDON

Sandona (x cent.); Sanduna (xii cent.); Saundon (xiii cent.).

Sandon is a parish of 4,060 acres lying high on the chalk. The level of the land over the greater part of the range upwards from some 400 ft. above the ordnance datum to 528 ft. in the immediate neighbourhood of the village, from which there is a gradual descent in a north-westerly direction to a level of only 240 ft. The soil is light, containing a considerable quantity of chalk, of which the subsoil is wholly composed. Arable land covers rather more than 3,000 acres, pasture nearly 700 acres, and the extent of woodland, which comprises small plantations at Roe Wood, Tichney Wood (possibly the 'Tichenho' Wood of 1222)[1] and Park Wood, is about 115 acres.[2] The Cat Ditch, a tributary of the Ivel, flows northwards through the parish. The village itself stands on the high ground at some distance from the main road. It consists of a few farms and cottages grouped irregularly about the church. There are several outlying hamlets. Roe Green,[2a] three-quarters of a mile to the south-west of the village, may be identical with 'the green at le Rothe' mentioned in 13th-century court rolls.[3] There is a Congregational chapel at Roe Green dating from 1868,[4] and representing a community which existed in the parish in the latter half of the 17th century.[5] In 1809 the house of Thomas Smith at Roe Green was licensed for worship.[6] The chapel was licensed for marriages in 1877.[7] The same minister serves the chapel of Red Hill, a hamlet in the extreme south-west of the parish.[8] The first chapel was built here in 1720, and in 1805 a new building was erected on ground given by Mr. Fordham.[9]

There are no important roads passing through the parish, but that part of the Icknield Way which forms the high road from Hitchin to Royston separates this parish from that of Ashwell, where the nearest railway station lies.

The open fields were inclosed in 1842.[10]

There are moated sites at Daniels Farm and at Hankins, about a mile to the south-west of the church, and a thickly planted moated tumulus on the east side of the village. Traditions are attached to the two latter. That relating to Hankins is that the owner, who has probably been wrongly identified with John Fitz Geoffrey, whose brass, dated 1480, is in the church, on his arrival from London one night found his home in flames and his wife and children slain by robbers. The other legend, which refers to

---

[15] Cussans, *Hist. of Herts. Odsey Hund.* 169.
[16] MS. in Linc. Cath. Mun. Room D ii, 86, i, communicated by Rev. Jas. Mearns; Chauncy, *Hist. and Antiq. of Herts.*
[17] *Annales de Dunstaplia* (Rolls Ser.), 158, 254, 342.
[18] MS. Linc. Cath. D ii, 86, i, 2, 4; Inq. a.q.d. file 79, no. 13.
[19] *Cal. Pat.* 1307-13, p. 207; *Abbrev. Rot. Orig.* i, 171.
[20] MS. Linc. Cath. D ii, 86, i.

[21] See Inst. Bks. P.R.O.
[22] Paper read by Rev. Jas. Mearns, *East Herts. Arch. Soc. Trans.* i (1), 82.
[23] Terrier in custody of Messrs. Hawkins of Hitchin, communicated by Rev. J. Mearns.

[1] Hale, *Dom. of St. Paul's* (Camd. Soc.), 13.
[2] *Statistics from Bd. of Agric.* (1905).
[2a] Chauncy's identification of this hamlet with the 'Rodenhangre' of Domesday Book is apparently incorrect (*V.C.H. Herts.* i, 333b, 343a).

[3] D. and C. of St. Paul's, Press B, Box 35, no. 7, Morrow of Trans. of St. Thos. Martyr, 12 Edw. I.
[4] Cussans, op. cit. *Odsey Hund.* 160.
[5] *Congregational Year Bk.* 1912, p. 228; Urwick, *Nonconf. in Herts.* 817-18.
[6] Urwick, *Nonconf. in Herts.* 817.
[7] *Lond. Gaz.* 5 Jan. 1877, p. 61.
[8] Inform. kindly supplied by the Rev. F. W. Low, vicar.
[9] Urwick, loc. cit.; Close, 1805, pt. xiv, no. 7.
[10] *Dep. Keeper's Rep.* xxvii, 25.

270

Rushden Church   The Nave looking East

Sandon Church   Easter Sepulchre North Side of Chancel

the Mount (Woodley Yards), is that the inhabitants were forewarned by a boy of an impending attack by robbers, which they successfully resisted, but the robbers, having caught the boy, flayed him alive.[11]

The canons of St. Paul's held MANORS SANDON in 1086. They had been in possession before the Conquest.[12] A charter, of which copies are preserved in registers of the dean and chapter,[13] purports to be a grant or confirmation made by King Athelstan (924–40) to the monastery of ten 'mansae' at Sandon with Rode (possibly Roe Green)[14] and other lands in Hertfordshire. The charter itself is a palpable forgery, but there may be truth in the tradition that the canons owed the gift of these lands to Athelstan. In 1086 Sandon was assessed at 10 hides, of which 5 hides were then in demesne, and half a hide was attached to the church[15] (q.v.). There was arable land sufficient for twenty ploughs. An extent of the manor taken in 1155 gives a detailed account of the stock. There were on the farm forty-four oxen, five horses and one cart horse, in addition to cattle and sheep.[16] Some of the services mentioned in an inquisition of 1222 are of interest.[17] Tenants of half-virgate holdings had to carry twenty-five loads to London. They also paid wood-silver and malt-silver, and provided two hens at Christmas and fifteen eggs at Easter. Holders of 10 and 5 acres rendered similar services in proportion to the extent of their holding. The manor of Sandon was not attached to any of the prebends, but formed part of the 'communa,' the revenue of which was appropriated to the support of all the officers of the cathedral.[18] Together with 'Rode' and Luffenhall it supplied the chapter with 'farm' or provisions for about ten weeks in each year.[19] Luffenhall was in fact taxed with Sandon for temporal purposes, but for spiritual purposes it was regarded as a part of Ardeley[20] (q.v.).

The lessee of Sandon was often one of the canons of the cathedral. Thus in 1155 the canon Alexander was appointed 'farmer' of this manor for life.[21] Towards the end of the next century Master Robert de Braundon, prebendary of Sneating,[22] had a life interest in the farm of the manor,[23] although Ralph de Diceto, the chronicler, who was dean from about 1181 to 1204, tried to secure that the lessee should always be the dean himself.[24] He apparently found two lay 'farmers' there, namely Richard the Red (*ruffus*) and Richard of Sandon.[25]

The manorial lands were let to John Newport in 1526[26] and the lease was renewed to him and his eldest son Robert in 1550.[27] Robert succeeded his father about 1552, but was disturbed in his possession by his younger brother Thomas and the latter's daughter Clare, who married her cousin John Newport of East Greenwich.[28] Moreover, in February 1559–60 Robert Dudley Earl of Leicester obtained from the dean and chapter a ninety-nine years' lease of the manorial rights with a reversionary interest in the lands let to Newport,[29] and conveyed his title to William Hyde of Sandon.[30] Consequently disputes arose between Hyde and Robert Newport, who feared that Hyde would oust him from his lease and also arrogated to himself the right of holding courts.[31]

After the abolition of cathedral chapters in 1641 the reversionary interest of the Dean and Chapter of St. Paul's was sold to Henry Scobell of London,[32] afterwards clerk of the Parliament and Secretary of State. At the Restoration it was recovered by the dean and chapter together with their other estates. In 1863 they sold the manor to Mr. John George Fordham of Royston.[33] From him it has descended to Mr. Francis John Fordham of Yew Tree House, Royston, the present owner.[34]

The house of the manor is mentioned in the early part of the 13th century, when its 'houses, ditches and closes' were repaired.[35] The present farm-house, called Sandon Bury, which stands on the south-east of the church, is a 17th-century brick building of three stories to which a wing has been added on the east side. It contains an original staircase. Near the house are two 17th-century barns and a 17th-century brick pigeon-house with a tiled roof, now much out of repair. Late in the 17th century the house called Sandon Bury was in the occupation of Edward Nicholas, son of the Dean of St. Paul's.

The Dean and Chapter of St. Paul's claimed their usual extensive liberties in this manor.[37] In 1247 they had a grant of free warren which was confirmed in 1316.[38] It appears, however, that until 1253 the men of Sandon had been accustomed to come to the sheriff's tourn twice a year, and in 1278 the township was ordered to be distrained because it had not come to the tourn.[39]

John son of William Fitz Geoffrey of Sandon released his right in 'Ladygrove' in Sandon to Stephen Cowherd in 1421.[40] This William appears to have been the grandfather of John Fitz Geoffrey of Sandon, who died in 1480, leaving a son and heir John.[41] The brasses of John Fitz Geoffrey the father and of his wife and children are still preserved in the nave of the church.[42] It appears that the Fitz Geoffrey estate was the reputed manor of *DANIELS*,

---

[11] *East Herts. Arch. Soc. Trans.* iii (1), 47.
[12] *V.C.H. Herts.* i, 317*a*.
[13] The charter is printed by Dugdale, *Hist. of St. Paul's*, 292; Birch, *Cart. Sax.* ii, 451; Kemble, *Cod. Diplom.* 1127. The jurors of 1274–5 stated that Sandon was ancient demesne of the Crown (*Hund. R.* [Rec. Com.], i, 193).
[14] Since the form in the charter is Rode or Rode, and the name 'Rothe' Green occurs in early court rolls (see above).
[15] *V.C.H. Herts.* i, 317*a*; cf. Hale, *Dom. of St. Paul's* (Camd. Soc.), 141.
[16] Hale, *Dom. of St. Paul's* (Camd. Soc.), 134.
[17] Ibid. 17 et seq.
[18] Ibid. p. iii.
[19] Ibid. p. xxxix.
[20] D. and C. of St. Paul's, Press B,
Box 35, no. 7, Thursday before St. Philip and St. James, 13 Edw. III.
[21] Hale, op. cit. 134.
[22] Dryden, *Hist. of St. Paul's* (1818), 274.
[23] *Plac. de Quo Warr.* (Rec. Com.), 290.
[24] D. and C. of St. Paul's, Press A, Box 40, no. 1402.
[25] Hale, *Dom. of St. Paul's* (Camd. Soc.), 111; the farmer in 1222 was John de St. Laurence (ibid. 13).
[26] Chan. Proc. (Ser. 2), bdle. 82, no. 19.
[27] Ibid.
[28] Ibid. bdle. 246, no. 5. They asserted that John Newport had assigned the lease to Thomas Newport in the church of Sandon.
[29] Chan. Proc. (Ser. 2), bdle. 246, no. 5. See Close, 1649, pt. li, no. 1.
[30] Chan. Inq. p.m. (Ser. 2), c, 48.
[31] Chan. Proc. (Ser. 2), bdles. 82, no. 19; 86, 26.
[32] Close, 1649, pt. li, m. 1.
[33] Cussans, *Hist. of Herts. Odsey Hund.* 147.
[34] See *V.C.H. Herts. Families*, 10.
[35] Hale, op. cit. 14.
[36] Inscription in the chancel (Dugdale, *Hist. of St. Paul's*, 228).
[37] Hale, op. cit. 13; Assize R. 325; *Plac. de Quo Warr.* (Rec. Com.), 290.
[38] Chart. R. 32 Hen. III, m. 5; *Cal. Chart. R.* 1300–26, p. 305; *Hund. R.* (Rec. Com.), i, 194.
[39] Assize R. 323.
[40] Anct. D. (P.R.O.), D 395.
[41] Chan. Inq. p.m. 20 Edw. IV, no. 53.
[42] See below.

SANDON

the Mount (Woodley Yards), is that the inhabitants were forewarned by a boy of an impending attack by robbers, which they successfully resisted, but the robbers, having caught the boy, flayed him alive.[11]

The canons of St. Paul's held MANORS SANDON in 1086. They had been in possession before the Conquest.[12] A charter, of which copies are preserved in registers of the dean and chapter,[13] purports to be a grant or confirmation made by King Athelstan (924-40) to the monastery of ten 'mansae' at Sandon with Rode (possibly Roe Green) [14] and other lands in Hertfordshire. The charter itself is a palpable forgery, but there may be truth in the tradition that the canons owed the gift of these lands to Athelstan. In 1086 Sandon was assessed at 10 hides, of which 5 hides were then in demesne, and half a hide was attached to the church [15] (q.v.). There was arable land sufficient for twenty ploughs. An extent of the manor taken in 1155 gives a detailed account of the stock. There were on the farm forty-four oxen, five horses and one cart horse, in addition to cattle and sheep.[16] Some of the services mentioned in an inquisition of 1222 are of interest.[17] Tenants of half-virgate holdings had to carry twenty-five loads to London. They also paid wood-silver and malt-silver, and provided two hens at Christmas and fifteen eggs at Easter. Holders of 10 and 5 acres rendered similar services in proportion to the extent of their holding. The manor of Sandon was not attached to any of the prebends, but formed part of the 'communa,' the revenue of which was appropriated to the support of all the officers of the cathedral.[18] Together with 'Rode' and Luffenhall it supplied the chapter with 'farm' or provisions for about ten weeks in each year.[19] Luffenhall was in fact taxed with Sandon for temporal purposes, but for spiritual purposes it was regarded as a part of Ardeley [20] (q.v.).

The lessee of Sandon was often one of the canons of the cathedral. Thus in 1155 the canon Alexander was appointed 'farmer' of this manor for life.[21] Towards the end of the next century Master Robert de Braundon, prebendary of Sneating,[22] had a life interest in the farm of the manor,[23] although Ralph de Diceto, the chronicler, who was dean from about 1181 to 1204, tried to secure that the lessee should always be the dean himself.[24] He apparently found two lay 'farmers' there, namely Richard the Red (*ruffus*) and Richard of Sandon.[25]

The manorial lands were let to John Newport in 1526 [26] and the lease was renewed to him and his eldest son Robert in 1550.[27] Robert succeeded his father about 1552, but was disturbed in his possession by his younger brother Thomas and the latter's daughter Clare, who married her cousin John Newport of East Greenwich.[28] Moreover, in February 1559-60 Robert Dudley Earl of Leicester obtained from the dean and chapter a ninety-nine years' lease of the manorial rights with a reversionary interest in the lands let to Newport,[29] and conveyed his title to William Hyde of Sandon.[30] Consequently disputes arose between Hyde and Robert Newport, who feared that Hyde would oust him from his lease and also arrogated to himself the right of holding courts.[31]

After the abolition of cathedral chapters in 1641 the reversionary interest of the Dean and Chapter of St. Paul's was sold to Henry Scobell of London,[32] afterwards clerk of the Parliament and Secretary of State. At the Restoration it was recovered by the dean and chapter together with their other estates. In 1863 they sold the manor to Mr. John George Fordham of Royston.[33] From him it has descended to Mr. Francis John Fordham of Yew Tree House, Royston, the present owner.[34]

The house of the manor is mentioned in the early part of the 13th century, when its 'houses, ditches and closes' were repaired.[35] The present farm-house, called Sandon Bury, which stands on the south-east of the church, is a 17th-century brick building of three stories to which a wing has been added on the east side. It contains an original staircase. Near the house are two 17th-century barns and a 17th-century brick pigeon-house with a tiled roof, now much out of repair. Late in the 17th century the house called Sandon Bury was in the occupation of Edward Nicholas, son of the Dean of St. Paul's.[36]

The Dean and Chapter of St. Paul's claimed their usual extensive liberties in this manor.[37] In 1247 they had a grant of free warren which was confirmed in 1316.[38] It appears, however, that until 1253 the men of Sandon had been accustomed to come to the sheriff's tourn twice a year, and in 1278 the township was ordered to be distrained because it had not come to the tourn.[39]

John son of William Fitz Geoffrey of Sandon released his right in 'Ladygrove' in Sandon to Stephen Cowherd in 1421.[40] This William appears to have been the grandfather of John Fitz Geoffrey of Sandon, who died in 1480, leaving a son and heir John.[41] The brasses of John Fitz Geoffrey the father and of his wife and children are still preserved in the nave of the church.[42] It appears that the Fitz Geoffrey estate was the reputed manor of *DANIELS*,

---

[11] *East Herts. Arch. Soc. Trans.* iii (1), 47.
[12] *V.C.H. Herts.* i, 317a.
[13] The charter is printed by Dugdale, *Hist. of St. Paul's*, 292; Birch, *Cart. Sax.* ii, 451; Kemble, *Cod. Diplom.* 1127. The jurors of 1274-5 stated that Sandon was ancient demesne of the Crown (*Hund. R.* [Rec. Com.], i, 193).
[14] Since the form in the charter is Rode or Rođe, and the name 'Rothe' Green occurs in early court rolls (see above).
[15] *V.C.H. Herts.* i, 317a; cf. Hale, *Dom. of St. Paul's* (Camd. Soc.), 141.
[16] Hale, *Dom. of St. Paul's* (Camd. Soc.), 134.
[17] Ibid. 17 et seq.
[18] Ibid. p. iii.
[19] Ibid. p. xxxix.
[20] D. and C. of St. Paul's, Press B, Box 35, no. 7, Thursday before St. Philip and St. James, 13 Edw. III.
[21] Hale, op. cit. 134.
[22] Dryden, *Hist. of St. Paul's* (1818), 274.
[23] *Plac. de Quo Warr.* (Rec. Com.), 290.
[24] D. and C. of St. Paul's, Press A, Box 40, no. 1402.
[25] Hale, *Dom. of St. Paul's* (Camd. Soc.), 111; the farmer in 1222 was John de St. Laurence (ibid. 13).
[26] Chan. Proc. (Ser. 2), bdle. 82, no. 19.
[27] Ibid.
[28] Ibid. bdle. 246, no. 5. They asserted that John Newport had assigned the lease to Thomas Newport in the church of Sandon.
[29] Chan. Proc. (Ser. 2), bdle. 246, no. 5. See Close, 1649, pt. li, no. 1.
[30] Chan. Inq. p.m. (Ser. 2), c, 48.
[31] Chan. Proc. (Ser. 2), bdles. 82, no. 19; 86, 26.
[32] Close, 1649, pt. li, m. 1.
[33] Cussans, *Hist. of Herts. Odsey Hund.* 147.
[34] See *V.C.H. Herts. Families*, 10.
[35] Hale, op. cit. 14.
[36] Inscription in the chancel (Dugdale, *Hist. of St. Paul's*, 228).
[37] Hale, op. cit. 13; Assize R. 325; *Plac. de Quo Warr.* (Rec. Com.), 290.
[38] Chart. R. 32 Hen. III, m. 5; *Cal. Chart. R.* 1300-26, p. 305; *Hund. R.* (Rec. Com.), i, 194.
[39] Assize R. 323.
[40] Anct. D. (P.R.O.), D 395.
[41] Chan. Inq. p.m. 20 Edw. IV, no. 53.
[42] See below.

since Francis Fitz Geoffrey son of John Fitz Geoffrey of Clapham (co. Beds.)[43] sold the 'manor of Daniels' to George Hyde of Throcking about 1541.[44] He bequeathed the manor to his younger son William Hyde,[45] who sold his life-interest to Sir John Perient, kt., and others, including Thomas Bowles the elder.[46] The conveyance was possibly in trust for Thomas Bowles the younger and Mary his wife, to whom a William Hyde (presumably the nephew and heir of the former William) and his wife Elizabeth transferred their rights in 1556.[47] By 1578 the estate had apparently reverted to William Hyde, the nephew, of Hyde Hall, since with his sons Leonard and George he then sold it to Thomas Morrison,[48] evidently the Thomas Morrison of Cadeby, co. Lincs., whose son Thomas lived at Sandon.[49] Charles son of Thomas Morrison of Sandon moved to Overstone, co. Northants, after the death of his first wife Elizabeth, and in 1650 sold the property to Thomas Flyer of Brent Pelham.[50] It descended to his son Francis,[51] who sold it in February 1720 to Sir Gregory Page[52] of Greenwich, bart., one of the directors of the East India Company.[53] His son Sir Gregory sold the property in 1729 to Sir John Jennings of Newsells.[54] Sir John's son George sold it to Mr. Edward King Fordham in 1786,[55] and from this date Daniels has descended with the manor of Gannock (q.v.).

The farm called Daniels is about a quarter of a mile south-east of Sandon Church, and one of the fields belonging to the farm is known as 'Mooresmead.' It appears possible, therefore, that Daniels and La More (q.v.) were once held as one property, and this theory is strengthened by the tenure of La More by a certain John Daniel about 1275.[56]

FITZ GEOFFREY. *Sable a bull passant or.*

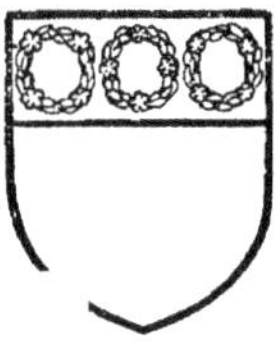

MORRISON of Sandon. *Or a chief gules with three wreaths or therein.*

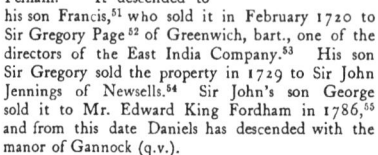

The reputed manor of GANNOCK is identical with lands held by the dean and chapter as of Sandon Manor by Warin de Bassingbourn of Wimpole, who died about 1348.[57] Land in Sandon had been held by two branches of this family since at least 1222, when Alan son of Alexander de Bassingbourn[58] was tenant of 3 virgates of freehold in addition to other land, and John de Bassingbourn had the custody of William 'Anglus' with 1 virgate of freehold and 3 acres of the demesne of Sandon.[59] In 1239–40 Aubrey (Albreda) de Bassingbourn joined in a settlement on Alexander de Bassingbourn of lands in Sandon and Kelshall and elsewhere.[60] Both John and Warin de Bassingbourn were presented as defaulters in the view of frankpledge of 1301.[61] It appears that the holding of John de Bassingbourn included the mill.[62] He was succeeded in 1320 by his brother Nicholas.[63] The tenement called Gannocks had been settled by Rosamond de Hoo (living in 1316)[64] upon Warin de Bassingbourn of Wimpole during her life with reversion to her own son Robert de Bassingbourn.[65] In 1324 another settlement had been made on Warin de Bassingbourn and his wife Amice and the heirs of Warin.[66] It was possibly on this pretext that Warin withheld the lands from Robert de Bassingbourn until his own death, after which they were restored to Robert.[67]

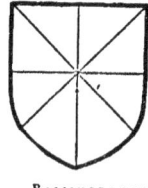

BASSINGBOURN. *Gyronny or and gules.*

The subsequent history of the Bassingbourn holding at Gannock is obscure. The 'manor' of Gannock was said to be held by John Sawyer at his death in 1525, when it descended to his daughter Elizabeth wife of John Clifford.[68] It was afterwards found that her father had sold it to Humphrey Monmouth, in whose favour a decree was issued in 1537.[69] Two years later the manor was sold by Richard Breame (possibly an agent of Monmouth) to John Newport, lessee of Sandon Bury, and Margery his wife.[70] John died seised of it in 1552 and left it to his eldest son Robert.[71] In 1600 Edward Newport son of Robert[72] conveyed the estate to Thomas Morrison.[73] The latter with his wife and son Charles[74] conveyed it in 1629 to Christopher

---

[43] *Visit. of Beds.* (Harl. Soc.), 26. This John may possibly be identical with the John mentioned above, who was aged nine at his father's death in 1480.
[44] B.M. Add. Chart. 35511; Feet of F. Herts. East. 33 Hen. VIII; cf. Feet of F. Herts. Mich. 37 Hen. VIII.
[45] *Visit. of Herts.* (Harl. Soc. xxii), 67; B.M. Add. Chart. 35511.
[46] B.M. Add. Chart. 35511.
[47] Feet of F. Herts. Trin. 2 & 3 Phil. and Mary. The first William died without issue (*Visit. of Herts.* loc. cit.). His nephew William of Hyde Hall and Throcking had a wife Elizabeth (Chan. Inq. p.m. [Ser. 2], cxciii, 69).
[48] Feet of F. Herts. East. 20 Eliz. (printed in *Herts. Gen. and Antiq.* ii, 223).
[49] *Visit. of Herts.* (Harl. Soc. xxii), 77.
[50] Close, 1650, pt. lxxiv, no. 36; cf. Chauncy, op. cit. 82.
[51] Exch. Dep. East. 3 Jas. II, no. 23; Berry, *Herts. Gen.* 146.
[52] Close, 6 Geo. I, pt. x, no. 10.

[53] G.E.C. *Baronetage,* V, 24.
[54] Feet of F. Herts. East. 2 Geo. II.
[55] Close, 27 Geo. III, pt. xxx, no. 5.
[56] *Cal. Close,* 1272–9, p. 229. See note 97 below. There is, however, no proof that this place lay in Sandon (see below).
[57] Chan. Inq. p.m. 22 Edw. III, no. 41.
[58] Among the records of St. Paul's is an undated acknowledgement of the receipt of the custody of Thomas and Alan 'sons of Alexander de Bassingbourn' together with their lands in Sandon (Liber A. fol. 45).
[59] Hale, op. cit. 13–15.
[60] Feet of F. Div. Co. 24 Hen. III.
[61] D. and C. of St. Paul's, B Box 35, no. 7, Morrow of St. Lawr. Martyr, 29 Edw. I.
[62] Ibid. Tues. after Mich. 8 Edw. II. Henry son of Richard held the site of the mill in 1222 (Hale, op. cit. 15).
[63] Ibid. Morrow of Trans. of St. Thos. 14 Edw. II.

[64] Liber A. St. Paul's, fol. 52.
[65] Chan. Inq. p.m. 22 Edw. III, no. 41. A Warin de Bassingbourn of Wimpole surrendered his lands in Sandon to the dean and chapter in 1316 (D. and C. of St. Paul's, A 28, no. 299), when Rosamond also surrendered her right in certain pasture (Liber A. fol. 52).
[66] Feet of F. Herts. 18 Edw. II, no. 391. John de Bassingbourn, parson of Abingdon, was agent in this settlement.
[67] *Cal. Close,* 1346–8, p. 480.
[68] Chan. Inq. p.m. (Ser. 2), xliii, 44.
[69] *L. and P. Hen. VIII,* xii (1), 1138.
[70] Feet of F. Herts. Trin. 31 Hen. VIII.
[71] Harl. MS. 758, fol. 27; cf. Chan. Inq. p.m. (Ser. 2), c, 48.
[72] Harl. MS. 758, fol. 27; cf. settlements quoted by Chauncy, *Herts.* 75.
[73] Feet of F. Herts. East. 42 Eliz., printed in *Herts. Gen. and Antiq.* iii, 272.
[74] *Visit. Herts.* (Harl. Soc. xxii), 76.

Vernon [75] of Hertingfordbury (q.v.). Francis son of Christopher Vernon and Eleanor his wife and another son Edmund [76] made a conveyance of the property in 1654 to Elias Harvey and John Prestwood,[77] possibly in trust for sale. By 1680 the manor had come into the possession of Henry Lawrence and Ann his wife, who conveyed it that year to Giles Lawrence [78] of Stepney, mariner. He bequeathed all his estates, including Gannock and 'Laomer' (i.e. La More) Farm in Sandon, to his wife Sarah and her heirs.[79] He had previously settled two-thirds of his estate on his wife for life with remainder to their children,[80] and in 1688 Mary wife of John Chappell conveyed her interest in two-thirds of the manors of Gannock and More to William Wakelyn and Richard Wildey.[81] This two-thirds was apparently acquired by Rene Tahourdin, who was in possession in 1746.[82] He died in 1751.[83] He was apparently succeeded by Richard Tahourdin, who with his wife Anne sold this estate to Edward Slater in 1778.[84] The subsequent history of this part of the property is unknown. It is said that Richard Lawrance of Lambeth Marsh was owner of the 'manor and estate of Gannock' (possibly the remaining third of the original manor) in 1761, and that it was sold by his brother Giles and his sister Cecily Courtenay and others to Mr. Elias Fordham of Sandon.[85] He sold it to his brother Mr. Edward King Fordham of Ashwell, who died in 1847. After this the estate came by will to his nephew John George Fordham of the Priory, Royston.[86] It now belongs to Mr. F. J. Fordham of Yew Tree House, Royston.

The present farm-house of Gannock lies to the north-west of the village near Gannock Green and is in the occupation of Mr. J. S. Sale.

The history of another reputed manor known as *GRENEHALL* is somewhat obscure. It was the subject of a plea in the King's Bench between Robert son of Nichola, who was wife of Adam Pigas, and Sir Thomas de Heslarton, kt., and his wife Alice. In 1345 Robert claimed the reversion of Grenehall in accordance with a settlement upon Adam and Nichola, which he affirmed had been made during the reign of Edward II.[87] The termination of the plea, which was still proceeding in 1350,[88] is unknown. In 1568 Grenehall Manor was conveyed by Edward Bridges and Frances his wife to Nicholas Fitz Hugh for the life of Frances.[89] In 1571 a settlement was made on Nicholas for twenty years from March 1569 with remainder to Richard Fitz Hugh,[90] who in 1584 conveyed the estate to George Edwards and his heirs.[91] Nothing more is known of Grenehall after this date.

The manor of *LA MORE* was held of the Dean and Chapter of St. Paul's.[92] Walter and William 'de Mora' were freehold tenants in Sandon early in the 13th century.[93] Robert 'atte More' was a tenant there about 1301.[94] The earliest known record of the manor is a conveyance by Robert Basset of Rushden and his wife Margaret to John de Preston and Thomas Semelegh.[95] In 1261 William Basset had been among the witnesses of a surrender to the dean and chapter by William son of James de Sandon of 1d. rent due from Theobald 'de la Mor' for land in Wodewellfeld.[96] Robert Basset also witnessed the surrender by Warin de Bassingbourn of his lands in Sandon in 1316.[97] Evidently the manor alienated by Robert Basset in 1384 was identical with the messuage and lands in Sandon held by the trustees of Sir Robert Belknap, kt., in 1390.[98] He had succeeded the Bassets as lord of Rushden (q.v.). With that manor Sir John Fray, kt., baron of the Exchequer, also acquired the manor of La More in Sandon.[99] He settled it upon his wife Agnes with remainder to their daughters Agnes and Katherine in succession.[100] The latter married Humphrey Stafford [1] and succeeded her sister, who died without issue.[2] Possibly La More was accounted an appurtenance of her manor of Rushden. It is not specifically mentioned among the lands of which she died seised in 1482,[3] but in 1654 [4] it was in the possession of Francis Vernon of Gannock, whose predecessor, Robert Newport, purchased Rushden in 1574.[5] Nevertheless, the house and land called 'the Moore' in Sandon was the property of Ralph Parker about 1600.[6] From 1654 onwards the manorial rights seem to have descended with Gannock (q.v.).

OLIVERS, known also as *HYDE HALL, EAST END* or *SOUTHALL*, was held of the Dean and Chapter of St. Paul's as Sandon Manor.[7] The family of Oliver were tenants of the manor in the 13th and 14th centuries. About 1277 William Oliver was sued in the court of Sandon in a plea of debt.[8] Towards the end of the same century Richard Oliver witnessed a conveyance of a grove in Sandon.[9] A Richard Oliver had land in Sandon and 'Somereshale' in 1312.[10] 'Magister' Ralph Oliver was in default at a court held at Sandon in 1322.[11] It was possibly he upon whom settlement was made in 1314 of two messuages and certain land in Sandon [12] for life with successive remainders to Alice and Nichola his sisters and to William Oliver

---

[75] Feet of F. Herts. Mich. 5 Chas. I.
[76] *Visit. Herts.* (Harl. Soc. xxii), 100.
[77] Feet of F. Herts. Trin. 6 Chas. II.
[78] Ibid. Trin. 32 Chas. II.
[79] P.C.C. 23 Cann.   [80] Ibid.
[81] Feet of F. Herts. Mich. 4 Jas. II.
[82] Recov. R. Hil. 20 Geo. II, m. 157.
[83] *Gent. Mag.* (1751), xxi, 139.
Feet of F. Div. Co. Mich. 19 Geo. III.
[85] Clutterbuck, *Herts.* iii, 581.
[86] Cussans, *Herts. Odsey Hund.* 155.
[87] De Banco R. 344, m. 78; 345, m. 118; 352, m. 130.
[88] Ibid. 363, m. 175 d.
[89] Feet of F. Div. Co. Trin. 10 Eliz.
[90] Ibid. East. 13 Eliz.
[91] Ibid. Herts. Mich. 26 & 27 Eliz.
[92] Inq. a.q.d. file 448, no. 22.
[93] Hale, op. cit. 15; D. and C. of St. Paul's, A Box 29, no. 366.

[94] Ibid. B 35, no. 7. View of frankpledge, 29 Edw. I.
[95] Feet of F. Herts. 7 Ric. II, no. 61.
[96] D. and C. of St. Paul's, A Box 29, no. 367; cf. p. 284 below.
[97] Ibid. A Box 28, no. 299. There is a possibility that the unidentified lands called 'La More,' which John Daniel sought to replevy against Sibyl widow of Richard la Tracie in 1275, lay in Sandon (*Cal. Close*, 1272–9, p. 229). See above under Daniels.
[98] *Cal. Pat.* 1388–92, p. 231. Thomas Semelegh was one of these trustees.
[99] Inq. a.q.d. file 448, no. 22.
[100] Chan. Inq. p.m. 1 Edw. IV, no. 28; Early Chan. Proc. bdle. 71, no. 40.
[1] Chan. Inq. p.m. 18 Edw. IV, no. 45 (file 67).

[2] Early Chan. Proc. bdle. 71, no. 40; cf. the account of Rushden Manor.
[3] *Cal. Inq. p.m. Hen. VII*, i, 230.
[4] Feet of F. Herts. Trin. 6 Chas. II.
[5] See the account of that manor.
[6] They are mentioned in his will of that date (*Herts. Gen. and Antiq.* iii, 350).
[7] Chan. Inq. p.m. 28 Edw. III, no. 45; (Ser. 2), cxciii, 69.
[8] D. and C. of St. Paul's, B Box 35, no. 7.
[9] Ibid. A 29, no. 368.
[10] Ibid. B Box 35, no. 7, Sat. after St. Andrew, 6 Edw. II.
[11] Ibid. Morr. of Trans. of St. Thos. Martyr, 16 Edw. II. At this court John Scutel was presented by the homage for having beaten William Oliver at 'Ikenild' (possibly on the Icknield Way).
[12] B.M. Add. Chart. 6248.

of Buntingford and his heirs. It seems probable that one of these sisters married Laurence de Ayot, lord of Ayot St. Lawrence. In 1353 he died seised of a tenement called Olivers in Sandon which he held of the inheritance of his son and heir William,[13] who was imprisoned for felony in the Bishop of Winchester's gaol at the time of his father's death.[14]

In 1457 Walter and Alice Freeman were holding the manor in right of Alice and granted a life-interest in it to Robert Oliver and his wife Elizabeth.[15] Possibly in consequence of the felony of William de Ayot the tenement had reverted to the other heirs under the settlement of 1314.[16] In 1490 this estate belonged to Matilda Exton in her own right, and she together with John Barbour, her son by a former marriage, conveyed it to Richard Fyfehid *alias* Lowe and other trustees,[17] who granted it in 1492 to Leonard Hyde of Throcking and others.[18] These appear to have been acting only as trustees. In 1506 they transferred the 'manor' to Sir Robert Drury, kt., and others, who in turn conveyed to Thomas Sandon.[19] It passed from his daughter Agnes to her daughter Rose wife of John Bird.[20] They sold the 'manor of Olivers or East End' to Simon Pratt, and his son John with his wife 'Etheldred'[21] (Audrey) made a conveyance of the estate to William Hyde of Throcking about 1522. George Hyde of Throcking had a release from Francis Fitz Geoffrey.[22] His grandson William son of Leonard Hyde conveyed the estate to his uncle William Hyde of Daniels, who reserved it in alienating Daniels.[23] William Hyde of Daniels died childless, and Olivers appears to have reverted to William Hyde of Throcking. He died in 1580, leaving to his son and heir Leonard the manor of Olivers, and a capital messuage called Hyde Hall to his wife for life.[24] After this date the manor is frequently called by the name of Hyde Hall.

HYDE of Throcking. *Azure a saltire engrailed or and a chief ermine.*

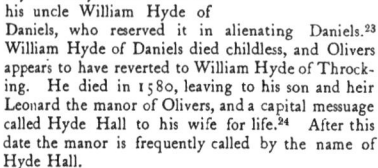

In 1607 Sir Leonard Hyde, kt., sold the manor of Olivers or Hyde Hall to Sir Thomas Cheeke, kt., of St. Martin's in the Fields,[25] who is said to have conveyed it two years later to the Earl of Exeter.[26] In 1612 he sold it to Sir Julius Adelmare *alias* Caesar.[27] This estate was settled on his son Sir John Caesar.[28] His eldest son John sold it in 1656 to William Franklyn. He died without male issue, and the manor passed to his only sister and heir Mary wife of Sir Nicholas Miller, kt.[29] They were succeeded by their son Franklyn, who married Jane daughter of Sir Reginald Forster.[30] She succeeded to the manor on the death of her husband in 1728. At her death four years later the estate passed to her grandson Nicholas Franklyn Miller.[31] He died at the age of nineteen, and the estate passed to his aunt Jane Northcliff, widow, his father's sister. Under her will the estate came to Edward Mundy[32] of Shipley, Derby, who had married Hester sister of her nephew Nicholas Franklyn Miller. From Edward Mundy the estate passed to his son Edward Miller Mundy,[33] and he sold it in 1789 to William Baker of Bayfordbury.[34] It has since descended in

BAKER of Bayfordbury.

his family, and the present owner is Mr. Clinton R. Baker[35] of Bayfordbury.

Hyde Hall is a 17th-century house much restored and altered. Two of the chimney-stacks and a part of one of the gables appear to be original. Near the house is a large 16th-century brick barn lighted by long narrow loops.

The church of ALL SAINTS consists CHURCH of chancel 36 ft. by 15 ft., nave 52 ft. 6 in. by 20 ft., north and south aisles 54 ft. by 9 ft. 6 in., south porch 12 ft. by 10 ft., west tower 12 ft. 6 in. by 12 ft., all dimensions being taken internally.

The chancel was rebuilt on the old foundations about 1348,[36] and the nave with its aisles was erected about 1360–70, the west tower and south porch

---

[13] Chan. Inq. p.m. 28 Edw. III, no. 45.
[14] Ibid.
[15] Chauncy, *Herts.* 81, quoting a fine levied 34 Hen. VI, which cannot now be found.
[16] Cf. Add. Chart. 6248.
[17] Feet of F. Herts. Trin. 5 Hen. VII.
[18] Chauncy, op. cit. 81, quoting title-deeds.
[19] Chauncy, op. cit. 81, quoting title-deeds, 'Carta penes Dom. Nich. Miller.'
[20] Ibid.
[21] Chan. Inq. p.m. (Ser. 2), lxxxi, 276.
[22] Chauncy, op. cit. 81.
[23] B.M. Add. Chart. 35551; cf.

Chauncy, loc. cit.; Recov. R. Mich. 4 Eliz. m. 818.
[24] Chan. Inq. p.m. (Ser. 2), cxciii, 69. For the pedigree see *Herts. Visit.* (Harl. Soc. xxii), 67–8.
[25] Close, 5 Jas. I, pt. xviii.
[26] Chauncy, loc. cit., quoting title-deeds.
[27] Close, 9 Jas. I, pt. xxv, no. 32.
[28] Chan. Inq. p.m. (Ser. 2), ccclxxxiv, 159.
[29] Chauncy, *Herts.* 81, quoting from 'Carta penes Dom. Nich. Miller.'
[30] Le Neve, *Pedigrees of the Knights* (Harl. Soc. viii), 354.
[31] Clutterbuck, *Hist. and Antiq. of*

Herts. 579, quoting from 'Evidences of late W. Baker of Bayfordbury.'
[32] Ibid.; cf. P.C.C. Will, 226 Lisle.
[33] Burke, *Landed Gentry* (1906), 1203.
[34] Close, 30 Geo. III, pt. xviii, no. 14.
[35] *V.C.H. Herts. Families*, 31.
[36] Among the muniments of the Dean and Chapter of St. Paul's is an agreement dated 11 July 1348 between Masters Alan de Hothom and John de Barnet, canons of St. Paul's, on behalf of the dean and chapter, and Thomas Rykelyng, stone-mason, by which the latter undertook to pull down the walls of the chancel of the church of Sandon and to rebuild

SANDON: CHURCH AND COTTAGES FROM THE SOUTH-WEST

SANDON CHURCH: THE NAVE LOOKING EAST

being later additions of about the first decade of the 15th century. The church, all but the tower, was repaired in 1832 and 1875 and the tower and south porch in 1909. The church is built of flint rubble with stone dressings, the chancel roof is tiled and the nave roof covered with lead.

The three-light traceried window in the east wall of the chancel is modern; in the north wall are two late 14th-century windows having two trefoiled lights with rectilinear tracery. Between them is a low-arched recess which was probably used as an Easter sepulchre; the arch has a richly crocketed label; it is of late 14th-century work. The two windows in the south wall are similar in detail and date to those on the north. In the south wall is a 14th-century triple sedile with a good deal of modern work, which does not appear to be *in situ*. The arches are trefoiled with crocketed heads and the shafts under have moulded capitals and bases. Adjoining the sedile is a trefoil-headed piscina of contemporary date but a good deal defaced. The chancel arch is of the latter part of the 14th century and has two hollow-chamfered orders, and the jambs have moulded capitals and bases. Parts of the roof trusses over the chancel appear to belong to the 14th century, the rest of the roof being modern.

The nave arcades are of four bays, the arches having two chamfered orders with labels on both sides of the walls; the piers are octagonal and have moulded capitals and bases; the bases vary in the north and south arcades. A small clearstory window at the east end on either side of the nave was inserted in the 15th century, probably to give additional light to the rood-loft.

In the east wall of the north aisle is a three-light window, nearly all of which is of modern stonework. Adjoining it, in the north wall, is a plain niche or recess with a segmental head, which possibly contained an image, or it may be part of the stairway to the rood-loft of which no other traces remain. In the south-east angle is a 15th-century piscina with cinquefoiled arch and moulded edges. The east and west windows in the north wall are of the late 14th century and have two trefoiled lights with a sixfoiled opening above; the other window is modern. The north doorway is of two moulded orders with grotesque head stops to the label.

In the east wall of the south aisle is an obtusely pointed window of three lights with flowing tracery of about 1360–70; adjoining it, in the south wall, is a 14th-century trefoiled piscina with credence shelf. The two windows in the south wall are of modern stonework, but the doorway of two moulded orders is original. There is an old iron ring handle on the door.

The south porch, of early 15th-century work, restored in 1908, has a two-light cusped window on either side, and the doorway is of two moulded orders with moulded capitals, all a good deal repaired.

The roofs over nave and aisles are chiefly modern, but some old timbers remain, and at the west end of the north aisle is a 15th-century moulded beam and carved boss.

The tower is of three stages. It was considerably restored in 1908. The four-centred tower arch is of three moulded orders, the inner order resting on engaged shafts with moulded capitals and bases. The west doorway and window above are modern. The second stage is pierced in the south by a narrow single light; the belfry windows are of two lights with a cusped opening in the heads, all much repaired.

The bowl of the font is modern, but the octagonal stem with its four flanking octagonal shafts and bases belongs probably to the 14th century.

SANDON: CHURCH TOWER AND SOUTH PORCH

The 15th-century oak rood-screen stands in its original position; the upper part is open with ogee arches and traceried heads, the lower panels are cusped, with carved spandrels and are separated by pilaster buttresses; some traces of colouring are visible.

The early 17th-century oak pulpit is richly carved; the reading-desk has some old linen panels in it. At the west end of the nave are some oak seats of the

them on the old foundations to a height of 17 ft. at the two sides. The east wall was to have a window containing three divisions, called 'dayes,' and each of the side walls two windows like the said chief window, but containing only two 'dayes' apiece. At each of the two chief angles there should be a buttress, 5 ft. in breadth and 1½ ft. in thickness, and a buttress of like size in each of the side walls. There was to be a suitable door on the south side. For this work the said Thomas was to have the stone of the chancel and 20 marks (*Hist. MSS. Com. Rep.* ix, App. i, 39).

A HISTORY OF HERTFORDSHIRE

15th century with poppy-head finials. In the windows of the aisles are some fragments of old painted glass. On the nave floor is the brass of John Fitz Geoffrey, lord of the manor of Daniels, who died in 1480, in armour, with his wife and six daughters; there are three shields, a fourth being missing. At the west end of the south aisle is a brass inscription, undated, but probably of the early 16th century, to Symond Pratt, lord of Olivers Manor, and his wife Jone. On the south chancel wall is a mural tablet to Edward Nicholas, who died in 1683, and an alabaster monument to Elizabeth Moryson of Daniels, who died in 1626. There is a slab on the nave floor to Edward Nicholas, 1683.

There are five bells: the treble (undated), second (1721), third (1728) and fourth (1709) by John Waylett; the tenor (1624) by Miles Graye.

The communion plate consists of cup and large paten, 1688, the gift of John Nicholas, Warden of Winchester College, and a pewter almsdish.[37]

The registers are in four books: (i) baptisms 1697 to 1749, marriages and burials 1678 to 1749; (ii) baptisms and burials 1750 to 1795, marriages 1750 to 1766; (iii) baptisms and burials 1796 to 1812; (iv) marriages 1767 to 1812.

ADVOWSON   The advowson of the church of Sandon belonged to the Dean and Chapter of St. Paul's,[38] and in 1155 it was let to farm with the manor to Alexander, one of the canons of the cathedral.[39] There was attached to the church half a hide of land which was geldable to the king.[40] The church was appropriated to the dean and chapter by Bishop Walter of Lincoln in 1183–4.[41] A vicarage was ordained in the time of Bishop Hugh Wells (1209–35)[42] and confirmed in 1406.[43] The advowson of Sandon remained with the Dean and Chapter of St. Paul's until the middle of the 19th century.[44] In 1845 the parish was transferred from the diocese of Lincoln to that of Rochester, and in 1850 the advowson was transferred to the bishop of the latter diocese.[45] In 1877, after the formation of the see of St. Albans, the patronage of Sandon was transferred to the Bishop of St. Albans,[46] in whose gift it now is.

CHARITIES   In the Parliamentary returns of 1786 it is stated that an unknown donor gave a rent-charge of £2 for bread to the poor. Bread to the value of £2 is provided annually by the tenant of Beckfield Farm and distributed by him at Christmas.

It is also stated in the same returns that an unknown donor gave £2 yearly for distribution to the poor. This sum is annually distributed by the tenant of 'Killhop Farm' to the poor in small sums.

In 1747 John Brett by his will gave a sum of money, now represented by £782 3s. 9d. consols with the official trustees, producing £19 11s. yearly, the interest to be applied towards the support or maintenance of the Protestant Dissenting Calvinist minister or ministers officiating at Redhill.

THERFIELD

Furreuuelde (xi cent.); Tirefeld (xii cent.); Terfeud, Tertefeud, Trefeud, Tirefeld, Therefeud, Tiresfeld (xiii cent.); Theresfelde, Torfeld (xvi cent.); Tharfield (xvii cent.).

Therfield is a parish of about 4,704 acres in the north of the county, stretching from the Cambridgeshire border some 4½ miles towards the south. It lies on a ridge of the Chilterns which slopes somewhat abruptly to the north and more gradually to the south. The highest part of this ridge is more than 500 ft. above the ordnance datum, while the low ground on the northern border has a height of about 235 ft., and in the south the ground slopes down to 365 ft. The Icknield Way marks the northern border of the parish and the straight line of Ermine Street forms the parish boundary on the east.

A by-road leads direct from the Icknield Way to Therfield village, which stands on the highest part of the ridge. The village, called locally the 'town,'[1] is small and built irregularly about an open green, the rectory and the church standing a little way back on the south-west.

To the north-west of the church there can be traced a fortified village with a mount and baileys, defended by a dry ditch. There is evidence of an inner ditch, and of a larger inclosure on the south.

The rectory lies to the south-east of the church. Its main building, which is of brick, appears from the registers to have been rebuilt about 1769, the library having been added in 1800.[2] On the east side is a building of two stories which dates from the 15th century, and which was probably a wing of the old building, foundations of a similar wing having been discovered on the west side of the main building.[3] The old wing is built of flint rubble covered with cement, and with clunch dressings; the roofs are tiled.

The ground stage of this wing consisted originally of one long room, running north and south, 30 ft. 8 in. by 11 ft. 3 in.[4]; at either end, on its eastern side, was a projecting wing, that on the north being 11 ft. 3 in. by 7 ft., that on the south 12 ft. 6 in. by 12 ft. Some time during the 17th century, probably in the time of Charles II, the south wall on the ground story of the

---

[37] There were formerly belonging to the church two silver flagons given in 1689 by John Nicholas, bearing date letter 1637–8, maker's mark R.C. and a pheon and the Nicholas arms, argent a fess wavy gules between three ravens or. They bore the inscription 'Donum Johannis Nicholas S.T.P. Coll. Beatæ Mariæ prope Winton custodis. Quid rependam Domino pro omnibus retributionibus ejus quas contulit mihi. Calicem salutarem accipiam et nomen Domini invocabo.' These flagons were sold in 1907 for £700 under a faculty and the sum utilized for the repair of the tower and porch of the church (*Herts. and Cambs. Reporter*, 5 June 1908).
[38] Hale, op. cit. 148.
[39] Ibid. 134.
[40] Ibid. 141, 148.
[41] *Hist. MSS. Com. Rep.* ix, App. i, 29b. For the confirmation by Bishop Henry in 1254 see ibid. 32; cf. also Liber A. St. Paul's, fol. 23.
[42] *Liber Antiquus Hugonis Wells*, 29.
[43] *Hist. MSS. Com. Rep.* ix, App. i, 39.
[44] Inst. Bks. (P.R.O.).
[45] See *East Herts. Arch. Soc. Trans.* iii (1), 43.
[46] *Lond. Gaz.* 13 July 1877, p. 4126.
[1] Rev. J. G. Hale, *St. Albans Archit. and Arch. Soc. Trans.* 1884, p. 20. The 'town house' was granted to Sir Robert Chester in 1553 (Pat. 7 Edw. VI, pt. iii, m. 18).
[2] Rev. J. G. Hale, op. cit. 27.
[3] Ibid.
[4] All dimensions are taken internally.

north wing was removed, and a beam put in to carry the wall above, and the east wall continued to the south wing, thus forming the two wings into one

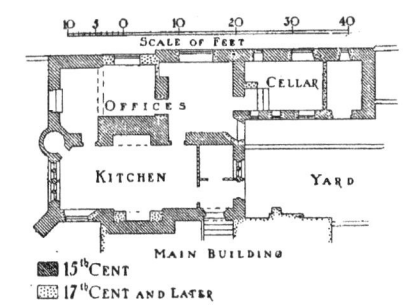

PLAN OF THERFIELD RECTORY

rectangular block. Projecting southwards from the south wing is a one-story building of the same date, 21 ft. by 8 ft. 8 in., beyond which are brick outbuildings and a brew-house of the 17th century; in the yard is an old deep well.

The principal room on the ground floor, which is now used as a kitchen, and may have been originally so used, has been reduced by a modern lobby at the south end, from which an original doorway with two-centred arch and moulded jambs gives access to the modern building. In the centre of the west wall of the kitchen is a fireplace, 9 ft. wide with straight lintel, now partly blocked; on the opposite wall is a wide round-arched recess, on either side of which is a low doorway with two-centred arch and moulded jambs, opening into the north and south wings respectively. At either end of the original room or kitchen is a four-light window with pointed cinquefoiled arches under a square head, with moulded label and head stops; the jambs and mullions are moulded, and a heavy mullion divides each pair of lights; the window at the south end has had one pair of lights cut down to form a doorway. In the north-east angle is the doorway to the turret stair to the upper floor, but the stair itself is gone; a portion of the circular stairway projects on the outer face of the wall. The north wing, now used as a scullery, had formerly a two-light window in its north wall, but this has been made into a doorway, only the outer moulding being retained. The 17th-century wall connecting the two wings is of brick, about 22 in. thick, the old walls adjoining being 2 ft. 6 in.

The south wing is entered from the enlarged north wing by a 17th-century opening under a four-centred arch, the original north doorway to the wing having been blocked by the east wall erected at that period. The window in the east wall of the wing is not original. A doorway of late date has been cut through the south wall to give access to the yard. The one-story building to the south has, on either side, a small circular quatrefoiled window of clunch; all the other windows are modern.

Above the north wing is a small room fitted up as a chapel, with traces of a pointed window in the east wall, now partly blocked and occupied by a sash window. In the north wall are two 15th-century windows, one of two lights, the other a single light, both now blocked. The chapel is lined with oak bolection moulded panelling of the time of Charles II; the door to the adjoining room on the south, which was part of the 17th-century extension, has its upper panels filled with the original squares of clear glass; this adjoining room has woodwork of the same period as that in the chapel, and the brass door handles and locks are cut and pierced with patterns.

Externally, the old portion, which projects about 10 ft. in front of the main rectory building, is covered by a roof, gabled at each end, running its whole length; over the east wall of the chapel is a smaller gable, the roof running into the main roof at right angles. On the upper floor in the room over the kitchen are two-light windows in the north and west walls, similar in detail to the north window of the kitchen underneath; the window in the west wall of the kitchen is modern. In the north gable is a small quatrefoiled opening set in a triangular moulded frame of clunch, and on the apex of the gable are small cusped gablets. The outer portion of the circular staircase on the north front is finished, under the springing of the gable, by a plain low pyramidal roof; there are some narrow loop lights in it, now blocked. Some heraldic painted glass, formerly in the old building, has been removed to the church.

At the foot of the sloping garden, on the south side of the house, is an old fish pond.

THERFIELD RECTORY: 15TH-CENTURY EAST WING FROM THE NORTH-WEST

A HISTORY OF HERTFORDSHIRE

In the village itself are one or two 17th-century houses, notably The Limes, the residence of Mrs. Hale, widow of the late rector, a house now used as the village reading-room, and, to the east of the church, a timber and plaster house with thatched roof divided into two cottages. The Elms, further north, is a two-storied house, partly of brick plastered and partly of timber and plaster. It dates from the early part of the 16th century, and has additions probably made at the beginning of the 18th century. It contains some original fireplaces and other fittings.

To the north-west of the village is Tuthill Farm, composed of several cottages, which at one time apparently formed a single 17th-century house. Barley Barn at Tuthill Farm was licensed as a place of worship for Protestant Dissenters in 1779.[5] Dissenters had a certified place of worship in the village from 1691 onwards, and generally met in buildings belonging to the family of Fordham,[6] who occupied the demesne lands of Therfield Manor.[7] The present Congregational Chapel, a little south-east of The Elms, dates from 1836, and a manse was established in 1854.[8] Schools were endowed about the year 1854.[9]

The parish is thinly populated, but there are a few outlying farms and cottages, and in the extreme south-east the village of Buckland has extended across the Ermine Street into Therfield. There are several homestead moats in outlying parts of the parish. These are at the manor-house of Mardley Bury near Reed End, and at the manor-farm called Hoddenhoo in the extreme south of the parish.[10] Bull Moat, in the south-east, is in Buckland village. Another moat lies opposite to Five Houses Farm, in the west. The name 'Fivehowses' occurs on the 17th-century Court Rolls.[11]

A notable feature of the parish is the large open common covered with short turf which extends along the whole of the northern border, and has an average breadth of half a mile. The surface of this common is undulating and forms a series of low hills. Five tumuli lie together in a single group, to the south of which is the only long barrow remaining in Hertfordshire. There are other round tumuli in the same neighbourhood. One barrow at Money Hill, now demolished, probably dated from the Bronze Period.[12] From the higher grounds there are extensive views of the Cambridgeshire plain, and on a favourable day the towers of Ely Cathedral and King's College Chapel, Cambridge, may be seen clearly. This common is generally known as Royston Heath, taking its name from the market town of Royston, part of which was formerly in Therfield parish.[13] The heath was a favourite hunting ground of James I while residing at Royston (q.v.), and is now a public recreation ground with golf links and rifle range, under the care of a body of conservators. There is a right of sheep feeding, but no other animals may be grazed. A portion of the heath is let for training racehorses. The southern edge is fringed with belts of wood, chiefly beech and larch. Similar woods occur in other parts of the parish, within which there are 113 acres of woodland.

There are several small greens. Hay Green and Washing Ditch Green to the south-east of the village and Collins Green in the west of the parish are mentioned in 16th-century Court Rolls.[14] The pound is situated at Hay Green near Haywood Lane. Chapel Green lies a mile to the south of the village. The open arable fields were inclosed in 1849,[15] the heath and greens in 1893.[16]

The soil is chalk, and the land is for the most part arable, but grass covers over 600 acres. The people are entirely agricultural, and turkey breeding is a source of considerable profit. There is a disused chalk-pit immediately to the north of the village.

Among estates released to the abbey of Ramsey in the 13th century were lands in 'Wellemadestot' and on 'le Watelrydie.'[17] The field called 'Eyhtacres' abutted on 'Sepwykestrate'[18]; and certain common pasture lay 'beyond Theuestrat' partly at 'Pyntte-sheggis,' partly on 'Astoneshel' and partly on 'Ordmarashel,'[19] which last abutted on the road to Buntingford (i.e. Ermine Street).[20] Other place-names which occur on the 16th-century Court Rolls are Rowkes nest (cf. the modern Rooksnest Farm), Moneycrofte,[21] Myldaynefeld, Gillarkes, and Snaylhorne peece.[22]

Among the outlying farms are Wing Hall, overlooking the heath, and Slate Hall in the occupation of Mr. Albert Drage.

A fair formerly held on the third Monday and Tuesday in July was abolished in 1873.[23]

MANORS Certain land, afterwards part of the manor of THERFIELD, was bought by Ethelric Bishop of Dorchester early in the 11th century (1016–34), and presented by him to the abbey of Ramsey.[24] It was said that the bishop purchased it from an unpopular Dane who feared that the villagers would murder him.[25] Thomas of Therfield evidently confirmed this land to the abbey in the time of Abbot Robert.[26] They were confirmed in their possession of this land by Edward the Confessor,[27] William I[28] and 'other kings,'[29] and by Edward III.[30]

In 1086 the abbot's holding at Therfield was assessed at 10 hides 1 virgate, and the manor was said to be and to have been (i.e. before the Conquest) the demesne of Ramsey Abbey.[31] Nevertheless the men of the Hundred Court declared in 1274–5 that

---

[5] Urwick, *Nonconformity in Herts.* 822.
[6] Ibid.
[7] See below.
[8] Close, 1854, pt. lxii, no. 21.
[9] Ibid. no. 22; cf. 1855, pt. xlv, no. 15; 1865, pt. xxxii, no. 12.
[10] See below.
[11] MSS. D. and C. of St. Paul's, B, box 41.
[12] *V.C.H. Herts.* i, 233.
[13] See the account of Royston.
[14] MSS. D. and C. of St. Paul's, B, box 39.
[15] Enrolled in Com. Pleas, Com. R. East. 12 Vict. m. 2.

[16] *Blue Bk. Incl. Awards,* 64.
[17] Anct. D. (P.R.O.), A 5412.
[18] Ibid. A 5411.
[19] Ibid. A 7262.
[20] Ibid. A 5432.
[21] See under Charities.
[22] Ct. R. *penes* D. and C. of St. Paul's, B, boxes 34–41.
[23] *Lond. Gaz.* 6 June 1873, p. 2742.
[24] *Chron. Abbat. Ramesei.* (Rolls Ser.), 140–3; *Cartul. Mon. de Ramesia* (Rolls Ser.), ii, 73.
[25] *Chron. Abbat. Ramesei.* (Rolls Ser.), 140–3; cf. the name Dane End near Reed End.

[26] *Cartul. Mon. de Ramesia* (Rolls Ser.), i, 101, 276; cf. *Chron. Abbat. Ramesei.* (Rolls Ser.), 341. The abbot was probably Robert Trianel (1180–1200).
[27] *Cartul. Mon. de Ramesia* (Rolls Ser.), i, 276.
[28] Ibid. ii, 94.
[29] Ibid. i, 276.
[30] Ibid. ii, 73.
[31] *V.C.H. Herts.* i, 316a, 299, 301. The measure of land on this manor was 64 acres equal to the virgate (*Cartul. Mon. de Ramesia* [Rolls Ser.], iii, 213). The 10 hides held in 1086 was land apart from the gift of Ethelric (cf. *Cartul. Mon. de Ramesia,* i, 276).

THERFIELD RECTORY: NORTH WINDOW OF KITCHEN

THERFIELD RECTORY: SOUTH WINDOW NOW PARTLY DOORWAY

THERFIELD

this manor was ancient demesne of the Crown, but that they knew nothing of its alienation.[32] Apparently there was no foundation for their statement.[33] The manor was kept in hand by the abbot and convent [34] until the dissolution of the monastery in 1539.[35] The service due to the Crown was that of four knights' fees.[36]

The 'farm' due from the manor of Therfield to the abbey was sufficient to sustain the monks for a whole fortnight.[37] It was rendered in October, February, April, and August.[38] It included flour, meal, malt, peas, cheese, bacon, honey, butter, herrings, eggs, hens and geese, sheep and lambs, and beef, in addition to a money payment.[39]

RAMSEY ABBEY. *Or a bend azure with three rams' heads argent thereon having horns or.*

It is recorded that Abbot Walter (1133–60) alienated portions of the demesne lands to his sister's son Ralph of Therfield, kt.[40] In 1386 the abbot added to the manor lands to the value of £20 in part satisfaction of a licence to acquire property to the value of £60 [41] which had been granted to the abbey by Edward II at the instance of his wife Isabel.

Among the records of this manor is a late 13th-century custumal.[42] The villein tenants were tallaged by the monks of Ramsey at £4, which was rated according to the property of each tenant, and was assigned to the cellarer by Abbot Hugh Folliot (1216–31).[43] They had numerous carrying services to Ramsey, Cambridge, Ware and London, and it is interesting to notice that the tenants were already beginning to compound for these and other services.

After the dissolution of Ramsey Abbey, Therfield Manor was seized by Henry VIII, and remained in his hands until 14 January 1540–1, when he gave it to his queen, Katherine Howard, as part of her jointure.[44] After her execution in February 1542 the manor reverted to the king,[45] and in June 1544 he granted it in frankalmoign to the Dean and Chapter of St. Paul's in exchange for certain manors in Essex and Middlesex.[46]

The first court of the dean and chapter was held in July 1544.[47] In 1642 the cathedral was closed and the Mayor and Aldermen of London were appointed sequestrators of the property of the dean and chapter.[48]

Therfield Manor was purchased from the trustees for the sale of the lands of deans and chapters in March 1649–50 by Samuel Pennoyer of London.[49] After the death of Pennoyer his widow Rose succeeded to the property and held courts in April 1655.[50] In the same year she evidently married Samuel Disbrowe, who was still holding in her right in 1657.[51] The manor was recovered by the Dean and Chapter of St. Paul's at the Restoration with their other confiscated estates.[52] They remained lords of the manor until 1872, when all their estates, including Therfield, were vested in the Ecclesiastical Commissioners.[53]

In 1542 Thomas Benett was tenant of the manorhouse, styled the 'manor or Bery Stede.' [54] It was afterwards held at will by John Wenham the elder, who surrendered it to the use of his brother John Wenham the younger in 1552.[55] The dean and chapter reserved right of accommodation for their receiver, steward and bailiff, when they should hold courts, and also a room for the use of the bailiff at the time of his rent-collecting.[56] In 1578 John Wenham conveyed his rights in the 'Bury Stede' to John Wood, who held it at his death in 1587. He left as heir his son John, aged three years.[57]

In the 17th century the site of the manor was let to members of the family of Fordham,[58] who have resided in the parish ever since.[59] Mr. F. J. Fordham of Royston is the present owner of Park Farm, which is in the occupation of his son, Mr. H. J. Fordham.

The Abbots of Ramsey had extensive liberties within their manors including Therfield. Under a confirmatory charter of Edward the Confessor they claimed soc and sac, toll, 'mundbryche, feardwite, fihtwite, blodwite, mischenninge, fritsocne, hamsocne, forstalle, forhpheang, withpheang, heangwite, gridbriche, uthleap, infangentheof, scipbriche, tol and team.' [60] William I added the right of gallows, and it is said of infangtheof.[61] King John granted view of frankpledge, amendment of the assize of bread and ale, tumbril and free warren,[62] To these privileges Henry III added freedom from scot or geld and exemption from the shire and hundred courts,[63] which the abbot's tenants at Therfield were wont to attend until about 1267.[64] The abbot proved his claim to all the above liberties within the manor of Therfield in 1287.[65]

The manor of HAY (la Haye, xiv cent. ; Heye or Haye, xvi cent.) was held of the main manor of Therfield.[66] Its early history is obscure ; it may be

---

[32] Hund. R. (Rec. Com.), i, 193.
[33] See, however, the carrying services mentioned below, which may point to its having been once ancient demesne.
[34] Add. R. (B.M.), 39473, 39584, 39656 ; cf. Mins. Accts. (Gen. Ser.), bdle. 108, no. 27 ; Cartul. Mon. de Rameseia, ii, 218 ; iii, 226, 325.
[35] Dugdale, Mon. ii, 550.
[36] Testa de Nevill (Rec. Com.), 270 ; Feud. Aids, ii, 444.
[37] Cartul. Mon. de Rameseia (Rolls Ser.), iii, 230.
[38] Ibid. 234–6.
[39] Ibid. 161–2, 168.
[40] Ibid. ii, 270, 275 ; cf. iii, 112 ; Pipe R. 6 John, m. 3 d.
[41] Cal. Pat. 1385–9, p. 233.
[42] Cartul. Mon. de Rameseia (Rolls Ser.), i, 45–8.
[43] Ibid. ii, 218.
[44] L. and P. Hen. VIII, xvi, p. 716.
[45] Courts were held in his name in 1542 (MSS. D. and C. of St. Paul's, B, box 39).
[46] L. and P. Hen. VIII, xix (1), g. 812 (32).
[47] MSS. D. and C. of St. Paul's, B, box 39.
[48] V.C.H. Lond. i, 417 ; courts were held in the name of the sequestrators in 1645 and 1648 (D. and C. of St. Paul's, B, box 41) ; in the name of the trustees in 1649 (ibid.).
[49] Close, 1650, pt. lxvi, no. 30.
[50] Pennoyer held courts there in 1653 (MSS. D. and C. of St. Paul's, B, box 41).
[51] Ibid.
[52] Cf. V.C.H. Lond. i, 430.
[53] Ibid.
[54] Therfield Ct. R. (MSS. D. and C. of St. Paul's, B, box 39).
[55] Ibid.
[56] Ibid.
[57] MSS. D. and C. of St. Paul's, B, box 39.
[58] Chauncy, Hist. Antiq. of Hertf. 86.
[59] See monumental inscriptions quoted by Clutterbuck (Hist. and Antiq. of Herts. iii, 593), and V.C.H. Herts. Families, 10.
[60] Cartul. Mon. de Rameseia (Rolls Ser.), ii, 76.
[61] Plac. de Quo Warr. (Rec. Com.), 287 ; but cf. the list of liberties including infangtheof quoted above from the (probably spurious) charter of the Confessor.
[62] Ibid. A new grant of free warren was made in 1251 (Cal. Chart. R. 1226–57, p. 366).
[63] Cartul. Mon. de Rameseia (Rolls Ser.), iii, 58.
[64] Hund. R. (Rec. Com.), i, 194.
[65] Plac. de Quo Warr. (Rec. Com.), 287.
[66] Chan. Inq. p.m. 14 Edw. III, 35 ; 7 Hen. IV, 52 ; Ct. R. penes D. and C. of St. Paul's, B, box 39.

A HISTORY OF HERTFORDSHIRE

identical with the place called 'Haia' associated with 'Bradenach,' co. Huntingdon, and mentioned in a 12th-century account of the increase in the lands of Ramsey Abbey.[67]

In the 14th century it was in the possession of the family of Scrope of Masham. Sir Geoffrey Scrope, kt., founder of that family and justice of the Common Pleas, was associated with Hertfordshire through his marriage with Laura daughter of Sir Gerard Furnival of Munden Furnival[68] (q.v.). In 1338 Thomas of Brancaster granted the manor of Hay to Sir Geoffrey Scope in return for 100 marks silver, and shortly afterwards Sir Geoffrey granted a life-interest to Thomas.[69] The latter is included among the tenants of Ramsey Abbey in Therfield who owed suit at Broughton.[70] The manor apparently reverted to Sir Geoffrey Scrope within a few years, for he held at his death before 1341 a tenement in Therfield with pleas of court and a capital messuage.[71] In or before the time of his son and heir Sir Henry Scrope, kt., of Masham, a sub-enfeoffment was possibly made to the family of Sir John Scrope,[72] a younger son of Sir Richard Scrope of Bolton, and great-nephew of Sir Geoffrey.[73] The rights of the Scropes of Masham as mesne lords had evidently lapsed by 1561.[74]

The tenant, Sir John Scrope, was succeeded by two daughters Joan and Elizabeth,[75] who married respectively Sir Richard Hastings, kt., and Thomas Clarell of Aldwark, co. Yorks.[76] Apparently Elizabeth Clarell succeeded in time to the whole of Hay,[77] for in 1474 it was evidently inherited in entirety by her daughter Elizabeth wife of Sir Richard Fitz William, kt. In that year a settlement was made on Sir Richard and Elizabeth for their lives with remainder to Sir Richard's third son Edward.[78] Probably a further settlement was made later, for the manor descended to Thomas Fitz William,[79] Sir Richard's eldest son, who was slain at Flodden Field in 1513.[80] His young son and heir William Fitz William died under age 26 August 1515, and was succeeded by his two sisters, Alice wife of James Foljambe and Margaret wife of Godfrey Foljambe.[81] Godfrey and Margaret Foljambe sold one moiety of the manor to Robert Pakenham of Streatham,[82] from whom it was purchased in February 1549-50 by the tenant, John Berners of Therfield.[83] Thomas Berners apparently united the two moieties by purchasing the second from George Gill in 1562.[84] Gill had acquired this moiety from Sir Godfrey Foljambe, kt.,[85] probably the eldest son of James and Alice Foljambe.[86]

John Berners, gent., resided in Therfield about 1641,[87] and probably retained this manor, but the subsequent history of the estate is unknown.

Hay Farm lies on the high ground to the east of the village, presumably on the site of the capital messuage held by Sir Geoffrey Scrope.[88] A windmill belonged to the manor in the 14th century.[89]

SCROPE of Masham.
Azure a bend or and a label argent.

GLEDSEYS, known also as *BUTLERS*,[90] was held of the main manor of Therfield[91] apparently by service of one-fourth of a knight's fee.[92] Abbot William of Ramsey (1267-85) assigned to the almoner of the abbey a tenement lately acquired from John of Gledsey.[93] About 1278 Joan wife of John of Gledsey demanded of Robert of Gledsey the custody of one quarter of a knight's fee in Therfield, the heir to which was still a minor.[94] Elias of Gledsey owed suit to the Abbot of Ramsey at Broughton early in the 14th century.[95] This Elias was witness to a lease of land in Therfield in 1333.[96] The tenement called Gledseys was occupied by John Butler in 1444.[97]

In the time of Henry VIII the Hyde family were in possession of this manor.[98] In 1544 John Hyde and Margaret his wife and Thomas their son conveyed it to John Gill and Margaret his wife.[99] John Gill was succeeded in 1546 by his son George.[100] The latter assigned this manor to his wife Anne as a portion of her jointure,[1] and died in 1568, leaving a son John as heir.[2] John Gill died in 1600 and the manor passed to his son George,[3] who sold it in 1607 to William Clerke.[4] In 1638 William Clerke, gent., was ordered in the court of the main manor to keep his flocks for Gledseys and Five Houses within the ancient bounds.[5] He was apparently succeeded by his son Thomas Clerke,[6] whose property was divided

[67] Cartul. Mon. de Ramescia (Rolls Ser.), iii, 226.
[68] Foster, *Yorks. Ped. N. and E. Riding*, ii, pedigree of Scrope.
[69] Feet of F. Herts. East. 12 Edw. III, no. 186, 187.
[70] Cartul. Mon. de Ramescia (Rolls Ser.), i, 41.
[71] Chan. Inq. p.m. 14 Edw. III, no. 35.
[72] Ibid. 16 Ric. II, pt. i, no. 28.
[73] Foster, loc. cit.
[74] Ct. R. *penes* D. and C. of St. Paul's, B, box 39 ; the last known record of the mesne lordship is the inquisition on the death of Sir Stephen son of Sir Henry Scrope of Masham (Chan. Inq. p.m. 7 Hen. IV, no. 52), when the service claimed was that of half a knight's fee. Probably this sub-feoffment, which seems to have been made after the Statute of 'Quia Emptores,' represents a sub-tenancy made before the Statute.
[75] Chan. Inq. p.m. 7 Hen. IV, no. 52.
[76] Foster, loc. cit.
[77] Sir Richard Hastings left no children (Chan. Inq. p.m. 15 Hen. VI, 58). Probably, therefore, Joan Hastings died childless.
[78] Feet of F. Div. Co. Hil. 13 Edw. IV ; cf. Foster, *Yorks. Ped. W. Riding*, i, pedigree of Scrope.
[79] Chan. Inq. p.m. (Ser. 2), xxix, 53.
[80] Foster, loc. cit.
[81] Chan. Inq. p.m. (Ser. 2), xlv, 87.
[82] Feet of F. Herts. Trin. 38 Hen. VIII.
[83] Ibid. Mich. 4 Edw. VI ; Close, 4 Edw. VI, pt. ii, no. 13.
[84] Feet of F. Herts. East. 4 Eliz. ; Ct. R. *penes* D. and C. of St. Paul's, B, box 39.
[85] Ibid.
[86] Foster, loc. cit.
[87] Lay Subs. R. bdle. 121, no. 342. Cussans and Clutterbuck misread Chauncy in stating that La Hay was acquired by the family of Turner before 1630.
[88] Chan. Inq. p.m. 14 Edw. III, no. 35.
[89] Ibid.
[90] Chan. Inq. p.m. (Ser. 2), cclxv, 77.
[91] Ct. R. *penes* D. and C. of St. Paul's, B, boxes 40, 41 ; A, box 64.
[92] Chauncy, *Hist. Antiq. of Herts.* 87.
[93] Cartul. Mon. de Ramescia (Rolls Ser.), ii, 233.
[94] Quoted by Chauncy, loc. cit.
[95] Cartul. Mon. de Ramescia (Rolls Ser.), i, 41.
[96] Ibid. iii, 116.
[97] MSS. D. and C. of St. Paul's, A, box 64.
[98] Herts. Gen. and Antiq. iii, 258.
[99] Feet of F. Herts. Trin. 36 Hen. VIII.
[100] Ct. R. *penes* D. and C. of St. Paul's, B, box 39.
[1] Chan. Inq. p.m. (Ser. 2), cli, 82 ; cf. Feet of F. Herts. Hil. 5 Edw. VI.
[2] Chan. Inq. p.m. (Ser. 2), cli, 82.
[3] Ibid. cclxv, 77.
[4] Ct. R. *penes* D. and C. of St. Paul's, B, box 40 ; Feet of F. Herts. Hil. 4 Jas. I ; nevertheless it was included (possibly in error) among the lands of which Sir George Gill, kt., died seised in 1619 (Chan. Inq. p.m. [Ser. 2], ccccvii, 95).
[5] Ct. R. *penes* D. and C. of St. Paul's, B, box 41.
[6] Thomas Clerke was a tenant of Therfield Manor in 1627 ; cf. Chauncy, loc. cit.

280

among his four daughters, Hester wife of Henry Meade, Elizabeth wife of Thomas [7] Sanford, Susan Clerke and Sarah wife of John Higham.[8] The Highams were dealing with their fourth of 'Butler's' manor in 1666.[9] By 1676 a part of the estate of Thomas Clerke in Therfield had been acquired from the four co-heirs by John Green of Thorpe.[10] After the death of Susan Clerke her sisters divided her portion of Gledseys Manor between them. Sanford held one-third in right of his wife and purchased another third. He was succeeded by his son John Sanford, who was in possession of two-thirds of the manor about 1700.[11] The remaining third was purchased by Ralph Baldwin, gent., whose son Ralph Baldwin inherited it in 1694.[12] The 'manor' of Gledseys was subsequently sold by Mr. B. Wortham to the late Mr. Phillips, who bequeathed it to the father of the present owner, Captain J. H. J. Phillips.[13] The lands of Gledsey Manor extend into Buckland parish.[14]

The manor of *HODDENHOO* or *HODDENHOO NEWHALL* was among the possessions of Royston Priory at its dissolution.[15] In 1086 Hoddenhoo was within the hundred of Edwinstree,[16] and the greater part of the manorial lands lie in Buckland parish,[17] but the manor-house of Hoddenhoo is within the boundaries of Therfield parish.

In the Domesday Survey Hoddenhoo is returned in two portions. The one consisting of 1 hide and half a virgate had been held before the Conquest by a sokeman of Earl Algar and three sokemen of Archbishop Stigand. In 1086 it was held by Odo Bishop of Bayeux by Osbern, tenant also of Buckland and of land in Throcking.[18] Possibly, therefore, this was the land in Hoddenhoo given with land in Throcking to the priory of Holy Trinity, Aldgate, by Roger son of Brian and his wife Maud and confirmed to the priory by Henry III in February 1226–7.[19]

The second portion consisted of a hide and a virgate held before the Conquest by two sokemen of Earl Algar. Tetbald held it of Hardwin Scales (*de Scalers*) in 1086.[20]

It is uncertain how Royston Priory acquired the 'manor of Newhall and Hoddenhoo in Buckland,'[21] which by process of exhaustion appears to be identical with Tetbald's holding. Probably it was given to the priory between 1189 and 1291, for it is not named in the confirmatory charter of Richard I of the former date,[22] and the priory had lands in Buckland worth £3 8s. at the latter date.[23]

In January 1512–13 the site of the manor was let on a sixty years' lease, and Laurence Pleydon was lessee in 1536, when the property of the priory had been surrendered to the Crown.[24] The courts were apparently held at Buckland.[25] In December 1540 Robert Chester, gentleman usher of the Chamber, received a grant of all the possessions late of Royston Priory including the manor of Newhall and Hoddenhoo.[26] He sold this manor to John Gill and his wife Margaret about the following Easter.[27] It remained with his direct descendants[28] at least until the death of Sir George Gill, kt., in 1619.[29]

Early in the year 1662 the lord was Ralph Freeman[30] (lord also of the manor of Aspenden). He had been preceded by John Putnam,[31] and the manor descended to his son Ralph Freeman.[32] Apparently a settlement was made on his son Ralph about 1700.[33] The latter's son William Freeman was dealing with the manor in 1730.[34] Dr. Ralph Freeman, his brother, succeeded in 1749.[35] It descended with his manor of Hamels in Standon to Philip third Earl of Hardwicke, and is now the property of the Hon. John Henry Savile, grandson of Lady Anne Yorke, eldest daughter of the Earl of Hardwicke mentioned above.

FREEMAN of Aspenden. *Azure three lozenges argent.*

The manor of *WEST REED* or *ALAN DE REDE*, sometimes called *MARDLEY BURY*, was held by the Priors of Royston.[36] The house at Mardley Bury with a carucate of arable land and certain meadow, pasture and rent was acquired by the priory in 1302 from Adam de Twynham.[37] The 'manor' of West Reed, 'formerly called Alan de Rede,'[38] held by the priory at the Dissolution, is in all probability identical with the tenement in the 'vill' of West Reed which a certain Alan de Rede held of the Earl of Gloucester rendering suit in the earl's court of Popeshall[39] (in the neighbouring parish of Buckland). Alan de Rede died about 1314 and left a son and heir Henry.[40] The priory of Royston had already in 1251 acquired from Elias son of Richard of West Reed a messuage and 51½ acres of land in West Reed.[41] How the priory obtained the manor of Alan de Rede is unknown. In 1358 Thomas Palfreyman of Royston, chaplain, alienated 80 acres of land in West Reed and Royston to the priory'.[42] The estates seized by

---

[7] Chauncy styles him William Sanford.
[8] Ct. R. May 1673 *penes* D. and C. of St. Paul's, W.C. 1, no. 13.
[9] Feet of F. Herts. Mich. 18 Chas. II.
[10] Ct. R. *penes* D. and C. of St. Paul's, W.C. 1, no. 13; possibly about the year 1671 (Feet of F. Herts. Trin. 23 Chas. II).
[11] Chauncy, loc. cit.
[12] Ibid.
[13] Inform. kindly supplied by Mr. J. Phillips of Royston.
[14] Chan. Inq. p.m. (Ser. 2), cli, 82.
[15] Mins. Accts. Hen. VIII, no. 1606.
[16] *V.C.H. Herts.* i, 310*b*, 340*a*.
[17] Cf. Anct. D. (P.R.O.), A 6845, 7052; Chan. Inq. p.m. (Ser. 2), cclxv, 77.
[18] *V.C.H. Herts.* i, 310*b*.
[19] Dugdale, *Mon.* vi, 153.
[20] *V.C.H. Herts.* i, 340*a*.

[21] Mins. Accts. Hen. VIII, no. 1606.
[22] Dugdale, *Mon.* vi, 405.
[23] *Pope Nich. Tax.* (Rec. Com.), 14; cf. *Inq. Nonarum* (Rec. Com.), 432.
[24] Mins. Accts. Hen. VIII, no. 1606.
[25] Ibid.
[26] *L. and P. Hen. VIII*, xvi, g. 379 (60).
[27] Feet of F. East. 33 Hen. VIII; cf. *L. and P. Hen. VIII*, xv, g. 733 (57).
[28] See the account of Gledseys above.
[29] Chan. Inq. p.m. (Ser. 2), lxxxvi, 97; cclxv, 77; ccccvii, 95; cf. Plac. de Banco, Mich. 1 & 2 Phil. and Mary, m. 1 *d*.
[30] Feet of F. Hil. 13 & 14 Chas. II; cf. Misc. Bks. (Duchy of Lanc.), lxii, fol. 55*a*.
[31] Misc. Bks. (Duchy of Lanc.), lxii, fol. 58 *d*.
[32] Ibid. fol. 55*a*, 58 *d*.; Feet of F.

Herts. Trin. 25 Chas. II; cf. Chauncy, *Hist. Antiq. of Herts.* 125.
[33] Feet of F. Div. Co. Hil. 11 Will. III.
[34] Recov. R. Hil. 4 Geo. II, m. 254; cf. Cussans, *Hist. of Herts. Edwinstree Hund.* 96.
[35] Recov. R. East. 23 Geo. II, m. 323.
[36] Mins. Accts. Hen. VIII, no. 1597.
[37] *Cal. Pat.* 1301–7, p. 36; cf. Inq. a.q.d. file 40, no. 5.
[38] Chan. Inq. p.m. (Ser. 2), lxviii, 14.
[39] Ibid. 8 Edw. II, no. 9; the Priors of Royston subsequently paid rent to Popeshall (Mins. Accts. Hen. VIII, 1597).
[40] Chan. Inq. p.m. 8 Edw. II, no. 9.
[41] *Cal. Chart. R.* 1226–57, p. 360.
[42] Chan. Inq. p.m. 32 Edw. III (2nd nos.), no. 55.

A HISTORY OF HERTFORDSHIRE

the Crown upon the surrender of the priory included the manor of West Reed with rents in Therfield and West Reed including the rent of Mardley Bury Close.[43]

In 1540 Henry VIII granted 'the manor of West Reed called Alan de Rede' with all the property of the late priory to Robert Chester.[44] Shortly afterwards this manor was purchased from Chester by John Bowles of Wallington and his son and heir-apparent Thomas.[45] John Bowles died seised of it in 1543, but his son Thomas was evidently already dead, for John's heir was his grandson Thomas son of Richard Bowles.[46] Thomas Bowles 'the younger' of Standon sold the manor of West Reed *alias* 'Alan de Rede' with its appurtenances in West and East Reed and Therfield (evidently including Mardley Bury) to William Hyde of Sandon about 1556.[47] In 1563 William Hyde conveyed the manor to Thomas Turner of West Reed in Therfield, yeoman, and John his son.[48] This Thomas Turner had learned to sing at Royston Priory and lived more than ninety-five years.[49] In March 1606-7 he was styled 'of Reed End in Therfield.'[50] William Turner is said to have sold the manor in 1630 to John Willymot.[51] His son John bequeathed it to his wife Anne, daughter of James Willymot of Kelshall, and she was holding it in 1700.[52] In 1714 it was acquired by John Fisher, and in 1721 it was the property of the Hon. Peregrine Bertie the younger and his wife Elizabeth.[53] In 1753 it was in the possession of Peregrine Bertie,[54] and Catherine Dorothy Bertie, Elizabeth Bertie and Mary wife of Samuel Lichigaray joined in a conveyance of it in 1783.[55] George Sutton was dealing with the manor in 1788.[56] It was bought in 1790 by James Free,[57] and from his grandson Clerke Free it was purchased by the Rev. Charles Moss, rector of Therfield and afterwards Bishop of Oxford. In 1839 his executors sold to the Hon. William Herbert, from whom the manor was purchased in 1853 by Thomas Henry Usborne of Staplehurst, co. Kent.[57a] He was succeeded by his son Captain Thomas Starling Usborne, who bequeathed it to his three daughters. Two-thirds of the estate together with the manorial rights were purchased from them by the present owner, the Rev. George Archer.[57b]

A farm-house and homestead moat still remain at Mardley Bury. The site of the house of 'Alan de Rede' is more difficult to locate. It certainly lay in West Reed, if it is to be identified with the manor-house of the priory of Royston at West Reed, and some, at least, of the 'fields' of West Reed were within the parish of Therfield.[58] They probably extended as far as 'Reed End.'

In 1275 it was returned that the men of West Reed had withdrawn their suit due to the honour of Richmond.[59] These were possibly the men of that hide in Reed which Alward had held of Count Alan in 1086.[60] The land had formerly been held by Turbern, one of Eddeva's men.[61] The fact that castle ward was due to the honour of Richmond from the collector of the rents of the Prior of Royston in West Reed and elsewhere[62] tends to prove that this hide was among the lands acquired by the priory in West Reed.

Before the time of the Domesday Survey Alric the priest held of the Abbot of Ramsey 3 virgates of land in Therfield.[63] These had passed by 1086 to Wigar, a tenant under Hardwin Scales.[64] The overlordship thus diverted from the abbey was still in the possession of the Scales family in 1303,[65] and was possibly attached to their neighbouring manor of Reed (q.v.). The tenant in 1303 was a certain John of Oclee.[66]

Manorial rights belong to the *RECTORY*. It was said in 1547 that courts leet and view of frankpledge were usually held at the rectory.[67] The rectory manor was let on lease with the parsonage in 1553.[68] The late incumbent, the Rev. J. G. Hale, was accustomed to hold courts yearly in the 'Court Room' of the rectory.[69] In 1336 Wymar de Corton conveyed a toft in Therfield to the parson for the enlargement of the rectory.[70]

The church of *ST. MARY THE CHURCH VIRGIN*, which consists of chancel, nave with north and south aisles, and west tower, was rebuilt in 1878, some of the old material being re-used. The windows in the chancel, all but the one in the east wall, are from the old church,[71] and in the modern roof are some carved figures of angels and bosses of the 15th century. The porch was added in 1906, and the tower, of which only the first story was built, was completed by the rector, the Rev. F. R. Blatch, in 1911.

In the south wall of the chancel the early 14th-century double piscina has been reset; it has moulded arches on shafted jambs with moulded capitals and bases. The sedilia adjoining, though chiefly of modern work, have some old stone in them. In the north chancel wall is an arched recess containing an ancient stone coffin.

In the vestry are many fragments of stone carving dating from the 13th to the 16th century, corbels, parts of tombs, including a curious effigy of a man lying with his head at right angles to his body and his legs crossed; in his right hand is a drawn sword; at the end of the stone are two small female figures, standing; on the end of the stone is a shield charged with a cross.

On the window sills in the chancel are some fragments of carvings, and underneath the tower are some carved oak figures of angels from the old roof.

There are some fragments of 15th-century heraldic glass in the church, until lately in the old rectory.

---

[43] Mins. Accts. Hen. VIII, 1597.
[44] L. and P. Hen. VIII, xvi, g. 379 (60).
[45] Ibid. g. 1308 (40); Close, 33 Hen. VIII, pt. i, m. 31.
[46] Chan. Inq. p.m. (Ser. 2), lxviii, 14.
[47] Pat. 2 & 3 Phil. and Mary, pt. v, m. 1; Feet of F. Div. Co. Mich. 3 & 4 Phil. and Mary. [48] Add. Chart. 27340.
[49] Exch. Dep. East. 5 Jas. I, no. 16.
[50] Ibid.
[51] Chauncy, *Hist. Antiq. of Herts.* 87.
[52] Ibid.; cf. Feet of F. Herts. Mich. 20 Chas. II; Recov. R. East. 1 Jas. II, m. 190.
[53] Clutterbuck, *Hist. and Antiq. of Herts.* iii, 586; cf. Feet of F. Herts. East. 7 Geo. I.
[54] Recov. R. East. 26 Geo. II, m. 407.
[55] Ibid. Hil. 23 Geo. III, m. 270.
[56] Ibid. Mich. 29 Geo. III, m. 179.
[57] Clutterbuck, loc. cit.
[57a] Cussans, *Odsey Hund.* 119.
[57b] Inform. kindly supplied by Mr. J. Phillips of Royston.
[58] Exch. Dep. East. 5 Jas. I, no. 16.
[59] Hund. R. (Rec. Com.), i, 194.
[60] V.C.H. Herts. i, 319.
[61] Ibid.
[62] Mins. Accts. Hen. VIII, 1597.
[63] V.C.H. Herts. i, 339a.
[64] Ibid. cf. p. 292.
[65] Feud. Aids, ii, 433.
[66] Ibid.
[67] Pat. 1 Edw. VI, pt. v, m. 24.
[68] Star Chamb. Proc. Phil. and Mary, i, 39; v, 36; Chan. Proc. (Ser. 2), clxxi, 21.
[69] Rev. J. G. Hale, 'Paper on Therfield,' *St. Albans Archit. and Arch. Soc.* 1884, p. 19 et seq.
[70] Cal. Pat. 1334-8, p. 333.
[71] Hale, op. cit. 26.

ODSEY HUNDRED — THERFIELD

The octagonal font belongs to the late 14th century; the basin is plain, with mouldings underneath, and mouldings to the base.

Underneath the tower is a large mural monument of cedar wood, flanked by carved figures, to Ann wife of Francis Turner, a former rector; she died 1677. The carved figure of Time is intact, but the skeleton, Death, is broken.

There are six bells: the treble by W. & P. Whitman, 1689 (recast in 1911); second and third (recast in 1911) by Miles Graye, 1626 and 1656 respectively; fourth by John Dier, 1597; fifth inscribed 'Fraies the Lord,' 1608; and tenor by John Waylett, 1707.

The communion plate consists of cup and two patens without hall mark, a small cup with handle, the hall mark erased, and a large silver-gilt flagon, 1667, the gift of Dr. Barwick, Dean of St. Paul's and rector of Therfield.

The registers are in six books: (i) baptisms from 1538 to 1662, burials 1539 to 1662, marriages 1538 to 1661; (ii) baptisms from 1662 to 1750, burials 1662 to 1681, marriages 1662 to 1749; (iii) burials from 1678 to 1750; (iv) baptisms and burials from 1750 to 1812, marriages 1750 to 1753; (v) and (vi) marriages from 1754 to 1796 and 1796 to 1812 respectively. There are some considerable gaps in book i.

ADVOWSON. The earliest definite record of the church is a papal bull of 1178 confirming the abbey of Ramsey in possession of it.[72] The successive abbots retained the right of patronage until the Dissolution,[73] after which the advowson was granted with the manor to the Dean and Chapter of St. Paul's.[74] They have retained the advowson to the present day.[75]

In 1392 the Abbot of Ramsey had licence to unite the church of Therfield with Shillington Church, co. Beds., notwithstanding that the advowsons of these churches were parcel of the respective manors of Shillington and Therfield.[76] The arrangement, if ever it was carried into effect, does not appear to have been permanent. A licence to appropriate Therfield Church was obtained by the Dean and Chapter of St. Paul's in 1547 upon condition that a perpetual vicar should be appointed to fulfil in all respects the office of rector, and that he should pay to the Bishop of Lincoln and Archdeacon of Huntingdon for procurations and synodals of the church of Therfield 11s. 6d., and should support all other burdens of the church excepting only the repairs of the chancel, for which the dean and chapter were to be responsible.[77] It was also stipulated that a suitable residence and an income of £20 should be provided for the vicar. It appears that the proposed ordination of a vicarage was never carried into effect.[78] The living is now a rectory in the gift of the Dean and Chapter of St. Paul's.

A pension of 4 marks was paid by this church to the monastery of Ramsey[79] and devoted to the office of sacrist.[80] Confirmations of this pension were made by Pope Honorius III in 1225[81] and by Pope Gregory IX in 1233,[82] by Richard Bishop of Lincoln in 1262,[83] by St. Hugh Bishop of Lincoln (1189–95),[84] and it was included in a general confirmation by Walter Archbishop of Canterbury of gifts to Ramsey Abbey in 1319.[85] William Burham, rector of Therfield, who was deprived for marriage about 1554,[86] refused to pay this pension.[87] Thomas Hewlet and another incumbent in the 16th century declared that the living was free of any such charge.[88]

Several men of note have been rectors of Therfield. Among these was John Yonge, Master of the Rolls and diplomatist, whose well-known monument stood in the Rolls Chapel, now the Record Office Museum. He was made Prebendary of Holborn in St. Paul's Cathedral in 1511, and three years later was presented to the rectory here. In the 16th and 17th centuries William Alabaster, a Prebendary of St. Paul's, Francis Turner, Bishop of Norwich, William Holder, a noted divine, and William Sherlock, Dean of St. Paul's, were successively appointed to this living. In 1604 John Overall, Bishop of Norwich, was rector, but the church was served by a curate.[89]

William Burham, the rector, deprived about 1554, had 'let to farm all the Rectory premises except one chamber in the west end of the parsonage house' to Andrew Meverell for six years. In August of the next year John Sapcote, a lessee of Burham's successor, John Whiting, clerk, entered upon the parsonage-house. It appears that Sapcote was occupying the rectory in 1561,[90] but Burham let to another lessee, Robert Newport.[91] The end of this dispute is unknown.

Elyn Colle, by will dated 1494, left £3 6s. 8d. for a new rood loft in the church within two years of her decease,[92] and in 1511 a bequest was made by William Chapman for the painting of this rood loft.[93] In 1503 Edward Shouldam, clerk, made provision for a priest to say mass in the church of Therfield.[94] In 1506 Richard Bentley left an offering to the altar of the chapel of SS. John and James, where he desired to be buried.[95] There were also altars of St. John the Baptist and St. Katherine,[96] and lights of our Lady of Pity,[97] St. Nicholas and St. Katherine.[98]

A devotional gild which paid 12d. yearly to Ramsey Abbey at the feast of St. Benedict was in existence not later than 1130.[98a] Two obits in Therfield Church were suppressed by Edward VI. One was given by John Bateman, and was of the value of 5s. yearly. This was to be paid out of the

---

[72] Cartul. Mon. de Ramesia, ii, 134, 150.
[73] The abbot recovered the right of presentation against John de Retford, clerk, about 1381 (Chan. Misc. bdle. 62, file 1, no. 14).
[74] L. and P. Hen. VIII, xix (1), g. 812 (32).
[75] Inst. Bks. (P.R.O.).
[76] Cal. Pat. 1391–6, p. 73.
[77] Pat. 1 Edw. VI, pt. v, m. 24.
[78] The living was a rectory in 1553 (Star Chamb. Proc. Phil. and Mary, bdle. 1, no. 39).
[79] Cartul. Mon. de Rameseia (Rolls Ser.), ii, 180.
[80] Ibid. 202; Dugdale, Mon. ii, 574.
[81] Cartul. Mon. de Rameseia (Rolls Ser.), i, 109.
[82] Ibid. 110.
[83] Ibid. ii, 181, 182, 207.
[84] Ibid. 180.
[85] Ibid. 183; see also 211.
[86] Star Chamb. Proc. Phil. and Mary, bdle. 5, no. 36.
[87] Augm. Off. Proc. xvi, no. 59.
[88] Chan. Proc. (Ser. 2), bdle. 111, no. 82.
[89] Dict. Nat. Biog.
[90] D. and C. of St. Paul's, Ct. R. Press B, box 39.
[91] Chan. Proc. (Ser. 2), bdle. 171, no. 21.
[92] P.C.C. Will, 20 Vox.
[93] Ibid. 6 Fetiplace.
[94] Ibid. 24 Blamyr.
[95] Ibid. 7 Adeane.
[96] Ibid. 20 Vox.
[97] Ibid.
[98] Ibid. 6 Fetiplace.
[98a] Cartul. Mon. de Rameseia (Rolls Ser.), i, 131.

rent of some 29 acres of land which he gave to the use of the poor.[99] The other was worth 8s. yearly, and arose from 8 acres of land given by John Chapman for that purpose.[100]

CHARITIES The School House charity, comprised in an indenture of 12 December 1670, in which it is recited that the house had from time out of mind belonged to the inhabitants and had been used as a dwelling-house for a schoolmaster, is regulated by a scheme of the Charity Commission dated 18 August 1905. The property consists of a cottage and 10 poles of land let for £5 yearly, and the scheme directs that the income shall be applied for the benefit of the poor. The income is distributed in sums of about 2s. 6d. each.

The Bateman charity, the date of the foundation of which is unknown, but comprised in a deed of 8 April 1644, is regulated by a scheme of the Charity Commission 3 January 1899. The endowment consists of 37 a. 2 r. 16 p. of land in Therfield and 2 roods in Kelshall producing £34 12s. yearly. The net income is applied in the purchase and distribution of coal to the poor.

In 1772 John Clerke by his will gave £2 yearly issuing out of a field called Moneycroft to be distributed in bread to the poor every three years. The last distribution was made in 1909.

WALLINGTON

Wallingtone (xi cent.); Waudlington or Wadlington (xii–xiv cent.); Wadelington (xv cent.).

The village of Wallington lies on the northern slope of the chalk hills about 3 miles south-east of Baldock station on the Cambridge branch of the Great Northern railway.

The single village street lies at right angles to the road from Sandon to Baldock. The village has a plentiful water supply, and the hill on which it stands is almost surrounded by the Cat Ditch, a tributary of the River Beane. At the head of the street, 466 ft. above the ordnance datum, is Wallington Bury, and just below it lie the church and rectory faced by the Manor Farm. Below these the street follows the slope of the hill in a north-easterly direction, and at its centre the road to Baldock turns westwards near the school.[1]

Wallington, like the adjacent parishes of Bygrave and Clothall, is still uninclosed, and it retains a few features of the mediaeval village community. The great open arable field, covering nearly two-thirds of the whole area of the parish (2,043 acres), lies on the sloping ground to the north of the village. Its wide expanse is unbroken by hedge or tree and only divided from the open fields of Bygrave by the Icknield Way and from those of Clothall by an open roadway. In its centre, at Metley Hill, is a tumulus of unknown date and origin. At the present day the villagers apparently claim no rights over the field, which is farmed by the occupiers of the Manor Farm, Wallington Bury and the Lodge Farm. The cottagers have, however, the right to keep a cow and a calf on the small common pasture in the south of the parish.[2] This district is well wooded and contains inclosed meadows and fields. The permanent grass increases and the population of the parish diminishes.[3] The inhabitants are almost entirely employed in agriculture.

In 1401 a house with 360 acres of land in Clothall and Wallington was purchased from Richard Martell of Dunmow by the Prior of Dunmow.[4]

The modern estate of Wallington MANORS was consolidated early in the 16th century by John Bowles, who acquired the three manors of Wallington, Monks and Montfitchets. These three were evidently identical with the two holdings of Robert Gernon and Goisbert de Beauvais at the time of the Domesday Survey.[5]

In 1086, however, there were three other holdings in Wallington. Wimund held 2 hides less 10 acres of Count Alan of Britanny, lord of the honour of Richmond. Before the Conquest this land had been held by two sokemen of Eddeva,[6] probably Edith the Fair.[7] It was possibly a part of the 'two hides and one virgate' in Wallington which with a virgate in Clothall was held in the 12th century by Robert of Abinger (*de Habingwurth, de Abbingburne*).[8] The mesne lord of the fee was then Ruald Pincerna.[9] The heir of Robert of Abinger was a leper and a minor, and therefore his inheritance was seized by the Crown about 1185.[10] One part of the fee was then in the occupation of the lords of the manors of Wallington and Monks, while Warin de Bassingbourn held a carucate 'by so much knight's service as pertains to a hide.'[11] It appears possible that the first portion became absorbed in the two manors of Wallington and Monks. In 1275 the bailiffs of Richmond Honour still took 12d. yearly from the tenement which had belonged to Theobald 'de Mora,'[12] and may have been that formerly held by Warin de Bassingbourn. 'William' of Abinger is said to have given two thirds of the tithes of Wallington to the priory of Bermondsey.[13] Evidently this gift was of two thirds of the tithes arising out of the 'Abinger fee' in Wallington. It gave rise to a dispute between William de Thorntoft, parson of Wallington, and the Abbot of St. Albans in 1308.[14]

Of the other Domesday holdings, one belonged to the fee of Hardwin de Scales, of whom it was held by Siward. It included 1½ hides and 26 acres, and had formerly been held by Wlware, a man of Anschil of Ware.[15] No later trace of this holding

---

[99] Chant. Cert. 27, no. 32. [100] Ibid.
[1] For the school see under Charities.
[2] Slater, *Engl. Peasantry and Encl. of Common Fields*, 45.
[3] Ibid. There were 213 inhabitants in 1831 (*Pop. Ret.* 248), and in 1901 there were 152 (ibid. 14), but this gave a slight increase on the population of 1891.
[4] *Cal. Pat.* 1399–1401, p. 539.
[5] See below.
[6] *V.C.H. Herts.* i, 319.

[7] Cf. *V.C.H. Essex*, i, 350.
[8] Stacey Grimaldi, *Rot. de Dominabus*, 35. The identification rests upon its extent. The other holding of about 2 hides was that of the Scales family (see below).
[9] It has not yet been possible to identify this Ruald, unless he may be Ruald the Constable of the honour of Richmond. See Gale, *Reg. Honoris de Richmond*, 32, 82.
[10] Stacey Grimaldi, loc. cit. [11] Ibid.

[12] Hund. R. (Rec. Com.), i, 193; cf. the account of 'La More' in Sandon.
[13] Dugdale, *Mon.* v, 97; according to the monks the gift took place in 1180; but in 1185 it was the heir of *Robert* of Abinger who was in the king's custody.
[14] Chauncy, *Hist. Antiq. of Herts.* 47, quoting 'Mich. Term 2 Edw. II Rot. 1, Cur. Receipt. Scac.' The original record of this plea cannot be found.
[15] *V.C.H. Herts.* i, 339.

ODSEY HUNDRED — WALLINGTON

has been found. It may have been attached to Hardwin's neighbouring manor of Reed (q.v.). It is not clear whether it was this same Siward who held a virgate in Wallington of Geoffrey de Mandeville.[16]

The manor of WALLINGTON seems to be identical with the 3 hides and 40 acres of land there which were held of Goisbert de Beauvais by a certain Fulk in 1086. The greater part of this holding was occupied before the Conquest by Edric, one of Earl Algar's men; but a small tenement of 24 acres was held by a sokeman of Eddeva the Fair, and subsequently came to Ralf Earl of Norfolk. It was amalgamated with the main manor before 1086, and probably before 1075, for it was not then held by the earl.[17]

In 1543 the manor was said to be held as of Little Wymondley[18]; this was probably an error for Great Wymondley, for a portion of the latter was held by Goisbert de Beauvais in 1086.[19] From the 13th century onwards the overlordship of Wallington Manor was held by the Argentines and their successors, lords of both Great and Little Wymondley (q.v.), of whom it was held by the service of half a knight's fee.[20]

The immediate tenants of this manor in the 12th and two following centuries took their name from Wallington. They may possibly have been descendants of Fulk, the tenant in 1086. William de Wallington appears to have held the manor in 1185.[21] He was probably the son of Robert de Wallington and the same William who gave the church to the monks of St. Albans.[22] William and Reginald de Wallington served as jurors with Richard of Clothall and others in 1200.[23] John de Wallington witnessed charters relating to neighbouring lands in 1279.[24] This or another John held the manor in 1303,[25] and was still living in 1324.[26] Apparently he was succeeded by Richard Monchesney,[27] the king's escheator in Hertfordshire,[28] who had grant of free warren in Wallington and also in Clothall,[29] where his interest was for life only.[30] Walter Monchesney, evidently the heir of Richard, seems to have conveyed the manor to Sir John Lee, kt., lord of the neighbouring manor of Botteles in Clothall, for a yearly rent of 100s.[31] Sir Walter Lee, kt., son of Sir John,[32] released all his rights in Wallington to Richard Ravensere and others in 1376,[33] evidently in trust for sale.[34]

The history of the manor during the next century is obscure. William Brid was holding it in 1428.[35] In 1455 it was settled on John Prisot, a judge and member of the commission for raising funds for the defence of Calais,[36] and his wife Margaret with remainder to the heirs of Margaret by her former husband William Walkern.[37] Richard Echingham and his wife Joan were parties to this settlement, and appear to have been the heirs of Margaret,[38] since the manor subsequently descended to Sir Edward Echingham of Ipswich, kt.[39] In February 1515–16 he sold Wallington Manor for 400 marks to John Bowles, gent., who already resided at Wallington.[40]

John Bowles purchased also the manors of Monks and Montfitchets (q.v.), thus consolidating in Wallington a considerable estate, which he settled upon his grandson Thomas.[41] The latter was aged thirteen at his grandfather's death, which took place in 1543.[42] In his time a single court was held for his manors in Wallington. In consequence even the tenants of his son and successor Thomas Bowles began to doubt the existence of two distinct manors of Monks and Wallington, while the existence of Montfitchets was almost forgotten.[43] Thomas Bowles the younger settled the Wallington estate on John son of his eldest son Lewis with remainders in succession to Lewis and to the latter's younger brothers, Charles, Thomas and others. Thomas Bowles died 10 September 1626,[44] and John, the grandson, on whom the estate had been settled, 28 January 1627–8,[45] leaving a brother and heir Thomas. Lewis Bowles survived till 1 February 1633–4, when his son Thomas was still living.[46] It is not clear whether this Thomas was to inherit under his grandfather's settlement. A Thomas son of Thomas Bowles and probably nephew of Lewis was dealing with the estate in 1659,[47] and was possibly the same Thomas who in 1671 sold it to the Rev. John Breton, D.D., Master of Emanuel College, Cambridge.[48]

The latter bequeathed it to Thomas Breton, a merchant of London, who was succeeded by his son Francis Breton. A life-interest was bequeathed by Francis Breton to his widow.[49] His daughter and heir, Alice Breton, married Sir John Jennings of Newsells in Barkway.[50] Their granddaughter Hester Elizabeth Jennings carried the estate in marriage to John (Peachey) Lord Selsey.[51] Their second son and ultimate heir Henry John Lord Selsey died childless

---

[16] V.C.H. Herts. i, 331a.
[17] Ibid. 336a.
[18] Chan. Inq. p.m. (Ser. 2), lxviii, 14.
[19] V.C.H. Herts. i, 335b.
[20] Feud. Aids, ii, 433, 447; Chan. Inq. p.m. 6 Hen. VI, no. 53.
[21] Stacey Grimaldi, Rot. de Dominabus, 35, where this William is associated with the monks of St. Albans, who were holding the manor of 'Monks' in Wallington.
[22] Dugdale, Mon. ii, 229.
[23] Rot. Cur. Reg. (Rec. Com.), ii, 275; cf. i, 169.
[24] MSS. D. and C. of St. Paul's, A, box 31, no. 597; cf. A, box 30, no. 453.
[25] Feud. Aids, ii, 433.
[26] Cal. Close, 1323–7, p. 81; Lay Subs. R. bdle. 120, no. 11.
[27] Feud. Aids, ii, 447.
[28] Cal. Pat. 1340–3, pp. 393, 479 et seq.
[29] Chart. R. 7 Edw. III, no. 23.
[30] See the account of Hauvills in Clothall.
[31] Cott. Chart. xxvii, 127.

[32] See Clothall; it is remarkable that Wallington is not mentioned in the inquisition on John Lee (Chan. Inq. p.m. 44 Edw. III, no. 37).
[33] Close, 50 Edw. III, pt. ii, m. 9, 12.
[34] Cf. Botteles in Clothall.
[35] Feud. Aids, ii, 447.
[36] Dict. Nat. Biog.; cf. the account of the altar tomb in the north chapel of the church.
[37] Feet of F. Herts. 33 Hen. VI, no. 175.
[38] Thomas Walkern held Netherwick in Wallington in right of his wife Joan about the middle of the 14th century (Assize R. 339).
[39] Close, 8 Hen. VIII, m. 8; it is notable that the manor of Barsham, co. Suff., which had belonged to the Wallington family and was held by Aymer de Wallington as late as 1346 (Feud. Aids, v, 40, 65, 67), also descended to the Echinghams (Suckling, Hist. of Suff. i, 37; Exch. Inq. p.m. [Ser. 2], file 639, no. 13).

[40] Close, 8 Hen. VIII, m. 8; Feet of F. Herts. Trin. 9 Hen. VIII.
[41] Chan. Inq. p.m. (Ser. 2), lxvii, 14.
[42] Ibid.
[43] Chan. Proc. Eliz. B. vi, 6; B. xiv, 7.
[44] Chan. Inq. p.m. (Ser. 2), ccclxviii, 14; ccclxxxvii, 111.
[45] Ibid. ccccxc, 84.
[46] Ibid.
[47] Recov. R. Mich. 1659, m. 126; since Thomas son of Lewis Bowles was aged eighteen in 1658 it is scarcely possible that he could have been succeeded by a son Thomas by 1659.
[48] Chauncy, Hist. Antiq. of Herts. 48.
[49] Ibid.; cf. Feet of F. Herts. Hil. 2 & 3 Jas. II; Recov. R. Hil. 2 & 3 Jas. II, m. 8.
[50] Clutterbuck, Hist. and Antiq. of Herts. iii, 365, 596; cf. Feet of F. Herts. East. 6 Anne; Recov. R. East. 6 Anne, m. 224; East. 15 Geo. II, m. 211.
[51] Clutterbuck, op. cit. iii, 596; cf. Recov. R. Mich. 47 Geo. III, m. 237.

10 March 1838.[52] The estate descended to his sister the Hon. Caroline Mary Peachey, who married the Rev. Leveson Vernon-Harcourt, and died without issue in 1871.[53] In accordance with her mother's will, Wallington then passed to Hugh Henry Rose, Lord Strathnairn of Jhansi, who had distinguished himself in the command of the Central India Field Force during the Sepoy Mutiny.[54] He died in 1885, and his estate was administered by his great-nephew Admiral the Hon. George Henry Douglas, who succeeded to the Wallington property.[55]

Apparently Mr. John Dorsett Owen of Plastyn Grove, Ellesmere, Salop, purchased the whole of the Wallington estate, which was held by his trustees after his death in March 1905. They sold to Mr. Philip Arnold. The estate has again been divided in recent years. The Manor Farm, with the manorial rights, was purchased by Mr. Hugh Rayner, junior, whose father has long been tenant of the farm. The Bury Farm was purchased in two lots by Colonel H. A. Remer and Mr. Pratt.[56]

Half a knight's fee in Wallington was held early in the 14th century as a separate tenement. Richard de Hoggeswell held it of the lord of Wallington in 1303.[57] He was still living at Wallington about 1322.[58] He seems to have been succeeded by William de Hoggeswell, but this holding evidently escheated to the lord of Wallington before 1428,[59] and was probably absorbed in the main manor.

MONKS' MANOR in Wallington and Clothall originated in grants of lands to the monks of St. Albans by William son of Robert de Wallington and several others.[60] These gifts were confirmed by Henry II between the years 1174 and 1182.[61] It was probably assigned to the use of the monks' kitchen, as was Wallington Church.[62] In 1291 the manor was worth £7 12s. 4d.[63] The lands, with reservation of the courts baron and view of frankpledge, were let to farm in the 16th century and were held by John Bowles,[64] who was also tenant of the monks' lands in Bygrave (q.v.).

The manor was purchased in June 1540 by John Sewster of Ashwell.[65] He alienated it in the same year to John Bowles,[65a] who thus completed the consolidation of the Wallington estate.

A field called 'Monks' Piece' still belongs to Wallington Manor.[66]

The manor of *MONTFITCHETS* is probably identical with 3 hides all but 20 acres held of Robert Gernon by a certain William in 1086. This land had been held by Alvric, a man of Goduin son of Ulestan.[67] It was probably acquired in the time of Henry I by William Montfitchet together with the estate at Letchworth held of Robert by the William of Domesday Book.[68] The overlordship apparently descended in the Montfitchet family. Richard Montfitchet (son of Gilbert and grandson of William) succeeded to the Letchworth Manor (q.v.) about 1190. The latter's son and heir died about 1258, and the fee of Montfitchet in Wallington was ultimately assigned to Margery Corbet, granddaughter of his sister Margery.[69] It was held by the service of a quarter of a knight's fee.[70] As in the case of Letchworth a sub-feoffment seems to have taken place, the actual tenant of Montfitchets being John Muschet,[71] a name which is possibly a corruption of Montfitchet.[72] With Letchworth the Wallington quarter-fee had certainly come by 1295 to a younger branch of the Montfitchet family.[73] It seems possible that the feoffment was made to a younger son of William Montfitchet during the 12th century, as in 1198 Richard son of William Montfitchet unjustly disseised Warin son of John of a tenement in Wallington.[74] Before 1295 the overlordship had been acquired by Philip Burnell, heir of the Bishop of Bath and Wells, and was assigned to his widow Maud.[75]

The subsequent history of Wallington Montfitchets is identical with that of Letchworth Montfitchets until 1539, when John Hanchet, gent., sold the former to John Bowles,[76] who had already purchased the main manor of Wallington. Thenceforward these two manors have been amalgamated.

The church of *ST. MARY* consists of chancel 27 ft. by 17 ft. 6 in., north chapel 24 ft. by 11 ft. 6 in., nave 47 ft. by 20 ft. 6 in., south porch 10 ft. 6 in. by 9 ft., west tower 11 ft. square; all internal dimensions.

The walls are of flint rubble, all covered with cement except the chancel, the dressings are of stone; the chancel roof is slated, that over the nave being covered with lead.

The general walling of the nave and chancel may be of the 14th century, but the absence of such early detail makes the date uncertain. The west tower belongs to the beginning of the 15th century, and the north chapel and north nave aisle were probably added shortly afterwards, and at the same time new windows were inserted throughout; the south porch is of late 15th-century date. In 1864 the chancel was almost entirely rebuilt and a new chancel arch inserted.

All the details of the chancel are modern with the exception of the arch opening into the north chapel, which dates from about 1440–50. It is four-centred and consists of two wave-moulded orders, the outer order being continuous, the inner resting on shafts with moulded capitals and bases.

The east window of the chapel is of three cinquefoiled lights with rectilinear tracery under a four-centred arch; the two windows in the north wall have each three lights under a four-centred arch. In the south wall are the remains of a piscina projecting from the wall on a semi-octagonal moulded pedestal;

---

[52] G.E.C. *Complete Peerage*, vii, 109.
[53] *P.O. Dir.* 1866, 1870; Burke, *Landed Gentry*.
[54] Cussans, *Hist. of Herts. Odsey Hund.* 82; G.E.C. op. cit. vii, 291.
[55] *Times*, 24 Dec. 1885.
[56] Inform. from the Rev. Charles W. Clarke, rector. [57] *Feud. Aids*, ii, 433.
[58] Lay Subs. R. bdle. 120, no. 11.
[59] *Feud. Aids*, ii, 447.
[60] Dugdale, *Mon.* ii, 229; Cott. MS. Nero D vii, fol. 95.

[61] Dugdale, loc. cit.
[62] Ibid. 232.
[63] *Pope Nich. Tax.* (Rec. Com.), 51b.
[64] Partic. for Grants (Augm. Off.), Hen. VIII, no. 982 (1).
[65] *L. and P. Hen. VIII*, xv, 831 (45).
[65a] Ibid. (49); Feet of F. Herts. Trin. 32 Hen. VIII.
[66] Inform. from the Rev. Charles W. Clarke, rector.
[67] *V.C.H. Herts.* i, 324a.
[68] Cf. the account of Letchworth.

[69] *Cal. Gen.* i, 224; *Cal. Close*, 1272–9, pp. 82, 84.
[70] *Feud. Aids*, ii, 433; 447.
[71] *Cal. Close*, 1272–9, pp. 82, 84.
[72] See under Letchworth.
[73] *Cal. Close*, 1288–96, p. 463; cf. Stansted Mountfitchet in Essex.
[74] *Rot. Cur. Reg.* (Rec. Com.), i, 15
[75] *Cal. Close*, 1288–96, p. 463.
[76] Feet of F. Herts. East. 31 Hen. VIII; Com. Pleas D. Enr. Mich. 31 Hen. VIII, m. 9 d.

WALLINGTON CHURCH: 15TH-CENTURY ALTAR TOMB

in the north-east angle, high up in the wall, is a stone roof corbel carved with an angel bearing a shield.

On the north side of the nave is an arcade of three bays with pointed arches of two moulded orders upon piers composed of four semicircular shafts separated by hollows; the shafts have moulded capitals and bases; the shafts on the east and west sides of each pier are larger than those on the north and south, and their capitals are deeper. In the east end of the south wall is a low-side window of two cinquefoiled lights under a square head, very similar in position and detail to that at Hinxworth Church, and belonging to the same period (about 1440). The two other windows in the south wall are of three plain lights under four-centred arches; these belong to the 15th century, as also does the south doorway of two moulded orders with label. In the north-east angle of the nave is the doorway to the stair to the rood loft. The roof over the nave is of the 15th century, plain.

In the north wall of the north aisle are three windows similar to those in the north wall of the chapel, and the west window in the aisle is like the east window of the chapel. The north doorway is blocked; it has a four-centred arch under a square head. The roof over the aisle is original, about 1440–50, and has moulded principals with carved bosses at the intersections; at the feet of the principals are carved figures of angels. The roof is carried to a point a little to the east of the chapel screen, the remainder of the chapel having a flat panelled modern roof.

The outer doorway of the south porch is of two moulded orders, the inner order forming the arch and resting on shafted jambs with moulded capitals and bases, the outer order being carried over square; the arch spandrels are pierced. On either side of the porch is a three-light window, most of the stone-work being modern. In the north-east corner are the remains of a stoup.

The tower arch is of three orders, a plain splay between two hollow chamfers; the semi-octagonal responds have moulded capitals and bases. The buttressed tower is of three stages; the west window in the first stage is of two trefoiled lights with quatrefoiled opening above; the second stage has a narrow single light on the south side; the belfry windows are each of two trefoiled lights with a quatrefoiled opening in the head, but are much decayed; the tower is finished with an embattled parapet.

A 15th-century oak screen separates the north aisle from the chapel; the open upper panels have traceried heads, and the lower closed panels are also traceried. The doorway has an ogee crocketed arch; a portion of the carved and moulded cornice remains.[77] There are some plain old pre-Reformation seats in the nave, and the oak communion table belongs to the early part of the 17th century.

In the north window of the chapel are some fragments of 16th-century glass with the arms of Piggot and Prysot.

In the chapel is a 15th-century altar tomb panelled alternately with cusped niches containing small figures of saints, and large cinquefoiled panels containing shields bearing the arms of Piggot and Prysot; on the west end one panel contains a shield, and the other a carving of a pelican in her piety. On the

WALLINGTON CHURCH FROM THE SOUTH-EAST

covering slab are indents of a man and his wife, four shields and a marginal inscription. In the nave floor is a slab to Richard Blow, who died in 1698. In the chapel are the indents of an early 16th-century brass of a man and his wife, with four sons and four daughters, also two shields and a representation of the Trinity, and in the south porch is the indent of a 15th-century brass of a priest or civilian.

In the churchyard are remains of the old font, which is much broken. The octagonal bowl is of the late 12th century, and has shallow arched sinkings on the sides; the clunch base is of the 15th century and is moulded with cusped panels.

[77] In 1495 Laurence Harrys left money for painting the rood loft and its images (P.C.C. Wills, 11 Vox).

A HISTORY OF HERTFORDSHIRE

There are five bells, all by John Briant, 1794.

The communion plate consists of a cup of 1754, paten of 1840, a modern plated flagon and two pewter almsdishes.

The registers are in three books: (i) baptisms and burials from 1661 to 1753, marriages 1661 to 1751; (ii) baptisms and burials from 1754 to 1812; (iii) marriages from 1754 to 1812.

ADVOWSON   The church was given to the monks of St. Albans with the manor of Monks by William de Wallington.[78] In 1218 Honorius III confirmed the assignment of Wallington and Bygrave Churches to the use of the kitchen of the monastery.[79] Apparently no appropriation took place, but an annuity of £1 was assigned to the abbot.[80] The right of presentation remained with successive abbots until the Dissolution, but the advowson for one turn was often granted by the abbot to private individuals.[81]

The subsequent history of the advowson is coincident with that of Monks Manor until 1660, when Thomas Bowles sold the advowson for one turn to Neville Butler.[82] Upon the death of his nominee, which took place in 1714, Francis Breton, to whom the advowson then reverted, gave it to the Master of Emanuel College, Cambridge, on condition that the incumbent should always be a Fellow of the College.[83]

The advowson was subsequently transferred to Mr. Owen, who died in 1905. It was purchased by the late Mrs. Clara Risdon.[84]

In 1645 the ejected minister, John Bowles, evidently a relative of Thomas Bowles, then patron of the living, assaulted William Sherwin, a Puritan divine of some note, who had been appointed to the living upon its sequestration.[85] Sherwin ceased to preach at Wallington either in 1660 or in 1662.[86]

CHARITIES   In 1736 the Rev. John Browne by his will gave £100 for a schoolmistress. The same testator also gave £20 for aged poor, the interest to be distributed every year on Easter Monday. These legacies were invested in £131 17s. 4d. consols with the official trustees, and in 1868 £106 13s. 4d. stock was sold to provide a cottage and premises for the residence of a schoolmistress. By an order of the Charity Commission, dated 5 August 1904, it was determined that the cottage and premises and a sum of £3 4s. 5d. consols should form the endowment of 'Browne's Educational Foundation,' and the residue £21 19s. 7d. consols should form the endowment of 'Browne's Charity for the Poor.'

Joseph Edmonds gave, but at what period is unknown, a sum of £5, the interest to be paid to the most constant communicants among the poor. This legacy was invested in £5 8s. 5d. consols in the name of the official trustees, producing 2s. 8d. yearly.

In the Parliamentary returns of 1786 it is stated that £30 was given many years ago by an unknown donor for the benefit of the poor. This sum was invested in 1864 in £32 18s. 7d. consols in the name of the official trustees, producing 16s. 4d. yearly.

The income arising from 'Browne's Charity for the Poor' and the two last-mentioned charities is distributed among poor communicants and those attending church.

---

[78] Cott. MS. Nero D vii, fol. 95; Dugdale, *Mon.* ii, 229.
[79] Dugdale, op. cit. 232.
[80] *Pope Nich. Tax.* (Rec. Com.), 37.
[81] Chan. Inq. p.m. 30 Edw. I, no. 69; *Cal. Pat.* 1301–7, p. 27; 1348–50, p. 306; Wethamstede, *Reg. Mon. S. Albani* (Rolls Ser.), ii, 4, 71, 88, 117, 165, 224.
[82] Inst. Bks. (P.R.O.); Cussans, *Hist. of Herts. Odsey Hund.* 85.
[83] Cussans, loc. cit.
[84] Inform. from the Rev. Charles W. Clarke, rector.
[85] Add. MS. 15669, fol. 186, 365.
[86] *Dict. Nat. Biog.*

THE HUNDRED OF BRAUGHING

CONTAINING THE PARISHES OF

BISHOP'S STORTFORD	HUNSDON	THUNDRIDGE
BRAUGHING	SAWBRIDGEWORTH	WARE
EASTWICK	STANDON	WESTMILL
GILSTON	STANSTEAD ABBOTS	WIDFORD
	THORLEY	

Braughing Hundred is large in area in proportion to the number of its parishes. Its boundary has changed little since the earliest records of it. Widford and Cockhamsted were both in Edwinstree Hundred in 1086, but assessments of the 14th century show that Widford had been transferred to Braughing before that date,[1] whilst Cockhamsted does not later appear to have had any separate entity either civil or ecclesiastic, but to have been included in the parish of Braughing in this hundred. Besides the vills of the Domesday Survey which correspond with the other civil parishes in the list of 1831,[2] there were then also Wickham[3] and Eia.[4] Wickham was a separate vill for judicial[5] and fiscal purposes as late as the 14th century, but four persons only were assessed under its name for a subsidy in 1307.[6] Later it was included in Bishop's Stortford. Eia must have lain not far from Wickham, for it seems to have been originally included in the same assessment (see below), but no further mention of it has been found, and there seems to be no survival of the name. Gilston is not mentioned in the Domesday Survey, and seems to have been then included in Sawbridgeworth. Thundridge, although assessed by itself in 1086,[7] does not seem to have had any

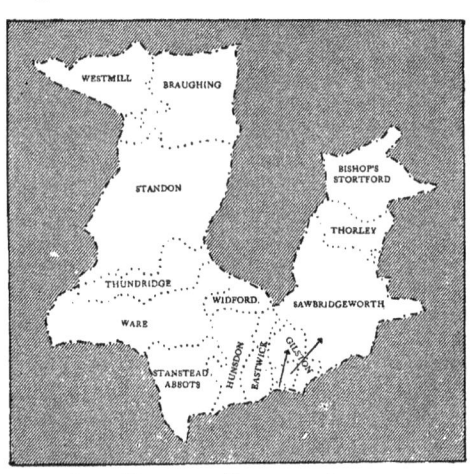

INDEX MAP TO THE HUNDRED OF BRAUGHING

---

[1] See Subs. R. bdle. 120, no. 8.
[2] *Pop. Ret.* 1831.
[3] *V.C.H. Herts.* i, 308*a*, 332*b*, 335*b*.
[4] Ibid. 311*a*.
[5] Assize R. 325 (15 Edw. I).
[6] Subs. R. bdle. 120, no. 8.
[7] *V.C.H. Herts.* i, 311*a*.

A HISTORY OF HERTFORDSHIRE

independent existence for civil purposes later,[8] and ecclesiastically was a chapelry to Ware.

The assessment of this hundred was evidently based on a 6-hide unit. This is shown clearly in the assessment of Bishop's Stortford[9] at 6 hides, Stanstead,[10] Eastwick[11] and Hunsdon[12] together at 24½ hides, Westmill[13] at 12 hides, Standon[14] and Thundridge[15] together at 12 hides, and Ware[16] at 24 hides. The total as it stands (counting Stanstead, Hunsdon and Eastwick at 24 hides, which must have been the original number) is 116 hides 3 virgates 21 acres. Evidently 3 hides and 9 acres had dropped out of an original assessment of 120 hides. These 3 hides and 9 acres, if distributed among Sawbridgeworth, Thorley, Braughing, Wickham and Eia (the only places in 1086 not corresponding with the 6-hide unit), bring up the assessment of Sawbridgeworth and Thorley together to 30 hides, Braughing to 6 hides, and Wickham and Eia together to 6 hides, which was probably the original apportionment.[17]

The conditions of tenure before the Conquest show comparatively few estates held in demesne by tenants of any importance, but a great number of holdings, some of very small extent, in the hands of 'men,' sokemen, or thegns of the larger landholders.[18] Thus Asgar the Staller had, besides a large estate formed of Sawbridgeworth and most of Thorley, men or sokemen at five different places; Earl Harold, who had no demesne lands in this hundred, had tenants also in five places, and six tenants of the king held land in the hundred. King Edward himself had no lands in demesne, but from the pre-Conquest tenants given in the Domesday Survey it seems probable that Braughing, Westmill, Hunsdon, and Eastwick were once in the king's hands, whilst the payment to the king's sheriff due from Stanstead Abbots points to that also having been once royal demesne. The result of the Conquest was a considerable simplification of tenure, most of the divided estates of 1066 being held in 1086 by some great Norman baron who had taken over, not only a pre-Conquest lord's own estate, but also those of his sokemen (cf. the holding of Asgar the Staller and his men in Stanstead, Sawbridgeworth, Thorley and Wickham acquired by Geoffrey de Mandeville and the holding of Alwin of Godtone and his men in Stanstead acquired by Ranulf). This may be compared with the tenurial conditions in Odsey Hundred, where the small, divided estates of the pre-Conquest period seem in many cases to have survived the changes in ownership (cf. particularly Hinxworth).[19]

---

[8] Its original assessment was evidently with Standon (see below), but later it was included for fiscal purposes in Ware (cf. Subs. R. bdle. 120, no. 8 [1 Edw. II], where the lord of the manor of Thundridge [Adam de Swillington] is assessed under Ware). See also Assize R. 325 (15 Edw. I), where it is called the 'hamlet of Thundridge.'

[9] *V.C.H. Herts.* i, 308*a*.   [10] Ibid. 326*b*, 332*a*, 335*a*, 343*b*.   [11] Ibid. 335*b*.
[12] Ibid. 344*b*.   [13] Ibid. 324*b*, 325*a*.   [14] Ibid. 343*b*.
[15] Ibid. 311*a*.   [16] Ibid. 326*b*.

[17] Sawbridgeworth was assessed at 24½ hides (*V.C.H. Herts.* i, 332*a*), Thorley at 4½ hides (ibid. 308*a*, 332*b*). These with 1 hide added make up 30 hides. Braughing needs 1 hide added to its 5 hides (ibid. 322*a*) to make up 6. Wickham (ibid. 308*a*, 332*b*, 335*b*) was assessed at 4 hides 1 virgate 21 acres, and Eia (ibid. 311*a*) at ½ hide. These with 1 hide and 9 acres added make 6 hides. These additions make up the 3 hides 9 acres.   [18] See Domesday Survey, *V.C.H. Herts.* i, 288.

[19] The numerous manors found in Standon and Ware in Braughing Hundred at a later date may perhaps represent arrangements made before the Conquest, the tenants of that date continuing to hold, but under the new Norman lord.

BRAUGHING HUNDRED

Very little information is to be found in regard to the hundred court. The hundred was a royal one,[20] and remained in the king's hands until granted by Elizabeth to Sir William Cecil in 1571.[21] The descent then follows that of Hertford Hundred (q.v.). The court must have been originally held at Braughing, which seems to have been a place of importance. It was probably part of the ancient demesne of the Crown,[22] and was the head of a deanery,[23] besides giving its name to the hundred. Whether the three weekly court continued to be held at Braughing is not clear from the evidence, but in the 14th century the sheriff's tourn was held at the neighbouring village of Puckeridge.[24]

The jurisdiction of the sheriff was limited by the usual private franchises. In 1287 no fewer than six lords claimed the right to hold view of frankpledge at Sawbridgeworth, three claimed it in Gilston, three at Thorley, and one at Ware.[25] Rather earlier the lord of Standon had been presented for non-payment of 16s. for sheriff's aid, 1 mark for view of frankpledge and for withdrawal of suit at the hundred and county court, which ought to have been rendered for the whole vill by the tenant of certain lands whose tenure made him responsible for rendering the suit.[26] The lords of Braughing and Eastwick were presented at the same time for similar encroachments, all of which were said to have been made within the last twenty years.[27] Bishop's Stortford, as a borough, was independent of the hundred in the appearance before the justices of assize, and sometimes also for purposes of local assessment.[28]

---

[20] Assize R. 325, m. 25 (15 Edw. I); *Hund. R.* (Rec. Com.), i, 190.
[21] Pat. 13 Eliz. pt. vii, m. 21.
[22] See Assize R. 6 Edw. I (Agard's MS. index, fol. 98*b*).
[23] The deanery was not coincident with the hundred. It included most of the places in Braughing Hundred, the greater part of Edwinstree Hundred, and a few parishes in Odsey.
[24] Ct. R. (Gen. Ser.), portf. 178, no. 41.
[25] Assize R. 325, m. 25 (15 Edw. I).
[26] *Hund. R.* (Rec. Com.), i, 188; cf. p. 193, where suit is said to be owed by the reeve and four men. Possibly the Geoffrey de Leukenure mentioned in the other passage was the reeve.
[27] Ibid. 191.
[28] See Subs. R. bdle. 120, no. 25 (14 Edw. III).

A HISTORY OF HERTFORDSHIRE

BISHOP'S STORTFORD[1]

Stortford (xi–xvi cent.); generally Bishop's Stortford after xvii cent; variants are found such as Storsurde (xvi cent.),[2] Startford and Stafford (xvii cent.).[3]

Bishop's Stortford is a parish of 3,284 acres, of which 13 are water. Nearly one half of the area is arable land, permanent grass is rather less than a third, whilst woods and plantations only cover about 160 acres.[4] These returns show a considerable change in proportion since the Domesday extent of the manor, which must have included most of the parish; the return of meadow was for one plough team only and of woodland for 300 swine. Hoggate's Wood to the north of the town, part of Bloodhound's Wood, High Wood, Great Plantains Wood on the west of the parish and part of Birchanger Wood on the east are now the only woods of any size. An inclosure award was made for the parish in 1826 under an Act of 1820.[5] The principal common fields were Prestley Field (Prestlaye, 1396; Priestlay, 1656), Hockerill Field, Bishop Field on the east, Apton or Appleton Field on the west, South Mill Field on the south, Broad Field and Common Down on the north.[6]

The navigable river Stort flows through the parish from north to south, forming for a little way the north-eastern boundary between Stortford and Birchanger. The parish is intersected by the road from London to Cambridge which runs north and south, and crossing this from east to west is a road partly coinciding with the Roman Stane Street, which connects Stortford with Great Dunmow on the east and Little Hadham and Braughing on the west, whilst a branch from it to the south runs through Standon to Ermine Street. Many fragments of Roman pottery have been found on the brickfield owned by Mr. J. L. Glasscock on the east side of the main road from Hockerill to Cambridge, and Roman coins of the Lower Empire have been found in Castle Garden. Of prehistoric remains there are two palaeolithic implements, the tusk and tooth of *elephas primigenius* found near Potters Street, and the skeleton of a horse attributed to the neolithic period. Two iron Anglo-Saxon spear heads have also been found.[7]

The town of Stortford is situated in the south of the parish on the River Stort. It must have been a little to the south of the Roman road if that road continued, as is probable, in a straight line across the Stort. The town evidently grew up round the ford, and it seems likely that the site of the castle was chosen so as to command the ford, which would account for its position on such low ground. This ford was possibly safer than the ford or bridge further north where the Roman road originally crossed the river, and so the old line of road was abandoned, and a loop line brought south across the second ford. This, the present road, passes in a westerly direction through the town, where it is called successively Hockerill Street, the Causeway, High Street and Windbill, then turns to the north and rejoins Stane Street to the west of the town. Intersecting this road and running from south to north is the road from London to Cambridge. The line of this road now follows a course to the east of the town, passing through Hockerill. But the earlier route was probably that of the road which, leaving the present London Road to the south of the town just before that road crosses the Stort,[8] runs right through the town where it is called South Street until its intersection with the road running east and west and is continued as North Street on the other side. At Northgate End it turns to the east, then to the north, and eventually rejoins the other line of the road to Cambridge. The town is also connected by road with Farnham to the north-west and Much Hadham to the south-west.

The four main streets of the town, North Street, South Street, Windbill and High Street, form a cross. The names North Street and South Street occur in the 13th century, whilst Cornmarket Street of that date possibly represents the present High Street. Fyl Street and Water Lane are also mentioned then.[9] With so many lines of communication Stortford was a place of great commercial activity as far back as we have any records of it. The Bishops of London seem to have had a prescriptive right to a market there, for no grant is on record. The market-place is in the centre of the town in the south-west angle at the intersection of the two roads. Converging on it were rows (probably of permanent booths) called the Fish Row,[10] the Spicery Row,[11] the Mercery,[12] the Buchery,[13] Shop Row,[14] Barley Hill and Wheat Hill.[15] The Fish Row or Market which branched off from High Street lay to the west of the present corn exchange.[16] Continuing to the south was Potters Hill or Potters Cross,[17] otherwise Pultry or Poultry Hill and later the Leather Market. A cross called Potters Cross stood here and was possibly the market cross.[18] Tanning and leather making were important industries of the town[19]; tanning was carried on in the 15th century in Water Lane.[20] The names of thirteen token issuers at Stortford during the second half of the 17th century are known. Nineteen

---

[1] In this account of Bishop's Stortford the writer has been much indebted to Mr. J. L. Glasscock for his help and suggestions.
[2] L. and P. Hen. VIII, viii, p. 339.
[3] Sess. R. (Herts. Co. Rec.), i, 159, 268.
[4] Statistics from Bd. of Agric. (1905).
[5] Blue Bk. Incl. Awards.
[6] Information from Mr. J. L. Glasscock.
[7] Evans, Anct. Stone Impl. 602; Evans, Arch. Surv. of Herts.; information from Mr. J. L. Glasscock.
[8] The earlier road is likely to have avoided the crossing, as the Saxons were not engineers.
[9] Rentals and Surv. R. 298.
[10] Glasscock, Rec. of St. Michael's, Bishop's Stortford, 94.
[11] Ibid. 140.
[12] Ibid. 4.
[13] Add. Chart. 5295.
[14] Rentals and Surv. R. 299; Glasscock, op. cit. 70.
[15] Sess. R. (Herts. Co. Rec.), i, 51.
[16] Glasscock, Anct. Crosses of Stortford, 25.
[17] See will of John Potter of Potter-crowshe, 1433; printed in Herts. Gen. i, 384.
[18] Glasscock, Anct. Crosses of Stortford, 25.
[19] Cf. the frequent occurrence of Tanner and Skinner as a surname on the court rolls, &c., and in Glasscock, Rec. of St. Michael's, Bishop's Stortford, 45, 70.
[20] Ibid. 102. A decree was made in the court baron at the beginning of the 17th century that no one having stalls or standing in the fish market should let them to any tanner or shoemaker on pain of 20s.

BISHOP'S STORTFORD : ST. JOSEPH'S, FORMERLY WIND HILL HOUSE
(From '*A History of the Families of Skeet, Somerscales and others*')

of their tokens are extant, of which the dated ones range from 1666 to 1669, and all of which were probably issued between 1665 and 1680.[21]

Fairs were held at Stortford three times a year, on the feasts of St. Michael, Ascension and Corpus Christi. Part of the fairs were held inside the churchyard until the end of the 16th century.[22] A schoolhouse stood near the churchyard in the 15th century, where a chantry school was probably carried on.[23] The grammar school founded by Margaret Dane in 1579 was a building abutting on the High Street on the north and on Church Lane on the west. The library adjoined the schoolhouse; this was collected chiefly by Dr. Thomas Leigh, vicar of Stortford. On the refounding of the school by Dr. Tooke, the Wheat Hill market-house was acquired in 1699, and a schoolhouse built on arches over the market-house with the west front looking over the churchyard.[24]

Destroyed either at the Reformation or during the Commonwealth were four crosses which stood in roads leading from the town of Stortford. Collin's Cross probably stood on the site still called by that name at the point where the road from Takeley joins the road leading from Hockerill to Stanstead. It was probably named from the family of Colin who were living here from the 13th century onward. The name also survives in Collin's Croft. Crabb's Cross stood on the road now called Rye Street leading from Stortford towards Manuden, probably at a four-want-way made by the intersection of this road with an ancient way (now a water-course) to Farnham. Crabb was a common surname in the parish, and the family has given its name to Crabb's Croft, Crabb's Croft Mead and Crabb's Field in the immediate neighbourhood of the site above indicated. A third cross was Wayte Cross, which stood at the junction of Maze Green Road with the old road from Stortford to Little Hadham on a site now occupied by the grounds of Westfield (the modern name for Waite Field) House. Close by was Waite Field,[25] and Wayte Strete[26] was probably the name of the road leading from the cross to the town. Maple Cross, the fourth cross, is said by Chauncy to have stood on the south of the town, probably on the old South Road leading from Stortford to London.[27] Its exact site and also the derivation of the name are uncertain.

Like other market towns with a powerful lord of the manor, Stortford had to some extent a burghal constitution, but there seems to be no truth in the story told by Chauncy and repeated by other historians of its having received this constitution from King John, for as far as is known he gave no charter to the town. It appears to have been a mesne borough held of the Bishops of London. At the beginning of the 14th century separate courts were held for the barony and the borough,[28] but later only manorial courts were held, at which the borough presented separately from the 'upland' by 12 burgesses and separate officers were elected.[29] The burgage tenants could alienate by charter, and on entering into a tenement they paid a variable sum ranging from 8d. to 20d. for the freedom of the borough. In 1344–5 the burgage rents amounted to 5s. 4d. for the year.[30] In the 13th and 14th centuries the township is found presenting separately from the hundred before the justices of assize,[31] and in a subsidy collected in 1340 it is classed as a borough with Hertford and assessed separately from the rest of the county.[32] As the head of the Bishop of London's barony it was important enough to send members to Parliament in the 14th century. Two members were summoned from it to the Parliaments held in 1311,[33] 1312, 1313, 1314–15, 1318, 1320, 1322,[34] and 1340–1.[35]

The number of inns which appear in the records of the town witness to its active commercial life.[36] Many of these are still standing, although most of them have been much altered. The White Horse Inn in North Street is a house of two stories built of brick and plastered timber, in plan the shape of an L. The overhanging upper story is plastered and decorated with square and diamond-shaped plaster panels containing ornamental designs. The Half Moon Inn in the same street is a timber house which was restored about thirty years ago. In High Street there is the Boar's Head Inn, built about 1600 of timber and plaster, but so much altered that the original plan is obscured. The projecting wings as well as the main building are gabled. In a few of the windows are still the old metal casements; the quarter-circle bay windows in the re-entering angles are an 18th-century addition. In the stables there has been inserted a moulded beam with a defaced carved boss of the 15th century. There is an embattled oak beam of the 15th century over the fireplace in the top room. The Grapes Inn in South Street is probably of the late 16th century. It is built of timber and plaster. An original angle bracket is hidden behind a square corner. On the other side of the same street is a house now known as the Reindeer Inn of the 16th or 17th century. This is not the Reindeer Inn of Pepys' fame, kept by the notorious Betty Ainsworth, which stood at the corner of Fish Street and High Street on the site now occupied by Messrs. Walker's Stores. In Bridge Street is the Black Lion Inn, a 16th-century timber and plaster rectangular house of two stories and an attic. The upper story overhangs on the north and east, and the attic again projects;

---

[21] Information from Mr. J. L. Glasscock.
[22] Sess. R. (Herts. Co. Rec.), i, 13.
[23] This and the Gatehouse, close by, paid a rent to the church (Glasscock, Rec. of St. Michael's, Bishop's Stortford, 4).
[24] V.C.H. Herts. ii, 81.
[25] Chauncy, Hist. and Antiq. of Herts. 170.
[26] Mins. Accts. bdle. 1140, no. 3; Ct. R. (Gen. Ser.), portf. 178, no. 65, 66. Wadeswyk is another name found in the 14th century (Ct. R. portf. 178, no. 66). This is probably the same word, for Wadesmill in Standon is found as Watesmill (Cott. MS. Nero, vi E, fol. 120).

[27] The account of these crosses is taken from Glasscock, Anct. Crosses of Stortford. Mr. Glasscock has found reference also to a 'Shyrte Cross' (Rentals and Surv. R. 299), which may possibly be another name for one of those above mentioned.
[28] MSS. of D. and C. of St. Paul's, Press A, box 64, no. 23.
[29] Ct. R. (Gen. Ser.), portf. 178, no. 65, 66.
[30] Mins. Accts. bdle. 1140, no. 10.
[31] See Assize R. 318 (32 Hen. III); 320 (39 Hen. III); 325 (15 Edw. I);

[a] see also Agard's MS. index to Assize R. 6 Edw. I.
[32] Lay Subs. R. bdle. 120, no. 25.
[33] This Parliament was first summoned in August 1311, but was prorogued and re-summoned in November 1311. At the second summons Stortford did not, so far as we know, return any members.
[34] Ret. of Memb. of Parl. i, 23; V.C.H. Herts. Families, 295.
[35] The names of these two members are given by Willis Browne in Notitia Parl.
[36] Glasscock, Rec. of St. Michael's, Bishop's Stortford; Rentals and Surv. R. 299; Ct. Rolls, &c.

293

on the north the upper story has a moulded sill with a twisted ornament and is carried on carved brackets. On the upper floor of the north front, on each side of two modern oriel windows, is a row of small lights with moulded oak frames and mullions. On the east there are also two small blocked windows with oak mullions. The house contains some 17th-century panelling. The Star Inn in the same street is a 17th-century house of timber and plaster, much restored. There is a carved bracket under the eaves.

Besides the inns there are a number of interesting old houses in the town, principally of the 17th century. St. Joseph's, formerly Wind Hill House, west of the church, is an early 17th-century L-shaped house of two stories and attics. It was apparently encased in the 18th century with brick walls, and was much altered in the following century. It contains a 17th-century heavy oak staircase, with moulded handrail, carved balustrade and panelled and moulded newels. The entrance hall on the east of the staircase was formerly part of the large hall and has the remains of an ornamental plastered ceiling. This house belonged in the 18th century to the Clapp family, and was probably used in connexion with the old Stortford School.[37] In 1806 it became the property of the Wilby family, who enlarged it and put in a fresh front. Mr. William Wilby of Wind Hill House died in 1827 and was buried in St. Michael's. His son Thomas died without issue in 1847, when the property passed to his nephew William, who also died without issue in 1866. His brother Thomas succeeded, and on his death the house descended to Mr. Frederick Wilby (lord of Piggotts Manor, q.v.). In 1903 it was acquired by the Provincial of the Redemptorist order for the Redemptorist Fathers, who since May 1900 had occupied a small house in the Portland Road, to which an iron church was attached. A church dedicated in honour of St. Joseph and the English Martyrs was built on the site of the stables of Wind Hill House, and opened by Cardinal Bourne, Archbishop of Westminster, in 1906. One of the stained glass windows has fragments of old glass said to have come out of St. Michael's Church. Previous to the arrival of the Redemptorist Fathers in the parish a small house of Belgian nuns (Sœurs de Ste. Marie) had been established in the Grange Road in 1896. The sisters afterwards bought Wind Hill Lodge, where they built a large convent by the side of the old house, and they now have a school there.[38] The house no. 12 North Street is probably of the 17th century and retains some of the old beams. In High Street there is a timber and plaster house of three stories (now divided into two dwellings, nos. 10 and 12) of the early 17th century. It has two gables and projecting upper stories, with carved brackets under the second floor. There are two oriel windows on the first floor, and all the windows have wooden frames and mullions. On the north side of Bridge Street, opposite the 'Black Lion,' is a 16th-century house with a hipped roof, now occupied

THE WHITE HORSE INN, BISHOP'S STORTFORD

[37] In 1768 Dr. Johnson's negro servant Francis Barker was at school at 'Mrs. Clapp's.' The Rev. Joseph Clapp was head master of the school; he died in 1767.

[38] Information supplied by Major F. Skeet.

by a saddler, in which is a ceiling ornamented with some plaster work similar to that in the hall at Wind Hill House.[39] Several other houses on the same side of the street have gabled roofs. An old house called Feckinghams or Fockinghams in Basbow Lane was pulled down between 1870 and 1880 by the owner, Mr. G. E. Sworder.[40]

The most important event in the later history of the town was the construction of the canal called the Stort Navigation by George Jackson (afterwards Sir George Duckett, bart.), under Act of Parliament passed in 1765.[41] The canal was begun in 1766 and finished in 1769. The improved water communication stimulated the manufacture of malt, which has always been the chief industry.[42] Between 1801 and 1891 the population increased about fifteen years ago by Messrs. Benskins. Other industries include brickfields, limekilns, coach and sacking works, a hatters' furrier manufactory, and a foundry. The corn exchange at the corner of Market Place was built in 1828.[44] The fairs held on Holy Thursday and Thursday after Trinity Sunday were abolished in 1893, but the corn market is still held in Market Square and cattle and poultry markets at Northgate End and North Street. The tolls have been recently given to the town by Sir Walter Gilbey, bart., lord of the manor, and are now collected by the urban district council.[45]

Petty sessions were held at Bishop's Stortford for that parish, Thorley and Sawbridgeworth before 1832, but it was not until that year that it was proposed to make a separate division of those parishes,

THE BLACK LION INN, BISHOP'S STORTFORD

from 2,305 to 6,595, an unusual increase for a rural parish.[43] The opening of the Great Eastern railway also increased the trade, and large quantities of malt are now exported to London. The old Stortford Brewery, which occupies a large site between Water Lane and Northgate End, was founded by Messrs. Hawker & Co. in the 18th century, and was bought which were then included in the division of Eastwick, but were said to comprise together more than one-third of the population of the hundred of Braughing.[46] Stortford was made the head of the new petty sessional division thus formed. The sessions are held at the police station. In 1866 the Local Government Act was adopted by the parish,[47] and a board

[39] Information supplied by Major F. Skeet.
[40] For this house see Com. Pleas D. Enr. Mich. 39 Eliz.; Hil. 6 Chas. I, m. 9.
[41] Glasscock, *Rec. of St. Michael's, Bishop's Stortford.* Sir George Duckett is buried in the churchyard. As George Jackson he was for many years secretary to the Navy Board and Admiralty. Port Jackson in New Zealand and Port Jackson in New South Wales were called after him by his friend Captain Cook the navigator. He was created a baronet in 1791, and in 1797 he obtained licence to take the name and arms of Duckett, his wife being an heiress of that family. See *Duchetiana,* by Sir G. F. Duckett, and G.E.C. *Baronetage,* v, 273.
[42] About 1636 the justices of the peace for Hertford returned that the maltsters of Stortford and other towns in the county were chiefly employed in making malt for the provision of the houses of the neighbouring gentry, who sent their own barley to them for this purpose (*Cal. S. P. Dom.* 1636–7, p. 323).
[43] *Herts. and Essex Observer,* 30 Mar. 1901.
[44] Cussans, *Hist. of Herts. Braughing Hund.* 109.
[45] Information from Mr. J. L. Glasscock.
[46] *Sess. R.* (Herts. Co. Rec.), ii, 338.
[47] *Lond. Gaz.* 7 Dec. 1866, p. 6835.

A HISTORY OF HERTFORDSHIRE

governed the town until 1894, when by the Local Government Act of that year it was replaced by an urban district council. The county court district of Stortford was formed in 1847.[48] Stortford is also the head of a union, the union buildings lying some way to the south-east of the town, off the Dunmow Road.[49] The isolation hospital of the Hadham and Stanstead rural district and the Sawbridgeworth urban district is also in this parish. In 1895 a hospital was given to the town by members of the Frere family and built on a site on the north of the town presented by Sir Walter Gilbey, who also built the King's Cottage Homes in South Street, to which an additional block has lately been added by Admiral F. Van der Meulen.

The ecclesiastical parish of Holy Trinity, New Town, was formed in 1860,[50] and the church in South Street built in 1859. A congregation of Independents was formed here in 1662.[51] In the 18th century they acquired a chapel in Water Lane,[52] and the present Congregational Church, built in 1859, is in that street. Incumbents of some note were Richard Rawlin, 1687–1759, and John Angus, 1724–1801.[53] A Wesleyan congregation was formed about 1823, and in 1866 a chapel was built in South Street. This was superseded by a chapel on the west side of the road, built about 1908. A Baptist chapel was built in Sandpit Field in 1819,[54] but was pulled down in 1899 and the present chapel built.[55] There were Friends in the parish as early as 1665, and a meeting-house (successor to a former one) was built in the New Town Road in 1709.[56] The meeting has now been discontinued, but the old house still stands on the north side of the road. Baron Dimsdale, the famous inoculator, was buried in the Friends' burial ground. The cemetery on the south of the town was made in 1855.

In Hadham Road is Bishop's Stortford Grammar School, representing the foundation of Margaret Dane of 1579. After its discontinuance for many years the school was revived in 1850, chiefly through the efforts of the vicar, the Rev. F. W. Rhodes.[57] His son, the Rt. Hon. Cecil Rhodes, was born at a house at the end of South Street, and was educated at the grammar school. The Nonconformist school now called the Bishop's Stortford College in Maze Green Road was opened in 1868 by the East of England Nonconformist School Company, who acquired the buildings and land of the Stortford Collegiate School, an unsectarian school opened in 1850 just before the old grammar school was revived. There are public elementary schools at Northgate End (built in 1839), in Apton Road (built in 1872), and in South Street (built in 1852), a County Council secondary school built in 1910 in Warwick Road, and a Technical Institute in Church Street. The Diocesan Training College for Schoolmistresses in Hockerill was opened in 1852.

Hockerill (Hokerhulle, xiv cent.)[58] forms a suburb of Bishop's Stortford and lies on the east side of the river at the intersection of the London Road and the Dunmow Road. Hockerill Bridge is mentioned in the 14th century.[59] Here also are a number of old houses, among which may be mentioned the 16th-century timber and plaster house which was once the Old Red Lion Inn. It is of two stories and has a projecting upper story carried on two carved brackets. It contains some 16th-century oak panelling. On the south side of the main road is a cottage probably of the early 17th century with original brick central chimney stack, and the Cock Inn, which is a timber and plaster house of about 1600 with carved barge-boards in the gables. At the Crown Inn, which stood on the south side of Hockerill, the manorial courts of Bishop's Stortford were held. This was an important inn in coaching days, as it was the second stopping place for coaches travelling from London to Cambridge and Newmarket. The premises now used as a malting were part of the stables.[60] The church of All Saints was built in 1852 and the vicarage in 1894. An elementary school for boys was built in 1868.

Plaw Hatch, about 1 mile east of Stortford, is the residence of Mr. C. J. Hegan, J.P.; The Grange, of Sir John Barker, bart., J.P.; Whitehall, of Mr. T. Gilbey, J.P.; and Westfield House, in the Hadham Road, of Mr. F. Wilby.

CASTLE AND MANORS
The manor of STORTFORD was held in the reign of King Edward the Confessor by Eddeva the Fair. After the Conquest it was sold by William I to William Bishop of London (1051–75),[61] and in 1086 it was held by Hugh Bishop of London. It was assessed in the Domesday Survey at 6 hides. There was land for ten ploughs, although there were only six plough lands under cultivation; two mills were then included in the extent of the manor.[62] Stortford remained part of the lands of the bishopric until 1868. It seems to have been usually farmed out by the Bishops of London. Occasionally the offices of keeper of the gaol, farmer of the manor, farmer of the market and mills, and farmer of the park were held by the same person,[63] but generally the custody of the gaol was held separately from the farm of the manor,[64] although accounts for 1346 show the custodian of the gaol also the farmer of the market and mills.[65] The farm of the whole manor, including courts, markets, fairs, &c., amounted in 1437–8 to £40, reservation being made by the lord of the

SEE OF LONDON.
Gules two swords of St. Paul crossed saltirewise.

---

[48] *Lond. Gaz.* 10 Mar. 1847, p. 990.
[49] The old workhouse mentioned in 1793 (see *Sess. R.* [Herts. Co. Rec.], ii, 177) stood on the south side of Hockerill Street and is now part of a malting (information from Mr. J. L. Glasscock).
[50] *Lond. Gaz.* 25 Jan. 1860, p. 292.
[51] See Urwick, *Nonconformity in Herts.* 700; *Sess. R.* (Herts. Co. Rec.), i, 207.
[52] Close, 19 Geo. II, pt vi, m. 12.
[53] See *Dict. Nat. Biog.*
[54] Urwick, op. cit. 767.
[55] *Herts. and Essex Observer*, 6 Apr. 1901.
[56] Urwick, op. cit. 706.
[57] *V.C.H. Herts.* ii, 81.
[58] Mins. Accts. bdle. 1140, no. 1.
[59] Ibid.
[60] *Herts. and Essex Observer*, 6 Apr. 1901. Paper by Mr. J. L. Glasscock.
[61] *V.C.H. Herts.* i, 308, 279. This William was a pre-Conquest bishop, who acquired a number of estates by purchase from William I.
[62] Ibid.
[63] Mins. Accts. bdle. 1140, no. 41.
[64] See ibid. no. 10.
[65] Ibid. no. 3. Two mills, as mentioned above, are given in the Domesday extent. The mill conveyed in Feet of F. Div. Co. 10 Hen. III, no. 44, may be another one.

BISHOP'S STORTFORD CHURCH: THE NAVE LOOKING EAST

BISHOP'S STORTFORD: WAYTEMORE CASTLE, SOUTH WALL OF KEEP FROM ENCLOSURE

BRAUGHING HUNDRED — BISHOP'S STORTFORD

advowson of the church, wood and underwood on the manor, warren, fishery, chattels of felons and fugitives. The park was accounted for separately, the profits of this arising from the agistment of cattle and the sale of the underwood.[66] The courts of the manor were held by the farmers.[67] Accounts for 1394–5 show four courts held in that year, at Michaelmas, Epiphany, Easter, and Trinity, and one view of frankpledge,[68] but in the next century, as appears from the court rolls extant at the Record Office,[69] only two courts were held in the year, one general court about Michaelmas, and a court and view of frankpledge usually on the morrow of the feast of Holy Trinity. Two constables were chosen at the view of frankpledge. The common fine payable by the chief pledges at the same court was 16d. A fine for recognition called 'Sadelselver' was levied from the customary tenants of the manor at the first court held after a vacancy of the bishopric. It was returned, however, in 1429 that all the customary lands had been resumed by the lord and re-granted at farm. These grants at farm for a period of years are very common on the court rolls at this date. In 1415 a tenement in South Street formerly belonging to the priory of St. James the Apostle of Thremhall, and then in the lord's hands by reason of the prior's refusal to pay the rent, was granted to Richard Pygdon for 100 years at a rent of 8d.[69a] There were, however, customary tenants on the manor in the 18th century, and such tenants were admitted at courts baron held for the manor at this date.[70] Thomas Hasler of Tilbury Fort, Essex, was the customary tenant of land near Goose Meade to which his son Thomas Hasler was admitted in 1705.[71] George Jackson of the Admiralty (afterwards Sir George Duckett, bart.) held a messuage on Goose Meade and land between Town Mill and Goose Meade.[72] Grants by the lord of pieces of the waste are common about this date.[73] After 1830 the headborough, ale-tasters, flesh and fish-tasters, and cattle drivers were appointed by the vestry instead of by the court leet, and so continued to be until 1872, when the officers were abolished.[74] Paid surveyors of the highway were first appointed in 1836, instead of those chosen by the town.[75] They were superseded by a Highway Board in 1856, which lasted until the adoption of the Local Government Act in 1866.

A lease of the manor for twenty-one years from 1614 was made by Richard Bishop of London to Queen Elizabeth, who assigned it to Sir Edward Denny in 1596.[76] The manor, together with the site, park, two watermills called Town Mills, and the fairs and markets, was sold in 1647 by the trustees for the sale of Bishops' lands to Richard Turner, a citizen and merchant tailor of London.[77] It reverted to the Bishop of London after the Restoration, and remained with the see until transferred to the Ecclesiastical Commissioners in 1868.

For the origin of the castle of Waytemore we have no exact date.[77a] It was probably one of the numerous castles raised by William I[78] whilst the manor was in his hands before the sale to William Bishop of London between 1066 and the bishop's death in 1075. The first mention of it seems to be in the charter (issued probably on the accession of Maurice Bishop of London in 1086) by which William I confirmed to the see the castle of Stortford and all the land which William Bishop of London had of the king.[79] At this date the castle must have consisted only of the earthworks, upon which were erected a timber keep and other timber defences.[80] It was not probably till the reign of Henry I, or later in the 12th century, that masonry works were commenced. The remains of the keep stand on the summit of an artificial mound about 42 ft. in height. The plan of the keep is roughly rectangular, the northern end forming a segment of a circle; the other three sides appear to have been straight, but the walls themselves have been broken down almost to the ground level, with the exception of some blocks at the south end; the whole of the outer and inner facings of the outer walls, except next the sunk chambers, have completely disappeared. The average dimensions within the inclosed area measure about 106 ft. from north to south and 57 ft. from east to west. At the north-east and south-east angles are chambers sunk about 7 ft. below the general surface level; they measure, respectively, about 18 ft. by 15 ft. 6 in. and 17 ft. 6 in. by 15 ft.; across the segmental northern end is a low wall about 2 ft. 6 in. thick, at the west end of which are traces of a circular turret; a break in the main south wall may indicate the former entrance. The outer and inner walling is built of flint rubble; the inner walls at the north end are bonded irregularly with Roman bricks, with mediaeval tiles in parts; no stonework remains *in situ*. The flint walling probably dates from the Norman period, but it is not possible to speak definitely on the point owing to the lack of detail. At the north end is a small collection of wrought stones, chiefly limestone, which have been found on the site; they comprise splayed window and door jambs and plinths; a moulded stone was also found, which may have supported an oriel or formed part of a deep string-course. These stones probably date from the 14th century, when a licence to crenellate was granted. Portions of leadwork from window glazing, spurs and fragments of pottery have also been picked up in the inclosure. A well still exists within the walled space, the depth of which is about 40 ft. The castle and grounds are now the property of the urban district council, which is taking proper care of the remains.

In 1137 Anselm Abbot of St. Edmund's, who was trying to obtain the bishopric of London, took possession of the castle. His election by a faction in opposition

---

[66] Mins. Accts. bdle. 1140, no. 20.
[67] Ibid. no. 9, 10.
[68] Ibid. no. 10.
[69] (Gen. Ser.), portf. 178, no. 65, 66.
[69a] Ibid. no. 66.
[70] Add. Chart. 27090–105.
[71] Ibid. 27090.
[72] Ibid. 27105. He had seisin in 1794. For details about him see note 41.
[73] See ibid. 27091, 27093, 27097.
[74] J. L. Glasscock, *Rec. of St. Michael's, Bishop's Stortford*, 87. At a court held in 1718 bread and butter weighers were among the officers elected.
[75] Ibid. 88.
[76] *Cal. S. P. Dom.* 1595–7, p. 295.
[77] Close, 24 Chas. I, pt. xxvi, no. 43.
[77a] It has been suggested that Waytemore may be identified with the Saxon Wigingamere, where in 921 a 'burg' was built by Edward the Elder (*Angl.-Sax. Chron.* [Rolls Ser.], ii, 31; i, 194; see also ii, 82). It may be noticed that the name Waytemore seems to be connected with the Wayte Field and Wayte Street also found in this parish (see above).
[78] See Round, 'Castles of the Conquest' (*Arch.* lviii).
[79] Dugdale, *Hist. of St. Paul's* (1658), 196. The charter is taken *ex codice MS.* of the Dean and Chapter of St. Paul's.
[80] For description and plan of earthworks see *V.C.H. Herts.* ii, 115.

A HISTORY OF HERTFORDSHIRE

to the dean was, however, shortly afterwards annulled.[81] In the intrigues of Stephen's reign the castle played a part of some importance, and it is probable that the masonry keep had been built by this time. From its position on the main road from London to Saffron Walden it cut the communication between those places for Geoffrey de Mandeville Earl of Essex. The possession of the castle was therefore an important object to the earl and formed part of the price demanded by him from the Empress Maud for his support. By her charter of 1141 or 1142 she promised that if she could acquire the castle from the Bishop of London by exchange she would grant it to him, but if she was unable to do this she would destroy it.[82] In the quickly changing events of the reign, however, neither the promise nor the threat was carried out. In 1189 the temporalities of the bishopric were in the king's hands, and on the Pipe Roll for that year is entered a payment to the custodian and porter of the castle.[83] William de St. Mere l'Eglise, who held the see of London in the reign of John, was one of the bishops who published the interdict in 1208 and was consequently obliged to leave the country; his property was seized by the king, who in 1211 dismantled the castle.[84] The next year the king was excommunicated. After his submission in May 1213 he restored the lands of the bishopric and in July of that year gave the bishop leave to rebuild the castle.[85] The bishop, however, was in a strong enough position to demand compensation, and a few months later obtained from the king an acknowledgement that he was bound to repair the castle and restore it to its former strength.[86] Rather more than a century after the rebuilding, licence was obtained by Ralph Stratford, then Bishop of London, to crenellate the castle and tower.[87]

There seems little evidence that the bishops ever used the castle as a residence. Stephen de Gravesend, Bishop of London, died at Stortford in 1338, but his death took place at the rector's house.[88] There was, however, a chapel in the castle, and a chantry was founded there by Ralph Bishop of London in 1352. The provost and chaplains had a plot of land in the castle assigned them on which to build a dwelling-house and licence for free entrance to and exit from the castle.[89]

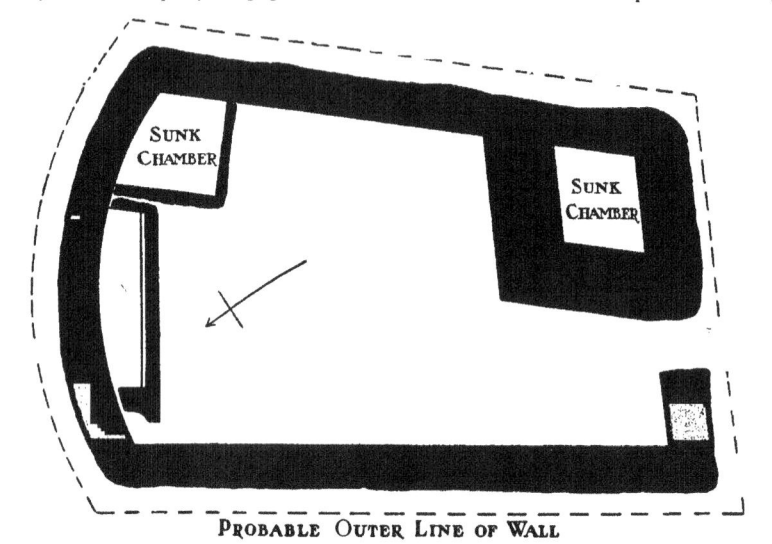

PLAN OF WAYTEMORE CASTLE, BISHOP'S STORTFORD

[81] Ralph de Diceto, *Opera* (Rolls Ser.), i, 25.
[82] Round, *Geoff. de Mandeville*, 167, 174.
[83] Hunter, *Gt. Roll of Pipe*, 1 Ric. I (Rec. Com.), 12.
[84] The date is given as 1213 in 'Annales Londonienses,' *Chron. of Reigns of Edw. I and Edw. II* (Rolls Ser.), i, 15, but the other date is probably the correct one (Walsingham, *Ypodigma Neustriae* [Rolls Ser.], 129). *Evertitur* and *destruitur* are the words used by the chronicler. The subsequent rebuilding of the *castrum* (the word used) refers probably to the buildings in the bailey as distinguished from the keep (*turris*).
[85] *Rot. Lit. Pat.* (Rec. Com.), 101. See note 84. [86] Ibid. 124.
[87] *Cal. Pat.* 1345–8, p. 61.
[88] *Chron. of Reigns of Edw. I and Edw. II* (Rolls Ser.), i, 367. A synod was held at Stortford c. 1150 (*Cart. of Colchester* [Roxburghe Club]), 174.
[89] *Cal. Pat.* 1350–4, p. 324.

298

BRAUGHING HUNDRED BISHOP'S STORTFORD

The prison in the castle was in existence early in the 13th century and probably before. In 1234 there is mention of a prisoner detained for murder 'in the king's prison at Stortford.'[90] Why it should be called the king's prison is not clear, for the see was not vacant at that date. The custody of the gaol was held by an officer of the bishop,[91] who, as mentioned above, was sometimes the same as the farmer of the manor or the farmer of the market. The gaol was used for all criminals within the liberty of the bishop in Hertfordshire,[92] but the greater number of prisoners were convicted clerks. The treatment was probably rigorous. A certain heretic named Ranulf, an apostate Franciscan, who disturbed London by his attacks on the Catholic faith in 1336, was imprisoned there by the bishop until the best method of proceeding against him should have been decided, but his death is recorded very shortly afterwards.[93] In September 1344 there were fifty prisoners in the gaol, and seven more were added during the year, and of these twenty-nine died. At the beginning of the year 1345 there were twenty-five prisoners, and nine of these died. In 1347–8 there were fifty prisoners, the cost of keeping them being reckoned at ¼d. a day each.[94] The accounts of the gaolers include such items as lights for visiting the prisoners at night, shackles, fetters, iron for staples, stocks, and so on.[95] In spite of all precautions, however, the prison does not seem to have been very secure, judging by the numerous notices of the escape of prisoners from it.[96] During the episcopate of Robert Braybrook (ob. 1404) batches of sixteen, eighteen, and ten prisoners escaped in succeeding years.[97] In each case the bishop received pardon from the king for the escape, but William Gray, bishop in 1429, seems to have been actually charged with a fine of £426 13s. 4d. for the escape of five clerks, who had carried off their gaoler with them. On information received by the king that these prisoners had been recaptured at great labour and expense while the bishop was abroad on an embassy a respite of the fine for ten years was allowed to him.[98] In 1539 the number of prisoners was eleven.[99] The prison was not in the keep of the castle, but stood with some of the other buildings on a site now occupied by the house called Castle Cottage, and was separated from the keep by the moat.[100]

By 1549 the castle was in ruins, only a few pieces of the walls remaining.[1] The prison survived and is mentioned by Norden, writing in 1598, as 'a dungeon deep and strong.'[2] The Jesuit lay brother Thomas Pound was imprisoned there by Bishop Aylmer in 1580 to prevent his infecting others by his conversation,[3] and in a letter to Sir Christopher Hatton gives a dismal description of it.[4] It was probably used until the time of the Commonwealth, after which prisoners were sent to the county gaol.[5] Channey says that the buildings were sold about 1649, and soon afterwards pulled down. An inn called Cherry Tree Inn was built on the site near the old gatehouse of the castle. This has been incorporated in the present Castle Cottage, formerly the residence of Mr. Edward Taylor.[6] The ground on which the castle stands was lately the joint property of several members of the Taylor family.[7] In 1907 it was acquired with the castle by the urban district council for public gardens.

The remains of the castle are close by the town, but separated from it by the River Stort. The land round it is very marshy, so that it is often spoken of as standing on an island. The entrance was probably on the south from the causeway across the marsh.

CASTLE COTTAGE, BISHOP'S STORTFORD

---

[90] *Cal. Close*, 1231–4, p. 403.
[91] John de Solio is called constable of the castle in 1305 (*Hist. MSS. Com. Rep.* ix, App. i, 39b).
[92] See Assize R. 325 (15 Edw. I), m. 25 d.
[93] *Chron. of Reigns of Edw. I and Edw. II* (Rolls Ser.), i, 365.
[94] Mins. Accts. bdle. 1140, no. 1, 3. A yearly rent of 3 quarters of wheat from two plots of land called Redynge and Bocmongerecroft was granted to the bishop in 1387 for the maintenance of the prisoners (*Cal. Pat.* 1385–9, p. 374).
[95] Mins. Accts. bdle. 1140, no. 1, 3. One pair of stocks was made 'in the free prison in the long bay,' so that there seems to have been some distinction in the treatment of prisoners.
[96] See Assize R. 320 (39 Hen. III), m. 26, for an instance of collusion between the Bishop and William de Say (a neighbouring lord), one of whose clerks had been imprisoned in the castle.
[97] *Cal. Pat.* 1391–6, pp. 45, 345; 1399–1401, p. 501. These prisoners were all clerks. Some of them may have been Lollards, for Braybrook was a vigorous opponent of heresy (see *Dict. Nat. Biog.*).
[98] *Cal. Pat.* 1422–9, p. 540; 1429–36, p. 35.
[99] *L. and P. Hen. VIII*, xiv (2), 242.
[100] *East Herts. Arch. Soc. Trans.* i (1), 45.
[1] Leland, *Itin.* quoted by J. L. Glasscock in *East Herts. Arch. Soc. Trans.* i (1), 45.
[2] *Descr. of Herts.* 23.
[3] Strype, *Life of Aylmer*, 46–7.
[4] See *Herts. and Essex Observer*, 3 June 1905. Paper by Major F. J. A. Skeet.
[5] Salmon, *Hist. of Herts.* 269.
[6] Information from Mr. J. L. Glasscock.
[7] Cussans, *Hist. of Herts. Braughing Hund.* 110.

299

A HISTORY OF HERTFORDSHIRE

The farm called Stortford Park and Park Cottages mark the site of the park of the Bishops of London. The site of the manor and the farm called Stortford Park were held on a lease by Dr. William Stanley, the precentor of St. Paul's, at the beginning of the 18th century.[8] After his death in 1827 the lease was sold, the premises then including 950 acres of land and quit-rents amounting to £13 13s.[8a] The farm, which now belongs to Mr. F. Wilby, dates from about 1600 and is built of timber and plaster, which was refaced with brick in the 18th century. It is composed of a main block and two wings; in the former is a square chimney stack with V-shaped pilasters.

Stortford Castle was the head of the barony of the Bishop of London.[9] The barony consisted of thirty-six and a third knights' fees lying in Hertford and Essex.[10] The service, however, appears to have been commuted for twenty knights in the early 13th century,[11] and by 1303 the whole barony is returned as responsible for the service of five fees only.[12] A similar reduction is noticeable in the assessment of Richmond Honour, which fell from 140 fees to five. Castle-ward rents were payable to Stortford by the lands of the barony; these like the rents of Rochester Castle were due on St. Andrew's Day.

The bishop's feodary held courts leet throughout these lands.[13] The places composing the bishop's liberty in Hertfordshire were Stortford, the two Hadhams, Albury, the three Pelhams, Meesden, Datchworth, Stevenage, Graveley and Chesfield. Castle-ward rents amounting to £5 15s. 4d. were still payable from lands within these parishes when Salmon wrote (1728). Sheriffs' warrants for execution within this area were directed to the bailiff of the liberty, who also had a right to strays and to toll of corn and cattle in the markets and fairs.[14]

The manor of *PICOTS, PIGGOTTS, PEKOTES* or *PICKETTS*, lying in the south-west of the parish, was evidently formed by subinfeudation from the manor of Stortford, of which it was held by a castle-ward rent.[15] A rental of Stortford of the late 13th century mentions 'tenementum Pycot' under the heading of North Street, but does not give any additional information.[16] In 1351 John de Mounteney of Stanford Rivers, co. Essex, released all his right in 'the land called Picottes' to James de Thame, citizen of London.[17] The latter possibly left two heiresses, for in 1377 Thomas Mounjoye and Alice his wife conveyed the manor to John Gemptyng and Agnes Grey and the heirs of Agnes, the quitclaim being from the heirs of Alice.[18]

PIGGOTTS, BACK VIEW, BISHOP'S STORTFORD

---

[8] Salmon, op. cit. 271; Feet of F. Herts. East. 5 Geo. II.
[8a] Particulars of sale communicated by Major F. Skeet. [9] *Feud. Aids*, ii, 434.
[10] *Red Bk. of Exch.* (Rolls Ser.), 187, 499; *Testa de Nevill* (Rec. Com.), 270. The number, probably by a scribal error, is given in the latter list as 26¼.
[11] *Red Bk. of Exch.* (Rolls Ser.), ii, 541.
[12] *Feud. Aids*, ii, 434.
[13] See Mins. Accts. bdle. 1140¹ no. 13, 26; Cott. Chart. xxvii, 46; *Bracton's Note Bk.* (ed. Maitland), no. 275; Chan. Inq. p.m. (Ser. 2), lx, 147; *Cal. Pat.* 1388–92, p. 443. [14] Salmon, op. cit. 279.
[15] Cussans says that this manor was held by the family of Picot by grand serjeanty (*Hist. of Herts. Braughing Hund.* 116), but he is probably confusing it with the manor of Heydon in Essex. Possibly this manor was held by the same family, but not by serjeanty.
[16] Rentals and Surv. R. 298. Mr. Glasscock suggests that this is the tenement which in the 15th century paid a rent of 15s. to the lord of Picots and which stood on the west side of North Street, on the site now occupied by the George Hotel (see *Herts. Gen. and Ant.* ii, 325).
[17] *Cal. Close*, 1349–54, p. 362.
[18] Feet of F. Herts. 1 Ric. II, no. 4.

BRAUGHING HUNDRED   BISHOP'S STORTFORD

Court rolls of the manor for 1396, 1417 and 1421 are extant, but the name of the lord is not given.[19] In 1427 a court was held for John Gaall and Agnes his wife, who were possibly the heirs of John and Agnes Gemptyng. In 1458 the court of John Leventhorp,[20] Robert Canfeld, Ralph Grey and their co-feoffees was held, and in 1470 the court of Henry Barlee (of Albury) and others.

In 1533 the manor was in the possession of Richard Apryce,[21] and a few months after it passed to his brother and heir Thomas.[22] In 1556 Roger Apryce conveyed it to John Ellyott, citizen and mercer of London.[23] He evidently left two daughters, for in Hilary 1573–4 Thomas Saunders and his wife Jane levied a fine of a moiety of the manor,[24] and in 1577 Robert Hall, jun., and his wife Anne together with Saunders and his wife conveyed the whole to Robert Hall, sen., and others.[25] This may have been for a settlement on Thomas Saunders and Jane, for in the next year they conveyed to Thomas Crabbe,[26] who held his first court in 1581.[27] In 1604 Thomas Crabbe was holding with Grace his wife, and in that year conveyed the manor to Francis Cutt of Debden, co. Essex, and John Cutt his brother (sons of Richard Cutt of Debden).[28] After the death of Francis within a year, John Cutt (called of London) sold the manor with the meadow called Pigotts Hatch, the two fields called the Leyes, &c., to Robert Salmon of Broxted, co. Essex,[29] who held his first court in 1606.[30] He granted the manor in 1622 to his son Robert,[31] who held his first court in 1649.[32] Later he joined in a sale with Nicholas Westwood of Farnham, co. Essex, and Sarah his wife, John Cleere the elder of Bengeo and Mary his wife, and John Cleere the younger and Sarah his wife to Edward Hawkins of Stortford. After the death of the latter it descended to his three daughters : Mary, who married Robert Dawgs, of Loughton, co. Essex ; Elizabeth, who married John Barrington, second son of Sir John Barrington, bart., and Susan, who married William Layer of Shepreth, co. Cambridge. In 1700 Mary Dawgs, then a widow, Susan Layer and her husband, and John Barrington, son of Elizabeth, and Anne, her daughter, wife of John Flacke of Linton, co. Cambridge, joined in a sale to John Lowe of St. Margaret's, Westminster.[33]

John Lowe left the manor by will of 1707 to his grandson John Lowe of Ashwell, co. Herts. From the latter's brother and devisee William Lowe of Henlow, co. Bedford, and of Basinghall Street, London, it came by will to Thomas Wheeler of Basinghall Street, who held it for life with remainder to his wife Susan for life, then to their four sons, William, Thomas, James Rivington, and Peter, as tenants in common. In 1801, after the death of Thomas Wheeler, Susan with her three sons sold the manor to her fourth son James Rivington Wheeler.[34]

PIGGOTTS FROM THE WEST

---

[19] Printed by Mr. Glasscock in the *Hertf. Gen.* ii, 266. The court for 1396 was held by . . . clerk, but this is probably not the name of the lord.
[20] John Leventhorp married Joan Barrington, daughter and heir of a Barrington who had grant of free warren in Thorley and Stortford in 1448 (Chart. R. 1–20 Hen. VI, no. 41). The Leventhorpes had Thorley.
[21] Recov. R. Mich. 25 Hen. VIII, rot. 434.
[22] Feet of F. Herts. Hil. 26 Hen. VIII.
[23] Ibid. East. 2 & 3 Phil. and Mary.
[24] Ibid. Hil. 16 Eliz.
[25] Ibid. East. 19 Eliz.
[26] Ibid. Trin. 20 Eliz.
[27] Ct. R. communicated by Major Skeet.
[28] Feet of F. Herts. East. 2 Jas. I.
[29] Deed communicated by Major F. Skeet. Dated Feb. 1604 (o.s.).
[30] *Herts. Gen.* ii, 377.
[31] Deed communicated by Major Skeet.
[32] *Herts. Gen.* ii, 378.
[33] Close, 12 Will. III, pt. vi, no. 9 ; Feet of F. Herts. Mich. 12 Will. III.
[34] Clutterbuck, *Hist. and Antiq. of Hertf.* iii, 253 ; Feet of F. Herts. East. 41 Geo. III.

On his death in 1834 the manor came by will to his nephew Henry James Wheeler for life, with remainder to his sons in succession; he died in 1860 and was succeeded by his son Henry James William Wheeler.[35] In 1875 Wheeler sold the manor to Lord Ellenborough, who mortgaged it to the Rev. Edward C. Dermer and others. They conveyed it in 1901 to Mrs. Helen Fitzgerald, who sold it in 1903 to Mr. Frederick Wilby, the present lord, whose family had for some generations been resident at Wind Hill House[36] (see above).

WILBY. *Gules a millrind argent and a border ermine.*

The old manor-house of Piggotts, now a farm-house occupied by the foreman to Mr. F. J. Lukies, farmer, of Shingle Hall, lies about a mile to the south-west of Bishop's Stortford. It is partly surrounded on the north and east sides by a moat containing stagnant water. The house itself is built of timber framing covered with lath and plaster, the plaster work having still the remains of a style of a decoration very common in the eastern counties during the 17th

PIGGOTTS, N° BISHOPS STORTFORD
GROUND PLAN. 17TH CENT. MODERN.

century. The surface of the walls is divided into large panels by means of slightly sunk mouldings, the panels being filled with roughly executed pattern, consisting of rows of arcs of circles placed one above another. The house is small, with gables at the front and back, and there is a long kitchen wing extending parallel with the house. The whole interior has been modernized, though the old wide kitchen fireplace still remains.

WICKHAM HALL (Weekham Hall, Wykeham Hall, xvi and xvii cent.), an estate on the north-west of the parish, apparently represents the 'Wickeham' of Domesday, where were several small holdings.[37] After 1086 it first appears about the end of the 15th century. In January 1491-2 Sir William Say conveyed his 'plot called Wykeham hall' and lands called Bryans, Bledeways and Thornes in Stortford and Farnham to Henry Freshwater for twelve years.[38] The property descended to Elizabeth daughter and co-heir of Sir William Say, who married William Blount, fourth Lord Mountjoy, and to her daughter and heir Gertrude, wife of Henry Courtenay Marquess of Exeter.[39] She was attainted in 1539, and in 1544 the farm of Wickham Hall with lands called Tolgrove, Lyvery Coppice, Whites Coppice, and Mawkins, were granted to Sir Henry Parker, Lord Morley.[40] He is said to have alienated it to John Elliott, and Elliott to have sold to William Goodwyn.[41]

In 1560 Goodwyn with Margaret his wife conveyed the farm to John Goodday.[42] In 1564 John Goodday sold it to John Gibbe,[43]s who died seised in 1597, having left his property in Stortford to his grandson George, son of his son William.[44] It descended to a William Gibbe, son apparently of Edmund, the eldest son of John Gibbe,[45] who died seised of it in January 1624-5,[46] his brother James being his heir. It was sold by James Gibbe in 1633 to Arthur Capell of Little Hadham, created Lord Capell in 1641, who also bought the manor of Wickham (from which the farm seems to have been separated, perhaps on the death of Sir William Say) from Edward Atkins. He turned the house known as Wickham Hall into a keeper's lodge. The estate descended with Little Hadham to George Devereux de Vere Capell, seventh Earl of Essex, who in 1900 sold it to Mr. Frank Stacey, the present owner.[47] The house is timber framed and plastered, of two stories with attics built on an L-shaped plan. It probably dates from the early 17th century, but has been much altered and restored. One original chimney stack remains. The brick cottage on the south of the house, formerly a pigeonhouse, is now used as a lodge.

CAPELL, Earl of Essex. *Gules a lion between three crosslets fitchy or.*

The lands of the church or *RECTORY MANOR* were held with the advowson by the precentor of St. Paul's. In 1651 the manor was sold by the trustees for the sale of church lands to William Alsop, a haberdasher of London, together with the manorhouse, fields called Brickhill Croft, Great and Little Kingsbridge, and Swinstead, a water-mill called Parson's Mill on the lower side of Great Kingsbridge, and woods called Chanters Woods and Pixsoe Wood.[48] Leases of the manor were made by the precentors in the 18th century. With their other lands it passed in 1867 to the Ecclesiastical

GILBEY, baronet. *Gules a fesse wavy with a horse rampant between two stars in the chief and the like in the foot all or.*

---

[35] Cussans, *Hist. of Herts. Braughing Hund.* 116.
[36] Information from Major F. Skeet, nephew of the present owner.
[37] *V.C.H. Herts.* i, 308*a*, 332*b*, 335*b*.
[38] Anct. D. (P.R.O.), D 967.
[39] G.E.C. *Peerage*.
[40] *L. and P. Hen. VIII*, xix (1), 278 (57).
[41] J. C. Geere, *Farnham, Essex, Past and Present*, 111.
[42] Exch. L.T.R. Memo. R. Mich. 3 Eliz. rot. 81.
[43] Com. Pleas D. Enr. East. 6 Eliz.
[44] Chan. Inq. p.m. (Ser. 2), ccxciii, 47; cccviii, 106.
[45] Geere, op. cit. 111.
[46] Chan. Inq. p.m. (Ser. 2), dxxxi, 138.
[47] Geere, op. cit. 111.
[48] Close, 1651, pt. xvii, no. 27. These are part of the present Birchanger Wood. Information from Mr. J. L. Glasscock.

Commissioners, who about 1900 sold it to Sir Walter Gilbey, bart., who has a minute book of the courts from 1656-1806. No courts are held now and the copyholders have been nearly all enfranchised.[49] The site of the manor was held on lease by the Denny family in the 18th century. It passed from them to the Sandfords, to the Bromes, to the Debarys, and is now owned and occupied by the Misses Lee, nieces of the late Rev. Thomas Debary.[50] The manor-house stands about three-quarters of a mile north-east of the church. It is of timber and plaster, of two stories with attic, and was built probably about 1600. It has, however, been almost completely encased with brick early in the 18th century. An original window remains with moulded wooden mullions. The house contains some 17th-century panelling.

CHURCHES
The church of ST. MICHAEL stands on rising ground close to the centre of the town, and consists of chancel 43 ft. by 22 ft., north chapel 43 ft. by 14 ft., south vestry and organ chamber, nave 85 ft. by 20 ft. 6 in., north aisle 84 ft. by 15 ft., south aisle 84 ft. by 14 ft., north porch 14 ft. 6 in. by 12 ft., south porch 12 ft. by 9 ft. 6 in., west tower 17 ft. by 16 ft.; all dimensions taken internally.

The church is built of flint with stone dressings; the walls are embattled; the roofs are covered with lead. The building belongs to the early part of the 15th century. In 1812 the spire and portions of the tower were taken down, the present belfry stage built, and a new spire erected; about the end of the 17th or beginning of the 18th century the chancel was lengthened eastwards by about 5 ft. 6 in.; in 1870 the north chancel aisle and south vestry were built; in 1885 the chancel clearstory was added, the chancel arch rebuilt, and an organ chamber erected on the south side of the chancel, and at various periods during the 19th century the whole church was thoroughly restored. The west tower and westernmost bay of the nave appear to be somewhat later than the rest of the church, as may be inferred from the churchwardens' accounts for 1431.[51]

In the east wall of the chancel is a large five-light modern window, and in the south wall one of three lights, the tracery of which has been renewed; in the south wall is a trefoil-headed piscina with a modern sill. The sedilia are modern. The truss roof appears to be of 15th-century work, the date 1668 appearing on one of the tie-beams probably refers to repairs only; the spandrels of the roof trusses are filled with tracery.

The nave is of six bays; the arches are of two moulded orders with a hollow between, and the label stops are carved; the piers are composed of four semi-octagonal shafts with moulded capitals and bases; the westernmost piers are wider than the others, and are each practically two responds, back to back with a vertical joint between them, these bays being probably built last as a connecting link between the tower and the nave. Over each arch of the nave arcades is a clearstory window of two lights, of modern stonework, but the inner jambs appear to be original. The low pitched king-post roof is of 15th-century date; the spandrels under the trusses are filled with tracery; the roof rests on stone corbels carved with figures of angels with shields and of saints with their emblems.

BISHOP'S STORTFORD CHURCH FROM THE SOUTH-WEST

On the south side of the north aisle at the east end is the turret which contained the stair to the roodloft; the stair is gone, but the upper and lower doorways remain. There are five windows in the north wall and one in the east, all of three lights of modern stonework, all but the inner jambs, which are original. The north doorway is original; the arch is moulded and the jambs have small moulded capitals. The head over the pointed arch is square and the spandrels are carved, one with the figure of a woman with an eye looking down on her, the other with an

---

[49] Information from Mr. J. L. Glasscock.
[50] Ibid.
[51] Payments made for covering, with straw and lead, the walls of church and tower, and of levelling the western part of the nave floor (see Glasscock, *Rec. of St. Michael's, Bishop's Stortford*, 1882).

303

angel holding a trumpet and a censer; the label stops are carved with the symbols of the four Evangelists. The two windows on either side of the porch, each of two lights, are of modern stonework externally, and most of the moulded outer doorway belongs to the 15th century.

The windows in the south aisle are similar to those in the north, but the east window has been replaced by an arched opening to the modern organ chamber. In the south wall at the east end is a small piscina with pointed arch, with plain round bowl partly damaged. The south doorway is of two moulded orders with some modern stonework.

The oak north and south doors are original but have been repaired. In the east wall of the south porch is a fragment of a stoup, and near it in the wall a piece of clunch rudely carved in the form of a horse-shoe. The truss roofs over both aisles are similar in character and date to that over the nave, with traceried spandrels, and rest on stone corbels carved with a most interesting series of figures, human and grotesque.

The west tower is of four stages with a stair turret, no longer used, in the north-west angle; a modern stair turret has been erected at the north-east angle, and the belfry and spire are modern. The lofty tower arch is of three moulded orders, separated by hollows, and the moulded responds have capitals and bases partly repaired. The west doorway has a pointed arch of three moulded orders, but the other openings in the tower are of modern stonework, except the doorway and loop-lights in the original turret.

The square bowl of the Purbeck marble font, which is of late 12th-century date, is ornamented on each side with four shallow round-arched sinkings; the stem is modern.

The 15th-century rood-screen still remains in its place; the lower panels are closed with traceried heads, the open upper panels have tracery in their arches; the cornice with its supporting groined canopy is modern.

In the chancel are eighteen oak stalls, with misericordes carved with representations of human heads, animals, birds, fishes, &c.; the fronts have traceried panels and pilaster buttresses and the ends have poppy-head finials; they are of 15th-century workmanship.

The hexagonal oak pulpit was erected in 1658[52]; the sides are carved and panelled; it stands on a hexagonal pillar and is supported by carved brackets. The communion table is modern, but it stands on the ancient altar slab.

In the vestry is an early 17th-century chest, with a hidden lock with fourteen bolts under the lid; there is a false lock with padlocks.

On the chancel floor are some brass inscriptions: one to Thomas Edgcombe, 1614; another on the same slab to an infant of the Edgcombe family; a third to Charles Denny, 1635, for twelve years senior fellow of King's College, Cambridge.

In the chancel are mural monuments to Mrs. Cordelia Denny, 1698, with arms, and to the children of Edward Maplesden, 1684-6.

There are ten bells: the treble, second (1820), third, seventh and ninth (all 1791), by John Briant; the fourth, fifth and sixth (1713), by John Waylett; the eighth a funeral bell, inscribed 'Statutum est omnibus semel mori' (1802), by John Briant; the tenor (1730), by John Waylett.

The communion plate consists of a cup, 1735; another, 1823; four patens, 1683 (?), 1711, 1772, and one modern; an almsdish, 1722; two large flagons, 1721 and 1731; also a knife and fork, 1823, and a spoon with marks erased.

The registers of baptisms, marriages and burials begin in 1561.

The church of *HOLY TRINITY* was built of stone in 1859 in 13th-century style. It consists of chancel, nave, transept and bell-turret. The living is in the gift of the vicar of Bishop's Stortford.

ALL SAINTS, Hockerill, was built of stone in 1852. It consists of a chancel, nave, with bellcot over north-east corner, baptistery, south porch, and vestries. The living is in the gift of the Lord Chancellor.

ADVOWSON
The church of Stortford was appropriated by the Bishops of London to the precentorship of St. Paul's. In 1243 the church was said to be in the gift of the bishop,[52] whereas in 1294 the precentor of St. Paul's is called the parson,[54] so that the appropriation may have been between these two dates. In 1352 the king gave licence for the appropriation of Stortford to the bishop's table instead of to the chantership, as its value was not great enough for an official of the precentor's importance,[55] but the change does not seem to have been made, for the rectory and advowson remained with the precentors until 1867, when they passed to the Ecclesiastical Commissioners. The advowson was made over by the Commissioners to the Bishop of St. Albans on the creation of that bishopric. Two endowments of great tithes have been made by the precentors to the vicarage, viz. the tithes from the farm called Stortford Park, which at the beginning of the 18th century was held on a lease for lives of the Bishop of London by Dr. William Stanley, precentor of St. Paul's, and a moiety of the great tithes of a piece of land called by Salmon 'the Earl of Essex Park,' which were given by Dr. Dibbing, precentor when Salmon wrote in 1728.[56] The great tithes of the rectory were leased out with the rectory manor.[57]

The chantry of Baldwin Victor[58] was founded in 1485 by his widow Marjory Victor. The chantry priest celebrated mass at the altar of St. John the Baptist.[59] The chantry was dissolved under Edward VI, when its property was valued at £8.[60] In 1583 the chantry priest's house and two messuages and land in Stortford, which had belonged to it, were in the possession of Oliver Godfrey and Elizabeth his wife, who conveyed them in that year to Thomas Bowyer.[61] He died seised of them in 1607, leaving a daughter and heir Helen Bowyer, then aged two.[62] The lands included some of the meadows between the river and

---

[52] It cost £5 (see Glasscock, *Rec. of St. Michael's, Bishop's Stortford*, 76).
[53] *Cal. Pat.* 1232-47, p. 355.
[54] Ibid. 1292-1301, p. 119.
[55] Ibid. 1350-4, p. 239.
[56] Cussans, *Hist. of Herts. Braughing Hund.* 271.
[57] Ibid.
[58] He was of Stanstead Mountfitchet, co. Essex.
[59] *Cal. Pat.* 1476-85, p. 498.
[60] Chant. Cert. 20, no. 67.
[61] Feet of F. Herts. East. 25 Eliz.
[62] Chan. Inq. p.m. (Ser. 2), dcxl, 50.

the road to Manewden,[63] a piece of land in 'Mochehalfacres' called Shortland *alias* Chantry Land *alias* Walter Blanks and Twyford Mill (given by Richard Wild).[64]

The house called the Chantry situated in the Hadham Road at the end of North Street probably marks the site of the priest's house.[65] It is a two-storied house of plastered timber with a tiled roof built in the latter part of the 16th century. It is L-shaped in plan with modern additions.

There were three gilds in the church of St. Michael, called the gilds of St. John the Baptist, St. Mary, and St. Michael. There are bequests to them in wills of the late 15th and early 16th centuries.[66] The gild of St. John the Baptist was connected with the chantry of Baldwin Victor, the priest celebrating at the altar of the gild chapel[67] (see above). This must have been at the east end either of the north or south aisle, both of which evidently contained altars.[68] In 1490 the collectors of the gild of St. Mary contributed a sum of £3 2*s*. 6*d*. towards church bells.[69] The latter gild was probably dissolved about 1540, for in the churchwardens' accounts for that year there is an entry for 8*d*. received for the stock of Our Lady gild.[70]

CHARITIES
The Poor's Estate which comprises the charities mentioned below is regulated by a scheme of the Court of Chancery 17 January 1851: namely, the charities of:—

1. Richard Pilston, founded by deed 1572, consisting of five almshouses at New Town, acquired by exchange under the Inclosure Act 1821 for two tenements originally given, an acre of land at Thorley let at £1 a year, and a rent-charge of 15*s*., portion of a rent-charge of £3 3*s*. issuing out of 'The Reindeer,' comprised in a decree made by a commissioner for charitable uses 3 June 1692, and secured by deed 3 April 1766 (enrolled).

2. Robert Adison *alias* Lustybludd's Charity, founded by will 1554, the bequest to be laid out in land.

3. Margaret Dane, founded by will of 1579, a legacy of £20 to be laid out in land.

4. Henry Harvey, LL.D., Master of Trinity Hall, Cambridge, founded by will of 1584, which consisted of a rent-charge of £6 to be divided between the poor of the parishes of Stortford and Littlebury, Essex.

5. John Dane, founded by deed of 1630, formerly part of workhouse.

6. Rowland Elliott, founded by will, date unknown, included in the inquisition of charitable uses above referred to and consisting of a rent-charge of £2 out of the manor of Walkers in Farnham, Essex.

7. William Ellis, founded by will of 1616, consisting of a rent-charge of 20*s*. out of premises in South Street.

8. Thomas Hoy, included in inquisition above referred to and consisting of a rent-charge of 6*s*. 8*d*. out of a messuage in Windhill.

9. John Gace and Richard Kirby, founded by wills recited in deed 11 April 1634, and now represented by a portion of the stock mentioned below arising from the sale of land in Common Down, awarded on the inclosure in 1820 in respect of original gifts.

The endowment of the Poor's Estate now consists of the five almshouses and land mentioned under Pilston's Charity, and the several rent-charges, and of a sum of £2,480 4*s*. 3*d*. consols with the official trustees, producing £62 a year in annual dividends, arising mainly from the sales of land from time to time.

The income is applied in the upkeep of the almshouses, which are inhabited by poor aged women in receipt of parochial relief, and in the distribution of coal to the poor. The amount distributed in coal averages about £50 a year.

The following charities are administered by the vicar and churchwardens, namely:—

1. The Church Estate, the donors of which are unknown, is regulated by a scheme of the High Court of Chancery 17 January 1851. The property consists of 1 a. 2 r. 27 p. of land called Little Field at Collins Cross let for £7 2*s*. yearly; the site of the old National school let for £1 yearly; a rent-charge of £3 out of 'Half Acres'; a rent-charge of £2 8*s*. out of 'The Reindeer' at Windhill; £1,584 7*s*. 6*d*. consols in the High Court of Chancery and £2,742 4*s*. 5*d*. consols in the name of the official trustees arising out of sales of land producing in annual dividends £108 3*s*. The income is applied in payment of the salaries of the organist, verger, &c., and insurance premiums.

2. Elizabeth Jones, who died in 1827 and bequeathed £500, the interest to be applied for the purpose of ornamenting and repairing the parish church. The endowment is now represented by a sum of stock producing £12 16*s*. yearly.

3. The same testatrix bequeathed £250, the interest to be distributed annually on New Year's Day in coals and clothing to the poor. The endowment is now represented by a sum of stock producing £6 16*s*. 4*d*. yearly.

4. Humphrey Hetherington, by his will without date, gave £100, the interest to be applied in bread for the poor. This sum was laid out in the purchase of land in Bishop's Stortford. The land was sold in 1885 and the proceeds invested in £278 19*s*. 5*d*. consols with the official trustees, producing £6 19*s*. 4*d*. yearly.

5. William Gibbs, by will recited in deed 9 April 1630, devised a piece of land called Long Hedge Piece, containing about 2 acres, the rent of which, amounting to £9 10*s*. 8*d*. yearly, is distributed in coal.

6. In 1862 John Baynes, by his will proved at London 21 May, gave £300, the yearly income to be applied towards repairing and ornamenting the parish church. The endowment is now represented by a sum of stock producing £7 18*s*. yearly in dividends.

7. In 1866 William Wilby, by will proved at London 23 June, gave £300, now represented by a

---

[63] Salmon, op. cit. 271.
[64] Glasscock, *Rec. of St. Michael's, Bishop's Stortford*, 68.
[65] The old chantry-house is described as at North Gate (Rentals and Surv. R. 299).
[66] P.C.C. 37 Milles, 16 Moone, 1 Bodfelde.
[67] See account of papers relating to the 'chantry and gild of St. John the Baptist' in Glasscock's *Rec. of St. Michael's, Bishop's Stortford*, 118.
[68] Only the piscina at the east end of the south aisle now remains, but there was formerly one in the north aisle.
[69] Glasscock, op. cit. 22.
[70] Ibid. 94. A rental of obit-lands and light-lands belonging to the church is printed by Mr. Glasscock (ibid. 48).

A HISTORY OF HERTFORDSHIRE

sum of £309 9s. 1d. consols, producing £7 14s. 8d. yearly, the interest to be applied in the purchase of clothing for distribution to the poor at Christmas.

The apprenticing charity of the Rev. Thomas Turner, founded by will 1706, consists of a close of land called Dovelees of about 7 acres, producing £11 4s. 6d. yearly.

In 1730 John Sandford by deed gave a rent-charge of £2 to the poor not in receipt of parochial relief. This charge is received from an estate at Collins Cross and appears to be distributed in money gifts.

The charity of Mrs. Anne Phillips, founded by deed 1744, towards the maintenance and support of the minister of the Water Lane Meeting House, consists of £610 5s. consols, in the name of the official trustees, producing £15 5s. yearly, arising from the sale in 1870 of land originally given.

The Educational Charities.[71]—Comprising the gifts of Margaret Dane, will 1579; the Rev. William Polhill, will proved in 1722; Exton Sayer, will 1730; and of the above-mentioned Elizabeth Jones. Also the Nonconformist school.[72]

BRAUGHING

Brachinges (xi cent.); Bracking, Braughinge, Brawyng (xiii cent.); Broughhynge (xvi cent.), and many other variants.

Braughing is a parish of 4,368 acres, of which 15 acres are water. Rather less than three-quarters of the area is arable land, about one-quarter grass, and a small proportion, about 252 acres, woods and plantations.[1] The parish lies high, the level for the most part being between 300 ft. and 400 ft. above the ordnance datum, and the valleys of the rivers about 100 ft. lower. The country is undulating and well wooded. The soil is mixed, the subsoil clay over chalk and gravel. Here and there the sand outcrops at the surface, and where this is the case springs of good water exist.

In 1812 an Act was passed for inclosing the common lands, then estimated at 1,300 acres, and certain Lammas lands consisting of 50 acres, also for freeing all lands within the parish from tithes by allotments to the rectors and vicar. Lammas Piece and Lammas Mead, adjoining the vicarage, were allotted to the vicar, whilst Lammas land in Langrey Mead and Sow Mead was allotted to the lord of Hamels, to whom a portion of the great tithes belonged.[2] The copyhold land has now been nearly all enfranchised.

The River Quin joins the Rib a little to the south-west of the village. To the north of this point the road to Cambridge crosses the Quin by a brick bridge of three arches, called Griggs Bridge,[3] built in 1769. Further on the road crosses the Rib on Ford Bridge, a county bridge, which in the 17th century was of wood,[4] was rebuilt in 1766[5] probably in brick, repaired in 1773,[6] and now consists of two brick arches. The New Bridge on the road to Buntingford crossing the River Rib on the west of the parish is also a county bridge.[7]

The Roman road called Stane Street, after passing through Little Hadham and then forming for a little way the boundary between Braughing and Standon, comes to an abrupt end at Horse Cross[8] in this parish. The course of the road, however, can be traced westward along the parish boundary, which follows a straight line as far as the River Rib. A little further to the west it must have crossed Ermine Street. There was a Roman settlement to the south-west of the village.[9] That Braughing was a place of importance in Saxon times is evidenced by the fact that it was the head of a hundred and also of a deanery. The Domesday Survey shows that the greater part of Braughing was held 'in alms' by a man of King Edward, and had been so held under his predecessors. There is, therefore, some reason to think that it was once royal domain, as the meeting-place of the hundred court very often seems to have been.[10] In the 10th century the church of Braughing is called 'monasterium,'[11] which possibly suggests a church of unusual importance.

The village of Braughing is situated a little to the east of Ermine Street in the valley of the River Quin. It is built on both sides of the river in the angle formed by the junction of the road to Cambridge and a road running north-east towards Furneux Pelham. The parish church of St. Mary stands about midway between these two roads, along which lie the two main streets of the village, Green End on the Cambridge road and The Street on the Pelham road. At the further end of The Street is a group of houses called Powell's Green. Green End is the main street of Braughing. At the south end of it is the village smithy. Braughing Hall close by was built in 1889; it is attached to the Congregational chapel and is used for social purposes. The rest of the village is grouped irregularly round the church, and owing to its trees and old houses and varying levels is very picturesque. Between the two main streets run three lanes, all of which cross the River Quin. These are called Malting Lane or Bridge, Fleece Lane or Bridge, and Ships Bridge.[12] Malting Lane, the southernmost, is so called from a malting at one end of it, and is also called Bell Lane from the Bell Inn at the other. The names of the other two lanes evidently recall the sheep washing which took place in the shallow part of the river here. Close to the church on the north-west is Braughing Bury, the old

---

[71] See article on the Herts. Schools, V.C.H. Herts. ii, 81. [72] Ibid. 82.
[1] Statistics from Bd. of Agric. (1905).
[2] Local and Personal Act, 52 Geo. III, cap. clxi. Copy lent by Mr. C. J. Longman.
[3] The road here was formerly called Grig's Case (Sess. R. [Herts. Co. Rec.], i, 41).
[4] Ibid. 91. [5] Ibid. 103, 105.
[6] Ibid. 127, 128, 132.
[7] Ibid. passim. Called New Bridge as early as 1667 (ibid. i, 201). Another bridge called Jennings Bridge is mentioned in 1665 (ibid. 172). Thomas Jennings had land in Braughing in the 16th century (Com. Pleas D. Enr. East. 6 Edw. VI, m. 5). See also will of Henry Johnson, 1569 (Herts. Gen. i, 238), which mentions a 'Mr. Jenyngs.'
[8] Hoare's Cross is another spelling. Hoare's Cross Field is close by. The Tithe Allotment of Standon spells it Whore's Cross.

[9] For the account of this see V.C.H. Herts. iv, 'Roman Remains.'
[10] Cf. Assize R. 6 Edw. I, Agard's MS. index, fol. 98b, where the jurors depose that it is ancient demesne.
[11] Birch, Cart. Sax. ii, 571. This is a bequest by a certain Æthelgiva of land charged with a rent in kind to the monasterium of Braughing.
[12] Shipes Bredg in 1642 (Sess. R. [Herts. Co. Rec.], i, 70).

306

manor-house, now divided into two houses. The house is approached by a fine avenue of trees. A moat to the east of it probably incloses the site of an older house. The vicarage is situated to the north of the church. Pentlows is a farm lying above it to the south, which takes its name from a 14th-century owner (see manor of Queenbury). To the west of the church is a house now divided into two, which was built about 1600, and was formerly the Rose and Crown Inn. It is a rectangular timber-framed building covered with plaster, with a projecting upper story and three brick chimney stacks. The plaster in front is divided into square and circular panels which are decorated in low relief. Another house south of the church, known as the 'Old Boys' School,' of similar date, is rectangular in plan, with herringbone brick nogging and tiled roof. It is gabled and the upper story projects. In the lane called the Causeway, to the south-west of the church, is another house of the same date. It is of red brick and timber with a plastered front with rusticated quoins in plaster, and still has its original window frames and fastenings.

The church hall at the end of the Causeway is a red brick building used for a men's club and similar purposes. It was built by Mr. H. Shepherd Cross in 1903 in place of a Memorial Hall which he had built in Ford Street in 1893 and which is now converted into cottages. The public elementary school was built in 1877 on a piece of ground called the Orchard (see under Charities). The north chapel of the church was used for a school,[13] which was carried on there until its removal to a building now used as a bakehouse at the end of Fleece Lane. It was again moved to the old house on the south of the church described above, and remained there until taken to its present site. There is a Congregational chapel to the north-west of the church dating back in origin to 1691, when Robert Billio, preacher, certified a place for Divine worship.[13a] There is also a Wesleyan chapel to the south of the church. A fair was held at Braughing within living memory, at which earthenware was one of the commodities sold.

To the south The Street is continued as Ford Street. Ford Street Farm is a 17th-century building, altered in the 18th century, of timber and plaster, the latter being decorated with comb-work. About a quarter of a mile north of Green End, on the Cambridge road, is the hamlet of Hay Street.[14] Further north still lies the hamlet of Dassels. On the east side of the road here is a farm-house, now divided into three tenements, dating from the early 17th century. It is L-shaped in plan, and is built of timber and plaster, the latter being decorated with the usual combed pattern. The roofs are tiled, and the shorter wing is gabled at both ends, while the other is hipped. It has the remains of old chimney stacks. A few of the original casements of the windows remain. At Dassels there is a Methodist chapel. Bozen Green, in the north-east of the parish, seems to preserve the name of Bordesdene of the Domesday

ROSE AND CROWN, BRAUGHING

[13] Parish Bk., 1720. There was a school before 1710 (see *V.C.H. Herts.* ii, 100).
[13a] Urwick, *Nonconformity in Herts.* 673.
[14] It is called Hay Street in the 17th century (Chan. Inq. p.m. [Ser. 2], ccccix, 25).

A HISTORY OF HERTFORDSHIRE

Survey, which lay for the most part within the parish of Little Hormead in Edwinstree Hundred, but which perhaps extended into Braughing. A little to the east of Bozen Green is a farm-house called Rotten Row. It is a two-storied building of timber and plaster, and was probably built in the 16th century,[15] but underwent considerable alteration in the 17th, 18th, and 19th centuries. It was apparently of the half H-shaped plan with interior space inclosed. The roof of the main block is covered with slate, and the wings are tiled, with hipped ends. The entrance passage and the parlour, with a 17th-century fireplace, formed the original hall. There is some 17th-century oak panelling in one of the rooms on the ground floor.

Place-names that occur in this parish are Netherstokkying, Aldithelee, Kingesho or Kingshohull, Enneworth, Fordmad (xiii cent.)[16]; Pumps Land and Sportlowfield (xvii cent.).[17] Near Sportlowfield was a loam-pit in the road to Furneux Pelham, for which the inhabitants of Braughing were indicted in 1683.[18]

MANORS Before the Conquest Braughing was held by two thegns; one, a man of King Edward, held 4 hides, and the other, a man of Asgar the Staller, 1 hide. In 1086 these holdings were united in the hands of Count Eustace of Boulogne. They were assessed at 5 hides, but there was land for eleven ploughs. A mill is mentioned in the extent.[19] The lands of the honour of Boulogne came by inheritance to Queen Maud, wife of Stephen, and the manor of Braughing was divided among several grantees. Between 1146 and 1148 Stephen granted 100s. rent in the manor to the priory of Holy Trinity, London, and at the same time he granted them 6 librates of land there in exchange for the mill and land which the queen had granted them near the Tower of London, where she had afterwards founded the hospital of St. Katherine; these 6 librates, as the charter explains, being that part of the manor left over after the rest had been granted away and including the site of the church and the market.[20] This charter was confirmed by the queen[21] and by her son Eustace Count of Boulogne.[22] Other 4 librates of land in the manor were given to Holy Trinity by Hubert the queen's chamberlain, to whom 16 librates had been granted by the king and queen.[23] The priory's lands formed the manor of *BRAUGHING* or *BRAUGHINGBURY*. The mill of Braughing was also given to the canons by Henry de Furneaux and Theobald de Braughing.[24] In 1291 their lands, rent and mill at Braughing were taxed at £37 6s. 5½d.[25] The prior had a grange there for the management of his estates.[26] By Stephen's charter he claimed to have soc, sac, toll, team and

THE MALTINGS, BRAUGHING

---

[15] It is mentioned by its present name in 1610 (Chan. Inq. p.m. [Ser. 2], cccxxii, 174).
[16] Anct. D. (P.R.O.), A 5794, 1049, 5459, 5454, 5110.
[17] Sess. R. (Herts. Co. Rec.), i, 125.
[18] Ibid. 328. [19] V.C.H. Herts. i, 322b.
[20] Cart. Antiq. N. 21; Anct. D. (P.R.O.), A 1051.
[21] Cart. Antiq. N. 22; Anct. D. (P.R.O.), A 1050; Dugdale, Mon. Angl. vi, 152.
[22] Cart. Antiq. N. 23. In 1141 Stephen had granted 100 librates of land in Anstey, Braughing and Ham to Geoffrey de Mandeville to the use of Ernulf his son (Round, Geoff. de Mandeville, 141). This he probably forfeited in 1143, and Ernulf was never restored to his father's lands.
[23] Anct. D. (P.R.O.), A 1043, 1042.
[24] Dugdale, Mon. Angl. vi, 153; Anct. D. (P.R.O.), A 1110, 6101. Henry de Furneaux owned seven parts of the mill.
[25] Pope Nich. Tax. (Rec. Com.), 14b.
[26] Assize R. 325 (15 Edw. I).

308

infangentheof over his tenants, and in that part of the manor held of the honour of Boulogne he claimed view of frankpledge 'by ancient custom of the honour, without charter,' each view being attended by the bailiff of the honour and the prior's bailiff, the former receiving 4s. as the part of the profits due to the royal officials. These liberties, together with gallows and assize of bread and ale, were allowed by the justices in 1278.[27]

In February 1531–2 the Prior of Holy Trinity surrendered to the Crown,[28] and in 1534 Braughing was granted to Sir Thomas Audley the chancellor,[29] afterwards Lord Audley of Walden.[30] In 1585 the manor was conveyed by Thomas Howard, second son of Lord Audley's daughter Margaret, who married Thomas Duke of Norfolk,[31] to John Steward of Marham, co. Norfolk.[32] John Steward died seised of the manor, with a mill, dovecote, and several fishery in Braughing, in February 1604–5.[33] John his son succeeded, but left no issue.[34] The manor appears to have passed to his brothers Humphrey and Francis Steward, and to have been divided between their sons, for Hoo Steward, son of Francis (who married Roberta Hoo), conveyed a moiety in 1668 to John Spicer and John Paltock.[35] The object of this conveyance is not clear, but before 1695 the manor (for this moiety seems to have included all manorial rights) had been sold to William Harvey of Chigwell, co. Essex,[36] M.P. for Essex in 1722. It descended to his son William, who died in 1742, and to William, son of William, who died in 1763.[37] William the eldest son of the last-named William died single and the manor came to his brother Eliab Harvey,[38] afterwards Sir Eliab Harvey, G.C.B., of the Royal Navy. He greatly distinguished himself at the battle of Trafalgar, where he commanded the *Téméraire*, celebrated in naval history and in art as the 'fighting *Téméraire.*' For his services there he was made a rear-admiral.[39] He died in 1830, leaving four co-heirs, of whom Maria, the wife of the Rev. William Tower, inherited the manor.[40] Her daughter and co-heir Maria Louisa married Col. Edward Goulburn, and their son Col. Henry Goulburn is the present lord of the manor. There are now no copyhold lands left.[41]

The other moiety of the manor seems to have consisted of the capital messuage called Braughing Bury which had been divided into two tenements.[42] Humphrey Steward (see above) left a son Humphrey,[43] and Francis Steward, apparently his son,[44] sold it to William Delawood.[45] Part of the Bury came with Hamells into the possession of Miss Mellish and was sold with that manor to Mr. H. Shepherd Cross in 1884,[46] the other part descended with Uphall and Gatesbury and was bought by Mr. C. J. Longman in 1896.[47] Both parts are now farms with barns and other farm buildings attached, although Mr. Longman's part is now let as a private house. The whole is a 17th-century plastered brick house. It contains some old panelling in the south parlour and a good oak staircase.

The manor of QUEENBURY[48] seems to have taken its name from Queen Maud and to have been the 16 librates of land which Stephen and Maud granted to Hubert de Anstey the queen's chamberlain.[49] Four of these he gave to the priory of Holy Trinity.[50] Richard and John, sons of Hubert de Anstey,[51] seem to have died without issue,[52] and his lands to have descended to his daughter Denise, who married Warin de Munchensey.[53] From her granddaughter Denise, who married Hugh de Veer,[54] the fee in Braughing passed to the former's cousin and heir Aymer de Valence, Earl of Pembroke, on whose death in 1324 it was assigned to Elizabeth Comyn, one of his co-heirs.[55]

Under Denise Munchensey this fee was held by Matthew Furneaux and Henry Pentelow, who were assessed for it in 1303.[56] Matthew Furneaux in Hilary term 1288–9 granted his 'manor of Braughing' to David le Grand for life.[57] Henry Pentelow seems to have been holding his quarter of the fee as late as 1331,[58] but Furneaux's moiety had apparently passed before that date to John Peverel,[59] and it was the latter which was known as the manor of Queenbury. In 1324 John Peverel granted the

HARVEY. *Or a chief indented sable with three crescents or therein.*

---

[27] *Plac. de Quo Warr.* (Rec. Com.), 278.
[28] Dugdale, *Mon. Angl.* vi, 125.
[29] *L. and P. Hen. VIII,* vii, 1610 (35); see ibid. xiii (2), 491 (6).
[30] Chan. Inq. p.m. (Ser. 2), lxxxvi, 100.
[31] Ibid. clxii, 167; clxi, 169.
[32] Feet of F. Herts. Mich. 27 & 28 Eliz.
[33] Chan. Inq. p.m. (Ser. 2), cclxxxvii, 86; cccclxxx, 114.
[34] *Visit. of Herts.* (Harl. Soc. xxii), 94. He had no children in 1634, when he was thirty-six years of age, and he was succeeded by his brothers, so the presumption is he left no issue.
[35] Feet of F. Herts. Trin. 20 Chas. II. According to Chauncy (op. cit. 223) Humphrey and Francis held a court in 1610, but John was still living in 1634 (*Visit. of Herts.* loc. cit.).
[36] Recov. R. East. 7 Will. III, rot. 200. The conveyance of 1668 can scarcely have been to William Harvey, for he would have been very young at that date, nor to his father Sir Eliab Harvey, for he lived until 1698, so that William would not have been holding in 1695.
[37] Morant, *Hist. of Essex,* i, 167; Recov. R. Trin. 24 Geo. II, rot. 280.
[38] Recov. R. East. 20 Geo. III, rot. 385.
[39] Cussans, *Hist. of Herts. Braughing Hund.* 190.
[40] See Feet of F. Herts. Trin. 1 Will. IV.
[41] Information from Mr. C. J. Longman.
[42] Com. Pleas D. Enr. East. 31 Geo. II, rot. 124.
[43] Chauncy, *Hist. Antiq. of Herts.* 223. Chauncy says that this Humphrey sold to William Delawood, but this seems to be an error.
[44] Called great-grandson of John.
[45] Com. Pleas D. Enr. East. 31 Geo. II, rot. 124.
[46] Information from Mr. H. Shepherd Cross.
[47] Information from Mr. C. J. Longman.
[48] Quinbury seems to be a modern form, owing to a false derivation from the River Quin.
[49] Anct. D. (P.R.O.), A 1043; *Red Bk. of Exch.* (Rolls Ser.), ii, 578. Mr. Round points out that the Anstey family held three knights' fees of the honour of Boulogne in Anstey, Hormead and Braughing, which must not be confused with the further grant made to them out of the demesne of the honour by Stephen and Maud (see Anstey).
[50] Anct. D. (P.R.O.), A 1043 (see above).
[51] Anct. D. (P.R.O.), A 1043.
[52] Richard was a minor at the time of his father's death (see *Testa de Nevill* [Rec. Com.], 269*b*).
[53] See V.C.H. *Surr.* iii, 222; *Feud. Aids,* ii, 435.
[54] *Abbrev. Plac.* (Rec. Com.), 252.
[55] *Cal. Close,* 1323–7, p. 272.
[56] *Feud. Aids,* ii, 435.
[57] De Banco R. 76, m. 21.
[58] *Cal. Close,* 1330–3, p. 199. The holders given for fees in such cases are not, however, always correct. Pentelow's property seems to be represented later by the estate called Pentlow's Farm.
[59] Ibid. 1323–7, p. 265.

A HISTORY OF HERTFORDSHIRE

manor to John de Preston and his wife Joan and Peter de Horseden for their lives.[60] In 1448 William Bradbury and his wife Margaret, holding in right of Margaret, conveyed it to Roger Ree and Thomas Gryme.[61] There seems to be no further record of the manor until 1527, when Richard Bishop of Norwich obtained licence to grant it to Trinity Hall, Cambridge.[62] The manor has since remained in the possession of the college. The house called Quinbury, now a farm, is situated to the south-east of Hay Street.

TRINITY HALL, CAMBRIDGE. *Sable a crescent in a border engrailed ermine.*

The manor of *TURKS* is first heard of at the beginning of the 15th century when it was in the possession of Robert Turk.[63] His daughter Joan married Roland Barley, who survived his wife and died seised of it in 1448, leaving a son Thomas.[64] Before 1527 this manor had come into the same hands as Queenbury and was given with that manor to Trinity Hall, Cambridge, in 1527,[65] in whose possession it has since remained.

Turks Wood on the north-east of the parish marks the site of this manor. Within the wood is a nearly circular homestead moat with an entrance on the south-west side.

In 1086 Count Eustace of Boulogne had an estate at *COCKHAMSTED* which was held in the time of Edward the Confessor by Gouti, one of Harold's thegns, and was assessed at 2 hides, with land for six ploughs. For a considerable time after this date there seem to be no records relating to this manor, but during this interval it was apparently granted to the priory of Anglesey, co. Cambridge. In 1291 the prior was assessed at £6 for his property in Standon, and, as the prior is not otherwise known to have held land there, this entry may refer to Cockhamsted in Braughing, which perhaps extended into Standon.[66] In 1346 Thomas de Chedworth[67] by licence of the Earl of Pembroke granted a messuage and 180 acres of land, with meadow, pasture and wood, formerly belonging to Sir Robert Scales, to the prior and convent.[68] Before this, however, the prior seems to have sub-enfeoffed a tenant of his other lands there, for the manor appears in the hands of lay lords who held of the priory. In 1319 Geoffrey de la Lee had a grant of free warren in his demesne lands in Braughing.[69] John de la Lee his son[70] had a similar grant in 1366 and also licence to inclose and impark 300 acres of land in Braughing and Albury.[71] From Sir Walter de la Lee, son of John, the manor of Cockhamsted passed to one of his sisters, Joan, who married John Barley,[72] and in February 1445-6 their son John Barley died seised of the manor held jointly with his wife Katherine of the Prior of Anglesey.[73] Henry his son was his heir. Henry was succeeded in 1475 by his son William Barley, who died seised of the manor held as above in March 1521-2.[74] It descended to his son Henry, and in 1529 to the latter's son William,[75] whose daughter and co-heir Dorothy married Thomas Leventhorpe of Sawbridgeworth,[76] and they levied a fine of it in 1570.[77] Their son Thomas[78] died before 1594, when the manor was divided between his daughters and co-heirs.[79] Of these Dorothy wife of Simeon Brograve seems eventually to have inherited the whole manor. In August 1611 George and Thomas Whitmore, who were the informers as to defective titles usually called 'fishing grantees,' obtained a grant from the Crown of the manor as lately belonging to the priory of Anglesey.[80] They conveyed their title to William Millett and Paul Mason, who again conveyed it to Zachariah Blackstock of London.[81] Simeon Brograve and Dorothy his wife seem, however, to have been able to show that the king only had a rent issuing from the manor which had formerly been paid to the Prior of Anglesey, who had parted with the manor and land, and that the manor was rightly theirs.[82]

The manor was settled on their fourth son Edward, and he settled it on his third son Edward.[83] The latter died without issue, and his widow Susan conveyed the manor to the heir-at-law Thomas Brograve,[84] who in 1716 conveyed it to Robert Colman, apparently in trust for Jacob Houblon[85] of Hallingbury Place, co. Essex. The latter settled it in 1758 on his son Jacob.[86] John Archer Houblon, son of the latter, sold Cockhamsted to John Larken of Braughing,[87] who devised it to his nephew the Rev. William P. Larken.[88] It was bought from Mr. Larken's representatives in 1894 by Mr. Robert Lanyon of Spitsberg, Kansas, U.S.A., whose son now holds it.

The moated house called Cockhamsted, situated on the east of the parish, is a farm occupied by Mr. Grigg.

GATESBURY seems to have originally formed part of the manor of Westmill[89] (q.v.), and to have been held under the Montfitchets and their successors by the family of Gatesbury. At the end of the 12th century it was held by John de Gatesbury,[90] who gave lands there to the monastery of Holywell in Middlesex.[91] Sir Richard de Gatesbury was holding

---

[60] Feet of F. Herts. 18 Edw. II, no. 394. [61] Ibid. 26 Hen. VI, no. 144.
[62] L. and P. Hen. VIII, iv (2), 3213 (26); Chan. Inq. p.m. (Ser. 2), xlvi, 111.
[63] Chan. Inq. p.m. 27 Hen. VI, no. 5. For an earlier Robert Turk (Turkys) see Assize R. 318 (32 Hen. III).
[64] Chan. Inq. p.m. 27 Hen. VI, no. 5.
[65] L. and P. Hen. VIII, iv (2), 3213 (26).
[66] Pope Nich. Tax. (Rec. Com.), 14b.
[67] In 1338 Thomas de Chedworth had received from Simon de Shyringe, called 'Cornmongere,' a messuage with a meadow and land in the field called Monecroft (Anct. D. [P.R.O.], A 5244).
[68] Anct. D. (P.R.O.), A 975; Inq. a.q.d. file 256, no. 2; *Cal. Pat.* 1345-8, p. 203.
[69] *Cal. Chart. R.* 1300-26, p. 417.

[70] See chart. quoted by Chauncy, *Hist. Antiq. of Herts.* 147.
[71] Chart. R. 39 & 40 Edw. III, m. 7, no. 21.
[72] Close, 50 Edw. III, pt. ii, m. 12, 9; Morant, *Hist. of Essex,* i, 393, 570.
[73] Chan. Inq. p.m. 24 Hen. VI, no. 29.
[74] Ibid. (Ser. 2), xxxviii, 24.
[75] Ibid. li, 5. [76] Ibid. ccxvii, 133.
[77] Feet of F. Herts. Trin. 12 Eliz.
[78] Chan. Inq. p.m. (Ser. 2), ccxvii, 133; Feet of F. Herts. Hil. 31 Eliz.
[79] Feet of F. Herts. Mich. 36 & 37 Eliz.; Hil. 38 Eliz.
[80] *Cal. S. P. Dom.* 1611-18, p. 70.
[81] Com. Pleas D. Enr. Mich. 9 Jas. I, m. 7; East. 10 Jas. I, m. 1.
[82] Ibid. East. 10 Jas. I, m. 1; *Cal. S. P. Dom.* 1611-18, p. 84.

[83] Chauncy, op. cit. 227.
[84] Ibid.
[85] Feet of F. Herts. East. 2 Geo. I; see Com. Pleas D. Enr. East. 31 Geo. II, m. 124.
[86] Recov. R. East. 31 Geo. II, rot. 304; Com. Pleas D. Enr. East. 31 Geo. II, m. 124.
[87] Clutterbuck, op. cit. iii, 152.
[88] Cussans, *Hist. of Herts. Braughing Hund.* 193.
[89] See *Cal. Close,* 1288-96, p. 463.
[90] For this John de Gatesbury as a witness to deeds see Anct. D. (P.R.O.), A 5823, 5824; B 1032 is a grant of land in Gatesbury by a John de Gatesbury, but this may be another John.
[91] Dugdale, *Mon. Angl.* iv, 393. Not the manor, as Chauncy says.

310

about a century later.[93] His son Richard de Gatesbury[93] received a grant of free warren in 1320.[94] In 1323 he settled the manor on his son John and John's wife Elizabeth and their issue with remainder to John's brothers Adam, Ralph, and Roger.[95] Richard was living in 1324,[96] but John had succeeded before 1328.[97] A further settlement was made by John on his brothers Adam and Roger, failing his own issue, in Hilary term 1330–1.[98] The manor seems to have remained in this family until the beginning of the 15th century, when an Adam de Gatesbury appears to have left two sisters and heirs, Joan, who married John Elveden, and Elizabeth, who married John Tuwe. He also left a widow Agnes, who married Thomas Tuwe.[99] In 1456 John Joskyn and Elizabeth his wife, kinswoman and co-heir of Adam de Gatesbury (and probably the above Elizabeth Tuwe or her daughter), and Henry Elveden of Gyng Mounteney, co. Essex, kinsman and another heir of the same Adam,[100] levied a fine of the manor of Maisters in Westmill and of lands in Braughing.[1] Henry Elveden was outlawed for a murder in 1462, and in 1463 his moiety was granted to John Sturgeon.[2] In 1472, however, he received a general pardon,[3] and he died seised of Gatesbury in 1498.[4] His son Henry had predeceased him in 1493,[5] leaving Denise his daughter and heir, then aged one year. She was her grandfather's heir, and in 1515 was married to Humphrey Fitz Herbert of Uphall.[6]

The tenure of the Fitz Herberts is marked by a series of lawsuits resulting from quarrels among themselves and with their neighbours. About 1535 Humphrey brought a suit in the Court of Requests against Sir Henry Parker, lessee of the other half of Gatesbury, for entering tenements belonging to Uphall and for cutting down trees on his half of Gatesbury.[7] In 1520 the vicar took proceedings in the court of Star Chamber against Humphrey Fitz Herbert for an attack made upon him in church, the immediate cause of quarrel being the presence of John Fitz Herbert, a priest, the defendant's brother, whom the defendant had brought to arbitrate between the vicar and the parishioners, and on whom, by the defendant's account, the vicar had laid violent hands, the defendant retaliating by an attack on the vicar.[8] After the death of Humphrey several actions were brought against Denise by copyholders of the manor for her refusal to admit them to their lands,[9] the reason given in one case being that the tenant's predecessor had forfeited the land for not taking off his cap when he met Humphrey in the streets of London.[10] In 1578 Denise, who was then about eighty-four years of age, brought an action in the same court against her eldest son John for evading the settlements made by Humphrey on herself and younger sons.[11]

John son of Humphrey and Denise seems to have left a son Thomas, who was holding this moiety in 1589, and in that year conveyed it to Thomas Hanchett, who was already seised of the other.[12] Thomas Hanchett conveyed it by fine of Hilary term 1608–9 to Sir Arthur Heveningham and two others,[13] apparently in trust for John Stone, who died seised of it in 1640, leaving a son and heir Richard.[14] In March 1656–7 Richard Stone, described as of Stukeley, co. Hunts., and John Stone of Uphall, his son and heir, sold the manor with lands called Gatesbury Green, Broom Hill, Brickhill (now Brick Kiln Hill), Sacombe, the Mawne (now the Malm), &c., a warren in Braughing, a water-mill and fulling mill called Gatesbury (Gaddesbury) Mill to Robert Dicer of London.[15] Through Dorothy, daughter and heir of Robert Dicer,[16] the manor passed to William Harvey,[17] and thereafter descended with Braughing until about 1890, when it was bought from the executors of Mrs. Tower by Mr. Robert Lanyon, a Cornishman by birth, who emigrated to America and there made a fortune. In 1896 he sold Gatesbury Mill and Farm to Mr. C. J. Longman, who resides at Upp Hall. Gatesbury Mill, on the River Rib, was pulled down in 1906. The mill-house has been converted into two cottages.[18]

The other half of the manor which descended to John Joskyn was forfeited by him in 1461 [19] and granted to Nicholas Harpisfield.[20] Later it was restored to Edward Joskyn, son of John.[21] Through an heiress named Elizabeth, possibly daughter of Edward, this half came to Richard Braughing, who died seised of it in January 1517–18, Richard his son succeeding.[22] Richard seems to have left two co-heiresses, for in 1559 Nicholas Fulham and Elizabeth his wife conveyed a fourth part of the manor to Thomas Hanchett.[23] A certain Thomas Braughing apparently also had some interest which he conveyed at the same time to Andrew Gray.[24] In 1583 Thomas Hanchett joined in a conveyance with Sir Arthur Heveningham and his wife Mary and Sir Thomas Barnardiston and his wife Elizabeth (Mary and Elizabeth being presumably the Braughing heiresses) and Andrew Gray to Andrew Paschall, sen., and Andrew Paschall, jun.[25] This was probably for assurance of title. Soon after Thomas Hanchett bought the other half (see above) and re-united the manor.

The house called Gatesbury is situated a little to the east of the Cambridge road where it branches off at Puckeridge. A wood called Gatesbury Wood lies to the north-east.

The manor of UPHALL first appears in the 15th century. Its name is probably derived from its situation on the high land to the south-east of the village. In 1461 it appears in the possession of John Joskyn (see Gatesbury) and was forfeited by him

---

[92] See Anct. D. (P.R.O.), A 5460; C 2034; Cal. Close, 1288–96, p. 463.
[93] See Anct. D. (P.R.O.), C 322.
[94] Cal. Chart. R. 1300–26, p. 431.
[95] Feet of F. Herts. 17 Edw. II, no. 367.
[96] Cal. Close, 1323–7, p. 330.
[97] De Banco R. 272, m. 46.
[98] Feet of F. Herts. 5 Edw. III, no. 117.
[99] Cf. Early Chan. Proc. bdle. 5, no. 128; Feet of F. Herts. 35 Hen. VI, no. 180. Agnes Tuwe afterwards became Agnes More.
[100] This Henry was son of Thomas Elveden (see Anct. D. [P.R.O.], A 1033).
[1] Feet of F. Herts. 35 Hen. VI, no. 180.
[2] Cal. Pat. 1461–7, p. 296.
[3] Ibid. 1467–77, p. 369.
[4] Chan. Inq. p.m. (Ser. 2), xxx, 47.
[5] Ibid. ix, 24.
[6] Ibid. xxx, 47.
[7] Ct. of Req. bdle. 3, no. 259.
[8] Star Chamb. Proc. bdle. 19, no. 319, 316.
[9] Chan. Inq. p.m. bdle. 20, no. 71, 67, 56.
[10] Ibid. no. 71.
[11] Ibid. bdle. 74, no. 92.
[12] Recov. R. Trin. 31 Eliz. rot. 31.
[13] Feet of F. Herts. Hil. 6 Jas. I.
[14] Chan. Inq. p.m. (Ser. 2), ccccxcv, 85.
[15] Com. Pleas D. Enr. East. 1657, m. 6 d.
[16] Morant, op. cit. 167.
[17] Recov. R. Trin. 24 Geo. II, rot. 280.
[18] Information from Mr. Longman.
[19] Parl. R. v, 477b, 588a.
[20] Cal. Pat. 1461–7, p. 356.
[21] Parl. R. vi, 33a.
[22] Chan. Inq. p.m. (Ser. 2), lxxix, 254.
[23] Feet of F. Herts. Mich. 1 & 2 Eliz.
[24] Recov. R. Trin. 1559, rot. 547.
[25] Feet of F. Herts. East. 25 Eliz.

A HISTORY OF HERTFORDSHIRE

and granted to Nicholas Harpisfield.[26] Edward Joskyn, who was reinstated, seems to have left one heiress Elizabeth (see above) and may have left a second Katherine, for by fine of Hilary term 1484-5 Thomas Grey and his wife Katherine (who were holding in her right) conveyed the manor to Ralph Josselin and others.[27] This seems to have been in trust for Robert Fitz Herbert, for he died seised in 1515.[28] His son was Humphrey Fitz Herbert, who married Denise Elveden, and Uphall then descended with the first half of Gatesbury (q.v.). With Gatesbury it was bought in 1896 by Mr. C. J. Longman. Mr. Longman's estate includes fields called the Malm, the Moad, Sibdale, Haven End Pasture, Old Field, Brick Kiln Field,[29] Hither and Further Tunnocks, Windmill Ley, Great and Little Readings and Hoare's Cross Field.[30]

LONGMAN of Upp Hall. *Gules three lozenge-shaped buckles or.*

BRAUGHING. UPP HALL GROUND PLAN — EARLY 17TH CENTURY / MODERN

Upp Hall, the residence of Mr. Longman, is situated on high ground about a mile south-east of the village, with which it is connected by a road. A considerable part of the late 16th or early 17th-century house still exists, although much added to and modernized. The house is built of the early 2-in. bricks, and a brick outside plinth runs round the walls of the old house, appearing inside where modern work has been added, making it possible to obtain an accurate plan of the original house, so much of it, at least, as has survived, as there are clear indications that the principal or west front has been shortened. The old part of the house consists of a long building of the usual two stories with attics, running north and south. At the south end is a wing projecting eastwards, and near the north end is a smaller projection which probably contained the staircase. The old building to the north of this has been swept away, and modern kitchen offices substituted.

The west front has two steep brick gables, with copings above the roof, and connected at their bases with a parapet; there are gables, but no parapets, on the south and east fronts. All the windows have straight brick drips or hoods over them, and the wide front windows are of six lights, and have the original oak mullions and transoms. The window to the drawing room is partly blocked by the large fireplace, but, as both appear to belong to the same period, the large window was probably inserted for the sake of symmetry, as it comes in the centre of a gable. The chimneys appear to have been rebuilt. The principal entrance is on the west front, and retains the original door, though the wooden portico is comparatively modern. The head of the door is formed by a four-centred arch, the door itself being made of two thicknesses of oak planks, and on the outside are fixed narrow fillet and cavetto mouldings dividing the door into three vertical panels. Two plain iron strap hinges appear on the outside.

On entering the house the old hall is on the right. It is still used as a hall, but a modern screen takes the place of the old one. The fireplace is 10 ft. wide, and has a straight lintel. At the back, adjoining the seats, are two small niches, probably made to hold flagons. Similar niches in the ingle-nooks may be found in many old houses and cottages in the county.

Beyond the hall is the drawing room, with the library forming the wing at the back. A modern passage, with staircase, has been formed behind the hall. To the left of the entrance is the dining room, in which is a very good but simple example of a wood chimney-piece of the time of Queen Anne. It is flanked by wide slightly-projecting plain pilasters carried up to the ceiling. The overmantel has a narrower plain pilaster in the centre. There is a moulded cornice at the top, broken round the pilaster. In the room over the dining room is a stone fireplace of the usual early 17th-century type.

The old gate piers which afforded entrance to the forecourt still stand facing the west entrance door, about 111 ft. west of the main building. The piers are built of brick, and are square on plan. They have stone cornices finished on the top with large stone balls. The southern inclosure of the forecourt, whether wall or buildings, has disappeared, and the modern avenue comes in on that side, but the inclosing building still remains on the north side. It is a very long and lofty barn of ten bays, built of brick, running east and west, the east end being within 50 ft. of the house itself. There appear at one time to have been two wide doorways with pointed arches on each side, but only one of those on the south side is in its original state, the others being built up in whole or part. The old window openings, of which a good number exist, are mere slits, 8 in. wide, splayed on the inner side.

On the north wall, outside, near the centre of the building, are two curious little aumbries, the use of which has not been satisfactorily explained. One is a plain sinking in the wall, about 13 in. wide and 15 in. deep, covered with a four-centred arch; the

---

[26] *Cal. Pat.* 1461-7, p. 356.
[27] *Feet of F. Herts.* 2 Ric. III, no. 4.
[28] *Chan. Inq. p.m.* (Ser. 2), xxx, 95.
[29] Bricks from this field are said to have been used for the foundations of Old Hall.
[30] Particulars for sale, 1890. Lent by Mr. C. J. Longman.

312

BRAUGHING HUNDRED
BRAUGHING

other is a little larger and has a curious little side cupboard or arm, 12 in. wide, running for about 2 ft. behind the brickwork.

The west end of the barn seems to have had a return building to the south, as the existing buttress has a partly built up narrow light in it, and has evidently been formed from the remains of a wall. Marks on the south wall of the barn show this returned building to have been 30 ft. wide. The barn is probably not earlier than the first half of the 17th century, though the burned-brick diapers in it might suggest an earlier date.

The house and barn stand within a moated inclosure. A portion of the moat on the east side of the house is still filled with water, and is about 25 ft. wide. In length it is about 245 ft., and it has a return westwards at its north end. There are indications in the ground that the moat extended to some 335 ft. in length on the north side, then turned southward past the west end of the barn. The west side seems not to run parallel with the east side, and this probably accounts for the skew end to the barn, which is parallel to the sinking in the ground indicating the position of the moat.

HAMELLS seems to have been part of the manor of Milkley in Standon which extended into Braughing, and does not appear as a separate estate until a house was built there by John Brograve,[31] who was attorney for the duchy of Lancaster under Elizabeth and James I and was knighted by James I.

He served as *custos rotulorum* for the county of Hertford for thirty years. He died in 1613 and was buried at Braughing.[32] His son Simeon Brograve, who succeeded him, obtained a grant of free warren

UPP HALL, BRAUGHING: OLD BARN FROM THE SOUTH-WEST

for his several fisheries within his Hertfordshire lands in 1617.[33] His brother John Brograve rebuilt the house at Hamells for him at his own expense.[34] Simeon Brograve, who was also attorney for the duchy of Lancaster and *custos rotulorum* for thirty-three years, died in January 1638–9 seised of the manors of Hamells *alias* Milkley Hamells and Cockhamsted.[35] He was succeeded by his son John, who was one of Cromwell's commissioners for the county of Hertford.[35a] Thomas Brograve, son of John, was created a baronet in March 1662–3. He was Sheriff of Hertfordshire from 1664 to 1665 and died in 1670 and was buried at Braughing. John his eldest son

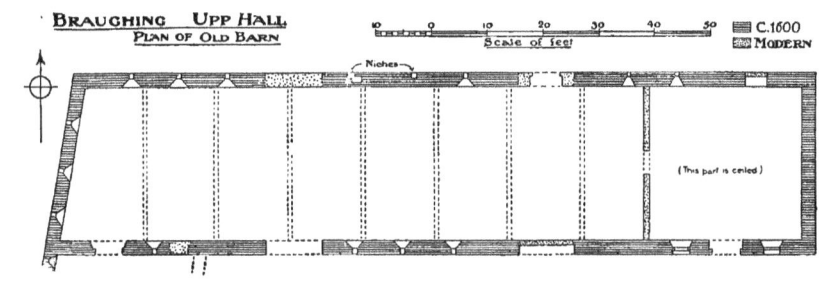

BRAUGHING UPP HALL
PLAN OF OLD BARN

died unmarried in 1691 and was also buried at Braughing, and Thomas brother of John died without issue and was buried there in 1707.[36]

[31] For a description of this house see Chauncy, op. cit. 226.
[32] *Dict. Nat. Biog.*
[33] Pat. 15 Jas. I, pt. xv, no. 4.
[34] M.I. at Braughing.
[35] Chan. Inq. p.m. (Ser. 2), ccccxci, 18.
[35a] See Urwick, *Nonconformity in Herts.* 670.
[36] G.E.C. *Baronetage*, iii, 272; M.I. at Braughing. See Recov. R. Mich. 1657, rot. 126.

313

A HISTORY OF HERTFORDSHIRE

The entail on the estates had been barred by Sir Thomas Brograve in 1691, and the manors had been settled to the use of himself and his heirs.[37] These heirs were his sisters Jemima Brograve and Honoria wife of John Stevenson. Jemima died before 1712. In that year the manor of Hamells with Masters, Mentley alias Milkley, and Westmillbury with Berkesdon, the capital messuage called Hamells with four pews in the churches of Braughing and Westmill, the water-mill in Braughing and the tenement called Pentlows there were sold by order of the Court of Chancery to Ralph Freeman, one of Sir Thomas Brograve's creditors.[38] Ralph Freeman, who was M.P. for the county in 1722, made extensive additions to the house and grounds at Hamells.[39] In the latter he planted great numbers of trees brought from Aspenden and other places ; he made a bowling-green, fenced in a warren, built a greenhouse, pigeon-house and beehouse, dug a pond in the park, re-fronted the east side of the house, set up iron gates before the west front, built a chapel, set up a great gate and a hunting gate in Langram Mead, and otherwise altered and 'improved' the estate.[40] Ralph Freeman died in 1742. His son William died in 1749, when the manors passed to the latter's brother, the Rev. Dr. Ralph Freeman,[41] prebendary of Salisbury. He devised them to his great-nephew Philip Yorke, son of Catherine daughter of William Freeman, who had married the Hon. Charles Yorke, for three days Lord Chancellor of England,[42] and had died in 1763. Philip Yorke, third Earl of Hardwicke, sold the property in 1796 to John Mellish of Albemarle Street,[43] who two years afterwards fell a victim to an assault by footpads on Hounslow Heath.[44] His daughter Catherine Martha Mellish[45] survived until 1880. She left the estate to the Rt. Hon. C. P. Villiers with reversion to Mr. H. F. Gladwin, and they in 1884 combined in a sale of the manors of Hamells cum Masters, Milkley and Westmill to Mr. H. Shepherd Cross, the present owner, who resides at Hamells Park.[46] The house stands in a park of 200 acres, which lies partly in

BROGRAVE of Hamells, baronet. *Argent three leopards gules.*

Westmill and partly in Braughing. The mill at Braughing mentioned above as part of the estate is no longer working.

The origin of the manor of *FRIARS* in Braughing is obscure, as no continuity can be traced between it and any monastic estate. It seems possible, however, that it represents the land held by the Priory of Haliwell in Braughing. Lands at Gatesbury were given to the nuns there in the reign of Richard I by John de Gatesbury,[47] and by a deed witnessed by John de Gatesbury Ralph de Langeford gave them all his land lying in the field called Sibbedellersfield.[48] In 1200 Henry Furneaux was in mercy for having unjustly disseised the prioress of her free tenement in Gatesbury.[49] The prioress contributed 10s. 4¼d., assessed on her goods at Braughing, towards a lay subsidy in 1307.[50] At the time of the Dissolution the convent had property at Braughing assessed at £4.[51] There seems to be no grant of this estate by Henry VIII, but if it may be identified with the manor of Friars[52] it had come by the end of the 16th century into the possession of the Newport family. Robert Newport suffered a recovery of Friars in 1580[53] and Edward Newport in 1586.[54] In 1603 Thomas Hanchett of Uphall was holding it and mortgaged it in that year to William Whettell of Thetford, co. Norfolk.[55] It is then described as the manor of Friars in Braughing and Albury, and as including a water corn-mill with the stream belonging to it in Braughing and *inter alia* 1½ acres in a field named Sibdale. The latter is evidently the 'Sibbedellersfield' of the grant mentioned above, which forms one link in the identification of Friars with the land held by Haliwell. The manor seems to have been conveyed by Thomas Hanchett to John Stone together with Gatesbury, for John Stone died seised of it in 1640,[56] and it then descended with Gatesbury (q.v.). The house called Braughing Friars is situated on the south-east of the parish.

The manor of *HOTOFTS* was the holding of the family of Hotoft, who had lands in Braughing in the 13th and 14th centuries.[57] In the 16th century it was held by a family named Greene. Richard Greene, son and heir of a John Greene, died in 1561 and was buried in the church.[58] Richard Greene, also buried in the church, died in 1610 seised of the manor of Hotofts, a capital messuage called Hotofts and another called Rotten Row, and 200 acres of land.[59] He was a bachelor, aged seventy-eight at the time of his death, and had bequeathed his property to his brother Henry Greene, with remainder to Ralph his brother and Francis Harvey, Justice of the King's Bench, his kinsman. These were both dead before the death of Henry in 1635, and Sir Stephen Harvey, son of Francis, had also died in 1630, so that the title descended to Francis son of Sir Stephen Harvey,

YORKE, Earl of Hardwicke. *Argent a saltire azure with a bezant thereon.*

---

[37] Close, 3 Will. and Mary, pt. ix, no. 22 ; Recov. R. Hil. 3 Will. and Mary, rot. 43.
[38] Chan. Decr. R. 1335, no. 6.
[39] For drawings of it see Add. MS. 32348, fol. 170.
[40] See Hardwicke Papers, vols. dcccxci–iii (Add. MS. 36239–41).
[41] See Recov. R. East. 23 Geo. II, rot. 323.
[42] G.E.C. *Peerage,* s.v. Hardwicke.
[43] Close, 36 Geo. III, pt. xxiii, no. 6.
[44] M.I. in Braughing Church.

[45] See Com. Pleas D. Enr. Mich. 7 Geo. IV, m. 20.
[46] Information from Mr. H. Shepherd Cross.
[47] Dugdale, *Mon. Angl.* iv, 391.
[48] Harl. Chart. 52 I. 12. The grant was made for his soul and the soul of his lord William Foliot.
[49] Dugdale, *Mon. Angl.* iv, 391.
[50] Lay Subs. R. bdle. 120, no. 8.
[51] *Valor Eccl.* (Rec. Com.), i, 394.
[52] The fact that this manor was called Friars would probably be no argument against its having been owned by a nunnery. 'Friars' seems to have been a generic name applied to any monastic estate.
[53] Recov. R. Hil. 1580, rot. 459.
[54] Ibid. Trin. 1586, rot. 9.
[55] Com. Pleas D. Enr. Hil. 1 Jas. I, m. 16.
[56] Chan. Inq. p.m. (Ser. 2), ccccxcv, 85.
[57] *Cal. Close,* 1339–41, p. 85 ; Harl. Chart. 52 I. 12.
[58] M.I. in the church.
[59] Chan. Inq. p.m. (Ser. 2), cccxxii, 174.

314

BRAUGHING : UPP HALL FROM THE WEST

BRAUGHING CHURCH FROM THE SOUTH

then aged seven.[60] Francis died seised in 1644, when the manor passed to his brother Richard.[61] It was sold soon afterwards to Sir Hoo Steward, who was holding it in 1668,[62] and remained with the Stewards until 1704, when Francis Steward conveyed it to Samuel Mason.[63] In 1733 John Mason conveyed it to Margaret Long, widow,[64] but possibly for life only, for in the settlement by Jacob Houblon of his property in Braughing on his son Jacob in 1758 Hotofts is included and is said to have been purchased of John Mason.[65] It then descended with Cockhamsted.

CHURCH The church of ST. MARY consists of chancel 34 ft. by 16 ft. 6 in., small north chapel now used as an organ chamber and vestry, nave 63 ft. by 16 ft. 6 in., north aisle 63 ft. by 12 ft. 6 in., south aisle 64 ft. by 15 ft., large south porch, west tower 14 ft. square, all internal dimensions. The walls are of flint, with stone dressings; the porch and tower are covered with cement, and the north chapel is built of red brick. The walls of the nave and south porch are embattled. The chancel belongs to the early part of the 13th century, about 1220; the nave with its aisles and porch and the west tower were rebuilt about 1416[66] and the north chapel was added early in the 17th century. In 1888 the church was thoroughly restored, the stonework of most of the windows having been renewed, and in 1901 the chancel was repaired.

The window in the east wall of the chancel is modern, but in the north wall are two 13th-century lancet windows, repaired; one is open, the other is blocked, but can be seen in the vestry. The windows and blocked doorway in the south wall are mostly of modern stonework; there is a low-side window near the chancel arch. The chancel arch is of 15th-century work, and has two splayed orders, the outer order being continuous; the inner has jambs with modern moulded capitals and bases. The roof is chiefly modern, but contains some old trussed rafters.

The eastern and larger part of the north chapel has its floor raised to cover a vault; it is now used as a vestry; the western portion contains the organ. The windows are modern, but some old timbers remain in the flat roof. A painted inscription on the wall plate records the erection of the chapel by Simeon Brograve, who died in 1639.

The nave has arcades of four bays of the 15th century. The arches are of two orders; the piers have four engaged shafts separated by hollow chamfers, and have moulded capitals and bases. In the small portion of wall at the east end of the north arcade is a small trefoiled opening, about 5 ft. from the floor, with splayed jambs next the nave. In the south-east angle of the nave is the stair turret to the rood-loft and to the roof above; the doorway is in the south aisle; the doorway to the rood-loft is blocked, and there is an upper one on to the roof, the turret being carried some height above the nave wall and embattled round the top; a quatrefoil opening in the aisle to light the stair is now blocked. The three-light clearstory windows are of modern stonework, all but their inner jambs, which are original.

The 15th-century roof has moulded ribs with carved bosses, and figures of angels at the feet of the intermediate trusses; the panels are plastered. The eastern bay is more richly treated and with painted decorations; the painting, however, has been renewed.

The eastern part of the north aisle is raised 6 in. above the nave floor. In the east wall is a three-light window, unglazed, opening into the north chapel; the jambs are original but the tracery is modern. The three windows in the north wall and one in the west wall are of three lights, with modern tracery under four-centred arches; the jambs are original. The north doorway, now blocked, has an arch of two moulded orders, and label with grotesque heads, all much worn.

The windows in the south aisle are similar to those in the north aisle. The south doorway has a moulded arch under a square head with traceried spandrels, and a label with defaced head stops. The 15th-century roofs over the aisles are of similar detail to the nave roof and rest on stone corbels carved with angels bearing shields.

The south porch has a parvise over it, and is a lofty structure, standing well above the aisle roof; at each of its southern angles are two buttresses with cusped gablets, and at each of its four angles is a crocketed pinnacle; the walls are embattled. The doorway has a two-centred moulded arch under a square head, with traceried spandrels; the side windows in the porch are of two lights with traceried heads. In the south-east corner is a stoup with a round basin, slightly broken. The inner door is not central with the porch; the greater wall space is on the east side, which was possibly the position of the ladder to the room above, there being no trace of a stone stair. The room over, the floor of which has been removed, was lighted by a large two-light traceried window with a square head, flanked on either side by a niche with cusped arch under a square head.

The west tower is of four stages with embattled parapet, and a slight timber spire, covered with lead. The tower arch is of three moulded orders, the two outer orders being continuous, the inner resting on jambs with moulded capitals and bases. It is of early 15th-century date. The west doorway has a two-centred arch under a square head; the arch mouldings are continuous and die on the tower basecourse; the spandrels are traceried. The doorway is flanked on either side by a niche for an image having a cusped and ribbed canopy with a carved finial. These are somewhat unusual features beside west doorways of Hertfordshire churches.[67] The corbels which supported the figures show remains of tracery. The three-light window above has modern tracery. The third stage has a quatrefoil opening in each of its north, west and south walls. The belfry has on each side a window of two cinquefoiled lights, with a quatrefoil in its head. These have all been repaired.

The font is modern, but the old one stands at the east end of the north aisle, and is of early 14th-century date. The sides of the octagonal basin have cusped panels, all much mutilated; the flat oak cover belongs to the early part of the 17th century.

---

[60] Chan. Inq. p.m. (Ser. 2), ccclxxx, 84; Ct. of Wards, Feod. Surv. no. 17.
[61] Chan. Inq. p.m. (Ser. 2), dxxiii, 50.
[62] Feet of F. Herts. Trin. 20 Chas. II.
[63] Ibid. Trin. 3 Anne.
[64] Ibid. 6 & 7 Geo. II.
[65] Com. Pleas D. Enr. East. 31 Geo. II, rot. 124.
[66] In 1416 John Kyllum of St. Stephen's, Walbrook, left £5 to the work of the body of the church (Will, P.C.C. Marche 33).
[67] The neighbouring church of Westmill has niches set in the jamb of the west doorway.

In the nave are some 16th-century seats with buttressed bench ends.

On the east wall of the south aisle are brasses of a civilian and his wife, without inscription, but of about 1485; on the floor is a brass inscription to Richard Grene, died 1561; another, with arms, to Richard Grene, died 1610; an inscription to Barbara Hanchett, died 1561, and the lower part of a lady's figure, probably of the late 15th century. On the north side of the chancel is a large monument to John Brograve, who died in 1625, and his younger brother Charles, who died in 1602. The monument is of marble and alabaster; on the panelled tomb, under a canopy supported by Corinthian columns, lie the two effigies in armour; on the cornice above is a cartouche bearing their arms, and behind the figures is an inscription. On the same side of the chancel is a mural monument to Simeon Brograve, who died in 1639, and his wife Dorothy, who died in 1645. On the south side of the chancel are mural monuments to Augustin Steward, with his bust in armour, with his arms above, who died in 1597, and to Sir John Brograve, who died in 1593, with arms above.

In the north aisle is a large painting of the Resurrection, probably of 17th-century work; it has only been recently discovered, and may have formed part of an altar-piece.

There are eight bells: the first three by Robert Catlin, 1745, presented by William Freman; the fourth by William Harbert, 1628; the fifth inscribed 'Deus in adiutorium meum intende I C,' 1562; the sixth, seventh and tenor by Miles Graye, 1615, 1653 and 1631 respectively.

The communion plate consists of cup, large paten, and flagon, 1718, and modern paten.

The registers of baptisms, marriages and burials begin in 1563.

ADVOWSON The church was granted to the priory of Holy Trinity by Queen Maud about the same time as the manor.[68] In 1217 the legate Gualo signified the approval of the Holy See for the papal sympathies shown by the priory during the Barons' War by confirming the church of Braughing,[69] and this was followed by a confirmation of William Bishop of London, whose charter reserved a vicarial portion for a priest, who was to be presented by the canons and to serve the parish with the help of a chaplain.[70] After the Dissolution the rectory and advowson descended with the manor of Braughing. On the division of the manor between Humphrey and Francis Steward, one-half descended with the manor of Braughing. The other half was sold by Francis Steward, grandson probably of Humphrey, to William Delawood,[71] who presented in 1680.[72] He bequeathed his property to Isaac and Abraham Houblon of London, merchants.[73] The families of these two brothers died out before 1758, when this moiety of the rectory and advowson had come to Jacob Houblon, grandson of their brother Jacob, who in that year made a settlement on his son Jacob.[74] The presentations were made by the Harveys and Houblons alternately until 1832, when the Rev. William Tower (see Braughing) bought the second moiety of the advowson.[75]

The chapel of ST. JAMES, GATESBURY, was probably founded by one of the Gatesbury family. It was granted by Richard de Gatesbury to the canons of Holy Trinity with its tithes and appurtenances, except the tithes of land called 'Little Reding' held by the nuns of Haliwell,[76] on condition that the canons celebrated four masses weekly in the chapel.[77] In 1487 Henry Elveden, successor of Richard de Gatesbury, commuted the masses to two, to be celebrated weekly in the chapel of Holy Trinity within the nave of the conventual church.[78] Probably the chapel fell into decay after this. The advowson was still mentioned in an inquisition on Henry Elveden in 1515.[79]

CHARITIES The charity of Thomas Jenyns, founded by will, 1579, is regulated by scheme of the Charity Commissioners 2 April 1867. The endowment consists of a yearly payment of £8 13s. 4d. by the Fishmongers' Company, a rent-charge of £3 issuing out of Ford Street farm, and a piece of land called 'The Orchard' with the school thereon. By an order of the Charity Commissioners 30 September 1904 it was determined that the Orchard and school together with a yearly sum of £3 15s. should form the endowment of 'Jenyns School Foundation.' The residue of the income is applied as follows: £2 12s. in bread to twelve poor widows, £1 to the parish council towards the repair of bridges, £1 to poor girls getting married, and the remainder in small sums to the poor on Old Christmas Day.

Thomas Blossom, as stated in the Parliamentary returns of 1786, gave a rent-charge of 10s. to the poor. This sum is paid out of land called Austen Wells and distributed in small sums to the poor on Old Christmas Day.

In 1595 Matthew Wall by his will gave a rent-charge of 20s. out of a house and about 12 acres of land at Green End in Braughing. This sum is applied as follows: 3s. 6d. to poor, 6s. 8d. to twenty school children, 4s. 10d. to sexton and clerk, and 5s. to the vicar and churchwardens for their trouble.

In 1612 William Bonest by will devised his tenement in Overbury to the churchwardens upon trust that they should place not more than four widows to dwell there rent free; and he also gave £1 yearly out of a field called Dassel Field to be distributed equally among the four poor widows.

In 1663 Edward Younge, D.D., by his will gave a yearly sum of 40s. to the poor. The annuity was redeemed in 1869 by the transfer to the official trustees of stock, now £67 consols, producing

---

[68] Cott. R. xiii, 18 (1).
[69] Ibid. (2); Cal. Papal Letters, i, 52.
[70] Cott. R. xiii (3); Lond. Epis. Reg. FitzJames, fol. 55. In 1432 the churchwardens and parishioners brought a suit against the vicar in the London consistory court for not maintaining a chaplain (Lond. Epis. Reg. Fitz James, fol. 126, 127).
[71] Com. Pleas D. Enr. East. 21 Geo. II, rot. 124.
[72] Inst. Bks. P.R.O.
[73] See his will quoted by Clutterbuck, op. cit. iii, 60.
[74] Com. Pleas D. Enr. East. 21 Geo. II, m. 324. The Henry Houblon mentioned in the deed must have been son of Isaac. Abraham had a son Richard and a daughter Anne, who married Henry first Viscount Palmerston (Berry, Essex Gen. 164; Visit. Essex [Harl. Soc. xiv], 633; Morant, op. cit. ii, 513). Abraham and Henry were holding the property jointly in 1703 (Recov. R. Trin. 2 Anne, rot. 134).
[75] Cussans, Hist. of Herts. Braughing Hund. 198.
[76] Anct. D. (P.R.O.), A 1111.
[77] Ibid. A 1033.
[78] Ibid.
[79] Chan. Inq. p.m. (Ser. 2), xxx, 47.

BRAUGHING HUNDRED

£1 13*s.* 4*d.* yearly, which is distributed to the poor in the same manner as Blossom's Charity.

In 1694 William Delawood by his will gave £5 yearly to the poor. The annuity is paid out of an estate called Hormead Hall, and is distributed to the poor in the same manner as Blossom's Charity.

By an award made in pursuance of an inclosure in 1812[80] a piece of land containing 2 a. 36 p. was allotted for a public stone and gravel-pit. The land was sold in 1854 and the proceeds invested in £109 14*s.* consols in the names of four trustees.

The annual dividends, amounting to £2 14*s.* 8*d.*, are applied towards the repair of the roads.

In 1710 Marmaduke Tenant, by his will dated 7 February, gave £4 yearly out of a farm called High Street Farm for instructing eight poor boys. This sum is received by the school managers.

The Congregational Chapel Manse and Trust Property comprised in indentures of 18 May 1803 and 13 November 1844, and indenture of 21 June 1888, is regulated by a scheme of the Charity Commissioners dated 3 June 1908.

EASTWICK

Esteuiche (xi cent.); Estuic (xii cent.); Estuick, Estwyk, Estwyke (xiii cent.); Estwyk atte Flore (xiv cent.); Eastuick (xvi cent.).

The parish of Eastwick is a narrow strip of land of 840 acres lying between the parishes of Gilston and Hunsdon. On the south it is bounded by the stream called Canons Brook, which here divides Hertfordshire from Essex. The height above sea level is greatest in the north, where it attains about 260 ft. in Eastwick Wood. The village stands about 135 ft. above ordnance datum and from it the land slopes still further to the banks of the Stort Navigation and Canons Brook, a district much liable to floods. In 1905 there were 422¾ acres of arable land, 152½ of permanent grass and 118 of woods and plantations in this parish.[1] The geological formation is London Clay.

There is no line of railway within the parish. The chief road is a branch road from the main road to Newmarket, which enters the parish at Eastwick village and thence runs westward along the valley of the Stort Navigation, to enter the parish of Hunsdon at its south-eastern corner. The village, which with the church is situated in the south of the parish near the Stort, is very small. The rectory stands close by the church; the manor-house of Eastwick Hall is considerably to the north. A road leads to it from the village and continues under the name of Cockrobin Lane to Eastwick Wood in the extreme north of this parish, and thence into Sawbridgeworth. In Eastwick Wood is the fragment of a homestead moat.

At the time of the Domesday Survey *MANOR* the manor of *EASTWICK* was held by Geoffrey de Bech, successor to Ilbert, the first Norman sheriff of the county.[2] It is not known who was the heir or successor of Geoffrey de Bech, but in 1138 Baldwin son of Gilbert de Clare gave the church of Eastwick to the abbey of Bourne in Lincolnshire, by his foundation charter to that monastery.[3] It seems reasonable to suppose that Eastwick Manor was also in his hands at that date, for early in the 13th century it is found forming part of the honour of Bourne (Brunne),[4] held by the Wakes, the descendants of the founder of Bourne Abbey through the marriage of Baldwin's daughter Emma to Hugh Wake.[5] Baldwin Wake, lord of Liddell in Cumberland and descendant of this Hugh,[6] was holding Eastwick in chief of the king at the time of the *Testa de Nevill*,[7] and died seised of it in 1282.[8] The overlordship descended with the barony of Wake[9] till the death of Edmund Earl of Kent in 1408 without issue, when the rights of overlordship in Eastwick, if not already lapsed, are no longer traceable.

WAKE. *Or two bars gules with three roundels gules in the chief.*

In 1086 the tenant in demesne at Eastwick under Geoffrey de Bech was Rainald,[10] of whom, however, nothing further is known. In the 12th century it was held by the family of Tany, of whom Ascolf de Tany is found holding land 'in Essex and Herts.' as early as 1131,[11] and various other members of the Tany family occur frequently with such holdings on the 12th-century Pipe Rolls and in the *Red Book of the Exchequer*.[12] The earliest specific mention of a Tany at Eastwick is, however, in 1194, when Richard de Tany, son of Reginald de Tany,[12] sued the Abbot of Bourne in Lincolnshire for the right of presentation to the church of Eastwick.[14] Early in the 13th century Richard de Tany held 'two fees in Eastwick and Bengeo of the honour of Bourne,'[15] and later in the century another Richard son of Peter was holding,[16] to whom Henry III made grants of free warren, a weekly market on Tuesday and a fair on the vigil, feast and morrow of St. Botolph, in 1253.[17] This

TANY. *Or six eagles sable.*

---

[80] Local and Personal Act, 52 Geo. III, cap. clxi.
[1] Statistics from Bd. of Agric. (1905).
[2] *V.C.H. Herts.* i, 335*b*, 273, 282.
[3] Dugdale, *Mon.* vi, 370.
[4] *Red Bk. of Exch.* (Rolls Ser.), 505. The date given of this charter is 1210–12.
[5] J. H. Round, *Peerage Studies*, 75; *Geoffrey de Mandeville*, 160.
[6] Dugdale, *Baronage*, i, 539.
[7] *Testa de Nevill* (Rec. Com.), 269, 280.
[8] Chan. Inq. p.m. 10 Edw. I, no. 439.
[9] Inq. a.q.d. file 25, no. 13; Chan. Inq. p.m. 29 Edw. I, no. 38; 11 Edw. II, no. 38; 15 Edw. III, no. 40; 23 Edw. III, no. 75; 26 Edw. III, no. 54; 20 Ric. II, no. 30; 1 Hen. IV, file 14, no. 56; see G.E.C. *Peerage*, viii, 35.
[10] *V.C.H. Herts.* i, 335*b*.
[11] Hunter, *Mag. Rot. Scacc. de* 31 *Hen. I* (Rec. Com.), 53. Eastwick was less than 10 miles as the crow flies from the manor of Stapleford Tawney in Essex.
[12] *Red Bk. of Exch.* (Rolls Ser.), 174, 319, 498, 507; Hunter, *Gt. R. of the Pipe* 2–4 *Hen. II* (Rec. Com.), 132; 1 *Ric. I*, 22, 24, 227.
[13] For Reginald see Bengeo in Hertford Hundred.
[14] *Rot. Cur. Reg.* (Rec. Com.), i, 4, 7, 69. See above on overlordship of Eastwick, also below on advowson of Eastwick.
[15] *Red Bk. of Exch.* (Rolls Ser.), 505.
[16] See Feet of F. Herts. 53 Hen. III, no. 615 (Temple Chelsen in Bengeo).
[17] *Cal. Chart. R.* 1226–57, p. 429.

317

A HISTORY OF HERTFORDSHIRE

Richard took a prominent part in the Barons' Wars. In 1266 we hear of him 'coming to the King's Court to treat of his peace with him.'[18] By the close of the year 1270 he had been succeeded by his son Richard,[19] of whom it was reported in 1274 that he 'held assize of bread and ale and view of frankpledge in Eastwick.'[20] He is almost certainly identical with the Richard de Tany who in 1295 was holding the manor of Eastwick, value £40, by the service of two knights' fees.[21] He was succeeded by his son Roger, who died seised of Eastwick Manor in 1301, leaving an infant son Lawrence to succeed him.[22] Lawrence was only nineteen when he died in 1317, leaving as heir to Eastwick his sister Margaret, then aged sixteen.[23] She married John de Drokensford, and they in 1329 received a quitclaim of the third of the manor held in dower by Margaret widow of Laurence de Tany, then wife of Thomas de Weston.[24] Margaret predeceased her husband, who held Eastwick 'by courtesy' until his death in 1341.[25] His son Thomas de Drokensford, who is styled 'knight' in 1346, in that year granted the manor to Nicholas le Blake of Ware and his wife Margery, to hold for life.[26]

Thomas de Drokensford died in 1361, leaving an only daughter and heir Anne, then aged four, who subsequently married Thomas Mandeville, son of Walter Mandeville of Black Notley in Essex.[27] Thomas son and heir of Thomas Mandeville died seised of Eastwick in 1400,[28] leaving as heirs his two sisters, Joan the wife of John Barry and Alice wife of Helmyngus Leget, both of full age. Eastwick fell to the share of Alice, on whom and her first husband (Leget) the manor was settled in 1408,[29] and on her and her second husband (Roger Spice) in 1413.[30] Alice survived her second husband, who seems to have been succeeded in the tenure of Eastwick Manor by Clement Spice, who was holding in 1428,[31] and after him by Roger Spice. The latter, in Michaelmas 1447, sold the manor of Eastwick to William Oldhall, kt.[32] William Oldhall purchased the neighbouring manor of Hunsdon either at or about this date, and for nearly two hundred years after this the two manors followed exactly the same descent.[33] Hunsdon being the larger and more important of the two, the Eastwick tenants attended the Hunsdon courts, the last separate court known to have been held for Eastwick being in 1527.[34] When Hunsdon Manor in 1532 became Hunsdon Honour, Eastwick formed part of that honour. The two properties are last found in the same hands in 1637, in which year Henry Earl of Dover, then of Hunsdon, conveyed Eastwick to trustees,[35] and it was shortly afterwards sold to Sir John Gore of Gilston, kt.,[36] probably in order to raise money for the Royalist cause. From him descended with the manors in Gilston (q.v.) to Mr. A. S. Bowlby, the present lord of the manor.

A mill worth 5s. is recorded in the Domesday Survey, but there is no mention again of a mill in Eastwick until 1607, when it may be concluded that of the two mills owned by the lord of Hunsdon and Eastwick one was an Eastwick mill.[37] Both the mills were acquired by Sir John Gore in 1641,[38] but only Hunsdon Mill is mentioned in the sale to John Plumer in 1701.[39]

CHURCH The church of ST. BOTOLPH was rebuilt, all but the west tower, in 1872, some of the old material being re-used; the stonework of the tower has been renewed. It consists of chancel, north organ chamber, nave with north porch, and west tower; all the walls are faced with flint and have stone dressings; the roofs are tiled.

The original 13th-century chancel arch has been re-erected in the church; it is of two richly-moulded orders, with three detached Purbeck marble shafts in the jambs, with moulded capitals and bases. On the sill of one of the north windows of the chancel is the bowl of a piscina, without sufficient detail to determine its date. The tower is of three stages, unbuttressed, with embattled parapet, but has been re-faced.

Under the tower is the recumbent effigy in stone of a knight with crossed legs; he is clad in chain mail and a long surcoat; on his left arm is a long shield. The plinth below the slab on which the effigy lies is modern. The figure belongs to the middle of the 13th century, and may be of Richard de Tany who died about 1270. It is in a very good state of preservation.

On the tower wall is a brass figure of a lady in Elizabethan costume, a shield and part of an inscription; the figure is that of Joan wife of Robert Lee, whose figure has disappeared. The remaining part of the inscription reads: 'which Robert died ye 23 day of January 1564 and the sayd Joan died the . . . day of . . .' Salmon also states that the brass is a palimpsest and gives the inscription.

There are three bells: the treble bears an inscription in English, illegible; the second is inscribed 'Vox Augustini sonet in aure dei,' without date; the third is by John Clark, 1601.

The communion plate consists of cup, 1719; one paten, 1705; another, 1735; and a modern flagon.

The registers of baptisms and burials begin in 1555, those of marriages in 1556.

ADVOWSON A priest is included among the tenants of Eastwick Manor at the time of the Domesday Survey.[40] In 1138 Baldwin son of Gilbert de Clare (see the manor) granted the church of Eastwick to Bourne Abbey, Lincolnshire, a house of his own foundation.[41] In 1194 a dispute arose between the Abbot of Bourne and Richard de Tany, lord of the manor of Eastwick, concerning the right of presentation,

---

[18] Cal. Pat. 1258–66, p. 575.
[19] Excerpta e Rot. Fin. (Rec. Com.), ii, 528.
[20] Hund. R. (Rec. Com.), i, 191; Assize R. 323 (6 Edw. I).
[21] Inq. a.q.d. file 25, no. 13.
[22] Chan. Inq. p.m. 29 Edw. I, no. 38.
[23] Ibid. 11 Edw. II, no. 38.
[24] Feet of F. Herts. 3 Edw. III, no. 32.
[25] Chan. Inq. p.m. 15 Edw. III, no. 40.
[26] Cal. Close, 1346–99, p. 71.
[27] Chan. Inq. p.m. 35 Edw. III, no. 74; Morant, Hist. of Essex, ii, 179, 443.
[28] Chan. Inq. p.m. 1 Hen. IV, no. 56. According to Morant this Thomas was a grandson of Anne, but this is impossible.
[29] Feet of F. Div. Co. Mich. 10 Hen. IV, no. 43.
[30] Ibid. Hil. 14 Hen. IV, no. 93; Early Chan. Proc. bdle. 22, no. 136.
[31] Feud. Aids, ii, 451.
[32] Feet of F. Herts. Mich. 26 Hen. VI, no. 139; Close, 37 Hen. VI, m. 9.
[33] For this descent see manor of Hunsdon.
[34] Ct. R. (Gen. Ser.), portf. 177, no. 44, 45. There are no Court Rolls in the P.R.O. for either manor after their separation in the 17th century.
[35] Feet of F. Div. Co. Mich. 13 Chas. I.
[36] Close, 17 Chas. I, pt. xxiii, no. 20.
[37] Recov. R. Mich. 5 Jas. I, rot. 187.
[38] Close, 17 Chas. I, pt. xxiii, no. 20.
[39] Ibid. 13 Will. III, pt. viii, no. 11.
[40] V.C.H. Herts. i, 335b.
[41] Dugdale, Mon. vi, 370. This grant was confirmed in 1327 (Chart. R. 1 Edw. III, m. 24, no. 41).

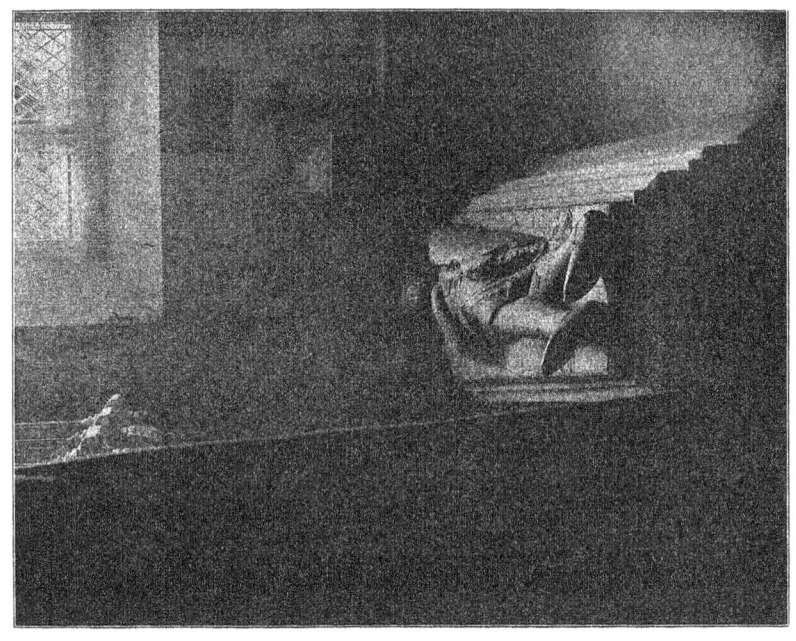

BRAUGHING CHURCH MONUMENT TO JOHN AND CHARLES BROGRAVE

EASTWICK CHURCH: 13TH-CENTURY EFFIGY

BRAUGHING HUNDRED

Richard de Tany claiming that such right had been exercised by his father Reginald de Tany, whose nominee had been forcibly ousted by the abbot.[42] The lord of Eastwick must have won his suit, for the advowson is included in an extent of the manor in 1300.[43] The living is given as a vicarage in 1535,[44] but seems to have been endowed with the tithes later. The advowson subsequently passed with the manor[45] until the purchase of the latter by Mr. Hodgson from Mr. Plumer-Ward in 1850, when the presentation to the living was retained by Mr. Plumer-Ward, who presented in 1852 and 1866. The advowson was purchased in 1870 by the incumbent, the Rev. J. R. Pursell,[46] who apparently sold it to Mr. John Hodgson, who presented in 1874.[47] It has since descended with the manor.

CHARITIES

In 1599 Sir George Carey, K.G., Lord Hunsdon, by his will proved in the P.C.C. 27 September 1603, gave a sum of money, which was afterwards invested in land situate in Great Parndon in Essex, to the poor of Eastwick and Hunsdon. The land was sold in 1906 and the proceeds invested in North-Eastern Railway 4 per cent. Guaranteed Stock in the name of the official trustees, and the parish of Eastwick receives the dividends, £6 12s. 10d. yearly, on a sum of £166, being a moiety of the stock. The charity is distributed to poor widows.

See also under the parish of Hunsdon.

In the Parliamentary Returns of 1786 it is stated that a donor unknown gave a house to the poor which was occupied by two poor families rent free.

GILSTON

Gedeleston (xii cent.); Godeleston, Gedeleston (xiv cent.); Godulston (xv cent.); Gelston (xvi cent.); Gilston (xvii cent.).

Gilston is a small parish of 984 acres, of which 10 are water. On the south-east it is bounded by the River Stort, which divides it from the county of Essex. It adjoins Sawbridgeworth on the east and there is a detached part of Sawbridgeworth on the south-west, whilst cut out from this on the extreme south is a small detached part of Gilston.[1] The parish is low lying, for the most part less than 200 ft. above the ordnance datum, and slopes down from north to south.

Of the total extent of Gilston about 330 acres are permanent grass, 260 acres arable land, and 70 acres woods and plantations.[2] The chief woods are Golden Grove on the north, Home Wood and Gibson's Shaw on the west, whilst Gilston Park occupies a large space on the south-west. Ditchingford, Solsden, Dunstalls, Start, Oxstid, Long Mead and Full Mead were common fields, but no inclosure award has been made.[2a] A stream called Fiddler's Brook runs south through the parish and joins the River Stort. The road from Eastwick runs in an easterly direction through the parish, ultimately joining the road from London to Sawbridgeworth. From this road another branches off at Pye Corner, and runs north past the church and Overhall Farm towards the parish of Widford.

Gilston is not mentioned in the Domesday Survey and was probably part of the vill of Sawbridgeworth. Besides the tenure of the manors, evidence of this is seen in the intermingling of the boundaries. The church of St. Mary and the manor-house of Overhall lie together on the high ground in the north of the parish; the village is at Pye Corner on the high road in the south of the parish. The Plume of Feathers Inn,[3] which stands here, is a 17th-century house of two stories. It is timber-framed and plastered outside with a central porch and a chimney stack with diagonal shafts. The rectory lies near the park, and the schools built in 1856 are close by. There was a fulling-mill in Gilston in the 13th century.[3a]

The Gilston and Eastwick Working Men's Club was built by Mr. A. S. Bowlby in 1908, in memory of his father Mr. E. S. Bowlby. To the south of the village is Terlings Park, the residence of Mr. R. E. Johnston. This estate takes its name from a family of Terling who had land in Gilston in the 15th century.[4] In 1602 the messuage called Terlings was sold by Robert Stephyn to John Howe.[5] From 1683 to 1847 it was in the possession of the family of Turvin.[5a]

MANORS

There is no mention of Gilston in the Domesday Survey, and it seems to have formed part of the manor of Sawbridgeworth held by Geoffrey de Mandeville. Before the end of the 12th century the Mandevilles had subinfeudated,[6] and Gilston was held as one knight's fee of the barony of Mandeville.[7] The overlordship passed through Beatrice, aunt and heir of William de Mandeville, to the Say family, and through Beatrice de Say, granddaughter of the elder Beatrice, to Geoffrey Fitz Piers, created Earl of Essex in 1199, and through their daughter Maud to Humphrey de Bohun. It descended with the Bohuns, Earls of Hereford and Essex,[8] until the marriage of Eleanor de Bohun brought it to Thomas Duke of Gloucester. His daughter and ultimate heir Anne married Edward Earl of Stafford. In 1420 Gilston was said to be held of the Countess of Stafford,[9] but after her death in 1438 its tenure seems to have been lost, for in 1444 it is returned as held of the king of the duchy of Lancaster.[10]

Under the Mandevilles and their successors Gilston was held in two moieties as the manors of Overhall and Netherhall, the names corresponding apparently

---

[42] *Rot. Cur. Reg.* (Rec. Com.), i, 4, 7, 69.
[43] Chan. Inq. p.m. 29 Edw. I, no. 38.
[44] *Valor Eccl.* (Rec. Com.), i, 452.
[45] See references under manor, also Inst. Bks. (P.R.O.).
[46] Cussans, *Hist. of Herts. Braughing Hund.* 66. [47] *Clergy List.*
[1] This part of Gilston is within the union of Ware, the rest is in the union of Bishop's Stortford.
[2] Statistics from Bd. of Agric. (1905).

[2a] Tithe Bk. of 17th cent. in parish chest, communicated by Mr. C. E. Johnston.
[3] In 1697 the justices refused to renew the licence of this house (*Sess. R.* [Herts. Co. Rec.], i, 427).
[3a] Assize R. 323, m. 35 (6–7 Edw. I).
[4] Early Chan. Proc. bdle. 56, no. 150; see also a Subsidy Roll of 1545 printed in *Herts. Gen.* ii, 273.
[5] Com. Pleas D. Enr. East. 44 Eliz.

[5a] Their tomb is in Gilston churchyard (see C. E. Johnston, 'Gilston Church,' *East Herts. Arch. Soc. Trans.* ii, 57).
[6] See *Rot. Cur. Reg.* (Rec. Com.), i, 167 and below.
[7] *Testa de Nevill* (Rec. Com.), 269.
[8] *Feud. Aids,* ii, 434; Chan. Inq p.m. 30 Edw. I, no. 58; 47 Edw. III, no. 30.
[9] Chan. Inq. p.m. 7 Hen. V, no. 19.
[10] Ibid. 22 Hen. VI, no. 28.

319

A HISTORY OF HERTFORDSHIRE

with their geographical position, Overhall occupying the higher ground in the north of the parish, Netherhall the lower ground further south.

The manor of OVERHALL was held in the 13th century by the family of Ros.[11] In 1287 Alice de Ros claimed view of frankpledge in the vill of Gilston,[12] and she was assessed for half a fee there in 1303.[13] She was presumably holding in dower, for a Robert de Ros is returned as holder of the fee in Gilston in the inquisition on Humphrey de Bohun in 1302,[14] and was among the tenants in Gilston assessed for a lay subsidy in 1307.[15] A John de Ros, probably son of Robert, succeeded, and died seised of the manor held jointly with his wife Alice in 1373, his heir being his grandson John, son of John de Ros, deceased.[16] Alice died two years afterwards; the inquisition taken at her death is unfortunately missing, but Morant, apparently quoting from it, says that the younger John died without issue and that his aunt Ellen, wife of Sir Geoffrey de Brockholes, was the heir.[17] Geoffrey de Brockholes was holding this half-fee under the Duke of Gloucester in 1397.[18] In 1419 Ellen Brockholes, his wife, died seised of the manor, leaving as heirs her daughter Joan, widow of Thomas Aspall, and her grandson John, son of John Sumpter and her daughter Mary.[19] Joan married as her third husband Robert Armeburgh.[20] John Sumpter, who died in 1420, left two sisters and heirs, Ellen wife of James Bellers and Christina wife of Thomas Bernard.[21] His moiety seems to have been settled on Ellen Bellers.[22] Ellen survived her husband and married secondly Ralph Holt,[23] with whom she brought a suit in Chancery against her father-in-law Ralph Bellers for the recovery of the manor, which had been settled on Ralph Bellers for payment of his son's debts.[24]

In 1444 Joan Armeburgh died seised of the other moiety of the manor,[25] held with Robert her husband under settlement [26] for their lives, with remainder to a certain John Palmer and his issue, and contingent remainder first to Palmer's sister Joan, then to Philip Thornbury and others in trust apparently for Ralph and Ellen Holt.[27] The Palmers' interest seems to have devolved on the Holts before 1453 or thereabouts, when they brought a suit in Chancery to recover the manor against Thornbury and the other feoffees.[28] In 1453 Ralph Holt and Ellen conveyed their moiety of the manor and the reversion of the other after the death of Robert Armeburgh to Thomas Ardern and others,[29] evidently in trust for Sir Peter Ardern. He left the manor by will for the endowment of a chantry in the church of Latton, co. Essex.[30] Licence was given to his executors to carry out the bequest in 1477.[31] The manor remained attached to the chantry until its dissolution in the reign of Edward VI. It was then granted to John Perient.[32] Elizabeth, Perient's widow, married Henry Poole, and they in 1567 had licence to alienate Overhall to John Chauncy.[33] John Chauncy appears in possession in 1568,[34] but the final conveyance by Henry and Elizabeth Poole does not seem to have been made until 1570.[35] In 1572 John Chauncy sold the manor to William Parker.[36] Parker conveyed it in 1577 to Humphrey Corbett,[37] who died seised at Newington, co. Middlesex, in 1609.[38] His kinsman and heir Rowland Corbett succeeded. He settled the manor on his son Richard on his marriage with Jane Fowler in 1624.[39] Rowland died at Grantham in 1634.[40] Before 1657 the manor had been sold to Sir John Gore,[41] and then descended with Netherhall (q.v.).

The old manor-house of Overhall is now a farm.

The manor of NETHERHALL was held under the Earls of Essex by the family of Goldington. There seems to have been a Thomas de Goldington holding about the middle of the 12th century, who was succeeded before 1199 by his son Peter de Goldington.[42] In 1287 Peter, son of a Peter de Goldington, claimed view of frankpledge in Gilston,[43] and he with Alice de Ros was assessed for half a knight's fee there held of the Earl of Hereford in 1303.[44] Goldington's interest passed to John Dyer, who was contemporary with John de Ros of Overhall (see above).[45] In the next century the manor was acquired by Sir William Estfield, kt., a citizen of London and lord mayor in 1429 and 1437.[46] His will is dated February 1446-7, and in it he makes a bequest to the church of Gilston.[47] His heir was his grandson John Bohun, son of his daughter Margaret wife of Humphrey Bohun,[48] to whom the manor of Netherhall passed.[49] Ursula daughter of John Bohun married Sir Robert Southwell, and they in 1494

---

[11] The subinfeudation probably took place considerably before this. The church was in existence in the first half of the 12th century and would probably not have been built until the manor was occupied by a tenant.
[12] Assize R. 325.
[13] Feud. Aids, ii, 439.
[14] Chan. Misc. file 61, no. 1. See also Rooshall in Sarratt; V.C.H. Herts. ii, 439.
[15] Subs. R. bdle. 120, no. 8.
[16] Chan. Inq. p.m. 47 Edw. III, no. 30.
[17] Morant, Hist. of Essex, ii, 536; Visit. Essex (Harl. Soc. xiv), 591.
[18] Chan. Inq. p.m. 21 Ric. II, no. 29 (on Thomas Duke of Gloucester).
[19] Ibid. 7 Hen. V, no. 19.
[20] Visit. Essex (Harl. Soc. xiv), 591; Morant, op. cit. ii, 536.
[21] Chan. Inq. p.m. 4 Hen. VI, no. 6, and see below.
[22] See Close, 15 Hen. VI, m. 6 d., where property in Essex only is mentioned as held by Thomas Bernard for life after the death of his wife Christina with reversion to James Bellers and Ellen.
[23] Early Chan. Proc. bdle. 9, no. 356.
[24] Ibid.
[25] Chan. Inq. p.m. 22 Hen. VI, no. 28.
[26] Feet of F. Div. Co. 22 Hen. VI, no. 13.
[27] Chan. Inq. p.m. 22 Hen. VI, no. 28; Early Chan. Proc. bdle. 205, no. 94.
[28] Early Chan. Proc. bdle. 205, no. 94; Close, 31 Hen. VI, m. 4 d.
[29] Feet of F. Herts. 32 Hen. VI, no. 169. [30] Inq. a.q.d. file 454, no. 6.
[31] Ibid.
[32] Pat. 3 Edw. VI, pt. vii, m. 8.
[33] Ibid. 9 Eliz. pt. vii, m. 38.
[34] Feet of F. Herts. Mich. 10 & 11 Eliz.
[35] Ibid. Trin. 12 Eliz.; see Chan. Proc. (Ser. 2), bdle. 215, no. 32. With the present amount of evidence it is quite impossible to explain satisfactorily the deeds quoted by Clutterbuck (op. cit. ii, 404) and Chauncy (op. cit. 187), which show various members of the family of Chauncy making settlements of the manor of Overhall whilst it was apparently in the possession of Latton Chantry. It is just possible that after Giffords (which belonged to the Chauncys at this date) was divided between two heiresses the two moieties were known as Overhall and Netherhall.
[36] Feet of F. Herts. Mich. 14 & 15 Eliz.
[37] Ibid. East. 20 Eliz.; Recov. R. Hil. 1577, rot. 752; Pat. 20 Eliz. pt. viii, m. 25.
[38] Chan. Inq. p.m. (Ser. 2), cccxiv, 129.
[39] Feet of F. Herts. Trin. 22 Jas. I; Recov. R. Trin. 22 Jas. I, rot. 37.
[40] Chan. Inq. p.m. (Ser. 2), ccclxxvi, 108.
[41] See Netherhall; see also Recov. R. Mich. 32 Chas. II, rot.127.
[42] Rot. Cur. Reg. (Rec. Com.), i, 167.
[43] Assize R. 325, m. 25.
[44] Feud. Aids, ii, 434; see also Chan. Inq. p.m. 30 Edw. I, no. 58.
[45] Feud. Aids, ii, 451.
[46] Johnston, 'Parish of Gilston,' Home Cos. Mag. iii, 193.
[47] Sharpe, Calendar of Wills enrolled in Court of Husting, ii, 509. [48] Ibid.
[49] Early Chan. Proc. bdle. 27, no. 37.

320

conveyed the manor to John Chauncy and William Colt, clerk.[50] John Chauncy died in 1510.[51] In 1533 his son John Chauncy received a quitclaim from Giles Heron and his wife Cicely,[52] but it is not clear what interest they had in the manor.

John Chauncy, who died in 1547, seems to have settled Netherhall on his second son Henry,[53] to whom a further quitclaim was made by Leonard Skillingham and Griselda his wife, James Frauncys and Alice his wife, and John Whypall and Winifred his wife in 1549.[54] Henry Chauncy (father of the John Chauncy who held Overhall) built the capital messuage of New Place in Gilston, having, it is said, been forced to leave Pishobury in Sawbridgeworth, which he held on lease and used as a residence, by a sale over his head to Walter Mildmay.[55] He attached to his new house 40 acres of land, part of the manor of Netherhall, and 80 acres of land, part of Giffords.[56] The manor of Netherhall was settled on his son Edward, but Edward never appears in possession, and immediately after the death of Henry in 1587 William his grandson and heir (son of John Chauncy) conveyed the manor to his uncle George Chauncy.[57] In 1615 George Chauncy sold it to Alexander Williams of the Pipe Office,[58] who married Elizabeth sister of Sir Dudley Carleton, ambassador at the Hague.[59] Their son Anthony died in 1632, and shortly afterwards his father sold Netherhall to John Gore,[60] Lord Mayor of London in 1624 and knighted in 1626, who died seised of it in 1636.[61] His son John Gore of Sacombe was Sheriff of Hertfordshire in 1639, and was knighted by Charles I in 1641. He fought on the king's side during the Civil War, but later he made his peace with the dominant party. He died in 1659,[62] having in 1657 settled the messuage or farm called Upperhall, a mill in Hunsdon, and the manors of Overhall, Netherhall and Giffords on his son Humphrey Gore, on the occasion of his marriage with Persis English.[63]

Humphrey Gore, who was knighted in 1660, inclosed the park at New Place.[64] He made a settlement on his son John in 1691,[65] but John died in his father's lifetime, and Humphrey was succeeded at his death in 1699 by his son Henry Gore.[66] In 1701 Henry Gore sold the manors to John Plumer of Blakesware.[67] He died in March 1718–19, and was buried at Eastwick. His second son William, who married Elizabeth Byde of Ware Park and was M.P. for Herts. in 1754, succeeded him here and at Blakesware,[68] and in 1760 settled the manors on his son William Plumer the younger,[69] who succeeded at his father's death in 1767 and lived at New Place. He was M.P. for Hertfordshire from 1768 to 1806. He died in 1822 and was buried at Eastwick, having left New Place to his widow Jane. The old house at Blakesware (q.v.) was then pulled down, and its most valuable contents brought to Gilston.[70] Mrs. Plumer (Lewin) married as her third husband Robert Ward, who assumed the name of Plumer. The latter, by profession a barrister, was also a novelist and politician of some note. After his marriage he lived at Gilston Park and acted as sheriff of the county in 1832. His wife died in 1831; he survived until 1846.[71] After Mrs. Ward's death Gilston Park had been left unoccupied and in 1851 the house was dismantled and the pictures and old furniture (including the marble busts of the Caesars immortalized by Lamb) were offered for sale. The old house was situated nearer the lake than the present one; the porch still remains on the lawn.[71a] Henry George Ward, only son of Robert Ward by a previous marriage, sold Gilston Park to John Hodgson, who built a new house there.[72] His brother William Hodgson succeeded in 1882, and died in 1886,[73] when the manor passed to his nephew Mr. Edward Salvin Bowlby. His son Mr. Arthur Salvin Bowlby succeeded in 1902, and is the present lord of the manor. The courts leet and baron for the manor were held in 1702 at New Place, but generally afterwards at the Plume and Feathers Inn.[74]

The manor of *GIFFORDS* was the holding of a family named Giffard or Gifford who appear in Gilston at the end of the 12th century, when Giffard de Gilston called Peter de Goldington to

CHAUNCY. *Gules a cross paty argent and a chief azure with a lion passant or therein.*

BOWLBY of Gilston. *Six pieces party fessewise wavy sable and argent with three hinds' heads razed in the sable and three rings in the argent all countercoloured.*

---

[50] Anct. D. (P.R.O.), A 644. According to a deed quoted by Clutterbuck (op. cit. ii, 404) a moiety of the manor was conveyed to John Chauncy in 1480 by Joan and Robert Horncliff. These probably represent a co-heiress either of Sir William Estfield or of John Bohun. The difficulty in the descent of Overhall explained in note 35 applies also to Netherhall as far as a deed quoted by Clutterbuck (loc. cit.) is concerned, whereby John Chauncy settled (*inter alia*) the manor of Netherhall on his son John in 1478.
[51] Chauncy, *Hist. Antiq. of Herts.* 187.
[52] Feet of F. Herts. Trin. 25 Hen. VIII.
[53] Chauncy, loc. cit. The eldest son Maurice became a monk at the Charterhouse, London (see 'Dom. Maurice Chauncy' by E. Burton, *East Herts. Arch. Soc. Trans.* iv [1], 105). Henry Chauncy and his sons Edward and George were in 1581 accused of 'seditious practices in favouring popery' (*Cal. S. P. Dom.* 1581–90, p. 36).
[54] Feet of F. Herts. East. 3 Edw. VI.
[55] Chauncy, loc. cit.
[56] Chan. Inq. p.m. (Ser. 2), ccxiv, 159. In 1574 he conveyed 'the site of the manor of Netherhall' to John Peter and Francis Wyndham (Feet of F. Herts. East. 17 Eliz.). This was perhaps a sale of the old house.
[57] Feet of F. Herts. Mich. 30 & 31 Eliz.; Recov. R. Mich. 29 Eliz. rot. 130; Chauncy, op. cit. 190.
[58] Feet of F. Herts. East. 13 Jas. I.
[59] Johnston, op. cit. A letter from Elizabeth to her brother written in 1616 and giving a description of Gilston (S. P. Dom. Jas. I, lxxxviii, 2) is printed here.
[60] Johnston, op. cit.
[61] Chan. Inq. p.m. (Ser. 2), ccclxxxi, 31.
[62] M. I.; Le Neve, *Pedigrees of the Knights* (Harl. Soc. viii), 100.
[63] Close, 3 Will. and Mary, pt. xvii, no. 5.
[64] Ibid. 9 Will. III, pt. v, no. 4.
[65] Recov. R. Trin. 3 Will. and Mary, rot. 177; Close, 3 Will. and Mary, pt. xvii, no. 5.
[66] Chauncy, op. cit. 189; Feet of F. Div. Co. Trin. 6 Will. and Mary; Recov. R. Mich. 9 Will. III, rot. 271.
[67] Feet of F. Herts. Mich. 13 Will. III; Close, 13 Will. III, pt. viii, no. 11.
[68] Salmon, *Hist. of Herts.* 256.
[69] Recov. R. East. 33 Geo. II, rot. 271.
[70] Johnston, loc. cit.
[71] *Dict. Nat. Biog.*
[71a] See *Illus. Lond. News*, 26 Apr. 1851; information from Mr. C. E. Johnston.
[72] Johnston, loc. cit.
[73] M. I.
[74] Johnston, loc. cit.

warrant to him a quarter of a virgate of land in Gilston which he had by charter of Thomas his father.[75] In 1307 Ralph Giffard was among the tenants at Gilston assessed for a lay subsidy,[76] and in 1324 this Ralph was in debt to Hugh le Despenser, jun., for £40, which were to be levied on his lands in Essex and Hertfordshire.[77] John Gifford made a settlement of two messuages, two mills, 240 acres of land with appurtenances in Gilston, Sawbridgeworth and Eastwick on himself and his wife Margaret in 1341.[78] William Gifford, possibly son of John, left a daughter and heir Margaret, who married John Channcy, and in 1418 a quitclaim of a moiety of the estate above mentioned was made to John and Margaret by William Johan of Hatfield Broadoak, co. Essex, and his wife Joan, who was presumably another heiress.[78a] John Channey, son of John and Margaret, died in 1479 seised of a messuage called Giffords in Gilston and Sawbridgeworth held of the manors of Overhall and Pishobury.[78b] He was succeeded by his son John, who acquired Netherhall, and the two manors then descend together.

The farm-house of Giffords was situated at the lower end of the lake. It was pulled down in the 19th century.[78c]

CHURCH The church of ST. MARY consists of chancel 25 ft. by 12 ft. 6 in., north vestry, nave 46 ft. by 12 ft. 6 in., north and south aisles 6 ft. wide, south porch, west tower 12 ft. by 11 ft.; all dimensions taken internally. The walls of the nave and chancel are of flint with stone dressings, the chancel walls being coated with cement; the tower is of brick; the roofs over nave and chancel, which are continuous, are tiled, those over the aisles being slated.

The church appears to have been rebuilt late in the 13th century, an early 13th-century doorway from the former church, which was probably without aisles, having been re-set in the north wall; the tower is mainly of late 16th-century work, and was probably rebuilt then. The church was thoroughly restored during the 19th century, the south aisle rebuilt, a north vestry added to the chancel, a new east window inserted and the stonework of most of the others renewed, a south porch erected, and the nave and chancel and aisles re-roofed.

The east window is modern; a single lancet in the north wall and two in the south wall belong to the 13th century; the westernmost windows on the south and north sides have low sills, about 2 ft. 8 in. from the ground, but the heads of all the windows are on the same level. In the south wall is a piscina and credence combined; it has two moulded 13th-century arches, having shafted jambs with moulded capitals and bases; the central shaft is of Purbeck marble; in the eastern opening is a nine-foiled bowl, the other being plain as a credence. At some later period, probably the 16th century, the two arches have been united under a pointed arch with a star-shaped ornament and a rose in the centre, all of plaster. There is no chancel arch.

The nave has north and south arcades of four bays; the arches are of two hollow-chamfered orders with moulded labels, with piers of four clustered

GILSTON CHURCH FROM THE SOUTH-EAST

---

[75] *Rot. Cur. Reg.* (Rec. Com.), i, 167.
[76] Subs. R. bdle. 120, no. 8. For Ralph Gifford see also Feet of F. Herts. 19 Edw. II, no. 431; 20 Edw. II, no. 438. [77] *Cal. Close,* 1323–7, p. 171.
[78] Feet of F. Herts. 15 Edw. III, no. 236.
[78a] Ibid. 6 Hen. V, no. 37; see charters given by Clutterbuck, op. cit. ii, 404, and Chauncy, op. cit. 187.
[78b] Chan. Inq. p.m. 19 Edw. IV, no. 32.
[78c] Information from Mr. C. E. Johnston.

GILSTON CHURCH: PISCINA AND CREDENCE

columns having moulded capitals and bases of the latter part of the 13th century.

The east window in the north aisle is modern. In the north wall is a two-light window of late 13th-century date; the other windows are of modern stonework. The north doorway, which is blocked, is a good example of early 13th-century work; it has a moulded arch and label and detached shafts in the jambs; the capitals have moulded abaci and bells carved with early leaf ornament; the bases are gone. The south aisle is modern.

The west tower has a modern embattled parapet and a small octagonal timber spire covered with lead; on the south side is an octagonal projecting turret stair, which is finished at the belfry stage with a brick roof. The tower arch is of late 16th-century date; the arch is of two splayed orders; the jambs are shafted and the capitals and bases roughly executed. The west doorway has a pointed arch of four moulded orders and shafted jambs; it is of late 13th-century work much worn. The west window is of two lights with old splayed jambs and a modern traceried head. In its head is a 15th-century painted glass shield with the arms of Sir William Estfield, Sheriff of London in 1422: Sable, a cheveron ermine between three maidens' heads cut off at the shoulders argent with hair dishevelled or, and the inscription 'Orate p [. . . . .] Willi Estfeld, militis.' The belfry windows are of two trefoiled lights with cusped opening in the heads; they have been repaired with cement and may be of 14th-century date.

The bowl of the font is of the 12th century; it is hexagonal and on each face are three shallow sunk plain panels; the bowl rests upon a 14th-century stem with moulded cap and base.

The oak chancel screen is of special interest, as it has incorporated with it remains of a late 13th-century screen. The old work consists of arches with trefoiled heads under pointed arches, with rosettes carved in the spandrels between the arches; the shafts are an inch in diameter and have moulded capitals and bases and central bands.

On the floor of the north aisle are two stone coffin lids, probably of 14th-century date; one bears a floreated cross in relief on its face with an illegible inscription; the cross of the other stone has been almost obliterated. On the north chancel wall is a large mural monument of marble to Sir John Gore, who died in 1659; on the south wall is another to Bridget Gore, his daughter, who died in 1657; a slab on the floor marks the place of her burial.

There are two bells; the treble by Anthony Bartlett, 1663; the tenor, inscribed 'Jesvs be ovr spede,' by Robert Oldfeild, 1628.

The communion plate consists of cup, 1562, and cover paten, the marks of which are erased; flagon, 1697, and paten of the 17th century.

The registers of baptisms, marriages and burials begin in 1558.

ADVOWSON Geoffrey de Mandeville, lord of Gilston and founder of the abbey of Walden in Essex, who died in 1144, included the church of Gilston in his foundation charter to that monastery.[79] It remained with Walden until the first half of the 13th century, when the right of the abbey was contested by the Bishop of London, and the arbitrators appointed to decide on the rival claims assigned the patronage to the Bishop of London and his successors.[80] The advowson remained vested in the see until 1852, when it was transferred to Rochester.[81] In 1874 it was transferred to St. Albans.[82]

CHARITIES In the Parliamentary Returns of 1786 it is stated that the following donations were given for bread to the poor and for teaching poor girls, viz.:—Thomas Gore, Sir John Gore, £50; Lady Tyrrell, £60.

The Gilston estate was charged in respect of these gifts with annuities of £2 12s. for bread and £3 for catechizing children. These charges were redeemed in 1869 by the transfer of stock to the official trustees, which with accumulated income now amounts to £243 13s. 5d. consols, producing £6 1s. 8d. yearly.

By an Order of the Charity Commissioners 15 July 1904 the sum of £120 consols was assigned to 'The Gore and Tyrrell Educational Foundation,' and £123 13s. 5d. consols to 'The Gore and Tyrrell Eleemosynary Charity.'

HUNSDON

Hunesdone (xi cent.); Honesdon, Hamesdun, Hunnesdon (xiii cent.); Hunsdon (xiv cent.).

Hunsdon parish lies on the high ground which divides the valleys of the Rivers Ash and Stort, having a southward slope from a height of about 266 ft. in the extreme north of the parish down to the latter valley, where the land is little more than 100 ft. above sea level. The area of the parish is 1,971 acres, nearly half of which is arable, about a third pasture and only a small portion woodland.[1] The soil is very varied, the subsoil chalk or gravelly loam. There is no line of railway in the parish, the nearest station being Roydon in Essex, on the Great Eastern railway, rather less than a quarter of a mile from the south-western boundary of Hunsdon parish.

The church lies close to Hunsdon House and the village is about a mile to the north on the road to Widford. There are a few houses along the road between the church and the village called Acorn Street, one of which is Nine Ashes, the property and residence of Mr. Samuel Shott Death. In the village are several 17th-century cottages of timber and plaster with tiled roofs. The Wheatsheaf Inn, now converted into two cottages, is an interesting timber and plaster gabled building with a tiled roof. Within there is a large fireplace bearing the date 1681 or 1687. The

---

[79] Harl. MS. 3697, fol. 18.
[80] Ibid. fol. 45 d.; London Epis. Reg. Stokesley, fol. lxxxvi or 121; Hist. MSS. Com. Rep. ix, App. i, 36a. The second of these is an inspeximus by Geoffrey, Dean of St. Paul's, who held that office from 1231 to 1241.

[81] Lond. Gaz. 4 June 1852, p. 1578.
[82] Ibid. 13 July 1877, p. 4126.
[1] Statistics from Bd. of Agric. (1905).

pound is at the cross roads near to Hunsdon Mill, which is on the River Stort in the south of the parish.

Hunsdon House, which is possibly on the site of the earlier manor-house, is said to have been built by Sir William Oldhall in 1447. In 1447, however, the Duke of York seems to have been holding the manor, and in May of that year received licence 'to build within his manor of Hunsdon a tower of stones, with lime and sand, and to embattle the same.'[2] Oldhall is not known to have been in possession until February 1448. He may have begun building directly after that date, but the house was apparently unfinished in 1453, for Oldhall having forfeited, a certain Walter Burgh, a servant of the king, then received a grant of 'stones called brick in Hunsdon and Eastwick late pertaining to William Oldhall,'[3] which looks as if the latter had been in the midst of building. The house seems to have come into the possession of Henry VIII with the manor before 1527, when he granted the custody of it to Henry Norris, squire of the body.[4] The place was a favourite one with Henry VIII, who carried on extensive buildings here. In February 1534 the 'master surveyor of the King's works at Hunsdon' reported on the expenditure of £2,900 applied to this purpose: 'for "parelles" of freestone for the chimneys in the King's watching chamber, palett chamber, privy chamber, and in the other chamber beneath the same; for lime, plaster, "rigge tyles," corner tiles, paving tiles and plain tiles; for timber, and for wood bought by the acre; for wainscoats, laths, pails, tile pins, hooks, hinges, locks, clasps, keys . . . new glass bought of Galyon Hone and "sett with symond," etc.'[5] In June 1528 the king appears to have fled here from the sweating sickness. Thomas Hennege writes from Hunsdon to Wolsey: 'Laud be Jesu, the King's grace is very merry since he came to this house, for there was none fell sick of the sweat since he came hither, and ever after dinner he shooteth to supper time'; but the postscript adds: 'This night as the King went to bed, word came of the death of William Carey.'[6] After the divorce of Katherine of Aragon, the Princess Mary was sent to Hunsdon (February 1536), and there are a number of letters of hers extant written from Hunsdon, both to her father and to Cromwell, on the subject of her reconciliation with the king.[7] Writing to Charles V on the subject of the princess's escape, Chapuys says of Hunsdon: 'The house where she is at present is much more inconvenient for the enterprise . . . there are a great many houses and people in the village where she now is.'[8] It was while in the service of the princess at Hunsdon (1538–40) that Lady Elizabeth Fitzgerald—'the fair Geraldine'—first met her admirer Henry Howard Earl of Surrey.[8a] Prince Edward also spent much of his infancy and youth at Hunsdon, whence it was written of him on one occasion: 'My lord Prince is in good health and merry. Would to God the king . . . had seen him last night. The minstrels played, and his Grace danced and played so wantonly that he could not stand still.'[9] After the accession of the prince to the throne as Edward VI the Princess Mary spent much of her time here. In 1559, however, Hunsdon House ceased to be a royal residence, for Queen Elizabeth granted it with the manor (q.v.) to Sir Henry Carey. In 1576 Queen Elizabeth and the Countess of Warwick stood godmothers to Elizabeth daughter of Sir George Carey, who was baptized at Hunsdon on 7 June. When Emmanuel son of Thomas Scrope (afterwards Lord Scrope) was baptized there on 26 August 1584 the queen again stood godmother. Henceforward manor and house followed the same descent, both being

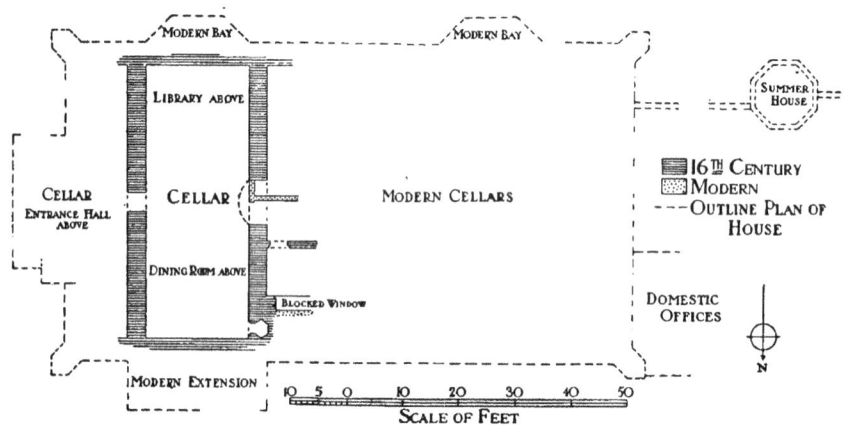

PLAN OF HUNSDON HOUSE

[2] Pat. 25 Hen. VI, pt. ii, m. 10.
[3] Cal. Pat. 1452–61, p. 34.
[4] L. and P. Hen. VIII, iv, g. 3622 (27). Ibid. vii, 250.
[5] Ibid. iv, 4403, 4408. He was father of Sir Henry Carey, to whom Elizabeth granted Hunsdon Manor in 1559.
[7] Ibid. i, 199, 307, 968, 991, 1022, 1083, 1108, 1109, 1129, 1133, 1136, 1186, 1203; see also vii, 1036.
[8] Ibid. x, 307.
[8a] Dict. Nat. Biog.
[9] L. and P. Hen. VIII, xiv (2), App. 9; v, 755; viii, 20.

purchased by James S. Walker of Hunsdonbury in 1858. Mr. Walker then sold the manor to Mr. Charles Phelips, but the house (in 1861) to Mr. James Wyllie, in whose family it remained until 1882, when it was purchased by Mr. Spencer Charrington. It is now the property of the latter's son, Mr. Edmund Knowles Charrington, and is the residence of his sister Mrs. Montgomerie.

The house consists of a large rectangular block with a low modern wing at the west end containing the domestic offices. The house is built of brick with embattled parapet and a flat roof. Judging from the dimensions given by William of Worcester,[9a] the original building must have been a very extensive structure; none of these dimensions, however, agree with the present house. After the manor came to the Crown (see below) Henry VIII made considerable additions[9b]; about 1743 the wings are said to have been pulled down,[10] and in 1805 Mr. Nicolson Calvert pulled a great part of the old house down and reconstructed most of what remained.[10a] Mrs. Calvert writes 16 April 1806[10b]: 'I hear there is hardly a bit of old Hunsdon House left standing . . . it will be nearly a new house.'

The oldest parts of the existing house are the cellars under the east end; they probably date from the 16th century. The largest cellar, which measures 48 ft. 6 in. by 18 ft. 6 in., runs transversely across the building, and appears to have formed a wing of a former house, as it projects northwards 8 ft. beyond the original north wall, which still remains visible in the basement, the present north wall standing about 9 ft. outside it; the lower part of a small hexagonal turret or closet still remains at the angle of the old walls. The cellar itself has a barrel vault of brick; the walls and vault are constructed of thin bricks. The turret, which has no trace of a stair, is entered by a low doorway with a four-centred arch. The adjoining cellars on the west are of the same date; one has a doorway with a four-centred arch, and in the original north wall is a window, now blocked. All the cellarage at the west end has been rebuilt with modern bricks. Mrs. Calvert writes 6 August 1805[11]: 'We have completed cellars and we think of adding to and repairing the old building'; this, she writes later, was eventually done.

The interior of the ground and upper stories is entirely a reconstruction of 1805, the only evidence of an earlier date being a 17th-century carved oak mantelpiece in the entrance hall; a stone fireplace with a four-centred arch and three blank shields under a carved wood mantel are probably all of 1805. The external walls are built chiefly of old thin bricks, but a large part appears to have been rebuilt and an embattled front added to the attic story in 1805; all the windows are modern. At each of the four angles of the house is a large diagonal buttress with keel-shaped face, carried up above the parapet and finished with a slated pinnacle; the upper parts are modern, but the buttresses are built of thin bricks; some of them have probably been rebuilt. The whole of the external brickwork has been covered with a thick coat of red colour-wash and 'tuck-pointed.' The main entrance is in a projection at the east end; the doorway, which has wide moulded jambs and four-centred arch, all executed in cement, is probably modern. In the garden wall to the west of the house

HUNSDON HOUSE FROM THE SOUTH-EAST

is an octagonal summer-house, all of modern brickwork. West of the house are modern stables and a large brick gateway with embattled parapet, which forms the entrance to the courtyard of the house; the gateway is modern, but some old bricks have been re-used in the upper part. A wooden lintel, now built in over the gateway between the garden and the stable yard, is inscribed 'H.H. 1593.' A moat which formerly surrounded the old house has been filled up.

In 1728 Salmon wrote that 'Robert Chester hath within a few years built a seat in this parish, and

[9a] *Itin. Will. de Worc.* (ed. Nasmyth), 89.
[9b] Chauncy, *Hist. Antiq. of Herts.* 197.
[10] Cussans, *Hist. of Herts. Braughing Hund.* 46.
[10a] Mrs. Warenne Blake, *An Irish Beauty of the Regency* (Hon. Mrs. Calvert), p. 50.
[10b] Ibid. 66.
[11] Ibid. 49.

inclosed it with a park.[11a] This was Briggens Park, situated in the south-western corner of the parish, on the banks of the River Stort, which Robert Chester had bought from the Feildes of Stanstead Abbots.[12] The house built by Chester occupied the site of two older messuages called Over Bredons and Nether Bredons or Great Briggens and Little Briggens.[13] Robert Chester died in 1732,[14] having left Briggens Park to his sister Jane Chester provided that she kept up the park, gardens and deer. Jane Chester died in 1736,[15] and was succeeded by her brother Henry (or by his son Henry), who in 1740 sold the property to Thomas Blackmore of Covent Garden.[16] He was succeeded in 1763 by his nephew Thomas Blackmore, who left a son Thomas and several daughters, one of whom, Mary, in 1792 married Rev. Charles Phelips, fourth son of Edward Phelips of Montacute. The death of Thomas Blackmore in 1824 resulted in Briggens Park passing into the hands of their son Charles Phelips. The latter died in 1870, when the estate was inherited by his son Charles James Phelips. Charles James Phelips died without issue in 1903, and Briggens Park fell to his nephew Gerald Edward Farquharson Phelips, whose trustees sold it with the manor in 1907 to the Hon. Herbert Cokayne Gibbs, the present owner, who resides there.[17] The house built by Chester forms the centre of the present house, and some of the 2-in. brick foundations of the older houses have recently been discovered.[18]

Hunsdonbury is now the property of Mr. E. Thomas, who bought it from Mr. John Henry Buxton in 1911. The latter purchased it in 1889 from Mr. Salisbury Baxendale.[19] It originally formed part of the estate of the Calverts, who resided there after 1840, and later passed to Mr. Walker,[20] who also lived there.[21] About half a mile south of the church is Brickhouse Farm, a 17th-century house built of 2-in. bricks.

Olives Farm is a moated house on the extreme west of the parish. It is of timber and plaster, with tiled roofs, and dates back to the 17th century, though it has considerable later additions.

Fillett's Farm, situated in the northwest of the parish, was in the 16th century in the possession of Sir Wimund Carew, whose son Thomas Carew sold it in 1551 to William Grave[22] of Stanstead Abbots. In 1575 Thomas Grave conveyed it to Edward Baesh.[23] Caddingtons is the name of another old house, which in the 15th century belonged to the Shelley family of Hunsdon.[24] In 1542 the king made John Carey keeper of the messuage called Caryngtons *alias* Cadyngtons.[25]

At the time of the *MANOR* Domesday Survey the manor of *HUNSDON* formed part of the lands of Hugh de Beauchamp, who had succeeded Ralph Taillebois (Tulgebos or Tailgebosch) in estates both in Hertfordshire and Bedfordshire. The manor comprised 4 hides, of which 1 had been taken by Ralph from the manor of Stanstead Abbots and attached to Hunsdon.[26] The Beauchamps continued to hold Hunsdon as part of their Bedford barony, Simon de Beauchamp in the 12th century granting certain tithes of this manor to Newnham Priory.[27] John de Beauchamp, the last feudal baron of Bedford, fell fighting against the king at the battle of Evesham

HUNSDON HOUSE FROM THE NORTH-EAST

[11a] Salmon, *Hist. and Antiq. of Herts.* 253.
[12] Information from Hon. H. C. Gibbs.
[13] In 1696 William Crowley of Briggens was buried at Hunsdon (ibid.).
[14] M.I.
[15] Ibid.
[16] Information from Hon. H. C. Gibbs.
[17] Ibid.
[18] Ibid.
[19] Information supplied by Mr. J. H. Buxton.
[20] See below on Hunsdon Manor.
[21] Cussans, *Hist. of Herts. Braughing Hund.* 46.
[22] Com. Pleas D. Enr. East. 4 Edw. VI, m. 10 d.
[23] Feet of F. Herts. Trin. 17 Eliz.
[24] Early Chan. Proc. bdle. 70, no. 34; Cal.Pat. 1476–85, p. 243; Add. MS. 32490, Q 44; *Cal. Inq. p.m. Hen. VII*, 204. Gilbert Shelley was buried at Hunsdon in 1548. (Information from Hon. H. Gibbs.)
[25] *L. and P. Hen. VIII*, xviii (1), 545.
[26] *V.C.H. Herts.* i, 344a, 283, 284.
[27] *Cal. Chart. R.* 1300–26, p. 358. Confirmation of this grant in 1317.

(1265), and Hunsdon went to Maud, one of his sisters and co-heirs, wife of Roger de Mowbray.[28] Her great-grandson John, third Lord Mowbray, is

BEAUCHAMP of Bedford. *Quarterly or and gules a bend sable.*

MOWBRAY. *Gules a lion argent.*

found as overlord of Hunsdon in 1358,[29] and the fourth Lord Mowbray is similarly described in 1367.[30] John, eighth Lord Mowbray, is so found in 1419 under his title of Earl Marshal of England.[31] Anne, only daughter and heir of the tenth Lord Mowbray, married Richard, younger brother of Edward V. Richard was murdered in the Tower in 1483, his child-wife having died some three years previously, and such rights of overlordship in Hunsdon as survived fell to the Crown.

The tenant in demesne at the time of the Domesday Survey was the daughter of Ralph Taillebois, who had succeeded Lewin, a thegn of Earl Harold, at the Conquest.[32] No under-tenant is known after this date until 1248, in which year Vitalis Engayne died seised of this manor, holding of the Beauchamps.[33] This Vitalis, son of Richard Engayne, is found earlier in the century holding the manor of Upminster in Essex.[34] His son and heir Henry[35] received a grant of free warren in the demesne lands of Hunsdon in 1253,[36] and died seised of the manor in 1271.[37] Henry's brother and heir John died similarly seised in 1296.[38] John Engayne, his son and heir, is found holding Hunsdon in the early years of the 14th century,[39] and Nicholas his son and successor made a settlement of the manor in 1318.[40] Nicholas Engayne was succeeded by his son John, a knight, who married Joan the daughter of Robert Peverel and died in 1358.[41] Thomas, their son and heir, died 'in parts beyond the sea' about

ENGAYNE. *Gules a fesse dancetty between six crosslets or.*

1367, when the Engayne inheritance was divided amongst his three sisters and co-heirs.[42]

Hunsdon fell to Joyce the wife of John Goldington, the latter dying some time previous to 1383,[43] when she was still living. John Goldington, son of Joyce and John, died seised of this manor in 1419, leaving Thomas his son and heir a minor.[44] Thomas must have died very shortly after, for in 1423 John Hinxworth of Ashwell was holding Hunsdon as the kinsman and heir of John Goldington, when he released all right in it to John Tyrell of Essex and others.[45] John Tyrell was still holding in 1428,[46] after which the immediate descent is not clear.

In 1445 view of frankpledge, waifs and strays, and other rights within the manor of Hunsdon were granted to William Estfeld, kt.[47] Possibly he was a trustee for Richard Duke of York, who was evidently lord of this manor in the autumn of 1445,[48] and who in May 1447 received royal licence to hold it to himself and heirs.[49] It was probably from him that Sir William Oldhall, kt., his chamberlain, obtained Hunsdon, either by grant or by purchase. Oldhall is described as 'of Hunsdon' in February 1448,[50] and 'late of Hunsdon' in April 1450.[51] He forfeited for complicity in the rebellion of Jack Cade, which took place in that year, and was formally attainted in Parliament in June 1453.[52] In May 1453 the manor of Hunsdon, with all appurtenances, was granted by the king to York's rival, Edmund Duke of Somerset.[53] In 1454 the York party returned to power and Somerset was imprisoned. It was not, however, until after the complete triumph of the Yorkists at the first battle of St. Albans, when Somerset was slain (May 1455), that Oldhall's attainder was reversed in Parliament (November 1455).[54] The fortunes of the Wars of the Roses brought about a second attainder for Oldhall in the autumn of 1459. In January 1459–60 his possessions were granted to Humphrey Duke of Buckingham,[55] but in February they were taken into the king's hands.[56] The accession of Edward IV a year later nullified this attainder, and Oldhall presumably held Hunsdon until his death, which took place before the end of 1460.[57] In his will, dated 15 November 1460, Oldhall left Hunsdon to his executors, to be sold by them for the payment of legacies.[58] The Archbishop of Canterbury, one of the executors, transferred the manor to trustees, who conveyed it to Laurence, Bishop of Durham, and others.[59] It seems that the latter were acting for the king, Edward IV, who was clearly in possession by 1476.[60] Richard III, at some time during his brief reign (June 1483–August 1485) granted Hunsdon to Sir

---

[28] *Feud. Aids,* ii, 435; G.E.C. *Peerage,* v, 410.
[29] Chan. Inq. p.m. 32 Edw. III, no. 27.
[30] Ibid. 41 Edw. III, no. 25.
[31] Ibid. 7 Hen. V, no. 7.
[32] *V.C.H. Herts.* i, 344a.
[33] Chan. Inq. p.m. 33 Hen. III, no. 70.
[34] *Excerpta e Rot. Fin.* (Rec. Com.), i, 6; Wrottesley, *Pedigrees from the Plea Rolls,* 478, 490.
[35] *Excerpta e Rot. Fin.* (Rec. Com.), ii, 46.
[36] *Cal. Chart. R.* 1226–59, p. 423.
[37] Chan. Inq. p.m. 56 Hen. III, no. 33.
[38] Ibid. 25 Edw. I, no. 46.

[39] Inq. a.q.d. file 40, no. 17; 126, no. 6; cf. *Feud. Aids,* ii, 435.
[40] Feet of F. Herts. 12 Edw. II, no. 303.
[41] Chan. Inq. p.m. 32 Edw. III, no. 27.
[42] Ibid. 41 Edw. III, no. 25; Add. Chart. 19979.
[43] Close, 7 Ric. II, m. 29 d.
[44] Chan. Inq. p.m. 7 Hen. V, no. 7.
[45] Close, 2 Hen. VI, m. 15 d.
[46] *Feud. Aids,* ii, 451.
[47] Chart. R. 23 Hen. VI, no. 25.
[48] Inq. a.q.d. file 450, no. 32.
[49] *Cal. Pat.* 1446–52, p. 77.
[50] Ibid. 233. He purchased the neighbouring manor of Eastwick in the autumn of 1447 (see Eastwick Parish).

[51] *Cal. Pat.* 1446–52, p. 324.
[52] *Dict. Nat. Biog.*
[53] *Cal. Pat.* 1452–61, p. 103; *Parl. R.* v, 266a. A general grant of Oldhall's lands to Jasper Earl of Pembroke in June 1452 (*Cal. Pat.* 1446–52, p. 557) did not take effect in regard to Hunsdon.
[54] *Parl. R.* v, 451; *Cal. Pat.* 1452–61, p. 282.
[55] *Cal. Pat.* 1452–61, pp. 282, 535.
[56] Ibid. 562, 572.
[57] C. E. Johnston, 'Sir Wm. Oldhall,' *Engl. Hist. Rev.* xxv, 715.
[58] Will, P.C.C. 21 Stokton.
[59] Anct. D. (P.R.O.), A 5235; Close, 15 Edw. IV, m. 1 d.
[60] *Cal. Pat.* 1467–77, p. 596.

A HISTORY OF HERTFORDSHIRE

William Stanley, kt., whose wavering support to the throne he was most anxious to secure.[61] Stanley afterwards maintained that Richard's substantial grants to him had been in exchange for 'other manors, lands and tenements of great value,' but the truth of this statement remains unproved. His execution in 1495 for complicity in the rising of Perkin Warbeck caused Hunsdon once more to revert to the Crown. In 1503 Henry VII made a life grant of this manor to his mother Margaret Countess of Richmond and her husband the Earl of Derby, elder brother of the late Sir William Stanley.[62] The earl died in 1504 and the countess in 1509.[63] On 1 February 1514 Hunsdon was granted to Thomas Howard, Earl of Surrey and Treasurer of England, on his creation as Duke of Norfolk.[64] The duke died in 1524. His son and heir Thomas Duke of Norfolk conveyed the manor in 1526 to Sir Henry Wyatt and others[65] evidently in trust for the king, who in 1529 granted it to Henry Norris, reserving the house and parks.[66] In 1531 the grant to Thomas Duke of Norfolk was recited and the manor was confirmed to the duke, his successor,[67] but this was probably only a formality, as in 1532 the manor was still in the king's hands.[68] On 15 January 1532 an Act of Parliament was passed whereby the manor became the honour of Hunsdon, to which various lands in Hertfordshire were attached.[69] In the same year Henry VIII granted an annuity out of this honour to Anne Boleyn on her creation as Marchioness of Pembroke,[70] but the manor remained under the control of his bailiffs or stewards.[71] In 1548 Edward VI granted Hunsdon Manor to the Princess Mary 'for her life, or until she is otherwise provided for,' this being in accordance with the will of their late father Henry VIII.[72] Mary, after she became queen, annexed the honour in 1558 to the duchy of Lancaster.[73]

In March 1558–9 (six months after her accession) Queen Elizabeth granted this manor, with house and lands, &c., to her cousin Sir Henry Carey, kt., and his heirs male,[74] she having already (January 1558–9) created him Lord Hunsdon. Carey died in 1596,[75] and was succeeded by his son George Lord Hunsdon, who died in 1603, leaving as heir his brother John, then over fifty years of age.[76] A neighbour wrote in 1616: 'Seven men are to be hanged for a robbery of £700 in the house of Lord Hunsdon, who is building a monument in Hunsdon Church for himself and family.'[77] John, third Lord Hunsdon, died in 1617,[78] and the manor was inherited by his son Henry, the fourth baron,[79] created Viscount Rochford in 1621 and Earl of Dover in 1628. He was Speaker of the House of Lords in 1641, and played a prominent part on the Royalist side in the Great Civil War. On the triumph of the Parliamentarians, Carey was accounted a 'delinquent, or malignant, or cavalier,' and his estates sequestrated.[80] He must have compounded for them before the sale of Hunsdon by him in March 1653 to William Willoughby, afterwards sixth Lord Willoughby of Parham.[81] Lord Willoughby made a settlement of Hunsdon Manor on himself and his wife Anne in 1666.[82] In 1671 he sold Hunsdon Manor to Matthew Bluck,[83] who was succeeded by his son and heir of the same name.[84] He was still holding in 1728,[85] and in 1743 a Matthew Bluck suffered a recovery of this manor.[86] Clutterbuck, writing in 1823, says that this was the occasion of the purchase of Hunsdon by Mr. Josias Nicolson of Clapham.[87] The latter's daughter and heir Christian married Felix Calvert of Furneux Pelham, their son Nicolson Calvert inheriting Hunsdon at his mother's death in 1759. He suffered a recovery of this manor in 1789,[88] and died in 1793. His nephew and heir Nicolson Calvert made a settlement of Hunsdon in 1806,[89] and was holding in 1823.[90] In 1858 Edmund Calvert, son of Nicolson, sold the manor to James S. Walker, who in turn sold it to Charles Phelips of Briggens Park in this parish.[91] On the latter's death in 1870 Hunsdon Manor descended to his son Charles James Phelips. He died in 1903, when his nephew Mr. Gerald F. Phelips succeeded, who in 1907 transferred the manor with the Briggens estate to the Hon. H. C. Gibbs. The existing rolls of the manor date from 1675.

CAREY, Lord Hunsdon. *Argent a bend sable with three roses argent thereon.*

---

[61] See *Cal. Inq. p.m. Hen. VII*, 204; *Parl. R.* vi, 316*b*. There are two inquisitions, dated respectively June 1481 and Nov. 1483, in which it is stated that the manor of Bengeo was then held of William Hussey 'as of his manor of Hunsdon' (Chan. Inq. p.m. 21 Edw. IV, no. 46; 1 Ric. III, no. 38). This is explained by a conveyance from the Bishop of Durham and other trustees to William Hussey (Anct. D. [P.R.O.], A 979), who held for the king (cf. *Cal. Pat.* 1471–85, p. 247).
[62] Close, 18 Hen. VII, no. 28.
[63] A mortgage of the manor by John Lord Berners to Sir William Capell in 1508 (Close, 23 Hen. VII, pt. ii, no. 9), is difficult to explain. Possibly Berners was a lessee.
[64] *L. and P. Hen. VIII*, i, 4694. His father had been created Duke of Norfolk in 1483, but the title had been forfeited in 1485.
[65] Feet of F. Herts. Trin. 18 Hen. VIII.
[66] *L. and P. Hen. VIII*, iv (3), 5336 (10). The Duke of Norfolk was at Hunsdon in July 1527, but he was probably in the train of the king, who was also there at that date (ibid. 3276, 3277, 3302).
[67] Pat. 22 Hen. VIII, pt. i, m. 17.
[68] *L. and P. Hen. VIII*, v, 730. See also 916. Probably the king came to some arrangement with the duke, for in 1538 the manor is mentioned among the lands which he sold to the king (ibid. xiii [2], 1215). Norris was probably compensated with lands elsewhere.
[69] Ibid. v, 720.
[70] Ibid. g. 1370 (3); 1274; g. 1499 (23).
[71] Ibid. xiii (1), p. 582; xv, g. 539.
[72] Pat. 2 Edw. VI, pt. v, m. 32.
[73] Pat. 4 & 5 Phil. and Mary, pt. ii, rot. 4.
[74] Pat. 1 Eliz. pt. ix; Duchy of Lanc. Misc. Bks. xxiii, 240. Sir Henry's mother Mary was the sister of Anne Boleyn.
[75] Chan. Inq. p.m. (Ser. 2) ccxlvi, 111.
[76] Chan. Inq. p.m. (Ser. 2), cclxxxvi, 170; Memo. R. Mich. 2 Jas. I, rot. 80.
[77] *Cal. S. P. Dom.* 1611–18, p. 378.
[78] Chan. Inq. p.m. (Ser. 2), ccclxxiv, 95. He was buried at Hunsdon 7 April 1617 and his wife on 7 April 1627 (notes from par. reg. supplied by the Hon. H. C. Gibbs).
[79] Pat. 10 Chas. I, pt. ii.
[80] Exch. Dep. Mixed Co. Mich. 36 Chas. II, no. 22. The Careys were certainly still at Hunsdon in 1644 (*Hist. MSS. Com. Rep.* App. vi, 39).
[81] G.E.C. *Peerage*, iv, 279.
[82] Feet of F. Herts. Div. Co. Hil. 18 & 19 Chas. II.
[83] Feet of F. Herts. East. 23 Chas. II.
[84] Recov. R. East. 12 Anne, rot. 158; Exch. Dep. Mich: 36 Chas. II, no. 22.
[85] Salmon, *Hist. and Antiq. of Herts.* 253.
[86] Recov. R. Mich. 17 Geo. II, rot. 379.
[87] Clutterbuck, *Hist. and Antiq. of Herts.* iii, 182.
[88] Recov. R. Hil. 29 Geo. III, rot. 23.
[89] Feet of F. Herts. Trin. 46 Geo. III.
[90] Clutterbuck, loc. cit.
[91] Cussans, *Hist. of Herts. Braughing Hund.* 44. Cussans does not give the date of the second sale, but Mr. Phelips was patron of Hunsdon living in 1859.

Hunsdon Church: 17th-century Oak Screen to South Chapel

PARKS

Henry Engayne, lord of the manor of Hunsdon, received a grant of free warren in the demesne lands of the manor in 1253.[92] A park was inclosed shortly afterwards, for in 1296 a commission was appointed 'touching the persons who entered the park of John Engayne at Hunsdon, hunted therein, and carried away deer.'[93] In 1445 it was reported that Richard Duke of York might safely 'inclose a way (100 virgates long and 16 ft. wide) called Jermynslane leading from Eastwick to Hunsdon, in his park of Hunsdon, making another road on the south of the park.'[94] The park also occurs in the life-grant of Hunsdon to the Countess of Richmond in 1503. It was, however, not included in the grant in tail-male to the Duke of Norfolk in 1514,[95] but was retained by the Crown. In 1529 there were three royal parks at Hunsdon: the 'old,' the 'new,' and 'Goodmanneshyde.'[96] Probably one of these was the same as 'Wyntrey Park,' where the king killed two stags in July 1532.[97] In the following month Stephen Gardiner wrote to Wolsey from Hunsdon: 'I have been hunting from morn till night by the king's commandment.'[98] The three parks of Hunsdon were granted with the manor to Sir Henry Carey in 1559 and continued with his successors. Henry Earl of Dover enlarged the park by the purchase of certain lands called the Spring, formerly Chauncy's Lands, in the parish of Eastwick. Other lands within the parks were the Brick Hills, the Nursery, Eastwick Lawn and Edward's Downs. The parks were disparked before 1684, when the boundaries were given as follows: Eastwick Hall and lands called Germans on the north-west, Hunsdon Mill Lane on the south, Hunsdon House on the south-west, Eastwick Woods on the north-east.[99]

A mill is included in the description of Hunsdon given in the Domesday Survey and 'a water mill worth 20s.' in an extent of 1297.[100] In 1508 the mill conveyed with the manor was called Wadesmill,[1] and another reference also occurs to 'Wardes Mill' in Hunsdon.[2] In 1607 two mills are included in the manor.[3] Probably one of these was in the parish of Eastwick, as the two properties were in the same hands at this date. Subsequently the Hunsdon Mill passed to the owners of Eastwick, and was sold with that estate by Henry Gore to John Plumer in 1701.[4] Situated in the south of the parish on the River Stort, it stands within a quarter of a mile of the boundary between Hunsdon and Eastwick parishes. The mill has been destroyed, but the house now forms part of the Briggens estate.

CHURCH

The church stands close to Hunsdon House, nearly a mile south of the village. Its dedication is uncertain, but is attributed to ST. DUNSTAN. It consists of chancel 43 ft. by 17 ft. 6 in., north chapel 22 ft. 6 in. by 13 ft. 6 in., nave 48 ft. 6 in. by 22 ft. 6 in., south transept or chapel 23 ft. by 22 ft. 6 in., west tower 12 ft. 9 in. by 11 ft., timber north porch; all the dimensions taken internally. The walls are of flint rubble with stone dressings, the south chapel being built of brick; the roofs are tiled; much of the stonework has been renewed and the building generally repaired. This church possesses some exceptionally good details of fittings of the 16th and 17th centuries.

The walling of the nave belongs probably to an earlier period than the rest of the building, but the indications are too slight to fix the date; the west tower and north porch belong to the early part of the 15th century; the chancel was rebuilt in the latter part of the 15th century; the north chapel was added about the middle of the 16th century, and the south chapel was built by Lord Hunsdon about 1616.

The chancel has a large five-light window in the east wall, one two-light window in the north, and two with a doorway between in the south wall; some of the jamb stones in the windows are original, the rest is modern stonework. The north doorway into the chapel has a four-centred arch with splayed jambs; the arch opening into this chapel, which is used as an organ chamber and vestry, is modern. In the south chancel wall is a piscina with hollow splayed jambs and pointed arch; adjoining it is a plain recess with a wooden seat. The chancel arch of two plain chamfered orders dates from the latter part of the 15th century.

The floor of the north chapel was raised about 4 ft. 8 in. in the 18th century for the construction of a vault beneath, and a small gabled projection at the east end was built to contain the short stair up from the chancel. The east window is of two cinquefoiled lights with a sexfoil opening in the head, and is of late 14th-century date, reset in this wall; the jambs have been repaired with cement. In the north wall is a window of two cinquefoiled lights chiefly of modern stonework. The plain collar-beam roof is probably original.

In the north wall of the nave are two three-light windows with cinquefoiled arches and tracery above, also a door with moulded arch and jambs and traceried spandrels; all these are of the 15th century, but the stonework has been much renewed. At the east end of the north wall are the lower and upper doors to the rood-loft set in a projecting portion of the wall. In the south wall is a wide arch of three moulded orders plastered, opening into the south transept or chapel. West of it are two three-light windows of modern stonework, the westernmost of which occupies the position of the old south doorway, done away with about 1830.[5] There are some old moulded timbers in the roof.

In the east and west walls of the south chapel is a five-light mullioned and traceried window of plastered brickwork and a four-centred doorway in the east; in the south wall are two single-light windows with

---

[92] *Cal. Chart. R.* 1226–59, p. 423.
[93] *Cal. Pat.* 1292–1301, p. 220.
[94] Inq. a.q.d. file 450, no. 32.
[95] See Manor.
[96] *L. and P. Hen. VIII*, iv, g. 5336 (10). A field called 'Godmundeshyde' in this manor occurs as early as 1297. It was then held by the lord of the manor of Humphrey Earl of Hereford (Chan. Inq. p.m. 25 Edw. I, file 80, no. 2).

[97] *L. and P. Hen. VIII*, v, 1206.
[98] Ibid. iv, 5831.
[99] Exch. Dep. Mixed Co. Mich. 36 Chas. II, no. 22.
[100] Chan. Inq. p.m. 25 Edw. I, no. 46.
[1] Close, 23 Hen. VII, pt. ii, no. 9.
[2] Rentals and Surv. portf. 8, no. 30. This took its name from the Warde family. John Warde had two mills in Hunsdon a little earlier (Chan. Proc. [Ser. 2],

xlii, 53). In the conveyance of 1508, which mentions Wadesmill as belonging to the manor of Hunsdon, appurtenances are given in Standon and Wadesmill. The latter is another Wadesmill, a hamlet in the parishes of Standon and Thundridge.
[3] Recov. R. Mich. 5 Jas. I, rot. 187.
[4] Close, 13 Will. III, pt. viii, no. 11. See Eastwick and Gilston.
[5] *East Herts. Arch. Soc. Trans.* ii, 50.

four-centred arches; they are all of early 17th-century date.

The upper part of the north porch is of open timber-work; the entrance has a pointed-arched opening flanked on either side by an opening with a cusped head; the barge-board has plain cuspings; the open sides have square bars at short intervals set diagonally; it is of early 15th-century work.

The early 15th-century tower, which is unbuttressed, is in three stages; the tower arch is of two orders, the inner order resting upon jambs with capitals and bases; above the arch may be seen the line of an earlier steep roof to the nave; the west doorway is of two moulded orders, the inner order forming a pointed arch, the outer being carried square over it; in the spandrels are shields, all repaired; above is a window of two cinquefoiled lights with cusped opening in the head. On the north and west faces of the second stage are two-light windows, and at the belfry stage on each face is a

The pulpit is hexagonal and of small dimensions; it has two tiers of plain moulded panels with a carved frieze above and a carved sounding-board over; it is of early 17th-century date.

In the chancel windows and in some of the nave windows are fragments of 15th-century glass, containing figures of six of the Apostles, white rose of York, fetterlocks, and Bowyers' flotes.

On the north side of the chancel is a recess with a depressed arch, having cusped and panelled sides and arch, and shields of arms to Francis Poynz, 1528. On the same side is a large canopied tomb to Sir Thomas Foster, with a recumbent effigy clothed in the judges' robes; he died in 1612. In front of the tomb is a richly worked railing of wrought-iron. The Fosters were a branch of the Northumberland family.

On the south side of the south chapel is a large monument to John Carey, third Lord Hunsdon, and his wife, the founder of the chapel erected by him during their lives about 1616; it is of marble and

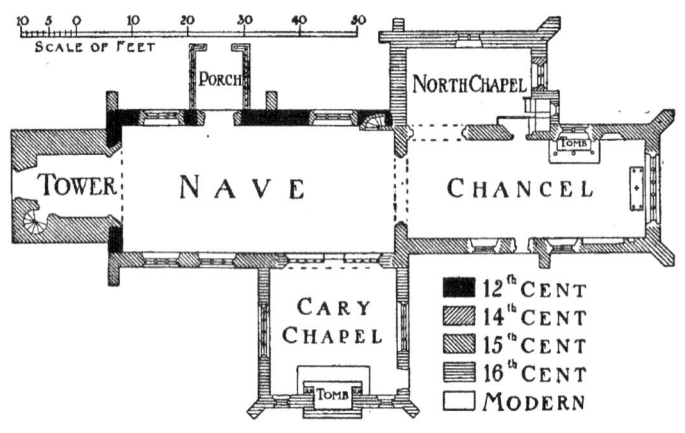

PLAN OF HUNSDON CHURCH

window of two trefoiled lights with cusped opening above. Above the embattled parapet is a slender spire covered with shingles. In the south-west angle of the tower is the circular newel stair to the belfry. The font, of clunch, is the original one recut, and is probably of 15th-century date. Under the chancel arch is the lower part only of the 15th-century rood screen with traceried panels.

Under the arch to the south chapel is a fine oak screen of about 1610. The lower part has moulded panels separated by fluted pilasters above which is a rail of richly carved arabesque patterns; the upper part consists of a series of open panels with round arches set in square frames separated by Ionic carved and fluted pillars, and having a moulded entablature with richly carved frieze; over the cornice, in the centre, in an open scroll-work setting is a shield containing the arms of the Careys and allied families.

The communion table and rails in the chancel are of early 17th-century date, and near the door is a plain 17th-century poor-box.

alabaster, with Corinthian columns and moulded entablature supporting an arched canopy, under which are the recumbent effigies of the knight and his wife; the dates of their death are omitted.

Two large early 18th-century monuments to the Calverts of Hunsdon House and to Robert Chester of Briggens were moved from the north wall of the chancel to the north chapel, and thence in 1911 to the nave.

In the nave is a brass to James Gray, park-keeper, who died 1591. The figures represent a hunter who has just shot an arrow into a stag, being himself killed by an arrow in the hand of Death, represented by a skeleton. Another brass on the north wall of the chancel is to Margaret Shelley, 1495; the figure is dressed in a shroud, and above is a representation of the Holy Trinity; portions of the brass are missing.

There are eight bells: the treble, second and third by Mears & Stainbank, 1883; the fourth inscribed 'Jesus be our spede, 1630,' by Robert Oldfeild; the fifth recast in 1883; the sixth, by

330

HUNSDON CHURCH: TOMB OF SIR THOMAS FOSTER

J. Briant, 1787; the seventh, dated 1668, and the eighth, 1652, both by Anthony Bartlett.

The communion plate consists of cup and cover paten, 1660, and modern chalice, paten and flagon.

The registers are in five books, as follows : (i) baptisms 1546 to 1675, burials 1546 to 1679, marriages 1546 to 1674 ; (ii) baptisms and burials 1679 to 1730, marriages 1680 to 1729 ; (iii) baptisms and burials 1734 to 1812, marriages 1734 to 1753 ; (iv) and (v) marriages 1754 to 1772 and 1772 to 1812.

ADVOWSON A priest is included among the tenants of Hunsdon Manor recorded in the Domesday Survey, and the church is mentioned in the taxation of Pope Nicholas (1291).[6] At this date Merton Priory possessed an annual pension of £8 from Hunsdon Church,[7] and in 1350 we find the lord of Hunsdon Manor (John Engayne) suing the Prior of Merton for the right of presentation to the living.[8] There is no record of the termination of the suit, but Merton continued to present until the Dissolution. The copy of a patent granting the advowson of Hunsdon Church to the Prior and convent of Merton Abbey is said to have been in the possession of Thomas Cromwell,[9] but no further trace of this patent has been found. The advowson seems to have passed to Sir Henry Carey with the manor,[10] and henceforward followed the same descent.[11] After the death of Mr. Charles James Phelips in 1903 Hunsdon advowson was sold to Mr. John Henry Buxton, the present patron.

CHARITIES The Poor's Land and Stock Charities are regulated by a scheme of the Charity Commissioners 17 January 1906. They comprise the charities of :

1. George, Lord Hunsdon, founded by will proved in P.C.C. 27 September 1603, under which he gave a sum of money which was invested in land for the benefit of the poor of Eastwick and Hunsdon.

2. Henry, Lord Hunsdon, founded by indenture dated 1 February 1615. The endowment of these two charities originally consisted of four pieces of land

HUNSDON CHURCH FROM THE NORTH-WEST

known respectively as Godfrey's Piece, Puke's Piece, the Town Lands and Oldburys, which were sold in 1905 and the proceeds invested in stock. The endowment for the parish of Hunsdon consists of £448 North-Eastern Railway 4 per cent. Guaranteed Stock, producing £17 18s. 4d. yearly, and £30 13s. 11d. consols, producing 15s. 4d. yearly. (See also under parish of Eastwick.)

3. Robert Chester, founded by will dated in 1730. The endowment originally consisted of land called Mallons, containing about 12 acres, which was sold

---

[6] *Pope Nich. Tax.* (Rec. Com.), 18.
[7] He still held this pension in 1428 (*Feud. Aids*, ii, 466), but there is no record of it at the Dissolution.
[8] De Banco R. 362, m. 39 d.; 363, m. 56.

[9] *L. and P. Hen. VIII*, vii, 923 (v).
[10] See Memo. R. Mich. 2 Jas. I, rot. 80 ; Duchy of Lanc. Misc. Bks. xxiii, 240.
[11] Chan. Inq. p.m. (Ser. 2), ccxlvi, 111 ; cclxxxvi, 170 ; ccclxxiv, 95 ; Feet

of F. Div. Co. Hil. 18 & 19 Chas. II ; Herts. East. 23 Chas. II ; Recov. R. Mich. 17 Geo. II, rot. 379 ; Hil. 29 Geo. III, rot. 23 ; Feet of F. Herts. Trin. 46 Geo. III ; Inst. Bks. (P.R.O.).

A HISTORY OF HERTFORDSHIRE

in 1900 and the proceeds invested in £190 4s. 7d. consols, producing £4 15s. yearly.

4. The Pound Piece, containing about 30 poles, which was sold in 1902 and the proceeds invested in £14 7s. 6d. consols, producing 7s. yearly.

The net income of the united charities is applied in pensions for the aged poor. The several sums of stock are held by the official trustees, who also hold £163 6s. 9d. consols arising from sale of glebe lands.

SAWBRIDGEWORTH

Sabrixteworda (xi cent.) ; Sebrichworde, Sebristeworda, Sabrytesworth (xii cent.) ; Sabrithtesworth (xiii cent.) ; Sabrisceworth, Sabrettesworth (xiv cent.) ; Sabresford or Sabrisworth (xv cent.) ; Sabridgeworth (xvi cent.) ; Sawbridgeworth (xviii cent.).

Sawbridgeworth is a large parish of about 6,638 acres in extent, divided from the county of Essex on the south and east by the River Stort, except for a projecting tongue of land forming the Hyde Hall estate which lies on the east of the river. On the south and east. From the main road here a view is obtained over the river into Essex. The chief crops are wheat, barley and beans, about half the area consisting of arable land. Large quantities of saffron were once grown in Sawbridgeworth, but cornfields had replaced the saffron fields before the 15th century.[4] Saffron Field on Great Beazleys Farm and Saffron Garden, south-west of Spelbrook, now both arable, preserve the name of this ancient industry. No inclosure award has been made for Sawbridgeworth,

THREE MILE POND FARM, SAWBRIDGEWORTH

west the boundary is formed by a small stream called Fiddler's Brook. The road from London to Newmarket passes through the parish in a north-easterly direction. To the south of the village it is known as the London Road, to the north as the Stortford Road. At Spelbrook in the north of the parish stood a turnpike gate where tolls were collected for the Hockerill trustees.[1] The road crosses the river and at the same time passes from Essex to Hertfordshire by the High Bridge, which is maintained by the county.[2] The old wooden bridge here was ruinous in 1771, and was replaced by one of brick.[3] A little to the east of the town is a railway station on the Cambridge line of the Great Eastern railway.

Sawbridgeworth lies on the London Clay. The ground reaches an altitude of about 300 ft. in the north, sloping down towards the valley of the Rib on but there were a great number of common fields in the parish. Townfield lay within the quadrangle formed by the four main streets of the town, North Field was on the north-west of the town, East Field on the south-east and on the east of the main road, Mill Fen was on the east of North Field, with the mill at its southern extremity, Eden Common adjoined the western side of the quadrangle, whilst White Post Field, Great Sayes Field, Manfield, Hoestock, Claveley, Bean Field, Brick Field, Belcomstead, Writhingales, Henley Hearn, Great Hollingson, Sidcup, Kingsey, and many other commons appurtenant to the numerous manors covered the greater part of the parish.[5] All these fields are now in separate ownership. Other field-names in Sawbridgeworth mentioned in 1838 are Goggles and Further and Hither Glices on Stonard's Farm, Numums Field on Redrick's Farm,

---

[1] *Sess. R.* (Herts. Co. Rec.), ii, 240.
[2] Ibid. 44, 45, 99, 109, 233, 238, 280, 426.
[3] Ibid. 119, 120, 271.
[4] See advowson.
[5] Apportionment of rent-charge in lieu of tithes, 1838. Returns and map at Bd. of Agric.

332

Rainbow Field and Parrot's Field on Rowney Farm, White Moor, White Field, and Mountain Mead on Blunt's Farm, Great and Little Battles (arable) and Battle Wood, part of Gilston Glebe.[6] Beanfield, now called Bell Mead, was left to the church for the purpose of growing beans to be strewn on the floor of the church.

An interesting agricultural enterprise was begun here by the late Mr. John Prout. In 1861 he acquired Blunt's or Blount's Farm, consisting of about 450 acres on the chalky boulder clay, and there applied the results obtained from the Rothamsted experiments to practical farming. The farm was laid out for the production of a continuous series of corn crops, and for this purpose was divided into fields of about 50 acres, each of which was dressed with chemical manures and cultivated by steam ploughs. Mr. John Prout carried on the farm until 1894, when he was succeeded by his son Mr. William Prout.[7] The nursery gardens of Messrs. Rivers & Sons date back to about 1720, when they were established by John Rivers, a native of Berkshire. Mr. Thomas Rivers, who succeeded to the business in 1827, formed his famous collection of roses here. He also introduced the 'Early Rivers' plum, which has done good service to English gardeners by extending the native fruit season. His son, Mr. T. A. H. Rivers, is the present head of the firm.

The town of Sawbridgeworth lies on the east of the parish near the Stort and on the London Road. It forms a parallelogram in shape, Barkers Lane (now called Station Road) and Cock Street (or Bell Street, as it is now generally called) running at right angles to the London Road (here called the Cambridge Road) and Knight Street forming the fourth side of the figure. The Newtown lies along Barker Laue, which is the north side of the parallelogram. The names Knight Street and Cock Street are as old at least as the 16th century.[8] A cross called Knight's Cross was apparently situated in the former street, whilst from it a road led to the Two Crosses (Le Toocrowches) which were in Sayesfield.[9] Church Street, a continuation of Cock Street, leads to the parish church of St. Mary. To the south-west of the church is the Square, which was once the market-place. There is now no market, but two fairs are still held on the Fair Green, one in April and the other in October. The vicarage lies to the south of the church. In the London Road is a Congregational chapel representing a dissenting community dating back as far as 1669. In 1814 a chapel for Independents and Baptists was certified at Sawbridgeworth; this was superseded by a new chapel built in 1862.[10] There are two elementary schools, one to the north and the other to the south of the church. To the north of the town is a corn-mill, probably occupying the site of the mill mentioned in the Domesday Survey. The eastern part of the town is for the most part occupied by malt-houses, malt-making being the chief industry.

A number of old houses still remain in and about the town. The Church House, situated at the churchyard gates, is an old building with good beams. This was formerly church property, and

SAWBRIDGEWORTH : HAND AND CROWN INN

[6] Apportionment of rent-charge in lieu of tithes, 1838. Returns and map at Bd. of Agric.
[7] *V.C.H. Herts.* ii, 138 ; *Dict. Nat. Biog.* s.v. John Prout.
[8] Ct. R. (Duchy of Lanc.), bdle. 77, no. 1000. Cherchegate Street, which occurs in 1378, is perhaps an earlier name for Cock Street, or may correspond with the present Church Street (Subs. R. bdle. 242, no. 19).
[9] Ct. R. (Duchy of Lanc.), bdle. 77, no. 1000.
[10] Urwick, *Nonconformity in Herts.* 686–7. One place of meeting for Presbyterians at the beginning of the 18th century was Hyde Hall, certified by Strange Jocelyn in 1715–16 (ibid.).

was used as a workhouse and afterwards as a school. It has lately been bought and given for a church house (see Charities, no. 1).[10a] On both sides of Bell Street are several 17th-century cottages built of timber and brick coated with cement and having projecting upper stories. A cottage on the south side has its original brick chimneys. There are also some pleasing 18th-century houses in the town. On the road to High Wych is the Hand and Crown Inn, a 16th-century gabled building of two stories which has been added to in the last century. It is of timber and plaster with a projecting upper story and a porch. There is an original window on the south side. On the Stortford Road, a little way past North End, is Three Mile Pond Farm, a 17th-century pargeted house. Clay Lane (now called West Road), leading west from the town, has also several old farm-houses. Great Beazleys, on the north of it, is now a small cottage, but incorporates a fragment of an earlier 17th-century timber-framed farm-house of two stories. On an interior

Successive grants of market (see manor) have never resulted in making Sawbridgeworth a commercial centre. Probably the neighbourhood of a flourishing market at Bishop's Stortford interfered with the success of the Sawbridgeworth market. From the number of inhabitants who contributed to the various local assessments, however, it would seem that the town has always been a thriving one, and in the 15th century there is record of burgage tenure there (see manor). In the 14th century the parish was divided for fiscal purposes into the districts of Cherchegate Street, Pyshoo Street, Nethynhoo, Westwood Street, Frere Street, Mynton Street, Smith Street, Chames Well Street, Haleynes Grene (Allen's Green), Brod Street, Spelbrok and Northende. Clutterbuck, writing in 1827, mentions that the parish contained three hamlets, Town Quarter, Spelbrook Quarter and Highway Quarter. In 1901 part of the parish of Sawbridgeworth was made into a new civil parish and urban district. The town is

THARBIES, SAWBRIDGEWORTH

beam is cut I.R. 1612. To the east of the house is an old barn built of sun-dried mud bricks. Crump's Farm, on the same side of the road, is a red brick building of two stories and attics, with the inscription $_I{}^K_A$ 1628 over the front door. Little Beazleys, on the south side, is a two-storied building with thatched roof and the date 1662 on the north front. Due north of Great Beazleys is Tharbies, now a modern farm-house occupied by Mr. J. L. Kirkby. Close to the house is a small square dove-house, timber-framed. The lower part is weather-boarded and the upper part covered with lath and plaster and ornamented with square flush panels. The pyramidal roof is tiled and has two small gables at the apex. About half a mile north of Tharbies there was an old moat marked on the ordnance map. This has been recently filled up by Mr. Kirkby and ploughed over.

now governed by an urban district council of twelve members.

The hamlet of High Wych lies on the road from Sawbridgeworth to Gilston, about half a mile south-west of Sawbridgeworth. It was formed into an ecclesiastical district in 1862.[11] St. James's Church stands on the north of the road. To the south of the church is the school, and on the other side of the road is the vicarage. Spelbrook[12] is another hamlet on the main road to the north of Sawbridgeworth. The school, which was built in 1891, is used for services on Sunday.

There is little of antiquarian interest in the history of the parish of Sawbridgeworth. Only one discovery of prehistoric remains has been made, that of two cinerary urns containing ashes or calcined bones found about 300 yards north of the Stort and 170 yards east of the high road from Sawbridgeworth

[10a] Information from Rev. H. A. Lipscomb.
[11] *Lond. Gaz.* 25 Mar. 1862, p. 1605.
[12] The name is found in the 13th century (see Assize R. 325 [15 Edw. I], which mentions ' Richard Faber de Spelebrok ').

to Harlow and fragments of pottery of the Romano-British period.[13] Historically Sawbridgeworth owes its interest to its manors, which furnish an unusually complete example of the processes of subinfeudation (see below).

The manor of *SAWBRIDGEMANORS WORTH*, assessed in 1086 at 24½ hides and consisting of land for forty ploughs, meadow for twenty plough-teams, pasture for the live stock, woodland for 300 swine and a mill then held by a tenant, must have comprised the whole of the present parish. In the reign of Edward the Confessor it had been held by Asgar the Staller, and after the Conquest it was acquired by Geoffrey de Mandeville, who held in 1086.[14] William de Mandeville, son and successor of Geoffrey, mortgaged the manor to the Crown, and it was granted by Henry I to Eudo Dapifer.[15] Geoffrey de Mandeville the younger, however, on obtaining a renewed grant of the earldom of Essex (conferred originally on his father Geoffrey de Mandeville, son of William, in 1156), also received all the lands held by Geoffrey his great-grandfather, including Sawbridgeworth, with a release of the mortgage held by Henry I on the manor.[16] The lands were to be held with soc, sac, toll, team and infangentheof. Geoffrey the second Earl of Essex died in 1166, when he was succeeded by his brother William de Mandeville, third Earl of Essex. He died in 1189, leaving no issue, and Sawbridgeworth passed to his aunt Beatrice de Say, daughter of William de Mandeville, and on her death to her younger son Geoffrey de Say. From this family the manor (reduced by 74 librates from its extent in 1086, see below under Pishobury) took the name of *SAYESBURY*.

MANDEVILLE, Earl of Essex. *Quarterly or and gules* which arms were assumed and borne by the SAYS.

In 1222 Geoffrey de Say, son of the last-mentioned Geoffrey, received the grant of a market to be held at Sawbridgeworth on Saturday.[17] By another grant the following year the day was changed to Friday.[18] William de Say, son and successor of Geoffrey, probably inclosed the park, for in 1237 he was allowed ten bucks from the king's forest of Essex to place in his park of Sawbridgeworth.[19] In 1245 he obtained a licence for free warren in his manor.[20] The extent taken at his death in 1272 mentions the park and warren.[21] William de Say, his son and successor, was presented before the commissioners of Edward I for having appropriated free warren on alien fees and on the lands of his tenants.[22] He claimed the liberties of gallows, view of frankpledge, assize of bread and ale, pillory, tumbrel and prison at Sawbridgeworth as belonging to the honour of Mandeville and exercised by his ancestors. These were allowed him.[23] William de Say died in 1295.[24] Geoffrey de Say, his son, was summoned to Parliament as Lord Say from 1313. In 1306 he obtained a renewal of the Friday market granted in 1223 and a grant of a yearly fair on the vigil and feast of the Nativity of the Virgin Mary (8 September).[25] He died in 1322[26]; his wife Idonia survived him and received a grant of the manor for life from her son Geoffrey.[27] Geoffrey the younger died in 1359[28] and was succeeded by his son William de Say. The extent of the manor taken at his death in 1375 gives a messuage with garden, 500 acres of arable land, 15 acres of meadow, 20 acres of pasture and 100 acres of wood. The rents from customary tenants included 1 lb. of wax and 3 gross of arrows.[29] John son and heir of William died a minor in 1382.[30] The manor passed to his sister Elizabeth, who made a settlement on herself and her first husband, Sir John de Falwesle, in 1388,[31] and on herself and second husband, Sir William Heron, in 1396.[32] Elizabeth Lady Say died without issue in 1399. Heron, who was summoned to Parliament as Lord Heron from 1393, and is generally considered to have been styled Lord Say,[33] obtained many of his wife's estates, including Sawbridgeworth. Maud Bosenho, daughter of Elizabeth de Alden, one of the co-heirs of Elizabeth de Say, quitclaimed her right in the manor to him in 1401.[34] He died seised in 1404,[35] his nephew John, son of his brother John, being his heir. The extent taken at his death mentions that the capital messuage was then ruinous. Sir John Heron died in 1420 and was succeeded by his son John,[36] who in 1460–1 settled Sawbridgeworth on himself and his wife Agnes in tail with contingent remainder to Brian Rowcliff and other feoffees.[37] John Heron died in 1468 without issue.[38] A few months afterwards the feoffees conveyed the manor to Sir John Say, who died seised of it in 1478.[39] His son Sir William Say died in 1529, leaving two daughters, of whom Mary wife of Henry Bourchier, Earl of Essex, inherited Sawbridgeworth.[40] Their daughter and heir Anne, wife of William Lord Parr, had livery of Sawbridgeworth on her father's death in March 1539–40.[41] Lord Parr, who was created Earl of Essex in 1543 and Marquess of Northampton in 1547, was attainted in 1553[42] and Sawbridgeworth came to the Crown.

---

[13] *East Herts. Arch. Soc. Trans.* i, 191.
[14] *V.C.H. Herts.* i, 332a.
[15] *Colchester Cartulary* (Roxburghe Club), 22. There may have been a former grant of the manor, as well as of the church, to Otwel Fitz Count (see advowson).
[16] See charter printed by Mr. J. H. Round in *Geoff. de Mandeville*, 235. See also article by Mr. Round in *Essex Arch. Soc. Trans.* (New Ser.), v, 245.
[17] *Rot. Lit. Claus.* (Rec. Com.), i, 514.
[18] Ibid. 540b.
[19] *Cal. Close*, 1234–7, p. 445.
[20] *Cal. Chart. R.* 1226–57, p. 282; *Abbrev. Rot. Orig.* (Rec. Com.), i, 7.
[21] Chan. Inq. p.m. 56 Hen. III, no. 37.
[22] *Hund. R.* (Rec. Com.), i, 188.

[23] Assize R. 323 (Mich. 6 Edw. I).
[24] Chan. Inq. p.m. 23 Edw. I, no. 49; *Cal. Pat.* 1292–1301, p. 188; Chan. Inq. p.m. 25 Edw. I, no. 10.
[25] *Cal. Chart. R.* 1300–26, p. 73. An exemplification of this charter and of the grant of free warren were obtained by the lord in 1531 (*L. and P. Hen. VIII*, 559 [31]).
[26] Chan. Inq. p.m. 15 Edw. II, no. 41.
[27] *Cal. Pat.* 1330–4, p. 310.
[28] Chan. Inq. p.m. 33 Edw. III, no. 37.
[29] Ibid. 49 Edw. III, pt. ii (1st nos.), no. 44 (file 251).
[30] Ibid. 6 Ric. II, no. 67.
[31] *Cal. Pat.* 1385–9, p. 407; Feet of F. Div. Co. 11 Ric. II, no. 93.

[32] *Cal. Pat.* 1391–6, p. 339; Feet of F. Div. Co. 19 Ric. II, no. 110.
[33] G.E.C. *Peerage*, s.v. Say.
[34] Close, 2 Hen. IV, pt. ii, m. 19 d.
[35] Chan. Inq. p.m. 6 Hen. IV, no. 21.
[36] Ibid. 8 Hen. V, no. 17.
[37] Feet of F. Div. Co. 39 Hen. VI, no. 457.
[38] Chan. Inq. p.m. 8 Edw. IV, no. 33. The heir was unknown. Agnes married David Malpas (*Cal. Pat.* 1476–85, p. 116).
[39] Chan. Inq. p.m. 18 Edw. IV, no. 43.
[40] Ibid. (Ser. 2), li, 50.
[41] Ct. of Wards, Feod. Surv. dlxxviii, fol. 372 d.; see *L. and P. Hen. VIII*, xvi, 1308 (16); Feet of F. Herts. Hil. 33 Hen. VIII.
[42] G.E.C. *Peerage*, s.v. Northampton.

A HISTORY OF HERTFORDSHIRE

In 1556 a lease of the manor for forty years was made to trustees for the benefit of Anne Lady Bourchier, whom Lord Parr had repudiated as his wife in 1543.[43] During her tenure a suit in Chancery was brought against her by copyholders of the manor whom she had turned out of their tenements on the plea that the lands had been granted by her father, who held the manor for life only. Judgement was given for the plaintiffs in 1565.[44] Anne died in 1571 without legitimate issue and the manor escheated to the Crown. In January 1572–3 the farm called Sayes Park was leased to William Lord Burghley,[45] and in 1609 a lease was made to Robert Earl of Salisbury (son of Lord Burghley) for the lives of himself, his son William Cecil and his daughter Frances Cecil.[46] The earl died in 1612 and his son in 1668. In February 1613–14 the manor and park were granted in fee to Lionel Cranfield,[47] a son of Thomas Cranfield of London. He filled successively the offices of Master of the Requests, Keeper of the Great Wardrobe and Master of the Court of Wards and Liveries, and in 1621 was made Lord Cranfield of Cranfield, co. Bedford. From 1621 to 1624 he was Lord High Treasurer and was created Earl of Middlesex in 1622. In May 1624, however, he was convicted of mismanagement and sentenced to lose all his offices and fined £50,000.[48] He seems to have surrendered the manor to the king, who in 1632 granted it with Sayes Park, the manor of Pishobury (except the park), Sawbridgeworth Mills and the rents of land called Alexander, late of Edward Leventhorpe, and of the manor of Glasmonhall, co. Cambridge (viz. 1 lb. of pepper and 1 lb. of corn from the first and 1 red sparrow-hawk from the second) to Arthur Brett and Nicholas Harman.[49] They in 1635 joined with the earl in conveying the manors to Thomas Hewett,[50] created a baronet in 1660, who resided at Pishobury.[51] He died in 1662 and was succeeded by his son Sir George Hewett of Pishobury, who for his services in Ireland was made Baron of Jamestown, co. Longford, and Viscount Hewett of Gowran, co. Kilkenny, in 1689. He died without issue in 1689.[52] His heirs were his four surviving sisters, Elizabeth wife of Sir Richard Anderson, bart., Arabella wife of Sir William Wiseman, Margaret wife of Sir Edward Farmer, and Mary wife of Sir Charles Crofts Read.[53]

In the same year Sir Charles and Lady Read settled their quarter of the manor of Sayesbury, of the farm called Sayes Park, closes called Church Close and Sayes Garden, a coppice called Sayes Coppice, the two water-mills called Sawbridgeworth Mills, one a corn-mill and the other a fulling-mill, and the manor of Pishobury on their three youngest children, Jane wife of Anthony Wroth, Bridget afterwards wife of Thomas Tarver, and Thomas.[54] In the division of Lord Hewett's lands made in 1691 the whole of the Sawbridgeworth estate seems to have been settled on Lady Read[55] and to have descended to her three younger children. Jane and Anthony Wroth conveyed their third about 1700 to William Betts,[56] and Bridget and Thomas Tarver their share some years later to Thomas Betts.[57] In 1709 Thomas and Bridget conveyed a sixth (their share after the death of Bridget's brother Thomas) to Robert Colman.[58] Each of the first two of these conveyances, and possibly the third, was in trust for Ralph Freeman.[59] Whether he acquired the remaining sixth of the lands is uncertain, as in 1709 Anthony Wroth settled it to his own use.[60]

The manors descended with Hamells in Braughing (q.v.) to Philip Yorke, third Earl of Hardwicke,[61] who, according to Clutterbuck, sold them in 1823 to Rowland Alston of Harrold House, co. Beds.[62] In 1851 they were purchased by John Hodgson of Gilston,[63] since which date they have descended with Gilston (q.v.), Mr. A. S. Bowlby being the present lord of the manors.

The manor-house of Sayesbury was long ago pulled down, and the demesne lands have been for the most part divided up into farms.[64] Sayes Park Farm, Park Field a large field to the west of Sayes Park Farm, Corn Park to the south of this and Grass Park to the north of it preserve the name of the ancient manorial park, and Dovehouse Field of the manorial dovecote.[65]

Some accounts for the manor at the end of the 13th century show that there were 8 virgates which paid ox-silver and sheep-silver to the lord (cf. Pishobury). The 'gavelerth,' of which each acre paid 6d., is also mentioned.[66] Burgage tenure is mentioned in a rental of 1433 of the lands of John Heron (15th century), where the rent of assize within the borough of Sawbridgeworth is said to amount to £4 9s. 6d. and the rent within the 'patria' to £3 17s. 9d.[67] A pedigree of the villeins of the manor taken by inquisition apparently in the 13th century[68] is printed by Professor Vinogradoff.[69]

The manor called *SAWBRIDGEWORTH* down to the end of the 13th century, and after that *PISHO* or *PISHOBURY* (Peyshoo, Pyssoubery, xiii cent.; Pyshobury, Spisshou, xiv cent.; Pishou, Pyshowe, xv cent.; Pyssowe, Pisshebury, Pishoo, xvi cent.; Pishebury, xvii cent.), originated in a grant of 74 librates of land at Sawbridgeworth, which Geoffrey de Mandeville the elder (ob. 1144) made to Warin and Henry Fitz Gerold, to hold by

---

[43] G.E.C. *Peerage*, s.v. Northampton; Pat. 3 & 4 Phil. and Mary, pt. xii, m. 42. He had apparently kept her lands.
[44] Chan. Proc. (Ser. 2), bdle. 139, no. 31; bdle. 136, no. 7; Chan. Decr. R. 30, no. 4.
[45] Pat. 15 Eliz. pt. i, m. 9.
[46] Ibid. 7 Jas. I, pt. iii, no. 9.
[47] Ibid. 11 Jas. I, pt. xiii.
[48] G.E.C. *Peerage*, s.v. Middlesex.
[49] Pat. 8 Chas. I, pt. ix, no. 20. This grant may have been in trust for the Earl of Middlesex, for his wife was Anne daughter of James Brett of Hoby, co. Lincoln.
[50] Feet of F. Div. Co. Mich. 11 Chas. I.
[51] See *Cal. S. P. Dom.* 1638–9, p. 586.

[52] G.E.C. *Peerage*, s.v. Hewett.
[53] Add. Chart. 44867; Feet of F. Div. Co. Trin. 5 Will. and Mary. Arabella and Mary were widows by the latter date (1693).
[54] Add. Chart. 44869; Feet of F. Div. Co. Hil. 1 Will. and Mary.
[55] See Feet of F. Div. Co. Trin. 5 Will. and Mary; Chauncy, *Hist. Antiq. of Herts.* 172.
[56] Feet of F. Herts. Mich. 12 Will. III; Mich. 13 Will. III.
[57] Ibid. Div. Co. Trin. 6 Anne; Recov. R. Mich. 6 Anne, rot. 77.
[58] Feet of F. Div. Co. Hil. 8 Anne; Recov. R. Hil. 8 Anne, rot. 124, 133.

[59] See Com. Pleas D. Enr. Hil. 8 Anne, m. 5.
[60] Ibid.
[61] See Recov. R. Hil. 4 Geo. II, rot. 254; Trin. 16 Geo. II, rot. 26; Com. Pleas D. Enr. East. 39 Geo. III, m. 42.
[62] Clutterbuck, *Hist. and Antiq. of Herts.* iii, 196.
[63] Cussans, *Hist. of Herts. Braughing Hund.* 78.
[64] See apportionment of rent-charge, 1838.
[65] Ibid.
[66] Mins. Accts. bdle. 868, no. 6.
[67] Ibid. no. 9; Rentals and Surv. R. 295.
[68] Ibid. portf. 8, no. 42.
[69] *Villeinage in Engl.* 143.

the service of one knight for each 20 librates.[70] Grants were made by Warin and Henry to Bury St. Edmunds and Reading Abbey (see Tednambury and Groves); the remainder of the land formed the manor of Pishobury. Henry, who survived his brother, left two sons, Warin and Henry. Margaret, daughter and heir of Warin, married Baldwin de Redvers, Earl of Devon, whom she survived, and secondly Falkes de Breauté, who forfeited in 1224. The manor was granted to Margaret during the king's pleasure.[71] In 1248 Margaret levied a fine with William de Say, by which it was agreed that William and his heirs were to have free warren throughout the vill of Sawbridgeworth including Margaret's demesnes, the warren to be kept by William's warrener, whilst Margaret and her heirs were to have free chase in her fee with dogs, birds or nets, and free fishery in the river where it adjoined her lands.[72] Baldwin de Redvers, Earl of Devon, son and heir of Margaret, died in February 1244-5 [73] and his son Baldwin in 1262,[74] leaving no issue. His widow Margaret had seisin of the manor.[75] She married Roger Aguilon,[76] and held the manor until her death in 1292.[77] It then passed to Isabella Countess of Albemarle, sister of Baldwin,[78] who died in 1293, having survived her only daughter Avelina, wife of Edmund Earl of Lancaster. Her cousin Hugh de Courtenay, great-grandson of Mary daughter of William de Redvers (father of the first-mentioned Baldwin), was her heir, but Warin Lisle (de Insula) had a grant of the issues of the manor in 1294 to hold until Hugh came of age,[79] and in 1310 his son Robert successfully claimed the manor against Hugh de Courtenay by descent from Henry the brother of Warin above mentioned (son of Henry Fitz Gerold), whose daughter Alice married Robert Lisle of Rougemont and was father of Robert, father of Warin, father of the plaintiff.[80]

REDVERS. *Or a lion azure.*

Robert Lisle was summoned to Parliament as Lord Lisle from 1311. Shortly before his death (in January 1342-3) he took religious orders, having previously in 1339 granted Pishobury with other manors to his daughters Alice, wife of Sir Thomas Seymour, and Elizabeth Peverel for life, with remainder to his son John, who quitclaimed to his sisters.[81] This grant was apparently made by Robert for the performance of certain alms.[82] In 1343, however, John obtained from Alice and Elizabeth a release of the manor for thirty years, with the exception of certain premises—viz. the house on the left-hand side within the second gate, which contained two chambers for habitation, and the park of Gedelesho, which belonged to the manor, John retaining 12 acres of underwood yearly with profits from the land called Vodeleye and housbote and heybote for the manor, the keeper of Gedelesho Wood to be chosen with the assent of both parties and to have his robe from Alice and his livery of corn, &c., from John.[83] John Lord Lisle died seised of the lease in 1356.[84] After his death Alice Seymour surrendered Pishobury to his son Robert, who was to assist her in the foundation of charities begun by Sir John Lisle for the soul of his father.[85] In 1368 Robert Lisle granted his knights' fees and the courts held for his tenants at Walbrook and Farningho, co. Essex, to the king.[86] This transaction has led to the inference that he had no legitimate issue, but one pedigree gives him a son William,[87] and a William Lisle granted Pishobury in March 1392-3 to Richard first Lord Scrope of Bolton,[88] this transaction being followed in 1394 by a quitclaim from Sir Robert Lisle.[89]

LISLE. *Gules a leopard argent crowned or.*

In 1393 Lord Scrope had licence to endow a chantry in his chapel in Bolton Castle with a rent of £33 6s. 8d. from the manor.[90] He died in 1403, his will being dated at Pishobury in 1400.[91] His son and heir Roger second Lord Scrope died in the same year. Richard third Lord Scrope, son of Roger, mortgaged the manor, and it was held by mortgagees at the time of his death in 1420.[92] His son Henry fourth Lord Scrope died seised in January 1458-9,[92a] and the manor was held successively by his son John fifth Lord Scrope, who died in 1498,[93] and by Henry sixth Lord Scrope, son of John, who died in 1506. Henry, the seventh

SCROPE of Bolton. *Azure a bend or.*

---

[70] *Red Bk. of Exch.* (Rolls Ser.), i, 356; iii, 731.
[71] *Rot. Lit. Claus.* (Rec. Com.), i, 617b.
[72] Feet of F. Herts. 32 Hen. III, no. 385.
[73] G.E.C. *Peerage,* s.v. Devon.
[74] Chan. Inq. p.m. 47 Hen. III, no. 37b.
[75] *Excerpta e Rot. Fin.* (Rec. Com.), ii, 384.
[76] See Assize R. 323 (Mich. 6 Edw. I), where Roger de Aguilon is said to hold three and a quarter knights' fees in Sawbridgeworth.
[77] Chan. Inq. p.m. 20 Edw. I, no. 139.
[78] *Cal. Close,* 1288-96, p. 236.
[79] Ibid. p. 357. A rental of the manor at this date shows that there were a capital messuage, 242 acres of arable land, 29 acres of meadow, 27 acres of several pasture, an inclosed wood of 156 acres called the Park, where was both several and common pasture, and a water-mill. The rents from the customary tenants included two called ox-silver and sheep-silver (Anct. Extents Exch. K.R. no. 81 [1]).
[80] Chan. Inq. p.m. 3 Edw. II, no. 60; file 27, no. 5; *Cal. Close,* 1307-13, pp. 273, 284. An extent of the manor of about this date is in Rentals and Surv. portf. 8, no. 43. The manorial buildings consisted of an outer court with barn, grange, dovecot, &c., and an inner court with hall and chapel and rooms built over them.
[81] Feet of F. Div. Co. 13 Edw. III, no. 70; *Cal. Close,* 1339-41, pp. 274, 332, 635, 647.
[82] See *Cal. Close,* 1343-6, p. 119.
[83] Ibid.
[84] Chan. Inq. p.m. 30 Edw. III, no. 40; *Cal. Close,* 1354-60, p. 255.
[85] *Cal. Close,* 1354-60, p. 630.
[86] Ibid. 1364-8, p. 494.
[87] G. F. Beltz, *Mem. of Order of Garter,* 44; see G.E.C. *Peerage,* s.v. Lisle; Baker, *Northants,* i, 620.
[88] Close, 16 Ric. II, m. 16d. This William may have been Robert's brother Sir William Lisle, who is said to have died without issue.
[89] Ibid. 18 Ric. II, m. 29d.
[90] *Cal. Pat.* 1391-6, p. 224.
[91] G.E.C. *Peerage,* s.v. Scrope.
[92] Chan. Inq. p.m. 9 Hen. V, no. 27. Accounts for the manor at this date exist at the Record Office. Among the tenants of the manor were seven molemen who did works amounting to 5s. 10d. and paid rents of assize (Mins. Accts. bdle. 839, no. 16).
[92a] Chan. Inq. p.m. 37 Hen. VI, no. 31.
[93] Ibid. (Ser. 2), xiii, 138.

A HISTORY OF HERTFORDSHIRE

lord, received an intimation through Cromwell in 1532 that the king wished to have the manor to annex it to the honour of Hunsdon.[94] Negotiations were begun, but the transaction was not completed when Lord Scrope died in December 1533. The exchange was effected by his son John eighth Lord Scrope in March 1533-4.[95] An extent of the manor of about this date, probably when it came into the king's hands, describes a park nearly 2 miles in circumference, well wooded, with game, deer and coneys, and a lodge on one side for the keeper, a moated house within the park, then somewhat fallen into decay, and a stable in good repair, with room for twenty horses.[96]

In 1534 Henry VIII granted the manor to his queen Anne Boleyn.[97] The Sawbridgeworth mills, which had been leased by Henry Lord Scrope to Robert Noddes, were in 1544 leased to Oliver Rigbye of Waltham Holy Cross.[98] In 1547 Edward VI granted the manor with Sawbridgeworth Mill and Pishoo Park to Sir Thomas Cawarden, Gentleman of the Privy Chamber,[99] who a few months later alienated it to Sir Wimund Carew of Blechingley.[100] Thomas son of the latter conveyed it in 1555 to Thomas Mildmay,[1] from whom it descended to his second son Walter Mildmay,[2] who was holding in 1576.[3] Rather later (about 1598) the manor was seized into the hands of the queen in satisfaction of a sum of £2,232 for which Sir Wimund Carew had been in debt to the Crown,[4] and was leased to Thomas Monke.[5] Mildmay died in February 1606-7, when the debt was still unliquidated, but Sir Thomas Mildmay, his son, was holding in 1610,[6] and in 1611 conveyed the manor, with the two mills and other appurtenances, to Lionel Cranfield,[7] who also acquired Sayesbury. The rest of the descent of the two manors is treated under Sayesbury (q.v.).

After the death of George Lord Hewett in 1689 the capital messuage of Pishobury was limited to his sister Lady Arabella Wiseman for a thousand years.[8] She sold it, according to Clutterbuck, to William Gardiner,[9] from whom it came to Edward Gardiner and then descended with Shingehall and Mathams (q.v.) to Rowland Alston. He sold it in 1847 to Francis Ede, after whose death in 1849 it was acquired by Mr. B. B. Colvin of Waltham, and his executors conveyed it in 1865 to Andrew Caldecott. It was bought from Caldecott by the late Mr. Francis W. Buxton, who sold it later to Col. F. Charrington, C.M.G., the present owner and occupier.[10]

The house, which lies within Pishobury Park immediately to the south of the town, is said to have been built in 1585 by Sir Walter Mildmay. Chauncy describes it as having 20 acres of ground on the east side then used as a paddock for deer, a bowling green in front raised 5 ft. high and inclosed with a brick wall, and two avenues about 4 furlongs in length from the house to the road.[11] Two of the avenues were removed and the third destroyed by Jeremiah Mills under the advice of 'Capability Brown,' who superintended the making of an ornamental lake.[12] The house was destroyed by fire and practically rebuilt by James Wyatt in 1782, who utilized some of the old material. It is a square brick building of three stories with embattled parapet, and a central courtyard, which is now roofed in. In the entrance hall is some 16th-century oak panelling. The dining room is panelled and has a carved stone fireplace with an iron fireback bearing the Stuart royal arms and dated 1635. Above is a carved oak overmantel of about the same date. In the servants' hall are a 16th-century fireplace and panelling. The stables and barns on the south of the house date from about 1600.

The manor of TEDNAMBURY, TEDENHAMBURY, or TEDENHOEBURY (Tydenham,[13] xiv cent.; Tydenhoubery, Tuddenhoburye, xvi cent.; Tuddinghoebury, xvii cent.), which lies on the north-east of the parish, was formed by 6 librates of land given to the monastery of Bury St. Edmunds (of which the name seems to be a corruption) by Warin Fitz Gerold (see under Pishobury) in the first half of the 12th century.[14] In the reign of Edward I the Abbot of St. Edmund's claimed gallows, view of frankpledge, and assize of bread and ale at Sawbridgeworth as among the liberties conferred on the abbey by Canute.[15] These were allowed him. The manor remained with St. Edmund's until the Dissolution, when the farm was worth £11 10s.[16]

In 1544 the manor was granted to Sir Henry Parker, Lord Morley, together with woods of 9½ acres called Sperthes Grove, Walters Grove and Patmore's Grove.[17] Lord Morley was succeeded in 1555 by his grandson Henry, who died seised in 1577,[18] when it descended to his son Edward Lord Morley, and at his death in 1618 to his son William Lord Morley and Mounteagle of Gunpowder Plot fame.[19] He died in

CHARRINGTON. *Gules a griffon's head razed between two crosses formy or with two flaunches wavy or and azure.*

BURY ST. EDMUND'S ABBEY. *Azure three crowns or each thrust through with a pair of arrows or saltirewise.*

---

[94] L. and P. Hen. VIII, v, 916; vi, 43, 348, 383.
[95] Stat. of Realm, iii, 488.
[96] Rentals and Surv. portf. 8, no. 35.
[97] L. and P. Hen. VIII, vii, 1498 (1).
[98] Ibid. xix (1), 1636 (59).
[99] Pat. 1 Edw. VI, pt. i, m. 37.
[100] Ibid. pt. iii, m. 41.
[1] Ibid. 1 & 2 Phil. and Mary, pt. i, m. 28.
[2] The pedigrees of the Mildmay families do not agree (cf. Harl. Soc. Publ. xiii, pt. i, 251; Berry, Essex Gen. 149; Morant, Hist. of Essex, ii, 4). But there seem to have been three generations called Thomas, and Walter seems to have been a son of the second Thomas who died in 1567.
[3] Recov. R. East. 1576, rot. 155.
[4] Egerton MS. 2644, fol. 105 (copy of commission to inquire as to its value).
[5] Chan. Inq. p.m. (Ser. 2), cccxcv, 85; Add. Chart. 25607.
[6] Feet of F. Herts. Trin. 8 Jas. I.
[7] Ibid. Mich. 9 Jas. I.
[8] Add. Chart. 44867.
[9] Hist. and Antiq. of Herts. iii, 201.
[10] Cussans, Hist. of Herts. Braughing Hund. 80; information from Rev. H. A. Lipscomb.
[11] Chauncy, Hist. Antiq. of Herts. 177.
[12] Cussans, Hist. of Herts. Braughing Hund. 80.
[13] Cal. Close, 1364-8, p. 494.
[14] Red Bk. of Exch. (Rolls Ser.), i, 356; Dugdale, Mon. iii, 139.
[15] Plac. de Quo Warr. (Rec. Com.), 290.
[16] Valor Eccl. (Rec. Com.), iii, 460.
[17] L. and P. Hen. VIII, xix (1), 278 (57).
[18] W. and L. Inq. p.m. xix, 91.
[19] G.E.C. Peerage, s.v. Morley. He was Lord Mounteagle in his mother's right.

338

BRAUGHING HUNDRED SAWBRIDGEWORTH

1622[20] and his son Henry Lord Morley in 1655. Thomas Lord Morley, son of the latter, conveyed it in 1657 to Robert Brudenell and others,[21] apparently trustees for Thomas Lindsey,[22] whom Chauncy gives as the purchaser. Lindsey had two daughters, Grace, who married Richard How, and Elizabeth, who married George Hocknell.[23] The manor was divided between them, but seems eventually to have become the property of the heirs of Grace. Her son Richard How died without issue[24]; his brother John was holding the manor in 1738,[25] in which year he conveyed it to William Taylor.[26] William Taylor How was in possession in 1756.[27] He died before 1779, leaving five sisters and co-heirs, Jane, Catherine and Anne Taylor, Elizabeth wife of James Stillingfleet and Sarah wife of Savile Read.[28] According to Clutterbuck it was assigned to Sarah and Savile Read, but was devised by the latter, who survived, to the three unmarried sisters, and was sold by Anne, who outlived the others, to Mrs. Rose Milles in 1799.[29]

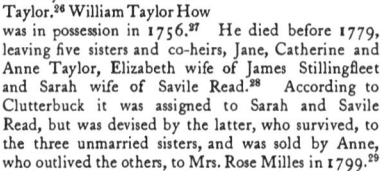

Tednambury descended with Shingehall and Mathams (q.v.) to Rowland Alston, who sold in 1842 to William Bigg of London. After his death in 1868 it was conveyed by trustees to Augustus Smith of Upper Norwood.[30] In 1867 John Hodgson of Gilston bought it.[31] It now belongs to Sir Walter Gilbey.

The manor of GROVES comprised the land given by Henry Fitz Gerold (see Pishobury) to the abbey of St. Mary, Reading, probably in the second half of the 12th century.[32] In 1287 the Abbot of Reading claimed assize of bread and ale, infangentheof, utfangentheof, chattels of fugitives and felons, and waif in his lands at Sawbridgeworth as among the liberties granted him by Henry I.[33] After the Dissolution the manor was granted in 1544 to William Gooding or Goodwin[34] of Writtle, co. Essex. He sold it in 1549 to Robert Gooday.[35] It descended to Thomas Gooday, who conveyed it in 1571 to Robert Hirst.[36] The latter died seised in 1548, his heir being his nephew Henry, son of his brother John.[37] Henry Hirst sold in 1594 to John Duke,[38] who held it until his death in 1606.[39] In the inquisition taken at his death the manor is called Sawbridgeworth *alias* Groves, the first time that the latter name appears. Robert Duke, his son, is said by Channcy to have granted the manor in 1628 to his own son John Duke, rector of High Roding, co. Essex, who married Joyce Bennet.[40] Robert son of John sold the manor in 1665 to his mother Joyce,[41] who in 1671 conveyed it to Thomas Rogers.[42] John Rogers, son of Thomas,[43] sold it in 1693 to Edmund Godwin[44] of Eastwick, and from the latter it was bought in 1702 by Anne Mary Godfrey, widow.[45] It descended to Peter Godfrey, and a Godfrey was holding when Salmon wrote (1728). In 1742 it was in the possession of Eliott Taylor,[46] of whose heirs it was bought by Thomas Nathaniel Williams, the owner in 1823.[47] It was sold, according to Cussans' descent, to Jones De'Ath by Williams's trustees in 1844.[48] Later it was acquired from the De'Ath family by Mr. E. B. Barnard, who sold it to Mr. Silva, the present owner. The house called Grove Lodge lies within a small park a little to the north-west of High Wych.

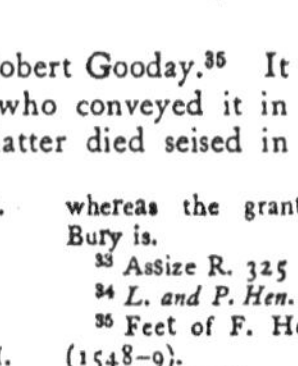

PARKER, Lord Morley. *Argent a lion passant gules between two bars sable with three harts' heads caboshed sable in the chief and three bezants on the bars.*

READING ABBEY. *Azure three scallops or.*

The manors of SHINGEHALL *alias* SHINGEHALL *alias* SHINGEY and MATHAMS seem to have been originally two separate properties which became amalgamated in the hands of the Matham family, from whom the second manor took its name. They were evidently formed by subinfeudation from the Mandeville manor, and were held of the honour of Mandeville. This descended not to the Says (as did the manor of Sayesbury) but to the Earls of Essex, descendants of William de Say, eldest son of Beatrice de Say, whose daughter Beatrice married Geoffrey Fitz Piers, created Earl of Essex in 1199, their son Geoffrey taking the name of Mandeville.[49] Through Maud, sister and heir of William de Mandeville, it passed to the Bohuns, Earls of Hereford, and eventually came to the Crown by the marriage of Mary de Bohun with Henry IV and was annexed to the duchy of Lancaster.[50] The manor of Mathams was the holding of a family of that name who had lands in Sawbridgeworth at an early date. A John de Matham appears as a witness to deeds at the end of the 13th century.[51] He had a daughter Christina[52] and a wife Isabel. John and Isabel were apparently both dead by 1304, when a conveyance took place of a piece of land charged with an annual rent of 2d. for celebrating two anniversaries for their souls.[53] Geoffrey de Matham[54] was holding lands in Sawbridgeworth in 1268.[55] He claimed view of frankpledge in 1278,[56] as held by his ancestors since the

[20] Chan. Inq. p.m. (Ser. 2), cccci, 16.
[21] Feet of F. Div. Co. East. 1657.
[22] See Chauncy, op. cit. 179.
[23] Ibid.
[24] Salmon, *Hist. of Herts.* 263.
[25] Feet of F. Herts. East. 11 Geo. II.
[26] Ibid.
[27] Recov. R. Mich. 30 Geo. II, rot. 225.
[28] Feet of F. Div. Co. Hil. 19 Geo. III.
[29] Clutterbuck, op. cit. iii, 210; Recov. R. Trin. 43 Geo. III, rot. 193.
[30] Cussans, *Hist. of Herts. Braughing Hund.* 83.
[31] Ibid.
[32] Dugdale, *Mon.* iv, 42. The gift is not mentioned in Henry's *carta* of 1166, whereas the grant to St. Edmund's Bury is.
[33] Assize R. 325 (East. 15 Edw. I).
[34] L. and P. Hen. VIII, xix (2), 690 (1).
[35] Feet of F. Herts. Hil. 2 Edw. VI (1548–9).
[36] Ibid. Mich. 13 & 14 Eliz.
[37] Chan. Inq. p.m. (Ser. 2), cc, 34.
[38] Feet of F. Herts. East. 36 Eliz.
[39] Chan. Inq. p.m. (Ser. 2), ccxcix, 131.
[40] *Hist. Antiq. of Herts.* 180.
[41] Ibid.
[42] Feet of F. Herts. Trin. 23 Chas. II.
[43] Chauncy, loc. cit.
[44] Feet of F. Herts. Mich. 5 Will. and Mary.
[45] Ibid. 1 Anne.
[46] Recov. R. Trin. 16 Geo. II, rot. 26.
[47] Clutterbuck, op. cit. iii, 210.
[48] Cussans, *Hist. of Herts. Braughing Hund.* 83.
[49] G.E.C. *Peerage*, s.v. Essex.
[50] Chan. Inq. p.m. 32 Edw. III (2nd nos.), no. 92; 5 Ric. II, no. 41; 2 Ric. III, no. 32.
[51] Add. Chart. 4718. Mr. Round points out that a Serlo de Matom is mentioned in the charter of the Empress Maud to Geoffrey de Mandeville (1141).
[52] Ibid. 4733.
[53] Ibid. 4749.
[54] He is witness to the above-mentioned conveyance.
[55] Feet of F. Herts. 52 Hen. III, no. 605.
[56] *Plac. de Quo Warr.* 278.

339

A HISTORY OF HERTFORDSHIRE

time of the Conquest. About 1301 he acquired the lands called 'La Syngledehall' from Geoffrey de la Mare,[57] and henceforth the two manors descend together. He seems to have been succeeded by Sampson Matham.[58] In 1365 Sampson and his wife Margaret granted all their lands in Sawbridgeworth to John Blode, a London fishmonger, to hold during their lives.[59] Hamelin son of Sampson succeeded to the property in Sawbridgeworth, and died seised of a messuage and 240 acres of land, 10 acres of meadow, 7 acres of pasture, 4 acres of wood and 16s. 4d. rent there in 1382.[60] He left two daughters, Elizabeth and Margaret,[61] who as Elizabeth wife of John Thorpe and Margaret wife of John Michell, a fishmonger of London, conveyed the manor called Mathams and lands in Sawbridgeworth to John Leventhorpe by fine of Hilary, 1413–14.[62]

John Leventhorpe was member for the county in 1413 and 1422.[63] He died in 1433 and was buried at Sawbridgeworth.[64] His son John Leventhorpe, also member for Hertfordshire in 1467,[65] had a grant of free warren in Sawbridgeworth, Thorley and Stortford in 1439.[66] In 1447 he obtained a grant of a market on Wednesdays and two fairs on the eve, day and morrow of the feasts of St. Denis and St. George the Martyr, and licence to inclose 400 acres of land, 40 acres of meadow and 80 acres of wood in Sawbridgeworth and Thorley for a park.[67] On his death in 1484 he was succeeded by his son Thomas, aged sixty,[68] who held the manor until his death in 1493.[69] John, his son, who was Sheriff of Hertfordshire in 1509,[70] died in 1511, when Shingehall and Mathams descended to his son Thomas,[71] who in 1517 received a confirmation of the grant of market, fair, and park made in 1447.[72] He died in 1527,[73] his son Edward in 1551,[74] and his grandson Edward in 1566.[75] John son of Edward was knighted at Theobalds in 1603, was Sheriff of Hertfordshire in 1593–4 and 1607–8, and was created a baronet in 1622. He married Joan daughter of Sir John Brograve of Hamells in Braughing and died at Sawbridgeworth in 1625.[76] Thomas, his second but eldest surviving son, succeeded. He died in 1636 and was buried at Sawbridgeworth.[77] His son John, a minor at his father's death,[78] died of smallpox in 1649, when the property passed to his brother Sir Thomas Leventhorpe, who had no male issue. Sir Charles Leventhorpe, his uncle and male heir, rector of White Roding, co. Essex, succeeded to the title in 1679, but the manors passed to Mary daughter of Sir Thomas Leventhorpe, who married John Coke of Melbourne, co. Derby.[79]

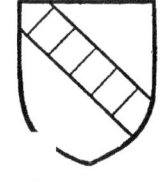

Thomas Coke, son of John and Mary, sold Shingehall and Mathams to Ralph Freeman, D.D.,[80] who conveyed them in 1755 to Edward Gardiner.[81] His daughter and heir Rose married Jeremiah Milles, and they were holding the manor in 1781.[82] Jeremiah died in 1797, whilst Rose Milles suffered a recovery of the manor in 1803,[83] and survived until 1835.[84] Rose, her daughter and co-heir, married Rowland Alston,[85] who acquired Sayesbury and Pishobury, after which the manors descend together (see under Sayesbury).

There is a homestead moat at Shingehall close to Trim's Green. The house is now a farm occupied by Mr. F. J. Lukies. The names Park Field and Mill Field on this estate (now both arable) point to the ancient park and mill.[86] On the north-west a moat marks the site of the old manor-house of Mathams.

The manor of *HYDE HALL*, which occupies the tongue of land on the east of the Stort, is an interesting example of an estate which has remained in the same family from the date of its first appearance until the present day. It appears first under the name of The Hyde and was held of the Earls of Essex, chief lords of the fee.[87] Early in the 13th century it was in the tenure of the Jocelyn family. A Ralph Jocelyn held land in Easton, co. Northants, in the reign of John, but there is no evidence of his holding The Hyde.[88] His son John, however, held it rather later.[89] Thomas son of John succeeded his father about the middle of the 13th century.[90] His son Thomas married Joan daughter of John le Blunt[91] (for this family see manor of Blunts). After the death of the younger Thomas[92] the rent from The Hyde was granted by the Earl of Essex to Sir Walter de Essex, who sold it in 1284 to Adam de Stratton to hold during the minority of the heir Thomas son of Thomas.[93] The next year Joan de la Lee, widow of Thomas, released her right of dower to Adam de

LEVENTHORPE of Shinglehall, baronet. *Argent a bend gobony gules and sable.*

JOCELYN, Earl of Roden. *Azure a circular wreath twisted argent and sable with four hawks' bells or affixed thereto.*

---

[57] Cott. Chart. xvii, 33.
[58] See *Cal. Close*, 1337–9, p. 262; 1354–60, p. 303; Chan. Inq. p.m. 32 Edw. III (2nd nos.), no. 92. His property in Sawbridgeworth is here called the manor of Eststede.
[59] *Cal. Close*, 1364–8, p. 70. Sampson was in money difficulties; see references in last note and ibid. 186.
[60] Chan. Inq. p.m. 5 Ric. II, no. 41.
[61] Ibid. ; *Cal. Pat.* 1381–5, p. 297.
[62] Feet of F. Herts. Hil. 1 Hen. V.
[63] *V.C.H. Herts. Families*, 290.
[64] There is a brass to him in the church.
[65] *V.C.H. Herts. Families*, 290.
[66] Chart. R. 1–20 Hen. VI, no. 41.
[67] Ibid. 25 & 26 Hen. VI, no. 13.
[68] Chan. Inq. p.m. 2 Ric. III. no. 32.

[69] Ibid. (Ser. 2), xxiii, 127.
[70] *V.C.H. Herts. Families*, 282.
[71] Chan. Inq. p.m. (Ser. 2), xxvii, 11.
[72] *L. and P. Hen. VIII*, ii (2), 3730.
[73] Exch. Inq. p.m. (Ser. 2), file 311, no. 2.
[74] Chan. Inq. p.m. (Ser. 2), xcv, 94.
[75] Ibid. cxlvi, 125.
[76] G.E.C. *Complete Baronetage*, i, 196; Chan. Inq. p.m. (Ser. 2), ccclxvii, 93.
[77] Chan. Inq. p.m. (Ser. 2), cccclxxx, 115.
[78] Ct. of Wards, Feod. Surv. no. 17.
[79] See Recov. R. East. 1 Anne, rot. 47.
[80] Cussans, *Hist. of Herts. Braughing Hund.* 82.
[81] Feet of F. Herts. Trin. 27 & 28 Geo. II ; Trin. 28 Geo. II (K.S.B.).

[82] Feet of F. Herts. Trin. 21 Geo. III.
[83] Recov. R. Trin. 43 Geo. III, rot. 193.
[84] M.I.
[85] Cussans, loc. cit.
[86] Apportionment of rent-charge, 1838 (Bd. of Agric.).
[87] Anct. D. (P.R.O.), A 5111.
[88] Harl. MS. 4944 (pedigrees and arms of Essex families), fol. 51b.
[89] Ibid.
[90] Ibid.
[91] Ibid.
[92] The pedigrees in Chauncy, op. cit. 82, and *Harl. Soc. Publ.* xiii (1), 225, leave out this Thomas.
[93] Anct. D. (P.R.O.), A 5111 (12 Edw. I).

Stratton.[94] A rental of the manor exists for this date. There was a house (*curia*) with garden and courtyard, 140 acres of arable land in the fields called Langeland, La Doune, Wrechewellefeld, Hallefeld, Hydewode, Suthfeld, and Wodeleye; nine free tenants, of whom four paid a yearly rent, other four paid a rent and owed suit of court, and one paid a rent and came to view of frankpledge on St. Andrew's Day and owed two capons at Christmas; six 'molmen' who paid a rent and owed suit of court, two of them being tallaged with the customary tenants; and four customary tenants who paid a rent and owed two works a week from Michaelmas to the Gules of August (forty-one weeks), and five works in the summer for mowing 2 acres of meadow, and sixteen works from the Gules of August to Michaelmas for cutting 4 acres of corn and 2 acres of oats, and also paid eight eggs and owed tallage and redemption of their blood and suit of court.[95]

Thomas Jocelyn (the third of the name) was succeeded by Ralph Jocelyn,[96] who died before 1323.[97] His widow Matilda was holding the manor with her second husband Roger de Berners in 1331.[98] Geoffrey son and heir of Ralph was living in 1360.[99] His son Ralph is mentioned as holding half a knight's fee in Hyde in 1373.[100] He died about 1383 and was succeeded by his son Thomas.[1] Geoffrey, called by Clutterbuck son of Thomas, was holding as late as 1403.[2] Thomas, his son apparently, had succeeded him before 1407, when he had a grant of the manor from Robert de la Rokell,[3] but he seems to have granted it in the same year to Geoffrey his brother and heir.[4] Geoffrey Jocelyn by will of 1424 left the manor to his son Thomas subject to his wife Joan's dower.[5] This Thomas inherited and was succeeded by his son George, who in 1457–8 granted it (for life apparently) to his uncle Ralph Jocelyn of London,[6] twice mayor of that city, who died in 1478.[7] In 1480 George settled the manor on his son Ralph, then about to marry Katherine daughter of Richard Martin of Faversham.[8] Ralph died in 1504, George, his son, being aged fourteen.[9] George had no issue, and in 1513 conveyed Hyde Hall to his uncle John Jocelyn,[10] to whom Gabriel, his brother and heir, released all right.[11] John died in 1525 and was succeeded by his son Thomas of High Roding, co. Essex,[12] created a Knight of the Bath at the coronation of Edward VI. At his death in 1585[13] the manor descended to his son Richard,[14] who died in 1605.[15] Robert his son succeeded him.[16] He was Sheriff of Hertfordshire in 1645–7. His third but eldest surviving son inherited Hyde Hall at his father's death in 1664, and was created a baronet in 1665. He was Sheriff of Hertfordshire in 1677–8.[17] In 1685 he settled Hyde Hall on his son Strange Jocelyn (by his wife Jane Strange), on the occasion of his marriage with Mary daughter of Tristram Conyers of Copped Hall in Epping.[18] He died and was buried at Sawbridgeworth in 1712, when Sir Strange Jocelyn succeeded.[19] After his death in 1734 the manor descended successively to his son Sir John Jocelyn, barrister-at-law, who died without issue in 1741, and to the latter's brother Sir Conyers, Sheriff of Hertfordshire 1745–6, who died in 1778, also leaving no issue. The estates and baronetcy passed to a cousin Robert Jocelyn, son and heir of Robert first Viscount Jocelyn and Lord Newport, Lord Chancellor of Ireland, son of Thomas, fifth son of the first baronet. Robert, who succeeded his father as Viscount Jocelyn in 1756, was M.P. for Old Leighlin from 1745 to 1756 and was Auditor-General in 1750. He was created Earl of Roden, co. Tipperary, in 1771. He died at Dublin in 1797. Robert, his son and heir, was also Auditor-General of the Exchequer. He died in 1820 at Hyde Hall and was succeeded by his son Robert, Auditor-General and M.P. for Louth 1806–7 and 1810–20, also *custos rotulorum* for the county of Louth. In 1821 he was created Baron Clanbrassil of Hyde Hall. He died at Edinburgh in 1870 and was succeeded by his grandson Robert, fourth Earl of Roden, who died single in 1880, when his uncle John Strange Jocelyn, fifth earl, inherited the property.[20] On his death in 1897 the title passed to his cousin William Henry Jocelyn, sixth earl, and at his death in 1910 to his brother Robert Julian Orde Jocelyn, seventh Earl of Roden. Hyde Hall is now held by Sophia Countess of Roden, widow of the fifth earl, but the house, which stands in a park of 300 acres, is the residence of the Earl of Arran. The old house was in the form of a quadrangle, but about the year 1806 the courtyard was roofed in to form an entrance hall.[21] Many new rooms were added and the exterior entirely altered, very little of the old house now remaining, but probably the walls once inclosing the courtyard and parts of the cellars are old. The present front is of a plain classic character and is coated with cement.

At the Record Office are a series of ministers' accounts for the manor from 12 Edward I to 19 Edward I, illustrating its domestic economy in the 13th century.[22]

The manor of *CHAMBERLAINS* alias *BURSTEAD*, which was held of the manor of Pishobury, seems to have been formed from two properties, one the holding of a family named Chamberlain and the other of a family named Burstead. The names of Simon le Chamberlain and his wife Isabel, holding land in Sawbridgeworth in 1323,[23] of Simon their son, living in 1355,[24] of John Chamberlain, living in 1354,[25] and of Walter Chamberlain, assessed for the poll tax in 1378,[26] have survived, whilst the name of Thomas Burstead occurs in 1426.[27] The estate seems to be first called a manor in the 16th

---

[94] Anct. D. (P.R.O.), A 5130.
[95] Rentals and Surv. portf. 8, no. 31.
[96] Harl. MS. 4944.
[97] Ibid.
[98] Ibid.
[99] Ibid.
[100] Ibid.
[1] Ibid.
[2] Ibid.
[3] Ibid.
[4] Ibid.
[5] Ibid.
[6] Ibid. Even if it was not a life grant the manor would have reverted to George as his uncle's heir.
[7] See inscription in church.
[8] Harl. MS. 4944; Exch. Inq. p.m. file 295, no. 6.
[9] Exch. Inq. p.m. file 295, no. 6.
[10] Feet of F. Herts. Trin. 5 Hen. VIII.
[11] Harl. MS. 4944.
[12] Chan. Inq. p.m. (Ser. 2), xliii, 21.
[13] Harl. MS. 4944.
[14] Ibid.; Feet of F. Mich. 27 & 28 Eliz.
[15] Morant, *Hist. of Essex*, ii, 466.
[16] Ibid.; see Add. Chart. 41717.
[17] G.E.C. *Complete Baronetage*, iv, 16.
[18] Ibid.; Feet of F. Herts. East. 1 Jas. II.
[19] G.E.C. *Complete Baronetage*, iv, 16.
[20] G.E.C. *Peerage*, s.v. Roden.
[21] Clutterbuck, op. cit. iii, 203. The original house is illustrated by Chauncy, op. cit.
[22] Mins. Accts. bdle. 868, no. 1–5.
[23] Add. Chart. 4952.
[24] *Cal. Pat.* 1354–8, p. 216.
[25] Add. Chart. 4775.
[26] Subs. R. bdle. 242, no. 19.
[27] Add. Chart. 4801.

century. John Shelley died seised of 'the manor of Chamberlains' in January 1523-4,[28] William Shelley, his son, a judge, being his heir. It appears in 1615 in the possession of Sir Thomas Bishop of Parham, co. Sussex,[29] who sold it in that year as the manor of Chamberlains *alias* Burstead to Thomas Draner of Hoxton, co. Middlesex. The latter died seised in 1632, having settled the manor on his nephew Sir William Halton (son of his sister Joan) with contingent remainder to his brother Robert Halton for life, then to Thomas son of Robert.[30] Thomas Halton was holding in 1661 [31] and Philip Halton in 1692.[32]

In 1743 Chamberlains was in the possession of Christopher Parker of St. George's, Hanover Square, who in that year settled it on his son Christopher and his issue.[33] In 1763 this entail was barred, the manor then being in the hands of mortgagees.[34] Christopher the elder died almost immediately afterwards, and in 1764 Christopher the younger (of St. Paul's, Covent Garden) paid off the mortgage by the sale of Bleches.[35] The manor was bequeathed by him to John Grimstead and Elizabeth his wife for their lives, with reversion to his cousin and heir Dorothy Parker.[36] He died before 1775.[37] Dorothy Parker conveyed her interest in 1786 to Robert Palmer.[38]

According to Cussans the farm called Bursteads was sold by Robert Lord Ebury to William Barnard of Sawbridgeworth in 1867.[39] It now belongs to Mr. E. B. Barnard, M.A., J.P., who lives at Fairgreen House in Sawbridgeworth.

The old manor-house, now used as a farm-house, which lies a little to the east of Trim's Green and is occupied by Mr. E. Stephens, is a small timber-framed house covered with lath and plaster, the plaster work being decorated with basket-work pattern probably of the middle of the 17th century. The main gables are weather-boarded, the apex of each being slightly hipped. The roofs are tiled. The house consists of a main block measuring about 37 ft. long by 24 ft. 6 in. in depth and is of two stories with attics. A massive brick chimney occupies the centre of the building, dividing the interior into two rooms, one of which is now subdivided. The entrance door is in the middle of the front and opens into a small lobby the width of the brick substructure of the chimneys (about 9 ft.), through which, as at Berkhampstead School and Rectory Farm, Pirton, a modern passage has been tunnelled to the stair at the back. The two small bay windows in front are modern, but all the other windows have oak mullions and transoms.

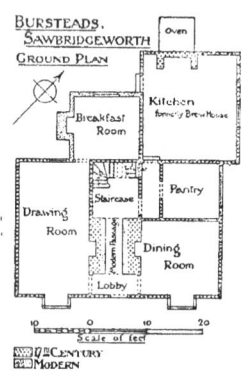

Adjoining the house is a very large and lofty thatched barn, probably erected during the 17th century.

The manor of *BLUNTS* originated in a grant of lands to Robert Blunt of London made by Warin Fitz Gerold (for whom see above under Pishobury) and confirmed by Geoffrey de Mandeville Earl of Essex, lord of the fee.[40] The names of John le Blunt,[41] who died before 1330,[42] Agnes his wife,[43] John (possibly their son),[44] who was living in

BURSTEADS: SOUTH-WEST FRONT

[28] Chan. Inq. p.m. (Ser. 2), xlvi, 40.
[29] Com. Pleas D. Enr. East. 13 Jas. I, m. 41.
[30] Chan. Inq. p.m. (Ser. 2), ccclxxiii, 34; *Visit. of Lincoln* (Harl. Soc.), ii, 446.
[31] Feet of F. Div. Co. Trin. 13 Chas. II.
[32] Recov. R. Mich. 4 Will. and Mary, rot. 12.
[33] Com. Pleas D. Enr. Hil. 3 Geo. III, m. 67.
[34] Ibid.
[35] Ibid. Trin. 4 Geo. III, m. 182.
[36] Ibid. 15 Geo. III, m. 256; Feet of F. Herts. Mich. 17 Geo. III.
[37] Com. Pleas D. Enr. Trin. 15 Geo. III, m. 256.
[38] Ibid. Hil. 26 Geo. III, m. 280.
[39] *Hist. of Herts. Braughing Hund.* 74.
[40] Sloane Chart. xxxii, 64; for facsimile of this charter see *Facsimiles of Charters in British Museum*, i, no. 43.
[41] Add. Chart. 4718.
[42] Ibid. 4757.
[43] Ibid. 4718, 4757.
[44] Ibid. 4761.

342

1341, Thomas, living in 1348,[45] and a Thomas, living in 1418,[46] occur in records of Sawbridgeworth. The services for their lands were owed in the 15th century to the lord of Mathams, to whom apparently they had been assigned at some earlier date by a lord of Pishobury.[47] Later the lands came either by escheat or purchase to the owners of Mathams. John Leventhorpe died seised in 1511 of the 'manor of Blunts,' and for a long time it descended with that manor[48] (q.v.). In 1861 it was bought by Mr. John Prout (see general description of parish) and now belongs to Mr. William Prout.

Other tenants of the lords of Pishobury and Mathams were the Vantorts,[49] whose holding in the 16th century is called the manor of *VANTORTS*. Margaret wife of Robert Vantort died in 1310 seised of lands in Sawbridgeworth, which descended to her son Thomas.[50] The name of Richard Vantort of Sawbridgeworth occurs in 1337 and 1348[51] and of John Vantort in 1378[52] and 1386.[53] A John Vantort was holding lands of John Leventhorpe of Mathams early in the 15th century.[54] In the 16th century the 'manor of Vantorts' was held with Mathams by the Leventhorpes[55] and subsequently became amalgamated with that manor. Vantorts Farm lies to the south-east of the town.

BLECHES, BLACHES, or *BLOTCHES* was the holding of a John Bleche, whose name appears in Sawbridgeworth at the end of the 14th century,[56] and who was living in 1404.[57] His lands, called the manor of Bleches, were held with Chamberlains (q.v.) in the 16th century by John Shelley. The estate descended with that manor until 1764, when it was sold by Christopher Parker the younger to raise money for paying off the mortgage on Chamberlains.[58] The purchaser was Edward Gardiner of Pishobury.

FRERES was similarly the holding of another local family. The name of Walter Frere occurs in 1220[59] and of William Frere in 1278.[60] Another Walter Frere and Alice his wife held lands in Sawbridgeworth in the 14th century.[61] They had sons John[62] and Robert.[63] Robert and his wife Cecilia were conveying lands in 1379,[64] and a Robert and his wife Katherine were living in 1418.[65] The chief holding seems to have been that of Thomas Frere, whose name occurs about the middle of the 15th century.[66] He held the property called Freres Place. By his wife Cecilia (who afterwards married Hamelin de Matham and died in 1410) he had two daughters, Joan, who married John son of John Burman of Stainby, co. Lincoln, by whom she had a son John aged three in 1418[67] (by which date she was dead),

and Alice, who married first Denis Lopham and secondly John Rodenhale.[68] In 1481 John Lymbard granted the manor of Freres to John Browne and John Jocelyn,[69] but whether any of these were beneficiary owners is uncertain. The estate next appears in 1509, when Clement Cotton and Constance his wife conveyed to Thomas Laurence,[70] after which no further record of it has been found. It seems to be represented by the present Fryars in the west of the parish.

A reputed manor called *ACTONS* was held in the 16th century by the Leventhorpes. John Leventhorpe was in possession in 1561.[71] In 1564 Edward Leventhorpe conveyed it to Thomas Leventhorpe,[72] who was holding it in 1570, when he granted it to Oliver Lord St. John and others,[73] probably trustees

BURSTEADS : INTERIOR OF GREAT BARN

in a sale. In February 1636–7 Sir John Fowle died seised of 'the manor or farm of Actons,' John, his eldest son, aged fourteen, being his heir.[74] This farm is situated on the west of the parish close to Fryars.

---

[45] *Cal. Close,* 1346–9, p. 611.
[46] Feet of F. Herts. 6 Hen. V, no. 35.
[47] Ibid. Or possibly they had lands held of both manors.
[48] It is mentioned in the documents dealing with Mathams as late as 1636 (Chan. Inq. p.m. [Ser. 2], ccclxxx, 115).
[49] See Feet of F. Herts. 6 Hen. V, no. 35 ; Chan. Inq. p.m. 4 Edw. II, no. 18.
[50] Chan. Inq. p.m. 4 Edw. II, no. 18.
[51] *Cal. Pat.* 1334–8, p. 401 ; *Cal. Close,* 1346–9, p. 611.
[52] Subs. R. bdle. 242, no. 19.

[53] Add. Chart. 4788.
[54] Feet of F. Herts. 6 Hen. V, no. 35 ; Early Chan. Proc. bdle. 75, no. 93.
[55] Chan. Inq. p.m. (Ser. 2), xlvi, 49 and later documents.
[56] Add. Chart. 4790.   [57] Ibid. 4793.
[58] Com. Pleas D. Enr. Trin. 4 Geo. III, m. 182.
[59] *Excerpta e Rot. Fin.* (Rec. Com.), i, 57.
[60] Assize R. 6 Edw. I (Agard's MS. index). For another William see Chan. Misc. bdle. 62, no. 42.
[61] Add. Chart. 4754, 4758, 4762, 4768, 4769, 4779.

[62] Ibid. 4774.   [63] Ibid. 4779.
[64] Ibid. 4783.
[65] Ibid. 4797, 4798.
[66] Ibid. 4771, 4773.
[67] For his proof of age see Chan. Inq. p.m. 19 Hen. VI, no. 47.
[68] Ibid. 5 Hen. V, no. 38.
[69] Harl. MS. 4944, fol. 51*b* et seq.
[70] Feet of F. Herts. Mich. 1 Hen. VIII.
[71] Ibid. Mich. 3 & 4 Eliz.
[72] Ibid. East. 6 Eliz.
[73] Ibid. Trin. 12 Eliz.
[74] Chan. Inq. p.m. (Ser. 2), ccclxxxiv, 153.

A HISTORY OF HERTFORDSHIRE

CHURCHES

The church of ST. MARY consists of chancel 44 ft. by 23 ft. 6 in., nave 58 ft. by 28 ft., north aisle 59 ft. by 11 ft. 6 in., south aisle (inclusive of south chapel) 73 ft. by 19 ft., south porch 12 ft. by 10 ft., west tower 19 ft. 6 in. by 17 ft.; all internal dimensions. The church is built of flint rubble with stone dressings, the chancel walls being coated with cement; the roofs are covered with lead.

It is probable that the main part of the chancel, nave and lower stage of the tower were built in the 13th century; the north and south aisles and the south chapel were added early in the 14th century; the clearstory was raised and the nave re-roofed in the 15th century, and probably about the same period the south porch was erected and the upper part of the tower built. In 1870 the whole church was repaired, much of the stonework renewed, and the chancel re-roofed.

In the east wall of the chancel is a large five-light window, one of two lights in the north wall, and two of three lights in the south are almost entirely of modern stonework. The partially blocked doorway on the north side is of 15th-century date, it probably opened into a vestry, now destroyed; the doorway has a four-centred arch with moulded jambs. The south chancel doorway is modern. At the west end of the south wall is a pointed arch of two richly-moulded orders, now blocked by the organ. The inner order is carried on moulded corbels; it is of about 1300. The chancel arch is of two splayed orders, with jambs of similar section; it is of 13th-century work, but the jambs, capitals and bases have been repaired.

The south chapel is used as a vestry, and is partly filled by the organ. The three-light east window is of modern stonework; in the south wall is a blocked window of 14th-century date. At the west end on the north side is the doorway to the rood stair; the upper doorway opens into the nave; the stair is partly blocked. The west end of the chapel opens into the south nave aisle without any structural division.

The nave has north and south arcades of three bays of pointed arches; the arches are of two moulded orders, with labels and head stops; the piers are of quatrefoil section and have moulded capitals and bases. The details of the two arcades differ, the north arcade being the richer, and is probably some twenty years earlier in date than the other. The clearstory windows are of two cinquefoiled arches under square heads, all of modern stonework. The roof is of 15th-century date, with moulded timbers and traceried spandrels, the trusses resting on carved stone corbels.

At the east end of the south wall of the north aisle is a recess, probably a piscina, with a cinquefoiled arch under a square head; it has been much renewed. The windows in the east and west walls are of three cinquefoiled lights, and those in the north wall of two lights, have moulded internal jambs and rear-arches; they have geometrical tracery under pointed arches, which has been partly renewed. The north doorway with its moulded arch has been largely renewed. Both the windows and the doorway are of 14th-century date. To the east of the doorway, internally, is a recess with square bracket under.

SAWBRIDGEWORTH CHURCH FROM THE SOUTH-EAST

344

SAWBRIDGEWORTH CHURCH : THE NAVE LOOKING EAST

SAWBRIDGEWORTH CHURCH : THE CHANCEL

The windows of the south aisle, with their tracery, are of modern stonework, but the internal jambs may be of 14th-century date. The south doorway is chiefly of early 14th-century date; the pointed arch is of three moulded orders; the moulded jambs appear to be earlier, and may be 13th-century work reset. The roofs of both aisles have moulded ribs and carved bosses, and are of 15th-century work; the spaces between the ribs are plastered. The trusses of the south aisle roof rest on carved stone corbels. To the east of the south doorway, internally, is a recess with cinquefoiled head and moulded jambs.

The stonework of the south porch is all modern, but it retains its 15th-century wooden roof.

The tower is of three stages without buttresses, and has an embattled parapet and a slender octagonal spire, lead covered, the lead ribs forming a lozenge-shaped diaper pattern. On the south side is a projecting stair turret of brick, finished with an embattled parapet below the belfry stage; it was probably built in the 16th century. The tower arch is of two splayed continuous orders of 14th-century date; the stonework of the jambs has been renewed. The 14th-century west door is of two splayed continuous orders, with a moulded label, and has been repaired; the 15th-century window above has three cinquefoiled lights under a four-centred arch.

The second stage of the tower has on the north and the south face a single pointed light; the belfry stage has on each face a two-light window of the 15th century, repaired with cement.

The octagonal font dates from about 1400, and has been repaired; on each side of the basin is a quatrefoil within a square panel; on the stem are traceried panels.

The 15th-century oak rood screen consists of three wide bays with pointed arches in the upper part; these are subdivided and the heads traceried; the lower close panels are also traceried.

The south door is panelled, the upper parts being traceried; it has been repaired. It retains its old ironwork, and is probably of late 14th-century date. Near it is an oak poor-box dating from about 1600. Under the tower is a large oak chest with five locks, probably of the 17th century, and incorporated with some of the seating are some early 16th-century bench ends and other woodwork. The oak pulpit is carved and panelled, and is inscribed 'Christe is all in all. 1632.'

At the north-east corner of the chancel is a tomb with the recumbent effigies of John Jocelyn, 1525, and his wife Phyllis; he is in plate armour and his wife is dressed in a long robe; the figures are much defaced. On the same wall is a large classical monument, with the figure of George Viscount Hewett, who died 1689. On the south wall of the chancel is a late 15th-century marble tomb without an inscription; the lower part has traceried panels with shields from which the brasses have been taken; above is a richly carved and traceried canopy supported on engaged shafts carved with a lozenge-shaped surface ornament. At the back, beneath the canopy, are indents of brasses of a man, his two wives and his children. In the south chapel is a large marble monument, with recumbent effigies of Sir John Leventhorpe, who died 1625, and his wife; they lie under a semicircular canopy with sculptured figures in the spandrels, and flanked by Corinthian columns supporting the cornice over which are his arms; kneeling figures of his fourteen children are in front.

On the east wall of the nave is a marble mural monument to Sir William Hewett, died 1637, and his wife, and under the tower is a monument to Sir Thomas Hewett, who died in 1662.

In the nave is a slab of Purbeck marble with an incised figure, apparently of a nun, probably of early 14th-century date, but the marginal inscription is illegible. Another slab in the nave bears the much-worn marginal inscription 'Hic jacet Thomas de Aungerville quondam Rector Ecclesie de Sabruchesworth, Non. Dec. 1333.'

In the south aisle is a stone slab with an illegible inscription of the 14th century.

On the chancel floor is a brass of Geoffrey Jocelyn, 1470, with figures of himself and his two wives; part of the inscription is gone.

In the nave is a slab with indents of a man, his two wives and four shields, the remaining shield bears the arms of Chauncy; another slab with brasses of twelve sons and six daughters with arms quarterly 1 and 4, on a chief a lion passant, 2 and 3 a lion rampant debruised by a bend.

On the floor of the south chapel are figures of a knight and a lady, with the arms of France and England quartered. The figures are said to be John Leventhorpe and his wife, about 1433; there is no inscription. In the south aisle is a figure of a lady in a mantle; three shields and arms of Leventhorpe. There is an indent of a man and another shield, but no inscription, said to represent Thomas Leventhorpe, who died in 1527, and his wife Joan; a brass with figures of a man in armour and a lady in Elizabethan dress, and inscription to Edward Leventhorpe, died 1551, and his wife Elizabeth.

In the north aisle are brasses of two shields and an inscription to William Channey, probably of the 15th century.

Beneath the tower is the figure of Mary wife of Edward Leventhorpe, died in 1566, with inscription; also of a man and a woman in shrouds, with a shield of France and England, probably to John Leventhorpe, who died in 1484. In the south aisle is the indent of a woman of 15th-century date. Other brasses belonging to Sawbridgeworth Church are now in the museum of Saffron Walden.

There are nine bells: the treble and second by John Taylor, 1872; the third by Thomas Lester, 1749; the fourth, fifth, sixth and seventh recast by Taylor, 1870; the tenor by John Briant, 1795; a small bell not in the peal, 1664.

The communion plate consists of modern chalice, paten and flagon.

The registers of baptisms, marriages and burials begin in 1558.

The church of ST. JAMES, HIGH WYCH, is a building of flint and stone in 13th-century style, consisting of chancel, nave of four bays, south aisle, south porch and south-west bell-turret.

ADVOWSONS A priest is mentioned among Geoffrey de Mandeville's tenants in 1086,[75] showing that the church was appurtenant to the manor. The tithes were given by Geoffrey de Mandeville to the church of St. Mary of Hurley, co. Berks., endowed by him at the end

[75] V.C.H. Herts. i, 332a.

A HISTORY OF HERTFORDSHIRE

of the reign of William I and granted to Westminster, to which church it formed a cell.[76] Early in the 12th century, probably while the manor was in the king's hands through a mortgage (see above), the church seems to have been granted by Henry I to Otwel Fitz Count (son of Hugh Earl of Chester), and after his death in the catastrophe of the *White Ship* in 1120 to have been given by the king to the abbey of Westminster.[76a] After the Mandevilles had regained possession, Geoffrey the first Earl of Essex (ob. 1144) granted the church of Sawbridgeworth to the abbey of Walden as part of its endowment.[77] Geoffrey de Mandeville the younger and William his brother are said to have looked with little favour on the numerous grants of churches made by their father to this abbey,[78] and this probably accounts for a renewal of the grant to St. Peter's, Westminster, made by William Earl of Essex (ob. 1189).[79] By an agreement made between Richard Abbot of Westminster and Eustace Bishop of London (1221–9) the advowson is said to have been transferred to the Bishops of London, who were to make annual payments to the Abbots of Westminster and Walden for the tithes.[80] In 1258 the king, who claimed the presentation during the vacancy of the abbey of Westminster, brought an action against the Bishop of London, recovered seisin of the advowson,[81] and presented John Maunsel, treasurer of York.[82] In 1266 the abbey recovered the presentation against Henry Bishop of London by assize of darrein presentment.[83] Licence for appropriation was granted by the king in 1331,[84] a mandate from Pope John XXII to the Bishop of London to carry out the appropriation having been obtained the year before.[85] The Bishop of London refused to appropriate, as appears by a second mandate of 1333[86] and also by a further renewal of the licence by Pope Clement VI in May 1351, the reason here given for the appropriation being that some of the abbey's houses had been burnt in the fire at the king's palace.[87] Apparently after the issue of these letters the abbey's proctor at the Roman Court renounced the abbey's right in favour of the Bishop of London, for in December of the same year the abbey agreed to pay the merchants of the society of Malbayl 800 florins if Sir Anthony Malbayl would obtain a renewal of the apostolic letters dated after the renunciation made by the abbey.[88] The appropriation seems to have been finally carried out in 1356, when a vicarage was ordained.[89] After the Dissolution the advowson was granted by Henry VIII to the Bishop of Westminster in 1541,[90] and by Edward VI, after the resignation of the Bishop of Westminster in 1550, to the Bishop of London,[91] with whom it remained until transferred to the see of Rochester in 1852. In 1877 it was again transferred to the Bishop of St. Albans, the present patron.[91a]

The rectory was granted by Henry VIII in 1542 to the Dean and Chapter of Westminster,[92] and after the dissolution of the abbey, temporarily refounded by Mary, was confirmed to them by Elizabeth.[93] The Ecclesiastical Commissioners are now the lay rectors. View of frankpledge was held by the parsons of Sawbridgeworth (previous to the appropriation) for their tenants in the parish,[94] and courts were held by the abbey of Westminster for the rectory lands as late as the 15th century.[95] In 1651 the trustees for the sale of church lands sold the parsonage-house to Patrick Carey with the site containing about 3½ acres, other lands including the Great and Little Orchard and Upper and Nether Stockwell, the first abutting on Parsonage Lane and the second on the field called Tedenhambury. These had been leased out by the dean and chapter.[96] A survey of the rectory taken in 1773 mentions the house with two barns, two stables, a cowhouse, a carthouse, a granary, a dovehouse and a large garden and field, also 118 acres of land and 14 acres in the common fields.[97] By an agreement with the tenant in 1791 the coalhouse, pantry and granary were to be taken down, the dairy, woodhouse, and barn rebuilt, and the parlour, brewhouse, servants' hall and the room above it to be repaired and tiled.[98] The moated house called Parsonage Farm, which has been recently pulled down, was situated a little to the north of the town. There is still a very large tithe barn with fine timbers in the roof. The thatched roof was replaced by a slate one a few years ago.

By the composition made in 1356 (see above) the vicar of Sawbridgeworth received a part of the revenues of the church, which then amounted to 43 marks yearly. For a long time the endowment was sufficient even for a cure of the size of Sawbridgeworth, and the vicars 'did not all only keep good hospitality, but also did so apply themselves to learning that they were able and did sufficiently do their duty.' A great part of their income was derived from the tithe paid for the saffron then grown in large quantities in the parish, but by the beginning of the 16th century the cultivation of saffron had been given up and the land used for corn; consequently the vicars' stipend had so decreased that they had to borrow from their parishioners and run into debt.[99] Matters were not much improved by 1704 when the vicar (Charles Pole) complained that the small tithes did not afford subsistence for himself and his family.[100]

In 1352 William Basset of Stowe St. Edward, parson of Toppesfield, had licence to grant a messuage in Sawbridgeworth to William de Stowe, parson of the church there, as a residence for two chaplains who were to celebrate in the church.[101] This was probably in connexion with a chantry.

---

[76] Dugdale, *Mon.* iii, 431.
[76a] J. A. Robinson, *Gilbert Crispin Abbot of Westminster*, 156. For this reference we have to thank Mr. J. H. Round.
[77] Dugdale, *Mon.* iv, 133.
[78] Ibid. 134.
[79] Cott. Chart. x, i. Yet the church was confirmed to Walden by Geoffrey de Mandeville the younger, by William, by Geoffrey Fitz Piers and by Stephen and Henry II (Harl. MS. 3697, fol. 18 [Cartulary of Walden]; Duchy of Lanc. Deeds, A 11).
[80] Cur. Reg. R. 160, m. 9 d.

[81] Ibid.; Westm. Abbey MSS. no. 8587; *Cal. Pat.* 1258–66, p. 81.
[82] *Cal. Pat.* 1247–58, p. 643.
[83] Ibid. 1258–66, p. 640.
[84] Ibid. 1330–4, p. 180.
[85] *Cal. Papal Letters*, ii, 350.
[86] Ibid. 394.
[87] Ibid. iii, 356. The vicar's portion was to be settled by the Bishop of Worcester.
[88] *Cal. Close*, 1349–54, p. 405.
[89] Westm. Abbey MSS. no. 8625.
[90] *L. and P. Hen. VIII*, xvi, 503 (33).
[91] Pat. 4 Edw. VI, pt. iv, m. 16.

[91a] *Lond. Gaz.* June 4 1852, p. 1578; July 13 1877, p. 4126.
[92] *L. and P. Hen. VIII*, xvii, 714 (5).
[93] Pat. 2 Eliz. pt. xi.
[94] Assize R. 325 (15 Edw. I).
[95] Some court rolls have survived (Ct. R. [Gen. Ser.], portf. 178, no. 28).
[96] Close, 1651, pt. xxxi, no. 23.
[97] Westm. Abbey MSS. no. 8648. For earlier surveys of the rectory lands see no. 8561–6.
[98] Ibid. 8650.
[99] Westm. Abbey MSS. no. 8625.
[100] Ibid. 8642.
[101] *Cal. Pat.* 1350–4, p. 221.

SAWBRIDGEWORTH CHURCH   TOMB OF SIR JOHN LEVENTHORPE AND HIS WIFE

BRAUGHING HUNDRED

The living of St. James, High Wych, is a vicarage in the gift of the vicar of Sawbridgeworth.

CHARITIES
The Sawbridgeworth United Charities are regulated by a scheme of the Charity Commissioners dated 6 March 1908. They comprise:—

1. The Church and Poor Lands (exclusive of the Sawbridgeworth Ecclesiastical Charity) comprised in an indenture dated 20 July 1652. The endowment consists of a moiety of the income derived from the following property:—

The bowling green, containing 3 r. 22 p., used as a recreation ground for boys;

Three cottages occupied as almshouses by three poor women who receive parochial relief;

Pishocroft Gardens, containing about 5 acres, near High Wych, let in allotments and producing about £9 10s.;

And a sum of £720 14s. 5d. consols in the name of the official trustees, producing £18 0s. 4d. yearly, arising from the sale in 1898 of a rood of land in Church Street, with the dwelling-house and school buildings thereon. The net income is distributed to the poor.

2. Charity of John Salmon for the poor, founded by will dated in 1729, whereby a yearly rent-charge of 20s. issuing out of a croft called Little Hempsall was devised for distribution in sums of 2s. at Christmas to ten poor families.

3. Charity of Richard King, founded by will dated in 1748, whereby a rent-charge of £1 issuing out of a messuage and land in Sawbridgeworth was devised to be distributed to twenty poor widows.

The Sawbridgeworth Ecclesiastical Charity.—By an Order of the Board of Charity Commissioners dated 17 March 1896 a moiety of the net income of the Church and Poor Lands was severed from the rest of the endowment and called the Sawbridgeworth Ecclesiastical Charity. The income is applied to church expenses. John Salmon also devised a sum of £1 yearly, issuing out of the croft called Little Hempsall, for beautifying and ornamenting the church. This sum is carried to the Church Expense Fund.

STANDON

In 1811 Mr. Orchard gave a sum of £25 stock, now represented by £25 consols with the official trustees, producing 12s. 4d. yearly, which sum is paid to the oldest widow in the parish.

In 1864 Daniel Brown, by will proved at London 5 May, gave £100 stock, the interest to be applied in keeping in repair the tomb of testator's family in the churchyard and any residue to be distributed to the poor on the first Sunday after Christmas Day. The dividends on the endowment amount to £2 5s. yearly.

In 1910 £1 7s. 6d. was spent in repairs to the tomb and twenty-six old people received 2s. each.

In 1895 Miss Frances Lane, by her will proved 8 October, gave £300 to be applied, so soon as land should be given for the purpose, in building and endowing an almshouse or almshouses for the benefit of married couples of sixty years and upwards. The legacy, less duty, was invested in consols, and the dividends are being invested in consols in augmentation of the principal sum, which in May 1909 amounted to £341 7s. 4d., in the names of the Rev. H. A. Lipscombe and two others.

The same testatrix bequeathed £100, the income arising therefrom to be applied in keeping the family tomb in the churchyard in repair, and any residue to be distributed to the poor; also a further sum of £100 to the Sunday school. These legacies, less duty, were invested in £161 11s. 5d. consols, producing £4 0s. 8d. yearly. In 1910 a sum of 18s. 9d. was spent in repairs to the tomb, £1 1s. 7d. was carried to the Sick and Needy Fund, and £2 0s. 4d. was paid to the treasurer of the Sunday school.

The same donor by her will also bequeathed a sum of money, the interest arising therefrom to be applied at the discretion of the vicar for the good of the district of Spelbrook. The legacy was invested in New Zealand 3½ per cent. Inscribed Stock, producing £14 6s. yearly in dividends. One moiety of this amount is applied to church expenses and the other to the church school.

STANDON

Standone (xi cent.); Staundon, Stondon, or Staunden (xiii cent. and later).

Standon is a large, irregularly shaped parish of about 7,738 acres, including 30 acres of water. Of this extent about half is arable land, rather less than half permanent grass, and the rest, about 500 acres, wood.[1] The soil varies, the subsoil being chalk and clay. The ground lies high with an altitude even in the Rib valley of from 200 ft. to 300 ft. above the ordnance datum, and rising to the east and west of the river. The highest point is 410 ft. in the extreme north-west of the parish. A very large proportion of the parish was covered by the numerous common fields before the inclosure award was made in 1835 under an Act of 1831.[1a] Among the common fields were the Half Acres, immediately to the east of the village, Pockendon, Pudding Dane, and Cobbin's Hill on the east of the river, Puckeridge, Stanboro, Shanfield, Widen, Barwick, Stapleford, Nimdell, Ragborough, Ody (Old Hall), Perry Field, and Herne Commons on the west of the river.[2] Other interesting field-names which occur are Great Bacchus, Upper Bacchus to the east of Colliers End, Bacchus north of this, Great and Little Artic, Strickups (once Strepock), the last three now part of the park of St. Edmund's College, Poundfield, Hop Ground, Hoppett and Colliers Croft (the last two part of Riggories Farm), all on the west of the parish in the neighbourhood of Old Hall Green; The Park,[3] Monk's Croft (south of Great Southey Wood), Thundermarsh (on the west bank of the river to the east of Youngsbury), Gunpowder Hill[4] (about half a mile north of Thundermarsh), Noah's Garden,[5] Old Field, close to Wadesmill, all on the south-west of the

---

[1] Statistics from Bd. of Agric. (1905).
[1a] Priv. Act, 11 Geo. IV & 1 Will. IV, cap. 15.
[2] Inclosure award map in the custody of the clerk to the parish council.
[3] This name is not now known; Knats Park to the west of Gravel Pit Wood may be the same. Information from Mr. F. C. Puller.
[4] Gunpowder Wood on the east bank of the river is in Thundridge.
[5] This is not now known, but there is a Noah's Ark in Thundridge.

347

parish on Mr. Giles Puller's estate; Fryer Field, Fryer's Farm, Knight's Spring, Knight's Leys, Fryer's Lawn, Fryery Croft and the Stove (reminiscent of the Knights Hospitallers), all in the neighbourhood of Standon Friars; Stags Park, evidently marking the site of the manorial park, to the west of the lordship, Park Hill on the east of the lordship, Old Lawn, Balsoms Park and Flax Ground in the neighbourhood of Lodge Farm, all probably once forming part of the demesne lands of Standon lordship.

On the south of the parish near the Rib, and to the east of the Roman Ermine Street, are two tumuli. One of these was opened by David Barclay (owner of Youngsbury, where they are situated) in 1788, and was found to contain Roman coins and pottery. The other was opened by Sir John Evans in 1889, and contained one of the largest sepulchral urns found in this country, with two bottles, one earthenware lords. The vineyard on the manor mentioned in 1086 probably indicates a residence of the lord at that time, and the dating of Letters Close and Patent at Standon in 1218, 1232, 1234 and 1305 is an argument in favour of the lords of Clare having a house there in the 13th and 14th centuries at which they entertained the king.

The lord of the manor of Standon *BOROUGH* had a prescriptive market which he farmed out at the beginning of the 13th century.[7] The position of Standon was scarcely a favourable one for a market, but it was encouraged at the expense of other towns. In 1366 a market and fair, which had been granted to Buntingford to replace one at a place called 'Newechepyng' near that town, were revoked because they injured the trade of Standon, where henceforth a market was to be held every Friday and a fair on the vigil, day, and

HIGH STREET, STANDON

and one glass. Tessellated pavement was also found about 300 yards north-west of the tumuli in 1736, and other remains which have since been brought to light show that this was the site of a villa. The existence of pre-Roman inhabitants in the neighbourhood is evidenced by copper coins of the reign of Cunobelinus (ob. 40 or 42 A.D.) found between Standon and Braughing.[6]

The village of Standon is situated on the Rib about half a mile east of Ermine Street. Although not possessing any particular advantages of situation, it was a place of importance in the middle ages, owing primarily to the fact that it was held by great feudal morrow of St. Peter ad Vincula.[8] Already in 1262 Standon was a borough governed by a reeve,[9] called the portreeve, who held it at a farm of 9 marks from the lord of the manor and divided with him the profits of fairs, shops and stalls. The borough had a separate court called the common court, of which the pleas and perquisites were divided between the lord and the reeve. At this court two bailiffs were chosen for the borough, and an ale-taster.[10] The burgage tenants held chiefly by money rents, but they also owed certain customs, viz. making and carrying hay in 'Broadmead' and doing one bedrip in autumn; they also owed tallage at the will of the lord on the

[6] *Arch.* lii, 287; Evans, *Coins of Ancient Britons*, 569.
[7] Mins. Accts. bdle. 1117, no. 13.
[8] Chart. R. 41 Edw. III, m. 2, no. 7;
Abbrev. Rot. Orig. (Rec. Com.), ii, 293.
[9] The reeve was apparently also the lord's official, for at the same date there is an Augustine Juvene, called bailiff of the Earl of Gloucester and Augustine the Portreeve (*Hund. R.* [Rec. Com.], i, 188, 191).
[10] Ct. R. (Gen. Ser.), portf. 178, no. 45.

BRAUGHING HUNDRED — STANDON

knighting of his eldest son and the marriage of his eldest daughter.[11] In 1399 there were twenty 'free tenants of the borough,' and among the names of those living in the town those of Fanmaker, Dyer, Lokyer, Couper, Tanner, &c., are common in the 14th century.[12] There is evidence also that maltmaking was carried on then.[13] New Street, which runs westward from the village at right angles to the northern end of the High Street, was made to facilitate communication with Ermine Street about the beginning of the 13th century, when the name appears in deeds.[14] In the 16th century a farm of 66s. 8d. was still paid by the burgesses as the fee farm of the borough.[15] At the present day the borough is distinct from the manor of Standon, and there still survive some copyholds which are held of the former.

The construction of railways is said to have struck the death-blow to the trade of Standon,[18] which after the lapse of the local market depended on the road communication with the neighbouring market towns. It is now only a country village, attractive in appearance from the wide main street, numerous trees and fine church. Some of the old houses still remain. The oldest is probably the house now used by Standon Endowed School south of the church. This is a brick and timber house of two stories with a projecting upper story and tiled roof. It has been much repaired, but probably dates back to the later mediaeval period. It is said to have belonged to the Knights Hospitallers, who, as rectors and lords of the manor of Standon Friars, may have had a court-house here after they had begun to grant leases of the manor in the 14th century. The school, which was founded

THE SCHOOL, STANDON

Standon market had lapsed before 1668, when Walter Lord Aston obtained a grant of a market to be held on Friday and two fairs, one on St. Mark's Day (25 April) and the other on 26 August.[16] This market, however, had also lapsed long before 1728.[17] The fair on St. Mark's Day is still held in the wide part of Standon Street (evidently the original marketplace) and in the meadow opposite the post office. There is a tradition that the August fair was a horse fair.

before 1612,[19] is now a public elementary school. The girls' school adjoining this is a modern building. On the east side of the main street is a row of two-storied 17th-century cottages, five of which have had the fronts renewed. One of these is the Wind Mill Inn. On the opposite side of the road is the Star Inn, a house of the same date. At the north end of the street opposite the flour mill is a block of timber cottages with thatched roofs and central chimney stack. A little further south is the smithy. The

---

[11] Chan. Inq. p.m. Hen. III, file 27, no. 5. For Broadmead see charter in Harl. MS. 1240, fol. 82 : grant of 1 acre of meadow 'in prato quod vocatur Brademed de longo in longum juxta regale chiminum quod ducit de foro de Staundon usque Zeyledonehulle' (probably early 14th century).

[12] Subs. R. bdle. 120, no. 8 ; Ct. R. (Gen. Ser.), portf. 178, no. 37, &c.
[13] Cal. Pat. 1388–92, p. 260 ; 1467–77, p. 336.
[14] Harl. Chart. 57921 ; Anct. D. (P.R.O.), A 1011, 1013.
[15] Mins. Accts. Herts. Hen. VII, no. 258 ; Hen. VIII, no. 1567.

[16] Pat. 20 Chas. II, pt. viii, m. 17, no. 7. [17] The date of Salmon's history.
[18] It is noticeable that in 1545 a larger number of inhabitants was assessed in Standon than in any other place in the hundred except Ware. See Subs. R. printed in Herts. Gen. ii, 272.
[19] See V.C.H. Herts. ii, 99.

349

A HISTORY OF HERTFORDSHIRE

parish on Mr. Giles Puller's estate; Fryer Field, Fryer's Farm, Knight's Spring, Knight's Leys, Fryer's Lawn, Fryery Croft and the Stove (reminiscent of the Knights Hospitallers), all in the neighbourhood of Standon Friars; Stags Park, evidently marking the site of the manorial park, to the west of the lordship, Park Hill on the east of the lordship, Old Lawn, Balsoms Park and Flax Ground in the neighbourhood of Lodge Farm, all probably once forming part of the demesne lands of Standon lordship.

On the south of the parish near the Rib, and to the east of the Roman Ermine Street, are two tumuli. One of these was opened by David Barclay (owner of Youngsbury, where they are situated) in 1788, and was found to contain Roman coins and pottery. The other was opened by Sir John Evans in 1889, and contained one of the largest sepulchral urns found in this country, with two bottles, one earthenware

lords. The vineyard on the manor mentioned in 1086 probably indicates a residence of the lord at that time, and the dating of Letters Close and Patent at Standon in 1218, 1232, 1234 and 1305 is an argument in favour of the lords of Clare having a house there in the 13th and 14th centuries at which they entertained the king.

BOROUGH The lord of the manor of Standon had a prescriptive market which he farmed out at the beginning of the 13th century.[7] The position of Standon was scarcely a favourable one for a market, but it was encouraged at the expense of other towns. In 1366 a market and fair, which had been granted to Buntingford to replace one at a place called 'Newechepyng' near that town, were revoked because they injured the trade of Standon, where henceforth a market was to be held every Friday and a fair on the vigil, day, and

HIGH STREET, STANDON

and one glass. Tessellated pavement was also found about 300 yards north-west of the tumuli in 1736, and other remains which have since been brought to light show that this was the site of a villa. The existence of pre-Roman inhabitants in the neighbourhood is evidenced by copper coins of the reign of Cunobelinus (ob. 40 or 42 A.D.) found between Standon and Braughing.[6]

The village of Standon is situated on the Rib about half a mile east of Ermine Street. Although not possessing any particular advantages of situation, it was a place of importance in the middle ages, owing primarily to the fact that it was held by great feudal

morrow of St. Peter ad Vincula.[8] Already in 1262 Standon was a borough governed by a reeve,[9] called the portreeve, who held it at a farm of 9 marks from the lord of the manor and divided with him the profits of fairs, shops and stalls. The borough had a separate court called the common court, of which the pleas and perquisites were divided between the lord and the reeve. At this court two bailiffs were chosen for the borough, and an ale-taster.[10] The burgage tenants held chiefly by money rents, but they also owed certain customs, viz. making and carrying hay in 'Broadmead' and doing one bedrip in autumn; they also owed tallage at the will of the lord on the

---

[6] *Arch.* lii, 287; Evans, *Coins of Ancient Britons,* 569.
[7] Mins. Accts. bdle. 1117, no. 13.
[8] Chart. R. 41 Edw. III, m. 2, no. 7;
Abbrev. Rot. Orig. (Rec. Com.), ii, 293.
[9] The reeve was apparently also the lord's official, for at the same date there is an
Augustine Juvene, called bailiff of the Earl of Gloucester and Augustine the Portreeve (*Hund. R.* [Rec. Com.], i, 188, 191).
[10] Ct. R. (Gen. Ser.), portf. 178, no. 45.

348

knighting of his eldest son and the marriage of his eldest daughter.[11]

In 1399 there were twenty 'free tenants of the borough,' and among the names of those living in the town those of Fanmaker, Dyer, Lokyer, Couper, Tanner, &c., are common in the 14th century.[12] There is evidence also that maltmaking was carried on then.[13] New Street, which runs westward from the village at right angles to the northern end of the High Street, was made to facilitate communication with Ermine Street about the beginning of the 13th century, when the name appears in deeds.[14] In the 16th century a farm of 66s. 8d. was still paid by the burgesses as the fee farm of the borough.[15] At the present day the borough is distinct from the manor of Standon, and there still survive some copyholds which are held of the former.

The construction of railways is said to have struck the death-blow to the trade of Standon,[18] which after the lapse of the local market depended on the road communication with the neighbouring market towns. It is now only a country village, attractive in appearance from the wide main street, numerous trees and fine church. Some of the old houses still remain. The oldest is probably the house now used by Standon Endowed School south of the church. This is a brick and timber house of two stories with a projecting upper story and tiled roof. It has been much repaired, but probably dates back to the later mediaeval period. It is said to have belonged to the Knights Hospitallers, who, as rectors and lords of the manor of Standon Friars, may have had a court-house here after they had begun to grant leases of the manor in the 14th century. The school, which was founded

THE SCHOOL, STANDON

Standon market had lapsed before 1668, when Walter Lord Aston obtained a grant of a market to be held on Friday and two fairs, one on St. Mark's Day (25 April) and the other on 26 August.[16] This market, however, had also lapsed long before 1728.[17] The fair on St. Mark's Day is still held in the wide part of Standon Street (evidently the original marketplace) and in the meadow opposite the post office. There is a tradition that the August fair was a horse fair.

before 1612,[19] is now a public elementary school. The girls' school adjoining this is a modern building. On the east side of the main street is a row of two-storied 17th-century cottages, five of which have had the fronts renewed. One of these is the Wind Mill Inn. On the opposite side of the road is the Star Inn, a house of the same date. At the north end of the street opposite the flour mill is a block of timber cottages with thatched roofs and central chimney stack. A little further south is the smithy. The

[11] Chan. Inq. p.m. Hen. III, file 27, no. 5. For Broadmead see charter in Harl. MS. 1240, fol. 82 : grant of 1 acre of meadow 'in prato quod vocatur Brademed de longo in longum juxta regale chiminum quod ducit de foro de Staundon usque Zeyledonehulle' (probably early 14th century).

[12] Subs. R. bdle. 120, no. 8 ; Ct. R. (Gen. Ser.), portf. 178, no. 37, &c.
[13] Cal. Pat. 1388–92, p. 260 ; 1467–77, p. 336.
[14] Harl. Chart. 57921 ; Anct. D. (P.R.O.), A 1011, 1013.
[15] Mins. Accts. Herts. Hen. VII, no. 258 ; Hen. VIII, no. 1567.

[16] Pat. 20 Chas. II, pt. viii, m. 17, no. 7. [17] The date of Salmon's history.
[18] It is noticeable that in 1545 a larger number of inhabitants was assessed in Standon than in any other place in the hundred except Ware. See Subs. R. printed in Herts. Gen. ii, 272.
[19] See V.C.H. Herts. ii, 99.

349

church of St. Mary is at the south end of the street, its local connexion being with the village and not with the manor-house, which is about half a mile distant to the south. The old vicarage was situated in the meadow opposite the post office. After 1811, when Richard Jeffreys resigned the living, the house, which was in a dilapidated condition, was made into two cottages which have now disappeared. The present vicarage in New Street was the private property of the Rev. Henry Law, successor of Mr. Jeffreys. On his resignation in 1856 he sold this house to Mr. Christopher Puller, the patron, whose son the Rev. Charles Puller, vicar of Standon, legally converted the house into a vicarage.[20] The Men's Institute near the school was opened in 1886. The bridge over the river at the northern end of the village is a county bridge. It was proposed in 1782 to replace the old wooden bridge by a brick one of five arches wide enough for the passage of carriages, so that it might combine with the recent widening of the road from Hadham to Braughing and Standon to improve the communication between Essex and Hertfordshire.[21] The present iron bridge of two arches replaced the brick bridge, which was destroyed by a flood, in 1858.[22] There is a disused windmill to the south of the village ; to the north of it close by the railway station is a large flour-mill, built in 1901, which is connected by electric wires with the old water-mill on the other side of the river where the water-power is now supplemented by steam. This was the manorial mill to which the copyholders owed multure.[23] Early in the 19th century there was a paper-mill at the south end of the village (probably on the site of the mill granted to the Hospitallers, see under rectory manor) which was owned in 1846 by John Parkinson of Lincoln's Inn Fields.[24] It was afterwards used as a saw-mill.[25] The house and water-wheel still remain and the name survives in Paper Mill Lane, Paper Mill Meadow and Paper Mill House. The almshouses at the south end of the village were originally part of the outbuildings of Standon Workhouse, which was disused after the Poor Law Act of 1834,[26] Standon being now included in Ware Union. The railway station on the Buntingford branch of the Great Eastern railway was opened in 1863.

About half a mile east of the village on the high ground near Well Pond Green is a farm called Standon Friars, probably the site of the preceptory of the Knights of St. John of Jerusalem which was established at Standon after the church and rectory manor had been granted to them by Gilbert de Clare (see rectory manor).[27] The names of the adjacent fields, Knights Spring, Knights Leys, Friars Lawn, &c., suggest this. The farm-house is modern, but among the out-buildings is a large late 16th-century barn. It is built on dwarf walls of old thin bricks, and is of timber, weather-boarded ; the roofs are tiled. A small wing of the same date projects at the south end, on its eastern side. The large barn measures internally about 144 ft. by 29 ft., and is divided into nine bays by dwarf walls of brick projecting about 7 ft. on either side internally, and carrying the main posts of the heavy roof trusses. There are no remains of any older buildings, but in the orchard and meadow adjoining the farm buildings on the north are some ditches and cuttings which may mark the site of a former house. The Hospitallers also had a grange at Papwell on the west side of the parish (see under rectory manor).

Weever writing in 1651 says that there was 'a little religious fabric of Austin Friars' near Sir Ralph Sadleir's house, a cell to the priory of Clare in Suffolk.[28] He evidently refers to Standon Friars, but confuses it with the chapel of Salbourne or Salebourne founded as a hermitage by Richard de Clare

STANDON FRIARS FARM : OLD BARN

---

[20] R. Wetherall, *Hist. of Standon*, 14.
[21] *Sess. R.* (Herts. Co. Rec.), ii, 150–2.
[22] Information from Mr. J. A. Brown.
[23] Information from Mr. J. Chapman.
[24] *Sess. R.* (Herts. Co. Rec.), ii, 439, 440.
[25] Information from Mr. J. Chapman.
[26] Ibid.
[27] See article on Religious Houses, *V.C.H. Herts.* iv. Human remains have lately been found near Standon Friars.
[28] *Ancient Funeral Monum.* 593.

and granted by him about 1175[29] to the monks of Stoke by Clare that they might celebrate divine service there in honour of St. Michael, St. John the Baptist, St. John the Evangelist and All Saints, for him and all his family.[30] For a time the hermit and brothers lived at Salbourne and received various grants of land,[31] but there seems to have been no community after the beginning of the 14th century.[32] At the end of the century, when the manor was in the king's hands, he appointed chaplains,[33] and in 1393 the chaplain of All Saints, Puckeridge (see below), received a grant of 'the chapel called a hermitage of St. Michael, Salbourne,' on condition that he stayed there and officiated.[34] From the 15th century the chapel and lands were farmed out by the Dean and Chapter of the collegiate church of Stoke for a rent of 30s.[35] They were held in the reign of Edward IV by John Field [36] (see Bromley Hall), and at the beginning of the 15th century by his widow Agnes Morton.[37] As only a rent of 30s. is entered to Stoke in the *Valor Ecclesiasticus*,[38] it is evident that the chapel property was still in the hands of tenants, who probably remained in possession after the Dissolution, as no grant of it is on record. The lands of John Field and his descendants included a close called Pound Hawe (otherwise Pond Croft), Crabs Croft, land in Highfield, a tenement called Buttons, and a messuage called Hallys (the last held of the manor of Milkley).[39] These descended with his other lands (see the Brickhouse, under manors) to Thomas Howe, who in 1544 conveyed the messuage called 'Hallys and Ducketts' with lands lying in the common field called Papwell Walk, Long Croft and Cock Croft, to John Gardiner.[40] The identity of these names with the names of lands afterwards in the possession of St. Edmund's College [41] points to the property of John Field and his descendants lying in the neighbourhood of Old Hall Green, and if the hermitage estate was included in that property, as seems probable, the cottage called the Hermitage at Old Hall Green, now belonging to the college, may mark the site of the original hermitage, local tradition having preserved the name.

Another chapel is recorded to have stood on Our Lady Bridge on the highway to Stortford, possibly where the road to the south of the village crosses the Rib. This, according to a survey of the 16th century, contained 'a lady [i.e. presumably an image of our Lady], and certain service thereunto did belong with divers offerings made unto her.' The offerings were received by the Prior of St. John of Jerusalem and were probably for the repair of the bridge, for which he was responsible. This chapel had fallen into ruins and been removed before 1590, and the bridge was then in decay.[42] The bridge may have had some connexion with the gild of our Lady in the church.

At Old Hall Green (Eldhallegrene, xiv cent.),[43] on a high ridge of ground to the west of the North Road, is the Roman Catholic College of St. Edmund. In 1749 a school (representing one at Twyford which had been closed since 1745) was established at Standon Lordship (then in the hands of the Roman Catholic family of Aston [44]) by a Douay priest named Richard Kendal. The school was afterwards moved to Hare Street in 1767, and in 1769 to Old Hall Green.[45] In 1772 Bishop Talbot bought the Hermitage with 20 acres of land there from John Hale Wortham, and in 1787 he purchased the Old Hall Estate, which he already held on a lease, from Sir George Jennings of Greenwich.[46] These properties were added to the school, which became known as the Old Hall Green Academy. St. Edmund's College also represents the English college at Douay (founded by Cardinal Allen in 1568, primarily for the education of clergy) which was suppressed with its offshoot the secular college of St. Omer during the French Revolution, when the professors and students from both colleges came to Old Hall Green (1793 and 1795) and took up their quarters in the 'Hermitage,' the 'Ship' and the 'School in the Garden,' now the carpenter's shop. The estate was increased by the purchase of Riggory's Farm in 1815 (see under manors) and of the Old Hall Farm [47] estate, purchased from the representatives of Ambrose Proctor by Bishop Poynter in 1826.[48] The old schoolhouse known as the Old Hall is a low red-bricked house separated by several acres of garden from the present college. A new building, forming the main block of the present college, was begun in 1795 by Dr. Stapleton, the first president, and opened in 1799.[49] After the Roman Catholic Relief Act of 1791 [50] a chapel called the 'old parish chapel' was built at the back of the Old Hall on the site of the present farmyard in 1792, and for a time this was used by the college.[51] A new parish chapel was built in 1818, which has been superseded by a building consecrated in December 1911. A college chapel, afterwards known as the 'old chapel' (now the senior study), and a refectory (now the college library) were built in 1805.[52] The present chapel, designed by A. W. Pugin, and containing a rood screen which is considered his masterpiece, was built in 1845-53.[53] In 1855-60 the wing containing the present refectory was built, and

---

[29] The charter is addressed to Gilbert Bishop of London, probably Gilbert Foliot, 1163-78, and was probably made after Richard de Clare succeeded his father, 1173.
[30] Cott. MS. App. xxi, no. 38; Add. MS. 6042, fol. 72.
[31] Add. MS. 6042, fol. 72.
[32] See article on Religious Houses, V.C.H. Herts. iv.
[33] Cal. Pat. 1381-5, p. 488.
[34] Ibid. 1391-6, p. 241.
[35] Harl. Chart. 44 I. 30-50.
[36] Ibid.
[37] Ibid.
[38] *Valor Eccl.* (Rec. Com.), ii, 469.
[39] See Chan. Inq. p.m. 17 Edw. IV, no. 56; (Ser. 2), xxxii, 88; Harl. Chart. 56 C. 43; Harl. Roll L. 33.

[40] Com. Pleas D. Enr. East. 36 Hen. VIII.
[41] Deeds communicated by Mgr. Ward, president of the college.
[42] *Sess. R.* (Herts. Co. Rec.), i, 2.
[43] Cott. MS. Nero, E vi, fol. 121.
[44] Lord Aston had shortly before moved to his Staffordshire seat at Tixall (see E. H. Burton, *Life and Times of Bishop Challoner*, i, 290).
[45] Ibid.; B. Ward, *Hist. of St. Edmund's College*, 35.
[46] Deeds communicated by the President. The conveyance was effected on Bishop Talbot's behalf by John Hollingworth, the penal laws preventing Roman Catholics from being able to purchase lands being still in force.
[47] The farm (now called Hake's Cottage) had until recently the date 1693 on the plaster.
[48] Deeds communicated by the President.
[49] Ward, *Hist. of St. Edmund's College*.
[50] Previous to this the Roman Catholics of the neighbourhood, who were numerous, had attended the private chapel at Standon Lordship, see Ward, *St. Edmund's College*, who shows that Standon was a Roman Catholic centre even before this date. In 1650, in the returns relating to popish recusants, nine names were given for this parish including that of Walter Lord Aston (*Sess. R.* [Herts. Co. Rec.], i, 304).
[51] Before this a chapel hidden in the loft of the 'Old Hall' is said to have been used.
[52] Information from the Rev. E. Burton.
[53] Ward, *St. Edmund's College Chapel*.

in 1905 the Divines' Wing with accommodation for fifty students was added.[54] St. Hugh's School was originally a house designed by Pugin for Mr. W. G. Ward, who in 1851 was appointed lecturer in moral philosophy at the college. After he moved to Northwood Park in 1858 the house became a preparatory school for the college. The fourth provincial council of Westminster was held at St. Edmund's College in 1873.[55]

The repair of the many roads in the parish was a heavy burden on the inhabitants of Standon. In 1389 a grant of pavage was made for repairing the highway from All Saints' Chapel, Puckeridge, to Lapdenbridge,[56] and in 1390 the bailiffs and constables of Standon, Puckeridge and Buntingford were allowed a similar grant for the road between Wadesmill and Buntingford and between Puckeridge and Braughing.[57] About 4 miles of this road was repairable by Standon, and was particularly liable to get into a bad state owing to the springs of water arising in the swallowing clay and sandy places.[58]

Situated on the North Road at a distance of about a mile from each other are the hamlets of High Cross.(Heghe Crouch), Colliers End (Colyersend, xvi cent.),[59] and Puckeridge (Pockerich). Part of Wadesmill, a hamlet on the road further south, is also in this parish.[60] These were settlements made possibly in the 12th or 13th century as the traffic increased along the main road. A grant of market and fair at Puckeridge (see Milkley Manor) in 1314 witnesses to the growing importance of that hamlet. Consequent on the numerous travellers along the road there were many inns in the village. The name of Chequers Inn dates back as early as 1473.[61] The Old George Inn remains on the west side of the street, a two-storied building of timber and brick nogging with a tiled roof and overhanging upper story on the north end of the street front, dating from the 17th century. Two cottages at the north end of the village now used as stables are probably of the late 16th century. They are built of timber with brick nogging and have tiled roofs. In the north front are two four-centred doorways, one with moulded edges and enriched spandrels. Thorpe Hall on the east side of the street, once an inn, is a 17th-century house of two stories. It is of plastered timber construction with tiled roofs, and has a timber gateway on the south side. Close by is the Crown and Falcon Inn, dating from about the middle of the 16th century. It is a timber house, plastered, with projecting upper story on the south and west sides and a timber gateway. Near this inn was the common pump.[62] The chapel of All Saints, Puckeridge, was founded as a chantry chapel by Richard de Gatesbury (for whom see Gatesbury in Braughing), who in 1320 had licence to endow it with lands and rent in Braughing, Puckeridge, Gatesbury and elsewhere.[63] These lands were unsuccessfully claimed as dower by Agnes wife of Thomas Tuwe, widow of Adam de Gatesbury.[64] The exact site of this chapel is not known, but it was situated on the main road.[65] There is still no church at Puckeridge, but a Congregational chapel was built in 1832.[65a] The Church of England school and lecture room were built in 1862.

The ecclesiastical district of High Cross was formed in 1845. It includes the hamlet of Colliers End and part of Wadesmill. The church of St. John the Evangelist, High Cross, was built in 1847 by Lady Giles-Puller and her son Mr. Christopher William Puller. High Cross elementary school was built in 1866. The church of St. Mary at Colliers End, a small red brick building, was built as a mission church in 1910 by Mr. E. E. Wickham of Plashes in memory of his wife. William Davies (1814–91), mineralogist and palaeontologist at the British Museum, had a residence at Colliers End, where he died in 1891.

MANORS In the reign of King Edward the Confessor the manor of *STANDON* was held by Archbishop Stigand, under whom were six sokemen each holding 1 hide. After the Conquest it was presumably acquired by Walter Giffard, lord of Longueville, for in 1086 it formed part of the possessions of Rohais his daughter, then wife of Richard de Tonbridge, lord of Clare. It was assessed at 11 hides, of which 6 were in demesne; and there was land for twenty-four ploughs, but only seventeen ploughs were on the manor. The extent included five mills and 2 arpents of vineyard.[66] The manor remained in the family of Clare. Gilbert son of Richard (grandson of Richard of 1086) was created Earl of Hertford about 1138. His nephew Richard de Clare married Amicia daughter and co-heir of William Fitz Robert Earl of Gloucester, and Gilbert de Clare, their son, was recognized as Earl of Gloucester about 1218.[67] He died in 1230; during the minority of the heir, Richard de Clare, the manor was granted to Gilbert Marshal, Earl of Pembroke, for his sustenance in the king's service.[68] In the following reign Richard de Clare was presented for withholding the payment for sheriff's aid and view of frankpledge for Standon, and also for withdrawing suit at the hundred and county courts which was said to be owed for the whole vill by Geoffrey de Leukenore by reason of his tenure of certain lands. The earl also claimed warren on the lands of his free tenants and had appropriated the common fishery in the river which he sold to the men of Standon.[69] His son Gilbert Earl of

CLARE. *Or three cheverons gules.*

---

[54] Information from Rev. E. Burton.
[55] Ward, *Hist. of St. Edmund's College*; *Dict. Nat. Biog.* s.v. Ward.
[56] For refusal to pay this pavage see Early Chan. Proc. bdle. 68, no. 201.
[57] *Cal. Pat.* 1388–92, p. 204.
[58] *Sess. R.* (Herts. Co. Rec.), i, 82, 68.
[59] This probably took its name from the colliers in the parish. Nicholas le Coliere was assessed at Standon in 1307 (Subs. R. bdle. 120, no. 87).
[60] This is described under Thundridge.
[61] P.C.C. Will, 9 Wattys.
[62] *Sess. R.* (Herts. Co. Rec.), ii, 26. There was an inn called the Falcon as early as 1444 (see will of Ralph Asteley in Cant. Archiepis. Reg. Stafford, fol. 135*b*).
[63] *Cal. Pat.* 1317–21, p. 428.
[64] Ibid. 1391–6, p. 633; 1401–5, p. 66; Plac. in Canc. file 23, no. 12; Early Chan. Proc. bdle. 69, no. 79. See also Early Chan. Proc. bdle. 7, no. 267, for another suit concerning the endowment of the chapel.
[65] *Cal. Pat.* 1388–92, p. 30.
[65a] Urwick, *Nonconformity in Herts.* 674.
[66] *V.C.H. Herts.* i, 343.
[67] G.E.C. *Peerage*.
[68] *Cal. Close*, 1231–4, p. 482.
[69] *Hund. R.* (Rec. Com.), i, 188; Assize R. 323.

STANDON THE HERMITAGE, OLD HALL GREEN

STANDON: ST. EDMUND'S COLLEGE, OLD HALL GREEN

BRAUGHING HUNDRED
STANDON

Gloucester claimed view of frankpledge, gallows, tumbrel and pillory, free market, amendment of the assize of bread and ale, quittance for himself and men of gelds, aids, sheriff's aids and sheriff's tourn.[70] From an extent of the manor taken on the death of Earl Richard in 1262 it appears that there were in demesne 250 acres of arable land, 15 acres of meadow, 9½ acres of pasture, 140 acres of poor (*debile*) pasture, a park[71] about 2 leagues in circumference, a fruit and herb garden (the remembrance of which may still survive in the name Balsoms Park, a field to the east of the lordship),[72] a fishery in defense, and another common fishery, whilst in villeinage were 209½ acres.[73] A later extent taken on the death of Joan, widow of Gilbert de Clare, mentions also the farm of a mill.[74]

Gilbert de Clare, son of Gilbert and Joan, was killed at Bannockburn in 1314,[75] when his estates were divided among his sisters. For a short time, however, Standon remained in the king's hands and the custody was granted to William de Trente.[76] In 1315 the king took venison from Standon Park for his larder at Westminster.[77] Eventually Standon was assigned to Gilbert's sister Elizabeth, who married John de Burgh. She died in 1360, having survived her son William de Burgh, Earl of Ulster, and was succeeded by her granddaughter Elizabeth, wife of Lionel, third son of Edward III, who after his wife's succession to the honour of Clare was created Duke of Clarence in 1362.[78] In the extent of the manor taken at the death of Elizabeth de Burgh are mentioned two water-mills, farmed out by the lord. One of these was called Latchford (Loteford) Mill, the other was a fulling-mill.[79]

The manor descended to Philippa, only daughter of Lionel Duke of Clarence and Elizabeth his wife,[80] who married Edmund Mortimer Earl of March. At this time the demesne lands of the manor were farmed out to the collector of the rents.[81] The Earl of March died in 1381, having survived his wife Philippa.[82] His son Roger succeeded on attaining his majority and held the manor until his death in 1398. The inquisition then taken mentions four water-mills on the manor. There were only six customary tenants remaining on the manor at this date,[83] the disappearance of the rest being probably due to the farming of the demesne

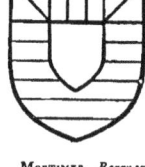

MORTIMER. *Barry or and azure a chief or with two piles between two gyrons azure therein and a scutcheon argent over all.*

lands[84] or to the Black Death. Edmund Mortimer, son of Roger, died without issue in January 1424–5, and was succeeded by Richard Duke of York, son of his sister Ann, who married Richard Earl of Cambridge.[85] For the duke's good service as the king's lieutenant in France and Normandy the officers of the household were excluded from taking live stock or crops, fuel or carriage within the parish of Standon, and the harbingers of the household from lodging there.[86]

About 1441 the manor was granted for life by the Duke of York to Sir William Oldhall, kt.[87] After the death of the duke in 1460 it descended to his son Edward Duke of York, who ascended the throne as Edward IV in 1461. In the same year he granted the manor to his mother Cicely Duchess of York as part of her jointure,[88] and the grant was confirmed by Richard III on his accession.[89] The custody of the park was granted by Cicely in 1476 to her servant John atte Field[90] (see Bromley Hall) and the office of bailiff of the lordship the next year to John Deryng.[91] The Duchess of York died in 1495. In 1509 the manor was granted by Henry VIII to the Princess Katherine of Aragon on the occasion of their marriage,[92] and it also formed

KATHERINE OF ARAGON. *Gules a castle or, for* CASTILE, *quartered with Argent a lion purpure, for* LEON.

JANE SEYMOUR. *Gules a pair of wings or.*

part of the jointure of Queen Jane Seymour, after whose death it reverted to the Crown.[93]

The Rt. Hon. Sir Ralph Sadleir, Gentleman of the Privy Chamber, was appointed keeper of the site, parker, bailiff of the manor and steward of the lordship in 1539.[94] In the same year he was visited there by Cromwell, through whose influence he rose to power and became principal Secretary of State.[95] In 1540 he obtained a grant of the manor with the park and warren in tail-male,[96] which in 1544 was changed to one in fee.[97] Two years later, while he was on an embassy in Scotland, his steward built a house for him in

---

[70] *Plac. de Quo Warr.* (Rec. Com.), 278.
[71] Cf. the name Stag's Park still surviving.
[72] Spelt Balsham on the ordnance map, but Balsoms Park in the tithe allotment.
[73] Chan. Inq. p.m. Hen. III, file 27, no. 5. The extent taken on the death of Gilbert de Clare, his son, in 1295, varies considerably (see ibid. 24 Edw. I, no. 107). Several references occur to the earl's 'vivarium' (see Harl. MS. 1240, fol. 82*b*).
[74] Ibid. 35 Edw. I, no. 47.
[75] Ibid. 8 Edw. II, no. 68.
[76] *Cal. Close*, 1313–18, p. 141.
[77] Ibid. p. 140.
[78] G.E.C. *Peerage*.

[79] See Mins. Accts. bdle. 1111, no. 24. Possibly the second was the mill called Lynchmelne mentioned in early charters (Harl. MS. 1240, fol. 82*b*, 83*b*). There was also the mill which the lords of Standon had rented from the Prior of St. John of Jerusalem (who held it by gift from Elizabeth's ancestor Gilbert de Clare) and which he released to Elizabeth de Burgh in 1337 (see rectory manor).
[80] Chan. Inq. p.m. 43 Edw. III, pt. i, no. 23.
[81] Mins. Accts. bdle. 1111, no. 24.
[82] Chan. Inq. p.m. 5 Ric. II, no. 43; see *Cal. Pat.* 1381–5, p. 93, for grant of park during minority of heir.
[83] Chan. Inq. p.m. 22 Ric. II, no. 74.

[84] See *Engl. Hist. Rev.* xv (1900).
[85] Chan. Inq. p.m. 3 Hen. VI, no. 32.
[86] *Cal. Pat.* 1436–41, p. 473.
[87] Ibid. p. 531.
[88] Ibid. 1461–7, p. 131.
[89] Pat. 1 Ric. III, pt. v.
[90] *Cal. Pat.* 1467–77, p. 598.
[91] Add. Chart. 15478.
[92] *L. and P. Hen. VIII*, i, 155; v, 330.
[93] Ibid. xii (2), 975.
[94] Ibid. xiv (2), 780 (42). He succeeded Sir William Coffyn, who died of the great sickness in 1538, and was buried in Standon Church (see ibid. xiv, 650).
[95] Ibid. 154.
[96] Ibid. xvi, 379 (26).
[97] Ibid. xiv (2), 166 (70).

A HISTORY OF HERTFORDSHIRE

Standon, on a much larger scale, it is said, than he wished,[98] and here he several times entertained Queen Elizabeth.[99] Sadleir was created knight banneret on the battlefield of Pinkie in 1547. He served as Lord Lieutenant of Hertfordshire, sat for the county in seven Parliaments and survived until 1587, having served with distinction in three successive reigns.[100] He was succeeded by his son Thomas, who was M.P. for Lancaster from 1572 to 1583 and Sheriff of Hertfordshire in 1595.[1] On 30 April 1603 James I came to Standon and having been met by the Bishop of London and a company of gentlemen 'in coats and chains of gold,' proceeded to Sadleir's house, where he stayed for a Sunday and knighted his host.[2] Sir Thomas Sadleir died in 1606.[3] His son Ralph, the 'noble Mr. Sadler' of Walton's *Compleat Angler*, was Sheriff of Hertfordshire in 1609–10.[4] He died in 1660, leaving no issue, and was succeeded in the manor by Walter Lord Aston, son of his sister Gertrude, who married Sir Walter Aston of Tixall, co. Stafford,

SADLEIR of Standon.
Or a lion parted fessewise azure and gules.

ASTON, Lord Aston.
Argent a fesse sable with three lozenges sable in the chief.

created a baronet on the institution of that order in 1611 and made Lord Aston of Forfar in 1627.[5]

The Astons were a Roman Catholic family.[6] Walter, second Lord Aston, was an adherent of Charles I, and after fighting on the king's side had to compound for his estates and live privately.[7] His son Walter, third Lord Aston, who succeeded him in 1678,[8] suffered as a victim of Titus Oates' plot. He was indicted for high treason in 1680 and was a prisoner in the Tower until 1685. On one occasion a mob came to plunder the Lordship while he was there, and he only escaped by hiding in a dovecot, whilst his valuables were packed in an iron chest and sunk in the Rib.[9] His fortunes changed under James II and he was made Lord Lieutenant of Staffordshire. He died in 1714 and was buried at Standon.[10] Walter, fourth Lord Aston, his son and successor, lived in retirement at Standon owing to the severity of the penal laws against Roman Catholics. He died at Tixall in 1748, but was buried at Standon. His son James, the last Lord Aston, left no male issue

on his death in 1751. The manor descended to his daughters Mary, who married her cousin Sir Walter Blount, bart., of Sodington, co. Worcester, and Barbara, who married the Hon. Thomas Clifford.[11] They in 1767 joined in a conveyance to William Plumer of Blakesware.[12] The conveyance included the park, the free fishery, the several fishery and view of frankpledge. William Plumer died in the same year and was succeeded by his son William. He by will of 1821 devised the manor to his wife Jane with remainder to her legatees.[13] After his death in 1822 his widow married (as her third husband) Robert Ward, who took the name and arms of Plumer.[14] He survived his wife and sold the manor in 1843 to Arthur, first Duke of Wellington, on whose death in 1852 it descended to his son Arthur Richard, second duke, then successively to his son Henry, third duke, in 1884, and to the latter's brother Arthur Charles, fourth duke and present lord of the manor, in 1900.

WELLESLEY, Duke of Wellington. *Gules a cross between twenty roundels argent,* for WELLESLEY, *quartered with Or a lion gules,* for COLLEY, *with an augmentation of the union device of the United Kingdom charged upon a scutcheon.*

The old manor-house was kept in repair until after the sale of the manor by William Plumer. In a letter written in 1733 to the Earl of Oxford by George Vertue is recorded a visit to 'Lord Aston's ancient house,' made especially to see a picture of Vicar-General Cromwell painted by Holbein, which he suggests was one of those done for Sir Thomas More at his house at Chelsea.[15] The original house, of which only a small part now remains, was built about 1546 by Sir Ralph Sadleir (see above), his initials and that date appearing on the front. The old house, of which a plan has been preserved, was of the courtyard type ; the main entrance, with flanking turrets both on the front and next the courtyard, faced the west ; the south wing probably contained the principal rooms and the north wing the domestic offices. On the east side of the courtyard was a long range of buildings at a different angle, stretching southwards beyond the main building, which may possibly have been built at a different period. The only portions now remaining of this once extensive building are the lower parts of the walls of the north end of the west wing, on which a modern building has been erected, the south end of the west wing, and a small part of the south wing. The foundations and some of the walling of the demolished wings still remain between the present

---

[98] Fuller, *Hist. of Worthies of Engl.* (ed. Nichols), ii, 41. It was probably built on the site of an earlier house, for inquisitions mention a capital messuage on the manor.
[99] Nichols, *Prog. of Queen Eliz.* i, 100 ; ii, 104.
[100] Information from Mr. T. U. Sadleir; Chan. Inq. p.m. (Ser. 2), ccxv, 259. For an account of him see the memoir by Sir Walter Scott in *State Papers and Letters of Sir Ralph Sadleir*, ed. A. Clifford, 1809 ; F. Sadleir Stoney, *Life and Times of Sir R. Sadleir*, 1877 ; article by T. U.

Sadleir in *East Herts. Arch. Soc. Trans.* iii (1), 79.
[1] *V.C.H. Herts. Families*, 283.
[2] Nichols, *Prog. of James I*, i, 106.
[3] Chan. Inq. p.m. (Ser. 2), ccxcvi, 95.
[4] *V.C.H. Herts. Families*, 283.
[5] G.E.C. *Peerage*.
[6] The first Lord Aston became a Catholic whilst acting as ambassador at the Spanish court.
[7] G.E.C. *Peerage*.
[8] For an account of the great state kept up by him at the Lordship see the account written by his grandson Sir Edw.

Southcote and published by Father John Morris in *Troubles of our Catholic Forefathers*.
[9] E. H. Burton, *Life and Times of Bp. Challoner*, i, 214.
[10] *East Herts. Arch. Soc. Trans.* iii (1), 67 et seq. [11] G.E.C. *Peerage*.
[12] Recov. R. Mich. 8 Geo. III, rot. 335; Feet of F. Herts. East. 7 Geo. III ; Trin. 7 Geo. III.
[13] Clutterbuck, *Hist. and Antiq. of Herts.* iii, 229. [14] Berry, *Herts. Gen.* i, 99.
[15] *Portland MSS.* (Hist. MSS. Com.), iv, 49.

354

house and the river. All the old work is built of thin bricks and the roofs are tiled. The modern portions of the building were erected about 1872. In the centre of the west front is the wide entrance gateway, now inclosed and forming an entrance hall, with four-centred arches covered with cement; the original semi-octagonal flanking turrets have been demolished nearly to the ground level, one of them having been formed into a bay window; the turrets next the courtyard still contain the oak newel stairs to the upper floor, but they have been shortened and re-roofed. A turret at the north-west angle of the building has also been lowered and re-roofed. On the south side of the entrance two of the original gables remain; they have moulded brick copings with square pinnacles set diagonally; these appear to be old, but according to an old view the gables had no copings. The upper parts of the chimneys have been

apparently granted by Richard Earl of Gloucester (ob. 1262) to a younger son Thomas de Clare. His son Gilbert de Clare died in 1307 seised of a manor in Standon held of Gilbert Earl of Gloucester by suit at the earl's manor of Standon.[16] He was succeeded by his brother Richard de Clare. Under the Clares this manor was held by Hugh Plessy, who died in 1301, leaving a son and heir Hugh, then aged five.[17] This Hugh probably died soon after, for before 1314 the manor had been resumed by Richard de Clare, and was in that year granted by him to Master Richard de Clare, clerk, for life.[18] Richard, the grantor, left a son Thomas, who died without issue in 1320–1, and was succeeded in the manor by his aunt Margaret (daughter of Thomas de Clare), who married Bartholomew de Badlesmere.[19] They held the manor jointly until the death of Bartholomew in 1322.[20] It descended to their son Giles de Badles-

STANDON LORDSHIP: WEST FRONT

rebuilt; they have square shafts set diagonally. All the window frames are modern. One of the rooms contains some 17th-century oak panelling, and in others are old stone fireplaces.

The house is now occupied by Mr. Herbert le Blanc Smith.

The manor of PLASHES (Plessetes, Plesiz, Plessy, Plesshes, xiv cent.; Pleshez, xv cent.) was composed of lands within the manor of Standon, which were

mere, who died without issue in 1338, when his lands were divided between his four sisters and co-heirs.[21] Plashes was assigned to his sister Elizabeth, wife of William de Bohun Earl of Northampton.[22] She with her husband in 1352 granted the reversion of the manor (held for life by Elizabeth widow of Giles de Badlesmere and then wife of Guy de Brien) to Master Richard Plessy, presumably heir of the above-mentioned Hugh.[23] In 1354 Guy and

[16] Chan. Inq. p.m. 1 Edw. II, no. 45. Previously a moiety of a third of the manor had come into the possession of Walter de Furneaux and his wife Alice. See under Rennesley, p. 360, note 35.

[17] Chan. Inq. p.m. 29 Edw. I, no. 54. Hugh Plessy subinfeudated certain lands called Le Hethe in Standon consisting of a capital messuage, 160 acres of arable land, 8 acres of meadow, 5 acres of pasture, 10 acres of wood, and 50s. rent of assize to Edmund Mauley, who died seised in 1314, when he was succeeded by his kinsman Peter Mauley (Chan. Inq. p.m. 8 Edw. II, no. 141; *Abbrev. Rot. Orig.* [Rec. Com.], i, 210).

[18] Duchy of Lanc. Deeds, L 1282. Richard de Clare is called in the charter 'lord of Tothomon.'

[19] G.E.C. *Peerage*.

[20] Chan. Inq. p.m. 2 Edw. III (2nd nos.), no. 23.

[21] Ibid. 12 Edw. III, no. 54a.

[22] A rent was payable from the manor to another sister Maud, wife of John de Veer Earl of Oxford (*Cal. Close*, 1360–4, p. 18; Chan. Inq. p.m. 34 Edw. III, no. 84).

[23] Feet of F. Herts. 26 Edw. III, no. 414.

355

A HISTORY OF HERTFORDSHIRE

Elizabeth de Brien exchanged their life interest for a rent of 20 marks.[24] Master Richard died about 1362. He left as co-heirs the three daughters of his brother John (called young John), viz. Alice Bysouthe, Joan, and Parnell wife of Stephen Stourde.[25] Before 1371 Alice was married to Thomas Veautrer and Joan to Hugh de Syreston. In that year these two co-heirs with their husbands conveyed two parts of the manor to Edmund de Mortimer, Earl of March, and his wife Philippa (lords of the manor of Standon in Philippa's right),[26] and a conveyance was also made to them about the same time by a certain Simon le Reve of Plashes, called son of 'Elder John' and nephew and heir of Master Richard Plessy.[27] After this date the manor follows the descent of Standon, and like that manor was farmed out by the lords.[28] Plashes Farm lies to the south-east of the hamlet of Colliers End and is now occupied by Mr. E. E. Wickham. Plashes Wood lies immediately to the north. In the grant by Simon le Reve mentioned above a mill called 'Cuttydmelle' is mentioned.

The manor of DOOS (Doucetts, Dowsetts) first appears as lands belonging to Roger D'Amorie, who probably obtained them from his wife Elizabeth daughter of Gilbert de Clare, on whom they were presumably settled as a marriage portion.[29] In 1320 Roger D'Amorie received a grant of free warren in his demesne lands in Standon.[30] The manor descended to his daughter Elizabeth, wife of John Bardolf, Lord Bardolf of Wormegay, co. Norfolk, of whose inheritance it was held for life by her stepmother Elizabeth de Burgh.[31] William Bardolf, son of John and Elizabeth, granted the manor to William Walcote for life in 1373, to hold by the rent of a rose and the office of his chief chamberlain.[32] Apparently Thomas Bardolf, his son, who succeeded him in January 1385-6, alienated the manor,[33] for in 1412 John Riggewyn died seised of it, leaving a son and heir John.[34] This John died in 1425, and was succeeded by his son, also John.[35] After this there seems to be no trace of the manor until the reign of Mary, when it was held by William Emerson, who died seised of it in February 1533-4.[36] He left a son and heir Richard Emerson, who held it until his death in 1562.[37] The manor then passed to James Hennage (son of Alice, paternal aunt of William Emerson, who married William Hennage),[38] and in 1569 was conveyed by him to Sir Ralph Sadleir,[39] lord of Standon, with which manor it thereafter descended.

Dowsett's Farm lies a little to the east of the North Road, and to the north-east of the hamlet of Colliers End.

Besides the manor of Doos John Riggewyn held at his death in 1412 tenements called Sotes, Gernon's and Riggewyns. In February 1427-8 John Riggewyn, his grandson, conveyed the messuage called SOTES or SUTES in Standon to John Fray and other feoffees.[40] The property apparently consisted of the capital messuage of the manor of Doos and part of the lands of the manor; it is called in subsequent conveyances 'the manor of Doos called Sotes' and sometimes Doos *alias* Sotes. The feoffees probably held in trust for Nicholas Ellerbek, as he died seised in 1472.[41] His daughter and heir Margaret married William Tendring, and they with Margaret's mother Ann, who after Ellerbek's death married John Digges, conveyed the manor in 1493 to Henry Marney and others,[42] probably for a settlement on William and Margaret. This Margaret survived a second husband,[42a] and at the age of fifty-seven, as Margaret Marzen, widow, seems to have intended a marriage with Richard son of Sir John Audley, kt.,[43] of Swaffham, co. Norfolk, but apparently the marriage never took place. William Tendring, who died about 1500, left two daughters, one of whom, Margaret wife of Robert Forster of Little Birch, co. Essex,[44] seems to have inherited the whole of Sutes. Robert and Margaret had a son George, who died in 1556, and a daughter Elizabeth, who married John Southwell of Barham, co. Suffolk,[45] and on whom the manor of Sutes was evidently settled. In 1550 John and Elizabeth Southwell conveyed the manor to Richard Wytherall.[46]

Denise, daughter and heir of Wytherall, married William Wrothe, son of Robert Wrothe of Enfield,[47] who held the manor jointly with his wife and died seised in January 1593-4.[48] The manor descended to Richard Wrothe, their son, whose will is dated 1596,[49] and to William son of Richard,[50] who is described as of London and of Heaven or Hatten End in Standon.[51] This William had eight children, of whom William Wrothe was the eldest. The will of William the elder is dated 1643.[52] William the younger died in 1677.

WROTHE. *Argent a bend sable with three lions' heads razed argent thereon having crowns or.*

---

[24] Feet of F. Herts. 28 Edw. III, no. 427*a*.
[25] Cal. Close, 1360-4, p. 430; Chan. Inq. p.m. 38 Edw. III, no. 37.
[26] Feet of F. Herts. 45 Edw. III, no. 624.
[27] Add. MS. 1240 (documents of the Earls of March), fol. 84. Evidently Richard Plessy had two brothers both called John.
[28] Mins. Accts. bdle. 1111, no. 24.
[29] The manor was held of Standon, so must have been formed by subinfeudation.
[30] Chart. R. 14 Edw. II, m. 8, no. 33.
[31] Chan. Inq. p.m. 34 Edw. III, no. 83. Roger D'Amorie was Elizabeth de Burgh's third husband.
[32] Close, 47 Edw. III, m. 22 d.
[33] Or possibly it was alienated after his death in February 1407-8 by his daughters Anne wife of Sir William Clifford, and Joan wife of Sir William Phelipp.
[34] Chan. Inq. p.m. 14 Hen. IV, no. 4; see Agard's Indexes (2nd no.), vii, 5.
[35] Cal. Pat. 1422-9, p. 252; Close, 2 Hen. V, m. 24.
[36] Chan. Inq. p.m. (Ser. 2), c, 49.
[37] Ibid. cxxxv, 76. He was buried in Standon Church.
[38] Ibid.
[39] Feet of F. Herts. East. 1569.
[40] Close, 6 Hen. VI, m. 6 d.
[41] Chan. Inq. p.m. 12 Edw. IV, no. 12.
[42] Feet of F. Herts. Trin. 8 Hen. VII.
[42a] See Early Chan. Proc. bdle. 337, no. 33. Anne Ellerbek is here said to be daughter of Ralph Baud; see also Berwick.
[43] See Anct. D. (P.R.O.), A 3358, for the marriage settlement, in which the manors of Sotes, Marshalls and Younges are mentioned. In 1534, however, Margaret was still Margaret Marzen, widow (Feet of F. Herts. Trin. 26 Hen. VIII), and according to the Audley pedigrees the only wife of Richard Audley was Catherine daughter of Richard son of Lord Scroop (see Blomefield, *Hist. of Norf.* [ed. Parkin], vi, 210).
[44] Morant, *Hist. of Essex*, ii, 184. The Tendrings had long been lords of Little Birch.
[45] Page, *Supp. to Suff. Traveller*, 566. According to Morant's pedigree, *Hist. of Essex*, ii, 184, Robert and Margaret had two daughters, Mary and Joan. If this is correct he must have left out a third daughter Elizabeth.
[46] Feet of F. Herts. Mich. 1550.
[47] *Visit. of Essex* (Harl. Soc. xiii), 132; Ct. R. (Gen. Ser.), portf. 998, no. 77.
[48] Chan. Inq. p.m. (Ser. 2), ccxliii, 64.
[49] P.C.C. 45 Drake.
[50] He was baptized at Thundridge in 1594. Information from Mr. W. C. Waller.
[51] Waller, *Loughton in Essex* (transcripts of Wills, 29, 31).
[52] Ibid. 31.

In the same year the manor was sold by his widow Margaret (described as mother of John Wrothe, deceased, heir of William) and her son Edward [53] to William and John Leake in trust for Robert Bird of Staple Inn.[54] It descended to his son John Bird, who died in 1732, leaving four co-heirs, the daughters of his brother Robert who predeceased him. Of these Elizabeth Bird conveyed her share in 1740 to her sister Jane Bird, who also acquired the share of her sister Martha, wife of George Jesson.[55] In 1744 Jane married David Poole, serjeant-at-law, and a settlement of the three undivided fourth parts was made on David for life, with remainder to Jane and their children. In 1745 David Poole bought the remaining fourth from the assignees of his wife's fourth sister Abigail, wife of Marmaduke Lilley, who died about 1737.[56] The manor then descended with Youngs (q.v.), and now belongs to Mr. C. B. Giles-Puller.

son James Henry Leigh conveyed the site in 1790 to David Barclay, and it thus became reunited with the manor.[60] The manor-house lies near the North Road, a little to the north of High Cross. It is an early 17th-century building, originally L-shaped, with a fragment of moat remaining. It has two stories, and is timber-framed with plastered walls and tiled roof. Two of the original chimney stacks remain. In the kitchen is the large original fireplace. Sutes Wood and Great and Little Southey Woods lie a little to the east.

The manor of *YOUNGS* took its name from a family of Juvene or Young, who held lands in Standon in the 13th and 14th centuries.[61] In 1426 Youngs is called a manor, and was released by John Oke to Henry Barton, William Crowmer and Thomas Holewell, who held it of the gift of Thomas Farndon.[62] In 1472 Nicholas Ellerbek died seised of it,[63] and it descended with Sutes (q.v.) to William Tendring.

SUTES MANOR-HOUSE, STANDON

The site of Sutes Manor was held separately from the demesne lands in 1692 by Thomas Nason.[57] His son Thomas sold it about 1704 to William Norcliffe,[58] who in 1719 conveyed it to Franklin Miller and Arnold Warren,[59] evidently in trust for Robert Lord of St. Martin's Lane. Robert Lord left two daughters and co-heirs, Mary, who married William Leigh, and Elizabeth, who married Thomas Wentworth. James Leigh, son of William and Mary, was heir of both his mother and aunt. His

After his death it was apparently divided between his two daughters, Margaret wife of Robert Forster and Dorothy wife of Francis Southwell.[64] In 1543 John Southwell, husband of Elizabeth, daughter of Robert and Margaret Forster, conveyed one-fourth of the manor to Richard Wytherall,[65] and at the same time her brother George Forster, between whom and Elizabeth this half seems to have been divided, conveyed another quarter to Wytherall.[66] In 1545 Wytherall acquired the other half from John Beaumont and his

[53] John, born in 1632, and Edward in 1640, were both baptized at Thundridge (notes from the registers lent by Mr. W. C. Waller).
[54] Feet of F. Herts. Mich. 29 Chas. II; deeds in possession of Mr. C. B. Giles-Puller of Youngsbury.
[55] Feet of F. Herts. Trin. 13 Geo. II; Div. Co. Mich. 16 Geo. II; deeds in possession of Mr. C. B. Giles-Puller.
[56] Will of David Poole, 1758; deeds in possession of Mr. C. B. Giles-Puller.

[57] Feet of F. Div. Co. Hil. 3 Will. and Mary.
[58] Exch. Dep. Trin. 6 Anne, no. 10.
[59] Feet of F. Div. Co. Mich. 6 Geo. I.
[60] Ibid. Herts. Mich. 2 Geo. II; deeds in possession of Mr. C. B. Giles-Puller.
[61] For John Juvene as a witness to deeds see Harl. Chart. 45911; *Cal. Pat.* 1446–52, p. 51. Augustine Juvene was bailiff to the Earl of Gloucester in 1275 (*Hund. R.* [Rec. Com.], i, 188).

[62] Close, 5 Hen. VI, m. 19 d.
[63] Chan. Inq. p.m. 12 Edw. IV, no. 12.
[64] So Dorothy's husband is given in Blomefield, *Hist. of Norf.* (ed. Parkin), x, 275, but according to Morant's pedigree (*Hist. of Essex*, ii, 184) she married George Southwell.
[65] Feet of F. Herts. Hil. 35 Hen. VIII.
[66] Com. Pleas D. Enr. Hil. 35 Hen. VIII, rot. 5; Feet of F. Herts. Hil. 35 Hen. VIII.

A HISTORY OF HERTFORDSHIRE

wife Anne,[67] to whom it had apparently passed from Francis and Dorothy Southwell.

The whole having thus come into the possession of Wytherall, the manor descended with Sutes to David Poole, who built the present house of Youngsbury.[68] After his death in 1758 his widow Jane and son Josiah sold the manor in 1769 to David Barclay,[69] who improved and enlarged the house. In 1793 it was bought by William Cunliffe Shawe, a mortgagee, who sold it in 1796 to Daniel Giles of London,[70] whose family came originally from Caen in Normandy. He was governor of the Bank of England in 1796 and died in 1800. Youngs descended to his son Daniel Giles, M.P. for St. Albans in 1809 and Sheriff of Hertfordshire in 1816. He died in 1831. His sister Mary married Joseph King of Taplow, and the manor went to her son Benjamin Giles King, who was succeeded in 1840 by his sister Louisa, widow of Sir Christopher Puller, kt., Chief Justice of Bengal in 1823. She died in 1857, when the manor passed to her son Christopher William, who in that year had licence to add the name Giles before his own surname, the licence extending to such of his descendants as should hold Youngsbury. He died in 1864, the manor descending to his son Arthur Giles Giles-Puller. The latter died without issue in 1885 and was succeeded by his brother the Rev. Charles Giles-Puller, at one time vicar of Standon, whose son

GILES. *Party chev- eronwise ermine and azure a lion counter- coloured with two crosses azure pointed and voided in the chief.*

PULLER. *Azure a bend invected and plain cotised between three scallops or and a chief or with a quatrefoil be- tween two scallops azure.*

Mr. Christopher Bernard Giles-Puller is the present owner of the manor and resides at Youngsbury.[71]

MARSHALLS, on the south-west of the parish to the north-west of the hamlet of High Cross, apparently originated in a property consisting of four messuages, 72 acres of land, 10 acres of meadow, 16 acres of pasture, 6 acres of wood, the site of a mill called Linchemill with a pond, and 24s. rent in Standon, which Robert Marshall (Le Mareschal) acquired from Elizabeth de Burgh, lady of the manor of Standon, in 1337, and of the reversion of a messuage, 200 acres of land, meadow and pasture and 4 acres of wood expectant on the death of Henry de Thrillowe,[72] Elizabeth his wife and Thomas their son, and also of the reversion of 150 acres on the death of Richard le Somenour, which they acquired at the same time.[72a] There was also a John Marshall, dead before 1338,[72a] and a John Marshall, his son, with a wife Margaret, both dead before 1353,[73] who held land in Standon. By 1474 the 'tenements called Marshalls' were in the possession of Nicholas Ellerbek and descended with Sutes and Youngs to William Tend- ring, then with Youngs to Richard Wytherall, and with both manors to David Barclay. It was separated from these manors before 1823, when Frederick Croker and his wife Anne conveyed it to John Martin Leake of Thorpe Hall.[74] He died in 1836 and was succeeded by his son John Martin Leake. On the death of John in 1862 it passed to his brother Stephen Ralph Martin Leake, and in 1865 to his son Stephen, barrister- at-law of the Middle Temple. He died in 1893,[75] and Mrs. Martin Leake, his widow, now holds the estate and resides there.

LEAKE. *Or a saltire engrailed azure with eight rings argent thereon and a quarter gules with a castle argent therein.*

The capital messuage or farm of Marshalls was separated from the manor in the 17th century. Roger Pavier of Uppington, co. Salop, died seised of it in February 1634–5, leaving as co-heirs his nieces Margaret wife of Ralph Kynaston, Elizabeth wife of Thomas Brees and Mary wife of Samuel Challoner.[76]

The manor of BERWICK or BARWICK (Berewyk, xiv cent.), an estate in the south-east of the parish on the River Rib, was held of the manor of Standon at the end of the 13th century by Eustace Fitz Thomas (of Hawstead, co. Suff., and Shenley, co. Bucks.), who died in 1272. The manor, called in this instance the manor of Hollenhac, was then seized into the king's hands.[77] Thomas Fitz Eustace succeeded his father and in 1292 received a grant of free warren in his demesne lands of Berwick.[78] He died in 1318–19,[79] when the manor descended to his son[80] Thomas Fitz Eustace,[81] and on the death of the latter in 1341 to his son, also Thomas Fitz Eustace, Agnes his widow having dower of a chamber and chapel adjoining at the upper door of the hall and land called Siguresgrove 'on the north of Berewykwood near the park.'[82] Thomas, the son, died in 1349.[83] During the minority of John his brother and heir, Sir John atte Lee held the manor by grant of Edmund de Mortimer, the overlord.[84] John at his death in 1369 left an infant son Philip. He apparently died soon afterwards, for the manor went to a cousin John Fitz Eustace, whose daughter Elizabeth married Robert Berland of Raithby, co. Lincoln.[85] They probably had a son William Berland, the father of Elizabeth

---

[67] Feet of F. Herts. Mich. 37 Hen. VIII. Another conveyance from John Southwell and Elizabeth took place in 1550 (ibid. Herts. Mich. 4 Edw. VI).
[68] Clutterbuck, op. cit. iii, 331.
[69] Feet of F. Herts. Trin. 9 Geo. III.
[70] Deeds in possession of Mr. C. B. Giles-Puller.
[71] Pedigree in possession of Mr. C. B. Giles-Puller.
[72] Cal. Pat. 1334–8, p. 490.

[72a] Cal. Close, 1337–9, pp. 388, 393; Cott. MS. Nero, vi, E, fol. 119b.
[73] Cal. Close, 1349–54, p. 595.
[74] Feet of F. Herts. Mich. 3 & 4 Geo. IV.
[75] Brass in High Cross Church.
[76] Chan. Inq. p.m. (Ser. 2), cccxxxiv, 109.   [77] Hund. R. (Rec. Com.), i, 188.
[78] Chart. R. 20 Edw. I, m. 10, no. 58b.
[79] Chan. Inq. p.m. 12 Edw. II, no. 15.
[80] The heir is called nephew in the above inquisition, but apparently by an error. See Gage, Hist. and Antiq. of Suff. 410.
[81] Fitz Eustace was henceforth used as a transmissible surname.
[82] Cal. Close, 1341–3, p. 496.
[83] Chan. Inq. p.m. 23 Edw. III, pt. ii, no. 122.
[84] Harl. Chart. 53 E. 43 ; Assize R. 339.
[85] Called Robert Eland in the pedigree in Gage, op. cit. 410, but Berland is the form given in Chan. Inq. p.m. 1 Hen. VI, no. 53.

Berland, who married John Baud.[86] He held the manor jointly with his wife and died seised in 1422.[87] William their son and heir succeeded and died about four years afterwards.[88] The manor then passed to his uncle Thomas Baud of Corringham, co. Essex, and Hadham, co. Herts., who died in 1430.[89] His son Thomas died in 1449. Ralph his son held the manor until 1483, when he died and was succeeded by his son Thomas.[90] In 1502 Thomas Baud conveyed Milkley (q.v.) to Sir William Say of Essendon, co. Herts., and Berwick was probably conveyed about the same time. Elizabeth daughter and co-heir of Sir William Say married William Blount Lord Mountjoy, and their daughter and co-heir Gertrude became the wife of Henry Courtenay Marquess of Exeter, who with his wife was attainted in the reign of Henry VIII.[91]

In 1543 the manor was leased by the king to Sir Ralph Sadleir.[92] It seems, however, to have been eventually restored to the Say family. Thomas, brother of Sir William Say, left a son William, who died a minor in 1508, and two daughters, Anne wife of Sir Robert Hussey of Linwood, co. Lincoln, and Elizabeth wife of William Clopton, second son of Sir William Clopton of Melford and Lutons, co. Suffolk. In 1575 William Clopton conveyed one half of the manor to Clement Newce,[93] and in the same year Dorothy daughter and co-heir of Sir Robert and Anne Hussey[94] and wife of John Massingberd of Gunby, co. Lincoln, also conveyed a twentieth part to him.[95] In 1576 he acquired another twentieth from John Mounson, son (apparently) of Mary Mounson sister of Dorothy, and Margaret Thoralde, widow, a third sister.[96] Clement Newce died seised of the whole in 1579,[97] and was succeeded by his son William, who died in February 1610–11.[98]

The Newces lived at Much Hadham in this county.[99] Thomas Newce died in 1623[100]; his son William conveyed the manor in 1648 to Edward Hide and Oliver Bromhall to be sold for the payment of his debts.[1] It was purchased, according to Chauncy, by Thomas Flyer of Brent Pelham,[2] and descended to his son Francis.[3] Thomas son of Francis died in 1743.[4] In 1746 the entail on the lands of Francis Flyer was barred and the estates divided between his daughters, Elizabeth wife of John Gibbs of Clapham, Judith and Catherine Flyer, and Anne wife of Angel Chauncy of Cottered.[5] According to Clutterbuck the manor was sold in 1764 to Ambrose Procter.[6] He devised it by will of 1803 to George Procter, eldest son of his nephew John Procter. After the death of George Procter, his son Leonard being an infant, the manor was sold under an Act of Parliament in 1831 to Daniel Giles of Youngsbury,[7] with which manor it has since descended.

The capital messuage or manor called *BIGGINGS*, to the east of Barwick, was held with that manor by Thomas Baud, who died in 1449,[8] and by his son Ralph Baud at his death in 1483. After the forfeiture of the Marchioness of Exeter it was apparently separated from that manor, for in 1547 Clement Newce acquired it from Sir Richard Lee.[9] Clement Newce died seised of it in 1579, but it was again separate from Berwick in 1591, when George Dyer conveyed it to William Newce.[10] In 1648 William Newce settled it on his son Thomas.[11] It is now included in the Berwick estate.

The manor of *MILKLEY* or *MENTLEY* (Melchlega, xii cent.; Melkeleia, Melkeleye, Melklegh, xiii cent.; Mylkeley, xv cent.) was held of the manor of Standon by the service of a knight's fee and a rent of 26s. 8d.[12] It appears first in the tenure of a family with a local designation. Robert son of John de Milkley appears on the Pipe Rolls in connexion with Hertfordshire in the reign of Henry II.[13] Richard de Milkley, who died before 1222, held a hide and 2 virgates in 'Melkeleia and Hungerhulla,' which descended to his son Richard.[14] Later in the century a John de Milkley was acquiring lands in Standon from Thomas le Verly and his wife Alice, daughter of John Pake, and others,[15] but the principal holding was probably that of Robert de Milkley, who in 1311 received a grant of free warren at Milkley.[16] The grant was made 'at the request of Bartholomew de Badlesmere,' and to William le Baud of Corringham, co. Essex, and his wife Isabel in conjunction

NEWCE of Much Hadham. *Sable two pales argent and a quarter ermine.*

---

[86] Chan. Inq. p.m. 1 Hen. VI, no. 53.
[87] Ibid.
[88] Ibid. 5 Hen. VI, no. 29.
[89] Minet, 'Baud Family of Corryngham and Hadham Parva' (*Essex Arch. Soc. Trans.* [new ser.], x, 145; Morant, *Hist. of Essex*, i, 241). In Thomas Baud's will (P.C.C. 18 Rous) Berwick was left to his son William, but there is no evidence as to William holding it. Possibly he died without issue.
[90] Chan. Inq. p.m. 1 Ric. III, no. 6. After the death of Thomas Baud a suit was brought against his widow Anne, then wife of Sir Edmund Lucy, by Margaret Marzen (see Sutes), who claimed to be the daughter of Anne Ellerbek, daughter and heir of Ralph Baud, and therefore entitled to the manors of Berwick, Milkley and Biggin. The suit was brought to recover the title deeds which were said to be in the possession of Lucy and his wife (Early Chan. Proc. bdle. 339, no. 33). There is no further evidence as to Margaret Marzen's kinship, and the presumption is that Thomas was son and heir of Ralph Baud as stated in the inquisition.
[91] G.E.C. *Peerage*.
[92] L. and P. Hen. *VIII*, i, 981 (22).
[93] Feet of F. Herts. Mich. 17 & 18 Eliz.
[94] Their only son Thomas died without issue in 1559. For pedigree see *Sketches Illust. of Topog. and Hist. of New and Old Sleaford* (1825), 108.
[95] Feet of F. Herts. Mich. 17 & 18 Eliz.
[96] Ibid. Trin. 18 Eliz.
[97] Chan. Inq. p.m. (Ser. 2), clxxxix, 92; Feet of F. Herts. Trin. 18 Eliz.
[98] Chan. Inq. p.m. (Ser. 2), cccxvii, 99.
[99] See the inquisitions.
[100] Chan. Inq. p.m. (Ser. 2), ccccxxix, 131.
[1] Com. Pleas D. Enr. East. 24 Chas. I, m. 31.
[2] *Hist. Antiq. of Herts.* 220.
[3] Recov. R. East. 28 Chas. II, rot. 96; Hil. 1 Geo. I, rot. 82.
[4] Clutterbuck, op. cit. iii, 230.
[5] Com. Pleas D. Enr. East. 19 Geo. II, m. 12; Recov. R. East. 19 Geo. II, rot. 142; Feet of F. Herts. East. 19 Geo. II.
[6] Op. cit. iii, 230. Clutterbuck gives the sale of 1764 as from Mary daughter and heir of Thomas Flyer, but this scarcely seems to be correct.
[7] Deeds in possession of Mr. C. B. Giles-Puller; Private Act, 5 Geo. IV, cap. 27.
[8] See P.C.C. Will, 18 Rous. Bigging was left to his son Thomas, who possibly died without issue.
[9] Pat. 1 Edw. VI, pt. viii, m. 8.
[10] Feet of F. Herts. East. 33 Eliz.
[11] Com. Pleas D. Enr. East. 24 Chas. I, m. 31.
[12] *Cal. Close*, 1323–7, p. 94.
[13] *Pipe R.* 22 Hen. II (Pipe R. Soc.), 9; 25 Hen. II, 55 *et annis seq.*
[14] *Bracton's Note Bk.* (ed. Maitland), ii, 163–4.
[15] Anct. D. (P.R.O.), A 1016, 1011, 1013, 1019, 1021, 1058; B 4014, 4153. The heir of this John and of Richard de Milkley was John's daughter Muriel (ibid. A 5127, 9598).
[16] *Cal. Chart. R.* 1300–26, p. 183. See also Subs. R. bdle. 120, no. 8, where he is assessed under Standon.

A HISTORY OF HERTFORDSHIRE

with Robert de Milkley, so that apparently they had some interest in the manor at that date, probably a grant of the reversion. In 1314 they received a grant (made again at the request of Bartholomew de Badlesmere) of a market on Thursday and a fair on the vigil, day and morrow of the Decollation of St. John the Baptist (29 August) at their manor of Puckeridge (by which name Milkley was then known).[17] Robert de Milkley was apparently still living at the manor, and after his death in 1315–16 a rent of 100s. was payable from the manor to Alice his daughter.[18]

William Baud forfeited in the rebellion of Thomas Earl of Lancaster,[19] and Milkley was not restored until 1327,[20] in which year a fresh grant of market and fair was made, the market to be held on Saturday and the fair on the vigil and day of St. Peter and St. Paul (29 June).[21] In 1331 William Baud made a settlement on his son John.[22] William died at Corringham in 1343 and John in Gascony in 1346.[23] Sir William Baud, son of John, died before 1388, when Milkley was in the possession of Thomas his third son.[24] He was Sheriff of Hertfordshire in 1446 and 1447.[25] In 1422 he granted the Tilehouse at the manor of Milkley with land and a pasture called Mayeshull and free entrance and exit for carrying tiles by three ways, viz. towards Puckeridge, Old Hall Green and 'Schakelocks Lane,' to William Colt for six years, a thousand tiles yearly being reserved for roofing the houses there.[26] Thomas Baud died in 1430 and his son Thomas in 1449.[27] The manor then descended to Ralph son of Thomas, and in 1483 to Thomas son of Ralph. In 1502 Thomas Baud conveyed it to Sir William Say of Essendon, to whom he was bound in a sum of £1,000.[28] Agnes his wife released her right to a third after his death in 1521.[29] With Berwick (q.v.) the manor was forfeited to the Crown under Henry VIII,[30] and in 1534 was granted to Sir Thomas Audley, afterwards Lord Audley of Walden.[31] It descended to his daughter

BAUD. *Gules three chevrons argent.*

Margaret, who married Thomas Duke of Norfolk, and was settled on Thomas Lord Howard, their second son, who in March 1583–4 conveyed it to Simeon Brograve, son and heir-apparent of John Brograve of Westmill.[32] It then descended with Hamells in Braughing (q.v.).

The house called Mentley, now a farm, lies a little to the north-west of Puckeridge. There are the remains of a homestead moat near it. A mill at Milkley is mentioned in 1342.[33]

The rolls of courts held at Milkley in 1516 and 1558 are at the Record Office.[34] Mention of the tile kiln at Milkley occurs in the former roll.

The manor of RENNESLEY (Reneslegh, Romesley, xiii cent. ; Ranesleye, xiv cent.), on the south of the parish near the Rib, was held about the middle of the 13th century by Walter de Furneaux and his wife Alice, who granted it to Adam de Cretinge. He in 1283 or soon after conveyed it to Anthony Bek, Bishop of Durham.[34a] Possibly Robert de Wyleby and John de Harecourt, the kinsmen and heirs of Anthony Bek, reconveyed the manor to Sarah daughter of Walter de Furneaux.[35] In 1317 a certain Gerard Daudenard and his wife Sarah conveyed a moiety of the manor held for the life of Sarah to John de Horneby,[36] who in 1321 acquired another moiety from Jordan de Beverley, called one of the heirs of Sir Roger de Scotre.[37]

There seems to be no further trace of the manor until 1517, when it was held by Thomas Bird.[38] In 1543 John and Nicholas Bird with their wives, both named Elizabeth, conveyed it to John Gardiner,[39] who died seised in 1550,[40] having bequeathed it to his son Thomas with a remainder to Richard Farnfield.[41] The latter was holding it at his death in 1609,[42] and it descended to his son Walter, who died in 1611, Thomas his brother and heir being then aged twelve.[43] Before 1676 it had come into the possession of Ralph Freeman,[44] who with his wife Elizabeth conveyed it in 1685 to Christopher Cratford and Henry Clarke,[45] probably in trust for Benjamin Gardiner, who was holding in 1700.[46] It descended to Sarah daughter of John Gardiner and wife of Thomas Kilpin. She joined with her daughter Martha in 1731 in a sale to John Jennings, whose

---

[17] Chart. R. 8 Edw. II, m. 20, no. 44.
[18] *Cal. Close,* 1323–7, p. 94.
[19] *Parl. Writs* (Rec. Com.), ii, App. 178.
[20] *Cal. Close,* 1327–30, p. 21 ; 1323–7, p. 94.
[21] Chart. R. 1 Edw. III, m. 22, no. 40.
[22] Feet of F. Div. Co. 5 Edw. III.
[23] Morant, op. cit. i, 241. For grants by John of land in Puckeridge, &c., see Anct. D. (P.R.O.), B 656, 2474 ; A 11517.
[24] See Minet, op. cit. 162–5.
[25] V.C.H. *Herts. Families,* 282.
[26] Anct. D. (P.R.O.), D 407.
[27] Minet, op. cit. 166.
[28] Close, 18 Hen. VII, no. 15.
[29] Feet of F. Herts. Trin. 13 Hen. VIII.
[30] L. and P. Hen. *VIII,* ix, 481.
[31] Ibid. vii, 587 (10) ; xiii (2), 491 (6). The manor (i.e. the rent from it) was annexed to the duchy of Lancaster in 1558 (Pat. 4 & 5 Phil. and Mary, m. 23).
[32] Com. Pleas D. Enr. East. 26 Eliz. ; Feet of F. Herts. East. 26 Eliz. At some date before 1628 a conveyance of the manor seems to have been made to the Crown, for in that year the king granted it to Edward Ditchfield and others (Pat. 4 Chas. I, pt. xxxv, rot. C, m. 1). They conveyed it to Edward Brograve (Close, 6 Chas. I, pt. vi, no. 32), and according to Chauncy it descended in his family until 1695, when Elizabeth Wyke, heir of Thomas Brograve, sold it to Sir Thomas Brograve of Hamells (Hist. *Antiq. of Herts.* 220). But all the conveyances dealing with Hamells, Westmill, &c., during this period mention Milkley also, and it seems more probable that Edward Brograve (who was of Gray's Inn) was acting in trust for Simeon Brograve, and that the whole transaction was for an alteration in tenure.
[33] Anct. D. (P.R.O.), B 2474.
[34] (Gen. Ser.), portf. 148, no. 18 ; 998, no. 77.
[34a] Harl. Chart. 48 I. 48. The tenure of this manor does not appear ; probably it was held of Standon.
[35] Adam de Creting had a son John, who in 1328 brought a suit against Alice le Boteler and her son John for one-third of the manor of Plessis which Walter de Furneaux and Alice had given to Adam de Creting and he to Anthony Bek, whose heirs apparently released it to Sarah daughter of Walter de Furneaux, whose son Walter granted it to Sarah Boteler and John (De Banco R. Trin. 2 Edw. III, m. 60). At first sight it would appear that this moiety of Plessis must be the same as the manor called Rennesley, but the date of the action when compared with the date at which it was acquired by John de Horneby (see text) makes this impossible.
[36] Feet of F. Herts. 11 Edw. II, no. 272.
[37] *Abbrev. Plac.* (Rec. Com.), 338.
[38] See Chan. Inq. p.m. (Ser. 2), xxxii, 88.
[39] Feet of F. Herts. Hil. 34 Hen. VIII.
[40] Chan. Inq. p.m. (Ser. 2), xciii, 107.
[41] Clutterbuck, op. cit. iii, 232.
[42] Chan. Inq. p.m. (Ser. 2), cccxi, 115.
[43] Ibid. cccxxv, 195.
[44] Feet of F. Div. Co. Trin. 28 Chas. II.
[45] Ibid. Trin. 1 Jas. II.
[46] Ibid. Mich. 12 Will. III.

BRAUGHING HUNDRED — STANDON

son George sold it to Ambrose Procter in 1786. He devised it to George Procter, son of his nephew John,[47] by whom it was sold in 1826 to Abel Smith of Woodhall. His son Abel Smith, M.P., was lord in 1873,[48] and the manor is now held by his son Mr. Abel Henry Smith.

To the south of Rennesley Garden Wood is a moated tumulus.

Another mesne manor held of the manor of Standon was BARTRAMS (Bertrammes, xv cent.) alias BARTRAMS LAND, situated on the east of the parish. It evidently took its name from a family of Bertram, one of whom, William Bertram, appears as witness to a 13th-century deed.[49] In the second half of the 14th century the manor was in the tenure of Robert Marshall, from whom it descended to his son Robert Marshall, who died seised of it in January 1402–3.[50] His heir was Richard Torell, son of his sister Elizabeth, who held the manor until his death about 1410.[51] His son Thomas succeeded on reaching his majority.[52] In 1436 Thomas Torell conveyed the manor to Ralph Asteley and four co-feoffees.[53] It descended to Nicholas Asteley, whose widow Cicely was holding it in 1503 together with two water-mills called Wades Mills.[54] In 1518 Robert Asteley and his wife Elizabeth conveyed it to Thomas Newce.[55] Another Thomas Newce was holding it in 1597.[56] He or possibly a son of the same name sold it in 1638 to William Fenn[57] of Harrow, co. Middlesex, who, according to Chauncy, was lord of the manor when he wrote (1700),[58] but this was more probably a son of the same name. George Fenn suffered a recovery of the manor in 1741.[59] In 1746 Mary Fenn, senior, and Mary Fenn, junior, conveyed the manor to William Waddilove,[60] possibly for a settlement on the younger Mary on her marriage with William Woodward, for he with his wife Mary was holding it the next year.[61] In 1754 William and Mary Woodward conveyed it to Henry Lewis.[62] In 1839 it was in the possession of Mary de Horne Hooper,[63] daughter of John Scott, the Quaker poet.

The manor of BROMETTS, BROMELLS, or BROMLEY HALL was held of the lord of Standon early in the 15th century by John Clerk, a netmaker of London.[64] His daughter and heir Margaret married William Walden of London,[65] but whether she held it is uncertain, as it seems to have passed to Nicholas Sterlyng,[66] and from him before 1462 to John Field, who in March of that year received an acquittance of homage 'for the lands and tenements of Bromeley' from Cecilia Duchess of York.[67] This John was possibly son of Roger atte Field, bailiff of the manor of Standon in 1362 and 1366.[68] The brass of John who died in 1477 is in Standon Church, also that of his son John (1474). No further record of this manor has been found until 1548, when Thomas Howe and Audrey his wife conveyed it as the manor of Bromley Hall to Philip Gunter.[69] In 1585 it was in the possession of Francis Gunter,[70] and Thomas Gunter was holding it in 1587.[71] In 1636 it was sold by Blanche James, widow, to Richard Spicer, M.D., and his wife Thomasine.[72] John Spicer, son of Richard, joined with Mary his wife and Steward Spicer, his eldest son, in a conveyance of the manor and of the capital messuage at Standon in which he lived to Henry Uthwhat of St. Margaret's, Westminster, in 1690.[73] Elizabeth daughter and heir of Henry Uthwhat married Edward Elderton, afterwards of Mile End, Stepney. They became bankrupt, and in 1718 the manor was sold to Francis Brownsword and Charles Cotton,[74] who conveyed it to Thomas Scott, a poulterer of London.[75] Thomas Scott died without issue and intestate in January 1738–9, leaving a wife Elizabeth and two sisters, Ann Wilkinson and Mary Easton. In 1741 proceedings in Chancery were taken by Ann Wilkinson to obtain a partition of the estate, her brother's widow having, according to her evidence, taken possession of the whole property by right of dower, and having with her agent Charles Easton, son of Mary, committed waste there. A decree for partition was obtained, but does not seem to have been carried out.[76] Mary Easton died in 1746, and left an undivided moiety to her younger son Charles Easton of Twickenham, co. Middlesex.[77] He by will of 1785, proved in 1786, left it to Charles Easton, son of his brother Robert.[78] In 1822 Charles Easton conveyed this moiety to Joseph Tringham of St. John's Wood.[79] Ann Wilkinson's moiety descended in 1757 to her daughter Ann, wife of Thomas Reynoldson. She

SMITH of Woodhall. *Or a cheveron cotised sable between three demi-griffons sable, the two in the chief facing one another.*

FIELD. *Gules a fesse argent between three eagles argent sprinkled with drops gules.*

---

[47] Clutterbuck, op. cit. iii, 232, quoting from deeds of George Procter.
[48] Cussans, *Hist. of Herts. Braughing Hund.* 173.
[49] Anct. D. (P.R.O.), A 5112. The names of Peter Bartram, Robert Bartram and Thomas Bartram also occur as witnesses to deeds (Harl. MS. 1240, fol. 82, 83b, 84).
[50] Chan. Inq. p.m. 5 Hen. IV, no. 19. It is here said to be held of the king owing to the minority of the Earl of March (see Foreign R. 12 Hen. IV, m. A).
[51] See Foreign R. 12 Hen. IV, m. A.
[52] Ibid.; Chan. Inq. p.m. 5 Hen: V, no. 19.
[53] Feet of F. Herts. 14 Hen. VI, no. 81.
[54] Anct. D. (P.R.O.), A 5507.
[55] Feet of F. Herts. Mich. 10 Hen. VIII.
[56] Ibid. Mich. 39 & 40 Eliz.
[57] Recov. R. Mich. 14 Chas. I, rot. 123.
[58] *Hist. Antiq. of Herts.* 221.
[59] Recov. R. Trin. 14 & 15 Geo. II, rot. 156.
[60] Feet of F. Herts. Mich. 20 Geo. II.
[61] Ibid. Mich. 21 Geo. II.
[62] Ibid. East. 27 Geo. II.
[63] Tithe apportionment.
[64] Harl. Chart. 45 G. 3.
[65] Cal. *Close*, 1422–9, p. 553. John Clerk is here called chandler, but is presumably the same.
[66] Harl. Chart. 45 G. 3. He may possibly have been only a feoffee.
[67] Add. Chart. 15476.
[68] Mins. Accts. bdle. 1111, no. 9, 11; see also Harl. Chart. 51 C. 55.
[69] Feet of F. Herts. Mich. 2 Edw. VI.
[70] Recov. R. Hil. 27 Eliz. rot. 76.
[71] Com. Pleas D. Enr. Mich. 29 & 30 Eliz. m. 34 d.
[72] Recov. R. Mich. 12 Chas. I, rot. 28.
[73] Feet of F. Herts. Hil. 3 Will. and Mary; Recov. R. East. 4 Will. and Mary, rot. 89; Close, 4 Will. and Mary, pt. v, no. 2.
[74] Com. Pleas D. Enr. Mich. 5 Geo. I, m. 27 d.
[75] Deeds in possession of Mr. Grosvenor Berry communicated by Mr. W. Minet.
[76] Ibid.
[77] P.C.C. Will communicated by Mr. W. Minet.
[78] Ibid.
[79] Deeds in possession of Mr. Grosvenor Berry communicated by Mr. W. Minet.

devised it by will proved in 1792 to her son Martin Reynoldson, whose daughter Ann Easton Reynoldson sold it in 1824 to William Tringham. Both moieties remained in the Tringham family until 1911, when the estate was bought by Mr. Grosvenor Berry, the present owner.[80]

WIGFRITH (also called *REGREY* or *REGRACYES*,[81] and now *RIGGORY'S*) was another reputed manor held of Standon. Robert Fitz Herbert died seised of it in 1515 and was succeeded by his son Humphrey,[82] whose son Sir John Fitz Herbert[83] sold it in 1551 to Henry Chauncy.[84] He conveyed it to William Holliland in 1562.[85] David Holliland sold it in 1598 to Richard Hale,[86] who died seised in February 1620–1,[87] William his son, aged fifty-two, being his heir. In 1706 Susan Baldwin, spinster, was holding one-third of the manor.[88] Later it was in the possession of the Jennings family, and was offered for sale by auction with other lands of George Jennings, son of Sir John Jennings of Greenwich, in 1786. It was bought by St. Edmund's College in 1815.[89] The farm lies to the south-west of Old Hall Green.

The *STONEHOUSE* alias *BRICKHOUSE* estate may perhaps be traced to John Field, who in 1477 died seised of nine messuages and other property in Standon including an inn called the New Inn alias the 'Swan' at Puckeridge.[90] His widow Agnes Morton died seised of the same in 1517,[91] when they descended to Dorothy wife of Sir William Filoll, kt., as daughter and heir.[92] A rental of Filoll's lands includes tenements scattered over the north-west of the parish,[93] and among them is one called 'Stonehaw in Stortford Street,' which probably represents the later form of Stonehouse. The property descended to Anne Filoll, daughter and heir, who married Sir Edward Willoughby. After the death of her husband she and her son Henry sold the 'manor of Standon alias the Stonehouse' to Thomas Howe in 1541.[94] In 1544 he alienated part of the estate called Hallys and Ducketts (see history of the chapel of Salebourne above) to John Gardiner, and in 1550 sold the 'manor of Standon alias the Brickhouse alias the Stonehouse' to Thomas Gardiner,[95] from whom it passed in 1552 to Guy Wade of London.[96] Wade's will is dated 1557.[97] His son and heir Samuel died without issue about 1562,[98] and in 1567 Samuel's paternal aunt and heir Marion wife of William Pickering of London sold the Stonehouse to Thomas Stanley.[99] It descended to his daughter and heir Mary, who married Sir Edward Harbert of Hendon, and they in 1583 conveyed it to Sir Ralph Sadleir,[100] with other lands called Palmers and Mylmans which Thomas Stanley had acquired from Thomas Wytton in 1567. It then follows the descent of Standon and is mentioned in conveyances of that manor as late as the reign of James I. If the stone house or brick house of this estate is the same as the tenement called the 'Stonehaw' (see above) which lay in Stortford Street, it is possible that this is the old manor-house described by Salmon as lying west of the town by the road leading to the main road to Ware.[1]

By an early 13th-century deed Ralph Child of Milkley settled a messuage in Standon and land in Milkley, Hanley and Northfield by Ruggeberwe (Ragborough) on his sister Isold.[2] John Child was assessed for property at Standon in 1307.[3] The Childs' property may be identified with the 'manor, capital messuage or farm called *CHILDS* alias *THE HOLLE*,' which belonged to Ralph Asteley at the beginning of the 15th century,[3a] and of which John Watts (see Mardocks in Ware) died seised in 1616.[4] Hole Farm, which corresponds with the situation of this estate,[5] may preserve the name.

The *RECTORY MANOR* alias *STANDON FRIARS* originated in a grant made by Gilbert de Clare son of Richard de Tonbridge, probably early in the 12th century, of the church of Standon, 140 acres of land and his vineyard there to the Knights of St. John of Jerusalem.[6] Roger de Clare his brother and successor further granted them 'the mill which is outside the gate of Standon towards the south.'[7] It was evidently this mill which the lords of Standon subsequently rented from the prior,[8] who in 1337 exchanged the rent with Elizabeth de Burgh for lands in West Peckham and Swanton, co. Kent.[9] The maintenance of a chantry 'in the chapel of the manor' was incumbent on the prior, and was probably a condition of the grant by Gilbert de Clare.[10] The Prior of St. John of Jerusalem had amendment of the assize of bread and ale from his tenants at Standon.[11] In 1330 the prior leased the manor to William de Langeford for ten years,[12] and in 1533 the manor and parsonage were leased to Richard Wytherall (for whom see Youngs).[13] After the Dissolution the manor and rectory were granted in 1540 to Sir Ralph Sadleir,[14] and they have since

THE KNIGHTS OF ST. JOHN. *Gules a cross argent.*

Hall Green property afterwards acquired by St. Edmund's College is given in 1677 as 'the land lately of Sir John Watts' (deed in possession of St. Edmund's College).
[6] *Cal. Rot. Chart.* 1199–1216 (Rec. Com.), 1.
[7] Dugdale, *Mon. Angl.* vi, 806.
[8] Add. MS. 6042, fol. 72 (Mun. of Mortimer Earl of March).
[9] Ibid.; Inq. a.q.d. file 240, no. 20.
[10] Ct. R. (Gen. Ser.), portf. 178, no. 37, 39; Cott. MS. Claud, E vi, fol. 10.
[11] Assize R. 323.
[12] Cott. MS. Nero, E vi, fol. 120.
[13] Land Rev. Misc. Bks. lvii, fol. 108. For other 16th-century leases see Cott. MS. Claud. E vi, fol. 10, 245 d.
[14] *L. and P. Hen. VIII,* xvi, 379 (26).

[80] Deeds in possession of Mr. Grosvenor Berry communicated by Mr. W. Minet.
[81] Chan. Proc. (Ser. 2), bdle. 2, no. 77.
[82] Feet of F. Herts. Hil. 32 Hen. VIII.
[83] Ibid. Mich. 5 Edw. VI.
[84] Ibid. Mich. 4 & 5 Eliz.
[85] Ibid. Hil. 40 Eliz.
[86] Chan. Inq. p.m. (Ser. 2), ccclxxxvii, 111.
[87] Recov. R. East. 5 Anne, rot. 145.
[88] Information from the Rev. E. Burton, D.D.
[89] Chan. Inq. p.m. 17 Edw. IV, no. 56.
[90] Ibid. (Ser. 2), xxxii; 38.
[91] Ibid.
[92] Harl. Roll L. 33.
[93] Com. Pleas D. Enr. East. 33 Hen. VIII, m. 7 d.; Feet of F. Trin. 33 Hen. VIII.
[94] Feet of F. Herts. Mich. 4 Edw. VI.
[95] Ibid. East. 6 Edw. VI.
[96] Add. Chart. 1996.
[97] Chan. Proc. (Ser. 2), bdle. 144, no. 29.
[98] Com. Pleas D. Enr. East. 9 Eliz. m. 21 d.; Feet of F. Herts. Trin. 9 Eliz.
[99] Com. Pleas D. Enr. Hil. 26 Eliz. m. 7; Feet of F. Herts. Mich. 25 & 26 Eliz.
[1] Salmon, *Hist. of Herts.* 238.
[2] Anct. D. (P.R.O.), A 5112.
[3] Subs. R. bdle. 120, no. 8.
[3a] Will of Ralph Asteley in Cant. Archiepis. Reg. Stafford, fol. 135b.
[4] Chan. Inq. p.m. (Ser. 2), cccliv, 135.
[5] One of the boundaries of the Old

STANDON CHURCH : THE NAVE LOOKING EAST

descended with Standon,[15] being now held by the Duke of Wellington.

Appurtenant to the manor of Standon Friars was a grange at a place called Papwell to which were attached the tithes of a part of the parish lying between Old Hall Green and Latchford.[16] The name Papwell does not seem to survive now, but in the 17th century the 'liberty of Poppwell or Papwell Walk' occurs as the name of a division of the parish for the collection of the hearth tax,[17] and from the fact that 155 householders were assessed there it seems that this district must have included the hamlet of Collier's End.[18] Papwell Walk also occurs as the name of a common field which seems to have lain between Collier's End and Old Hall Green (see above). There is no further record of this grange, but part of the Old Hall estate acquired by Bishop Talbot in 1787 consisted of copyhold held of the rectory manor.[19] The 'parsonage of Standon and Papwell' mentioned in a 16th-century lease shows that there was still a distinction between the tithes of the two districts.[20]

The abbey of Croyland had a small estate in Standon. According to the forged history of Ingulph the abbey had 5 hides there confirmed by charters of Edred and Edgar, and a house is said to have been built there in 1032 by the Abbot Brichtmer.[21] The abbey certainly had lands there in the 13th century.[22] John Field had a lease of these lands in 1470, and later his widow Agnes and her husband Robert Morton held them.[23] At the time of the Dissolution the farm of the lands was 26s.[24]

In the 10th century a certain Ethelgiva devised lands in Standon to the abbey of St. Albans, but there is no further trace of them after this date.[25]

The church of ST. MARY, situated CHURCH in the middle of the village, consists of chancel 38 ft. 6 in. by 20 ft. 6 in., north vestry, south chamber, nave 71 ft. 6 in. by 22 ft., north and south aisles 73 ft. by 12 ft., south porch 9 ft. 6 in. by 7 ft. 6 in., west porch 14 ft. 6 in. by 12 ft., south-east tower 14 ft. square, all internal dimensions. The walls are of flint with stone dressings; the tower is covered with cement.

The earliest part of the existing church is the chancel, which dates from about 1230–40. The nave appears to have been rebuilt about the middle of the 14th century, but the west doorway is earlier, about 1320–30. The north and south aisles are of the same date as the nave. The west porch and a detached tower to the south of the chancel were added in the 15th century. The unusual position of the tower is probably due to the existence of the west doorway of an earlier date. In 1864 the church was thoroughly repaired, much of the external stone was replaced, the whole building re-roofed, a vestry built north of the chancel, the upper part of the tower repaired with brick and cemented, an organ-chamber erected on the south side, connecting the chancel with the tower, and a timber south porch added.

This church presents several interesting features unusual in the Hertfordshire churches. The chancel has a considerable elevation above the floor of the nave. The floors of both nave and chancel have a perceptible inclination upwards towards the east; this is probably partly due to the slope of the ground, and there is a belief, which, however, has never been investigated, that a vault exists under the chancel. The other unusual features are the detached tower on the south, now connected with the chancel, and the west porch.

The chancel is approached from the nave by a flight of eight steps, the full width of the chancel, most of them projecting into the nave; the rise is 4 ft. 1 in. There is another flight of five steps, also the width of the chancel, from the floor of the chancel to the foot pace round the communion table, with a rise of 2 ft. 3 in.; there is also a slight slope in the floor upwards towards the east.

The three single lights in the east wall are modern. To the south of these lights is a moulded bracket supported by an angel bearing a shield. In the north wall are two modern lancet windows and a doorway to the modern vestry. In the south wall are a single-light window and an arched opening to the organ-chamber, both modern. In the same wall is a blocked doorway. The fine chancel arch dates from about 1230–40. The arch is of two richly moulded orders, with the dog-tooth ornament between. The jambs are moulded, and have modern detached shafts of red Devonshire marble. The moulded bases and the capitals of carved foliage are original. The wall on either side of the chancel arch is pierced by a squint with pointed arch; it was originally open down to the floor, but the lower part was subsequently built up. These openings have been repaired, but appear to be coeval with the chancel arch.

The nave has north and south arcades of five pointed arches. The arches are of two moulded orders with moulded labels next the nave. The piers, of oolite,[26] are of four grouped semi-octagonal shafts separated by a fillet. The capitals and bases are moulded; they date from about 1340–50. Over each pier is the clearstory window of two lights, the inner jambs of which belong to the early 15th century, the rest of the stonework being modern.

The west doorway is of early 14th-century date, with moulded clunch arch and jambs of oolite. The west window has four lights, with flowing tracery of about 1340–50.

The east window of the north aisle is of three cinquefoiled lights with flowing tracery. The west window is also of three lights with flowing tracery. The four windows in the north wall are of two lights with traceried heads. All the windows are of mid-14th-century date, repaired. On the east wall of the aisle is a bracket for an image, square with a plain

---

[15] There is a grant to Tipper and Dawe, fishing grantees, in 1592 (Pat. 34 Eliz. pt. vii, m. 1 [2nd pt. of roll]).
[16] Cott. MS. Nero, E vi, fol. 121. These may have possibly been the endowment of an ancient chapel.
[17] Lay Subs. R. bdle. 248, no. 23 (1663).
[18] The term 'liberty' is probably used on account of the earlier connexion with the Hospitallers.
[19] Information from the Rev. E. Burton, D.D. [20] Cott. MS. Claud, E vi, fol. 10.
[21] 'Hist. Croyland Ingulphi,' Rerum Anglicanim Scriptorum veterum, i, 61; Dugdale, Mon. Angl. ii, 96.
[22] Assize R. 6 Edw. I, Agard's MS. index, fol. 46.

[23] Harl. Chart. 44 C. 59–64, 44 D. 1–12.
[24] Dugdale, Mon. Angl. ii, 124.
[25] Cott. MS. Nero, D. 7; Thorpe, Cod. Dipl. 497.
[26] The jambs of the north, south and west doorways are also of shelly oolite, the arches are of clunch.

splay under. In the south-east corner is a piscina with a pointed head and splayed edge ; the bowl is in a projecting part of the sill. A moulded string-course on the inside wall at the sill level is broken only by the blocked north door, which has a pointed arch of two moulded orders of 14th-century date.

The windows in the south aisle are similar to those in the north, the section of the inner label in the windows in the south wall being different. The east window, which opens into the modern organ-chamber, is unglazed. The stair to the rood-loft is placed in the north-east corner of the aisle ; the 15th-century four-centred doorway is set in a splay in the aisle ; the upper doorway to the rood-loft, also with a four-centred arch, opens into the nave. In the south wall near the east end is a mid-14th-century piscina with pointed head and moulded jambs. The wall string carried round the arch forms the label. A little to the west of this a large modern ogee-arched recess contains an ancient stone coffin without a lid.

The 14th-century south doorway has a pointed arch of two moulded orders, with richly moulded inner arch having a moulded label and head stops. The south porch is modern.

The west porch has a pointed entrance moulded archway which has been repaired. The side windows are filled with modern tracery. The porch is of 15th-century date.

The south-east tower is of three stages, with doorways on the north and west sides. The second stage is pierced by loops. In each face of the belfry stage is a two-light window with traceried head. The tower is finished with an embattled parapet and a small leaded spire.

The font has an octagonal basin, round which are carved in relief two rows of continuous foliage, probably of early 13th-century work ; the stem is modern, but the original bases of detached shafts remain.

All the other fittings are modern.

In the organ-chamber is a large chest bound with many iron bands and with six handles ; it is probably of 16th-century date. Another chest, in the vestry, bears the letters R.S. and the crest of the Sadleir family.

On the north side of the chancel is a large marble monument to Sir Thomas Sadleir, who died in 1606, and Gertrude his wife. Their recumbent effigies lie under a semicircular canopy supported by columns ; above the cornice are their arms. The knight is in armour and the lady clad in a long robe with ruff ; in front are the kneeling figures of a son and daughter.

On the south side of the chancel is the monument to Sir Ralph Sadleir, who died in 1587. His recumbent effigy, in armour, lies in an arched recess, above which is a cornice supported on Ionic columns ; in front of the base are the kneeling figures of three sons and four daughters ; above the cornice are his arms. Above the tomb, on iron brackets, are two helmets, a sword, stirrups, halbert and spurs, also a long standard pole, bound spirally with strip iron, said to have been captured by Sir Ralph at the battle of Pinkie[27] ; the banner itself is modern, the old one having dropped to pieces.[28]

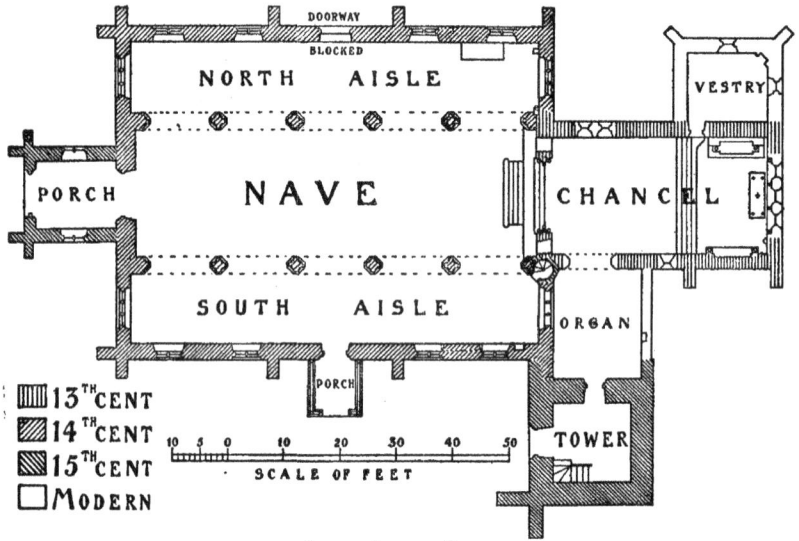

PLAN OF STANDON CHURCH

[27] This pole was for a time removed to Gilston Park (see *Illus. Lond. News*, 26 Apr. 1851). There is a legend that it was the pole of the Royal Standard of Scotland, which Sadleir is said to have captured (see memoir of him by Sir Walter Scott in *State Papers and Letters of Sir R. Sadleir* [ed. A. Clifford, 1809], p. xix, and *Life and Times of Sir R. Sadleir* by F. Sadleir Stoney [1877], 112).

[28] Some armour, including a breastplate and helmet, pistol, spurs, and an instrument for stringing a cross-bow, which were over Sir Ralph's tomb, and a piece of horse armour which had hung over Sir William Coffyn's, are now in the possession of Rev. Franc Sadleir. Information from Mr. T. U. Sadleir.

STANDON CHURCH: MONUMENT TO SIR RALPH SADLEIR

In the north aisle is an altar tomb with stone sides, having indents of three shields; on the top is a marble slab, round the top edge of which is an inscription, part of which is lost, but said to be to John Field, who died in 1477. On the slab is his brass, a figure clothed in the robes of an alderman. He has a double chain of gold round his neck and a rosary and a purse hanging from his girdle; below are small figures of two sons and a daughter. On the same slab is the brass of his son John, in an elaborate suit of armour, with his tabard emblazoned with his arms; the date of his death is missing. Below are the figures of two sons and two daughters. Above the figure of the alderman is a shield of the arms of the city of London, and below is one charged with a merchant's mark; the shield above his son has the arms of the Staple of Calais, the arms of Field being on another shield below.

In the vestry is a mural tablet to Ann daughter of Sir Edward Coke, Lord Chief Justice of the Common Pleas, and wife of Ralph Sadleir of Standon, who died in 1660.

In the east wall of the chancel, outside, is the undated tomb of Richard Sadleir.

On the nave floor, near the east end, are four slabs with brasses; one to Sir William Coffyn, of the household of King Henry VIII, died in 1538, a shield with his arms above. Another brass is of a civilian, the inscription and paternal coat of arms are gone; the maternal shield bears the arms of Wade. The third brass has the figure of a man in armour, with inscription and arms of — Wade, impaling another, died 1557; under the inscription are the old arms of the Merchant Taylors' Company. The fourth brass has inscription only to Richard Emerson, who died in 1562. On the south wall is a brass inscription to John Riggewyn, 1412, and his wife.

There are six bells: the treble by Thomas Mears; the second and fourth by Miles Graye, 1630, presented by Ralph Sadleir; the third by Mears & Stainbank, 1868; the fifth by J. Briant, 1792; the tenor by Pack & Chapman, 1778.

The communion plate is modern.

The registers of baptisms and burials begin in 1671, and of marriages in 1672; there are no marriage registers from 1719 to 1728.

ADVOWSON The church of Standon was granted by Gilbert de Clare to the Knights Hospitallers probably at the beginning of the 12th century (see rectory manor). Before 1280 the church was served by a vicar, and in that year the vicarage was formally endowed by the prior with a messuage and 3 acres of land.[29] After the Dissolution the advowson was granted with the rectory and rectory manor to Sir Ralph Sadleir,[30] and descended with Standon until conveyed by the Duke of Wellington to Christopher Puller of Youngsbury. In 1896 it was sold to Mr. E. S. Hanbury, the present patron.[31]

At the beginning of the 16th century there was a brotherhood of our Lady in Standon Church. Various bequests made to it occur in wills of that date.[32]

CHARITIES The Parochial Charities are regulated by a scheme of the Charity Commissioners 10 April 1894. They comprise the charities of:

1. John de Standon, by deed 1658, consists of 32 a. 3 r. 8 p., acquired by exchange under the Inclosure Act 1830 and producing £32 5s. 5d. yearly.
2. Thomas Fysher, by deed 1614, consists of 29 a. 2 r. 25 p. and a sum of £262 14s. 10d. consols, producing altogether about £76 8s. 4d. yearly.
3. George Crowch, by deed 1554, trust fund, £427 £2 10s. per cent. annuities, producing £10 13s. 4d. yearly.
4. William Haynes, by deed 1635, consists of an allotment of 2 a. 0 r. 5 p., part of Puckeridge Common, producing £2 11s. 2d., and a sum of £218 19s. 10d. consols, producing £5 9s. 4d. yearly.
5. David Thomas, by deed 1702, consists of an allotment of 2 a. 1 r. 35 p., part of Puckeridge Common, producing £2 4s. yearly.
6. Henry Gutteridge, established by admittance entered on the Court Rolls of the manor of the borough of Standon 17 December 1766, consists of an allotment of 1 a. 3 r., part of Puckeridge Common, producing £1 11s. 11d. yearly.
7. Matthew Roe, by deed 1700, consists of 10 a. 3 r. 27 p., producing £13 5s. 3d., and £109 5s. 9d. consols, producing £2 14s. 8d. yearly.
8. The town charities of Richard Sadleir, established as to an annuity of £1 6s. 8d. by deed 1612 and as to an annuity of £5 by deed 1676, now consists of a sum of £211 15s. consols, producing £5 5s. 8d. yearly.

The scheme divides the charities into:

(*a*) The educational branch, consisting of five-ninths of the net income of Thomas Fysher's charity and two-thirds of the net income of Matthew Roe's charity being applicable in connexion with the public elementary schools.[33]

(*b*) The eleemosynary branch, consisting of two-ninths of the net income of Thomas Fysher's charity, one-third of the net income of Matthew Roe's charity, and the whole of the net income of the charities of George Crowch, William Haynes, David Thomas, Henry Gutteridge and Richard Sadleir which are applicable in subscriptions to any dispensary, &c., or provident club, or provision for nurses.

(*c*) The general branch, consisting of the net income of the charity of John de Standon, which is made applicable towards the easement of the common charges and expenses of the inhabitants and parishioners, including the maintenance of a public elementary school.

The remaining two-ninths of the net income of Thomas Fysher's charity is directed to be paid to Christ's Hospital, London.

For the year ended Lady Day 1911 the educational branch received £46 13s. 8d., the eleemosynary branch received £44 2s. 1d., the general branch received £28 9s. 6d., and Christ's Hospital £15.

In 1878 Thomas Chapman, by his will proved at London 29 June, gave a sum of money, now represented by £427 7s. 1d. consols, the annual dividend, amounting to £10 13s. 8d., to be applied in January

---

[29] Cott. MS. Nero, E vi, fol. 119.
[30] *L. and P. Hen. VIII*, xvi, 379 (26).
[31] Information from Mr. W. Minet.
[32] Consistory Ct. of London, 1514–20, fol. 39 d.; P.C.C. 34 Bennett.
[33] See also article on Herts. Schools, *V.C.H. Herts.* ii, 99.

A HISTORY OF HERTFORDSHIRE

in food, clothing or fuel to poor. In 1909 blankets were distributed to forty recipients.

In 1875 Thomas Ginn, by his will proved at London 12 June, gave £100 consols, the dividends arising therefrom to be applied in or towards the maintenance of Standon National Schools.

In 1878 William Rolph Thornell, by his will proved 23 October, left a legacy, now represented by £212 9s. 8d. consols, the annual dividends amounting to £5 6s. to be applied at Christmas in providing a bun and 6d. to each poor child attending the public school, and any surplus to be distributed among old widows of Standon almshouses.

In 1852 Miss Abigail Pratten, by her will proved at London 13 August, gave £1,000, now represented by £1,007 9s. 5d. consols, producing £25 3s. 8d. yearly, the income to be applied in fuel and bread at Christmas and Easter to poor widows and other deserving persons. In 1909 coal was distributed to seventy recipients.

The almshouses at Wadesmill were founded by Rachel and David Barclay by indenture dated 19 May 1794. The endowment consists of a sum of £720 London, Brighton and South Coast Railway 5 per cent. consolidated guaranteed stock, producing £36 yearly. The almshouses are inhabited by four poor widows, who receive 3s. weekly.

The several sums of stock belonging to the charities in this parish are standing in the name of the official trustees.

STANSTEAD ABBOTS

Stanstede (xi cent.); Stanstede Abbatis, Abbotts or Abbot (xiv cent.); generally Stansted Abbots after xvi cent.

Stanstead Abbots is a parish of 2,612 acres, bounded on the north-west by the River Ash, which joins the Lea in this parish, on the south-west by the Lea and River Lea Navigation, and on the south by the Stort. Owing to so many rivers there is a large amount of permanent grass in the parish, about two-fifths of the whole extent.[1] There are large patches of wood in the higher part of the parish : Easneye Wood on the north-west, Newgate Wood and Black Bushes on the north-east. The parish lies on the London Clay, the chief crops being wheat, barley and beans.

The old church of St. James and the manor-house of Stanstead Bury lie on high ground at some distance to the south-east of the village, which is situated near the river on the road to Hertford. The neighbourhood of Hertford and Ware probably brought a considerable amount of traffic through Stanstead, which may account for the seven burgesses there recorded in the Domesday Survey. Stanstead never had a market, as far as is known, nor is there any specific mention of burgage tenure later, but a 14th(?)-century conveyance of a messuage and land 'vendere, dare, legare vel assignare'[2] may, perhaps, point to a survival of privileged tenure. To remedy the inconvenient distance of the church from the village the school was used as a chapel on Sundays in the 17th century and served by a minister of its own.[3] It was probably from this circumstance that Chapel Lane (so called in 1712)[4] took its name.

The main street of the village is the High Street. This at one end is continued as the road to Hertford, and at the other end makes an angle with the Roydon road, which just past the village branches north to Hunsdon and south to Roydon. At the east end of the street is the old Clock School, a 17th-century two-storied building with a tiled roof. The school was founded by Sir Edward Baesh as a free grammar school for the sons of inhabitants in 1635. Although it has been much altered and repaired, the schoolroom on the ground floor still has the original beams in the ceiling and oak-mullioned windows. Under the Endowed Schools Act of 1879 the endowment was separated from the rest of Sir Edward Baesh's charities, and by a scheme under the same Act was devoted, under the name of the Baesh Scholarship Endowment, to maintaining two scholarships of £10 in Ware Grammar School for boys from elementary schools in Stanstead Abbots. When Ware Grammar School was abolished these scholarships were made payable at Hertford Grammar School.[5] The public elementary school opposite the corn-mill was built in 1869 on a site presented by Mr. T. F. Buxton. In the middle of the village is the Red Lion Inn, an early 17th-century building much altered. The date 1538, however, in modern form of figures appears in the middle gable. The house is tiled and has a projecting upper story and five gables ; in spite of the rough-cast with which it is coated, there is visible some plaster ornament in low relief of early 17th-century date. Further along the Roydon road at the bottom of Cat's Hill (Ketteshell, xiv cent.) are Sir Edward Baesh's almshouses, built by the terms of his will proved in 1653. They consist of six brick cottages of two stories under one tiled roof and still retain the original door-posts and moulded window frames of oak. Netherfield, at the top of Cat's Hill, is the residence of Mr. H. L. Prior, J.P. In the village are a number of maltings, the manufacture of malt being the chief industry here as at Ware. The corn-mill, probably occupying the site of the mill mentioned in the Domesday Survey, is situated in Roydon Road. The present mill is a flour-mill, which succeeded an old timber-mill burnt down some years ago. The Mill Race is carried from the Lea through the town, and joins the Lea again to the south of the village, but the present mill is worked by gas power. In Chapel Lane is St. Andrew's Church, built by Mr. T. F. Buxton, consecrated in 1881, and constituted the parish church in 1882,[6] and the chapel of the Countess of Huntingdon's Connexion, dating from about 1809,

---

[1] Cf. the Domesday Survey (V.C.H. Herts. i, 293), which records meadow sufficient for sixteen plough-teams.
[2] Harl. MS. 4809 (cartulary of Waltham), fol. 155 d. From the account of Stanstead in the Domesday Survey it seems probable that it was once ancient demesne, which might account for the burgage tenure.
[3] Chan. Surv. of Church Livings printed in Hern. Gen. and Antiq. i, 28.
[4] Sess. R. (Herts. Co. Rec.), ii, 42. There was, however, an early chapel in the parish. At the end of the 13th century John son of John son of Robert Clericus had licence from the abbot to build a chapel in honour of the Virgin Mary (Harl. MS. 4809, fol. 151b).
[5] V.C.H. Herts. ii, 95.
[6] East Hertn. Arch. Soc. Trans. ii, 28.

but rebuilt in 1874.[7] To the north of the church is Hill House, the residence of Mr. B. Richardson, and Warrax, that of Mr. E. H. Barlow. The vicarage in the Roydon road is part of the Baesh trust,[8] and is held on lease by the vicar.

The south-west part of the parish between the Lea and the Stort lies very low, and the Rye Meads adjoining the Stort are liable to flood. Apparently in the 15th century the state of flood was permanent, for the district round the Rye House was then known as the Isle of Rye.[9] The extent of the island, which was imparked by Sir Andrew Ogard in 1443, seems to have been about 157 acres,[10] from the Lea on the west to the ditch running from the Stort to the Lea on the east. It thus included Rye Farm, about mid-way along this ditch, and the fields formerly called the Warren, now used as a sewage farm for Ware.[11] The lord of Rye Manor maintained a bridge over the Lea, and he also kept up a causeway through the Rye Meadows, which was used by coaches, &c., travelling to and from Norfolk and Suffolk (via Stortford) as a more direct way than the main road, for the use of which they paid a toll to the lord.[12] The present road across the meadows was made by Sir Charles Booth, and the tolls are now taken by the owners of the Netherfield estate.

The chief historical interest in Stanstead Abbots attaches to the Rye House. Richard Rumbold, a maltster and old army officer, one of the most desperate of the conspirators in the famous plot within a plot, was lessee of the Rye House in 1685. One suggestion which he is said to have made for the assassination of the king and Duke of York was to blow up the playhouse when they were both inside ; a plan rejected by the other conspirators, who probably remembered the failure of Guy Fawkes in a similar attempt. When other proposals fell through he suggested the use of the Rye House for the murder, as from its lonely situation and high inclosures it seemed to offer a suitable shelter for the conspirators. Forty of these were to hide in the Rye House and waylay the king on his return from Newmarket. After the murder they were to retire into the house, which, being guarded with a moat and brick walls, could easily be defended against the country people.[13] Travellers from Newmarket, after crossing the Rye Meadows, would have to pass along a narrow lane with a thick hedge and ditch on one side and a long range of buildings belonging to the Rye House on the other, past which were the moat and garden wall, and further on a bridge over the Lea and another over the New River. It was proposed to place a body of horse and foot in the outer courtyard, who, when the king and duke arrived, were to issue out into the lane, this having been previously blocked by an overturned cart.[14] The plan was frustrated by the unexpected return of the king and Duke of York to London owing to a fire at Newmarket, and before another opportunity occurred the plot was revealed by Joseph Keeling, one of the conspirators, and the king's vengeance fell on the whole Whig party.[15] Rumbold escaped, and fought in the rising in Scotland under Argyle. He was taken prisoner when Argyle's forces were routed, and although mortally wounded was executed at Edinburgh, 'the pleasure of hanging him,' as Macaulay said, being 'one which the conquerors could not bear to forego.'[16] The contemporary official account of the plot gives a plan of the house.[17] North of the gatehouse, which occupies the south-east angle of the site, were two small rooms and a kitchen ; on the west there was a small staircase, and next to it a hall 30 ft. by 24 ft.[18] In the north-west angle was a well staircase. There was a great parlour 35 ft. by 20 ft. at the west end and a smaller one 17 ft. by 16 ft., also other apartments and passages. The house was apparently built round a court (*claustrum*) of brick, and outside had an inner and outer court, the whole being surrounded by a moat.[19] Of the main part of the building only the gatehouse remains. This was used as a workhouse for the parish before the Poor Law Act of 1834, when the inmates were removed to Ware. In 1904 it was acquired by Messrs. Christie & Co. (see Rye Manor). It is now used as a show place, and an inn built in the forecourt of the house is a famous resort of excursionists and anglers. . The 'great bed of Ware,' apparently immortalized by the reference to it in Shakespeare's *Twelfth Night*, was brought here from the Saracen's Head at Ware. It bears the date 1463, but it did not probably exist before the latter part of the 16th century. It is a four-post bedstead of carved oak, and measures 11 ft. square and 8 ft. high.

Easneye Wood (Isneye, Hysenhey, xiii cent.) in the north-west of the parish contains a tumulus. This was opened in 1899, but only calcined bones of pre-Roman date were found.[20] In 1253 the Abbot of Waltham Holy Cross had licence to make two roads through the wood in place of two other roads outside it,[21] and in 1332 another licence was obtained for imparking it.[22] A lease of the lodge in the park with the lands belonging, of the Lady Grove, Stanstead Grove *alias* Almond's Frith, and all the woods in the manor of Stanstead Abbots was made to John Rodes of this parish for fifty-seven years in 1526.[23] The farm of these lands was granted with that of the manor to Anne Boleyn in 1532.[24] In the reign of Elizabeth John Raymond had a lease of Isney Park together with the Great Farm of Stanstead.[25] When the estate was acquired by Thomas Buxton (see manor

---

[7] Urwick, *Nonconformity in Herts.* 691 ; see Close, 50 Geo. III, pt. xliii, no. 11, 12.
[8] See under Charities.
[9] In the 13th century a number of persons were responsible for the upkeep of bridges in 'La Rye' (see *Plac. de Quo Warr.* 285, 286).
[10] See Sir Andrew Ogard's licence to impark in descent of manor.
[11] See *East Herts. Arch. Soc. Trans.* ii, 32.
[12] Salmon, *Hist. of Herts.* 250.
[13] *A true account and declaration of the horrid conspiracy against the late king*, &c. (3rd ed. 1686).

[14] *East Herts. Arch. Soc. Trans.* ii (1), 32, quoting from *A true acct.*, &c.
[15] Drawings of the Rye House and prints of Keeling, Algernon Sidney and the Duke of Monmouth are in Illustr. of Herts. (Add. MS. 32, 352).
[16] Macaulay, *Hist. of Engl.* i, 276. Macaulay gives him a high character and condones his share in the Rye House plot.
[17] Reproduced in an article in the *East Herts. Arch. Soc. Trans.* ii, 32.
[18] This must be the 'aula' whose measurements are given as 34 ft. by 24 ft. in the *Itin. of William of Worcester* (ed. Nasmyth), 86.

[19] Ibid.
[20] *East Herts. Arch. Soc. Trans.* i, 137.
[21] *Cal. Chart. R.* 1226–57, p. 427. The name Adam de Isneistrete occurs in 1279 (*Cal. Pat.* 1272–81, p. 349). Possibly the road skirting the wood was so called.
[22] Inq. a.q.d. file 205, no. 7 ; *Cal. Pat.* 1330–4, p. 259.
[23] Anct. D. (P.R.O.), A 640.
[24] *L. and P. Hen. VIII*, v, 1499 (23).
[25] Chan. Proc. (Ser. 2), bdle. 113, no. 47.

of Stanstead Abbots) Isney was still a thick wood. He built the present house, now the residence of Mr. J. H. Buxton, in 1869.[26] This house stands in a park of 133 acres and is approached by an avenue of trees nearly a mile long. In the abbot's manor were also some lands called Joyses after a family of Joce who had them in tenure in the 14th century.[27] In 1304 the abbot leased a dwelling-house and land assigned to the pittancer of the convent to Master John de Manhale, clerk, for life,[28] and in 1525 Roger Rodes had a lease of the land called the Pitansry or Joyses for twenty-one years at a rent of 5 marks payable to the pittancer.[29] These lands came with the manor to the Crown at the Dissolution and the name survives in Pitansey Meadow.[30] Other place-names occurring about the 13th century are Danesthemaneswode, Sturtereshull, Newstrate, Bokkeberwefeld, Alfladesfelde, Kyngesfeld and Alfeyesholsme. The frequent occurrence of 'holms' in this parish is noticeable.

Newgate, the site of which is marked by Newgate Wood, was an estate held in the middle of the 15th century by Andrew Ogard, lord of the manor of Rye, and sold in 1558 by George Ogard to Robert Grave.[31] Bonningtons, about 3 miles north-east of the church, formerly belonging to the Calvert family (see Hunsdon), who made the pond there, and afterwards the seat of Mr. Salisbury Baxendale,[32] is for the most part a modern two-storied house, but has an east wing which may date from the 17th century. In Moat Wood, on the north-east of the parish, there are traces of a homestead moat, but nothing is known of its history.[33]

One inhabitant of Stanstead Abbots of more than local fame was Joyce Trappes, daughter of Robert Trappes, a goldsmith of London, who married first Henry Saxaye, a London merchant, and, secondly, William Frankland of the manor of Rye. Her memory is famous from her numerous gifts for educational endowment. Jointly with her son William, who was a student at Gray's Inn, she founded junior fellowships and scholarships at Caius and Emmanuel Colleges, Cambridge. William, to whom there is a brass in the church, was killed whilst riding an unbroken horse in 1581, aged twenty-three.[34] In memory of him his mother founded the free school at Newport Pond, Essex, and by will of 1586 gave money and houses to Brasenose College to increase the emoluments of the principal and fellows and for the foundation of a fellowship. Her name was included in the grace after meat in the college hall, and the principal and fellows of Brasenose erected a monument to her memory in the church of St. Leonard's, Foster Lane, where she was buried. There is a portrait of her in the hall of Brasenose College and another in the master's gallery in the combination room at Caius College, Cambridge.[35] Thomas Bradock (1576–1604), who translated Bishop Jewell's confutation of the attack of Thomas Harding on Jewell's *Apologia Ecclesiae Anglicanae*, was vicar of Stanstead Abbots from 1591 to 1593.[36]

MANORS

The manor of STANSTEAD, called later STANSTEAD ABBOTS, STANSTEAD BURY, and sometimes STANSTEAD BAESH, was held in 1086 as 17 hides by Ranulf brother of Ilger. It was then composed of two separate estates, one consisting of 11 hides which had been held in the time of the Confessor by Alwin of Godtone and which after the Conquest had been given by Ralf Taillebois to Ranulf as a marriage portion with his niece (one other hide which had belonged to the estate he attached to his manor of Hunsdon), and the other of 7 hides which had been held by fourteen sokemen, four of them the men of Anschil of Ware and the other ten the men of Alwin. On Ranulf's estate in 1086 there were 13 hides in demesne with two ploughs, whilst the tenants of the manor had eight ploughs, although there was land and also meadow for sixteen plough-teams. There was pasture on the manor for the live stock of the vill, woodland for a hundred swine, and a mill. Among the tenants are mentioned seven burgesses, who paid 23s., including dues of meadow and wood.[37] With other lands of Ranulf[38] Stanstead was acquired by the Clares, lords of Chepstow and Earls of Pembroke,[39] by whom it was held as two knights' fees.[40] After the manor was acquired by Waltham (see below) Richard de Clare released the abbey from all knight service, and the king also released him from the same service.[41] This Richard, son of Gilbert the first earl, left a daughter Isabel de Clare, who married William Marshal, afterwards Earl of Pembroke. His sons all died without issue, and the rent from the manor payable by the abbey to the overlords after the mesne lordship lapsed descended to his daughter Joan, who married Warin de Munchensy, and to her daughter Joan, wife of William de Valence Earl of Pembroke.[42] Through Isabella, sister and heir of Aymer son of William de Valence and wife of John de Hastings, the rent came to Laurence de Hastings, their son, created Earl of Pembroke in 1339.[43] His grandson John Earl of Pembroke died without issue,[44] his heir being his kinsman Reginald de Grey de Ruthyn, who levied a fine of the rent in 1400.[45] Philippa, widow of John de Hastings and afterwards wife of Richard Earl of Arundel, held, however, 44s. in dower[46] (i.e. one-third of £6 13s. 4d., or 10 marks), and later 5 marks (one-half of £6 13s. 4d.) was in the possession of

---

[26] Cussans, *Hist. of Herts. Braughing Hund.* 27.
[27] See *Abbrev. Rot. Orig.* (Rec. Com.), i, 249a; *Cal. Pat.* 1317–21, p. 280; Chan. Inq. p.m. Edw. II, file 93, no. 21.
[28] Anct. D. (P.R.O.), A 5716.
[29] L. and P. Hen. VIII, v, 1499 (23).
[30] See Charities.
[31] Com. Pleas D. Enr. Trin. 1 Eliz. m. 5 d. For some of this family see will of Elizabeth Grave, probably mother of this Robert (*Herts. Gen.* i, 35).
[32] Cussans, *Hist. of Herts. Braughing Hund.* 45.
[33] *V.C.H. Herts.* ii, 120.
[34] A rubbing of the brass is at the British Museum (Add. MS. 32490, RR, 17).
[35] *Dict. Nat. Biog.*; *East Herts. Arch. Soc. Trans.* ii, 29.
[36] *Dict. Nat. Biog.*
[37] *V.C.H. Herts.* i, 326b. Two other small holdings are mentioned separately (ibid. 332a, 343b).
[38] Cf. Stagenhoe in Walden St. Paul.
[39] This branch was descended from Gilbert de Clare, a younger son of Gilbert son of Richard de Tonbridge. His son Gilbert was created Earl of Pembroke in 1138.
[40] *Testa de Nevill* (Rec. Com.), 269, 270.
[41] Ibid.
[42] G.E.C. *Peerage*; see *Cal. Chart. R.* 1226–57, p. 462. The money was raised by rent charged on certain lands within the manor. Thus we find in the 13th century that certain tenements paid a rent of 4s. to the 'veterem firmam' of Stanstead and 2s. to the pittancer of the convent (Harl. MS. 4809, fol. 145 d.).
[43] Chan. Inq. p.m. 22 Edw. III, no. 47.
[44] Ibid. 13 Ric. II, no. 30; 14 Ric. II, no. 134.
[45] Feet of F. Div. Co. Mich. 2 Hen. IV, no. 16.
[46] Chan. Inq. p.m. 21 Ric. II, no. 2; 2 Hen. IV, no. 54.

BRAUGHING HUNDRED STANSTEAD ABBOTS

Joan de Beauchamp, wife of Lord Abergavenny and sister of Thomas Earl of Arundel son of the above Richard [47]; this descended to her son Richard Earl of Worcester, to Richard's daughter Elizabeth de Beauchamp, who married Sir Edward Nevill, and to their son George Nevill Lord Abergavenny.[48] After this there seems to be no further trace of it.

VALENCE. *Burelly argent and azure an orle of martlets gules.*

HASTINGS. *Or a sleeve gules.*

At the beginning of the 12th century the manor was held under the Earls of Pembroke by Roger de Wancy, who mortgaged it to Bruno, a Jew of London, for a debt of £280 17s. 4d. His son Michael de Wancy, in order to obtain release from the debt, conveyed half of the manor to the king (Henry II), who granted it in free alms to the Abbey of Waltham Holy Cross. The other half was also given to the abbey by Michael at a rent of £12.[49] The grant was confirmed by William Marshal, the overlord, with a proviso that, if by escheat the fee should come to him or his successors, nothing should be exacted from them except the £12 reserved by Michael de Wancy,[50] the services due to the overlord being extinguished as stated above. The rent was paid by the abbey to Michael's heir Henry de Wancy, 'a Norman,' who seems to have forfeited at the beginning of the reign of Henry III, when it was granted by the king to Henry de St. Owen for his expenses whilst in Gascony with the king's brother Richard Earl of Cornwall.[51] Afterwards it was paid to the overlords as above.[52]

WALTHAM ABBEY. *Argent a cross engrailed sable with five crosslets fitchy or thereon.*

In 1253 the abbey obtained a grant of free warren in their demesne lands.[53] The liberties enjoyed by the abbey in their lands were as full as 'royal power could make them.' In Stanstead they had *inter alia* toll, team, soc, sac, infangentheof, utfangentheof, chattels of thieves, amercements of murders, pleas of *namii vetiti*, free fishing in the Lea throughout their demesne lands, and free warren. Their men were quit of shires and hundreds, ward, scot, geld, sheriff's aids, toll in markets and fairs and in crossing bridges, roads and seas, and anyone accused had the right to take his plea to the court at the Holy Cross and answer there according to civil law.[54] In 1522 the abbey leased the manor for sixty-one years (reserving the manorial rights) to John Rodes of London and his wife Margaret.[55] The manor was obtained from the abbey by Henry VIII in 1531, who granted it in exchange the site of the monastery of Blackmore in Essex, the priory manor and other lands.[56] The next year the king gave the farm and reversion of the manor to Anne Boleyn on her creation as Marchioness of Pembroke.[57]

After the death of Anne Boleyn in 1532, Stanstead Abbots remained in the Crown until 1559, when Queen Elizabeth granted it to Edward Baesh of London,[58] who in 1577 had licence to impark 300 acres of land there with a grant of free warren.[59] Edward Baesh died in 1587, when the manor descended to his son Ralph. The inscription to Edward in the church calls him general surveyor of victuals for the royal navy and marine affairs in England and Ireland during the reigns of Henry VIII, Edward VI, Mary and Elizabeth. Ralph died in 1598 and was succeeded by his son Edward.[60] On the death of Edward in 1653 the manor passed to his cousin Ralph, whose son Edward conveyed it in 1678 to Edward Byde and Ralph Skynner,[61] probably in trust for Thomas Feilde. Thomas was knighted in 1681[62] and died in 1689, when Edmund his son succeeded.[63] Edmund's three sons, Thomas, Edmund and Paul, held the manor successively and died without issue.[64] It passed to their cousin Thomas Feilde, rector of Eastwick, to his son William Henry Feilde and to the latter's son of the same name.[65] William Henry Feilde, jun., sold it to Philip Hollingsworth of Thundridge, who bequeathed it to his sister. She directed that at her death it should be sold for the benefit of the children of Paul Meyers of Forty Hill, Enfield. It was bought by Dr. Abraham Wilkinson of Enfield, whose son sold it to Thomas Powell Buxton.[66] Mr. Henry Buxton, his grandson, is the present lord of the manor.

At the beginning of the 19th century the manorhouse of Stanstead Bury was the residence of Captain Jocelyn, R.N., descended from Sir Robert Jocelyn, bart., of Hyde Hall in Sawbridgeworth. He died in 1806 and was succeeded by his son Robert Salusbury Jocelyn of Stanstead Bury.[67] Later the manor-house was used as a hydropathic establishment, and is now the property and residence of Mr. Spencer Trower.[68]

---

[47] Chan. Inq. p.m. 14 Hen. VI, no. 35. The original amount seems to have been £12 (Cart. Antiq. M. 22). Out of this £6 were granted by Walter Marshal, Earl of Pembroke, to William Joymer, who released this sum to the convent (Harl. MS. 4809, fol. 139b, 140). After this the rent is generally given as £6 13s. 4d. (see text), but sometimes as £8 (Cal. Chart. R. 1226–57, p. 462; Feet of F. Div. Co. 2 Hen. IV, no. 16).
[48] Chan. Inq. p.m. 16 Edw. IV, no. 66.
[49] Cart. Antiq. M. 22.
[50] Ibid. 23.
[51] Rot. Lit. Claus. (Rec. Com.), ii, 21b.
[52] See Feet of F. Herts. 53 Hen. III, no. 612 (a composition between the abbot and William de Valence).
[53] Cal. Chart. R. 1226–57, p. 427. Their lands were increased by many small grants (see cartulary of Waltham, Harl. MS. 4809, fol. 138 et seq.).
[54] Plac. de Quo Warr. (Rec. Com.), 283.
[55] Harl. MS. 303, fol. 10.
[56] L. and P. Hen. VIII, v, 452, 622.
[57] Ibid. 1274 (6), 1499 (23).
[58] Pat. 2 Eliz. pt. viii, m. 8.
[59] Ibid. 19 Eliz. pt. xii, m. 14.
[60] See Feet of F. Herts. Mich. 43 & 44 Eliz.
[61] Ibid. Trin. 30 Chas. II.
[62] Shaw, *Knights of Engl.* ii, 256.
[63] Feet of F. Herts. Trin. 12 Will. III; Recov. R. Trin. 12 Will. III, rot. 82.
[64] Clutterbuck, *Hist. and Antiq. of Herts.* iii, 244; Recov. R. Hil. 3 Geo. III, rot. 225.
[65] Clutterbuck, loc. cit.; Feet of F. Herts. Trin. 6 Geo. IV.
[66] Cussans, *Hist. of Hertf. Braughing Hund.* 27.
[67] Inscriptions in church.
[68] It had for some time been held by his family on lease before he became the freehold tenant (information from Miss Trower).

It is a building of two stories with attics, and is partly built of brick and partly of timber framing covered with cement. It was probably originally a house of late 16th-century date, but it has been so much altered and added to in the 17th and 18th centuries that the old plan is lost. The west side is the oldest part, and the cellar under this appears to be the only 16th-century work remaining. In one of the cellars is a blocked window in the east wall, probably originally an outside wall; in the south wall of the same cellar are two small triangular-headed niches, similar to those at Watton Place, Wymondley Bury, and other old houses in the county. In an angle on the west front is a timber-framed staircase, cemented externally, probably of 17th-century date. The north, south and east fronts are mainly additions of the early 18th century. In the window of a room on the west side is some old heraldic glass; one portion shows a sheaf of corn flanked by the initials I.F. of a member of the Feilde family. There is also a shield of arms with the date 1563 above.[69]

The manor of RYE may be identified with the half hide which was held in 1086 by Geoffrey de Bech.[70] There seems to be no further record of it until 1443, but doubtless it followed the descent of Thele in Hertford Hundred (q.v.), for in that year Sir Andrew Ogard had licence to inclose the site of his manor of Rye *alias* the Island of Rye and 50 acres of land, 10 acres of meadow, 80 acres of pasture and 16 acres of wood within the island, to make a park and have free warren, and to crenellate the house.[71] Sir Andrew Ogard was by birth a Dane, who received letters of denization in England in 1436.[72] He was a 'knight, chamberlain, and councillor' of John Duke of Bedford, the regent,[73] who granted him the keepership of the castle of Prudhoe in Northumberland and made him one of his executors.[74] Later he was appointed captain of the castle and town of Caen in Normandy.[75] He had estates in Norfolk and Hertfordshire, and acted several times as J.P., commissioner, &c., for the latter county.[76] According to a contemporary account the purchase of the manor of Rye cost £1,100; the building of the inner court with brick and of the rooms and inclosure (*claustrum*) cost 11,000 marks, whilst the granary and storehouse with 16 horses and 30 cows were worth 2,000 marks. It also relates that whilst in England Ogard had a chapel in his house with priests, clerks, and choristers.[77] Apparently his expenditure was on a lavish scale, and he is known to have been very rich when he died. This was in 1454, when his son Henry was four years old.[78] The custody of the heir was granted by Edward IV to Lawrence Bishop of London,[79] and in 1463 the manor was granted during the heir's minority to the king's brother, George Duke of Clarence.[80]

Henry Ogard bequeathed the manor of Rye to his son Andrew,[81] who died seised of it in 1526, leaving a son and heir George.[82] In 1559 George Ogard (of Ormesby, co. Norfolk) sold the manor to William

STANSTEAD BURY FROM THE NORTH-WEST

---

[69] It seems impossible to identify this coat or to connect it with any owner of the house.   [70] *V.C.H. Herts.* i, 335.
[71] Chart. R. 21–4 Hen. VI, no. 44.
[72] *Cal. Pat.* 1429–36, p. 288.
[73] Ibid. 1436–41, p. 80.
[74] Ibid. 189.
[75] Ibid. 1446–52, p. 537.
[76] Ibid. 382, 388; 1441–5, p. 471.
[77] *Itin. of William of Worcester* (ed. Nasmyth), 86. The wording is somewhat obscure: 'custodiebat capellam in domo sua de presbiteris, clericis et choristis, qualibet die 16 cum 4 presbiteris,' so that there must have been a large number altogether.
[78] Chan. Inq. p.m. 33 Hen. VI, no. 25.
[79] *Cal. Pat.* 1461–7, p. 12.
[80] Ibid. 226.
[81] P.C.C. Will, Bennett, 38.
[82] Chan. Inq. p.m. (Ser. 2), xlv, 104.

370

Frankland of London, clothworker.[83] He settled it on himself and his intended wife Joyce Saxaye, whom he married in February 1565-6.[84] William died in 1576[85] and Joyce in 1587.[86] A settlement had been made on William's eldest son William for life with reversion to Hugh Frankland, his nephew, for life, and then to the issue male of William. In 1606 Hugh Frankland conveyed his interest in the manor to William Frankland his nephew, William Frankland the elder having died without issue.[87] In 1619 William Frankland and Lucy his wife sold it to Sir Edward Baesh, together with the capital messuage where William Frankland lived, the farm close by, and fields called the Pond, Sayres Mead, Nunneholm, the Little or Hither Park and the Further Park.[88] The manor descended with Stanstead Abbots to the Feildes. Miss Feilde, who inherited the property, married Captain Upton, and soon afterwards the estate was broken up. Part of it, the Netherfield estate, was sold to Sir Charles Booth, bart., and descended to his niece, who married Mr. H. L. Prior.[89] The Rye House with 50 acres of land was sold about 1864 to Mr. William Henry Teale, and from him was acquired in 1904 by Messrs. Christie & Co.[90]

The church of ST. ANDREW, CHURCHES erected in 1881, superseded St. James's as the parish church; it is built of brick faced with dressed flint, and is a cruciform building in 15th-century style.

The old church of ST. JAMES, which is still used for services, consists of chancel as at present 10 ft. long by 17 ft. wide, north chapel 41 ft. 6 in. by 15 ft. 6 in., nave as at present 69 ft. by 17 ft. 6 in., west tower and timber south porch, all internal dimensions. The walls are chiefly of flint rubble, but parts are of brick with stone dressings; the roofs are tiled.

The earliest detail is of the 13th century, but it is probable that the nave walls are older. The chancel was built during that period and windows inserted in the nave. The west tower is of early 15th-century date, the south porch late in the same century, and the north chapel was built of brick in 1577. The original length of the nave was 47 ft., that of the chancel being 32 ft., but at some period, probably when the north chapel was built, they were altered to their present dimensions. There is no chancel arch or structural division between nave and chancel, and externally one unbroken roof covers both, the original chancel being marked internally by the lower part of the rood screen, now forming the back of a pew, and by the mouldings on the roof timbers.

The east window has three cinquefoiled lights under a four-centred arch, and is of late 15th-century date. In the north wall is an arcade of four bays opening into the north chapel. The three western arches belong to the arcade erected in 1577. They are pointed arches with double ogee mouldings and with octagonal piers and responds and moulded capitals and bases; the westernmost arch is narrower than the other two. The easternmost arch has a plain splay and square jambs, and probably was opened at a later date. The whole of the arcade is plastered. In the south wall are two windows of two lights; they are of 15th-century date, but most of the stonework is modern. There are traces of some 13th-century lancet windows in the wall. Near the east wall is a double piscina with two splayed lancet arches, and a ledge at the back which supported a credence shelf; they belong to the 13th century.

On a stone in the east wall of the north chapel, outside, is inscribed the date 1577; it was built by Edward Baesh. In the east wall is a window of three cinquefoiled lights under a four-centred arch, and in the north wall are two windows of two lights under square heads; all the windows have been restored.

There are no window openings in the north wall of the nave, but there are remains of a blocked north doorway. The wall is not in a straight line from chancel to tower, and appears to have been altered or rebuilt at some period—perhaps when the chancel was erected—in order to suit its width. In the south wall are three windows of two cinquefoiled lights with tracery; they are probably of 15th-century work, but most of the stonework has been renewed. The westernmost window appears to be a 13th-century lancet window enlarged in the 15th century; parts of the inner splays of the earlier window remain. The south doorway consists of two continuous splayed orders and is of 13th-century date.

The 15th-century south porch is of plain open timber work, the lower part of the sides is boarded, the upper part open; the gabled front has a cusped barge-board and the arch over the entrance is three-centred.

The roofs retain their 15th-century king-post trusses and tie-beams, but the rafters are plastered.

The west tower is in two stages, with angle buttresses at the west; the parapet is embattled and the wood spire is lead-covered. At the south-east angle a projecting octagonal stair-turret rises to above the parapet. The tower arch is of two moulded orders, the inner stopping upon shafted jambs with moulded capitals and bases. The west doorway is of two moulded orders, the inner one forming a pointed arch, the outer being carried square over it. The west window is of three cinquefoiled lights with tracery in the head. The belfry windows are of two lights.

The basin of the font is of 13th-century date; it is circular, and on the rim are the original iron staples for securing the cover; on the south-west side is a small incised cross. The base appears to be of 13th-century date, reversed, but the octagonal stem belongs to the 15th century.

The lower part of a 15th-century rood screen now forms the back of a pew in the nave. Under the tower arch is a screen made up from the 16th-century canopy formerly over the pulpit.[91]

The oak pulpit is of 16th-century work and the communion table of the late 17th century; the high plainly-panelled pews belong to the 18th century.

In the east window of the chapel are some remains of old glass with the royal arms of Elizabeth's time

[83] Recov. R. East. 1559, rot. 447.
[84] Ct. of Req. bdle. 65, no. 34.
[85] Chan. Inq. p.m. (Ser. 2), clxxviii, 15.
[86] P.C.C. Will, Spencer, 17.
[87] Feet of F. Herts. Trin. 4 Jas. I.
[88] Com. Pleas D. Enr. Trin. 17 Jas. I, m. 34; Mich. 17 Jas. I, m. 47; Feet of F. Herts. East. 18 Jas. I. His father Ralph Frankland joined in the sale (Com. Pleas D. Enr. Mich. 17 Jas. I, m. 47).
[89] Information from Mr. H. L. Prior.
[90] Information from Mr. W. Davies of Bachelor's Hall.
[91] East Herts. Arch. Soc. Trans. ii, 28.

and the date 1573 ; in the north window are fragments of Baesh's arms with his motto 'Boulde in God' and other lettering. On the north and east walls are remains of painted inscriptions only partly legible.

In the chapel is the monument of Sir Edward Baesh, died 1587 ; he is represented in armour, his wife being opposite to him, both kneeling. Above them is a round-arched canopy flanked by classical columns supporting a cornice on which are his arms ; below are the kneeling figures of his children.

On a slab against the south chancel wall is the brass of a knight in armour of late 15th-century date. On the chancel floor is the brass of William Saxaye, who died in 1581 ; he is represented in robes and with a ruff. On the nave floor near the pulpit is a small brass of a man and woman with their hands joined together ; there is no inscription, but it is of the middle of the 16th century. On a large slab is a shield with the arms of Boteler, and on another a

co. Surrey.[92] The priory also held a carucate of land in right of the church,[93] which in 1291 was assessed at £20.[94] The church was appropriated and a vicarage ordained before the end of the 12th century.[95] The tithes were leased out by the priory, and after the Dissolution were granted for twenty-one years to John Carye.[96] In 1553 the rectory and advowson were granted to Thomas Sidney and Nicholas Halswell,[97] probably trustees for Edward Baesh. The advowson subsequently descended with the manor[98] (q.v.) until 1847, when it was purchased by W. K. Thomas, from whom it passed into the hands of trustees.[99]

CHARITIES

The charity of Sir Edward Baesh, founded by deed 10 November 1635, and by his will proved in P.C.C. 28 May 1653, consists of the vicarage-house and grounds containing 1 a. 33 p ; land in Chapel Lane containing 11 p. 3 yds., producing £2 yearly ; alms-

STANSTEAD ABBOTS CHURCH : SOUTH PORCH

shield of arms not identified. In the churchyard near the porch is a mutilated coffin slab with remains of a cross.

There are three bells : the treble by John Briant, 1790 ; the second inscribed 'God save the King, 1617' ; the tenor of 1605, both by Robert Oldfeild.

The communion plate consists of one cup and three patens, all of 1714.

The registers are in four books as follows : (i) baptisms 1695 to 1774, burials 1678 to 1774 ; (ii) marriages 1754 to 1772 ; (iii) baptisms and burials 1774 to 1812 ; (iv) marriages 1774 to 1812.

ADVOWSON   The advowson of the church of St. James was given by Roger de Wancy to the priory of Merton,

houses with 30 p. of land ; also the Railway Hotel, let at £70 yearly ; also property formerly described as 'a piece of meadow ground called the Pitansey Meadow alias Parentase,' now consisting of (a) gas works, cottages and land containing 2 a. 3 r. 23 p. ; (b) maltings, private dwelling-house and pounds containing 2 a. 1 r. 31 p. ; and (c) a meadow containing 3 a. 1 r. 7 p., the whole producing £43 yearly. Also a rent-charge of £25 issuing out of the manor of Stanstead Baesh ; the block-house and yard containing 3 p. 5 yds., producing £7 16s. yearly, and land in Netherfield Lane containing 2 a. 1 r. 15 p., producing £3 yearly. The official trustees also hold the sum of £219 2s. 5d. consols, producing £5 9s. 4d. yearly, arising from sale of land and accumulations.

[92] Dugdale, Mon. vi, 247.
[93] Abbrev. Plac. (Rec. Com.), 54.
[94] Pope Nich. Tax. (Rec. Com.), 18 ; also Feud. Aids, ii, 459.
[95] See Merton Cartulary, Cott. MS. Cleop. cvii, fol. ccxix.
[96] L. and P. Hen. VIII, xviii, p. 556.
[97] Pat. 7 Edw. VI, pt. iv, m. 1.
[98] Inst. Bks. P.R.O. sub annis 1660, 1682, 1767, 1781.
[99] East Herts. Arch. Soc. Trans. ii, 28.

STANSTEAD ABBOTS OLD CHURCH FROM THE SOUTH-WEST

STANSTEAD ABBOTS OLD CHURCH: THE NAVE LOOKING EAST

BRAUGHING HUNDRED

The vicarage-house and grounds and the land in Chapel Lane designated the ecclesiastical charity of Sir Edward Baesh is regulated by a scheme of the Charity Commissioners dated 3 June 1902. The vicarage-house is for the use of the vicar of Stanstead Abbots, subject to the payment of 12d. yearly to the non-ecclesiastical branch, and the yearly income derived from the land in Chapel Lane is applied towards the salary of the clerk to the parish church.

In 1908 the net income of the non-ecclesiastical branch was applied in payment of 7s. weekly to the six poor widows in the almshouses, and a premium of £9 8s. was paid for apprenticing a poor boy.

Sir Edward Baesh by the above-mentioned deed also gave a rent-charge of £20 out of the manor of Stanstead Baesh for a schoolmaster of a free grammar school in Stanstead. This sum is annually paid to the governors of Hertford Grammar School.[100]

In 1802 Randle Cheney gave a sum of £20 3 per cent. reduced annuities, now a like sum of consols in the name of the official trustees, producing 10s. yearly, the interest to be applied in the repair of the tomb in the churchyard of the testator's wife and any surplus to the poor.

The dividends are accumulated and distributed from time to time among the poor.

THORLEY

Torlei (xi cent.); Thorleia (xii cent.); Thorley (xiii cent.).

Thorley is a small parish of 1,536 acres adjoining the county of Essex on the east.[1] The road from Sawbridgeworth to Bishop's Stortford passes through the east of the parish. The parish lies on the London Clay and consists for the most part of agricultural land, the chief crops being wheat, barley and beans. Thorley Wood in the south-east is the only wood of any size. From the road the ground slopes upward towards the west, this higher part lying about 300 ft. above the ordnance datum. On the high ground about three-quarters of a mile from the road are situated Thorley Hall (now a farm-house) and the church of St. James. Thorley Hall stands in a moated inclosure to the east of the church. It is a building of two stories, the older parts of which on the west are timber-framed and plastered. It probably dates from the early part of the 16th century. It now consists of the southern end of the old hall, with a south wing and a projecting staircase in the internal angle. The south wing contains the old parlour; the north end of the hall and probably a north kitchen wing have disappeared. The eastern part of the south wing is modern and the whole of the south front has been encased with brick. The hall was originally open to the roof, part of which remains, but a floor is now inserted under it. The original roof, of which only one queen-post truss remains, has a span of about 25 ft.; the tie-beam, which is 12 in. square, has been cut away between the queen-posts, which stand on coarsely moulded octagonal bases, the profiles of which resemble capitals more than bases. The tie-beam and straining-beam above are supported by curved brackets and the purlins are strutted; the tie-beam with the brackets and wall-pieces under is splayed; the roof is ceiled on the rafters and at the level of the straining-beam. There is a wide fireplace with ingle seats at the south end of the hall, now the kitchen, and above the tiled roof is a large early 17th-century brick chimney stack of square shafts set diagonally.

THORLEY HALL: WEST FRONT

---

[100] See above and article on 'Schools,' V.C.H. Herts. ii, 95.

[1] The manor of Thorley lies partly in Essex.

373

BRAUGHING HUNDRED

The vicarage-house and grounds and the land in Chapel Lane designated the ecclesiastical charity of Sir Edward Baesh is regulated by a scheme of the Charity Commissioners dated 3 June 1902. The vicarage-house is for the use of the vicar of Stanstead Abbots, subject to the payment of 12d. yearly to the non-ecclesiastical branch, and the yearly income derived from the land in Chapel Lane is applied towards the salary of the clerk to the parish church.

In 1908 the net income of the non-ecclesiastical branch was applied in payment of 7s. weekly to the six poor widows in the almshouses, and a premium of £9 8s. was paid for apprenticing a poor boy.

Sir Edward Baesh by the above-mentioned deed also gave a rent-charge of £20 out of the manor of Stanstead Baesh for a schoolmaster of a free grammar school in Stanstead. This sum is annually paid to the governors of Hertford Grammar School.[100]

In 1802 Randle Cheney gave a sum of £20 3 per cent. reduced annuities, now a like sum of consols in the name of the official trustees, producing 10s. yearly, the interest to be applied in the repair of the tomb in the churchyard of the testator's wife and any surplus to the poor.

The dividends are accumulated and distributed from time to time among the poor.

THORLEY

Torlei (xi cent.); Thorleia (xii cent.); Thorley (xiii cent.).

Thorley is a small parish of 1,536 acres adjoining the county of Essex on the east.[1] The road from Sawbridgeworth to Bishop's Stortford passes through the east of the parish. The parish lies on the London Clay and consists for the most part of agricultural land, the chief crops being wheat, barley and beans. Thorley Wood in the south-east is the only wood of any size. From the road the ground slopes upward towards the west, this higher part lying about 300 ft. above the ordnance datum. On the high ground about three-quarters of a mile from the road are situated Thorley Hall (now a farm-house) and the church of St. James. Thorley Hall stands in a moated inclosure to the east of the church. It is a building of two stories, the older parts of which on the west are timber-framed and plastered. It probably dates from the early part of the 16th century. It now consists of the southern end of the old hall, with a south wing and a projecting staircase in the internal angle. The south wing contains the old parlour; the north end of the hall and probably a north kitchen wing have disappeared. The eastern part of the south wing is modern and the whole of the south front has been encased with brick. The hall was originally open to the roof, part of which remains, but a floor is now inserted under it. The original roof, of which only one queen-post truss remains, has a span of about 25 ft.; the tie-beam, which is 12 in. square, has been cut away between the queen-posts, which stand on coarsely moulded octagonal bases, the profiles of which resemble capitals more than bases. The tie-beam and straining-beam above are supported by curved brackets and the purlins are strutted; the tie-beam with the brackets and wall-pieces under is splayed; the roof is ceiled on the rafters and at the level of the straining-beam. There is a wide fireplace with ingle seats at the south end of the hall, now the kitchen, and above the tiled roof is a large early 17th-century brick chimney stack of square shafts set diagonally.

THORLEY HALL: WEST FRONT

[100] See above and article on 'Schools,' *V.C.H. Herts.* ii, 95.

[1] The manor of Thorley lies partly in Essex.

373

A HISTORY OF HERTFORDSHIRE

The old parlour adjoining the south end of the hall is lined with early 17th-century oak panelling with a fluted frieze. The room above projects about 18 in. on the west; its orginal fireplace, now in a passage, is built up. The external plastering on the west front is in flush-beaded panels decorated with combed work. Close to the house is a large barn of pre-Reformation date; it measures externally about 146 ft. by 33 ft., and is divided into nine bays; there are two large transeptal entrances on the east side. The building is timber-framed and weather-boarded and rests on dwarf walls of thin bricks; the roof is tiled, and the end gables are slightly hipped.

The stocks and whipping-post stand in the churchyard protected by an iron railing. The rectory and school (built in 1875) lie a little to the north-east. Close by are some gabled cottages of two stories with tiled roofs (once forming one house) of about 1600. This is all the village of Thorley there is, if village it can be called. Probably Thorley was originally part of the vill of Sawbridgeworth.[2] Thorley Street is a hamlet on the main road.

Thorley Place is the residence of Mr. G. S. Streeter, the lord of the manor; Stone Hall, close by, is the residence of Mrs. Clark. Thorley House is the property of Mr. Laurie Frere. On the east of Thorley Street a group of buildings is formed by Twyford House, Twyford Bury, and Twyford Mill. Twyford House is the residence of Mr. Laurie Frere. It came into the Frere family through the marriage of Elizabeth Raper Grant (daughter of William Grant and Elizabeth daughter of John Raper who married Elizabeth daughter of William Hale of Twyford House) with George Frere, who died in 1854. His son Mr. Bartle John Laurie Frere, who died in 1893, was of Twyford House. Twyford Bury is the residence of Mr. T. Cornwell.

No inclosure award has been made for the parish, but there were common fields when the tithe commutation award was made. Thorley Common lay on the north-east of the parish, Limestead Common to the west of Butler's Hall on the south side of the road leading from Thorley Place to that house, Dunnings Common on the north side of the same road, Harris Common to the south-east of Butler's Hall.[3] Appurtenant to Thorley Hall were lands in some of the Sawbridgeworth common fields adjoining Thorley,[4] an additional argument in favour of the intimate connexion between the two parishes. Other place-names found in Thorley are the Vineyard, a field north of the road leading from the main road to the church, Further Park near Thorley Houses, the Moors, Church Field west of the churchyard, Mill Field (marking the site of the mill) on the north of the church, Alderbury Pasture opposite the rectory, and Sedgwick, a very large field on the north of Thorley Place.[5]

MANORS

The manor of *THORLEY* was held in the reign of Edward the Confessor by a certain Godid, a 'man' of Asgar the Staller. After the Conquest it was purchased from the king by William Bishop of London, to whom Godid remitted her right. Before 1086, however, it had been acquired by Geoffrey de Mandeville (elsewhere the successor to the lands of Asgar the Staller), and he was holding it at the time of the Domesday Survey, although the Bishop of London was still trying to make good his claim.[6] The manor was then assessed at 4 hides and had land for eight ploughs, of which four were on the demesne; a mill is mentioned in the extent.[7] The overlordship descended with the honour of Mandeville.

Pain and Ernald de Thorley were landholders in Thorley at the end of the 12th century,[8] and were possibly tenants of the manor. Richard de Thorley was defendant in an action of common fishery at Thorley in 1230,[9] and Arnold son of Richard was holding the manor later in the century.[10] He conveyed it to William Gerbergh of Yarmouth (Gernemuth), who in 1269 was forcibly ejected by William de Clifford,[11] who claimed free warren in Thorley in 1275.[12] About the same time, however, judgement was given for William Gerbergh in an action brought by him against William Clifford.[13] Shortly afterwards Margery daughter of Arnold de Thorley quitclaimed the manor to William Gerbergh,[14] whose son Thomas claimed view of frankpledge and assize of bread and ale as liberties pertaining to the manor as part of the honour of Mandeville in 1278.[15] In 1311 Theobald de Merk, who in 1303 was assessed with Thomas Gerbergh and the Prior of Merton (for whom see below) of a third of a knight's fee in Thorley, conveyed his 'manor of Thorley' to John Gerbergh and his wife Alice.[16] John was succeeded by Thomas Gerbergh, who died before 1379, when his widow Alice was holding the manor.[17] She married secondly Stephen Wyvele,[18] and in 1389 released all right in the manor.[19] In Hilary term 1389–90 William son of Roger Gerbergh conveyed the manor to Thomas de Pinchbeck and others,[20] probably for a settlement. A later conveyance to the same in 1393[21] seems to have been in trust for John Corbet, who had a grant of free warren in the manor in 1395.[22] Thomas son of John Corbet granted it in 1414 to Richard Marshall,[23] evidently in trust for John Leventhorpe, to whom John son of Thomas Pinchbeck remitted his right in 1419.[24] John Leventhorpe obtained an inspeximus of the grant of free warren in 1438.[25]

From this date the manor descended in the Leventhorpe family with Shinglehall and Mathams in

---

[2] They were both held before the Conquest by Asgar the Staller, but Asgar had put a tenant into Thorley. The assessment of 1086 also shows that it was once part of a larger area (see account of hundred).
[3] Tithe commutation at Bd. of Agric. (Thorley).
[4] Ibid. (Sawbridgeworth).
[5] Ibid. (Thorley).
[6] *V.C.H. Herts.* i, 332.
[7] Ibid.
[8] *Rot. Cur. Reg.* (Rec. Com.), i, 171.
[9] *Cal. Close,* 1224–31, p. 575.
[10] *Abbrev. Plac.* (Rec. Com.), 188.
[11] So deposed before the justices itinerant in 1275 (*Hund. R.* [Rec. Com.], i, 188).
[12] Ibid.
[13] *Abbrev. Plac.* (Rec. Com.), 188. The result of the action is here given with the enrolment of the charter of conveyance.
[14] Ibid. 190.
[15] *Plac. de Quo Warr.* (Rec. Com.), 277, 288. A certain William de Thorley had half the manor at this date, possibly a life interest in it.
[16] *Feet of F. Herts.* 5 Edw. II, no. 106. Letitia widow of William le Madle was holding one-third in dower.
[17] Close, 3 Ric. II, m. 27 d.
[18] Ibid. 11 Ric. II, pt. i, m. 21 d.
[19] Ibid. 12 Ric. II, m. 8 d.
[20] *Feet of F. Herts.* 13 Ric. II, no. 110.
[21] Ibid. 17 Ric. II, no. 151.
[22] Chart. R. 18 & 19 Ric. II, m. 14, no. 9.
[23] Close, 2 Hen. V, m. 3.
[24] Ibid. 7 Hen. V, m. 15 d, 14 d.; see Chan. Misc. bdle. 62, no. 23.
[25] *Cal. Pat.* 1436–41, p. 235.

374

Sawbridgeworth (q.v.) until 1672, when Sir Thomas Leventhorpe, bart., conveyed it to William Kiffen.[26] In 1691 William Kiffen, Henry Kiffen, merchant, and Rachel his wife joined in a sale to John Billers,[27] a haberdasher of London, after whose death in 1712 his son William sold it in 1714 to Moses Raper of London.[28] Raper died in 1748,[29] and was succeeded by his brother Matthew, who married Elizabeth sister (or daughter) and heir of Sir William Billers. Matthew died the same year,[30] and the manor descended to his son Matthew Raper, F.R.S. Raper left no issue, and devised Thorley (by will of 1775) to his brother John, who had married Elizabeth daughter of William Hale of Twyford House in this parish, and who succeeded in 1778. Elizabeth daughter and heir of John Raper married William Grant, M.D., a Scotchman, but died in 1778 before her father, whose heir at his death in 1783 was his grandson John Peter Grant, then an infant.[31] The latter suffered a recovery in 1805.[32] His trustees sold the manor in 1810 to Edward Law, first Lord Ellenborough.[33] It descended to the fourth Lord Ellenborough, who in 1895 sold the manorial rights to Charles Gayton of Much Hadham. In 1906 they were bought by Mr. G. S. Streeter, the present lord of the manor.[34]

LAW, Lord Ellenborough. *Ermine a bend engrailed between two cocks gules with three pierced molets or on the bend.*

One half-hide in Thorley still remained to the Bishop of London in 1086 after his dispossession of the rest by Geoffrey de Mandeville, and was held of him by a tenant named Roderi.[34a] This is probably the 'manor of Thorley in Stortford ' which was held of the Bishop of London in 1294 by Hugh de Birne, who then died seised leaving a brother John.[34b] As there seems to be no further trace of this estate, it was probably afterwards attached to the Bishop of London's manor of Stortford.

MOORHALL was a small estate of the priory of Merton in Thorley. The grantor is unknown, but in 1291 the lands of the Prior of Merton were taxed at £4 7s. 2d.[35] The prior claimed view of frankpledge in 1278, but as he could only show the general charters to his house his claim was not allowed.[36] In 1535 the 'rent of assize with rents and farms in Morehall in Thorley' held by Merton was assessed at £5 6s. 8d.[37] The estate was granted as the manor of Morehall to Sir Henry Parker, Lord Morley, in 1544,[38] who in the same year alienated it to Clement Newce.[39] It descended with the Newces[40] (see Berwick in Standon) until as late as 1611, when William Newce died seised of it,[41] and it appears to be the Morehall held with Tedenhoebury in Sawbridgeworth by the Taylor family in 1779.[42] It now belongs to Mr. A. N. Gilbey of Swakeleys, Uxbridge.

In 1468 William Wetenhale died seised of a tenement called *MAUNDEVILE*, consisting of 20 acres of arable, 4 acres of meadow and 6 acres of pasture, held of John Leventhorpe by suit of court.[43] These from their name were apparently some lands which the Mandevilles had for a time kept in their own hands.

In 1555 the messuage called Maundevile with lands and rent in Thorley was conveyed by George Whetenhall to John Elliot, merchant of London.[43a]

CHURCH

The church of *ST. JAMES* consists of chancel 31 ft. by 20 ft. 6 in., small north vestry, nave 43 ft. by 23 ft. 6 in., south porch, and west tower 12 ft. 6 in. by 11 ft., all internal dimensions.

The walls are probably of flint rubble and are coated with cement, the dressings are of stone.

The nave and chancel were built in the early part of the 13th century, but the south doorway, of 12th-century work, remains. The chancel arch appears to have been rebuilt in the 14th century and the west tower added early in the following century. In the 19th century the church was repaired and the vestry and south porch were built and all the walls covered with cement.

The three-light east window in the chancel is modern. In the north wall are two 13th-century lancet windows, one of which has been restored, and a doorway of the same period. In the south wall is another 13th-century lancet. There are two other windows with modern tracery. In the same wall is a piscina with cinquefoiled head and moulded jambs, and adjoining it is a triple sedile with ogee-arched heads, moulded and cusped, all under a square moulded label with head stops, and with cusped spandrels; both sedilia and piscina belong to the late 14th century. The 14th-century chancel arch is of two chamfered orders with semi-octagonal responds and moulded capitals and bases.

At the east end of the north nave wall is the doorway to the rood stairs, and above is the doorway formerly giving access to the loft. Of the three windows on each side of the nave the central one is a 13th-century lancet, the others are probably of the 15th century with modern tracery. The south doorway is of 12th-century work and has been much restored; the arch is semicircular of two cheveron-moulded orders, the outer one having a double cheveron; the jambs have twisted shafts with scalloped capitals. In the south wall at the east end is a trefoiled recess, chiefly of cement, which was probably a piscina.

The west tower is of three stages, unbuttressed, and is finished with an embattled parapet and slender wood spire. At the south-east angle is a projecting stair turret which is carried up to the belfry level; the doorway to this stair, which is inside the tower, has a four-centred moulded arch. A filleted roll in the jamb mouldings has a foliated capital supporting an upper member which dies into the arch. The

---

[26] Feet of F. Herts. Mich. 24 Chas. II.
[27] Ibid. Mich. 3 Will. and Mary.
[28] Salmon, *Hist. of Herts.* 268.
[29] M. I. in church.
[30] Ibid.
[31] Cussans, *Hist. of Herts. Braughing Hund.* 100.
[32] Recov. R. Trin. 45 Geo. III, rot. 229.

[33] Feet of F. Herts. Mich. 51 Geo. III.
[34] Information from Rev. J. E. I. Procter. [34a] *V.C.H. Herts.* i, 308a.
[34b] Chan. Inq. p.m. 22 Edw. I, no. 14.
[35] *Pope Nich. Tax.* (Rec. Com.), 15.
[36] *Plac. de Quo Warr.* (Rec. Com.), 289.
[37] *Valor Eccl.* (Rec. Com.), ii, 49.
[38] *L. and P. Hen. VIII*, xix (1), 278 (57).

[39] Ibid. 610 (116), p. 385.
[40] Chan. Inq. p.m. (Ser. 2), clxxxix, 92.
[41] Ibid. dxxvii, 99.
[42] Feet of F. Div. Co. Hil. 19 Geo. III.
[43] Chan. Inq. p.m. 8 Edw. IV, no. 4. He left an infant son William.
[43a] Feet of F. Herts. East. 1 & 2 Phil. and Mary.

tower arch is of three moulded orders and moulded jambs, the inner members of which have moulded capitals and bases. The west doorway has a two-centred arch with continuous mouldings, under a square moulded label, with head stops. In each spandrel is a quatrefoiled circle containing a shield; the shield on the north is charged with a mitre, that on the south with three leopards. To the south of the doorway is a small plain recessed stoup. The tracery of the three-light west window is modern. On each face of the belfry stage is a two-light window with quatrefoil in the head, nearly all in cement.

The basin of the font is square, and on each side are five shallow round-headed panels; it belongs to the 12th century and stands on a modern base.

Under a window-sill on the south wall of the nave is a brass inscription to John Duke, farmer at Thorley Hall, who died in 1606.

There are three bells: the first inscribed 'John White, James Cramphorn, Churchwardens, 1682'; the second, 'God save the King, 1628' by Robert Oldfeild; the third, by William Wightman, 1682.

The communion plate consists of cup and cover paten, 1562, one paten, 1809, another, 1818, a flagon, 1839, and a pewter flagon.

The registers are in three books, as follows: (i) baptisms, burials and marriages 1539 to 1750; (ii) baptisms and burials 1750 to 1812, marriages 1750 to 1754; (iii) marriages 1754 to 1812.

ADVOWSON The church of Thorley was part of the endowment of Walden Abbey, founded by Geoffrey de Mandeville (ob. 1144).[44] It was appropriated to the office of pittancer for the garments of the monks in 1336.[45] Apparently before this date the advowson had been acquired by the Bishop of London,[46] probably in the same way as Sawbridgeworth[47] (q.v.). If the appropriation ever took place, the living was a rectory in 1535,[48] from which the Abbot of Walden received a pension of 53s. 4d. This was surrendered to the Crown in 1538[49] and granted in the same year to Sir Thomas Audley.[50] The advowson remained with the see of London until the latter part of the 19th century. The patronage is now vested in the see of St. Albans.[51]

Francis Burleigh, presented by Queen Elizabeth during a vacancy of the see of London in 1594, was one of the translators of the Authorized Version of the Bible.[52]

Thomas Turner, who was rector from 1680 to 1689, was in 1688 elected president of Corpus Christi College, Oxford, where his tenure of office was marked by the erection of Turner's, now called Fellows' Buildings.[53]

CHARITIES In 1686 Thomas Hoy by his will gave a rent-charge of 6s. per annum to the poor. This sum is received out of a farm called Rumbold's and is applied in bread given to a poor widow.

In 1706 the Rev. Thomas Turner, S.T.P., a former rector, by his will gave a sum of £50 to be laid out in land, the rents and profits to be applied in binding a poor child apprentice to some honest trade. A piece of copyhold land containing about 3 acres situate in the common field called North Field was purchased, which produces £4 yearly, and a child is

THORLEY CHURCH FROM THE SOUTH-EAST

[44] Harl. MS. 3697, fol. 18.
[45] Ibid. fol. 244.
[46] The Bishop of London presented in 1327 (see Cussans, *Hist. of Herts. Braughing Hund.* 104).
[47] Hurley, the cell to Westminster, had part of the tithes of Thorley (*Pope Nich. Tax.* [Rec. Com.], 18; see Sawbridgeworth).
[48] *Valor Eccl.* (Rec. Com.), i, 452.
[49] Feet of F. Herts. East. 30 Hen. VIII.
[50] *L. and P. Hen. VIII*, xiii (1), 575.
[51] It came subsequently to Henry Higham (see Chan. Inq. p.m. [Ser. 2], ccxvii, 105).
[51] Information from Rev. J. E. I. Procter, rector; see Sawbridgeworth.
[52] Ibid.
[53] *Dict. Nat. Biog.*

THORLEY CHURCH: THE SOUTH DOORWAY

apprenticed from time to time, a premium of £10 being paid in 1907.

In 1884 Mrs. Georgiana Martha Vander Meulen by declaration of trust gave a sum of £115, the interest to be paid to the rector for the time being for the upkeep of the churchyard. This charity was augmented in 1909 by Admiral F. Vander Meulen by a sum of £100, the two gifts being represented by £244 17*s*. 11*d*. 2½ per cent. annuities with the official trustees. The annual dividends, amounting to £6 2*s*. 8*d*., are applied in the upkeep of the churchyard.

THUNDRIDGE

Tonrich (1086); Tunrigge, Thanrugge, Thornrugge (xiii cent.); Thunrigge, Thunrych, Thurrich (xiv and xv cent.); Thundriche (xvi cent.).

Thundridge is a small parish of 2,206 acres bounded on the north-west by the River Rib, which divides it from the parish of Standon, and on the north-east by the Nimney Bourne. The main road to Buntingford intersects the parish on the west. Of the total area rather more than half is arable land, but there is a considerable amount of pasture in the valley of the Rib. The chief woods are Sawtres Wood on the north in the bend of the river, Steere Wood further south, and Buckney Wood to the south of this. Gardiner's Spring, a small wood to the west of Buckney Wood, preserves the name of the 17th-century owners of the manor. The land rises from the valley of the Rib on the north and is for the most part between 200 and 300 ft. above the ordnance datum. The soil varies, the subsoil being gravel and clay. No inclosure award has been made for the parish. Burleigh Common and Halfyard Common are still in several ownership, but Ashridge Common, which from its name must have been an open field, is now owned by one person only. All three are arable.[1]

There is no village of Thundridge properly speaking ; all that remains of the original settlement are a 17th-century chimney stack of brick which belonged to the manor-house called the Bury (pulled down in 1812),[2] the ruins of a cottage which once formed part of the stables of the Bury, and the tower of the old church, all situated close together in a bend of the river about half a mile east of the Buntingford road. The church is surrounded by fine chestnut trees, pines and yews, and in summer the spot is beautiful in spite of its deserted appearance. To the south of the church is Thundridge Hill, the slope of which is occupied by a long field planted with lines of elm trees. Leading to the church from the west is an avenue of elms known as the Causeway. This at the further end is continued to Wadesmill by a picturesque path along the side of the river.

The hamlet of Wadesmill is built along the road to Buntingford and lies partly in the parish of Thundridge and partly in High Cross (formed from the ancient parish of Standon), the bridge over the Rib forming the boundary. The part of the village on the eastern bank of the river is known locally as Thundridge. The church of St. Mary occupies a good position on high ground further along the road to the south. The vicarage stands some little distance from it in Poles Lane. The main street of the village was the street parallel with the main road, now known as Back Street. The main road is said to have run along here before it was diverted to its present route, this new part of it being still known as New Road.[3] In Back Street is the old White Hind Inn and next to it stood the smithy, now pulled down. A row of cottages on the same side as the 'White Hind' was built by Mr. Hanbury in 1888. The mixed elementary school on the other side of the road was built in 1900, superseding one opposite the church which is now used as a reading-room. The infants' school near the church was opened in 1894, taking the place of one which stood in front of the present house. The situation of the hamlet on the main road to Cambridge brought much traffic through it when travelling was by coach. At the beginning of the 19th century more than 100 horses were often stabled at the Feathers Inn on the other side of the bridge. The turnpike at Wadesmill was one of the first three put up in the county.[4]

Poles, on the north-west of the parish, is the seat of Mr. E. S. Hanbury ; the house, which is modern, stands in a park of about 100 acres. Swangle's Farm, to the south-east of the old church, preserves the name of a family of Swangle who appear in the neighbourhood in the 14th century.[5] On the south-east of the parish is a farm called Castlebury. The original form of this name is Casewellbury. At the end of the 15th century there is record of a mill called Casewell Mill,[6] and in 1694 half a messuage or farm called Casewelbury, or Carswelbury, was sold by Humphrey Taylor, citizen and mercer of London, to Sir Henry Wincombe of Bucklebury, co. Berks., bart.[7] From Castlebury a by-road runs south-west to Newhall Green in Ware parish and east to Baker's End in Thundridge. Baker's End[8] communicates by road with Nobland Green on the north-east and with Rush Green on the north by a road which passes through Halfyard Common. The number of these small greens in the neighbourhood is noticeable.

Anastasius Cottonus Jacksonus Lightfoot, son of John Lightfoot, rector of Great Munden, the Hebrew scholar and Biblical critic (and named after his father's friends Sir Rowland Cotton and Sir John Jackson), became vicar of Thundridge in 1661. Another divine of some note, William Webster, was instituted in 1740. He was a voluminous writer, chiefly of theological works, but in 1740 he published a pamphlet on the woollen manufactory from materials furnished by a merchant in the trade called *The Consequences of Trade to the Wealth and Strength of any Nation, by a Draper of London*, which had a large sale ; this he followed next year by a refutation of his own arguments called *The Draper's Reply*.

---

[1] Information from Mr. F. C. Puller.
[2] *Midd. and Herts. N. and Q.* ii, 151; view in *Gent. Mag.* lxxxi, 609.
[3] If this is so the present road must be a return to the original course of Ermine Street.
[4] J. H. Hinde, 'The Old North Road,' *Arch. Aeliana*, iii, 237.
[5] Cott. MS. Nero E vi, fol. 122*b*.
[6] Early Chan. Proc. bdle. 159, no. 22.
[7] Close, 7 Will. III, pt. v, no. 37.
[8] Other spellings are Cassullbery on a map of 1648 and Cassalbery on Norden's map.
Bequest to Christopher Bedle of Baker's End, 1572 (Herts. Gen. i, 370); house and land called Gymmes at Baker's End (ibid. ii, 85).

A HISTORY OF HERTFORDSHIRE

MANORS Before the Conquest the manor of THUNDRIDGE, sometimes called WADESMILL, was held by Alnod under Stigand, Archbishop of Canterbury. In 1086 it formed part of the possessions of Odo Bishop of Bayeux, of whom it was held by Hugh de Grentmesnil. It was assessed at 1 hide only. There was land for four ploughs, but there were only three on the manor, one of which was on the demesne; there was meadow for four plough-teams, woodland for sixteen swine, and a mill [9] (possibly on the site of Wadesmill). After the forfeiture of the Bishop of Bayeux the manor was held of the king in chief by the successors of Grentmesnil, and this tenancy follows the descent of the manor of Ware (q.v.).

In the 13th century the immediate tenants of the manor were the family of Dive of Balderton, co. Nottingham, and Kingerby, co. Lincoln. It was held by William de Dive, who died before 1251, when his heir John was under age and a third of the manor was held in dower by his widow Ermentrude.[10] In 1277 John Dive obtained a grant of free warren in his demesne lands of Thundridge.[11] John died seised in 1292–3, leaving two sisters, Joan then the wife of Ralph de Trehamtone and apparently widow of Sir William Disney,[12] and Elizabeth, then wife of John D'Aubyn.[13] The extent of the manor is given as a messuage and dovecote, 1 carucate of land, 10 acres of meadow, 30 acres of wood, 40 acres of pasture, with rents of assize and rents from customary tenants.[14] In the following year Elizabeth died holding half the manor,[15] leaving a son Sir Hugh de Bussy, kt., by a former marriage. Apparently this half was acquired by the other heirs, for there seems to be no further trace of it. In 1303 Joan the second heir, then a widow, conveyed her part of the manor to Adam de Swillington for life.[16] Afterwards, before 1312, she married Adam de Swillington [17] (of Swillington, near Leeds), with whom she was jointly seised. He obtained a grant of free warren in February 1327–8 [18] and died in or before 1330.[19] The manor then passed to Sir William Disney, apparently the son of Joan by her first marriage. He in 1347 settled it on

WADES MILL, THUNDRIDGE

his son and daughter-in-law William and Joan Disney.[20] From William the younger it passed to Sir William Disney, his son,[21] to John of Norton Disney, co. Lincoln, son of William, who was killed at Towton in 1461,[22] and to his grandson and heir William, who died seised of it in 1540.[23] Richard, his son and heir, conveyed it in 1543 to John Gardiner of London and his wife Joan.[24] John Gardiner died in 1555. His son Thomas died without issue and the manor passed to his brother Henry, who had two sons Henry and James. After the death of Henry, James conveyed it to his

---

[9] *V.C.H. Herts.* i, 311a.
[10] Cur. Reg. R. 145, m. 17 d.
[11] *Cal. Chart. R.* 1257–1300, p. 204.
[12] *Gen.* iii, 375; Thoroton, *Nottinghamshire*, i, 359.
[13] Chan. Inq. p.m. 21 Edw. I, no. 42.
[14] Ibid.
[15] Ibid. 22 Edw. I, no. 44.
[16] Feet of F. Herts. 31 Edw. I, no. 374.
[17] See ibid. 5 Edw. II, no. 84.
[18] Chart. R. 2 Edw. III, m. 28, no. 29.
[19] *Cal. Pat.* 1330–4, p. 29.
[20] De Banco R. 352, m. 311; Feet of F. Div. Co. 21 Edw. III, no. 12.
[21] For fine levied by him in 1411 see Feet of F. Div. Co. 12 Hen. IV, no. 71.
[22] Chan. Inq. p.m. (Ser. 2), xxiii, 105; *Gen.* loc. cit.
[23] Ibid. xliv, 120; *Gen.* loc. cit.
[24] Feet of F. Herts. Mich. 35 Hen. VIII; Recov. R. Hil. 35 Hen. VIII, rot. 126.

378

nephew Edward Gardiner, son of his sister Elizabeth by Simon Gardiner her first cousin.[25] Edward was sheriff of the county in 1628[26]; he died in 1650, leaving a son Edward, who also served as sheriff in 1657.[27] On his death in 1664 Thundridge descended to a younger son John, and then, according to Chauncy, to his son Henry, who died in 1693, and to Henry son of Henry, the owner in 1700.[28] Clutterbuck, however, gives a rather different account, making the manor descend to John, the fourth son of the abovementioned John, to John his son, who died in 1760, to another John his son, and then to Gilbert son and heir of John. Gilbert Gardiner sold part of the estate called Poles, and later another part called Downfield[29], and in 1811 he with Dorothy Gardiner, widow of John, sold the manor with the mill at Wadesmill to Daniel Giles of Youngsbury.[30] It then descended with Youngsbury in Standon (q.v.), and Mr. C. B. Giles-Puller of Youngsbury is the present lord of the manor.

GARDINER. *Party or and gules a fesse between three hinds tripping all counterchanged.*

The manor of *SAWTRES* (Sawtrey, Sawtrees), an estate on the north of the parish, situated in the bend of the River Rib, was held of the manor of Ware. At the beginning of the 15th century it seems to have belonged to Sir Nicholas Thorley, kt., and to have passed from him to his kinsman and heir Walter Estoft, who conveyed it in 1451 to John Viscount Beaumont and others.[31] In 1533 Walter Wadeland and Thomas Montgomery conveyed it to Richard Welles and others.[32] Francis Roberts died seised of it in 1632, his grandson Sir William Roberts, son of his son Barn, being his heir.[33] Sir William Roberts, called of Willesden, co. Middlesex, sold the manor and capital messuage in 1638 to Robert Turner, D.D., canon residentiary of St. Paul's Cathedral,[34] excepting three copyholds in Ware and an acre of land in Ware Park. It descended to Thomas Turner, Dean of Canterbury, and to his son Francis Turner, Bishop of Rochester 1683–4, Bishop of Ely in 1684 (afterwards suspended from the latter bishopric for refusing to take the oath of allegiance to William and Mary), who in 1695 sold the manor to Richard Crawley of London.[36] After this the descent of the manor is fragmentary. Jane Smith suffered a recovery of it in 1732,[36] Edmund Pepys and his wife Sarah did the same in 1765,[37] and Lee Steere Steere in 1824.[38] It was acquired from the Steere family

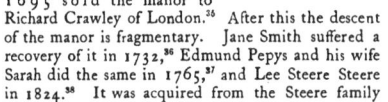

TURNER. *Or a lion between three crosses paty gules.*

about forty years ago by Mr. Arthur Giles-Puller, and has since descended with the Youngsbury estate (Standon, q.v.).

CHURCH

The church of *ST. MARY* at Wadesmill consists of chancel 26 ft. 9 in. by 20 ft. 9 in., north vestry, nave 56 ft. 9 in. by 25 ft., and west tower; all internal dimensions. The church was built in 1853 of squared rubble with stone dressings, to take the place of the old church, of which only the tower remains.

The old church was pulled down in 1853 on the erection of the church at Wadesmill. There was a chapel here in the time of Hugh de Grentmesnil, who was tenant in 1086.[39] The dedication is given variously as *ALL SAINTS*[40] and *ST. MARY*. Chauncy says it was called Little St. Mary's.[41] The tower is built of flint rubble with stone dressings, and is of three stages, with angle buttresses on the west; it was erected in the 15th century. The tower arch is blocked and the stonework much defaced. Under the arch has been inserted a 12th-century doorway with semicircular arch, with cheveron and billet mouldings, all much decayed; above the doorway a 14th-century window has been inserted. It has two trefoiled lights with tracery under a square head; it is in good condition. Both doorway and window appear to have come from the old church. On the south wall, in the first stage, is a square panel inclosing a quatrefoil piercing with a rose in the centre; in the west wall is a doorway with a four-centred arch under a square head, with tracery in the spandrels, and above it is a window of three cinquefoiled lights under a four-centred arch. The second stage has narrow single lights on the north, south and west faces and a sundial on the south. Each face of the belfry stage has a window of two trefoiled lights with a quatrefoiled opening in the head, under a four-centred arch. The tower has been buttressed on the east, and the upper stages are secured with iron bolts.

The bells, of which there are four, are now in the modern church. The treble is inscribed 'Johannes est nomen ejus' by an unknown founder; the second is dated 1623; the third 1631, both by Robert Oldfeild; the fourth by John Dier, 1580.

The communion plate consists of flagon, 1775, cup, 1837, and paten, 1837.

The registers are in five books as follows: (i) baptisms, burials and marriages 1556 to 1670; (ii) baptisms, burials and marriages 1682 to 1738; (iii) baptisms and burials 1738 to 1812, marriages 1738 to 1751; (iv) marriages 1754 to 1806; (v) marriages 1806 to 1812.

ADVOWSON

The advowson of the old church of *ST. MARY* follows the descent of the advowson of Ware (q.v.), to which church it was a chapel. Hugh de Grentmesnil gave both church and chapel to the Priory of Ware. In the composition made between the parishioners of Ware and Thundridge and the Prior of Ware in 1231 (see advowson of Ware) it was agreed that the Prior and vicar of Ware should serve the church daily by

---

[25] Clutterbuck, *Hist. and Antiq. of Herts.* iii, 278; Feet of F. Herts. Mich. 11 Jas. I.
[26] List of *Sheriffs* (P.R.O.), 64.
[27] Ibid.
[28] Chauncy, *Hist. Antiq. of Herts.* 213.
[29] Clutterbuck, loc. cit.
[30] Deed in possession of Mr. C. B. Giles-Puller of Youngsbury.
[31] Close, 32 Hen. VI, m. 15.
[32] Feet of F. Herts. Trin. 25 Hen. VIII.
[33] Chan. Inq. p.m. (Ser. 2), ccclxv, 65.
[34] Com. Pleas D. Enr. East. 14 Chas. I, m. 10.
[35] Close, 7 Will. III, pt. vii, no. 17.
[36] Recov. R. Mich. 6 Geo. II, rot. 184.
[37] Ibid. East. 5 Geo. III, rot. 203.
[38] Ibid. Trin. 5 Geo. IV, rot. 197.
[39] See advowson.
[40] Lond. Epis. Reg. Gilbert, fol. 170.
[41] *Hist. and Antiq. of Herts.* 214.

A HISTORY OF HERTFORDSHIRE

a chaplain, who should reside there and who should be provided by the parishioners with a house, 4 acres of arable land, 1 d. every Sunday with blessed bread, 2 s. in Christmas week or bread to that value, and 3 s. 2 d. per annum.[42] After the Dissolution the advowson came with that of Ware to Trinity College, Cambridge. The church was served by a vicar of its own until 1781, when the vicarage was consolidated with that of Ware.[43]

In 1810 the parsonage and glebe land were sold for the redemption of the land tax with which the vicarage was charged, and the house was then pulled down.[44] When the church of St. Mary was built by Mr. Hanbury in 1853 the Master and Fellows of Trinity College gave him the advowson, reserving the great tithes. The vicarage was then again separated from Ware and a residence built for the vicar.[45] Mr. E. S. Hanbury is the present patron.

CHARITIES The charity of Jane Wall, founded by will dated in 1573, is regulated by schemes of the Charity Commissioners 1862 and 1875. The property originally consisted of about 19 a. of land in Thundridge and 4 a. 2 r. of land in Much Munden. The land at Thundridge was exchanged under the Act of 1 & 2 George IV for 25 a. 1 r. 37 p. of land situate near Nobland Green. The real estate has been sold from time to time, and the trust fund now consists of £2,126 9s. 9d. consols with the official trustees, producing £53 3s. yearly.

The charity of an unknown donor, which is regulated by a scheme of the Charity Commissioners 14 December 1909, consists of an annual rent-charge of 40s. issuing out of the Youngsbury estate.

The income of these two charities was applied in 1909 as to £22 10s. in clothing tickets to about forty-eight families, £18 in bread tickets to fifty families, £5 to parish nurse, and £9 10s. in scholarships and assistance to children leaving school.

In 1908 Miss Katharine Jane Green, by her will proved at London 24 November, gave £40 consols, the interest to be applied in coals to be given at Christmas, and equally divided between the six oldest poor women, either widows or spinsters. The stock is held by the official trustees.

WARE[1]

Waras (xi cent.); Wares (xii cent.); Warre (xiii cent.).

Ware is a large parish now divided into the civil parishes of Ware Urban and Ware Rural, the latter including an area of about 4,208 acres, of which 31 acres are water, whilst Ware Urban comprises the town of Ware and has an area of 628 acres, of which 16 are water. Thus the town occupies but a small part of the ancient parish, being surrounded by open country, but the population is almost entirely massed in the town, except for that part of it scattered in the hamlets of Widbury, a mile to the east, Fanhams Hall, a mile north-east, and Wareside, 2 miles north-east. An inclosure award for Ware Marsh was made in 1861 and one for Ware Wengeo Common in 1854.[2]

The parish is intersected by the main road from London to Cambridge through Buntingford and Royston, from which the Watton Road branches off immediately to the west of the town, whilst the road to Hertford forms the boundary for a little way on the south. The Broxbourne and Hertford branch of the Great Eastern railway has a station in the town, and at Mardocks is a station on the Buntingford branch of the same line. On the west the parish is bounded by the River Rib, which joins the Lea at a point on the south-west of the parish near Ware Park Mill.

The River Lea, which joins the Thames at Blackwall about 20 miles distant, has always played an important part in the history of Ware. It has long formed the principal means of communication between the eastern side of Hertfordshire and London, and it was therefore of great importance for the carriage of corn and other commodities to the capital. The efforts of Hertford to preserve the monopoly of this trade and of Ware to secure it caused an acute rivalry between the two towns. Disputes constantly arose with regard to obstructions in the river at Ware, made in order to block the passage of the Hertford ships. In 1275 the lord of the manor prevented ships from passing up and down by the erection of a weir between Ware and Hertford,[3] and in 1300 a commission was appointed for removing obstructions caused by mariners and boatmen placing their vessels across it.[4] Obstruction to navigation was frequently caused by the weirs, mills, pools, stakes and kiddles erected in the river, and after the statute of 25 Edward III commissions were periodically issued for the removal of all those erected later than the reign of Edward I and for preventing tolls being taken from the boats at these weirs, &c.[5] In 1439 the river seems to have been completely stopped up by these impediments.[6]

Efforts to improve the navigation of the river were made in the 16th century and later. An Act of Parliament was passed in 1571 for bringing the Lea (or Ware) River to the north of London by means of a new cut to be made by the City. This was to serve for barges and other boats carrying corn, victuals and articles of merchandise between Ware and London and also for 'tytlebotes' and wherries carrying passengers. The part of the river between Ware and this new cut was to be cleansed and made deep enough for the passage of barges.[7] In 1739 an Act was passed for improving the navigation from Hertford to Ware and from Ware to the new cut,[8] and a further Act, passed in 1767, for improving the navigation from Hertford to the Thames empowered the trustees to make new cuts between Hertford and Ware at

---

[42] Lond. Epis. Reg. Gilbert, fol. 170.
[43] Clutterbuck, *Hist. and Antiq. of Herts.* iii, 280.
[44] Clutterbuck, loc. cit.
[45] Cussans, *Hist. of Herts. Braughing Hund.* 163.
[1] The writer is indebted in this history of Ware to Mr. R. T. Andrews of Hertford, who kindly lent his bibliography of Ware.
[2] *Blue Bk. Incl. Awards.*
[3] *Hund. R.* (Rec. Com.), i, 188, 190.
[4] *Cal. Pat.* 1292–1301, p. 547.
[5] Ibid. 1377–81, p. 474; 1381–5, pp. 144, 472; 1422–9, pp. 402, 551; 1429–36, pp. 350, 356; 1436–41, pp. 83, 371, 453; 1476–85, pp. 22, 344; *Parl. R.* iv, 292, 332, 381; L. *and P. Hen. VIII,* ii, 2138.
[6] *Cal. Pat.* 1436–41, p. 371.
[7] *Stat. of Realm* (Rec. Com.), iv (1), 553.
[8] Local and Personal Act, 12 Geo. II, cap. 32.

380

THUNDRIDGE OLD CHURCH: THE TOWER

WARE CHURCH FROM THE NORTH-EAST

the places where the old channel was stopped up.[9] Manifold Ditch and Black Ditch, now filled with stagnant water, formed the original channel of the Lea.[10] The management of the river is vested in thirteen conservators chosen by different representative bodies, including the Corporation of London and the Metropolitan Water Board. The fishing rights are held by the conservators.

Half a mile distant from the town is the head of the New River, which is fed by a spring in the meadow called Chadwell[10a] in this parish and by some deep wells in the parish of Great Amwell, as well as by a cut from the Lea using part of the old Manifold Ditch. The scheme for making this river was proposed by Hugh Middleton, commissioner for the water supply of London in the reign of James I, with the object of supplying fresh water to the north of London. An Act of Parliament empowering the corporation of the city of London to make the trench was passed in 1605.[11] Middleton had offered to bear all the expense, but long before it was finished he had to petition for a royal grant, and the king in 1612 promised to pay half the expenses. The river was finished in 1613, and in 1619 the shareholders were incorporated.[12]

Palaeolithic implements and a neolithic celt have been found in Ware.[13] Ermine Street ran through the parish on the west, and many Roman coins and antiquities have been found in Bury Field, close by Ware lock, whilst excavating for Messrs. Allen & Hanbury's factory in 1899.[14]

The town is situated on the west side of the parish on the River Lea, a little to the east of the line of Ermine Street. The main road to Buntingford and Royston runs through it, forming the High Street and the continuation of it called Baldock Street (Baldokstrete 1512).[15] High Street is the chief street of the town, and contains many 17th and 18th-century houses. The detached groups of houses on the north side seem to be encroachments on the market-place, which, now a square space in front of the town hall, may have been originally a rough triangle in shape with the base at the church.[16] The market dates back to 1199, and must have been of considerable importance in the development of the town. The oldest houses are probably those on the south of the market-place which have back premises extending down to the river. Later extension of the town has been almost entirely on the north, first between High Street and Musley Lane and then north of Musley Lane.

In the High Street probably the oldest house is no. 65, formerly the Christopher Inn,[17] but now a house and shop occupied by Mr. Harradence. The main building facing on the road has been much altered in the 18th and 19th centuries. It has a large archway with late 15th-century details opening into a courtyard. The wing running south in the east side of the courtyard seems to have formed part of two 15th-century timber and plaster houses, which had a narrow alley between them running through what is now a coal cellar in the middle of the wing. The upper stories of these houses project and were apparently connected by a bridge from which a gallery ran on the west side of the south house. There are many 15th-century details still remaining in the building. Near this house is a plastered timber and brick house with the date 1624, but altered in the 18th and 19th centuries. It contains some good panelling and two fine overmantels. In an upper room are the initials $_{I}{}^{H}{}_{S}$ and the date 1624. On the north side of the High Street is a 17th-century house of timber and brick with a tiled roof known as the Blue Boot Store. It has been considerably altered to adapt it for a shop, but two interesting plaster ceilings remain, bearing shields of arms (two lions passant between three crosslets). Another 17th-century house on the north side is Gilpin House, called in memory of the famous ride. At Blue Coat Yard, formerly Place House, a little off the High Street, is an 18th-century house which was till 1760 a branch house of the Blue Coat School or Christ's Hospital, London. This house stands in a courtyard which is entered by a brick gateway of the 18th century. Over the gateway is a niche which formerly contained a figure of a blue coat boy now moved to the Blue Coat School at Hertford. On the west side of the courtyard are twelve picturesque cottages of about the middle of the 17th century and on the east some 18th-century buildings formerly belonging to the school. There is a group of 17th-century houses with overhanging stories on the north side of Ware Bridge.

In Baldock Street is a 16th-century house (no. 23), which has been much altered in the 18th and 19th centuries. It has an archway leading to the yard behind the house. On the east side of Wadesmill Road is a 17th-century house now covered with plaster and on the west side a group of red brick maltings of the 17th century, one with a brick mullioned window. In Crib Street are several 17th-century houses including the Green Dragon, the Albion and Red Cow Inns. They are all of timber and plaster with tiled roofs and mostly with overhanging upper stories.

The present iron bridge over the Lea was built in 1845 by G. Stephenson. There was a bridge over the river, probably on the site of the existing bridge, as early as 1191. It is mentioned then as having been broken down by the men of Hertford[18] who were trying to force all traffic to make the passage of the Lea at Hertford instead of taking the more direct route through Ware. The bailiff of Hertford claimed rights over the bridge as appurtenant to the borough of Hertford, and the early bridge was kept closed to carts by a bar, the keys of this and also of a chain across the adjoining ford being held by the king's bailiff of Hertford. It was not until the Barons' War in the reign of John that the bridge was opened to traffic.[19] The tolls were then constantly disputed

---

[9] Local and Personal Act, 7 Geo. III, cap. 51.
[10] R. T. Andrews, ' Navigation of River Lea,' *St. Albans and Herts. Archit. and Arch. Soc. Trans.* 1888, p. 51.
[10a] One of the wells called after St. Chad.
[11] At first the water was conveyed through wooden pipes. Some of these could recently be seen in Oxford Street. Andrews, 'Chadwell Spring, *East Herts. Arch. Soc. Trans.* i, 7.
[12] Local and Personal Act, 3 Jas. I, cap. 18 ; 4 Jas. I, cap. 12 ; Cussans, *Hist. of Herts. Braughing Hund.* 131 ; *Cal. S. P. Dom.* 1611–18, p. 517.
[13] *V.C.H. Herts.* i, 227.
[14] *East Herts. Arch. Soc. Trans.* i, 187.

[15] Ct. R. (Gen. Ser.), portf. 178, no. 71.
[16] A 'house in the old market place,' bequeathed in 1572, points to encroachments before this date (*Herts. Gen.* i, 334).
[17] Information from Mr. Harradence ; see Exch. Dep. East. 14 Chas. II, no. 30.
[18] Pipe R. 3 Ric. I, m. 12 d.
[19] Assize R. 313 (32 Hen. III), m. 6 d.

between the bailiff of Hertford and the lord of the manor of Ware.[19a] Finally the borough asserted its right and the tolls were afterwards farmed with the borough, or occasionally leased apart by the king.[20] In 1258 the townsmen of Hertford again broke down the bridge, dug a channel in the ford and blocked up the London road with a ditch.[21] But in spite of all their efforts it was impossible permanently to prevent the traffic from taking the more direct route.[21a]

There are still a great number of inns in Ware surviving from the time when the main road brought many travellers through the town. The 'White Hart,' mentioned in 1511,[22] the 'Saracen's Head' about the same time, the 'Bull' referred to in 1547[23] are all in the High Street; the 'George' in Amwell End is mentioned in 1622.[24] The great bed of Ware was kept at the 'Saracen's Head' before its removal to Rye House (see under Rye House). Other early inns are the 'White Horse,' mentioned in 1626,[25] the 'Bell' in 1616,[26] the 'Bear' in 1494,[27] the 'Crown' in 1603[28] and 1725.[29] In 1681 a certain Thomas Collup was presented before the justices of the peace as owning an inn called the 'King's Head,' worth £100, which he would not sell, or let, or live in, and allowing the house to drop down for want of repair and the timber to be stolen, whilst he begged his bread from door to door and his wife and daughter were chargeable to the parish.[30] A hostel or inn called the 'Katherine Wheel,' whose site is unknown, belonged in the middle of the 15th century to William Pery,[31] a maltman of Ware,[32] and remained in his family for some generations.[33]

The parish church of St. Mary is at the west end of High Street, on which the churchyard abuts. At the corner close by the church is a smithy. The Priory estate lies between the High Street and the River Lea. The priory was founded as a house of Grey Friars in 1338 by Thomas Lord Wake of Liddell, who granted the friars a messuage and 7 acres of land on which to build an oratory, houses, and other buildings.[34] After the Dissolution the site was granted to Thomas Birch (see manorial descents). Besides the friary there was an alien house at Ware, founded as a cell to St. Evroul when that monastery was endowed with the church of Ware and land in the parish by Hugh de Grentmesnil. He or one of his successors also gave certain lands for the board of himself and his heirs whenever they stayed at the monastery, and Joan de Bohun, lady of the manor (q.v.), ensured accommodation by building a house for herself in the close of the priory.[35] On the suppression of alien houses it was granted by Henry V to his new foundation at Sheen.[36] There are no remains of the priory, but the old rectory (now called the manor-house) may possibly mark the site of the monastic buildings.

The girls' school at the School House, Amwell End (which used to be known as Amwell House, and was the residence of the Quaker poet John Scott), represents the old Ware Side School. This was founded before 1633, when Humphrey Spencer left £100 to the feoffees for teaching four of the poorest children of Ware Upland to read and write. It was built on part of the site of Corpus Christi Barn[37] in Dead Lane, which by some unknown donor had been devised to the poor of Ware. The school was rebuilt in 1747. It was an elementary school in 1834, but had become by usage a grammar school before 1866. In 1889 it was amalgamated with the Chuck Memorial School, founded by Mrs. Elizabeth Moore Chuck in memory of her husband in 1857. A grammar school was then established under thirteen governors appointed by the Hertford County Council. This was converted into a girls' school in 1906, and Amwell House was bought for its accommodation.

Another early school was Ware Free School, which in 1612 is described as carried on in the Town House. In the 17th century it was called a grammar school. The schoolhouse was a wooden building, and stood in a corner of the churchyard by the old brewery; the lower room was let as a beer cellar. The noise and fumes which reached the school caused its removal before 1872.[38] In 1889 it was amalgamated with the Wareside and Chuck Memorial School.

The elementary school near the church was built in 1844[39] and the one in New Road about 1860.[40] In the New Road is Christ Church, built and endowed by Robert Hanbury of Poles,[41] to which an ecclesiastical district, formed from Ware and Great Amwell, was assigned in 1858.[42]

Malt-houses occupy the greater part of the town to the north of High Street as far as Musley Lane.

[19a] Duchy of Lanc. Misc. Bks. xii, fol. 56; Hund. R. (Rec. Com.), i, 190.
[20] See Hertford; Abbrev. Rot. Orig. (Rec. Com.), ii, 256; Duchy of Lanc. Misc. Bks. xiii, fol. 9; Mins. Accts. bdle. 1094, no. 10. Within recent years the tolls have been acquired by the urban district council (Dawes, Rec. of Ware).
[21] Abbrev. Plac. (Rec. Com.), 148.
[21a] There were other bridges also in Ware. The Abbot of Waltham was responsible for the upkeep of two bridges between Ware and Hertford in Lokmead. The king, whenever he proposed to hawk in the neighbourhood, would issue injunctions to the repair of the bridges round Hertford and Ware on those chargeable for it (Cal. Close, 1307–13, p. 557; 1346–9, p. 397). Later, in the 17th century, many indictments were made in the court of quarter sessions against the persons responsible for the repair of the numerous bridges in Ware which were constantly allowed to fall into decay (Sess. R. [Herts. Co. Rec.], i, 105, 107, 108, 124, 134, 196, 368; ii, 23, 27).
[22] P.C.C. Will, Fetiplace 5; Ct. of Req. bdle. 103, no. 53; Aug. Off. Proc. bdle. 31, no. 29; bdle. 94, no. 41.
[23] Feet of F. Herts. Trin. 1 Edw. VI.
[24] MSS. of Gaweley Family (Hist. MSS. Com.), 114.
[25] Recov. R. Trin. 2 Chas. I.
[26] Pat. 3 Jas. I, pt. vii.
[27] P.C.C. Will, Vox 11.
[28] Hist. MSS. Com. Rep. xi, App. iv, 450. See p. 290 of this volume for the accounts of Lady Rutland for a supper at Ware.
[29] Ibid. xv, App. iv, 81.
[30] Sess. R. (Herts. Co. Rec.), i, 313, 337.
[31] Early Chan. Proc. bdle. 153, no. 6.
[32] Son of John Pery (see Anct. D. [P.R.O.], A 5218).
[33] Anct. D. (P.R.O.), A 5193, 1134, 5203, 5202, 1133, 978, 1088; Feet of F. Herts. East. 6 Edw. VI.
[34] Cal. Pat. 1338-40, p. 14. 'Le Freire Crosse' is mentioned in the court rolls of the manor (see Ct. R. portf. 178, no. 71). The tenants within the town were bound to make a bridge there. The site of this cross is not known.
[35] De Banco R. no. 44 (12 Edw. I), m. 97. It is this house (not the friary) which in early records is known as Ware Priory.
[36] Pat. 3 Hen. V, pt. ii, m. 30.
[37] This probably had some connexion with the gild of Corpus Christi (see under the church).
[38] V.C.H. Herts. ii, 88. In 1661 Thomas Gaudey of Ware was indicted in the court of quarter sessions for keeping a school at Ware without the bishop's licence (Sess. R. [Herts. Co. Rec.], i, 140).
[39] See Close, 1844, pt. cx, no. 13.
[40] Ibid. 1861, pt. xi, no. 15.
[41] Cussans, op. cit. Braughing Hund. i, 155; Close, 1857, pt. cxv, no. 9.
[42] Lond. Gaz. 7 Sept. 1858, p. 4052.

Further north still, between Musley Hill and High Oak Road, are the buildings of the Union (superseding the old workhouse in Crib Street which was sold in 1841), and on Musley Hill are the waterworks of the Ware Urban District.

BOROUGH

Although Ware primarily owed its importance to advantages of situation, its history is closely bound up with the manor, which for a long time was held by powerful lords such as the Earls of Leicester. It was to Robert de Quincy as lord of the manor that the grant of a market was made in 1199 (see manor). The lords of the manor also tried to establish two additional markets for cattle and corn on Wednesday and Friday, the market days of Hertford. These were held for some time before the proceedings under *Quo Warranto* by Edward I, when they were probably stopped.[43] As in other market towns, there is early trace of burgage tenure in Ware. The origin of this is perhaps to be found in the charter of Robert Earl of Leicester,[44] by which he granted to the men of Ware that all who had received or should receive a dwelling from his court at Ware[45] should hold that dwelling from him and his heirs in free burgage at a rent of 2s. This charter was confirmed by Roger de Quincy and a royal *inspeximus* was obtained by the men of Ware in 1447.[46] The area of burgage tenure probably corresponded with the manor of Ware Infra.[47] No doubt a great impulse to trade was given by the opening of the bridge to traffic at the beginning of the 13th century, when the road through Ware became the normal route to the north. It is said to have been after this date that weavers and dyers of cloth began to settle in the town.[48] Various local assessments show that from the 13th century Ware has always been the largest place in the hundred,[49] far outrivalling in importance the neighbouring borough of Hertford, which is spoken of in 1343 as 'Hertford by Ware.'[50] There is abundant evidence of the trade carried on at that period, chiefly in corn and malt,[51] the River Lea forming the waterway for the carriage of these to London. The toll (*avalagium et karkiam batellorum*) from the boats at Ware was granted by the king to the Countess of Leicester, lady of the manor (q.v.), in 1207, but, later, disputes arose between Margaret Countess of Leicester and the bailiffs of Hertford, who claimed the right of providing ships for foreign merchants and others and of taking toll (*fretum*) from them, and tried to limit the countess's right to providing ships for her own use and that of the men of her manor, merchants and others, the bailiffs taking the toll. A compromise was made by which the tolls from all ships laded at Ware, or at any place where the king or countess was entitled to the customs, were to be divided between the countess and the bailiffs, reserving, however, free carriage to the countess for her corn, hay and similar articles, and to the men of Hertford free passage for their ships laded at Hertford.[52] About the same date the countess granted to the canons of Holy Trinity, London, free carriage of their corn by ship from Ware to London at the same price as they had paid in the time of her father and mother, viz. 1d. on a quarter of hard corn.[53] Although the term 'foreign merchants' used above probably only means merchants from other towns, there were a number of aliens (chiefly from the Low Countries) living in Ware in the 15th century,[54] and possibly some of the malt manufacturers were foreigners.[55]

The town seems to have been governed by royal bailiffs in addition to the bailiffs of the manor.[56] Later the constables took over the administrative functions of the bailiffs.[57] Although often called a borough it never had any charters besides the one mentioned above, neither did it send members to Parliament nor appear before the itinerant justices by jurors separately from the hundred. On the other hand, besides the burgage tenure mentioned above, there is evidence of corporate action on the part of the inhabitants.[58] Certain feoffees were seised at the beginning of the 16th century of two messuages called the White Hart and the Saracen's Head for meeting the common expenses of the town, such as providing soldiers, paying taxes and tallages, maintaining a beacon beside the Lea and the bridge over it.[59] These houses had once been the property of the brotherhood of Jesus, so that perhaps this brotherhood (which is treated below) may have had some share in the government of the town.

Ware ceased to be called a borough after about the 16th century. In 1849 it was placed under the control of a Local Board; now by the Local Government Act of 1894 it is governed by an urban district council. Ware Union, formed in 1835, comprises fifteen parishes. The town is also the head of a petty sessional division.

The position of Ware on the road to London brought many travellers to the town. Visits to it were paid by Henry III, Edward I, Edward II, and Edward III, who were probably entertained by the lord of the manor.[60] In 1238 the king issued a prohibition of the tournament proposed to be held at Ware on Monday after Ascension Day,[61] but in 1241 a tournament was held there, at which Gilbert Marshal Earl of Pembroke met with injuries of which he died at Hertford Priory on 27 June.[62]

---

[43] *Hund. R.* (Rec. Com.), i, 188; Assize R. no. 323, m. 6 d.
[44] It is uncertain which earl this is. The last Robert Earl of Leicester died in 1204.
[45] 'Omnibus qui mansuram de curia mea de Ware acceperunt vel accipient.' *Cal. Pat.* 1446–52, p. 51.
[46] *Cal. Pat.* 1446–52, p. 51.
[47] The area of the borough must have been a definite one; see Ct. R. portf. 178, no. 71, for an agreement by the homage that anyone whose pigs were found coming (transeuntes) into the 'borough' by the sub-bailiff should pay 4d.
[48] Assize R. 318, m. 6 d.
[49] See also Assize R. 336 (for gaol delivery at Ware) and *Cal. Close,* 1341–3, p. 220.

[50] *Cal. Pat.* 1340–3, p. 460.
[51] For conveyances of shops, &c., see Anct. D. (P.R.O.), A 5222, 5191, 5192, 5207, 5209; see also *Cal. Pat.* 1377–81, p. 429.
[52] Cur. Reg. R. 94, m. 17 (Hil. 10 Hen. III).
[53] Anct. D. (P.R.O.), A 1089.
[54] *Cal. Pat.* 1429–36, pp. 548, 551, 575, 578, 586.
[55] In 1339 the bailiffs received an order to restore malt to a certain Master Reymond Peregrini (*Cal. Close,* 1339–41, p. 135; see also 1323–7, p. 50). In a will of 1504 is a bequest to 'the Dutchman, the beer brewer' (P.C.C. 4 Holgrave).

[56] See *Cal. Close,* 1323–7, p. 50. Unless these are the bailiffs of Hertford.
[57] See Early Chan. Proc. bdle. 5, no. 105, 106.
[58] In 1338 acquittance of the fifteenth was made 'to the men of the town of Ware' (*Cal. Pat.* 1338–40, p. 111).
[59] Aug. Off. Misc. Bks. xiv, fol. 127 et seq.
[60] See Letters Patent and Close dated there, *Cal. Pat.* 1216–25, pp. 371, 384; 1281–92, pp. 486, 516; 1301–7, pp. 124, 126, 127, 314; 1317–21, pp. 37, 89; 1345–8, p. 18; *Cal. Close,* 1302–7, pp. 20, 239; 1343–6, p. 676.
[61] *Cal. Pat.* 1232–47, p. 236.
[62] G.E.C. *Peerage,* s.v. Pembroke.

A HISTORY OF HERTFORDSHIRE

The men of Hertford were summoned to meet the king (Edward III) at Ware in 1337 when war with France was imminent, and Giles de Badlesmere and three others were sent to lay before them the decisions of the council and the king's plans for defence.[63] Again, in 1339 the Sheriff of Wilts. was directed by Richard II to go to Ware with sixty knights and esquires and 100 archers to join the Duke of York, Lieutenant of England, who was fighting for the king.[64] The town was a rendezvous for the county in 1569, when the sheriff and justices met there and signed the articles for the uniformity of public worship.[65] James I came to the town for hawking in 1606,[66] and later paid it several visits on his way to or from Theobalds.[67] Of more historical interest is the rising of William Parr Marquess of Northampton (lord of the manor of Waters Place) in the reign of Mary. He assembled 500 men there and proclaimed Lady Jane Grey as Queen of England. He was indicted at Ware, and afterwards sentenced to be drawn from the Tower to Tyburn and there hanged and quartered, but was ultimately pardoned by the queen.[68] Here too in 1647 Lilburne's mutinous regiment defied the authority of Parliament, and was only reduced by Cromwell and Fairfax seizing fourteen of the mutineers, of whom one was executed.[69] In the reign of Henry VIII Ware was made one of the post towns,[70] the postal arrangements being under the control of the postmaster, supported by the constables.[71]

There is little of importance to record in the later history of the town. Malt-making has always been the principal industry, and Ware one of the chief malt-producing towns in England. In 1788 a riot was caused by the oppressive conduct of the excise officers, who, on the plea of obstructions caused by the inhabitants in the collection of revenue, brought troops into the town and caused a number of persons to be arrested. A petition on behalf of the town was made to Pitt by William Plumer and Lord Grimston, which resulted in the Board of Excise being ordered to remove the objectionable supervisor of excise and the troops being recalled. The inhabitants were let off with a warning to allow the revenue to be peaceably collected. It was then stated that there were thirty-three maltings in the town, in which 1,370 quarters of malt were made every week, seventy men being employed in them.[72] At the present day many of the maltings are disused owing to the depression in the trade. Brewing and brick-making are carried on in the parish; the brickfields are to the west of the town near the river. Messrs. Allen & Hanbury have a chemical manufactory close by Ware Lock.

The market is now no longer held. About forty years ago an attempt was made to establish a corn market (as successor to one which had been held at Ware but had been discontinued owing to the market at Hertford), and a house was built for a corn exchange. The project failed, however, and the house is now used as the town hall. Fairs held under the charter made to Robert de Quincy in 1254 (see manor) are still kept.

In the 17th century the field called Bury Field or Berry Close, near the river, was used by the inhabitants of Ware as a shooting ground and any 'musterynge or trayninge of the country' generally took place there.[73]

The highways of the parish were under the control of three surveyors, two for the town (Ware Infra) and one for the upland (Ware Extra). The upland surveyor was responsible for the repair of 3 miles of highway from Ware Town's End to Widford Mill[74] and other cross roads, and the town surveyors for the highways leading to Wadesmill and Westmill. Great difficulty was experienced by these surveyors from the refusal of the inhabitants to do their share in mending the roads.[75] The road from Ware to London was proverbially bad,[76] owing to the clay soil and to the heavy loads of malt carried along it. In 1631 the justices of the peace for Hertfordshire reported that the repair of the highway would be of little use unless the king ordered that wagoners between Royston and London should use carts with two wheels and not more than five horses with one cart, and that malt should be brought on horseback from Royston to Ware between Michaelmas and May.[77] This order was carried out, but the maltsters did their best to evade it.[78]

Among the inhabitants of Ware may be mentioned William Warre, Guaro, or Varon, S.T.P. (fl. c. 1300), who was born in this parish, from which he took his name. He spent most of his life in Paris, where he is said to have taught Duns Scotus, who mentions him twice in his works.[79] William Vallans, poet and friend of Camden, was born in the neighbourhood in 1578. His poem 'A Tale of Two Swannes' (1590), one of the earliest examples of blank verse outside the drama, is chiefly descriptive of the towns of Hertfordshire.[80] The musician Simon Ive was also born at Ware, and baptized in the church 20 July 1660.[81] In the parish registers are many entries relating to the Fanshawe family, and the most famous member of it, Sir Richard Fanshawe, diplomatist and author, is buried in St. Mary's chapel in Ware Church, to which his body was removed by Lady Fanshawe, who bought a site there for the purpose. Lady Fanshawe, well known by her *Memoir*,[82] was buried beside her husband, and their son Richard,

---

[63] *Cal. Pat.* 1334–8, p. 504.
[64] Ibid. 1401–5, p. 61.
[65] *Cal. S. P. Dom.* 1547–80, p. 351.
[66] Ibid. 1603–10, p. 329.
[67] Ibid. p. 506; Nichols, *Prog. of Jas. I,* iii, 493; MSS. *of Lord Montagu of Beaulieu* (Hist. MSS. Com.), 96.
[68] Warr. for Gt. Seal, Chan. Ser. bdle. 16, file 979.
[69] *Hist. MSS. Com. Rep.* vi, App. 210a; V.C.H. Herts. ii, 32. See *A remonstrance from his Excellency Sir Thomas Fairfax and his councell of Warre,* 1647.
[70] *Hist. MSS. Com. Rep.* xiv, App. viii, 25.
[71] See *Cal. S. P. Dom.* 1581–90, p. 367; *Sess. R.* (Herts. Co. Rec.), i, 421; H. Joyce, *Hist. of Post Office.*
[72] *Verulam MSS.* (Hist. MSS. Com.), i, 136.
[73] Exch. Dep. Trin. 20 Jas. I, no. 4.
[74] This was before the road was diverted (see under Widford). Widford Mill was pulled down some years ago.
[75] *Sess. R.* (Herts. Co. Rec.), i, 85, 86, 30, 46, 315; ii, 263, 264. A curious indictment was made in the court of quarter sessions in 1838, when Richard Blow, a yeoman, was accused of digging ten ditches, erecting ten stiles, ten gates, ten stone walls, ten mounds of earth, 100 posts and 100 rails, and planting 1,000 trees and 1,000 shrubs, and ploughing up the public highway leading from Tatling Town to Fanham Hall Lane and also the old footpath from Tatling Town along Black Bush Lane and a close called Cranefield into Fanham Hall Lane (ibid. ii, 387).
[76] See MSS. *Lord Montagu of Beaulieu* (Hist. MSS. Com.), 137; *Cal. S. P. Dom.* 1619–23, p. 495.
[77] *Cal. S. P. Dom.* 1631–3, pp. 66, 409.
[78] Ibid. 1633–4, pp. 232, 305, 478.
[79] *Dict. Nat. Biog.*
[80] Ibid.   [81] Ibid.
[82] Ed. Nicolas, 1829.

second baronet, was also buried there in 1694.[83] Several of the incumbents of Ware have been men of some note. Charles Channey (1592-1672), a distinguished Oriental and classical scholar and professor of Greek at Trinity College, Cambridge, was presented to the vicarage in 1627. As an opponent of Laud, he was accused of making a schism in Ware and was imprisoned by the high commission in 1634.[84] He submitted, but afterwards wrote a retractation before sailing for America in 1637. During the Commonwealth he was invited home by his old parishioners at Ware, but was persuaded by the overseers of Harvard College to become their second president, a post which he held until 1672. He was married at Ware to Catherine Eyre in 1630, and his eldest son Isaac, afterwards a Nonconformist minister, was baptized there in 1632.[85] William Webster, a voluminous writer, was instituted to the vicarage in 1740, and held the living until his death in 1758.[86] Another Greek professor at Cambridge, Thomas Francklin, became vicar in 1759. He was a popular preacher, and in 1767 was made a royal chaplain. He was also a friend of Dr. Johnson and Sir Joshua Reynolds, and through their influence was made chaplain to the Royal Academy. He vacated Ware on being appointed rector of Brasted in 1777.[87] Joseph W. Blakesley, a distinguished scholar and tutor at Trinity College, Cambridge, was vicar from 1845 to 1872. He was well known as the 'Hertfordshire Incumbent' from his letters to the *Times* on social and political subjects ; he was appointed Dean of Lincoln in 1872. John Trusler (1735-1820), a man of most eccentric genius, was curate at Ware in the early part of his life. Among many wild schemes projected by him was one of sending circulars to every parish in England and Ireland proposing to print in script type 150 sermons at the price of 1s. each, in order to save the clergy both study and the trouble of copying. This plan is said to have met with considerable success.[88] From 1778-9 William Godwin, author of *Political Justice*, was a minister at Ware. Alexander Cruden, compiler of the famous Concordance, was a tutor there in his youth. The antiquary John Nickolls, son of a Quaker miller in the parish, was born at Ware in 1710 or 1711. He acquired the letters formerly in the possession of John Milton, which he published as *Original letters and papers of state addressed to Oliver Cromwell 1649-58*. His collection of 2,000 prints of heads at his house at Queenhithe, collected from the bookstalls about Moorfields, furnished the material for Joseph Ames's *Catalogue of English Heads*.[89]

The hamlet of Wareside on the east of the parish, which is served by Mardocks railway station, was formed into a consolidated chapelry in 1844,[90] the church of Holy Trinity having been built in 1840. The National infants' school was built in 1895 and the mixed school in 1872. To the west of Wareside is Reeves Green, to the north-east of it are two other greens, Babb's Green and Helham Green, joined by Hogtrough Lane, while to the north-west of it is Newhall Green. Fanhams Hall on the main road about half a mile west of Newhall Green is a brick house covered with rough-cast with stone dressings. The roofs are tiled. The principal rooms are panelled and some of them have elaborate plaster ceilings.[90a] From Newhall Green Long Lane runs south to Bulters Green, passing Morley Ponds. Morley House, close by, has a moat. There was also a moat (now not much more than a vallum) at Prior's Wood Farm to the west of Waters Place.

At the time of the Domesday Survey MANORS WARE was a large and important manor rated at 24 hides and valued at £45, whilst under King Edward it had been worth the exceptionally large sum of £50.[91] Before the Conquest it had been held by Anschil of Ware, and was evidently his seat.[92] In 1086 it was held by Hugh de Grentmesnil, who probably acquired it in exchange for land in Bedfordshire of Ralph Taillebois,[93] who elsewhere appears as the grantee of Anschil's lands.[94] At the time of the Survey there was land for thirty-eight ploughs, meadow sufficient for twenty plough-teams, woodland to feed 400 swine, two mills worth 24s. and 375 eels, an inclosure for beasts of the chase and 4 arpents of vineyard newly planted.[95] The last two appurtenances of the estate point to a residence there of Hugh de Grentmesnil.[96] The chief estates of this powerful lord were in Leicestershire, and there is an early connexion between his family and that of the Beamonts, Counts of Meulan and afterwards Earls of Leicester. According to Ordericus Vitalis, Ivo son of Hugh de Grentmesnil was one of the four lords of the town of Leicester and, being in disgrace at court, he pledged his share (apparently the largest one) to Robert Count of Meulan, who about 1107 received a grant of the county of Leicester and is generally considered the first Earl of Leicester. According to the chronicler, Robert never made any restoration to Ivo's son and heir. It is possible that this son was Hugh de Grentmesnil, and that he was the father of Parnel de Grentmesnil, who in 1168 married Robert Earl of Leicester, grandson of the above-mentioned Robert, who thus acquired the vast estates of the Grentmesnils,[97] and among them the manor of Ware.[98]

Earl Robert, Steward of England, died on a voyage to Jerusalem in 1190, when he was succeeded by his second son Robert, called Fitz Parnel, who in 1199 received the grant of a weekly market on Tuesdays at Ware.[99] This grant was made shortly after he had acted as steward at the coronation of King John. He died without issue in 1204 ; his mother, Parnel Countess of Leicester, survived him, and apparently held the manor of Ware in dower, for in 1207 the king granted her *avalagium et karkiam batellorum* and a market and bridge at Ware for her life as Earl Roger had them.[100] Parnel

---

[83] *Notes Gen., &c., of the Fanshawe family* ; *Dict. Nat. Biog.*
[84] *Dict. Nat. Biog.* ; see *Cal. S. P. Dom.* 1629-31 ; 1634-5.
[85] *Dict. Nat. Biog.*
[86] Ibid. [87] Ibid. [88] Ibid.
[89] Ibid.
[90] *Lond. Gaz.* 30 Apr. 1844, p. 1454.
[90a] See *Archit. Rev.* Dec. 1905 (July 1905–Dec. 1905, p. 242).
[91] *V.C.H. Herts.* i, 326b.
[92] Ibid. 326b, 383.
[93] On the fief of Hugh de Beauchamp (the successor of Ralf Taillebois) in Bedfordshire were several estates 'held in exchange for Ware' (*V.C.H. Herts.* i, 283).
[94] Anschil is probably identical with Aschil, a thegn of King Edward, who held Stotfold and who was succeeded there by Ralf Taillebois (ibid.).
[95] *V.C.H. Herts.* i, 326b.
[96] Ibid. 283.
[97] G.E.C. *Peerage*, s.v. Leicester.
[98] The manor was in the king's hands by forfeiture of the Earl of Leicester in 1173, when the sheriff accounted for £19 5s. spent in stocking it (*Pipe R.* 19 *Hen. II* [Pipe R. Soc.], 20).
[99] *Cal. Rot. Chart.* 1199-1216 (Rec. Com.), 5b.
[100] *Rot. Lit. Pat.* 1201-26 (Rec. Com.), 69h.

A HISTORY OF HERTFORDSHIRE

evidently died before 1212, when seisin of the manor of Ware was allowed to Saer de Quincy Earl of Winchester,[1] who between 1168 and 1173 had married Margaret the younger sister and co-heir of Robert Earl of Leicester.[2] The Earl of Winchester was Justiciar of England from 1211 to 1214. He was one of the twenty-five barons who were guardians of Magna Carta, and took an active share in bringing over Prince Louis in January 1215–16, to whom he adhered even after the accession of Henry III, being joint commander of the barons' army April–May 1217. Two years later he joined the Crusade during the siege of Damietta, and died abroad on 3 November 1219. He was buried at Acre.[3] Whilst still in favour with John, in 1205–6, he had obtained a grant that he and all lands and fees of the honour of Leicester should be quit of shires and hundreds and sheriff's aids.[4] A view of frankpledge was therefore held by the lords of Ware,[5] and the area of their jurisdiction is called a liberty. His son and heir Roger Earl of Winchester granted the manor of Ware in 1253 to his brother Robert de Quincy,[6] to hold of him and his heirs at the yearly rent of half a mark and by service of a knight's fee.[7] The Earls of Winchester held it of the king by three parts of a knight's fee.[8] The overlordship remained with the earl and his descendants. Roger died without male issue in 1264, leaving three daughters, Margaret wife of William Ferrers, fifth Earl of Derby (her stepmother's father), Elizabeth or Isabel, who married Alexander Comyn Earl of Buchan, and Helen or Ela, who married Sir Alan la Zouche of Ashby-de-la Zouch.[9] Ware was for a time held of all the heirs jointly,[10] but ultimately became vested in the Ferrers. Margaret had as part of her inheritance the manor of Groby, co. Leicester, to which Ware was appurtenant, and this she settled on her second son William.[11] William, son of William, was summoned as a baron, Lord Ferrers, to Parliament in 1300, and was the ancestor of the Lords Ferrers de Groby,[12] with whom the overlordship of Ware descended.[13]

QUINCY. *Gules seven voided lozenges or.*

FERRERS. *Vairy or and gules.*

In 1254 the king by a charter dated at Bordeaux granted to Robert de Quincy, the tenant, a yearly fair at his manor of Ware on the eve and day of the Nativity of the Virgin Mary and the three days following.[14] Robert died in 1257, leaving two daughters, Joan and Hawise.[15] Joan, who married Humphrey de Bohun, died seised of Ware in 1284,[16] when it passed to Hawise widow of Baldwin Wake of Liddell, co. Cumberland. The custody of John Wake, son and heir of Hawise, and of the manor of Ware was granted to Queen Eleanor in 1285.[17] John Wake did homage for his lands in 1290, and was summoned to Parliament as Lord Wake in 1295.[18] In 1297 he granted Ware to the king, who regranted it to him and his wife Joan in fee-tail, with reversion to the king.[19] John Lord Wake died in 1300. During the minority of his son Thomas the king assigned the custody of the manor and town to William Trente for three years, in discharge of a debt due to him for wine purchased from him by the king's butler, Henry de Say, and for money advanced by him on the king's behalf to Gilbert de Clare Earl of Gloucester.[20] Later the custody was granted to Queen Isabella.[21]

Thomas Lord Wake was one of the barons who took part with the queen against Edward II, and was by her made justice of all forests south of the Trent and Constable of the Tower of London. In the reign of Edward III he was made Governor of Hertford Castle and also of the Channel Islands. He took part with Edward Balliol in his claim to the crown of Scotland in 1329.[22] Later, in 1342, he served in the French wars. His wife was Blanche second daughter of Henry Earl of Lancaster, who after his death in 1349[23] held the manor in dower[24] and granted 4 acres from it to the Friars Minor of Ware.[25] The extent of the manor at this date was 576 acres of arable land, 48 acres of meadow, 40 acres of meadow in the park, 36 acres of wood, a watermill and a fulling-mill, perquisites of court worth £5 (an exceptionally large sum), a fishery from 'Stretende' to 'Newemededych' and half a fishery from 'Stretende' to 'Bemsford.' Thomas Lord Wake had no issue and his heir was his sister Margaret, widow of Edmund Earl of Kent, the youngest son of Edward I. She died in 1349, and was succeeded by her second son and heir John Earl of Kent, who also died before Blanche, in 1352.[26] His heir Joan Lady Wake married Thomas de Holand Earl of Kent, and after his death in 1360 she married Edward Prince of Wales and was the mother of Richard II. Her son and heir by her first husband, Thomas de Holand Earl of Kent, succeeded to her estates in 1385.[27] He died seised of Ware in 1397, and it then

---

[1] *Rot. Lit. Claus.* (Rec. Com.), i, 118.
[2] G.E.C. *Peerage*, s.v. Winchester.
[3] Ibid.
[4] Hunter, *Rot. Selecti*, 9.
[5] See Assize R. 325.
[6] Saer de Quincy had two sons named Robert: the eldest, who died v.p. in 1217, and the fourth, who is mentioned in the text (*Dict. Nat. Biog.* s.v. Quincy).
[7] Feet of F. Div. Co. 37 Hen. III, no. 77.
[8] *Testa de Nevill* (Rec. Com.), 265, 269*b*. The Countess of Leicester, however, is said to have held Ware as 6 carucates of land for the service of one knight (ibid. 279).
[9] G.E.C. *Peerage*, s.v. Quincy.
[10] Chan. Inq. p.m. 7 Edw. II, no. 36.
[11] Ibid. 12 Edw. I, no. 27.
[12] G.E.C. *Peerage*, s.v. Derby.
[13] Chan. Inq. p.m. 23 Edw. III, no. 75; 46 Edw. III (2nd nos.), no. 37 ; 9 Ric. II, no. 54 ; 11 Ric. II, no. 26 ; 17 Ric. II, no. 24 ; 20 Ric. II, no. 30, and other inquisitions given below.
[14] *Cal. Pat.* 1247–58, p. 324; Chart. R. 37 & 38 Hen. III, m. 7.
[15] *Cal. Gen.* (ed. Roberts), i, 112.
[16] Chan. Inq. p.m. 12 Edw. I, no. 27 ; *Cal. Close*, 1279–88, p. 250.
[17] *Cal. Pat.* 1281–92, p. 180.
[18] G.E.C. *Peerage*, s.v. Wake.
[19] *Cal. Pat.* 1292–1301, pp. 296, 303, 304.
[20] *Cal. Pat.* 1307–13, p. 218 ; *Cal. Close*, 1307–13, p. 39; *Abbrev. Rot. Orig.* i, 169.
[21] *Cal. Close*, 1318–23, p. 77.
[22] G.E.C. *Peerage*, s.v. Wake.
[23] Chan. Inq. p.m. 23 Edw. III, no. 75.
[24] *Cal. Close*, 1349–54, p. 53. She died in 1380 (Chan. Inq. p.m. 4 Ric. II, no. 59).
[25] Chan. Inq. p.m. 46 Edw. III (2nd nos.), no. 37.
[26] Ibid. 26 Edw. III, no. 54.
[27] Ibid. 9 Ric. II, no. 54.

descended to his son Thomas Earl of Kent[28] (created Duke of Surrey in 1397), who two years later was taken prisoner and beheaded by the populace at Cirencester during the contest with Henry IV. His lands were forfeited, and Henry IV granted Ware, the manor, town and lordship, to his son John. These were valued at £120 a year.[29] Later the manor was restored to Edmund Earl of Kent, brother and heir of Thomas, who died without issue in 1408.[30] His heirs were his sisters, of whom Eleanor, the wife of Thomas de Montagu Earl of Salisbury, inherited Ware. The extent of the manor taken on the death of the earl, who survived his wife, included a capital messuage, 70 acres of arable land, 80 acres of meadow, 30 acres of pasture, a water-mill let for 100s., rents of free tenants amounting to £30, perquisites of court worth 6s. 8d., and the park worth nothing beyond the fee of the parker and the keeping of the deer.[31]

HOLAND, Earl of Kent. *ENGLAND with the difference of a border argent.*

Alice, only daughter and heir of the Earl of Salisbury and Eleanor, married Sir Richard Nevill, afterwards Earl of Salisbury. Their son Richard succeeded on his marriage to the Warwick estates, and was confirmed as Earl of Warwick in 1449. He was the 'Kingmaker' of the Wars of the Roses, and was slain at Barnet in 1471, leaving no male issue. His daughter Anne married first Edward Prince of Wales, who was killed after the battle of Tewkesbury, and secondly, about a year afterwards, Richard Duke of Gloucester, who became King Richard III in 1483.[32] The king in 1485 granted an annuity of £10 from the issues of Ware to William Porter, a yeoman of the Crown.[33] Sir Robert Brackenbury, Constable of the Tower, was appointed steward of the manor.[34] Queen Anne died in 1485; her heir was Edward Earl of Warwick, son of Isabel, sister of Anne and co-heir of Richard Earl of Warwick, who, having spent all his life in prison,[35] was condemned for conspiring high treason with Perkin Warbeck, a fellow prisoner, and was executed on Tower Hill in 1499, aged twenty-four. He, however, never held Ware,[36] for after the death of Richard III King Henry VII granted it to

NEVILL, Earl of Salisbury. *Gules a saltire argent with a label gobony argent and azure.*

his mother, Margaret Countess of Richmond (who had already received a grant of the nomination of officers within the lordship), for life.[37] After her death in 1509 it came into the hands of the king, who in the same year appointed Sir Thomas Lovell, treasurer of the household, steward of the manor.[38] The next year William Compton, groom of the stole, was made bailiff of the town and manor, keeper of the park, meadows, fishery, and two mills.[39]

In 1513 Lady Margaret Pole, sister and heir of Edward Plantagenet Earl of Warwick, was reinstated as Countess of Salisbury.[40] Two inquisitions were taken on the manor of Ware,[41] after which it was restored to her. Accounts for the manor about this date show that the fishery called the truncage was leased with the park for £8 13s. 4d., the mill for £26 13s. 4d. During the year 1515 four views of frankpledge and four other 'little courts' were held, the perquisites amounting to £2 9s. 3d., whilst the perquisites of the court of pie-powder amounted to 14s. 2d. for that year. The extent included the site of the manor called Le Bury, a capital messuage with a grange called Kydeswell, and a wood called Wolkechyn, all leased out at farm.[42] As the last remaining member of the old royal house of England, the Countess of Salisbury aroused the jealousy of the king and was attainted in 1539 and beheaded in 1541, two years after her eldest son Henry Pole Lord Montagu had suffered the same fate.[43] The manor thus came again into the hands of Henry VIII, who in 1539 granted the fishery and 'custom called troncage' in the water at Ware to John Noode, a yeoman of the guard.[44] In 1542 Thomas Wrothe was appointed bailiff of the manor and keeper of the park in reversion after Oliver Frankeleyn, who held these offices by grant from the Countess of Salisbury.[45] Leases of 'the stable within the close called Le Bury,' of the meadows called Chaldewell and Berymede, of Newnney Wood, and the field called Newnney or Woodfeld were made by the king at different times,[46] and in 1544 he leased the two corn-mills to Thomas Lennard of Ware for forty years.[47]

In 1548 the manor and park were granted by King Edward VI to his sister, the Lady Mary, for life.[48] On her accession as queen, Mary granted them to Francis Earl of Huntingdon and his wife Katherine,[49] who was daughter of Henry Pole, son of the Countess of Salisbury, and who with her sister and co-heir Winifred were restored in blood and honours by Act of Parliament in 1554–5.[50] Katherine received a confirmation of Ware from Queen Elizabeth in 1570, with the exception of the park, mills, and fishery[51]; the park and fishery were, however, granted to her son Henry Earl of Huntingdon two years afterwards.[52] Later the countess sold the manor to Thomas Fanshawe of Fanshawe Gate, co. Derby,

---

[28] Chan. Inq. p.m. 20 Ric. II, no. 30; G.E.C. *Peerage*, s.v. Wake.
[29] *Cal. Pat.* 1399–1401, p. 195.
[30] Chan. Inq. p.m. 10 Hen. IV, no. 51.
[31] Ibid. 7 Hen. VI, no. 57.
[32] G.E.C. *Peerage*, s.v. Salisbury.
[33] *Cal. Pat.* 1476–85, p. 529.
[34] Ibid. 521.
[35] See Stat. 5 Hen. VIII, cap. 12.
[36] In a later inq. (Ser. 2, xxviii, 71) he is said to have held it until his death, but this is probably wrong. It was claimed and kept as Crown property owing to Richard III having held it (T.R. Misc. Bks. 155, m. 17), although Richard, as shown above, only held it in right of his wife.
[37] Pat. 2 Hen. VII, pt. i, m. 21; T.R. Misc. Bks. 155, m. 17.
[38] *L. and P. Hen. VIII*, i, 276.
[39] Ibid. 992, 1395.
[40] *Dict. Nat. Biog.*
[41] Exch. Inq. (Ser. 2), file 299, no. 9, 10; Chan. Inq. p.m. (Ser. 2), xxviii, 71.
[42] Mins. Accts. Hen. VIII, 1593 and 6869.
[43] G.E.C. *Peerage*, s.v. Salisbury.
[44] *L. and P. Hen. VIII*, xiv (2), 1354 (15).
[45] Ibid. vii, 1251 (15).
[46] Ibid. xv, 282 (112); xviii, 449 (78); xix (1), 610 (4); Pat. 36 Hen. VIII, pt. xxii, m. 6; *L. and P. Hen. VIII*, xix (1), 812 (45, 112).
[47] *L. and P. Hen. VIII*, xix (2), 166 (19).
[48] Pat. 2 Edw. VI, pt. v, m. 32.
[49] Ibid. 1 Mary, pt. vii, m. 20.
[50] G.E.C. *Peerage*, s.v. Montacute.
[51] Pat. 12 Eliz. pt. x.
[52] Ibid. 14 Eliz. pt. iii.

A HISTORY OF HERTFORDSHIRE

reserving to herself a yearly rent of £80. In 1575 he acquired the park and piece of ground where the disused fish weir had been from the earl,[53] who in 1581 sold him also the reserved rent,[54] and in 1587 he bought the two water-mills and a fulling-mill from Robert Lennard.[55]

Fanshawe was Remembrancer of the Exchequer, was M.P. for Rye in 1571, in the five succeeding Parliaments for Arundel, and in 1597 for Much Wenlock in Shropshire. He died in 1601 at his house in Warwick Lane, London.[56] His son Henry Fanshawe, M.P. for Westbury, co. Wilts., in 1588, and for Boroughbridge, co. Yorks., in 1597, succeeded him as Remembrancer of the Exchequer. He was a friend of Prince Henry, and was knighted in 1603.[57] His garden at Ware became famous for its fruit, flowers, and herbs,[58] and many of the trees in the park were planted by him. He was also a collector of pictures, prints, drawings, medals, and stones, which he placed first in his house at Warwick Lane, but by his will of 1600 bequeathed to Ware Park, to be placed in the gallery or other fit place and not to be dispersed.[59] He died at Ware, and was buried in the church, March 1615–16,[60] when the manor descended to his eldest son Thomas, who also held the office of Remembrancer of the Exchequer. He was made a Knight of the Bath at the coronation of Charles I in February 1625–6,[61] and was M.P. for the county of Hertford in 1661. During the Civil War he fought on the king's side, and his property was sequestrated by Parliament. He was allowed to compound for Ware upon the Articles of Barnstaple, having resided in the town and garrison within seven months of the surrender of the garrison.[62] Charles II shortly after his accession raised him to the peerage as Viscount Fanshawe of Dromore in Ireland,[63] but the sequestration of his property had nearly ruined him, and in 1668 he sold the manor to Sir Thomas Byde,[64] M.P. for Hertford in 1672. Sir Thomas Byde, the eldest son of Thomas, died in 1684–5 during his father's lifetime. Thomas son of Skinner succeeded to the manor; he married Katherine daughter of John Plumer of Blakesware.[65] His son, Thomas Plumer Byde, suffered a recovery of the manor in 1749.[66] The latter's sons, Thomas Hope Byde and John Hope Byde, did the same in 1774.[67] Thomas Hope Byde built the present manor-house on the site of the older one.[68] John Hope Byde, who succeeded him, by will of 1829 devised the manor to trustees

FANSHAWE. *Or a cheveron between three fleurs de lis sable.*

for sale; a decree in Chancery was obtained for this purpose, but it was not until 1846 that Ware was bought by James Cudden of Norwich. He sold the manor in 1853 to Daniel de Castro, who died in 1867. Two years later it is said by Cussans to have been conveyed by his trustees to George Rastwick of Woking,[69] but it is doubtful whether this is correct. Mr. William Parker was owner in 1858 or earlier, and was succeeded by his son Mr. J. H. E. Parker. His son, Mr. W. F. Parker, is the present lord of the manor.[70]

The manor-house, an 18th-century building, stood in Ware Park, which lies on high ground and contains very fine avenues of elms and limes. The house was destroyed by fire in 1911 and is now being rebuilt. The estate is skirted by the mill stream, the mill being situated at the junction of this stream with the Lea and Rib.

A full list of the liberties belonging to the lord of the manor appears upon a *quo warranto* brought against Thomas Fanshawe in 1585, when he claimed *inter alia* market, court of pie-powder, view of frankpledge, assize of bread, wine, ale, and other victuals, election and nomination of constables and other officers in the court leet, waif and stray, pillory and tumbrel, park, free warren, goods and chattels of felons, deodands, treasure trove, return of writs of the Exchequer and of the Pleas of the Crown.

A book containing copies of the court rolls of Ware from 1665 to 1706 is among the additional manuscripts at the British Museum.[71] Separate courts were held (on the same day) for Ware Infra and Ware Extra. Possibly the former was originally held for the burgage tenants. At the view of frankpledge held for Ware Extra, the tithings of Ware Extra, Thundridge, and Ware Upland presented; a constable and headborough were chosen for each of these tithings. At the view held for Ware Infra a constable and headborough were chosen, also two aleconners. A custom of the manor was for tenants to grant customary lands from three years to three years up to nine years. It was also customary for tenants to cut down and carry away trees growing on their lands without leave from the lord. There are still two manors of Ware Infra and Ware Extra, but no courts have been held of late years.

All the manors described below were held of the manor of Ware.

BLAKESWARE (Blakysware, Blacksware, Blakys, Blacks, Blages), an estate lying on the north-east of Ware, took its name from the family of Blake, who belonged to this parish. Stephen le Blake was assessed at Ware in 1307.[72] John le Blake, sen., John le Blake, jun., and Nicholas le Blake were all of some note locally at the beginning of the 14th century.[73] Nicholas le Blake had leases of the manor

---

[53] Close, 17 Eliz. pt. x (m. not numbered).
[54] Ibid. 28 Eliz. pt. xi; Feet of F. Herts. Mich. 23 & 24 Eliz.
[55] Feet of F. Herts. Hil. 29 Eliz. The fulling-mill was perhaps the windmill concerning which Thomas Cox brought a suit against Robert Lennard in 1570 (Chan. Proc. [Ser. 2], bdle. 11, no. 72).
[56] *Dict. Nat. Biog.*; Chan. Inq. p.m. (Ser. 2), cclxxvii, 103.
[57] Shaw, *Knights of Engl.* ii, 104.

[58] *Dict. Nat. Biog.*; Cussans, op. cit. *Braughing Hund.* 40 (quoting Sir Henry Wotton's description of the garden).
[59] *Notes, &c., of the Fanshawe family,* 45.
[60] Chan. Inq. p.m. (Ser. 2), ccclix, 111.
[61] Shaw, *Knights of Engl.* i, 163.
[62] *Cal. S. P. Dom.* 1648–9, p. 322; *Cal. Com. for Comp.* 1864.
[63] *Cal. S. P. Dom.* 1661–2, p. 68.
[64] Feet of F. Herts. East. 20 Chas. II; Recov. East. 20 Chas. II, m. 153.

[65] Berry, *Herts. Gen.* 11.
[66] Recov. R. Trin. 22 & 23 Geo. II, m. 40.
[67] Ibid. 15 Geo. III, m. 427.
[68] Cussans, op. cit. *Braughing Hund.* 140.
[69] Ibid.
[70] Information from Mr. R. T. Andrews.
[71] No. 27977.
[72] Subs. R. bdle. 120, no. 8.
[73] See *Inq. Non.* (Rec. Com.), 432; *Cal. Close*, 1346–9, p. 513.

388

of Newhall (q.v.) from the Abbot of Waltham Holy Cross in 1344 and 1365. He, or his son Nicholas, was alive in 1380, when letters of protection for him were revoked because he had not gone to Calais to join in the defence of that town as he had purposed.[74] In 1387 'Nicholas Blake the younger' was grantee in a conveyance of lands in Ware.[75]

The holding of the Blakes came before 1479 into the possession of Thomas Braughing, when it was held by him of the lord of Ware Manor as the 'manor called Blakes.' He in that year made a settlement on his son Thomas and his wife Joan; Thomas the younger died seised of the manor in 1496.[76] John son of Thomas was holding in 1519[77] and Richard Braughing and Elizabeth his wife in 1522.[78] The latter conveyed it to John Yeolyn and others, probably trustees, for in 1560 Simon Clare and John Clare levied a fine of the manor.[79] The next year Simon Clare and Agnes his wife conveyed it to Sir Thomas Venables of Kinderton, co. Chester.[80] After his death Anne Brooks, the mother of his son Thomas, married Ralph Davenport,[81] and held the manor with reversion to Thomas, who was attainted in 1580.[82] His lands, however, seem to have been restored to him, for he was carrying on transactions with the Crown concerning the reversion in 1583.[83] After Anne's death, however, the profits were taken by Thomas Harris, to whom Venables released all right in 1597.[84] Harris conveyed Blakesware to John Goodman.[85] Goodman, sen., with John Goodman, jun., levied a fine (Hilary 1616–17) with Katherine Tirrel, widow,[86] who two years afterwards joined with John Goodman and Grace Goodman, widow, in a conveyance to Moses Tryon.[87] Tryon with Elizabeth his wife conveyed to George Hanger in 1620–1.[87a] It was acquired from George and John Hanger in 1635 by John King, D.D., canon of Christ Church, Oxford, whose son John King sold it in 1655 to Heneage Featherstone, created a baronet in 1660. By Featherstone it was conveyed in 1664 to Sir Thomas Leventhorpe, who rebuilt the house, and afterwards in 1678 sold the estate to Sir Thomas Clutterbuck, kt.,[88] English consul at Leghorn and afterwards commissioner for victualling the Mediterranean fleet, for which he was knighted. He died in February 1682–3, and was buried in Ware Church. After his death the estate was conveyed to John Plumer, Sheriff of Hertfordshire in 1689, from which date it descended with Gilston (q.v.) to Sir Henry George Ward, who sold it in 1850 to Martin Hadsley Gosselin of Ware Priory.[89] After his death in 1868 the estate was held by his widow until her death in 1892, when it devolved on her eldest son Sir Martin Le Marchant Hadsley Gosselin, Assistant Under-Secretary for Foreign Affairs from 1898–1902 and minister plenipotentiary at Lisbon from 1902 to 1905. He died at Busaco, Portugal, in 1905 and was succeeded by his son Captain Alwyn Gosselin, the present owner.

The manor-house built by Sir Thomas Leventhorpe was pulled down by Mrs. Plumer after William Plumer's death in 1822, Mr. Plumer having some years previous to his death moved to Gilston.[90] It was a fine brick mansion situated on the south of the Blakesware estate, with a large courtyard and terraced gardens, with the Quarters and the Wilderness to the rear.[91] Charles Lamb, whose grandmother Mrs. Field was housekeeper in the Plumer family and who used to stay with her at Blakesware during his childhood, describes it in one of his essays under the name of Blakesmoor. There are drawings of the ruins among the Additional Manuscripts at the British Museum.[92] The present house was built by Mrs. Hadsley Gosselin, grandmother of the present owner, in 1878. The chapel was built by her son Sir Martin Gosselin and was opened by the Cardinal Archbishop of Westminster in 1896.

GOSSELIN. *Gules a cheveron between three crescents ermine.*

Blakes Bushes and Little Blakesware also preserve the name of Blake.

WIDBURY alias GRIMBOLDS alias WHITE-BOROUGH HILL lies on the east of Ware. The name occurs as Witerberwe in 1308[93] and survives in Widbury Hill, Widbury Hill Farm and Widbury Wood. The estate took its first name from a family of Grimbold (Grymbaud), who were living at Ware in the 14th century.[94] In 1353 Juliana Grimbold released a moiety of a messuage situated in Ware to John son of William atte Water.[95] The Grimbolds' lands in Ware came later, about the end of the 15th century, into the possession of Thomas Rede, a citizen of London. His daughter and co-heir Agnes married Robert Lytton, whose son William died seised of half the manor of Grimbolds in 1517.[96] Robert his son and heir was aged five; he had livery of seisin in 1533. Another quarter of the manor was held in 1520 by John Smith and his wife Joan, who was perhaps a daughter of Rede's other co-heir. They conveyed it in that year to Richard Hill and others.[97] Gilbert Hill was in possession in 1579.[98] He was said to hold a third part of the manor of Grimbolds and a capital messuage called Whitborowe Hill.[99] There is no further trace of the remaining parts of the manor, so that probably he had the manorial rights. In a rental of his lands a dove-house and pond are mentioned, and he received quit-rents from 'The Bear,' 'The Bull,' 'The Checker,' and from a

---

[74] *Cal. Pat.* 1377–81, p. 530.
[75] Anct. D. (P.R.O.), A 5195.
[76] Chan. Inq. p.m. (Ser. 2), xi, 94. By his will (P.C.C. 22 Horne) he desired to be buried in the Lady chapel of the parish church. He made a bequest to the brotherhood of Jesus in the same church.
[77] Feet of F. Herts. Mich. 11 Hen. VIII.
[78] Ibid. Trin. 14 Hen. VIII.
[79] Ibid. Div. Co. East. 2 Eliz.
[80] Recov. R. Hil. 1561, m. 658; Feet of F. Herts. Trin. 4 Eliz.
[81] Com. Pleas D. Enr. East. 25 Eliz. m. 10.
[82] Chan. Inq. p.m. (Ser. 2), ccvii, 106.
[83] Com. Pleas D. Enr. East. 25 Eliz. m. 10.
[84] Feet of F. Herts. Trin. 39 Eliz.
[85] Fine in the same term.
[86] Feet of F. Herts. Hil. 14 Jas. I.
[87] Ibid. East. 16 Jas. I.
[87a] Ibid. Hil. 18 Jas. I.
[88] Deeds in possession of Mr. Gosselin.
[89] Cussans, op. cit. *Braughing Hund.* 142.
[90] See Ainger, *Charles Lamb*, 20, 119; *Essays of Elia* (ed. Ainger), 400.
[91] Cussans, op. cit. *Braughing H.* 142.
[92] Add. MS. 32352, pp. 90, 91.
[93] *Cal. Pat.* 1307–13, p. 169.
[94] Ibid. 1330–4, p. 132; De Banco R. 273, m. 99 d.; 274, m. 124; 269, m. 48; 270, m. 12 d.; Chan. Misc. bdle. 62, no. 36, 81.
[95] Anct. D. (P.R.O.), A 966.
[96] Chan. Inq. p.m. (Ser. 2), xxxiii, 5.
[97] Feet of F. Herts. Trin. 12 Hen. VIII.
[98] Ibid. Mich. 21 & 22 Eliz.
[99] Ct. of Wards, Extents, &c., no. 618.

A HISTORY OF HERTFORDSHIRE

house against the market-place occupied by John Lennard.[100]

Gilbert Hill died in 1583, his son Richard being aged four.[1] During Richard's minority his sisters Philippa wife of Edward Meade and Elizabeth wife of Thomas Calvert held his Ware estate.[2] After attaining his majority he sold the manor to James Stanley,[3] who died seised of it in 1611.[4] His son Thomas apparently sold it to Alexander Weld, who was holding it in 1665.[5] His son Alexander[6] possibly left a daughter Sarah, who married Robert Jones; they held it (in Sarah's right) in 1710,[7] and later Robert Jones joined with George Bruere and Anthony Thompson, the heirs of Alexander Weld, in selling it to Walter Plumer, called of Cavendish Square.[8]

Widbury House (as it is now called) was burnt down about ten years ago. It was rebuilt by the present owner, Mr. J. H. Buxton of Easneye.

The manor of *WATERS* alias *MARTOCKS*, now *MARDOCKS* (Mattocks, Mallocks, Maddocks, Mardocks, Mardox), on the east of the parish, probably took its first name from its situation in a bend of the River Ash. The family of Atte Water held land in Ware in the 14th century and later. There is record of John atte Water in 1331,[9] of Robert son of William in 1348,[10] of John son of William in 1353 and 1354,[11] of William in 1356, 1398 and 1408,[12] of Richard son of William, who granted the lands settled on him by his father to Thomas Braughing and other feoffees in 1324,[13] of William atte Water in 1401, 1403 and 1420,[14] and of Thomas atte Water of Ware, 'gentilman,' in 1427.[15] The manor of Waters, held of the manor of Ware, first appears by name in the reign of Henry VII, when it was in the possession of Sir Thomas Bourchier, kt., who died seised of it in 1492. His nephew Henry Earl of Essex succeeded him.[16] He apparently retained the capital messuage called Waters Place (see below), but alienated the manor of Waters, which in 1505 is said to have been in the possession of Hugh Chapman and Agnes his wife.[17] They

BOURCHIER. *Argent a cross engrailed gules between four water-bougets sable.*

seem to have acquired it from Margaret Martok, against whose executors they brought a suit in Chancery for having kept back the title deeds. In this suit it is called the manor of John at Waters.[18] This accounts for the alternative name of Martocks, which began to be used in the 16th century.

From Hugh Chapman the manor descended to his son Robert, to John son of Robert, to Henry son of John, and then to John, probably son of Henry.[19] In 1590–1 (Hilary Term) John Chapman conveyed it to Theophilus Adams,[20] probably in trust for John Watts,[21] who in 1601 settled it on his son John on his marriage with Mary daughter of Adam Bayninge of Little Bentley, co. Essex.[22] Sir John Watts (knighted in 1603),[23] alderman of London, died in 1616.[24] His son John died before 1652, when Mary Watts, widow, with John Watts, evidently her son, conveyed the manor to John Buck of Hamby Grange in Leverton, co. Lincoln,[25] created a baronet in 1660.[26] In 1664 Sir John Buck conveyed it to Sir Cyril Wich and Matthew Pinder,[27] evidently trustees for Thomas Bird, who was in possession in 1666.[28] It descended to his nephew and heir Richard, who sold it in 1701 together with the capital messuage called 'Mattox,' the mill, and fields called Bridge Mead, Down Mead, Dickholm Mead, Grimswood Mead and Queach Valley[29] to Arthur Windus. In 1711 the heirs of Windus joined with mortgagees of the manor and creditors of Windus in conveying it, with the mill belonging, to the trustees of Felix Calvert of Hunsdon, for a settlement on Felix and his wife Elizabeth, with reversion to their eldest son Peter.[30] He, according to Clutterbuck, sold it in 1767 to Norton Hutchinson, whose eldest son the Rev. Julius Hutchinson succeeded.[31] The latter conveyed the estate to Ambrose Procter, by whom it was devised to his great-nephew George Procter.[32]

In 1814 George Procter rebuilt the manor-house near the mill and afterwards (1818) let it to Sir James Mackintosh, who had been appointed professor of law and general politics at Haileybury College and who lived there until 1824, when he resigned the professorship.[33] In 1826 Procter sold the manor to Dr. Abraham Wilkinson of Forty Hall, Enfield, who lived there for a short time and then let it to William Tugwell Robins, solicitor in the case of Wellesley v.

---

[100] Rentals and Surv. (Gen. Ser.), portf. 8, no. 45.
[1] Chan. Inq. p.m. (Ser. 2), cclxvi, 116.
[2] Ct. of Req. bdle. 136, no. 49.
[3] Feet of F. Herts. Mich. 43 & 44 Eliz.; Trin. 2 Jas. I.
[4] Chan. Inq. p.m. (Ser. 2), cccxliii, 179.
[5] Feet of F. Herts. Trin. 17 Chas. II.
[6] Ibid. Mich. 12 Will. III.
[7] Ibid. Herts. East. 9 Anne.
[8] Com. Pleas D. Enr. Hil. 13 Geo. II, m. 1; Feet of F. Herts. Hil. 13 Geo. II. In this conveyance (1739) it is called the manor, capital messuage, or farm of Grimbalds alias Whitborough Hill.
[9] Cal. Close, 1330–3, p. 303.
[10] Ibid. 1346–9, p. 513.
[11] Ibid. 1349–54, p. 523; Chan. Inq. a.q.d. file 312, no. 11; Anct. D. (P.R.O.), A 966.
[12] Cal. Close, 1354–60, p. 325; Anct. D. (P.R.O.), A 5195, 5196, 5216.
[13] Anct. D. (P.R.O.), C 3420, 3388.

[14] Cal. Pat. 1401–5, pp. 66, 147; Anct. D. (P.R.O.), A 1073.
[15] Cal. Pat. 1422–9, p. 372.
[16] Chan. Inq. p.m. (Ser. 2), vii, 3. Sir Thomas Bourchier by his will (P.C.C. 1 Dogett) desired to be buried in the parish church of Ware, and the bones of Isabel, his late wife, to be taken up and laid by his bones. He left many ornaments to the church.
[17] Ct. of Req. bdle. 4, no. 84; bdle. 16, no. 60.
[18] Early Chan. Proc. bdle. 128, no. 6.
[19] See Notes of F. Div. Co. East. 7 Eliz.; Chan. Proc. (Ser. 2), bdle. 31, no. 75; bdle. 70, no. 22; bdle. 224, no. 65; bdle. 227, no. 55; bdle. 223, no. 81.
[20] Feet of F. Herts. Hil. 33 Eliz.
[21] For Thomas Watts of Ware, yeoman, probably father of this Thomas, see will printed in *Herts. Gen.* i, 369.
[22] Feet of F. Herts. Mich. 43 & 44 Eliz.
[23] Shaw, *Knights of Engl.* ii, 128.
[24] Chan. Inq. p.m. (Ser. 2), cccliv, 135.

[25] Recov. R. Mich. 1652, m. 35; East. 1656, m. 228.
[26] G.E.C. *Baronetage*, iii, 141.
[27] Feet of F. Herts. Hil. 15 & 16 Chas. II.
[28] Com. Pleas D. Enr. East. 19 Chas. II, m. 2; see also Feet of F. Herts. East. 22 Chas. II; Com. Pleas D. Enr. East. 10 Will. III, m. 6; Recov. R. Mich. 11 Will. III, m. 42.
[29] Close, 1 Anne, pt. vi, no. 11.
[30] See Feet of F. Herts. Trin. 12 Will. III; Recov. R. Trin. 12 Will. III, m. 118; Feet of F. Mich. 10 Anne; Com. Pleas D. Enr. Mich. 10 Anne, m. 10. For dealings with it by the Calvert family see Feet of F. Herts. Hil. 9 Geo. I; Recov. R. Hil. 9 Geo. I, m. 77; Feet of F. Herts. Trin. 28 Geo. II; Recov. R. Hil. 7 Geo. III, m. 234.
[31] See Recov. R. East. 19 Geo. III, m. 47.
[32] Clutterbuck, op. cit. iii, 305. See Berwick in Standon.
[33] *Dict. Nat. Biog.*

390

BRAUGHING HUNDRED

Mornington. He resided there until 1835, after which the house was occupied by Edward Downs of Lincoln's Inn for ten years and subsequently by Captain Moorsom, C.E., of Birmingham. It was then left unoccupied until 1863, when being in a state of decay it was pulled down. The manor was sold in 1865 by Edward Smith Wilkinson to Thomas Fowell Buxton of Easneye in Stanstead Abbots.[34] Mr. J. H. Buxton is the present owner. Mardocks Mill, now pulled down, was situated on the River Ash.

Henry Bourchier Earl of Essex, who apparently retained the capital messuage and some of the lands of the manor of Waters (see above), which henceforth was known as the manor or tenement of *WATERS PLACE*, died without male issue in March 1539–40. On his death the viscounty of Bourchier became extinct.[35] His daughter Anne married William Lord Parr, and a settlement of Waters Place was made on them in 1542.[36] In 1543 Lord Parr was created Earl of Essex, although he had that same year repudiated his wife and obtained an Act of Parliament declaring her children bastards.[37] He was created Marquess of Northampton in February 1546–7, but was attainted in 1553. Waters Place came to the Crown, where it remained until 1563, when Elizabeth granted it to the marquess for the maintenance of Anne.[38] After her death without legitimate issue in January 1570–1 the queen granted it to Walter Devereux Viscount Hereford[39] (great-grandson of John Devereux, husband of Cicely, sister of Henry Bourchier Earl of Essex), who was one of the few peers of the old blood who remained faithful to the queen during the conspiracy of the Duke of Norfolk and who was made Earl of Essex in 1572.[40] In that year he conveyed Waters Place to William Garnett,[41] from whom it was acquired in 1573 by Ralph Baesh.[42] He died in 1598, leaving a son Edward, aged four.[43] After this, apparently, it was owned by Robert Hellam in 1643 and by John Andrewes in 1652.[44] Waters Place is now owned with Mardocks by Mr. J. H. Buxton.[45]

The estate of *COSYNS* or *COUSYNS*, sometimes called a manor, was held in the reign of Henry VI by John Hotoft.[46] His widow Joan had it at her death in 1445.[46] With Waters Place it was settled on Lord Parr and his wife Anne in 1542,[47] and descended to Ralph Baesh, who died seised of it. In the survey of his lands it is mentioned as the 'farm called Cosyns.'[48] The house now called Great Cousins, near Fanhams Hall, is the residence of Mr. Henry Page Croft, M.P., J.P.

BRAUGHYNS was the holding of another local family. Thomas Braughing was one of a number of grantees of land from Richard atte Water in 1444.[49] He or his son Thomas died seised of the 'manor called Braughyns' in 1490, leaving a son Thomas, aged forty.[50] There is no further trace of this estate as a manor.

In 1326 John de Hengham, clerk, granted all his tenements in the vill of Ware called *LE NEWEHALLE*,[51] viz. two messuages, 200 acres of land, 7 acres of meadow, 1½ acres of wood, to the Abbot and convent of Waltham Holy Cross,[52] to hold of the chief lords of the fee by the customary services. This estate remained in the possession of the convent until the Dissolution. Leases of it were granted to Nicholas le Blake in 1344 and 1365.[53] After the Dissolution it was granted (in 1543) under the name of the manor and tenement called Newhall, with two woods called Abbottes Gardeyn containing 1½ acres, and Tyle Wood, containing 3 acres, to Richard Andrewes and Nicholas Temple,[54] probably trustees, as they immediately alienated it to John Dodyngton.[55] He died seised of it in January 1544–5, leaving a son and heir John, aged twenty-two,[56] who conveyed it in 1548 to Thomas Thorogood.[57] No further trace of it has been found until 1783, when William Ward and Anna Maria Gardiner, spinster, conveyed it to William Leake.[58] The estate is now owned by Mrs. Croft of Fanhams Hall. The house and farm buildings are inclosed by a homestead moat, one side of which is now filled up.[58a]

The manor of *HALFHIDE* or *WESTMILL* is said to have been held by a family of Halfhide,[59] of whom a pedigree is given by Chauncy, who, moreover, wrongly identifies it with the Westmill held by Ralph de Tany in 1086.[60] In 1483 this manor was in the possession of Richard Bull and his wife Anne in right of Anne,[61] and they conveyed in that year to Robert Gobye and Thomas Bacon. In 1651 George Bromley was holding of it.[62] According to Chauncy, George son and heir of George Bromley sold it to Thomas Feltham, and it descended to Ralph Feltham, who was holding in 1722.[63] In 1743 Ralph Feltham conveyed the manor to Crowley and John Hallet,[64] trustees, apparently in trust for Thomas Hall,[65] whose brother and heir Humphrey Hall was holding in 1766.[66] It is said by Cussans to have been sold in 1770 to John Scott, the Quaker poet, and after the death of his daughter Maria de Horne Scott, who married Joseph Hooper,

---

[34] Cussans, op. cit. *Braughing Hund.* 143.
[35] G.E.C. *Peerage*, s.v. Essex.
[36] Feet of F. Div. Co. Hil. 33 Hen. VIII.
[37] G.E.C. *Peerage*.
[38] Pat. 5 Eliz. pt. ii, m. 20.
[39] Ibid. 13 Eliz. pt. x, m. 36.
[40] G.E.C. *Peerage*, s.v. Essex.
[41] Recov. R. 1572 Trin. m. 1018.
[42] Feet of F. Herts. East. 15 Eliz.
[43] Chan. Inq. p.m. (Ser. 2), ccliii, 81; Ct. of Wards, Feod. Surv. no. 17.
[44] Sess. R. (Herts. Co. Rec.), i, 76.
[45] Information from Mr. R. T. Andrews.
[46] Chan. Inq. p.m. 24 Hen. VI, no. 31.
[47] Feet of F. Herts. Hil. 33 Hen. VIII.
[48] See ref. under Waters Place.
[49] Anct. D. (P.R.O.), C. 3388.
[50] Chan. Inq. p.m. (Ser. 2), vi, 78.
[51] There was apparently also an Old Hall in Ware. The name survives as late as 1599, when presentment was made that the highway between Ware and Widford, near 'Old Hawle,' was very ruinous (*Sess. R.* [Herts. Co. Rec.], i, 30). There was also an Old Hall Mead south of Hartham in Hertford.
[52] Chan. Inq. a.q.d. file 184, no. 9; Cal. Pat. 1324–7, p. 277; Add. Chart. 17671, 17672.
[53] Add. Chart. 17678, 17681.
[54] *L. and P. Hen. VIII*, xviii (1), 981 (56).
[55] Ibid. 981 (64).
[56] Chan. Inq. p.m. (Ser. 2), lxxiv, 102.
[57] Feet of F. Herts. Hil. 1 Edw. VI.
[58] Ibid. Mich. 24 Geo. III.
[58a] See 'Moated houses, moats and remains of moats,' by R. T. Andrews, *Herts. Mercury*, 8 Nov. 1902.
[59] A John de Halfhide and Joan wife of Walter de Halfhide were assessed at Ware in 1307 (Subs. R. bdle. 120, no. 8). Alexander and Walter Halfhide were jurors in the inquisition on Blanche de Wake in 1380 (Chan. Inq. p.m. 4 Ric. II, no. 59).
[60] *Hist. Antiq. of Herts.* 209.
[61] Feet of F. Herts. 22 Edw. IV, no. 66. In 1452 there is a conveyance of a manor of Halfhide from John and Alice Shipton to Richard Merston (ibid. 30 Hen. VI, no. 157); but there is no proof that this manor was in Ware. Alice and Anne may, however, have been co-heirs.
[62] Ibid. Div. Co. East. 1651.
[63] Recov. R. Hil. 9 Geo. I, rot. 13.
[64] Feet of F. Herts. Hil. 17 Geo. II.
[65] Cussans, op. cit. *Braughing Hund.* 145.
[66] Recov. R. Mich. 7 Geo. III, rot. 29.

A HISTORY OF HERTFORDSHIRE

to have been sold by trustees to Robert Hanbury.[67] After Robert Hanbury's death in 1884 it descended to his son Mr. R. C. Hanbury, whose son Mr. E. S. Hanbury is the present owner. The manor-house of Westmill was near the Watton Road.[68]

On the foundation of the GREYFRIARS at Ware their house was endowed with 7 acres of land by Thomas Lord Wake,[69] and later Blanche Lady Wake granted them an additional 4 acres from the manor of Ware.[70] Probably other grants were made to them. After the Dissolution the site of the priory with the orchard, gardens, and ponds was farmed by Robert Birch for 20s. The 'osierhope' was farmed for 20d.[71] In 1544 the site and the 'osierhope' were granted to Thomas Birch, a yeoman of the Crown,[72] who died seised of these and of a messuage called the Sign of the Bear in 1550.[73] His grandson Thomas Birch sold the site and osierlands to Job Bradshaw in 1623.[74] The descent, as given by Cussans,[75] is that it passed from Bradshaw to Richard Hator, and in 1685 became the property of Robert Hadsley of Great Munden, whose son Robert died without issue, having bequeathed the estate to Jeremiah Rayment, who took the name of Hadsley. On his death in 1778 it passed to his widow for life, then to his daughter Maria Hadsley, on whose death in 1847 it devolved on Martin Hadsley Gosselin, son of Admiral Thomas Le Marchant Gosselin and Sarah daughter of Jeremiah Rayment. After Martin Gosselin's death in 1868 it was sold by his widow to Clement Morgan of St. John's Wood, London. Later it was bought by Mr. J. Gwyn Jeffreys, the conchologist, on his retirement from the practice of law. While he lived there it was a meeting-place for many British and foreign artists. He was J.P. for Hertford and sheriff of the county in 1877. After the death of his wife he moved to Kensington and in 1881 sold the priory to Mr. Robert Walters, J.P., the present owner.[76]

HANBURY. *Or a bend engrailed vert plain cotised sable.*

The house, which is a residence of two floors with attics, lying a little to the south of the church, is constructed out of nearly the whole of the southern range of the cloisters of the Franciscan friary, not quite half of the western range, and the great hall which runs westward at right angles to the western range. A small two-storied wing projects on the south side of the south range. The rubble walls of the house are plastered and have stone dressings; the roofs are tiled. Nothing earlier than late 15th-century work survives. The modern additions are of brick and timber plastered.

In the south-west angle of the cloisters, which were about 8 ft. wide, a modern porch has been erected, which forms, with the two ends of the cloisters, the present entrance hall of the house.

The south wall of the southern range, on the ground floor of which is the drawing room, is not original. On the first floor of this range are bedrooms formed out of the ancient frater. The small wing projecting southward contains a smoking room on the ground floor and bedrooms above. The modern staircase is at the western end of the southern range, and beyond it are the kitchens and offices. On the ground floor of the western range is the dining room with bedrooms above. The undercroft of the great hall is now occupied by six rooms and a corridor. The hall over it, measuring 48 ft. by 22 ft., was in four bays with an open timber roof.[76a] Above the rooms now occupying this space are attics formed by the insertion of a floor at the level of the old tie-beams. The north side of the southern range has six of the original cloister windows of three cinquefoiled lights, but these have been much altered, and some of them are blocked. In the northern range only two of the cloister windows remain; one of them, which lights the dining room, has been almost entirely renewed. The end window in this and the southern range having had their tracery removed are now arches between the modern porch and the entrance hall. One other window in this part of the house is old, but it is now blocked. It is on the west side of the kitchen, between it and the modern pantry where its external label shows. In the hall wing are six original windows of detail like those of the cloisters; all have been plastered and restored. One is on each floor on the south side of the wing, three are on the upper floor of the north side; one on this side is so considerably above the ground floor level that it has the appearance of an old stairway window. The rest of the windows of the house are modern, those on the north side of the hall wing being imitations of the original windows. Of the thin ashlar buttresses which divided this wing into four bays four remain, three on the south and one on the north side. The inside of the house has been so greatly altered that little original work is visible. There is, however, a 15th-century doorway in the south-west corner of the cloisters, a little niche survives in the north-east corner of the hall, an old doorway, now blocked, is in the cross wall of the undercroft, and most of the roof timbers about the house appear to be old.

The houses of Holy Trinity, London, St. Paul's, St. Helen's Within Bishopsgate, and Bermondsey, also had lands in the parish.[77]

CHURCHES

The church of ST. MARY stands in the middle of the town. It consists of chancel 40 ft. 6 in. by 23 ft., south chapel 25 ft. by 15 ft. 6 in., vestry and organ chamber on the north, north and south transepts, each 23 ft. by 22 ft., nave 78 ft. by 22 ft., north and south aisles, each 13 ft. wide, west tower 15 ft. square and south porch, all internal dimensions. The walls are of flint with stone dressings, the roofs are lead covered.

The church, consisting of chancel, nave and transepts, was probably erected in the 13th century; the

---

[67] Cussans, loc. cit.
[68] Information from Mr. R. T. Andrews; C. E. Dawes, *Records of Ware*, 19.
[69] *Cal. Pat.* 1338–40, p. 14.
[70] Chan. Inq. a.q.d. file 378, no. 9.
[71] Mins. Accts. Hen. VIII, no. 1617; 32 & 33 Hen. VIII, no. 71, m. 2.

[72] *L. and P. Hen. VIII*, xix (1), 610 (68).
[73] Chan. Inq. p.m. (Ser. 2), xc, 124.
[74] Com. Pleas D. Enr. Hil. 4 Chas. I, m. 5 d.
[75] Op. cit. Braughing Hund. 154.

[76] *Dict. Nat. Biog.*
[76a] For the roof see *The Builder*, vii, 342 (21 July 1849).
[77] Anct. D. (P.R.O.), A 5441; *Hist. MSS. Com. Rep.* ix, App. i, 70a; Mins. Accts. bdle. 1107, no. 11; *Cal. Pat.* 1391–6, p. 156.

392

west tower and perhaps the nave aisles were built about the middle of the 14th century; the south chapel dates from the close of the 14th century; the clearstory was added about 1410, and the nave arcades appear to have been rebuilt at the same time, and probably also the south porch and the old vestry, now part of the organ chamber; the rest of the organ chamber occupies a chapel built late in the 15th century between the old vestry and the north transept. During the 19th century the present vestry was partitioned off and the whole of the external stonework renewed and a great deal of stonework internally.

The five-light traceried east window of the chancel is modern. In the north wall is a 15th-century doorway opening into the vestry, with continuous mouldings to arch and jambs, with carved heads inserted at the springing of the arch. The oak door is original, but has been painted; the door had originally three stock locks of oak, one of which is still in position and another is in the vestry cupboard. To the west of the doorway is a coarsely moulded arch of late 15th-century work opening into the organ chamber. In the south wall is a modern three-light window. Adjoining it is a large round-headed arch, subdivided beneath into two lancet arches resting on a central shaft of Purbeck marble; the arches are well moulded and the spandrels of the inner arches are filled with tracery. The central shaft is composed of four grouped shafts separated by hollows; the work is of the late 14th century. Part of a 13th-century window still remains to the east of the arch. The chancel arch is of two moulded orders, the outer one continuous, the inner one carried on grouped shafts with moulded capitals and bases; it appears to have been rebuilt in the early part of the 15th century. The 15th-century clearstory has three windows on each side, of two cinquefoiled lights, much of which is modern stonework. On the south side of the chancel is a 15th-century piscina with moulded jambs and arch under a square head. The chancel roof is modern.

In the east wall of the south chapel is a five-light traceried window, and in the south wall are two three-light windows, all of which are of modern stonework. In the south wall is a late 14th-century cinquefoil-headed piscina, which has been restored. Adjoining it is a sedile with cinquefoiled head; the moulded label forms an ogee arch over piscina and sedile.

The nave has north and south arcades of five bays; those opening into the transepts are wider and loftier than the others. Both the eastern angles of the nave are splayed to receive the doorways to the stairs—of which there are two—to the rood-loft and roof above. Both turrets are carried well above the roof and are finished with embattled parapets. The north turret has still the lower and roof doorways, but that to the rood-loft is blocked; the south turret doorways are blocked. The arches of the arcades are of two moulded orders, the outer being continuous, the inner carried on shafted jambs with moulded capitals and bases. On each side of the nave are four clearstory windows, each of three lights under a segmental arch, but most of the stonework is modern, only the inner jambs and arches being original. The roof belongs to the 15th century, but has been restored; the trusses have traceried spandrels, supported on stone corbels carved with half-figures of saints or apostles. There are some heraldic shields as bosses at the intersection of the timbers.

In the north wall of the north transept is a large five-light traceried window, nearly all of which is of modern stonework; the inner jambs are original and have an early 14th-century wave moulding with stops.

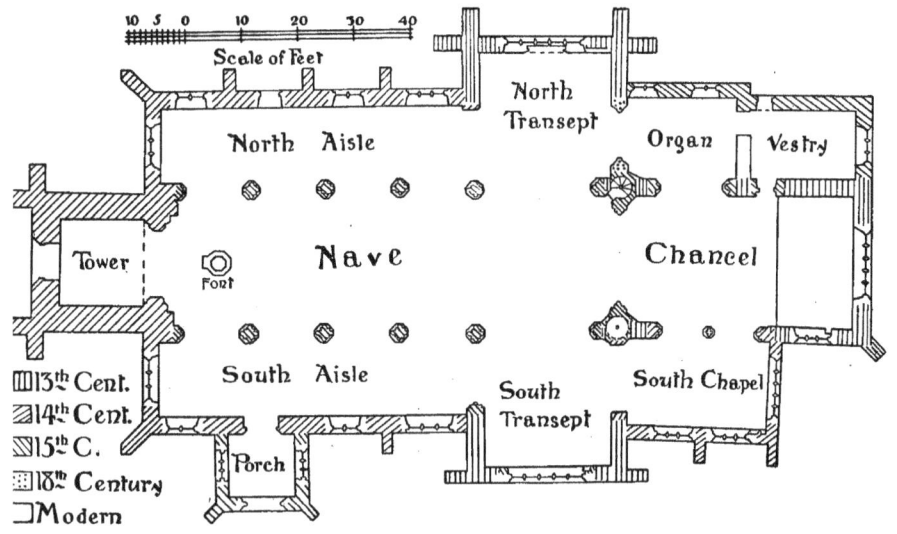

PLAN OF WARE CHURCH

Beneath the window are two recesses; the first is about 3 ft. 6 in. in width, 2 ft. 7 in. to the springing of the arch, and 3 ft. from the floor. The arch is segmental and cinquefoiled with leaf sub-cuspings. Over the arch is an ogee crocketed label with head stops and foliated finial. The jambs are shafted with carved capitals and moulded bases. Part is much decayed. It may possibly have once formed a reredos over an altar in the east wall. The other recess is 6 ft. 3 in. wide with moulded jambs and segmental arch; this was probably a recess for a tomb. Both recesses are of 15th-century work. An 18th-century arch in the east wall opens into the organ chamber, and opposite is an arch of two chamfered orders opening into the north aisle. The clearstory is modern.

The five-light window in the south wall of the south transept is of modern stonework, all but the inner jambs and rear arch, which have a 15th-century double ogee moulding. A late 14th-century arch with two chamfered orders opens into the south chapel, and on the west side is a plain arch opening into the south aisle. In the south wall is a small piscina with a moulded cinquefoiled arch of the 14th century; there is no bowl, and the mouldings are much decayed. The clearstory is modern.

The three side windows and the west one of each aisle are all of modern stonework, as are also the north doorway and the windows and archway to the south porch; the south doorway is of 14th-century work, repaired. The roofs of aisles and south porch retain many of their original 15th-century timbers.

The west tower is of five stages with buttressed angles, with embattled parapet and small lead-covered spire. The tower arch is of three hollow-chamfered orders, with splayed jambs having moulded capitals and bases; it is of the 14th century. The west doorway is of modern stonework, and above it is a window with two cinquefoiled lights. The third stage has narrow loop-lights on three of its faces; the fourth stage has a window of two trefoiled lights on the north and east faces and clocks on the other two. On each side of the belfry is a window of two cinquefoiled lights with cusped opening in the head.

The font is a fine example of the work of about 1380; the bowl is octagonal, and each side has a sunk and moulded arched panel with crocketed label and contains a figure in high relief. The figures represent the Annunciation (two panels), St. Margaret, St. Christopher, St. George, St. Katherine, St. James and St. John the Baptist; at each angle are half figures of angels, four with emblems of the Passion and four with musical instruments; behind each angle is a crocketed pinnacle. Each face of the stem has a square quatrefoiled panel; the base is moulded and is enriched with a running floral ornament.

The oak pulpit is of the late 17th century; it is hexagonal with raised lozenge-shaped panels flanked by beaded pilasters. The oak screen under the western arch of the chapel is partly modern, but has some good 15th-century tracery. In the south chapel are some carved panelling of the late 17th century and the communion rail (c. 1640) formerly in Benington Church.

On the east wall of the north transept is a brass with the figure of a lady with inscription to Helen daughter of John Cook, 1454, and also to her two husbands William Bramble and Richard Warburton, and her son William Bramble. In the south transept is a brass of William Pyrry (Pery) and his two wives with inscription and portion of date 147–; below each wife are five sons and five daughters. On the north transept floor are the brass of a lady without inscription, but c. 1420, a slab with indents of a civilian and his wife under a canopy, c. 1400, and a slab with indent of a floreated cross of the 14th century, said to be from an altar tomb formerly in the north transept. On the east wall of the south transept is a large marble monument to Sir Richard Fanshawe, bart., 1666; he was ambassador to Spain in the reign of Charles II. In the south chapel is a monument to Agnes wife of Sir Richard Fanshawe, 1680.

There are eight bells: the treble by R. Phelps, 1735; the second and sixth by T. Mears, 1826; the third and fifth by J. Briant, 1792; the fourth and seventh by R. Phelps, 1731; the eighth by T. Mears, 1834.

The communion plate consists of a cup, 1618, paten, 1806, small cup, 1806, two modern chalices and patens, a spoon, a Sheffield plate paten, 1755.

The registers are in six books as follows: (i) all entries 1577 to 1653; (ii) all 1653 to 1730; (iib) burials 1678 to 1706; (iii) baptisms and burials 1730 to 1776, marriages 1730 to 1754; (iv) baptisms and burials 1776 to 1812; (v) marriages 1754 to 1764; (vi) marriages 1764 to 1812.

CHRIST CHURCH consists of chancel, nave, north and south aisles, porches and tower with spire, containing one modern bell, and is built of stone in the style of the 13th century. The living is in the hands of trustees.

HOLY TRINITY, Wareside, is a small building of white brick with stone facings, in the 12th-century style, consisting of apsidal chancel and nave, transepts and north tower containing one bell. The advowson belongs to the vicar of Ware.

ADVOWSON Hugh de Grentmesnil, who founded the monastery of St. Evroul in Normandy, gave the church of Ware and the chapel of Thundridge with the tithes and 2 carucates of land to the monks there.[78] This grant was confirmed by Robert Fitz Parnel Earl of Leicester, who granted also the whole tithe from the park, viz. of sales [of wood], pannage, herbage, stud, hunting, and of all crops and profits, and the tithe of food from his kitchen at Ware, the tithe also of all sheep, lamb's wool, cheeses, young of geese, poultry and sheep, and of wine belonging to the earl and countess.[79] The church was attached to the priory of Ware founded as a cell to St. Evroul. A vicarage was ordained before 1231, when, a dispute having arisen between the parishioners and the Prior of Ware, who had not seen to the proper serving of the church, the matter was referred to the pope, who appointed Roger [Niger] Bishop of London and the Dean of St. Paul's to arbitrate. The prior had to quitclaim a pension of 10 marks which he had been trying to make the vicar pay, whilst it was settled that if this pension were ever again claimed by a prior the vicar was to claim the tithes of all mills in Ware and Thundridge, the tithes of the park, and of sheaves from certain specified portions of arable land. The vicar was to have the small tithes and tithes of wood

---

[78] Dugdale, *Mon.* vi, 1049.   [79] *Cal. Doc. of France* (ed. Round), 229.

Ware Church: The Font, East Face

Ware Church: The Font, West Face

and the 'priest's messuage' and garden which had been the prior's.[80]

At the Taxation of 1291 the church was valued at £40 and the vicarage at £2 13s. 4d.[81] The advowson was often in the king's hands together with the other temporalities of the priory by reason of wars with France.[82] On the suppression of alien priories it was granted by Henry V to the Carthusian monastery of Sheen.[83] It was farmed out by the monks for £40.[84] After the Dissolution the rectory and advowson of the vicarage and all lands belonging were granted by Henry VIII to Trinity College, Cambridge,[85] with whom they have since remained, Trinity College being now the lord of the rectory manor.

The church is mentioned as a collegiate church in 1504,[86] but there seems to be no evidence as to when the college was formed. Master Edward Haseley was dean of the college at that date.

The chantry of Helen Bramble was founded in 1470. Helen Bramble, whose brass is in the north transept of the church, was the daughter of John and Margery Cook and married first William Bramble and secondly Richard Warburton of London. By her will proved 9 September 1454 she desired to be buried in the parish church of Ware next the tomb of Margaret her mother. She left 12d. to the clerk and 12d. to the sub-clerk or sacrist, 5 marks to the fabric of the church, and after several other bequests the rest of her property to works of charity and the repair of altars.[87] The chantry was founded by Brian Roucliff, baron of the Exchequer, and John Marchall. Mass was to be celebrated at the altar in the chapel of St. Mary for the present and future kings of England, for Brian and John and Master William Graunger, and for the souls of Helen, her two husbands, of William Bramble her son, and of her parents. The chantry was endowed with lands to the value of £10.[88] Thomas Beal left 3s. 4d. to the repair of the chantry by his will proved in 1506,[89] and lands were left to its use by Richard Shirley (will proved 1510).[90] When the chantry was dissolved in the reign of Edward VI it had rents accruing to it from the inns called the 'Cardinal's Hat' in Amwell and the 'Bull's Head,' a tenement in the Myddel Row with a garden in Kybislane, a tenement called Wodehouse in Gardiner Lane and a croft called Sowrecroft, amounting to £9 14s. 8d. and goods and ornaments valued at 7s. 4d.[91] The chantry priest's chamber was granted in 1549 to Sir John Perient and Thomas Reve.[92] At this time the serving of the church fell entirely on the chantry priest and the curate hired by the vicar, although the parish contained at least 1,200 inhabitants.[93] This led to the inhabitants appointing a 'morrow mass priest,' whose wages were collected from among them, some giving 2d., some 4d. and some 8d., according to their devotion; if a sufficient sum was not collected the deficit was made up from the common fund.[94]

There were at least two gilds or brotherhoods in the church, the brotherhood of Jesus and the brotherhood of Corpus Christi. Bequests to these date from about 1490.[95] Thomas Ware, whose will was proved in 1505, left a brass pot of four gallons, a brass pan and three spoons of silver to the latter fraternity.[96] The brotherhood of Jesus had an alderman and four masters; it met every year on the feast of Jesus, when the masters rendered their account to the alderman and brethren, and a new alderman and masters were chosen. This gild was entirely dependent on the voluntary gifts of inhabitants of the town and strangers; these gradually decreased in value, and the gild was dissolved about 1525. Its possessions then included a large brass pot, a little silver cup for wine, twelve silver spoons, and three velvet coats embroidered with gold for the image of Jesus in the church.[97]

There was also an obit founded by William Kinge (date unknown), which at the Dissolution was maintained by a yearly sum of 10s. paid by Thomas Kinge, of which 6s. was paid to the poor.[98]

St. Joseph's Roman Catholic Church, founded by the late Mr. Constantine Ketterer and served from Hertford, is in Church Street. The registrations by the archdeacon of early Nonconformist meeting-places are lost, but a number of registrations before the magistrates are recorded from 1672 onwards.[99] There are now two Congregational chapels, one in Church Street, built in 1778, and representing a cause dating from 1662, and the other, in High Street, founded in 1811 and rebuilt in 1859. In the New Road are a Wesleyan [100] and a Baptist chapel. The Salvation Army have quarters in Baldock Street built in 1907. A place of meeting was certified for Quakers in 1699,[1] but the Meeting House, which was in Kibes Lane, fell into disuse after the death of Mrs. Hooper (daughter of John Scott), who was its chief supporter.[2] In the hamlet of Wareside is a Wesleyan Methodist chapel.

CHARITIES The history of the Free School and Wareside School has already been traced.[3]

The combined charities are regulated by a scheme of the Charity Commissioners dated 26 January 1909. They comprise:

1. Almshouses of Lawrence Armatridinge.—These consist of five tenements in Crib Street inhabited by ten poor women. The date of foundation is unknown, but an old benefaction table in the church dated 5 July 1722 records that Lawrence Armatridinge gave twenty twopenny loaves of bread to twenty widows out of the rent of these five tenements.

2. The Bell Close.—An indenture of feoffment dated 20 March 1612 recites that a donor unknown

---

[80] Lond. Epis. Reg. Gilbert, fol. 169, 170.
[81] *Pope Nich. Tax.* (Rec. Com.), 14.
[82] *Cal. Pat.* 1334-8, p. 519; 1381-5, pp. 364, 384; 1405-8, p. 184.
[83] Pat. 3 Hen. V, pt. ii, m. 30.
[84] *Valor Eccl.* (Rec. Com.), ii, 53.
[85] Pat. 38 Hen. VIII, pt. vi, m. 19; see Pat. 3 Jas. I, pt. xvii.
[86] P.C.C. Will, 8 Holgrave.
[87] P.C.C. 1 Stokton.
[88] *Cal. Pat.* 1467-77, p. 420.
[89] P.C.C. 10 Adeane.
[90] Ibid. 29 Bennett.
[91] Chant. Cert. 27, no. 6; Aug. Off. Misc. Bks. lxvii, fol. 726.
[92] Pat. 3 Edw. VI, pt. vii, m. 8.
[93] Chant. Cert. 27, no. 6.
[94] Aug. Off. Misc. Bks. xiv, fol. 127.
[95] P.C.C. 22 Horne; 17 Bennet; 13 Ayloffe; 25 Porch; 24 Milles; 5 Dogett; 6 Vox; 4 Adeane.
[96] Ibid. 4 Adeane.
[97] Aug. Off. Misc. Bks. xiv, fol. 127 et seq.
[98] Chant. Cert. 27, no. 51.
[99] Urwick, op. cit. 718.
[100] See Close, 27 Geo. III, pt. xxix, no. 3.
[1] Urwick, loc. cit.
[2] Dawes, *Records of Ware*, 19.
[3] See *V.C.H. Herts.* ii, 83.

gave the Bell Close, containing about 4 acres, for the benefit of the poor. This produces £27 10s. yearly.

3. James Birch's Almshouses.—The benefaction table also records that James Birch gave two almshouses near the north gate of the churchyard for the dwelling of two poor widows. The inmates are in receipt of parochial relief.

4. Charity of Ellen Bridge, founded by deed dated in 1628, consists of a garden formerly known as Pope's or Doulton's Pightle situate in Watton Road and producing £10 yearly.

5. John Burr's Charity, founded by will dated in 1814, whereby testator gave £400 3 per cent. Bank annuities, now a like sum of consols, producing £10 yearly, the interest to be distributed to poor widows in sums not exceeding 2s. 6d. each.

6. Corpus Christi Barn.—The indenture of feoffment of 1612 above referred to also recites that a donor unknown gave to the poor a piece of ground whereon formerly stood a barn called Corpus Christi Barn.

7. Hellum or Elm Green Almshouses.—A deed of feoffment dated in 1788 recites that two almshouses were given by a donor unknown. These are inhabited by four widows who receive parochial relief.

8. Paul Hogge's Charity.—The origin of this charity is unknown, but a rent-charge of 6s. 8d. is paid out of a close called Hogg's Close in Great Amwell.

9. Mill Lane Almshouses.—The indenture of 1612 further recites that a donor unknown gave two almshouses in Mill Lane. The property now consists of eight almshouses in Mill Lane with garden ground in the rear let for £2 15s. yearly.

10. Sir William Roberts's Charity.—By a feoffment dated 8 April 1788 it appears that Sir William Roberts gave three almshouses in Mill Lane and pasture land known as Widow's Mead and Mill Mead containing 8 a. 3 r. 3 p. and producing £22 yearly. The rents are divided among the inmates.

11. The 'Saracen's Head.'—The indenture of 1612 further recites that a donor unknown gave a messuage or inn called the 'Saracen's Head' together with a piece of land called the Netherhoe to the poor. The land was sold in 1891 and the proceeds invested in £247 6s. 8d. consols. The stock has since been increased to £276 2s. 10d. by the investment of balance of premium on lease of the 'Saracen's Head.' The 'Saracen's Head' is let for £130 per annum and the stock produces £6 18s. yearly.

12. Charity of Humphrey Spencer, founded by will dated 26 June 1630, consists of a cottage in Kibes Lane producing £9 2s. yearly.

13. The White Hart Estate.—The indenture of 1612 further recites that a donor unknown gave a messuage or inn called the 'White Hart' with appurtenances. The 'White Hart' was pulled down many years ago, and the property now consists of two shops in High Street, Ware, producing £88 yearly and a slaughter-house producing £20 yearly.

14. Charity of Frederick Harrison, founded by will proved in London 8 June 1907.—The property consists of two almshouses erected on a part of the Bell Close called the Harrison Almshouses and £94 13s. 5d. New South Wales 3½ per cent. stock (1924), £400 Great Northern Railway 3 per cent. preference stock, 1898, and £200 London and South Western Railway 3½ per cent. preference stock, producing altogether yearly £22 6s. 2d. and called the Harrison Fund.

It appears there are fourteen almshouses in Crib Street under the control of the trustees of the combined charities, including the almshouses of Lawrence Armatridinge and James Birch.

The scheme directs that the Harrison almspeople shall be two married couples and each couple shall receive a stipend of not less than 7s. 6d. or more than 10s. weekly. In the case of a couple possessing a properly secured income from other sources the trustees may pay a smaller stipend, provided that the total income shall not be less than 7s. 6d. a week.

The remaining income of the charities is directed to be applied in the payment of pensions of not less than 5s. weekly and for the general benefit of the poor, subject, however, to the continuance for ten years after the date of the scheme of certain accustomed payments which have been made for a period of at least three years next before the date of the scheme.

For the year ended 31 March 1911 the widows in the almshouses received £24 13s. 6d., eighty widows received 2s. 6d. each (John Burr's Charity), 211 recipients received £121 amongst them, two pensions at 2s. a week for thirty-five weeks, and £23 5s. was paid in stipends in respect of the Harrison bequest.

In 1619 George Mead, M.D., by his will gave £5 yearly issuing out of the George Inn, Ware, to the poor. This payment is now received out of a house in High Street, Ware, called Riverslea, and there is a sum of £133 16s. 3d. consols, representing accumulations and producing £3 6s. 8d. yearly. The income is distributed to poor housekeepers, £6 10s. being distributed among five recipients in 1908.

In 1622 John Elmer by his will gave a house afterwards called Baldock House for the benefit of the poor of Ware and Stevenage. The property was sold in 1906, and the part of the proceeds applicable to Ware invested in £414 7s. 3d. consols, producing £10 7s. yearly, which is distributed among the poor of St. Mary's parish, Christ Church parish, and Wareside. In 1908 the sums of £5 5s., £3 10s. and £1 15s. were distributed in the respective parishes.

In 1722 Dame Margaret Tufton by her will gave £260, the interest to be applied in coats to six poor men and gowns to six poor women once every two years and in teaching four boys and four girls to read and write and say the catechism.

In 1749 Anne Ball by her will gave £40 to be applied to the same purposes as Dame Margaret Tufton's bequest.

These legacies were invested in £286 8s. 3 per cent. Bank annuities, now a like sum of consols.

Under an Order of the Charity Commissioners dated 26 July 1904 a sum of £160 consols was placed to a separate account to form Tufton and Ball's Educational Foundation. The dividends on this sum, amounting to £4 yearly, are paid to the managers of the Ware National Schools.

The residue of £126 8s. consols forms the endowment of Tufton and Ball's Eleemosynary Charity, and the income, amounting to £3 3s. yearly, is applied every two years in overcoats for six old men and material for dresses to six old women.

In 1739 Mary Evans by her will gave £100, now represented by £110 9s. 11d. consols, producing £2 15s.

yearly, the income to be distributed in sums of 5*s.* to poor widows.

In 1825 William Murvell by his will gave £300, the dividends arising therefrom to be applied in the upkeep of testator's monument and the residue, together with the interest on £100, in the relief of five poor women of sixty years and upwards. These two sums were invested in consols, and are now represented by £499 12*s.* 8*d.* India 3 per cent. stock, producing £14 19*s.* 8*d.* yearly.

The same testator gave £666 13*s.* 4*d.* consols, the interest arising therefrom to be applied in the relief of six poor men of sixty years and upwards. This stock is now represented by £660 13*s.* 10*d.* India 3 per cent. stock, producing £19 16*s.* 4*d.* yearly. In 1907 £2 2*s.* was spent on the monument and £30 5*s.* 10*d.* was distributed among six men and five women.

The Parish Clerk's Charity.—Four acres of land in Wainges Field, Ware, have been appropriated from time immemorial to the use of the parish clerk, being the gift of a donor unknown. The land is let for £13 yearly, which sum is paid to the parish clerk.

The Nursing Fund.—Frederick Harrison above mentioned likewise bequeathed £200, the interest arising therefrom to be applied in aid of the Ware Parish Church Nursing Fund. The endowment is now represented by £213 15*s.* 5*d.* India 3½ per cent. stock, producing £7 9*s.* 8*d.* yearly in dividends.

In 1857 Charles Brunton, by his will proved in P.C.C. 9 May, bequeathed £100, the interest to be divided equally between and amongst all widows of the Upland division of Ware annually on 1 January. The legacy was invested in £109 17*s.* 10*d.* 3 per cent. annuities, now a like sum of consols, producing £2 14*s.* 8*d.* yearly.

The several sums of stock above mentioned are held by the official trustees.

The Old Independent Chapel endowment consists of two houses in New Road, Ware, known as Cambridge Villa and Hope Villa, which are stated to have been purchased with bequests of Diminsdell in 1759, Hannah Tew in 1838 and Mrs. Flack. The houses produce £50 yearly, and of this £37 is paid to the minister and the remainder is applied in the upkeep of the houses.

WESTMILL

Westmele, Westmel (xi and xii cent.); Westmelne,[1] Westmill, Westmelle (xiii cent.); Westmylne, Westmulle (xiv cent.).

Westmill including Wakeley (which was formerly an extra-parochial liberty of Aspenden (q.v.) and was added to Westmill by Local Government Board Order in 1883) is a parish of 2,663 acres of land, of which about three-quarters at a rough estimation are arable. The River Rib runs through the parish and forms for a little way its eastern boundary, but the land for the most part lies high and the extent of meadow land has always been small; at the time of the Domesday Survey there was enough for six plough-teams only. The commons were inclosed by an award of 1819 under an Act of 1813.[1a] High Field, Hunsdon, Albury and Mill Field were among the common fields.[2] The chief patch of woodland in the parish is formed by Coles and Knights Hill with Millcroft on the east. Part of Hamells Park also lies in this parish on the south, but the house is in the parish of Braughing. The Buntingford branch of the Great Eastern railway has a station in the village.

Westmill is intersected on the east by Ermine Street. In 13th-century deeds this road is alluded to as Erningstrat, Hernigstrate, the mediaeval forms of Ermine Street, and also as Stanstrate.[3] In 1729 two Roman *amphorae* were found in Lemonfield (Lemannsfeld, xiv cent.).

It is not possible now to locate the mill from which the parish took its name. There were three mills in 1086, but there are now none surviving within the bounds of the parish. Millcroft Wood and Upper and Lower Mill Field must, however, have taken their name from a mill in their neighbourhood.[4] Among the early place-names in the parish were Burgcys, Aldburg, Adthelingo, Staplys,[5] Mannefeld,[6] Mannemad,[7] Tunmannemade[8] and Tounhallefeld.[9] Of these the only one that seems to survive is Auldbury or Albury, the name of a field (formerly a common field) to the north-west of Millcroft Wood, near the river. Other names frequently occurring in 13th-century deeds are Admundeslane, Rogeneyehefeld or Ruwenhofeld, Lindley, Dedemannesot, Pandulveswelle, Pekeswellemed,[10] Purtewellehul, Sudpurtewelle, and a wood called Albertisgrave. None of these names seem to survive.[10a] Lands called Hammondes in 1521[11] were so named after a family of Hamond, whose name occurs constantly in wills, deeds, inquisitions, &c., of the 15th, 16th and 17th centuries.[12] This family has died out in Westmill since the beginning of the 19th century.[13] Another local family who have left their name in a field called after them are the Chipereviles or Chiperfields, who can be traced back to the 13th century.[14] John Chiperfield, by will of 1507, bequeathed 10*s.* to building a 'church house' in the churchyard.[15] Among the place-names still surviving in the parish are Great and Little Ridgeway Field to the south of the road leading to Westmill Green, Norwich Grove and Close to the north-east of Coles, Allen's Mead near Westmill Lodge, and Church Field to the north of the church.[16]

---

[1] The form with the 'n' is the Norman spelling of the name.
[1a] *Blue Bk. Incl. Awards*; Priv. Act, 53 Geo. III, cap. 72.
[2] Information from Mr. T. T. Greg of Coles.
[3] Anct. D. (P.R.O.), A 10415, 5229, 5251. Tenants of the manor called Atte Strate appear in Court Rolls of the 13th century.
[4] 'Melefield' occurs in a 13th-century deed (Anct. D. [P.R.O.], C 2613).
[5] Mins. Accts. bdle. 873, no. 3, 4, 5.
[6] Anct. D. (P.R.O.), A 1078, 1072.
[7] Ibid. A 5251.
[8] Ibid. A 5229, 968.
[9] Chan. Inq. p.m. 1 Ric. II, no. 163.
[10] Land here was given to the church by Alice de Overton for lights and masses (Anct. D. [P.R.O.], A 1083; A 1077).
[10a] The present Portal Shot on the Coles estate may be a modern form of Purtewelle Shot.
[11] Will, P.C.C. 22 Maynwaryng.
[12] Early Chan. Proc. bdle. 206, no. 50; Anct. D. (P.R.O.), D 1074; Chan. Inq. p.m. (Ser. 2), cccxxviii, 110; P.C.C. 34 Bodfelde; 3 Logge.
[13] Information from Mr. T. T. Greg.
[14] See Anct. D. (P.R.O.), A 1185.
[15] P.C.C. 23 Adeane.
[16] Information from Mr. T. T. Greg.

The village of Westmill is situated on low ground near the River Rib, a little under half a mile to the west of Ermine Street, with which it communicates by roads running north-east and south-east. There is one main street in the village, which ends towards the east in a village green. The church of St. Mary is situated on the north side of this street and the old manor-house of Westmillbury (now a farm) on the south. The only inn in the village, the 'Sword in Hand' (probably so called from the crest of the Greg family), is an old house, which by local tradition was for a time the residence of the Scottish family of Bellenden. The second Lord Bellenden was a partisan of James II and was an exile in Holland. His son John, the third baron, was married at Radwell in Hertfordshire to Mary Parnell of Baldock, and came to live at Westmill, where eight of his children were born,[17] and where most of them were buried. Lord Bellenden died in 1741 and was succeeded by his eldest son Ker, of the Royal Navy, who died at the age of twenty-seven. The tombs of the second baron and his wife and of the third baron and his eldest sister, Jane Miller, are in front of the altar in Westmill Church.[18] At the east end of the street, on the south side, are seven cottages built early in the 18th century by Samuel Pilgrim, who belonged to a family of Pilgrim or Pegram, who are well represented in the parish at the present day.[19] Kent's Corner, to the back of these cottages (now being pulled down), preserved the name of the Kent family (see charities). Opposite the church is a cottage called the Woolpack. A barn which adjoins the church and forms a prominent feature of the village when viewed from the west may occupy the site of a sheepfold and threshing-floor mentioned in the 13th century.[20] At right angles to the main street on the west runs the road to Aspenden, in which is the public elementary school built about 1829.[21]

Wakeley (see under Aspenden) forms a roughly triangular-shaped projection on the west of the parish; the hamlet, which is about 2 miles from Westmill village, consists of a farm and a few cottages and the site of the church of St. Giles.

Half a mile south of the village is Coles, the property and residence of Mr. T. T. Greg, J.P. This includes three separate estates, Knight's Hill, Coles, and Tillers End, which were copyhold of the manor of Westmill. The house was rebuilt about 1847 in the Elizabethan style, and has a park of about 140 acres.

A house called Button Snap at Westmill Green,[22] about a mile and a half south-west of the village, is of interest as having belonged for three years to Charles Lamb, the only landed property which he ever possessed. The house is thatched with straw and has diamond-paned windows. He relates that as he strode over his 'allotment of three quarters of an acre with its commodious mansion in the midst' he enjoyed for the first time the 'feeling of an English freeholder that all betwixt sky and centre' was his own. The property came to him from his uncle Francis Field of Holborn, the 'most gentlemanly of oilmen,' who bought it in 1779. His widow conveyed it in 1812 to Charles Lamb. The name Button Snap was probably given to it by Lamb, as it is not found before. In 1815 Lamb joined with his aunt in conveying it to Mr. Thomas Greg,[23] and so it passed 'into more prudent hands.' Cherry Green consists of a few cottages about a mile from the village. The name is evidently derived from a family of Cherry who had land here.[24]

Nathaniel Salmon (1675–1742), the historian and antiquary, was for some years a curate at Westmill. He resigned on the accession of Anne, to whom he refused to take the oath of allegiance, and practised as a doctor at St. Ives in Huntingdon and afterwards at Bishop's Stortford. Later he took to literature and published his *History of Hertfordshire* in 1728. He is said to have been buried at St. Dunstan's. A rector of Westmill of some fame was Henry Pepys, who was appointed to the living in 1827 and held it until he became Bishop of Sodor and Man in 1840. He was made Bishop of Worcester in the following year.

The Domesday Survey gives WEST-
MANORS MILL as being held in the time of
King Edward the Confessor by Achi, a thegn of Earl Harold, and in 1086 forming part of the lands of Robert Gernon, of whom it was held by Anschitil, probably Anschitil of Ware. It was assessed at 7 hides 1 virgate, and there were fourteen ploughs on it, four of which were on the demesne. Three mills are mentioned on the manor.[25] With the other estates of Robert Gernon, Westmill was acquired in the reign of Henry I by William de Montfitchet,[26] of whom it was held as one knight's fee by Ralph Fitz Haselin and Richard Westmel.[27] William was succeeded by Gilbert de Montfitchet, who paid £10 for the farm of Westmill for several years preceding 1165–6.[28] After that year until 1176–7 the farm is accounted for by the sheriffs among the purprestures and escheats.[29] Whether this is due to a forfeiture by Gilbert is not certain, but Richard de Montfitchet, who seems to have succeeded Gilbert in the latter part of the reign of Henry II, appears in possession,[30] and the *Testa de Nevill* gives this Richard or his son holding three and one-sixth fees in Westmill and Gatesbury.[31] The younger Richard died in 1258[32]; his lands were divided among his three sisters, Westmill probably falling to the share of Margery wife of Hugh de Bolebec. She left four daughters and heirs,[33] who probably conveyed Westmill to Robert Burnell, Bishop

---

[17] The two eldest were baptized at Walkern.
[18] J. A. Ewing, *The Story of the Bellendens*.
[19] Information from Mr. T. T. Greg.
[20] See Maisters in manorial descents. For architectural description see below under Westmill Manor.
[21] See Close, 9 Geo. IV, pt. lxxxvi, no. 4.
[22] The name Westmill Green is marked on the map, but does not seem to be well known locally. The green is mentioned in the 14th century (Mins. Accts. bdle. 873, no. 3).
[23] T. T. Greg, 'Charles Lamb as a landed proprietor' (*Athenaeum*, 5 Jan. 1901).
[24] John Cherry is the name of a tenant in the 15th century (Ct. R. [Gen. Ser.], portf. 178, no. 77).
[25] *V.C.H. Herts.* i, 324*b*.
[26] Cf. Ayot St. Peter in Broadwater Hund. and Stanstead Montfitchet in Essex.

[27] *Red Bk. of Exch.* (Rolls Ser.), i, 349.
[28] *Pipe R.* 8 *Hen. II* (Pipe R. Soc. v), 70, et annis seq.
[29] Ibid. 13 *Hen. II* (Pipe R. Soc. xi), 153, et annis seq.
[30] *Red Bk. of Exch.* (Rolls Ser.), ii, 498, 505, 731; i, 66, 78, 95, 141.
[31] *Testa de Nevill* (Rec. Com.), 269.
[32] Banks, *Dorm. and Extinct Peerage*, i, 140.
[33] See *Cal. Close*, 1272–9, p. 82.

BRAUGHING HUNDRED
WESTMILL

of Bath and Wells.[34] From Robert the fees descended to his nephew Philip,[35] and after his death were held in dower by his widow Maud.[36] The overlordship then probably followed the descent of Burnells in Stanstead Montfitchet, which became vested in the Earls of Oxford.[37]

Holding under the Montfitchets in the time of Henry II was a family named Zoing, Szuyn or Zon. In 1178 Hubert le Zoing paid 100 marks for seisin of Westmill, and his brother Jordan is mentioned in 1183.[38] In 1226 Geoffrey le Zoing received a grant of a market to be held at Westmill on Friday and a fair on the vigil and day of St. Lawrence.[39] After his death[40] his widow Amice granted the third part of lands and a messuage in Westmill, which she held in dower, to the Prior of Holy Trinity, London.[41] William le Zoing is mentioned as holding a knight's fee in Westmill and Gatesbury in 1274.[42] In 1284 John, son and heir of William le Zoing, granted the manor to Sir Thomas de Leukenore, kt., apparently in confirmation of a previous grant made by William.[43] This is probably the Thomas son of Sir Nicholas de Leukenore who appears in a number of deeds concerning lands in Westmill.[44] After this the history of the manor becomes rather confused. In 1293 Margery and Violet, daughters of William de Say, brought an action against John de Lovetot for the manor, which John claimed to hold for life of the grant of Thomas de Leukenore.[45] John de Leukenore was assessed for fees in Westmill in 1303,[46] and in 1311 a fine was levied between Walter de Huntingfield and John de Leukenore of 2 acres of land, an acre of meadow and the advowson of the church.[47] Possibly John de Leukenore was in debt and gradually parted with his lands, for in 1309 Aymer de Valence Earl of Pembroke had a grant of free warren for lands extending into Westmill,[48] and the next year Sir Walter de Huntingfield granted him pasturage for three cows in the pasture of Westmill and Braughing before Sir Aymer's gate in Westmill, 'as far as the river between the manors of Sir Aymer and John de Leukenore.'[49] It may have been the agents of John de Leukenore who in 1315, while the earl was fighting in the marches of Scotland, broke into his houses at Westmill at night and burnt them and his goods,[50] for, although the earl seems to have acquired the whole manor before 1324,[51] apparently John de Leukenore tried to retain his hold on it. In 1328 he was in mercy in an action brought against him by Mary widow of Aymer de Valence for two parts of the manor,[52] but after this he does not appear again except as in receipt of a pension of 40s. paid out of the manor.[53] The extent of the manor as held by the countess included a capital messuage, 515 acres of land, 22 acres of meadow, 16 acres of pasture, and a water-mill.[54] The countess at one time formed a plan for settling the reversion of the manors of Westmill, Meesden and Little Hormead on a Carthusian priory to be founded in one of these parishes,[55] but she afterwards altered her intention and gave the reversion after her death to the Cistercian abbey of St. Mary Graces by the Tower (founded by Edward III in 1349),[56] obtaining Letters Patent for the purpose in 1376.[57]

Westmill remained with the abbey until 1538, when it was conveyed by the abbey and convent to Sir Thomas Audley, Chancellor of England, to hold of the king by fealty and a rent of £3 4s.[58] Audley was the grantee of a great number of monastic lands, *inter alia* the monastery of Walden, co. Essex. In 1538 he was made Lord Audley of Walden, and died in 1544 at the priory of Holy Trinity, London. He left two daughters Mary and Margaret.[59] Mary died unmarried, Margaret married first Lord Henry Dudley, who died without issue in 1557, and secondly Thomas Howard, fourth Duke of Norfolk, who survived her and held the manor until his attainder in January 1571–2.[60] Westmill came to the Crown, but was restored to Thomas Lord Howard de Walden, his son by Margaret, who conveyed it as the manor of Westmill *alias* Westmill Bury to John Brograve in 1583.[61] The manor has since descended with Hamells in Braughing (q.v.).

Westmill Bury has been occupied as a farm since the beginning of the 18th century. It is a modern building, but has a large barn of pre-Reformation date. This barn is built of timber-framing on low walls of thin bricks; the sides are weather-boarded and the roof covered with thatch. The total length of the building covered by the long unbroken roof is about 237 ft., but one end of it is partitioned off from the present barn, which is 30 ft. wide internally and about 165 ft. in length, and is divided into ten bays; some of the timbers are carefully wrought and have splayed edges.

Another tenant holding under the Montfitchets in Westmill was a certain Nicholas le Mestere or Maystre, from whom the manor of *MAISTERS* took its name. Various deeds of his of the time of Henry III remain: one, by which he grants to Thomas de Leukenore, son and heir of Sir Nicholas, a sheepfold with threshing-floor and land by the churchyard of Westmill; another by which with Amabilia his wife he granted the same Thomas a rent of 10s.; and another by which he gave rent from land in 'Nethersuhtfeld,' 'Mannefeld' and Benham to the Prior of Holy Trinity, London.[62] Before 1303 his fee had passed to Richard de Gatesbury[63]

---

[34] See Ayot St. Peter and Stanstead Montfitchet in Morant, *Hist. and Antiq. of Essex*, ii, 576; *Cal. Close*, 1279–88, p. 57.
[35] Chan. Inq. p.m. 22 Edw. I, no. 45.
[36] *Cal. Close*, 1288–96, p. 463; *Abbrev. Plac.* (Rec. Com.), 258.
[37] Morant, op. cit. ii, 578.
[38] Pipe R. 24, 25, 26, 27, 28, 29 Hen. II, s.v. Essex and Herts. For Jordan see also Anct. D. (P.R.O.), A 5823, 5824.
[39] *Rot. Lit. Claus.* (Rec. Com.), ii, 129.
[40] He was living in 1234, when he was witness to a deed (Anct. D. [P.R.O.], A 1090).
[41] Anct. D. (P.R.O.), A 1084.
[42] *Cal. Close*, 1272–9, p. 82.
[43] De Banco R. 55, m. 112 d. (Mich. 12 & 13 Edw. I). See also Assize R. 6 Edw. I (Agard's MS. index, fol. 25*b*), which suggests that Nicholas father of Thomas may have previously held.
[44] Anct. D. (P.R.O.), C 2035; A 5219; C 1434. He may be the Thomas who is supposed to be buried in the church, the father of Nicholas, buried close by.
[45] De Banco R. 100, m. 42 d. (East. 21 Edw. I).
[46] *Feud. Aids*, ii, 434.
[47] Feet of F. Herts. 4 Edw. II, no. 64.
[48] Chart. R. 2 Edw. II, m. 8, no. 23.
[49] Anct. D. (P.R.O.), A 5220.
[50] *Cal. Pat.* 1313–17, p. 417.
[51] Mins. Accts. bdle. 873, no. 3.
[52] De Banco R. Mich. 2 Edw. III, m. 306 d.
[53] Mins. Accts. bdle. 873, no. 5.
[54] Chan. Inq. a.q.d. file 365, no. 18.
[55] Ibid.
[56] Dugdale, *Mon.* v, 717.
[57] Pat. 50 Edw. III, pt. ii, m. 16; *Cal. Pat.* 1429–36, p. 415; 1461–7, p. 162.
[58] *L. and P. Hen. VIII*, xiii (2), 967 (33), 969.
[59] Chan. Inq. p.m. (Ser. 2), cxxxvi, 100.
[60] Ibid. clxii, 167.
[61] Feet of F. Herts. East. 25 Eliz.; Com. Pleas D. Enr. Hil. 25 Eliz.
[62] Anct. D. (P.R.O.), C 1921; A 1334, 10415; see also A 9232.
[63] *Feud. Aids*, ii, 434.

399

A HISTORY OF HERTFORDSHIRE

of Gatesbury in Braughing. In 1317 Richard son of Richard de Gatesbury released to his lord Aymer de Valence Earl of Pembroke his right in a moiety of a mill, land and 4s. rent in Westmill.[64] This is, perhaps, the mill mentioned in the extent given above of Westmill Manor. The manor descended with Gatesbury (q.v.), and with that manor was divided between Joskyn and Elveden.

Joskyn's part came with one half of Gatesbury to Thomas Hanchett, who in 1584 conveyed it to John Brograve.[65] The other half came to Thomas Fitz Herbert, who conveyed it in 1588 to John Brograve,[66] after which the whole manor followed the descent of Hamells in Braughing (q.v.). The estate became amalgamated with Hamells, which in later documents is called Hamell-cum-Masters.[67]

The manor of *BARKESDEN*, which belonged to the Priory of Holy Trinity, London, lay partly in Aspenden and partly in Westmill.[68] The early history of this manor is treated under Aspenden (q.v.). In 1578 that part of the manor which lay in Westmill was separated from the rest of the manor and was sold by Edward Halfhyde and his wife Anne to John Brograve.[68a] He soon afterwards acquired Westmill *alias* Westmillbury, and the two manors have since become incorporated under the name of Westmill-cum-Barkesden.

Besides Robert Gernon's estate at Westmill in 1086 there were also 4 hides and 3 virgates there held by Ralph de Tany, and under him by 'Roger.' These had been held before the Conquest by Sexi, a house-carl of King Edward. In 1086 there was attached to them a virgate of land which a sokeman of Anschitil of Ware had held in the time of King Edward, and which formerly had not belonged to the manor. There were nine ploughs on the land, two of which were on the demesne, meadow for two plough-teams only, sufficient pasture, and woodland for sixty swine.[69] This estate descended with the Tany family. Luke de Tany in the reign of Henry III granted all the land in Westmill which he held from his granddaughter Amphelisa, daughter of Hugh de Marines, except an acre of meadow in Tunmannemade, to the convent of Holy Trinity.[70] The family of Marines held under the Tanys in Westmill, and many deeds of theirs are extant. The grantors include Gwerric de Marines and Hugh de Marines his brother, Hugh son of Gwerric, John and Theobald, brothers of Hugh, and Theobald son of Hugh.[71] Hugh de Marines, son of Gwerric, fell into debt, and mortgaged 15 acres of his demesne land in Westmill to Thomas de Nevill, Chancellor of Lichfield, for ten years,[72] and other lands there he mortgaged to certain Jews.[73] In 1275 he was presented for making a purpresture on the high road of half an acre.[74] About 1264 John de Marines, presumably John brother of Hugh, granted the manor of Westmill,

WESTMILL CHURCH FROM THE SOUTH-WEST

---

[64] Anct. D. (P.R.O.), C 322.
[65] Feet of F. Herts. Mich. 26 & 27 Eliz.
[66] Ibid. Hil. 31 Eliz.
[67] See Com. Pleas D. Enr. Mich. 7 Geo. IV, m. 20.
[68] Possibly it lay originally wholly in Aspenden and all the land in Westmill was added to it later. There are numerous grants to the priory of lands in Westmill about the 13th century (Anct. D. [P.R.O.], A 5214, 1070, 1069, 1085, 1093, 5215, 1082, 5230, 1076, 1080, 1087, 1358).
[68a] Pat. 21 Eliz. pt. vi, m. 29.
[69] *V.C.H. Herts.* i, 325a.
[70] Anct. D. (P.R.O.), A 5229, 1163. By a deed of 1247 Master Walter de Tany, Archdeacon of Nottingham, granted land in Stanstead to the Abbot of Waltham. This deed was witnessed by Lord Peter de Tany and Luke de Tany (Add. Chart. 35518). The relationship of these different members of the Tany family is not clear.
[71] See *Cal. of Anct. D. passim*; Cur. Reg. R. no. 39, m. 3 d. Their holding is here called the manor of Westmill.
[72] Anct. D. (P.R.O.), A 8907.
[73] Cott. MS. Nero, C. iii, fol. 194.
[74] *Hund. R.* (Rec. Com.), i, 191.

400

together with common of pasture in the demesne lands of Hugh de Marines, to Sir John le Moine, son of Sir Nicholas le Moine,[75] and by a later agreement John le Moine undertook to find food and clothing and all necessaries for John de Marines and his wife Amabilia in Moine's own house as long as Marines lived, Marines giving up his life interest in the estate.[76] Shortly afterwards John le Moine, called of Selford, granted his tenement and capital messuage in Westmill, with the rents of his tenants and two parts of the tithes from the demesne of the late Sir Hugh de Marines, to Holy Trinity, London,[77] and later it appears that Holy Trinity held these lands by the service of finding ' 1 *saccum cum una broch*' for Ralph de Tany, and that Ralph held the serjeanty of the king by providing one sergeant as often as the king should go with his army into Wales.[78] This estate probably became united with the rest of the lands of Holy Trinity in the parishes of Westmill and Aspenden.

TANY. *Or six eagles sable.*

The church CHURCH of ST. MARY consists of chancel 25 ft. by 15 ft., north vestry, nave 41 ft. 6 in. by 21 ft., north aisle 42 ft. 6 in. by 12 ft., south porch, west tower 14 ft. square; all the dimensions are internal. The church is built of flint rubble with stone dressings, and at the south-east angle of the nave is some long-and-short work; the roofs are tiled.

The plans of nave and chancel are probably pre-Conquest; the walls may be of the 13th century, as there are details of that period, and the north aisle was erected earlier in that century; the chancel arch has details of the middle of the 14th century, and the west tower is of late 15th-century work. The church was thoroughly repaired in 1875, the stonework of most of the windows renewed, a south porch and north vestry were added, the chancel and aisle were re-roofed, and all the walls but those of the tower refaced with flint.

The three-light traceried window in the east wall of the chancel is modern; a single lancet in the north wall and two in the south are of modern stonework. The south doorway is mainly modern, but the internal jambs are probably part of the original 14th-century work; above it is a narrow blocked single light with a square head of the 13th century, it shows as a recess externally. The 14th-century chancel arch is of two moulded orders, with a label on both sides of the wall; the jambs consist of three large engaged shafts with rolls between, and have moulded capitals and bases.

The south-east external angle of the nave is built of pre-Conquest long-and-short work, but the splayed plinth on which it stands is of later date; other long-and-short stones have been re-used in a buttress to the north aisle. The north arcade consists of two early 13th-century pointed arches with chamfered edges and having labels on both sides; between the arches is a wide rectangular pier with moulded abaci which vary slightly in the two arches, and which are cut flush with the face of the wall; beneath the abacus on the east respond is a small plain niche. A modern

WESTMILL CHURCH : THE NAVE LOOKING WEST

[75] Anct. D. (P.R.O.), A 1089.   [76] Ibid. 1075.   [77] Ibid. 6184.   [78] Assize R. 323 (6 Edw. I).

A HISTORY OF HERTFORDSHIRE

opening has been cut through the east end of the wall, and above it is the blocked doorway to the rood-loft. The three-light window and the doorway in the south wall are modern. The roof is probably of 15th-century date and is plain.

In the north wall of the aisle are two modern windows; in the west wall is a two-light window with modern mullions and tracery; the outer four-centred arch is of brick of the early 16th century with hollow-chamfered edge and label over.

The west tower is of three stages with embattled parapet; the roof is pyramidal and slated and is crowned with a small octagonal leaded spire. The tower arch is very lofty and consists of three splayed continuous orders which are stopped on a splay at the base. The west doorway has a two-centred arch, with moulded label forming a square head over it; the arch and jamb are continuously moulded and on each side is a niche for an image, with crocketed canopy, and at the apex are carved figures of two angels; in the spandrels are carved figures of angels holding censers; the doorway is much decayed and has been repaired with cement. The west window is of three cinquefoiled lights with traceried head, and has been repaired with cement; the belfry windows are also much decayed; they are of two cinquefoiled lights with traceried heads. Their moulded labels are returned round the tower as a string-course. The angle buttresses of the tower terminate at the belfry stage.

The octagonal font is of clunch and dates from the latter part of the 15th century; the south side of the bowl is plain, the others have traceried panels; the stem is plain.

At the west end of the nave and aisle and in the chancel are some 16th-century benches and standards; the communion rail is of late 17th-century date and has twisted balusters.

There are five bells: the treble by Thomas Mears, 1838; the second by Lester & Pack, 1757; the third is inscribed 'Sancta Margareta Ora Pro Nobis'; the fourth by William Rofford, undated, but probably c. 1350; the fifth by Miles Graye, 1616.

The communion plate consists of a cup, 1562, a cover paten without hall marks, dated 1630, a large paten, 1713, a modern paten and a plated cup.

The registers are in four books as follows: (i) baptisms 1580 to 1730, burials 1565 to 1736; (ii) baptisms 1562 to 1730; (ii) baptisms and burials 1731 to 1775, marriages 1750 to 1753; (iii) baptisms and burials 1776 to 1812; (iv) marriages 1755 to 1812.

ADVOWSON The advowson of the church was appurtenant to the manor of Westmill held by the Leukenores. In 1311 John de Leukenore conveyed it to Walter de Huntingfield,[79] from whom it was evidently acquired by Aymer de Valence Earl of Pembroke.[80] It descended with the manor of Westmillbury until 1796, when it was reserved in the conveyance of the manor by Philip Earl of Hardwicke to John Mellish.[81] The living is now in the gift of Mr. T. T. Greg of Coles.

A meeting-place for Quakers was certified in Westmill in 1693, and one for Protestants in 1820.[82] There is now no Nonconformist place of worship in the parish.

CHARITIES In 1826 Philip Earl of Hardwicke, by deed dated 13 November, gave the land tax or annual sum of £28 charged upon the parsonage-house of Westmill for the benefit of the National school.

In 1736 Jane Francis by her will charged a messuage and garden in the village with 10s. a year for the poor.

WIDFORD

Wideford, Wydeford, Wydford (xi–xvi cent.); Wodeford (once in xiv cent.); generally Widford after xvi cent.

Widford is a small parish of 1,167 acres, of which about two-thirds are arable land and about one quarter pasture.[1] The commons, which were extensive, were inclosed under an award of 1856.[2] The only wood of any size is Lily Wood to the west of the village; Marshland Wood, which adjoined Eastwick Wood in the neighbouring parish of Eastwick, was cut down about 1877. The River Ash, sometimes called Widford River, runs in a westerly direction through the northern part of the parish. From north to south the parish is intersected by the road from Hadham to Hunsdon and Stanstead Abbots, whilst at right angles with this another road joins the village with Ware on the west. The Great Eastern railway has a station on the Buntingford branch at Widford, at some distance to the west of the village.

The meadows occupying the low ground by the Ash on the north of the parish are pleasant, the banks of the stream being lined with willows. The ground rises steeply to the south of the river. On the east and west the parish is flat and uninteresting. The soil is mixed, the subsoil clay and chalk.

On a hill on the north-west of the parish are two barrows of unknown date, one of which was opened by the Hon. Richard Braybrook in 1851. It has been suggested that the names Godwyn's Wood and Battles Wood in the neighbourhood may traditionally preserve the history of some local event.[3] Barrow Farm, to the north, takes its name from the tumuli.[4] Nether Street is the name of a road, lately re-made and planted with trees, which enters the parish on the east and, after running in a curiously straight line for some distance, is continued as a lane on to the river, and is traceable for some way on the other side, passing close by Barrow Hill. It then joins another lane which here for a little distance

---

[79] Feet of F. Herts. Hil. 4 Edw. II, no. 64.
[80] See Inq. a.q.d. file 365, no. 18.
[81] Close, 36 Geo. III, pt. xxiii, no. 6.
[82] Urwick, op. cit. 724.
[1] Statistics from Bd. of Agric. (1905).
[2] *Blue Bk. Incl. Awards*, 65.
[3] *East Herts. Arch. Soc. Trans.* ii, 130.

Flint implements have been turned up at Widford Glebe close to Lily Wood (information from Rev. G. Traviss Lockwood). In the Blakesware title deeds the wood is called Goodwin or Goldings Wood, and there was a neighbouring field called Goddens Field in Ware parish.

The deeds also mention a house called Goodwyns (1631–96), which was probably in this field (information from Mr. H. Gosselin Grimshawe).
[4] Atteberwe and De la Berwe are the names of tenants on the manor in the 13th century

402

forms the parish boundary. Both these lanes are probably ancient trackways. Another old by-road called Crackney Lane or Watery Lane (also ancient, as it forms the parish boundary) ran south from Barrow Farm, passed Crackney Wood, and ran through the south-east corner of the Blakesware estate. This was closed by order of Quarter Sessions in 1878, when a new by-road was made from Widford station. At the same time part of the old main road from Ware to Widford was closed, which to the east of Scholars Hill followed a line to the north of the present road. This was made when the new house at Blakesware was built. The old road joined the present main road a little to the west of Widford station.[4a]

The village is situated along the road to Hunsdon on the high ground to the south of the river. The church of St. John the Baptist and Widford Bury (now a farm) lie further down the hill a little to the west. The rectory is close by the church. At the top of the road leading from the church to the village is Walnut Tree House, the residence of Mr. G. S. Pawle, J.P. The village is built in a straggling way along the main road. There are a good many new cottages and several inns. At the north end of the main street is a smithy. The public elementary school was built in 1875. Considerably to the south of the village, in the main road, is a Congregational chapel, built in 1898. Bourne House, to the north of the village, is the residence of Mr. G. M. Horsey.

The churchyard at Widford is the burial-place of Mary Field, grandmother of Charles Lamb and subject of his poem 'The Grandame.' She was housekeeper at Blakesware, which adjoins Widford on the north-west. The tombstone records her death in 1792. Mrs. Elizabeth Norris, widow of Lamb's friend Randal Norris of the Inner Temple, her son Richard and her daughter Elizabeth, widow of Charles Tween, were also buried here. The original of Lamb's 'Rosamund Gray' is said to have been a native of Widford.[5] John Eliot, the 'Indian Apostle,' was baptized at Widford in 1604; his father was Bennett Eliot, a yeoman and landowner in the neighbourhood. The version of the Bible in the language of the Massachusetts Indians made by Eliot was printed in 1661 by Samuel Green, successor of Stephen Daye, the first American printer, and is therefore of typographical as well as philological interest.

Before the Conquest *WIDFORD* was *MANOR* held by Edred, a thegn of King Edward. It was the land of the Bishop of London in 1086, when it was assessed at 3 hides, 2 of which were in demesne. There were two ploughs on the demesne and three others on the manor. There was meadow for two plough teams, woodland for fifty swine[6] and a mill.[7] Another hide was held of the Bishop of London by a certain Tedbert, the successor of Alward, who had held of Archbishop Stigand in the time of King Edward.[8] These are the only entries given in the Domesday Survey, but whether they refer to the land which was afterwards given to the abbey of Bermondsey by Ivo de Grentmesnil is not clear. It has been suggested that the 'Wadford' which was given in exchange by Hugh de Witvile to Hugh de Grentmesnil for five houses in the city of Leicester[9] is Widford in Hertfordshire.[10] Widford, however, does not seem to be elsewhere spelt Wadford[11]; also there is no hint of such a transaction in the Survey under Hertfordshire, and there is nothing to account for the disappearance of the Bishop of London's estate. But the manor seems to have been acquired in some way by Ivo de Grentmesnil, son of Hugh, and to have been given by him to Bermondsey in exchange for 'Andretesbury.'[12] It was confirmed in 1118 by Robert Earl of Leicester, to whom part of the Grentmesnil estates were pledged.[13]

The manor remained with Bermondsey until the Dissolution. The prior and convent had view of frankpledge there, assize of bread and ale, infangentheof, quittance of shires and hundreds, sheriff's tourns and sheriff's aids.[14] It was one of the estates of which the notorious Adam de Stratton obtained a grant from the convent in the reign of Edward I. He was evicted in 1277 because he had no royal confirmation of this grant,[15] but the next year he again obtained possession, this time to hold at a rent of 1d., whilst by Ivo de Grentmesnil he quitclaimed to the prior a rent of £100 in which the prior was bound to him.[16] Ultimately he was convicted for forging charters which would give him the fee simple of the land; it was held in fee farm of the priory.[17] Widford then came to the Crown and was granted back to Bermondsey, with a rebuke for having 'indiscreetly and improvidently' leased it to Stratton.[18] In 1317 the manor was leased to Geoffrey de Stokes and his wife Alice for their lives at a rent of 12 marks.[19] The convent was heavily in debt about twenty years later to William de Cusancia, keeper of the king's wardrobe, and obtained licence to lease the manor again for a sum to be paid in advance or at a yearly farm, in order to relieve their estate.[20] It was accordingly leased in 1342 to Richard de Wylughby and his wife Joan for their lives.[21] The monastery surrendered in January 1537-8. The extent of the manor as given in the Valor of 1535 included 32 acres of wood.[22]

In 1544 the king granted Widford to Sir Richard Southwell[23] of Horsham St. Faith, co. Norfolk,[24] one

---

[4a] The last piece of this road (running due south) was diverted to the west when the railway was made about 1864. The older road passed through a ford, of which the piles could be seen in the river until a few years ago. It joined the present line of road at Widford station (plans, &c., lent by Mr. H. Gosselin Grimshawe).
[5] Ainger, *Charles Lamb*, 40.
[6] This is a large amount of woodland as compared with the present extent.
[7] *V.C.H. Herts.* i, 306a.   [8] Ibid.
[9] *Dom. Bk.* (Rec. Com.), fol. 230a.
[10] Manning and Bray, *Hist. and Antiq. of Surr.* i, 193.

[11] It is, however, spelt *Wodeford* (see *Cal. Pat.* 1338-40, p. 543).
[12] See confirmation of Henry III printed by Dugdale in *Mon.* v, 110.
[13] Ibid. 88.
[14] *Plac. de Quo Warr.* (Rec. Com.), 382.
[15] Ibid. 282.
[16] De Banco R. 31, m. 95 d.; Feet of F. Div. Co. Mich. 7 & 8 Edw. I, no. 92.
[17] *Red Bk. of Exch.* (Rolls Ser.), iii, p. cccxxv. His first conviction was for assault on Roger Goodman of Bermondsey, who was attacked by Adam's servants at Widford and robbed of his horses and merchandise. Adam tried unsuccessfully to prove that Roger was a fugitive bondsman (ibid.).

[18] *Cal. Pat.* 1281-92, p. 338.
[19] Ibid. 1317-21, p. 62; Inq. a.q.d. file 128, no. 4.
[20] *Cal. Pat.* 1338-40, p. 543. William de Cusancia had apparently already had a mortgage of the manor (*Cal. Close*, 1337-9, p. 166).
[21] *Cal. Pat.* 1340-3, p. 432.
[22] *Valor Eccl.* (Rec. Com.), ii, 59.
[23] *L. and P. Hen. VIII*, xix (1), 80 (11).
[24] Le Neve, *Pedigrees of the Knights* (Harl. Soc.), 496.

of his councillors. In the same year Thomas Lewyn, clerk, who was apparently a trustee for Southwell, had licence to alienate the manor to the use of Mary Leech, wife of Robert Leech, alderman of Norwich ; also a field called Newnneye Wood *alias* Woodfield beside Newnneye (Nimney) Wood in Ware.[25] This Mary Leech, who in another place is called Mary Darcy *alias* Leech, must have been Mary daughter of Sir Thomas Darcy of Danbury, co. Essex, who afterwards became the second wife of Sir Richard Southwell.[26] In 1558 she as Mary Darcy *alias* Leech of Horsham St. Faith, co. Norfolk, alienated the manor to Robert Adams, a yeoman of Widford,[27] who died seised of it in 1580. In 1589 his son and heir Henry Adams conveyed it together with forty messuages, a water-mill, free warren, free fishery and view of frankpledge to Bartholomew Barnes, sen., and Bartholomew Barnes, jun.[28] A Bartholomew Barnes, probably the younger, citizen and mercer of London, settled it in 1608 on Elizabeth, one of his three daughters, the wife of Roland Backhouse,[29] also citizen and mercer of London. Their grandson, William Backhouse (son of Nicholas, a younger son of Roland), created a baronet in 1660, sold it with the water-mill, warren, fishery, and frankpledge to William Bird[30] of Martocks in Ware. Thomas Bird, according to Chauncy, was lord of the manor in 1700.[31] Before 1741 it was acquired by William Parker of Haling in Croydon,[32] whose daughter Elizabeth married her cousin William Hamond.[33] Their son, William Parker Hamond of Haling, died in 1812 ; his son of the same name suffered a recovery in 1814,[34] and in 1829 sold the manor to Nicholas Parry of Little Hadham. It descended to his son Nicholas Segar Parry,[35] who devised to Mr. H. D. Parry-Mitchell of Merivale, Atherstone, Warwick, the present lord.[36]

Widford Bury was sold by Mr. Parry-Mitchell to Sir Martin Gosselin in 1889 and is now the property of Capt. Alwyn Gosselin of Blakesware. It is an L-shaped building, with timber-framed walls covered with plaster ; there is little of interest in the house, which probably dates from the 17th century. A little to the north-west of the house is an early 17th-century dove-house ; it is of brick, octagonal on plan and has a thatched roof. None of the cots now remain. Between the house and the churchyard is an old brick wall about 65 yards in length, part of which formed the outer wall of what may have been the eastern wing of the Bury ; it appears to be of 16th-century date. At the north end, beside the stile into the churchyard, the wall is returned westwards. A four-centred arched doorway and part of a moulded brick window, now blocked, are visible on the east side ; on the west face are a large fireplace and a wide four-centred arch. The wall is now about 8 ft. high. At the south end of the wall is a round-arched gateway of brick with moulded arch and imposts. The gateway is flanked by plain pilasters, with remains of a frieze and moulded cornice above. The pilasters have moulded plinths, and the capitals also are moulded, but they appear to have belonged to narrower pilasters. The wall at this

WIDFORD : OLD GATEWAY IN CHURCHYARD WALL

---

[25] *L. and P. Hen. VIII*, xix (1), 812 (114).
[26] See pedigree in Fosbrooke's *Gloucestershire*, i, 496 ; Blomefield, *Hist. of Norf.* 277.
[27] Pat. 4 & 5 Phil. and Mary, pt. xv, m. 12 ; Feet of F. Herts. East. 4 & 5 Phil. and Mary.
[28] Pat. 32 Eliz. pt. xiv, m. 27 ; Feet of F. Herts. East. 32 Eliz.
[29] Feet of F. Herts. East. 6 Jas. I ; Com. Pleas D. Enr. Hil. 14 Jas. I.
[30] The fine (Mich. 20 Chas. II) was levied to William Bird, but according to Chauncy the sale was to Thomas Bird.
[31] Op. cit. 200.
[32] See Recov. R. Trin. 14 & 15 Geo. II, rot. 53.
[33] Ibid. Hil. 16 Geo. III, rot. 53.
[34] Ibid. Mich. 55 Geo. III, rot. 250.
[35] Cussans, *Hist. of Herts. Braughing Hund.* 55.
[36] J. Traviss Lockwood, *Widford and Widford Church*, 5.

point is 3 ft. in thickness. The gateway is probably of early 17th-century date, but some old materials may have been re-used in its construction.

Widford Mill, mentioned in the conveyances recited above, was situated just outside Widford in the parish of Ware, close to the site of old Blakesware.[37] It was pulled down about twenty years ago. There was an earlier one, which seems to have been within the parish of Widford, the site of which is probably marked by Mill Mead on the south side of the river close to the flood-gates.[38]

The church of ST. JOHN THE CHURCH BAPTIST consists of chancel 21 ft. by 18 ft., small north organ chamber, nave 43 ft. by 18 ft. 6 in., north vestry, south porch, and west tower 11 ft. square, all internal dimensions. The church is built of flint with clunch dressings, except those of the tower, which are of Barnack stone ; the roofs are tiled.

A church stood here in the 12th century, but the only details of that period still existing are some fragments now built into the walls, though portions of the nave walls may belong to the older building. The chancel and west tower are chiefly of 14th-century date. During the 15th century the tower arch was reconstructed and windows inserted in the chancel. During the 19th century the church was repaired several times, the spire rebuilt, and the organ chamber, vestry and south porch erected.

The three-light window [39] in the east wall of the chancel is modern. In each of the side walls is a window of two cinquefoiled lights, with rectilinear tracery, of the 15th century. The south doorway of the same period has a four-centred arch, over which is a modern label. In the south wall an early 12th-century cushion capital set on a shaft now forms a credence shelf. This fragment of the former church, along with several others now in the nave, was discovered near the tower arch during repairs early in the 19th century. In the same wall is a recess 4 ft. 3 in. wide, with splayed edge and pointed segmental arch, which may have inclosed a tomb ; it is of 14th-century work. On the chancel walls are some remains of distemper paintings. On the east wall, north of the window, is the figure of a knight.

South of the window is the figure of a bishop in cope and mitre, carrying a crozier.[40] On the north wall is a figure seated on a rainbow, with a sword placed horizontally above his uplifted hands ; beside it is a small figure of an angel with a Tau cross. There is no chancel arch.

The only old window in the nave is the most easterly one in the south wall, which is of two cinquefoiled lights with flowing tracery, of about 1350 ; one other window in the same wall and one in the north wall are of modern stonework. The north doorway, which now opens into the modern vestry,

WIDFORD CHURCH FROM THE SOUTH-EAST

is of late 14th-century work and has an arch of two moulded orders. The oak door with its ironwork is of the same period. On the north wall outside is a projection which contained the stair to the rood-loft, but no opening is visible inside. The south doorway is similar to that in the north wall ; built into the wall above it are some fragments of a 12th-century arch with zigzag moulding. Near the eastern end of the south wall is a small roughly formed piscina

---

[37] Information communicated by Mr. G. M. Horsey.
[38] Information from Mr. H. Gosselin Grimshawe.
[39] The glass was inserted in memory of John Eliot.
[40] See illus. in Cussans, op. cit. *Braughing Hund.* facing p. 56.

A HISTORY OF HERTFORDSHIRE

with credence shelf; it is of brick, cemented, and is of early 16th-century work. The nave roof retains some old tie-beams.

The west tower is of three stages, unbuttressed, and is finished with an embattled parapet and modern copper-covered spire; a turret stair at the south-east angle gives access to the belfry. The tower arch, of the full width of the tower, is of three continuous moulded orders. The 14th-century west doorway is of two moulded orders and label with returned stops; of the same date is the window above, of two cinquefoiled lights with a cusped opening in the head. On each face of the belfry stage is a window of two trefoiled lights, all of modern stonework.

The font dates from about 1420; it is octagonal, and on each side of the bowl is a square panel containing a cusped circle, the centres being carved with various devices such as the head of a nun, a lion, flower ornaments, &c.

In the tower is a slab with indents of a half-figure with shields and inscription.

The paintings on the chancel ceiling were executed by Miss F. C. Hadsley Gosselin between 1881 and 1883.[41]

There are six bells: the treble by Mears & Stainbank, 1890; the second recast by John Taylor, 1869; the third by Robert Oldfeild, 162- (incomplete date); the fourth is a 15th-century bell inscribed 'Sancta Katerina Ora Pro Nobis'; the fifth by Robert Oldfeild, 1624; the tenor by Lester & Pack, 1766.

The communion plate consists of a chased cup, 1562, a cover paten without a hall mark and a modern flagon.

The registers are in four books as follows: (i) baptisms 1562 to 1644, burials 1558 to 1676, marriages 1558 to 1660; (ii) baptisms 1674 to 1762, burials 1674 to 1757, marriages 1674 to 1752; (iii) baptisms and burials 1763 to 1812; (iv) marriages 1754 to 1812.

ADVOWSON The advowson of the church of St. John the Baptist was appurtenant to the manor until the sale of the latter by William Parker Hamond to Nicholas Parry, when it was reserved by Hamond. It was bought about five years ago by Captain Alwyn Gosselin, and the last presentation was made by trustees, he as a Roman Catholic being unable to present.[42]

A burial-ground for Roman Catholics was made near the churchyard by Sir Martin Gosselin shortly before his death in 1905.[43]

CHARITIES In 1808 Mary Mason by her will gave £300 for the benefit of the poor. The legacy is now represented by a sum of £372 15s. 7d. consols with the official trustees, producing £9 6s. 4d. yearly.

The Parliamentary Returns of 1786 state that a donor unknown gave lands to the poor. The parish is in possession of 13 a. 2 r. of land lying in the common fields and producing £12 4s. yearly.

The income from these charities was in 1910 applied as to £5 as a subscription to a nursing fund, £3 in outfits to five girls, £3 to eight widows, 15s. to two aged men and £5 5s. for special cases.

The Congregational chapel and trust property comprised in an indenture dated 25 January 1898 is regulated by a scheme of the Charity Commissioners dated 27 April 1906.

---

[41] For a description of them see J. Traviss-Lockwood, *Widford and Widford Church, with an explanation of her recently completed painting by F. C. Hadsley Gosselin*.

[42] Information from the Rev. J. H. Hart. The Crown presented in 1765 by reason of the lunacy of William Parker (Guildhall MS. 481). In 1806 H. Partridge presented, probably *pro hac vice* (ibid.).

[43] Information from Mr. H. Gosselin Grimshawe.

406

THE HUNDRED OF HERTFORD

CONTAINING[1] THE PARISHES OF

PARTS OF ALL SAINTS AND ST. JOHN'S,
HERTFORD, including the liberties of
BRICKENDON and LITTLE AMWELL
GREAT AMWELL
BAYFORD
BENGEO
LITTLE BERKHAMPSTEAD
BROXBOURNE WITH HODDESDON
CHESHUNT ST. MARY

ESSENDON
HERTINGFORDBURY
ST. ANDREW RURAL
STANSTEAD ST. MARGARET'S
STAPLEFORD
TEWIN
WORMLEY

AND HERTFORD BOROUGH

Hertford Hundred lies in the valley of the Lea, for the most part to the south of the borough of Hertford, which it almost encircles. Little is known of the spot where the courts were held, but it was apparently customary for the sheriff's tourn to be held at Ware Bridge in the 14th century.[2] The hundred adjoins the counties of Essex and Middlesex on the east and south respectively.

The hundred in 1086 was somewhat more extensive than at the beginning of last century. It originally included Bramfield on the north-west.[3] Four men and the reeve together with the whole township (*villata*) of Bramfield were wont to plead and to be geldable with the rest of the king's 'foreign' (*forinsec*) hundred of Hertford; but about 1260 Abbot John of St. Albans annexed Bramfield to his liberty,[4] and thenceforward it was accounted part of the abbots' hundred of Cashio.[5] The Domesday Survey also locates the unidentified holdings of Stiuicesworde and Bricewold within the hundred of Hertford.[6] The royal jurisdiction here as elsewhere was considerably diminished by the liberties exercised by religious houses over their lands. The Abbot of Westminster claimed exemption from suit at the hundred

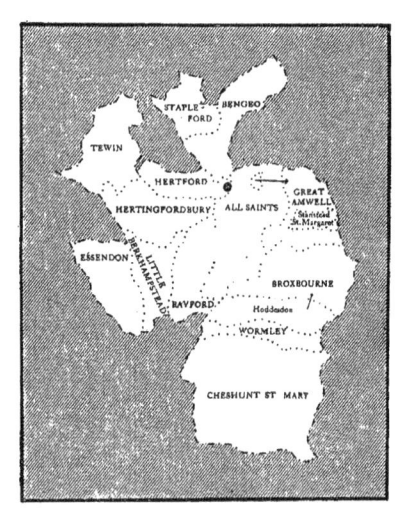

INDEX MAP TO THE HUNDRED OF HERTFORD

---

[1] This list represents the extent of the hundred in 1831 (*Pop. Ret.* 1831, i, 248). In the arrangement of the parishes of Hertford Borough the boundaries adopted under the Municipal Corporations Act of 1835 have been used.
[2] Chan. Inq. p.m. 50 Edw. III (1st nos.), no. 3; Anct. D. (P.R.O.), D 641.
[3] *V.C.H. Herts.* i, 341*a*.
[4] *Plac. de Quo Warr.* (Rec. Com.), 290.
[5] *V.C.H. Herts.* ii, 320.
[6] Ibid. i, 331, 341.

407

A HISTORY OF HERTFORDSHIRE

court for his tenants at Amwell, the Knights Templars for theirs in Bengeo. The tenants of Waltham Holy Cross had a similar exemption in the liberty of Brickendon and at Wormley. The men of the hospital of St. Bartholomew at Tewin, and those of Hertford Priory, Merton Priory and the priory of Holy Trinity Aldgate, had all withdrawn their suit from the hundred by 1278.[7]

The hundreds of Hertford and Braughing were usually farmed jointly by a single bailiff.[8] The value of Hertford Hundred in 1278 was £10 yearly.[9] Early in the year 1319 inquisition was made as to the possibility of severing these two hundreds from the body of the county; but their value was uncertain, since the sheriff accounted for the whole county in gross.[10] In 1335 the petition of Edmund 'de Bolestroda,' a servant (*valet*) of Henry of Lancaster, who desired to hold the two hundreds severally at farm, was rejected, as it was proved to the Council that they were of the body of the county and could not be separated.[11] No such consideration weighed with Queen Elizabeth, who in 1571 granted these and other hundreds to William Cecil Lord Burghley and his heirs, to hold in fee farm.[12] Burghley's son, Robert Earl of Salisbury, bequeathed them to his son and heir William,[13] and they have descended with the earldom of Salisbury.

[7] *Plac. de Quo Warr.* (Rec. Com.), 276 et seq.; cf. *Hund. R.* (Rec. Com.), i, 190.
[8] Assize R. 318, m. 18; Hardy, *Sess. R.* (Herts. Co. Rec.), i, 28, 54, 64, 319; Memo. R. (Exch. L.T.R.), Hil. 11 Jas. I, 'Recorda,' m. 294. In 1297 John of Bayford farmed these two hundreds and also Broadwater and Hitchin. [9] Assize R. 323.
[10] Memo. R. (Exch. L.T.R.), Hil. 12 Edw. II, 'Brevia,' m. 78. [11] *Parl. R.* ii, 93a.
[12] Pat. 13 Eliz. pt. vii, m. 25 (grant begins m. 21). [13] Will P.C.C. 49 Fenner.

HERTFORD HUNDRED

Parts of ALL SAINTS and ST. JOHN'S, HERTFORD, including the liberties of BRICKENDON and LITTLE AMWELL.

The following account deals with the district comprising the modern civil parishes of Brickendon Rural, St. John Rural and Little Amwell, all of which lie immediately south and east of Hertford Borough. They were for the most part either in the ecclesiastical parish of All Saints, the church of which belonged to Waltham Abbey, or in the parish of St. John, a church belonging to Hertford Priory.[1] The benefices of All Saints and St. John were amalgamated about 1640,[2] and Little Amwell was constituted a separate parish in 1864.[3] This district lies on the southern edge of the Hertfordshire Chalk beds, and the arable land and pasturage are about equal in quantity.

The present parish of Brickendon Rural includes about 1,348 acres immediately south of All Saints' Church. A large part lay within the liberty of Brickendon, also belonging to the abbey of Waltham.[4] Brickendon Bury, the capital messuage of the manor of Brickendon, lies within Brickendon Rural. It stands on the summit of rising ground about a mile south of Hertford. The present house dates from the early 18th century, but the interior has been completely modernized and additions have been made to the rear. The plastered north or entrance front, which is two stories in height with an attic, remains more or less in its original condition and presents, with its central pediment and Corinthian pilasters, an elevation correct in detail but poor in design. Considerable portions of the moat remain on the west and south, where it is still filled with water. A large find of Roman coins was discovered in making a sunk bed to the south-east of the house. On the Hertford side the house is approached by a magnificent avenue of trees nearly three-quarters of a mile in length, known as 'Morgan's Walk.' On the well-wooded slopes to the south are Brickendon Green and Grange. A part of this district was at one time held by the equally powerful Abbots of Westminster.[5] Fanshaws, a little to the north of Brickendon Green, is the property of Mrs. Kingsley. The house was built by Mr. H. Demain-Saunders, Mrs. Kingsley's first husband, who acquired property at Brickendon Green (including Fanshaws Farm), formerly part of the manor of Brickendon.

St. John Rural is a purely agricultural district immediately east of Brickendon. It covers some 1,662 acres and includes only one considerable house, viz. Jenningsbury, at which there is a moat. The manorial lands of Jenningsbury extend into the ecclesiastical parishes of All Saints, St. Andrew and St. John, Hertford, and also into Broxbourne and Great Amwell.[6] Balls Park, the estate of Sir George Faudel Faudel-Phillips, bart., is a detached portion of Little Amwell, lying between the parishes of Brickendon Rural and St. John. It was the property of Sir John Harrison about 1640, when in endowing the joint vicarage of All Saints and St. John he excepted the tithes of his own estate.[7] At Dalmonds, near Hoddesdon, there are fragments of a homestead moat.

The civil parish of Little Amwell contains about 495 acres and lies between St. John Rural and the parish of Great Amwell. On its north-west is a detached portion of Great Amwell. There is reason to believe that Little Amwell was included within the holding of Amwell in 1086,[8] and that it subsequently became distinct, both for ecclesiastical and other purposes, through its acquisition by the monks of Waltham.[9]

The village of Little Amwell stands on high ground between Hertford and Great Amwell, near the junction of Ermine Street with the Hertford road. The modern church is a little south of the village, which is small, consisting of a few scattered houses and the farm buildings of Amwellplace. On the Ermine Street, about half a mile north of the village, is the small hamlet of Rush Green with a moated homestead at Gamels Hall. Late in the 14th century John son of Robert Gamel held the land formerly 'Gameles' jointly with seven other tenants of the lord of Great Amwell Manor.[10] A barrow of unknown date lies beyond 'Thieves Lane' on the borders of the detached portion of Great Amwell parish.[11]

The main road from Hertford to Ware traverses the northern part of the parishes of St. John and Little Amwell. The famous spring at Chadwell near this road is the head of the New River, the water-supply brought to London by 'one man's industry, cost and care.' As early as the 13th century the monks of Waltham had been induced by Philip of Hertford to improve the supply from Chadwell Spring, doubtless for local use.[12] Under Queen Elizabeth an Act was passed for the conveyance of water from any part of Middlesex or Hertfordshire to the city.[13] The Acts of 1605 and 1606 mention the springs of Chadwell and Amwell as the source of the projected supply.[14] The works were begun by Sir Hugh Myddelton 20 February 1608, and the 'keeper of Amwell-head' took a conspicuous part in the pageantry on Michaelmas Day 1613, when the water was first admitted to the great cistern at Islington.[15] On a pedestal at the spring is an inscription to the memory of the great engineer of the river.

The *LIBERTY OF BRICKENDON MANORS* lay outside the borough of Hertford. Before the Conquest Brickendon already belonged to Waltham Abbey, to which it had been

---

[1] See under Hertford Borough.
[2] Ibid.
[3] *Lond. Gaz.* 2 Aug. 1864, p. 3809.
[4] See under Hertford Borough and below.
[5] See below.
[6] Com. Pleas D. Enr. Trin. 30 & 31 Geo. II, m. 50.
[7] Chauncy, *Hist. of Herts.* 258.
[8] See under Great Amwell.
[9] See below.
[10] Add. R. (B.M.), 26828.
[11] See under Great Amwell.
[12] Harl. MS. 4809, fol. 167.
[13] Stow, *Survey* (ed. Strype, 1720), i, 25.
[14] Loc. and Personal Acts, 3 Jas. I, cap. 18; 4 Jas. I, cap. 12.
[15] Stow, op. cit. i, 26.

A HISTORY OF HERTFORDSHIRE

confirmed by Edward the Confessor.[16] Between 1174 and 1184 Henry II confirmed the manor to the monks who had replaced the canons at Waltham.[17] He gave with it freedom from geld and toll and the forfeitures of criminals,[18] thus establishing the 'liberty.' The Abbot of Waltham duly claimed and obtained freedom from tallage in 1227.[19] The estate at Brickendon, having no church, was regarded as belonging to the parish of All Saints.[20]

The liberty was held by the monks until the Dissolution.[21] Henry VIII granted it to Thomas Knighton,[22] with the advowson of All Saints' Church, and it descended with All Saints[23] (q.v.) to Sir William Soame, who conveyed it to Edward Clarke in 1682.[24] Clarke's son Thomas held the manor in 1728[25] and 1730.[26] On his death in 1754 he is said to have left the manor to Mrs. Jane Morgan, his niece, whose youngest son John died in 1792 and left half to his sister Jane and the other half to the representatives of his aunt Anne Freke. From Jane's son, Sir Charles Morgan, the one moiety passed finally to his grandchild Selina Rose Catherine wife of the Rev. W. T. Marsh Lushington-Tilson.[27] The other moiety came to Anne Freke's two granddaughters—Mary wife of the Rev. Edward Lewis and Fanny wife of the Rev. Francis Lewis.[28]

In 1881 the representatives of Mary and Fanny Lewis joined with Mrs. Lushington-Tilson in a sale of the whole manor to Messrs. Paine & Brettell of Chertsey. It was afterwards acquired from them by Mr. Hill of Nottingham, who sold it to Mr. George Pearson, father of Mr. Ernest Pearson, the present owner.[29]

Three virgates in Brickendon which had been held by three brothers before the Conquest were held by Baldwin, a serjeant of the king, at the time of the Domesday Survey.[30] This holding was probably identical with the 1 carucate in Brickendon which Miles de Somery (d. about 1229)[31] held by serjeanty at the king's storehouse (*de dispensa*).[32] Among the co-heirs of Adam grandson of Miles de Somery was John son of Ela Monchensey.[33] It is therefore possible that it was over the holding of Miles de Somery that Richard Monchensey had a grant of free warren in 1333.[34]

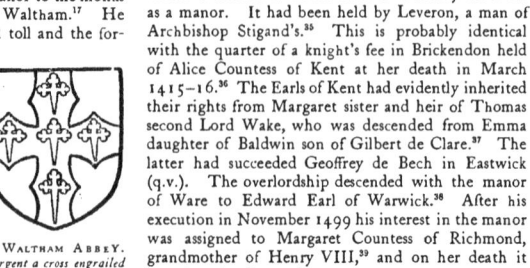

WALTHAM ABBEY.
Argent a cross engrailed sable with five crosslets fitchy or thereon.

Another holding of 1086 consisted of 5 virgates which a certain Isenbard held of Geoffrey de Bech as a manor. It had been held by Leveron, a man of Archbishop Stigand's.[35] This is probably identical with the quarter of a knight's fee in Brickendon held of Alice Countess of Kent at her death in March 1415–16.[36] The Earls of Kent had evidently inherited their rights from Margaret sister and heir of Thomas second Lord Wake, who was descended from Emma daughter of Baldwin son of Gilbert de Clare.[37] The latter had succeeded Geoffrey de Bech in Eastwick (q.v.). The overlordship descended with the manor of Ware to Edward Earl of Warwick.[38] After his execution in November 1499 his interest in the manor was assigned to Margaret Countess of Richmond, grandmother of Henry VIII,[39] and on her death it lapsed to the Crown.[40]

Of the actual tenants of this holding little is known. About 1282 the tenant was possibly one of the name of 'Bellere.'[41] A 'manor of Brickendon' was held in January 1250–1 by Philip Darcy, who had a grant of free warren within it at that date.[42]

The third holding in the Domesday Survey was 1 virgate which Walter held of Geoffrey de Mandeville.[43] It had previously been held by Oswi, one of the men of Asgar the Staller. It is possible that this is a part of the knight's fee in Amwell (and Brickendon) subsequently held by the Abbot of Westminster of Hugh de Oddingselles.[44] This fee was probably attached to the manor of the abbey at Great Amwell, which included lands in Brickendon.[45] The monks of Westminster produced Saxon charters purporting to be the gift of Brickendon to the abbey by a certain Aelfhelm Polga and the confirmation of the same by Bishop Dunstan and King Edgar,[46] but the latter is certainly, and the former probably, a forgery.[47]

The Grange estate originated in copyhold and freehold land of the manor of Brickendon Bury, purchased by Benjamin Cherry of Hertford, gent., and by him bequeathed to his brother John Cherry. The mansion now known as the Grange was built by Benjamin son of John Cherry about the middle of the last century. The property has recently been sold by Mr. B. L. Cherry, grandson of Benjamin Cherry, to Mr. John Trotter, who resides at the Grange.[48]

The manor of JENNINGSBURY (Juveneles or Juvenelisbury, xiv cent.; Jenaldesbury 'la Mote' or Jovenellesbury, xv cent.; Genyngisbury, xvi cent.) was held as one knight's fee by Aymer de Valence Earl of Pembroke in 1303.[49] The manor was always held in chief, but the service is recorded as that of a quarter of a fee in the 15th century.[50] The

---

[16] *V.C.H. Herts.* i, 317; Dugdale, *Mon.* vi, 61.
[17] Cart. Antiq. M. 2, 115.
[18] Ibid. For the disputes of the abbots with the burgesses of Hertford with regard to jurisdiction in the hamlet of West Street see under Hertford Borough.
[19] *Rot. Lit. Claus.* (Rec. Com.), ii, 176.
[20] Ibid.
[21] Ct. R. (Gen. Ser.), portf. 173, no. 30–1; *Plac de Quo Warr.* (Rec. Com.), 283; Ct. R. (Gen. Ser.), portf. 178, no. 21.
[22] *L. and P. Hen. VIII,* xvi, 878 (61).
[23] Com. Pleas D. Enr. East. 6 Edw. VI, m. 8 d.; Chan. Inq. p.m. (Ser. 2), clvii, 81; Pat. 28 Eliz. pt. xiii, &c.
[24] Feet of F. Herts. Trin. 34 Chas. II.

[25] Salmon, *Hist. of Herts.* 40.
[26] Deeds *penes* Mr. B. L. Cherry.
[27] Ibid.; Cussans, *Hist. of Herts.* ii, 67.
[28] Cussans, loc. cit.
[29] Deed *penes* Mr. B. L. Cherry; information from Mr. C. E. Johnston.
[30] *V.C.H. Herts.* i, 342*b*.
[31] Ibid. ii, 266.
[32] *Testa de Nevill* (Rec. Com.), 279*b*.
[33] *Cal. Inq. p.m.* 1–19 Edw. I, 448.
[34] Chart. R. 7 Edw. III, no. 23.
[35] *V.C.H. Herts.* i, 334*a*.
[36] Chan. Inq. p.m. 4 Hen. V, no. 51.
[37] See under Eastwick.
[38] Chan. Inq. p.m. (Ser. 2), xxviii, 71.
[39] Ibid.   [40] Ibid.
[41] *Cal. Inq. p.m.* 1–19 Edw. I, 262.
[42] *Cal. Chart. R.* 1226–57, p. 351.

Walter del Acre had £20 land in 'Brechened' (*Testa de Nevill* [Rec. Com.], 281), but it is uncertain whether this entry relates to Brickendon. The form 'Breckendon' has not been found.
[43] *V.C.H. Herts.* i, 331*b*.
[44] *Feud. Aids,* ii, 433. The identification, however, rests only on the absence of later history of the 'Mandeville' holding and the fact that the Mandeville family were benefactors of Westminster.
[45] Add. R. (B.M.), 26828.
[46] Birch, *Cart. Sax.* iii, 1050; Kemble, *Cod. Dipl.* 967.   [47] *V.C.H. Lond.* i, 434*b*.
[48] From information and deeds kindly supplied by Mr. B. L. Cherry.
[49] *Feud. Aids,* ii, 434.
[50] Ibid. 443, 450.

410

HERTFORD HUNDRED

family of Juvenal was connected with this neighbourhood about the year 1228, when William Juvenal, as guardian of the heir of Alexander Alders (de Alno), had the custody of the half of 2 carucates in Brickendon and Hoddesdon.[51] Aymer de Valence died in 1324,[52] and this manor was committed to the custody of Hugh le Despenser the younger[53] during the minority of Lawrence de Hastings (afterwards Earl of Pem-

VALENCE. *Burelly argent and azure an orle of martlets gules.*

HASTINGS. *Or a sleeve gules.*

broke), who was Valence's grand-nephew and one of his co-heirs.[54] In February 1326-7, shortly after the forfeiture of Despenser's land, the king assigned Jenningsbury to Juliane widow of John de Hastings, the father of Lawrence, in dower.[55] She had married Sir Thomas Blount, kt.,[56] and afterwards became the wife of William de Clinton Earl of Huntingdon.[57] In 1345 Lawrence Earl of Pembroke, Juliane's son and heir, released to her third husband and his heirs all right in the manor of Jenningsbury.[58] It thus descended to the Earl of Huntingdon's nephew John Lord Clinton after the death of Juliane in 1367.[59]

In 1391 the manor was in dispute between Reginald de Grey, grandson of Elizabeth, aunt of Lawrence Earl of Pembroke, who had died without issue, and Richard Talbot and others, representatives of the second sister of Lawrence's great-uncle, Aymer de Valence.[60] In accordance, however, with the settlement of 1345 Jenningsbury remained in the Clinton family until William Lord Clinton, grandson of John Lord Clinton mentioned above, enfeoffed Simon Stratford and others.[61] The feoffees transferred the manor to Richard Clitherow and John Chamberleyn, chaplain.[62] The tenant in 1402 was returned as John

CLINTON. *Argent six crosslets fitchy sable and a chief azure with two pierced molets or therein.*

ALL SAINTS AND ST. JOHN'S, HERTFORD

Clitherow,[63] and Richard Clitherow of Kent, esq., conveyed to Richard Claidich and others on 3 April 1415, evidently in trust for his son and heir Richard, upon whom the feoffees settled the manor in 1443.[64] William Lord Clinton was returned as tenant in 1428,[65] and, as in the case of Pirton (q.v.), his son and successor John apparently attempted to oust Roger son of Richard Clitherow from Jenningsbury.[66] Roger died on 12 March 1455, and the manor apparently passed to his daughter Eleanor wife of John Norres[67] of Goldstone, co. Kent.[68] A John Norres, apparently the younger brother of William Norres, who succeeded John in Goldstone,[69] held Jenningsbury jointly with his wife Isabel. He died on 12 October 1485, and his widow married Henry Marney.[70] Edmund Norres, son and heir of John and Isabel, probably sold the manor to Edward Sulyard,[71] who bequeathed it to his wife Anne and their heirs.[72] He died on 30 March 1516, leaving a son and heir William.[73]

The manor passed by sale to the family of Gardiner. Henry son of Henry Gardiner of London and Mary his wife were dealing with it in 1552.[74] Their son John was styled 'of Jenningsbury,'[75] and the manor descended to his son Henry Gardiner of Jenningsbury,[76] whose daughter and ultimate heir married Henry Dunster.[77] 'Henry Dunster of Jenningsbury, esq.,' was indicted for not repairing a footbridge on a footway from Hertford to Ware in 1671,[78] and in 1683 refused to pay his quota of the rate for building a house of correction.[79] His wife survived him.[80] Upon her death in 1718 her estates descended to her son Giles.[81] He died childless in 1724, and was succeeded by his nephew Henry Dunster.[82] Upon the death of the latter without issue in 1754 the estate of Little Amwell with Jenningsbury passed to his nephew Henry Dunster, who died on 23 August 1791.[83] In accordance with Henry Dunster's will the manor was sold to George Townshend Earl of Leicester, from whom it was purchased by Lord John Townshend[84] of Balls Park, great-grandfather of the sixth Marquess Townshend, who is the present owner.[85]

The manor of LITTLE AMWELL, sometimes known as LITTLE AMWELLBURY or RUSHEN,[86] was among the possessions of the abbey of Waltham Holy Cross at its dissolution on 23 March 1540.[87]

GARDINER of Jenningsbury. *Party gules and or a fesse between three hinds tripping countercoloured.*

---

[51] Cal. Close, 1227-31, p. 92; cf. Feet of F. Div. Co. 24 Hen. III, no. 157.;
Excerpta e Rot. Fin. (Rec. Com.), i, 109.
[52] G.E.C. Complete Peerage, vi, 208.
[53] Cal. Close, 1327-30, p. 75.
[54] Plac. in Canc. file 16, no. 16; Chan. Inq. p.m. 15 Ric. II, pt. i, no. 179.
[55] Cal. Close, 1327-30, pp. 12, 39, 75.
[56] Ibid.
[57] Chan. Inq. p.m. 41 Edw. III (1st nos.), no. 34.
[58] Feet of F. Herts. Trin. 19 Edw. III, no. 300; Cal. Pat. 1343-5, p. 474.
[59] Chan. Inq. p.m. 41 Edw. III (1st nos.), no. 34; cf. ibid. 28 Edw. III, no. 39.
[60] Plac. in Canc. file 16, no. 16; Chan. Inq. p.m. 15 Ric. II, pt. ii, no. 179.
[61] Chan. Inq. p.m. 33 Hen. VI, no. 29.

[62] Ibid.
[63] Feud. Aids, ii, 443.
[64] Close, 21 Hen. VI, m. 14 d.
[65] Feud. Aids, ii, 450.
[66] Chan. Inq. p.m. 33 Hen. VI, no. 29; Close, 30 Hen. VI, m. 30 d.
[67] Chan. Inq. p.m. 33 Hen. VI, no. 29.
[68] Hasted, Hist. of Kent, iii, 677.
[69] P.C.C. Will quoted by Hasted, loc. cit.
[70] Exch. Inq. p.m. (Ser. 2), file 290, no. 4.
[71] He sold Pirton to Alice Say and John Leche in Jan. 1507-8 (Close, 23 Hen. VII, no. 28).
[72] Chan. Inq. p.m. (Ser. 2), xxxi, 97.
[73] Ibid.
[74] Feet of F. Herts. Hil. 6 Edw. VI; cf. Herts. Visit. (Harl. Soc.), 57.

[75] Ibid.
[76] Ibid.; Recov. R. East. 3 Chas. I, m. 36.
[77] Chauncy, Hist. Antiq. of Herts. 264.
[78] Sess. R. (Herts. Co. Rec.), i, 225.
[79] Ibid. 330.
[80] Chauncy, loc. cit.
[81] Clutterbuck, Hist. and Antiq. of Herts. ii, 183.
[82] Ibid.
[83] M.I. quoted by Cussans, op. cit. Hertford Hund. 81.
[84] Clutterbuck, loc. cit.
[85] See under Balls Park.
[86] Mins. Accts. Hen. VIII, R. 964; Pat. 32 Eliz. pt. xiv.
[87] Mins. Accts. Hen. VIII, R. 964; V.C.H. Essex, ii, 170.

A HISTORY OF HERTFORDSHIRE

It was distinct from the neighbouring manor of Brickendon, which with its members had been held by the canons since the foundation of their house.[88] It probably had its nucleus in the lands given to Waltham by Gilbert Monk ('Monacus') in the latter part of the 12th century.[89] These were the tenements of Henry the Salter ('Salinarius'), Siward Claud and Edward Felleden in Amwell near Brickendon and certain meadow lying in Broadmead, Caldwell and 'Hoco' (? Hook).[90] Gilbert's brother John confirmed this grant,[91] and Richard I included the land 'at Brickendon' (sic) given by Gilbert the Monk in his confirmatory charter to the abbey on 14 March 1189–90.[92] The land in the hamlet of Rushen came to the abbey by grant of Walter de Wyteberuwe (Widbury) and his wife Beatrice.[93] Other land in Amwell was held by the abbey of the fee of Philip son of Galien of Hertford,[94] who held of the Prioress of Cheshunt land acquired from Galien son of Joseph.[95] Philip and his wife Beatrice gave to the abbey Chadwell (Chaldewell) Grove and 'Chadwell holme' with a part of his meadow which was of the fee of Berkhampstead, desiring that the monks would improve the water supply from Chadwell Spring.[96] The abbey also acquired other small tenements in Amwell from various donors.[97]

The 'manor' of Little Amwellbury was let for forty years to Nicholas Nortes in 1536.[98] After the surrender of Waltham Abbey on 23 March 1540 this manor was purchased from the Crown on 17 June 1542 by Richard Andrews of Hailes, co. Glouc., and Leonard Chamberlain of Woodstock.[99] They immediately obtained licence to convey to John Knighton of Aldbury the elder and to his son John Knighton the younger.[100] In 1576 John Knighton the elder of Bayford conveyed the manor to John son of George Knighton.[1] In 1590 George Knighton and his son John Knighton the younger had licence to alienate a moiety of the manor to John Knighton the elder, gent.[2] This last was evidently the son of Sir George Knighton of Bayford. He held a court for Little Amwell in 1614[3] and was the last of his name.[4] He is said to have given the manor to Henry Gardiner of Jenningsbury, a gentleman 'knowing and ingenious in the management of the affairs of this country,' who had married his niece Mary Spring.[5] Little Amwell was thus united to the neighbouring manor of Jenningsbury, with which it has descended to the present Marquess Townshend.

The Abbot of Waltham obtained a grant of free warren in Amwell and elsewhere on 30 March 1253.[6] He had extensive liberties, including sac and soc, infangtheof and utfangtheof, and quittance from shires and hundreds throughout all his lands.[7] Thus the abbey had its 'liberty' of Little Amwell distinct from its 'liberty' of Brickendon; but it appears that Rushen was a tithing of Brickendon,[8] and it was to Brickendon that Gilbert the Monk and his heirs sent for the rent due for the lands with which he had endowed the abbey.[9]

The manor of Hertford Priory was styled in 1637 'the manor of Hertford Priors otherwise called the manor of the Priory of Hertford and now or late called or known by the name of the manor of Amwell or called and known by the name of the fee of Amwell.'[10] This was probably due to the close connexion between the Limesy fee in Hertford and Amwell.[10a] The founder of Hertford Priory, Ralph de Limesy the elder (vetus), also endowed it among other holdings with a free tenement in Amwell,[11] evidently part of the fee which he held in 1086.[12] The priory had charters concerning this land from Ralph's uncle and from John de Limesy.[13] In the time of Richard I Ralph de Limesy, possibly the grandson of Geoffrey de Limesy and tenant of Great Amwell under the elder branch of the family,[14] attempted to exact from the priory aid towards scutage contrary to the effect of these charters.[15] The lands and rents of the priory in Amwell were valued at £1 0s. 2d. in 1291.[16] They may perhaps be identical with the estate held by the priory now known as *BALLS PARK*, which is a detached portion of the parish of Little Amwell,[17] surrounded by the parishes of St. John Rural and Brickendon Urban and Rural.[18] The name 'Balls' also exists in 'Balleshoke,' a meadow adjoining the footway from Hertford to Ware, near a former footbridge called 'High Bridge.'[19] Balleshoke was among the possessions of Hertford Priory in 1462. In that year Prior Thomas Walden failed to credit himself with various sums received to the use of the priory. These included 6s. 8d. paid by Thomas Blak and John Sadiller for hay crops at Balleshoke.[20] The capital messuage called 'Balles' was evidently included in those 'members' of the manor of Hertford Priory which lay in Hertford. It was held with the manor by Richard Willis at his death 16 October 1625,[21] and descended from him to Thomas Willis of Fen Ditton.[22] He sold with the priory manor to John Harrison of London in 1637 the mansion-house and farm called Balls 'and two other little tenements thereto belonging and now decayed.'[23]

Harrison rebuilt the house at Balls Park, where he was visited in 1643 by John Evelyn the diarist.[24]

---

[88] See above.
[89] Harl. MS. 391, fol. 80b; 4809, fol. 166.
[90] Ibid. 391, fol. 80b, 81b; 4809, fol. 166b. [91] Ibid. 391, fol. 81b.
[92] Ibid. fol. 42; cf. Cart. Antiq. RR, 7.
[93] Harl. MS. 3809, fol. 174b, 175, 177b. [94] Cal. Bodl. Chart. Midd. R. 1.
[95] Harl. MS. 4809, fol. 171, 181b.
[96] 'De cursu aque fontis de Chaldewelle suam conditionem meliorare' (ibid. fol. 167).
[97] Cott. MS. Tib. C ix, fol. 90, 92; Harl. MS. 4809, fol. 166 et seq.
[98] Mins. Accts. Hen. VIII, R. 964.
[99] L. and P. Hen. VIII, xvii, 443 (39).
[100] Ibid. (46).
[1] Memo. R. (Exch. L.T.R.), Hil. 19 Eliz. 'Recorda,' m. 27.

[2] Pat. 32 Eliz. pt. xiv.
[3] Chauncy, Hist. and Antiq. of Herts. 264.
[4] M. I. quoted by Clutterbuck, op. cit. ii, 44.
[5] Chauncy, op. cit. 264, 269; cf. Herts. Visit. (Harl. Soc.), 57.
[6] Cal. Chart. R. 1226–57, p. 427.
[7] Plac. de Quo Warr. (Rec. Com.), 283.
[8] Ct. R. (Gen. Ser.), portf. 178, no. 21; 174, no. 42.
[9] Harl. MS. 391, fol. 80b.
[10] Close, 13 Chas. I, pt. xxxviii, no. 17.
[10a] See under Great Amwell and Hertford Borough.
[11] Fines, 10 Ric. I and Rot. Cur. Reg. (Pipe R. Soc. xxiv), 219.
[12] See under Great Amwell.
[13] Fines, 10 Ric. I, &c., loc. cit.

[14] See under Great Amwell.
[15] Fines, 10 Ric. I, &c., loc. cit. The priory also held Great Amwell Church. This plea may therefore refer to the church endowment.
[16] Pope Nich. Tax. (Rec. Com.), 15.
[17] See above.
[18] Sir John Harrison, kt., in effecting the union of the parishes of All Saints and St. John, Hertford, reserved the tithes of his own lands, i.e. of Balls Park (Chauncy, op. cit. 258).
[19] Sess. R. (Herts. Co. Rec.), i, 203, 224, 368.
[20] Mins. Accts. bdle. 865, no. 15.
[21] Chan. Inq. p.m. (Ser. 2), ccccxviii, 64.
[22] See under Hertford Borough.
[23] Close, 13 Chas. I, pt. xxxviii, no. 17.
[24] Evelyn, Diary (ed. Bray), i, 39.

HERTFORD HUNDRED

He was one of the farmers of the customs [25] in 1640–1 and M.P. for Lancaster.[26] Charles I knighted him in 1640 in reward for advancing £50,000 on the security of the subsidies; but it was with difficulty that he overcame the scruples of the Long Parliament regarding the payment of interest.[27] He supported the Royalist cause until August 1645, when he tried to surrender to Parliament.[28] His estates had been sequestrated, Balls Park was in the hands of a certain Mr. Rolles, who left it empty, making scarcely any use of the orchard and gardens, and Lady Harrison and her children were homeless.[29] Harrison fled to France and only recovered his estates in 1648 by paying a fine of £1,000.[30] After his death in 1669 Lady Mary retained Balls Park for life. She died in 1705.[31] The estate was inherited by her son Richard,[32] and ultimately passed to his third son Edward Harrison, who had served the East India Company as Governor of Fort St. George in 1711 and was appointed postmaster-general in 1726.[33] His daughter and heir Audrey wife of Charles third Viscount Townshend was the brilliant and witty friend of Horace Walpole[34] and the mother of Charles Townshend, chancellor of the Exchequer,[35] who doubtless inherited from her his eloquence and facility of repartee. Her uncle George Harrison lived at Balls until his death in 1759.[36] She died 5 March 1788, having bequeathed the estate to her grandson Lord John Townshend.[37] It descended to his son John, who became Marquess Townshend in 1855 upon the death of his cousin George, the third marquess.[38] Balls Park was one of the principal seats of his son, the fifth marquess.[39] The present owner is Sir George Fandel Faudel-Phillips, bart., who purchased the estate (where he had already resided for some time) in 1901.

HARRISON. *Or a cross azure with five pheons or thereon.*

FAUDEL-PHILLIPS, baronet. *Paly ermine and azure a chief gules with a squirrel or therein.*

The house is an early and interesting example of the purer type of design which the influence of the work of Inigo Jones was beginning to make fashionable towards the end of the first half of the 17th century. Built, so far as can be ascertained, soon after the year 1640 (see above), the elevations have so completely lost the characteristics of the preceding Jacobean style as to appear at a little distance contemporary with the large sash-windows by which the original casement frames were replaced early in the 18th century, when the house was enlarged by the addition of a kitchen wing on the west. The original house, which is square on plan with a central court, perhaps originally open, but now covered in, is of two stories elevated on a basement, with an attic floor in the roof, and is built of narrow red bricks, the courses varying in depth from 2¼ in. to 2½ in., with occasional dressings of stone. All four elevations are of equal length and height, and are crowned by uniform slated roofs, hipped at the angles, and having projecting eaves supported by large and widely-spaced console brackets of wood. An elaborate string-course of moulded brick, which marks the level of the first floor, runs round the whole building, and the architraves of the windows are also of moulded brick, while the angles are emphasized by rusticated quoins of the same material. The walls set back from the face of the basement with a bold inverted cyma. The entrance doorway in the centre of the principal or north front has elaborate dressings of stone, from which the paint has recently been removed. It has a semicircular head and is flanked by Tuscan pilasters, from which spring bold consoles of considerable projection supporting a balcony above. Their design and that of the ornament above the keystone of the doorway betray their early 17th-century origin. The first-floor window over the doorway has also a semicircular head with a continuously moulded architrave, and is flanked by Ionic pilasters, each with a swag depending between the volutes. In the tympanum of the pediment which crowns the design is the shield of Harrison, with the crest of a cuffed arm holding in the hand a broken dart. The centres of the elevations on either side of the doorway are accentuated by semicircular heads to the first-floor windows, which with those of the ground floor are elsewhere square-headed. The basement is lighted by semicircular-headed openings with rusticated dressings of moulded brick. The south front has a central doorway with a porch supported by fluted Ionic columns. This feature is clearly shown to be an addition of the Queen Anne period as well by its greater purity of design as by the method in which the moulded brick string-course at the first floor level is rudely cut away for its insertion—a strong contrast to the workmanlike way in which it is stopped in stone for the dressing of the entrance doorway on the north front. Above is a semicircular-headed window flanked by sham 'œils-de-bœuf.' The east and west elevations are of similar type, with the exception that each stage has pilasters at the angles. The later additions on the west partly conceal this elevation.

The entrance doorway leads by a short passage directly into the central court, known as the vestibule, which has recently been panelled with oak in the Jacobean style, replacing a painted scheme of wall decoration dating from the Queen Anne reconstruction of the house. The fireplace here, which is of Jacobean date, was brought from elsewhere. To the east of the entrance, occupying the remainder of the

---

[25] *Cal. S. P. Dom.* 1641–3, p. 491.
[26] *V.C.H. Lancs.* ii, 234.
[27] Gardiner, *Hist. of Engl.* 1603–42, ix, 254.
[28] *Cal. Com. for Comp.* 1523.
[29] Ibid.
[30] Ibid.
[31] M. I. in All Saints' Church quoted by Clutterbuck, *Hist. and Antiq. of Herts.* ii, 157.
[32] Ibid. 158.
[33] Ibid. Some letters from Harrison to his son-in-law Lord Townshend are preserved among the Townshend papers (*Hist. MSS. Com. Rep.* xi, App. iv, 348, 349, 350).
[34] Walpole, *Letters* (ed. 1905), xiv, 69, passim. [35] *Dict. Nat. Biog.*
[36] M. I. in All Saints quoted by Clutterbuck, op. cit. ii, 158; cf. *Hist. MSS. Com. Rep.* xi, App. iv, 357.
[37] *Gent. Mag.* lviii, 275.
[38] G.E.C. *Complete Peerage*, vii, 418.
[39] Ibid.

413

south front on this side, is the dining room, the walls of which are lined with painted panelling. The original kitchen probably occupied the corresponding portion of this front to the west of the entrance. The offices are now principally contained in a building added to this side of the house at the 18th-century reconstruction. South of the dining room and separated from it by the main staircase hall is the oak parlour, the ceiling of which appears to be of the original date. Opposite the main entrance, leading out of the hall or vestibule, is a short passage connecting with the south or garden entrance. Some 17th-century panelling is preserved here. Over the fireplace of the small room to the east of the garden entrance is a view of the house, painted, to judge from the figures introduced into the foreground, about the middle of the 17th century. The lay-out of the surrounding gardens has completely disappeared, but in other respects the house presents much the same appearance as now, with the exception that casement frames take the place of the sashes inserted later. The remaining rooms on the ground floor contain little of architectural interest. A later staircase has been formed on the west side of the court. The satin drawing room, over the entrance on the north, and the long gallery on the east, over the dining room and oak parlour, are more nearly in their original condition than any of the principal rooms on the ground floor. Their panelling is divided into compartments by fluted Corinthian pilasters, having the lower third of their shafts enriched with arabesque designs. The panelling of the long gallery is now painted, and, with the exception of the pilasters, is probably 18th-century work. The ceiling of the drawing room, with its wreaths of fruit and flowers in comparatively shallow relief, appears to be of original date with the house. In the principal bed room on the south side of the house is a fine marble chimney-piece of the late 18th century, which was formerly in the vestibule. The corridor communicating with the apartments here has an original plaster ceiling on which is the Harrison crest. Generally the interior has been much modernized, but sufficient detail remains to show that the building is substantially that which was erected by Sir John Harrison about the year 1640.

CHURCH The church of HOLY TRINITY, Little Amwell, was built and endowed about the year 1863. It is in 13th-century style, and consists of chancel, nave, transept, north porch and eastern spire. The advowson is vested in trustees.[40]

The history of the parish church of All Saints and the charities for that parish are given under the borough.

GREAT AMWELL

Emmewell or Emwell (xi–xiv cent.); Ammewell, Amewell or Amwell (xiii–xiv cent.); Amwell Magna, Much Amwell or Great Amwell (xvii cent.).

The parish of Great Amwell lies on the right bank of the River Lea to the south of Ware and the south-east of Hertford. A detached part surrounded by the civil parishes of Little Amwell and St. John's Rural lies to the north-west of Little Amwell. It includes Gallows Plain, and its boundary passes through a tumulus of unknown origin on the western side of 'Barrow Field.'[1]

The parish contains 2,264 acres, but was formerly of greater extent. A considerable portion of the hamlet of Hoddesdon lay within the ecclesiastical parish of Great Amwell[2] until 1844, when Hoddesdon itself was consolidated into a separate parish.[3] This part of Hoddesdon was known as 'Amwell hamlet in Hoddesdon.'[4] The 'vill' of 1086 apparently included a part of Hoddesdon[5] and the lands of Ralf de Limesy in Hertford.[6] The hamlet of Amwell End, notorious for a disorderly fair established without licence in 1768,[7] was transferred to the civil parish of Ware in 1858.[8]

About one-quarter of the parish is arable land. The woods at Amwell Bury, Hertford Heath and Hailey cover some 500 acres. Richard of Hailey gave 5 acres of woodland in Amwell to the friars of Easton, co. Wilts.,[9] in 1301. Characteristic features of the parish are the meadows or 'holmes' of the Lea Valley. Several of these were attached to houses in 'Nethenhostret' in the 14th century.[10] Star Holme belonged to the house called 'the Star' in Ware.[11] Hedenhoo Marsh and Amwell Marsh also provided considerable pasturage.[12]

The parish lies at the junction of the Chalk with the Reading Bed of clay and pebble.[13] The surface soil is clay, chalk and gravel. The village is situated on the western slope of the valley of the Lea, a little to the east of the main road to London from Ware, where Izaak Walton promised to meet 'Venator' for an otter-hunt.[14] The village is on an 'outlier' of the Reading Bed. On the hill-side above is the church with the stocks now much repaired, and close by are the vicarage, Home Lodge, the residence of Rev. R. S. Mylne, F.S.A., and the school built in 1875. The Quaker poet John Scott built a grotto near his father's house at Amwell End and entertained among others Dr. Johnson.[15] The grotto is in the grounds of a house called the Grotto, now the residence of Mr. Sidney Harrington. In writing of Great Amwell Scott describes how the

'Roofs of russet thatch
Rise mix'd with trees, above whose swelling tops
Ascends the tall church tow'r and loftier still
The hill's extended ridge.'[16]

Another poet connected with Amwell is William Warner, author of *Albions England*, who died suddenly in the parish 1 March 1608–9.[17]

---

[40] *Lond. Gaz.* 2 Aug. 1864, p. 3809.
[1] Palaeolithic flint instruments of pointed form have been found at Amwell (*V.C.H. Herts.* i, 227).
[2] The remainder lay in Broxbourne parish, under which the account of Hoddesdon is given.
[3] *Census Rep.* 1901, *Herts.*, 5.
[4] *L. and P. Hen. VIII*, xiv (1), 652 (M 10).   [5] See Broxbourne.
[6] See Hertford.
[7] *Sess. R.* (Herts. Co. Rec.), ii, 123.
[8] *Lond. Gaz.* 7 Sept. 1858, p. 4052.
[9] *Cal. Pat.* 1292–1301, p. 599.
[10] Add. R. 26828.
[11] Chan. Proc. Eliz. H. xv, 50. Linche Holme, Marsh Holme, Locke Holme and Mill Holme are mentioned in the agreement as to tithes in 1399 (Lond. Epis. Reg. Grindall, fol. 95).
[12] Add. R. 26828; Aug. Off. Proc. i, 65.   [13] See *V.C.H. Herts.* i, 13 et seq.
[14] *Complete Angler* (ed. Bohn), 88.
[15] *Dict. Nat. Biog.*
[16] J. Scott, *Amwell* (ed. 1776), 18.
[17] *Dict. Nat. Biog.*

HERTFORD : BALLS PARK FROM THE SOUTH-EAST

HERTFORD : BALLS PARK, THE ENTRANCE FRONT

HERTFORD HUNDRED
GREAT AMWELL

At Amwell Magna Cottage there is let into the wall a triangular panel bearing the date 1606 and surmounted by a crown and thistle and the letters I. R. 6. A. R., the initials of James I and his queen, Anne of Denmark, and the king's favourite motto *Beati pacifici*. This stone was formerly above the central arch of Netherbow Port, Edinburgh,[18] and was placed in its present position by Mr. Robert William Mylne, F.R.S., of the Home Lodge, architect and antiquary. The latter's grandfather, Robert Mylne, F.R.S., architect to the Dean and Chapter of St. Paul's (where he is buried), and designer of the bridge at Blackfriars opened in 1769, settled in Amwell about 1770. He was engineer to the New River Company for forty years, and was succeeded by his son, William Chadwell Mylne of Amwell, who also was engineer to the company, and effected the alterations in the works of the New River Company after the Metropolis Waterworks Act, 1852.[19]

Immediately below the village is 'Emma's Well,' a spring utilized by Sir Hugh Myddelton as one of the sources of the New River. It is said to have been named after Emma wife of Cnut.[20] It seems to have been called 'Amwell Well' in the 14th century.[21] On an island in the New River is a stone bearing a legend to this spring. On another island is a monument to Sir Hugh Myddelton. Beyond the river the Hertford branch of the Great Eastern railway traverses the parish. The River Lea, which forms the eastern boundary, was doubtless the mediaeval route from Amwell to London. There is record of the swamping of a boat on the way to Westminster about 1289.[22] The Lea evidently served also to turn the manorial mill which existed in 1086.[23] It was damaged by the erection of a new sluice by the Abbot of Waltham in 1281,[24] and was still in need of repair in 1289.[25]

Amwell Bury lies to the north-west of the village. Between Amwell Bury and Ware is Presdales,[26] a modern house, the residence of Mr. A. G. Sandeman, J.P.

Hailey is a hamlet in the south of the parish separated from Amwell village by Goldings Wood and the parish of Stanstead St. Margaret's. Hailey Hall, on the main road from Hoddesdon to Ware, is a modernized house with a homestead moat. Near it are brick-works, and the clay on the opposite side of the road is still worked. The hamlet includes Haileybury College, which stands on high ground near the beautiful woodland of Hertford Heath. The heath is crossed by Ermine Street. The college was opened in 1809 for the training of civil servants of the East India Company.[27] After the abolition of the company the building was temporarily used as a barracks for its army. In 1862 the college was converted into a public school.[28] It is built in the classical style after the designs of Mr. William Wilkins, architect of the National Gallery. The buildings, which are of brick with stone dressings, surround a large quadrangle, having the chapel, library and head master's house on the south. The chapel, which was completed in 1877, occupies the centre of this range. The chancel is on the north, projecting into the quadrangle, and is surmounted by a lofty octagonal dome. The southern portion of the chapel is contained within the walls of the older buildings. To the east is the library, a plain, well-proportioned room, which formed the original chapel. The south front of this range, facing on the terrace, forms the principal elevation of the college, and, seen from Hailey Lane, presents an imposing appearance. The centre is marked by a hexastyle portico of the Ionic order, above which rises the chapel dome, and near either end of the elevation are tetrastyle porticoes of the same order. The original perspective drawings for the terrace front, both as first proposed and as actually erected, are preserved in the library, having recently come into the possession of the school authorities. Among the many alterations and additions made to the buildings since 1862 the Bradby Hall, to the east of the great quadrangle, designed by Mr. Reginald Blomfield and erected in 1887, is the most important from an architectural point of view. It is a building of brick in the quasi-Jacobean style of that period. In 1907 additional class rooms were built on the west side of the quadrangle. Hailey House, an 18th-century building of brick, is now incorporated into the premises of the school.

The southernmost point of the parish is the little hamlet of Woolensbrook, where there is a mission church served from Great Amwell. The 15th-century form of this name was 'Wowelond.'

Before the Conquest AMWELL, MANORS AMWELLBURY or GREAT AMWELL was a 'berewick' or outlying estate attached with two others at Hertford and Hoddesdon to Earl Harold's manor of Hatfield Broadoak.[29] All three berewicks were evidently included in the 14½ hides at Amwell which constituted the holding of Ralf de Limesy in 1086.[30] This holding probably extended over what is now Little Amwell, part of which with Ralf's lands in Hertford formed the endowment of his priory at Hertford.[31] Ralf's holding at Hoddesdon was probably identical with the manor of Geddings and other lands held of the manor of Great Amwell.[32]

About 1130 Ralf de Limesy was succeeded in his Hertfordshire lands by his son Alan.[33] Gerard son of Alan owed scutage for lands in Hertfordshire in 1161.[34] His widow Amice had two sons living in 1185.[35] The elder was John de Limesy.[36] Either this John or one of his predecessors seems to have

---

[18] In the centre of the stone above it was the spike on which were placed the heads of executed criminals. This stone is now in Greyfriars churchyard, Edinburgh (inform. kindly supplied by the Rev. R. S. Mylne, F.S.A.).
[19] *Dict. Nat. Biog.*; inform. kindly supplied by the Rev. R. S. Mylne.
[20] *East Herts. Arch. Soc. Trans.* i, 33.
[21] Add. R. 26827. [22] Ibid.
[23] *V.C.H. Herts.* i, 325.
[24] *Cal. Close*, 1279–88, p. 132; *Cal. Pat.* 1281–92, p. 103.

[25] Add. R. 26828.
[26] There is mention of the field 'del prestesdene' in an account of Amwell Manor, 1289–90 (Add. R. 26827).
[27] *V.C.H. Herts.* ii, 97–9. [28] Ibid.
[29] *V.C.H. Essex*, i, 429*b*. Possibly the Hertford 'berewick' was 'Limesy fee' in which was built the Priory of Hertford (see the account of the Borough).
[30] *V.C.H. Herts.* i, 325*b*; cf. ibid. 299; *V.C.H. Essex*, i, 338.
[31] See under Little Amwell; cf. Dugdale, *Mon.* iii, 300.

[32] Add. R. 26828. The manor of Hoddesdonbury and the other manor at Hoddesdon held before the Conquest by Asgar the Staller were dealt with under Broxbourne, in which parish lay Hoddesdonbury.
[33] Hunter, *Great R. of the Pipe*, 31 *Hen. I* (Rec. Com.), 60.
[34] *Red Bk. of Exch.* (Rolls Ser.), 29, 693; cf. Dugdale, *Mon.* iii, 300.
[35] Stacey Grimaldi, *Rot. de Dominabus*, 27.
[36] Ibid.; cf. Dugdale, loc. cit.

made a sub-enfeoffment of Amwell Manor to a younger branch of the family, the descendants of Geoffrey, who was evidently a younger son of Ralf de Limesy of the Domesday Book.[37] Ralph de Limesy, grandson of this Geoffrey, left a daughter Felise, who apparently married Robert the son of her guardian Ralph son of Nicholas.[38] Robert son of Ralph son of Nicholas with his wife 'lady Felicia' had licence,[39] and made an agreement in 1252 with the Prior of Hertford to build a free chapel in their 'court' at Amwell.[40] Felise died without issue,[41] and her cousin Ralph, the son of Alan her father's brother, sold Amwell Manor in or shortly before 1270 to Richard of Ware, Abbot of Westminster,[42] reserving a rent of a clove gillyflower.[43] His nephew and heir Peter de Limesy[44] released all right in the manor as mesne lord to the abbey in 1317.[45] The abbot owed knight's service of one fee to the chief lord,[46] which in 1303 was due to Hugh de Oddingselles,[47] grandson of Basile, one of the co-heirs of John de Limesy.[48] Hugh afterwards sold to the abbey all his rights in Amwell as chief lord.[49] A rental of the late 14th century shows that the abbey exacted the service of a half-fee from Robert son of Robert de Gedding, who was then holding one-quarter of the vill,[50] and of another half-fee from the seven tenants of land which had been held by Nicholas Usshel and John Percival, and also of a quarter-fee from the nine tenants of the holding formerly of Stephen de Aldingbourne.[51]

Abbot Richard promised to assign Amwell Manor to the convent, from the goods of which he had paid Ralph de Limesy 700 marks of silver[52]; but it was not until 1288 that Abbot Walter de Wenlak definitely assigned it to the cellarer of the abbey.[53] In 1535 the treasurer of outlying estates received the profits.[54]

In 1289 the reeve accounted for the manor including the courts, and Brother Richard de Waltham

WESTMINSTER ABBEY. *Gules St. Peter's keys or crossed with St. Edward's ring or in the chief with its gem azure.*

visited Amwell four times yearly to receive the profits.[55] Early in the 14th century Sir William de Goldington, kt., lord of the neighbouring manor of Goldingtons,[56] had a lease of the manor for life.[57] The courts were usually reserved in leases of the demesne lands,[58] and in 1398 the profits of the courts were farmed separately by a collector of rents.[59] In 1537 a reversionary lease of the demesne lands, contingent upon the death of Gilbert Rooks, was made to Thomas Leigh, Master of the Hospital of Burton St. Lazars, and to his nephew William Leigh, a mercer of London, in survivorship.[60]

The abbey surrendered to the Crown in January 1539-40,[61] and in the following August Sir Anthony Denny, kt., of Cheshunt, the favourite of Henry VIII and an ardent supporter of the Reformation,[62] had a grant in tail-male of all the estate of the late abbey at Amwell.[63] Dame Joan, Sir Anthony's beautiful and accomplished widow, purchased from William Leigh his interest in the manor in March 1552-3,[64] and after her death her executor John Tamworth transferred to Henry Denny of Dalonce, co. Essex, the remaining years of Leigh's lease.[65]

DENNY, Earl of Norwich. *Gules a saltire argent between twelve crosses formy or.*

Under the terms of the grant to Sir Anthony the manor descended in tail-male to his son Henry Denny of Cheshunt[66] and his grandson Robert, a minor at his father's death.[67] The latter was succeeded in 1576 by his brother, Sir Edward Denny, kt., who was created Lord Denny of Waltham in 1604 and Earl of Norwich in 1636.[68] In 1600, desiring to build in a place with good air, Sir Edward wished to cut off the entail and purchase the reversionary rights of the Crown in the manor.[69] Having met with opposition from his uncle, he apparently changed his plans.[70] Sir James Hay, kt., his extravagant son-in-law,[71] obtained a grant of the Crown rights in the manor 11 February 1605-6,[72] and in 1607 joined with Sir Edward in a sale to Thomas Hobbes the elder of Gray's

---

[37] Wrottesley, *Ped. from Plea R.* 530, 538. The same family held also of the elder branch in Yardley, co. Worc. (Bracton, *Note Bk.* [ed. Maitland], iii, 347-9).
[38] *Excerpta e Rot. Fin.* (Rec. Com.), i, 177; Wrottesley, loc. cit.
[39] Doc. of Westm. Abbey, Press 17, shelf 4, box 76, no. 4248.
[40] Feet of F. Herts. 36 Hen. III, no. 413. [41] Wrottesley, loc. cit.
[42] The fine between the abbot, who was probably a native of Ware, and Ralph is dated Feb. 1269-70 (Doc. at Westm. no. 4246, cf. no. 4214, 4197), and the charter was enrolled in 54 Hen. III (Pat. 54 Hen. III, m. 26 d.). But Henry III granted liberties to the abbot in his manor of Amwell in May 1262. (see the confirmation by Edward I, Westm. Doc. 4243; cf. Assize R. 323, m. 45). The purchase was undoubtedly made by Richard of Ware, and must therefore have taken place after 1259, when he became abbot (*V.C.H. Lond.* i, 455).
[43] Pat. 54 Hen. III, m. 26 d.

[44] Wrottesley, op. cit. 538.
[45] Doc. at Westm. no. 4196; cf. De Banco R. 199, m. 116 d.; *Cal. Close*, 1313-18, p. 204; 1313-15, p. 343. The family of Limesy were tenants of the abbey in the 14th century (Add. R. 26828, 26829).
[46] Pat. 54 Hen. III, m. 26 d.; *Feud. Aids*, ii, 433.
[47] *Feud. Aids*, ii, 433.
[48] See the account of Caldecote.
[49] Doc. at Westm. 4230. About the same time Juliane daughter of Simon of Offley conveyed to her son Robert all her right in the vill (ibid. 4199).
[50] Add. R. 26828. This was possibly the manor of Geddings in Hoddesdon which was held as of Amwell Manor (Chan. Inq. p.m. [Ser. 2], li, 50). See under Broxbourne.
[51] Add. R. 26828.
[52] *Cal. Pat.* 1281-92, p. 416; Doc. at Westm. no. 4246.
[53] *Cal. Pat.* 1281-92, p. 416; cf. *Cal. Close*, 1307-13, p. 24; Mins. Accts. bdle. 1109, no. 4; *V.C.H. Lond.* i, 449.

[54] *Valor Eccl.* (Rec. Com.), i, 415.
[55] Add. R. 26827.
[56] See under Stanstead St. Margaret's.
[57] Doc. at Westm. no. 4231; cf. no. 4219.
[58] Harl. Chart. 80, F. 26; Add. R. 26829.
[59] Add. R. 26829.
[60] Harl. Chart. 80, F. 26. William Rook of Berden had been a tenant within the manor in 1378 (*Cal. Pat.* 1377-81, p. 219).
[61] *V.C.H. Lond.* i, 447.
[62] *Dict. Nat. Biog.*
[63] *L. and P. Hen. VIII*, xv, 1027 (25).
[64] Harl. Chart. 80, F. 26.
[65] Ibid.
[66] Chan. Inq. p.m. (Ser. 2), xc, 115.
[67] Ibid. clxix, 85.
[68] G.E.C. *Complete Peerage*, vi, 100.
[69] *Cecil MSS.* (Hist. MSS. Com.), x, 26; *Cal. S. P. Dom.* 1598-1601, p. 386.
[70] *Cecil MSS.* (Hist. MSS. Com.), x, 26, 80.
[71] G.E.C. *Complete Peerage*, iii, 63.
[72] Pat. 3 Jas. I, pt. xvi.

GREAT AMWELL CHURCH FROM THE SOUTH-EAST

HERTFORD HUNDRED — GREAT AMWELL

Inn.[73] Thomas Hobbes, possibly the son of the last-named Thomas, settled the remainder of the manor, failing his own children, on those of his sister Martha Peyton.[74] He left an only daughter Susan, who was aged ten at his death in February 1631–2.[75] She married John Fiennes, second son of William first Viscount Saye and Sele.[76] Upon his death in 1696 Amwell Manor passed to his son-in-law Thomas Filmer of the Inner Temple, who had purchased the reversion of it.[77] He died in 1701 and was succeeded by his two daughters, Susan wife of Robert Eddowes and Mary afterwards married to Edward Trotman.[78] They sold the Amwell estate to Thomas Burford,[79] and it descended to his brother John Burford of King's College, Cambridge.[80] Upon his death it was purchased by Bibye Lake of Edmonton, whose only daughter and heir Anna Maria took it in marriage to Colonel Charles Brown.[81] At his death in 1836 it descended to his son Captain Henry Brown, who had distinguished himself in the Peninsular War.[82] His widow, Mrs. Mary Anne Brown, held it after his death, which took place in November 1873.[83] It was inherited by Captain Brown's only child, Mrs. Charrington, from whom the lordship of the manor was purchased by the governors of Haileybury College.[84]

A hall existed at Amwell in 1289.[85] It may have been the 'capital messuage' with lands in 'Hallefeld' held by Andrew de Godesfeld, one of the successors of Stephen de Aldingbourne, in the latter half of the 14th century.[86] In 1398 the 'house' had to be repaired after a strong wind.[87] Sir Edward Denny's desire to build at Amwell implies that there was probably no considerable house there in 1600. The present Amwell Bury lies among woods about half a mile to the north-west of the village. It has a modern pigeon-house, the walls of which evidently encase a late 17th-century building. The house is now the property of Mr. E. S. Hanbury of Poles.

Henry III granted to the Abbot of Westminster in Amwell all the extensive liberties which he possessed in his other lands.[88] By virtue of this charter, and a confirmation of it by Edward I,[89] the abbey had return of writs, exemption from the sheriff's tourn, view of frankpledge, amends of assize of bread and ale and other royalties[90] within the 'liberty' of Amwell.[91]

A striking result of the abbot's privileges was the difficulty experienced by the tenants of the manor in bringing pleas of land against their lord. Hence a plea between Peter de Limesy and the abbot in 1313 became a test case as to the right of the sheriff to enter a liberty in the case of default upon the part of the officers of its lord.[92]

There was a fishery in the mill-pond in 1289–90.[93] This was probably the fishery farmed by Ellen de Limesy in 1398.[94] At the present day the subscription waters of Amwell Magna Fishery, which have been sold to the Metropolitan Water Board, are among the best in the River Lea.

In 1086 Geoffrey de Bech held 2 hides at *HAILEY* (Hailet, xi cent. ; Heilet, xii cent. ; Heyle, xiv cent. ; Heyleghe, xv cent.). They had formerly been held by Wlwin, a man of Earl Harold,[95] and with the rest of Geoffrey's fief had subsequently been in the hands of Ilbert, the first Norman sheriff of the county.[96] In 1086 the lord of the manor of Great Amwell claimed woodland which Ilbert had attached to this manor, and the canons of Waltham, probably as lords of Brickendon,[97] also laid claim to woodland in Hailey.[98]

Ralf the Butler ('Pincerna')[99] appears to have succeeded Geoffrey de Bech in Hailey, Cockenhatch and Bengeo. In the time of Henry I, Ralf sub-enfeoffed Aubrey de Vere, possibly the father of the first Earl of Oxford, who died in 1141,[100] of all the land which had been held of him by Roger de Burun in Hailey, Cockenhatch and Bengeo.[1] Robert de Burun, possibly the son of Roger, was to recover the tenancy under Aubrey de Vere upon payment of £32.[2] The 2 hides of Geoffrey de Bech and the land held under Ralf the Butler in Hailey apparently included the manor known later as Goldingtons in Thele.[3] Of the interest of Ralf the Butler nothing further is known,[4] but the successive Earls of Oxford retained the overlordship of the manors of Revells Hall in Bengeo and Goldingtons in Thele.[5] There was in 1700 no distinct manor of Hailey,[6] but a reputed 'manor' of Hailey was held with Goldingtons by Sir Andrew Ogard, kt., in the 15th century[7] and was acquired with that manor by William Frankland in 1560.[8] It probably became absorbed in the neighbouring manor of Goldingtons.

---

[73] Feet of F. Herts. Hil. 4 Jas. I; Trin. 5 Jas. I; Recov. R. Trin. 5 Jas. I, m. 81; Add. Chart. 13582; Chauncy, *Hist. Antiq. of Herts.* 283.
[74] They were Robert, Edward and John Peyton and Anne Lawrence; Chan. Inq. p.m. (Ser. 2), ccclxxxiii, 85; cf. Recov. R. East. 22 Chas. I, m. 37.
[75] Chan. Inq. p.m. (Ser. 2), ccclxxxiii, 85.
[76] G.E.C. *Complete Peerage*, vii, 69.
[77] Chauncy, loc. cit.; cf. Recov. R. Trin. 21 Chas. II, m. 49.
[78] Title-deeds quoted by Clutterbuck, *Hist. and Antiq. of Herts.* ii, 11.
[79] Feet of F. Herts. Hil. 5 Geo. I.
[80] Clutterbuck, loc. cit.
[81] Cussans, op. cit. *Hertford Hund.* 123; Recov. R. Mich. 23 Geo. III, m. 205; Feet of F. Herts. East. 40 Geo. III; Mich. 54 Geo. III.
[82] Cussans, loc. cit.; cf. Recov. R. Mich. 54 Geo. III, m. 195.
[83] Cussans, loc. cit.
[84] Inform. kindly supplied by the Rev. R. S. Mylne, F.S.A.

[85] Add. R. 26827.
[86] Ibid. 26828; the name 'Haulfeefelide' is mentioned in the settlement concerning tithes in 1399 (Lond. Epis. Reg. Grindall, fol. 95).
[87] Add. R. 26829.
[88] Doc. at Westm. no. 4243.
[89] Ibid.
[90] *Hund. R.* (Rec. Com.), i, 190; *Plac. de Quo Warr.* (Rec. Com.), 276.
[91] Add. R. 26828.
[92] De Banco R. 199, m. 116 d.
[93] Add. R. 26827.
[94] Ibid. 26829.
[95] *V.C.H. Herts.* i, 334a.
[96] Ibid. 273.
[97] See above.
[98] *V.C.H. Herts.* i, 334a.
[99] Possibly the Ralf of Oversley who was butler to Robert Earl of Leicester (Dugdale, *Baronage*, i, 594).
[100] Round, *Geoff. de Mandeville*, 389.
[1] Harl. Chart. 46, I, 30.
[2] Ibid.
[3] See under Stanstead St. Margaret's.
[4] Possibly his descendants failed to assert their right to service from such powerful mesne tenants as the Earls of Oxford. But about 1314 a quarter-fee in Hailey was said to be held of Alan la Zouche, lord of Ware, by the Abbot of Westminster (*Cal. Inq. p.m.* 1–9 *Edw. II*, 253), and a quarter-fee was also held of him in Bengeo by the Earls of Oxford, and the manor of Chelsin Temple there by the Knights Templars. It is possible that the interest of Ralf the Butler was subsequently acquired by the Earls of Leicester (lords of Ware), in whose family Ralf the Butler of Oversley and his descendants held office. In this case the jurors, who returned the Abbot of Westminster as tenant of the quarter-fee, had possibly failed to distinguish between the two holdings in Hailey.
[5] *Feud. Aids*, ii, 433; Chan. Inq. p.m. (Ser. 2), ccclxxiii, 15.
[6] Chauncy, op. cit. 283.
[7] Chan. Inq. p.m. printed by Cussans, op. cit. *Hertford Hund.* 135; cf. Chart. R. 21–4 Hen. VI, no. 44.
[8] Feet of F. Herts. East. 2 Eliz.

A HISTORY OF HERTFORDSHIRE

A part of Hailey lay within the lordship of Great Amwell.[9]

The church of ST. JOHN BAPTIST CHURCH stands in the village and consists of a round apsidal chancel 25 ft. by 16 ft., nave 39 ft. by 22 ft. 6 in., west tower 12 ft. by 10 ft. 6 in., and vestry; all internal dimensions.

The chancel and nave date from the close of the 11th century,[10] the west tower was built about 1420–30, the vestry is modern. The church was restored in 1866. The walls are of flint rubble with stone dressings; the roofs are tiled.

In the north wall of the chancel is a narrow window of the 11th century, with deeply splayed jambs both inside and outside; it is round-arched, but a slight point has been given to the outer arch at some later period. The other windows of the chancel are all modern lancets. The doorway to the vestry in the north wall has a massive 15th-century oak frame with four-centred head. Two recesses, one on either side of the east window, now used as sedilia, are of modern stonework. There is a modern piscina in the south wall with an old basin, part of which has been cut away. The chancel arch is round, of two plain square orders towards the west, square jambs and grooved and splayed abaci not returned on east or west faces; it is probably of late 11th-century date. On either side of the chancel arch is a round-arched squint, recently enlarged, set diagonally in the wall. The roof retains one tie-beam of the 15th century; the eastern part of the apse roof is domical and above it is a gabled roof.

A sloping recess in the north wall of the nave at the east end marks the position of the stair to the rood-loft. In the north wall are two windows, one of three lights with traceried head and the other a single traceried light. In the south wall are a 13th-century lancet with splayed jambs and a window of three lights of 15th-century character. All these windows are of modern stonework externally, but their inner jambs are old. In the south wall is a 14th-century piscina with trefoiled head and moulded edges; part only of the basin is original. The roof is modern.

The tower is of three stages with an embattled parapet; the octagonal timber spire is modern. The tower arch is of the 15th century; the arch is moulded, the outer mouldings being continuous, the inner resting on engaged shafts with moulded capitals and bases. The west doorway has a moulded arch with a square head and traceried spandrels; in the inner jambs are the holes for the old wooden bar. The door, which is of 15th-century date, has tracery in the head. The west window is of three cinquefoiled lights under a four-centred arch; the mullions are of modern stonework. A newel stair is carried up in the south-west corner of the tower. The second stage has loop lights on each face but the east; on each face of the belfry stage is a two-light window with traceried head under a four-centred arch, the mullions of which have been repaired.

The font is modern. The oak communion table is of early 17th-century date. The octagonal pulpit is of oak with lozenge-shaped panels flanked by herms; the cornice bears the date 1696, but the rest of the work appears to be earlier in the century. It is said to have originally belonged to the chapel of the archiepiscopal palace at Croydon.[11] In the tower is a modern screen in which are incorporated 15th-century traceried doors from a former screen.

On the north wall of the nave is a brass with the figure of a civilian with his two wives and seven children; the head of the male figure is missing and there is no inscription. On the east wall of the nave is the figure of a priest of 15th-century date, in alb and hood, without inscription.

There are three bells: the treble has neither date nor inscription; the second is by Robert Oldfield, dated 1612; the tenor is undated, but in it is set an Elizabethan shilling.

The communion plate consists of cup and cover paten, 1620, and another paten, 1736.

The registers before 1812 are as follows: (i) all entries 1559 to 1657; (ii) baptisms and burials 1683 to 1791, marriages 1683 to 1753; (iii) baptisms and burials 1792 to 1812; (iv) marriages 1754 to 1793; (v) marriages 1793 to 1812.

ADVOWSON A priest was among the tenants of Ralf de Limesy at Amwell in 1086.[12] The church of Amwell with all its tithes was apparently given to Hertford Priory by Ralf. It was confirmed to the priory by Alan son of Ralf as the gift of his father,[13] but was not definitely mentioned in the foundation charter of the priory.[14] A vicarage was ordained between 1291 and 1349.[15] In 1399 a new agreement was made between the priory and John Bodlet, then vicar.[16] This was possibly the result of a recent agreement between the Prior of Hertford and the Bishop of London, impropriator of Broxbourne, as to the exact limits of the two parishes.[17] Henry Johnson, vicar of Amwell, in 1539 successfully asserted the right of the vicar to certain tithes under the composition of 1399.[18]

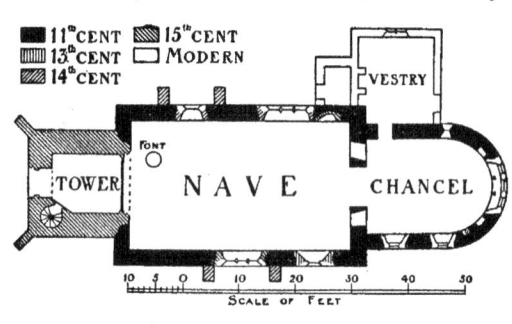

PLAN OF GREAT AMWELL CHURCH

Key: 11th CENT / 13th CENT / 14th CENT / 15th CENT / MODERN

[9] Add. R. 26827, 26828.
[10] A south porch is mentioned in the register 11 Oct. 1626.
[11] Rev. W. J. Harvey, *Great Amwell, Past and Present*, 1896.
[12] *V.C.H. Herts.* i, 325.
[13] Dugdale, *Mon.* iii, 300.
[14] Ibid. 299.
[15] *Pope Nich. Tax.* (Rec. Com.), 18; *Cal. Pat.* 1348–50, p. 399.
[16] Lond. Epis. Reg. Grindall, fol. 95.
[17] Newcourt, *Repertorium*, i, 810.
[18] Lond. Epis. Reg. Grindall, fol. 95.

GREAT AMWELL CHURCH : THE NAVE LOOKING EAST

HERTFORD HUNDRED

BAYFORD

In February 1537-8, shortly after the dissolution of Hertford Priory, Anthony Denny and his prospective wife, Joan Champernown, obtained a grant of the advowson and rectory of Amwell [19]; they descended with the manor of Great Amwell to Sir Anthony's grandson Edward, who sold them in 1577 to John and Thomas Skinner.[20] They alienated them to Isaac Woder of Gray's Inn, gentleman, in 1599.[21] In the same year he transferred the presentation for one turn to William Hutchinson, S.T.D.,[22] and apparently parted with the advowson and rectory shortly afterwards, as in 1616 they were bequeathed by Geoffrey Elwes, alderman of London, to his son Silvius,[23] who died in 1638.[24] The advowson and rectory evidently passed to his executor, who was his brother Jeremy.[25] The latter's grandson Jeremy Elwes of Throcking was presented to the living in 1683, and was succeeded by his brother Robert.[26] The advowson descended in the direct line of this family until 1833,[27] when Robert Cary Elwes of Great Billing, great-grandson of the last-named Robert,[28] sold it to the Rev. Mordaunt Barnard, from whom it was purchased by William McNab.[29] His only daughter married the Rev. R. Parrott, who became vicar in 1864. The advowson descended to their daughter, Mrs. W. J. Harvey, wife of the present vicar. The rectorial tithe was not included in the sale to William McNab, and is at present vested in trustees.[30]

On the parish borders near the heath is a chapel belonging to the Countess of Huntingdon's Connexion, built in 1900 in memory of Dr. Reynolds of Cheshunt College. There were certificates for a Quaker meeting-house in 1691, a meeting-place for Anabaptists in 1692, and for Primitive Methodists in 1850.[31]

CHARITIES — The charities of this parish have been consolidated and are regulated by a scheme of the Charity Commissioners 8 May 1908. They comprise the charities of:

1. William Purvey, founded by will proved 28 October 1617, consisting of a yearly rent-charge of 13s. 4d., issuing out of an estate called Wormley Bury at Wormley.

2. William Hill, will (date unknown) referred to in Parliamentary Returns of 1786 as a rent-charge of 20s. A sum of £1 6s., supposed to represent the endowment, is paid in respect of two cottages in Ware Valley in this parish.

3. Sylvester (*alias* Silvius) Elwes, will proved 1639. The endowment now consists of £797 7s. 5d. consols, arising from the sale in 1870 of land originally purchased with a legacy of £40.

4. Elizabeth Spranger, by deed 1686, being a rent-charge of 50s. out of Hailey Hall Farm.

5. William Plomer, will 1727, trust fund £310 5s. consols, arising from the sale in 1870 of land originally purchased with a legacy of £30.

The sums of stock are held by the official trustees, producing £27 13s. 8d. yearly, the total income of the charities amounting to £32 3s., which under the scheme is applied for the benefit of the poor of the ancient parish, mainly in the distribution of money and coal.

BAYFORD

Begesford (xi cent.); Begeford, Beiford (xii cent.); Beyford, Byfordberi (xiii cent.).

The parish of Bayford has an area of 1,852 acres, of which 398 acres are arable land, 1,028 acres permanent grass and 425 acres woods.[1] The parish in the north, where it extends to the River Lea, stands at about 140 ft. above the ordnance datum ; the ground rises gradually in a southerly direction and reaches a height of 402 ft. near Ashendene in the extreme south of the parish. A small stream which rises near Ashen Grove forms part of the eastern boundary of the parish and flows through the grounds of Bayfordbury into the Lea, which forms the northern boundary. Another tributary of the Lea divides Bayford on the west from Little Berkhampstead.

Bayfordbury, the residence of Mr. H. W. C. Baker, the lord of the manor, lies, with its park of 270 acres, in the north-east of the parish. The house is three stories in height with a basement, consisting, as originally designed in 1759, of a square central block with isolated office wings on either side. A view in the possession of the owner shows that the walls were then faced with red brick. In the early 19th century the wings were connected with the main portion of the house by the erection of a large room on the west for the reception of the portraits of the Kit Cat Club, which had been moved here from Barn Elms, and the corresponding library on the east. At the same time the exterior of the whole house was stuccoed. The chimney-pieces and doorcases of the earlier date are excellent examples of the mid-18th-century style. The later additions are well designed in the Greek manner of their period. A number of fine cedars standing near the house were planted in 1765. The celebrated collection of portraits of thirty-nine members of the Kit Cat Club, a political association numbering among its members most of the Whig celebrities of the early part of the 18th century, includes those of Addison, Steele and Pope ; they are mostly by Kneller. Sir William Baker married Mary daughter of Jacob Tonson, who was nephew and heir of Jacob Tonson, the secretary of the Kit Cat Club, and the portraits came to his son William Baker in 1772 on the death of Richard Tonson, the last of the Tonsons.[1a]

The village of Bayford lies on high ground on the road leading to Hertingfordbury on the north and

---

[19] L. and P. Hen. VIII, xiii (i), 384 (47).
[20] Pat. 19 Eliz. pt. iv, m. 5.
[21] Feet of F. Herts. Mich. 41 & 42 Eliz.
[22] Lond. Epis. Reg. Grindall, fol. 333*b*.
[23] Cussans, op. cit. *Hertford Hund.* 130.
[24] V.C.H. *Northants Families*, 63.
[25] Ibid.
[26] Inst. Bks. (P.R.O.).
[27] Ibid. ; Feet of F. Herts. Trin. 17 Geo. III.
[28] V.C.H. *Northants Families*, 80.
[29] Cussans, op. cit. *Hertford Hund.* 130.
[30] Inform. kindly supplied by the Rev. R. S. Mylne.
[31] Urwick, op. cit. 481–2.
[1] Statistics from Bd. of Agric. (1905).
[1a] See article on Bayfordbury by J. J. Baker in *East Herts. Arch. Soc. Trans.* iii, 264.

HERTFORD HUNDRED

BAYFORD

In February 1537-8, shortly after the dissolution of Hertford Priory, Anthony Denny and his prospective wife, Joan Champernown, obtained a grant of the advowson and rectory of Amwell [19]; they descended with the manor of Great Amwell to Sir Anthony's grandson Edward, who sold them in 1577 to John and Thomas Skinner.[20] They alienated them to Isaac Woder of Gray's Inn, gentleman, in 1599.[21] In the same year he transferred the presentation for one turn to William Hutchinson, S.T.D.,[22] and apparently parted with the advowson and rectory shortly afterwards, as in 1616 they were bequeathed by Geoffrey Elwes, alderman of London, to his son Silvius,[23] who died in 1638.[24] The advowson and rectory evidently passed to his executor, who was his brother Jeremy.[25] The latter's grandson Jeremy Elwes of Throcking was presented to the living in 1683, and was succeeded by his brother Robert.[26] The advowson descended in the direct line of this family until 1833,[27] when Robert Cary Elwes of Great Billing, great-grandson of the last-named Robert,[28] sold it to the Rev. Mordaunt Barnard, from whom it was purchased by William McNab.[29] His only daughter married the Rev. R. Parrott, who became vicar in 1864. The advowson descended to their daughter, Mrs. W. J. Harvey, wife of the present vicar. The rectorial tithe was not included in the sale to William McNab, and is at present vested in trustees.[30]

On the parish borders near the heath is a chapel belonging to the Countess of Huntingdon's Connexion, built in 1900 in memory of Dr. Reynolds of Cheshunt College. There were certificates for a Quaker meeting-house in 1691, a meeting-place for Anabaptists in 1692, and for Primitive Methodists in 1850.[31]

CHARITIES — The charities of this parish have been consolidated and are regulated by a scheme of the Charity Commissioners 8 May 1908. They comprise the charities of:

1. William Purvey, founded by will proved 28 October 1617, consisting of a yearly rent-charge of 13s. 4d., issuing out of an estate called Wormley Bury at Wormley.

2. William Hill, will (date unknown) referred to in Parliamentary Returns of 1786 as a rent-charge of 20s. A sum of £1 6s., supposed to represent the endowment, is paid in respect of two cottages in Ware Valley in this parish.

3. Sylvester (*alias* Silvius) Elwes, will proved 1639. The endowment now consists of £797 7s. 5d. consols, arising from the sale in 1870 of land originally purchased with a legacy of £40.

4. Elizabeth Spranger, by deed 1686, being a rent-charge of 50s. out of Hailey Hall Farm.

5. William Plomer, will 1727, trust fund £310 5s. consols, arising from the sale in 1870 of land originally purchased with a legacy of £30.

The sums of stock are held by the official trustees, producing £27 13s. 8d. yearly, the total income of the charities amounting to £32 3s., which under the scheme is applied for the benefit of the poor of the ancient parish, mainly in the distribution of money and coal.

BAYFORD

Begesford (xi cent.); Begeford, Beiford (xii cent.); Beyford, Byfordberi (xiii cent.).

The parish of Bayford has an area of 1,852 acres, of which 398 acres are arable land, 1,028 acres permanent grass and 425 acres woods.[1] The parish in the north, where it extends to the River Lea, stands at about 140 ft. above the ordnance datum; the ground rises gradually in a southerly direction and reaches a height of 402 ft. near Ashendene in the extreme south of the parish. A small stream which rises near Ashen Grove forms part of the eastern boundary of the parish and flows through the grounds of Bayfordbury into the Lea, which forms the northern boundary. Another tributary of the Lea divides Bayford on the west from Little Berkhampstead.

Bayfordbury, the residence of Mr. H. W. C. Baker, the lord of the manor, lies, with its park of 270 acres, in the north-east of the parish. The house is three stories in height with a basement, consisting, as originally designed in 1759, of a square central block with isolated office wings on either side. A view in the possession of the owner shows that the walls were then faced with red brick. In the early 19th century the wings were connected with the main portion of the house by the erection of a large room on the west for the reception of the portraits of the Kit Cat Club, which had been moved here from Barn Elms, and the corresponding library on the east. At the same time the exterior of the whole house was stuccoed. The chimney-pieces and door-cases of the earlier date are excellent examples of the mid-18th-century style. The later additions are well designed in the Greek manner of their period. A number of fine cedars standing near the house were planted in 1765. The celebrated collection of portraits of thirty-nine members of the Kit Cat Club, a political association numbering among its members most of the Whig celebrities of the early part of the 18th century, includes those of Addison, Steele and Pope; they are mostly by Kneller. Sir William Baker married Mary daughter of Jacob Tonson, who was nephew and heir of Jacob Tonson, the secretary of the Kit Cat Club, and the portraits came to his son William Baker in 1772 on the death of Richard Tonson, the last of the Tonsons.[1a]

The village of Bayford lies on high ground on the road leading to Hertingfordbury on the north and

---

[19] *L. and P. Hen. VIII*, xiii (i), 384 (47).
[20] Pat. 19 Eliz. pt. iv, m. 5.
[21] Feet of F. Herts. Mich. 41 & 42 Eliz.
[22] Lond. Epis. Reg. Grindall, fol. 333*b*.
[23] Cussans, op. cit. *Hertford Hund.* 130.
[24] *V.C.H. Northants Families*, 63.
[25] Ibid.
[26] Inst. Bks. (P.R.O.).
[27] Ibid.; Feet of F. Herts. Trin. 17 Geo. III.
[28] *V.C.H. Northants Families*, 80.
[29] Cussans, op. cit. *Hertford Hund.* 130.
[30] Inform. kindly supplied by the Rev. R. S. Mylne.
[31] Urwick, op. cit. 481-2.
[1] Statistics from Bd. of Agric. (1905).
[1a] See article on Bayfordbury by J. J. Baker in *East Herts. Arch. Soc. Trans.* iii, 264.

419

Northaw on the south. The village smithy, the school, the vicarage and the Manor House lie close together at the junction of this road with Stocking Lane, which is an old road running north-west and south-east through the parish. Opposite the school is a large pond. Most of the cottages here are of brick and date from the 18th and early 19th centuries. The cottage now used as the post-office appears to date from the first half of the 17th century. It is of brick, two stories in height, with diagonal brick chimney-shafts, and is now weather-boarded. The church stands in an isolated position about a quarter of a mile north-west of the village. South of the village a road branches off westwards to Little Berkhampstead, and still further south another turns east to Broxbourne, passing Ashendene, the residence of the Rev. Charles Edward Hornby, M.A., J.P. Bayford Hall, a short distance north-west of the church, is the residence of Admiral Alexander Plantagenet Hastings, C.B., J.P., and the Misses Randolph reside at Bayford House at the south end of the village. Mr. Leonard Marlborough Powell resides at Bayford Grange and Mrs. Cuninghame at the Warren. The Manor House, near the vicarage, is the seat of Mrs. Barclay. It was originally built in the 17th century, but received many additions and alterations in the 19th century. The original staircase and some 17th-century panelling still remain.

The nearest railway station is Hertingfordbury, about 2 miles north of the village.

The subsoil of the parish in the north is chalk. A belt of Woolwich and Reading Beds runs across the centre and the subsoil in the south is London Clay.

Place-names that occur in Bayford in the 15th century are: Lindhawes (now How Claypits Farm), Westhalegrove, Stroutershacche, Smoggefeld, Walbournes and Crosfeldes. In the middle of the 18th century the following are mentioned: Lobb's Pound, Stockinmead, Boarded Bridge Pastures, Moonfield, Lay Breech, Dendrige Hill, Great and Little Chace, Quaker's Mead, Little Brickhills, Sallinger's Wood, Duricke Lane, Eldenburymore, Weepine Wood, Abbs Close, Haddons Mead, Gidnes, Cramphorne Croft, Stangells, Sluttswell Field, Warborne Spring, Black Fan Wood.

MANOR The manor of BAYFORD was part of the lands of the Saxon kings, and Edward the Confessor held it in demesne on the day he died. During the reign of Harold Bayford was held by Earl Tosti or Tostig, his brother, but after the Conquest it again formed part of the royal demesne, and in 1086 was held by King William. It was then assessed at 10 hides,[2] but this assessment probably included Essendon.[3] William I granted the manor to Peter de Valognes, Sheriff of Hertfordshire,[4] and it was afterwards granted to his son Roger in 1141 by the Empress Maud to hold to him and his heirs.[5] After the death of Roger de Valognes, however, Bayford seems to have returned to the Crown, for Henry de Essex paid 76s. 4d. as the farm of Bayford for half a year in 1154–5.[6] Towards the end of the 12th century the recognized farm of the manors of Bayford and Essendon was £20 annually. Richard the Treasurer (Thesaurarius) returned half this amount in 1177, presumably for half a year, and the whole £20 for some years after.[7] In 1194 the Bishop of London, Richard Fitz Neal, owed 100 marks for having the two manors, 'as he had previously had them,' for life.[8] At the death of the bishop in 1199 the payments of £20 were resumed by William the Treasurer, who then paid for a quarter-year.[9] In 1211 he was succeeded as farmer by John Fitz Hugh,[10] who gave place to John de Bassingburn in 1214,[11] and payment was made by Falkes de Breauté from 1218 to 1221.[12] Richard de Argentein, sheriff of the county, was the farmer in 1226.[13]

In 1228 the manor of Bayford was committed to Raymond de Burgh,[14] and in 1230 to John de Burgh.[15] Raymond paid no farm during the two years he held it, but was pardoned the debt thus incurred in 1230.[16]

In 1247 the king granted the keepership of the manor to his half-brother William de Valence, and in 1249 granted the manor itself to him for life, with reversion to the Crown.[17] William forfeited his lands after the battle of Lewes in 1264, but was restored in 1266, after the defeat of the barons at Evesham,[18] and held Bayford until his death in June 1296,[19] after which in 1297 the issues of the manor were granted to Philip de Wiloughby, Dean of Lincoln, for the remainder of that year and the whole of the next.[20] A little later Edward I granted the manor for life to his second queen, Margaret of France,[21] whom he married in 1299; she held it until her death in 1318,[22] after which it was held for life by Isabella, queen of Edward II,[23] who survived her husband for some years. In 1360 Bayford was granted by Edward III to John of Gaunt, then Earl of Richmond,[24] and his heirs male, and it was confirmed to him in 1376 under his new title of King of Castile and Leon and Duke of Lancaster.[25] William de Louthe was appointed steward there in 1359,[26] and remained

JOHN OF GAUNT, Duke of Lancaster. OLD FRANCE quartering ENGLAND with the difference of a label ermine.

[2] V.C.H. Herts. i, 304b.
[3] Ibid. 278. [4] Cart. Antiq. K. 22.
[5] Ibid. K. 24 ; Round, Geoff. de Mandeville, 236 ; Dugdale, Mon. iii, 346. See Hertford Manor.
[6] Red Bk. of Exch. (Rolls Ser.), ii, 651.
[7] Pipe R. 23 Hen. II (Pipe R. Soc.); 24 Hen. II ; 25 Hen. II.
[8] Pipe R. 6 Ric. I, m. 3.
[9] Ibid. 1 John, m. 7.
[10] Ibid. 13 John, m. 6.
[11] Ibid. 16 John, m. 1.
[12] Ibid. 2 Hen. III, m. 6a, &c.
[13] Rot. Lit. Claus. (Rec. Com.), ii, 116–18b.

[14] Cal. Pat. 1225–32, p. 199.
[15] Ibid. 348 ; cf. the descent of Hertford Castle.
[16] Cal. Close, 1227–31, p. 455 ; Cal. Pat. 1247–58, p. 1.
[17] Cal. Pat. 1247–58, p. 46 ; see also Cal. Chart. R. 1226–57, p. 351.
[18] Dict. Nat. Biog.
[19] Ibid. ; D. of Lanc. Misc. Bks. xii, fol. 56 d.; Assize R. 323, 325. His son Aymer de Valence seems to have claimed the manor, for it appears in the inquisition taken at his death in 1323–4. This was evidently in virtue of the grant to him of Hertford Manor (q.v.).

[20] Chan. Inq. p.m. 17 Edw. II, no. 75 ; Cal. Pat. 1292–1301, p. 316 ; Duchy of Lanc. Misc. bdle. 11, no. 25 ; Duchy of Lanc. Misc. Bks. xii, fol. 56 d.
[21] Duchy of Lanc. Misc. Bks. xii, fol. 58.
[22] Ibid.
[23] Duchy of Lanc. Royal Chart. no. 342 ; Chan. Inq. p.m. 10 Edw. III, no. 47 ; 11 Edw. III, no. 46.
[24] Great Cowcher, fol. 228, no. 1.
[25] Duchy of Lanc. Royal Chart. no. 342, 343.
[26] Abbrev. Rot. Orig. (Rec. Com.), ii, 255 ; Mins. Accts. bdle. 862, no. 19.

HERTFORD HUNDRED

BAYFORD

in office until 1361,[27] when the Abbot of St. Albans received a grant of the manor at farm. John of Gaunt died early in 1399, and his son Henry became king in the same year as Henry IV; thus Bayford returned once more to the Crown, and was granted for life to Henry's second queen, Joan of Navarre.[28] Henry VI, upon his accession in 1422, granted the manor in dower to his mother Katherine of France,[29]

KATHERINE of France. *Azure three fleurs de lis or.*

ELIZABETH WOODVILLE. *Argent a fesse and a quarter gules.*

queen of Henry V, and his successor Edward IV gave it to his queen Elizabeth Woodville for her life.[30]

In 1489 Henry VII leased the manor-house of Bayford and the demesne lands to Robert Markham for seven years,[31] at the end of which term he received the lease for another seven years,[32] and in 1504 a further term of twenty years was granted to Robert's widow, Agnes Markham.[33]

In 1544 Henry VIII granted to John Knighton 'all the manor of Bayford, with members and appurtenances, to be held of the king and his successors as of the duchy of Lancaster by the service of one-fortieth of a knight's fee.'[34-43] John Knighton died in 1586, leaving the manor of Bayford or Bayfordbury to his eldest son George,[44] who died in 1612, leaving a son John and a daughter Anne.[45] John Knighton held the manor until his death in 1635, when it passed to his nephew Knighton Ferrers, son of his sister Anne and Sir John Ferrers.[46] Knighton Ferrers mortgaged Bayford to Edmund Knight in 1638 for £2,000, and died in 1640, leaving the debt to his wife Katherine, who was to pay it off and hold the manor for her life, after which it was to pass to their daughter Katherine.[47] Katherine the younger, when twelve years old, married Thomas Fanshawe, afterwards Viscount Fanshawe[48] of Dromore, and was holding Bayford in 1651,[49] but in 1655 they conveyed it to John Mayo,[50] who was succeeded by his son Israel Mayo in 1675.[51] Israel Mayo, who died in 1715, sold the manor in 1713[52] to Charles Kent and Joseph Wright,[53] trustees for Henry Long, whose daughter and heiress Jane was lady of the manor in 1728.[54] Jane married Charles Adelmare or Caesar the younger[55] of Bennington, and had two daughters —Jane, who married Charles Cottrell in 1755,[56] and Harriet, who later married Robert Chester.[57] After the death of Charles Caesar in 1740 (his wife had died in 1737)[58] Bayford was divided between Jane Cottrell and Harriet,[59] who joined in conveying their moieties of the manor to Sir William Baker in 1758.[60] Sir William was succeeded in 1770 by his son William Baker, M.P. for Hertfordshire,[61] who died in 1824[62] and whose grandson and successor William Robert held the manor and died in 1896.

BAKER of Bayfordbury. *Party ermine and gules a running greyhound between two bars invected and three quatrefoils all counter-coloured.*

William Clinton Baker, son of the latter, inherited Bayford and died in 1903, and his son Mr. Henry William Clinton Baker is the present lord of the manor.[63]

The liberties of sac, thol, theam and infangentheof were granted to Roger de Valognes with his lands by the Empress Maud[64] in 1141. When the manor was in the king's hand view of frankpledge and other courts were held together with Essendon.[65] Court leet, view of frankpledge, amendment of the assize of bread and ale and free warren were included in the grant of Bayford Manor to John Knighton in 1544.[66]

In 1278 it was stated that the men of Bayford had been accustomed to fish in their waters with 'boterell' and other small engines until William de Valence had hindered them some twenty years before.

---

[27] Esch. Enr. Accts. 35 Edw. III, 8, m. F; Duchy of Lanc. Misc. Bks. xii, fol. 58.
[28] Ct. R. (Gen. Ser.), portf. 77, no. 997.
[29] D. of Lanc. Misc. Bks. xviii (2), fol. 49.
[30] Feet of F. Div. Co. Edw. IV, file 76, no. 102.
[31] Duchy of Lanc. Misc. Bks. xxi, fol. 171.
[32] Ibid. 172.
[33] Ibid. 174 d. By his will of 1503 Robert Markham desired to be buried in Bayford Church (P.C.C. 13 Holgrave).
[34-43] D. of Lanc. Misc. Bks. xxii, fol. 194 d.
[44] Chan. Inq. p.m (Ser. 2), ccxi, 191.
[45] Ibid. cccxliii, 143.
[46] Ibid. ccclxxvi, 129.
[47] Ibid. cccxciv, 59.
[48] G.E.C. *Complete Peerage*.
[49] Feet of F. Div. Co. Hil. 1651.
[50] Recov. R. East. 1655, rot. 163.
[51] M. I.
[52] Ibid.
[53] Recov. R. Trin. 12 Anne, rot. 63; Close, 12 Anne, pt. vi, no. 13.
[54] Salmon, *Hist. of Herts.* 29.
[55] Recov. R. East. 8 Geo. II, rot. 19.
[56] Close, 32 Geo. II, pt. vi, no. 20.
[57] M. I. at Hertingfordbury.
[58] M. I.
[59] Recov. R. Hil. 28 Geo. II, rot. 143; Mich. 30 Geo. II, no. 217.
[60] Close, 32 Geo. II, pt. vi, no. 20.
[61] Clutterbuck, *Hist. of Herts.* ii, 43.
[62] M. I.
[63] Burke, *Landed Gentry* (1906).
[64] Round, op. cit. 286.
[65] Ct. R. (Gen. Ser.), portf. 77, no. 996, 997.
[66] Duchy of Lanc. Misc. Bks. xxii, fol. 194 d.

The right of such fishery was then restored to them.[67] Free fishery is mentioned as parcel of the manor in the various conveyances.

Of the two mills mentioned in 1086 one seems to have been in Bayford. The tithes of it were granted in 1226 to Richard de Argentein.[68]

The park of 270 acres which surrounds the manor-house of Bayfordbury was inclosed by Sir William Baker between 1758 and 1762, at about the same date that he built the house (see above).[69]

In 1316 another manor of BAYFORD, now represented by the estate of Bayford Hall, and then described as two messuages, 150 acres of land with appurtenances, was conveyed by Richard le Rous and his wife Mabel to Henry le Scrope.[69a] In 1330 it is mentioned that a messuage and carucate of land in Bayford were held of the king by Henry le Scrope by a yearly farm of 8s. 11½d. and 30 other acres by certain day works of ploughing, reaping, weeding, mowing meadows and carrying hay or payment of 11s. 3¼d. In that year, however, the king remitted all these services and substituted a yearly rent of 1d., payable at Christmas.[70] Henry le Scrope died in 1336, leaving a son William,[71] who died without issue in 1344.[71a] In 1346 Cecily, widow of William le Scrope and re-married to John Clopton, received in dower the Bayford lands with reversion to Richard le Scrope of Bolton, brother and heir of William and at that time a minor in the custody of Queen Philippa.[72] Sir Richard le Scrope conveyed his manor of Bayford to John Staunton apparently towards the end of the 14th century.[73] He granted it to Peter de St. Paul, an alien and serjeant-at-arms to Queen Isabella (who became the second queen of Richard II in 1395). Peter de St. Paul was never naturalized, and his lands in England were thus legally forfeited to the Crown. He, however, granted the manor to William de Neweton, who conveyed it to John and Milicent Pomye and William Chelmsford, seemingly for the purpose of settling it on himself and his wife Maud, to whom his feoffees regranted it. Afterwards he conveyed it to John Brampton, vicar of All Saints, Hertford, Richard Wyndesore and Richard Sampson, who in turn granted it to Roger Bokenham and Maud. Roger conveyed the property to William Fromond, chaplain, and John Ecleshale, who enfeoffed John Chambre, citizen and fishmonger of London, and Catherine his wife. John died and Catherine married, secondly, Robert Wydyton, citizen and grocer of London, who sold the estate to John Wodehous and John Dalton. All these proceedings had taken place without royal licence. Wodehous and Dalton obtained a pardon in 1415, but were dispossessed apparently in 1417 because of the alleged forfeiture of Peter de St. Paul for not having been naturalized. Henry V then granted the custody of 'le Halle' to John Sauton, but upon the appeal of Wodehous and Dalton it was restored to them in 1426.[74] In 1439 John Tewkesbury, goldsmith of London, held the 'manor of Bayford called Halle Place' in right of his wife Agnes and in that year conveyed it to Alexander Orable and others.[74a] Orable seems to have sold the manor to Sir John Fortescue (who bought the manors of Gacelyns and Ponsbourne in 1448), for later it was (with Ponsbourne) in the possession of John Fortescue, who died seised in 1517, leaving a son Henry.[75] It seems to have passed with Ponsbourne to Sir Thomas Seymour, and in spite of a suit brought by Henry Fortescue, who claimed it as a separate manor from Ponsbourne,[76] to have descended with that manor until the death of Sir John Ferrers in 1640. It was apparently settled on a younger son Charles, whose son Charles Ferrers in 1678 sold 'the messuage or farm called Bayford Hall' to Israel Mayo, lord of Bayfordbury,[76a] with which it has since descended.

A third manor or capital messuage of BAYFORD (held of the principal manor) appears at the beginning of the 16th century in the possession of the Knighton family. Thomas Knighton settled it in 1529 on his heirs by his second wife Joan Colloppe with reversion to his younger son John, to whom it actually passed at the death of Thomas in 1545.[77] This John had received a grant of Bayfordbury in 1544, and the two manors then descended together.

The manor of Gacelyns in Hatfield extended into Bayford and was partly held of the manor of Bayford.[78]

CHURCH

The church of ST. MARY stands about a quarter of a mile north of the village and consists of chancel, with octagonal eastern end, 40 ft. by 18 ft., south chapel 18 ft. by 10 ft., nave 51 ft. by 21 ft., north vestries and south porch; all internal dimensions. The church was built in 1870 close to the site of the old church, which has disappeared, but some of its fittings are preserved in the present church.

In a recess on the north side of the chancel is a white marble monument of George Knighton, who died in 1612. On the tomb is the recumbent effigy of a knight in armour; underneath are two panels, one containing an inscription, the other contains arms. At the back of the recess three brasses have been fixed; one, with a figure of a knight in armour, is supposed to represent Thomas Knighton, who died in

---

[67] Assize R. 323, m. 46 d.
[68] Rot. Lit. Claus. (Rec. Com.), ii, 153.
[69] Clutterbuck, op. cit. ii, 43; quoting evidences of William Baker.
[69a] Feet of F. Herts. 10 Edw. II, no. 239. Part of this holding extended into Little Berkhampstead, and a meadow there was called Scropesmead as late as 1468 (Herts. Gen. and Antiq. ii, 148).
[70] Cal. Pat. 1327–30, p. 495.
[71] Chan. Inq. p.m. 10 Edw. III, no. 47; G.E.C. Complete Peerage.
[71a] Chan. Inq. p.m. file 75, no. 16.
[72] Cal. Close, 1346–9, p. 168; Chan. Inq. p.m. 19 Edw. III, Add. no. 87.
[73] Cal. Pat. 1413–16, p. 307.
[74] Ibid.; Cal. Pat. 1422–9, p. 326.

See also Early Chan. Proc. bdle. 16, no. 104.
[74a] Feet of F. Herts. Hil. 17 Hen. VI, no. 95. Orable is said to have been Wydyton's heir (Partic. for Grants, Aug. Off. no. 674), so Agnes may have had only a right of user.
[75] Chan. Inq. p.m. (Ser. 2), xxxiii, 126. See also entry in the survey printed in Herts. Gen. and Antiq. ii, 148. John Wenlok, kt. (who in 1462 had a grant of the lands forfeited by Sir John Fortescue, the late chief justice), holds Danelond (now known as the Deans, which Mr. Johnston tells us has always formed part of the Bayford Hall estate), lately in the tenure of John Fortescue, kt., and before

of Alexander Orable. Sir John Fortescue (father of the John Fortescue who died in 1517 and said to be nephew of the chief justice [see Lord Clermont's edition of Fortescue's Works, ii, 51; Pedigrees of Devon Families, Harl. MS. 1538, fol. 74.]) died seised of lands in Hertingfordbury, Bayford and Essendon held of the king, but the manor is not mentioned by name (Chan. Inq. p.m. [Ser. 2], xv, 3).
[76] Aug. Off. Proc. bdle. 27, no. 65.
[76a] Close, 30 Chas. II, pt. i, no. 141.
[77] Chan. Inq. p.m. (Ser. 2), lxxxiii, 126.
[78] Ibid. 1 Edw. III, no. 85; 11 Edw. III, (1st nos.), no. 46. See also Chan. Proc. (Ser. 2), bdle. 205, no. 15.

HERTFORD HUNDRED — BENGEO

1545; it is a palimpsest and on the back are parts of a shrouded figure; the second has also a figure of a knight in armour, without inscription, but possibly representing John Knighton, who died in 1586; the third is a shield of arms: barry of eight, on a canton a tun, for Knighton, impaling quarterly (1) and (4) on a pale a conger's head, for Gascoigne, (2) and (3) three picks, for Pickett or Pigott. Hanging on a bracket close by is part of the brass of a lady, said to be the wife of Thomas Knighton above mentioned; this brass and the shield are also palimpsests, and have both been cut from a Flemish brass of an ecclesiastic.

The octagonal font is of late 15th-century date; the panelled sides of the bowl are ornamented with Tudor roses, the base is moulded.

The two bells are modern.

The communion plate consists of chalice, 1869, paten, 1871, and flagon, 1869.

The registers before 1812 are as follows: (i) all entries 1538 to 1713; (ii) baptisms and burials 1713 to 1775, marriages 1713 to 1754; (iii) baptisms and burials 1775 to 1812; (iv) marriages 1755 to 1812.

ADVOWSON Bayford Church, which is mentioned as early as 1222,[79] was a chapelry pertaining to the rectory of Essendon[80] until 1867, and the advowson therefore followed that of Essendon[81] (q.v.). In 1867 it was made a vicarage in the presentation of the lord of the manor, and was endowed out of the Common Fund.[82]

In 1366 the people of Bayford appealed for right of sepulture at their own chapel, owing to the inconvenience of having to go to Essendon. They stated that the distance between their chapel and Essendon Church was about 3 miles and that the vill of Little Berkhampstead lay between them. The bodies had to be carried past a water-mill on a stream of which one bank was in the demesne of Berkhampstead and the other in Essendon, wherefore 'the carts going with bodies are often brought to grief in the river, and the people attending annoyed with attachments in passing through Berkhampstead.'[83]

In 1503 the church had an image of St. Nicholas, for the mending of which Robert Markham left 6s. 8d.[84]

CHARITIES In 1607 Sir George Knighton, kt., by will gave 10s. yearly towards the reparation of the chapel in Bayford Church and 10s. yearly for the poor. The annuities were redeemed in 1863 by the transfer to the official trustees of £33 6s. 8d. consols, who also hold a further sum of £30 16s. 3d. consols, arising from accumulations of income. The dividends on the stock, amounting to £1 12s. yearly, are distributed to the poor periodically.[85]

In 1840 Edward Jones, by his will, bequeathed a legacy, now £459 3s. 8d. consols, the annual dividends, amounting to £11 9s. 4d., to be applied in keeping in repair the family vault, and the residue to be distributed triennially among male labourers, being housekeepers and over twenty-five years of age, not having received parish relief. In 1907 a sum of £29 8s. was divided among twelve labourers.

In 1853 William Yarrell, by will, bequeathed £500 consols, the annual dividends, amounting to £12 10s., to be applied, subject to the repair of the family vault, for the benefit of the poor. In 1908 twenty-two persons received sums of 7s. 6d. or 10s. each.

The sums of stock are held by the official trustees.

The Baker Foundation, under the will of Miss Charlotte Amelia Baker, proved 8 February 1836, consists of £431 8s. 9d. Leicester Corporation 3 per cent. stock, held by the official trustees, producing £12 18s. 10d. yearly. By a scheme of the Board of Education 13 December 1904 the income, wholly or in part, is made applicable for the benefit of any public elementary school in the parish, and the residue (if any) in maintenance of exhibitions at a secondary school or institution of technical or industrial instruction.

BENGEO

Belingehou (xi cent.); Beneggho, Beningho (xiii cent.); Bengeho (xv cent.); Benjow (xvi cent.).

The parish of Bengeo lies north of Hertford and west of the parish of Ware, from which it is separated by the River Rib. Under the provisions of the Local Government Act of 1894 the old parish of Bengeo was divided into two parts. The northern or rural part has an area of 2,778½ acres, consisting mainly of arable land, which forms about two-thirds of the whole area, and a few scattered woods. The greater part of the parish has an elevation of over 200 ft., but there is lower-lying land in the eastern part near the River Rib which is liable to flood. The soil is gravel, the subsoil clay, and the chief crops are wheat, barley and turnips. The district is thinly populated, the population being concentrated for the most part in the hamlets of Tonwell and Chapmore End. A road from Hertford passes through the parish, dividing into two branches; one branch leading north-east crosses the road from Ware to Stevenage, which also passes through Bengeo, the other branch continues in a northerly direction.

The southern or urban parish of Bengeo is bounded on the east by the River Beane. It has an area of 275 acres and lies on either side of the road from Hertford, of which borough it forms part. The church of St. Leonard stands in the eastern corner of Bengeo urban parish near the junction of the Beane with the Lea; near it is Bengeo Hall, the old manor-house, and their position suggests that

---

[79] *Cal. Pat.* 1216–25, p. 328.
[80] The church served by the priest mentioned among the tenants of the manor in 1086 must have stood in that part of its territory now comprised by Essendon.
[81] *Cal. Pat.* 1216–25, p. 328; Bacon, *Liber Regis*, 518.
[82] *Lond. Gaz. Index*, 118; Cussans, op. cit. *Hertford Hund.* 152.
[83] Linc. Epis. Reg. Mem. Bp. Buckingham, 289.
[84] P.C.C. 13 Holgrave.
[85] Sir George Knighton also charged his capital messuage in Bayford with the maintenance of his almshouses, respecting which, however, nothing is known in the parish.

423

A HISTORY OF HERTFORDSHIRE

the earliest settlement grew up near the water-ways, at some distance from the high road. Bengeo Hall was bought on the sale of the Byde property in 1846 by Admiral Thomas le Marchant Gosselin, who had already occupied it for some time previously, and it is now the property and residence of his grandson Mr. H. R. H. Gosselin-Grimshawe, J.P. In front of the house are two stones with initials K.B. and T.P.B. (probably Katherine Byde and Thomas Plumer Byde), and the date 1745, which seem to have been inserted into an earlier building. St. Leonard's, on the south side of the church, was formerly the vicarage. It was acquired by W. R. Best in 1849, and sold by him in 1863 to Miss Charlotte Gosselin, from whom it descended in 1892 to her nephew Mr. H. R. H. Gosselin-Grimshawe, the present owner. It is a 17th-century house of two stories and an attic with additions and alterations of the 19th century. Near St. Leonards are some cottages and a field called 'The Vineyard.' The field is described in 1767 as having lately been used as a vineyard by Thomas Dimsdale, the owner, who is said to have planted the vines.[1]

The modern parish church of Holy Trinity lies further west in the more thickly populated part of the parish. Tonwell, a hamlet on the road from Ware to Stevenage, has a chapel of ease built with the adjoining school by Mr. Abel Smith in 1857. Chapmore End, another hamlet, lies south-west of Tonwell. Near Chapmore End is the Lammas land belonging to the parish; it consists of 20 a. 3 r. 28 p. and yields £30 a year, which is divided amongst the householders. Waterford, a hamlet in the north-western part of Bengeo rural parish, was formed into an ecclesiastical parish in 1908.

There is a homestead moat at Bengeo Temple.

An inclosure award was made for Bengeo, Sacombe and Stapleford in 1852.[1a]

MANORS   The manor of *BENGEO* appears to have been the manor in this parish that was held by Hugh de Beauchamp at the time of the Domesday Survey.[2] In 1092 the monks of Bermondsey received a grant of lands which they afterwards sold in order to buy the 'manor of Richmond in Bengeo' for 160 marks,[3] and as, according to Dugdale, this manor was bought from Payn de Beauchamp,[4] it was probably the same as that previously held by Hugh de Beauchamp. In 1204 the Prior of Bermondsey paid 5 marks for having inquisitiou as to what lands were in his demesne in Bengeo when he delivered the land of Bengeo at farm to Ralph de Quenhay, who was said to have alienated those demesnes.[5]

During the 13th century the family of Tany (see Temple Chelsin below) established a claim to the manor; perhaps it was mortgaged or leased to them by the monks, to whom they afterwards made a formal grant of it apparently merely for purposes of settlement on one of their own family, for in 1272 Reginald and Richard de Tany gave the manor of Bengeo or Richmond to the monks of Bermondsey,[6] and in 1276 Richard and Margery de Tany quitclaimed the manor to Luke de Tany as his by right of the gift of Henry, late Prior of Bermondsey, whilst John Prior of Bermondsey, who had succeeded Henry in 1276,[7] acknowledged Luke's claim, the monks of Bermondsey retaining only the advowson of the church.[8] There is no evidence to show whether Luke de Tany had more than a life interest in the manor. He died in 1283.[9] In 1290 Edward I granted to the monks of Bermondsey the manor of Richmond with other manors and lands which had come into the king's hands by reason of the felony committed by Adam de Stratton, to whom the manors in question had been demised at farm.[10] Dugdale says that the manors were demised a second time to Adam de Stratton, forfeited in 1302, and again restored to the convent, which obtained a further confirmation of them from Edward II and continued in possession of them until the Dissolution.[11] As far as Bengeo was concerned, however, the descent after 1290 shows that the monks had alienated all except the advowson.

In 1303-4 John son of John Fitz Simon died seised of the manor of Bengeo. It is described in the inquisition as held of John Engayn.[12] The overlordship was therefore evidently attached to the manor of Hunsdon, which in 1272 Henry Engayn held of the heirs of Sir William de Beauchamp of Bedford.[13] The Fitz Simons held the manor for several generations, the descent being identical with that of Almshoe in Ippollitts, Hitchin Hundred (q.v.). Eventually Elizabeth, the Fitz Simon heiress, married Thomas Brockett,[14] and he held the manor —which is described as held of William Hussey as of the manor of Hunsdon—jointly with his wife and in her right. Thomas Brockett died in 1477; his wife survived him, and his brother Edward Brockett was his heir.[15]

The manor was probably sold by the Brocketts to Sir William Say, as he died seised of it in 1529. His property was inherited by his daughter Mary Countess of Essex, and by his granddaughter Gertrude, daughter of Elizabeth Lady Mountjoy,[16] who married the Marquess of Exeter. On the attainder of Gertrude in July 1539 the manor of Bengeo was forfeited to the Crown,[17] and in 1546 it was granted to Nicholas Throckmorton,[18] who in 1555 conveyed it to William Sharnbrook.[19] The latter died in 1563, leaving a son and heir Nicholas as well as younger sons.[20] The manor of Bengeo probably formed part of the provision for the widow and younger sons, for in 1571 Joan Sharnbrook, widow, and John Sharnbrook released all their right in the manor to Robert Spencer and Frances his wife,[21] and in 1594 it was

---

[1] Information from Mr. H. R. H. Gosselin-Grimshawe.
[1a] *Blue Bk. Incl. Awards.*
[2] *V.C.H. Herts.* i, 327.
[3] Harl. MS. 231, fol. 6. The name Richmond does not occur for this manor after the 13th century. The manor may perhaps have included the virgate which in 1086 Count Alan of Britanny, lord of Richmond, held in Bengeo (see *V.C.H. Herts.* i, 338).
[4] Dugdale, *Mon. Angl.* v, 86.
[5] Pipe R. 6 John, m. 3 d.

[6] Harl. MS. 231, fol. 42.
[7] Ibid. fol. 43.
[8] Feet of F. Herts. 4 Edw. I, no. 49.
[9] *Cal. Pat.* 1281-92, p. 43.
[10] Harl. MS. 231, fol. 45; see Anct. D. (P.R.O.), A 6239, 1008.
[11] Dugdale, *Mon. Angl.* v, 87.
[12] Chan. Inq. p.m. 32 Edw. I, no. 56.
[13] See Clutterbuck, *Hist. and Antiq. of Herts.* iii, 177.
[14] *Visit. Essex* (Harl. Soc. xiii), 30.
[15] Chan. Inq. p.m. 17 Edw. IV, no. 47.

[16] Ibid. (Ser. 2), clvii, 82.
[17] Ibid. lxxiii, 93. Lady Anne Bourchier, daughter of Mary Countess of Essex, appears to have inherited the right to half the manor, but what became of her interest is not clear (see ibid. clvii, 82).
[18] Pat. 38 Hen. VIII, pt. viii.
[19] Ibid. 1 & 2 Phil. and Mary, pt. i; Feet of F. East. 1 & 2 Phil. and Mary.
[20] Chan. Inq. p.m. (Ser. 2), cxxxv, 80.
[21] Add. MS. 27979 (Ware, co. Herts. Abstract of Evidences, 1570-1668), fol. 19.

424

BENGEO CHURCH FROM THE SOUTH-EAST

HERTFORD HUNDRED

BENGEO

sold by John Spencer to Thomas Fanshawe[22] of Ware Park, in Ware, Braughing Hundred. From this point the descent is the same as that of Ware. Mr. William Francis Parker of Ware Park is the present lord of the manor.

The manor of *TEMPLE CHELSIN* (Chelse, xiii cent.) was evidently one of the manors held by Geoffrey de Bech in Bengeo in 1086,[23] for the overlords in the 13th century, the Tanys, held under the lords of Bourne, who had succeeded Geoffrey de Bech elsewhere.[24] In 1210–12 Richard de Tany held two fees in Eastwick and Bengeo of the honour of Bourne.[25] By the middle of the 13th century the manor was held by the Knights Templars, who received a grant of free warren in their demesne lands in 1253.[26] From a fine levied in 1269 it appears that the Tanys had previously enfeoffed the Abbot of Warden of the manor, to hold by a rent of £12; the abbot had enfeoffed Simon Fitz Adam of Almshoe, to hold by the same rent, whilst the latter in his turn had enfeoffed the Master of the Knights Templars to hold also by a rent of £12. By the fine of 1269 the rent was released to Imbert de Peraud, Master of the Knights Templars,[27] who was henceforth to hold the manor of the king by the service of half a knight's fee. It is possibly this transaction that is spoken of in the Hundred Rolls as the sale of Chelsin to the Templars by Peter de Tany, the father's name being mentioned instead of that of the son.[28] In 1278 and 1287 the Templars claimed, with other liberties, view of frankpledge, amendment of assize of bread and ale, and gallows in their demesne lands in Chelsin.[29] In 1313 a mandate was issued in compliance with the decision of Pope Clement V and of the Council of Vienne for the delivery of the English possessions of the Templars to the Hospital of St. John of Jerusalem.[30]

At the time of the Dissolution the manor was held at farm of the Hospitallers by Nicholas Thurgood, under a lease made in 1524 for forty years.[31] In 1542 it was granted by Henry VIII to Sir Ralph Sadleir, one of the king's chief secretaries.[32] Sir Ralph Sadleir died in 1587, leaving the manor to his son Henry, with remainder to his son Thomas and heirs,[33] and in 1595 Henry Sadleir sold the manor to Sir Philip Boteler.[34] When the latter died in 1606 the manor passed to his grandson and heir Robert Boteler,[35] who was succeeded in 1622 by his daughter Jane, then three years old.[36] In 1637 a warrant was issued to the judges of the Common Pleas to admit Jane, who had married John Belasis, to levy fines and suffer recoveries, by her guardian, of Temple Chelsin and other manors, for the payment of the debts of her father and mother.[37] John Lord Belasis sold the manor, probably about 1650,[38] to Sir John Gore, from whom it passed by sale in 1688 to trustees for Sir Thomas Rolt,[39] who had been President of the East India Company at Surat.[40] From Sir Thomas Rolt the manor descended to Edward Rolt, his son, and from the latter to Thomas Rolt, who possessed it in 1728.[41] The elder son and daughter of Thomas Rolt died unmarried, and he was succeeded by his younger daughter Mary, who married Timothy Caswall. On the death of Mary's son George Caswall in 1825 the estate was sold to Samuel Smith, from whom it has descended to Mr. Abel Henry Smith,[42] the present lord.

The manor-house, now a farm-house standing off the road to Ware, is a 17th-century building of timber and plaster.

The manor of *CHELSIN alias SMEREMONGERS* appears first in the 15th century; in 1469 John Shelley, citizen and mercer of London, received licence to grant the manor of Chelsin, held in chief, to John Say and others to hold to the use of John Shelley and heirs.[43] A settlement was again made in 1483, when the manor was granted to trustees for the use of John Shelley, the son, and Elizabeth his wife, and their heirs.[44] John Shelley, the son, died in January 1526–7, leaving a son and heir William Shelley, who was a justice of the Common Pleas,[45] and was knighted in 1529.[46] By the will of the latter, which was proved in February 1548–9, the manor of Chelsin was left for life to Thomas,[47] his fifth son.[48] The reversion of the manor after the death of Thomas belonged to John Shelley, the eldest brother of Thomas, who by his will proved in 1551 left it to be held by his executors until the majority of his son William Shelley.[49] The Shelleys, however, appear to have forfeited the manor, for in 1573, when it was leased to John Bedingfield, it was described as being in the Crown by the forfeiture of Thomas Shelley.[50] After this there is no trace of the manor until 1625, when Robert Hemming, yeoman, died seised of the manor of Chelsin *alias* Smeremongers held of the Crown in socage, his heir being his son Samuel.[51] The latter died in 1639, leaving an heir John Hemming. The descent of the manor from this point is very obscure. By 1698 it had apparently passed to George Nodes.[52] Eventually by 1802 the manor of Chelsin or Smeremongers, passing with Temple Chelsin, was held by George Caswall.[53]

The manor of *REVEL'S HALL* first appears mentioned as a manor at the end of the 15th century. It probably formed part of Geoffrey de Becb's lands

SADLEIR. *Or a lion parted fessewise azure and gules.*

---

[22] Add. MS. 27979 (Ware, co. Herts. Abstract of Evidences, 1570–1668), fol. 19; Feet of F. Herts. Trin. 36 Eliz.
[23] See *V.C.H. Herts.* i, 334.
[24] See Eastwick.
[25] *Red Bk. of Exch.* (Rolls Ser.), ii, 505.
[26] *Cal. Chart. R. 1226–57*, p. 415.
[27] Feet of F. Herts. 53 Hen. III, no.615.
[28] See *Hund. R.* (Rec. Com.), i, 191.
[29] *Plac. de Quo Warr.* (Rec. Com.), 281, 291.
[30] *Cal. Pat. 1313–17*, p. 52.
[31] Mins. Accts. 31 & 32 Hen. VIII, no. 114, m. 36.

[32] L. and P. Hen. *VIII*, xvii, g. 220 (48).
[33] Chan. Inq. p.m. (Ser. 2), ccxv, 259.
[34] Feet of F. Mich. 37 & 38 Eliz.
[35] Chan. Inq. p.m. (Ser. 2), ccxcvii, 149.
[36] Ibid. ccccli, 144; Ct. of Wards, Feod. Surv. 17.
[37] *Cal. S. P. Dom.* 1637–8, p. 19.
[38] See Close, 1650, pt. lxviii, no. 4, which records the sale of lands in Bengeo, but does not mention the manor.
[39] Close, 4 Jas. II, pt. v, no. 10.
[40] Chauncy, *Hist. Antiq. of Herts.* 269.
[41] Salmon, *Hist. of Herts.* 46.
[42] See Cussans, *Hist. of Herts. Hertford Hund.* 36.

[43] *Cal. Pat.* 1467–77, p. 182.
[44] Ibid. 1476–85, p. 347.
[45] Chan. Inq. p.m. (Ser. 2), xlvi, 40.
[46] Shaw, *Knights of Engl.* ii, 47.
[47] P.C.C. 25 Populwell.
[48] For the Shelley family see Berry, *Sussex Gen.* 62.
[49] See will of John Shelley, P.C.C. 12 Bucks.
[50] Crown Lease Pipe, 15 Eliz. pt. ix.
[51] Chan. Inq. p.m. (Ser. 2), ccccxxxiii, 27; dxxxvi, 30.
[52] Recov. R. Mich. 10 Will. III, rot. 73.
[53] Ibid. Mich. 43 Geo. III, rot. 7.

in Bengeo at the time of the Domesday Survey.[51] Geoffrey de Bech seems to have been succeeded here by Ralph the Butler (Pincerna), who at the end of the reign of Henry I granted two knights' fees, consisting of the manor of Cockenhatch and lands in Hailey (Heilet) and Bengeo, which were held under him by the family of Burun, to Aubrey de Vere. The latter was to hold the knights' fees in demesne until Robert de Burun paid him £32, after which Robert was to hold of Aubrey and Aubrey of Ralph.[55] The knights' fees are described as being formerly held by Roger de Burun,[56] and it is possible that the latter was the son of the Roger who held 5½ virgates of Geoffrey de Bech in Bengeo in 1086.[57] The materials giving evidence of the descent of these knights' fees are scanty. Roger de Burun, grandson of Robert, was holding land in Bengeo in 1206, when he made an agreement about 1 carucate of land with Thomas de Herlawe.[58] It is probable that ultimately the Burns granted their holding in Bengeo to the Revels, from whom the manor afterwards took its name, for before 1194 Robert de Burun had granted certain lands in Cockenhatch to William son of Andrew de Revel.[59] The Revels were holding land in Bengeo in 1303, when Geoffrey Revel was returned for half a fee in Bengeo held of the Earl of Oxford.[60] There is no evidence to show how long the Revels held it or who succeeded them, but in 1495 Thomas Babthorpe died seised of the manor of Revels in Bengeo in demesne, and it was taken into the king's hands,[61] probably on account of the minority of the heir. It was evidently restored to the family of Babthorpe, as it appears to have passed from Nicholas Babthorpe to William Caldwell,[62] whose daughter and heir Joan conveyed it in marriage to Sir George Knighton. Their son John Knighton succeeded on his father's death in 1613. He gave the manor to his sister's daughter Mary, who married Henry Gardiner. Mary Gardiner, who survived both her sons and held a court in 1658, was succeeded by her daughter Mary wife of Henry Dunster. Mary survived her husband and was lady of the manor in 1700.[63] On her death the manor passed to her son Giles, who, dying without issue, left it to his nephew Henry Dunster, possessor of the manor in 1728.[64] It remained with the family of Dunster[65] until the death of Edward Dunster in 1791, when it was sold to Thomas Hope Byde. Afterwards it came by purchase together with the principal manor to William Parker of Ware Park.[66]

Revel's Hall, the farm-house north-east of St. Leonard's Church, probably marks the site of the old manor-house. The present house is a 17th-century timber-framed building with additions on the south side.

The ancient church of ST. LEONARD CHURCH consists of a chancel measuring internally 24 ft. by 19 ft. 6 in., with round apsidal east end, nave 44 ft. by 21 ft., west bellcote and south porch. It is built of flint with stone dressings; the nave is coated with plaster and the roofs are tiled.

The church is of early 12th-century date; windows have been inserted in later periods and a south porch was added in the 18th century; the bellcote is modern. The interior of the nave is now dismantled and the chancel arch boarded up; the chancel is still used for services.

The east window of the chancel is a single light with splayed inner jambs of 12th-century date, and splayed light with square head of the 13th century. In the north wall is a single original light, now blocked. In the south wall are three windows; the most easterly is a window of two cinquefoiled lights under a square head, and is of 15th-century date, but the inner jambs belong to an earlier window; the inner sill has been cut down to form a sedile. The next window is a single pointed light of 13th-century date, and the third is a single light with square head of the same period. In the same wall is a blocked doorway of the 15th century, with four-centred arch. Much of the external stonework of windows and doorway has been renewed. Next the east window on the south is a rough recess about 2 ft. 3 in. wide, which may have been used as a locker; adjoining the two-light window is a small piscina with cusped head, but it is fragmentary; further west is a larger piscina with pointed arch and hollow-chamfered edge. The portion of stone now forming the sill allows the old grooved water drain to be seen. On the north side of the chancel are two roughly cut openings through the wall, now concealed by sliding doors in the internal panelling; these are about 2 ft. in width and 2 ft. 6 in. apart; they are about 4 ft. 6 in. in height and appear to have been cemented inside. It has been suggested that one of these openings (the other appears to have been only a recess) was cut to enable an anchorite to obtain access to the church from a cell outside. The chancel arch is semicircular, with a span of

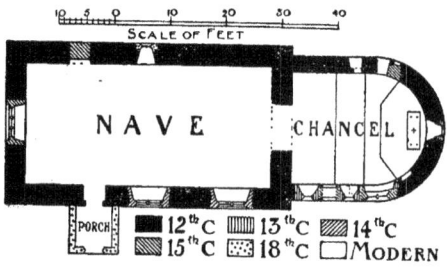

PLAN OF BENGEO CHURCH

■ 12th C ▥ 13th C ▨ 14th C
▧ 15th C ▦ 18th C □ MODERN

---

[54] See *V.C.H. Herts.* i, 334.
[55] Harl. Chart. 46, I, 30. Geoffrey de Bech held Hailey and lands in Cockenhatch at the time of the Survey. See *V.C.H. Herts.* i, 333–4, and see further under Hailey for a possible subsequent devolution of Ralph the Butler's interest.
[56] Harl. Chart. 46, I, 30.
[57] See *V.C.H. Herts.* i, 334b.
[58] Abbrev. Plac. (Rec. Com.), 49.
[59] Dugdale, *Mon. Angl.* v, 87.
[60] *Feud. Aids*, ii, 433. The other half of the knight's fee held by William de Goldington appears to be Thele, which is mentioned in the inquisition on William de Goldington in 1319 (see *Cal. Inq. p.m.* 10–20 *Edw. II*, 113).
[61] Chan. Files, 1623 (old numbering).
[62] Feet of F. East. 33 Hen. VIII.
[63] Chauncy, *Hist. Antiq. of Herts.* 268–9.
[64] Salmon, *Hist. of Herts.* 45.
[65] See Recov. R. Trin. 24 Geo. III, rot. 43.
[66] Cussans, op. cit. Hertford Hund. 36.

BENGEO CHURCH: CHANCEL ARCH LOOKING FROM THE NAVE

HERTFORD HUNDRED — LITTLE BERKHAMPSTEAD

about 8 ft.; it has a large edge-roll on the west side and is square on the east. The west jambs have engaged shafts with carved capitals and moulded bases. It is of 12th-century date. Portions of the jambs have been cut away. The roof of the chancel is modern.

In the north wall of the nave is a single-light window with 12th-century inner jambs and arch and brick exterior. There is a north doorway, now blocked. In the south wall is a window of two trefoiled lights with tracery under a square head, of late 14th-century date, repaired with cement; the other window is also of two lights, but has been renewed in cement. The south doorway is of 12th-century date, with an inner round arch and a flat lintel on the outside, and moulded imposts; the brick south porch is of 18th-century date. In the west wall is a window of three cinquefoiled lights under a square head; it is of 15th-century date and has been repaired with cement. The open collar-beam roof over the nave appears to be old, but the timber bellcote is modern. The south doorway has an old oak door which may date from the 14th century. On the jambs of the west window on the south side of the chancel are some faint remains of distemper paintings of figure subjects in which the figure of a bishop can possibly be discerned, and on the east wall of the nave are other indications of figures, one of which is crowned; on the chancel walls is a red chequer pattern under which is a much older masonry pattern. Under the communion table are a number of 14th-century tiles, much worn.

There is one bell, dated 1636, by Robert Oldfeild. The plate consists of a cup and paten, 1626, a flagon, two chalices, and two patens, 1862.

The registers before 1812 are as follows: (i) baptisms 1538 to 1696, burials 1547 to 1696, marriages 1539 to 1696; (ii) baptisms 1696 to 1782, marriages 1696 to 1754; (iii) burials 1678 to 1812; (iv) baptisms 1783 to 1812; (v) marriages 1754 to 1797; (vi) marriages 1797 to 1812.

The modern church of HOLY TRINITY was erected in 1855 of squared rubble with ashlar dressings, and consists of a chancel with organ chamber and vestry, nave with aisles, and western tower.

ADVOWSON — A priest is mentioned in the Domesday Survey as holding land of Geoffrey de Bech.[67] In 1156 the church of Bengeo was granted to the monks of Bermondsey by Reginald de Tany. The grant was confirmed by Henry II in 1159 and by Richard de Tany in 1272.[68] The monks of Bermondsey retained the rectory and advowson of the vicarage until the Dissolution.[69] They may, however, have mortgaged part, for in 1268 a fine was levied, by which Richard Michelefeld and Alexandra his wife acknowledged the advowson of a fourth part of the church of Bengeo to be the right of Michael Testard.[70] The king presented in 1338 and 1378, when the temporalities of the priory were in the hands of the Crown by reason of the war with France.[71] In 1553 Edward VI granted the rectory and church of Bengeo to Edward Walter of London,[71] and in 1563 they were sold by Henry Walter to George Horsey,[72] whose son Sir Ralph Horsey sold them to Henry Fanshawe in 1596,[74] from which date they followed the descent of the manor of Bengeo[75] until the sale of the Byde property in 1845. They were then bought by Mr. Abel Smith, whose son Mr. Abel Smith endowed the vicarage with the great tithes in 1848.[76a] The living was declared a rectory in 1867. Mr. Abel Henry Smith is the present patron.

Meeting-places for Protestant Dissenters were certified in 1810, 1812, 1813, 1817 and 1831.[76]

CHARITIES — Mrs. Clarke, as stated in the Parliamentary Returns of 1786, gave land for the poor. The charity is known locally as Shaw's Charity. The land is 4½ acres in extent and is let at £9 a year, which is distributed in bread.

In 1870 Captain William Rayner Best bequeathed £200, now represented by £215 6s. 2d. consols, in the names of trustees, the annual dividends amounting to £5 7s. 6d. to be applied, subject to the repair of tomb, in the distribution of money or articles in kind.

The almshouses, the origin of which is unknown, consist of six almshouses occupied by six poor widows without children.

The Lammas lands consist of 20 a. at Chapmore End let in allotments, producing in 1908 about £33 a year, which was divided in sums of 1s. 3d. among 577 recipients.

LITTLE BERKHAMPSTEAD

Berchehamstede (xi cent.).

The parish of Little Berkhampstead is bounded on the north by the River Lea, which separates it from the parish of Hertingfordbury. The area of the parish is 1,581 acres of land and 6 acres of water. The soil is of clay and gravel, the subsoil clay and chalk, and the chief crops are grass and wheat. The village, standing at a height of nearly 400 ft., is situated on a road which runs north to the Lea and south to Tyler's Causeway, which forms part of the southern boundary of the parish, and is continued as the road to Cheshunt. The church lies at the north end of the village, and a little further along the road is the old manor-house of the Welds. The house is a timber and plaster building of the early part of the 17th century, with a tiled roof. It has an open timber porch on the east side and a bay window with moulded wooden transoms and mullions on the north. Most of the internal details are modern, but part of the original hall ceiling still exists decorated with roses and other flowers in low relief. The house is the property of Mr. A. Hale, and is now used as a cyclists' resort.

---

[67] V.C.H. Herts. i, 334b.
[68] Dugdale, Mon. Angl. v, 89; Harl. MS. 231, fol. 18, 42.
[69] Dugdale, op. cit. v, 102.
[70] Feet of F. Herts. 52 Hen. III, no. 603.
[71] Cal. Pat. 1338–40, p. 60; 1377–81, p. 277.
[72] Add. MS. 27979 (Ware, co. Herts. Abstract of Evidences, 1570–1668), fol. 16.
[73] Add. MS. 27979, fol. 16; Feet of F. Herts. East. 5 Eliz.
[74] Add. MS. 27979, fol. 16; Feet of F. Mich. 38 & 39 Eliz.
[75] Inst. Bks. P.R.O.; Recov. R. East. 20 Chas. II, rot. 153.
[76a] Information from Mr. H. Gosselin-Grimshawe.
[76] Urwick, Nonconf. in Herts. 484.

A HISTORY OF HERTFORDSHIRE

The modern house called the Manor House, further north, is the residence of Mr. Cornelius Hanbury.

On the north side of Berkhampstead Lane and close to the church and village are the rectory and Little Berkhampstead House. The latter was formerly the property of Owen Lloyd, stationer, of Temple Bar, who died in 1756, and left it to his nephew Samuel Gibbons. It was acquired early in the last century by Thomas Daniell, grandfather of the present owner, Mr. A. E. Daniell. Pondfield, the residence of Mr. Percival Bosanquet, stands in a park about half a mile north-east of the church. At the southern end of the village stands the Village Hall, which was built in 1888, and south of the hall is the school.

About a quarter of a mile east of the church is The Gage (formerly the Gaze or Gaze Place), a late 16th-century house, much altered subsequently. It is of brick and timber with tiled roofs and contains some late 17th-century panelling. In the grounds on high land is a circular tower built mainly of 17th-century bricks in 1789 by John Stratton as an observatory. The house belonged to John Bentley at the end of the 17th century. It was acquired by John Stratton in 1780, and is now the property of his grandson Colonel J. H. Stratton. At Woodcock Lodge Farm are the remains of a homestead moat. This house belonged in the early 17th century to William Smithsby, groom of the Privy Chamber to Charles I. He sold it to William Priestley of Camfield (see Essendon), in whose family it remained until the death of Meliora Priestley, widow, in 1761. It afterwards came into the possession of William Baker of Bayfordbury.

Little Berkhampstead is said to have been the birthplace of Thomas Ken, Bishop of Bath and Wells, who was born in 1637.[1a]

Epping Green, a hamlet, lies 1 mile south of the village, and another hamlet, Howe Green (probably Le Hoo of the 15th century), lies a mile to the north. Epping House, to the west of Epping Green, was the property of William Horne, attorney-general, who died in 1860. It now belongs to Mr. B. H. Henderson.[1b]

An inclosure award was made in 1842.[2] Ashfield, Sprowsefield and Mill Field were the principal common fields.

Hardwin de Scales held *LITTLE MANOR BERKHAMPSTEAD* at the time of the Domesday Survey, when it gelded at 5 hides. Before the Conquest 2 hides of the manor were held by Semar, a priest, 2 hides by a certain widow, Levefa, and 1 hide by Uluric. According to the testimony of the shire-moot these lands were of the 'alms' of King Edward and his royal ancestors.[3] The manor descended in the Scales family to Geoffrey de Scales,[4] who in 1223 granted it to Falkes de Breauté and his heirs to hold by the service of rendering one pair of gilt spurs or 6d. at Easter, for all service except foreign service.[5] Falkes de Breauté forfeited his possessions to the Crown in 1224,[6] and the houses in Little Berkhampstead which had belonged to him were removed to the castle of Hertford.[7] The manor, which should have been restored to the Scales family, was apparently kept by the king, who in 1225 gave orders that the old court, chapel, brewhouse and 'marescalcia' were still to be left at Little Berkhampstead for John Marshall, to whom he had granted Falkes's lands in Little Berkhampstead during pleasure. In 1226, however, the sheriff was ordered to move the 'domus marescalciae' from Little Berkhampstead to the castle of Hertford whenever the carriage of it should cause least inconvenience to the neighbourhood.[8] The manor was granted by the king in 1226 to Nicholas de Moels[9] during pleasure, a grant afterwards changed into one in fee.[9a] His son Roger held it in 1278[10] and received a grant of free warren in 1290.[11] Roger, who died before July 1295, was succeeded by his son John,[12] summoned to Parliament as Lord Moels. Extents of the manor at this date mention a water-mill. On the death of John in 1310 the manor went to his son Nicholas,[13] who, by a fine with Philip de Courtenay in 1313, settled it on himself and his wife Margaret and their heirs.[14] When Nicholas Lord Moels died before 12 March 1315–16 his heir was his brother Roger.[15] Roger de Moels died without issue in 1325, and was succeeded by his brother John,[16] who in 1328 obtained a licence to exchange some of his other lands for the life interest of Margaret, his sister-in-law, in the manor of Little Berkhampstead.[17] As John had no male heir, on his death in 1337 the barony of Moels fell into abeyance and his lands were divided between his daughters Muriel and Isabel. Isabel, who had married William de Botreaux, received Little Berkhampstead in 1347 as part of her share of the inheritance.[18]

William Lord Botreaux, son of Isabel, was under age when his father died in 1349,[19] and his estates remained in wardship until 1359.[20] He leased the manor in 1375 to Edmund de Hyndon for the term of the latter's life,[21] and in 1384 to William Framelyngham, citizen and skinner of London, for twenty years.[22] William Lord Botreaux died in 1391 and

MOELS, Lord Moels. *Argent two bars gules with three roundels gules in the chief.*

---

[1] In 1755 Mrs. Priestley created a rentcharge of £16 10s. on the house, of which £10 were to be applied for the schooling of the poorest girls of the parish of Bow and £6 for providing twenty sixpenny loaves on the first Sunday of the month for nineteen of the poorest inhabitants who should attend divine service most regularly (Close, 29 Geo. II, pt. vi, no. 5).
[1a] *Dict. Nat. Biog.*
[1b] The history of the different houses in the parish has been kindly supplied by Mr. C. E. Johnston.
[2] *Blue Bk. Incl. Awards*, 63.
[3] *Dom. Bk.* (Rec. Com.), i, 142a.
[4] For the descent of the family of Scales see Challers in Reed, p. 248.
[5] Feet of F. Herts. 7 Hen. III, no. 63.
[6] *Dict. Nat. Biog.* ii, 1158.
[7] *Rot. Lit. Claus.* (Rec. Com.), ii, 34.
[8] Ibid. 48b, 130.
[9] Ibid. 131.
[9a] *Cal. Chart. R.* 1226–57, p. 80. The Charter Roll is now defective (see C. E. Johnston, *Early Hist. of Little Berkhamstead*, 270).
[10] Assize R. 323.
[11] *Cal. Chart. R.* 1257–1300, p. 365.
[12] Chan. Inq. p.m. 23 Edw. I, no. 59; *Feud. Aids*, ii, 434.
[13] *Cal. Inq. p.m.* 1–9 Edw. II, 104.
[14] Feet of F. Herts. 7 Edw. II, no. 133; *Cal. Pat.* 1307–13, p. 528.
[15] *Cal. Inq. p.m.* 1–9 Edw. II, 384.
[16] G.E.C. *Complete Peerage*, v, 321.
[17] *Cal. Pat.* 1327–30, p. 262.
[18] *Cal. Close*, 1346–9, p. 298.
[19] *Abbrev. Rot. Orig.* (Rec. Com.), ii, 202b.
[20] G.E.C. *Complete Peerage*, i, 388.
[21] Chan. Inq. p.m. 49 Edw. III, pt. ii (2nd nos.), no. 28; Close, 49 Edw. III, m. 26.
[22] Chan. Inq. p.m. 15 Ric. II, no. 6.

428

LITTLE BERKHAMPSTEAD CHURCH FROM THE NORTH

HERTFORD HUNDRED

LITTLE BERKHAMPSTEAD

was succeeded by his son William,[33] who survived him less than a year, leaving a son, another William, under age.[34] By 1402 the manor had passed, probably by sale, to John Norbury,[25] who had already in 1388 acquired the manor of Bedwell with lands and tenements in Little Berkhampstead,[26] and who in 1406 received a grant of free warren and licence to make a park in these manors.[27]

From 1402 the manor of Little Berkhampstead must have followed the descent of Bedwell in Essendon (q.v.), as it formed part of the possessions of the Marquess of Exeter which were granted to Sir Anthony Denny in 1547.[28] In 1600 it was sold by Sir Edward Denny, grandson of Sir Anthony, to Humphrey Weld, citizen and alderman of London.[29] From Sir Humphrey Weld it passed in 1610 to his son John (afterwards Sir John) Weld,[30] and the latter, dying in 1623, left it to his son Humphrey, who was a minor.[31] Humphrey suffered a recovery of the manor in 1639.[32] In 1645 it was sold by Frances Weld, widow of Sir John Weld, to Phineas Andrews, a London merchant.[33] In 1655 Phineas Andrews sold the manor to George Nevill[34] of Staple Inn, London, who died in 1679, leaving as heir a daughter Elizabeth, the wife of Cromwell Fleetwood.[35] She died without issue in 1692,[36] when the manor passed to her cousin John Nevill's son George,[37] who sold it in 1713 to Sir John Dimsdale.[38] He died in 1726 and his widow was owner of the manor in 1728.[39] As Sir John Dimsdale left no issue, the heir under his will was his cousin Thomas Dimsdale,[40] who in 1768 was made a baron of the Russian Empire. He died in 1800, leaving the manor to his second son Nathaniel, who had received a title similar to his father's. Nathaniel, dying unmarried in 1811, left the manor to his sister Anne Dimsdale, who was the possessor in 1817.[41] When she died unmarried in 1832 the manor went by will to her nephew Thomas Robert fourth Baron Dimsdale, on whose death without male issue in 1865 it passed to his wife. On her

BOTREAUX, Lord Botreaux. *Argent a griffin gules.*

DIMSDALE. *Argent a fesse dancetty azure with three besants thereon between three molets sable and an augmentation of a scutcheon or with an eagle's wing sable thereon.*

death in 1874 it was vested in her sons-in-law, Vice-Admiral Sir Walter Tarleton, K.C.B., and Colonel David Henry Mackinnon, as trustees for her four daughters, Lucinda widow of Major George Darby Griffith, Ann widow of the Rev. Henry Dawson, Finette Esther wife of Sir Walter Tarleton, and Caroline Mrs. Mackinnon.[42] The present lords of the manor are Mr. A. M. Mackinnon and Mr. A. H. Tarleton.

The church of *ST. ANDREW* stands about the centre of the village, and consists of chancel 22 ft. by 16 ft., north chapel 13 ft. by 11 ft. 6 in., nave 39 ft. 6 in. by 20 ft., north aisle 24 ft. by 15 ft., south porch and wooden bell-cote; all the measurements are internal. The walls are faced with Kentish rag.

The church is said to have been rebuilt about 1647 on the site of an older building, but the only remains of that date are parts of the east and west walls, the rest of the church being modern. In the chancel are some late 17th-century floor-slabs to the families of Pendred, Nevill and Fleetwood.

There are three bells: the first, by John Waylett, dated 1718; the second inscribed 'Ave Maria gracia plena dominus tecum benedicta tu in mulieribus' in Lombardic lettering; the third, dated 1621, cast by Robert Oldfeild.

The communion plate consists of a cup of 1565, a cover paten of 1576, another paten, 1721, an almsdish with handles (silver), 1791, a plated flagon (Sheffield), c. 1790, and two pewter almsdishes, c. 1720.

The registers before 1812 are as follows: (i) baptisms, burials and marriages 1647 to 1708; (ii) baptisms 1712 to 1762, burials 1721 to 1762, marriages 1714 to 1747; (iii) baptisms and burials 1769 to 1812; (iv) marriages 1756 to 1812.

ADVOWSON Hugh de Scales, lord of the manor in the 12th century, gave the church of Little Berkhampstead to the priory of Lewes, and the grant was confirmed by Henry his son and Hugh his grandson.[43] In 1397 the king presented 'by reason of his wardship of the land and heir of William Botreaux, kt., tenant-in-chief,'[44] and he also presented in 1399[45] and again in 1444,[46] but by what title does not appear. In 1538 the advowson of the church of Little Berkhampstead was granted to Thomas Cromwell with the priory of Lewes.[47] In 1612 Robert Earl of Salisbury died seised of the advowson,[48] and the advowson was retained by his descendants,[49] the Marquess of Salisbury holding the patronage at the present day.

A house was licensed as a Presbyterian meeting-place in Little Berkhampstead in 1672, and one at

---

[23] Chan. Inq. p.m. 15 Ric. II, no. 6.
[24] G.E.C. op. cit. i, 389.
[25] *Feud. Aids,* ii, 443; see Feet of F. Herts. Trin. 3 Hen. V, no. 34, which is a fine levied by Sir William Botreaux to John Norbury in 1415. This was probably for assurance of title after Lord Botreaux came of age.
[26] Anct. D. (P.R.O.), D 448.
[27] Chart. R. 6 & 7 Hen. IV, no. 5.
[28] Pat. 1 Edw. VI, pt. ix.
[29] Feet of F. Herts. printed in *Herts. Gen. and Antiq.* ii, 321; Close, 42 Eliz. pt. xxiii. Reservation was made of the demesne lands which had been inclosed in Bedwell Park.

[30] Chan. Inq. p.m. (Ser. 2), cccxxii, 173.
[31] Ct. of Wards, Feod. Surv. 17.
[32] Recov. R. Trin. 15 Chas. I, rot. 60.
[33] Close, 21 Chas. I, pt. x, no. 32. For details about Andrews see Johnston, op. cit. 66.
[34] Close, 1655, pt. xlii, no. 20.
[35] M.I.
[36] Ibid.
[37] C. E. Johnston, op. cit. 67.
[38] Feet of F. Herts. East. 12 Anne.
[39] Salmon, *Hist. of Herts.* 26.
[40] Clutterbuck, *Hist. and Antiq. of Herts.* ii, 33.
[41] Ibid. 34.

[42] Cussans, *Hist. of Herts. Hertford Hund.* 168.
[43] Dugdale, *Mon. Angl.* v, 3.
[44] Cal. Pat. 1396–9, p. 59. There is no other evidence that the lord of the manor had any right in the advowson at this date (De Banco R. Trin. 23 Ric. II, m. 324).
[45] Ibid. 1399–1401, p. 38.
[46] Ibid. 1441–6, p. 274.
[47] L. and P. Hen. VIII, xiii (1), g. 384 (74).
[48] Chan. Inq. p.m. (Ser. 2), ccclviii, 108.
[49] See Inst. Bks. (P.R.O.); Recov. R. East. 9 Geo. II, rot. 194.

429

Epping Green was certified as a place of worship for Protestant Dissenters in 1810.[50]

CHARITIES

In 1730 Maurice Hunt, by will, bequeathed £600 in trust for the use of the poor. The legacy is now represented by £558 5s. consols with the official trustees, producing £13 19s. yearly, which, in pursuance of a decree of the Court of Chancery, is distributable in November among the poor. In 1911 twenty-four persons received gifts of money varying from 10s. to 20s.

BROXBOURNE WITH HODDESDON

Brochesborne (xi cent.); Brokesburn.

The civil parish of Broxbourne,[1] which has an area of 1,932 acres, contains 509 acres of arable land, 658 acres of permanent grass and 686 acres of wood.[2] The ground slopes downward from the west of the parish, which lies at more than 300 ft. above the ordnance datum, to the east, where the elevation is less than 100 ft., on the banks of the River Lea, which forms the boundary between Broxbourne and Nazeing, the neighbouring parish in Essex. The Spital Brook, which runs into the Lea on the east of the parish, forms the boundary between the civil parishes of Broxbourne and Hoddesdon for a little way before the junction. The main road from London to Ware and the north passes through the eastern end of the parish and forms the main street of the village of Broxbourne. In this street are a few old houses, notably The Gables at the south end of the village, which is a two-storied house dating from the early part of the 17th century. It is a timber-framed house now covered with plaster, with a modern front. The chimney-stack and one fireplace are probably original. The Bull Inn, in the middle of the village on the west side of High Street, is also a 17th-century timber and plaster house. Opposite the Bull Inn are the Monson Almshouses erected in 1728. They are contained in a plain two-storied building of brick, with sash-windows, and a crowning cornice of moulded brick. Over the entrance doorway is the following inscription:—

'This Building is Erected at the Sole | charge of Dame Laetitia Monson | Relict of Sr William Monson Bart | and was Daughter of John Lord Poulett | of Hinton St George in the County of Somersett, which Gift is for the Relief | and Benefitt of poore Widows of the | Parish of Broxborne in Hartfordshire | in the year of our Lord 1728.'

Above on a lozenge are the arms of Monson impaling Poulett.

The Cedars in the High Street, although an 18th-century house, contains an early 17th-century staircase. From the main street Pound Lane and Mill Lane run eastward, the latter passing the church of St. Augustine and the vicarage, and leading to the Broxbourne mill, which is picturesquely situated on the old stream of the River Lea. To the west two lanes turn off. The lower leads to Baas manor-house, an early 17th-century brick and plastered timber building now divided into two tenements, Cold Hall and Cold Hall Green, and the higher to Broxborne Bury, the seat of the lord of the manor. Broxborne Bury is a 16th-century house of red brick and stone with roofs partly tiled, slated and leaded. It was probably built by John Cock, who received a grant of the manor in 1544. In the following century an addition was made to the west side of the house, and in the 19th century it was much altered and largely rebuilt. Some of the chimney-stacks appear to be original, and there is a fireplace on the first floor, which is also of the 16th century. The windows are of the 18th century or modern.

The western half of the parish is largely covered by beautiful woods, chiefly of oak, beech and hornbeam.

The Great Eastern railway runs through the parish parallel to the main street and between it and the river. The station is situated at the end of Pound Lane and Station Road. It is doubtless due to the railway that the new quarter of the town to the north of the church, consisting mainly of villa residences and practically continuous with the southern extension of Hoddesdon, has grown up within the last fifty years.

The subsoil of the parish is London Clay, with the exception of a narrow strip of Alluvium on the banks of the Lea. The chalk is not far below the clay on the lower lands. There is a disused gravel-pit east of Broxborne Bury Park.

The inclosure award was made in 1843 and 1850, and is in the custody of the clerk of the peace.[3]

The civil parish of Hoddesdon, formed from those of Broxbourne and Great Amwell, has an area of 2,685 acres, which on 1 January 1895 was divided into the parishes of Hoddesdon Urban, 1,575 acres, and Hoddesdon Rural, 1,110 acres.[4] The combined parishes contain 563½ acres of arable land, 912½ acres of permanent grass, and 724 acres of wood.[5]

The elevation of the western half of the parish is over 200 ft. above the ordnance datum, with the exception of a small area by the Spital Brook, where it falls to 170 ft. In the east the ground slopes downward towards the Lea, which forms the eastern boundary of the parish. The town of Hoddesdon continues up the main road from Broxbourne, and is hardly separated from that village. About the middle of the town the road divides into Amwell Street and Burford Street, both running north to Ware, the Clock House being situated at the junction in the open space in front of the Maidenhead Inn. Amwell Street, on the west side of which there are some 17th-century cottages, passes the church of St. Paul and the vicarage, and meets the road from Hertford a little further north. Burford Street, which is part of the Stanstead Road, has two roads branching off to the east, Rye Road leading to the suburb of Rye Park, and Essex Road, the more southerly of the two, which crosses the New River, passes Geddings and goes on to the Lea. South of the town hall two roads run

---

[50] Urwick, Nonconf. in Herts. 487, 488.
[1] The ecclesiastical parish of Broxbourne in 1831 included the present civil parishes of Hoddesdon and Broxbourne. Hoddesdon chapelry was formed in 1844 (see below).
[2] Statistics from Bd. of Agric. (1905).
[3] Blue Bk. Incl. Awards, 63.
[4] Stat. 56 & 57 Vict. cap. 73.
[5] Statistics from Bd. of Agric. (1905).

430

HERTFORD HUNDRED — BROXBOURNE WITH HODDESDON

west from the High Street, Lord Street (formerly Lord's Lane), the most northerly, leading past High Leigh, the residence of Mr. Robert Barclay, J.P. Opposite Lord's Lane was the old market cross which stood at least until the end of the 17th century. A little south of the cross was the market-house, built about 1634. The market-place occupied the space between the cross and the present clock-house. The market-house was pulled down in 1833, and the market soon after ceased to be held. The cattle market now held on a site to the south of the old cross was founded in 1886.[5a] Eastwards from the High Street Conduit Lane runs down to Lynch mill pond, from which the stream called the Lynch flows to the Lea. Lynch mill pond is mentioned in 1569 as 'a pond anciently called "le Lince" where is now built a water mill.'[5b] The Wollans Brook, which flows through Box Wood and the north of the parish, falls into the Lea.

In the High Street are many old houses. Rawdon House, now St. Monica's Priory, a convent of the canonesses of the Augustinian order, on the east side was built by Sir Marmaduke Rawdon in 1622, as appears from a stone over the porch and many rain-water heads bearing this date and the initials M.R. The house is a large red brick rectangular building with stone dressings and a tiled roof, to which a wing was added in 1880. It is of two stories with an attic and has a porch and bay windows, both of two stories, in front, and a central tower, in which is the staircase, at the back. The hall has a ceiling ornamented with fleurs de lis, roses, &c., and a fireplace with plaster figures. There are a fine oak staircase with heraldic figures and some good old doors and panelling, but many of the original fittings were sold by the canonesses, three of the fireplaces being purchased by Sir Charles Wittewronge and set up at Rothamsted House, Harpenden. A little to the north of St. Monica's Priory on the same side of the road is Stanboroughs House, now the Conservative club, the main part of which was built about 1600 of timber and plaster work and a wing of brick added in 1637, according to a date upon the rain-water heads. A good deal of the woodwork within is original, including a fine oak staircase in the added wing and some oak panelling and doors. On the same side of the road is Hogges Hall, originally built probably in the 15th century. The exterior of the house is modern, but some of the internal details, including the timber ceiling of the hall and a wooden doorway, are of the 15th century. There is also some 16th and 17th-century panelling which is not in its original position.

On the west side of the road is the Grange (once an inn called the 'Cock'), a brick house of two stories, built in 1657, but almost rebuilt in the 18th century. It contains some 17th century panelling and an overmantel of the same period, together with three doors of the early part of that century.

There have always been many inns in the town. The 'Black Lion' (now the 'Salisbury Arms') was held in the 16th century of the manor of Geddings.[6] Henry Barrell or Burwell, serjeant-at-arms and tenant of the 'Black Lion,' died in 1562, leaving a widow Jane, who afterwards married Christopher Lyster. His son Henry Barrell entered upon the tenement at his father's death, but died in 1566 and was succeeded by his brother George.[7] Another inn called the 'George' was held before 1464 by Richard Riche[8] and remained in his family until 1528, when it was sold by Thomas son of Thomas and Rachel Riche to Sir Thomas Baldry, alderman, and John Garwey, mercer of London.[9] In the 17th century it was held by George Taylor and afterwards by John Marshall. In 1702 it was sold by Matthew Clarke to Edward Browne.[10] The Golden Lion Inn stands on the west side of the High Street and is a two-storied house of plastered timber and brick with an overhanging story built in the early part of the 17th century, but much altered at a later date. The Old Swan Inn is a similar house built in the latter part of the 17th century, and the Griffin Hotel contains some woodwork possibly of the same century. Another inn called the 'Bull,' the front of which appears to date from the 18th century, projects over the pathway, the two upper floors being carried on Ionic columns. Near the southern end of High Street is some good Georgian work. A house on the east side three stories in height, with a moulded brick string-course and cornice, has a good Doric doorcase with elaborate fretwork in the metope of the frieze containing in Roman characters the date 1746.

At Connals Farm is the stone conduit-head presented to the town by Sir Marmaduke Rawdon in the early part of the 17th century. It formerly stood at the town well in the High Street, and represents the three-quarter length figure of a woman carrying a pitcher. The old 'Thatched House,' immortalized by Izaak Walton, stood on the site of the brewery offices of Messrs. Christie & Co., adjoining the brewery in the High Street. The clock-house itself stands on the site of the ancient chapel of St. Catherine. In it is hung a bell, probably from that chapel, which was cast by Thomas Bullisdon at the beginning of the 16th century and bears the inscription 'Sancta Aña ora pro nobis.'[11]

In the west of the parish, which is thickly wooded, runs the Ermine Street, a Roman way, which crosses the Spital Brook and passes through the Hoddesdon Woods. There is a tumulus at Hoddesdonbury on the south side of the road. The hospital of St. Laud and St. Anthony, of which the first record seems to be in the 14th century, has left its name in Spital Brook, near which it stood. The hospital (which survived the Dissolution) fell into decay towards the end of the 16th century, and the Spital House was then adapted for the use of the free grammar school founded by Queen Elizabeth by charter of 4 January 1559–60. By the same charter the queen incorporated the town of Hoddesdon under the style of a bailiff and warden of the town and school, and eight assistants, and granted the tolls of the market and of two fairs to the corporation. The school, however, was apparently discontinued before 1595, and nothing further is heard of the corporation.[11a]

[5a] Tregelles, *Hist. of Hoddesdon*, 243 et seq.
[5b] Ibid. 252, where a history of the mill is given.
[6] Chan. Inq. p.m. (Ser. 2), cli, 59; clxi, 81; cclvii, 91.
[7] Ibid. There is a brass in the church said to be that of John Barrell, serjeant-at-arms to Henry VIII (see under church).
[8] P.C.C. 4 Godyn.
[9] Feet of F. Herts. Hil. 19 Hen. VIII.
[10] Close, 1 Anne, pt. ix, no. 9.
[11] For an account of many other houses and inns see chapter on Roads and Ways and Inns and their Signs in Tregelles's *Hist. of Hoddesdon*.
[11a] See article on Religious Houses, V.C.H. Herts. iv; Tregelles, op. cit. 229 et seq.; Pat. 2 Eliz. pt. iii, m. 31.

A HISTORY OF HERTFORDSHIRE

The Great Eastern railway passes through the east of the parish and Rye House station is in the extreme north-east.

The subsoil of the parish is chiefly London Clay on chalk, but in the east this gives place to Woolwich and Reading Beds, beyond which is a strip of Alluvium by the Lea. In the north-east a wedge of Chalk separates the two latter. There are many gravel-pits in the parish.

The inclosure award was made in 1855, and Lampits Field was inclosed in 1841. Both awards are in the custody of the clerk of the peace.[12] The chief common fields were Lowefeld, Westfeld, Middlefeld (or Ditchfeld), Estfeld (or Ryefeld), Lampitfeld, and Southfeld. The chief common meadows were Dole Mead, Ditch Mead, Chaldwell Mead and South Mead.[12a]

Other place-names that occur in Broxbourne and Hoddesdon are Phelippesholm, Flodgate Bridge, Huttescroft, Beggers-grene, Gosewellehelle, Algoresholme, Loffeld (xiii cent.); Hathell, le Newelonde, Coppethorne (xiv cent.); Pikottes, Sawells, Sampsons, Broderedyng, Longhedge and Stockinges (xv and xvi cent.); Tunefield, Harfield, Cockabury Stable (xvii cent.); Morsforlong, Sparewynesmade, Lawefeld, Godewelleacre, Blakemad, Safoghel and Curstmarsh.

MANORS The manor of BROXBOURNE was held in the time of Edward the Confessor by Stigand, Archbishop of Canterbury, whose reeve held half a hide of it as a sokeman. In 1086 it was held by Adeliza wife of Hugh de Grantmesnil, and was assessed at 5½ hides.[13] Ivo de Grantmesnil, son and heir of Hugh,[14] gave Broxbourne to the abbey of Bermondsey, but as a consequence of his having previously mortgaged his estates to Robert Count of Meulan and first Earl of Leicester to defray the expenses of his journey to the Holy Land and dying on the way, Robert is said to have taken possession of Broxbourne with the consent of the monks of Bermondsey.[15] Robert died in 1118, and Waleran, his eldest son, took his father's Norman lands and became Count of Meulan, while Robert, the second son, became Earl of Leicester and inherited the English estates.[16] Robert Earl of Leicester, son of the latter, married in 1168 Parnell or Petronilla, the heiress of the Grantmesnils and apparently granddaughter of Ivo,[17] shortly after which Robert and Parnell, with the consent of their sons William and Robert, gave the manor of Broxbourne to the Knights Hospitallers.[18] King John confirmed this grant in 1199,[19] and the manor remained in the hands of the Hospitallers until the dissolution of their order in

THE KNIGHTS HOSPITALLERS. *Gules a cross argent.*

1540.[20] In 1331 the king confirmed a charter of the late prior, Thomas Larcher, by which he granted the manor, reserving the lordship and royalty of his tenants there, to Edward de St. John for life, at a rent of 10 marks for the first five years and of 5 marks for the rest of the term.[21] In 1539 it was leased to John Sargeante, dyer, of London, for twenty-nine years.[22]

In 1544 Broxbourne Manor, with woods of 70 acres called Broxbourne Wood, Broderedyng, and Longehedge, was granted to John Cock,[23] who died seised of it in 1557, leaving it to his wife Anne as jointure, after whose death it passed to his son Henry.[24] Sir Henry Cock died in March 1609-10, leaving two daughters, Frances, the wife of Sir Edmund Lucy, and Elizabeth, who married first Robert West and secondly Sir Robert Oxenbridge.[25] Broxbourne was apportioned to Elizabeth, who married thirdly Sir Richard Lucy about 1617, and died in 1645.[26] Sir Richard survived her and continued to hold the manor until his death in 1667, when it passed to Ursula Oxenbridge, daughter of Elizabeth Cock by her second husband.[27] Ursula was the wife of Sir John Monson, bart., K.B., who died in 1683, and was succeeded by his grandson Henry.[28] Sir Henry Monson died childless in 1718 and his brother William died in March 1726-7, when Broxbourne passed to his nephew John, son of a third brother George.[29] This Sir John Monson was created Lord Monson of Burton in 1728 and lived until 1748.[30] His son John died in 1774,[31] and his grandson, also named John, joined with his mother Theodosia Dowager Lady Monson in selling the manor of Broxbourne in 1790 to Jacob Bosanquet.[32] The latter was succeeded in 1830 by his son George Jacob Bosanquet, whose daughter and only child Cecily married Horace James Smith, second son of Samuel George Smith of Sacombe.[33] Upon becoming lord of the manor of Broxbourne in right of his wife in 1866 Mr. Horace Smith assumed the surname of Bosanquet.[34]

COCK of Broxbourne. *Quarterly gules and argent.*

MONSON, Lord Monson. *Or two cheverons gules.*

BOSANQUET. *Or a tree on a mount vert and a chief wavy gules with a crescent between two six-pointed molets argent therein.*

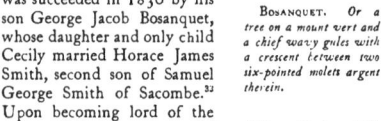

[12] Blue Bk. Incl. Awards, 64.
[12a] Tregelles, Hist. of Hoddesdon, 90 et seq., where the position of these fields is described. See also p. 184 et seq. for many other field-names.
[13] V.C.H. Herts. i, 344a.
[14] G.E.C. Complete Peerage.
[15] Dugdale, Mon. v, 87.
[16] G.E.C. op. cit. [17] Ibid.
[18] Cal. Rot. Chart. 1199-1216 (Rec. Com.), 16. [19] Ibid.
[20] Assize R. 323; Dugdale, Mon. vii, 799-800.
[21] Cal. Pat. 1330-4, p. 101. See also Tregelles, Hist. of Hoddesdon, 76.
[22] Misc.Bks.Land Rev.Rec.vii,fol.192a.
[23] L. and P. Hen. VIII, xix (1), 80 (48).
[24] Chan. Inq. p.m. (Ser. 2), iii, 82.
[25] Ibid. cccxix, 200.
[26] N. and Q. (Ser. 2), vii, 37; Recov. R. Herts. Mich. 15 Jas. I, rot. 111.
[27] N. and Q. loc. cit.
[28] G.E.C. Complete Baronetage; Chauncy, Hist. Antiq. of Herts. 289.
[29] Ibid.; Recov. R. Mich. 10 Geo. I, rot. 165. [30] G.E.C. Complete Peerage.
[31] Ibid.; Recov. R. East. 24 Geo. II, rot. 153.
[32] Close, 30 Geo. III, pt. xiv, no. 10.
[33] Cussans, Hist. of Herts. Hertford Hund. 187, 201.
[34] Ibid. 177; Burke, Landed Gentry (1906).

432

HERTFORD HUNDRED — BROXBOURNE WITH HODDESDON

He died in 1908 and was succeeded by his son Mr. George Smith-Bosanquet, who is the present possessor.

Broxbourne possessed a mill in 1086,[35] which passed with the estate of the Knights Hospitallers. The mills were granted with the manor in 1544 to John Cock, together with 'le lokk' upon the River Lea, through which water was carried from the river to the mills.[36] John Cock in the same year granted the lock and the mills to William Garnett and Agnes,[37] and in 1550 the mills were granted as 'parcel of the lands of William Garnett' to Ralph Sadleir and Laurence Wennyngton and the heirs of Ralph, being then or late in the tenure of Richard Stansfeld.[38] William Garnett, however, died seised of them in 1559, leaving a son William.[39] At the end of the 16th century the mills and lock were held by Robert Garnett, who died in 1600 or shortly after, leaving his property to his daughter Elizabeth, who was then the wife of Abraham Hartwell. She soon afterwards married Robert Bennett, and died in 1610, when she was succeeded by John Hartwell, her son by her first husband.[40] John Hartwell died in 1644 seised of two water-mills called Broxbourne Mills and two other mills, and also the lock, all of which passed to his cousin Henry Hartwell, son of Abraham Hartwell's brother Alexander.[41] In 1671 the vicar of the parish sued the occupier of the water-mills, then Thomas Pryor, for his tithe. This had been fixed at one peck of the best wheat meal weekly, for which a former vicar in 1662–3 had compounded for £4 a year. It was then stated that there were three water corn-mills under one roof.[42]

In 1547 'the sewer called a Weyre, and a fishery called the Weyre, and one island called the Islande and the shrubbery and wood,' and two meadows in Broxbourne and Nazeing (the neighbouring parish of Essex) were granted to Sir William Herbert and his heirs, having been part of the possessions of the Knights Hospitallers.[43] This weir and fishery with the island were subsequently held by Elizabeth Bennett, the heiress of the Garnetts,[44] and descended with the mills.[45]

In 1670 Sir John Monson obtained a licence to make a park of 320 acres, and to 'enjoy franchise and liberty of free chace and free warren within the same,' and to store it with deer and coneys.[46] It is mentioned in 1751, but is said to have been disparked in the time of the last Lord Monson who held Broxbourne, and to have been converted partly into a grazing farm and partly cultivated.[47] A park of about 330 acres still surrounds the Bury.

Besides the manor of Broxbourne there were in 1086 several holdings in Hoddesdon, whose assessment made a total of about 10 hides.[48] Of these one holding assessed at 2 hides and 3 virgates was in the hands of Alan Count of Britanny and formed a berewick of his manor of Cheshunt, and another, consisting of 1 hide, was held of Geoffrey de Mandeville[49] by a certain Ralph.

The manor of BAAS was formed out of lands held of both these fees.[50] Early in the 13th century this manor seems to have been in the tenure of John de Burgh, and he enfeoffed of it Henry de Baa or Ba (Bathonia),[51] from whom it takes its name. The manor was recovered against Henry by the king as an escheat on the ground that Henry was a Norman, but in 1257 it was confirmed to him and his wife Aline.[52] Aline, widow of Henry de Baa, died about 1274 seised of a messuage, 120 acres of arable land, 3½ acres of meadow, 10 acres of pasture, 8 acres of wood, 19s. 4d. rent of assize, and a fishpond in Broxbourne, held of the Earl of Hereford (representing Geoffrey de Mandeville) by scutage for a quarter of a knight's fee and of the Count of Brittany by a rent of 20d., with small services to other lords.[53] Henry left a son and heir John, who conveyed the manor to John Pykard and Joan his wife, niece of John Baa.[54] In 1297 John Pykard, keeper of the king's forests in the county of Huntingdon, exchanged the manor with Richard Chertsey.[54a] John Chertsey is recorded as the holder of a quarter of a fee in Broxbourne in 1303,[55] and in 1394–5 the 'manor of Bas' was settled on John Chertsey and Isabel his wife.[56] In 1402–3 it held by Richard Spice, who seems to have been the second husband of this Isabel, for he leased the manor to John Chertsey (apparently the son and heir of the above-mentioned John) 'for the term of the life of Isabel wife of the said Richard.'[57] After the death of Isabel the manor evidently came to John Chertsey and descended to his son, also John, for in 1418 'Johns, son and heir of John Chertsey,' conveyed Baas to Robert Hackeston and John Newelton.[58]

The manor seems to have remained in the hands of trustees for some time. In 1426–7 one William Rotse surrendered his right in the manor to William Lochard and others,[59] and in 1430–1 Edmund Chertsey, son and heir of John Chertsey, released his right to Nicholas Dixon and others.[60] Probably these transactions were for the purpose of a mortgage to Thomas Gloucester, for the latter held courts at Baas from 1433 onwards,[61] although it does not seem to have been formally conveyed to him until 1438. It was then surrendered by William Chertsey and Lettice his wife.[62] Ten years later

BAAS. *Gules a cheveron between three roundels argent.*

---

[35] V.C.H. Herts. i, 344a.
[36] L. and P. Hen. VIII, xix (1), 80 (48).
[37] Chan. Inq. p.m. (Ser. 2), cxxvii, 6.
[38] Pat. 4 Edw. VI, pt. iv, m. 21.
[39] Chan. Inq. p.m. (Ser. 2), cxxvii, 6.
[40] Ibid. cccxvi, 19.
[41] Ibid. dxxxi, 78.
[42] Exch. Dep. Mich. 23 Chas. II, no. 3.
[43] Pat. 1 Edw. VI, pt. iv, m. 24.
[44] Chan. Inq. p.m. (Ser. 2), cccxvi, 19.
[45] Ibid. dxxxi, 78.
[46] Cal. S. P. Dom. 1660–70, pp. 337, 563; Recov. R. East. 24 Geo. II, rot. 153.
[47] Paper among Sir J. Evans's MSS. Herts. Co. Museum, St. Albans.
[48] V.C.H. Herts. i, 320a, 322, 330, 331, 342b.
[49] Ibid.
[50] Chan. Inq. p.m. 2 Edw. I, no. 1.
[51] Cal. Chart. R. 1226–57, p. 467.
[52] Ibid.
[53] Chan. Inq. p.m. 2 Edw. I, no. 1.
[54] Tregelles, Hist. of Hoddesdon, 24 (quoting deed at Hatfield).
[54a] Ibid.
[55] Feud. Aids, ii, 433. The fee is said to be held of the Earl of Oxford, but there is probably some mistake as to the tenure.
[56] Close, 18 Ric. II, m. 11 d.
[57] Ibid. 4 Hen. IV, m. 9, 19.
[58] Feet of F. Herts. 6 Hen. V, no. 38. Apparently the father was still living at this date, for a little later there is mention of John Chertsey the elder (Anct. D. [P.R.O.], B 567).
[59] Close, 5 Hen. VI, m. 19.
[60] Ibid. 9 Hen. VI, m. 3, 4.
[61] Ct. R. (Gen. Ser.), portf. 177, no. 60, 61.
[62] Feet of F. Herts. 16 Hen. VI, no. 89.

it was conveyed to John Say by John Edward and Joan his wife,[63] brother and sister-in-law of Thomas Gloucester. Sir John Say died seised of Baas in 1478 and was succeeded by his son William,[64] after whose death in 1529 it passed to his daughter Mary and her husband Henry Earl of Essex,[65] and thence to their daughter Anne, the wife of William Lord Parr, created Marquess of Northampton in 1547.[66] The marquess was attainted in 1553 and his lands forfeited.[67] Queen Mary granted the manor to the Earl of Arundel and others in 1553, to hold during pleasure, apparently to the use of Anne Marchioness of Northampton.[68] Elizabeth granted it in 1569 to Sir William Cecil,[69] who also obtained releases of title from Anne Parr[70] and other heirs of Sir William Say.[71] From that time Baas descended in the Cecil family[72] and eventually became amalgamated with the manor of Hoddesdonbury. It is mentioned separately as late as 1820.[73] Courts held at Baas are recorded from 1404 onwards.[74]

The manor of HODDESDONBURY seems to have been also formed of lands held of the fees of Mandeville and Richmond. Those held of the latter fee owed a service of a quarter of a knight's fee to the Earls of Richmond, 1s. 6d. rent for the ward of the castle of Richmond and the service of inclosing 11 perches of hedge belonging to Cheshunt Park.[75] The Mandeville fee descended to the Earls of Hereford through Maud, heiress of the Mandevilles, who married Henry de Bohun Earl of Hereford, who

MANDEVILLE. Quarterly or and gules.

BOHUN. Azure a bend or cotised argent between six lions or.

died in 1220.[76] A half fee in Hoddesdon remained in the hands of the Bohuns[77] until the death of the last Humphrey de Bohun in January 1372-3,[78] when it passed to his elder daughter Eleanor, who married Thomas of Woodstock Duke of Gloucester and died in 1399.[79] Eleanor left three daughters: Joan, who also died in 1399,[80] Isabel, who became a nun in 1402, and Anna, who married first Thomas Earl of Stafford and secondly his brother Edmund Earl of Stafford,[81] and inherited her sister's lands. At the death of Edmund in 1403[82] a redistribution of the estates took place between the heirs of Eleanor and Mary, daughters of Humphrey de Bohun, and Hoddesdonbury fell to Mary's son and heir Henry, who ascended the throne as Henry V. The overlordship thus became vested in the Crown, and the view of frankpledge at Hoddesdon was granted by Henry VI to his mother Katharine in dower in 1422.[83] The rolls of the courts of the honour of Mandeville, parcel of the duchy of Lancaster, held there in 1539 and later are preserved at the Record Office.[84]

The sub-tenant of the Mandeville fee at Hoddesdon before the Conquest was Godid, and in 1086 it was held of Geoffrey de Mandeville by Ralph.[85] The next sub-tenants of whom there is record are the Bassingburn family, who probably acquired the manor towards the end of the 12th century. The first to be mentioned in Hoddesdon are Humphrey de Bassingburn and his mother Aubrey, who appear in 1242.[86] This Aubrey was probably identical with Aubrey the wife of John de Bassingburn, who was holding the manor of Woodhall in Hatfield in 1198.[87] Humphrey was apparently succeeded by another John de Bassingburn,[88] perhaps his brother John, who is mentioned in 1243.[89] John died about 1276,[90] and was succeeded by Stephen de Bassingburn, whose son John was in possession by 1301-2.[91] About 1323 Agnes de Bassingburn, mother of this John, died seised of Hoddesdon Manor, which she held for the term of her life 'from the inheritance of Agnes, daughter of John, son of the deceased Agnes.'[92] The granddaughter Agnes, who was aged five in 1323, may have been assigned the manor by her father, but in this case must have died young, for Stephen de Bassingburn, son of John, was holding Hoddesdon in 1333. Joan, widow of John de Bassingburn, was then holding a third in dower.[93]

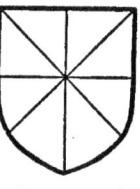

BASSINGBURN. Gyronny or and gules.

Later in the same century the manor was held by Thomas de Bassingburn. He was holding Astwick (in Hatfield) in 1370, and presumably Hoddesdon at the same time, for he is mentioned later as having held it.[94] He died before 1397, leaving an infant son John, whose wardship he had sold to Alexander

---

[63] Feet of F. Herts. 27 Hen. VI, no. 146; Ct. R. (Gen. Ser.), portf. 177, no. 63; Mins. Accts. bdle. 862, no. 16, 17.
[64] Chan. Inq. p.m. 18 Edw. IV, no. 43. For accounts of the manor during Sir John Say's tenure see Tregelles, Hist. of Hoddesdon, 35.
[65] Chan. Inq. p.m. (Ser. 2), li, 50.
[66] Ct. of Wards, Misc. Bks. dlxxviii, fol. 372 d.; Feet of F. Herts. Hil. 33 Hen. VIII.
[67] G.E.C. Complete Peerage.
[68] Pat. 1 Mary, pt. ii, m. 11. She was holding Geddings, one of the manors similarly granted, in 1569 (Chan. Inq. p.m. [Ser. 2], cli, 59).
[69] Pat. 11 Eliz. pt. viii.
[70] Feet of F. Div. Co. Hil. 12 Eliz.
[71] Ibid. Hil. 14 Eliz.; Chan. Inq. p.m. (Ser. 2), clvii, 82.
[72] Chan. Inq. p.m. (Ser. 2), cccxlii, 123; Recov. R. East. 13 Chas. II, rot. 194; East. 9 Geo. II, rot. 194.
[73] Recov. R. Mich. 1 Geo. IV, rot. 223.
[74] Ct. R. (Gen. Ser.), portf. 177, no. 58-63; 227, no. 82.
[75] Chan. Inq. p.m. 16 Edw. II, no. 42.
[76] G.E.C. Complete Peerage.
[77] Plac. de Quo Warr. (Rec. Com.), 293; Chan. Inq. p.m. 30 Edw. I, no. 58.
[78] Chan. Inq. p.m. 46 Edw. III, no. 10.
[79] Ibid. 21 Ric. II, no. 29; 1 Hen. IV, no. 50. [80] Ibid. 1 Hen. IV, no. 49, 51.
[81] G.E.C. Complete Peerage.
[82] Chan. Inq. p.m. 4 Hen. IV, no. 41.
[83] Duchy of Lanc. Misc. Bks. xviii (2), fol. 49.
[84] Ct. R. (Gen. Ser.), portf. 171, no. 14.
[85] V.C.H. Herts. i, 331 b.
[86] Red. Bk. of Exch. (Rolls Ser.), i, p. xlvii.
[87] Feet of F. Herts. 9 Ric. I, no. 21.
[88] Chan. Inq. p.m. Incert. temp. Hen. III, no. 15.
[89] Feet of F. Herts. 27 Hen. III, no. 305.
[90] Clutterbuck, Hist. of Herts. ii, 344, quoting Plac. Hil. 5 Edw. I; Plac. de Quo Warr. (Rec. Com.), 276, 285; Assize R. 323.
[91] Chan. Inq. p.m. 30 Edw. I, no. 58; Cal. Pat. 1307-13, p. 472.
[92] Chan. Inq. p.m. 16 Edw. II, no. 42.
[93] Feet of F. Div. Co. Trin. 7 Edw. III, no. 135.
[94] Chan. Inq. p.m. 1 Hen. IV, no. 50; 4 Hen. IV, no. 41; 21 Ric. II, no. 29.

HERTFORD HUNDRED

BROXBOURNE WITH HODDESDON

Besford for 100 marks. The wardship was duly delivered to Alexander by Thomas Arundel, Archbishop of York, and Edward Earl of Rutland, but he afterwards entered into an agreement to deliver the child up to Ralph Hamelyn and Ralph son of Richard upon payment of 200 marks. A little later, however, in spite of this, Alexander granted the wardship of the infant John to Robert Whytington and others. The two Ralphs gave up the child to Robert's servants, but afterwards Ralph Hamelyn 'chased the servants and took away the child by force.'[95] In 1457 apparently another John de Bassingburn and Katherine his wife conveyed the manor of Hoddesdonbury to trustees,[96] probably for the purpose of a settlement, for John de Bassingburn was lord of the manor in 1477, and two of the same feoffees granted it to John's son Thomas Bassingburn and his wife Katherine in 1493.[97] In the following year Thomas Bassingburn conveyed Hoddesdonbury to Sir William Say,[98] his wife's brother. At the death of Sir William Say in 1529 the manor descended to his daughter Mary and her husband Henry Earl of Essex,[99] whose daughter and heir Anne Bourchier married William Parr, afterwards Marquess of Northampton.[100] Sir William Parr was attainted in 1553 and his lands forfeited to the Crown. The reversion of Hoddesdonbury after the expiration of a grant made in favour of Anne was granted by Queen Elizabeth in 1566 to Robert Earl of Leicester,[1] who in the following year conveyed it to Sir William Cecil, afterwards Lord Burghley, who obtained releases from the Marchioness of Northampton and other possible heirs of Sir John Say.[2] From him it passed to his second son Robert Cecil,[3] who was created Earl of Salisbury in 1605 ; it has since descended in that family,[4] the Marquess of Salisbury being the present lord of the manor.

Stephen de Bassingburn claimed a park in Hoddesdon in 1277 of ancient custom.[5] Hoddesdon Park Wood probably marks the site of it. Stephen de Bassingburn also claimed by charter of King John free warren, gallows, and waif.[6]

In 1533 Henry Earl of Essex petitioned for a licence to change the day of the fair at Hoddesdon, which, he said, would be 'a great ease for the inhabitants.' This evidently referred to the fair originally granted to Richard de Boxe in Hoddesdon in 1253 (see below). The date, that of the vigil, feast and morrow of St. Martin (in winter), 11 November, was changed to the vigil, day and morrow of the Translation of St. Martin in summer (3–5 July).[7] The charter of Queen Elizabeth granted two fairs to the corporation, one beginning on the vigil of St. Martin in winter (11 November) and the other on the vigil of St. Peter (29 June).[8] In 1792 the fair was held on 29 June as a toy fair,[9] and a pleasure fair is still held on 29 and 30 June. A market, to be held on Thursdays, originally granted to Richard de Boxe,[10] was also confirmed to Henry Earl of Essex at the same time as the fair. By Queen Elizabeth's charter the tolls (the ownership of which was said to be unknown) were granted to the corporation. The market is now held on Wednesdays.

In 1086 the manor received twenty-two eels from the weir.[11] A water-mill which it was hardly possible to use except in winter is mentioned in 1323.[12] In 1277 Stephen de Bassingburn was expected to provide a bridge in Rutholm, 16 ft. by 6 ft.[13] In 1656 it was presented that the town of Hoddesdon was destitute of stocks, and that the parishioners of Broxbourne ought to provide them.[14]

Another manor of Hoddesdon may perhaps be identical with a hide in Hoddesdon held before the Conquest by Asgar the Staller, later by Ingelric, and in 1086 by Count Eustace of Boulogne.[15] The sub-tenant of Asgar the Staller in this hide was Godid, but it was given soon after the Conquest to the canons of St. Martin-le-Grand, London, probably by Ingelric, their founder, predecessor of Count Eustace, of whom the canons held it in 1086.[16] It had been confirmed to them by William the Conqueror in the second year of his reign.[17] The church still had demesne lands in Hoddesdon in 1290, when the dean, William de Luda, had licence to stock his park there from the forest of Essex,[17a] but probably most of their lands had been already granted in sub-fee, for in 1287[18] certain privileges exercised by the canons in their lands were claimed by John le Sarmonner, who was apparently holding under them. The hide was confirmed to them as late as 1422–3, and at the end of the 15th century suit was still owed to the leet of St. Martin by tenants in Hoddesdon.[19]

The earliest sub-tenants of the manor apparently were a family of Boxe, who took their name from Boxe in Walkern and Stevenage and who held that manor. Alan de Boxe, nephew of a Hugh de Boxe, is mentioned as holding land in Hoddesdon in 1198.[20] In 1253 Richard de Boxe had a grant of free warren in his demesne lands of Boxe (i.e. Boxe in Walkern) and Hoddesdon and a weekly market on Thursdays at Hoddesdon and a yearly fair on the vigil, feast and morrow of St. Martin (11 November).[21] In 1256 he had licence to inclose and build on a space of ground between the two high roads and the cross of Hoddesdon.[22] He was apparently succeeded by John le Summoner or Sarmonner, who is mentioned in Hoddesdon in 1276,[23] and in 1287 claimed view of frankpledge and assize of bread and ale at Hoddesdon as among the liberties belonging to the Dean and canons of St. Martin's, London

---

[95] Early Chan. Proc. bdle. 69, no. 11.
[96] Feet of F. Herts. 35 Hen. VI, no. 182 ; Mins. Accts. bdle. 862, no. 17.
[97] Anct. D. (P.R.O.), D 769 ; B 1600.
[98] Feet of F. Herts. Hil. 9 Hen. VII.
[99] Pat. 27 Hen. VIII, pt. i.
[100] Ct. of Wards, Misc. Bks. dlxxviii, fol. 372 d. ; Feet of F. Herts. Hil. 33 Hen. VIII.
[1] Pat. 8 Eliz. pt. vii, m. 28.
[2] Clutterbuck, *Hist. and Antiq. of Herts.* ii, 59 (quoting deed at Hatfield House) ; Feet of F. Div. Co. Hil. 12 Eliz. ; Hil. 14 Eliz.
[3] Feet of F. Herts. Hil. 45 Eliz. In 1602 there was a grant of the manor to Roger Houghton and Richard Langley. These were presumably fishing grantees (Pat. 44 Eliz. pt. xiii, m. 9).
[4] Chauncy, *Hist. Antiq. of Herts.* 287 ; Salmon, *Hist. of Herts.* 22.
[5] *Plac. de Quo Warr.* (Rec. Com.), 276.
[6] Ibid.
[7] *L. and P. Hen. VIII*, vi, p. 611 ; viii, g. 962 (6).
[8] Pat. 2 Eliz. pt. iii, m. 31.
[9] *Rep. on Market Rts. and Tolls*, i, 170.
[10] *Cal. Chart. R.* 1226–57, p. 416 ; Pat. 8 Edw. IV, pt. ii, m. 4.
[11] *V.C.H. Herts.* i, 331*b*.
[12] Chan. Inq. p.m. 16 Edw. II, no. 42.
[13] *Plac. de Quo Warr.* (Rec. Com.), 285.
[14] *Sess. R.* (Herts. Co. Rec.), i, 115.
[15] *V.C.H. Herts.* i, 322*a*. [16] Ibid.
[17] Dugdale, *Mon.* viii, 1324.
[17a] *Cal. Close*, 1288–96, p. 64.
[18] Assize R. 325.
[19] Dugdale, loc. cit. ; Tregelles, *Hist. of Hoddesdon*, 66.
[20] *Rot. Cur. Reg.* (Rec. Com.), i, 175, 168.
[21] *Cal. Chart. R.* 1226–57, p. 416.
[22] *Cal. Pat.* 1247–58, p. 473.
[23] Anct. D. (P.R.O.), A 1030 ; Assize R. 325.

A HISTORY OF HERTFORDSHIRE

(see above).[24] He was living in 1290,[24] but before 1303 his lands seem to have been divided between heirs. These were apparently Thomas Langton and Richard de St. Edmund, then both minors.[25] In 1307 Mabel widow of Thomas de Langton conveyed her share of the manor to Robert de Langton, clerk, probably for a settlement.[26] This part of the manor continued as the manor of Langtons, whilst the part of Richard de St. Edmund, which seems to have descended to an heiress Margery wife of Ralph de Foxton,[27] became known as Foxtons.

The part of the manor known as LANGTONS descended to John de Langton,[28] who was son of Robert de Langton, and may have been nephew of Thomas and Mabel.[29] From John de Langton it descended to his daughter and heir Alice wife of Sir Robert Corbet, whose only child Agnes married John Halle, citizen and goldsmith of London. In 1429 John and Agnes conveyed one year's rent of 60s. from lands in Hoddesdon called 'Langtonnesland' to Richard Benyngton and William Burton.[30] In the same year the 'manor' of Langtons was acquired by Thomas Gloucester, who held courts there from that year until about 1442.[31] It then came into the hands of John Edward, brother of Thomas Gloucester, and Joan his wife, and they conveyed it in 1448 to Sir John Say,[32] who in 1468 obtained an inspeximus of the grant of free warren and the market and fair granted to Richard de Boxe.[32a] He died seised of it in 1478.[33] His son and heir Sir William Say became lord of the manor of Hoddesdonbury,[34] in which this small estate seems to have afterwards become absorbed.

The quarter fee of FOXTONS, held in 1325 by Ralph de Foxton in right of Margery his wife,[35] had come into the same hands as Langtons by 1380,[36] and follows the same descent.[37]

The manor of BOXES was a part of the holding of the Boxe family, which seems to have become separated from the larger holdings in the divisions of the 14th century. In 1376 a messuage and 30 acres called 'Le Boxes' with rents and services in Hoddesdon were held by Simon son of Imbert.[38] After his death these tenements were acquired by the Langtons[39] and thenceforth descended with their manor.[40] In the inquisition on William Say in 1529 it is mentioned as the manor of Boxes.[41]

MARIONS formed part of the lands of the Knights Hospitallers,[42] to whom a rent was payable from the manor. Under the Hospitallers the manor was held in the 15th century by John Edward and Joan his wife, who conveyed it to Sir John Say in 1448, together with Langtons and Foxtons and other manors,[43] whose descent it follows. Maryons Manor House stood west of the high road above Spital Brook.[43a]

The 'manor' of HALLE or HALLES was another holding in Hoddesdon which by the 14th century had given its name to a family of Halle. Richard and John atte Halle were holding lands in Hoddesdon of the manor of Great Amwell at the end of the 14th century.[44] There is a rental of the manor made in the reign of Henry VI.[45] In 1448 it was in the possession of John Edward and Joan his wife. They conveyed it in that year to Sir John Say,[46] and it followed the same descent as the above manors.[47]

The manor of GEDDINGS probably formed part of the berewick of Hoddesdon, which was originally appurtenant to the manor of Hatfield Broadoak in Essex,[48] and which in 1086 seems to have been included in the manor of Great Amwell, then held by Ralph de Limesi.[49] With that manor (q.v.) it came into the possession of the Abbot of Westminster. Lands in Hoddesdon were held under the abbot in the 13th century by a family of Gedding. William de Gedding is mentioned at Hoddesdon during the abbacy of Richard of Ware,[50] who held that office from 1258 to 1283.[51] A Richard de Gedding is mentioned in Hertfordshire in 1287. In 1327 Edmund de Gedding received a grant of free warren in his demesne lands of Amwell and Hoddesdon.[52] He died before 1331, when the wardship of Robert de Gedding, son and heir of Edmund, was granted by the Abbot of Westminster to Richard and William of Hailey.[53] In 1332 Beatrice widow of Edmund de Gedding was assigned in dower one-third of a messuage in Hoddesdon.[54] Robert son of Robert de Gedding was returned as holding a fourth of the vill of Amwell by half a knight's fee in the latter part of the 14th century,[55] and this must have included his lands in Hoddesdon. In 1378 Reynbroun de Gedding, son of Robert, conveyed a messuage, 300 acres of arable, 25 acres of meadow, 6 acres of pasture and 40 acres of wood and 100s. rent in Hoddesdon to Philip de Melreth,

---

[24] Cal. Close, 1288–96, p. 138. He seems to have held some of his lands of the manor of Great Amwell (see Anct. D. [P.R.O.], A 1030).

[25] cf. Feud. Aids, ii, 430 and 433. The overlordship both here and in later records is given as vested in the overlords of the manor of Boxe in Walkern, and evidently some of the lands forming this fee were held with that manor of the Balliols and their successors, lords of Bennington (cf. deed quoted in Tregelles, Hist. of Hoddesdon, 69).

[26] Feet of F. Herts. 35 Edw. I, no. 432.

[27] See Cal. Close, 1323–7, p. 296; Chan. Inq. p.m. 18 Edw. II, no. 62.

[28] Chan. Inq. p.m. 18 Edw. II, no. 26.

[29] cf. Feet of F. Herts. 35 Edw. I, no. 432; Chan. Inq. p.m. 50 Edw. III (2nd nos.), no. 55.

[30] Close, 8 Hen. VI, m. 11.

[31] Tregelles, Hist. of Hoddesdon, 68; Ct. R. (Gen. Ser.), portf. 177, no. 59–61.

[32] Auct. D. (P.R.O.), B 241; Feet of F. Herts. 27 Hen. VI, no. 146; Mins. Accts. bdle. 862, no. 16, 17; Cal. Pat. 1446–52, p. 253.

[32a] Cal. Pat. 1467–77, p. 123.

[33] Chan. Inq. p.m. 18 Edw. IV, no. 43.

[34] Ibid. (Ser. 2), li, 50.

[35] Cal. Close, 1323–7, p. 296.

[36] Ct. R. (Gen. Ser.), portf. 177, no. 56–61.

[37] Feet of F. Herts. 27 Hen. VI, no. 146; Mins. Accts. bdle. 862, no. 16, 17; Chan. Inq. p.m. 18 Edw. IV, no. 43; (Ser. 2), li, 50.

[38] Chan. Inq. p.m. 50 Edw. III (2nd nos.), no. 35. [39] Ibid.

[40] Ct. R. (Gen. Ser.), portf. 177, no. 56.

[41] Chan. Inq. p.m. (Ser. 2), li, 50.

[42] Feet of F. Herts. 27 Hen. VI, no. 146; Chan. Inq. p.m. 18 Edw. IV, no. 43; (Ser. 2), li, 50; Mins. Accts. bdle. 862, no. 16, 17.

[43a] Tregelles, Hist. of Hoddesdon, 23.

[44] Add. R. 26828. See also Chan. Inq. p.m. 50 Edw. III (1st nos.), no. 3, for John atte Halle.

[45] Rentals and Surv. Herts. portf. 8, no. 27.

[46] Feet of F. Herts. 27 Hen. VII, no. 146.

[47] Mins. Accts. bdle. 862, no. 16, 17; Chan. Inq. p.m. (Ser. 2), li, 50; Feet of F. Div. Co. Hil. 12 Eliz.; Hil. 14 Eliz.

[48] V.C.H. Essex, i, 429b.

[49] V.C.H. Herts. i, 325b; Doc. at Westm. Press 17, shelf 4, box 85, no. 4733; box 76, no. 4247; Chan. Inq. p.m. (Ser. 2), li, 50.

[50] Doc. at Westm. Press 17, shelf 4, box 85, no. 4732.

[51] Dugdale, Mon. i, 2; Assize R. 325, m. 4 d.

[52] Chart. R. 1 Edw. III, m. 29, no. 50.

[53] Doc. at Westm. Press 17, shelf 4, box 85, no. 4733.

[54] Ibid. box 76, no. 4247.

[55] Add. R. 26828.

Broxbourne Church: The Font

Broxbourne Church: Tomb of Sⁱ William Say

HERTFORD HUNDRED

BROXBOURNE WITH HODDESDON

clerk, and his heirs.[56] In the next century these lands were in the possession of Edward Chertsey, who in 1430–1 granted them as the manor of Geddings to Nicholas Dixon and others,[57] after which the manor follows the same descent as the manor of Baas (q.v.).

The reputed manor or tenement of BERNARDES or BARNETTS belonged about the middle of the 16th century to the family of Castell. Thomas son of Dorothy Castell mortgaged Bernardes about 1559 to Henry Brograve, who sold the property to William Frankland of London.[58] In 1582 William and Hugh Frankland (for this family see Thele Manor in Stanstead St. Margaret's) conveyed the 'manor,' then called Barnetts, to Bernard Dewhurst and Thomas Bennett.[59] Within the next ten years the two latter sold it to Sir William Cecil, lord of the manor of Geddings,[60] after which it follows the same descent as that manor.[61]

Before the Conquest nearly 6 hides in HODDESDON (Odesdone, Dodesdone) were held by Gode of Queen Edith, wife of Harold, as two manors.[62] In 1086 the larger of these, assessed at 3¾ hides, was held by Edward the Sheriff of Salisbury.[63] The other, of the extent of 2 hides, was held of the king by Peter, a burgess. The latter was evidently identical with the Peter of St. Olave, Southwark, who in 1096 gave his lands at Hoddesdon to the monks of Bermondsey.[64]

About 1180 these lands or part of them seem to have been held by Robert de Hurtford in chief, for in that year he is entered as owing 2 marks for 3 hides in Hoddesdon,[65] and in the following year the same amount for 2 hides, of which he had 'not yet had right.'[66] He died three years later without having obtained it.[67] In 1210–12 Simon son of Gilbert held a quarter fee in Hoddesdon of the king in chief,[68] which perhaps represents this estate.

The RECTORY MANOR of Broxbourne was held with the church by the Bishops of London,[69] who seem to have generally farmed it out.[70] In 1651 the rectory and glebe lands were sold by the trustees for the sale of bishops' lands to Edmund Lewin and his heirs for £522.[71] The Bishop of London regained it at the Restoration, and in 1728 it was leased to the lord of the manor,[72] and was probably acquired by him together with the advowson in 1868.

CHURCHES

The church of ST. AUGUSTINE stands a little to the east of the village. It consists of chancel 35 ft. by 17 ft., north and south chapels, each 34 ft. by 10 ft., nave 68 ft. 6 in. by 17 ft., north and south aisles, each 69 ft. by 10 ft., vestry, with upper room, adjoining the north chapel, south porch and west tower, all internal dimensions.

The church was entirely rebuilt and enlarged in the 15th century, and no detail now remains of the former nave and chancel, which appear to have been added to from time to time. The north aisle was the earliest addition, then the two east bays of the south aisle and the west bay of the south chapel; shortly afterwards the south aisle was extended westwards the full length of the nave and the south chapel eastwards to the east wall of the chancel; the west tower was erected about the close of the 15th century, the north chapel and vestry are dated 1522, and the south porch was added in the early 17th century.

The walls are of flint rubble, except the north chapel and vestry, which are faced without and within with squared limestone ashlar. The nave and chancel roofs are tiled, the others lead-covered.

In the east wall of the chancel is a 15th-century window of three cinquefoiled lights with traceried head; hidden behind the table of the Commandments on the north side of the window are some remains of the splayed jamb of an earlier window; on each side of the chancel is an arcade of two bays with arches of two moulded orders and jambs of four engaged shafts with moulded capitals and bases.

The north chapel east window is of three cinquefoiled lights with traceried head under a four-centred arch; in the north wall are two similar windows with the door to the vestry between them. The doorway has a splayed four-centred arch and jambs, and retains its original oak door and ironwork. In the east wall of the vestry are two small recesses under four-centred arches; in each of the north and west walls is a small two-light window under a square head; in the chamber over the vestry are two similar windows; a third window, now blocked, opened into the church. The north chapel and vestry, both built in 1522, have an ornamental parapet carried round outside on which is carved the inscription 'Pray for the welfayr of Syr Wylyam Say knyght wych fodyd yis chapel in honor a ye trenete the yere of our Lord God 1522.' Stags' heads and traceried panels with the arms of Say are carried at intervals above the parapet; the upper parts of the panelled and crocketed buttresses are set diagonally.

The south chapel has a two-light window with traceried head in the east wall and two traceried windows of three lights under four-centred arches in the south wall; the junction between the earlier and later 15th-century work can be seen outside. In the south wall between the windows is a large recess for a tomb under a four-centred arch, with moulded jambs and arch. In the same wall is a piscina belonging to the earlier portion of the chapel, partially destroyed by the later tomb recess; the jambs of the piscina are moulded and have a ball-flower ornament. The four bays on either side of the nave are continuations of the arcades between chancel and chapels, and their detail is similar, though they are somewhat earlier in date. At the east end of the north wall of the north aisle is a semi-octagonal stair turret projecting on the outside leading to the rood-loft and roof over the aisle; the doorway to the rood-loft is blocked. In the north wall of the aisle are four windows, each of two cinquefoiled lights with traceried head under a pointed arch; the external stonework has been renewed. In the west wall is a

---

[56] Close, 1 Ric. II, m. 4 d.
[57] Ibid. 9 Hen. VI, m. 3, 4.
[58] Chan. Decree R. bdle. 31, no. 6.
[59] Feet of F. Herts. Mich. 24 & 25 Eliz.
[60] Ibid. East. 35 Eliz.
[61] Chan. Inq. p.m. (Ser. 2), ccclviii, 108.
[62] V.C.H. Herts. i, 342, 330.
[63] Ibid. 330a.
[64] Ibid. 342; Dugdale, Mon. Angl. v, 96. The connexion was shown by Mr. Tregelles in his Hist. of Hoddesdon, 58.
[65] Pipe R. 26 Hen. II, m. 1.
[66] Ibid. 27 Hen. II, m. 7.
[67] Ibid. 30 Hen. II.
[68] Red Bk. of Exch. (Rolls Ser.), ii, 499; Testa de Nevill (Rec. Com.), 270.
[69] Lond. Epis. Reg. Gravesend and Baldock, fol. 41.
[70] Ibid. Braybrook, fol. 345–6.
[71] Close, 1651, pt. xxxi, m. 3.
[72] Salmon, Hist. of Herts. 16.

splayed loop light. In the south wall of the south aisle are four windows similar to those in the north aisle; there is no window in the west wall. The south doorway has continuously moulded jambs and four-centred arch. In the east jamb of the doorway, in the porch, are remains of a roughly executed stoup, and in the south aisle, a little to the east of the doorway, is a plain recess, probably for a stoup. The south porch has a semicircular arched doorway with flanking pilasters and pediment over, and above is a shield charged with arms.

The roofs over the chancel and chapels have flat panelled ceilings of early 16th-century date; those over the nave and aisles are of the 15th century, but have been much restored. Over the east end of the nave is a painted inscription recording that the ceiling and decoration of the chancel roof was done by John Bryce.

octagonal plinth; it is of late 12th-century date. In the chamber over the north vestry are two oak chests, one belonging to the 14th, the other to the 17th century. In the south-east window of the south chapel is some 15th-century heraldic glass.

On the south side of the chancel is the Purbeck marble altar-tomb of Sir John Say and his wife, dated 1473. The sides of the plinth are panelled and traceried panels, three of which contain shields which retain some of their original colouring. On the moulded slab are fine brasses of

SAY of Broxbourne. *Party azure and gules three cheverons or voided party gules and azure.*

BROXBOURNE CHURCH FROM THE NORTH-EAST

The west tower is of three stages and is buttressed; at the south-west angle is a turret staircase; both tower and turret are finished with embattled parapets. The four-centred tower arch is of two moulded orders; the jambs have engaged shafts with moulded capitals and bases. The west doorway has a two-centred arch under a square head with traceried spandrels. The west window is of four cinquefoiled lights with tracery under a two-centred arch; the stonework is much decayed. On the north and south faces of the second stage of the tower are narrow trefoiled lights with square heads; on the west is a clock face. The belfry windows are of two cinquefoiled lights under square heads.

The font has an octagonal bowl of Purbeck marble, on each face of which are two plain sunk panels with round heads; the bowl rests on a circular shaft with eight smaller ones under the angles of the octagon; the shafts have moulded bases and stand on a plain

the knight and the lady; the knight is in plate armour with surcoat charged with his arms, the figure is now headless. The lady wears a sideless surcoat and a mantle charged with her arms. The figures are elaborately engraved and retain much of the original coloured enamelling. Two shields still remain with the arms of Say, and a brass inscription, parts of which are missing, runs round the margin. On the north side of the chancel is the altar-tomb of Sir William Say, the builder of the north chapel; it is of early 16th-century date. The plinth is ornamented with square moulded and cusped panels set diagonally, in which are shields bearing indents of missing brass figures. On the plinth is a slab of Purbeck marble. Above the tomb, supported on octagonal columns, is a canopy, the soffit carved with pendants and fan vaulting; under the east end is a slab with indents of a knight and a lady. In the south chapel is the tomb of Sir Henry Cock and his wife, 1609, with recumbent effigies, in alabaster, under a semicircular canopy with panelled soffit over which is the achievement of arms ; on the plinth below are the kneeling figures of two daughters and their children. In the chancel is a mural monument to William Gamble *alias* Bowyer, 1646, with inscription and arms. In the north chapel is a mural monument to Sir R. Skeffington, 1646, and another to John Baylie, 1609. There are several 17th-century floor slabs to members of the Monson and Rawdon families ; in the south aisle is a tablet in memory of John Loudon McAdam, the great road maker, who was buried at Moffat in 1836.

On the chancel floor is the brass of a priest in chasuble and holding a chalice ; it is without inscription, but is of late 15th-century date ; another of a priest in cassock and amice is also without inscription. At the corners are symbols of the Evangelists, and part of an inscribed scroll remains ; it belongs to the early 16th century. In the nave are indents of a knight and a lady ; a portion of the knight's figure remains. In the centre of the nave is a shield, vair bordered crusilly, and dated 1630 ; also the brass of a knight clad in armour and holding a mace, said to be that of John Barrell, serjeant-at-arms to Henry VIII. This brass was recovered from Roding in Essex in 1892.

There are eight bells : the treble, second, third and sixth are dated 1903 ; the fourth, fifth and seventh by Robert Oldfeild, 1615, and the eighth by John Hodson, 1670.

The communion plate consists of cup and cover paten, 1606, a paten, 1633, a cup and cover paten, 1824, and two flagons.

The registers before 1812 are as follows: (i) baptisms, burials and marriages from 1688 to 1741 ; (ii) baptisms and burials from 1741 to 1812, marriages 1741 to 1754 ; (iii) marriages from 1754 to 1812.

The church of *ST. PAUL*, Hoddesdon, near the centre of the town, was built in 1732 and repaired in 1822 and 1849 ; in 1865 the building was enlarged by the addition of a chancel with north and south chapels or aisles ; in 1888 the brick tower and spire were added. It now consists of chancel 35 ft. 6 in. by 21 ft., north and south chapels or aisles, each 34 ft. by 19 ft. 6 in., nave 61 ft. 6 in. by 31 ft., vestry and semi-detached tower, east of the south nave wall ; all the dimensions are internal. The church is built of brick with stone dressings. There are eight bells in the tower hung in 1901. The plate consists of three chalices, two patens and a flagon, all modern.

ADVOWSONS   The advowson of the church of St. Augustine originally belonged to the lords of the manor of Broxbourne and was granted together with that manor to the Knights Hospitallers by Robert Earl of Leicester.[73] In 1190, however, Garner of Naples, Prior of the Hospitallers, granted the church of Broxbourne to the Bishop of London for a yearly payment of 4 marks.[74] The advowson remained in the hands of the Bishops of London until 1852, when it was transferred to the Bishop of Rochester.[75] In 1868 it was acquired by Mr. Smith-Bosanquet, lord of the manor,[76] and is now in the hands of trustees.

Sir John Say left 200 marks in 1478 for a priest to sing mass for his soul for twenty years,[77] and his son Sir William Say built the chapel of our Lady within the parish church of Broxbourne as a chantry for his family (see above). He also left to the chapel a chalice of silver gilt and 'a payer of cruets of silver parcel gilt with other ornaments as shall be necessary for the chapel.' The salary of the priest belonging to the chapel was to be paid out of Sir William's lordship of Bengeo.[78] In 1578 it was reported that until about thirty-three years before two priests had been accustomed to sing mass in 'Sir William Saye's chapel,' and received £10 a year for it. It was also stated that until thirty-five or thirty-six years before 'there was usually set up a hearse in the midst of the church, furnished with lights and torches, and bells were rung.'[79]

There was a chapel at Hoddesdon in the 14th century which seems to have been appurtenant to the manor of Hoddesdon. It was the subject of a dispute in 1242-3 between Alexander de Swereford, Treasurer of St. Paul's, and Humphrey and John de Bassingburn.[80] Alexander acknowledged the right of the Bassingburns to the advowson, and Humphrey and John granted that the chapel should be moved back to its former situation by the side of the road which led to the court of Alexander de Swereford and near to the court of Humphrey de Bassingburn. Humphrey and John also agreed to supply a chaplain to celebrate service daily for their souls and that of Alexander and of their ancestors, and they confirmed all lands previously belonging to the chapel.[81] This chapel seems to have fallen into disuse, for in 1336 William de la Marche obtained licence to build a chapel in honour of St. Catherine on a 'void place' in Hoddesdon, 30 ft. by 20 ft., and to alienate it in mortmain when built to a chaplain or religious man.[82] In the time of Henry IV witnesses declared that the chapel lay in the parish of Great Amwell,[83] and in 1650 it was said to be partly in Amwell and partly in Broxbourne. It was then suggested that it could be conveniently constituted a parish church for Hoddesdon[84] ; the suggestion, however, was not carried out. At the end of the 17th century the chapel was pulled down, with the exception of the clock-tower, which remained until about 1836.[85]

In 1844 the parish of St. Paul, Hoddesdon, was formed as a consolidated chapelry out of Broxbourne and Great Amwell.[86] The living is a vicarage, and the patronage goes with that of Broxbourne.[87] There is a mission church at Rye Park, served from the parish church.

The priory of St. Monica at Hoddesdon is now used as a convent of the order of Canonesses Regular of St. Augustine.[88] There are also Congregational, Wesleyan, and Baptist chapels there, as well as meeting places of the Society of Friends[89] and Plymouth

---

[73] Chart. R. 1 John, pt. i, m. 106, 10. 111.
[74] *Hist. MSS. Com. Rep.* ix, App.'i, 32*a*.
[75] *Lond. Gaz. Index,* 264.
[76] *East Herts. Arch. Soc. Trans.* i, 293.
[77] P.C.C. 35 Wattys.
[78] Ibid. 6 Thorver.
[79] *Exch. Spec. Com.* no. 1027.
[80] *Red Bk. of Exch.* (Rolls Ser.), i, p. xlvii.
[81] Feet of F. Herts. 27 Hen. III, no. 305.
[82] *Cal. Pat.* 1334-8, p. 259.
[83] Doc. at Westm. Herts. Amwell.
[84] *Chan. Surv. of Church Livings,* i, p. 35.   [85] *Herts. Const. Mag.* ii, 96.
[86] *Lond. Gaz. Index,* 827.   [87] Ibid.
[88] *Catholic Dir.*
[89] For a history of the Quakers in Hoddesdon see Tregelles, *Hist. of Hoddesdon,* 217 et seq.

A HISTORY OF HERTFORDSHIRE

Brethren. Meeting-places for Protestant Dissenters were certified in Broxbourne in 1813, and at Hoddesdon in 1689, 1691, 1692, 1704 and 1821.[90]

Broxbourne: The Free school, founded in 1667 by will of Sir Richard Lucy, bart.[90a]

The Girls' school at Baas Hill.[91]

The following eleemosynary charities are regulated by scheme of the Charity Commissioners 3 October 1899. They comprise the charities of:

(1) Lady Lucy, gift about 1676, consisting of 4 a. 0 r. 29 p., situate at Roydon, of the annual letting value of £6.

(2) Roger Marsh, deed, 1635, being a rent-charge of £2 4s. 5d. issuing out of Hailey Hall estates in Great Amwell.

(3) William Purvey, will, proved in 1617, being a rent-charge of 3s. 4d. out of Wormley Bury estates.

(4) George Swaine, will, proved in 1829; trust fund £125 consols, with the official trustees, producing £3 2s. 4d. yearly; and

(5) William Thorowgood, will, proved 25 February 1603, being a yearly sum of £1 4s. issuing out of Hoddesdon vicarage.

In 1909 the income was applied as to £1 in surgical aid, £5 towards coal and clothing clubs, £2 in money gifts and the balance in the distribution of calico and bread.

The ecclesiastical charity of William Thorowgood consists of £107 13s. 5d. consols, in the names of the Rev. John Salwey and two others, producing £2 13s. 8d. yearly, representing the redemption of an annuity of £2 to the vicar for preaching six sermons, and an annuity of 16s. for repairing the windows in the church.

The almshouses erected by Dame Letitia Monson for six poor widows, and endowed by her will, dated in 1729, are regulated by a scheme of the Charity Commissioners 6 January 1888. The present endowment consists of £2,663 6s. 9d. Bank of England stock, which produced in 1909 £254 10s. 11d., and a sum of £519 10s. 9d. consols, producing £12 19s. 8d. yearly; the former sum of stock is standing in the name of the Paymaster-General in the High Court of Justice, and the latter is held by the official trustees.

In 1909–10 the sum of £163 16s. was paid to nine inmates, £7 4s. 9d. for gowns, £34 9s. for wood and coal, 5s. to the vicar for gloves and £10 for prayers and services.

The charity of Catherine Augusta Baroness of Sternberg, founded by will, proved in 1859, consists of £504 16s. 1d. consols, with the official trustees, producing £12 12s. 4d. yearly, which is in pursuance of a scheme of the Charity Commissioners 10 February 1882, applied for the benefit of the poor by the district visitors.

The Cecilia Smith-Bosanquet Memorial Trust, founded by deed 15 December 1904, for providing a nurse for the sick poor, is endowed with £2,500 New South Wales 3½ per cent. stock, with the official trustees, producing £87 10s. yearly.

The official trustees also hold a sum of £100 2½ per cent. stock, arising from the sale in 1891 of land known as the Clock Half-acre, the income of which is applicable for the winding, &c., of the church clock.

Hoddesdon: The following eleemosynary charities are regulated by scheme of the Charity Commissioners 3 October 1899. They comprise the charities of:

(1) Lynch Mill Corner, founded by an agreement, dated 21 April 1679, in consideration of the inclosure of certain Lammas land, being a yearly sum of £2 15s.

(2) Roger Marsh, by deed, 1635, being a rent-charge of £4 8s. 11d. issuing out of Hailey Hall estates in Great Amwell.

(3) William Purvey, will, proved in 1617, being a rent-charge of 10s. out of Wormley Bury estates.

(4) George Swaine, will, proved in 1829, trust fund, £375 consols, with the official trustees, producing £9 7s. 4d. yearly.

(5) William Thorowgood, will, proved 25 February 1603, being a yearly sum of £4 issuing out of the land now occupied by Hoddesdon vicarage, for distribution of bread.

(6) William Thorowgood, for distribution of beef and bread, consisting of a rent-charge of £4 4s. issuing out of Balls Park, near Hertford.

(7) Unknown donor—but stated in the Parliamentary returns of 1786 to have been given by Lady Oxendon in 1635—being a yearly sum of £1 6s. 8d. issuing out of the Grange, Hoddesdon.

In 1909 the sum of £4 was paid to the clothing and coal clubs, £1 to the dispensary and £25 applied in the distribution of meat and bread to 220 recipients.

In 1818 Easter Jones purchased land and erected a school thereon for girls, and endowed the same with £1,000 consols.

The income of a sum of £450 consols, the gift of — Game, is also applicable for educational purposes.

The Priscilla Manser Fund consists of £508 12s. Local Loans 2½ per cent. stock and £400 East Indian Railway 3 per cent. stock, in the names of Robert Barclay and four others, producing £27 5s. yearly.

In 1907 £11 14s. was paid to three inmates of the homes, and the balance added to the fund for their upkeep.

Samuel Dunn's Charity for the organist is endowed with a piece of meadow land near Hoddesdon, let at £4 a year.

In 1910 William Alfred Pryor, by his will, proved at London 12 October, left £50, now represented by £60 Great Northern Railway 3 per cent. stock, the annual dividends, amounting to £1 16s., to be applied for the benefit of the poor of the Congregational church.

Hoddesdon, St. Catherine: In 1885 George Ringrose, by his will, proved at London 25 September, left a legacy, now represented by £90 11s. 4d. consols, with the official trustees, the annual dividends, amounting to £2 5s., to be distributed to the poor in coal, bread, or money.

---

[90] Urwick, *Nonconf. in Herts.* 496.   [90a] See article on 'Schools,' *V.C.H. Herts.* ii, 100.   [91] Ibid.

CHESHUNT

Cestrehunt (xi, xii, xiii cent.); Chesthunt (xiv, xv, xvi cent.).

Cheshunt is an extensive parish containing about 8,479 acres. The urban part lies at the eastern end, east of the New River, which flows through the parish; the rural and more thinly-populated district is found in the western, higher-lying ground, and consists chiefly of scattered farms and parks, with Cheshunt Common extending to the western border. The surface of the parish is undulating and its physical aspect varies. Large areas are devoted to fruit culture, roses, horticultural nurseries, and market gardens.

The River Lea or one of its streams forms the eastern boundary, which has been the cause of many disputes between the Abbots of Waltham and the lords of Cheshunt; the former maintained that the Small River Lea flowing half a mile west of Waltham was the dividing line, and that all the adjacent meadows belonged to Waltham; the latter tried to prove that the River Lea itself, flowing through the town of Waltham, was the county boundary, and that the land west of it belonged to the manor of Cheshunt. Peter of Savoy, when lord of the manor, quitclaimed to Simon the abbot his right to the meadows and marshes in question, but the dispute broke out again, and at the time of the Dissolution was undetermined between Robert, the last abbot, and the lord of Cheshunt.[1] The quarrel was carried on by the two neighbouring towns,[2] and in the middle of the 19th century was still unsettled.[3] The present boundary appears to be a compromise, the southern part being formed by the Small River Lea, the northern by the River Lea itself.

Cheshunt Common covers a large area to the extreme west of the parish. An inclosure award made in 1804 and enrolled in 1806 is in the custody of the vestry clerk of the parish of Cheshunt. By a further local Act an allotment of 100 acres of common was made.[4]

Under the provisions of the Local Government Act of 1894 the parish is now governed by an urban district council of twelve members and divided into three wards—that is, the Northern, Central and Southern Wards, known for parochial purposes as Waltham Cross, Cheshunt Street and Woodside Wards.

The original settlement was probably at St. Mary's Church, now called Churchgate, off the Roman road (Ermine Street) on the east side. At an early date, however, a road settlement must have been established along the present high road which replaced the Roman road some time before the Conquest, for by 1086 there was already a trading community of ten merchants at Cheshunt, who would naturally be on the line of traffic.

At Churchgate is Cheshunt College, a large building standing south-east of the church. It was originally founded at Trevecca in 1768 by Selina Countess of Huntingdon as a training college for the ministry of the Countess of Huntingdon's Connexion, and moved to its present site in 1792. In 1905 it was converted into a theological college of the Church of England, and is now known as Bishop's College. Although largely added to during the 19th century, there still exists a small block of the original building, which is of red brickwork, with plain arched window openings. Above the upper floor windows is a moulded brick cornice with dentil course, surmounted by a brick parapet. On one side is an old lead rainwater head on which is a crest of a unicorn, and

OLDER PART OF CHESHUNT COLLEGE

above is the date 1746, which is probably the date of the erection of the building.

Not far from Bishop's College is a 17th-century brick house, now divided into three tenements. To the north is Dewhurst School, a brick house with brick mullioned windows and a tiled roof, built in 1640 by Robert Dewhurst, whose arms and initials and this date are on the east wall. The upper story and the interior of the house have been modernized and a large new school added on the north side. On the east side of the church are many 17th-century houses and cottages of half-timber and brick with tiled roofs; among them is the Green

---

[1] Fuller, *Hist. of Waltham Abbey*, 265.
[2] *Cal. S. P. Dom.* 1591–4, pp. 499–501.
[3] Brown, *Cheshunt in the Olden Times*, 17.
[4] *East Herts. Arch. Soc. Trans.* ii, 110–13.

A HISTORY OF HERTFORDSHIRE

Dragon Inn, a timber-framed house now cased with brick.

Westward lies the Lordship, the residence of Mr. Wyndham Birch, near to which is the moated site of Cheshunt Manor House. On the west side of the island formed by the moat are the remains of the abutments of a bridge. North of this homestead moat on the opposite side of the road to Goff's Oak is the Great House. Externally the house is not very interesting, having been recased in brick (all but the north front) by John Shaw in 1750, and in 1801 a large part was pulled down, having become ruinous. According to an early 18th-century print it was at that time quadrangular, inclosing a courtyard, and there are indications of a wing having been removed from the north end of the west front. The south wing has also been pulled down. The house was originally of the latter part of the 15th century and was of two stories with a tiled roof. The south, west, and east fronts of the part that remains are of plain red brickwork, with a parapet at the top, over which the tops of the old tiled roofs may be seen. The south front has a four-centred arch of stone to the entrance doorway and a round-arched brick window above, all built in 1750. Part of the north front, however, has not been touched, for the old walling of narrow bricks, rising 10½ in. in four courses, still remains, and in the gable is a three-light window with stone mullions, now bricked up, and above are the bases of three diagonal brick chimneys, probably of early 17th-century date.

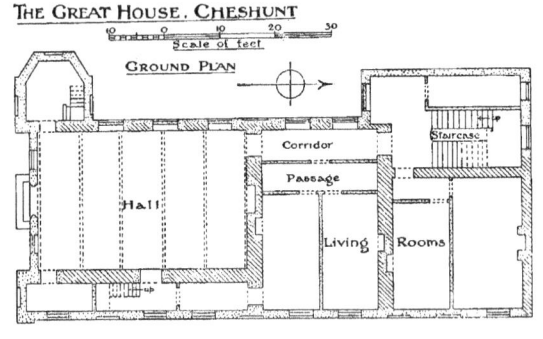

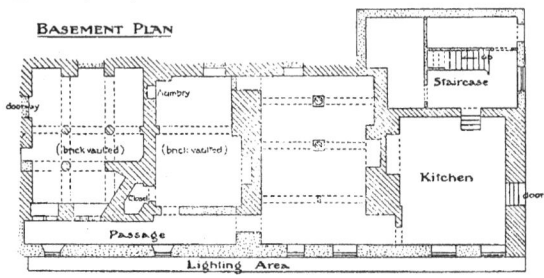

The interior of the building is much more interesting, though greatly altered and modernized. It consists of a large hall on the ground floor, at the back of which are some rooms and a staircase, and underneath the whole is a large basement. The hall is open up to the roof, but the rooms behind have a second and attic floor over them. The basement is very interesting, but it is not easy to indicate the uses of some of the places in it. Though now lighted only from the east side by means of a modern sunk area, there are built-up windows in the west wall showing that it was lighted from the courtyard also. It is entered at the north end of the building by a doorway in the external wall, the ground level being only a few steps up from the floor. This north room or kitchen, the ceiling of which is lath and plaster, has also a door to the staircase. The next room is somewhat similar; it has also a large, plain fireplace. The floor above is supported by three old oak beams, each supported in the centre by a circular pier, 15 in. in diameter, built with 2¼ in. bricks; these piers have no capitals, but have small moulded octagonal bases resting on square brick plinths, about 2 ft. 6 in. high. One of the piers has gone, its place being taken by a wooden post. There are two windows in the east wall and a built-up window in the west wall. There are two openings in the south wall; one, at the western end, is a vaulted passage, now partly bricked-up, leading to a vaulted place beyond, the other is a doorway leading to a passage along the east main wall, which gives access to the vaults under the hall. The first of these, at the northern end, measures about 23 ft. by 15 ft. and is covered by a brick vault, elliptical in section, in one span. On the south side is a curious, small, irregularly-shaped closet, which, perhaps, had a window to the passage at one time. The doorway to this has a low four-centred arch. In the same wall is a small arched recess or aumbry. There is a built-up window in the west wall and a fireplace in the north wall, with moulded four-centred arch and jambs.

The adjoining vault is curious. There is no sign of any doorway between it and the rest of the existing building; the only doorway is a built-up opening in the main south wall of the building, which gave access to the former south wing. It is not known what is beyond this doorway, but there is a tradition of a stair down to a lower basement, indications of which can be traced by tapping the floor, and it is possible that the stair went up to the hall above. This apartment is covered with three elliptical brick vaults running east and west, separated into nine compartments by moulded brick ribs resting

442

CHESHUNT: THE GREAT HOUSE, VAULT

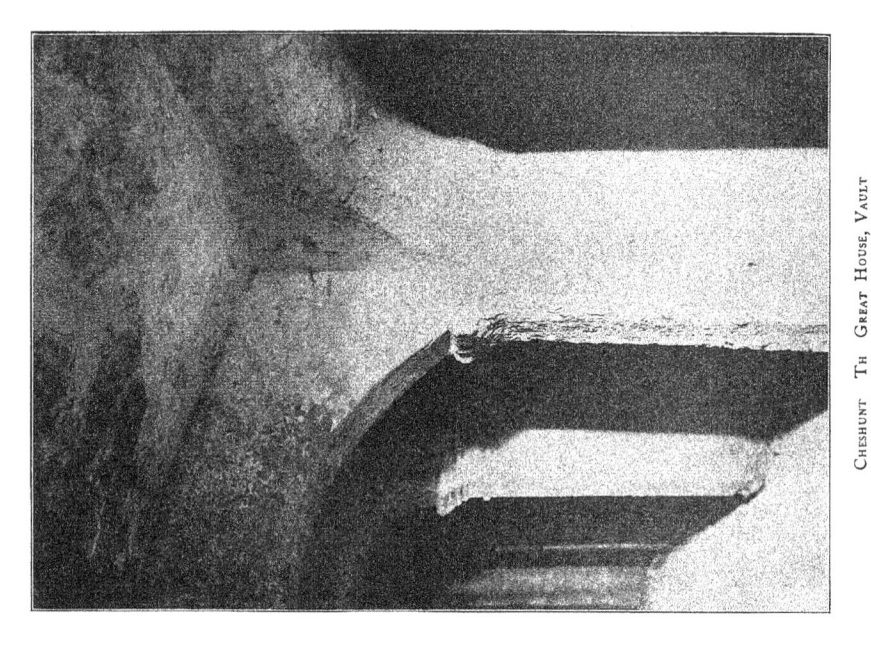

CHESHUNT: THE GREAT HOUSE, STAIRCASE

HERTFORD HUNDRED

on octagonal piers. The small closet previously mentioned projects into this apartment at its north-east corner. Two of the piers are of clunch, with 15th-century moulded capitals and small bases; the other piers and all the vaults and arches are of brick covered with plaster. In the east wall are two groups of windows into the passage. One group consists of two lights, each 2 ft. wide, with sills 2 ft. 6 in. from the floor and wide seats inside, the wall here being 3 ft. 2 in. thick; these openings have four-centred arches over them. The adjoining group consists — though now much decayed—of four lights, each about 10 in. wide, having pointed arches. All these are of brick with splayed jambs and arches and have been plastered. There is a fireplace, now partly bricked-up, in the south wall and a built-up window in the west wall. It is difficult to say to what use this vault was put, as, although it is locally known as the chapel, there are no indications that it was ever used for that purpose, and it probably owes its name to its semi-ecclesiastical appearance.

On the ground floor the principal entrance door, which is modern, opens directly into the south end of the old hall. The hall itself measures about 37 ft. 6 in. long by 24 ft. 6 in. wide and is open up to the roof. The old minstrels' gallery and screen underneath at the south end have disappeared, but the old opening from the stair-turret on the west side still exists, though the stair and turret belong to the rebuilding of 1750. The roof is original and is a simple open one, having curved principals with collars near the apex and resting on carved corbels, some of which, however, have disappeared. Of the four remaining corbels two represent angels holding shields and two human heads. The floor of the hall is paved with large square slabs of black and white marble. The fireplace is of stone, and both it and the panelling round the walls belong to the middle of the 18th century.

A doorway at the north-west corner of the hall leads to a corridor, off which are now two rooms which probably originally formed one. Beyond the corridor is a good mid-18th-century oak staircase, with turned and moulded balusters. There are three balusters to each step, each of the three of different design, and all repeated in succession. The ends of the steps are carved. There is not much of interest in the rooms on the ground and upper floors, though in one is a well-carved 18th-century chimney-piece.

In College Road is Water Lane Farm, a mid-16th-century house of brick and timber, covered with rough-cast, with a tiled roof. On the north side is a 19th-century addition.

The main part of the village lies along the North Road. The southern part is in Waltham Cross, which was formed into a separate ecclesiastical parish in 1855, with the church of Holy Trinity built in 1832. The road, here called the High Street, enters the parish at the county boundary, at which are the 'Spital Houses,' originally built in 1625 but rebuilt in 1908. As may be expected along a main high road, there are throughout the 2¼ miles of the road which Cheshunt and Waltham Cross cover numerous inns and taverns, one or two of which, such as the Four Swans Inn, near Waltham Cross, may date back to the 17th century, but the greater number are of the 18th century and later.

Waltham Cross stands at the junction of Waltham High Street with Eleanor Cross Road, and, although much restored, is one of the best preserved of the twelve Eleanor crosses, of which only three survive. Eleanor, the first wife of Edward I, died at Harby, co. Notts., 7 miles west of Lincoln, on 28 November 1290. Apparently the body rested at St. Albans on the night of 12 December and was carried thence to Waltham on the following day, where it rested for the night at Waltham Abbey and arrived in London on 14 December. Of the twelve Eleanor crosses Waltham Cross was the only one which was designed by a foreigner, 'Nicholas Dymenge de Reyns,' or 'Dymenge de Legeri.' It was begun in 1291 and completed before Christmas 1292. The sculptors engaged upon it were Roger de Crundale, Alexander le Imaginator or Imagemaker and Robert de Corf,[b]

CHESHUNT GREAT HOUSE: NORTH END OF THE HALL

[b] *V.C.H. Dorset*, ii, 335, n. 38.

the last of whom came from the Purbeck quarries and made the shafts, capitals and rings (verg. capit. et anul.). The stone was brought from Caen and the total cost was £95.[6] The cross is a fine specimen of architecture of the 13th century, although the four basement steps and the two upper stages are modern, having been extensively restored, and, indeed, almost wholly rebuilt in 1833 under the direction of Mr. W. B. Clark, and again, the soft Bath stone having decayed, in 1887-9 by Mr. C. E. Ponting. The lowest stage is original. It is hexagonal with panels of two 'lights,' having tracery in pointed heads under crocketed gables with finials, set against a diapered background which is surmounted by a sculptured cornice very much weathered. In the panels are shields suspended from foliage and carved with the arms of England, Castile and Leon, and Ponthieu. At the angles are small pinnacled buttresses. The second stage has six elaborately gabled and crocketed canopies with pinnacles between them. They contain three statues of the queen, said to be original, except the head of that on the west, which has been renewed.

The third stage, which is also hexagonal, rises from a plinth set in the space inclosed by the heads of the canopies below it, and masked on the centre of each side by tall heavy crocketed pinnacles with finials not too happily designed. The plinth has a foliated cornice at its base, and the panels on the sides of the stage, with the buttresses at the angles, are of a design practically repeating that of the canopies of the second stage, but solid. Above this is a low hexagonal plinth supporting a tall pinnacle, crocketed on its six angles, and surmounted by a cross. Practically the whole of the second stage is of the restoration of 1833, and the upper stages are also very much renovated. The general features of the old work have, however, been carefully preserved, much old stone laid aside in 1833 having been reintroduced in 1887-9. An addition to the width of the roadway, for the better preservation of the monument, was secured by the purchase and demolition of the Falcon Inn by the late Sir Henry Meux, bart., and completed in 1892.

Beyond Waltham Cross High Street the road is called Turner's Hill. On the west side is a row of ten almshouses, founded in 1620. They are plain erections of brick of one story, with mullioned windows, and appear to have been a good deal restored. There is no inscription on them. On Turner's Hill there still remains the old watch-house built in 1789. Further on is the New Road, from which branches off Blindman's Lane, an old road containing a 17th-century farm-house, now converted into a shop. At the corner of the lane is a row of three brick gabled cottages, two stories in height with tiled roofs. Northward of New Road is Cheshunt Street, in which are several old houses and cottages. One of these is now converted into a shop. At the northern end on the east side is a brick house with steep twin gables at the end. On the front, over the shop, is a brick panel in which are the initials G.K.M. and the date 1689. There is a moulded architrave round the panel, with a swelled frieze above, broken in the centre with a human head, above which is a moulded cornice and curved and broken pediment, in the centre of which is a shield with coat of arms: a cheveron between three garbs with a fleur de lis for difference. Immediately to the north is the Anchor Inn, a brick two-storied house of about the same date, whilst on the same side of the road, further south, adjoining Hill View, is a good two-storied house of the early 18th century.

Further northward along the same road is the hamlet of Turnford, where there are the large nursery gardens at Turnford Hall and elsewhere. A farm-house beside the railway stands on the site of the Cheshunt or Turnford Nunnery, of which nothing

OLD HOUSE, CHESHUNT STREET

[6] *Arch.* xxix, 184. Extracts.

Cheshunt Waltham Cross

Arthur V. Eisden, photo

HERTFORD HUNDRED

now remains except some old garden walls, which may be old inclosure walls, and a fragment of a moat which may have surrounded the monastery. As early as 1183 Lucius III exempted the site from payment of tithes.[7] The nunnery, or part of it, appears to have been destroyed by fire between the granting of a charter by Henry III in 1240 and 1315, when the nuns stated in a petition to the king that the charter had been burnt.[8] The fire must have taken place about 1290, in which year the nuns sought help from the king because they were impoverished by a fire.[9] In 1312 indulgence was granted for the fabric of the church of the house of the nuns of Cheshunt for their dormitory and other places.[10] The last remains of the nunnery were taken down early in the 19th century.[11] Eastward of Turnford is Hell Wood, which contains a good example of a homestead moat inclosing two islands.

Flamstead End is a hamlet north of Churchgate, and is approached from the Great North Road by Brookfield Lane, which skirts the reservoir formed by the New River Water Company. The hamlet is built at the meeting of four roads. There are here some nursery grounds, cottages and one or two inns, including the Plough Inn, a 17th-century timber-framed house, now plastered, with a projecting upper story on the south side.

In Church Lane near to the Great North Road is a row of 17th-century cottages. This lane continues under the name of Andrews Lane, probably so called from the manor of Andrews, of which the Great House is the manor-house, to Burton Grange, the residence of Mrs. Mason, to which is attached a small park.

Goff's Oak, formed into a district chapelry in 1871 with the church of St. James built in 1861, is a hamlet on the west side of the parish which communicates with the village of Cheshunt by Goff's Lane. The early tradition as to this name being taken from a certain Sir Theodore Godfrey, a follower of William the Conqueror, or from a Saxon personal name, seems to be baseless.[12] The remains of an ancient oak tree still exist opposite Goff's Oak public-house, but Goff is not an uncommon surname in the parish. William Goff had a ninety-nine years lease of Cheshunt Park in 1650, and there is a 19th-century monument to a member of the family in the church. It is probably from a member of this family that the oak was called. On the east side of Goff's Oak, a little off the road on the north side, is a homestead moat. In Goff's Lane is 'Claramont,' a modernized house, to which is attached a small park. Southward of Goff's Lane is Silver Street, which forms the northern boundary of Woodgreen Park, the house of which was built by Mr. James Bentley, D.L., in 1840, and is now the residence of Mr. Edmund T. Doxat, J.P.

Other hamlets are Hammond Street and Appleby Street in the north of the parish and Bury Green

CHESHUNT

hamlet in the south. At some distance south of the village and church lies Theobalds Park, through which the New River flows. A description of the house will be found later. As might be expected in a low-lying district, there are many homestead moats in the parish. Besides those already referred to there are others at Factory Farm, near Theobalds Park Farm, and near Cheshunt station.

Cheshunt has numbered amongst its inhabitants at different times many people of historical importance. Queen Elizabeth lived for several years at Sir Anthony Denny's house at Cheshunt before she came to the throne, and when Roger Ascham succeeded Grindal as her tutor in 1548 he too took up his residence at

GOFF'S OAK, CHESHUNT

Cheshunt.[13] John Tillotson, afterwards Archbishop of Canterbury, who was curate of Cheshunt from 1661 to 1663, lived with Sir Thomas Dacres 'at the great house near the church.'[14] Richard Cromwell on his return to England in 1680 stayed with Serjeant (afterwards Chief Baron) Pengelly in a house near the one now called Pengelly House close to the church. This was a 17th-century house, which was burnt down in 1888, after which the site was covered with cottages. Richard Cromwell died at Cheshunt

---

[7] Dugdale, *Mon. Angl.* iv, 328.
[8] *Cal. Pat.* 1313–17, p. 292.
[9] *Parl. R.* i, 53.
[10] Linc. Epis. Reg. Dalderby, Mem.
[11] Dugdale, *Mon. Angl.* iv, 329.
[12] See Cussans, *Hist. of Herts. Hertford Hund.* 206, citing Shirley Hibberd's *Brambles and Bay Leaves,* 120–34.
[13] *Dict. Nat. Biog.*
[14] Ibid.

445

A HISTORY OF HERTFORDSHIRE

in 1712.[15] Dr. Watts spent the latter part of his life with Sir Thomas and Lady Abney at Theobald's Park.[16]

No trace of permanent Roman occupation has been proved to exist at Cheshunt.[17] The boundary bank, known as 'Above and Below Bank,' which runs through Theobalds Park over Beaumont Green to Nine Acres Wood and is now hardly distinguishable from the field banks, is said to have formed the boundary between Mercia and Essex.[18] In connexion with this bank a curious custom of land tenure exists. In cases of intestacy all copyhold property on the west side, 'or above bank,' goes to the eldest son, all on the east side, or 'below bank,' to the youngest son. The greater part of the parish is 'below bank.'

A mill is mentioned in the Domesday Survey. It appears to have been included, later, within the manor of Periers.[19]

MANORS *CHESHUNT*, which, with its berewick Hoddesdon, had been held in the time of King Edward by Eddeva the Fair,[20] was one of the many manors granted by the Conqueror to Count Alan of Britanny, who held it in 1086, when it was assessed for 20 hides and had land for thirty-three ploughs. A little later than this the count built the castle of Richmond, and his lands were formed into the honour of Richmond,[21] the descent of which Cheshunt followed as a rule. Peter de Braine, who married Alice daughter of Constance of Britanny, daughter and heir of Conan Count of Britanny, had seisin of the manor in his wife's right in 1217.[22] He forfeited in 1227, and the manor was granted to Walter, Bishop of Carlisle, to hold until the king should restore it to Peter Count of Britanny or his heirs.[23] By renouncing his homage to Henry III in 1234 the Count of Britanny finally forfeited his English possessions,[24] and in 1241 the manor of Cheshunt was granted to Peter of Savoy[25] with the honour of Richmond. In 1244 Peter received a grant of a weekly market on Monday at his manor of Cheshunt and a yearly fair on the vigil, feast and Assumption of St. Mary[26] (15 August), the days of the fair being changed in 1257 to the morrow of the Exaltation of the Cross (14 September) and the three days following.[27] In 1268 Cheshunt was again in the hands of the Crown, Peter of Savoy having left the honour of Richmond to his niece Queen Eleanor, who sold it to her husband. The latter granted it to the descendants of Peter de Braine, whose grandson[28] John of Britanny in 1278 claimed view of frankpledge, assize of bread and ale, gallows and free warren in Cheshunt.[29] In 1335 John Duke of Britanny, great-nephew of the above,[30] received a grant of a weekly market at his manor of Cheshunt.[31] In 1341 the earldom of Richmond was again in the hands of the Crown after the death of John de Britanny Earl of Richmond, Queen Philippa being appointed to the custody of the lands.[32] In 1342 John of Gaunt was created Earl of Richmond.[33] A weekly market at Cheshunt was granted to him in 1344,[34] and he appears to have held Cheshunt and the other lands of the earldom until 1372, when he surrendered them to the king.[35] In the same year the earldom of Richmond was granted to John de Montfort Duke of Britanny (son of John de Montfort, half-brother and heir male of the last-mentioned John de Britanny), who had married as his second wife Joan half-sister of Richard II.[36]

On the death of the Duke of Britanny in 1399[37] Ralph Nevill Earl of Westmorland received a life grant of the earldom of Richmond.[38] He granted, for his own life, the manor of Cheshunt with the knights' fees, parks, warrens, franchises and liberties to John Norbury and his heirs. In 1412 Henry IV confirmed the grant to John Norbury for life, with successive remainders to Elizabeth his wife, Henry their son, the king's godson, and John the brother of Henry.[39] Ralph Earl of Westmorland died in 1425,[40] and in 1433 it was enacted that the manor of Cheshunt should go to the Duke of Bedford after the deaths of Elizabeth Norbury, Henry and John.[41] The Duke of Bedford died without surviving issue in 1435,[42] and in 1447, on petition from the Commons, the reversion of the manor of Cheshunt after the death of Elizabeth and Henry Norbury was granted in frankalmoign to the college of St. Mary and St. Nicholas, Cambridge.[43] By the Resumption Act of 1455, however, the

BRITANNY. *Ermine plain.*

PETER DE BRAINE. *Checky or and azure with a border of ENGLAND and a quarter of BRITANNY.*

NEVILL, Earl of Westmorland. *Gules a saltire argent.*

NORBURY. *Sable a cheveron engrailed between three bulls' heads caboshed argent.*

---

[15] *Cheshunt in the Olden Times*, 36.
[16] *Dict. Nat. Biog.*
[17] *Hist. Monum. Com. Rep. Herts.* 76.
[18] Ibid. 5.
[19] See Ct. R. portf. 177, no. 63; Cal. S. P. Dom. 1591–4, p. 501.
[20] *V.C.H. Herts.* i, 320.
[21] G.E.C. *Complete Peerage*, vi, 343.
[22] *Rot. Lit. Claus.* (Rec. Com.), i, 325*b*.
[23] *Cal. Chart. R.* 1226–57, p. 52.
[24] G.E.C. *Complete Peerage*, vi, 350.
[25] *Cal. Chart. R.* 1226–57, p. 259.
[26] Ibid. p. 281.
[27] Ibid. p. 469.
[28] G.E.C. op. cit. vi, 352.
[29] *Plac. de Quo Warr.* (Rec. Com.), 290.
[30] G.E.C. op. cit. vi, 353.
[31] *Chart. R.* 9 Edw. III, no. 50, no. 6.
[32] *Cal. Pat.* 1340–3, p. 236.
[33] G.E.C. *Peerage*, vi, 354.
[34] *Chart. R.* 18 Edw. III, m. 4, no. 13.
[35] Duchy of Lanc. Misc. Bks. xiii, fol. 8.
[36] G.E.C. op. cit. vi, 355.
[37] Ibid. 356.
[38] Ibid.; see *Feud. Aids*, ii, 443.
[39] *Cal. Pat.* 1408–13, p. 404.
[40] *Chan. Inq. p.m.* 4 Hen. VI, no. 37.
[41] *Parl. R.* iv, 462.
[42] G.E.C. op. cit. i, 295.
[43] *Parl. R.* v, 133.

446

HERTFORD HUNDRED

CHESHUNT

reversion returned to the Crown.[44] The manor continued to be held by Elizabeth Lady Say, widow of John Norbury, whose life interest was regranted to her in 1461[45] by Edward IV, and was exempted from the Resumption Act of 1461.[46] In the same year the reversion after the death of Elizabeth Lady Say was granted for life to Sir John Clay, Joan his wife, and John his son.[47] In spite of this grant, after the death of Elizabeth Lady Say the manor was granted in 1465 to George Duke of Clarence and heirs of his body.[48]

On the attainder of Clarence in 1477 his estates passed to the Crown,[49] and in 1484 Richard III granted the manor of Cheshunt for life to Walter Devereux Lord Ferrers,[50] who was killed at Bosworth in 1485.[51] In 1487 it was granted for life by Henry VII to Margaret Countess of Richmond,[52] who held it until her death in 1509.[53] In 1517 two annuities of £10 each were provided out of the issues of the lordship of Cheshunt for Katharine wife of Leonard Pole, nurse to the Princess Mary,[54] and in 1525 the manor, with many others, was granted to Henry Fitzroy Duke of Richmond,[55] who died without heirs in 1536. In 1538 Joan Brignan, widow, received a grant of an annuity of 5 marks out of the manor of Cheshunt in consideration of her services to Henry Duke of Richmond in his childhood.[56] Edward VI in 1547 granted the reversion of the site of the manor, then held by Henry Sell, yeoman, pricker of the king's buckhounds, with the manor itself, to Sir John Gates,[57] who was executed for treason in 1553.[58] The manor, having reverted to the Crown once more, was granted in 1554 to Sir John Huddleston,[59] who immediately sold it to John Cock of Broxbourne.[60] From this date the manor of Cheshunt followed the descent of Broxbourne (q.v.) until 1782, when it was sold by John third Lord Monson to George Prescott. It descended to his son George William Prescott, Sheriff of Herts. in 1793–4, created a baronet in 1794, who died in 1801, then to his son Sir George Beeston Prescott, who died in 1840, then to the latter's son Sir William Prescott, and in 1850 to Sir George Rendlesham Prescott, fourth baronet,[61] whose son Sir George Lionel Lawson Bagot Prescott succeeded in 1894[62] and is the present owner.

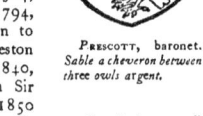

Cheshunt Park is mentioned in 1339, when John Duke of Britanny complained of trespass in his park at Cheshunt.[63] The keepership of Cheshunt or Brantingshey Park appears to have been held as a rule with the office of bailiff of the manor of Cheshunt.[64] In 1519 Cardinal Wolsey received a grant of it, from the death of William Bedell, with 4d. a day out of the issues,[65] and in 1538 a grant of the office in survivorship was made to Anthony Denny and Sir Thomas Hennage.[66] Cheshunt Park was apparently separated from the manor of Cheshunt before 1570, in which year it was conveyed by John Harrington to Sir William Cecil.[67] In 1607 it passed with Theobalds to the Crown.[68] It appears subsequently to have followed the descent of the manor of Theobalds, with which it is now held.[69] The house, a mid-Victorian stuccoed building, is the residence of Mr. F. G. Debenham.

The manor of *THEOBALDS* is first mentioned in 1441, when it was confirmed by Henry VI to John Carpenter, clerk, master of the hospital of St. Anthony, London, John Somerset, chancellor of the Exchequer, and John Carpenter the younger, citizen of London. The manor, which is described as being late of John Hylton, clerk, with a messuage, 1½ virgates of land and 5 acres of meadow in Cheshunt, was to be held as of the manor of Cheshunt of Elizabeth, Henry and John Norbury, and, after their deaths, of the king by fealty and the rent of a bow worth 2s. or of 2s. and a barbed arrow worth 3d. or of 3d. yearly for all suits and services and secular demands.[70] A grant was also made to these tenants of quittance from all shires, leets, hundreds and sheriffs' tourns, from service on juries and inquisitions and from seizure of goods by royal officials without payment.[71] These grantees were probably feoffees to uses. The manor seems to have come to Edward Green (see Cressbrokes), for in 1497 it was conveyed by William Craythorn and Cecilia his wife, Edward's heir, to William Denton, Clement Carsey and his heirs, and William Embroke,[72] possibly for purposes of settlement, as Cecilia Bedell died seised of it in 1521. Cecilia left a son and heir Thomas Burbage,[73] in whose family the manor appears to have remained[74] until it was finally conveyed by Robert Burbage in 1564 to Sir William Cecil,[75] created Lord Burghley in 1571.

Under its new owner Theobalds became historically important. The original site of the manor, according to Lysons, was a small moated house, the traces of which were still visible in Sir George Prescott's park in 1796.[76] Cecil appears either to have added to this or to have built on another site a house which, it is

PRESCOTT, baronet. *Sable a cheveron between three owls argent.*

CECIL, Lord Burghley. *Barry of ten pieces argent and azure six scutcheons sable with a lion argent in each.*

---

[44] *Parl. R.* v, 306.
[45] *Cal. Pat.* 1461–7, p. 20. For this Elizabeth see Little Berkhampstead.
[46] *Parl. R.* v, 471.
[47] *Cal. Pat.* 1461–85, p. 92.
[48] Ibid. p. 388.
[49] *Parl. R.* vi, 194b.
[50] *Cal. Pat.* 1476–85, p. 513.
[51] G.E.C. *Peerage,* iii, 331.
[52] *Pat.* 2 Hen. VII, pt. i.
[53] Chan. Inq. p.m. (Ser. 2), lxxxiii, 313; G.E.C. *Peerage,* vi, 357.
[54] L. and P. Hen. VIII, ii, 3429.
[55] Ibid. iv (1), 1500 (p. 673 n.).
[56] Ibid. xiii, 1309 (38).
[57] *Pat.* 1 Edw. VI, pt. ii, m. 2.
[58] *Dict. Nat. Biog.*
[59] *Pat.* 1 & 2 Phil. and Mary, pt. ii, m. 20.
[60] Chan. Inq. p.m. (Ser. 2), iii, 82.
[61] Cussans, op. cit. *Hertford Hund.* 209.
[62] G.E.C. *Complete Baronetage,* v, 293.
[63] *Cal. Pat.* 1338–40, p. 285.
[64] See *Cal. Pat.* 1476–85, p. 68; *L. and P. Hen. VIII,* i, 349, 4637.
[65] *L. and P. Hen. VIII,* iii, 485.
[66] Ibid. xiii (2), g. 734 (10).
[67] Com. Pleas D. Enr. Trin. 12 Eliz.
[68] See *Cal. S. P. Dom.* 1580–1625, p. 498.
[69] Cussans, op. cit. *Hertford Hund.* 214, 217. [70] *Cal. Pat.* 1436–41, p. 510.
[71] Ibid. p. 551.
[72] Feet of F. Div. Co. Hil. 13 Hen. VII.
[73] Chan. Inq. p.m. (Ser. 2), lxxx, 11.
[74] See Feet of F. Herts. Mich. 2 & 3 Eliz.
[75] Ibid. Hil. and Trin. 6 Eliz. A John Eliott and Eleanor his wife joined in the conveyance. Eleanor possibly had a right of dower.
[76] Lysons, *Environs of Lond.* iv, 31.

said, he intended to be the residence of his younger son,[77] and which eventually became a palace.

> If my buildings mislike them [wrote Burghley, in 1585, with regard to slanders raised against him by his enemies] I confess my folly in the expenses, because some of my houses are to come, if God so please, to them that shall not have land to match them : I mean my house at Theobalds ; which was begun by me with a mean mesure ; but encreast by occasion of her Majesty's often coming ; whom to please, I never would omit to strain myself to more charges than building it. And yet not without some especial direction of her Majesty. Upon fault found with the smal mesure of her Chamber, which was in good mesure for me ; I was forced to enlarge a room for a larger chamber : which need not be envied of any for riches in it, more than the she w of old oaks and such trees with painted leaves and fruit.[78]

Elizabeth first visited Theobalds in 1564, and it was probably before her second visit, in 1566, that the house was enlarged,[79] although building was going on there in 1568.[80] Elizabeth again visited Theobalds in 1571 (when some verses and a picture of the house were presented to her), 1572, 1573, 1575, 1577, 1578, 1583, 1587, 1591, 1593, 1594 and 1596.[81] In May 1583 the queen stayed five days and brought with her a large retinue.[82] Foreigners and ambassadors sometimes came to the queen at Theobalds 'where she hath byn sene in as great royalty, and served as bountifully and magnificently, as at anie other tyme or place, all at his Lordship's chardg.'[83] Norden was much impressed by the beauty of Theobalds. 'A most stately house,' he says, ... 'To speak of the state and beauty thereof as large as it deserveth, for curious buildings, delightfull walkes, and pleasant conceites within and without, and other things very glorious and ellegant to be seene would challenge a great portion of this little treatise, and therefore least I should come shorte of that due commendation that it deserveth, I leave it, as indeed it is, a princely seate.'[84] A contemporary biographer of Cecil says : 'He greatlie delighted in making gardens, fountaines and walkes ; which at Theobalds were perfected most costly, bewtyfully, and pleasantly. Where one might walk twoe myle[s] in the walks, before he came to their ends.'[85] Paul Hentzner, describing his visit to England in 1598, gives the following description of Theobalds :

> In the gallery was painted the genealogy of the Kings of England ; from this place one goes into the garden, encompassed with a ditch full of water, large enough for one to have the pleasure of going in a boat and rowing between the shrubs ; here are great variety of trees and plants ; labyrinths made with a great deal of labour ; a jet d'eau with its bason of white marble ; and columns and pyramids of wood and other materials up and down the garden. After seeing these we were led by the gardener into the summer-house, in the lower part of which, built semi-circularly, are the twelve Roman emperors in white marble . . . . . W were not admitted to see the apartments of this palace, there being nobody to show it, as the family was in town attending the funeral of their Lord.[86]

Burghley died in 1598, and the manor passed to his younger son Robert Cecil, created Earl of Salisbury in 1605. In May 1603 James I, on his way from Scotland, came to Theobalds, where the lords of Elizabeth's Privy Council awaited his coming and did homage, and where he stayed four days 'with entertaynment such and so costly as hardly can be expressed.'[87] He visited Theobalds again in February 1604, August 1604 and in May and July 1606.[88] In July he was accompanied by the King of Denmark, and Ben Jonson wrote an entertainment for the occasion. Sir John Harrington, who was present, writing to Mr. Secretary Barlow in 1606, gives a description of the revels :

> One day a great feast was held ; and after dinner the representation of Solomon's temple and the coming of the Queen of Sheba was made, or (as I may better say) was meant to have been made, before their Majesties, by device of the Earl of Salisbury and others. But, alas ! as all earthly things do fail to poor mortals in earthly enjoyments, so did prove our presentment thereof. The lady who did play the Queen's part did carry most precious gifts to both their Majesties ; but forgetting the steps arising to the canopy, overset her caskets into his Danish Majesty's lap and fell at his feet, though I rather think it was in his face. Much was the hurry and confusion . . . His Majesty then got up and would dance with the Queen of Sheba ; but he fell down and humbled himself before her, and was carried to an inner chamber and laid on a bed of state. . . . The entertainment and show went forward, and most of the presenters went backward or fell down ; wine did so occupy their upper chambers.[89]

In 1607 the manor of Theobalds, with the house, park and neighbouring manors, was surrendered to the Crown[90] and settled on the queen, the Earl of Salisbury receiving Hatfield and other manors in exchange.[91] Ben Jonson wrote a masque to be acted at the formal surrender of Theobalds to the queen, which took place on 22 May 1607.[92]

In July 1607 the king, having spent some time at Theobalds and found it a suitable place for sports, decided to make some alterations there and appointed the Earls of Suffolk, Worcester and Salisbury, with the officers of the works, to supervise the proposed improvements.[93] The alterations in question appear to have involved the enlargement of Theobalds Park and the inclosure of Cheshunt Park.[94] The process was both long and expensive. By September 1608 320 acres of land belonging chiefly to the manors of Theobalds and Periers had been included in the park.[95] On 17 February 1612 warrants were issued for the payment of £11,070 13s. 6d. for the purchase of inclosed lands from neighbouring landowners, of whom the chief were Sir Robert Wroth and Sir Thomas Dacre.[96] Several freeholders, apparently, held back before consenting to sell their lands and caution was necessary.[97] 'Mr. [Richard] Hale,' wrote Sir Fulk Greville, 'refuses His Majesty's offer of buying his house and land for more than its value ; but he is old and will soon be out of the way.'[98] The Earl of Suffolk and Sir Fulk Greville reported in 1617 that they had met with much opposition from the people in taking in ground for the enlargement of the park,[99] some apparently objecting to surveys of their lands being made,[100] and the inhabitants of Waltham Forest being fearful of the

---

[77] Lysons, *Environs of Lond.* iv, 31 ; Peck, *Desiderata Curiosa*, i, 25. Norden describes the house as being erected from its first foundation by Cecil.
[78] Nichols, *Progresses of Queen Eliz.* i, 205.
[79] Ibid. 291.
[80] *Cal. S. P. Dom.* 1547–80, p. 310.
[81] Nichols, op. cit. i, 291.
[82] Ibid. ii, 400.
[83] Lysons, *Environs of Lond.* iv, 32.

[84] Norden, *Descr. of Herts.* (ed. 1598), 31.
[85] Peck, *Desiderata Curiosa*, i, 26.
[86] *A Journey into England in the year 1598* (ed. 1758), 54.
[87] Stow, *Annals*, 822.
[88] Nichols, *Progresses of James I*, i, 319, 454 ; ii, 48, 63.
[89] Jesse, *Court of Engl. under the Stuarts*, i, 44.
[90] Feet of F. Div. Co. Trin. 5 Jas. I.

[91] *Cal. S. P. Dom.* 1603–10, pp. 354, 358, 359, 385.
[92] Ben Jonson, *Works* (ed. 1616), i, 885–7.
[93] *Cal. S. P. Dom.* 1580–1625, p. 498.
[94] Ibid.
[95] Exch. Spec. Com. 1 Chas. I, no. 5343.
[96] *Cal. S. P. Dom.* 1611–18, p. 120.
[97] Ibid. p. 461.
[98] Ibid. p. 462.
[99] Ibid. p. 466.
[100] Ibid. p. 462.

HERTFORD HUNDRED
CHESHUNT

commons being inclosed. By July 1617 the arrangements for the inclosure of neighbouring lands seem to have been concluded. 'All is paid for,' wrote the Earl of Suffolk and Sir Fulk Greville, 'and the king will find that he pays like a king for his pleasure.'[1] In September the Council mentioned the enlarging of Theobalds as one of the items of the extraordinary expenditure which would swallow up the £120,000 borrowed from the City and Merchant Strangers for the payment of the king's debts.[2] The surrounding of the park with a wall[3] 9 miles long involved further expenditure in 1620-2,[4] and in July 1623 Lord Brook reported to Secretary Conway that the 3 miles of wall which required coping at Theobalds Park could not be completed that year without heavy additional expense.[5] The building of this wall appears to have led to riots at Cheshunt in 1623, the commoners rising against the inclosure of part of the common near Theobalds.[6] In July 1624 a warrant was issued for the payment of £5,700 and upwards to the paymaster of the works for a new chapel, bedchamber, rooms and tennis court to be built next spring at the king's house at Theobalds,[7] and warrants had already been issued in June for the payment of persons appointed by Sir Patrick Murray to store the fish-ponds at Theobalds and to keep the herons, French fowls, elks, silkworms, partridges, pheasants, &c.[8] In 1620 the keeping of Theobalds House and Park was granted to William Earl of Salisbury, whose son, Charles Lord Cranborne, received a similar grant for life in 1629.[9]

James I spent a great deal of time at Theobalds.[10] It was there that he received the ambassador of the Princes of the Union in February 1620,[11] and that the Council met in July 1623 to hear the articles of the proposed Spanish marriage.[12] On Sunday 27 March 1625 James died at Theobalds, and the Lords of the Council with many others presently assembled together, penned and signed a proclamation, and instantly at the Court Gate proclaimed Prince Charles king.[13]

Charles I seems to have been less fond of Theobalds than his father, although he visited it occasionally.[14] It was at Theobalds that the last petition of Parliament concerning the militia was presented to him on 1 March 1642,[15] and from Theobalds on 3 March he set out for Royston on his way to Nottingham.[16]

In 1650 Theobalds House and Park were in the possession of the Parliamentary trustees,[17] but in April 1652 Major William Packer is described as one of the proprietors.[18] 'This Packer,' says George Fox, 'was a Baptist. . . . He set up a great meeting of the Baptists at Theobalds Park ; for he and some other officers had purchased it. They were exceedingly high, and railed against Friends and truth and threatened to apprehend me with their warrants if ever I came there. Yet . . . I was moved of the Lord God to go down to Theobalds, and appoint a meeting hard by them.'[19] Most of the buildings and the wall of the park appear to have been demolished during the Commonwealth and the materials to have been sold.[20] When Anne Countess of Bristol petitioned in 1660 for a lease of Theobalds Park she urged that the walls and tenements were so much out of repair that it was not likely to be again used for pleasure.[21] In the survey of 1650 the trustees recommended that 'the Spittle,' an almshouse for the entertainment of lame, impotent and decayed persons of the parish, should be continued as such.[22] A chapel was left standing and used by the Presbyterians as late as 1689.[23]

In 1661 the manor and park of Theobalds, excepting mines royal and the passage of the New River, were granted to George Duke of Albemarle, his wife and heirs male.[24] In 1667 Charles II promised that, if the Duke of Albemarle and his son Christopher Lord Torrington should die without heirs, he would create the Earl of Bath Duke of Albemarle and grant him the house and park of Theobalds.[25] When, however, Christopher Duke of Albemarle died without issue in 1688[26] the estate of Theobalds reverted to the Crown, and in 1694 James II issued a warrant from St. Germains granting it to James Duke of Berwick and his heirs male with remainder to his brother Henry Fitz James, Grand Prior of England,[27] whom he created Duke of Albemarle in 1696.[28] This warrant apparently was not carried into effect, as both the brothers were outlawed in 1695 ; the Earl of Bath, too, seems to have given up his claim.[29] The manor, separated from the park and house, passed to Elizabeth widow of Christopher Duke of Albemarle ; she married as her second husband Ralph Earl of Montagu, to whose son by his first wife, John Duke of Montagu, the manor came in 1709.[30] In 1736 the latter sold the manor to Mrs. Letitia Thornhill,[31] who died without issue. On her death the manor went to the granddaughters of Sir Robert Thornhill, Sarah wife of Richard Cromwell, and Eleanor Hinde, widow. Both moieties of the manor finally passed to the daughters of Sarah Cromwell, and then, as they all died unmarried, to their cousin

MONK, Duke of Albemarle. *Gules a cheveron between three lions' heads razed argent.*

---

[1] *Cal. S. P. Dom.* 1611–18, p. 475.
[2] Ibid. p. 485.
[3] Part of the original wall may be seen at Aldbury Farm (Hist. Monum. Com. Rep. Herts. 79).
[4] *Cal. S. P. Dom.* 1619–23, pp. 151, 262, 424.
[5] Ibid. 1623–5, pp. 86, 87.
[6] Ibid. p. 10.
[7] Ibid. p. 307.
[8] Ibid. p. 280. In 1618 the keeper of the garden had been paid £50 for making a place for the silkworms and providing mulberry leaves (*Cal. S. P. Dom.* 1611–18, p. 592).
[9] Parl. Surv. Herts. no. 26.
[10] S. P. Dom. Jas. I, *passim*.
[11] *Cal. S. P. Dom.* 1619–23, p. 125.
[12] Ibid. 1623–5, p. 30.
[13] Ibid. 1625–9, p. 1.
[14] Ibid. 1635–6, p. 523 ; 1636–7, p. 138 ; 1637–8, p. 523.
[15] Clarendon, *Hist. of the Rebellion*, iv, 322 n.
[16] Ibid. note.
[17] Sess. R. (Herts. Co. Rec.), i, 147.
[18] *Cal. S. P. Dom.* 1651–2, pp. 209, 214, 218.
[19] *Journal* (ed. 8), pp. 212–13. The campaign which followed was lively, but Geo. Fox appears to have been satisfied with the result.
[20] Earle, *Palace of Theobalds*, 23 ; *Cal. S. P. Dom.* 1660–1, p. 70.
[21] *Cal. S. P. Dom.* 1660–1, p. 289.
[22] Parl. Surv. Herts. no. 24.
[23] Earle, *Palace of Theobalds*, 23.
[24] *Cal. S. P. Dom.* 1660–1, p. 523 ; 1663–4, p. 502.
[25] *Stuart Papers* (Hist. MSS. Com.), i, 2.
[26] G.E.C. *Complete Peerage*, i, 59.
[27] *Stuart Papers* (Hist. MSS. Com.), i, 88. [28] G.E.C. *Complete Peerage*, i, 59.
[29] Feet of F. Div. Co. Hil. 10 & 11 Will. III.
[30] Cussans, *Hist. of Herts. Hertford Hund.* 214.
[31] B.M. Add. MS. 9434, fol. 46.

Oliver Cromwell. The latter died at Cheshunt Park in 1821, leaving an only daughter, Elizabeth Oliveria, wife of Thomas Artemidorus Russell.

On the death of the latter in 1858 the manor of Theobalds, with Cheshunt Park, came by will to his third son Thomas Artemidorus Russell for life, with remainder to the testator's daughters Elizabeth Oliveria, wife of Frederick Joseph Prescott, Letitia Cromwell Whitfield, wife of Frederick Whitfield, and Emma Bridget Warner, wife of Richard Warner. On the death of Thomas Artemidorus Russell the younger in 1863 the manor came to his sisters Mrs. Elizabeth Prescott and Mrs. Emma Warner.[32] It thus came to the Prescott family, and is now owned by Sir George Lionel Lawson Bagot Prescott, bart., of Isenhurst, Sussex. The estate now comprises little more than the manors of Cullings *alias* Tongs and Crossbrokes *alias* Darcies.

CROMWELL. *Sable a lion argent.*

The house and park of Theobalds descended separately from the manor. After reverting to the Crown on the death of Christopher Duke of Albemarle they were granted by William III to William Bentinck Earl of Portland. From the latter they descended to William Henry Cavendish, third Duke of Portland, who sold them in 1763 to George Prescott, by whom the present house was begun. He was succeeded in 1790 by his son George William Prescott, created a baronet in 1794. From this date Theobalds house and park passed like the manor of Cheshunt (q.v.) to Sir George Beeston Prescott, who sold them to Sir Henry Meux, bt.[32a] His son Sir Henry, who died in 1883, was succeeded by his son Sir Henry Bruce Meux. He died in 1900 and left the estate to his wife Valerie Susie. Lady Meux died in 1910, leaving by her will Theobalds Park to Sir Hedworth Lambton, who took the name of Meux, and is the present owner.

MEUX, baronet. *Paly or and asure a chief gules with three crosses formy or therein.*

Of the original house built in 1564–71 by Lord Burghley scarcely anything remains, owing to the dismantling of the house in the time of the Commonwealth. It consisted of two great quadrangles, 86 ft. and 110 ft. square respectively. On the east side of the former was a cloister, and there was a black and white marble fountain in the centre. The second quadrangle had cloisters, with galleries over, on the east and west sides, and a chapel on the south. There were two large gatehouses, one between the two quadrangles, and on the south side of the house was an open cloister, with paintings, inscriptions and pedigrees. This cloister existed till 1765, though the palace was for the most part demolished in 1651. The existing remains consist of a strip of walling, about 2 ft. wide and 15 ft. high, in the south side of the gardener's cottage at Old Palace House, of clunch in its lower portion, with a moulded plinth, and a moulded string at the top, much decayed, and in its upper half of red brick with clunch quoins. This appears to have been the south-west angle of the palace. Just to the north-east of this is a wide three-light window with moulded stone jambs and mullions under a brick four-centred arch; it is set in an old brick wall, but it is uncertain whether this is its original position or whether it is re-used material, as in the case of two stone-mullioned windows in Old Palace House. The original garden wall of red brick survives in several places, the most perfect being the lengths which inclose the gardens of Old Palace House and Grove House on the north side. In the dividing wall is a rectangular peep-hole rebated for a shutter, and having chamfered jambs and head. In the west wall of the Old Palace House garden are several niches, and one in the south wall. They are all about 2 ft. 6 in. above the ground, 1 ft. 9 in. high, 1 ft. wide, and 10 in. deep, and some have small holes at the bottom. They appear to have been used for charcoal fires, as the mortar joints above them are blackened by smoke. The west wall is carried on to the north of the garden of Grove House, and at its north and south ends are remains of circular angle-turrets. At the south-east of the 'Cedars,' the third house on the site, which takes its name from two large trees probably contemporary with the palace, is another wall, with returns for the central east gateway, and there is another piece of wall running eastward towards the London road, as well as a few other fragments.

Old Palace House, the residence of Mr. Frederick W. Lane, was built in 1768 on the site of the gardens and terraces. The garden walks still remain as formerly. The old banqueting-table is at the Old Palace House.[33]

The present house at Theobalds Park is a large red brick building with stone dressings begun in 1768, the wings being added at a later date. There are extensive gardens and grounds and in the park an ornamental lake formed from the New River. This house stands about three-quarters of a mile westward of the old palace.

The north-west gateway of Theobalds Park is formed by old Temple Bar removed from the Fleet Street entrance to the City in 1878, and re-erected in its present position in 1888 by Sir Henry Meux, bart., to whom it had been given. It was built in 1672 from Sir Christopher Wren's design, of stone with rusticated joints, and has a large central gateway with a three-centred arch having a carved projecting keystone and moulded imposts, flanked by smaller gateways with round heads. Above is an upper stage with a frieze and cornice, surmounted by a curved pediment, and divided on each face by shallow Corinthian pilasters. In the end bays are round-headed niches, containing, on the outer side, statues of Charles II and Queen Anne, and on the inner side of James I and Charles I. In the middle bay and at each end are round-headed windows.

---

[32] Cussans, loc. cit.; Add. MS. 9434, fol. 46; Feet of F. Herts. Trin. 30 & 31 Geo. II (K.S.B.); Recov. R. East. 25 Geo. III, rot. 307; Trin. 6 Geo. IV, rot. 12.

[32a] Sir George Beeston Prescott is called of Theobalds in 1837 (*Sess. R.* [Herts. Co. Rec.], ii, 370) and Sir Henry Meux is so described in his M.I. in Cheshunt Church, 1840. See also *Sess. R.* (Herts. Co. Rec.), ii, 458.

[33] *Hist. Monum. Com. Rep. Herts.* 79.

450

CHESHUNT   TEMPLE BAR AT THEOBALDS PARK

Arthur V. Eisden, photo

HERTFORD HUNDRED

CHESHUNT

Walter Culling in 1303 held a fourth part of a knight's fee in Cheshunt of the Earl of Richmond.[34] In 1383 a tenement called *CULLINGS* in Cheshunt, held, with a tenement called Mores, by William atte More, was valued for debt.[35] It is first described as a manor in 1387, when Baldwin de Radyngton, kt., and others received licence for the alienation in mortmain of the manor of Cullings, held of the manor of Cheshunt, to the Abbot and convent of Waltham Holy Cross,[36] who in 1428 held the fourth part of a knight's fee formerly held by Walter Culling.[37] The convent of Waltham Holy Cross continued to hold Cullings until its dissolution in 1540, when Robert Fuller, formerly abbot, received a life-grant of the manor.[38] In 1544 Cullings was granted to Thomas Blanke and others[39] in return for money lent to the king on condition that the grant was to be void if the loan should be repaid within a year.[40] In 1552 the manor passed by a fine from Henry Beecher and Alice his wife to Edward Baeshe,[41] who conveyed it to Sir William Cecil in 1573,[42] since which date it has followed the descent of Theobalds.

TONGS was one of the properties of which Theobalds was composed, but of its existence as a separate manor there is practically no evidence. Cussans says that in the latter part of the 13th century it belonged to the family of Fitz Bernard,[43] but he is confusing it with the manor of Tonge in Kent.[44] He identifies it with the manor of Cullings, which, according to Lysons, was afterwards called Tongs, then Theobalds, and was made over to William de Tong in 1385 by William atte More in payment of debt.[45] In no documents, however, is Cullings described as Tongs until it appears as one of the *aliases* of Theobalds. Possibly both estates were originally in the hands of William atte More, and this one, having come to William de Tong, took the name of Tongs.

The manor of *DARCIES* or *CRESSBROKE*[46] apparently gained its first name from John first Lord Darcy of Knaith, co. Lincoln, who in 1347 owned two messuages called Cressbroke and Tunsted,[47] which descended to his son John Lord Darcy. On the death of the latter in March 1355-6 his heir, John Darcy, was a minor, consequently the manor, which was held of the earldom of Richmond in socage, was taken into the king's hands. John Darcy the younger died in 1362, apparently having still a minor, and his brother and heir, Sir Philip Darcy, did not come of age until 1373.[48] He was succeeded by his son John in 1398, and the latter in 1411 by his son Philip, who died without male issue in 1418.[49] In 1434 John Darcy, brother and heir male of Philip, released to Sir John Stiward, Alice his wife and their heirs all right in the manor of Cressbroke.[50] In the following year Sir John Stiward and Alice granted the manor to John Stopynden, clerk, and Thomas Weston, citizen and fishmonger of London,[51] who were probably acting as trustees for a settlement. In 1441 the two daughters of Philip Lord Darcy,[52] Elizabeth wife of James Strangeways and Margery wife of John Conyers, conveyed the manor to Richard Appleby, clerk, Henry Holden and Robert Fountenys,[53] evidently the trustees of John Clay, for by a settlement made in 1446 the manor passed from these to other trustees, who, acting in compliance with the will of John Clay, confirmed the manor to his widow Joan and his son John.[54] In 1480 Cecily daughter of John Clay,[55] wife of Sir Robert Green and formerly wife of John Acton, died seised of the manor of Cressbroke.[56] Her son and heir Edward Green was a minor at the time of her death, and the manor with a messuage called Clays Place was taken into the king's hands. Edward Green died in January 1491-2, and was succeeded by his sister Cecily, the wife of William Burbage.[57] Cecily Burbage seems to have married again twice, as in 1498 William Craythorne and Cecily his wife were holding the manor,[58] and in 1521 Cecily Bedell died seised of the manor of Cressbroke, leaving a son and heir Thomas Burbage.[59] From this time the manor appears to have been held with Theobalds.

In the survey of 1650 the boundaries of the manor are given: 'The aforesaid Mannor extends itselfe to Walthamcrosse on the east and to Enfield on the south, and Wormely on the north and to Northall on the west, being also intermingled with the lands belongeing to Sir Richard Lucy called the Mannor of Cheshunt.' Courts were then held for the manor at the manor-house.[60]

The manor of *PERIERS* appears to have taken its name from a family who owned land in Cheshunt in the 13th century. At some date between 1275 and 1292 Richard de Periers granted 1 mark of yearly rent with 6 acres in Cheshunt Meadow to Robert Burnell, Bishop of Bath and Wells,[61] and in 1317 Richard de Periers and his heirs received a grant of free warren in Wormley and Cheshunt.[62] When Richard de Periers died in 1335 his lands were divided between his three sons, the eldest, Richard, receiving the Cheshunt property, which consisted of a messuage, land and rent, including two parks containing 40 acres, held of John Duke of Britanny by service of a quarter of a knight's fee.[63] It was still in the hands of the Periers family in 1430, when William Periers granted his manor of Periers to Thomas

DARCY of Knaith. *Azure crusilly and three cinqfoils argent.*

---

[34] *Feud. Aids*, ii, 453.
[35] Chan. Inq. p.m. 7 Ric. II, no. 147.
[36] *Cal. Pat.* 1385-9, p. 356.
[37] *Feud. Aids*, ii, 450.
[38] *L. and P. Hen. VIII*, xvi, p. 715.
[39] Ibid. xix (2), g. 166 (43).
[40] Ibid. (1), 891.
[41] Feet of F. Herts. Mich. 6 Edw. VI.
[42] Ibid. East. 15 Eliz.
[43] *Hist. of Herts. Hertford Hund.* 219.
[44] See *Cal. Close*, 1302-7, p. 421.
[45] *Environs of London*, iv, 29.
[46] John de Cressebrok (Kersebrok) is mentioned in connexion with Cheshunt in 1324 and Henry de Cressebrok in 1337 (see *Cal. Inq.* 10-20 *Edw. II*, 318; *Cal. Pat.* 1334-8, p. 446). Probably their lands comprised part of this manor.
[47] Chan. Inq. p.m. 21 Edw. III, no. 54.
[48] Ibid. 47 Edw. III, no. 11.
[49] Dugdale, *Baronage*, i, 373.
[50] Close, 13 Hen. VI, m. 14.
[51] Feet of F. Herts. 13 Hen. VI, no. 72.
[52] *Visit. of Yorks.* (Harl. Soc. xvi), 91-2.
[53] Feet of F. Herts. 19 Hen. VI, no. 107.
[54] Clutterbuck, *Hist. and Antiq. of Herts.* ii, 104.
[55] Will P.C.C. 6 Godyn.
[56] Chan. Inq. p.m. 20 Edw. IV, no. 24.
[57] *Cal. Inq. p.m. Hen. VII*, i, 330.
[58] Feet of F. Div. Co. East. 13 Hen. VII.
[59] Chan. Inq. p.m. (Ser. 2), lxxx, 11. One copy of the inquisition describes her as Cecilia wife of William Burbage.
[60] Parl. Surv. Herts. no. 20.
[61] Anct. D. (P.R.O.), B 3521.
[62] *Cal. Chart. R.* 1300-26, p. 334.
[63] *Cal. Inq. p.m.* 1-9 *Edw. III*, 453.

A HISTORY OF HERTFORDSHIRE

Gloucester and William Thornton.[64] John Edward, brother and heir of Thomas Gloucester, conveyed the manor to Lord Sudeley and others, who in 1448 demised it to John Say and certain co-feoffees.[65] Sir John Say died seised of it in 1478.[66] The manor of Periers then followed the descent of Baas and Hoddesdon, and with them came into the possession of Sir William Cecil in 1572.[67] For some years it was held with Theobalds.

In connexion with a dispute about the River Lea, which was referred to the judges in 1594, it was stated that the honour of the manor of Theobalds paid £1 6s. 8d. a year to the lord of the manor of Periers for the course of the water going through his ground from Lea to Cheshunt Mill until both the manors came to the Lord Treasurer.[68] In 1608 part of the manor of Periers was inclosed in the king's park,[69] the residue of the manor with the manor-house being leased in the same year for thirty-one years[70] to Thomas Dewhurst,[71] son of Barnard Dewhurst, formerly English secretary to Lord Burghley.[72] Thomas Dewhurst did not live for the term of his lease, and in the survey of 1622 the manor of Periers was included in the manor of Theobalds.[73] In 1629 the site of the manor was leased to Sir William Gardiner for twenty-one years.[74] The subsequent descent of the manor is not very clear. It was granted in 1661 to George Duke of Albemarle with Theobalds,[75] with which it was still held in 1699.[76] In 1774, however, it was held with the manor of Beaumond Hall by Hannah, Mary and Robert Sax.[77] It subsequently passed by marriage to — Griffenhoofe, whose devisees sold it in 1842 to Matthew son of Isaac and Judith Munt of Kingston, Jamaica. In 1851 Mr. Munt sold it to James Fort, who was the possessor in 1874,[78] since when it has passed to Mr. G. F. H. Grant.

Cussans suggests that the manor of *BEAUMOND HALL* derives its name from Robert Beaumont, third Earl of Leicester, who during the reign of Richard I gave the adjoining manor of Broxbourne to the Knights Hospitallers.[79] As, on the eve of the Dissolution, the manor of Beaumond Hall formed part of the possessions of the hospital of St. Mary without Bishopsgate,[80] it was more probably identical with the lands in Cheshunt which were granted to the hospital of St. Mary by Richard de Periers in 1297.[81] That this was the case is further suggested by the survey of 1650, which describes the manor as being 'intermixed with . . . . the Mannor of Periers.'[82] In 1540 the manor of Beaumond Hall was granted by Henry VIII to Thomas Wrothe of Enfield.[83] The latter appears to have sold it in 1572 to Sir William Cecil.[84] It evidently followed the descent of Theobalds, in which manor it was included with Periers in the survey of 1622, when it belonged to the Crown.[85] In 1639 the manor of Beaumond Hall was granted to Richard Barnard for eight years.[86] It was included in the survey of the king's lands in 1650, at which date Beaumond Hall and Periers were separate manors. The boundaries of Beaumond Hall are given in the survey: 'The Boundes of the Manno^r aforesaid extend to Wormeley Woodd on the North and on the River Leigh on the East And on the Lande of the Earle of Salisbury called Bassetts on the West and unto the Landes of Thomas Dacres on the South.'[87] For some time after this the manor was apparently held with Theobalds; that was the case in 1699, when it is described as 'Beaumonts and Periers,'[88] and in 1734.[89] By 1774, however, it had become separated from Theobalds and was held jointly with Periers,[90] with which it subsequently descended.

St. Mary's Hospital without Bishopsgate. *Party argent and sable a mill-rind cross counter-coloured with a martlet gules in the quarter.*

CLARKES alias LOCKEYS alias TEBBS was a tenement or farm-house, let to Joan Ireton for life in 1618. It was included in the manor of Beaumond and Periers in 1622[91] and in Periers in 1650,[92] but by 1699 it had apparently become merged in Theobalds.[93]

The manor called *LA MOTE* first appears in the 14th century, held of the Earls of Richmond and of other neighbouring lords, by the family of Valence, Earls of Pembroke. Aymer de Valence Earl of Pembroke died seised of it in 1324, and Mary his widow held the manor for life after the death of her husband, and died seised in 1377.[94] The heir was John de Hastings, descendant of Isabel, sister of Aymer de Valence. John de Hastings Earl of Pembroke died in 1389 seised of the manor of La Mote, and as he died without issue his heir was Reginald de Grey, whose grandmother Elizabeth was daughter of Isabel de Hastings, sister and co-heir of Aymer de Valence.[95] In 1414 Reginald de Grey conveyed the manor to Robert Bishop of London and others,[96] who were probably trustees, as by 1439 the manor had become divided into moieties,[97] held apparently by two heiresses. One moiety, which was conveyed by Robert Ellerbek and Agnes his wife to John Fray in 1439, seems to be the manor de la Mote which in 1507 Hugh Clopton and Katherine his wife surrendered by a fine to Edmund Denny and others,[98]

---

[64] Close, 9 Hen. VI, m. 10. Apparently it was subsequently granted to John Halle, who may have been acting as trustee for Gloucester (see Close, 25 Hen. VI, m. 9).
[65] Anct. D. (P.R.O.), B 241 (see Ct. R. [Gen. Ser.], portf. 177, no. 63).
[66] Chan. Inq. p.m. 18 Edw. IV, no. 43; *Cal. Pat.* 1476–85, p. 116.
[67] Feet of F. Div. Co. Hil. 14 Eliz.
[68] *Cal. S. P. Dom.* 1591–4, p. 501.
[69] Exch. Spec. Com. 1 Chas. I, no. 5343.
[70] Pat. 5 Jas. I, pt. xv.
[71] *Cal. S. P. Dom.* 1603–10, p. 406.
[72] M.I.
[73] Land Rev. Misc. Bks. ccxvi, fol. 33.
[74] Pat. 5 Chas. I, pt. viii.
[75] *Cal. S. P. Dom.* 1660–1, p. 523.
[76] Feet of F. Div. Co. Hil. 10 & 11 Will. III.
[77] Ibid. Herts. Trin. 14 Geo. III.
[78] Cussans, *Hist. of Herts. Hertford Hund.* 219.
[79] Ibid. 218.
[80] Dugdale, *Mon. Angl.* vii, 626.
[81] B.M. Add. Chart. 10647b.
[82] Parl. Surv. no. 15.
[83] *L. and P. Hen. VIII,* xv, 733 (64).
[84] Feet of F. Hil. 15 Eliz.
[85] Land Rev. Misc. Bks. ccxvi, fol. 33.
[86] Pat. 14 Chas. I, pt. ix.
[87] Parl. Surv. no. 15.
[88] Feet of F. Hil. 10 & 11 Will. III.
[89] Recov. R. Hil. 8 Geo. II, rot. 189.
[90] Feet of F. Herts. Trin. 14 Geo. III.
[91] Land Rev. Misc. Bks. ccxvi, fol. 36.
[92] Parl. Surv. no. 30.
[93] Feet of F. Hil. 10 & 11 Will. III.
[94] *Cal. Inq. p.m.* 10–20 *Edw. II,* 318; Chan. Inq. 51 Edw. III, no. 28.
[95] Chan. Inq. p.m. 15 Ric. II, pt. ii, no. 179.
[96] Feet of F. Div. Co. 2 Hen. V, no. 16.
[97] Ibid. 17 Hen. VI, no. 108; 19 Hen. VI, no. 96.
[98] Feet of F. Herts. Mich. 23 Hen. VII.

HERTFORD HUNDRED   CHESHUNT

and which passed in 1520 to Thomas son of Edmund,[99] and later to John son of Thomas. John Denny exchanged it in 1544 with George Dacres,[100] who already held the other moiety of the original manor.[1] This other moiety was conveyed in 1440 by Roger Ree and Rose his wife to John Walsh and others[2]; it is in association with this moiety that the manor of *ANDREWS* first appears, both being held in 1474 for life by Margaret widow of John Walsh,[3] and from this time the moiety in question and the manor of Andrews are always associated. In 1487 a court was held for the latter in the name of John Walsh and Christine his wife.[4] This John Walsh, who was probably the son of the former owner, conveyed the manor of Andrews with a moiety of the manor of 'Moteland' to John More and others in 1500 as feoffees to the use of his last will.[5] The feoffees transferred the property to Henry Stafford Earl of Wiltshire and Lucas Langland[6]; the latter appears to have been acting for Cardinal Wolsey, who by 1519 had bought up the claims of John Rufford and Michael Nevill, nephews of John Walsh,[7] Alice wife of William Chesyll, his sister,[8] and others.[9] On the attainder of Wolsey in 1529 the manor of Andrews and a moiety of the manor of 'la Mote' were forfeited to the Crown and granted to Henry Duke of Richmond, who died without heirs in 1536.[10] In 1531 Henry Earl of Worcester and Elizabeth his wife received a grant in survivorship of the estate[11]; but in 1538, before the death of the Earl of Worcester, it was granted in fee to Robert Dacres of London,[12] to whom the Earl of Worcester released his interest.[13] Robert Dacres was succeeded in 1543 by his son George,[14] who united the two moieties of the Mote (see above).

On the death of George Dacres in 1580 the manors went to his son Sir Thomas Dacres,[15] who died in 1615, leaving a son and heir Thomas Dacres.[16] The latter, outliving his eldest son, was succeeded by his grandson Sir Robert Dacres, who sold the property in 1675 to James Cecil third Earl of Salisbury.[17] By the end of the 17th century the manors are described as the manor of Andrewes le Mote, for which courts were held in 1690 and 1691 in the name of James Earl of Salisbury.[18] In 1692 the latter conveyed the manor to Sir Edward des Bouverie,[19] who, dying in 1694, left directions in his will that the manor should be sold by his sons William and Jacob; it was bought by Sir John Shaw, second baronet, who was the possessor in 1700.[20] Sir John Shaw lived until 1721,[21] but by 1715[22] the manor had come by settlement to William Shaw, the eldest son of Sir John and his second wife.[23] In 1750 William Shaw, barring the entail, conveyed the estate to trustees for the use of his son John Shaw and Meliora Huxley, the latter's future wife. On the

CHESHUNT GREAT HOUSE FROM THE NORTH-WEST

[99] Chan. Inq. p.m. (Ser. 2), xxxv, 49.
[100] *L. and P. Hen. VIII*, xix (1), 25 (cap. xxiii).
[1] Chan. Inq. p.m. (Ser. 2), lxxiii, 89.
[2] Feet of F. Herts. 19 Hen. VI, no. 108.
[3] Ibid. 14 Edw. IV, no. 98.
[4] Ct. R. portf. 177, no. 28.
[5] Anct. D. (P.R.O.), A 6801.
[6] Ibid. A 6729.
[7] Ibid. A 6730, 6733, 1157.

[8] Ibid. A 6715.
[9] Ibid. A 6731, 6732. La Mote seems to have been acquired by Wolsey for a grant to Cardinal College, Ipswich (see *L. and P. Hen. VIII*, iv [2], 4229 [4] [7]).
[10] Chan. Inq. p.m. (Ser. 2), lxxxii, 88.
[11] *L. and P. Hen. VIII*, v, g. 220 (13).
[12] Ibid. xiii (2), g. 734 (37).
[13] Feet of F. Div. Co. East. 31 Hen. VIII.
[14] Chan. Inq. p.m. (Ser. 2), lxxiii, 89.

[15] Ibid. cxcv, 56. [16] Ibid. ccclix, 119.
[17] *A Brief Hist. of Cheshunt Great House*, 6.
[18] Stowe MSS. 847, fol. 37b, 94b.
[19] Feet of F. Herts. Mich. 4 Will. and Mary.
[20] Chauncy, *Hist. Antiq. of Herts.* 301.
[21] G.E.C. *Baronetage*, iv, 13.
[22] Salmon, op. cit. 11.
[23] *A Brief Hist. of Cheshunt Great House*, 6.

453

A HISTORY OF HERTFORDSHIRE

death of John Shaw in 1772 the property went to Meliora, and at her death in 1788 to Anne widow of William Shaw, jun., third son of William Shaw, sen. According to the will of William Shaw, jun., the manors and estate were to come, after the deaths of his widow, Anne Shaw, and his two sisters, to the Rev. Charles Mayo, grandson of Rebecca daughter of Sir John Shaw and his second wife. Charles Mayo, who had previously been a lessee of the estate, succeeded to the property in 1824, and when he died without issue in 1858 he was succeeded by his nephew William Herbert Mayo. On the death of the latter in 1888 the estate passed to his nephew, the Rev. Herbert Harman Mayo,[34] who dying in 1900 was succeeded by his son the Rev. Charles Edward Mayo.[35]

SHAW, baronet. *Argent a cheveron between three lozenges erminees.*

In 1240 Henry III granted the lands of the canons of Cathal to the nuns of Cheshunt,[26] which lands became known as the manor of *CHESHUNT NUNNERY*. In 1352 Edward III granted the nuns exemption from payment of tenths, fifteenths, aids and tallages,[27] and in 1358 free warren in all their lands of Cheshunt,[28] a grant which was confirmed by Richard II and Henry VI.[29] In 1536 the site of Cheshunt Nunnery, or the priory of the nuns of St. Mary de Swetmannescrofte, was granted to Sir Anthony Denny.[30] The latter was succeeded by his eldest son Henry Denny, who in 1564 sold the estate to Richard Springham, Anthony Throckmorton and Richard Davys. In 1590, however, Edward Denny, younger brother of Henry, bought back the estate, which he sold in 1592 to Sir William Cecil.[31] Cheshunt Nunnery then probably followed the descent of Theobalds until in 1608 it was leased by the Crown to Thomas Dewhurst for thirty-one years.[32] In 1614 it was granted to Robert Dewhurst,[33] who settled the estate upon his great-nephew Robert Gill. On the death of the latter it came to his brother William Gill, who in 1675 conveyed it to Mark Mortimer, by whom it was sold in 1713 to Samuel Benson. The latter conveyed it in 1714 to Robert Benson Lord Bingley, who left it by will in 1729 to Robert son of Samuel Benson, who released it to William Jansen.[34] Catherine Ann, the daughter of William Jansen, had married John Blackwood, and in 1776 Cheshunt Nunnery was settled upon her.[35] From her it passed to the Hon. Lionel Damer and Williamza his wife, only surviving daughter and heir of William Jansen. In 1804 the Nunnery was released to William Butt of Corney Bury, and he in 1811 sold it to John Early Cook, who was the owner in 1821.[36] At the present time the property is in the possession of the devisees of the late Thomas Rochford.

After the Dissolution the rectory of Cheshunt, to which was attached an estate called the *RECTORY MANOR*, became part of the possessions of the Dean and Chapter of Westminster,[37] who in 1544 received licence to alienate it to Anthony Denny. From the latter it passed by exchange in the same year to George Dacres, who at the same time acquired the manor of Mote.[38] By 1612 the rectory had come into the possession of Henry Atkins, physician in ordinary to James I and Charles I,[39] who in that year received £700 from the Crown for the surrender of tithes arising from land lately inclosed in Theobalds Park.[40]

DEAN AND CHAPTER OF WESTMINSTER. *Azure a cross paty between five martlets or and a chief or with a pale quarterly of FRANCE and ENGLAND between two Tudor roses.*

In 1632 Henry Atkins conveyed the rectory to Sir Edmund Scott; from the latter it passed with the parsonage-house and two water-mills to his brother Sir Stephen Scott,[41] whose youngest surviving son sold them to Sir Edward des Bouverie.[42] The latter, dying in 1695,[43] left the rectory to be sold, and it was bought by his elder son William des Bouverie, who was the possessor in 1700.[44] He left it to his son Sir Edward, who sold it to Thomas Martin before 1728.[45] The rectory manor appears to have been still in the hands of the Martin family in 1814.[46] In 1855 it came by purchase to James Bentley of Woodgreen Park.[47] His estate was sold in 1881, and the present owner of the manor of the rectory is Mr. Edmund Theodore Doxat, but there is now no copyhold land.

CHURCHES

The church of *ST. MARY* stands a little to the west of the town, and consists of chancel 45 ft. by 21 ft., south chapel, north chapel or vestry, nave 74 ft. by 22 ft., south porch, north and south aisles, each 75 ft. by 9 ft. 6 in., and west tower 16 ft. square; all internal dimensions. The walls are cemented, probably on flint rubble; the east wall and the modern portions are faced with flint, and the west tower is built of ashlar.

It appears from a brass in the church to Nicholas Dixon, rector, that the whole of the church was rebuilt by him between 1418 and 1448, and no structural work of an earlier date now remains. The south chapel, north vestry and south porch are modern, and the church generally was extensively restored during the latter part of the 19th century.

The five-light traceried window in the east wall of the chancel is almost entirely modern, only the inner

---

[34] *A Brief Hist. of Cheshunt Great House*, 7.
[55] Burke, *Landed Gentry* (1906).
[26] *Cal. Chart. R.* 1226–57, p. 253.
[27] *Cal. Pat.* 1381–5, p. 56.
[28] Chart. R. 32 Edw. III, m. 3, no. 5.
[29] *Cal. Rot. Pat.* (Rec. Com.), 198, 276.
[30] *L. and P. Hen. VIII*, ii, g. 519 (12).
[31] Clutterbuck, *Hist. and Antiq. of Herts.* ii, 108.
[32] Pat. 5 Jas. I, pt. xv.

[38] Ibid. 12 Jas. I, pt. xxiii.
[34] Clutterbuck, loc. cit. citing private deeds.
[35] Ibid.; Feet of F. Herts. East. 16 Geo. III.
[36] Clutterbuck, loc. cit.
[37] *L. and P. Hen. VIII*, xvii, 714 (5). See under advowson.
[38] Ibid. xix (1), 25 (cap. xxiii).
[39] M.I. in church.
[40] *Cal. S. P. Dom.* 1611–18, p. 121.

In 1620 the vicar of Cheshunt also received a grant of £21 a year as compensation (see ibid. 1619–23, p. 53).
[41] Chan. Inq. p.m. (Ser. 2), ccccxc, 76.
[42] Chauncy, *Hist. Antiq. of Herts.* 301.
[43] Harl. MS. 5802, fol. 13.
[44] Chauncy, op. cit. 302.
[45] Salmon, op. cit. 10.
[46] Recov. R. East. 54 Geo. III, rot. 370.
[47] Cussans, *Hist. of Herts. Hertford Hund.* 242.

454

CHESHUNT: THE GREAT HOUSE FROM THE SOUTH-WEST

CHESHUNT CHURCH FROM THE SOUTH-EAST

HERTFORD HUNDRED

jambs being original. The north and south arcades are modern, the former being blocked. In the south wall is a 15th-century piscina with cinquefoiled arch under a square head, and traceried spandrels; part of the bowl has been cut away. The triple sedilia now detached, in the first bay of the arcade, are 15th-century work restored. The chancel arch is of two moulded orders. The jambs have engaged shafts with moulded capitals and bases; it is of 15th-century date. The north and south arcades of the nave are of five bays, with arches of two moulded orders; the piers consist of four engaged shafts of Purbeck marble and have moulded capitals and bases. The wide eastern respond of the north arcade is pierced with a small opening with three traceried lights of 15th-century date; in the south arcade is a modern copy, and above it is the doorway to the former rood-loft. The clearstory windows, of two cinquefoiled lights under a square head, retain much of their original stonework.

In the north aisle wall are five windows of three cinquefoiled lights with traceried heads; these have all been repaired with cement. The window in the west wall is now blocked by an 18th-century monument. The windows in the wall of the south aisle are similar to those in the north; two of these are of 15th-century date, the other two are modern copies. At the east end of the south wall is a plain piscina of rude workmanship, which may belong to an earlier period. The roofs are almost entirely of modern work, but the carved corbels under the trusses are of 15th-century date.

The west tower is of three stages, the lower stage only being buttressed. At the south-east angle is an octagonal turret rising above the embattled parapet of the tower; the turret is entered by a doorway from the nave. The lofty moulded tower arch rests upon engaged shafts with moulded capitals and bases; in each of the north and south walls of the first stage is a window of two cinquefoiled lights with traceried head. The west doorway has a pointed arch under a square head with traceried spandrels; the west window above is of three cinquefoiled lights with a traceried head. The first stage is vaulted with stone; the vaulting is modern, but the shafts from which it springs are 15th-century work. The second stage has a window of two cinquefoiled lights under a square head in the north, south and west walls; the belfry stage has a similar window on each face. The stonework of all the windows of the tower is much decayed.

The font has a late 12th-century octagonal bowl; on each face are trefoiled panels of a later date or modern; the stem and eight small flanking shafts are modern. In the tower is an iron-bound chest with three locks of late 16th or early 17th-century date. There are some fragments of 15th-century glass with white and gold roses in one of the windows in the north aisle.

On the north side of the chancel is a large tomb to Robert Dacres, 1543; it also bears the names of his son George Dacres, 1580, his grandson Sir Thomas Dacres, 1615, and of their wives. The tomb was repaired by Sir Thomas Dacres in 1641. It has a canopy upon Ionic columns, surmounted by a coat of arms. In the south chapel is a small altar tomb with canopy to Henry Atkins, physician in ordinary to James I and Charles I; he died in 1635. Under the communion table is a brass to Nicholas Dixon, rector, who died in 1448; the remains consist of a portion of a crocketed canopy, two shields charged with fleurs de lis and a Latin inscription which records the rebuilding of the church. At the north-east of the nave is a brass to William Pyke, 1449, and his wife Ellen; the head of the male figure is missing. In the north aisle is a small brass with the kneeling figure of Elizabeth Garnett, wife of Edward Collen, 1609; another brass of the late 15th century, with figure of a woman and indents of a man, children and inscription; another, also of a woman without inscription, of the 15th century; there is also a slab with indents of a knight and shields, probably of the late 15th century. On the wall above these brasses is a brass inscription to Constance wife of John Parr, 1502; there is also an inscription to Agnes Luthyngton, 1468. In the south-east of the churchyard is an ancient stone coffin.

The six old bells were recast and two new ones added by Gillett & Johnston of Croydon in 1911.

The communion plate includes cup and flagon, 1638, and a paten, 1672.

The registers before 1812 are as follows: (i) all entries 1559 to 1610; (ii) 1611 to 1651; (iii) 1651 to 1678; (iv) 1678 to 1688; (v) 1688 to 1736; (vi) 1747 to 1792; (vii) baptisms and burials 1792 to 1812; (viii), (ix) and (x) marriages 1754 to 1776, 1776 to 1793 and 1793 to 1812.

The church of *ST. JAMES*, Goff's Oak, is a cruciform building of brick and stone in 13th-century style, consisting of chancel, nave, transept, north porch, vestry and north tower.

HOLY TRINITY, Waltham Cross, is of brick in 15th-century style, consisting of chancel, nave with two crocketed turrets at the west end, and small bell turret.

ADVOWSON — The church of Cheshunt appears to have been appendant to the manor of Cheshunt and to have formed part of the earldom of Richmond, as Conan Duke of Britanny granted it to the canons of Fulgeres[48] between 1146 and 1171.[49] This grant later gave rise to a controversy with the church of St. Paul, who apparently claimed some right, Constance of Britanny and her second husband, Ralph Earl of Chester, each petitioning Richard Bishop of London that the canons of Fulgeres should be allowed to remain in undisturbed possession of the gift of Conan.[50] The matter was finally settled by a compromise; it was arranged that the canons of Fulgeres should have perpetual right in the church of Cheshunt on the following conditions: they were to pay to the church of St. Paul a pension of 8 marks a year, payable at Michaelmas and Easter, and they were to endow a vicarage, of which they were to be the patrons.[51] The church of Cheshunt was again a subject of dispute in 1219, the rival claimants being the abbey of Fulgeres and Alice daughter of Constance.[52] Probably as a result of this dispute the advowson of Cheshunt again became part of the earldom of Richmond, for in 1305 it was in the king's gift by reason of the lands of John, late Earl of Richmond, being in his hands.[53] The church

---

[48] Cott. Chart. xi, 45.
[49] G.E.C. *Complete Peerage*, vi, 345.
[50] Cott. Chart. xi, 44, 45.
[51] Newcourt, *Repert.* i, 817.
[52] *Coll. Topog. et Gen.* i, 143.
[53] *Cal. Pat.* 1301–7, p. 410.

A HISTORY OF HERTFORDSHIRE

remained appendant to the manor from this date until the 16th century, the rectors, as a rule, presenting to the vicarage.[54] In 1479 Edward IV granted the advowson of the parish church of Cheshunt to the Dean and canons of St. George's Chapel, Windsor, with licence for them to appropriate the church in mortmain, on condition that the vicarage of the church should be sufficiently endowed and a sufficient sum of money should be distributed yearly amongst the poor parishioners of the church.[55] As a result, however, of an action brought by Margaret Countess of Richmond, who claimed in right of her grant of the manor, the Dean of St. George's Chapel quitclaimed his right in the church in 1497,[56] and the Countess of Richmond presented to the rectory in 1492 and 1494.[57] She granted the advowson to the Abbot of Westminster,[58] who presented as rector in 1503 and 1526,[59] and whose right to the advowson was confirmed by the Act of 1530–1 which confirmed the manor of Cheshunt to Henry Duke of Richmond.[60] The advowson of the vicarage was granted by Mary in 1554 to the Bishop of London,[61] in whose hands it apparently remained until it was assured by Act of Parliament in 1606 to Robert Earl of Salisbury and his heirs.[62] From this time it followed the descent of the manor of Theobalds. The Marquess of Salisbury is patron at the present day. The descent of the rectory is traced under the descent of the rectory manor (q.v.).

The chapel known as 'Saint Laurence in the Busshe of Wormeley' was in the parish of Cheshunt, and was probably founded in the 13th century.[63] It belonged to the canons of Thetford, and in 1538 the chapel, with lands belonging to it, was granted to William Cavendish.[64]

The living of St. James's, Goff's Oak, is a vicarage in the gift of the vicar of Cheshunt, as is also that of Holy Trinity, Waltham Cross.

During the 17th century Cheshunt was a stronghold of Nonconformity,[65] licences being granted for meeting-places from 1672. The tendency was probably increased by the establishment of Cheshunt College in 1792. The Congregational Church in Crossbrook Street, representing a cause dating from 1600, was built in 1705 and the present building was erected in 1857 on the old site. The Wesleyans also have a chapel in Crossbrook Street. There are two churches of the Countess of Huntingdon's Connexion, one in High Street, which was rebuilt in 1889 ; the other at Turnford was built in 1834. The Primitive Methodist chapel at Goff's Oak was built in 1868. A licence was granted to a Baptist teacher at 'Cheston' in 1672.[66] A Baptist chapel was opened in Cheshunt in 1909.

In Waltham Cross is the Roman Catholic Church of the Immaculate Conception and St. Joseph, and a Baptist chapel (1895) in King Edward Road.

CHARITIES The Beaumont Trust comprises a considerable part of the charitable endowments of the parish, the principal parts of the lands lying at a place called Beaumont Green, whence, it is conjectured, the title was derived. The endowments consist of the Beaumont Farm, containing 22 a. 3 r. ; the Curtis Farm, Nazeing, containing 18 a. ; Boundary Lodge, Waltham Cross, 2 a. or thereabouts ; Colesfield Farm, Cheshunt, 13 a. ; and house and land at Cheshunt, 5 a. 3 r. ; the rental to Lady Day, 1910, being £240 17s. ; a rent-charge of 13s. 4d. out of Wormley Bury, gift of William Purvey, 1677 ; and the following sums of stock :—£5,187 7s. 5d. Local Loans 3 per cent. stock, £13 6s. 8d. consols, representing redemption of a rent-charge of 6s. 8d. formerly paid by the governors of St. Thomas's Hospital under will of Mrs. Elizabeth Friend, 1562, and £1,199 17s. 9d. New Zealand 3½ per cent. stock, producing together in annual dividends £197 19s.

The trust properties had their origin for the most part from the following sources, namely, the compensation of King James I for inclosing a large piece of common for increasing Theobald's Park, £500, £180 of which was expended in the erection of almshouses at Turner's Hill and the balance of £320 in the purchase of Curtis Farm, Nazeing ; legacy of £100 for the almshouses by will of Lady Jane Mico, 1670 ; £200 by will of Humphrey Flint, 1610 ; £200 by will of Sir Edmund Scott, 1638 ; £900 stock, gift of Mrs. Sarah Gwilt, 1783 ; £2,000 by will of Samuel Brookland, 1799.

In 1810 Frances Leeson, niece of the said Samuel Brookland, also bequeathed to the trustees of the Beaumont Charity £400 stock for the poor in the almshouses on condition that £1 1s. be paid to the clergyman on 1 June yearly, 10s. 6d. to the clerk and 2s. 6d. to the sexton, and that her burial-place be kept in repair.

In 1620 Richard Coulter by his will left £100, which was invested in a house in Cheshunt Street, 10s. to be given yearly to the vicar for a sermon on the first Sunday in Lent and the residue to forty aged poor.

In 1814 Elizabeth Auber, by deed, gave £500 stock, the interest to be distributed amongst the inmates of the almshouses.

The income of the Beaumont Trust, after providing for the ecclesiastical payments above mentioned and for the Beaumont educational trusts after mentioned, is applied for the benefit of the almshouses at Turner's Hill for ten poor widows and the almshouses, known as the Spital Houses, for five poor widows, the origin of which is not precisely known.

The following charities are likewise administered by the Beaumont trustees :—

The Dewhurst Almshouse Charity founded in 1642 by Robert Dewhurst. By an order of the Charity Commissioners 7 February 1905 the governors of the Free school were authorized to pay to the Beaumont trustees a yearly sum of £13 to be applied in payment of 6d. a week to the ten inmates of Turner's Hill almshouses, and a yearly sum of £8 for providing coals for the same inmates.

In 1880 Dr. William Buchanan, by deed, gave £105, now represented by £102 9s. 6d. Local

---

[54] Clutterbuck, op. cit. ii, 109–11.
[55] Cal. Pat. 1476–85, p. 142.
[56] MSS. of D. and C. of Westm. no. 4688 (press 17, shelf 4, box 84).
[57] Clutterbuck, op. cit. ii, 110 ; Newcourt, Repert. i, 819.
[58] MSS. of D. and C. of Westm. no. 4695 (press 17, shelf 4, box 84).
[59] Clutterbuck, op. cit. ii, 111.
[60] Priv. Act, 22 Hen. VIII, cap. 17.
[61] Pat. 1 Mary, pt. iv, m. 19.
[62] Stat. of the Realm (Rec. Com.), iv (2), 1133.
[63] Anct. D. (P.R.O.), B 886.
[64] L. and P. Hen. VIII, xiii, g. 734 (8); xvi, 1308 (34).
[65] Urwick, Nonconf. in Herts. 509–12.
[66] Ibid. 507.

HERTFORD HUNDRED

Loans 3 per cent. stock, the annual dividends, amounting to £3 1s. 4d., to be applied in the purchase of wearing apparel for distribution on the first Monday in October to the widows at Turner's Hill almshouses.

In 1882 Henry Timson and Philip Augustus Browne, by deed, gave £540, now represented by £516 0s. 11d. Local Loans 3 per cent. stock, the annual dividends, amounting to £15 9s. 8d., for the benefit of inmates of Turner's Hill almshouses and of the Spital almshouses.

In 1584 Mildred Lady Burghley, by deed, granted an annuity of £10 payable by the Haberdashers' Company, whereof £2 13s. 4d. is payable to the vicar for sermons on the first Sunday after Michaelmas Day, and at Christmas, Easter and Whitsuntide, and the remainder in the distribution of bread and meat.

In 1794 Samuel Brookland, by deed, gave an annuity of £3 10s. payable out of a house in the High Street, £3 thereof to be distributed among the inmates of the workhouse and 10s. to the master for his trouble. The rent-charge is duly paid.

Allotment in lieu of common rights. By an inclosure award, 14 May 1804, 100 acres, part of Cheshunt Common, were inclosed for the benefit of cottagers having right of common ; the land is let producing £150 a year or thereabouts. In 1909–10 the net income, amounting to £125 5s. 7d., was paid to persons entitled to common rights. There was also a sum of £250 on deposit account at the bank.

The Cottage Hospital, founded about 1890, is supported partly by voluntary contributions and partly from endowments of about £80 a year derived from gifts by the late Lady Meux, J. and C. Docwra, Mrs. Baker, Mrs. Gayler and Thomas Leigh, and

ALMSHOUSES, TURNER'S HILL, CHESHUNT

In 1725 Joseph Alcock by his will gave £4 yearly to be distributed equally among forty poor men and women, 10s. to the inmates of the ten almshouses, and 10s. to the vicar for a sermon on the Sunday before Christmas. These sums are paid out of a house in the High Street.

In 1725, as recorded on a tablet in the church, Mrs. Nicholls gave the dividends for ever upon £54 10s. 4 per cent. stock to be laid out in bread for the poor. This sum, with accumulations, is now represented by £70 consols, producing £1 15s. yearly.

In 1793, as recorded on the same tablet, Mrs. Elizabeth Cook, and in 1794 Mrs. Sarah Cook, gave £50 each, the interest to be distributed in bread. These gifts, with accumulations, are now represented by £144 9s. 7d. consols, producing £3 18s. yearly. These charities are duly applied.

from legacies under the wills of Miss Sanders, Mrs. Hird, John Crawter and W. Stevens.

In 1854 John Britten, by deed, gave £1,000, represented by £1,060 0s. 9d. consols, in the names of John Crawter and others, producing £26 10s. yearly, of which £5 is payable every fifth year for the repair of a vault in the parish church, as an ecclesiastical charity, two-thirds of the remaining income being applicable in the distribution of money, food, clothing or fuel, and the remaining one-third as an educational charity.

In 1880 James Bentley, by will proved at London 7 December, bequeathed £1,000 consols upon trust that out of the dividends £10 should be distributed among five boys at the Dewhurst Free School (see under Educational Charities below), and that the remaining income should be distributed among the

A HISTORY OF HERTFORDSHIRE

poor of the ecclesiastical district of St. Mary. By an order of the Charity Commissioners 21 June 1904 £400 consols has been set aside as the educational branch and £600 consols as the eleemosynary branch of the charity. In 1909 gifts of 7s. 6d. each were made to thirty-nine labourers.

Educational Charities :

The Free school was founded in 1642 by Robert Dewhurst.[67]

By an order of the Charity Commissioners 10 February 1905, made under the Board of Education Act, 1899, a sum of £100 Local Loans 3 per cent. stock was set aside, producing £3 yearly, for providing dinners for boys attending the school, in respect of the gift in 1762 by John Gwilt for that purpose.

In 1880 Dr. William Buchanan, by deed, gave £105, now represented by £102 14s. 10d. Local Loans 3 per cent. stock, the annual dividends, amounting to £3 1s. 8d., to be applied in books or other articles as prizes on the last Monday in February to boys at the school.

In 1904 John Earley Cook, by will proved 28 September, left £200 for the benefit of the school, subject to repair of family tombs in Cheshunt churchyard. The legacy was invested in £223 8s. 3d. Cape of Good Hope 3 per cent. stock, producing £6 14s. yearly.

Mrs. Elderton by her will (date not stated) gave £100 for the use of the Sunday school at Cheshunt. The endowment now consists of £200 consols ; the annual dividends, amounting to £5 a year, are under a scheme of the Charity Commissioners of 3 November 1863 expended in prizes at Sunday school.

See under charity of John Britten above.

James Bentley's educational charity (see above) consists of £400 consols, the annual dividends of which, amounting to £10, are distributed among five boys at the Dewhurst School for good conduct and attainments.

Goff's Oak, St. James : In 1880 James Bentley by his will bequeathed £1,000 consols, now represented by £932 17s. 5d. Local Loans 3 per cent. stock with the official trustees, the annual dividends, amounting to £27 19s. 8d., to be applied as to £10 for the vicar and the remainder to be distributed to the poor of this district not in receipt of parochial relief.

ESSENDON

Essendene (xi cent.) ; Isendene (xiii cent.) ; Esyngden (xvi cent.).

The parish of Essendon is bounded on the north for some distance by the River Lea, which crosses its north-west and north-east corners. Near the southern border of the parish the land reaches a height of 400 ft., from which it slopes down towards the north, where the lower-lying land near the river is liable to floods. The parish contains 2,331 acres, of which nearly a half consists of permanent grass, arable land forming about one-third.[1] The soil is clay and gravel, the subsoil clay and chalk. Grass and corn are the chief crops. The greater part of the parish is farm land with a few scattered farms and gravel or chalk-pits. The woodland does not form any great continuous extent, the woods consisting for the most part of narrow belts and small plantations. An extent of the manor of Essendon made in 1332 states that there were 8 acres of wood, worth 2s. an acre, which might be felled every eighth year for faggots,[1a] but in 1439 there was no fuel that year from the king's woods at Essendon.[2] One of the privileges of the rectors of Essendon, granted or confirmed by Edward III, was the right to have a log from the wood at Essendon for their hearth every year at Christmas.[3]

The village stands on a hill overlooking the valley of the River Lea. The church, rectory and part of the village lie west of the Hertford road near the point at which it is joined by a road leading from Hatfield. The church is situated on the east side of a triangular green. Essendon Bury, the old manor-house, now a farm, lies about half a mile to the north of the church. East of the Hertford road are the school and a reading room and working men's club which was opened in 1896. A water-mill stands by the river, due north of the village. The present building comprises a 17th-century house now encased with brick but originally of timber and plaster. It stands probably on the site of the king's mill which was granted with the manor of Essendon, and to which reference is made in the extent of 1332 and in other mediaeval records.[4] In 1279, when a jury presented that men of Essendon were accustomed to fish in the waters of Essendon 'with boterell and other small engines' until William de Valence prevented them, a verdict was given against the lord of the manor.[5]

Essendon Place, a little to the south of the village, was until lately the seat of the Barons Dimsdale. Thomas, first Baron Dimsdale, was the son of John Dimsdale of Theydon Garnon, co. Essex, and came of a family of medical men. In 1766 he published a tract on the treatment of small-pox by inoculation, and in 1768 he was invited to Russia to inoculate the Empress Catherine. For his services there he was made a baron of the Russian Empire.[6] After his return to England he served as M.P. for Hertford from 1780 to 1790.[7] He died in 1800 and was succeeded by his son John, second Baron Dimsdale. Robert, third Baron Dimsdale, brother and heir of John, was succeeded by his son Thomas Robert, the fourth baron, who bought Camfield Place (q.v.). He died there in 1865. A little later Essendon Place was acquired by the family, and Charles John, the fifth baron, died there in 1872. The property is owned by the present baron, but is now occupied by Mrs. Edgar Lubbock. The house is a stuccoed building of the early 19th century.

Near Essendon Place was an old house called Bird's Place, pulled down in 1833,[8] which at the beginning

---

[67] See article on 'Schools,' V.C.H. Herts. ii, 99.
[1] Statistics from Bd. of Agric. (1905).
[1a] Duchy of Lanc. Misc. Bks. xii, fol. 59.
[2] Duchy of Lanc. Mins. Accts. bdle. 42, no. 825.   [3] Cal. Rot. Pat. (Rec. Com.), 176.
[4] Duchy of Lanc. Misc. Bks. xii, fol. 59; xxi, fol. 171.
[5] Assize R. 323, m. 46 d.
[6] See V.C.H. Herts. Families, 9.
[7] Ibid. 293.
[8] Cussans, op. cit. Hertford Hund. 159.

HERTFORD HUNDRED — ESSENDON

of the 17th century belonged to Henry Darnall, who died in 1607.[9] His wife was Marie daughter of William Tooke (second son of William Tooke, lord of the manor of Essendon), one of a Hertfordshire family of whom several members are buried in Essendon Church. Early in the 19th century Bird's Place was the seat of the Clitherow family. Christopher Clitherow died in 1807,[10] and Bird's Place came soon after to Robert Parnther, who lived there and who died in 1822. His daughter Isabella married John Currie of Bedwell Park.[11]

In the south-west of the parish is Camfield Place, which took its name from a family of Camvile or Canvile, who were holding lands in Essendon from the 13th to the 15th century (see below under Bedwell Lowthes).[12] In 1601 the estate was sold by Sir Edward Denny to William Brockett,[12a] who in 1611 died seised of a messuage, mansion-house and farm called Camfield which he held by knight service of the king in chief 'by gift and grant of Edward now Lord Denny and Lady Mary his wife.'[13] In 1618 William Brockett, his son, sold Camfield to William Priestley, who died seised of it in 1622,[14] and whose son William acquired the manor of Bedwell Lowthes in 1627. Camfield Place was then held with Bedwell Lowthes, and was the seat of the Browne family, and was bought in 1832 by Thomas Robert fourth Baron Dimsdale (see above). It is at present the property and residence of Mr. F. V. McConnell.

The house called Wild Hill is just within the parish of Hatfield, but the estate is generally spoken of as lying within the parish of Essendon. In the 15th century the 'hamlet of Wyldehelle' in the parish of Essendon is mentioned,[15] and the names 'Wyldegrene' and 'Wildefeld' also occur, both lying in Essendon.[16] The Priestleys, lords of the manor of Bedwell Lowthes, lived here in the 17th and 18th centuries.[17] There is a homestead moat near Coldharbour Farm.

Amongst the place-names which occur in the parish are the following: Panther's Wood, Hoppett's Wood, Poundfield Wood, Gobonescroft and Frydayfelde.

There is no railway station in the parish; the nearest stations are Cole Green, 2 miles to the north on the Hertford and Hatfield branch line, and Hatfield, lying 4 miles west on the main line of the Great Northern railway.

Wulsin, 'a great and wealthy man,' MANORS is said to have given ESSENDON to the monks of St. Albans,[18] probably during the 10th century, but there is no evidence of the date. There is, however, no further trace of the monastery holding land there. No mention is made of Essendon in the Domesday Survey, but from its subsequent history it was probably then included in the royal manor of Bayford. It was probably included with the manor of Bayford in the grant to Peter de Valognes,[19] as the Empress Maud confirmed it to Roger son of Peter.[20] It appears, however, to have reverted to the Crown (see Bayford). In 1214, 1218, and succeeding years Essendon was tallaged as part of the king's demesnes,[21] and in 1228 the men of Essendon and Bayford successfully asserted their claim to pay no share of a fine which had been assessed on the county as a whole.[22] The manor appears to have been, as a general rule, held at farm by the warden of the castle of Hertford. For these grants at farm see Bayford, with whose history that of Essendon is identical for about the next three centuries.

In 1489 Henry VII leased the site of the manor, with the fishery and water-mill, to Sir William Say for ten years.[23] Henry VIII granted Essendon in 1545 to Giles Bridges, citizen and wool merchant of London, and Thomas Harris in fee simple, with all the manorial rights,[24] but it again reverted to the Crown, for in the same year the king granted it to Sir Robert Southwell, Master of the Rolls, and his wife Margaret.[25] In the same year Sir Robert and Margaret Southwell exchanged it with the Crown for other manors.[26] In 1547 Edward VI granted Essendon with its appurtenances to Sir William Paulet Lord St. John to hold in chief for one-tenth of a knight's fee,[27] and a few months later Sir William Paulet received licence to alienate it to William Tooke, Auditor of the Court of Wards, and his heirs.[28] William Tooke died in 1588, having settled the manor of Essendon on his son William in consideration of the marriage of the latter with Mary Tichborne.[29] Until the middle of the 17th century the manor remained with the descendants of William Tooke.[30] It was probably sold by Ralph Tooke to John Middleton, serjeant-at-arms, who in 1666 petitioned for the restoration of his 'setting dog taken from him with affronting language' by Viscount Cranborne, and who is described in the petition as being seised of the manor of Essendon.[31] He was probably the 'John Middleton of Essendon, esq.,' who in 1665 was presented with others at quarter sessions for 'riotous assembly and entry into the close of Richard Pooley at Essendon and stealing firewood the property of Lancelot Stavesley, esq.'[32] In 1682 the manor was acquired from the Middleton family by T. Lechmere and J. Stanley, who the next year conveyed it to the Earl of Salisbury.[32a] It remained in the hands of the Cecil family,[33] and the Marquess

TOOKE. *Party cheveronwise sable and argent three griffons' heads rased and countercoloured.*

---

[9] M. I. in church; Chan. Inq. p.m. (Ser. 2), cccex, 42.
[10] M. I. in church.
[11] Ibid.
[12] Anct. D. (P.R.O.), A 5248; B 3738; A 1035, 5408.
[12a] Feet of F. Herts. Hil. 43 Eliz.
[13] Chan. Inq. p.m. (Ser. 2), cccxvi, 29.
[14] Close, 16 Jas. I, pt. xviii, no. 38; Chan. Inq. p.m. (Ser. 2), ccclxxxv, 34.
[15] Anct. D. (P.R.O.), B 1445; see also for an earlier occurrence of the name ibid. B 1448.
[16] Ibid. A 11514; B 1447.
[17] M. I. in church.
[18] Cott. MS. Nero, D 7, fol. 90.
[19] Cart. Antiq. K 10, no. 22.
[20] Ibid. no. 24.
[21] Pipe R. 16 John, m. 1 d.; 2 Hen. III, m. 7; repeated 3 & 4 Hen. III.
[22] Cal. Close, 1227–31, p. 29.
[23] Duchy of Lanc. Misc. Bks. xxi, fol. 171.
[24] Ibid. xxii, fol. 198.
[25] Close, 36 Hen. VIII, pt. v, no. 26.
[26] Feet of F. Herts. East. 36 Hen. VIII; L. and P. Hen. VIII, xx (1), g. 282 (20).
[27] Pat. 1 Edw. VI, pt. ii, m. 36.
[28] Ibid. pt. i, m. 42.
[29] Chan. Inq. p.m. (Ser. 2), ccxlvi, 124; see Feet of F. Herts. Mich. 36 & 37 Eliz.
[30] Chan. Inq. p.m. (Ser. 2), ccxlvi, 124; ccclxix, 149; cccc, 65; cccexcviii, 10.
[31] Cal. S. P. Dom. 1666–7, p. 171.
[32] Sess. R. (Herts. Co. Rec.), i, 173.
[32a] Information from Mr. R. T. Gunton.
[33] Recov. R. Hil. 7 Anne, rot. 115; East. 9 Geo. II, rot. 194; Mich. 1 Geo. IV, rot. 223.

459

A HISTORY OF HERTFORDSHIRE

of Salisbury is lord of the manor at the present day.

A court leet was held at Essendon once a year on the Thursday in Easter week [34] by the lord of the manor, who also had the right to view of frankpledge, free warren and the goods and chattels of felons, fugitives and outlaws. In the reign of Edward IV suit of court was paid to the manor of Essendon for the manors of Bedwell and Bedwell Lowthes,[35] but in 1652 it was asserted that the tenants of Bedwell were in the jurisdiction of the sheriff's tourn and of no other court leet.[36] As early as 1332 the demesne lands appear to have been granted out, the tenants paying rent and claiming to be bound to no other service except suit of court every third week.[37]

BEDWELL is not mentioned in Domesday Book, and the fact that in the reign of Edward IV it was held of Essendon [38] suggests that at the time of the Survey it was included, with Essendon, in Bayford. It does not appear to be described as a manor until 1388, when it was released, with lands and tenements in Essendon and Little Berkhampstead, to John Norbury and others by Peter Wisebech and William Hedyndon,[39] who were probably feoffees of Norbury. The latter in 1406 received a licence to inclose 800 acres of land and wood 'of his own soil' adjoining his manors of Bedwell and Little Berkhampstead, to make a park which was to be held to him and his heirs for ever.[40] This John Norbury married Elizabeth daughter of Sir Thomas Boteler of Sudeley, the widow and second wife of Sir William Heron, and he is known to have died before 1433.[41] Elizabeth de Say, Baroness Say in her own right, who had married Sir William Heron as her second husband, being his first wife, had died without issue in 1399, and after her death Sir William Heron continued to be summoned to Parliament till his death.[42] He died in 1404, having married secondly Elizabeth Boteler aforesaid.[43] After his death Elizabeth his widow married, as above mentioned, John Norbury, but she retained the title of Lady Say till her death in 1464.[44] She was married again to Sir John Montgomery at some date unknown before 1433,[45] and after 1412, when she is named as the wife of John (not Henry) Norbury [46] and widow of Sir William Heron.[47] Her heir was her grandson John Norbury, who in 1465 received licence to enter into all possessions that came into the hands of Henry VI or Edward IV by the death of John Norbury the elder, or of Elizabeth Lady Say his wife.[48] In Hilary Term 1465-6 John Norbury the younger conveyed the manor to Sir John Say,[49] who died in 1478 seised of the manors of Bedwell and Little Berkhampstead, and was succeeded by his son William Say.[50] During the ownership of the latter in 1522 Mary Tudor appears to have stayed at Bedwell.[51]

Sir William Say had two daughters, Elizabeth, who married William Blount Lord Mountjoy,[52] and Mary, who married Henry Bourchier second Earl of Essex. On the death of Sir William Say in 1529 the manor of Bedwell, in accordance with a settlement made in 1506, passed to Lord Mountjoy, who was to hold it for life and to be succeeded by his daughter Gertrude wife of Henry Courtenay Marquess of Exeter. On the attainder of Gertrude Marchioness of Exeter in 1539 the manor came into the hands of the Crown.[53] In the same year the stewardship of the manor, the keepership of Bedwell Park, of the hunt of deer and of the 'King's mansion of Bedwell with a little garden thereto annexed or adjoining' were granted to Sir Anthony Denny, 'a gentleman of the King's Privy Chamber,'[54] to whom in 1547 Edward VI granted the manor itself 'in support of his dignity' as Chief Groom of the Chamber.[55] Sir Anthony died in 1549, having settled the manor on his third son Charles.[56] On the latter's death without issue it passed to his elder brother Henry, who died in 1574, leaving a son Robert.[57] Robert Denny died in 1576 and was succeeded by his younger brother Sir Edward Denny,[58] who, being in debt to the queen,[59] sold the manor of Bedwell, with Bedwell Lowthes, in Hilary Term 1600-1, to William Potter,[60] to whose family it seems to have passed already leased.[61] Bedwell Park and part of the demesnes were sold by William Potter to Sir Henry Atkins,[62] after whose death in 1638 [63] they passed to his wife and then to one of his younger sons, Thomas Atkins, who was the owner of Bedwell in 1700.[64] On the death of Thomas Atkins in 1701 [65] Bedwell Park was sold to Richard Wynne,[66] who was M.P. for Boston in 1698 and 1705 and who died in 1719.[67] From the descendants of Richard Wynne Bedwell passed by sale to Samuel Whitbread, who sold it in 1807 to Sir Culling Smith, bart.,[68] to whose son, Sir Culling Smith, and grandson, Sir Culling Eardley Smith, the estate passed in succession. The latter assumed the name of Eardley. On his death in 1863 Bedwell was left to his eldest

---

[34] Duchy of Lanc. Misc. Bks. xii, fol. 59.
[35] Duchy of Lanc. Mins. Accts. bdle. 862, no. 20.
[36] Exch. Dep. East. 1652, no. 4.
[37] Duchy of Lanc. Misc. Bks. xii, fol. 59.
[38] Duchy of Lanc. Mins. Accts. bdle. 862, no. 20.
[39] Anct. D. (P.R.O.), D 448 ; see also B 408.
[40] Chart. R. 6 & 7 Hen. IV, no. 5.
[41] When his widow was the wife of Sir John Montgomery (see note 45).
[42] G.E.C. *Complete Peerage*, vii, 63.
[43] She is said to have been widow of Sir Henry Norbury (ibid.).
[44] Ibid.
[45] *Cal. Pat.* 1429-36, p. 296.
[46] Ibid. 1408-13, p. 404.
[47] Close, 12 Hen. IV.
[48] *Cal. Pat.* 1461-7, p. 459.

[49] Com. Pleas De Banco R. Hil. 5 Edw. IV, rot. 278 d. The order for the distraint in 1474 of John Norbury for entrance into Bedwell after the death of Lady Say (Ct. R. portf. 177, no. 32) is evidently only a repetition of an order at an earlier date.
[50] Chan. Inq. p.m. 18 Edw. IV, no. 43. See Rentals and Surv. Herts. R. 269.
[51] *L. and P. Hen. VIII*, iii (2), 3375 (p. 1409).
[52] Elizabeth Lady Mountjoy was buried in Essendon Church (see will of Lord Mountjoy quoted by Cussans, op. cit. *Hertford Hund.* 157).
[53] Chan. Inq. p.m. (Ser. 2), clxxvii, 82 ; *L. and P. Hen. VIII*, xiv (2), g. 780 (27). For a fuller account of the Norbury's and Say's see 'Hist. of Little Berkhampstead,' by C. E. Johnston, in *Home Cos. Mag.* xi, 275 et seq.

[54] *L. and P. Hen. VIII*, xiv (2), g. 780 (27).
[55] Pat. 1 Edw. VI, pt. ix, m. 30. See Johnston, op. cit. *Home Cos. Mag.* xiii, 64.
[56] Chan. Inq. p.m. (Ser. 2), xc, 115.
[57] Ibid. clxix, 85.
[58] G.E.C. *Complete Peerage*, vi, 100.
[59] *Cecil MSS.* (Hist. MSS. Com.), ix. 63.
[60] Feet of F. Herts. Hil. 43 Eliz.
[61] M. I. cited by Chauncy, *Hist. Antiq. of Herts.* 279.
[62] Chauncy, op. cit. 277.
[63] M. I. in church.
[64] Chauncy, loc. cit.
[65] M. I. in church.
[66] Cussans, *Hist. of Herts. Hertford Hund.* 157.
[67] M. I. in church.
[68] Cussans, loc. cit.

460

daughter, Frances Selena Eardley, who in 1865 married Mr. Robert Hanbury, M.P. for Middlesex, the latter adding the name of Culling to his surname.[69] Mrs. Culling-Hanbury is the present owner of Bedwell Park, which is now occupied by Mr. Charles George Arbuthnot.

In 1543 the king's park at Waltham was supplied with deer from Bedwell Park,[70] and amongst the privileges granted with the manor of Bedwell were the herbage and pannage of the park and free warren, both within the park and without, in the parishes of Essendon and Little Berkhampstead.[71] Within the park were inclosed lands called Ponsbourne Mead, which belonged to the manor of Ponsbourne in Hatfield, and were bought from Lord Wenlock (grantee of Sir John Fortescue's forfeited lands) by Sir John Say.[71a]

BEDWELL LOWTHES appears to have been originally a separate manor from Bedwell.[72] Roger de Louth or Luda (who founded the chantry in the church at Bishop's Hatfield) held four messuages and 3 carucates of land in Essendon and Bishop's Hatfield in 1333.[73] In 1351 William de Louth and Agnes his wife held lands in Essendon which formerly belonged to John de Walden.[74] John son and heir of Roger son of Roger de Louth (who held Hornbeamgate in Hatfield) also held lands in Essendon,[75] and these descended with that manor to Robert de Louth, who in 1409 granted a field of land called 'le Wildefeld,' with the moor belonging to it, to Peter Cheyne and Alice his wife.[76] Alice was the daughter of John Camville, who also held lands in Essendon.[77] Her sister Joan married William Basset, who seems to have acquired most of the lands formerly belonging to John Camville,[78] as well as the land owned by Peter Cheyne.[79] In 1466 Sir John Say acquired the manors of Hornbeamgate and Blounts (see Bishop's Hatfield) and lands in Essendon and Hatfield from Robert Louth,[79a] and in 1474 William Basset released lands in Essendon to Sir John Say.[80] In the same year the latter was fined for suit of court at Essendon for 'lands and tenements called Lowthes.'[81] The estate followed the descent of Bedwell,[82] from which it is not generally separately mentioned, until 1627, when William Potter sold Bedwell Lowthes to William Priestley,[83] who already held the house known as Camfield Place,[84] and whose son Thomas Priestley held it in 1668.[85] From the latter it appears to have passed to his son William Priestley,[86] who died without issue in 1744.[87] In 1759 the manor was held by Thomas Methwold,[88] nephew of William Priestley,[89] and was sold by him in 1760 to Thomas Browne,[90] whose son[91] William Browne held it in 1815.[92] On the death of the latter's widow in 1832[93] the manor was sold to Thomas Robert fourth Baron Dimsdale.[94] In 1866 the executors of the fourth Baron Dimsdale sold the manor, with Camfield Place, to Edmund Potter, eldest son of the late James Potter of Manchester.[95]

In 1614 Robert Earl of Salisbury died seised in fee simple of lands in the parish of Hatfield which are described as being 'once parcel of the manor of Bedwell Lowthes' and which he purchased in 1610 from William Potter and Dorothy his wife.[96] These lands, which descended with the manor of Essendon, are also called Bedwell Lowthes in later deeds.

CHURCH The church of *ST. MARY*, standing in the middle of the village, consists of chancel 25 ft. by 19 ft., north chapel, south organ chamber and vestry, nave 50 ft. by 21 ft.

ESSENDON CHURCH: WEST TOWER

6 in., north and south aisles, and west tower 14 ft. by 12 ft., all internal dimensions. The walls are built of flint with stone dressings.

The church appears to have been largely rebuilt in the 17th or 18th century, and in 1883 the whole of

---

[69] Cussans, loc. cit.
[70] L. and P. Hen. VIII, xviii (1), 436.
[71] Ibid. xiv (2), g. 780 (27).
[71a] *Herts. Gen.* ii, 147; C. E. Johnston, *Collector's Acct. for 1475 for Bedwell*, &c.; Anct. D. (P.R.O.), B 412.
[72] Ct. R. portf. 177, no. 7. It was held of the manors of Essendon and Hatfield (see C. E. Johnston, *Collector's Acct.*, &c.).
[73] Feet of F. Herts. 7 Edw. III, no. 137.
[74] Add. Chart. 1988; see also 5291.
[75] Anct. D. (P.R.O.), B 4213, 4215.
[76] Ibid. A 11514; B 1451; D 675.
[77] Ibid. A 5408, 1035.
[78] Ibid. A 1131.
[79] Ibid. A 5421.
[79a] Feet of F. Herts. 6 Edw. IV, no. 14; Anct. D. (P.R.O.), B 1443.
[80] Anct. D. (P.R.O.), A 1190.
[81] Ct. R. portf. 177, no. 32. The Bedwell Lowthes estate seems to have included under this name the manors of Hornbeamgate and Blounts in Hatfield and Essendon, which are not separately mentioned after the 15th century. There is a Hornbeam Lane in Essendon leading from Camfield towards Newgate Street.
[82] See Ct. R. portf. 177, no. 7; Feet of F. Herts. Hil. 43 Eliz.
[83] Feet of F. Herts. Mich. 3 Chas. I.
[84] See above.
[85] Feet of F. Div. Co. Hil. 19 & 20 Chas. II.
[86] Feet of F. Herts. Mich. 6 Will. and Mary.
[87] Clutterbuck, *Hist. of Herts.* ii, 129.
[88] Feet of F. (K.S.B.) Herts. East. 33 Geo. II.
[89] Clutterbuck, loc. cit.
[90] Ibid.
[91] Ibid.
[92] Recov. R. East. 55 Geo. III, rot. 44.
[93] M. I. in church.
[94] Cussans, op. cit. *Hertford Hund.* 154.
[95] Ibid.
[96] Chan. Inq. p.m. (Ser. 2), cccxlii, 123; Com. Pleas D. Enr. Trin. 8 Jas. I, m. 46. See also note 81.

A HISTORY OF HERTFORDSHIRE

the church with the exception of the west tower was again rebuilt.

The west tower is of 15th-century date with work of the 17th century and renewed stonework of 1883; it is of two stages with an embattled parapet and a small leaded spire. The tower arch has been much restored; in the west doorway are two of the original moulded jamb stones.

The font, made by Wedgwood in 1780, is interesting and somewhat uncommon. It consists of a circular bowl of basalt ware—a kind of black porcelain—about 21 in. in diameter, the exterior ornamented with festoons of drapery. The base is moulded; it stands on a square wooden pedestal which tapers downwards. The sides are fluted and the upper part is decorated with painted masks and festoons in the Adam style. A small round cylinder of porcelain, about 8 in. high, with moulded capital and base, stands inside the bowl to support a smaller basin for the water.

On the south aisle wall is a large monument to William Priestley, 1664, with twisted pilasters supporting the cornice, on which are his arms. There are also several 17th-century floor slabs. On the south aisle wall is a brass to William Tooke, 1588, and his wife Ales. The figures are kneeling at a table. Behind the man are figures of nine sons, and behind the woman three daughters. Above are three shields of arms; in the middle (1) the arms of Tooke with their crest, a griffon's head party cheveronwise razed and holding in its beak a sword erect; (2) Tooke impaling Barlee; (3) Barlee quartering Bibbesworth. On a floor slab with shield of arms, with the crest and arms of Tooke with quarterings, the inscription is missing. On the south wall are three brasses of shields, all similar; quarterly: (1) France quartering England, all within a border quarterly of England and France; (2) Courtenay; (3) Say; (4) Redvers. According to a modern inscription underneath these brasses were taken from a gravestone below in 1778. The arms are perhaps intended to represent those of Henry Courtenay Marquess of Exeter, beheaded in 1539.

There are six bells: the treble by Thomas Pack, 1769; the second and fourth (1685) and sixth (1681) by Richard Chandler; the third (1894) and the fifth (1903) by Mears & Stainbank.

The communion plate consists of cup and cover paten, 1569; large paten, 1692; silver flagon, 1769; baptismal dish, 1778; modern silver paten and glass flagon.

The registers before 1812 are as follows: (i) baptisms, burials and marriages from 1653 to 1731; (ii) baptisms and burials from 1729 to 1761, marriages 1729 to 1751; (iii) baptisms and burials from 1762 to 1812; (iv) marriages from 1754 to 1789; (v) marriages from 1789 to 1795; (vi) marriages from 1795 to 1812.

ADVOWSON The advowson of the rectory has always followed the descent of the manor.[97] In 1650 Essendon was described as a sequestered living worth £90 with the living of Bayford.[98] In 1725 the lord of the manor, James Cecil Earl of Salisbury, presented.[99] The advowson remained with his descendants, and the rectory of Essendon is in the gift of the Marquess of Salisbury at the present day.

There is evidence of Nonconformity in Essendon during the 17th century. In 1646 George Stallybrasse, who was rector of Essendon, signed the Hertfordshire ministers' petition to Parliament in favour of the Covenant. In 1674 the churchwardens were summoned before the archdeacon for neglect of duty, and in 1682 it was reported that at Essendon they lacked both surplice and prayer book.[100] In 1817 the chapel of James Pond was certified as a place of worship for Protestant Dissenters, and a Baptist chapel was built in 1885.

CHARITIES In 1761 Meliora Priestley, by a codicil to her will proved in the P.C.C. 27 June, left £100, now £133 6s. 8d. consols, with the official trustees, the annual dividends, amounting to £3 6s. 8d., to be distributed to the poor in bread each month.

In 1795 Samuel Whitbread, by a codicil to his will, bequeathed £533 6s. 8d. 3 per cent. reduced annuities, now represented by a like amount of consols, with the official trustees, producing £14 10s. 10d. a year, of which £5 a year is payable to the rector for administering the sacrament at least eight times during the year, and the residue in the distribution of bread. A sum of £200 consols has been set aside as the ecclesiastical charity and £333 6s. 8d. consols as the eleemosynary charity.

HERTINGFORDBURY

Herefordingberie (xi cent.); Hertfordburia, Hertfordingebyre, Hertfordiggebiry (xiii cent.).

The parish of Hertingfordbury has an area of 2,644 acres, of which 1,223 acres are arable land and 750½ acres are permanent grass.[1] The greater part of the parish lies at an altitude of over 200 ft. above the ordnance datum, reaching 264 ft. in the west, but in the east of the parish and along the northern border, in the valleys of the Lea and Mimram, the ground is below 200 ft. The road from Hatfield to Hertford runs through the parish in an easterly direction until it reaches St. Mary's Church, where it turns off at right angles, and is joined by the road running due north from Bayford. The village is situated at this corner and along the Hatfield road to the north. The last house in the parish is Epcombs, the residence of Mr. Charles Leslie, which is just on the boundary between Hertingfordbury and St. Andrew, Hertford, but a few houses on the other side of the boundary seem to belong to Hertingfordbury. The mill stands a little south of it on the same side of the road. The rectory is situated to the east of the village and north of the church. The old parsonage, which stands in the middle of the village, is an early 17th-century building of brick, most of it plastered externally; it is L-shaped on plan, and has

[97] See Pat. 6 Hen. III, m. 3; *Cal. Chart. R.* 1226–57, p. 351; Duchy of Lanc. Misc. Bks. xxii, fol. 198.
[98] Chan. Surv. of Church Livings, i, 35.
[99] Inst. Bks. (P.R.O.).
[100] Urwick, *Nonconf. in Herts.* 516, 517.
[1] Statistics from Bd. of Agric. (1905).

462

HERTFORD HUNDRED   HERTINGFORDBURY

tiled roofs. On the side facing the street is an old chimney, the lower intakes of which are concealed by stepping the brickwork in front of the sloping portion —a common mode of construction in Hertfordshire. The infants' school to the north of the church is a brick two-storied building of the same date, with a good central chimney stack surmounted by four octagonal shafts.

The southern half of Panshanger Park is included in this parish, the River Mimram, which runs through the centre of the park, forming part of the boundary. At the south-western corner of Panshanger Park, on the Hertford road, is the hamlet of Cole Green. Birch Green and Staines Green are farther along the road towards Hertingfordbury. From Cole Green a road goes south to Letty Green and Woolmers Park, the latter the residence of Mr. Charles Edward Wodehouse, M.A., J.P. In Woolmers Park, to the east of the house, is a spring known as Arkley or Acherley Hole. The water surface is about 70 ft. long and 40 ft. wide, and the depth is said never to have been found. It rises directly through the chalk, and in wet weather adds a large volume to the River Lea, whilst in dry weather it ceases to flow. Eastend Green and Roxford, now a farm at which is a homestead moat, lie about a mile to the west. Birchall, where there is also a homestead moat, is situated in the west of the parish, beyond Cole Green, and Hertingfordbury Park, the residence of Mr. Robert William Partridge, is in the extreme east.

There are two railway stations on the Hertford branch of the Great Northern railway, one at Cole Green and the other a short distance south-east of the village of Hertingfordbury.

The subsoil of the parish is chalk superimposed on the south side by traces of the Woolwich and Reading Beds, London Clay and brick earth, and there are many disused chalk-pits and gravel-pits to the west of Panshanger Park. At Birchall occurs an extensive outlier of the Woolwich and Reading Beds.

The inclosure award was made in 1813, the authorizing Act being passed in 1801.[2] Both are in the custody of the clerk of the peace. Lampits Field was inclosed in 1841.

Place-names which occur in the parish are: Talbottesland, Bauleys, Leverounhull, Stockenhull, Knyhteslond, Halpanyhache, Sampsoneshache (xiv cent.); John Amores,[3] Gorberyshot, Chilwelfeld, Flamstead, Beryfeld and Chapmans (xvi cent.); Copthall, Slabridge, Foxwell, Aldermaster, The Thorpe, Hanging Grove and Wytchfield (xvii cent.).

MANORS
The manor of HERTINGFORD-BURY was held before the Conquest by Alwin, a thegn of Earl Harold, and was given by William the Conqueror to Ralph Baynard or Bangiard before 1086, when it was assessed at 5 hides.[4] Juga Baynard was probably Ralph's widow and Geoffrey Baynard her son and heir.[5] A William Baynard succeeded, who forfeited under Henry I, when his barony was granted to Robert son of Richard son of Gilbert de Clare, ancestor of the Fitz Walters.[6] Hertingfordbury does not seem, however, to have been included in this grant, and was possibly given to Peter de Valognes, for it was in the possession of Agnes de Valognes, widow of Peter's son and heir Roger,[7] in 1185.[8] At the death of Robert son of

OLD PARSONAGE, HERTINGFORDBURY

Roger about 1194 Hertingfordbury came to his daughter and heir Gunnora de Valognes,[9] who married Robert Fitz Walter.[10] Their daughter Christine,[11] wife of William de Mandeville, died without issue, and the Valognes estates were divided between her three heirs, Lora de Baliol, Isabel Comyn and Christine de Maune, daughters of Philip de Valognes, cousin of Gunnora.[12] Hertingfordbury came eventually to Christine, the wife of Peter de Maune or Maule,[13] and passed before 1294 to Henry

---

[2] *Blue Bk. Incl. Awards*, 64.
[3] The house standing in the fork of the road to Cole Green and that towards Bayford is called Amores, and probably dates back to the 14th century (information from Mr. Andrews). The name John Lety (cf. Letty Green) occurs in 1341 (*Inq. Non.* [Rec. Com.], 431).
[4] *V.C.H. Herts.* i, 326a.
[5] Dugdale, *Mon. Angl.* vi, 147. The editor of the *Monasticon* calls Juga sister of Ralph, but apparently without any foundation. See also Dugdale, *Baronage*, s.v. Baynard; Morant, *Hist. of Essex*, ii, 427; *Gent. Mag.* 1826, pt. i, 418. Juga was lady of Little Dunmow (co. Essex), the chief holding of the Baynards, at the beginning of the 12th century.
[6] Dugdale, *Mon.* loc. cit.; *Baronage*, loc. cit.
[7] Dugdale, *Mon.* iii, 346.
[8] S. Grimaldi, *Rot. de Dominabus*, 36.
[9] *Abbrev. Plac.* (Rec. Com.), 3. See Bennington.
[10] *Testa de Nevill* (Rec. Com.), 269b; *Rot. de Oblatis et Fin.* (Rec. Com.), 424.
[11] See *Plac. de Quo Warr.* (Rec. Com.), 281; Cott. MS. Claud. dxiii, fol. 137, 183.
[12] See Bennington; Feet of F. Div. Co. 25 Hen. III, no. 48.
[13] Chan. Inq. p.m. 7 Edw. I, no. 42; *Testa de Nevill* (Rec. Com.), 281b. She is said to be holding it jointly with John Comyn as late as 1287 (see *Plac. de Quo Warr.* [Rec. Com.], 290; Assize R. 325).

463

de Maule, probably her son, who enfeoffed Agnes de Valence,[14] daughter of William de Valence. The king acknowledged the conveyance, which had been made without royal licence, in 1294,[15] but the transaction was not completed until 1297.[16] Agnes continued to hold the manor until her death in 1309–10,[17] when it passed to her brother Aymer de Valence Earl of Pembroke, who died in 1323 without issue.[18] His heirs were his nephew John de Hastings, son of his sister Isabel, Elizabeth Comyn, and Joan wife of David de Strathbolgi, daughters of his second sister Joan.[19] Elizabeth Comyn, to whom Hertingfordbury was assigned,[20] married Richard Talbot,[21] who in 1332 granted the manor to Roger de Chauntecler of London as security for a debt.[22] In 1345 Richard and Elizabeth surrendered the manor to the king in exchange for various lands in Herefordshire,[23] and it was granted in the following year to Queen Isabella, the king's mother, for her life.[24] Isabella died in 1358, and William de Louthe was appointed steward in 1359.[25]

In 1376 the king granted this manor with others in tail-male to his son John of Gaunt.[26] John of Gaunt died in February 1398–9, and Hertingfordbury again fell to the Crown with the duchy of Lancaster upon the accession of his son Henry in 1399 as Henry IV.[27] In 1422 Henry VI granted Hertingfordbury in dower to his mother Queen Katharine[28] and afterwards to his own queen, Margaret of Anjou.[29] Edward IV also granted it for life to his queen Elizabeth Woodville.[30] After this it seems to have remained in the possession of the Crown until Edward VI granted it in 1553 to his sister Princess Mary.[31] It remained in the hands of Queen Mary and Queen Elizabeth,[32] and in 1619 was granted by James I to Sir Henry Hobart and other feoffees for ninety-nine years to the use of Charles Prince of Wales.[33] In 1627 the feoffees transferred the remainder of the term to Christopher Vernon for a rent of £26 0s. 3d., the grant being confirmed by the king in the same year, whilst the reversion of the manor in fee simple was granted to William Downhall and John Darnell.[34] The latter grant was probably in trust for Christopher Vernon and his wife Elizabeth, daughter of John Darnell.[35] Christopher died in 1652 and was succeeded by his son Francis,[36] and Hertingfordbury remained in the Vernon family[37] (descendants of the Vernons of Haddon Hall) until 1690, when it was sold to James Selby.[38] James Selby was holding it in 1700[39] and his widow in 1728,[40] after whose death it descended to their son Thomas James Selby.[41] In 1785 Ellen Wells and Henrietta the wife of Dixie Gregory, the heirs apparently of Thomas James Selby,[42] joined with Sir Rowland Alston, bart., in conveying the manor to Joseph Hill,[43] probably in trust for George Earl Cowper, whom Clutterbuck gives as the purchaser. Hertingfordbury has since descended with the earldom,[44] and is now held by Countess Cowper, widow of the seventh earl.

VERNON of Hertingfordbury. *Argent fretty sable a quarter gules with a molet or therein.*

The park of Hertingfordbury is first mentioned in 1285.[45] In 1359–60 William de Louthe the keeper accounted for three men who were employed for five days at 3d. a day in inclosing and cutting wood in the park.[46] It was granted together with the manor to Princess Mary by Edward VI in 1553.[47] In 1604, when Sir Michael Stanhope was keeper of the park for James I, he was commanded to forbear killing any deer there for three years.[48] Later in the same year a special commission was appointed which certified that the extent of the park was 205 acres of very hard soil 'after the nature of Hertfordshire,' which would keep 150 deer and no more, and that 160 out of 200 deer kept there had died in one year.[49] In 1623 a buck from it was given by the king to Sir Henry Marten, judge of the Admiralty Court.[50] The park continued with the manor[51] until 1626, when Prince Charles's feoffees granted the remainder of their ninety-nine years' lease to John Purefey and John Graunt.[52] In the following year the king granted the reversion to Anthony Lowe, Christopher Vernon, Arthur Lowe and John Coxe. The park then contained 237 acres besides a meadow of 3 acres called 'le deere meadowe,' and 1 acre of osier woods. Free chase and free warren in it were granted at the same time.[53] In 1628 John Walter, Sir Henry Hobart and the others granted £20 rent from the park, which they had reserved from their earlier grant, to Richard Brownelowe, and this was confirmed in the same year to his son John Brownelowe by the king.[54]

[14] *Cal. Close*, 1288–96, p. 352.
[15] Ibid.
[16] Feet of F. Div. Co. 25 Edw. I, no. 28.
[17] *Feud. Aids*, ii, 434; Chan. Inq. p.m. 3 Edw. II, no. 37.
[18] Chan. Inq. p.m. 17 Edw. II, no. 75.
[19] Ibid.
[20] *Abbrev. Rot. Orig.* (Rec. Com.), i, 287.
[21] Chan. Inq. p.m. 20 Edw. II, no. 11.
[22] *Cal. Pat.* 1330–4, p. 305; Assize R. 337, m. 4 d.; Feet of F. Herts. 6 Edw. III, no. 107. The Fine and Patent R. say that the grant to Roger was for life, but according to the Assize R. it reverted to Talbot after seven years.
[23] Feet of F. Div. Co. 20 Edw. III, no. 89; Chan. Inq. p.m. 46 Edw. III, no. 66.
[24] *Cal. Pat.* 1345–8, p. 123; Mins. Accts. (Gen. Ser.), bdle. 865, no. 17.
[25] *Abbrev. Rot. Orig.* (Rec. Com.), ii, 255; Mins. Accts. (Gen. Ser.), bdle. 865, no. 18; Enr. Accts. F. 35 Edw. III, no. 8.
[26] *Cal. Pat.* 1377–81, p. 25; *Abbrev. Rot. Orig.* (Rec. Com.), ii, 346.
[27] G.E.C. *Complete Peerage*.
[28] Duchy of Lanc. Misc. Bks. xviii (2), fol. 49.
[29] Mins. Accts. (Gen. Ser.), bdle. 1093, no. 14.
[30] Feet of F. Div. Co. bdle. 294, file 76, no. 102.
[31] Duchy of Lanc. Misc. Bks. xxiii, fol. 86.
[32] Duchy of Lanc. Ct. R. bdle. 73, no. 906; *Cal. S. P. Dom.* 1547–80, p. 398.
[33] Pat. 17 Jas. I, pt. i.
[34] Ibid. 3 Chas. I, pt. xviii, no. 4.
[35] *Visit. Herts.* (Harl. Soc. xxii), 100.
[36] Clutterbuck, *Hist. and Antiq. of Herts.* ii, 205, quoting monumental inscription; Com. Pleas Recov. R. Hil. 4 Chas. I, m. 11.
[37] Feet of F. Herts. Hil. 25 Chas. II.
[38] Chauncy, *Hist. of Herts.* 272.
[39] Ibid.
[40] Salmon, *Hist. of Herts.* 52. She is said by Cussans (*Hist. of Herts. Hertford Hund.* 103) to have been the daughter of Sir Rowland Alston, bart.
[41] Clutterbuck, op. cit. ii, 199.
[42] See Clutterbuck, loc. cit.
[43] Feet of F. Herts. Hil. 25 Geo. III.
[44] Recov. R. Hil. 42 Geo. III, rot. 146.
[45] Coram Rege R. 92, m. 2.
[46] Mins. Accts. (Gen. Ser.), bdle. 865, no. 18.
[47] Duchy of Lanc. Misc. Bks. xxiii, fol. 86.
[48] *Cal. S. P. Dom.* 1603–10, p. 141.
[49] Duchy of Lanc. Spec. Com. no. 674.
[50] *Cal. S. P. Dom.* 1623–5, p. 46.
[51] Pat. 3 Chas. I, pt. xviii, no. 4.
[52] Ibid. pt. i, no. 2.
[53] Ibid. pt. xxxv.
[54] Ibid. pt. i, no. 2.

HERTFORD HUNDRED — HERTINGFORDBURY

Before 1643 Hertingfordbury Park was purchased by Thomas Keightley,[55] who seems to have built a house there, where he received a visit from his cousin John Evelyn the diarist in March 1643.[56] He was succeeded by his son William Keightley,[57] whose widow Amy married secondly John Belson and continued to live at the house during her lifetime.[58] After her death the park descended to her son Thomas Keightley, who sold the estate in 1681 to John Cullinge.[59] John Cullinge, son of the latter, was holding it in 1700,[60] but died childless shortly after, his lands passing to his sister Elizabeth, whose heirs sold Hertingfordbury Park to Spencer Cowper before 1727.[61] The latter died in 1727[62] and was succeeded by his son William, and his grandson of the same name in 1740.[63] The latter died in 1769, and his widow Maria Frances Cecilia joined with William son of William Cowper in conveying the park to Richard Baker in 1773.[64] Richard Baker, who died in 1780, bequeathed it to his brother William Baker of Bayfordbury. The latter gave it to his younger brother Samuel, who lived there until his death in 1804, and later it was occupied by William's eldest son William, who died in 1863.[65] His son was the heir of William Baker of Bayfordbury, and also held the manor of Roxford, with which Hertingfordbury Park subsequently descended. The old house at Hertingfordbury Park was pulled down in 1816, with the exception of part of the kitchens and cellars, which were left until the present house was built by Mr. R. W. Partridge, who resides there.

Christine de Valognes claimed in Hertingfordbury sac and soc, thol, theam and infangentheof, by charter of Henry I, and also view of frankpledge, amendment of the assize of bread and ale, and tumbrel 'of ancient custom.' Christine de Maule claimed also free warren, and made a claim to have gallows, which was not allowed.[66] Agnes de Valence obtained a fresh grant of free warren in 1309.[67] In 1446–8 John Treoylian was farmer of the 'warren of conies' for Queen Margaret at 70s. yearly,[68] and in 1517 Sir Edward Benstede was granted an annuity of £3 from it.[69]

Hertingfordbury possessed two mills in 1086,[70] but only one is mentioned later. In 1247 Peter de Maule and Christine de Valognes his wife granted their mill to Henry de Neketon, saving to themselves free multure for the use of their household in their manor of Hertingfordbury, also the meadows adjoining the mill and the fishery in the mill-pool.[71] They seem to have paid 20s. rent from the mill to the Master of the Hospital of St. Mary Magdalene at Hertford, for Christine bought back this rent in 1279.[72] Possibly a grant of the mill had been made to the hospital at the time of its endowment, and the lords of the manor had subsequently rented the mill from the hospital. In 1354–5 a rent was still paid to the same hospital.'s The farm of the mill and fishery adjoining amounted to 43s. 4d. in 1383–4.[74] In 1491 the king leased it to Edward Benstede for seven years,[75] and again for a term not stated in 1501–2.[76] In 1619, when the manor was granted by James I to his son Prince Charles, the mill was reserved,[77] and seems to have been let to Thomas Docwra.[78] In 1633 the king granted it, at the request of Sir John Heydon, to William Scriven and Philip Eden and their heirs, at which date it was worth £4 yearly.[79] The mill is situated on the River Mimram at the northern end of the village. There is a tradition that a second mill stood on the Lea 300 yds. north-east of Water Hall Farm, where there was a house within living memory and where there is still a floodgate.

Before the Conquest ROXFORD (Rochesforde, xi cent.; Rokesforth, Rokkysford, Roxeforth, xvi cent.) was held by Goduin, a thegn of King Edward; in 1086 it formed part of the lands of Geoffrey de Bech, of whom it was held by Guy the Priest, and was assessed at half a hide.[80] With other lands of Geoffrey de Bech this fee came to the Wake family,[81] and the overlordship descended with Stapleford[82] (q.v.).

In the 13th century lands in Roxford were held by the families of Moyne and Valognes,[83] but the manor of Roxford seems to be the eighth of a fee held in 1303 by Lady Wake by Nicholas de Paris.[84] In 1304 he conveyed his lands there with the advowson of the chapel of Roxford to Herman de Brickendon,[85] who in 1330 settled them on his son and daughter-in-law, Philip and Hawise.[86] The immediate successors of Philip de Brickendon are not known,[86a] but in the following century the estate seems to have come into the possession of the Louth family. A Robert de Louth, who was M.P. for Herts. in 1382, was holding land in Hertingfordbury in 1406,[87] and is again mentioned in connexion with the parish in 1434.[88] It is probable that this Robert held Roxford, as another Robert de Louth died seised of it in 1484. He left three sisters and co-heirs, Gille the wife of John Gryme, Christine, aged thirty-four and unmarried, and Alice the wife of John Wigge.[89] The manor seems to have been divided between these three, but apparently Christine sold her share to Alice and John Wigge, for Thomas Wigge, son of Alice and John, sold two-thirds of the manor in

---

[55] *Dict. Nat. Biog.*
[56] *Diary of J. Evelyn* (ed. Will. Bray), i, 39.
[57] *Dict. Nat. Biog.*
[58] Close, 33 Chas. II, pt. vi, no. 34.
[59] Ibid.
[60] Chauncy, *Hist. of Herts.* 272.
[61] Salmon, loc. cit.
[62] M. I. in church.
[63] Berry, *Herts. Gen.* 168, 170. See Thele.
[64] Feet of F. Herts. Mich. 14 Geo. III.
[65] See article on Bayfordbury by J. J. Baker in *East Herts. Arch. Soc. Trans.* iii, 264.
[66] *Plac. de Quo Warr.* (Rec. Com.), 281, 290; Assize R. 325.
[67] Chart. R. 2 Edw. II, m. 8, no. 23.

[68] Mins. Accts. (Gen. Ser.), bdle. 1093, no. 14.
[69] Duchy of Lanc. Misc. Bks. xxii, fol. 41 d.
[70] *V.C.H. Herts.* i, 326a.
[71] Feet of F. Herts. 31 Hen. III, no. 332.
[72] Chan. Inq. p.m. 7 Edw. I, no. 42.
[73] Mins. Accts. (Gen. Ser.), bdle. 865, no. 17.
[74] Ibid. bdle. 1272, no. 7.
[75] Duchy of Lanc. Misc. Bks. xxi, fol. 171 d.
[76] Ibid. fol. 174.
[77] Pat. 17 Jas. I, pt. i.
[78] Ibid. 9 Chas. I, pt. viii.
[79] Ibid.
[80] *V.C.H. Herts.* i, 335a.

[81] *Feud. Aids*, ii, 434; Chan. Inq. p.m. 4 Hen. V, no. 51.
[82] Chan. Inq. p.m. (Ser. 2), xxviii, 71.
[83] Anct. D. (P.R.O.), A 5257, 5259, 5256, 5260, 1031; Assize R. 325, m. 5.
[84] *Feud. Aids*, ii, 434.
[85] Feet of F. Herts. 32 Edw. I, no. 380.
[86] Ibid. 4 Edw. III, no. 52.
[86a] Possibly the female heirs who seem to have inherited Panshanger (in St. Andrew Rural) in succession to the Brickendon family may have held Hertingfordbury, for Matthew Lety, the husband of Margaret, is called 'of Hertingfordbury.'
[87] Anct. D. (P.R.O.), B 4024.
[88] *Cal. Pat.* 1429–36, p. 318.
[89] Chan. Inq. p.m. (Ser. 2), ii, 20.

A HISTORY OF HERTFORDSHIRE

1542 to Hugh Mynors.[90] In 1550 Mynors conveyed them to William Southwood.[91] In the following year William Southwood sold the property to William Caldewell,[92] who before 1557 conveyed it to William Coventry.[93] The last William left directions in his will that the two thirds of the manor should be sold after his death, and they were accordingly sold to John and Anne Myston, in spite of the protests of William's daughter Joan.[94] The Mystons, however, did not keep the estate for long, as in 1569 they sold it to William Kympton.[95] The two thirds then or subsequently seem to have been divided between John Baylie and William Kympton, William keeping one third, including the manor-house, for life, with remainder to John Baylie,[96] the other third being delivered to John by George Kympton in 1605.[97] John Baylie the elder died in 1611 and was succeeded by his son John, then a minor.[98] John was holding the two thirds in 1622,[99] but before 1651 there must have been a sale to Thomas Fanshawe, since the latter had united these two thirds with the other third and was holding the whole manor in that year.[100]

Of the third of Roxford apportioned to Gille and John Gryme nothing is known for a hundred years following. In 1586 John Knighton died seised of it, having settled it upon his son George,[1] after which it descended in his family in the same manner as Bayford[2] (q.v.) and came before 1651 to Thomas Fanshawe.[3] The Fanshawes appear to have sold the manor soon after to John Cox,[4] who presumably conveyed it to George Chalncombe.[5] In 1700 Frances Chalncombe, widow of George, joined with her daughter Frances, wife of Patrick Crawford, in conveying Roxford to John Brassey.[6] Nathaniel Brassey, successor of John, was succeeded in 1765 by his son Nathaniel,[7] who died in 1798.[8] Richard John Brassey, son of the latter, sold the manor in 1801 to William Baker[9] of Bayfordbury (q.v.), in whose family it has since descended.

WOOLMERS PARK evidently took its name from the family of Wolmer. John Wolmer is mentioned in Hertingfordbury between 1285 and 1289[10] and Thomas Wolmer in 1358.[11] In 1518 Woolmers was said to be held of the king as of his duchy of Lancaster,[12] so that it had probably always been held of the manor of Hertingfordbury. Sir Edward Benstede, who died in 1518, held a 'tenement or farm called Woolmers,' which he left to Joyce his wife for her life with remainder to his niece Alice Ferrers, daughter of his sister Katherine.[13] Joyce married secondly William Purdy, and was still living in 1531.[14] If Alice Ferrers died without issue the property was to pass to her elder brother John Ferrers, who was Sir Edward Benstede's nearest male heir, but there is no evidence to show whether it did so. Woolmers is not heard of again until the beginning of the 19th century, when it was in the possession of Francis Duke of Bridgewater. He died in 1803, leaving it to his nephew George Granville Earl Gower and Duke of Sutherland,[15] who died in 1833.[16] It is said to have been afterwards sold to Sir John St. Aubyn, bart., and to have been subsequently possessed by Sir Gore Ouseley, bart., and Rear-Admiral the Hon. George Frederick Hotham.[17] In 1842 it was bought by Mr. William Herbert Wodehouse,[18] who in 1903 was succeeded by his son Mr. Charles Edward Wodehouse, the present possessor.[19]

The manor of *BIRCHHOLT* now *BIRCHALL* was composed of lands granted at various dates to the Prior and convent of the Holy Trinity, London,[20] including the service owed by Roger de Essendon for land in Birchholt granted by John de Rocheford between 1316 and 1325.[21] These continued in the hands of the convent of the Holy Trinity until its surrender in 1531,[22] after which Birchholt was granted in 1534 to Sir Thomas Audley[23] of Walden, Lord Chancellor. About 1539 the latter conveyed it to William Cavendish and Margaret his wife.[24] It seems to have been re-conveyed to the Crown, for in 1599 Queen Elizabeth granted it to Henry Best and Robert Holland.[25] They sold it shortly afterwards to Sir Robert Wroth,[26] from whom it descended to John Wroth and Maud his wife[27] in the same manner as Tewin (q.v.). The latter sold it in 1621 to Sir Thomas Trevor,[28] afterwards chief baron of the Exchequer. He died in 1656,[29] leaving a son Thomas Trevor, baronet and knight of the Bath, who died childless in 1676,[30] after which the history of the estate is lost.

The estate called *EPCOMBS* (Epecaumpe, Epecombes) is thought to be the half hide in 'Thepecampe'[31] held both before and after the Conquest by a priest, in alms, of the king. An estate of 100 acres in Epcombs is said to have been held in the reign of Richard I by one Lyving, and to have descended to Luke son of William of Hertingfordbury, who claimed it in 1281.[32] Early in the 16th century it was in the possession of the Lawrence family, and in 1529 was held by Richard Lawrence and Agnes his wife and William Lawrence.[33] The latter, who was the son of John Lawrence, had a son William,[34] who died leaving

---

[90] Plac. de Banco, Mich. 34 Hen. VIII, m. 4; Feet of F. Herts. Mich. 34 Hen. VIII.
[91] Com. Pleas D. Enr. East. 4 Edw. VI, m. 1.
[92] Ibid. Mich. 5 Edw. VI, m. 11 d.
[93] Chan. Proc. (Ser. 2), bdle. 122, no. 18. [94] Ibid.
[95] Feet of F. Herts. Hil. 11 Eliz.
[96] Ct. of Wards, Feod. Surv. no. 17.
[97] Ibid. Trin. 3 Jas. I.
[98] Chan. Inq. p.m. (Ser. 2), cccxxxix, 196; Ct. of Wards, Feod. Surv. no. 17.
[99] Recov. R. Mich. 20 Jas. I, rot. 75.
[100] Feet of F. Div. Co. Hil. 1651.
[1] Chan. Inq. p.m. (Ser. 2), cxxi, 191.
[2] Ibid. (Ser. 2), cccxliii, 143; cccclxxvi, 129; cccxciv, 59.
[3] Feet of F. Div. Co. Hil. 1651.
[4] Close, 42 Geo. III, pt. xxxv, no. 1.

[5] See Clutterbuck, op. cit. ii, 201, who appears to have mixed up the two parts of the manor.
[6] Feet of F. Herts. East. 12 Will. III.
[7] Clutterbuck, Hist. of Herts. ii, 208, quoting monumental inscription.
[8] Ibid.; Recov. R. Mich. 14 Geo. III, rot. 351–2.
[9] Close, 42 Geo. III, pt. xxxv, no. 1.
[10] Anct. D. (P.R.O.), A 5247.
[11] Duchy of Lanc. Anct. D. (P.R.O.), L 258.
[12] Chan. Inq. p.m. (Ser. 2), xxxiv, 35.
[13] Ibid.; P.C.C. 25 Ayloffe.
[14] L. and P. Hen. VIII, v, g. 166 (57).
[15] P.C.C. 226 Marriott.
[16] G.E.C. Complete Peerage.
[17] Cussans, op. cit. 106. Sir Gore Ouseley is buried in the church.
[18] Ibid.

[19] Burke, Landed Gentry (1906).
[20] Anct. D. (P.R.O.), A 5256, 5260, 1031, 5257, 5259, 5221, 5250, 5249, 5241, 1121; B 4024.
[21] Ibid. A 1029, 5245.
[22] Dugdale, Mon. vi, 150.
[23] L. and P. Hen. VIII, vii, g. 1601 (35).
[24] Ibid. xiv (2), g. 619 (4).
[25] Pat. 41 Eliz. pt. xix, m. 1.
[26] Chan. Inq. p.m. (Ser. 2), ccxciv, 87.
[27] Feet of F. Div. Co. East. 19 Jas. I.
[28] Ibid.
[29] Burke, Extinct Baronetcies.
[30] Ibid. [31] V.C.H. Herts. i, 343.
[32] Assize R. 323, m. 12. One of the jurors for the 'inquisitio nonarum' for Hertingfordbury in 1341 was Robert Epcombe (Inq. Non. [Rec. Com.], 431).
[33] Feet of F. Herts. Hil. 21 Hen. VIII.
[34] Visit. Herts. (Harl. Soc. xxii), 72.

466

HERTFORD HUNDRED — HERTINGFORDBURY

four daughters—Susannah wife of John Darnell, Anne wife of John Jeve, Elizabeth wife of Rowland Hall, and Alice—between whom the property was divided.[35] Alice, who was a lunatic, and her three sisters were all living in 1606,[36] but it is not known to whom Epcombs afterwards descended. Susan Darnell had four daughters, of whom the eldest, Elizabeth, married Christopher Vernon,[37] lord of the manor of Hertingfordbury, and it is therefore possible that Epcombs thus became united with the main manor.

LAWRENCE. *Argent a ragged cross gules.*

In 1877 it was the residence of Mrs. Fenwick,[38] and is now occupied by Mr. Charles F. H. Leslie.

In 1086 there was a mill at 'Thepecampe.'[39]

The RECTORY MANOR has always been held by the rectors of the parish.[40] As a rule the records of only one court a year survive, held at various times; where the records of two survive they took place in May and October. In the reign of Edward III as many as four are recorded in a year, but this is exceptional. In 1638 the rents from the manor amounted to 9s. annually, besides six capons and various customary works.[41]

The church of ST. MARY, CHURCH which stands at the south-east end of the village, consists of chancel 38 ft. 6 in. by 21 ft., north chapel 22 ft. by 13 ft., south vestry and organ chamber, nave 50 ft. 6 in. by 23 ft., north aisle 50 ft. 6 in. by 11 ft. 6 in., south porch and west tower. These measurements are all internal. The church is built of flint rubble with stone dressings. The roofs are tiled.

The church was extensively restored and altered in 1845, and in 1890 it was practically rebuilt. The chancel and possibly the nave walls were built in the 13th century, the north aisle and west tower being added in the 15th century.

The three 13th-century grouped windows in the east wall of the chancel consist each of a single lancet having moulded arches and shafted jambs with moulded capitals and bases. The moulded labels have head stops. The external stonework is modern. In the chancel is a double piscina, part of the eastern jamb of which is original; it is of 13th-century date and has moulded and shafted jambs enriched with the dog-tooth ornament. The head and jamb stones of two windows in the north aisle, which are each of two cinquefoiled lights with a quatrefoil opening in the head, are of 15th-century date, as are parts of another window in the same wall, of two lights under a square head; a similar window in the south wall opposite is probably a little later.[42] Two jamb stones of the south doorway and the lofty four-centred and moulded tower arch are also of 15th-century date. The buttressed tower is of three stages with embattled parapet and leaded spire. Some parts of the belfry windows may be original. All the other detail in the church is modern.

On the north side of the tower is an altar tomb to Anne wife of George Calvert, 1622. On the tomb is an alabaster effigy of a lady, with mural cornice above supporting three shields of arms. On the south side of the tower is an altar tomb to William Harrington and his wife; it is of early 17th-century work. On a black marble slab are two recumbent shrouded effigies of alabaster; an arched cornice above, supported on pilasters, bears the arms of Harrington, eighteen quarterings in all. In front is the kneeling figure of a child. Over the pulpit is a mural tablet to Christopher Vernon, 1652, with his arms above. In the north aisle is a mural slab to Thomas Keightley, 1662, and his wife, 1682; and in the chancel are floor slabs to Robert Mynne, 1656, and Helen Mynne, 1659. On the north wall of the tower is a brass with inscription and shield of arms to Thomas Ellis, 1608, and his wife, 1612.

HERTINGFORDBURY CHURCH : WEST TOWER

There are five bells : the first by John Waylett, 1706; the second by T. Lester, 1750; the third by John Briant, 1823; the fourth and fifth by John Hodson dated 1656.

---

[35] *Visit. Herts.* (Harl. Soc. xxii), 72; Chan. Inq. p.m. (Ser. 2), clxxxvii, 77.
[36] Ct. of Wards, Feod. Surv. no. 17.
[37] *Visit. Herts.* (Harl. Soc. xxii), 72.
[38] Cussans, op. cit. *Hertford Hund.* 107.
[39] *V.C.H. Herts.* i, 343.
[40] Ct. R. Edw. I–Edw. VI, in the possession of Mr. F. Seebohm, Hitchin.
[41] *Herts. Gen. and Antiq.* iii, 178–9.
[42] Sir Edward Benstede desired in his will, proved in 1519, that his executors should make a window in the wall on the south side of the church and glaze it with images of St. Alban and St. 'Amphiabell,' setting two escutcheons therein with the arms of himself and his wife Joyce. He also left money for tapers before the image of our Lady of Acon, and directed that his body should be buried before that image (P.C.C. 25 Ayloffe).

A HISTORY OF HERTFORDSHIRE

The plate includes a cup with cover, a standing paten, and a flagon of 1675.

The registers before 1812 are as follows: (i) baptisms, burials and marriages from 1679 to 1744; (ii) baptisms and burials from 1745 to 1767, marriages from 1745 to 1762; (iii) baptisms from 1767 to 1812; (iv) burials from 1768 to 1812; (v) marriages from 1763 to 1812.

ADVOWSON The advowson of the church belonged to the lords of the manor[43] until Richard and Elizabeth Talbot surrendered the manor to the king in 1346, when they reserved the advowson.[44] Probably, however, they sold it to the king soon after, for they did not die seised of it, and it appears to have been granted to John of Gaunt Duke of Lancaster, and so passed to the Crown in the person of his son Henry IV. The presentation has ever since been made by the king in his capacity of Duke of Lancaster.[45]

In 1638 there was a 'parsonage house built of timber covered with Tile two storyes high, the lower storyes disposed into these roomes, a parlour, a hall, a kitchin, a milkhouse, a brewhouse, a mealehouse, a buttrye, and all these roomes are chambred over and boarded except the brewhouse and the mealehouse.'[46] The glebe lands amounted to 54½ acres.

A chapel of the Blessed Virgin Mary at Roxford is mentioned in 1304[47] and in 1330.[48] The advowson belonged to the lord of the manor.

The chapel of ease of *ST. JOHN BAPTIST* at Letty Green, built in 1849-50 and enlarged in 1890, is served from the parish church.

Meeting-places for Protestant Dissenters in the parish were certified in 1788 and 1811.[49]

CHARITIES In 1613 Grace Ellis, by her will proved in the P.C.C. 20 March, gave 40s. yearly for the poor, charged upon property in Norton Folgate, London. The annuity was redeemed in 1863 by the transfer to the official trustees of £66 13s. 4d. consols, now producing £1 13s. 4d. yearly, which is distributed in bread biennially to the value of 2s. to each recipient.

In 1708 Walter Wallinger by his will directed that £400 should be laid out in the purchase of a rent-charge to be applied in apprenticing sons and daughters of poor housekeepers not in receipt of parochial relief. The legacy, with interest, was laid out in the purchase of a fee-farm rent of £6 issuing out of Middle Mills, Colchester, a fee-farm rent of £5 out of Foxearth Hall Farm, Long Melford, Suffolk, and a fee-farm rent of £10 from Easthampstead Park, Berkshire. The last-mentioned was redeemed in 1904 by the transfer of £400 consols to the official trustees. The income has been found more than sufficient for the objects of the charity, and the surplus has from time to time been accumulated and invested in consols. The stock now amounts to £4,152 6s. 6d. consols with the official trustees and £115 19s. 6d. consols in the names of C. E. Wodehouse and two others, the annual dividends amounting together to £106 3s. 8d. The premiums usually amount to £12 10s.

In 1870 Thomas Newman, by his will proved 11 March, left a legacy, now represented by £582 4s. 2d. consols with the official trustees, the annual dividends, amounting to £14 11s., to be applied in aid of the schools.

ST. ANDREW RURAL

The civil parish of St. Andrew Rural is one of the outlying parts of the borough of Hertford and was separated from the urban parish of St. Andrew by the Local Government Act of 1894. It comprises an area of 1,040 acres, of which 1,022 acres are land and 18 water. The district is entirely rural, the western part being occupied by Panshanger Park, which covers an area of 900 acres and extends into the parish of Hertingfordbury. The southern boundary is formed by the River Mimram, which divides St. Andrew Rural from Hertingfordbury. The road from Bayford to Hertingfordbury, on which the village of Hertingfordbury is situated, is continued through this parish as Thieves Lane, and a little further north adjoins the main road from Hertford to Welwyn.

Sele Grange, now the residence of Miss E. Robertson, is situated on the extreme east of the parish, where it adjoins St. Andrew Urban. There is a wood called Selebroom at some distance to the north-west.

MANORS The manor of *BLAKEMERE* (Blachemene, xi cent.; Blackmere, xv cent.) was held in chief in 1086 by Geoffrey de Bech.[1] It probably came with Eastwick (q.v.) (also held by Geoffrey de Bech in 1086) into the possession of the Clares, and through Emma daughter of Baldwin de Clare to the Wake family, for in 1282 Baldwin de Wake was found to have been overlord of the quarter of a knight's fee in Blakemere.[2] The descent of the overlordship then follows that of Gobions in Stapleford[3] (q.v.).

In the time of Edward the Confessor Blakemere constituted the holdings of two thegns who had the right to sell. It was held in 1086 under Geoffrey de Bech by a single mesne tenant Geoffrey Runevile, and was assessed at 1 hide. It was said to contain land for two ploughs; there was one upon the demesne and there could be another. There was sufficient meadow for two plough teams. The unfree tenants were one villein and two bordars. The pasture sufficed for the live stock and the woodland for the feeding of forty swine.[4]

The tenant of Blakemere in 1281-2 was Robert (?) de Blakemere[5] and in 1303 John de Blakemere.[6] Before 1326 Blakemere had come into the same hands as Panshanger, which was evidently the more

---

[43] Chan. Inq. p.m. 17 Edw. II, no. 75; Cal. Close, 1323-7, p. 275.
[44] Feet of F. Div. Co. 20 Edw. III, no. 89.
[45] Cal. Pat. 1436-41, p. 351; Inst. Bks. (P.R.O.); Bacon, Liber Regis, 518.
[46] Herts. Gen. and Antiq. iii, 177-9.
[47] Feet of F. Herts. 32 Edw. I, no. 380.
[48] Ibid. 4 Edw. III, no. 52.
[49] Urwick, Nonconf. in Herts. 551.
[1] V.C.H. Herts. i, 335a.
[2] Cal. Inq. p.m. 1-19 Edw. I, 262.
[3] Feud. Aids, ii, 434; Chan. Inq. p.m. 23 Edw. III, pt. i, no. 75; 26 Edw. III, no. 54; 20 Ric. II, no. 57; 20 Ric. II, no. 30; 4 Hen. IV, no. 51; 7 Hen. VI, no. 57; (Ser. 2), xxviii, 71.
[4] V.C.H. Herts. i, 335a.
Cal. Inq. p.m. 1-19 Edw. I, 262.
[5]
[6] Feud. Aids, ii, 434.

468

HERTFORD HUNDRED

ST. ANDREW RURAL

important holding of the two. In that year William de Lodewyk received a grant of the manor of Panshanger and of 80 acres of arable land, 7 of meadow and 4 of wood in Blakemere.[7] Later conveyances of Panshanger mention these lands in Blakemere,[8] and the inquisition on Walter Chival (see Panshanger) gives the manor of Blakemere as well as that of Panshanger.[9] In 1474 the manor of Blakemere was conveyed with Panshanger,[10] but in 1492 lands only are mentioned,[11] and after this date it apparently became amalgamated with Panshanger.

The manor of *PANSHANGER* (Penneshanger, Paneshanger, Pensangre, xiii cent.; Peneshangre, xiv cent.; Pansangre, xiv and xv cent.; Passanger, Passhanger, Pansanger, xvi, xvii, and xviii cent.) is described in 1247 as 1 carucate of land.[12] In 1289 suit for it was owed every three weeks at the court of Robert de Hoo of Knebworth.[13] Robert de Hoo's rights in Blakemere descended with the manor of Knebworth, and had passed by 1428 to John Hotoft.[14] The latter's daughter and heir Idonea married Sir John Barre, kt., of Knebworth, of whom Panshanger was held in 1446,[15] and who died in 1483. His property descended to his daughter Isabel,[16] widow of Humphrey Stafford Earl of Devon, who was beheaded in 1469, and wife of Thomas Bourchier, kt., younger son of the Earl of Essex. She died childless in 1489,[17] and there is no later trace of rights in Panshanger which she had inherited.

Panshanger was held immediately in the first half of the 13th century by Walter de Gynney or Gisney, whose wife was Elizabeth. He made a feoffment thereof to his daughter Joan and her husband Philip de Mardley, who accordingly held in 1247–8 after his death. Walter had three other daughters, Eleanor, Nichola, and Philippa who married Robert Fitz William; and in 1247–8 John the son of Eleanor together with Philippa and her husband unsuccessfully claimed as their inheritance a moiety of 1 carucate of land in Panshanger.[18] Philip de Mardley was dead in 1274. In that year Joan his widow received from Philip his son a life grant of 1 carucate of arable land, 30 acres of meadow, 15 acres of wood and 32s. of rent in Panshanger.[19] In 1289 the younger Philip conveyed the manor of Panshanger to William de Burneton to be held for the rent of one clove gillyflower rendered to himself and his heirs and for all services due to the chief lords except suit at the court of Robert de Hoo at Knebworth which the grantor was to do during William's life.[20] William de Burneton in 1293 alienated the property, described at this date as a messuage, 300 acres of land and appurtenances in Panshanger, to William de Melksop and Maud his wife,[21] and this William in 1302 received a grant of free warren in his demesne lands of Panshanger.[22] He was succeeded by his son William about 1317. The latter was lord of the manor of Digswell in Broadwater Hundred, and it therefore seems probable that Stephen de Waltham, parson of the church of Digswell, and Ralph de St. Denis were acting for him when in 1326 they conveyed the manor of Panshanger to William de Lodewyk.[23] This William was succeeded by John de Lodewyk (see Ludwick Manor in Hatfield, Broadwater Hundred), who is given as the tenant of Blakemere in 1349[24] and 1352.[25] Later the manor appears to have passed to Felicia de Brickendon.[26] Felicia's husband was Herman de Brickendon, and he had a son Philip (see Roxford), but whether Panshanger was held by Philip is not certain. It passed ultimately to female heirs, for in 1369 a fine was levied between Matthew Lety of Hertingfordbury and his wife Margaret, and William de Tyringham and his wife Joan, by which it was settled on Nicholas son of Joan and Alice daughter of Margaret and the heirs of their bodies, a life interest being reserved to Matthew and Margaret Lety.[27] In 1370 Matthew and Margaret received a quitclaim of a moiety of the manor from Simon Clerk and his wife Agnes, who probably had a right of dower.[28] In 1397–8 Margaret, who was then the wife of William Kilmyngton, granted her life interest in the manor of Panshanger and lands in Blakemere to Nicholas Chival, citizen and vestment maker of London, and his heirs,[29] who may have been the Nicholas son of Joan Tyringham mentioned above. The heir of Nicholas was his son Walter, who died in 1434. His heirs were his sisters Joan and Alice, the wives in 1446 of Edmund Wykes and of Thomas Walssh, then holders in their right.[30] Thomas Walssh made a feoffment of the manors of Panshanger and Blakemere to William Walssh, Roger Bere and William Canwyk of Stevenage, and in 1474 the latter conveyed them to Thomas Birch and Ellen his wife.[31] In 1492 Thomas and Ellen conveyed Panshanger Manor and lands in Blakemere to Simon Paxman and Nicholas Larwood, with warranty against themselves and the heirs of Ellen.[32] This was probably in trust for Sir William Say; for Gertrude granddaughter and heir of Sir William Say of Broxbourne, daughter of William Blount Lord Mountjoy by Elizabeth Say, and widow of Henry Courtenay Marquess of Exeter, who was beheaded in 1539,[33] was found at her attainder in the same year to have forfeited to the Crown her reversionary right after the death of William Bruer[34] to the manor of Panshanger, by which name the early holdings in Panshanger and Blakemere were at this date both known.

In 1546 the manor was granted by the king to the famous Nicholas Throckmorton, then sewer to Queen Katherine.[35] He in 1555 conveyed it as the

---

[7] Feet of F. Herts. 20 Edw. II, no. 443.
[8] Ibid. 43 Edw. III, no. 600; 44 Edw. III, no. 614; 21 Ric. II, no. 183.
[9] Chan. Inq. p.m. 24 Hen. VI, no. 24.
[10] Close, 14 Edw. IV, m. 28.
[11] Feet of F. Herts. 8 Hen. VII, no. 41.
[12] Assize R. 318, m. 5.
[13] Feet of F. Herts. 17 Edw. I, no. 243.
[14] *Feud. Aids*, ii, 450. According to these returns John Hotoft's fee was that formerly held by Ralph Boteler, but apparently Panshanger has been confused here with Sele.
[15] Chan. Inq. p.m. 24 Hen. VI, no. 24.
[16] See account of Knebworth.
[17] G.E.C. *Complete Peerage*, iii, 105.
[18] Assize R. 318, m. 5, 17.
[19] Feet of F. Herts. 2 Edw. I, no. 30.
[20] Ibid. 17 Edw. I, no. 243.
[21] Ibid. 21 Edw. I, no. 294.
[22] Chart. R. 30 Edw. I, m. 4, no. 17.
[23] Feet of F. Herts. 20 Edw. II, no. 443.
[24] Chan. Inq. p.m. 23 Edw. III, pt. i, no. 75.
[25] Ibid. 26 Edw. III, no. 54.
[26] Ibid. 20 Ric. II, no. 30. See Roxford in Hertingfordbury.
[27] Feet of F. Herts. 43 Edw. III, no. 600.
[28] Ibid. 44 Edw. III, no. 614.
[29] Ibid. Ric. II, no. 183.
[30] Chan. Inq. p.m. 24 Hen. VI, no. 24.
[31] Close, 14 Edw. IV, m. 28.
[32] Feet of F. Herts. 8 Hen. VII, no. 41.
[33] G.E.C. *Complete Peerage*, iii, 107.
[34] Chan. Inq. p.m. (Ser. 2), lxxiii, 93.
[35] *L. and P. Hen. VIII*, xxi (1), g. 1166 (42).

A HISTORY OF HERTFORDSHIRE

manor, messuage or farm called Panshanger with its appurtenances to John Forster,[36] at whose death in 1558 it passed to his son Humphrey, a minor.[37] He alienated the manor in 1567 to Edward Skeggs,[38] who conveyed it in 1578 to John Matthew.[39] The latter in 1585 made conveyance of it to certain feoffees,[40] who granted it in 1587 to James Smyth.[41] He in 1588 conveyed to Humphrey Weld the manor and its appurtenances and five messuages, one dovecote, five gardens, 300 acres of arable land, 60 acres of meadow, 100 acres of pasture, 40 acres of wood and as much of furze and heath and of moor, in Panshanger, Swinhoe, Hertford St. Andrew and Hertingfordbury.[42] Humphrey was probably identical with the alderman of London of that name who was knighted in 1603[43] and who married Mary the daughter of Sir Stephen Slaney, Lord Mayor of London in 1596.[44] He died as holder of Panshanger in 1610 and had for heir a son John,[45] who was knighted, and who, at his death in 1623, was succeeded by his son Humphrey, a minor.[46] The latter was holder in 1642,[47] but probably alienated the manor in that year or subsequently. A conveyance of it took place in 1693 from George Hitchcock and his wife Elizabeth to Sir Gervase Elwes, bart., and Sir John Elwes, kt., with warranty against the heirs of Elizabeth.[48] This was probably in trust for Sir John,[49] who may be identified with Sir John Elwes, younger brother of the baronet, who was knighted in 1665 and who was of Grove House, Fulham, where he died in 1702. His wife was Elizabeth daughter and co-heir of Sir Walter Raleigh of West Horsley.[50] In 1719 there was a conveyance of Panshanger from John Elwes to Thomas Woodford,[51] afterwards executor to the first Earl Cowper,[52] which was probably in trust for the earl or his son and heir.

The Lord Cowper in question was the distinguished Lord Chancellor who held office from 1707 to 1710 and from 1714 to 1718, and who since 1706[53] or an earlier date had lived, when in the country, in the house which he had built at Cole Green in Hertingfordbury. This was for the remainder of the 18th century the mansion-house of Panshanger. It was sometimes the residence, while her husband was in London, of Mary Lady Cowper, second wife of the chancellor, Lady of the Bedchamber to the Princess of Wales, and author of a well-known diary.[54] Campbell states that the chancellor personally took no part in country affairs, yet there are extant certain of his instructions to his gardeners : ' The weeds in the orchard to be mowed. The little kitchen garden in the corner to be cleaned. The gooseberry and currant bushes trimmed. The fig-trees, mulberry-trees and such as seem decaying, but not desperate, watered. Stir and clean the borders. Remove trees which are to be removed.'[55] After his final retirement from office Lord Cowper spent much time at Cole Green and in this period acquired Panshanger. It seems that he did not find his rural leisure an unmixed blessing. ' It is cruelty in you to tantalize a poor countryman with the life of state and pleasure you describe,' he wrote in June 1720 to his wife, then in attendance on the Princess ; ' I could be content as I am if I did not hear of such fine doings.'[56] And in a letter to her in April 1722 he says, ' The country is

COWPER, Earl Cowper. *Argent three martlets gules and a chief engrailed gules with three rings or therein. The crest is a lion's paw or razed and holding a branch of a cherry tree in its proper colours. The supporters are two dun horses.*

excessively pleasant, but I am sensible while it pleases it dulls me, and in these few days I have contracted a great degree of indolence and an aversion to all cares but the little ones of this place.'[57] He died at Cole Green in 1723.[58] His son William, the second earl, was a Lord of the Bedchamber from 1733 to 1747, became lord lieutenant and *custos rotulorum* for Hertfordshire in 1744, and was a Fellow of the Royal Society. He died at Cole Green in 1764[59] and was succeeded by his son George Nassau,[60] who had been member for Hertford from 1759 to 1761. He spent much of his time in Florence, and through the influence of the Grand Duke of Tuscany was created

---

[36] Pat. 1 & 2 Phil. and Mary, pt. i ; Feet of F. Herts. East. 1 & 2 Phil. and Mary ; Com. Pleas D. Enr. East. 1 & 2 Phil. and Mary.
[37] Chan. Inq. p.m. (Ser. 2), ccxviii, 64 ; Recov. R. Trin. 1564, rot. 515.
[38] Feet of F. Herts. Mich. 9 & 10 Eliz. ; Recov. R. Mich. 1567, rot. 1247 ; see Com. Pleas D. Enr. Mich. 8 & 9 Eliz.
[39] Pat. 30 Eliz. pt. xii.
[40] Feet of F. Herts. Hil. 27 Eliz.
[41] Pat. 30 Eliz. pt. xii.
[42] Feet of F. Herts. Mich. 30 & 31 Eliz.; Pat. 31 Eliz. pt. vi.
[43] Shaw, *Knights of Engl.* ii, 128.

[44] Cussans, *Hist. of Herts. Hertford Hund.* 71. Hence presumably the error by which Chauncy and Clutterbuck state that Stephen Slaney held the manor.
[45] Chan. Inq. p.m. (Ser. 2), cccxxii, 173.
[46] Ibid. cccii, 132 ; Ct. of Wards, Feod. Surv. no. 17.
[47] Recov. R. Trin. 15 Chas. I, rot. 60 ; East. 18 Chas. I, m. 18.
[48] Feet of F. Herts. Mich. 5 Will. and Mary.
[49] Chauncy, op. cit. 266, calls him John Elwes, merchant of London, and says he was holding in 1700.
[50] Le Neve, *Ped. of the Knights* (Harl. Soc.), 199 ; Wotton, *Baronetage of Engl.*

ii, 23 ; Faulkner, *Hist. Acct. of Fulham,* 443.
[51] Feet of F. Herts. Trin. 5 Geo. I.
[52] *V.C.H. Herts. Families,* 138.
[53] Campbell, *Lives of the Lord Chancellors,* iv, 308.
[54] *Diary of Mary Countess Cowper* (ed. the Hon. Spencer Cowper).
[55] Campbell, op. cit. iv, 406 and note.
[56] Ibid. 410.   [57] Ibid. 411.
[58] Ibid. 412.
[59] *V.C.H. Herts. Families,* 139.
[60] Recov. R. Mich. 2 Geo. III, rot. 284 ; Trin. 12 Geo. III, rot. 15 ; East. 18 Geo. III, rot. 423 ; Mich. 19 Geo. III, rot. 47.

St. Andrew Rural: Panshanger House from the South-East

[Arthur V. Elsden, photo

a prince of the Holy Roman Empire by Joseph II, a title which George III empowered him to accept in 1785.[61] In his obituary notice in the *Gentleman's Magazine* it is stated, however, that the dignity was necessarily territorial, and that Lord Cowper was therefore correctly only prince of the Milanese in the empire.[62] He died in 1789 and was succeeded by his son George Augustus, who came of age in 1797. That event was celebrated in the traditional manner by the roasting of an ox whole at Cole Green :—

> The beast was put down in a pit, fastened by an iron chain to a wooden axletree between two cart-wheels, before a large wood fire, at two in the morning, and after being turned by two men suitably habited and decorated with ribbons, who were the same that assisted at this ceremony on that day 21 years, being his lordship's birthday, was cut up and distributed, with a proportionable quantity of strong beer, to an innumerable crowd of spectators, at two in the afternoon ; at which time his lordship, who had previously received the compliments of the neighbouring nobility and gentry at his steward's house on the edge of the green, was mounted on one of the beer buts, and received the homage of the multitude in nine successive cheers. . . . The whole festivity concluded with a display of fireworks from the front of the steward's house.[63]

In the following spring Lord Cowper, said to have been a young man of great promise, had a fall from his horse from which he never completely recovered. He caught cold while serving with the Hertfordshire militia, in which he was a captain, and died at Cole Green in 1799.[64] His heir was his brother Peter Leopold,[65] a student of the Middle Temple in 1794.[66] Of him Lord Campbell said : 'He had too much delicacy of sentiment to take a leading part in public life, but to the most exquisitely pleasing manner he joined a manly understanding and a playful wit. From him I received kind and encouraging notice when I was poor and obscure, and his benevolent and exhilarating smile is one of the most delightful images in my memory of pleasures to return no more.'[67]

This Lord Cowper in 1801 pulled down the house at Cole Green, and built that which is now at Panshanger,[68] and which had in 1808 recently undergone improvement and alteration.[69] He died in 1837, and had for heir a son George Augustus Frederick. In 1855 the house was considerably damaged by fire, and narrowly escaped destruction.[70] In the next year George Lord Cowper was succeeded by his son Francis Thomas de Grey, who in 1865 was envoy-extraordinary for the investiture of King Christian IX of Denmark with the order of the Garter, and from 1880 until 1882 Lord Lieutenant of Ireland. He died in 1905 at Panshanger, and left no children. The house is now the seat of his widow Katrine Cecilia Countess Cowper, who has in it a life interest.[71] It stands in a picturesque and well-wooded park, about 2½ miles due west of Hertford and 1½ miles to the north-east of Cole Green. It is a long stone and stucco building of two stories and attics, designed with battlements and angle turrets in the Gothic taste of the early years of the 19th century ; a central tower of three stories projects slightly from the garden front. From the top of a slope it overlooks the park and the little River Mimram, at this point artificially enlarged into a small lake, and faces nearly south-west.

The main entrance is by a spacious porch, projecting from the north front and opening into a well-proportioned hall hung with some valuable ancient tapestries and several examples of the art of Burne-Jones. Here is a fine Italian mantelpiece of carved stone, and opposite to the entrance is the well-known bust of Clytie, by G. F. Watts. On the south-east of the entrance hall is the inner hall, whence rises the grand staircase ; opening out of it is a lobby leading to the picture gallery, which occupies the south-east end of the house, and the north library. The picture gallery is a stately room, wherein are many treasures of furniture and china, together with the more important of the pictures collected by George Nassau, third Earl Cowper, during his long residence in Italy.

Next to the picture gallery, and entered from the lobby between it and the inner hall, is the library, lighted by windows on its south side, and giving beautiful views across the park. The most notable picture in this room is a grand portrait group, painted by Vandyck in 1634, of John Count of Nassau and his family ; it formerly hung in the old house at Cole Green. West of this room and opening out of it is the ante-library, where are three fine Knellers, a portrait of Admiral van Tromp by Lely, and one of William Prince of Orange by Wissing. Beyond the ante-library is the drawing room, a pleasant room lighted by a great south bay window, and containing many choice examples of English, foreign and oriental porcelain. The pictures are mainly by English portraitists ; among them three by Reynolds and a portrait of William Cowper the poet by Jackson are specially noteworthy.

Across a long corridor on the north side of the drawing room is the great dining room, which lies to the west of the entrance hall. This lofty room, lighted by windows in its north wall, is panelled in walnut, and has a great marble mantelpiece at either end. Here hang three portraits by Lely, two perfect Reynoldses of the Viscountess Melbourne with her son, and the children of the first Viscount Melbourne, and other notable pictures.

In the corridor stand several fine cabinets of European and oriental workmanship, and on the walls are portraits of Auverquerque and Nassau, ancestors of Henrietta Countess Cowper.

Beyond the drawing room on the south side of the house, and entered at the western end of the corridor, is the small dining room, which has on its south side a bay window similar to that in the drawing room. Its walls and ceiling are of good moulded plaster work. On the walls hang a few admirable Dutch paintings.

In the corridor leading westward from this part of the house to the late earl's study and the offices are many fine pieces of oriental china and Delft. The china cupboard near the garden entrance contains a valuable collection of dessert and dinner services, and other pieces of French, English and oriental porcelain.

The north-east corner of the house is occupied by the north library, a long room entered from the inner hall and hung with family portraits of Lambs, Cowpers and Auverquerques. An interesting portrait

[61] *V.C.H. Herts. Families,* 140.
[62] *Gent. Mag.* lix, 1213.
[63] Ibid. lxvii, 706.
[64] Ibid. lxix, 174.
[65] Recov. R. Hil. 42 Geo. III, rot. 146.
[66] *V.C.H. Herts. Families,* 141.
[67] Campbell, op. cit. iv, 420.
[68] Cussans, op. cit. *Hertford Hund.* 72.
[69] Brayley, *Beauties of Engl. and Wales,* vii, 269.
[70] Cussans, op. cit. *Hertford Hund.* 72 n.
[71] *V.C.H. Herts. Families,* 142–4.

A HISTORY OF HERTFORDSHIRE

by Zoffani of the third Earl Cowper is to be seen outside the door in the inner hall.

On the grand staircase are a fine Tintoretto and a portrait of Queen Mary by an unknown hand. The Queen's Room, entered from the landing at the head of the stairs, with its dressing room next door, is furnished with a remarkable suite of rosewood inlaid with ivory. Next to it is the Japanese room, with wonderful hangings of embroidered silk, and westward of this is the Indian room, with blue silk hangings and furniture of ebony and ivory.

Hard by the house is the famous Panshanger oak, a tree of noble growth, though now somewhat past its prime. Many other oaks of grand proportions are standing at the Cole Green end of the park.

The manor of SELE (Sela, xi cent.; Sella, xiii cent.) was held in 1086, like Blakemere, of Geoffrey de Bech, and the overlordship passed with that of Blakemere.[71a] The mesne tenant in the reign of Edward the Confessor and in 1086 was a certain Godwin, and he held half a hide. It contained land for one plough, which was there, and meadow enough for one plough team. There were two serfs, wood sufficient for the fences, and pasture for the live stock. The annual value in 1086 and before the Conquest was 10s. The tenant was able to sell. One-eighth of a fee was held in 1282 of Baldwin Wake by a certain tenant of the name of Sele, probably Hugh de la Sele, who in 1287 acknowledged that he had stopped up the way leading to Hertford, to the annoyance of the free tenants and of Peter, parson of St. Andrew's Church.[72] Rather later Sele seems to have come to the Peletots, for Eudo de Peletot was holding part of a fee in Blakemere of Joan Wake in 1303,[73] and in 1347 his son Philip Peletot (see Watton Woodhall) conveyed the manor to Ralph Boteler and his wife Katherine, Philip's daughter, with remainder to William and Thomas, the sons of Philip.[74] It descended in the line of the Botelers of Watton Woodhall,[75] and passed with that manor until it was bought in 1791, on the death of Sir Thomas Rumbold, by the second Marquess of Downshire. He in 1801 sold it to Peter Leopold Earl Cowper.[76]

There was in 1086 a mill in Sele, presumably a water-mill on the River Beane, which was of the annual value of 2s.[77] In the time of Henry VIII there was a paper-mill at Hertford, which belonged to John Tate, whose father was mayor of London. This is said to have been the first papermill in England, and to have been situated on Sele Manor. As late as 1785 a meadow in Sele and beside the Beane was known as Paper Mill Mead. A mill was erected on it in 1700, and was noted as the first in which the fine flour called Hertfordshire White was made.[78]

The church of St. Andrew is dealt with under the borough of Hertford.

STANSTEAD ST. MARGARET'S

The earliest name of this parish seems to be Thele (Thele, xi cent.; Theele, xiii cent.; Le Ele, xiv cent.; Theyle, the Yle, xvi cent.). At the end of the 13th century it took an alternative name from the bridge over the Lea and was called Pons de Thele, Punt de Tyull, Pons Tegule or Pons Tegleri[1] (Pontherigg, xiv cent.). In the 16th century it begins to be called St. Margaret's Theale (Margarthele, 1535) and Stanstead Thele, the first from its church and the second from the fact that the village of St. Margaret's adjoins the village of Stanstead Abbots, from which it is divided by the bridge over the Lea. Stanstead St. Margaret's is a modern form of the name. The parish has also been known by the name of Lea Vale and Old Stanstead.[2]

Stanstead St. Margaret's is a small parish, containing only 407 acres. About one-half of it consists of arable land and one-third of permanent grass, while there are about 60 acres of woodland.[3] This lies chiefly in the extreme west of the parish where Golding's Wood is situated. The soil is mixed on a subsoil of chalk and gravel. The River Lea forms the eastern boundary of the parish. In 1858 a bronze spear-head was found in the river here.[4] In this part of the parish the land is about 100 ft. above the ordnance datum and rises towards the south-west to about 300 ft. The Great Eastern railway has a station called St. Margaret's, lying north of the village in the parish of Great Amwell.

Stanstead St. Margaret's seems to have been originally a part of the parish of Great Amwell, in the middle of which it lies. There is no mention of it in the Domesday Survey, but it had acquired a separate parochial existence by the middle of the 13th century.

The bridge called in early records the Punt de Tyall or Pons Tegule, from which the parish possibly took one of its names, carries the main road to Hertford over the Lea. There was a bridge here early in the 12th century, when the manor of Stanstead Abbots (on the other side of the bridge) appears under the name of 'manerium de Stanstede et Pontis

---

[71a] *V.C.H. Herts.* i, 335a; *Cal. Inq. p.m.* 1–19 *Edw. I*, 262.
[72] *Abbrev. Plac.* (Rec. Com.), 213.
[73] *Feud. Aids,* ii, 434.
[74] *Feet of F. Herts.* 21 Edw. III, no. 331.
[75] Ibid. Div. Co. 10 Hen. IV, no. 49; Chan. Inq. p.m. 8 Hen. V, no. 78; 6 Hen. VI, no. 30 (calendar); P.C.C. Will, 8 Holder; Feet of F Div. Co. Mich. 11 Jas. I; Mich. 18 Jas. I; Recov. R. Hil. 21 Jas. I, rot. 19; Com. Pleas D. Enr. Mich. 3 Anne, m. 33; Feet of F. Herts. Mich. 3 Anne; Recov. R. Mich. 3 Anne, rot. 254; Hil. 15 Geo. III, rot. 387; Mich. 20 Geo. III, rot. 487.
[76] Clutterbuck, *Hist. of Herts.* ii, 196.
[77] *V.C.H. Herts.* i, 335a.
[78] Ames, *Typog. Antiq.* i, 197–201. See article on Paper Making in *V.C.H. Herts.* iv.

[1] The origin of this name is uncertain. There is no evidence that there was ever a brick bridge (*Pons Tegule*) here, although it is possible, but not probable, that there was one at the date at which the name first occurs. It is unlikely that there was a Roman bridge here, as it is not on the line of any known Roman road, and, so far as we know, there is no site near from which Roman bricks can have been obtained. It may have been called from tile works in the neighbourhood, or the name may be a corruption of a word unconnected with 'tegula.' The earliest form of reference to the bridge is 'Pons de Thele' (Cartae Antiq. M 22). Possibly the later form Pons Tegule is a wrong interpretation of Thele (taking it as tile).
[2] Norden, *Descr. of Herts.* 24.
[3] Statistics from Bd. of Agric. (1905).
[4] *Proc. Soc. Antiq.* iv, 279; Evans, *Anct. Bronze Implements of Gt. Britain,* 315.

472

STANSTEAD ST. MARGARET'S CHURCH FROM THE SOUTH-WEST

de Thele.'⁵ In 1247–8 it was deposed that the men of London had built a granary at Thele (*ad Pontem Tegule*) in which they placed corn which they carried to London in their own ships instead of in the king's ships.⁶ At the end of the 13th century the dues from the bridge of Thele were taken by the warden of Hertford Castle, and in 1299, in a suit brought by the monastery of St. Albans against the warden of that castle concerning tolls which he had taken in St. Albans and Barnet, it was stated as an analogous case that Henry III and his predecessors and William de Valence Earl of Pembroke, whom Henry had appointed governor of the castle (q.v.) in 1250, had always taken tolls at the bridge of Thele.⁷ In 1331 Aymer de Valence Earl of Pembroke, governor of the castle, died seised of the tolls of the bridge of Thele,⁸ and the bridge remained attached to the castle until the death of Queen Isabella, when the castle (q.v.) reverted to the Crown, and the king in 1359–60 granted the bridge of Thele with the bridge of Ware to John Lucas of Ware.⁹ It was afterwards acquired by John of Gaunt, to whom the castle of Hertford (q.v.) was granted in 1360, and descended with the castle, except for occasional leases.¹⁰ When in 1630 the castle and manor of Hertford were finally alienated from the Crown, the bridge of Thele passed with them to William Cecil Earl of Salisbury.¹¹ The bridge was a wooden one until 1873, when an iron bridge was built.¹²

The village of St. Margaret's is a continuation of Stanstead Abbots, on the west side of the Lea, along the road to Hertford. From this a road runs south to meet the main road from London to Ware, which passes through the parish on the west, and along this road are situated the church and manor-house, with St. Margaretsbury (so named only about twenty years ago), now the residence of Mr. Septimus Croft, lying to the west. At the junction of the two roads is a pair of framed timber cottages with thatched roofs, probably not earlier than the first half of the 19th century.

No record of THELE occurs in the MANOR Domesday Survey, and it was probably included at that date in the manor of Hailey in Great Amwell. The woodland mentioned in the extent of that manor in 1086.¹³ may be the woods in St. Margaret's, for Hailey itself is very bare. Hailey in 1086 was held by Geoffrey de Bech.¹⁴ In the early part of the 12th century it had come to Ralph Pincerna, of whom it was held by the Buruns,¹⁵ and that the Buruns held land in Thele is evident, for Roger de Burun granted a tenement on the banks of Thele to the abbey of St. Albans.¹⁶ In the reign of Henry I Aubrey de Vere appears as mesne lord in Hailey between Ralph Pincerna and the Buruns,¹⁷ which also tends to show that Thele was originally included in Hailey, for Aubrey de Vere's descendants, the Earls of Oxford,¹⁸ appear as overlords of the manor of THELE *alias* GOLDINGTONS¹⁹ (Thele, xiii cent. ; Goldingtons Thele *alias* St. Margaret's Thele *alias* Stanstead Thele, xvi cent.). By the end of the 13th century, apparently, the manor and advowson had become divided among the following co-heirs of a tenant under the Earls of Oxford : Lucy wife of Henry Chacepork,²⁰ Alice wife of William le Marchand,²¹ Mabel wife of Nicholas le Mareschal, and possibly Margaret wife of John de Lovetot. Between 1274 and 1276 John de Lovetot and Margaret his wife²² seem to have acquired the interests of the other co-heirs²³ and in 1277 obtained a grant of free warren in their demesne lands here and elsewhere.²⁴ They also received a quitclaim from Mabel de Waunford in 1287, who held in dower.²⁴ᵃ In 1281 John de Lovetot received a grant of a weekly market at Thele on Thursday and an annual fair there on the vigil, the feast and the morrow of the Nativity of St. John Baptist and the six days following.²⁵ Joan wife of Humphrey de Bohun (lord of Ware) quitclaimed to John in 1281 all right to hold view of frankpledge,²⁶ and later he claimed assize of bread and ale and gallows.²⁷

In 1303 William de Goldington was holding a fee of the Earl of Oxford,²⁸ half of which was in Bengeo,²⁹ and the other half probably in Thele. William de Goldington was holding the manor in 1313³⁰ and died seised before 3 February 1318–19.³¹ He was succeeded by his son John,³² who received a grant of free warren in his demesne lands of Thele in 1328³³ and settled the manor on himself and his wife Katherine in tail in the following year.³⁴ He died about 1338, when the manor remained with Katherine for life.³⁵ She married as her second husband John Fermer, who died holding the manor in her right in 1354.³⁶ Accounts for the manor while it was in his hands include the farm of the fishery, valued at 5*s*. 6*d*.³⁷ Katherine died in 1358 and was succeeded by her son John de Goldington, aged twenty-six.³⁸ He had a son John Goldington, and the latter a son, also John Goldington,³⁹ who died seised of the manor in 1419.⁴⁰ His son Thomas, then aged fifteen,⁴¹ survived him only a short time and Thele passed to his cousin and heir John Hinxworth of Ashwell, who was

---

⁵ Cartae Antiq. M 22, 23 ; RR 7.
⁶ Assize R. no. 313, m. 6 d.
⁷ Walsingham, *Gesta Abbatum Mon. S. Albani* (Rolls Ser.), ii, 43.
⁸ *Cal. Inq. p.m.* 10–20 *Edw. II*, 318.
⁹ *Abbrev. Rot. Orig.* (Rec. Com.), ii, 256.
¹⁰ See p. 502.
¹¹ Ibid.
¹² Ibid. 134 n.
¹³ *V.C.H. Herts.* i, 334.
¹⁴ Ibid.
¹⁵ Harl. Chart. 46, I, 30.
¹⁶ Cott. MS. Nero, D vii, fol. 92*b*.
¹⁷ Harl. Chart. 46, I, 30.
¹⁸ For descent see G.E.C. *Complete Peerage*, s.v. Oxford.
¹⁹ Feet of F. Herts. 2 Edw. I, no. 33 ; *Cal. Inq. p.m.* 10–20 *Edw. II*, 113 ; Chan. Inq. p.m. 32 Edw. III (1st nos.), no. 38 ; 34 Edw. III, no. 84 ; 45 Edw. III, no. 45 ; 1 Hen. IV, no. 52 ; 7 Hen. V, no. 7 ; (Ser. 2), civ, 156 ; ccclxxiii, 15.
²⁰ Feet of F. Herts. 55 Hen. III, no. 637.
²¹ Ibid. 2 Edw. I, no. 33.
²² Add. R. 26828.
²³ Feet of F. Div. Co. 4 Edw. I, no. 41 ; 5 & 6 Edw. I, no. 66 ; 15 Edw. I, no. 212.
²⁴ *Cal. Chart. R.* 1257–1300, p. 203.
²⁴ᵃ Feet of F. Herts. 15 Edw. I, no. 212.
²⁵ *Cal. Chart. R.* 1257–1300, p. 252.
²⁶ Feet of F. Herts. 9 Edw. I, no. 126.
²⁷ *Plac. de Quo Warr.* (Rec. Com.), 291.
²⁸ *Feud. Aids*, ii, 433.
²⁹ Ibid.
³⁰ See *Cal. Pat.* 1313–17, p. 56.
³¹ *Cal. Inq. p.m.* 10–20 *Edw. II*, 112.
³² Ibid.
³³ Chart. R. 2 Edw. III, m. 1, no. 5 ; see Feet of F. Div. Co. 3 Edw. III, no. 41.
³⁴ Feet of F. Div. Co. 3 Edw. III, no. 41.
³⁵ See Chan. Inq. p.m. 12 Edw. III (1st nos.), no. 38 ; *Cal. Close*, 1337–9, p. 507.
³⁶ Chan. Inq. p.m. 28 Edw. III, no. 29 ; see *Cal. Close*, 1354–60, p. 38.
³⁷ Mins. Accts. bdle. 1118, no. 11.
³⁸ Chan. Inq. p.m. 32 Edw. III (1st nos.), no. 38.
³⁹ Weever, *Ancient Funerall Monuments*, 550.
⁴⁰ Chan. Inq. p.m. 7 Hen. V, no. 7.
⁴¹ Ibid.

holding it in 1423.[42] John Hinxworth released all right in the manor in 1436 to John Fray and others,[43] who appear to have been trustees for Sir Andrew Ogard, kt., who died holding it jointly with his wife Alice in 1454, leaving as his heir his son Henry, aged four.[44] Henry Ogard was knighted, and by his will proved in 1511 he left the manor of Thele to his son Andrew,[45] who held it until his death in March 1525–6, when it passed to his son George.[46] In 1553 George Ogard leased the manor of Thele to Thomas Fleminge of Stanstead for ninety-nine years. He died shortly afterwards, bequeathing the remainder of the lease to Agnes his wife, who married John Thorowgood.[47]

In 1560 George Ogard sold the manor to William Frankland, clothworker of London,[48] who died in 1576, leaving Goldingtons to his son William for life with reversion to his nephew Hugh for life.[49] Hugh died in January 1607,[50] and in 1623 William Frankland his nephew with Lucy his wife conveyed the manor to Simon Adams, citizen and draper of London.[51] Simon Adams in 1637 settled the manor for the purpose of the payment of an annuity to Sarah his wife,[52] and in 1651 his son Simon Adams of Aston upon the Wall (co. Northants), clerk, sold it together with the messuage lately built upon a parcel of land called Quitchells *alias* Cutchills and the right of feeding one cow on Amwell Marsh to Henry Lawrence of St. Ives (co. Hunts.) for £1,090.[53] This Henry Lawrence was a relative of Oliver Cromwell and a member of the Commonwealth Council of State; his learning received the praise of Milton. On the death of the Protector he declared Richard Cromwell his successor, but on the return of Charles II he retired to Thele, where he died in 1664.[54]

The manor was soon afterwards sold to Thomas Westrow,[55] and after his death in 1675[56] it was held by his widow Elizabeth.[57]

In 1689 it was purchased of her by Francis Roston, who was holding it in 1700.[58] It passed to Richard Kynnesman of Broughton (co. Northants),[59] who sold it in 1714 to Spencer Cowper of Hertford Castle (co. Herts.).[60] On the death of Spencer Cowper in 1727[61] the manor descended to his son William Cowper, from whom it passed to a son of the same name, and from him to his son, also William Cowper.[62] The latter died without issue in 1798, and the manor of Thele was in-

COWPER. *Argent three martlets gules and a chief engrailed gules with three rings or therein.*

herited by his brother Charles,[63] on whose death it passed to his sister Frances Cecilia.[64] She married the Rev. Joseph Stephen Pratt,[65] and died in 1849, when the manor descended to her son the Rev. Charles Pratt, rector of St. Margaret's.[66] He held it until his death, and in 1889 it was bought of his executors by Mr. Septimus Croft,[67] who is the present lord of the manor and resides at St. Margaretsbury.

The site of the manor and the demesne lands of the manor were sold separately from the manor by George Ogard in 1559 to John Thorowgood and Agnes his wife, who were then holding a lease of the manor[68] (q.v.). John Thorowgood died in February 1568–9, and his lands descended to his son and heir Thomas.[69] At the end of the 17th century the capital messuage appears to have been divided between co-heirs, for in 1685 Thomas Wale, citizen and goldsmith of London, sold one-quarter and one-third of a quarter of it to Robert Peter the elder, citizen and girdler of London.[70] In 1782 the site of the manor was held by Anna Maria Lake, spinster.[71]

The manor-house on the west bank of the New River, opposite to and a little south of the church, has been much restored, but appears to date from the 17th century. It is a timber-framed building with a tiled roof. There are 18th-century iron gates at the principal entrance. These are surmounted by a shield charged with the arms of Lake with the coat of augmentation, beneath which is the motto 'Un Dieu un Roy un cœur.'

The church of ST. MARGARET CHURCH consists of chancel measuring internally 35 ft. by 19 ft., nave, which has no structural division from the chancel, 32 ft. by 19 ft., and two modern north vestries, the westernmost containing a stair to the modern west gallery. The walls are of flint rubble coated with cement and have stone dressings. The roof is tiled. The church was made collegiate about 1316.[71a]

The nave was built in the early part of the 12th century and the chancel about the middle of the 14th century; a north chapel and aisle were also erected at this period, but these were subsequently pulled down. The church is now a rectangular building with the two modern vestries on the north side.

In the east wall of the chancel is a 14th-century window of four trefoiled lights with geometrical tracery in the head; it has been much restored. On each side of the window is a tall shallow niche with cinquefoiled arch and crocketed canopy; the sills are supported on grotesque heads. In the north wall is a small and plain stone bracket, perhaps for a light. In the sill of the easternmost window in the south wall is a plain bowl of a piscina. On

---

[42] Close, 2 Hen. VI, m. 15.
[43] Feet of F. Herts. 15 Hen. VI, no. 85.
[44] Chan. Inq. p.m. 33 Hen. VI, no. 25.
[45] P.C.C. 38 Bennett.
[46] Chan. Inq. p.m. (Ser. 2), xlv, 104.
[47] Ibid. 156.
[48] Feet of F. Herts. East. 2 Eliz.; East. 3 Eliz.
[49] Chan. Inq. p.m. (Ser. 2), clxxviii, 15.
[50] Ibid. ccxcviii, 36.
[51] Feet of F. Herts. East. 21 Jas. I; Cussans, op. cit. *Hertford Hund.* 136.
[52] Deeds in possession of Mr. Septimus Croft.
[53] Ibid.; Close, 1651, pt. xxi, no. 28.

[54] *Dict. Nat. Biog.*
[55] Chauncy, op. cit. 284; see Recov. R. Trin. 36 Chas. II, rot. 79.
[56] Cussans, op. cit. *Hertford Hund.* 138.
[57] Chauncy, loc. cit.; see Feet of F. Herts. Trin. 3 Jas. II.
[58] Chauncy, loc. cit.
[59] Clutterbuck, op. cit. ii, 210.
[60] Close, 1 Geo. I, pt. v, no. 3.
[61] Cussans, op. cit. *Hertford Hund.* 109.
[62] See Clutterbuck, loc. cit.; Recov. R. East. 19 Geo. III, rot. 365–6; East. 23 Geo. III, rot. 282; Com. Pleas D. Enr. East. 23 Geo. III, m. 95.
[63] Clutterbuck, loc. cit.

[64] Cussans, loc. cit.
[65] Ibid.; see Feet of F. Herts. Mich. 1 & 2 Geo. IV; Mich. 2 & 3 Geo. IV.
[66] Cussans, loc. cit.
[67] *East Herts. Arch. Soc. Trans.* ii, 24.
[68] See Chan. Inq. p.m. (Ser. 2), clv, 156.
[69] Ibid.
[70] Com. Pleas D. Enr. Trin. 1 Jas. II, m. 15. Peter died in 1701 (see M. I. in church).
[71] Recov. R. Mich. 23 Geo. III, rot. 205.
[71a] Rev. R. S. Mylne, F.S.A., suggests that the present church formed the chancel only of the collegiate church.

STANSTEAD ST. MARGARET'S CHURCH : THE CHANCEL

HERTFORD HUNDRED   STANSTEAD ST. MARGARET'S

the north side of the chancel are two bays of arcading, now buried in the wall; part of one of these columns was recently exposed during a restoration, but was covered up again. The columns were of four engaged shafts separated by a roll moulding, the capitals were moulded; the windows inserted in these bays are modern. In the south wall of the chancel are two 14th-century windows, each of two lights with cusped opening in the head; between them is a blocked 14th-century doorway; a slight break in the wall to the west marks the junction of the 14th-century work with the original 12th-century wall. There is no chancel arch.

On the north side of the nave two bays of the arcade are buried in the wall; the apex of a third, the westernmost arch, is exposed. It is of two wave-moulded orders, and forms the head of the doorway to the gallery; in the built-up arches are inserted a modern window and doorway. In the east end of the south wall is a 14th-century window of two lights with a cusped opening in the head, much restored; a little to the west of it, on the outside, are the jamb stones and round arch of a narrow light, now blocked, of the original 12th-century nave; the arch is cut from a single stone. The south doorway is of 14th-century date with arch of two moulded orders and jambs with hollow moulding between ogees and fillets; parts of the stonework have been renewed. The west window is modern. The nave roof retains three late 15th-century trusses with king-posts and cambered tie-beams. Over the west end is a small modern bellcote.

All the fittings are modern.

Beside the stair to the gallery is a slab with indents of a foliated cross, shields and remains of an illegible inscription; in the chancel is a slab with indents of a half-figure of a priest of 15th-century date. There are several inscribed floor slabs to members of the Lawrence and Cresset families of 17th-century date.

The single bell is by John Briant. The date on it is 'mvcccxx.'

The communion plate consists of two cups, 1808, a paten, 1713, also plate, stand and paten of Sheffield plate.

The registers before 1812 are as follows: (i) baptisms from 1697 to 1784, burials 1706 to 1784, marriages 1703 to 1784; (ii) burials from 1772 to 1800, marriages 1774 to 1800.

ADVOWSON The earliest record of the church occurs in the year 1271 when it was divided between the four heiresses as already mentioned.[72] About 1316 Sir William de Goldington, then lord of the manor, founded a college of a warden and four chaplains who were to celebrate mass at the altar of St. Mary in the church of St. Margaret for the souls of Sir William and of Margaret his wife, their heirs and ancestors, and also for the soul of Robert de Vere Earl of Oxford, his heirs and ancestors. Sir William endowed the college with various lands in Thele, Amwell and Bures Giffard and the advowsons of the churches of Thele and Aldham. Licence to appropriate the church, the revenues of which were said to be insufficient for the support of a rector, was shortly afterwards granted to the college.[73] The college remained on this basis throughout the 14th century, receiving a few other grants of land,[74] but by the beginning of the 15th century it had become exceedingly poor, many of its lands had been alienated, and it consisted of only one priest.[75] Accordingly in 1431 licence was granted for its lands to be alienated to the hospital of St. Mary 'Elsyngspittel' in London, the prior of which was to supply two regular canons for the college of Thele.[76] On the dissolution of the hospital in 1530[77] the rectory of Thele came to the Crown, and from this time it has been a lay donative. In 1536 Henry VIII granted it to Roger Poten, the late prior of the hospital,[78] and in 1539 he granted

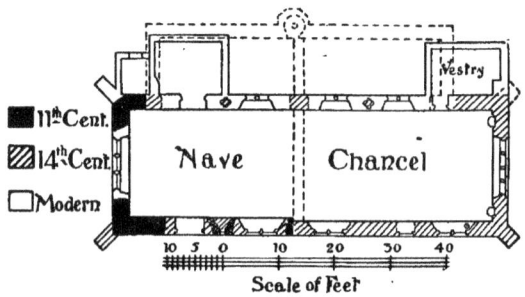

PLAN OF STANSTEAD ST. MARGARET'S CHURCH

the reversion of the rectory with the lands pertaining to Richard Higham.[79] The following year Richard Higham received licence to alienate it to Philip Parys.[80] Philip was knighted at the coronation of Queen Mary in 1553,[81] and died in 1558, when his heir was his kinsman Robert Parys, aged five.[82] In 1561 the advowson was held by Ferdinand Parys of Linton, co. Cambridge, who sold it in that year to Nicholas Baesh.[83] In 1563 Nicholas settled the rectory and mansion-house on his wife Dorothy and their heirs male.[84] Nicholas Baesh died in February 1590–1 and was succeeded by his son Edward,[85] who shortly afterwards sold the rectory to his mother, Dorothy, and her second husband[86] Robert Booth.[87] After Dorothy's death Robert mortgaged the rectory to Sir Reginald Argall, kt., of Higham Hill, co. Essex, into whose hands it finally passed.[8]

---

[72] Feet of F. Herts. 55 Hen. III, no. 637; 2 Edw. I, no. 33; Div. Co. 4 Edw. I, no. 41.
[73] Lond. Epis. Reg. Braybroke, fol. 199–200; Inq. a.q.d. file 118, no. 1; *Cal. Pat.* 1313–17, p. 434.
[74] See *Cal. Pat.* 1348–50, p. 100; 1350–4, p. 433.
[75] Newcourt, *Repertorium*, i, 891–2.

[76] *Cal. Pat.* 1429–36, p. 146. See *V.C.H. Lond.* i, 536–7.
[77] Dugdale, *Mon.* vi, 704.
[78] *L. and P. Hen. VIII*, xiii (1), p. 574.
[79] Ibid. xiv (1), g. 403 (70).
[80] Ibid. xv, g. 831 (35).
[81] Shaw, *Knights of Engl.* ii, 67.
[82] Chan. Inq. p.m. (Ser. 2), cxvi, 7.

[83] Feet of F. Herts. Mich. 3 & 4 Eliz.; Recov. R. Trin. 1561, rot. 405.
[84] Chan. Inq. p.m. (Ser. 2), ccxcix, 104; cf. Pat. 8 Jas. I, pt. xii, no. 16.
[85] Chan. Inq. p.m. (Ser. 2), ccxcix, 104.
[86] *Visit. of Herts.* (Harl. Soc. xxii), 126.
[87] Pat. 8 Jas. I, pt. xii, no. 16.
[88] Ibid.; Chan. Proc. (Ser. 2), bdle. 332, no. 19.

475

A HISTORY OF HERTFORDSHIRE

The history of St. Margaret's rectory after this date becomes very obscure. In 1626 it was held by Dorothy Lacy, widow of Matthew Lacy of Melton Mowbray, co. Leicester, and on her death in that year it passed to her six daughters and co-heirs.[89] They must have sold it, for in 1650 it was held by Sir Thomas Stanley, kt.,[90] but some time afterwards it passed to the lord of the manor of Goldingtons, and in 1684 was held together with that manor by Thomas Westrow.[91] From this date it has descended with the manor[92] (q.v.). In 1899 by an Act of Parliament abolishing all donatives it became presentative.[93]

A meeting-place for Protestant Dissenters in the parish was certified in 1700.[94]

CHARITIES An unknown donor — as stated in the Parliamentary Returns of 1786 — gave land for teaching one child. The land, known as Red Marsh, was sold in 1861 and the proceeds invested in £108 13s. 11d. consols, with the official trustees, subsequently augmented by accumulations to £153 15s. 6d. consols, producing £3 16s. 8d. yearly, which is applied in paying the apprenticeship premium for a poor boy, when there is sufficient money for the purpose.

In 1908 a premium of £25 was paid.

STAPLEFORD

Stapelford (xii cent.); Stapilford-by-Watton (xiii cent.).

Stapleford is a small parish containing about 1,354 acres. Arable land occupies more than half of it, while about one-third consists of permanent grass.1 There is very little woodland, and what there is lies chiefly in the higher ground in the west, where the ground rises to an altitude of from 250 ft. to 300 ft. The River Beane waters the east of the parish; the land here on the west bank is low and liable to floods. The soil is gravel, clay and chalk, on a subsoil of clay and chalk. The church, rectory, schools (built in 1872) and a few cottages stand on the north-east border of the parish on the east side of the River Beane on a by-road to Bengeo, but the principal part of the village lies scattered along the main road from Hertford to Stevenage a little to the west of the church. The road from the village to the church now crosses the River Beane by a bridge, probably on the site of the ford from which the parish takes its name. Stapleford has always been but a small village. In 1334 it is described only as a hamlet,[2] and in 1428 it is said to have contained only nine inhabitants.[3]

Wheat, barley, beans and oats form the principal crops. The nearest railway station is at Hertford, 3½ miles to the south.

MANORS Stapleford appears to have been included in the Domesday Survey in the large area comprised at that date by Bengeo, which encircles it on the east and south. Several of the holdings given under the name of Bengeo cannot be traced there after 1086. One of these was that of Geoffrey de Mandeville. This holding in 1086 was rated at 3 hides and 1 virgate and included a mill,[4] and may apparently be identified with the manor of *STAPLEFORD*, which has always formed part of the honour of Mandeville,[5] and with that honour the overlordship passed on the death of William de Mandeville Earl of Essex without heirs male in 1227 to his sister Maud, widow of Humphrey de Bohun.[6] It descended with the Bohuns[7] until 1373, when on the death of Humphrey de Bohun it passed to his daughter Eleanor wife of Thomas Duke of Gloucester.[8] Edmund Earl of Stafford,[9] husband of her daughter Anne, died seised of it in 1403,[10] and after his death there is no further record of the overlordship.

In 1192 John le Moyne, apparently tenant in fee of Stapleford Manor, was holding a knight's fee in Stapleford which he had inherited from his mother.[11] Stapleford remained with this family,[12] whose descent is difficult to trace, until the end of the following century, when John le Moyne granted it to Robert Aguillon. This was before 1278, in which year Robert claimed view of frankpledge in his manor of Stapleford, which he held by the gift of John le Moyne.[13] In 1286 Robert Aguillon died seised of 7½ acres of meadow in Stapleford, 11s. 6d. rent of assize, together with other rents and a water-mill, which he held of John le Moyne by the service of a clove gillyflower.[14] Probably before this date a subfeoffment had been made of the greater part of the manor, this part becoming the manor of Waterford Hall (see below). Isabel, the wife of Hugh Bardolf, was Robert Aguillon's heir,[15] and in 1303 Hugh Bardolf was holding a knight's fee in Stapleford with Anselm Gobion.[16] Bardolf was lord of the neighbouring manor of Watton Woodhall, and after this date the lands in Stapleford were attached as a

AGUILLON. *Gules a fleur de lis argent.*

---

[89] M. I. in church.
[90] Recov. R. Mich. 1650, rot. 36.
[91] Ibid. Trin. 36 Chas. II, rot. 79.
[92] See Feet of F. Herts. Trin. 3 Jas. II; Close, 1 Geo. I, pt. v, no. 3; Recov. R. East. 19 Geo. III, rot. 365–6; East. 23 Geo. III, rot. 282; Com. Pleas D. Enr. East. 23 Geo. III, m. 95; Feet of F. Herts. Mich. 1 & 2 Geo. IV; Mich. 2 & 3 Geo. IV.
[93] *East Herts. Arch. Soc. Trans.* ii, 24.
[94] Urwick, *Nonconf. in Herts.* 552.

[1] Statistics from Bd. of Agric. (1905).
[2] *Cal. Close,* 1330–3, p. 8.
[3] *Feud. Aids,* ii, 456.
[4] *V.C.H. Herts.* i, 331b.
[5] *Plac. de Quo Warr.* (Rec. Com.), 279.
[6] G.E.C. *Complete Peerage,* s.v. Essex.
[7] *Cal. Inq. p.m.* 10–20 *Edw. II,* 272; *Feud. Aids,* ii, 434; Chan. Inq. p.m. 46 Edw. III, no. 10.
[8] Inq. p.m. 21 Ric. II, no. 29; 1 Hen. IV, no. 50.

[9] G.E.C. *Complete Peerage.*
[10] Chan. Inq. p.m. 4 Hen. IV, no. 41.
[11] Pipe R. 4 Ric. I, m. 1 d.
[12] Robert le Moyne is entered in the *Testa de Nevill* as holding a knight's fee of Geoffrey de Mandeville (p. 264), which may be Stapleford.
[13] *Plac. de Quo Warr.* (Rec. Com.), 279.
[14] *Cal. Inq. p.m.* 1–19 *Edw. I,* 361.
[15] Ibid.
[16] *Feud. Aids,* ii, 434.

476

HERTFORD HUNDRED

STAPLEFORD

tenement to the manor of Watton[17] and eventually became merged in it.[18]

The manor of *WATERFORD HALL* was held of the lords of the manor of Stapleford in socage,[19] and was evidently formed from that manor as mentioned above. At the beginning of the 14th century Waterford was held by Geoffrey de la Lee, who is found holding property in Stapleford in 1305, when his houses and goods there were burnt.[20] In 1310 he received a grant of free warren in all his demesne lands of Stapleford and elsewhere,[21] a grant which was confirmed to him and his heirs in 1320.[22] By a fine of 1316 he charged the manor of Waterford with a rent of 10 marks to Robert Baard for the term of his life.[23] He appears to have been succeeded by his son Thomas Lee (de la Lee), whose bailiff and receiver in Stapleford was committed to the Fleet Prison in 1341.[24] Thomas was succeeded by his brother Sir John Lee, kt., who died in 1370, when his lands in Stapleford passed to his son Walter.[25] In 1379 Perceval Symeon, whose interest in the manor was through his wife Joan, probably the widow of Sir John Lee, quitclaimed all right in it to Walter Lee and his son Thomas.[26] Thomas died before his father, and on the latter's death in 1395 his three sisters became his co-heirs.[27] The manor of Waterford fell to

NEWPORT. *Argent a fesse between three crescents sable.*

PARKER, Lord Morley. *Argent a lion passant gules between two bars sable charged with three bezants and in the chief three harts' heads caboshed sable.*

the share of Margery, who married Robert Newport.[28] From her it descended to William Newport, who died seised of the manor in 1434.[29] His heir was his son George,[30] who died in 1474.[31] Waterford Hall afterwards came into the possession of Robert Newport, who died seised of it in 1518, when his lands were inherited by his son John.[32] John Newport died in 1524. His only child Grace, the wife of Henry Parker, son and heir of Henry Lord Morley, was his heir.[33]

Henry Parker died in 1551, and his son and heir Henry Parker succeeded his grandfather as Lord Morley in 1555.[34] In 1564 Lord Morley conveyed the manor of Waterford Hall to Sir John Boteler of Watton Woodhall,[35] who sold it the same year to George Grave, yeoman, who already held it on lease.[36] The sale included all courts, view of frankpledge and free fishery.[37] George Grave held the manor[38] until his death in 1597,[39] when it passed to his son Edward, who died in 1603.[40] His lands were inherited by his son Edward, aged seven years,[41] who in 1619 sold the manor of Waterford Hall to William Reeve, haberdasher.[42] On the death of William Reeve in 1625 it passed to his daughter and heir Margaret, who married George Bromley.[43] George Bromley died at the beginning of the Civil War,[44] and was succeeded by his son George,[45] who had to compound for his estates in 1644,[46] and receiving, as is said, no recompense from Charles II was finally compelled in 1696 to sell Waterford Hall to Thomas Feltham of Ware Westmill, co. Herts.[47]

Thomas Feltham was succeeded by his son John, who was lord of the manor in 1700.[48] From John Feltham the manor passed to Charles Feltham, brewer, of London, whose son Ralph sold the manor in 1743 to Peter Walley and Thomas Sheppard[49] in trust for Thomas Hall.[50] On the death of Thomas the manor descended to his son Humphrey of Manaton, co. Devon, who sold it with the capital messuage and the lands belonging and the fields called Fillies *alias* Phillhouse or Phillhorse Close, the Warren called the Great Warren and the Little Warren, in 1775 to John Kenrick of Berners Street, co. Middlesex.[51] He in 1778 sold it to William Hewlett of the Strand, ironmonger,[52] apparently in trust for Richard Emmott.[53] In 1811 Emmott sold it to Samuel Smith of Watton Woodhall[54] (q.v.). It descended in this family to Mr. Abel Henry Smith, who is the present lord of the manor. The house called Waterford Hall lies east of the main road from Hertford to Stevenage, at the point where it enters the parish of Stapleford, and is partly

---

[17] Chan. Inq. p.m. 3 Edw. III, no. 66; Cal. Inq. p.m. 1–9 Edw. III, 175; Abbrev. Rot. Orig. (Rec. Com.), ii, 44, 326; Close, 50 Edw. III, pt. i, m. 11, &c. In 1378 William Bardolf's lands are called 'the manor of Watton and Stapleford' (Cal. Pat. 1377–81, p. 207).

[18] In the later inquisitions relating to Watton only the advowson of Stapleford is mentioned.

[19] Chan. Inq. p.m. 44 Edw. III (1st nos.), no. 37.

[20] Cal. Pat. 1301–7, pp. 349, 354.

[21] Chart. R. 4 Edw. II, m. 22, no. 65.

[22] Ibid. 13 Edw. II, m. 5, no. 11.

[23] Feet of F. Herts. 9 Edw. II, no. 232.

[24] Cal. Pat. 1340–3, p. 287.

[25] Chan. Inq. p.m. 44 Edw. III (1st nos.), no. 37. See manor of Albury, Edwinstree Hundred.

[26] Close, 2 Ric. II, m. 7 d.; Feet of F. Herts. 2 Ric. II, no. 15.

[27] Berry, Herts. Gen. 74; Morant,

Hist. of Essex, i, 393. Morant quotes an inquisition of 18 Ric. II which is now apparently lost. For the Lees see Albury.

[28] Ibid. See Feet of F. Herts. 8 Hen. IV, no. 42, 59; 9 Hen. IV, no. 60; 11 Hen. IV, no. 82.

[29] Chan. Inq. p.m. 12 Hen. VI, no. 36.

[30] Ibid.

[31] Weever, Anct. Funerall Monuments, 548.

[32] Chan. Inq. p.m. (Ser. 2), xxxiv, 96.

[33] Ibid. xlii, 96.

[34] G.E.C. Complete Peerage, s.v. Morley.

[35] Recov. R. Trin. 1564, rot. 419.

[36] Com. Pleas D. Enr. Mich. 6 & 7 Eliz. m. 9; Feet of F. Herts. Mich. 6 & 7 Eliz.

[37] Com. Pleas D. Enr. Mich. 6 & 7 Eliz. m. 9.

[38] See Feet of F. Herts. Mich. 35 & 36 Eliz.

[39] Chan. Inq. p.m. (Ser. 2), cccxxxv, 12.

[40] Ibid.

[41] Ibid.

[42] Feet of F. Herts. Mich. 17 Jas. I; see Chan. Proc. (Ser. 2), bdle. 323, no. 22.

[43] Chan. Inq. p.m. (Ser. 2), ccccxlviii, 115; Visit. of Herts. (Harl. Soc. xxii), 34.

[44] Cussans, op. cit. Hertford Hund. 27.

[45] See Recov. R. Mich. 26 Chas. II, rot. 291; Feet of F. Herts. Trin. 29 Chas. II; Hil. 30 & 31 Chas. II; Trin. 2 Will. and Mary.

[46] See Cal. Com. for Comp. ii, 847.

[47] Chauncy, Hist. and Antiq. of Herts. 270.

[48] Ibid.

[49] Close, 17 Geo. II, pt. xiv, no. 17.

[50] Com. Pleas D. Enr. Hil. 15 Geo. III, m. 159.

[51] Ibid.

[52] Ibid. Trin. 19 Geo. III, m. 147.

[53] See Clutterbuck, Hist. o Herts. ii, 215.

[54] Ibid.

in Stapleford and partly in Bengeo. It is a small brick house of c. 1600, two stories in height with a floor in the roof. On plan the house consists of a large entrance hall, out of which a passage has been taken in modern times, with a central newel stair, contained within a projection at its north-west corner. There is a single room on the west side of the hall, and on the east a low two-storied office wing. The beams supporting the first floor have interesting leaf chamfer-stops of renaissance character, and the central newel of the stairs terminates above with a well-carved baluster finial. The original door-frames survive in many cases and their chamfers have leaf-stops of similar character to those of the beams. Externally the western end-gable has moulded brick kneelers. The original window openings have for the most part been enlarged and sash frames inserted. Those in the west wall have been blocked. Sufficient traces survive to show that they were low and mullioned and had moulded labels. On the north side of the house is a fine chimney stack surmounted by a pair of diagonal shafts with capitals and bases of moulded brick.

The manor of GOBIONS (Gybeouns, Gobyons, xiv cent.) like the manor of Stapleford (q.v.) must have originally been part of Bengeo. It is probable that it was derived from one of the numerous holdings of Geoffrey de Bech in that place in 1086.[55] With Eastwick it came into the possession of the Clares, and by the marriage of Emma daughter of Baldwin de Clare with Hugh Wake the overlordship passed to the Wakes.[56] It descended with the Wakes and Holands until 1408,[57] when Edmund de Holand Earl of Kent died without issue. It was inherited by his sister and co-heir Eleanor Countess of Salisbury.[58] Her daughter Alice carried it in marriage to Richard Nevill, afterwards Earl of Salisbury, and it descended to their granddaughter Isabel, who married George Duke of Clarence.[59] In 1499 his son Edward Earl of Warwick and of Salisbury was executed for high treason,[60] and the overlordship escheated to the Crown.

The earliest known tenant in fee of the manor of Gobions is William Loreng, who was holding half a hide of land in Stapleford of Baldwin Wake in 1282.[61] A John Loreng was holding land in Stapleford in 1295,[62] but the manor appears shortly afterwards to have been acquired by Henry Gobion, who was holding half a knight's fee in Stapleford in 1303.[63] There was also an Anselm Gobion holding part of a fee there at the same date.[64] This family held the manor for over a century and gave it its name, but very few records of them exist. The manor appears to have come to William Gobion, whose son William was holding it in 1389.[65] He was then in financial difficulties and had to raise money on his manor of Stapleford.[66] In 1390 he conveyed the manor to Simon de Burgh and William Ashwell.[67] It was sold by trustees in 1412 to John Perient,[68] whose son John was assessed for William Gobion's fee in Stapleford in 1428.[69] By 1444.[70] Gobions had descended to Edmund Perient, who died seised of it in 1474.[71] His son Thomas succeeded him,[72] and held the manor till his death in 1539, when it passed to his son Thomas,[73] on whom he had settled it in tail-male.[74] Thomas Perient died in 1546, and, as he had four daughters but no son, Gobions passed by terms of the settlement to his brother's family,[75] and in 1597 was held by his nephew [76] George Perient, who in that year conveyed it to Richard and Nicholas Boteler and others,[77] evidently in trust for Sir Philip Boteler,[78] lord of the manor of Woodhall in Watton. From this time Gobions has descended with that manor (q.v.), the present owner being Mr. Abel Henry Smith. The farm-house called Gobions lies in the north-west part of the parish, about a mile west of Stapleford village.

The earliest record of the manor of PATCHENDEN (Pachyndon, xv cent.) occurs in 1376, when it was held by Sir Walter Lee, kt., lord of the manor of Waterford Hall.[79] It descended with that manor (q.v.) until 1564, when Sir John Boteler, kt., sold the manor of Waterford Hall, but retained Patchenden in his own hands. Sir John was lord also of the manor of Woodhall in Watton, and from this time Patchenden has descended with that manor (q.v.). The present owner is Mr. Abel Henry Smith. The site of the manor-house of Patchenden, and a farm-house which bears this name, lie north of the church and west of the main road from Hertford to Stevenage shortly before it enters the parish of Watton at Stone.

Clutterbuck has identified lands at 'Waterford' and 'Beorouleam,' given to St. Albans Abbey by Edwin de Cadingdon,[80] with Waterford in Stapleford, but there is little doubt that the former of these places is Watford on the western side of the county, and the latter refers to other lands in Cashio Hundred. A later grant to St. Albans, however, by Agnes Fay and Ralph her son of the old mill of Stapleford with the adjacent pond, the marsh on each side of the river, and 60 acres of land which was confirmed to the monks by Henry II and Edward IV [81] possibly refers to a property called BULLS MILL alias BENWICK HALL.[82] In 1532 the manor of Benwick Hall was held of the abbey by Charles Bull, and there was a water-mill attached to it.[83] Charles Bull died seised of the manor, and it descended to his son Richard Bull, who held it until his death in 1585, at which time the water-mill was called Bull's Mill.

---

[55] V.C.H. Herts. i, 334.
[56] Red Bk. of Exch. (Rolls Ser.), ii, 505.
[57] Cal. Inq. p.m. 1–19 Edw. I, 262; Feud. Aids, ii, 434; Chan. Inq. p.m. 23 Edw. III, no. 75; 26 Edw. III, no. 54; 2 Ric. II, no. 57; 20 Ric. II, no. 30; G.E.C. Complete Peerage, s.v. Wake.
[58] Chan. Inq. p.m. 7 Hen. VI, no. 57.
[59] Ibid.; Chan. Inq. p.m. (Ser. 2), xxviii, 71; G.E.C. op. cit. s.v. Salisbury.
[60] Chan. Inq. p.m. (Ser. 2), xxviii, 71; G.E.C. loc. cit.
[61] Cal. Inq. p.m. 1–19 Edw. I, 262.
[62] Cal. Close, 1288–96, p. 448.

[63] Feud. Aids, ii, 434.
[64] Ibid.
[65] Close, 12 Ric. II, m. 22 d., 20 d.
[66] Ibid.
[67] Feet of F. Herts. East. 13 Ric. II, no. 113; see Close, 13 Ric. II, pt. ii, m. 22, 24 d., 22 d.
[68] Close, 14 Hen. IV, m. 8, 11, 13; 1 Hen. V, m. 19, 18 d.
[69] Feud. Aids, ii, 450; see Digswell in Broadwater Hundred.
[70] See Feet of F. Herts. Mich. 23 Hen. VI, no. 125.
[71] Chan. Inq. p.m. (Ser. 2), iv, 367.
[72] Ibid.

[73] Ibid. lxiii, 61.
[74] Ibid. lxxiii, 89.   [75] Ibid.
[76] See Visit. of Herts. 156.
[77] Recov. R. East. 1597, rot. 31.
[78] See Ct. of Wards, Feod. Surv. no. 17.
[79] Close, 50 Edw. III, pt. ii, m. 9, 12, 13.
[80] Clutterbuck, op. cit. i, App. 5; Dugdale, Mon. iii, 219.
[81] Ibid.
[82] Benwick or Benwith is an alternative name for the River Beane; cf. Ct. of Wards, Feod. Surv. no. 17; Sess. R. (Herts. Co. Rec.), ii, 175.
[83] Chan. Inq. p.m. (Ser. 2), lxi, 78.

Richard Bull left Benwick Hall to his wife Alice for life with remainder to his son Henry Bull.[83a] Towards the end of the 17th century George Goldesborough held Benwick Hall,[84] and in 1698 it was in the possession of Edward Goldesborough, who conveyed it to Elisha Burgess and Richard Edwards.[85] After this date its descent is lost for a time, but in 1779 it was the property of Elizabeth Willson, widow.[86] In 1784 William Willson and his wife Mary conveyed it to Richard Emmott,[87] lord of the manor of Waterford Hall. This sale included free fishing in the water of Stapleford. In 1803 Richard Emmott pulled down the house called Benwick Hall to erect a dog kennel.[88] It was then described as being 'a complete handsome strong brick house.'[89] Its exact site is difficult to determine, but it probably stood near Bull's Mill. Some old apple trees here suggest the site of the orchard of the hall.[90] Besides the general right of commons Benwick Hall had attached to it 2 several acres in Netherfield Common and a strip of 2 acres in Brocket's Bush.[91] Between 1795 and 1803 Thomas Blore, the well-known topographer, resided at Benwick Hall for several years. He collected a vast mass of material referring to the topography and antiquities of this county, which was afterwards used by Clutterbuck in his history.[92]

A manor to which one or two references occur, which lay partly in Stapleford and partly in Bengeo and Hertford, is the manor of *RUSSELLS*. This in 1750 was in the possession of William Willson and his wife Elizabeth, who were holding in the right of Elizabeth.[93] Elizabeth Willson, widow, and William Willson, junior, suffered a recovery of this manor with that of Stapleford in 1779,[94] and William Willson conveyed it to Richard Emmott in 1784.[95]

CHURCH The church of ST. MARY THE VIRGIN stands a little to the east of the village. It consists of chancel 19 ft. by 14 ft. 6 in., large south vestry 19 ft. 6 in. by 16 ft., nave 52 ft. by 19 ft., north transept 15 ft. by 12 ft. 6 in., and north porch, over which is a tower; all the dimensions are internal. The walls are of flint rubble covered with cement with stone dressings; the roofs are tiled.

The eastern part of the nave was built in the 12th century, and perhaps the chancel also. In the early part of the 16th century the chancel arch was rebuilt, the church re-roofed and new windows inserted. In 1874 about 20 ft. was added to the west end of the nave, a north transept and south vestry built, and a north porch with tower and timber spire above erected. The window of three cinquefoiled lights in the east wall of the chancel is modern. In the north wall is a modern blocked doorway, and a blocked window of 18th-century character outside, but within are the jambs and arch of an earlier window, possibly of the 13th century. In the south wall is a modern door to the vestry. The two-centred chancel arch is of two chamfered orders with jambs of the same section; the capitals are moulded; it is of early 16th-century date.

In the north wall of the nave is a modern arch to the transept, and in the modern extension of the

STAPLEFORD CHURCH: NORTH DOORWAY

nave is a single-light window. The north doorway is of mid-12th-century date, and has a semicircular arch of two orders, the outer having a vertical cheveron moulding, the inner a horizontal cheveron; the jambs have circular engaged shafts and capitals carved with leaf ornaments; the bases are moulded; the doorway is in a good state of preservation. The east end of the south wall has a thickness of about

---

[83a] Chan. Inq. p.m. (Ser. 2), ccxi, 188.
[84] *East Herts. Arch. Soc. Trans.* iv, 100.
[85] Feet of F. Herts. Hil. 9 Will. III; *Sess. R.* (Herts. Co. Rec.), ii, 8.
[86] Recov. R. East. 19 Geo. III, rot. 297.
[87] Feet of F. Herts. East. 24 Geo. III.
[88] *East Herts. Arch. Soc. Trans.* loc. cit.
[89] Ibid.
[90] Ibid.
[91] Ibid.
[92] *Dict. Nat. Biog.*
[93] Feet of F. Herts. Trin. 24 & 25 Geo. II. The manor is mentioned much earlier (see Chan. Inq. p.m. [Ser. 2], ccxi, 188), but the owner is not mentioned.
[94] Recov. R. East. 19 Geo. III, rot. 297.
[95] Feet of F. Herts. East. 24 Geo. III.

A HISTORY OF HERTFORDSHIRE

4 ft., which probably marks the position of the former rood-stair. To the west of this is a window of two cinquefoiled lights with tracery under a four-centred head; it is of mid-15th-century date and has been much repaired. In the upper part are some fragments of old glass of the same period. The other windows in the south wall are modern. The roof of the eastern part of the nave retains the 16th-century king-post trusses and timbers; the rafters are plastered underneath.

There are two bells in the modern open timber belfry, but they bear no mark or date.

The communion plate consists of cup and cover paten, 1712 (the paten had a new rim put on in 1824), another paten, 1822, and a modern plated flagon.

The registers before 1812 are as follows: (i) baptisms, burials and marriages from 1578 to 1670; (ii) baptisms and burials from 1671 to 1746, marriages 1671 to 1747; (iii) baptisms from 1747 to 1812, burials 1748 to 1812; (iv) marriages from 1755 to 1812.

ADVOWSON The earliest record of a church in Stapleford occurs in 1285,[96] when the patronage was in the hands of the lord of the manor, Robert Aguillon.[97] Through his daughter and heir Isabel it came to the Bardolfs and descended with the manor of Watton until the middle of the 16th century.[98] In 1550 John Brown died seised of Watton Manor and the advowson of Stapleford,[99] but soon afterwards they appear to have become separated. Edmund Hynde was holding the advowson in 1573.[100] In 1625 Sir William Sherard of Stapleford presented, in 1634 Oliver Harvey, in 1664 Arthur Spark of Hertford, and in 1677 Martha Williams, widow.[1] The advowson then came to Thomas Winford of Lincoln's Inn,[2] who was created a baronet in 1702 with special remainder—failing his own issue—to that of his brother Henry Winford.[3] He died the same year and was succeeded by his nephew Thomas Cookes Winford, who presented in 1717, 1723 and 1731.[4] He died childless in January 1743.[5] His widow survived him and left the advowson of Stapleford by her will of 1751 in trust for her niece Elizabeth Milward.[6] In 1755 Elizabeth Milward sold it to Anne Deane, widow, of Witchampton, co. Dorset,[7] who presented in 1756.[8] She left it by will to her nephew Robert Pargeter,[9] from whom it descended to his son Robert Thomas Deane Pargeter,[10] who sold it in 1794 to the Rev. Archibald Stevenson, rector of Littleham, co. Devon.[11] The following year the Rev. Archibald Stevenson sold the advowson to Robert Hamilton of Leman Street, Goodman's Fields.[12] In 1798 it was purchased by Paul Bendfield of Watton Woodhall,[13] who was declared bankrupt the same year,[14] and in 1804 Benjamin Brooks, who had apparently bought the advowson from him, presented.[15] In 1816 George Vansittart of Bisham Abbey, co. Berks., acquired the advowson,[16] which he sold in 1819 to Samuel Smith,[17] who held the manor of Waterford Hall (q.v.), and from this time the advowson has descended with the manor.

CHARITIES In 1674 Philip Boteler by his will gave 40s. yearly to the poor, issuing out of a field called Church Field; 20s. thereof to be distributed on St. Thomas's Day and 20s. on Good Friday. There are usually six recipients at each distribution.

TEWIN

Tewinge (xi cent.); Thewinge, Tywyng (xiii cent.); Tewinge, Tuyng (xvi cent.).

The parish of Tewin has an area of 2,694 acres, of which 1,305 acres are arable land and 537 acres permanent grass.[1] The valley of the Maran or Mimram crosses the centre of the parish from west to east. The ground there is about 170 ft. above the ordnance datum, and rises to the south to 266 ft. and towards the north to 400 ft. The main road from Hitchin to Hertford runs parallel to the river, and to the north of this on the high ground the village is situated, connected with it by a branch road. The village of Tewin is in two parts, the most southerly portion, known as Lower Green, being grouped round a triangular green where three roads meet. On the west side of the green is the parish room, and on the south are the post office and the school. The cottages surrounding the green are of the 18th and 19th centuries. The Rose and Crown Inn is a small brick building of mid-18th-century date retaining internally some plain panelling. The rectory and church are situated still further south towards the river. The rectory is a brick house of 18th-century date. On the east side is part of a former house which dates from the 17th century; it is timber-framed and covered with plaster; part of the chimney stack is original; the roofs are tiled. There is some 17th-century panelling in one of the upper rooms, and in the kitchen is a wide fireplace with a recess on one side. Adjoining the house is a 17th-century barn, timber-framed and weather-boarded, the roof of which is thatched. The stable, which is built of timber and brick, appears to date from the same period. The other portion of the village, known as Upper Green, lies a short distance north of the main part, where the road forks to

---

[96] Clutterbuck (Hist. of Herts. ii, 217) says that the Prior and convent of St. Catherine, Lincoln, presented in 1229, but this must have been to the church of Stapleford in Lincolnshire.
[97] Cal. Inq. p.m. 1–19 Edw. I, 360.
[98] See references under the manors of Stapleford and Watton.
[99] Chan. Inq. p.m. (Ser. 2), xciii, 80. By this date the manor of Stapleford (q.v.) was included in the manor of Watton.
[100] Feet of F. Herts. Trin. 15 Eliz.

[1] Clutterbuck, loc. cit.; Inst. Bks. (P.R.O.).
[2] Clutterbuck, loc. cit.
[3] G.E.C. Complete Baronetage, iv, 187.
[4] Inst. Bks. (P.R.O.).
[5] G.E.C. loc. cit.
[6] Ibid.; see Com. Pleas D. Enr. East. 29 Geo. II, m. 24.
[7] Ibid.
[8] Inst. Bks. (P.R.O.).
[9] Com. Pleas D. Enr. Mich. 36 Geo. III, m. 76; Inst. Bks. 1780, 1784, 1790.

[10] Com. Pleas D. Enr. Mich. 36 Geo. III, m. 76.
[11] Ibid. Trin. 34 Geo. III, m. 2; Inst. Bks. 1794.
[12] Com. Pleas D. Enr. Mich. 36 Geo. III, m. 76; Inst. Bks. 1797.
[13] Clutterbuck, loc. cit.
[14] Cussans, op. cit. Broadwater Hund. 170.
[15] Inst. Bks. P.R.O.
[16] Clutterbuck, loc. cit.
[17] Com. Pleas D. Enr. 59 Geo. III, m. 87.

[1] Statistics from Bd. of Agric. (1905).

HERTFORD HUNDRED

right and left. That to the left leads to Burnham Green (in Datchworth), while the right-hand road leads past Tewin Hill to Queenhoo Hall, the residence of Sir Clement Lloyd Hill, K.C.B., K.C.M.G., M.P , in the north-east of the parish.

To the south of the village at Archer's Green the river is fordable. Further east a new bridge has lately replaced the old wooden one which carried the path leading to Marden Hill, now the residence of Sir Henry J. Lowndes Graham, M.A., K.C.B., and Lady Margaret Graham.

A road also turns south from the main road to Attimore Hall, in the south-west of the parish. Tewinbury, a farm-house rebuilt of brick in the first half of the 19th century, lies a short distance south of the church. Tewin Water, lying further to the west and surrounded by a park, is the residence of Mr. Otto Beit.

The subsoil of the parish is chiefly chalk, with a little London Clay and Woolwich and Reading Beds in the north. There are many disused chalk-pits in the parish and an old sand-pit not far from the rectory.

The nearest railway station is Welwyn, 2 miles north-west, on the Great Northern main line.

Place-names which occur in Tewin are Muspratts, Westlie Wood, Post Lane, Gore Croft, Wadling, Swannell Grove, Punchehed Coppyes, Phipkins Mare, Bushylees, Rayfield and the Bratches.

MANORS In the time of King Edward the Confessor TEWIN was held by Aldene, a thegn of the king. After the Conquest, according to the statement of Aldene himself, King William regranted the manor to him and his mother ' for the soul of his son Richard.'[3] This was William's second son, ' who was cut off in the New Forest by a sudden and mysterious stroke while the wearied stag was fleeing for its life before him.'[3] Peter de Valognes the sheriff, however, maintained in 1086 that he held the manor of the gift of the king, and Aldene is recorded as holding it of him. It was then assessed at 5½ hides.[4]

The overlordship of Tewin descended in the Valognes family, and, being apportioned about 1240 to the youngest of the co-heirs Isabel Comyn, followed the descent of the manor of Sacombe in Broadwater Hundred[5] (q.v.).

By 1166 the lands of Aldene had become divided into two half-fees held respectively by Godfrey and Brian de Tewin.[6] Godfrey de Tewin's half-fee, which seems to be the manor of Tewin, descended to his son Richard before 1211,[7] and to Godfrey de Tewin, son of Richard,[8] by 1246.[9] This Godfrey de Tewin granted his lands or a part of them to Alexander de Swereford, baron of the Exchequer and treasurer of St. Paul's, apparently that he might grant them to the Prior and convent of St. Bartholomew, Smithfield. Godfrey confirmed them to the prior upon the death of Alexander,[10] and died leaving two sons, John, who was mesne lord of the manor in 1279 [11] and left a widow Amabel, and Guy, to whom the lands held by Amabel in dower reverted at her death.[12] This mesne overlordship seems to have died out on the death of Guy, for in 1303 the half-fee was held immediately of John Comyn by John Godefrei, Prior of St. Bartholomew, Roger de Louth, John de la Penne, and John the chaplain (Capellanus).[13] In 1347 the portion of Roger de Louth was conveyed to the prior by Richard de Burton and Roger de Creton.[14] In 1428 the half-fee was held by the prior and his coparceners.[15]

The manor of Tewin was entered among the possessions of the monastery in 1540, the farm of it amounting to £20.[16] Upon the dissolution of the priory in that year the manor was granted for life to Robert Fuller, the late prior,[17] who evidently did not long survive, for in 1544 it was granted in fee to John Cock of Broxbourne.[18] John, however, in the same year conveyed Tewin to his brother-in-law Thomas Wrothe and Mary his wife.[19] Sir Thomas Wrothe died in 1572–3, leaving the manor to his widow Mary for life, with successive remainders to his son Robert and his younger sons. Robert died in 1606, having settled Tewin upon his son Robert upon his marriage with Mary daughter of Robert Lord Sydney of Penshurst.[20] Robert the younger was succeeded before 1617 by John Wrothe,[21] who sold the manor in 1620 to Beckingham Butler.[22] The latter mortgaged the capital messuage in 1622 to John Manyngham, who died in the same year, leaving a son Richard.[23] The Butlers are said to have conveyed the manor soon after to Richard Hale, who sold it to William second Earl of Salisbury.[24] From the latter it descended to his younger son William, who was holding it with his son Robert in 1687.[25] Robert's son William [26] sold Tewin to James Fleet, who was in possession in 1728 [27] and died in 1733.[28] He left the manor and capital messuage of Tewin Water, which he had 'repaired and beautyfyed' (after the death of his wife), to his great-nephew John Bull, with remainder to his brothers.[29] In 1746 the manor was held by Edmund Bull,[30] presumably one of these brothers. Later the reversion of the manor was sold to George third Earl Cowper,[31] in whose family it has since remained,[32] Katrine Cecilia Countess Cowper, widow of the seventh earl, being the present lady of the manor.

WROTHE. *Argent a bend sable with three lions' heads rased argent having golden crowns.*

---

[3] V.C.H. Herts. i, 338.
[3] Ibid. 298. [4] Ibid. 338.
[5] Red Bk. of Exch. (Rolls Ser.), i, 361 ; Feud. Aids, ii, 434 ; Inq. a.q.d. file 283, no. 4.
[6] Red Bk. of Exch. (Rolls Ser.), i, 361.
[7] Abbrev. Plac. (Rec. Com.), 81.
[8] Chart. R. 6 Ric. II, no. 7.
[9] Feet of F. Herts. 31 Hen. III, no. 329 ; Testa de Nevill (Rec. Com.), 271b.
[10] Feet of F. Herts. 31 Hen. III, no. 329 ; Plac. de Quo Warr. (Rec. Com.), 279 ; Assize R. 325.

[11] Feet of F. Herts. 7 Edw. I, no. 74.
[12] Anct. D. (P.R.O.), A 1065.
[13] Feud. Aids, ii, 434.
[14] Inq. a.q.d. file 283, no. 4.
[15] Feud. Aids, ii, 450.
[16] Dugdale, Mon. vi, 297.
[17] L. and P. Hen. VIII, xvi, 715.
[18] Ibid. xix (1), g. 80 (48).
[19] Ibid. 507, g. 812 (114).
[20] Chan. Inq. p.m. (Ser. 2), ccxcix, 87.
[21] Feet of F. Herts. Trin. 15 Jas. I.
[22] Recov. R. Mich. 18 Jas. I, rot. 99 ; Feet of F. Herts. Trin. 18 Jas. I.

[23] Chan. Inq. p.m. (Ser. 2), cccxcix, 137.
[24] Clutterbuck, Hist. of Herts. ii, 221.
[25] Feet of F. Div. Co. Trin. 3 Jas. II.
[26] Ibid. Herts. Hil. 9 Anne.
[27] Salmon, Hist. of Herts. 49.
[28] Clutterbuck, op. cit. ii, 230, quoting monumental inscription.
[29] P.C.C. 149 Price.
[30] Feet of F. Div. Co. Trin. 19 & 20 Geo. II.
[31] Clutterbuck, op. cit. ii, 221.
[32] Cussans, op. cit. Hertford Hund. 16.

A HISTORY OF HERTFORDSHIRE

In 1278 the Prior of St. Bartholomew, Smithfield, claimed in Tewin, as in his other lands, sac and soc, thol and theam, flemenesfrith, frithsoken, mundbriche, miskennig, utlop (utlagh?), wesgeldethef and hamsoken in breach of the peace, arson and bloodshed. He also claimed to be quit of tolls, sheriff's aid and shire and hundred courts, and to have view of frankpledge.[33] In 1287 he claimed and was allowed utfangentheof, infangentheof, flemenesfrith, gallows, amendment of the assize of bread and ale, and view of frankpledge.[34] Court leet and view of frankpledge were included in the grant to John Cock in 1544.[35] In 1086 there was one mill in Tewin,[36] which was later given with the manor to St. Bartholomew, Smithfield.[37] In 1368 two are mentioned, perhaps both under the same roof, for they were called 'la Solo.'[38] They were granted with the manor to John Cock in 1544.[39] The mill, which was on the River Mimram, was pulled down in 1911.

The half-fee held of Robert de Valognes in 1166 by Brian de Tewin[40] presumably descended to his son Ralph before 1211.[41] Later it seems to have been held by Eudo de Hameley.[42] If this is the half-fee in Tewin which afterwards appears among the possessions of Aymer de Valence,[43] it must have been assigned by Henry de Maule, co-heir of the Valognes barony, to Agnes de Valence with the manor of Hertingfordbury. After the death of Aymer de Valence this half-fee was assigned in 1326 to David de Strabolgi and his wife Joan,[44] niece and co-heir of Aymer de Valence. David de Strabolgi, grandson of the above, died seised of it in 1375, leaving no male heirs.[45] Some time before 1323 this estate had been given to the priory of St. Mary at Little Wymondley,[46] who held it of Aymer de Valence and the Strabolgis. It remained in the possession of Wymondley until the middle of the 16th century, and in 1520 was leased by them for fifty years to Roger Wrenne, a weaver of Tewin, and Christine his wife.[47] At the dissolution of the priory the reversion of this lease was granted to James Needham,[48] together with the site of the priory. In 1537–8 the value of the property was £3 17s. 4d.[49]

A quarter-fee in Tewin, which again may represent the holding of Brian de Tewin, was held in 1303 by Robert de Kersebroc.[50] It had perhaps been previously possessed by John de Kersebroc, who is mentioned in Tewin at the beginning of the 13th century.[51] Robert de Kersebroc had a son Henry who was living in 1331,[52] but nothing more is known of his family.

In the 14th century another manor of Tewin appears which was held of the lords of Walkern (Broadwater Hundred). This in 1365 was divided between Elizabeth the wife of William Chelmersford[53] and Joan the wife of John Cook,[54] and by them was granted to John Spendlove and Joan his wife for the term of Joan's life.[55] In 1377 the reversion of the manor after the death of Joan was conveyed by trustees to the Prior and convent of St. Bartholomew, Smithfield,[56] and appears in their possession as a quarter-fee in 1428.[57] It presumably became united with the main manor of Tewin already in their hands.

The manor of MARDEN (Muridene, Meryden, Merden) was probably identical with the land at 'Cyrictiwa' or Tewin which was held about 1050 by Tova, widow of Wihtric. Tova at that time made an agreement with Leofstan, Abbot of St. Albans, by which she and her son Godwin were to hold the land for their lives, paying yearly to the abbot at the feast of St. Peter ad Vincula (1 August) one sextar, 32 ounces of honey, and that after the death of both the monastery of St. Albans was to take possession 'without contradiction.'[58] It remained with St. Albans[59] until 1529, when it came to the Crown by the conviction of Thomas Wolsey Cardinal of York, then Abbot of St. Albans, under the Statute of Praemunire.[60] He was, however, pardoned in 1530 and his possessions restored.[61] The abbey was surrendered in 1539, and in 1540 the manor of Marden was granted to William Cavendish and Margaret his wife.[62] Later it came into the possession of Edward North, whose son Edward succeeded his father in 1606.[63] Edward the younger died in 1653.[64] His son Hugh, who built a house at Marden Hill,[65] left two daughters—Mary, who married Arthur Sparke, and Sarah, who married Marmaduke Rawdon.[66] These sisters, who were holding the manor in 1672,[67] are said to have sold it to Edmund Field, after which it was acquired by Edward Warren, who was holding it in 1700,[68] and whose son Richard succeeded before 1728.[69] The latter died in 1768 and was succeeded by his son Arthur,[70] who is said to have sold Marden in 1785 to Robert Macky,[71] who was holding it with his wife Elizabeth in 1810.[72] He sold it soon after to Richard Flower,[73] from whom it was acquired in 1817 by Claude George Thornton.[74] The latter died in 1866 and his son George Smith Thornton in 1867, when Marden came to Godfrey Henry Thornton, son of the last-named, who was holding it in 1877.[75] It has since been acquired by the Earls Cowper, the Countess Cowper being the present owner.

The reputed manor of QUEENHOO HALL (Queenhawe, Quenehagh) lay partly in the parish of

---

[33] Plac. de Quo Warr. (Rec. Com.), 279.
[34] Assize R. 325.
[35] Pat. 35 Hen. VIII, pt. x, m. 18.
[36] V.C.H. Herts. i, 338.
[37] Feet of F. Herts. 7 Edw. I, no. 79.
[38] Campb. MSS. viii, 16.
[39] Pat. 35 Hen. VIII, pt. x, m. 18.
[40] Red Bk. of Exch. (Rolls Ser.), i, 361.
[41] Abbrev. Plac. (Rec. Com.), 81.
[42] Testa de Nevill (Rec. Com.), 271b.
[43] Chan. Inq. p.m. 17 Edw. II, no. 75.
[44] Cal. Close, 1323–7, p. 447; Chan. Inq. p.m. 1 Edw. III, no. 85.
[45] G.E.C. Complete Peerage; Chan. Inq. p.m. 14 Ric. II, no. 139b.
Chan. Inq. p.m. 17 Edw. II, no. 75.
[47] L. and P. Hen. VIII, xiii (1), g. 887 (13).
[48] Ibid.; see Little Wymondley.
[49] Dugdale, Mon. vi, 555.
[50] Feud. Aids, ii, 434.
[51] Anct. D. (P.R.O.), A 5873.
[52] Wrottesley, Ped. from Plea R. 13.
[53] Feet of F. Herts. 39 Edw. III, no. 548.
[54] Ibid. 49 Edw. III, no. 662.
[55] Ibid. 47 Edw. III, no. 651.
[56] Inq. a.q.d. file 390, no. 16.
[57] Feud. Aids, ii, 450.
[58] Matt. Paris, Chron. Maj. (Rolls Ser.), vi, 29.
[59] Dugdale, op. cit. ii, 252.
[60] Misc. Bks. (Aug. Off.), cclxxiv.
[61] Dugdale, op. cit. ii, 207.
[62] L. and P. Hen. VIII, xv, g. 282 (108).
[63] Chan. Inq. p.m. (Ser. 2), ccxcviii, 80.
[64] Clutterbuck, op. cit. ii, 228, quoting monumental inscription.
[65] Chauncy, Hist. of Herts. 276.
[66] Ibid.
[67] Feet of F. Herts. Mich. 24 Chas. II.
[68] Chauncy, op. cit.
[69] Salmon, op. cit. 49.
[70] Clutterbuck, op. cit. ii, 229, quoting monumental inscription; Recov. R. Hil. 9 Geo. III, rot. 30; Feet of F. Herts. East. 16 Geo. III.
[71] Clutterbuck, op. cit. ii, 224.
[72] Feet of F. Herts. Mich. 50 Geo. III.
[73] Clutterbuck, loc. cit. The date of conveyance here given is 1809, but this must be at least a year too early.
[74] Ibid.
[75] Cussans, op. cit. Hertford Hund. 13.

Tewin: Queenhoo Hall from the South-west

Tewin: Queenhoo Hall from the North-west

Bramfield in Cashio Hundred and perhaps originally formed part of the manor of Bramfield. There is no mention of the tenure until 1609, when it was said to be held of the king as of his castle of Hertford by fealty in socage.[76]

The first mention of Queenhoo occurs in 1223–4, when William Kilvington of Stebenhithe surrendered to Richard Hamme of Havering all right in the lordship called 'Queenhawe.'[77] Before 1281 it had come into the possession of Ralph de Ardern and Catherine his wife, for in that year they granted 9 marks rent in Queenhoo 'of their own fee' to Westminster Abbey.[78] This rent, held of the abbey, came soon after into the hands of the Goldingtons and descended with the manor of Thele.[79] Lands in Queenhoo were held at the beginning of the 13th century by Geoffrey de la Lee, who received a grant of free warren there in 1310,[80] and in 1376 Walter de la Lee granted 'land called Quynehawes' to Richard Ravensere and others.[81] These lands were, perhaps, only appurtenances of the neighbouring manor of Waterford held by this family.

In 1502 the manor of Queenhoo was conveyed by Henry Hammys and Elizabeth his wife to Sir Reginald Bray and others.[82] Sir Reginald died before 1510, and his lands descended to his niece Margery wife of Sir William Sandys, afterwards Lord Sandys.[83] In that year Margery and her husband were holding Queenhoo together with Reginald's widow.[84] In 1536, however, Margery and Lord Sandys conveyed it to John Malt,[85] merchant tailor of London, who died before 1552, leaving two daughters and co-heirs. One of these, Bridget, the wife of John Scutte, sold her moiety in that year to John Forster,[86] who died seised of it in 1558.[87] His son and heir Humphrey conveyed it in 1567 to Edward Skegges.[88] The other moiety of Queenhoo came into the possession of Sir Edward Bray and Mary his wife, who was probably the other daughter of John Malt. In 1569 they conveyed it also to Edward Skegges,[89] who thus became possessed of the whole manor. Joan Skegges, his widow,[90] and John Mathew, apparently her son by another husband,[91] sold it in 1584 to John Smyth. His son and successor James leased it in 1589 to Aphabell Partriche, goldsmith of London, for thirty years at a yearly rent of £21. Aphabell sold his interest to Julian Cotton in trust for Henry Butler, a younger son of Henry Butler of Bramfield, to whom James Smyth had sold the reversion of the property.[92] Sir Henry Butler died seised of it in 1609 and was succeeded by his son John[93] first Lord Butler of Brantfield (Bramfield). John Butler's lands passed to his son William,[94] an idiot, whose heirs were his five sisters, Audrey Lady Dunsmore, Lady Eleanor Drake, Jane Duchess of Marlborough (afterwards wife of William Ashburnham), Olive Porter, and Anne Countess of Newport, and Thomas Howard, his nephew, son of a sixth sister.[95] In 1637 the manor was divided among the six claimants[96] and remained so at least until 1668,[97] but eventually the whole estate was vested in the descendants of Audrey, the elder sister, who married Francis Lord Dunsmore, in 1644 created Earl of Chichester.[98] Their daughter married George Villiers Viscount Grandison, who was holding the whole of Queenhoo in 1684.[99] His grandson John Earl Grandison was holding it in 1728.[100] Later it came with Bramfield (q.v.) to the Smith family of Watton Woodhall. Mr. Abel Henry Smith is the present owner.

Queenhoo Hall stands on high ground about a mile and a half north-east of Tewin Church, commanding extensive views over the valley towards the south. It is a small house of red brick, very little altered, and there are no indications that it has ever been larger. It was built probably about 1550 or a little later, possibly by Edward Skegges. The principal front faces south-east and is about 57 ft. in length. At either end is a small rectangular projecting bay, with gable over, carried up to the same height as the wide main gables; the bays therefore stand well above the eaves of the main roof. The lower story of the south-western bay acts as a porch, through which access is gained to the parlour, now the drawing-room. The main entrance is a little out of the centre of the south-east front and has a straight brick lintel resting on a heavy oak door-frame. Each bay is finished at the top with a gable, having a moulded saddle-back coping of brick, with brick finials at the apex and base of the gable. These finials have circular moulded bases, with a brick or terra-cotta shaft above, cut with a honeycomb pattern. All the windows have moulded mullions covered with cement, those on the two lower stories having transoms. The roofs are tiled. There are three chimney-stacks on the back wall, all being finished with square detached shafts of brick, set diagonally, without any moulded work, and apparently dating from the first half of the 17th century. Between the upper floor windows in the principal front and in the lower parts of the end gables is a diamond-pattern ornament formed in blue bricks, similar to that on the front of Dean Incent's school at Berkhampstead, a building erected in 1544. An old brick wall surrounds the small garden in front of the house.

Hanging on the front and back walls were two cast-lead sundials, now removed, which were evidently not in their original positions. The dial at the back was circular, about 12 in. diameter, with the sun's face surrounded by rays in the centre, a very extended nose acting as the gnomon, the hours in Roman numerals round the margin, and at the top the date 1812 inscribed under what appears to be 'welcome sunshine. synce 12.' The sundial on the front

---

[76] Chan. Inq. p.m. (Ser. 2), cccviii, 113.
[77] Close, 8 Hen. III, m. 34, 35.
[78] Cal. Pat. 1272–81, p. 446.
[79] Chan. Inq. p.m. 12 Edw. II, no. 52; 32 Edw. III, no. 38; Mins. Accts. bdle. 1118, no. 11.
[80] Cal. Chart. R. 1300–26, p. 138.
[81] Close, 50 Edw. III, pt. ii, m. 13.
[82] Feet of F. Herts. Hil. 17 Hen. VII
[83] Ibid. Mich. 2 Hen. VIII.
[84] Ibid.
[85] Ibid. Mich. 28 Hen. VIII.
[86] Ibid. East. 6 Edw. VI.
[87] Chan. Inq. p.m. (Ser. 2), cxviii, 64.
[88] Feet of F. Herts. Mich. 9 & 10 Eliz.
[89] Ibid. Trin. 11 Eliz.
[90] See V.C.H. Herts. ii, 344.
[91] Chan. Proc. (Ser. 2), bdle. 234, no. 6.
[92] Ibid.
[93] Chan. Inq. p.m. (Ser. 2), cccviii, 113.
[94] Visit. Herts. (Harl. Soc. xxii), 112.
[95] Ct. of Wards, Feod. Surv. no. 17.
[96] Feet of F. Div. Co. Hil. 1658;

Herts. Mich. 16 Chas. II; Div. Co. East. 17 Chas. II. Ralph, step-uncle and male heir of William Butler, is referred to as 'Ralph Butler of Queenhoo Hoo' (Cal. S. P. Dom. 1628–9, p. 566), but seems to have been merely a resident there.
[97] Feet of F. Herts. East. 20 Chas. II.
[98] G.E.C. Complete Peerage.
[99] Feet of F. Herts. Hil. 35 & 36 Chas. II.
[100] Salmon, Hist. of Herts. 49.

measured about 18 in. by 14 in.; at the top was a representation of a coach and horses, below which was the inscription 'Time is flying, the coach is going,' and another, now indecipherable.

The main entrance door opens into a passage leading through the house to the staircase at the back. To the left of the passage, through a modern partition, is the old hall, now used as the dining room, and beyond the hall is the drawing room or parlour; both these rooms have the original stone fireplaces with moulded jambs and four-centred arches. A modern external doorway with a small porch has been formed on the north-west side of the hall. To the right of the central passage is the kitchen, with a fireplace 8 ft. 6 in. wide. There is an old external door to the kitchen and a cellar under the kitchen. The stair occupies a projecting wing at the back of the building, and is an interesting

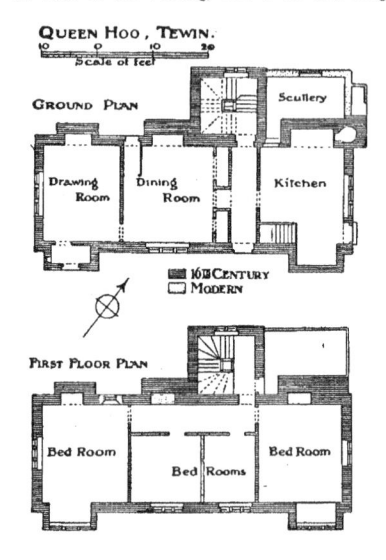

QUEEN HOO, TEWIN.

GROUND PLAN

FIRST FLOOR PLAN

example of the transition between the old solid newel stair and the later open well stair. The staircase is about 15 ft. square internally, the stair being constructed of oak, with winders at the angles. The central newel is 2 ft. 6 in. square, but instead of being solid is constructed of timber framing, the interior being divided vertically into a series of small cupboards or recesses at different heights of the stair. The first floor had originally three rooms corresponding to those below, and the fireplaces are over those on the ground floor; a modern passage has, however, been formed out of the room over the hall to connect the two end rooms, but the built-up fireplace still remains in the passage. The bedroom over the kitchen has an old stone fireplace, with a four-centred moulded arch very similar to many others in the county, but in this instance all the mouldings follow the arch, the square above being marked by a slight sinking, and instead of the usual ornamented stop there is a single splay. The old fireplaces in the passage and in the bedroom over the drawing room are of the more usual type, having the inner and the outer mouldings and the ornamental stops. They have, however, the peculiarity that instead of the arches being formed by four segments of circles the mouldings are in four straight lines, the usual proportions of a four-centred arch being retained. Over the last-named fireplace is an interesting distemper painting very much decayed. The picture is about 5 ft. 6 in. wide by 3 ft. 3 in. high and appears to represent a scene in some mystery play. On the right is a large figure of a man clothed in a long tunic, above which is a shorter garment like an ephod, and a girdle is tied about his waist. He has a mitre on his head and in his right hand he holds a censer. Opposite to him and kneeling with folded arms is another large figure with flowing beard, wearing a long robe over which is a cape and round his neck is a lace collar. Behind him are a number of indistinct figures, some wearing ruffs round their necks. Between the two principal figures, but further in the background, is a standing figure apparently naked except for a cloth round his loins; his right hand rests on what looks like a large viola. Behind him is a smaller figure with arms extended above his head. There are traces of colour remaining, chiefly greens and reds.

The capital messuage called *TEWIN HOUSE* was bought from the lord of the manor of Tewin by Thomas Montford, who died possessed of it in 1632, leaving a son John.[1] The latter died in 1651,[2] leaving a widow Joan and three daughters, Anne Layfield, Elizabeth Francklyn and Mary Rainsford.[3] Tewin House is said to have come to Mary Rainsford, who sold it to Sir George Butler.[4] At the death of the latter without issue in 1657[5] the property passed to his nephew Francis Butler,[6] who died in 1690, leaving two daughters, to the elder of whom, Isabella wife of Charles Hutchinson, Tewin House came. Isabella and Charles are said to have sold it to William Gore, at whose death in 1709 it passed to his grandson Henry.[7] Henry Gore conveyed it in 1715 to Gen. the Hon. Joseph Sabine,[8] who died in 1739 and was succeeded by his eldest son John.[9] John's son Joseph Sabine is said to have sold Tewin House to Robert Macky, who sold it to Charles Schreiber.[10] He died possessed of it in 1800, and his son William sold it in 1804 to Peter fifth Earl Cowper.[11] The earl pulled down the house, and the property became absorbed in the main manor.

Free fishery in the river of Tewin was included with the property.[12]

Two and a half hides in 'Theunge' held before and after the Conquest by the Abbot of Westminster are entered under Broadwater Hundred in the Domesday Survey, but seem to have been in this

---

[1] Chan. Inq. p.m. (Ser. 2), ccclxviii, 41.
[2] Cussans, op. cit. *Hertford Hund.* 17, quoting monumental inscription.
[3] Feet of F. Div. Co. Hil. 1651.
[4] Cussans, op. cit. *Hertford Hund.* 12.
[5] Ibid. 18, quoting monumental inscription. [6] Close, 2 Geo. I, pt. viii, no. 5.
[7] Cussans, loc. cit.
[8] Close, 2 Geo. II, pt. viii, no. 5.
[9] Cussans, op. cit. *Hertford Hund.* 21, quoting monumental inscription.
[10] Clutterbuck, op. cit. ii, 224.
[11] Ibid.
[12] Chan. Inq. p.m. (Ser. 2), ccclxviii, 41; Feet of F. Div. Co. Hil. 1651; Close, 2 Geo. I, pt. viii, no. 5.

TEWIN: LEAD SUNDIAL FORMERLY AT QUEENHOO HALL

TEWIN: LEAD SUNDIAL FORMERLY AT QUEENHOO HALL

parish. They formed a 'hardwich' of Stevenage,[13] to which manor they remained appurtenant.[14]

The church of ST. PETER stands about a quarter of a mile to the south-west of the village; it consists of a chancel 28 ft. 6 in. by 15 ft., north vestry, nave 36 ft. 6 in. by 18 ft. 6 in., south aisle 38 ft. 6 in. by 7 ft., south porch 12 ft. by 9 ft., and west tower 12 ft. square. These measurements are all internal. The walls are built of flint rubble covered with cement and have stone dressings; the roofs are tiled.

The nave, and probably the chancel, were erected in the late 11th or early 12th century. Early in the 13th century the chancel was altered and possibly partly rebuilt; later in the same century or early in the next the south aisle was added and clearstory windows inserted above the arcade.[15] The west tower was built about the end of the 15th century and the south porch added in the 16th century. The church was repaired during the 19th century, and in 1902 it was carefully restored; a number of ancient features were brought to light and a modern vestry was erected on the north side of the chancel.

In the east wall of the chancel is a late 15th-century window of three cinquefoiled lights, most of which is of modern stonework. The only opening in the north wall is the modern doorway to the vestry. In the south wall are two early 13th-century lancet windows, with deeply splayed jambs and chamfered rear-arch. West of these is a window of two cinquefoiled lights with a square head, of late 15th-century date. At the east end of the wall is a piscina with splayed edge and pointed trefoiled head, with a scroll-moulded label, probably of late 13th or early 14th-century date; the projecting basin has been cut away. In the same wall is a blocked modern doorway. The chancel arch is of two chamfered orders which die upon splayed jambs.

In the north wall of the nave close to the east end is the eastern jamb and part of the rear-arch of an early blocked window; west of this are two late 15th-century windows, each of two cinquefoiled lights under a square head; between them, high up in the wall, is a narrow round-headed window, now blocked, of late 11th or early 12th-century date. The north doorway with single splayed edge is almost entirely of modern stonework; above is a small square window probably inserted to light a gallery erected in 1864, now removed. On the south side of the nave is an arcade of three bays of the 13th century. The arches are of two splayed orders; the piers are octagonal with moulded capitals and damaged bases; the chamfers have been omitted on the south side of the western bay of the arcade. On the north-west face of the eastern pier is a small pointed niche with a hole in the stonework underneath, probably for a bracket to support a light. Over the piers are two blocked clearstory windows contemporary with the arcade; they are circular on the outside and have round-headed rear arches inside; they are now covered by the aisle roof, which is a continuation of that over the nave. In the south wall of the aisle are two 13th-century lancet windows; in the east wall is a window of two cinquefoiled lights under a square head, of late 15th-century date. The south doorway has moulded jambs and arch of mid-14th-century date, with label stops outside much defaced. On the eastern jamb of the doorway outside is an oval recess, formerly the stoup. The south porch is built of timber and brick and is of 16th-century date; a large 18th-century monument to General Joseph Sabine, Governor of Gibraltar, and one of Marlborough's generals, blocks the original entrance, but a modern doorway has been opened in the west side.

In the west wall of the aisle, high up, is a small square-headed window of 18th-century date. The nave roof is of 15th-century date; the rafters are plastered underneath, but the moulded tie-beams are exposed.

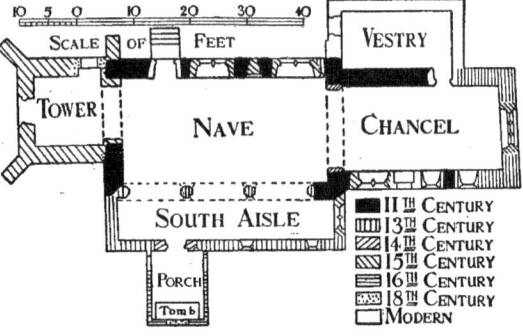

PLAN OF TEWIN CHURCH

11TH CENTURY
13TH CENTURY
14TH CENTURY
15TH CENTURY
16TH CENTURY
18TH CENTURY
MODERN

The west tower is of two stages, with diagonal buttresses on the west; the centre line of the tower is about 3 ft. 6 in. north of that of the nave, the two north walls being nearly in a line. The tower arch is of two splayed orders which die upon square jambs. The west doorway is modern. In the north wall is a blocked 18th-century door. Over the west doorway is a single pointed light. The belfry stage has windows of two cinquefoiled lights; the parapet is embattled, and above is a low timber spire.

The communion table appears to be of late 17th-century date. In the chancel is a slab of Purbeck marble inscribed 'Orate pro anima Walteri de Louthe.' He was instituted rector of the church early in the 14th century. There are several 17th-century slabs in the chancel to members of the Butler family of Queenhoo Hall. In the south aisle is a small brass, with figure, inscription and arms, to Thomas Pygott, 1610.

There are five bells: the treble by John Briant, 1799; the second, third, fourth and fifth by Anthony

[13] V.C.H. Herts. i, 312b.
[14] Ct. R. portf. 178, no. 51–4.
[15] It may be for this alteration that an indulgence was granted in 1315 for the construction or repair of the church of Tewin (Linc. Epis. Reg. Dalderby, fol. 317).

Chandler, 1673, the third being inscribed 'Praise the Lord. A.C. 1673.'

The communion plate consists of a cup of 1564, paten, 1662, large paten, 1687, flagon, 1688, and almsdish, 1702.

The registers before 1812 are as follows : (i) baptisms and marriages from 1559 to 1718, burials 1559 to 1717; (ii) baptisms and burials from 1718 to 1812, marriages from 1719 to 1727; (iii) marriages from 1755 to 1775; (iv) marriages from 1776 to 1812.

ADVOWSON The advowson belonged to the lord of the manor from an early date. In 1211 it was the subject of a dispute between Richard son of Godfrey de Tewin and Ralph son of Brian de Tewin, respective holders of half-fees in Tewin. Richard was successful in making good his claim.[16] Before 1246 the advowson was given by Alexander de Swereford to the monastery of St. Bartholomew, Smithfield, and was confirmed to them by Godfrey and his son John.[17] It remained with St. Bartholomew until its dissolution, and afterwards continued with the manor of Tewin[18] until it was sold by John Wrothe and others to Thomas Montford of Tewin House, who died seised of it in 1632.[19] It then continued in the possession of the owners of Tewin House and came to Sir Francis Butler,[20] whose daughter Isabella Hutchinson sold it to Jesus College, Cambridge,[21] who presented in 1728,[22] and in whose possession it has since remained.[23] In 1638 the glebe lands amounted to 40 acres.[24]

In 1330 Roger de Louthe alienated in mortmain various lands in the parish of St. Andrew, Hertford, to the Prior and convent of St. Mary, Little Wymondley, to find a chaplain to sing mass daily in the church of Tewin for the good estate of the souls of Roger and Joan his wife and their ancestors.[25]

Meeting-places for Protestant Dissenters in the parish were certified in 1706, 1707 and 1772.[26]

Tewin School[27] : The property *CHARITIES* demised by will of Dr. Yarborough, 1773, for the benefit of the parish clerk and a schoolmaster was sold in 1896 in consideration of a yearly rent-charge of £8 8s. upon property in Bishop's Hatfield, which was redeemed in 1904 by the transfer to the official trustees of £336 consols, of which £252 consols was set aside as the endowment of ' Dr. Yarborough's Educational Foundation,' producing £6 6s. yearly, and £84 consols, producing £2 2s. for the parish clerk. In 1783 Lady Cathcart by deed gave £166 13s. 4d. East India 3 per cent. annuities for providing coals for the school. These endowments are now attached to the endowed school founded under the will of Henry Cowper in 1838, which is endowed with government stocks producing £62 a year or thereabouts.

TEWIN CHURCH FROM THE SOUTH-EAST

[16] *Abbrev. Plac.* (Rec. Com.), 81.
[17] Feet of F. Herts. 31 Hen. III, no. 329 ; 7 Edw. I, no. 79 ; Chart. R. 6 Ric. II, no. 7.
[18] *L. and P. Hen. VIII*, xix (1), g. 812 (114) ; g. 80 (48) ; Feet of F. Herts. Trin. 15 Jas. I.
[19] Chan. Inq. p.m. (Ser. 2), ccclxviii, 41.
[20] Bacon, *Liber Regis*, 518 ; Inst. Bks. (P.R.O.).
[21] Salmon, op. cit. 50.
[22] Inst. Bks. (P.R.O.).
[23] Ibid. ; *Clergy List.*
[24] *Herts. Gen. and Antiq.* iii, 337–8.
[25] *Cal. Pat.* 1330–4, p. 17. In the same year he founded a chantry in Hatfield Church.
[26] Urwick, *Nonconf. in Herts.* 556.
[27] *V.C.H. Herts.* ii, 102.

HERTFORD HUNDRED   WORMLEY

In 1610, as stated in the Parliamentary returns of 1786, — Piggott by his will gave a stall in the market-place to the poor. The charity is now represented by £133 6s. 8d. consols with the official trustees, producing £3 6s. 8d. yearly, which is distributed biennially in money doles to about eighty recipients.

Dr. Layfield's Charity, founded by will of the Rev. Charles Layfield, D.D., dated 10 February 1710, for apprenticing in Tewin and four other parishes, is endowed as to this parish with a sum of £273 9s. 3d. consols with the official trustees, producing £6 16s. 8d. yearly. In 1907-8 a premium of £9 was paid for apprenticing.

Charity of Sir Francis Butler.—See under Bishop's Hatfield. This parish is entitled to nominate one poor widow for the benefit of this charity.

In 1748 Margaret Sabine by deed poll gave £200, now represented by £191 5s. consols with the official trustees. The annual dividends, amounting to £4 15s. 4d., are applicable—subject to keeping in repair the tomb of donor's husband—in clothing poor boys. The income is accumulated and applied from time to time in supplying boys with suits of clothes and boots.

Almshouses—as appears from an old parish register, dated in 1717—were built out of the poor's money on the Lower Green, of which £30 was given by will of William Gore and £20 by Dr. Fulk Tudor, the rector. The almshouses were converted into the parish workhouse.

In 1841 Henry Cowper, by his will proved in the P.C.C. 4 January, founded a Sunday Savings Bank, the endowment of which now consists of £1,807 8s. 8d. consols with the official trustees, producing £59 18s. 4d. yearly. The income is applied in augmenting the savings of poor married persons, poor widows or widowers. Subscriptions of not less than 6d. and not more than 2s. a week to be paid every Sunday, the bonus being one-fourth of the amount subscribed.

In 1909 there were thirty-six depositors, the amount deposited was £180 10s., and the bonus paid £45 2s. 6d.

WORMLEY

Wormley (Wurmelea, Wermelai, xi cent.; Wermele, xiii and xvi cent.) is a long, narrow parish stretching east and west and wooded at its western end. On the east it is bounded by the River Lea. The New River flows through the eastern end of the parish, and east of the river and parallel with it is the main road leading from London to Hoddesdon. The parish is 946 acres in area, and the proportion of arable is about one-sixth of the total area.[1] The soil is loam, the subsoil sandy loam, and the chief crops are wheat, oats, barley and roots.

The original settlement lies almost surrounded by Wormley Bury Park, about half a mile off the high road from London to Hoddesdon. It now consists of the church and Wormley Bury, the Manor House, the seat of Mr. Henry North Grant Bushby, J.P. (built by Mr. Bushby in 1908), the Bury Farm, Hill House, occupying the site of an older house called Fernbeds, the rectory and one or two farms and cottages. Wormley Bury is a three-storied brick house with an Ionic portico on the principal or north front, built by Abraham Hume in 1767. It was decorated by Adam and Angelica Kauffmann. Probably at an early date the village migrated to the high road along which it now lies. On the west side of the road is a 17th-century house called the Manor Farm House. It is timber framed, coated with rough-cast, and is of two stories with attics. The public elementary school, which was built in 1864 and enlarged in 1877 and 1899, stands in the village.

West End, a hamlet consisting of a farm (called Manor Farm, but modern) and some cottages, lies about 1 mile to the west of the Manor House. Here is Westlea, the residence of Lady Georgiana Peel.

An inclosure award was made in 1858 and amended in 1859.[2]

WORMLEY MANOR was one of the manors which were granted by Harold son of Godwin to the canons of Waltham Holy Cross.[3] At the time of the Domesday Survey, when it gelded at 5 hides, it was still held by the canons of Waltham. Two other manors are mentioned in the Survey; Wormley, 1½ hides, which Wimund held of Earl Alan and which had been previously held by Alsi, one of Eddeva's men, who could sell it. This land is described as belonging to Cheshunt. The remaining manor, 2¼ hides, was held by Alwin Dodesone of the king. It had been formerly held by Ulward, one of Asgar the Staller's men, who could sell it, and it was sold for 3 marks of gold after King William came. This manor may have been identical with the 2¼ hides in Wormley which were granted to Westminster Abbey by Edward the Confessor,[4] and which are not mentioned amongst the possessions of the abbey in the Survey. The other estate perhaps became absorbed in the Waltham manor, or it may have been attached to the manor of Beaumont Hall in Cheshunt which had appurtenances in Wormley. This manor was held by the monastery of Waltham until the Dissolution. In the reign of Henry II, when the secular canons were expelled by Pope Alexander III, the king granted Wormley with the church to the regulars of the Augustinian order who replaced them, and the grant was confirmed by Richard I.[5] In 1220 the canons of Waltham constructed a conduit for carrying water from Wormley to the monastery.[6] The Quo Warranto returns of 1278 show that the abbots of Waltham, under the charters of Henry II, Richard I and Henry III, claimed the following privileges in Wormley and their other lands in Hertfordshire : sac, soc, thol, theam, infangentheof, utfangentheof, flemenesfrith, grithbriche, forstal, hamsokene, blodwyte, ordeal and oreste, view of frankpledge and return of writs, and liberty from shire and hundred courts and all payments.[7] In 1287 the abbots further claimed in their manor of Wormley gallows and right of assize of bread and ale.[8] For 1 carucate in Wormley the Abbot of Waltham was obliged to

---

[1] Statistics from Bd. of Agric. (1905).
[2] Blue Bk. Incl. Awards.
[3] Dugdale, Mon. Angl. vi, 56.
[4] Cott. MSS. vi, 2. The grant is of doubtful authenticity.
[5] Cart. Antiq. M 2 ; RR 7.
[6] Harl. MS. 391, fol. 1–6, 13–15b.
[7] Plac. de Quo Warr. (Rec. Com.), 283.
[8] Assize R. 325.

487

make three bridges, one in Chaumberleynesholm (in Wormley) and two in Melholm (in Wormley ?).[9] A grant of free warren was made to the convent in 1253.[10]

In 1541 the manor of Wormley, with the advowson of the rectory and parish church, was granted, as part of the possessions of Waltham Holy Cross, to Edward North, Treasurer of the Court of Augmentations,[11] who in the same year received licence to alienate it to William Woodliffe, mercer, of London.[12] William Woodliffe had two daughters: Ann, who married John Purvey, and Angelette,[13] who married Walter Tooke.[14] On the death of their father in 1548 they appear to have been co-heirs, Angelette receiving Purvey the manor in 1553.[15] John Purvey, who survived his wife, died in 1583, and at his death was seised of the manor-house of Wormley with right of alternate presentation to the church.[16] He was succeeded by his son William Purvey, who appears to have been in possession of the whole manor by 1597.[17] William Purvey died without issue in 1617, having settled the manor and manor-house of Wormley, with right of alternate presentation to the rectory, on his wife Dorothy, sister of Edward Lord Denny, who survived him.[18] Ralph Tooke, son and heir of Angelette, is mentioned in the inquisition as his heir. Dorothy Purvey re-married, her second husband being George Purefoy of Wadley, Berks.,[19] and in 1621 the manor and advowson of Wormley passed to John Tooke, brother of Ralph,[20] and his heirs.[21] Courts were being held in the name of Ralph and John Tooke in 1633. On the death of John Tooke in 1634 the manor was left to his brother Thomas Tooke for sixty years for performance of John's will, with remainder to the male heirs of Ralph Tooke.[22] Ralph died without issue,[23] and the manor appears then to have gone to his remaining brothers, George and Thomas Tooke.[23a] George Tooke sold his moiety of the manor to Richard Woollaston, who died in 1691, leaving a son John, who survived him for a year only. John Woollaston was succeeded by his eldest son Richard.[24] In 1669 Thomas Tooke devised his moiety of the manor to trustees for the payment of his debts, and after his death it was sold successively to William Hastings, Elizabeth Reynolds, and, finally, to Thomas Winford, who bought it in 1684 or earlier.[25] In 1692 Thomas Winford conveyed to Richard Woollaston his moiety of the manor,[26] with the exception of the manor-house of Wormley Bury, with appurtenances, which he sold to William Wallis of Holborn in 1697.[27] In this way Richard Woollaston became lord of the whole manor.

Richard Woollaston conveyed the manor to William Fellowes, whose eldest son Coulston Fellowes was the possessor in 1728[28]; from the latter the manor passed in 1733 by sale to John Deane,[29] who in 1739 sold it to Alexander Hume. The latter, dying in 1765, left the manor to his youngest brother, Abraham Hume,[30] who was made a baronet in 1769[31] and was succeeded in 1772 by his son Abraham Hume.[32] The second baronet died in 1838, leaving no issue, his two daughters, Amelia Baroness Farnborough and Sophia Baroness Brownlow, having died during their father's lifetime.[33] The manor came to Viscount Alford and the Hon. Charles Henry Cust, children of Lady Brownlow. In 1853 they jointly sold the manor to Henry John Grant, on whose death in 1861 it came to his widow, Mary Grant.[34] In 1880, under the will of Henry John Grant, the manor passed to his cousin Henry Jeffreys Bushby, father of the present lord of the manor, Mr. Henry North Grant Bushby. The latter, who succeeded his father in 1903, is on the side of his mother Lady Frances, second daughter of Francis sixth Earl of Guildford, the tenth in direct descent from Sir Edward North, to whom the manor was granted by Henry VIII.[35]

BUSHBY of Wormley. *Vair a chief gules with five passion crosses argent therein.*

The manor of *OATES*, which first appears in 1611, was held of the manor of Baas and followed the descent of Broxbourne [36] (q.v.).

The church of *ST. LAWRENCE CHURCH* consists of a chancel 35 ft. by 19 ft., nave 48 ft. by 21 ft., south aisle 47 ft. by 11 ft. 6 in., small vestry and wooden south porch; all the dimensions are internal. The walls are of rubble flint with stone dressings, and are covered with cement all but the aisle; the roofs are tiled. The nave is of early 12th-century date. The chancel, which has undergone extensive alterations and has no old detail, is practically modern. During the 19th century the west wall of the nave was rebuilt and a bellcote erected, the chancel arch was rebuilt and a south aisle and a small vestry added. In 1911 a larger vestry was built on the south of the chancel.

In the east wall of the chancel is a group of three lancet windows; in each of the north and south walls are two lancets. All the windows are modern, as is also the chancel arch.

In the north-east angle of the nave is the doorway, partly blocked, and stair to the former roodloft. In the north wall are two 15th-century windows; one is a single trefoiled light under a square head, the other has two cinquefoiled lights: these windows have been repaired. Further west is a narrow 12th-century window with round head and

---

[9] *Plac. de Quo Warr.* (Rec. Com.), 285.
[10] *Cal. Chart. R.* 1226–57, p. 427.
[11] *L. and P. Hen. VIII*, xvi, g. 503 (50).
[12] Ibid. 878 (50).
[13] Chan. Inq. p.m. (Ser. 2), lxxxvi, 102.
[14] Fine R. 1 Mary, m. 44.
[15] Ibid.
[16] Chan. Inq. p.m. (Ser. 2), cci, 71.
[17] Feet of F. Div. Co. Trin. 39 Eliz.
[18] Chan. Inq. p.m. (Ser. 2), ccclxix, 165.
[19] *Visit. Herts.* (Harl. Soc. xxii), 161.
[20] Ibid. 167.
[21] Feet of F. Herts. Trin. 19 Jas. I.
[22] Chan. Inq. p.m. (Ser. 2), dxv, 83.
[23] *Visit. Herts.* 167.
[23a] Courts were being held in the name of George and Thomas in 1653. In 1661 they were being held by Thomas alone. Ct. R. communicated by Mr. H. N. G. Bushby.
[24] Chauncy, *Hist. Antiq. of Herts.* 292.
[25] *Hist. MSS. Com. Rep.* xi, App. ii, 309.
[26] Close, 2 Anne, pt. viii, no. 35.
[27] Ibid. 8 Will. III, pt. vi, no. 8.
[28] Salmon, *Hist. of Herts.* 14.
[29] Feet of F. Herts. Hil. 7 Geo. II.
[30] Clutterbuck, *Hist. and Antiq. of Herts.* ii, 234.
[31] G.E.C. *Complete Baronetage.*
[32] See Recov. R. East. 33 Geo. III, rot. 157.
[33] G.E.C. *Complete Baronetage.*
[34] Cussans, *Hist. of Herts. Hertford Hund.* 250.
[35] From information supplied by Mr. H. N. Grant Bushby.
[36] Chan. Inq. p.m. (Ser. 2), cccxix, 200; Cussans, loc. cit.

WORMLEY CHURCH FROM THE NORTH-WEST

HERTFORD HUNDRED — WORMLEY

deeply splayed jambs; the splayed sill appears to have been lowered. The north doorway has a round-headed arch of two orders with edge-rolls; the shafts and scalloped capitals are restorations. The window of three cinquefoiled lights in the west wall is modern, as are also the south arcade and aisle. In the south wall have been reset the inner jambs of a 12th-century window and also portions of a single splayed pointed south doorway, which is mainly of 13th-century date. The nave roof retains its 15th-century moulded and embattled tie-beams and other timbers. The hexagonal panelled pulpit is of early 17th-century date.

The font has a large cylindrical bowl of the 12th century; it has four large and four small rectangular panels surrounded by a cable moulding. In the centre of each of the larger panels is a leaf ornament; the smaller are carved with bands of leaf ornament. The upper part of the font has a border of leaves, the base is modern.

Over the communion table is a painting of the 'Last Supper,' attributed to Jacopo Palma; it was presented to the church in 1797 by Sir Abraham Hume, and came from a convent of regular canons in a village near Verona which had been suppressed.[37]

In the chancel is a large marble monument to William Purvey, 1617, and Dorothy his wife, with recumbent effigies; over them is a canopy flanked by pilasters; on the cornice are the arms. On the front of the tomb is the kneeling figure of a lady. There are some 17th-century slabs to members of the Sheere and Tooke families.

In the chancel is a brass to John Cok, yeoman, with figures of the man, the lower part of which is missing, his wife and nine sons. Above is a small representation of the Trinity, and beneath is a strip of brass with trees and a dog pursuing a hare, and a cock. There are remains of a marginal inscription, the date is about 1470. There are also a brass to Edmond Howton, with the figures of his wife Anne, five sons, and part of an inscription, 1479; a brass of a man, his wife, eight sons and four daughters, with shield of arms of Tooke impaling Woodliffe, with no date, but of about 1590; an inscription only to John Cleve, rector of Wormley, died 1404.

The two bells without date or founder's stamp are apparently modern.

The communion plate consists of a flagon, 1625, a pewter almsdish, 1699, a cup and paten, 1873, and another paten.

The registers before 1812 are as follows: (i) baptisms from 1674 to 1783, burials 1676 to 1783, marriages 1685 to 1753; (ii) baptisms from 1783 to 1812; (iii) burials from 1783 to 1812; (iv) marriages from 1754 to 1812.

A meeting-place for Protestant Dissenters in the parish was certified in 1838.[38]

ADVOWSON The church of Wormley with the manor was in the possession of the monks of Waltham Holy Cross in the reign of Henry II,[39] and it appears to have been retained by the monastery until the Dissolution. In 1541 the advowson of the rectory was granted with the manor to Sir Edward North.[40] From this time the advowson followed the descent of the manor until 1853, the representatives of the co-heirs of William Woodliffe exercising alternately the right of presentation.[41] The advowson was not included in the sale of the manor in 1853, but was afterwards sold to Horace James Smith-Bosanquet. He conveyed it in 1881 to Henry Jeffreys Bushby, and it thus became re-united to the manor.[42]

The old chapel or oratory which was known as 'the Chapel of St. Laurence in the Busshe of Wormley' lay apparently in the parish of Cheshunt.[43]

CHARITIES In 1670 Thomas Tooke by his will directed (*inter alia*) that land producing £3 a year should be purchased, the rent to be applied in providing coats, petticoats and stockings for six poorest boys and girls, and the residue to the most aged men and women. The endowment consists of 6 a. 2 r. of land at Cheshunt, let at £18 a year, which is duly applied.

It is stated in the Parliamentary returns of 1786 that an unknown donor gave land for the poor. The property consists of an acre of land now called 'Searangle Corner' in Cheshunt let at £3 a year.

Charities of Richard Tooke and others: By a decree of the Court of Chancery made 5 November 1684 (36 Charles II) in a cause between Thomas Gentle, complainant, and Nicholas Bigg and another, defendants, stating that several sums had been given by several persons to the poor of the parish, it was ordered that an estate at Great Parndon in the county of Essex, containing 15 acres, should be purchased for the use of the poor of Wormley. The land is let at £16 a year.

In 1710 Sir Benjamin Maddox, bart., by deed conveyed to trustees 16 acres of land called Oakells in Codecote upon trust that out of the rents £6 yearly should be paid to the rector of Wormley and the residue be paid to the poor. The land is let at £11 a year. This and the two preceding charities are administered together. In 1909 boots were distributed to eighteen men and twenty-four women, also 90 yards of flannel and 120 yards of calico.

In 1688 Richard Woollaston by a codicil to his will directed that lands to the value of £100 a year should be settled for providing £20 a year for clothing in the parish of Woolmer, £30 a year in the parish of Whitchurch, and £50 a year in six parishes in Leicestershire.

This charity was the subject of proceedings in Chancery at the instance of the Attorney-General against Jonathan Woollaston, the personal representative of John Woollaston, the executor, and others, and in the result, under an order of the Court 26 August 1704, certain lands in the county of Essex were purchased of the value of £100 a year to be applied for the benefit of the parishes referred to and in the like proportions.

The property now consists of freehold land at Latchingdon, Essex, and ground rents in Berlin Road and Bromley Road, Catford, in the metropolitan borough of Lewisham, producing £180 a year or thereabouts.

In 1909–10 the sum of £32 was applied in Wormley in suits, serge, flannel and calico to poor, distressed people.

---

[37] Notes of vestry meeting 9 Aug. 1797, communicated by Mr. Bushby.
[38] Urwick, *Nonconf. in Herts.* 559.
[39] Cart. Antiq. M 2.
[40] L. *and* P. *Hen. VIII*, xvi, 503.
[41] Chan. Inq. p.m. (Ser. 2), ccclxix, 165.
[42] Information from Mr. Bushby.
[43] L. *and* P. *Hen. VIII*, xiii (2), g. 734 (8); Newcourt, *Repert.* i, 912.

A HISTORY OF HERTFORDSHIRE

In 1660 Josiah Berners by his will gave £5 yearly out of Wormley Bury Estate for apprenticing. The sum of £1 is deducted for land tax; the sum of £4 a year and the annual dividends on a sum of £344 3s. 8d. consols, amounting to £8 12s., is applied in apprenticing. In 1909 one premium of £20 was paid.

In 1764 Rebecca Ward by her will bequeathed £150, now represented, with accumulations, by £318 14s. consols, producing £7 19s. 4d. yearly, which is applicable in the distribution of beef on old Michaelmas Day to the poor. About 720 lb. of beef are distributed annually. The two sums of stock are standing in the names of James John Deller and two others, who also hold a sum of £118 13s. 7d. consols, derived under the will of Sir Abraham Hume, proved in 1838. The annual dividends of £2 19s. 4d. are distributed in coal.

In 1613 William Purvey by his will gave £20 yearly to the rector for preaching twenty sermons. The charge is payable out of the manor of Wormley.

The recreation grounds consist of 1 acre acquired under an order of the Inclosure Commissioners, 1871, in exchange for two parcels of land awarded to the churchwardens and overseers in 1858.

In 1880 Mrs. Mary Grant, by her will proved at London 7 December, left £200, less legacy duty, now represented by £181 16s. 4d. consols, with the official trustees, the annual dividends, amounting to £4 10s. 10d., to be applied for the benefit of the schools established in 1863, and for the maintenance therein of the Established Church.

BOROUGH OF HERTFORD[1]

Heortforde, Heorotforda (x cent.); Hertforde (xi cent.); Hurtford (xiii cent.).

The borough of Hertford is situated 2 miles west of the main Cambridge road. From it a road runs north-eastwards to Ware and north-westwards to Watton at Stone. To the west of the town a branch from this road leads to Welwyn and another runs south-westwards to Hatfield, where it joins the Great North Road. The road between Watton and Hertford would seem to be an ancient road from the fact that it forms for a little way the parish boundary. The ford by which the road crossed the Lea was evidently the ford from which Hertford took its name and was presumably a little to the south of the present bridge, the situation of which now causes a deflection in the road.

Hertford is divided by the River Lea into two distinct portions; the principal thoroughfares follow the shape of a large Y, with Fore Street for its main limb running east and west. A small triangle of streets forms its western termination and connects it on the south with Castle Street and on the north with a street known as the 'Wash,' which leading northwards over the river by Mill Bridge takes a westward inclination and joins St. Andrew's Street at Old Cross. Along Fore Street and between it and the Lea the greater part of the town is grouped, the northern portion consisting mainly of the houses which compose St. Andrew's Street, on the south side of which stands the rebuilt church from which it takes its name. All Saints' Church, which is also entirely modern, stands in a large churchyard a little to the south of Fore Street. The castle is situated on the south bank of the River Lea, to the south-west of the town, and gives its name to Castle Street, which skirts the original line of the moat on the south side.

To the north-west of the parish church of All Saints is the old rectory, a plastered half-timber building of the early 17th century. On the front door is the date 1631. The plan is of the H type, but modern alterations have obscured the original arrangement. At the north-east of the churchyard is Hale's Grammar School, a one-storied brick building with an attic floor and tiled roofs, lighted by modern brick-mullioned windows. Worked in nails upon the door is the date 1667; the door itself, however, appears from its style to be contemporary with the school building, which was erected about the year 1617 by Richard Hale of London.[2] The school was amalgamated with Ware Grammar School in 1905, and an increase in the endowment having been made by Earl Cowper a new building was added at the rear to extend the accommodation in 1907. Bayley Hall, situated to the west of the rectory, is now used as the residence of the head master of the grammar school. It is a fine Queen Anne house of three stories and a basement, square on plan, with a large central staircase hall. Much good panelling remains internally; the panelled dado to the stairs is of mahogany with occasional inlaid ornament. The elevations are designed in the dignified manner of the period, with moulded brick string-courses and gauged brick pilasters. A modern addition has been made on the east. To the north-west of the house is a stable building of the same date, the basement of which has a brick vault, supported by a small circular column of the same material.

The Shire Hall, where the assizes and quarter sessions are now held, stands on the north side of Fore Street in the centre of the market-place. By the charter of James I the corporation received the grant of 'a house on the royal waste called the Town Hall,' with a reservation of the right to hold sessions of the peace there.[3] The erection of a new Shire Hall was proposed in 1767,[4] and the present building was completed in 1769.[5] It is a symmetrically planned building of stock brick, from the designs of the brothers Adam.[6] Among the paintings in the Council Chamber are portraits of King William III, George II, Queen Caroline and other members of the royal family, presented by the third Earl Cowper in 1768. The corn exchange and public hall were built on the site of the old Butchers Market in 1857.[7] To the west of the Shire Hall, upon the same side of

---

[1] The bounds of the borough as laid down by the Act of 1832 have been taken as most convenient for arrangement.
[2] V.C.H. Herts. ii, 89. A school called Hertford Grammar School existed in 1557. In an account of Hertford Priory in 1497 is a reference to 26s. 8d. paid for the pension of the scholars. This, however, probably refers to the priory scholars at Oxford.
[3] Pat. 3 Jas. I, pt. iii, m. 8.
[4] Sess. R. (Herts. Co. Rec.), ii, 105.
[5] Ibid. 112.
[6] Ibid. 111.
[7] Cussans, Hist. of Herts. Hertford Hund. 62.

490

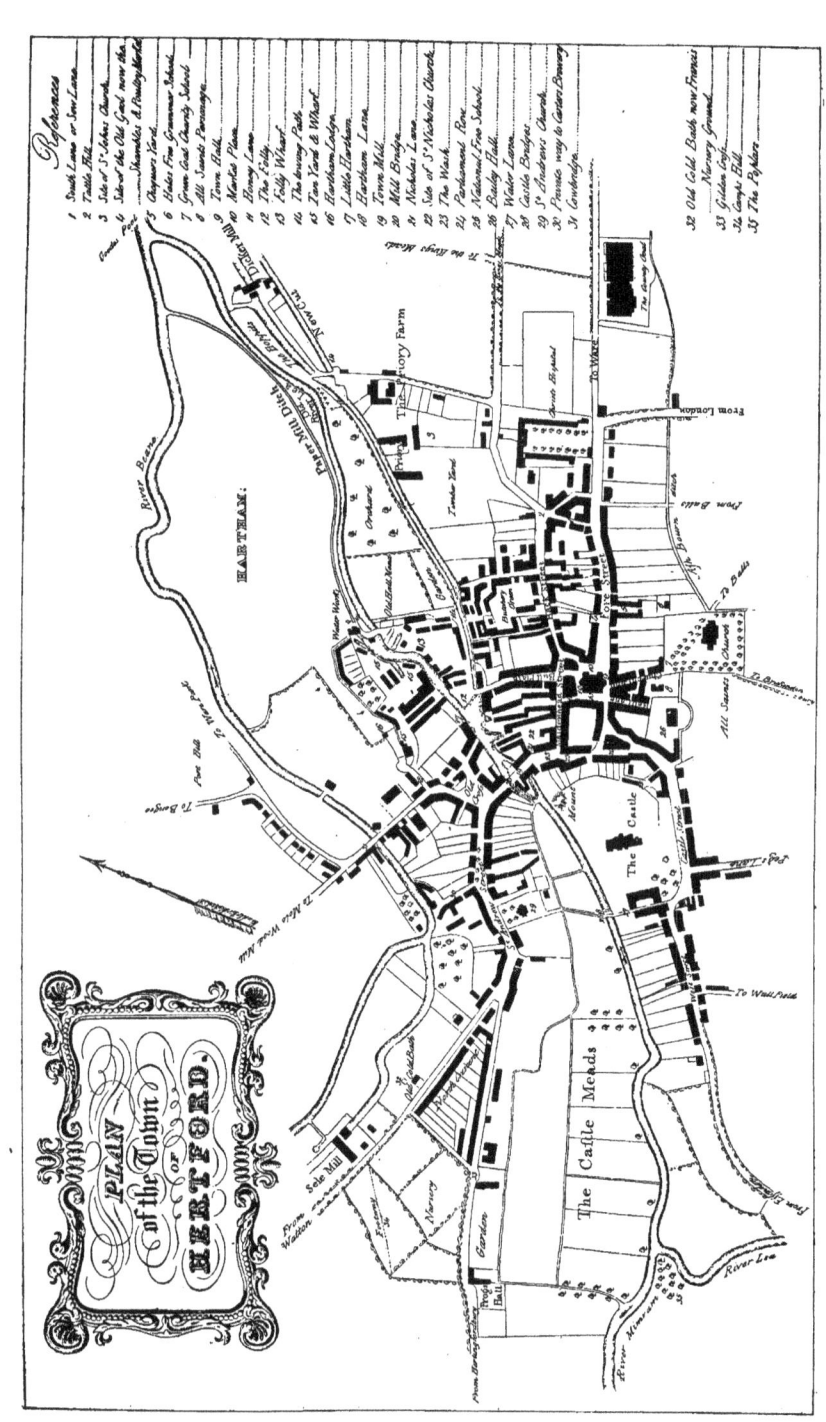

PLAN OF THE TOWN OF HERTFORD.
(*From Lewis Turnor's "History of Hertford"*)

HERTFORD HUNDRED

Fore Street, is an interesting pargeted house of the latter half of the 17th century. It is flush-fronted and of three stories with an attic and tiled roofs. The walls are decorated with well-modelled plaster panels, arranged in three bands, and each having a scroll ornament of acanthus foliage. The window openings have for the most part been enlarged in the 18th century, and the ornament has been much disturbed by subsequent alterations. The ground floor has been given over to shop windows. At the north-east corner of the market-place is the 'White Hart,' an early 17th-century building with 18th-century additions. Of a similar date is the house on the north side now occupied by the Hertfordshire County Council Education Office. On the west side are two good early 18th-century houses with an enriched modillion cornice of wood. The 'Salisbury Arms,' on the south side of Fore Street opposite the Shire Hall, dates from the early 17th century. The buildings are of brick and timber and surround a central courtyard. The front has been rebuilt, but the elevation towards Church Street remains nearly in its original condition. The main staircase, in its lower part, is original. The raking balusters are square moulded and the square newels have pierced finials. On the east side of the Shire Hall, at the corner of the market-place and Fore Street, is a three-storied building of the same date, the upper stories of which are supported at either end by Ionic columns. The whole of the intervening part of the ground stage is occupied by modern shop windows. No. 56, on the south side of Fore Street, a little distance to the eastward, is a gabled half-timber building of the late 16th century. Some original panelling remains internally.

The buildings of the girls' school of Christ's Hospital stand at the west end of Fore Street, which forms the southern boundary of its site. Of the original buildings which were completed in 1689 for use as a preparatory school for boys as well as for girls, only the schoolroom and steward's house adjoining, together with the entrance gateways and portions of the boundary walls, now remain. The buildings as then laid out inclosed a long tree-planted rectangular courtyard with the schoolroom at the north end, the entrance gateway on the south, placed axially with the schoolroom, and a block of ten cottages on either side converted in 1760 into ten wards. The original girls' school block, which faces Fore Street on the west side of the entrance gates, and the head master's house at the south-east of the courtyard were erected after 1766; they are not shown on the plan of Hertford by J. Andrews and M. Wren, published in that year. In 1800 the dining hall adjoining the schoolroom on the west was built. The site was extended westwards to South Street by the purchase in 1897 of the adjoining brewery buildings, together with the site of Brewhouse Lane which divided the two premises,[8] the Blue Boy Inn being, however, left standing at the south-west. On the removal of the boys to Horsham in 1902 and the reservation of the school for the girls only, the old wards were demolished and new buildings planned on modern principles were erected in their place. The schoolroom is a plain building

BOROUGH OF HERTFORD

with a pedimented centre slightly broken forward, lighted by large square-headed windows and crowned by a tiled hipped roof. The south front has been re-faced with red brick to correspond with the new buildings. The interior is quite plain, with a coved plaster ceiling and a later bay on the north side divided by columns from the main room. Over the entrance doorway is a niche containing the oaken figure of a 'blue boy' brought hither from the former school at Ware. The steward's house at the north-east corner of the courtyard indicates the character of the elevations of the wards which have been pulled down. The dining hall to the west of the schoolroom, erected in 1800, is a plain building of stock brick, lighted by large semicircular-headed windows. Like the schoolroom its south front has been re-faced with red brick. Some shields and panelling from the demolished hall of Christ's Hospital in Newgate Street, London, are preserved here. The entrance gateway, with its stone piers, surmounted by leaden figures of 'blue boys,' is of the original date. These figures are known to have been placed in their present position in 1689.[8a] The original girls' school block is a long two-storied building of brick, with a large schoolroom in the centre extending the whole height and surmounted by a pediment. It is lighted on the south front by a large 'Venetian' window, flanked externally by semi-circular-headed niches, each containing an excellently modelled figure of a blue-coat girl. Among the many interesting relics preserved in the buildings is the monument to Thomas Lockington, Treasurer of Christ's Hospital from 1707–16, which was brought here from the church of St. Mary Magdalene, Great Fish Street, destroyed by fire in 1888. In the modern chapel is a fine brass almsbox inscribed 'The Gift of a Governour Sept. 21st 1787.'

In Maidenhead Street, which runs parallel with Fore Street on the north side of it, are some good early 17th-century houses. At the corner of Honey Lane,[8b] which connects Maidenhead Street with the market-place, is the Old Coffee House Inn, a Jacobean building of two stories with an attic. The roof has projecting eaves finished with a plain plaster cove, and between the windows of the upper story are elaborate baluster pilasters. The window openings have all been altered. Next door, in Honey Lane, is the 'Highland Chief,' a much modernized house of the same date. Bull Plain is a short wide street leading northwards from Maidenhead Street to Folly Bridge, containing some 17th and 18th-century work. No. 16 is a brick two-storied house of the latter date, with a wood modillion cornice and moulded brick string-course. Some panelling remains inside. Fronting southwards upon Bull Plain, the back bordering upon the branch of the River Lea which is crossed here by Folly Bridge, is Lombard House,[8c] a plastered building of timber and brick two stories in height, dating from about the year 1600. The front appears to have been rebuilt of brick in the early 18th century, but the back with its five gables, overhanging upper story and wood-mullioned windows remains in its original condition. In the entrance

---

[8] This was formerly called Meeting-house Lane from the fact of the first Nonconformist chapel being in it, the site of which was sold to the authorities of the hospital in the 17th century.

[8a] *Rep. of Royal Com. on Hist. Monum. of Herts.* 114.

[8b] Honey Lane is a corruption of Oson Lane, a variant of Hosen Lane, which with Glove Street was the locality of the glovers and hosiers.

[8c] Formerly called Malloryes from the fact that Robert Mallory lived there temp. Hen. VI and could dispense £10 per annum.

491

A HISTORY OF HERTFORDSHIRE

hall is a carved oak chimney-piece surmounted by the arms and crests of Tooke and Tichborne.[9] In Bull Plain, nearly opposite Lombard House, is a plastered brick mid-17th-century house, now three cottages, with a recessed gabled centre and two projecting wings crowned by bold modillion cornices.

'The Walnuts,' on the south side of Castle Street, is a two-storied 17th-century house, the walls pargeted in plain panels. In Peg's Lane, so named from a W. Pegg who first built there, is a row of framed and weather-boarded cottages of the 18th century. The house attached to the brewery in West Street, as the continuation of Castle Street is called, bears the date on a brick panel 1719, above which are the initials C.I.C. On the south side of West Street is Bridgeman House, a brick building of the first half of the 17th century, two stories in height, with a tiled hipped roof and a large square panelled central stack. The elaborately framed and panelled front door is of original date. The house is now converted into cottages. A door belonging to the premises at the rear of the yard next to no. 17 on the north side of Castle Street bears the date 1654. In Parliament Row, said to be so named from having been occupied by the members of the Court at the time of the Plague, are three plastered half-timbered cottages of the early 17th century. The 'Waggon and Horses' on the east side of Old Cross is a plastered two-storied building, probably of the early 17th century. No. 6 St. Andrews Street is a late 16th-century building of brick and timber rebuilt in the early 18th century. A chimney stack surmounted by two octagonal chimney shafts of brick, one of which is elaborately panelled, is the only detail remaining of the earlier date. At the north-east of St. Andrew's churchyard is a good early 17th-century cottage of brick and half-timber with an oversailing upper story. Opposite the church is a mid-18th-century house with a door-case in the Gothic taste of the Batty Langley school. On the same side of the road a little distance to the east of the church is a very fine brick house of the first quarter of the 18th century, three stories in height, now occupied by the Hertfordshire Imperial Yeomanry. Between the second and third stories is an entablature of gauged and moulded brickwork supported at either end of the elevation by Ionic pilasters. The central doorway and the window of the first floor immediately over are accentuated by entablatures and curved pediments supported by small pilasters of the same order. On the south side of the road, a little further eastward, is a plainer house of the same type and date.

The Roman Catholic church, built in 1860,[10] stands in St. John's Street near the Lea. The Congregational chapel in Cowbridge represents a congregation dating from 1673,[11] but the present building (succeeding one on the same site) dates only from 1862.[12] The Baptist chapel, at the junction of the North and Hertingfordbury roads, was built in 1842, and the Wesleyan Methodist chapel in the Ware Road in 1865.[13] Quakers are found in Hertford from an early date,[14] and though much diminished in numbers have a meeting-house in Railway Street at the present day.

The old county gaol, now superseded by the prison at St. Albans, stood on the south side of the Ware road. At the end of the 12th century there was a gaol at Hertford, entries for the repair of which appear on the Pipe Rolls,[15] but in 1225 a mandate was issued to the sheriff to build a new gaol there.[16] This, however, also seems to have fallen into disuse, for in 1290 the inhabitants of Hertfordshire petitioned for a prison in Hertford,[17] and licence was granted to them to build one there at their own cost on the site of the old one.[18] The castle had evidently been used as a prison, for William de Valence, the governor, opposed the building of the new gaol.[19] The prison stood on the north side of Fore Street on the site of the present corn exchange.[20] At the beginning of the 18th century many complaints were made of its insanitary state and of the prevalence of gaol fever there.[21] After the Act of 1700[22] a proposal was made for the erection of a new building,[23] but the old one was patched up for the time being,[24] and it was not until more than fifty years later that the work was actually begun.[25] The borough prison, which had up to that time occupied a building in Back Street, was then amalgamated with it.[26]

It is impossible to suggest when the site of the town of Hertford was first settled. In 673 an important council was held at 'Heorutford' or 'Herutford,' which has generally been identified with Hertford. The council was held by Theodore, Archbishop of Canterbury, and Bisi, Bishop of the East Angles; there were also present St. Wilfrid of York and other great churchmen. It was the first synod of the united English Church, and dealt with various important matters, such as the date of Easter, the status of the bishops, marriage and divorce, and other points of great moment at the time.[27] Hertford, however, first undoubtedly appears in history

---

[9] William Tooke of Hertford Town, ob. 12 Feb. 1611, married Mary daughter of Nicholas Tichborne of Roydon, co. Essex, ob. 29 Aug. 1611 (*Visit. of Herts.* [Harl. Soc. xxii], 167).
[10] W. F. Andrews, *Hertford during 19th Cent.* 5.
[11] Urwick, *Nonconformity in Herts.* 542.
[12] Andrews, loc. cit.
[13] Ibid.
[14] See Urwick, op. cit. 532.
[15] *Pipe R.* 24 Hen. II (Pipe R. Soc.), 133; 25 Hen. II, 52; see also *Rot. Cur. Reg.* (Rec. Com.), i, 203.
[16] *Rot. Lit. Claus.* (Rec. Com.), ii, 34a.
[17] *Parl. R.* i, 61b.
[18] *Cal. Pat.* 1281–92, p. 473.
[19] *Parl. R.* i, 61b.
[20] Cussans, op. cit. 62.
[21] *Sess. R.* (Herts. Co. Rec.), ii, 69, 95, 104, 129.

[22] An Act to enable justices of the peace to build and repair gaols in their respective counties (Stat. 11 & 12 Will. III, cap. 19).
[23] A warrant was issued for the levying of a rate (*Sess. R.* [Herts. Co. Rec.], ii, 31, 33).
[24] Ibid. 79, 82, 127.
[25] Cussans gives the date as 1776, Gough in his edition of Camden (*Britannia*, i, 344) as 1778. In 1777 the contractor was paid £1,500 (*Sess. R.* [Herts. Co. Rec.], ii, 139). The building was still unfiled in 1790 (ibid. 168).
[26] Cussans, op. cit. 62.
[27] Birch, *Cart. Sax.* i, 49. A doubt as to the identification arises because Wina, Bishop of London, in whose diocese Hertford was then apparently situated, was not present, and, as it seems from the wording of the proceedings that Bisi was presiding with Theodore, it might be expected that 'Heorutford' was in Bisi's diocese of Dunwich, afterwards Norwich. It therefore seems possible that Heorutford may be Hereford (now spelt Hartford) in Huntingdonshire. For the extent of the East Anglian diocese see the diocesan maps in G. Hill's *English Dioceses* and p. 63 of the same work, where it is pointed out that Huntingdonshire may once have been included in it. It may also be noticed that the name Heorutford is capable of other developments besides Hertford. In the neighbouring parish the name was Hereford(ingbury) in the 11th century, and although in this case the name reverted to a form nearer the original one, in another case the Herefordtun of the 10th century has now become Harvington (co. Worcester).

HERTFORD OLD COFFEE HOUSE INN
[Arthur V. Elsden, photo

HERTFORD OLD HOUSES IN BULL PLAIN
[Arthur V. Elsden, photo

HERTFORD HUNDRED

BOROUGH OF HERTFORD

in the 10th century,[28] for some years being brought into a position of prominence as the administrative centre of the district. About 913[29] Edward the Elder, during his campaign against the Danes, established a 'burh' between the Rivers Maran, Beane and Lea. This site formed an important defensible position on the north side of the Lea, with a river protection on three sides.[30] On the completion of the work the king left Hertford for Maldon in Essex in order to superintend the building of the 'burh' at Witham. In the following year, however, some of his force returned to Hertford and 'wrought the burh' on the south side of the Lea,[31] with the object presumably of guarding both sides of the ford. We thus have at Hertford one of those double towns built upon the opposite banks of a river, such as arose at this time at Bedford, Stamford, Buckingham, York and elsewhere. What these 'burhs' were we do not exactly know.[32] At first they may have been purely military stations. They were evidently erected for the purpose of subduing the surrounding country, for it is stated in connexion with the building of Witham and Hertford that 'a good deal of the folk submitted to him [Edward] who were before under the power of Danish men.' From a military post it is only a step for Hertford to have become an administrative centre, to which the county, formed probably in the time of Edgar (957–75), was assigned and from which it took its name.[33] It was probably under the legislation of Edward the Elder limiting trade to boroughs that Hertford became a double market town and a mint town, at which coins were struck from the time of Edward II (975–8) to that of Edward the Confessor (1042–66). It was apparently governed as a royal town by one or more king's reeves,[34] to one of whom, who had a house in the town, there is a reference in the Domesday Survey.[35] By 1086 there was only one borough and one township, but for some time a survival remained of the two settlements in the two market-places, the one on the north side of the Lea at the Old Cross,[36] and that on the south at the market-place round the town hall. The prosperity of the town did not long survive the Conquest. It was off the main line of traffic, which at an early date passed from the Roman Ermine Street to the present north road nearer the Lea, and, although it retained its importance as the administrative centre of the county, its trade diminished.

BOROUGH

The ancient borough, according to the earliest description we have of it, comprised an area in which were about 166 houses belonging to burgesses and about thirty houses held by large neighbouring landowners.[37] The earliest surviving delimitation of the boundary belongs to 1621, when it was set out as follows :—

From a post at the west end of the town in the road to Hertingfordbury at the end of Castlemead to the corner of Scalefield ; then it meets the highway from Hertford to Watton, thence to a post near Papermillgate, and to the north side of the river at the east end of Papermill meade ; thence down the river to Cowbridge ; along the north side to the Lea at the east end of Hartham ; thence along Priory or Hoppitts mead, along the mill stream to Butchery green, thence to Back Street . . . thence to a pile of stones near St. John's churchyard gate, and thence to the high road from Hertford to Ware ; thence to Stonehall Close ; then it turns back to the east stile of All Saints excluding the churchyard, thence to the 'Bell' ; then it bounds on the tenements of the manor of Baylyhall, meets the highway of Castle Street, thence to a post in the street, and to the outermost ditch of the now decayed castle ; along the outside of the ditch to the millstream of Hertford, along Castle Mead and to the post.[35]

The borough thus comprised the whole of the civil parish of All Saints[39] and parts of the parishes of St. John and St. Andrew.[40] This was the area of the borough proper or of burgage tenure, but Hertford as a vill included a large area of surrounding territory. In 1428 the parishes which paid subsidy in the borough were the 'parish of the monks' (St. John), St. Andrew, St. Mary, St. Nicholas, and All Saints with Brickendon Holy Cross.[41] For lay taxation, however, Brickendon and Blakemere (afterwards Panshanger) were assessed separately from the borough.[42] The estate of Waltham Abbey, the 'Liberty of Brickendon,'[43] had belonged to the abbey with high immunities since the 11th century, but the abbey seems to have encroached on the bounds of the borough. It acquired much property in West Street,[44] and apparently drew this district into the Liberty. In 1274 the burgesses claimed that the 'hamlet of West Street had been withdrawn from the borough by the abbot.'[45]

The Abbot of Waltham was responsible also for the blurring of parochial boundaries. In the 12th and 13th centuries he acquired an estate at Rushen (in the parish of Amwell),[46] which became known as Little Amwell. As it entered the abbot's liberty it lost its connexion with Amwell parish, and from the 16th century was regarded as part of All Saints' parish.

---

[28] A settlement like Hertford on an old road does not generally belong to any ancient Saxon type. The more ordinary Teutonic form of settlement would be at Hertingfordbury. It may be noticed that, besides the relation between the two places suggested by their names, the position of Hertingfordbury village, which extends into the parish of St. Andrew, Hertford, may point to a time when Hertingfordbury and Hertford were comprised within one territorial area, in which case Hertingfordbury may have been the original settlement. This would be an argument against Hertford being old enough to be the meeting-place of the council.

[29] *Angl.-Sax. Chron.* (Rolls Ser.), ii, 78. Some historians place the date a little later.

[30] It was off the natural line of road communication to London and the north,

but, what was perhaps more important at the time, it commanded the water communication by the rivers just mentioned with the fertile lands to the west.

[31] *Angl.-Sax. Chron.* (Rolls Ser.), ii, 78.

[32] Allcroft, *Earthworks of England,* 383.

[33] *V.C.H. Herts.* i, 295 ; ii, 2. The county is first mentioned in the *Angl.-Sax. Chron.* in 1011.

[34] As to the authority of king's reeves in royal towns see Chadwick, *Studies on Angl.-Sax. Institutions,* 251, &c. Henry the reeve is mentioned in 1168 (*Pipe R. 14 Hen. II* [Pipe R. Soc.], 40).

[35] *V.C.H. Herts.* i, 300.

[36] Turnor, *Hist. of Hertford,* 283.

[37] *V.C.H. Herts.* i, 300.

[38] Hertf. Corp. Papers, v, no. 65. Thanks are owing to the corporation for permission to inspect these papers,

and to Mr. R. T. Andrews for his kindness in showing them.

[39] The civil parish of All Saints is a small area on the south of the river, the boundary of which coincides on the east and south and as far as Castle Street with the boundary of the ancient borough. It is to be distinguished from the ecclesiastical parish of All Saints, which includes the district of Brickendon.

[40] See *Parl. Papers, Boundary Rep. and Plans* (1832), ii, 243.

[41] *Feud. Aids,* ii, 456–7, 461.

[42] *V.C.H. Herts.* i, 317*b*, 331*b*, 334*a*, 342*b*, 335 ; Subs. R. bdle. 120, no. 5.

[43] Q.v.

[44] Harl. MS. 4809, fol. 166 ff.

[45] *Hund. R.* (Rec. Com.), i, 188*b*. In this connexion the name of Wall Field Alley which formerly ran parallel to the hamlet on the south is suggestive.

[46] Harl. MS. 4809, fol. 166 ff. (Ct. R.).

493

The Prior of Hertford tried to set up an immunity like that of Waltham. In 1273-4 the burgesses complained that the Prior of Hertford had withdrawn certain men who used to follow the court of the king at Hertford and be there for view of frankpledge.[47] In the 15th century the priory and its lands called Limesy Fee were considered to be outside the borough (see below under Manors).

The boundary of 1621 includes a small area, and the burgesses aimed at expansion. In 1678 ' in Bayliehall Street, Castle Street, West Street, and the street from Cowbridge to Porthill the inhabitants [had] a great trade and [paid] no scot or lot to the borough, whereby trade was removed into those streets and the freemen impoverished.'[48] The parishioners of St. John, on the contrary, complained that so many poor had settled in the borough part of the parish that overmuch poor rate fell upon the ' uplanders,' who lived in the parish outside the town.[49] The bounds were much enlarged by the charter of 1680.[50] ' They run from the furthest edge of Kingsmead to the Ware high road, then including the highway to a common place called London Crosse Hill ; thence to Falling Cross Gate, then including the church and cemetery of All Saints to the west side of West Street ; then to the Lea and to a post in the highway to Hertingfordbury ; thence to the foot of Porthill ; thence including the stream to the extreme edge of Kingsmead.'[51]

Thus West Street and the castle and All Saints' Church were brought within the borough. In 1610 the south side of Castle Street was scarcely built up ; houses extended to Cowbridge and to St. Andrew's. Fore Street, the present Maidenhead Street, and the blocks where the Shire Hall and the old market stood, were all built up.[52] By 1766 there was little change except that the row of houses along the outer castle ditch was beginning to rise.[53]

In 1832 the bounds of the parliamentary borough (which had been coincident with the ancient borough) were extended to include the larger area known as the out-borough, the extension comprising parts of the parishes of St. John and St. Andrew and of the liberties of Brickendon and Little Amwell,[54] and these boundaries were adopted as the municipal boundary under the Municipal Corporations Act of 1835.[55] In 1888 the borough was divided for the first time into a St. Andrew's Ward and an All Saints' Ward for the election of county councillors.[56] Four years later the boundary was enlarged to include parts of the parishes of St. Andrew, Brickendon and Bengeo, so that the wards for the election of town councillors became the Town Ward and Bengeo Ward.[57] In 1894 the borough portion of Bengeo was split off from the rest of the parish, under the name of Bengeo Urban. St. John's parish and St. Andrew's were similarly treated. In 1900 the whole urban part of the borough was made one civil parish ; its area is 1,098 acres of land and 36 of water.[58]

Under Edward the Confessor there were 146 burgesses in Hertford who belonged to the soke of the king. Eighteen other burgesses were the men of Earl Harold and Earl Lewin.[59] The term ' soke ' implies that the king held a court for the burgesses, but it is uncertain if the earls had the like jurisdiction over their tenants. It does not appear how the earls obtained their burgages or whether the holders of such burgages could ' go whither they would.'[60] In 1086 the burgesses of the earls passed to William the Conqueror.[61] These, it is mentioned, all rendered dues. Besides the burgesses proper there were a number of houses in the borough held by non-residents, the landowners of the neighbourhood. The dues on these houses were clearly not equally heavy all over the town. Some of the houses ' rendered dues and do so still ' in 1086, one rendered no dues, and twenty-one paid none except geld. The dues probably included multure, which appears in a charter of William I, a payment for the burgess's house in the nature of gafol, and possibly something for pasture rights.[62] There may have been other dues, of which all trace is lost. The profits arising from the town probably included also the tolls of Ware, St. Albans, Barnet, Thele and Hatfield.[63] In any case the ' dues ' do not seem to have been a fixed or essential part of burgage tenure. The burgess of 1086 was probably, as afterwards, the man who held a house within the borough with the land and pasture belonging, and resided there.

No attempt seems to have been made by the burgesses to obtain a permanent grant of the borough at fee farm. They seem to have farmed it in 1225 and 1226.[64] After this time the farm was either paid in by the sheriff[65] or by the warden of the town and castle.[66]

The aids formed a periodical burden on the borough. The full assessment in the 12th century seems to have been £10, of which a part, generally a half, was frequently remitted.[67] In the aid for marrying Maud eldest daughter of Henry II to the Duke of Saxony in 1168 eleven burgesses accounted for £18 10s.[68] Wiger and Henry the Reeve head the list, accounting for 100s. and 8 marks respectively ; each of the burgesses accounting is apparently responsible for a definite amount. Possibly the eleven were the principal burgesses who collected the tax from the body of burgesses. After this date for a time[69] the aids and tallages were collected and paid by the sheriff.[70] In 1218 it is the burgesses who under the name of the ' men of Hertford ' paid and apparently collected

---

[47] Hund. R. (Rec. Com.), i, 194b.
[48] Hertf. Corp. Papers, i, no. 40.
[49] Sess. R. (Herts. Co. Rec.), i, 282.
[50] Pat. 32 Chas. II, pt. iii, no. 22. The bounds are called ' the old limits,' and are defined because ' they have hitherto been nowhere clearly expressed.'
[51] Ibid.
[52] Speed, Engl. and Wales (1610), plate xxiii.
[53] Add. MS. 32350.
[54] Stat. 2 & 3 Will. IV, cap. 64, sched. O. See map in Parl. Papers, Boundary Rep. and Plans (1832), ii, 243. The bounds of the out-borough seem to have been those fixed by the charter of 1680.
[55] Stat. 5 & 6 Will. IV, cap. 76, sched. A.
[56] Local and Personal Act, 55 & 56 Vict. cap. 222.
[57] Ibid.
[58] When the new parish of Little Amwell was formed from the old liberty in 1864 parts of St. John's parish were added to it.
[59] V.C.H. Herts. i, 300.
[60] Ibid.
[61] Ibid.
[62] Cf. infra ' common rights.'
[63] Cf. infra ' forinsec tolls.'
[64] Rot. Lit. Claus. (Rec. Com.), ii, 38, 139b.
[65] Pipe R. 25 Edw. I, m. 23.
[66] Abbrev. Rot. Orig. (Rec. Com.), i, 101, 30 ; ii, 1.
[67] Magn. Rot. Scac. de 31 Hen. I (Rec. Com.), 62-3 ; Madox, Hist. of Exch. i, 601 ; Gt. R. of the Pipe, 1155-8 (Rec. Com.), 19.
[68] Pipe R. 14 Hen. II (Pipe R. Soc.), 40.
[69] Pipe R. 21 Hen. II, rot. 6, m. 1 ; 20 Hen. II, rot. 6, m. 1.
[70] Pipe R. 23 Hen. II (Pipe R. Soc.), 154, 155, 156.

[Arthur V. Elsden, photo
HERTFORD: 17TH-CENTURY PARGETTED HOUSE IN FORE STREET

the tallage.[71] The same entry is repeated some years later.[72] A tallage was taken in 1227, which was possibly collected by the burgesses themselves,[73] but after this date the tallages cannot be traced.

The early constitution of the borough is obscure. It has been already suggested that before the Conquest the town was governed by the king's reeves; these officers continued till towards the close of the 12th century and possibly later. The exact date when the reeve gave place to the bailiff, which probably marks an increase of burghal rights, is not known. In 1296 the 'community of the vill,' to use the favourite 13th-century phrase, was paying 40s. 'yearly to have the election of the bailiff and other customs.'[74] This custom was known as 'Felst,' which may be connected with the Anglo-Saxon *Felsan*, to recompense; if this is so, the payment may imply the purchase of some rights of self-administration in the 12th century. The name may be older than the right to elect the bailiff; other privileges may have been bought in the 12th century, which were forgotten in the 13th.[75] The most likely time for the purchase of such a right as the election of the bailiff would be the prosperous years of the early part of the 13th century, c. 1226, when it was the bailiffs and not the reeve who held the farm of the borough and seem to have acted as the elected representatives of the burgesses.[76] In 1296 the election was claimed as a custom,[77] which is thus described in 1331: 'the bailiff . . . ought to be elected by the community of the vill, and they make the election each year in the next court after Michaelmas, both of the bailiff and of all other officials,'[78] e.g. sub-bailiff and ale-tasters. But the chief bailiff still received a yearly sum for a robe from the king.[79] The plural address of the writ of 1226 implies two bailiffs,[80] but one bailiff was usual throughout the 13th and 14th centuries; the sub-bailiff occurs for the first time in 1331.[81]

Other royal officials appeared in the 14th century. In 1359 the king appointed William de Louth his steward in the court of the vill of Hertford and in the manor,[82] and William accounted for the farm of the borough in the next year.[83] John of Gaunt kept a bailiff only,[84] and the steward disappears—for a time at least.[85] Although the constables, ale-tasters and minor officers do not appear in records, they must have been chosen at the borough court.[86]

Of the burgesses themselves we know little until the 13th century. We then find record of the payment of the house gafol, called Hagavel and fixed at 14s.[87] This commutation (doubtless bought) must have involved a re-partition by the burgesses among themselves. The 40s. of 'Felst' was possibly assessed among the burgesses in a similar way.[88] Multure and market dues, and perhaps other works,[89] must also have been due. Corresponding privileges would be trade rights, freedom from tolls, pasture and fishing. The right of burgesshood evidently lay with the burgage tenants, the holders of the ancient messuages, who resided in the borough. On such the exercising of their rights and duties was obligatory, for the earliest Court Roll (1362) states that 'six men should be burgesses and are not.'[90] The qualification hinted at is presumably the ownership of a burgage, the confirmation the taking of the burgess's oath. The burgess paid no fine on entry, but the tenant who held a messuage in the borough and did not reside within it paid a fine of 4d.[91] Thus we read 'Andrew Body, citizen of London, comes and shews a charter for tenements in the borough of Hertford in the parish of St. Mary the Less. Because he is a foreigner (*extrinsecus*) and not a burgess he gives 4d. fine and does fealty.'[92] It was possible, however, for new burgesses to be elected. These were apparently the residents in the out-parishes of the borough—the 'foreigners.' Such were constituted burgesses 'to guard and maintain all the liberties and customs of the vill,' and they gave 3s. 4d. each for the liberty.[93]

In the 15th century, for the first time, there is plenty of evidence as to the constitution of the borough. Power was falling into the hands of a group. The burgesses shared in the market and pasture rights, but took less and less part in the town government. In 1461 the whole community of the vill, with the assent of the chief pledges, elected the officials,[94] and so again in 1465.[95] In 1472 'all the chief pledges' made the election, a practice which recurred in 1475 and 1481.[96] The chief pledges always elected the new burgesses and even chose the new chief pledges.[97] The extension of burgess privilege mentioned above could not be allowed in the election of burgesses. To allow non-burgesses to elect would have been absurd. Hence in this the chief pledges act as the old 'community' and represent the burgess core of the court. The officials included the bailiff and sub-bailiff; two constables, two weighers of bread, two ale-tasters, two supervisors of meat, two of fish, and two of hides were usually chosen in the same manner and time.[98] The bailiff presumably was responsible to the steward and receiver of the duchy.[99]

The 15th century gives the first clear view of the borough court. Its work was of four kinds. Lands were seized and distraints levied to show entry; charters of conveyance were inspected, fealty taken, and a fine, if the purchaser was not a burgess. Conveyances of land in the borough out of court were treated as invalid. In other words, the court guarded and registered the transfer of borough land, which passed freely among burgesses only. This close treatment is probably very ancient, and necessary because of the position of property as a burgess qualification.

---

[71] Pipe R. 2 Hen. III, m. 6a, 7.
[72] Ibid. 8 Hen. III, m. 63.
[73] *Rot. Lit. Claus.* (Rec. Com.), ii, 184.
[74] Anct. Ext. Exch. Q.R. no. 45.
[75] Such as rights to pasture or the commutation of the toll.
[76] *Rot. Lit. Claus.* (Rec. Com.), ii, 139b.
[77] Anct. Ext. Exch. Q.R. no. 45.
[78] Survey of 1331 in Chauncy, op. cit. 238.
[79] Ibid.
[80] *Rot. Lit. Claus.* (Rec. Com.), ii, 139b.
[81] See above.

[82] *Abbrev. Rot. Orig.* (Rec. Com.), ii, 255.
[83] Mins. Accts. (Gen. Ser.), bdle. 865, no. 16.
[84] Duchy of Lanc. Mins. Accts. bdle. 53, no. 998, 999, 1000.
[85] The castle officials acted sometimes as 'supervisors of the town.'
[86] Mins. Accts. (Gen. Ser.), bdle. 865, no. 16; Duchy of Lanc. Mins. Accts. bdle. 53, no. 998.
[87] Anct. Ext. Exch. Q.R. no. 45; Chauncy, op. cit. 238.
[88] Ibid.

[89] Ibid.; cf. Cart. Antiq. K 10, 23.
[90] Hertf. Corp. Papers, v, no. 33.
[91] Ct. R. (Gen. Ser.), portf. 177, no. 37.
[92] Ibid.
[93] Ibid.
[94] Ibid.
[95] Ibid.
[96] Ibid.
[97] Ibid.
[98] Duchy of Lanc. Mins. Accts. bdle. 42, no. 825; Ct. R. (Gen. Ser.), portf. 177, no. 37.
[99] Duchy of Lanc. Mins. Accts. bdle. 42, no. 825.

A HISTORY OF HERTFORDSHIRE

Besides this the chief pledges presented offences against the a.sizes, assaults, neglect of frankpledge, defects of the watches, or disobedience to the borough officers. The court seems to have overstrained its jurisdiction in the 13th century, for in 1278 the suitors were presented for an illegal process against a thief.[100] Further, there were the elections of the officials and the burgesses. Finally, a few pleas of debt and trespass came into court—so few that the sessions must have been far less important as a tribunal than as a local government council.

Such was the constitution until the grant of a charter by Mary in February 1554.[1] The borough was incorporated under the style of a bailiff and fifteen burgesses with power to have a common seal and to act in courts of law. The bailiff was to be elected by the burgesses from their number on the Thursday after Michaelmas in each year, and was to take the oath. The bailiff and burgesses were to appoint constables and all other officials, and were also to choose new burgesses, as need might arise, from the 'tenants and inhabitants' of the borough.[2] Thus the charter placed the bailiff to some extent under the control of the new body of burgesses. Possibly the chief pledges may have developed some consultative functions before this time, for the new burgesses represent the pledges more than anything else. The 'whole community' were the chief losers in giving up the election of the bailiff to the fifteen burgesses.

The charter granted by Elizabeth in 1589 set the borough government on the lines along which it developed. The executive was in the hands of eleven chief burgesses, forming the common council, and a bailiff.[3] The former were co-opted from the assistants, the latter was elected from the common council by the assistants and chief burgesses annually upon St. Matthew's Day. The bailiff-elect took the corporal oath and entered on office at the following Michaelmas. The chief burgesses lost their office if they lived away from the borough for six months. The assistants were a body of sixteen, chosen from the inhabitants by the bailiff and chief burgesses ; their only work was to vote at the bailiff's election. The powers of the bailiff and chief burgesses were legislative and executive. They had power to make ordinances at a court held in the town hall as often as they deemed convenient ; and their ordinances might be enforced by fine and imprisonment. The bailiff and burgesses had power to deal with these fines and with those proceeding from the market. They appointed the constables and minor officers. They also chose the chief steward of the court ; the steward of the borough was still apparently appointed by the Crown.

These stewards were both associated with the bailiff and one of the chief burgesses in the holding of the borough court of record every Monday. Its competence extended over personal actions within the borough where the sum sought was under £50. The bailiff alone had certain executive powers ; he was clerk of the market *virtute officii* and he appointed the serjeant-at-mace.

This charter governed the borough for sixteen years. In 1605 James I reincorporated the town under the new style of the mayor, burgesses and commonalty.[3a] The mayor was merely the bailiff of 1589. He was elected by the chief burgesses and assistants from the common council (or chief burgesses). The latter body was to consist of ten of the best men inhabiting within the borough (including the mayor). Each chief burgess was elected for life by the rest of the council and the mayor, who was given a certain control in the power of removing chief burgesses. The sixteen assistants were to be elected by the mayor and chief burgesses from the commonalty. The common council could also remove them. The powers of the assistants in the mayoral election were defined. On St. Matthew's Day the mayor and chief burgesses presented two candidates from their number, of whom the assistants chose one, who took the usual oath and came into office at Michaelmas following. The legislative powers of the old common council passed to the mayor and chief burgesses. Their executive powers were extended. They were to choose the chief steward of the borough, after the death of the Earl of Salisbury, who was appointed to the office by the king. They also chose the steward of the court (a lawyer), the town clerk, and the serjeants-at-mace ; the admission of burgesses was placed in their hands. Judicial powers were divided between the mayor and steward. The court of record, to be held by the mayor and steward of the court, was transferred to Tuesday, and the limit of damages brought down to £40. The mayor and steward and one burgess were to be justices of the peace for the borough, but their jurisdiction seems not to have excluded that of the county magistrates.

The defect of this charter is the excess of trust left in the mayor and chief burgesses, who were irresponsible in their town government. The evil effects were quickly felt in the administration of the common pasture, if nowhere else.[4] Moreover, the corporation fell into lazy ways. In 1635 penalties were ordained for those who did not come, or did not come properly dressed, to official meetings,[5] and for those who gave the mayor or officers 'opprobrious words' or disclosed counsel.[6] At the same time it was ordered that four chief burgesses should attend the weekly court of record. The council met at 'monthly courts,' to which the chief burgesses and officials were to be summoned. The ancient array of flesh and fish tasters, ale-tasters and bread-weighers was still kept up, with four constables, four viewers of the streets and two of the commons.[7] The regulations made for the cleanliness of the streets prove that the corporation did something at least in the public interest.

Town government was complicated by the uncertainty of the bounds within which the charter applied[8] ; and this was the chief argument of the movers for the new charter obtained in 1680.[9] The style of the incorporation was then altered to the 'mayor, aldermen and commonalty.' The mayor was chosen from the common council by the same form of double election as before and on the same tenure. The ten aldermen were elected from the assistants by the common council (including the

---

[100] See Assize R. 323, m. 46 d., 47 d. (6 & 7 Edw. I); see also ibid. 325, m. 33, 34, as to the relations between the bailiff of the vill and the constable of the castle, whose respective provinces in administrative work do not seem to have been very clearly defined.
[1] Pat. 1 Mary, pt. ix, m. 1.
[2] Ibid. 31 Eliz. pt. xi, m. 3.
[3a] Corp. Mun.
[3] Ibid.
[4] *Cal. S. P. Dom.* 1628–9, p. 560.
[5] Hertf. Corp. Papers, i, no. 37.
[6] Ibid. [7] Ibid. no. 57. [8] Ibid. no. 40.
[9] Pat. 32 Chas. II, pt. iii, no. 22. See under boundaries.

Arthur V. Elsden, photo

HERTFORD: BAYLEY HALL

HERTFORD: COTTAGE AT NORTH-EAST OF ST. ANDREW'S CHURCHYARD

HERTFORD HUNDRED

mayor). The sixteen assistants were chosen by the mayor and aldermen from the commonalty. Their powers were extended, in so far as they were to help in all the business of the borough, and limited in the election of the mayor, for the mayor, aldermen, recorder and chamberlain joined with them in the final vote. The recorder, indeed, assisted the mayor and aldermen in most of their functions. He took the place of the old steward of the court, and was elected by the common council. He assisted in the making of by-laws and in the choice of the two serjeants-at-mace. He paired with the mayor in his judicial work in the borough court, which was to be held on Wednesdays. The limit of damages was raised to £60. The mayor, recorder and one freeman, chosen by the mayor and aldermen, were to be the borough justices, and the mayor, in virtue of the older charter, remained clerk of market. The charter created an official, the chamberlain, who had long been wanting. He was elected by the mayor and aldermen, to hold office during their pleasure, giving account when they required. He collected the fines and amercements, made payments and managed the borough finance. The chief steward, the Earl of Salisbury, was to hold his place for life, after which it was to be filled by election, as in the charter of 1605.

This was the form of the constitution until 1835. The charter repeated the mistake of 1605. The mayor and aldermen had a monopoly of power without responsibility. The assistants, who shared in the making of by-laws,[10] were chosen, and perhaps removable, by the mayor. The usual life tenure of office increased the irresponsibility of the corporation.

The ordinances preserved resemble for the most part those of 1635, with an increasing tendency to the prescription of banquets.[11] Possibly the corporation was careless, if not corrupt, if the treatment of the pastures from 1645 to 1709 is a fair instance. In 1834 the mayor and council were unpopular rather for their politics than for any malpractice.[12]

During the 18th century practices untouched by charter hardened into customs. Thus in 1834 'the junior alderman who had not passed the chair' was usually elected mayor.[13] Otherwise no changes had taken place among the borough authorities. Even the two serjeants-at-mace still stood at the head of the police force; but there were seven constables chosen by the parishes, and watchmen and patrol under the Paving Act of 1787.[14]

The salient feature of the report of 1834 is the decay of the borough courts. The Wednesday court of record had fallen into disuse by 1782. In 1827 the inhabitants petitioned for its revival, and it was duly held in 1828. As, however, there were then only twenty-three summonses, and from 1830 to 1833 an average of three a year,[15] the court was not worth holding. The quarter sessions likewise did a very inconsiderable business. The petty sessions on Wednesdays was apparently the court of most resort.

Under the Municipal Corporations Act (1835) Hertford lost its archaisms. The ratepayer burgesses elected twelve councillors, who chose four aldermen, aldermen and councillors composing the council.[16] This body elected the mayor.

When the borough boundary was extended in 1892, and two wards formed, twelve councillors were given to the town ward and three to Bengeo, and one alderman was added to the council.[17]

The borough court of record has not survived. The quarter sessions of the borough justices were continued under the Act of 1835,[18] and are still held. The petty sessions are now held for the county every fortnight on Saturdays, and by the borough magistrates every Thursday.

The tenurial qualification for burgesshood had been weakened by 1605, when burgesses to the number of three were admitted from the out-portions of St. John's and St. Andrew's by the charter. Nevertheless, it left definite traces. An out-burgess might join in municipal elections and the giving of counsel, but he could not be mayor. Deeper traces remained in the pasture rights. In 1621 the rights of pasture were said to belong to the 'ancient messuages,' thus following the burgage tenements. Later the right was claimed for all cottages above thirty years old; but in 1719 the commoners were still regarded as the 'owners of burgage tenements,' and in 1737 are described as the inhabitant householders of the ancient borough.

With regard to the freedom of the borough, as far as we can judge, the 16th-century qualification was seven years' apprenticeship to a freeman. The direct evidence for it only dates from 1655[19]; it was still the usual one in 1834. As early as 1598 the freedom could be bought[20]; the payment varied in the early 19th century from £5 to £25. The eldest sons of aldermen took up their freedom on paying 1s. to the mayor and the usual fees.

In the 17th century the corporation treated applicants very fairly. Apprentices' indentures were entered on the rolls, and they could not be denied the freedom on payment of 1s. and the fees, after the completion of their service. The most important privilege was the exclusive right to trade and manufacture in the borough. It was re-asserted in the by-laws of 1692, 1731 and 1752,[21] and was maintained in 1834.[22] The corresponding duty was the 'quarterage,' apparently a payment for stalls in the market,[23] comparable with the earlier stall pence. Until 1731 the rate was higher for freemen dwelling outside the borough than for those dwelling within it[24]; in 1635 the former paid 4d. a quarter, the latter 1d.[25] After 1624 the freeman, like the inhabitant householders, had the Parliamentary vote,[26] and this right was guarded in the Reform Act.[27] By 1834 almost all qualified as freemen voted either as £10 householders or as inhabitant householders within the ancient borough.[28] In 1839 there were only 366 freemen in a population of 5,631.[29] The privilege was clearly not worth preserving.

---

[10] Hertf. Corp. Papers, i, no. 37; Rep. on Munic. Corp. (1835), v, 2885.
[11] Ibid.; Hist. MSS. Com. Rep. xiv, App. viii, 159, 163.
[12] Rep. on Munic. Corp. (1835), v, 2890.
[13] Ibid. 2885.
[14] Ibid.
[15] Ibid. 2886-8.
[16] Stat. 5 & 6 Will. IV, cap. 76.
[17] Local and Personal Act, 55 & 56 Vict. cap. 222.
[18] Stat. 5 & 6 Will. IV, cap. 76, sched. A.
[19] Sess. R. (Herts. Co. Rec.), i, 110.
[20] Carew, Rights of Election, i, 275 et seq.
[21] Hertf. Corp. Papers, i, no. 57; Hist. MSS. Com. Rep. xiv, App. viii, 160.
[22] Rep. on Munic. Corp. (1835), v, 2886.
[23] Hertf. Corp. Papers, iv, no. 430.
[24] Ibid. i, no. 37.
[25] Ibid.
[26] See below.
[27] Rep. on Munic. Corp. (1835), v, 2886.
[28] Ibid.
[29] Parl. Papers, 1839, xviii, 671.

A HISTORY OF HERTFORDSHIRE

Hertford first sent representatives to the Parliament of 1298.[30] Its two members were present in subsequent Parliaments from 1301 to 1311.[31] After this time St. Albans or Bishop's Stortford frequently sent members, and the representation of Hertford became very uncertain. Its members sat in 1313,[32] 1315,[33] and from 1319 to 1322.[34] In 1336, 1373 and 1376 they also appeared, but from this time the right to separate representation fell into desuetude.

The claim to return two members was made in 1621, and the right was proved to the satisfaction of a select committee in 1624.[35] The Speaker refused to define the franchise, and the controversy over the vote of non-resident burgesses raged in a series of petitions from 1681.[36] In 1705 a select committee resolved that the vote was in the inhabitants,[37] freemen resident at the time of their admission, and the three chartered out-burgesses.[38] On this followed a second series of petitions accusing the fairness of the mayor as returning officer,[39] a matter on which two opinions were hardly possible. The borough vote was a very saleable commodity,[40] and bribery, comically flagrant, was rife in Hertford in 1833.[41] It was not, however, until 1867 that Hertford lost one member.[42] The Redistribution Act of 1885 merged the borough representation in that of the county.[43]

The rights of common held by the burgess by ancient custom are first described in 1295–6.[44] The 'community' used the pasture of Hartham (20 a.) throughout the year, each burgess paying 4d. a head for horses, 3d. for oxen and cows, 1½d. for calves and 1d. for sheep. Kings Mead was subject to the same rights, except when it was fenced for hay every third year.[45] A third meadow (included in Kings Mead in 1331) lay open once in three years.[46] The custom may well be more ancient than the burgesses believed, and the rights a survival of Saxon arrangements.

No change is noticed in 1331, but in 1384 'foreigners' are described as putting their cattle on the pasture at a rate of 1d. a head higher than that of burgess-kine.[47] As this usage is referred to ancient custom, it may well have existed, although unrecorded, in 1331.

The rates remained unchanged throughout the 15th century,[48] but burgesses and foreigners hardly grazed a dozen cattle among them in the later years.[49]

After the grant of the charter in 1554 the question arose whether the common of pasture belonged to the tenants of the manor of Hertford or the inhabitants of the town.[50] The custom alleged was that the meadows should be inclosed from 2 February to 1 August, when they were thrown open to the inhabitants residing in Hertford; the Prior of Hertford also had common rights by agreement.[51] The owners, not being inhabitants, had put their beasts on the meadows, Kings Mead, Halles Holmes, Wrengdon's Mead, Halle's Cowlees, Hall's Horselees, Thurland and Chawdell Mead.[52] The case was apparently won by the inhabitants.

The difficulty was that many of the common lands lay outside the borough. Three kinds of commons were distinguished by the jury of 1621: Hartham and Kings Mead belonging to the borough; 'foreign' meadows lying outside the borough—Thurland, Hither Cowmead, Middle Cowlees, Heathe's Cowlees, Halles Hook, Horselees and Hoppitts[53]—which were common from 31 July to Candlemas; finally, fields belonging to other manors, and common for all manner of cattle at all times—Middle Field, Cockbush Field, High Field and others.[54] The last two classes of common rights appear here suddenly and cannot be traced. They may be omitted from earlier surveys as involving no payment to the Crown.

In November 1627 the corporation bought Kings Mead from the Crown for the use of the poor.[55] Disputes once more arose between the occupiers of the ancient burgage tenements and of the newer houses and cottages. The matter was finally referred to the Privy Council, who decided that the tenants of the newly-erected cottages should enjoy a life interest only, and that all right in the commons should then revert to the ancient burgagers.[56]

The mayor and his successors paid small sums to the poor and larger ones to the corporation, and kept no account.[57] In consequence of an investigation in 1709 the corporation were obliged to repay £15 11s. 10d. for every year since 1645, and the meadow was put into trust.[58] The corporation considered that they had no further jurisdiction, and the common rights were so little guarded that in 1737 fifty-three of the inhabitants agreed to impound cattle and take proceedings in defence of the poor.[59] In 1773 the same complaint was raised.[60] The commoning in Hartham was then still kept up, and was regulated by the mayor.[61] The agistments of this meadow, at the rate of 1s. a head of cattle, formed part of the borough income in 1834.[62]

Common rights over the meadow called Hoppitts or Le Holmes were disputed between the burgesses and the Prior of Hertford in December 1312.[63] The prior was evidently trying to free his lands altogether from jurisdictional and economic ties to the borough. The dispute was compromised. In the 16th century the commoning was still shared between the inhabitants of the borough and the prior (but

---

[30] *Return of Memb. of Parl.* i, 8.
[31] Ibid. 13, 16.
[32] Ibid. 41.
[33] Ibid. 48.
[34] Ibid. 57–64.
[35] J. Glanvil, *Rep. of Certain Cases*, 87 et seq.; Carew, op. cit. i, 275 et seq.
[36] Ibid.
[37] Apparently only those within the ancient borough (*Rep. on Munic. Corp.* [1835], 9, 2886).
[38] Carew, op. cit. i, 275 et seq. The non-inhabitant freemen are not mentioned in the *Boundary Rep.* (*Parl. Papers*, 1832, ii, 243).
[39] Carew, loc. cit.
[40] Cf. *Hist. MSS. Com. Rep.* xi, App. iv, 352.
[41] Cockburn and Rowe, *Controverted Elections*, 184–223; Perry and Knapp, *Controverted Elections*, 541.
[42] Stat. 30 & 31 Vict. cap. 102.
[43] Ibid. 48 & 49 Vict. cap. 23.
[44] Anct. Ext. Exch. Q.R. no. 45.
[45] Ibid.; Chauncy, op. cit. 238.
[46] Ibid.
[47] Duchy of Lanc. Mins. Accts. bdle. 53, no. 998.
[48] Ibid. no. 1010; bdle. 42, no. 825.
[49] Ibid.
[50] Duchy of Lanc. Dep. lxv, m. 1; cf. also under burgesshood.
[51] Ibid.
[52] Ibid.
[53] See below.
[54] Hertf. Corp. Papers, v, no. 65.
[55] Aug. Off. Fee Farm Rents, file 42, no. 261; Hertf. Corp. Papers, v, 35.
[56] Turnor, *Hist. of Hertf.* 97. See also *Cal. S. P. Dom.* 1628–9, p. 560. For continuance of the controversy see Turnor, op. cit. 116. The victory remained with the inhabitants of the borough.
[57] Hertf. Corp. Papers, v, no. 35.
[58] Ibid.
[59] Ibid. iv, no. 323.
[60] Ibid.
[61] Ibid.
[62] *Rep. on Munic. Corp.* (1835). App. v, 2888.
[63] *Hist. MSS. Com. Rep.* xiv, App. viii, 159.

498

HERTFORD CHRIST'S HOSPITAL

[*Arthur V. Elsden, photo*

HERTFORD HUNDRED

not by his tenants),[64] and in 1621 it is mentioned again.[65]

Hertford was one of the towns which escaped 'waste' at the Conquest,[66] so that its economic history between 1065 and 1086 is continuous. The town was prosperous, at least in the eyes of King William and his officials, who found that it had paid much less than it could afford.[67] Its 164 burgesses imply that Hertford held a position in the county which it did not keep up. Ware, the rival of later days, had 125 householders, both free and unfree[68]; St. Albans had forty-six burgesses and forty-two unfree inhabitants[69]; Cheshunt had ten merchants, and the remaining fifty-three were villeins.[70] The facts point to a pre-Conquest prosperity which steadily declined during the Middle Ages. Saxon Hertford may have been in reality the most important market of the shire.

From the Conquest to the end of the 12th century the records of Hertford are blank, just at the time when we should like to know something of the condition of the market and whether the tolls of Ware, Hatfield and St. Albans were already charged with the farm. When the men of Hertford were amerced in 1191 for breaking the bridge of Ware[71] they were probably asserting their monopoly of the passage of the Lea.

Hertford must have suffered both directly and indirectly in the war of 1215–16, for the castle was besieged and taken more than once, and the district around was the seat of war.[72] At the tallage of 1217–18 Hertford, whose assessment was two-thirds that of Colchester in 1176,[73] was assessed at one-third the amount demanded from the latter town, and paid about twice as much as the two rural manors of Essendon and Bayford.[74] The borough paid tallage on the same basis in 1219 and in 1223–4.[75] It evidently did not stand out much above the neighbouring vills, and was not in the same class as a commercial centre like Colchester. If the assessment of 1217 was adequate, the town must have prospered in spite of its difficulties, for in 1227 it paid £10 to the tallage,[76] which probably bore an unusually close relation to real values.[77] Indeed, this sum was accepted instead of £16 18s. 2d., the original assessment, 'so that the poor and the greatly injured might be relieved.'[78]

In 1226 the provisional grant of a fair further points to the fact that the burgesses could afford some amount of municipal independence. The secret of this prosperity lay in situation. Hertford was the natural market to which would come the produce of the valleys of the Maran, the Beane and the Rib, country which was especially rich in corn land. The town was situated on the Lea, just above the southern bend which brings the river straight down into the Thames at London. The economic attraction of London must not be overlooked, for it caused a struggle against the exclusive rights of the borough early in the 13th century. This attack came from the metropolis as well as from the local competitors —Ware, Chipping Barnet, Hatfield and Cheshunt.

In the early part of the 13th century the transport of corn to London had been by boats belonging to Hertford, but about 1247–8 the men of London built a granary further down the Lea at Thele, and shipped the corn in their own bottoms.[79] Unfortunately the issue of the quarrel is unknown.

The neighbouring towns suffered from the monopoly claimed by the burgesses, who held that the Lea must be crossed at their town bridge. But the direct route from Royston to London passed the water at Ware, a rising town. In the 12th century Hertford must have asserted its rights, for until John's reign the bailiff of Hertford held the keys of the bridge and ford of Ware, so that carts could only pass with his licence.[80] During the war of 1215–16 the men of Ware disregarded the custom, and carts passed freely over the bridge and ford, nor had the burgesses recovered their rights by 1247.[81]

For a town which owed its existence to a monopoly of trade and traffic rights the matter was vital, especially as Ware had attacked the Hertford market by holding illegal markets on Wednesdays and Fridays.[82] In 1258 the men of Ware sued the burgesses, complaining that they had forcibly broken the bridge and dug a channel in the ford, so that no one, even on foot, could pass it. They had also cut the London road by digging a ditch across it.[83] The cause of these aggressions was clearly the fact that the men of Ware had either made or restored the road between Ware and Hoddesdon, thus leaving Hertford outside the main line of traffic.[84] The burgesses pleaded the orders of their lord, William de Valence, but the jury ascribed the whole affair to their desire to have the passage (of the Lea) through the middle of their town.

This check damped the enterprise of the men of Hertford. Five years later the aggression was on the side of Ware.[85] By 1274 the 'turning aside of the high road which used to go from Hertford to Ware' had become a fact, much 'to the detriment of the vill of Hertford.'[86] The bailiffs of Ware tried also to cut off communication by water by 'occupying the weirs, so that no ship might pass.'[87] The tolls at Ware due to the bailiff of Hertford were not paid in 1277,[88] but after this time they seem to have been rendered. In 1296 the 'tolls of the passage of Ware' and of Hertford were separately valued at 40s. a year,[89] but the steady increase in the tolls of Ware shows that the main traffic passed through the direct route.

Hertford had lost to Ware the passage of the Lea and the possession of the main road, and this constituted the best capital of the borough. If it had ever been an industrial centre it had lost its position before

---

[64] Duchy of Lanc. Dep. lxv, m. 1.
[65] See above.
[66] V.C.H. Herts. i, 300.
[67] Ibid. [68] Ibid. 327.
[69] Ibid. 314.
[70] Ibid. 320a.
[71] Madox, Hist. Exch. i, 564.
[72] 'Ann. Lond.' Chron. of Edw. I and Edw. II (Rolls Ser.), i, 17; Roger of Wendover, Flor. Hist. (Rolls Ser. lxxxiv), ii, 200.
[73] Pipe R. 23 Hen. II (Pipe R. Soc.), 154, 155.
[74] Pipe R. 62, m. 6a, 7 (2 Hen. III).
[75] Ibid. 63 (8 Hen. III).
[76] Rot. Lit. Claus. (Rec. Com.), ii, 184.
[77] Stubbs, Const. Hist. ii, 40.
[78] Rot. Lit. Claus. (Rec. Com.), ii, 184.
[79] Assize R. 218, m. 6 d.
[80] Ibid.
[81] Ibid.
[82] Ibid.
[83] Abbrev. Plac. (Rec. Com.), 148.
[84] Apparently before this the line had passed through Hertford to Hatfield and joined the Great North Road there or had gone via Potthill to Wadesmill and there joined Ermine Street.
[85] Hund. R. (Rec. Com.), i, 190b.
[86] Ibid. 188, 190b.
[87] Ibid.
[88] Assize R. 323.
[89] Anct. Extents Exch. Q.R. no. 45.

A HISTORY OF HERTFORDSHIRE

1247–8, when the men of Hertford complained that before 1215–16 there were no weavers or dyers of cloth in Ware, but that 'now' there were. If this is true it may explain the prosperity of Hertford earlier in the century. The cloth industry cannot have been very vigorous. A document of 1290 gives few trade names beyond the ordinary carpenter, smith, miller, carter, fisher and butcher; the mustarder and the merchant being the only suggestive names.[90] In 1307 there are cutlers, a dyer, two 'chapmen,' and a mustarder.[91] Of course these casual mentions can be regarded only as clues. It is more significant that there is no trace of a craft or merchant gild.

Hertford was falling behind its neighbours. In 1290 St. Albans had more and richer taxpayers,[92] and even Cheshunt was larger than Hertford.[93] In 1308 the borough paid £7 16s. 8d., against £12 11s. 4d. from Cheshunt and £14 4s. 5¼d. from Ware.[94] The burgesses brought forward their old complaints against Ware without success.[95] In 1338 the taxable value was only half that of Ware.[96]

The history of the markets and fairs (q.v.) enforces the evidence of court rolls and accounts that Hertford decayed rapidly during the 14th century and more rapidly during the 15th. It seemed rather a village than a borough, and economic documents tend to treat it rather as a rural manor than as a town. The depopulation caused by the Black Death evidently gave an impetus to the decline. In 1428 there were not ten householders in the parish of St. Nicholas or that of St. Mary Minor.[97] The auditors began to allow the bailiff increasing sums for decay of rent.[98] Probably the last quarter of the 15th century was the apogee.

During this time there is naturally little development of trades. Brewing and baking are the most prominent, with the other provision businesses, fishmongers, butchers and chandlers; tanning and glovemaking also occur.[99]

About the beginning of the 16th century new conditions caused a new prosperity in the borough. The working classes were now no longer themselves corn growers, and the question of their corn supplies was a new problem, especially acute in London. The provisioning of London taxed the energies of the Privy Council.[100] Hence, while many towns were emptying their workers into the country, Hertford found more and more buyers in the corn market. It was important that the market should not be monopolized by speculators, and in 1588 the privy councillors interfered to prevent it.[1] Their object was to keep back some of the grain for the small local buyer, but this was difficult in the face of dealers from London. In 1595 the supply (between 140 and 200 qrs. of grain) was sold within an hour of the ringing of the market bell, and bought not by the poor, but by bakers from London and local millers who bought for the London market.[2] At this time there were above forty water-mills alone within 10 miles of Hertford.[3] Many of these probably served the London trade.

Hertford hardly kept its position in metropolitan markets as supplies came in from more distant areas, but it remained the trade centre both for corn and other goods for the district lying north of the town. Corn and malt, the chief articles in the market in 1728,[4] are the staple commodities to-day. The trade of Hertford has changed rather in volume than in kind.

Hertford has probably had a market since the Saxon King Edward first built his 'burh' there, but there is no historical evidence of it until the reign of John,[5] when it is spoken of as though it were already established by ancient custom. The market days were Wednesday and Friday throughout the 13th and for the greater part of the 14th century,[6] but in this latter period the value of the market was sinking. In 1359–60 the whole tolls of the market for nine months were only 16s. 8d.[7] In 1383 the Wednesday market was transferred to Thursday by royal grant,[8] probably an attempt to catch custom, and the tolls went up.[9] The improvement was brief. In 1397–8 the tolls and pleas sank to 20s., and 'no more because merchants forsake the market for others on every side.'[10] Henry IV confirmed the grant of Edward III,[11] and pardoned the burgesses the 26s. at which the tolls were estimated for ten years,[12] and in 1438–9 Henry VI was only receiving 10s. 6d. from the market.[13] It seems to have become almost valueless by the end of the century. The Thursday market was still held early in Elizabeth's reign, but it suffered from the competition of the market at Hoddesdon.[14]

The Elizabethan charter gave to the corporation the market to be held on Saturday,[15] which has remained the market day for Hertford ever since.[16] The charter of Charles II revived the Wednesday market,[17] which survived in 1888 as a small cattle market, held in alternate weeks.[18] The corporation have taken the tolls of the market since 1589.[19]

The Hertford fairs originated in the time of the minority of Henry III. In 1226 the men of Hertford received a provisional grant until the king came of age of a week's fair from the Sunday before the Feast of SS. Simon and Jude (28 October) until the following Sunday.[20] Whether by prescription or by a grant in confirmation, the fair continued throughout the 13th and 14th centuries. In 1295 the tolls were worth 10s.[21] Before 1331 a fair on 15 August had been acquired by the burgesses, and

---

[90] Lay Subs. R. Herts. bdle. 120, no. 2.
[91] Ibid. no. 5.
[92] Ibid. no. 2.
[93] Ibid.; cf. also no. 5.
[94] Ibid. no. 8.
[95] Survey of 1338 printed in Chauncy, op. cit. 238; Duchy of Lanc. Misc. bdle. 4, no. 6.
[96] Cal. Pat. 1336–40, p. 111.
[97] Feud. Aids, ii, 461.
[98] Duchy of Lanc. Mins. Accts. bdles. 733, no. 12043; 53, no. 1010.
[99] Ct. R. (Gen. Ser.), portf. 177, no. 37.
[100] Cunningham, Growth of Engl. Ind. and Commerce, ii (1), 51, 318, 23 ff.

[1] Acts of P.C. 1580–1, p. 301.
[2] Cal. S. P. Dom. 1595–7, p. 126.
[3] Ibid. 336; cf. Duchy of Lanc. Plead. cxcvii, no. C 2.
Salmon, Hist. of Herts. 1.
[5] Assize R. 218, m. 6 d.
[6] Ibid.
[7] Duchy of Lanc. Mins. Accts. bdle. 365, no. 16; Hertf. Corp. Papers, i, no. 2.
[8] Cal. Pat. 1381–5, p. 274.
[9] Duchy of Lanc. Mins. Accts. bdle. 53, no. 998.
[10] Ibid. no. 1000.
[11] Hertf. Corp. Papers, i, no. 4.

[12] Duchy of Lanc. Mins. Accts. bdle. 42, no. 825.
[13] Ibid.
[14] Duchy of Lanc. Dec. Lib. 2 Eliz. fol. 305a.
[15] Pat. 31 Eliz. pt. xi, m. 3.
[16] J. Norden, Description of Herts. (1598), 1; Pat. 3 Jas. I, pt. iii, m. 8; Rep. on Markets and Fairs, xiii (1), 124.
[17] Pat. 32 Chas. II, pt. iii, no. 22.
[18] Parl. Papers, 1888, liv, 46.
[19] Pat. 31 Eliz. pt. xi, m. 3.
[20] Rot. Lit. Claus. (Rec. Com.), ii, 111b.
[21] Anct. Ext. Exch. Q.R. no. 45.

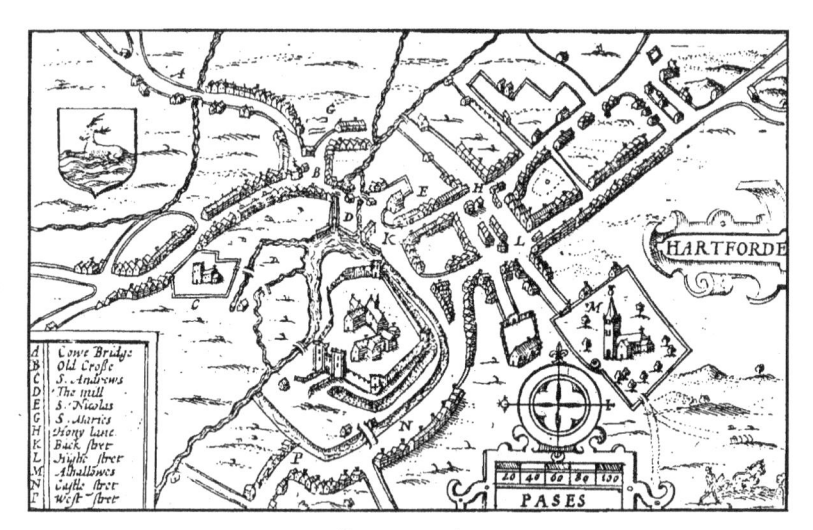

HERTFORD IN 1611
(*From Speed's Theatre of the Empire of Great Britain*)

HERTFORD HUNDRED

the two fairs brought in £2 10s. yearly.[22] One of these fairs seems to have been a horse fair held outside the town in the 15th century.[23] The Master of the hospital of the Holy Trinity held a fair on 22 July and paid half the tolls to the king's bailiff; he did so at least from the last quarter of the 14th century.[24] The amount was always small.[25] These three fairs continued until the end of the 15th century, suffering a gradual decay. The bailiff was compelled to admit that the merchants had given up the Hertford round. The proof lay in the disappearing tolls. In 1437–8 the October fair brought in 6s. 8d. instead of 11s. 8d. as it had done forty years before[26]; the July fair made no profits at all.[27] In 1444–5 the farmer of the market and fairs obtained a respite of payment, possibly in consequence of the paucity of his takings.[28]

Without some improvement in the 16th century the burgesses would hardly have troubled to obtain the three fairs granted by Queen Mary. One was to be held in the parish of St. Andrew from 23 to 25 June; the other two in the town on 27 to 29 October and on Passion Sunday with the Saturday and Monday.[29] The local distinction was probably derived from the three extinct fairs. Elizabeth re-granted these three fairs and added another, to be held in the parish of St. Andrew from 7 September to 9 September.[30] But the dates seem to have been changed and the duration shortened very soon, as in 1598 the fairs took place on 24 October, 4 September, 24 June, and the Friday before Passion Sunday.[31] Seven years later a fair lasting from 30 April to 2 May was substituted for that in September.[32] The charter of Charles II re-granted this fair and confirmed the others.[33] At the present day the dates of the fairs are 12 May, 5 July, 8 November, and the third Saturday before Easter.

Courts of pie-powder appear in the accounts of the town for the first time in 1384–5,[34] although they were probably held earlier. They were granted to the burgesses by the charter of Queen Mary with stallage and picage.[35] Charles II re-granted these rights for all the fairs.[36]

Besides the tolls of the market and fair[37] there were the more interesting forinsec tolls. They are first mentioned in the reign of Henry III as existing under King John.[38] The tax was 2d. on carts of merchants, ½d. on pack-horses, and ¼d. on pedlars.[39] In 1296 the account is fuller. The 'through toll' was taken at the bridges of Ware, Hertford and Thele, at the 'Barre' of Hatfield and Barnet,[40] and at the two 'heads' of St. Albans.[41] The Abbot of St. Albans acquired the tolls of his own town and of Barnet,[42] but the tolls of Ware, Hatfield and Thele remained in the king's hands and were generally accounted for as part of the farm of the town,[43] although occasionally during the 14th and 15th centuries they were leased apart.[44]

This arrangement of tolls may be one for the sheriff's convenience, or a survival from the time when Hertford was the shire market with a monopoly over buying and selling and passage. The lowey or *leucata*, the district outside a town over which the borough officers had certain rights, existed in varying degrees of importance around many towns. It occurred at London and Durham, and there is an excellent instance of it in the confirmation by Henry II of the customs of Nottingham. By this the burgesses of Nottingham were to have the tolls from all those who crossed the Trent as far as Newark, as fully as in the borough of Nottingham. The charter continues: 'The men of Nottinghamshire and Derbyshire ought to come to the borough on Friday and Saturday with their carts and loads, nor ought anyone to work dyed cloths for 10 leagues round, save in the borough.' Similar rights evidently occurred at Hertford, where the king claimed the tolls for merchandise carried through places within 7 miles of Hertford.[45] This liberty was apparently one of the rights which belonged to the pre-Conquest king's reeve at a time when Hertford as a *villa regalis* was the administrative centre for the district.

The right to have a common seal was first given to the bailiff and burgesses by the charter of Mary,[46] and was confirmed by the subsequent charters.[47] The British Museum has no specimen of an early date, presumably that made under the Jacobean charter. It shows a rosette of five double leaves, barbed and seeded, within a border. The legend is 'Burgus de Hertford, 1608.'[48] A later type (probably that used after 1680) shows the hart in the ford with a cross between the antlers; behind to the right a castle with three towers, to the left a tree on a low mound.[49]

CASTLE, HONOUR AND MANOR

The vill or manor of *HERTFORD* was demesne of the Crown and was granted by William I as the 'lordship of Hertford,'[50] together with the mills of Hertford and the manor of Bayford, to Peter de Valognes, Sheriff of Hertfordshire.[51] A confirmation of the two mills of Hertford *cum suo alio feodo* with multure and works (*operatione*) of the burgesses, was made to Valognes by Henry I,[52] and the Empress Maud confirmed the manors of Essendon and Bayford and the mills of Hertford to Roger de Valognes, son of Peter.[53]

[22] Extent of 1331 printed in Chauncy, op. cit. 238.
[23] Hertf. Corp. Papers, i, no. 5.
[24] Duchy of Lanc. Mins. Accts. bdle. 53, no. 998.
[25] Ibid. [26] Ibid. bdle. 42, no. 825.
[27] Ibid.
[28] Ibid. bdle. 733, no. 12043.
[29] Pat. 1 Mary, pt. ix, m. 1.
[30] Ibid. 31 Eliz. pt. xi, m. 3.
[31] Norden, op. cit. 1.
[32] Pat. 3 Jas. I, pt. iii, m. 8.
[33] Ibid. 32 Chas. II, pt. iii, m. 22.
[34] Duchy of Lanc. Mins. Accts. bdle. 53, no. 998.
[35] Pat. 1 Mary, pt. ix, m. 1.
[36] Ibid. 32 Chas. II, pt. iii, m. 22.
[37] See above.

[38] Assize R. 218, m. 6 d.
[39] *Hund. R.* (Rec. Com.), i, 194*b*; Assize R. 323.
[40] Anct. Ext. Exch. Q.R. no. 45; Duchy of Lanc. Misc. bdle. 11, no. 25; Pipe R. 25 Edw. I, m. 23.
[41] Anct. Ext. Exch. Q.R. no. 45.
[42] *V.C.H. Herts.* ii, 331.
[43] Chauncy, op. cit. 238; Duchy of Lanc. Mins. Accts. bdle. 53, no. 998–1000.
[44] *Abbrev. Rot. Orig.* (Rec. Com.), ii, 256; Duchy of Lanc. Misc. Bks. xiii, 9; Mins. Accts. (Gen. Ser.), bdle. 1094, no. 10; Duchy of Lanc. Dec. Lib. 2, Hen. VI, fol. 74*a*; Duchy of Lanc. Mins. Accts. bdle. 733, no. 12043; Cussans, *Hist. of Herts. Hertford Hund.* 55.

[45] Document quoted by Cussans, op. cit. 55 n. The tolls must have been of considerable value, as the rent reserved by the lease was £33 6s. 8d.
[46] Pat. 1 Mary, pt. ix, m. 1.
[47] Ibid. 31 Eliz. pt. xi, m. 3; 32 Chas. II, pt. iii, no. 22; 3 Jas. I, pt. iii, m. 8.
[48] *Cat. of Seals*, no. 4998.
[49] Ibid. 4999.
[50] The lordship evidently included the borough, which was farmed by Peter de Valognes in 1086 (*V.C.H. Herts.* i, 300).
[51] Cart. Antiq. K 10, 22. The grantor is Willelmus Rex Anglorum, the witnesses S. bishop and H. sheriff, probably Stigand and Haimo.
[52] Ibid. 23. [53] Ibid. 24.

501

A HISTORY OF HERTFORDSHIRE

These two latter grants probably did not include the lordship.[54] The grant to Roger seems to have been for life only, for in 1154–5 Henry de Essex, the sheriff, was accounting for the manor of Bayford[55] as well as for the farm of the borough of Hertford.[56] The terms 'manor,' 'borough' and 'vill' are used interchangeably at this date when the whole of the lordship is meant.[57]

In 1249 Henry III granted the vill of Hertford to William de Valence for life.[58] On the death of William in May 1296 the vill reverted to the king.[59] He entrusted it to a succession of farmers,[60] who were continued until Edward I gave it to Queen Margaret.[61] The queen transferred it to Aymer de Valence, who obtained a royal confirmation in 1309 and in 1317 a grant of Hertford in fee.[62] His widow surrendered it ten years later and gave up all claim to it.[63] The vill and honour were assigned at once to Queen Isabel in increase of her dower,[64] and after her fall she received a re-grant.[65] In 1360 Edward III granted Hertford to John of Gaunt, then Earl of Richmond,[66] a gift which was confirmed by Edward III in 1376[67] and by Richard II in 1377.[68] The manor and vill descended

VALENCE. *Burelly argent and azure an orle of martlets gules.*

JOHN OF GAUNT. *The royal arms of EDWARD III with the difference of a label ermine.*

DUCHY OF LANCASTER. *ENGLAND with a label azure.*

with the duchy of Lancaster[69] into the hands of Henry IV, and after his death were held in dower by Queen Joan.[70] In the reign of Henry VI they were granted to the dowager Queen Katherine,[71] and later to Henry's queen, Margaret.[72] Edward IV granted them to Queen Elizabeth Woodville,[73] who held her first court at Michaelmas 1465.[74] In 1553 Edward VI granted the manor and castle of Hertford

KATHERINE of France and MARGARET of France. *Azure three fleurs de lis or.*

ELIZABETH WOODVILLE. *Argent a fesse and a quarter gules.*

to Princess Mary for her life.[75] Prince Charles received a grant of the castle and manor in October 1609[76]; and after his accession he granted them in 1630 to William Earl of Salisbury,[77] whose successors have since held the manor.[78]

These grants of the manor include the king's rights over the borough. An extent of the manor taken in 1331 begins with 'the castle of Hertford and the borough there held of the king in chief.'[79] The profits include the fishery belonging to the borough, the *fluctus aquae* from Hertford to Waltham, the meadows called King's Meads, the two water-mills, the rent called hawgavel (see above), the custom called 'aletol,' the profits of the market and the tolls at Ware, Thele and Hatfield, the fairs and the court leet.[80] The 'issues of the manor' are first distinguished about the middle of the 15th century,[81] probably for convenience in accounting. The grant to the Earl of Salisbury included the fishery of the demesne water of Hertford, the meadow called Castle Mead, ten osier beds in the river and the tolls appurtenant to the castle and honour.[82] The water-mills (which were then held on lease) were excepted,[83] also the tolls of the market

CECIL, Marquess of Salisbury. *Barry of ten pieces argent and azure six scutcheons argent with a lion sable in each with the difference of a crescent.*

---

[54] Peter de Valognes' 'other fee' was probably his own private property (see below).
[55] See Bayford.
[56] *Red Bk. of Exch.* (Rolls Ser.), 651.
[57] Cf. ibid. 774; Pipe R. 8 Hen. III, s.v. Herts. (account of Faikes de Breauté).
[58] *Cal. Pat.* 1247–58, p. 46; see also *Cal. Chart. R.* 1226–57, p. 351; Assize R. 325.
[59] Duchy of Lanc. Misc. Bks. xii, fol. 56 d.
[60] *Abbrev. Rot. Orig.* (Rec. Com.), i, 101; *Cal. Pat.* 1292–1301, p. 316; *Abbrev. Rot. Orig.* (Rec. Com.), i, 301.
[61] Duchy of Lanc. Misc. Bks. xii, fol. 58.
[62] *Cal. Pat.* 1307–13, p. 153; 1317–21, p. 47; *Cal. Inq. p.m.* 10–20 Edw. II, 318.
[63] *Cal. Close,* 1327–36, p. 109.
[64] *Cal. Pat.* 1327–30, p. 67.
[65] Ibid. 1330–4, p. 195.
[66] Misc. Exch. bdle. 5, no. 3; Gt. Coucher, fol. 228, no. 1.
[67] Duchy of Lanc. Royal Chart. 342–4.
[68] *Cal. Pat.* 1377–81, p. 26.
[69] Duchy of Lanc. Mins. Accts. bdles. 53, no. 1000; 42, no. 825.
[70] Duchy of Lanc. Misc. Bks. xvi, fol. 26 d.
[71] *Parl. R.* iv, 187*b*.
[72] Ibid. v, 118*b*; Duchy of Lanc. Misc. Bks. xviii, 49 (pt. ii).
[73] *Parl. R.* v, 628*a*.
[74] Ct. R. (Gen. Ser.), portf. 177, no. 37.
[75] Duchy of Lanc. Misc. Bks. xxiii, fol. 56.
[76] Pat. 7 Jas. I, pt. i.
[77] Hertf. Corp. Papers, v, no. 3; Pat. 6 Chas. I, pt. x, no. 1.
[78] Harl. MS. 6708, fol. 4; Aug. Off. Fee-Farm Rents, file 42, no. 261; Recov. R. Hil. 7 Anne, rot. 115; East. 9 Geo. II, rot. 194.
[79] Duchy of Lanc. Misc. Bks. xii, fol. 58 d. The tenure was by knight service until James I changed it to socage. See Turnor, op. cit. 66; Cussans, op. cit. 60.
[80] Duchy of Lanc. Misc. Bks. xii, fol. 58 d.
[81] Duchy of Lanc. Mins. Accts. bdles. 733, no. 12043; 53, no. 1010.
[82] Pat. 6 Chas. I, pt. x, no. 1.
[83] The mills were often leased separately from the manor (see Duchy of Lanc. Misc. Bks. xvii, fol. 39 [pt. iii]; xvii, fol. 91; xxi, fol. 175, 174 d., 171, 171 d.; xxiv, fol. 60, &c.). In the first of these grants (1416) the mills are called the Chastell Mills, in the last (1634) they are described as grain mills. The park was also leased separately (see *Cal. S. P. Dom.* 1603–10, p. 164; Cussans, op. cit. 52).

502

BOROUGH OF HERTFORD

and fair, of which a grant had been made to the mayor by James I.

The soil and fishing of the Beane 'from the east end of Paper Mill Mead to Goodes Pool and in the waters called Black Ditch, Manifold Ditch and the other ditches to the east of Chadwell Mead' were granted to the mayor and burgesses by Charles I in 1627.[84] Of the paper mill Cussans says 'the site of the mill was probably near the old waterworks, for the channel through which the water flows to the River Beane is still known as Paper-mill Ditch.'[85] A paper-mill is mentioned in 1498, and was probably the earliest set up in England (see Sele Mill in St. Andrew Rural).[86]

The court held at Hertford in the 14th and 15th centuries did the work of a manorial court while choosing burgesses and guarding burgess right.[87] There was no distinction between the jurisdictional area of town and manor. The charters of Elizabeth and James gave the borough a weekly court of record,[88] with which the older courts were probably fused. This explanation at least fits the contemporary statement 'that there are certain courts leet and baron held, and the mayor has used to be instead of the (lord's) bailiff time out of mind'[89] (1621). After 1630 these manorial courts were held for the 'manor and castle' by the officials of the Earl of Salisbury,[90] in accordance with the theory that a manor must have courts leet and baron. There is record of these courts as late as 1773.[91]

The castle of Hertford is situated on the flat, low-lying land on the south bank of the River Lea.[92] It seems to have been one of the castles thrown up after the Conquest to form a ring of defence round London. The earthwork defences consisted of a double ditch on three sides, the space between them widening considerably on the south-west to form an outer ward. The ditches communicated at either end with the main course of the Lea, which sufficiently defended the north-west face. There was also a small artificial mound which still exists at the extreme northern angle of the curtain wall, but there is no evidence that this was ever surrounded by a separate moat. The masonry parts of the castle under the name of the castle of Hertford and the king's houses in it, which would probably include the keep, the curtain wall and the houses in the bailey, were apparently begun by Henry II in 1170.[93] They were under the charge of Henry the Chaplain or Henry the Deacon, William the Parker, Wigar, Azur, and Robert Crassus, the three last of whom were burgesses of Hertford.[94] Large sums of money were paid out by the sheriff on the building operations during the years 1171,[95] 1172,[96] 1173,[97] and 1174.[98] In 1173 the work was so far advanced that the castle was fully provisioned against the insurrection of young Henry, the king's eldest son,[99] and in the following year occurs the last payment for building operations for some years, so that the work was evidently then com-

pleted. This is confirmed by the fact that the castle was in this year garrisoned by knights and sergeants.[100] Lesser sums, probably for repairs, were paid in 1182[1] and 1183.[2] A shell keep similar to that at Berkhampstead evidently crowned the mound already referred to. With the exception of portions on the southern side the ditches are now all filled in and levelled, but their extreme limit outwardly is marked by St. Andrew's parish boundary, and the total area of the castle site is about 7¾ acres.

The existing remains belong entirely to the inner ward, which was in form an irregular pentagon surrounded by a curtain. This wall, built of flint rubble, much patched and re-faced with red brick, is still standing on the eastern and southern sides. It varies greatly in thickness from 5 ft. to 6 ft. upwards, and with the exception of the parapet is standing to its full height. It terminates at the southern angle in a small octagonal tower (internally 12 ft. in diameter), partially ruined, and evidently built to defend the postern which adjoins it on the east. The postern has a pointed arch quite devoid of ornament and dating from the 13th century. The curtain is probably somewhat earlier in date. In the centre of the western face stands the Tudor gate-house, a rectangular structure of red brick with octagonal projecting turrets at the four corners, that on the south-east being carried up above the roof. This building forms the northern half of the house known as Hertford Castle and has been much altered in the 18th century, when the southern wing was added on the line of the curtain wall. The windows are all of that date, as is the pseudo-Gothic corbelling and embattled parapet. Traces of the western or outer arch of the gate-house are to be seen behind the modern porch, and above it is a sunk stone panel bearing a coat of arms (said to be that of the Tudors, but now too much decayed to be identified) with supporters, and surmounted by a crown. The inner or eastern arch of the gate-house is now transformed into a window.

The internal arrangements of the castle are preserved in an Elizabethan plan at the Public Record Office, prepared by Henry Hawthorne about 1582 or 1592, when the courts of law were temporarily moved to Hertford owing to the prevalence of the Plague in London. The plan is unfortunately mutilated and what remains is in two fragments,[2a] but the main apartments are shown grouped round a central courtyard with the great hall on the eastern side. With the exception of the fireplace backs and chimneys the walls are shown so thin as to imply a timber-framed building carried on dwarf walls, traces of which have from time to time come to light under the present lawn and garden. The hall was an aisled building of three bays with screens and two porches at the northern end and a square oriel and a fireplace at the southern. On the plan it bears a close resemblance to the great hall at Ashby Castle (Leicestershire). The offices at the northern end are by no

---

[84] Turnor, op. cit. 62. This grant does not seem to be among the patents of the year.
[85] Op. cit. 53. [86] Ibid. 52, 53.
[87] Ct. R. (Gen. Ser.), portf. 177, no. 37; Hertf. Corp. Papers, v, no. 33.
[88] Pat. 31 Eliz. pt. xi, m. 3.
[89] Hertf. Corp. Papers, v, no. 65.
[90] Harl. MS. 6708; Ct. R. (Gen. Ser.), portf. 227, no. 82.

[91] Hertf. Corp. Papers, iv, no. 388.
[92] Its general disposition is excellently shown in a small inset view of the town in Speed's map of Herts. (1610), the accuracy of which is attested by documentary evidence.
[93] Pipe R. 17 Hen. II (Pipe R. Soc.), 118.
[94] They paid aid in 1168 (Pipe R. 14 Hen. II [Pipe R. Soc.], 40).

[95] Ibid. 17 Hen. II, 118.
[96] Ibid. 18 Hen. II, 40.
[97] Ibid. 19 Hen. II, 13.
[98] Ibid. 20 Hen. II, 67.
[99] Ibid. 19 Hen. II, 13.
[100] Ibid. 20 Hen. II, 67, 73.
[1] Ibid. 28 Hen. II; 98.
[2] Ibid. 29 Hen. II, 19.
[2a] S. P. Dom. Edw. VI, xviii, 43; Chas. I, lxxxix, 29.

503

A HISTORY OF HERTFORDSHIRE

means clear, and the only apartment with a fireplace large enough for the kitchen is that marked Court of Requests.[2b] To the south of the hall is a square courtyard, surrounded on three sides by an open timber cloister, and with a small oratory projecting into the court at the south-east angle. The great chapel probably occupied the first floor of one of the wings shown projecting eastward from the main building. The great angle bastion on the curtain wall has now completely disappeared. It was, however, still standing in 1772, and is shown in a view in Gröse's *Antiquities*.[3] On plan it formed the segment of a circle about 60 ft. in external diameter. The brick wall built across the gorge is still in part standing and is of the time of Henry VIII. On the outer face are traces of the newel stair with a sunk brick handrail.

and the chapel is mentioned in 1202.[3a] No doubt the castle suffered severely in the siege at the end of the reign of John, which would account for a sum of £10 from the farm of the vill being assigned to the constable for the repair of the gate in 1225.[4] In April of the same year a mandate was issued to the sheriff to pull down the houses which had belonged to Falkes de Breauté[5] at Little Berkhampstead, and to build them up again in the castle of Hertford.[6] The old hall, the old chapel, the brewery, and the marshalsea (*marescalcia*) were left at Little Berkhampstead, but in July of the following year the king ordered that the *domus marescalcie* should also be brought to Hertford and built up there.[7] In 1300 the hall, chamber, wardrobe, kitchen and paling were repaired, in 1301 the bakehouse and other houses,

HERTFORD CASTLE THE GATE-HOUSE

The second fragment of the MS. plan shows the bakehouse and other buildings in connexion with another angle bastion, in this case open at the gorge. It seems impossible to place it anywhere else but on the site of the earlier keep, in which case the keep ditch, if it ever existed, must have been filled in and the keep itself destroyed late in the Middle Ages.

These plans and the existing remains are explained and illustrated by documentary evidence. The residential part of the castle had been built before 1199, when a sum of £5 was spent in repairing the hall,

the walls and bridge, and in 1302 the houses, bridges, outer gates and the chamber over the gate.[8]

From the 14th to the 17th centuries there are a series of surveys of the castle. The earliest of these, dated 1327,[9] is a survey of the defects with the estimated cost of their repair. Mention is made of (1) a certain chamber without the outer bridge in the entry of the castle and a certain other chamber adjoining the outer gate; (2) the middle bridge with a certain chamber adjoining the outer gate of the same bridge; (3) a certain bakehouse against the

---

[2b] Marked kitchen in the accompanying plan.
[3] F. Grose, *Antiquities of Engl.* (1777), ii.
[3a] Pipe R. 1 John, m. 7; *Rot. Canc.* (Rec. Com.), 145.
[4] *Rot. Lit. Claus.* (Rec. Com.), ii, 88*a*, 88*b*, 139*b*.
[5] He forfeited in 1224.
[6] *Rot. Lit. Claus.* (Rec. Com.), ii, 34.
[7] Ibid. 130. The sheriff was to bring it 'whenever the burden of carriage should weigh least heavily on the neighbourhood.'
[8] *Cal. Close*, 1313–18, p. 515.
[9] *Exch. Accts.* bdle. 465, no. 15.

504

same gate and a granary adjoining the bakehouse; (4) the great chamber called the King's Chamber with two chapels adjoining the same, the kitchen and the lesser hall; (5) the great hall of the king with two chimneys adjoining the same and two garderobes; (6) a certain chamber without the postern and the drawbridge beyond the same postern; (7) the stone wall in the circuit with the tower of the same castle and the two chimneys of the two chambers aforesaid; (8) the wooden stockade next the outer ditch, 'which is in many places prostrate on the ground.'

The next two surveys are couched in general terms and give little information as to the buildings of the castle. That of 1522-3,[10] however, mentions that there is 'a fayre river runnynge alonge by the Northside of the said Castell and the water of the same Ryver serveth for and to all the houses of Office within the same Castell and arere a very litle garden grounde, but there is a fayre courtyarde and large which is almost finished rounde aboute with fayre [houses].'

The survey of 1558-9[11] refers only to the general dilapidation of the buildings, 'as well in timber work as in tiling, glazing and leading, dawbing, sealing and ironwork,' and computes the cost of repairs at £80.

Thirty years later the castle buildings were again in a bad state of repair, and a fourth survey[12] (dated 1587-8) indicates that many of the apartments required entire rebuilding. Mention is here made of the privy kitchen, the serving place with the scullery, the bakehouse, the rooms over the pantry, the passage between the court and the bakehouse, the shed towards the kitchen, timber for the chapel end, the lodging where my Lord Treasurer did lie in the term, the bridge towards St. Andrews, the house in the castle yard next the water with the chimney and the west gable end, the old gate-house in the castle yard. Many of these buildings may be identified on the Elizabethan plan and the majority of them appear to have been of timber. The 'Castle Yard' was evidently the inner bailey and the 'bridge towards St. Andrews' is distinctly indicated on Speed's view.

The greater part of the buildings were pulled down early in the reign of James I. In a survey of the extent of the castle dated 1609-10[13] it is stated that 'there are standing upon part of the site of the said castle one fair gatehouse of brick, one tower of brick and the old walls of the said castle and also three old houses without the walls.' The site contained 7 acres and 3 roods, part called the 'Castle yard' being fenced with stone and part unfenced called the 'Castle ditches'; 'the utter bryme of the utter ditch' being bounded by the king's highway called Castle Street on the south and east. With the exception of the three old houses and the tower of brick, evidently the south-east bastion, this survey represents fairly accurately the still existing remains of the castle.

The most important period in the history of the castle was the Civil War in the reign of King John. Hertford and Berkhampstead were both taken by the barons in 1215 and were held until the following year. The defection from Louis of France then began and was followed by the surrender of the castles.[14] At the end of the same year Hertford was besieged by Louis. The castle seems to have been bravely defended by the constable Walter de Godarvile, but after a siege of nearly a month it surrendered,[15] probably having no further supply of provisions.

The castle was used as an occasional residence by most of the kings of England whilst it remained a royal castle.[16] After the grant in dower made to Queen Isabel in 1327 (see above) she stayed at the castle from time to time and died there on 22 August 1358.[17] The next year King John of France was lodged there during his captivity in England.[18] John of Gaunt received a grant of the castle at the same time as the manor (see above) in 1360, and bought large stores of timber from his neighbours, who did not dare to refuse him, in order to fortify it. According to the chronicler Walsingham, one of his grievances when he retired from court in 1377 was that the king had taken possession of the castle of Hertford, where he had meant to spend most of his time.[19] The castle was, however, confirmed to him by a grant of the same year.[20] It seems to have been chiefly between 1396 and 1399 that he used it as a residence.[21] The castle came again to the Crown on the accession of Henry IV, and in 1428 was appointed one of the summer residences of the Crown.[22] In 1424 there is mention of the Bishop of Durham surrendering the great seal in 'the great chamber in the castle of Hertford.'[23]

In the itineraries of Henry VIII Hertford Castle appears with the royal houses of Hunsdon and Hatfield.[24] The Princess Mary was staying there when Wriothesley brought her a proposal of marriage from Philip Duke of Bavaria, nephew of the Count Palatine, in December 1539.[25] Prince Edward was at the castle at the time of Henry's death. The news of this event was for a time kept secret from the public, but the Earl of Hertford (afterwards Duke of Somerset) and Sir Anthony Browne hastened to Hertford, took Prince Edward secretly to Enfield, and there told him and the Princess Elizabeth of the prince's accession to the throne.[26]

In 1563, 1581 and 1592 the law courts were removed to Hertford Castle owing to the Plague in

---

[10] Exch. Accts. bdle. 465, no. 16.
[11] Duchy of Lanc. Special Com. no. 2.
[12] Ibid. no. 416.
[13] Duchy of Lanc. Special Com. no. 813. For notices of works at the castle occurring in 1357, 1397, 1424 and 1560 see *Cal. Pat.* 1354-8, p. 583; 1396-9, pp. 148-9; 1422-9, p. 193; *Cal. S. P. Dom.* 1547-80, p. 166.
[14] 'Ann. Lond.' *Chron. of Edw. I and Edw. II* (Rolls Ser.), i, 17, 21.
[15] Matthew Paris, *Chron. Maj.* (Rolls Ser.), iii, 5.
[16] See Letters Patent dated there, *Cal. Pat.* 1232-47, 1247-58, 1301-7, 1307-13, 1330-4, 1334-8, 1338-40, 1343-5, 1345-8, 1348-50, 1354-8, 1377-81, 1401-5, 1405-8, 1413-16, 1436-41, 1461-7, 1476-85, passim.
[17] For her household accounts there in 1357-8 see Cott. MS. Galba, E xiv. See Cussans, op. cit. 51.
[18] *Cal. Close*, 1354-60, p. 572.
[19] Walsingham, *Hist. Angl.* (Chron. Mon. Sci. Albani, Rolls Ser.), i, 339.
[20] *Cal. Pat.* 1377-81, p. 26.
[21] See numerous letters dated there, *Cal. Pat.* 1396-9, passim, also of Henry Duke of Hereford. The Duke of Lancaster spent Christmas there in 1390 (Walsingham, op. cit. 195).
[22] *Proc. of P.C.* iii, pp. lii, 295.
[23] Ibid. vi, 346.
[24] See *L. and P. Hen. VIII*, xvi, 677.
[25] Ibid. xiv, 696-7. There is a letter of hers dated there in 1536 (ibid. xi, 526).
[26] P. Fraser Tytler, *England under reigns of Edward VI and Mary* (1839), i, 16. See also Burnet, *Hist. of Reformation* (1865), ii, 37, where it is shown from Edward's Diary that he was at Hertford, not Hatfield.

A HISTORY OF HERTFORDSHIRE

London.[27] Queen Elizabeth stayed at Hertford on several occasions,[28] but James I does not seem to have been there, and in the next reign the castle ceased to be a royal one, being included with the manor in the grant to the Earl of Salisbury (see above).

Gaol delivery for the county took place at Hertford Castle.[29]

Down to the end of the 12th century the constableship of the castle seems to have been held by the sheriff of the county. The grant to Peter de Valognes, sheriff under William I, of the 'lordship of Hertford' was evidently considered later to include the constableship, for the enrolment of the charter among the 'cartae antiqnae' is headed 'Charter of Robert Fitz Walter,'[30] and it was evidently one of the charters which Robert Fitz Walter (who married Gunnora, the Valognes heir) showed to the king in order to prove his right to the constableship.[31] There is evidence that Geoffrey Fitz Peter, who was sheriff from 1190 to 1192, held the constableship,[32] and he continued to hold it until August 1202, when he received a mandate to deliver the castle to Robert Fitz Walter, who apparently claimed it in right of his wife.[33] In the same year, however, Richard de Montfitchet made fine with the king for the custody of the county and of the castle of Hertford.[34] In 1212 John Fitz Hugh was custodian and in August of that year was ordered to give up the custody to John de Bassingbourn, leaving behind the wines and other supplies bought with the king's money.[35] During the temporary peace following the signing of Magna Carta Robert Fitz Walter, who had been serving as marshal of the barons' army, obtained another grant of the custody in succession to John de Bassingbourn.[36] This was in June 1215, but in August of the same year war broke out again, and Robert Fitz Walter went over to France to offer the crown to Louis. The castle had meanwhile been taken by the barons, who held it until 1216 (see above). After its surrender to the king, John appointed Walter de Godarvile, a follower of Falkes de Breauté, governor,[37] and he was holding it during the siege by Louis.[38] Whilst it was in Louis' hands Robert Fitz Walter put in a claim to the custody which he claimed by 'ancient right,' but Louis, according to the chronicler, refused on the somewhat ungenerous plea that Englishmen who had been traitors to their own king were not worthy of any office of importance.[39]

During the next reign a constant succession appears in the appointment of constables. Before December 1223 the custody had been held by Falkes de Breauté; in that month it was granted to William de Eynesford.[40] On 7 January 1224 it was granted to Stephen de Segrave,[41] on 22 January of the same year to Richard de Argentein, the sheriff,[42] who held it until August 1228.[43] At the latter date it was granted to Raymond de Burgh, before 23 January 1230 to William de Culworth, on that date to Raymond de Burgh again,[44] on 3 July 1230 to William de Culworth, the sheriff,[45] and on 25 September 1230 to John de Burgh,[46] from whom apparently it passed to Hugh de Burgh, for he in 1232 was ordered to deliver it to Stephen de Segrave.[47] In May 1234 it was held by Robert Passelewe, who was then superseded by William de Culworth,[48] sheriff in that year, and he held it until the appointment of the next sheriff, Peter de Tany, in May 1236.[49] In 1242 Richard de Montfitchet was appointed sheriff and custodian of the castle,[50] holding the office until 1246.[51] In 1247 the king's brother William de Valence had a grant of the custody of the castle and mills,[52] to which the vill was added a few days later[53]; this was converted into a life grant in 1249.[54] From this date the castle descended with the vill or manor (q.v.).

The *LIMESY FEE* afterwards the MANORS *PRIORY MANOR* was the property of Hertford Priory. In 1086 Ralph de Limesy was holding lands in Hertfordshire and elsewhere which had been held by Earl Harold, and among these apparently was an estate at Hertford appurtenant to the manor of Hatfield Broadoak in Essex.[55] Ralph de Limesy founded the priory of St. Mary of Hertford as a cell to St. Albans and endowed it with a hide of land at Hertford and a church which he had built there.[56] The place where the friary stood was known as Limesy Fee and was outside the area and jurisdiction of the borough.[57]

After the Dissolution the manor and site of the priory were granted to Anthony Denny in February 1537–8.[58] They descended in

D E N N Y. *Gules a saltire argent between twelve crosses formy or.*

---

[27] Stow, *Annales*, 656, 695, 764. See *Cal. S. P. Dom.* 1581–90, pp. 71, 75; 1580–1625, pp. 79, 80; *Acts of P.C.* 1592, pp. 273, 274, 275.
[28] For councils held there see *Acts of P.C.* 1575–7, pp. 191, 192, 193, 195. For a visit in 1576 see *Hist. MSS. Com. Rep.* vii, App. i, 629a.
[29] Assize R. 336; *L. and P. Hen. VIII*, xvii, 443 (40), &c.
[30] Cart. Antiq. K 10, 22.
[31] *Rot. Cur. Reg.* (Rec. Com.), ii, 185.
[32] *Rot. Lit. Pat.* (Rec. Com.), i, 17.
[33] Ibid.; *Rot. Cur. Reg.* (Rec. Com.), ii, 185.
[34] *Rot. de Oblatis et Fin.* (Rec. Com.), 93. It is uncertain whether this was before or after August, for it is dated 'terminum infra annum (2 John)' only.
[35] *Rot. Lit. Pat.* (Rec. Com.), i, 94b. For writ carried to Hertford in 1226 see *Rot. Lit. Claus.* (Rec. Com.), ii, 117b. The first mandate to John Fitz Hugh of 21 August was followed by another one of 29 August, threatening him with the imputation of bad faith if he did not at once surrender the castle (*Rot. Lit. Pat.* [Rec. Com.], i, 95).
[36] *Rot. Lit. Pat.* (Rec. Com.), i, 144b.
[37] Matthew Paris, *Chron. Maj.* (Rolls Ser.), ii, 641.
[38] Ibid. iii, 5.
[39] Ibid.
[40] *Cal. Pat.* 1216–25, p. 418.
[41] Ibid. 420.
[42] Ibid. 425.
[43] Ibid. 1225–32, p. 199.
[44] Ibid. 322.
[45] Ibid. 347.
[46] Ibid. 348.
[47] Ibid. 496.
[48] Ibid. 1232–47, p. 50.
[49] Ibid. 144.
[50] Ibid. 286, 294.
[51] Ibid. 477.
[52] Ibid. 1247–58, p. 1.
[53] Ibid. 2.
[54] Ibid. 46. A similar grant was made in 1251 (*Cal. Chart. R.* 1226–57, p. 351).
[55] *V.C.H. Essex*, i, 429; see *V.C.H. Herts.* i, 299. The only possessions in Hertford belonging to Harold mentioned under Hertford in the Domesday Survey are eighteen burgesses who in 1086 belonged to King William. This can scarcely be the estate above mentioned, which appears not to be noticed in the Survey (except under Essex), but is perhaps included in Ralph de Limesy's manor of Amwell. The close connexion between the two estates (Hertford and Amwell) is shown by the style of the priory manor in 1637, 'the manor of the priory of Hertford and now or late called the manor of Amwell or the fee of Amwell' (Close, 13 Chas. I, pt. xxxviii, no. 17).
[56] See article on Religious Houses, *V.C.H. Herts.* iv.
[57] See Agard's MS. Index to Assize R. vii (2nd nos.), fol. 21 d. (Hil. 7 Hen. V).
[58] *L. and P. Hen. VIII*, xiii (1), 384 (47).

506

THE WASH

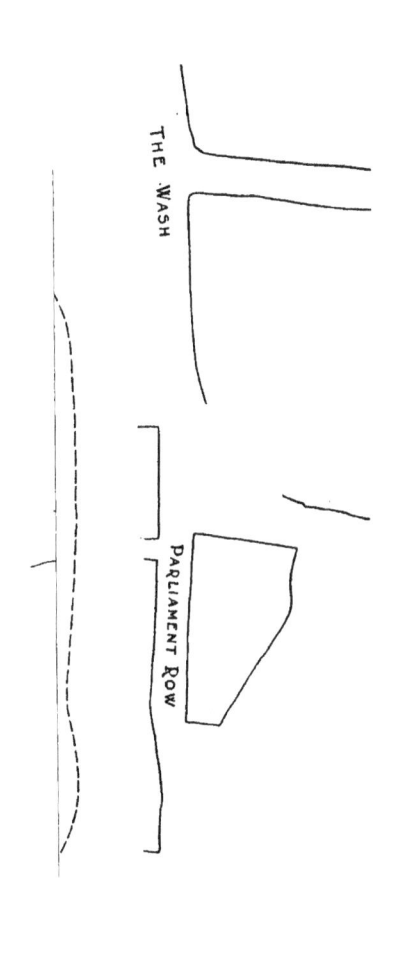

PARLIAMENT ROW

A HISTORY OF HERTFORDSHIRE

London.[27] Queen Elizabeth stayed at Hertford on several occasions,[28] but James I does not seem to have been there, and in the next reign the castle ceased to be a royal one, being included with the manor in the grant to the Earl of Salisbury (see above).

Gaol delivery for the county took place at Hertford Castle.[29]

Down to the end of the 12th century the constableship of the castle seems to have been held by the sheriff of the county. The grant to Peter de Valognes, sheriff under William I, of the 'lordship of Hertford' was evidently considered later to include the constableship, for the enrolment of the charter among the 'cartae antiquae' is headed 'Charter of Robert Fitz Walter,'[30] and it was evidently one of the charters which Robert Fitz Walter (who married Gunnora, the Valognes heir) showed to the king in order to prove his right to the constableship.[31] There is evidence that Geoffrey Fitz Peter, who was sheriff from 1190 to 1192, held the constableship,[32] and he continued to hold it until August 1202, when he received a mandate to deliver the castle to Robert Fitz Walter, who apparently claimed it in right of his wife.[33] In the same year, however, Richard de Montfitchet made fine with the king for the custody of the county and of the castle of Hertford.[34] In 1212 John Fitz Hugh was custodian and in August of that year was ordered to give up the custody to John de Bassingbourn, leaving behind the wines and other supplies bought with the king's money.[35] During the temporary peace following the signing of Magna Carta Robert Fitz Walter, who had been serving as marshal of the barons' army, obtained another grant of the custody in succession to John de Bassingbourn.[36] This was in June 1215, but in August of the same year war broke out again, and Robert Fitz Walter went over to France to offer the crown to Louis. The castle had meanwhile been taken by the barons, who held it until 1216 (see above). After its surrender to the king, John appointed Walter de Godarvile, a follower of Falkes de Breauté, governor,[37] and he was holding it during the siege by Louis.[38] Whilst it was in Louis' hands Robert Fitz Walter put in a claim to the custody which he claimed by 'ancient right,' but Louis, according to the chronicler, refused on the somewhat ungenerous plea that Englishmen who had been traitors to their own king were not worthy of any office of importance.[39]

During the next reign a constant succession appears in the appointment of constables. Before December 1223 the custody had been held by Falkes de Breauté; in that month it was granted to William de Eynesford.[40] On 7 January 1224 it was granted to Stephen de Segrave,[41] on 22 January of the same year to Richard de Argentein, the sheriff,[42] who held it until August 1228.[43] At the latter date it was granted to Raymond de Burgh, before 23 January 1230 to William de Culworth, on that date to Raymond de Burgh again,[44] on 3 July 1230 to William de Culworth, the sheriff,[45] and on 25 September 1230 to John de Burgh,[46] from whom apparently it passed to Hugh de Burgh, for he in 1232 was ordered to deliver it to Stephen de Segrave.[47] In May 1234 it was held by Robert Passelewe, who was then superseded by William de Culworth,[48] sheriff in that year, and he held it until the appointment of the next sheriff, Peter de Tany, in May 1236.[49] In 1242 Richard de Montfitchet was appointed sheriff and custodian of the castle,[50] holding the office until 1246.[51] In 1247 the king's brother William de Valence had a grant of the custody of the castle and mills,[52] to which the vill was added a few days later[53]; this was converted into a life grant in 1249.[54] From this date the castle descended with the vill or manor (q.v.).

MANORS The *LIMESY FEE* afterwards the *PRIORY MANOR* was the property of Hertford Priory. In 1086 Ralph de Limesy was holding lands in Hertfordshire and elsewhere which had been held by Earl Harold, and among these apparently was an estate at Hertford appurtenant to the manor of Hatfield Broadoak in Essex.[55] Ralph de Limesy founded the priory of St. Mary of Hertford as a cell to St. Albans and endowed it with a hide of land at Hertford and a church which he had built there.[56] The place where the friary stood was known as Limesy Fee and was outside the area and jurisdiction of the borough.[57]

After the Dissolution the manor and site of the priory were granted to Anthony Denny in February 1537–8.[58] They descended in

DENNY. *Gules a saltire argent between twelve crosses formy or.*

---

[27] Stow, *Annales*, 656, 695, 764. See *Cal. S. P. Dom.* 1581–90, pp. 71, 75; 1580–1625, pp. 79, 80; *Acts of P.C.* 1592, pp. 273, 274, 275.
[28] For councils held there see *Acts of P.C.* 1575–7, pp. 191, 192, 193, 195. For a visit in 1576 see *Hist. MSS. Com. Rep.* vii, App. i, 629a.
[29] Assize R. 336; *L. and P. Hen. VIII*, xvii, 443 (40), &c.
[30] Cart. Antiq. K 10, 22.
[31] *Rot. Cur. Reg.* (Rec. Com.), ii, 185.
[32] *Rot. Lit. Pat.* (Rec. Com.), i, 17.
[33] Ibid.; *Rot. Cur. Reg.* (Rec. Com.), ii, 185.
[34] *Rot. de Oblatis et Fin.* (Rec. Com.), 93. It is uncertain whether this was before or after August, for it is dated 'terminum infra annum (2 John)' only.
[35] *Rot. Lit. Pat.* (Rec. Com.), i, 94b. For wine carried to Hertford in 1226 see *Rot. Lit. Claus.* (Rec. Com.), ii, 117b. The first mandate to John Fitz Hugh of 21 August was followed by another one of 29 August, threatening him with the imputation of bad faith if he did not at once surrender the castle (*Rot. Lit. Pat.* [Rec. Com.], i, 95).
[36] *Rot. Lit. Pat.* (Rec. Com.), i, 144b.
[37] Matthew Paris, *Chron. Maj.* (Rolls Ser.), ii, 641.
[38] Ibid. iii, 5.
[39] Ibid.
[40] *Cal. Pat.* 1216–25, p. 418.
[41] Ibid. 420.
[42] Ibid. 425.
[43] Ibid. 1225–32, p. 199.
[44] Ibid. 322.
[45] Ibid. 347.
[46] Ibid. 348.
[47] Ibid. 496.
[48] Ibid. 1232–47, p. 50.
[49] Ibid. 144.
[50] Ibid. 286, 294.
[51] Ibid. 477.
[52] Ibid. 1247–58, p. 1.
[53] Ibid. 2.
[54] Ibid. 46. A similar grant was made in 1251 (*Cal. Chart. R.* 1226–57, p. 351).
[55] *V.C.H. Essex*, i, 429; see *V.C.H. Herts.* i, 299. The only possessions in Hertford belonging to Harold mentioned under Hertford in the Domesday Survey are eighteen burgesses who in 1086 belonged to King William. This can scarcely be the estate above mentioned, which appears not to be noticed in the Survey (except under Essex), but is perhaps included in Ralph de Limesy's manor of Amwell. The close connexion between the two estates (Hertford and Amwell) is shown by the style of the priory manor in 1637, 'the manor of the priory of Hertford and now or late called the manor of Amwell or the fee of Amwell' (Close, 13 Chas. I, pt. xxxviii, no. 17).
[56] See article on Religious Houses, *V.C.H. Herts.* iv.
[57] See Agard's MS. Index to Assize R. vii (2nd nos.), fol. 21 d. (Hil. 7 Hen. V).
[58] *L. and P. Hen. VIII*, xiii (1), 384 (47).

PLAN OF HERTFORD CASTLE

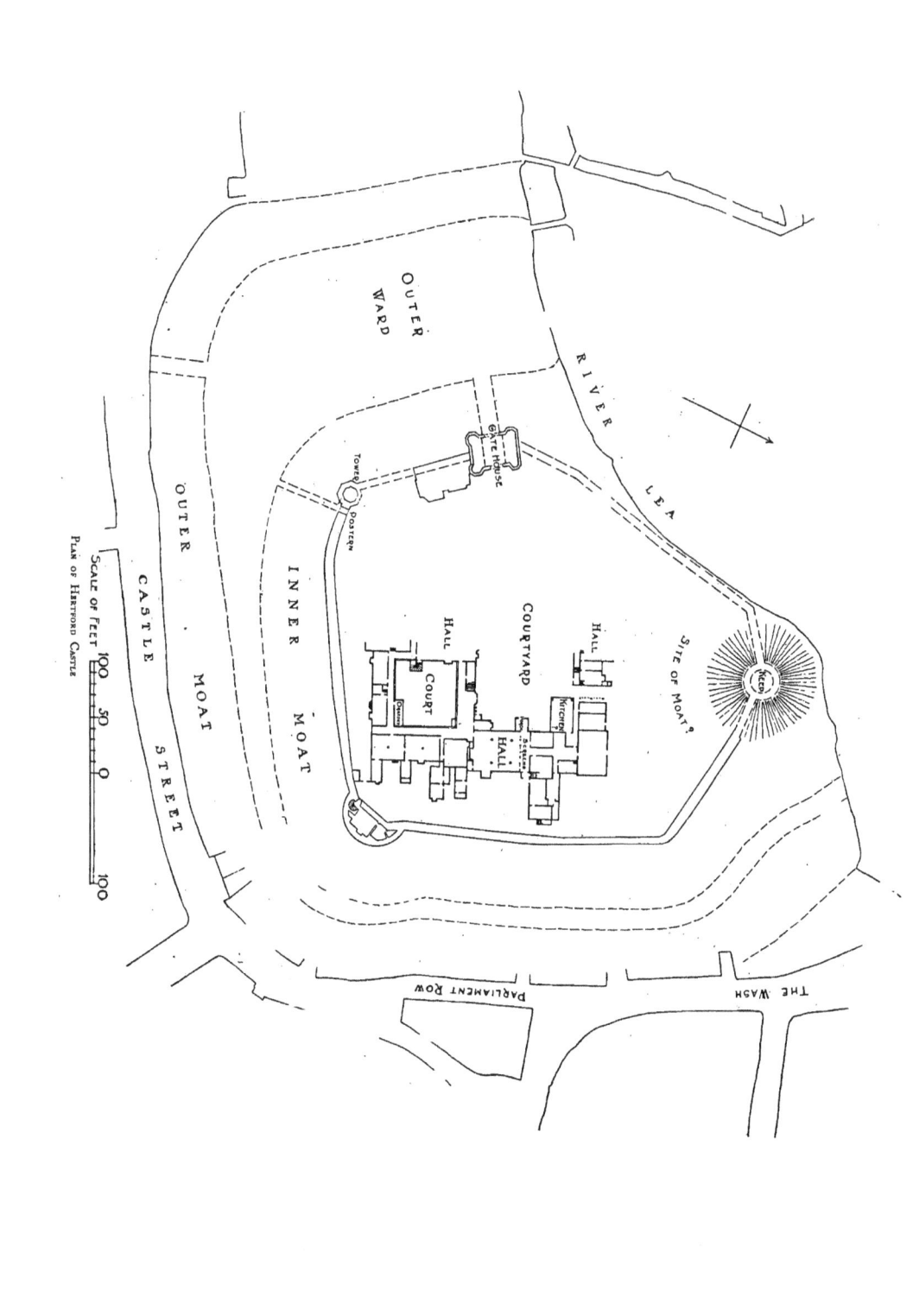

HERTFORD HUNDRED

the Denny family[59] until 1587, when Edward Denny and Margaret his wife conveyed them to Henry Colthurst.[60] They seem to have been conveyed to Martin Trott probably about 1590.[61] Trott sold them to Richard Willis in 1617,[62] who died seised in 1625,[63] leaving a son Thomas under age.[64] In 1637 Thomas Willis sold the manor to John Harrison of London,[65] and it descended with Balls Park in Little Amwell (q.v.) until the latter was sold to Sir G. F. Fandel-Phillips, bart. Hertford Priory is still in the possession of Marquess Townshend. In 1624 there are mentioned as appurtenant to this manor the water-mill called Lyckermill or Dickermill and the close called 'the churchyard of St. John the Evangelist or the Mill Close.'[66]

TOWNSHEND. *Azure a cheveron ermine between three scallops argent.*

The origin of the BOURNE FEE in Hertford is probably to be found in the property of Geoffrey de Bech, who in 1086 had three houses there.[67] Like the manors of Eastwick (in Braughing Hundred) and Bengeo this probably came to Baldwin de Clare, lord of Bourne, and through his daughter Emma to the Wakes. Later we find the court of the honour of Bourne (Broune, Brunne) being held at Hertford, to which the neighbouring tenants of the Wakes owed suit.[68]

WAKE. *Or two bars gules with three roundels gules in the chief.*

Another court held at Hertford was the court of the HONOUR OF MANDEVILLE. In 1086 Geoffrey de Mandeville had property at Hertford which had been held by Asgar the Staller, and he had also seven houses which rendered no dues except geld.[69] Humphrey de Bohun, Earl of Hereford and Essex, successor of Geoffrey de Mandeville, was presented in the reign of Edward I for withdrawing his suit from the borough.[70] In the 13th century and later one of the courts of the honour (called the court of knights)[71] was held at Hertford,[72] and to this we find a Middlesex tenant of the earl's doing suit in 1297.[73]

The VALOGNES FEE in Hertford can also be traced back to 1086, when Peter de Valognes (who was farming the borough) held two churches and a house which he had bought of Ulwi of Hatfield.[74] Roger de Valognes, son of Peter, received a grant of

MANDEVILLE. *Quarterly or and gules.*

BOHUN. *Azure a bend or cotised argent between six lions or.*

the mills of Hertford (see above) and 'the service of Alban de Hairon and all other lands and tenements as his father held them.'[75] In the reign of Edward I Christine de Maune, one of the Valognes heirs, was presented for withdrawing her suit at the borough court.[76] The Valognes family held the manor of Hertingfordbury which in 1086 had been held by Ralph Baniard, and it is probable that Ralph Baniard's Domesday holding of two houses in Hertford also came to them with that manor. In the 13th century the advowson of the hospital of St. Mary Magdalene is found descending with the manor of Hertingfordbury,[77] and it seems probable that the Valognes' lands in Hertfordshire were given to that monastery. The hospital of St. Mary Magdalene was taken over by the Crossed Friars of the order of Holy Trinity,[78] and after the Dissolution the messuage called 'Le Trinitie' was granted to Anthony Denny.[79] In 1577 Edward Denny alienated to John Spurling the close of pasture called Trinity Close on which Trinity House stood, 8 acres of arable land adjoining, 'Friers Grove' containing 8 acres and another grove of 6 acres.[80]

VALOGNES. *Paly wavy argent and gules.*

CHURCHES

The church of ST. ANDREW was erected on the site of the former church in 1869[81]; it consists of an apsidal chancel, nave with aisles, north and south transepts and west tower. It is built of flint with stone dressings in the style of the early 14th century.

The north doorway is part of the old church, and is of late 15th-century date, with moulded arch under a square head, and with quatrefoils in the

---

[59] Recov. R. Mich. 1574, rot. 818; Pat. 21 Eliz. pt. v, vi; 22 Eliz. pt. vii, viii and ix; 26 Eliz. pt. x.
[60] Pat. 29 Eliz. pt. iii; Feet of F. Hil. 29 Eliz.
[61] By fine of 1590 (Trin. 32 Eliz.) Colthurst conveyed the rectory of St. John's to Trott, but the manor is not mentioned. Chauncy says that Martin Trott held a court in 1577, which is difficult to explain unless he was a mortgagee. He was in possession in November 1590 (see Duchy of Lanc. Dec. and Ord. xxi, 191).
[62] Recov. R. East. 15 Jas. I, rot. 20.
[63] Chan. Inq. p.m. (Ser. 2), ccccxviii, 64.
[64] Ct. of Wards, Feod. Surv. no. 17.
[65] Close, 13 Chas. I, pt. xxxviii, no. 17; Recov. R. Mich. 14 Chas. I, rot. 109.
[66] Ct. of Wards, Feod. Surv. no. 17. For the removal of Dickermill to lower ground in order to get enough water after the position of the Queen's mills had been altered see Duchy of Lanc. Dec. and Ord. xxi, 191.
[67] V.C.H. Herts. i, 300.
[68] Chan. Inq. p.m. 9 Ric. II, no. 54; 20 Ric. II, no. 30; 15 Edw. III, no. 40.
[69] V.C.H. Herts. i, 300.
[70] Hund. R. (Rec. Com.), i, 194.
[71] Cal. Inq. p.m. 1–19 Edw. I, 442.
[72] Chan. Inq. p.m. 37 Edw. III, no. 10; 21 Ric. II, no. 29; 1 Hen. IV, no. 50;
Parl. R. iv, 136a; Duchy of Lanc. Misc. Bks. xviii, fol. 49.
[73] Cal. Inq. p.m. 1–19 Edw. I, 442.
[74] V.C.H. Herts. i, 300. One of these churches was probably All Saints (see advowson), the other one is uncertain.
[75] Cart. Antiq. K 10, 24.
[76] Hund. R. (Rec. Com.), i, 194.
[77] Feet of F. Herts. 31 Hen. III, no. 332; Div. Co. 20 Edw. III, no. 8 Chart. R. 20 Edw. III, m. 4, no. 14.
[78] See article on Religious Houses, V.C.H. Herts. iv.
[79] L. and P. Hen. VIII, xv, 1027 (25).
[80] Pat. 33 Eliz. pt. i, m. 19.
[81] For a description of the old church and its monuments see Turnor. op. cit. 250.

507

A HISTORY OF HERTFORDSHIRE

spandrels; the labels have stops carved with angels holding shields. On the west side of the doorway are the remains of a stoup.

Under the communion table in the north chapel is an old stone altar slab, discovered on the site of the former church of St. Mary the Great in 1888; the slab measures 3 ft. 5 in. by 2 ft. 2 in. and is about 5 in. thick. It bears five incised crosses, and in the centre is a rectangular cavity about 3 in. by 2 in. and 1½ in. deep, probably to contain relics. The communion table in the chapel has twisted legs and may be late 17th-century work.

On the nave floor is a brass inscription to Bridget Whitgifte, wife of Robert Collingwood, one of the sons of Sir Cuthbert Collingwood, kt., 1610. There is a floor slab to Arthur Sparke, 1665, with arms.

The church of *ALL SAINTS* was erected in 1895 on the site of the former church, which was burnt down in 1891; it consists of chancel, north organ chamber and vestry, south chapel, nave with aisles, north transept and west tower. It is built of squared Runcorn sandstone and has a tiled roof.

The old church consisted of chancel, nave, north and south aisles, north and south transepts, and west tower.[82] The only fittings which escaped destruction were two brasses, now placed in the modern church. In the north transept are the feet only of a man's figure and inscription in Norman French to John Hunger, master cook to Katherine wife of Henry V, 1435; the other is an inscription only to Thomas Boole, 1456.

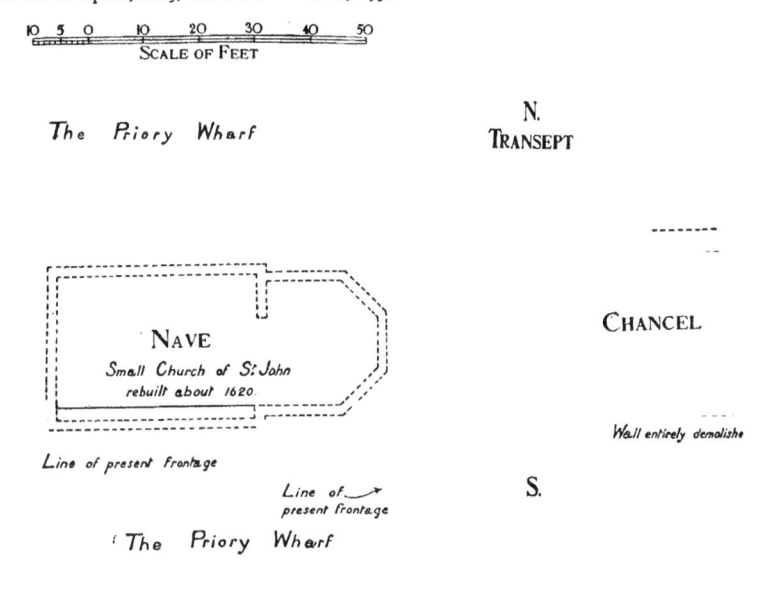

PLAN OF ST. JOHN'S CHURCH, HERTFORD

There is a ring of eight bells: the first, second and fourth of 1782, the fifth and eighth of 1797, and the sixth and seventh of 1793, are all by John Briant of Hertford; the third is by Mears & Stainbank, 1876.

There is an early Spanish chalice and a paten given by Canon Wigram in 1879, and an 18th-century chalice and paten given by Mr. Charles Butler in 1880.

The registers previous to 1812 are as follows: (i) baptisms 1560 to 1653, burials and marriages 1561 to 1653; (ii) baptisms 1653 to 1723, burials 1653 to 1721, marriages 1653 to 1724; (iii) baptisms 1724 to 1791, burials 1724 to 1796, marriages 1724 to 1753; (iii*b*) baptisms 1791 to 1811, burials 1797 to 1812; (iv) marriages 1755 to 1782; (v) marriages 1782 to 1812.

The bells were ten in number, the first and second by John Briant of Hertford, 1791, and the remaining eight by Pack & Chapman, 1771. They have been recast by Mears & Stainbank.

The communion plate consists of flagon, dated 1680; cup and cover paten, 1696; paten, 1725; large paten without hall mark; two chalices, 1874, and two modern spoons.

The registers previous to 1812 are as follows: (i) baptisms 1559 to 1641, burials 1559 to 1648, marriages 1560 to 1652; (ii) baptisms and burials 1653 to 1675, marriages 1653 to 1674; (iii) all entries 1675 to 1729; (iv) baptisms and burials

[82] For description of it and the monuments see Turnor, op. cit. 185. In 1763 the old church was greatly damaged by a storm (see *Sess. R.* [Herts. Co. Rec.], ii, 99).

508

HERTFORD HUNDRED

1730 to 1779, marriages 1730 to 1754; (v) marriages 1754 to 1837; (vi) baptisms 1780 to 1844; (vii) burials 1780 to 1858.

CHRIST CHURCH, in Port Vale, was built in 1868 by Mr. Abel Smith. It is a cruciform building of stone, in 13th-century style, consisting of chancel, nave of three bays, aisles and transepts, south porch and west bell turret. The parish was created in 1869.[83] The living is a vicarage, and the patron is Mr. Abel H. Smith.

Of the church of *ST. MARY* very few records have survived. In 1428 there were less than ten inhabitants in the parish.[84] The church[85] adjoined the Old Cross; it appears to have fallen into ruins in the 16th century.[86] During the excavations for the public library in 1888 many of the old stones were found[87]; some of these were used in the construction of a memorial fountain near the library, and consist of the greater part of a window of clunch of 13th-century date. The arch is moulded, and the jambs are shafted, with moulded capitals and bases. Both arch and jambs are enriched with the dog-tooth ornament. Other fragments are preserved in the library.

A messuage called St. Mary Churchyard was included in the grant of the manor to the Earl of Salisbury in 1630.[88]

The other parish churches originally in Hertford, namely, St. John the Evangelist[89] and St. Nicholas, have disappeared. *ST. JOHN'S* was built before the beginning of the 13th century,[90] and seems to have been pulled down before 1624, when the churchyard formed the mill close of Lyckermill.[91] It is said to have been rebuilt by Thomas Willis, the patron, in 1629,[92] and to have been demolished about fifty years later, after the parish was united to All Saints.[93] The church stood at the east end of the town, to the north of the present buildings of Christ's Hospital, upon the site now occupied (1912) by the timber yard of Messrs. Ewen & Tomlinson. The foundations (which have since been covered in) were excavated during the course of building operations in 1893, and reveal the ground plans both of the original church and of the smaller church erected upon its site in the 17th century. The former was a large cruciform building, having an aisleless nave measuring internally about 87 ft. by 29 ft., north and south transepts, each 30 ft. 4 in. by 20 ft., and a chancel 24 ft. in width, the eastern foundations of which cannot now be traced. At the angle formed by the west wall of the south transept with the south wall of the nave are signs of the existence of a stair-turret. The thickness of the walls, about 4 ft., indicate that the remains are at least as early as the 12th century. Several tiles of the 13th and 14th centuries were found on the site. One of these, of the later date, has a vigorously drawn hart upon it.

The church of *ST. NICHOLAS* existed in 1291, when the Prior of Wilford (Kent) had a pension of £1 in it.[94] The advowson of the rectory belonged to the alien priory of Wilford,[95] and hence came to the Crown.[96] St. Nicholas was parochial, but the extent of the parish is unknown. In 1428 it had less than ten inhabitants (householders).[97] In 1487

TILE FROM ST. JOHN'S CHURCH, HERTFORD

there is a will of John Lombard of London, by which he wished to be buried in the parish church of St. Nicholas, Hertford.[98] The living had been united to that of St. Andrew by 1535,[99] so that probably the church was then already disused.[100] The building is described by Chauncy as standing 'near St. Nicholas Street, at the west end of Back Street, towards the mills in the back yard to the Maidenhead Inn, where the ruins of the church are yet to be seen.'[1] Moulded stones are occasionally found on the north side of Maidenhead Street where the church stood.

In the grant of the manor to the Earl of Salisbury in 1630 the ruined and decayed church with the cemetery called St. Nicholas is mentioned.[2]

---

[83] *Lond. Gaz.* 22 June 1869, p. 3549.
[84] *Feud. Aids*, ii, 461.
[85] Chauncy (p. 261) calls this church St. Mary the Great, and other historians have followed his example and have called the priory church St. Mary the Less. There seems to be no documentary evidence to support this. The priory was certainly known as St. Mary Monachorum (*Cal. Pat.* 1381–5, p. 207), and there was a parish church of St. Mary Minor (see references to the parish of St. Mary Minor on pp. 495[b], 500[a]). But the parish church belonging to the priory seems to have been St. John the Evangelist (see below). It seems most probable from the present amount of evidence that the church of St. Mary (*Feud. Aids*, ii, 461) or St. Mary the Virgin (*Valor Eccl.* [Rec. Com.], iv, 277) was sometimes called St. Mary Minor to distinguish it from the priory church and was this church near the Old Cross.
[86] It had been annexed to St. Andrew's before 1535 (*Valor Eccl.* [Rec. Com.], iv, 277).
[87] See *Herts. Mercury*, 6 Oct. 1906.
[88] Pat. 6 Chas. I, pt. i, no. 1.
[89] For account of the discovery of foundations see *Herts. Mercury*, 2 Dec. 1893.
[90] See below under advowson.
[91] Ct. of Wards, Feod. Surv. no. 17.
[92] Chauncy, op. cit. 257. This second church is supposed to be the small church whose foundations have been found within the area of the larger nave of the earlier one (see *Herts. Mercury*, 2 Dec. 1893).
[93] Turnor, op. cit. 247. Willis is said to have dedicated his church in honour of St. John the Baptist, but all the documents dealing with this later church refer to it as St. John the Evangelist.
[94] *Pope Nich. Tax.* (Rec. Com.), 37. Possibly this was one of the churches held by Peter de Valognes in 1086 and was given by him or a successor to Wilford.
[95] This was a cell to Bec Hellouin (*Cal. Pat.* 1350–4, p. 503).
[96] Ibid. 1327–30, p. 3; 1350–4, p. 503; 1399–1401, p. 443.
[97] *Feud. Aids*, ii, 461.
[98] P.C.C. Will, Milles, 10. A bequest was made to the repairs of the church in 1495 (ibid. Vox, 30).
[99] *Valor Eccl.* (Rec. Com.), iv, 277.
[100] Several funeral monuments are given by Weever.
[1] See also Speed (1610), *Engl. and Wales*, plate xxiii.
[2] Pat. 6 Chas. I, pt. x, no. 1.

509

A HISTORY OF HERTFORDSHIRE

ADVOWSONS St. Andrew's Church is first mentioned by name in 1208, when King John granted it to Master Adam of Essex, his clerk, for life.[3] The grant mentions a perpetual vicarage, which never reappears.[4] The advowson of the rectory descended with the manor until the alienation of the latter to the Earl of Salisbury. It still belongs to the Crown in right of the duchy of Lancaster.[5]

The church of All Saints was probably one of those held by Peter de Valognes in 1086,[6] for Robert de Valognes gave it to Waltham Abbey.[7] The gift was confirmed by Richard I in December 1189, when the invocation is first mentioned.[8] The church was confirmed to the abbey in 1227,[9] and a vicarage ordained at the beginning of the 13th century.[10] The convent granted two turns of the presentation to Richard Heyham just before the Dissolution,[11] after which the king gave the rectory and advowson of the vicarage to Thomas Knighton.[12] Knighton's widow brought it to John Alleyn, who held it in 1545,[12] and on her death in 1551 it descended to her nephew, Andrew Baynton.[14] His heir Anne[15] seems to have married William Anstee, with whom she conveyed it to Richard Roberts in 1580,[16] possibly in trust for Christopher Aleyn, who died seised in 1588, and whose heir, Edmund Aleyn,[17] transferred it to Stephen Soame in 1589.[18] Sir William Soame, son of Stephen, conveyed the rectory in 1626 to certain feoffees,[19] who may have been trustees for Gabriel Barber, who bought the advowson for the purpose of uniting the living with that of St. John's and endowing it with the impropriate tithes. The king was to be patron of All Saints, presenting alternately with the patron of St. John's.[20] The arrangement was annulled by the House of Lords before 1649, the patronage being then claimed by the heirs of Mr. Barber[21]; but it must have been re-asserted, perhaps at the Restoration.[22] The alternate presentations from 1709 to the present day have been made by the Crown.[23]

A Fraternity of St. John celebrated in the church of All Saints, and had a chaplain there in 1495.[24] After the dissolution of the brotherhood its property passed to the Crown. In 1575 a 'ruinous house' in the north of All Saints' churchyard, which had been given for an obit and lamp, and the site of another house called the Guildhall or church house were granted to John Herbert and Andrew Palmer.[25]

Ralph de Limesy founded the priory of Hertford and endowed it with the church which he had built there.[26] It seems probable that this was the church of St. John, which was situated on the priory estate to the north of Christ's Hospital.[27] The church of St. John belonged to the monks at the beginning of the 13th century, when a vicarage was endowed.[28] It seems to be the church which served the parish known as the 'parochia de Monachorum' or Monkenchurch,[29] or the parish of the priory,[30] and to be the parish church within the priory mentioned in 1497.[31] After the Dissolution the rectory and advowson of the vicarage of the church of St. John the Evangelist were granted in 1538 to Antony Denny[32] and descended with the priory manor (q.v.).

In 1640 the vicarage was united to that of All Saints,[33] and it was proposed by Sir John Harrison to endow it with the impropriate tithes. Sir John Harrison was to have alternate presentation with the king.[34] Apparently the endowment did not stand, for the rectory appears to have descended with the advowson.[35] This with the priory manor is now in possession of Marquess Townshend.

CHARITIES The poor's estate comprises the charities of John Browne, Alderman Card, the King's Mead, Standon Green End Farm, the Herbage Money, and the charity of Ann Dimsdale, which were formerly under the administration of trustees for the poor created under a decree of commissioners for charitable uses 13 September 1708.

In 1909 the gross income amounted to £290, or thereabouts, of which £70 was derived from the rent of 101 acres known as the Green End Farm, Standon, co. Herts., £112 from rent of the post office, £23 from the King's Mead, and £83 10s. from other land. A fixed payment of £1 a year is also received from Balls Park and £2 1s. 10d. from the Lea Conservancy Board.

In 1889 the 'Talbot Arms' was sold for £1,000, and part of the Dimsdale Arms Inn for £300, and the proceeds invested in stock with the official trustees, which was subsequently sold out for effecting improvements in the property and towards the cost of building the post office. The official trustees now (1910) hold £460 16s. 3d. consols, which is accumulating for the purpose of replacing a sum of £315 3s. 11d. consols, also £305 17s. 5d. consols for the replacement of £1,289 11s. 5d. consols by annual instalments of £29, and £21 5s. 5d. consols to replace £74 11s. 7d. consols by annual instalments of £4 5s.

---

[3] *Rot. Lit. Pat.* (Rec. Com.), i, 79a; *Cal. Rot. Chart.* 1199–1216 (Rec. Com.), 175a.
[4] *Cal. Rot. Chart.* 1199–1216 (Rec. Com.), 175a.
[5] *Cal. Pat.* 1225–32, p. 190; 1232–47, p. 467; 1301–7, p. 139; 1435–41, p. 63; Chauncy, op. cit. 238; Inst. Bks. (P.R.O.); Bacon, *Lib. Reg.* 517.
[6] *V.C.H. Herts.* i, 300.
[7] Dugdale, *Mon.* vi, 67.
[8] Cart. Antiq. M 15. The church is called 'of the king's demesne.' This is probably because the king was lord of the borough.
[9] *Cal. Chart. R.* 1226–7, p. 27.
[10] *Liber Antiquus Hugonis Wells* (ed. A. Gibbons), 29.
[11] Aug. Off. Dec. and Ord. v, fol. 209b.
[12] *L. and P. Hen. VIII,* xvi, 878 (61).
[13] Ibid. xx (2), 1068 (52).

[14] Chan. Inq. p.m (Ser. 2), cxxxiii, 100.
[15] Ibid. clvii, 81.
[16] Feet of F. Herts. Hil. 22 Eliz.
[17] Chan. Inq. p.m. (Ser. 2), ccxvi, 63.
[18] Feet of F. Herts. Hil. 31 Eliz.
[19] *Hist. MSS. Com. Rep.* iv, App. 12.
[20] Chan. Surv. of Ch. Livings, i, fol. 25.
[21] Ibid.
[22] In any case before 1662 (Inst. Bks. [P.R.O.]), when Sir John Harrison presented to the united livings.
[23] Inst. Bks. (P.R.O.); Bacon, *Lib. Reg.* 517.
[24] Wills, P.C.C. 30 Vox; cf. also 5 Fetiplace; Archd. of St. Albans, W 140 d.
[25] Pat. 17 Eliz. pt. iii, m. 28 (grant begins on m. 9).
[26] Dugdale, *Mon.* iii, 299.
[27] See *Herts. Mercury,* 2 Dec. 1893.
[28] *Liber Antiquus Hugonis Wells* (ed. A. Gibbons), 29.

[29] *Pope Nich. Tax.* (Rec. Com.), 37; *Feud. Aids,* ii, 461.
[30] Aug. Off. Proc. bdle. 3, no. 92.
[31] Rentals and Surv. R. 277. Whether there was another church attached to the priory used by the monks themselves is not quite certain, or whether the monks used the parish church. By will of 1525 John Purfote desired to be buried in the priory church (P.C.C. 1 Porch), but this may only mean the church belonging to the priory.
[32] Pat. 14 Chas. I, pt. x, no. 1; 16 Chas. I, pt. viii.
[33] Chan. Surv. of Ch. Livings, i, fol. 35.
[34] Recov. R. Trin. 20 Chas. II, rot. 124; Feet of F. Herts. East. 2 Anne; Recov. R. Mich. 1 Geo. I, rot. 26; East. 5 Geo. IV, rot. 215.

HERTFORD HUNDRED — BOROUGH OF HERTFORD

In addition to these repayments a sum of £42 9s. was in 1909 applied towards the repayment of a loan from a building society, and a sum of £172 19s. 6d. was apportioned out of the income of the charity for the benefit of the poor, as follows: £76 16s. for the poor of St. John's, £55 5s. 6d. for St. Andrew's, £19 15s. for All Saints, and £21 3s. for the district of Brickendon.

Residence for a Wesleyan minister, comprised in deed 7 December 1896. In 1908, with the sanction of the Charity Commissioners, the residence was sold for £510, and the balance, after payment of liabilities, was invested in £104 2s. 3d. consols with the official trustees.

Educational Charities.—The grammar school was founded in 1616 by Richard Hale.[36]

The Greencoat school was founded in 1760 by Gabriel Newton, including the gifts of George Butteris, Lady Grimstone, Mrs. Skinner, and Benjamin Cherry.[37] This school was afterwards merged with the Cowper Testimonial School.

By will of 1649 Mary Pettyt, widow, gave two tenements near Cowbridge for as many poor widows. These were exchanged in 1824 for other houses in St. Andrew's Street occupied by eight poor widows nominated by the churchwardens of St. Andrew's.

The charity of Sir John Harrison, kt., will, 1669, augmented by his son, Richard Harrison, consists of certain fee-farm rents purchased with a sum of £108 13s. 4d. and conveyed by deed 14 March 1676. The properties charged having been subdivided, difficulties arose in obtaining payment of the several charges, and a sum of £5 only appears to be now received which is regularly distributed in bread among the poor of All Saints and St. John's. The official trustees also hold a sum of £17 10s. consols, producing 8s. 8d. yearly, arising from investment of balance of arrears of fee-farm rent of £2 11s. 2d. charged on the rectory and manor of Abbots Langley.

In 1625 Roger Daniel by his will (among other bequests) devised an annuity of £10, of which £5 was payable for a monthly sermon, £4 for fourteen poorest householders of All Saints and six of the parish of St. Andrew, 12s. for bread and drink for poor prisoners in the 'Maine Gaol,' and 8s. for a breakfast for the administering trustees. The annuity of £10 is duly received from the Merchant Taylors' Company, London—£5 is paid to the vicar for a monthly lecture, £4 for twenty poor widows, the 12s. for prisoners is paid into the Post Office Savings Bank, the amount of which exceeds £20, and the 8s. breakfast money is carried to the general church account.

Endowments for organist.—In 1698 Mrs. Elizabeth Cranmer, by will, left £200, which was laid out in the purchase of a rent-charge of £8 issuing out of land at Springfield near Chelmsford.

In 1724 Robert Dimsdale, M.D., by his will, devised a rent-charge of £15 issuing out of a house in the market-place, Hertford. The annuities are duly paid to the organist, who also receives under the will of Miss Dionisia Battell, 1730, the sum of £30 year, the rent of a house in Fore Street, Hertford, formerly known as the 'Blue Anchor.'

Thomas Noble, by his will dated 14 August 1662, devised a messuage in the parish of All Saints, at a place there called Bayley Hall Style, for the use of the poor. These premises are situated in Castle Street, producing £65 a year or thereabouts, which together with a rent-charge of £15 a year issuing out of an estate at Bennington derived under the will of the same donor is distributed among the poor of All Saints.

In 1909 a sum of £19 15s. was likewise applied for the benefit of the poor of All Saints in respect of the poor's estate for the borough.

In 1817 Charles Saunders by will bequeathed £500 consols, the dividends to be distributed in bread.

In 1844 Thomas Cheek by will bequeathed £200 consols, the dividends to be distributed in bread on Christmas Eve to the poor of All Saints and St. Andrew's, or either of them.

In 1872 John Davies, M.D., by will proved at London, left £53 17s. 6d. consols, the dividends to be applied for any charitable purpose the trustees should think fit. The annual dividends, amounting together to £18 16s. 8d., are distributed by the vicar and churchwardens chiefly in bread.

In 1854 six almshouses in All Saints parish were built by Marquess Townshend for poor widows and others.

In 1875 Miss Hannah Smith, by will, bequeathed a legacy represented by £275 10s. 3d. consols, the annual dividends amounting to £6 17s. 8d.—subject to repair of tomb in cemetery for sixty years after death of testatrix—in augmentation of the income of Herts. County Infirmary, at the expiration of the term the stock to be transferred to that institution.

In 1885 George Ringrose, by will, left a sum of money, now represented by £187 11s. consols, the annual dividends of £4 13s. 4d. to be distributed in coals, bread, or money to the poor.

In 1897 Henry Rayment, by will proved at London, left a sum of money, represented by £176 18s. 11d. consols, the annual dividends, amounting to £4 8s. 4d., to be divided on 8 February among three poor widows.

The several sums of stock are held by the official trustees.

---

[36] V.C.H. Herts. ii, 89.

[37] Ibid. 101.

511

Lightning Source UK Ltd.
Milton Keynes UK
UKOW05f1109031016

284340UK00001B/285/P